CONTAMINATED LAND

SECOND EDITION

CONTAMINATED LAND

SECOND EDITION

Stephen Tromans
M.A. (Cantab), Barrister, 39 Essex Street

and

Robert Turrall-Clarke
M.A. (Oxon), Barrister

London
Sweet & Maxwell
2008

First edition 1994

Published in 2008 by
Sweet & Maxwell Limited
of 100 Avenue Road, London NW3 3PF
http://www.sweetandmaxwell.co.uk

Typeset by LBJ Typesetting Ltd, Kingsclere
Printed and bound in Great Britain by
TJ International Ltd, Padstow, Cornwall

No natural forests were destroyed to make this product;
only farmed timber was used and re-planted.

British Library Cataloguing in Publication Data

A CIP catalogue record for this book
is available from the British Library

ISBN 978 0421 96620 8

PREFACE TO THE SECOND EDITION

This edition of our work brings together two main texts: *Contaminated Land*, which was published in 1994, and *Contaminated Land: the New Regime*, published in 2000. In trying to synthesise these two works, we have sought to strike a reasonable balance within the constraints of producing a manageable text, between the statutory regime specifically dealing with contaminated land, Part IIA of the Environmental Protection Act 1990, and other relevant areas of law. Whilst Part IIA (we have resisted the gratuitous purported Arabic renumbering by Circular 01/2006) is the natural focus of the attention of lawyers, the fact is that its effects in dealing with contaminated land have tended to be indirect rather than direct. Other areas of law covered, such as water pollution, waste management, town and country planning law, common law and the law relating to commercial transactions, may in many cases be of equal if not more importance for the practitioner. We have retained within the work the text of Part IIA and the vital statutory guidance, as in our experience it is useful to be able to refer to the relevant wording in conjunction with our commentary.

As the law has developed, there is now, it seems to us, a distinction between the legislation which prospectively seeks to prevent contamination occurring (and to require its rectification where it does occur) and that which is addressed to the retrospective remediation of identified contamination which does not arise from current activities on the land, but which may have occurred many decades ago. The two types of regime are not completely watertight in legal terms, but do require a different policy approach, and increasingly there is a need to consider carefully how they may relate in respect of a specific site. Equally, contaminated land cannot be considered in isolation from the law and policy on land use generally; particularly in a country as small and as subject to development pressures as the UK.

We hope, therefore, that this book will provide the reader, whether student, academic or practitioner, with not only a hopefully clear guide through the complex legislation concerning contaminated land, but also a broader understanding of where the subject sits within the wider framework of environmental law, its history, and where it may be heading next. This involves consideration of the commercial issues, the relevant science, and related subjects such as insurance and valuation, all of which we have attempted to include. It is also helpful to refer to experience in other countries with developed systems on contaminated land, since there are many common issues. We have, as with the first edition, therefore included some comparative material.

As well as those who have made the very substantial contributions to this edition, which are acknowledged below, we wish to thank a number of colleagues who have been kind enough to read parts of the text in draft and offer helpful comments and encouragement. A number of colleagues at 39 Essex Street took the time to comment on areas of the text within their particular expertise. In particular, Colin McCaul QC considered drafts of Chapters 12, 14 and 15 on Health and Safety and Tort, and we are most grateful for the insights from his expertise and experience in these dynamic areas of law. Justine Thornton kindly commented on Chapters 7 (Water), 8 (Waste) and 13 (EC Developments) and Richard Harwood read and made valuable comments on Chapter 16 (Planning Permission). Paul Davies, partner at Macfarlanes, was kind enough to comment on the Chapters dealing with Transactional Issues. We also gratefully acknowledge the assistance of Antony Turck of Argyll Environmental who provided most helpful comments in Chapter 23 (Insurance) and Peter Wyatt, Reader in Land Management at the University of the West of England, who very kindly read and commented on Chapter 24 on Valuation. We are also indebted to Simon Boyle and Chris Taylor of Argyll Environmental Ltd for use (with kind permission of the publishers) within Chapter 22 of material from their article on Information Sources published in PLC Environment and to those who have contributed material to Section 8 on Comparative Regimes, and who are acknowledged at the start of each Chapter.

So far as possible, the law is stated as at 1st November 2007.

Stephen Tromans

Robert Turrall-Clarke

ACKNOWLEDGEMENTS

It would not have been possible to produce this Second Edition without the able and expert help we have received from a number of contributors, which we are pleased to be able to acknowledge here.

Professor Stuart Bell, LL.B, Barrister, and **Laurence Etherington**, LL.B, Ph.D., Solicitor, both of York Law School, University of York, who updated and produced a revised first draft of our original text on Part IIA to take account of amendments, case-law and its extension to radioactively contaminated land.

Daniel Lawrence, Solicitor, and a number of his colleagues in the Environment, Planning and Regulatory Group at Freshfields Bruckhaus Deringer, who reviewed and updated the transactional Chapters 18–20, the Commercial Precedents, contributed new material on the Environmental Liability Directive in Chapter 13, and who facilitated the provision of the comparative material in Chapters 25–29 and the new Chapter 22 on Information Sources and Environmental Reports.

Valerie Fogleman, Consultant, Stevens & Bolton, Professor of Law at Cardiff University and Visiting Professor of Law at the University of Ghent, who produced the new and much expanded Chapter 23 on Insurance.

Peter Leonard, Principal at SLR Consulting Ltd, and **Mike Quint,** Associate Director at ARUP, who together produced a first draft of the new Chapter 21 on Technical Issues.

Responsibility for any errors of course remains with us as co-authors.

CONTENTS

FULL TABLE OF CONTENTS

SECTION 3. OTHER REGIMES

TABLE OF CASES

TABLE OF STATUTES

TABLE OF STATUTORY INSTRUMENTS

TABLE OF EC LEGISLATION

SECTION 1
INTRODUCTION AND OVERVIEW

Chapter 1

CONTAMINATED LAND GENERALLY

Causes of contaminated land

Contamination of land may arise from a wide variety of activities. One **1.01**
category is the intentional deposit of material on land, whether as a means
of disposing of that material, or in connection with development or
construction activities. Examples of this are landfill sites, tips, lagoons for
industrial effluent, deposits of dredgings, "made ground" and filled dock
basins, and the deposit of sewage sludge or other materials on agricultural
land. Another category is contamination arising incidentally in the course
of industrial activity, including spillages and leaks of materials from
storage tanks and drums, escapes of materials such as dust and liquids in
the course of the activity itself, and contamination resulting from deposition of airborne particulate matter. As well as contamination in the course
of ordinary industrial activity, incidents such as floods, fires and explosions
may give rise to significant contamination. Lax practices during the
decommissioning and demolition of industrial facilities are another possible cause of contamination. Many pollutants are, by their nature, mobile
and so capable of migration, whether in gaseous, liquid or particulate
form—a site may therefore become contaminated without itself having
been used for a contaminating purpose.

Various attempts have been made to compile lists of uses of land which **1.02**
are prone to cause contamination. In a report in 1990, the House of
Commons Environment Committee listed 19 categories of use, which were
said to represent the most common contaminating uses.[1] The categories
were as follows:

> waste disposal sites
>
> gas works
>
> oil refineries and petrol stations
>
> power stations
>
> iron and steel works
>
> petroleum refineries
>
> metal products, fabrication and finishing
>
> chemical works

[1] House of Commons Environment Committee, Session 1989–90, *First Report*, Contaminated
Land, Vol.I, para.12. (HC 170–I)

textile plants

leather tanning works

timber treatment works

non-ferrous metals processing

manufacture of integrated circuits and semi-conductors

sewage works

asbestos works

docks and railway land

paper and printing works

heavy engineering installations

processing radioactive materials.

Problems of contamination

1.03 The range of potentially harmful contaminants is wide. Toxic metals such as cadmium, lead, arsenic and mercury may present risks to human health if ingested directly or indirectly. Direct ingestion can arise, for example, by young children playing in contaminated soil. Where food plants and crops are grown in contaminated soil, elements such as cadmium, arsenic, copper, fluorine and lead may accumulate in the edible portions of the plant, making it unsafe to consume plants grown in such soil over a long period of time. There may also be a risk to livestock grazing on herbage grown on contaminated soil. Tars, oils, acids, corrosive and other chemical substances may cause problems on direct dermal contact, where workers or occupants of land are directly exposed to contaminated soil. Other metals such as copper, nickel and zinc may prevent or inhibit plant growth.

1.04 Contamination may involve combustible substances which could give rise to persistent underground fires. Some wastes may degrade to produce flammable gases such as methane, which may then migrate and present a risk of explosion; toxic or asphyxiating gases may also be generated. Some contaminants, such as sulphates, chlorides and acids, may have an aggressive effect on building materials, concrete foundations, and services. Fibrous or fine particulate contaminants such as asbestos may present dangers from inhalation, as may some volatile substances which produce vapours which enter houses or confined spaces. Contaminated land may have significant effects on surface water quality, both of internal waters and of estuarial and even coastal waters.[2]

---

[2] A striking example was given in the Royal Commission on Environmental Pollution on Freshwater Quality. *16th Report of the Royal Commission on Environmental Pollution on Freshwater Quality*, p.87. Cm. 1966 (June 1992) where it is suggested that two former waste sites at Slacky Lane and Bentley Mill Lane, Walsall between them contribute about 6 tonnes a year of copper and 15 tonnes of nickel to the River Tame; this amounts to about one-sixth of the loads of these metals of the Tame at its confluence with the Trent.

Substances such as oils, tars, phenols and chlorinated solvents may present serious problems in terms of contamination of water supplies, either through groundwater, or in some cases by causing deterioration of service mains. Groundwater is a valuable resource, and many parts of the UK are dependent upon it as the principal source of potable water. Contamination of an aquifer may be an extremely difficult problem to eradicate and solutions, if possible at all, may be available only at extremely high cost.

The aesthetic effects of soil contamination are frequently overlooked, **1.05** but may be difficult to eradicate and may have a serious effect on the value and marketability of property. Even relatively small quantities of oily or tarry substances may have a significant visual effect and may produce unpleasant and detectable odours. Such effects may be apparent at much lower concentrations than would be necessary to present a significant risk to health.

How big a problem?

A country with the long industrial history of the UK may be expected to **1.06** have a substantial legacy of contaminated sites. However, it is only comparatively recently that serious attempts have been made to estimate the extent of contaminated land in the UK. As was pointed out in 1990 by the House of Commons Environment Committee in its report, "Contaminated Land",[3] in contrast to a number of other western countries, the UK had, at that stage, never actively sought to identify contaminated sites and assess the amount of contaminated land comprehensively. There had been partial work, such as the survey of contaminated land in Wales, undertaken by Liverpool University for the Welsh Office and Welsh Development Agency, and suggesting that there might be 746 contaminated land sites in Wales covering some 10,000 acres.[4] Some work had also at that stage been carried out by Her Majesty's Inspectorate of Pollution, in conjunction with local authorities, to identify and locate waste disposal landfill sites generating gas; this work had led to an estimate of 1,400 such sites potentially emitting gas in sufficient quantities to present hazards of fire and explosion. Apart from these two specific examples, the Committee was referred to no firm figures on contaminated land in Great Britain.

When the Government published its Environmental White Paper, *This* **1.07** *Common Inheritance: Britain's Environmental Strategy*[5] in September 1990, the position was presented even more tentatively. In the brief section of the White Paper dealing with "derelict and contaminated sites", reference was made to the 1988 Derelict Land Survey which showed that, despite reclamation of 14,000 hectares since 1992, large areas of land required action. A total of about 40,000 hectares was derelict, three-quarters of which justified reclamation measures. In relation to contamination, as opposed to dereliction, all that the Government was able to say in the White Paper was[6]:

---

[3] House of Commons Environment Committee, Session 1989–90, First Report, Contaminated Land, 1990. Vol.I, para.22. (HC 170–1).

[4] Survey of Contaminated Land in Wales (1988) (Welsh National Digital Archive of Datasets (NDAD) Reference CRDA/15/DD/1/2).

[5] Cm. 1200.

[6] House of Commons Environment Committee, Session 1989–90, First Report, Contaminated Land, 1990. Vol.I, para.6.62. (HC 170–1).

"Contamination of land by chemicals and waste products is hard to define and measure exactly, but surveys suggest that over half of derelict land might be contaminated, and contamination is also found on other land. The nature of contamination and the possible risks to health and ground water supplies vary widely, and the Government needs better assessments of the scale of the problem."

1.08 What was clear, however, by 1990 was that in some cases contamination was presenting serious threats. The House of Commons Environment Committee received evidence of a number of sites where serious problems had occurred as the result of contamination and other examples were reported elsewhere. The list given below is indicative of the types of problems which were being unearthed at that time:

Amber Valley, Derbyshire: various sites within the area were contaminated by lead, acid leachates, dioxins and gasworks residues. Select Committee Report, Vol.I, para.32.

Chemstar Site, Greater Manchester: contamination of former solvent recovery works where explosion and fire occurred in 1981; asbestos contamination removed at cost of £530,000; problems remaining of contamination of site and nearby gardens by solvents and up to 400 chemicals. Select Committee Report, Vol.I. paras. 34–35.

Thamesmead, London Borough of Greenwich: housing estate built on filled quarry; contamination by toxic metals and "blue billy" gasworks waste. Remedial measures (partly funded by Derelict Land Grant) cost £250,000 at 1979 prices. Select Committee Report, Vol.I, para.36.

Hayle, Cambourne and other villages in Cornwall: garden soils with arsenic levels reportedly more than one part per hundred as a result of 18th and 19th century mining and smelting. No health effects apparent. *The Observer*, March 8, 1992.

Lumsden Road, Portsmouth: contamination of housing estate resulting from former "Glory Hole" site used for dumping wastes from naval yards between the wars; arsenic, asbestos, cadmium, and mercury among the substances. Residents evacuated. *The Independent*, November 2, 1991.

Neston Tank Cleaners, Queensferry, Clywd, Wales: contamination by oils, tars and solvents from tar distillery and tank farm. Area compulsorily purchased by local authority for remediation. *Environment Business*, June 1993, p.4.

Former Laporte Works, Ilford: contamination of site of old gas-mantle factory by mildly radioactive thorium and radium. Programme of remedial works expected to cost in excess of £11m. Select Committee Report, Vol.I, para.37.

Great Cambridge Road, Enfield: retail site contaminated by materials including low-level radium 226 from former instrument-dial factory. *Environment Business*, March 24, 1993.

Loscoe, Derbyshire: explosion of gas generated by putrescible matter disposed of in quarry, which destroyed a bungalow. Report of non-statutory inquiry of Derbyshire County Council, Vols I and II, 1987.

Callywhite Lane Industrial Site, Dronfield, Derbyshire: former tip developed in 1970s; signs of underground fire noticed in 1984. Subsequently affected safety of buildings. Local authority ordered to take remedial action under statutory nuisance provisions of Public Health Act 1936 at a cost of £600,000. Select Committee Report, Vol.I, para.33; *The Guardian*, February 1, 1990.

Powys, Wales: underground fire at tyre dump smouldered for four years; cost of extinguishing it by injection of liquid nitrogen followed by excavation, estimated at £4 million. Threat of water pollution; plans to divert local stream. *Sunday Telegraph*, January 16, 1994; *The Surveyor*, January 27, 1994.

Armley, Leeds: contamination of housing estate by asbestos dust from asbestos products factory; up to 258 houses (90 per cent of the estate) affected. Early estimates of decontamination costs put at £6.3m or £7,500 per house. *The Independent*, August 8, 1992.

Helpston, near Peterborough, Cambridgeshire: contamination of public drinking water supplies by pesticide wastes from local disposal sites leading to the closure of a borehole source. Activated carbon unit fitted at costs of £0.5 million. *The Independent*, February 13, 1992.

Luton and Dunstable: pollution of chalk aquifer by chlorinated solvents, discovered in 1988, requiring air-stripping equipment to be installed at three abstraction boreholes of Lee Valley Water Company, thought to be caused by solvent leakages from automotive companies and other users. ENDS Report 213, October 1992.

Pollution of River Fal system, Truro, Cornwall: metal contaminated water from Wheal Jane tin mine; serious effects on water quality, amenity and local economy. *The Guardian*, February 14, 1992.

The first detailed official attempt to estimate the scale of contaminated **1.09** land in Britain was research commissioned from WS Atkins in the mid-1990s, at the time of the Environment Bill. This study was not published at the time, but was later reported.[7] It estimated the area of contaminated land at 360,000 hectares, some 208,000 hectares of which had been redeveloped but could still present problems. The costs of assessment and remediation of contaminated sites were estimated at £15.2 billion. The greatest cost was attributed to an estimated 120,000 petrol station sites, but other significant activities were engineering works (43,000 sites), coal preparation works (1,800 sites), landfills and other waste sites

---

[7] ENDS Report 303, June 2000, pp.4–5.

(5,500 sites), gasworks (2,000 sites), railway land (175 sites), airfields (1,370 sites), chemical works (4,100 sites), printing works (10,000 sites) and textile and dye works (11,200 sites).

1.10　More recently, in August 2005, the Environment Agency published a report, Indicators for Land Contamination,[8] which covered England and Wales. This used study areas in conjunction with local authorities, which were extrapolated to regional level and compared with other sources such as the National Land Use Database, Coal Authority, Regional Development Agencies, English Partnerships, and major landowners. It suggested that 325,000 sites, covering 300,000 hectares, had been used for contaminating activity at some point in their history. Of this, 67,000 hectares of land (33,500 sites) was regarded as requiring some degree of remedial action, of which about two-thirds by area had undergone some degree of remediation. The study looked separately at radioactive contamination, and found that radioactive material had been used, stored or disposed of at 53,000 sites covering 27,000 hectares, of which between 100 and 1,000 might require consideration for action.

Current position

1.11　Since 1990, it is fair to say that contaminated land has been taken much more seriously as a problem. The development of the Pt IIA regime to identify and secure remediation of contaminated land is discussed in the next chapter. While progress in implementing the regime since 2000, when it came into force, has been modest, the existence of a statutory scheme of liabilities specifically for contaminated land has had an effect in encouraging voluntary remedial action, often in conjunction with redevelopment of sites. It has also raised awareness of the importance of investigating land condition as part of property transactions, which has led to more useful information being generated on specific sites.

1.12　The re-use of previously developed and often contaminated land has itself been encouraged through evolving planning policy. Various reports have stressed the importance of recycling urban land,[9] and the current target on an annual basis is for at least 60 per cent of new housing to be built on previously developed land.[10] Some of the most problematic sites are being tackled with public support and funding through partnerships between the private sector, English Partnerships and the Regional Development Agencies, for example the former Avenue Coking Works near Chesterfield, closed in 1992 and causing serious pollution by coal tars and other effluents for many years,[11] and the former Phurnacite smokeless fuel plant at Cynon Valley in South Wales, closed in 1990 after 48 years of

---

[8] Science Report SC030039/SR.

[9] See, e.g. Lord Rogers' Urban Task Force Report (1999); *The Barker Report on Land Use Planning* (2006), paras 2.13 and 2.14; Government White Paper. *Planning for a Sustainable Future*. HMSO, 2007. Cm.7120, para.1.6.

[10] See Planning Policy Statement 3: Housing (PPS3), November 2006, para.41. See further, Ch.16.

[11] See ENDS Report 376, *Clean-up to start at 'Europe's most contaminated site'*, May 2006, p.18.

operation, leaving residues of mercury, asbestos, phenols, ammonia, hydro-carbon gas and tars.[12] Further developments in contaminated land policy and possibly in law are likely to arise from EU initiatives in terms of the Water Framework Directive,[13] the Environmental Liability Directive,[14] and the proposed Soil Protection Directive.[15] In addition, since 1990 the stringency of environmental controls applying to potentially contaminating activities such as landfill, industrial processes and other matters such as the storage of fuel oil has increased significantly, so that new contamina-tion should be less likely to occur, or if it does, should not go undetected and unremedied.

Therefore there is reason to be encouraged in the progress made since **1.13** the first edition of this book was published in 1994, but not cause for complacency. The presence of contamination can still present risks to individuals, and where it affects them can have a very serious effect on their well-being. One of the problems is that knowledge is constantly developing and what may have been thought an acceptable solution or practice even relatively recently may no longer be thought so in future. By way of example, the contamination which occurred at the tannery site of Eastern Counties Leather in the 1980s, as the result of spillages of perchloroethylene (PCE), was originally viewed as a deep groundwater pollution incident, leading to civil proceedings which reached the House of Lords, and to clean-up action in conjunction with the National Rivers Authority. It was only some 16 years later, in 1999, that it was realised that hot spots of PCE remained in the shallow groundwater, in proximity to housing (some of which was only built in 1993) and that PCE vapour could potentially affect the indoor air quality of those houses.[16] Indoor air quality was also the issue with a site at Weston, near Runcorn, Cheshire, where in January 2000, 16 families had to be moved out of their homes because of potential contamination by hexachlorobutadiene (HCBD) which had been disposed of in a nearby quarry operated by the Castner-Keller Alkali Company (a predecessor of ICI) between 1917 and 1952.[17]

Moreover, there are numerous examples of sites where development has **1.14** taken place over contaminated infill, or having utilised ash or other contaminated material in the development process; such problems are not easily referable to information on past uses, and will continue to come to light, causing potentially serious financial consequences for the current owners.[18] Also, like many environmental problems, the full effects of

---

[12] See further, Chapter 17.

[13] See para.3.66 ff.

[14] See para.13.0 ff.

[15] See para.13.47 ff.

[16] See ENDS Report 293, June 1999, pp.5–6.

[17] ENDS Report 301, February 2000, pp.4–5. The issue came to light in the course of a programme set up by ICI in 1993 to investigate soil and groundwater contamination around its Runcorn site.

[18] See for example, [2004] Land Contamination & Reclamation Vol 12, 402–3: referring to arsenic being found at St Michael's public golf course in Widnes (constructed in 1970s over a chemical tip); arsenic and lead found at allotments in Cardiff, possibly originating from having mixed the soil with ash; cyanide at former Pinegrove Country Club, Sheffield (up to 300 barrels of sodium cyanide thought to have been buried illegally in late 1960s and early 1970s).

exposure to contaminated land may not become apparent for some considerable time. In January 2006 it was reported that a class action had been commenced by parents of 30 children born with malformed upper limbs in the Corby area, alleging that these birth defects are attributable to exposure to lead, zinc and other toxic substances during the course of the clean-up of the former Corby steel works between 1985 and 1999.[19] Nor is it the case that the planning system and Pt IIA can be assured to deal effectively with all these potential problems. There will remain tensions between the two systems, particularly where there is no obvious appropriate person to be made liable for remediation, and where redevelopment proposals are controversial. In April 2007, it was reported that such difficulties were arising in relation to a site at Cinderhill, near Belper, Derbyshire, which was an opencast clay works used for disposing of acid tar wastes from 1972–1979; leaving a number of pits containing tar, ash and tarry silts. It was reported that there were differences in views between the Environment Agency and the local authority as to whether action should be taken under Pt IIA or the site dealt with in the context of proposed development for housing by capping the pits. Local residents were reported as opposing the development of the site and as wanting the contamination excavated and removed. In many such cases there will be no ready answer to what is the correct solution and, in turn, the most appropriate means of achieving it.

[19] ENDS Report 372, January 2006, p.17.

Chapter 2

THE EVOLUTION OF PART IIA

General issues

It is clear that contaminated land presents problems to legislators and **2.01** policy makers that are somewhat different to other types of environmental issues. This is by virtue of the fact that land is permanent, may be put to many different uses, and may be subject to numerous successive owner-ships or current interests. The issues that need to be considered are essentially:

(a) When is land to be regarded as "contaminated" so as to require remedial action to be taken?

(b) If it is regarded as contaminated, then to what standard does it need to be cleaned up, or what other actions are required?

(c) Over what timescale should those measures be undertaken?

(d) Who should bear the legal and financial responsibility for under-taking those measures?

Whilst capable of being simply stated, these are complex and controver- **2.02** sial questions, which other countries such as The Netherlands, Germany and the USA have found difficult to answer.[1] There are in fact no easy answers, and an important function of Pt IIA of the Environmental Protection Act 1990 is to introduce a framework of public law to tackle these problems and answer these questions. However, before outlining the scheme of Pt IIA, it may be helpful to describe briefly the policy background which led to its enactment.

Pressure for action and the section 143 registers

At the end of the 1980s, concern was focused on contaminated land in two **2.03** reports of the House of Commons Select Committee on the Environment dealing with toxic waste and contaminated land: Toxic Waste[2] and Contaminated Land.[3]

---

[1] For comparative discussion of other national regimes, see Chs 26–29.
[2] House of Commons Select Committee on the Environment. *Second Report on Toxic Waste*. Session 1988/89. (HC 22 I–II).
[3] House of Commons Select Committee on the Environment. *First Report on Contaminated Land*. Session 1989/90. (HC 170 I–III). See also para.1.02.

11

In the second of these Reports, the Select Committee recognised the difficult policy issues raised by any statutory scheme of liability, but suggested that nonetheless action was needed:

> ". . . urgent attention [must] be given to the question of creating statutory liability for damage caused by contamination to land— particularly where this causes damage to neighbouring property or to the environment. We recognise that this will raise complex questions as to retrospection, insurance cover and limitation periods in particular, but we believe that the present lack of clarity in relation to civil liability hampers the development of appropriate policies on the issue of contaminated land."

2.04   The initial response of the Government was not to address the issue of statutory liability directly, but to introduce a provision (s.143 of the Environmental Protection Act 1990) for public registers of land which had been subject to a "contaminative use", i.e. a use which might cause land to be contaminated with noxious substances. This approach was intended, with "minimal demands" on local authority resources,[4] to provide a means of alerting interested parties to the possible existence of contamination without "extending planning blight in those areas of the country with a legacy of industrial land use".[5]

2.05   This proved to be a somewhat optimistic assumption. Section 143 was intended to be implemented late in 1991. But, following an initial consultation exercise as to the range of uses to be prescribed as "contaminative", the Government announced on March 10, 1992 that it was postponing the introduction of the registers in view of the concerns that had been expressed over them, relating to the likelihood of serious blight in an already depressed property market.

2.06   A second consultation process ensued, with a markedly reduced list of contaminative uses, and with a proposed timetable which would have led to the opening of the registers to public inspection in about April 1994. This exercise enabled the Government to identify three serious grounds for criticism of the proposed registers. First, because they were to be based on current or former uses of land rather than actual contamination, they would include a number of sites which were not actually contaminated, whilst excluding others which were. Furthermore, the logical consequence of a register based on historical fact as to land use would have been the inability to have the entry removed from the register following completion of clean-up. Finally, the system would have left it unclear what action should be taken and by whom, i.e. whether the land should be cleaned up and, if so, who should pay and how much. The registration system was therefore essentially designed to alert the parties interested in a given site to a potential problem, leaving them to address it within a contractual relationship; the wider public interest in ensuring the land was actually cleaned up was not necessarily recognised.

---

[4] *Hansard*, HL Vol.520, col.2269.
[5] Department of the Environment News Release, No.279, April 30, 1990.

Withdrawal of the registers and further consultation

These misgivings over s.143 led the Government to withdraw the proposal **2.07** for registers, a decision announced by then Secretary of State for the Environment, Michael Howard, on March 24, 1993. Further, he announced the institution of a "wide-ranging review" of the legal powers of public bodies to control and tackle contaminated land, to be conducted by an inter-departmental group under the chairmanship of the Department of the Environment. Following similar consultation exercises in Scotland, the Secretary of State for Scotland announced an equivalent review on the same date.

As part of this review process, the Government's first step was to issue **2.08** the consultation paper, *Paying for our past: the arrangements for controlling Contaminated Land and Meeting the Cost of Remedying Damage to the Environment* (March 1994). In Scotland, a similar though not identical consultation paper entitled Contaminated Land Clean-up and Control (March 1994) was issued by the Scottish Office Environment Department. Its conclusions did not differ in any material respect from those of the consultation paper issued in England and Wales. Neither paper presented any firm proposals but rather set out a number of "preliminary conclusions" and posed a series of questions for respondents, grouped under seven issues:

(a) What should the policy objectives be?

(b) How should the statutory framework meet the objectives?

(c) What relationship should the statutory framework have with the common law and civil liability?

(d) Should there be any extension of strict liability?

(e) Who should pay for putting right any damage?

(f) How should markets be provided with information?

(g) What roles should public sector bodies have?

"Framework for Contaminated land" and new legislation

The March 1994 Consultation Papers, inconclusive even by consultation **2.09** standards, instituted another phase of the debate, which culminated on November 24, 1994 with the publication of the outcome of the review, *Framework for Contaminated Land* (and in Scotland, *Contaminated Land Clean-up and Control: Outcome of Review*) and the subsequent passage of the Environment Act 1995 s.57, which introduced into the 1990 Act a new Pt IIA dealing with contaminated land. The central planks of the Framework, which were mirrored by those of its Scottish counterpart, were said to be:

(1) The maintenance of the "suitable for use" approach, requiring remedial action only where the contamination poses unacceptable actual or potential risks to health or the environment, and where there are "appropriate and cost-effective means to do so, taking into account the actual or intended use of the site".

(2) To deal with "urgent and real problems, but in an orderly and controlled fashion with which the economy at large and individual business and land-owners can cope".

(3) The creation of greater clarity and certainty than the law currently provides, so as to assist in the development of an efficient market in land which is contaminated and in land which has been subject to remedial works.

(4) Replacing the existing statutory nuisance powers, which "have provided an essentially sound basis for dealing with contaminated land", with a modern, specific contaminated land power. Here the position in Scotland differed, and the *Outcome of Review* indicated that the introduction of the contaminated land regime was to coincide with the extension to Scotland of the statutory nuisance provisions already existing in England and Wales, replacing existing provisions. This extension is achieved by s.107 of and Sch.17 to the Environment Act 1995.

2.10   Time will no doubt tell to what extent the actual drafting of the relevant provisions achieves those objectives. At the date of this second edition of the work, there have been only two cases which have reached the higher courts on the construction and operation of Pt IIA.[6] Substantial amendments were made to the provisions during the Parliamentary process, in response to concerns expressed by the industrial, financial, land-owning and legal communities. Taken together, these amendments have had the effect of mitigating somewhat the harshness of the proposed liability regime and perhaps making its provisions more palatable. Nonetheless, the fact remains that the new sections constitute a regime of strict and retroactive liability for historic contamination, and that liability can extend in certain circumstances not only to the original polluter, but also to an "innocent" landowner or occupier.

2.11   As mentioned throughout this work, much reliance is placed on Government guidance as a means of mitigating the potentially harsher elements in operation of the legislation, for example what degree of contamination or risk is sufficient to justify action, and how liability is to be apportioned between a number of potentially liable parties. At the time of the passage of the 1995 Act, none of this guidance was in final form, and much had not emerged even in draft. The shape of the guidance was only to become clear over the next five years.

Uncertainties after enactment

2.12 The heavy dependence of the new regime on statutory guidance for such fundamental questions as what constitutes contaminated land and how liability for clean-up is to be allocated and apportioned, meant that

---

[6] *Circular Facilities London Ltd v Sevenoaks DC* [2005] EWHC 865; [2005] Env. LR 35 (see para.5.33); and *R (on the application of National Grid Gas Plc, formerly Transco Plc) v Environment Agency* [2007] UKHL 30 (see para.5.65).

implementation was unlikely to be rapid or straightforward. It certainly proved to be neither. Various informal consultations took place on draft statutory guidance, which was ultimately issued for formal consultation in September 1996. In the meantime, the Royal Commission on Environmental Pollution published its Nineteenth Report, Sustainable Use of Soil[7] which included consideration of contaminated land issues, and the House of Commons Environment Select Committee published a short report on the new legislation.[8] A research project was commissioned by the Department of Environment to assess how the draft Guidance would work in practice[9] and various seminars with interested parties took place.

Further progress was halted temporarily by the 1997 General Election, **2.13** followed by a period during which the new Administration considered whether the legislation enacted by its predecessor did indeed provide "broadly the right framework" for the future,[10] concluding that it did.[11] However, it was announced in December 1997, by way of letter from the Minister for the Environment to the Chairman of the House of Commons Select Committee, that there were a number of "points of detail" (some quite substantial) where changes to the approach in the draft guidance could be expected.[12] The question of resources also became involved, with the cost of implementing the new duties on enforcing authorities being addressed as part of the 1997–1998 Comprehensive Spending Review, the results of which were announced in July 1998.[13] The outcome was provision of £14 million for implementation of Pt IIA by local authorities in 1999–2000, rising to £18 million for each of the following two years. Sums of £14 million (1999–2000), £15 million (2000–2001) and £15 million (2001–2002) were allocated for capital funding on contaminated land. The Environment Agency was allocated £13 million additional funding over the three years, at least in part to support its role in dealing with "special sites" and providing technical guidance to local authorities. A selective consultation exercise on the revised draft guidance followed in October 1998, on substantive and presentational changes to the 1996 version. It was, however, not until October 1999 that the Government proceeded to formal consultation on the full package of statutory guidance, regulations and associated material, with the intention of bringing the new regime into force from April 1, 2000.

The scheme of the legislation

The provisions of Pt IIA follow a sequence from the initial identification of **2.14** contaminated land to securing its remediation. The relevant sections are as follows:

[7] Royal Commission on Environmental Pollution. *19th Report Sustainable Use of Soil*. Cm. 3165, 1996.
[8] House of Commons Select Committee on the Environment. *Second Report on Contaminated Land*. Session 1996/97,HC 22–I, December 11, 1996.
[9] *A Study of the Effectiveness of the Liability Regime in the Draft Statutory Guidance on Contaminated Land*, Stanger Science and Simmons & Simmons, March 1997.
[10] Department of the Environment, Transport and the Regions, News Release 539, December 22, 1997.
[11] See *Hansard*, HC Written Answer, December 22, 1997, col.439.
[12] The letter is summarised in Environmental Law Bulletin No.42, (London: Sweet & Maxwell, February 1998) p.22.
[13] *Comprehensive Spending Review 1997–1998*. Chancellor of the Exchequer, July 1998. Cm. 4011.

Section 78A—Definitions.

Section 78B—Duty of local authorities to inspect their area to identify contaminated land, and notification to relevant persons.

Section 78C—Identification and designation of "special sites".

Section 78D—Referral of disputed decisions as to whether land is a "special site" to the Secretary of State.

Section 78E—Duty to require the remediation of contaminated land by service of a "remediation notice".

Section 78F—Determination of who is the appropriate person to bear responsibility for remediation.

Section 78G—Grant of rights of entry or other rights for the purpose of complying with a remediation notice, and compensation for the grant of such rights.

Section 78H—Restrictions and prohibitions on service of a remediation notice.

Section 78J—Restrictions on liability in relation to pollution of controlled waters and water from abandoned mines.

Section 78K—Provisions with respect to contaminating substances which escape to other land.

Section 78L—Appeals against remediation notices.

Section 78M—Offences of non-compliance with a remediation notice.

Section 78N—Powers of enforcing authorities themselves to carry out remediation.

Section 78P—Powers for enforcing authorities to recover and secure their costs incurred in carrying out remediation under s.78N.

Section 78Q—Procedures relating to special sites.

Section 78R—Public registers.

Section 78S—Exclusion from registers of information affecting national security.

Section 78T—Exclusion from registers of commercially confidential information.

Section 78U—Publication by the Environment Agencies of reports on the state of contaminated land.

Section 78V—Provision of site-specific guidance by the Environment Agencies.

Section 78W—Provision of guidance to the Agencies by the Secretary of State.

Section 78X—Miscellaneous supplementary provisions dealing with sites having a combined effect, land outside the area of a local authority which affects its own area, and the protection of insolvency practitioners.

Section 78Y—Application of provisions to the Scilly Isles.

Section 78YA—Procedures for the issue of guidance by the Secretary of State.

Section 78YB—Interaction of contaminated land provisions and other provisions relevant to contaminated land.

Section 78YC—Application of provisions to harm caused by radioactivity.

However, these statutory provisions are in many senses only the starting **2.15** point. The Contaminated Land (England) Regulations 2006 deal with various important procedural matters, including the content and service of remediation notices and the appeals process. The vast DETR Circular 01/2006, Contaminated Land (September 2006)[14] is also vital to the working of the new regime. It contains some six Annexes, the most important of which is Annex 3. This contains the statutory guidance in accordance with which enforcing authorities are required to act. Annex 1 comprises a general statement of Government policy, Annex 2 a description of the new regime, and Annex 4 a guide to the Regulations. Annex 5 is a brief guide to the commencement order, and Annex 6 is a glossary of the somewhat arcane terminology of Pt IIA and the Guidance.

Relationship of Part IIA and previous law

During the passage of the 1995 Act, the Government was anxious to stress **2.16** on a number of occasions that the provisions on contaminated land were not intended to create new categories of liability, and simply reflected the pattern of powers and duties under previous law, most notably statutory nuisance.[15] Certainly the scheme of liability bears many striking similarities to that for statutory nuisance, with the primary responsibility resting with the originator of the contamination (the person "responsible for the nuisance") and residual liability with the current owner or occupier. Whether it was wise to frame legislation intended to deal with the complex issues presented by contaminated land on the basis of a statutory nuisance code remains open to doubt.

---

[14] Replacing Circular 02/2000, which was issued when the regime came into force.
[15] See, for example, *Hansard*, HL Vol.560, col.1461; and *Hansard*, HL Vol.562, col.1054.

2.17   Specifically, steps have been taken to restrict liability where the harm or risk presented by the contaminated land takes the form of water pollution.[16] Here liability does not extend to the owner or occupier purely in their capacity as owner or occupier; this accords broadly with the position under s.161 of the Water Resources Act 1991 (or, in Scotland, under s.46 of the Control of Pollution Act 1974) which refers to those causing or knowingly permitting pollution but not to the owner or occupier.[17] Similarly, restrictions apply in relation to remediation in respect of water from abandoned mines, so as to reflect the position under the Water Resources Act 1991 (or, in Scotland, under the Control of Pollution Act), as modified by the Environment Act 1995.

2.18   Indeed, the then Conservative Government could with some justice point out that there were safeguards such as the requirements for consultation before service of a notice, the role of Government guidance and the provisions on financial hardship, which made Pt IIA preferable to statutory nuisance from the perspective of anyone facing potential liability.[18] There is also no provision in Pt IIA corresponding to that in s.82 of the 1990 Act, which permits any person aggrieved by the existence of a statutory nuisance to take proceedings by way of complaint direct to a magistrates court. Similarly, the line taken in Annex 1 of the Circular is that although Pt IIA is new, it largely replaces existing regulatory powers and duties, with their origins in the mid-nineteenth century legislation which created the concept of statutory nuisance.[19]

2.19   Despite these similarities and safeguards, Pt IIA cannot with entire credibility be presented as nothing more than a mere extension to the ambit of previous law. The new provisions on liability exist within an overarching framework of statutory duties to seek out, identify, prioritise and remediate contaminated land as such. If those duties are not performed, or are perceived by local residents or an environmental group as being performed inadequately, they may well provide the basis for actual or threatened judicial review proceedings. Overall, it seems unlikely simply to be "business as usual" so far as contaminated land is concerned.[20] This was certainly the view of Baroness Hilton of Eggardon in debate on the Bill:

> "For the first time local authorities will have an explicit duty to inspect their areas in order to identify contaminated land. The existing provisions, which are much more vague and tenuous, require only that they identify nuisances."[21]

2.20   One measure of the significance of this new explicit duty is to consider the extent to which local authorities had in place active programmes to identify contaminated land prior to the introduction of the regime. A

---

[16] 1990 Act s.78J.

[17] See House of Commons Standing Committee B, May 23, 1995, col.354.

[18] See *Hansard*, HL Vol.56, col.1055.

[19] Annex 1, para.23.

[20] The duty to inspect has been described as "undoubtedly an innovation [which] . . . if duly observed, will lead to the realisation of liabilities which might otherwise have remained notional". Christopher Miller, *Environmental Rights: Critical Perspectives* (London; Routledge 1998), p.156.

[21] *Hansard*, HL Vol.565, col.1499.

survey of local authorities in England and Wales by the Chartered Institute of Environmental Health (CIEH), to which 303 out of a total of 405 responded, indicated that only 64 out of the 303 respondents had such a programme in 1993–1994.[22]

Broader policy context

One of the problems of a regime which takes as long as Pt IIA to come into **2.21** force, is that in the meantime the overall policy context may have moved on. This is reflected in the statement of Government policy which forms Annex 1 to the Circular. This statement seeks to set the new provisions in the overall context of current Government thinking on sustainable development. As para.6 points out, the existence of contamination presents its own risks to sustainable development:

(a) it impedes social progess, depriving local people of a clean and healthy environment;

(b) it threatens wider damage to the environment and to wildlife;

(c) it inhibits the prudent use of land, in particular by obstructing the recycling of previously developed land and increasing development pressures on greenfield areas; and

(d) the cost of remediation represents a high burden on companies, home and land owners, and the economy as a whole.

The Government's stated objectives, set out at para.7 of Annex 1, are **2.22** threefold:

(a) to identify and remove unacceptable risks to human health and the environment;

(b) to seek to bring damaged land back into beneficial use; and

(c) to seek to ensure that the cost burdens faced by individuals, companies and society as a whole are proportionate, manageable and economically sustainable.

These three objectives feed into the "suitable for use" approach, which the Government considers the most appropriate way to achieve sustainable development in this field.

The suitable for use approach

Annex 1 to the Circular goes on to describe the "suitable for use" approach **2.23** as based on a site-specific assessment of risk. Paragraph 10 ascribes to it three distinct elements:

---

[22] Chartered Institute of Environmental Health, *Report on Environmental Health*, 1993/1994.

(a) Ensuring that land is suitable for its current use, so that the acceptability or otherwise of the risks presented by the land are assessed on the basis of its current use and circumstances. The use of the word "circumstances" is important here, since land can present risks to vulnerable targets offsite, regardless of what use the land itself happens to be put.

(b) Ensuring the land is made suitable for any new use, as planning permission is given for such use. This is primarily the role of the planning and building control systems rather than Pt IIA.

(c) Limiting requirements for remediation to the work necessary to prevent unacceptable risks to human health or the environment in relation to the current use or any future use for which planning permission is being sought. This approach, of relating risk to actual rather than hypothetical uses, is distinguished from the "multifunctionality" approach, of seeking to clean up land to a standard suitable for the most sensitive uses. That approach risks carrying out premature work (so distorting priorities) or unnecessary work (so wasting resources).

2.24 The thrust of the approach is therefore to avoid wasting resources by cleaning up land so as to make it fit for any purpose for which it might conceivably be needed in future. At one level, this is about risk assessment, but more fundamentally it is about the differing philosophical approaches of pragmatically doing enough for present purposes as against a complete and comprehensive solution here and now. The difficulty with the latter approach is partly one of uncertainty as to whether such complete solutions can ever be achieved at all, and partly one of sheer expense, as countries which have taken that approach have found.

2.25 Annex 1 indicates that there is an exception to the "suitable for use" approach, which applies where contamination has resulted from a specific breach of an environmental licence or permit. In such circumstances it will generally be appropriate for the polluter to remove the contamination completely (para.15). Otherwise the regulatory regimes which are aimed at preventing new contamination would be undermined.[23]

Objectives of the new regime

2.26 The Government's primary objectives for introducing the new regime, set out at para.26 of Annex 1 to the Circular, are:

(a) improving the focus and transparency of the controls, and ensuring authorities take a strategic approach to the problem;

(b) enabling all problems resulting from contamination to be handled as part of the same process, rather than by separate regulatory action to protect human health and the water environment;

---

[23] See further paras 3.77–3.79 on cases where remediation may be required by permit.

    (c) increasing the consistency of approach taken by different author-
        ities; and

    (d) providing a more tailored regulatory mechanism, including lia-
        bility rules, which is better able to reflect the complexity and
        range of circumstances found on individual sites.

To achieve most, if not all of these objectives, the Guidance is essential, as
providing a detailed set of principles or rules to be applied to the individual
circumstances of each site.

An important secondary objective of the creation of a detailed liability **2.27**
framework is to encourage voluntary remediation. The Government wishes
to see 60 per cent of new housing built on previously developed land. The
hope is that landowners and investors, faced with a clearer liability regime,
will be able to assess the likely requirements of the enforcement authorities and make their own plans to carry out remediation in advance of
regulatory intervention. Such plans may well involve redevelopment in
order to provide the funds to meet the costs of clean up.[24]

These aims of the Labour Government in bringing the legislation into **2.28**
effect are, it will be appreciated, not widely different from the aims of the
previous Conservative Government in enacting it, as described above. It is
however important to keep these general policy statements in perspective.
What matters ultimately are the words of the statute, and of the Guidance
which has statutory force under it. How the present Government views the
objectives of legislation which it did not enact cannot affect the meaning of
that legislation as a matter of law; nor for that matter can the Guidance
promulgated by the present Government widen the ambit or alter the
effect of the primary legislation from which it derives its legitimacy and
force. Such policy statements do however provide the context within which
the legislation will operate and (subject to challenge on administrative law
grounds) will no doubt have an influence on the way in which decisions by
the relevant regulatory bodies are taken.[25]

A further political development between the enactment of Pt IIA and its **2.29**
implementation has been devolution for Scotland and Wales. The ministerial functions of making the regulations and guidance necessary to bring
the new regime into force and to determine its effect in practice rest with
Scottish ministers under s.53 of the Scotland Act 1998 and with the Welsh
Assembly under s.22 of the Government of Wales Act 1998. This has
resulted in separate Regulations and Guidance in Scotland and in Wales.
The text does not attempt to provide references in each case to the
Scottish and Welsh regimes; the detail of the secondary legislation and
Guidance is essentially the same (at least in present versions) as for
England. Where there are material differences, these are noted in the
text.[26]

---

[24] See further, Chs 16 and 17.
[25] On the approach of the courts to determining the meaning and application of policy, see
   James Maurici [1998] J.R. 85.
[26] For Scotland, see also the comparative material at Ch.25.

Outline of the effect of Part IIA

2.30 This Chapter concludes, by way of introduction to the more detailed analysis in Section 2, with a brief overview of the effect of Pt IIA.

1. *Background and Introduction*
   Part IIA of the Environmental Protection Act 1990 formulated a regime for dealing with the problems arising from contaminated land. It imposed duties on local authorities to inspect their areas so as to identify contaminated land, and creates a complex scheme of strict and retrospective liability for remediation of land identified as contaminated. Part IIA came into force in England on April 1, 2000 by SI 2000/340.

2. *The Ambit of the Regime: What is "Contaminated Land"?*
   The term "contaminated land" is used in a specific sense in Pt IIA. The definition is given at s.78A(2) and is based on two main criteria: significant harm and the pollution of controlled waters. In applying those criteria, to determine whether land is in fact contaminated, local authorities must act in accordance with guidance issued by the Secretary of State. The approach of the Government is based on the twin pillars of the "suitable for use" test and the application of risk assessment; this approach is reflected in the Guidance. The Guidance also introduces the concept of a "pollutant linkage", that is the relationship between the potentially harmful substances, available pathways, and vulnerable receptors. This concept is a recurrent theme in much of the Guidance.
   Certain situations are excluded from the Pt IIA regime entirely and as such are "off limits" to local authorities acting under those powers. These are, specifically, situations relating to processes subject to integrated pollution control, waste management licensing, fly-tipped waste, consented discharges to controlled waters, and radioactive contamination.

3. *Enforcing Authorities*
   The contaminated land regime is enforced by local authorities at unitary and district level, except for "special sites", where the enforcing authority is the Environment Agency or SEPA. The environmental Agencies have powers of direction on a site-specific basis in cases where they are not the enforcing authority. A strong level of central control is exerted through the ability of the Secretary of State to issue guidance which is mandatory in effect. Generally remediation notices are served by the local enforcing authority. Where however a "special site" has been designated, the notice is served by the Environment Agency or SEPA.

4. *Inspection of Land*
   Section 78B places local authorities under a duty to cause their area to be inspected from time to time for the purpose of identifying contaminated land and deciding whether, if it is

contaminated, it is a "special site". This function is to be performed in accordance with guidance issued by the Secretary of State.

5. *Identifying Land as Contaminated*

The process of inspection may lead to the local authority identifying land as contaminated land, in which case it must give notice of that fact to the appropriate Agency and to the owner, occupier and any other person who it appears may be liable for remediation.

The Guidance addresses the criteria for making that determination, and the process by which the determination is made. The determination must be made in accordance with that Guidance.

6. *Special Sites*

Certain types of contaminated land are required to be designated as "special sites"; the effect being that the Environment Agency or SEPA, rather than the local authority, is the enforcing authority.

The descriptions of contaminated land which are required to be designated as special sites are set out in the Contaminated Land (England) Regulations 2006. These categories relate to the presence of certain types of substance, or to certain types of use or occupation, or to certain types of effects, such as serious water pollution. The presumption is that these types of site are likely to present particularly difficult or serious problems.

7. *Relationship with Other Powers*

The application of the statutory duties on contaminated land should be seen in the context of other provisions which may have potential application to contaminated land situations. In particular, these are powers in relation to water pollution, statutory nuisance, and land use planning.[27]

8. *Remediation Notices: Introduction*

At the heart of the system under Pt IIA is the statutory duty to require the remediation of land which has been identified as contaminated, by service of a remediation notice. It is the remediation notice which states what should be done, and who should do it. The key issues are the determination of the remediation requirements and the "appropriate person" or persons to be responsible for complying with the notice. Remediation can include assessment and monitoring actions, as well as actual clean-up. Government guidance plays an important role in setting the remediation requirements, and a determinative role in deciding who should be liable and to what extent.

---

[27] See Chs 7 and 16.

9. *Consultation before Service of Remediation Notice*

Before serving a remediation notice the enforcing authority must reasonably endeavour to consult those who may be responsible for remediation. This requirement is coupled with a moratorium of at least three months following (in broad terms) the decision that the land is contaminated, intended to allow time for such consultation to take place. No remediation notice can generally be served within that period. Consultation and the three-month moratorium may be dispensed with where it appears that there is imminent danger of serious harm or pollution.

10. *Restrictions on Serving Remediation Notices and Procedure where a Notice Cannot be Served*

There are a number of instances where the enforcing authority is precluded from serving a remediation notice. These are set out in s.78H(5). Examples are where nothing could be required to deal with the contamination which would not involve unreasonable expense or where the authority itself would be obliged to carry out the remediation and would not be able to recover costs, e.g. on grounds of hardship. Where these circumstances apply, then the legislation provides for either a remediation statement to be prepared and published by the responsible person (indicating what is going to be done by way of remediation) or a remediation declaration to be prepared and published by the enforcing authority (indicating why the authority is precluded from serving a notice).

11. *Drafting and Serving Remediation Notices*

Unless one of the circumstances set out in s.78H(9) applies, the enforcing authority is under a duty to serve a remediation notice on each "appropriate person". The notice must specify what the recipient is to do by way of remediation and the period within which he is to do each of the things specified. The authority is subject to constraints under s.78E(4) and (5) as to what a remediation notice may require. By s.78E(6), the requirements as to form, content and procedure are otherwise as set out in Regulations.

12. *The "Appropriate Person"*

A remediation notice must be served on each "appropriate person", i.e. any person who should bear responsibility for any thing which is to be done by way of remediation in relation to the land in question. Who is an appropriate person is to be determined in accordance with s.78F, which contemplates two main categories of appropriate persons. The first category (described in the Guidance as "Class A") are the persons who have caused or knowingly permitted the relevant contaminated substances to be in, on or under the land. The second category ("Class B") comprises the current owners and occupiers; this category is only responsible where no person falling within Class A can be found. Once the appropriate persons have been ascertained then, if there is more than one such person, the enforcing authority will have to apply the rules on exclusion of persons from liability and on apportionment.

13. *Exclusion of Parties from Liability*

Where two or more persons are appropriate persons to be served with a remediation notice in relation to the same remediation action, s.78F(6) requires the enforcing authority to determine, in accordance with statutory guidance, whether any of them should be treated as not being an appropriate person in relation to that thing. The Guidance provides six tests for this purpose for Group A persons and a single test for Group B persons.

14. *Apportionment of Liability*

Where two or more persons are appropriate persons in relation to any particular remediation action, they shall be liable to bear the cost of doing that thing in proportions determined by the enforcing authority (and stated in the remediation notice) in accordance with statutory guidance. The Guidance deals with three separate issues: apportionment within a Class A liability group; apportionment within a Class B liability group; and attribution of responsibility between different liability groups.

15. *When the Local Authority is Itself an Appropriate Person*

A local authority may well find itself in the position of an appropriate person, either in relation to land which it has itself contaminated in the past (for example as a municipal waste disposal facility or transport depot) or as the current owner or occupier of land. Particular care is needed in such cases in relation to the legal framework, and in managing situations of potential bias or conflict of interest which may arise where the authority is also the enforcing authority for the purpose of Pt IIA. Such notices may be subject to appeal by one or more of the recipients, which may in turn lead to the remediation declaration requiring reconsideration.

16. *"Orphan Sites" and "Orphan Linkages"*

The term "orphan site" has no precise meaning and can encompass a range of situations. The basic concept is of a site in respect of which the necessary remediation works, in whole or in part, cannot be attributed to any appropriate person, thereby leaving remediation in the hands of the enforcing authority. The Guidance uses the term "orphan linkage" to describe the situation where either no owner or occupier can be found for some land, or where those who would otherwise be liable are exempted by one of the statutory provisions.

17. *Enforcement*

By s.78M, failure to comply with a remediation notice without reasonable excuse constitutes an offence. As well as prosecuting, options open to the enforcing authority include the use of civil proceedings, and carrying out remediation itself with powers of cost recovery and charging orders. In seeking to recover its costs, the authority must take account of the Guidance on the issue of hardship to the appropriate person or persons concerned.

18. *Appeals against Remediation Notices*

    A 21–day period is allowed by s.8L within which to appeal against a remediation notice. Appeals against all notices served in England or Wales now go to the Secretary of State or the Welsh Assembly. In Scotland appeals against notices served by local authorities go to the sheriff by way of summary application and those against notices served by SEPA go to Scottish Ministers.

19. *Challenging Remediation Notices otherwise than by Appeal*

    There is a statutory process for appealing against remediation notices. Apart from this appeal system, there may (depending on the circumstances) be the possibility of challenging a remediation notice by judicial review proceedings, or by way of defence to a criminal prosecution for alleged non-compliance with the notice or as a defence to subsequent cost recovery proceedings by the authority. However, there are a number of potential difficulties in relation to all of these alternative courses, which will need to be considered carefully by those advising the recipient of the notice.

20. *Registers and Information*

    Enforcing authorities are required to maintain public registers containing various information relating to their functions under Pt IIA. The duty is subject to restrictions on including information on two grounds: national security and commercial confidential information. Additionally, the Environment Agency/SEPA is required to publish reports on the state of contaminated land generally.

21. *Commercial Implications*

    Liability for contaminated land is not a new risk. Increasingly, it has been recognised as a factor in commercial transactions during the 1990s. The new regime of Pt IIA however heightens the risks and necessitates reconsideration of previous practices in terms of drafting contracts and other commercial instruments.[28]

---

[28] See Chs 19 and 20.

SECTION 2

PART IIA OF THE ENVIRONMENTAL PROTECTION ACT 1990

Chapter 3

INVESTIGATION AND IDENTIFICATION OF CONTAMINATED LAND

PART 1: THE DEFINITION OF "CONTAMINATED LAND"

Problems of definition and the "suitable for use" approach

In Pt IIA, "Contaminated land" is used in a particular sense—namely **3.01** whether by virtue of substances present, in, on or under land there is an unacceptable risk of harm. This immediately invites a number of questions, however:

    (a) Harm to what?

    (b) What constitutes harm?

    (c) What level of risk is acceptable?

    (d) Within what context is risk to be judged? The land in its current use, or likely future uses, or all possible uses?[1]

These are the issues which will need to be considered in relation to **3.02** specific sites within the framework of legislation and guidance provided by Pt IIA, and the answers to which may have very significant legal and financial effects. The Government's stated intention[2] is that the definition and supporting guidance are consistent with the "suitable for use" approach, which recognises that risk needs to be assessed on a site-by-site basis, and which limits remediation costs to what is necessary to avoid unacceptable risks.

On these principles, what matters is the current use of the land in **3.03** question, or the actual presence of vulnerable receptors. Where a change of use is proposed, the planning and building control regimes will continue to play a vital role. The focus is on the range of uses to which the land is actually likely to be put.

What is "contaminated land"?

"Contaminated land" is defined by s.78A(2) as meaning: **3.04**

---

[1] See the discussion at para.2.23 ff.
[2] DEFRA Circular 01/2006, *Contaminated Land*, Annex 1 paras 9–15.

". . . any land which appears to the local authority in whose area it is situated to be in such a condition, by reason of substances in, on or under the land, that:

(a) significant harm is being caused or there is a significant possibility of such harm being caused; or

(b) pollution of controlled waters is being, or is likely to be, caused;[3] and, in determining whether any land appears to be such land, a local authority shall . . . act in accordance with guidance issued by the Secretary of State . . . with respect to the manner in which that determination is to be made."

3.05   It will therefore be appreciated first that the definition is a technical one, and may well exclude land which in a broad sense would be regarded as contaminated. Secondly, Government guidance has a critical role to play in the determination of the issue. Effectively, the legislation makes an implicit distinction between land which is contaminated, and land which is so contaminated that it requires clean-up in the public interest.

3.06   It is also important to read the definition in conjunction with the supplementary provisions of s.78X, which allows the effects of two or more sites to be considered together, and which deals with the situation where land adjoining or adjacent to the boundary of the relevant local authority is contaminated.

The "pollutant linkage" concept

3.07 The concept of risk assessment is fundamental to the determination of whether land is "contaminated land".[4] In particular, the Guidance applies existing principles of considering whether there is a contaminant, a relevant receptor (target), and a possible pathway between the two.[5] The contaminating substances in question are the potential source of harm, and the receptor is the living organisms, ecological systems or property which may be harmed, or the controlled waters which may be polluted. The pathway is the route or means by which the receptor is being exposed to or affected by the contaminants, or by which it could be so exposed or affected. The Guidance states that the pathway may be identified on the basis of a reasonable assessment of the general scientific knowledge without the need for direct observation.[6] The source and the receptors must be specific and actual, not hypothetical.

3.08   The relationship between the contaminant, the pathway and the receptor are termed by the Guidance "a pollutant linkage". Without the identification of all three elements of a pollutant linkage, land should not be identified as contaminated.[7]

---

[3] This definition is subject to an amendment under the Water Act 2003 (not yet in force in England and Wales) which introduces a new second "limb" to the definition of contaminated land for the purposes of Pt IIA as being where "significant pollution of controlled waters is being caused or there is a significant possibility of such pollution being caused", see Water Act s.105(3)(5) and further para.3.66ff. below.

[4] DEFRA Circular 01/2006, *Contaminated Land*, Annex 3 paras A.9–A.22.

[5] DEFRA Circular 01/2006, *Contaminated Land*, Annex 3 paras A.10–A.21. See also the explanation at Annex 2 para.2.6.

[6] DEFRA Circular 01/2006, *Contaminated Land*, Annex 3 para.A.15.

[7] DEFRA Circular 01/2006, *Contaminated Land*, Annex 3 para.A.17.

The Guidance makes it clear that there may be more than one pollutant **3.09** linkage on any given piece of contaminated land.[8] This follows from the fact that a single polluting substance may potentially affect a number of different potential receptors, and may do so through various pathways. The situation can be made more or less complex by the specificity with which the source, pathway and target are described. The Guidance refers to this issue only briefly, stating that, for the purposes of determining whether a pollutant linkage exists and for describing such linkage, the local authority may treat two or more substances as being a single substance, in any case where they are compounds of the same element, or have similar molecular structures, and where it is the presence of that element, or type of molecular structure, that determines the harmful effect on the relevant receptor.[9]

This ability to take a broad approach to identifying the substance in **3.10** question may be helpful where compounds are present in a combination which together gives rise to a harmful effect which might not be caused by each separate compound in isolation. However, the authority is not required to take that approach, which may in some cases be unhelpful. A good example is the case involving St Leonard's Court, St Albans,[10] where the determination by St Albans DC in 2002 identified separate linkages for bromate and bromide, originating from the site of a former chemical works. Bromides are simple compounds consisting of a negatively charged atom of bromine, combined with a positively charged atom of some other element. Bromate (BrO_3) consists of one atom of bromine combined with three atoms of oxygen, and can be reduced to a bromide ion where the oxygen is lost. As events showed, it would not have been appropriate to regard bromide and bromate as a single substance, since the Agency's later decisions on remediation distinguished between these substances both in terms of identifying who were the appropriate persons and the relative priority of the substances as drivers for remedial action.

In relation to harm attributable to radioactivity, the Guidance suggests **3.11** that the authority may treat two or more substances as being a single substance, in any case where they contain radionuclides,[11] the rationale presumably being that it is the radioactivity rather than the chemical composition of the substance which is relevant. However, whether it is sensible to amalgamate substances in this way will depend on the circumstances, e.g. whether different persons are responsible for distinct substances containing radionuclides or whether different approaches to remediation would or might be appropriate.

Substances

The presence of a substance or substances is the starting point of the **3.12** statutory definition. "Substance" is defined by s.78A(9) as meaning: "any natural or artificial substance, whether in solid or liquid form or in the

---

[8] DEFRA Circular 01/2006, *Contaminated Land*, Annex 3 para.A.17.
[9] DEFRA Circular 01/2006, *Contaminated Land*, Annex 3para.A.18.
[10] See further, para.5.190.
[11] DEFRA Circular 01/2006, *Contaminated Land*, Annex 3 para.A.18A.

form of a gas or vapour". The definition is comprehensive, and could for example cover methane or other gases deriving from biological processes affecting degradable materials. In the context of establishing liability, s.78F(9) expressly contemplates the possibility that it may be the secondary substances arising from chemical reactions or biodegradation which in fact give rise to the harm.

3.13 It is also clear that no distinction is drawn between natural or artificial substances in the definition. This is of potential significance, since in some instances significant harm may be presented by naturally occurring substances. There is nothing in the legislation to confine its scope to substances which are present as a result of human activity, although in s.78F(2) the draftsman clearly had it in mind that someone would have caused or knowingly permitted them to be present. The point is of potential significance since the legislation "bites" first on an "appropriate person" who caused or knowingly permitted the substance to be present; but if no such person can be found, then the current owner or occupier may be responsible.[12]

Land

3.14 "Land" is not a defined term in Pt IIA, and so the definition in Sch.1 to the Interpretation Act 1978 will be relevant: this provides that land ". . . includes buildings and other structures, land covered with water, and any estate, interest, easement, servitude or right in or over land".

3.15 For the purposes of the above definition of contaminated land, "land" would in principle include the sub-soil to any depth; this could include disused deep mineshafts which may have been utilised for waste disposal or which may produce hazardous gases.[13] The issue of deep contamination arose in the parliamentary debates on the Bill, where the Government indicated that its intention was that in general, where contamination existed in sub-surface mine workings, it would be the owner of the mine or mineral rights who would be regarded as "owner" (and thus potentially an appropriate person) rather than the surface owner.[14]

3.16 River beds or ponds with contaminated silts would be included within the definition, as would the seashore, which for these purposes would fall within the local authority's area.[15] Accretions from the sea and into the sea (for example, reclaimed land) will also fall within the jurisdiction of the local authority in this respect.[16] Docks and harbours may be the subject of private Acts, which may make express provision to the same effect.[17]

---

[12] See Ch.5 generally.

[13] See for example *R. v British Coal Corp Ex p. Ibstock Building Products Ltd* [1995] Env. L.R. 277, a case on environmental information relating to the possible disposal of wartime munitions into a mineshaft.

[14] *Hansard*, HL Vol.562, cols 165–166.

[15] The seaward boundaries of local authority areas will in general either be fixed by local acts, or by reference to the limit of median tides, or by statutory instrument under s.70 of the Local Government Act 1972.

[16] Local Government Act 1972 s.72; see also *R. v Easington DC Ex p. Seaham Harbour Dock Co Ltd* (1999) 1 L.G.L.R. 327.

[17] *R. v Easington DC*, at note 16.

This definition of land also includes buildings and other structures.[18] **3.17** "Other structures" are presumably man-made by either building or engineering works, but would not appear to include plant or equipment which is not of a structural nature, for example oil drums or parked vehicles.

"In, on or under the land"

Contaminated land is often thought of as land where contaminants are **3.18** directly present in the soil or groundwater. However, the use of the words "in, on or under", combined with the fact that the term "land" can include buildings or structures, means that the definition is in principle sufficiently wide to catch substances present in underground or surface structures or containers, provided the relevant conditions of harm or risk of harm are fulfilled. Examples might include exposed and friable asbestos within a building, harmful substances within drainage systems, chemicals stored in corroded drums, or oil stored in a leaking underground tank. The corroded drums would not themselves be "land", but they and their contents are present on the land. What has to be considered is the condition of the land by reason of the substances present on it: does that condition involve a significant risk?

"Appears to the local authority"

The definition of contaminated land, with its use of the words "appears to **3.19** the local authority", seems on its face to be a subjective judgment for the local authority.[19] The appearance of subjectivity is deceptive, given the requirement to act in accordance with Government guidance as to the manner in which the determination is made, and the requirement to determine the key questions in accordance with such guidance.[20]

Harm

"Harm" is defined in s.78A(4) to mean "harm to the health of living **3.20** organisms or other interference with the ecological systems of which they form part and, in the case of man, includes harm to his property".[21] The question of whether or not that harm is "significant" is to be determined in accordance with guidance. The potential for harm is the subject of rather more convoluted wording: "there is a significant possibility of such harm (i.e. significant harm) being caused". The phrase "significant possibility of such harm" requires a judgment as to the degree of potential for harm. It is a different question from that which may arise in the context of civil

---

[18] See, e.g. Town and Country Planning Act 1990 s.331.

[19] The word "appears" indicates that something less than complete certainty may be sufficient—see *Ferris v Secretary of State for the Environment* [1988] J.P.L. 777, considering the word in the context of planning enforcement proceedings.

[20] 1990 Act s.78A(2).

[21] Where harm is attributable to radioactivity the definition extends to harm and the significant possibility of such harm being caused: the Radioactive Contaminated Land (Modification of Enactment) (England) Regulations 2006 reg.4. See further Ch.9.

proceedings as to whether the harm in question is too remote in terms of foreseeability. In any event, the question whether the possibility of significant harm being caused is "significant" is a matter for guidance—see s.78A(5)(b) discussed below.

3.21 The definition of "harm" set out above is important. The word "health" and "living organisms" are not defined, but could clearly include micro-scopic organisms which can be said to be "living". The definition goes on to deal with interference with ecological systems of which living organisms form part. Thus in particular the ecological systems supporting mammals, fish, birds, insects, and other fauna and flora would be included. However, the property contemplated in the section is specifically man's property; for example unowned property, the general natural or built heritage, or an area of outstanding natural beauty or nature conservation interest do not as such fall within this definition of "property". They may of course still be protected by the legislation in the sense of being the habitat or ecological support systems of plant or animal life.

3.22 "Organism" is a term used in biological science to denote animals, fungi and micro-organisms. As such it is a very broad term and will cover such organisms at all stages of development including embryos.

3.23 There is also the question of the scope of "other interference with ecological systems of which they form part". Such interference is clearly something other than direct harm to living organisms. It presumably includes interference which diminishes their access to breeding or feeding grounds in terms of area or of available fodder, or which affects their corridors for migratory movements. Whether that type of harm would be "significant" will depend on criteria set out in the Guidance.[22]

3.24 Where a natural habitat is protected under Community Law, either as a special protection area under the Wild Birds Directive 79/4009 or as a special area of conservation under the Habitats Directive 92/43, the UK is under a general obligation to take appropriate steps to avoid the deterioration of natural habitats and the habitats of relevant species at any stage of their biological cycle.[23] This may conceivably entail addressing contamination which is contributing to such deterioration. The relevance of European protected status to the "significance" of contamination is reflected in the Guidance.[24]

3.25 Government guidance does not deal with the definition of "harm". It is whether the harm is "significant" which the Guidance addresses, and in this respect it can provide for different degrees of importance to be assigned to different descriptions of living organisms or ecological systems or for certain such descriptions to be disregarded—see s.78A(6).

Significant harm: generally

3.26 The word "harm" is defined in s.78A(4), and the question of whether certain types of harm are to be regarded as "significant" will be deter-mined in accordance with guidance (s.78A(5)). However, without prejudice

---

[22] 1990 Act s.78A(6)
[23] See Habitats Directive Arts 1(f), 6(2) and 7.
[24] See paras 3.29 and 3.32.

to this general guidance, there may be further and more detailed guidance making provision for different degrees of importance to be assigned to, or for the disregard of:

(a) different descriptions of living organisms or ecological systems;

(b) different descriptions of places; or

(c) different descriptions of harm to health or property, or other interference.

The word "descriptions" in s.78A(6) presumably means "categories" as **3.27** described in the guidance. If the word "categories" is inserted in place of the word "descriptions" then this section becomes the more readily intelligible.

The Guidance seeks to identify and set priorities so that there comes a point at which the interference with the ecological system in question is so important that it becomes "significant harm", or alternatively it may require certain types of harm to be disregarded as being less than significant. The same applies to interference with living organisms. This is primarily an area for the environmental scientist and ecologist rather than the lawyer, and may turn for example, upon whether the living organism or ecological system would be capable, having suffered the harm, of renewing itself, or whether the damage would be irreparable and permanent; and if so, whether such loss is significant, taking into account other ecological systems of the same type which would not be affected. For example, if there are millions of beetles of a particular species within ecological systems throughout the country, damage to a few of their number may not be "significant" in the overall context. These are the types of issues which the Guidance is intended to address.

What harm is to be regarded as "significant"

What harm is and is not to be regarded as "significant" is to be determined **3.28** in accordance with statutory Guidance.[25] The relevant Guidance is given in the form of a table (Table A) which lists types of receptors and describes in relation to each those types of harm which are to be regarded as significant. The authority should regard as significant only harm which is both:

(a) to a receptor of a type listed in Table A; and

(b) within the description of harm specified for that type of receptor.[26]

The types of receptor listed are: **3.29**

1. human beings;

2. ecological systems, or living organisms forming part of such systems, within certain listed types of location, such as SSSIs,[27]

---

[25] DEFRA Circular 01/2006, *Contaminated Land*, Annex 3 Ch.A Pt 3.
[26] DEFRA Circular 01/2006, *Contaminated Land*, Annex 3 Ch.A Pt 3 para.A.23.
[27] Notified under the Wildlife and Countryside Act 1981 s.28.

national nature reserves,[28] marine nature reserves,[29] European Sites within the Conservation (Natural Habitats, etc.) Regulations 1994[30] or Areas of Special Protection for Birds[31];

3. property in the form of crops; timber; produce grown domestically or on allotments for consumption; livestock; other owned or domesticated animals; or wild animals that are the subject of shooting or fishing rights; and

4. property in the form of buildings.[32]

3.30 The types of effects which are relevant in each case are listed in Table A and are described generically as:

(a) human health effects;

(b) ecological system effects;

(c) animal or crop effects; and

(d) building effects.

3.31 In each case, it is clear that the intention is to confine the scope of the legislation to what are clearly, and by any standards, serious effects. So for humans, the types of harm in question are death, disease, serious injury, genetic mutation, birth defects, or reproductive impairment. "Disease" is to be taken to mean an unhealthy condition of the body or part of it, and by way of example can include cancer, liver dysfunction, or extensive skin ailments, but not mental illness, except insofar as it is attributable to the bodily effects of a pollutant on the person concerned.[33]

3.32 Ecological system effects means harm resulting in "an irreversible adverse change, or in some other substantial adverse change, in the functioning of the ecological system within any substantial part of that location". It also covers harm which affects any species of special interest within that location, and which endangers the long-term maintenance of the population of that species at that location. Additionally, in the case of a designated or candidate European Site, it covers any harm which is

---

[28] Declared under the 1981 Act s.35. Also covered are nature reserves established under the National Parks and Access to the Countryside Act 1949 s.21.

[29] Designated under the 1981 Act s.36.

[30] SI 1994/2716. This will cover European Special Areas of Conservation and Special Protection Areas. Candidate or potential areas which are protected as such under PPS9, on Nature Conservation are also covered, i.e. cSACs, pSPAs and listed Ramsar sites (see para.6).

[31] Established under the 1981 Act s.3.

[32] This includes any structure or erection and any part of a building, including any part below ground level; but not plant or machinery comprised in a building, see the Town and Country Planning Act 1990 s.336(1).

[33] The stress of living close to a known contaminated site has been shown to result in adverse impacts on stress levels and mental health in some cases, for example causing vulnerability to a range of disorders not specifically related to exposure to any chemical—see Judith Petts, Thomas Cairney, Mike Smith, *Risk Based Contaminated Land Investigation and Assessment* (Chichester: John Wiley & Son, 1997), p.13.

incompatible with the favourable conservation status of habitats at that location, or species typically found there. The enforcing authority should have regard to the advice of the relevant national nature conservation agency for this purpose, and to the requirements of the Conservation (Natural Habitats, etc.) Regulations 1994.[34]

3.33 In relation to animal or crop-effects, the issue is whether there is a substantial loss in yield or substantial diminution in value resulting from death, disease or physical damage. A substantial loss in value should be regarded as occurring only when a substantial proportion of the animals or crops are dead or no longer fit for their purpose.[35] For domestic pets, death, serious disease or serious physical damage is enough; loss of value is not relevant. A benchmark of 20 per cent diminution in value or loss in yield is suggested as indicating what constitutes a substantial diminution or loss, though this is not phrased in absolute terms.[36]

3.34 For building effects, reference is made in Table A to structural failure, substantial damage or substantial interference with any right of occupation. "Substantial damage" or "substantial interference" in this sense is said to refer to cases where any part of the building ceases to be capable of being used for the purpose for which it is or was intended.[37] This might cover the situation where, for example, a house becomes uninhabitable because of the risks presented by explosive vapours or gases.

3.35 It will be appreciated that contamination may have many adverse effects which will not fall within those categories of "significant harm". In particular, where property is concerned, actual physical harm or interference with enjoyment is necessary—the fact that property may be seriously and adversely affected by stigma or blight is not relevant. The Guidance makes it clear that "significant" harm is limited to the receptors and to the types of harm mentioned in Table A: for example, harm to ecological systems other than those referred to as "ecological system effects" should be disregarded.[38]

3.36 The Guidance again stresses the "suitable for use" approach in applying Table A, in that the authority should disregard any receptors which are not likely to be present, given the "current use" of the land, or any other land that might be affected.[39] "Current use" means any use currently being made or likely to be made of the land, which is consistent with any planning permission or is otherwise lawful under planning legislation. This principle is qualified by the Guidance in four respects[40]:

[34] Though it may be noted that these are regulations which modify various statutory regimes so as to give effect to the EC Habitats Directive , do not make express reference to Pt IIA.
[35] Food should be regarded as not fit for its purpose when it fails to comply with the provisions of the Food Safety Act 1990.
[36] See DEFRA CLAN 4/04 Contamination of Agricultural Land and Pt IIA of the Environmental Protection Act 1990 (August 2004) which points out that it will be a matter for judgment as to the scale at which the 20% diminution is to be assessed; i.e. the worst affected area or the whole field or indeed farm. It also points out in respect of loss of livestock that it would be very unusual for acute effects of contamination to result in a loss of 20% of a flock or herd.
[37] In the case of scheduled ancient monuments the test is whether the damage significantly impairs its historic, archaeological or other cultural interest.
[38] DEFRA Circular 01/2006, *Contaminated Land*, Annex 3 Ch.A Pt 3 para.A.24.
[39] DEFRA Circular 01/2006, *Contaminated Land*, Annex 3 Ch.A Pt 3 para.A.25.
[40] DEFRA Circular 01/2006, *Contaminated Land*, Annex 3 Ch.A Pt 3 para.A.26.

3.37   (a) Current use is taken to include any temporary use permitted under planning law to which the land is being put, or is likely to be put, from time to time.

(b) Current use includes future uses which do not require a new or amended grant of planning permission.

(c) Nonetheless, current use also includes any likely informal recreational use, whether authorised by the owners or not.[41] A prime example would be children trespassing on waste land. However, in considering the likelihood of such use, due attention should be paid to measures taken to prevent or restrict access.[42]

(d) For agricultural land, the current agricultural use should not be taken to extend beyond the growing or rearing of the crops or animals "habitually grown or reared on the land". This principle could prove problematic. It is possible that particular types of crops could be especially sensitive to certain types of pollution: an example would be tomatoes grown hydroponically which are affected by contamination of water. The hypothetical possibility of growing such crops ought not, it is submitted, to be regarded. But what if the farmer genuinely decides to start growing such crops, and they are actually affected? It is not clear why this harm should be disregarded simply on the basis that there has been a change in farming practice.

Significant possibility of significant harm: generally

3.38 The question of whether the possibility of significant harm being caused is itself significant is to be determined in accordance with statutory guidance.[43] The Guidance requires the authority to take into account the following factors in deciding whether the possibility of significant harm being caused is significant[44]:

(a) the nature and degree of harm;

(b) the susceptibility of the receptors to which the harm might be caused; and

(c) the timescale within which the harm might occur.

---

[41] On the basis of this test, the risks presented to unlawful residential occupants of contaminated land could be disregarded since this goes beyond "informal recreational use". This may be an area where the Guidance comes into conflict with the Human Rights Act 1998, since the right to life (Art.2) and the right to respect for home and family life (Art.8) are not dependent on the occupation of the land being lawful. See, for example, *Öneryildiz v Turkey* (2005) 41 **EHRR** 20 (European Court of Human Rights: Grand Chamber) considering unlawful slum-dwellers on a municipal refuse tip, killed by a methane gas explosion and landslip.

[42] Though not expressly stated, the likelihood of such measures being breached or circumvented should also be taken into account.

[43] The question of what is significant is essentially one of risk assessment, as to which see Ch.21 on Technical Issues.

[44] DEFRA Circular 01/2006, *Contaminated Land*, Annex 3 para.A.28.

The general principle stated in the Guidance is that the more severe the **3.39** harm would be, or the more immediate its effect, or the greater the vulnerability of the receptor, the lower is the degree of possibility to be regarded as significant. A relatively low possibility of harm might, therefore, be regarded as significant if it would affect a substantial number of people, or if it would be the result of a catastrophic single incident or exposure. The Guidance provides a Table which for various types of harm seeks to express conditions for there being a significant possibility of such harm.[45] These in turn, refer to notions of acceptability or unacceptability of levels of risk, either from exposure to toxicological properties, or the risk of harm by, for example, fire or explosion. For other types of harm, the proposed test is "more likely than not". In all cases, reference is made to the need to make the assessment in relation to relevant, appropriate, authoritative and scientifically based information.

Given that this assessment of the local authority is likely to be subject to **3.40** scrutiny and possible challenge, it is important that the authority is able to demonstrate how they have applied the Guidance in reaching their decision. The form of instructions to any consultants or other advisers will be vital in this respect.

Guidance on what possibility of harm is significant

The Guidance provides a table which in relation to the various types of **3.41** significant harm listed in Table A, sets out the conditions for there being a significant possibility of such harm. The authority should regard as significant any possibility which meets the relevant conditions.[46]

Table A subdivides human health effects into those arising from the **3.42** intake of, or direct bodily contact with, a contaminant and, secondly, all other human health effects (particularly by way of explosion or fire). For the first category the question is whether the intake or exposure would be unacceptable when assessed in relation to relevant information on the toxicological properties of the contaminant. Effectively, this requires risk assessment of the likely exposure and its effects, based on what is known of the toxicological properties of the substance or substances.[47] Such an assessment should according to Table B take into account:

(a) the total likely intake or exposure to the polluting substance or substances from all sources, including the pollutant linkage in question;

(b) the relative contribution of the pollutant linkage in question to the likely aggregate intake or exposure; and

(c) the duration of the intake or exposure resulting from the pollutant linkage.

It will be appreciated therefore that the issue is not simply the extent to **3.43** which the contaminated land may expose an individual to toxic substances—cumulative effects must also be considered. Toxicological

---

[45] DEFRA Circular 01/2006, *Contaminated Land*, Annex 3 para.A.28 Table B.
[46] DEFRA Circular 01/2006, *Contaminated Land*, Annex 3 para.A.30.
[47] Discussed further below.

properties are for this purpose stated to include carcinogenic, mutagenic, teratogenic, pathogenic, endocrine-disrupting and other similar properties.

3.44 For all other human health effects, the issue is whether the probability or frequency of occurrence of the significant harm is unacceptable, assessed on the basis of relevant information, and taking into account the levels of risk which have been judged unacceptable in other similar contexts. Weight should be given to cases where the harm would be irreversible, would affect a substantial number of people, would result from a single incident, or would be likely to result from less than 24–hour exposure. An obvious example here would be the risk of death or injury caused by an explosion from a build-up of landfill gas. The issue therefore is what is the scientifically-based probability of that consequence, and whether that level of risk is deemed "acceptable".[48]

3.45 For ecological system effects the test is whether the relevant harm is more likely than not to result, taking into account the relevant information for the type of pollutant linkage in operation, particularly in relation to ecotoxicological effects. This test then appears to be on the balance of probabilities, i.e. a chance of more than 50 per cent and as such a very different standard to the "acceptable risk" used for human effects. However, a second limb of the test is whether there is a reasonable possibility of such harm, and if such harm occurred whether it would result in damage to the features of special interest such that they would be beyond any practicable possibility of restoration. The data available on ecotoxicological effects is likely to be far from complete, and to involve many uncertainties.

3.46 For animal and crop effects and for building effects, the test is whether the relevant harm is more likely than not to result. In the case of buildings, the relevant period for that assessment is over the maximum expected economic life of the building.[49] No such period is stated for animal or crop effects (or for that matter, ecological effects). Obviously the longer the period in question the higher the probability of harm may such be (e.g. persistent exposure of an ecosystem to leaching chemicals).

3.47 As indicated above, in the case of human health effects, particular weight should be given to harm which is irreversible, or affects large numbers of people, or would result from a single incident such as fire or explosion, or from short-term (less than 24–hour) exposure. These criteria essentially go to the acceptability of risk, and are the type of circumstances which the public are likely to regard as particularly unacceptable in those terms. Paragraph A.32 of the Guidance requires that a similar approach be adopted for other types of harm, in that where the harm would result from a single incident or less than 24–hour exposure, the test of "more likely than not" becomes one of "reasonable possibility". Again, this accords with common perceptions of risk, in that most people would regard the reasonable possibility of their building being destroyed by an explosion as "significant", even if it were less than a 50 per cent risk. The cumulative effect of the terms of Table B and this aspect of the Guidance for non-human effects is a two-tier test: reasonable possibility for some types of harm, balance of probabilities for others.

---

[48] See further on risk assessment Ch.21.

[49] For ancient monuments, the relevant period is the foreseeable future.

"Relevant information"

Table B refers to taking into account relevant information for the type of **3.48**
pollution linkage in question. Paragraph A.31 defines such information as
that which is:

(a) scientifically-based;

(b) authoritative;

(c) relevant to risk assessment; and

(d) appropriate to the determination under the Guidance, in that it is
consistent with providing the level of protection from risk set out
in the Table B criteria. The issue of such information, in terms of
literature and numeric guidelines, is discussed below.

Possibility of harm and the relevance of the current use of land

When considering whether harm from contaminants is a possibility it is **3.49**
vital to be clear as to the circumstances and assumptions against which the
determination is being made. In particular, is the possibility to be taken
into account that the current use of the land (or of adjoining land) may
change in such a way as to increase or decrease the risk of harm? The
Guidance seeks to answer this question in a number of ways. First,
receptors which are not present or likely on land in its current use are to
be disregarded.[50] Secondly, in considering the timescale within which harm
might occur, the authority is to take into account any evidence that the
current use of the land will cease in the foreseeable future.[51] Thirdly, the
possibility of significant harm being caused as a result of a use of any land
which is not the current use is not to be regarded as significant.[52] Fourthly,
in considering future uses, the assumption should be that any future use
will be in accordance with any extant planning permission: accordingly it
should be assumed that any remediation required by planning conditions
will be carried out, and that the planning authority will exercise any
powers of approval under the conditions to ensure adequate remediation.[53]

The intention behind these statements is to avoid arguments that land **3.50**
should be judged as contaminated (and accordingly cleaned up) if it fails to
meet standards based on highly-sensitive hypothetical end uses. Consequently it becomes crucial to define clearly what is meant by "current use",
as explained above, both for the contaminated land itself and for any
adjoining land which may be affected. Uses which would require any new
or amended grant of planning permission will in general fall outside the
definition of "current use" in the Guidance. The reasoning behind this

---

[50] DEFRA Circular 01/2006, *Contaminated Land*, Annex 3 para.A.26.
[51] DEFRA Circular 01/2006, *Contaminated Land*, Annex 3 para.A.29.
[52] DEFRA Circular 01/2006, *Contaminated Land*, Annex 3 para.A.33.
[53] DEFRA Circular 01/2006, *Contaminated Land*, Annex 3 para.A.34.

formulation is no doubt that if a use of land which is more sensitive than the current use is proposed, and requires planning permission, then under current policy such permission is not likely to be forthcoming unless the risks from contamination can be reduced to an acceptable level, and then only subject to conditions to ensure that the appropriate steps are taken. In some cases, development or a change of use may take place without planning permission (e.g. under permitted development rights) in which case such alternative use will be relevant.

3.51   The reference in the Guidance to the possibility that a current use of the land may cease in the foreseeable future sits somewhat uncomfortably with this reasoning: cessation of the use may or may not involve the extinguishment of existing use rights,[54] and if those rights are not extinguished there is no reason why the use should not be resumed at any time. Also, even where land has planning permission it may still be unlikely that the permission will be implemented because of access or infrastructure constraints, or restrictive covenants.

3.52   What the Guidance means in practice is that an adjoining landowner who is concerned that the development potential of his land is blighted by contamination on neighbouring land will find it difficult to secure the use of the Pt IIA provisions as a means of alleviating that blight, where receptors on the land in its current use are not affected. His redress, if any, will lie at common law.[55]

Risk assessment and generic guidance

3.53   Essentially, and at the risk of over simplification, there are two main approaches to assessing the risks of contaminated land: generic and site-specific.[56] The generic approach involves the use of numerical values set by an authoritative body and intended to assist the exercise of appropriate professional judgment. Such values have the advantages of being convenient and of aiding consistency; however they will not be available for all contaminants and cannot always cater for unusual circumstances such as mixtures of contaminants or high local background levels. If qualitative risk assessment involving such generic guidelines is used, then it is vital to understand the basis for those values and the assumptions within them which may be conservative or "worst case" in nature. Moreover, such an approach is unlikely to be acceptable as the sole means of making decisions on specific source-pathway-target scenarios under Pt IIA, and indeed confusion on the issue has contributed to delay in effectively implementing the new regime.[57]

3.54   Similarly, the approach of risk ranking or semi-quantified risk assessment, which involves a scoring system to give an indication (rather than an assessment) of relative risk is unlikely to be an appropriate method for Pt IIA, helpful though it may be as an aid to commercial decision making.

---

[54] See S. Tromans and R. Turrall-Clarke, *Planning Law, Practice and Precedents* (London: Sweet & Maxwell, 1991), paras 2.03 et seq.

[55] See Ch.14.

[56] Judith Petts, Tom Cairney and Mike Smith, *Risk Based Contaminated Land Investigation and Assessment* (Chichester: John Wiley & Sons, 1997), p.22; see also Peter E.T. Douben (ed.), *Pollution Risk Assessment and Management* (Chichester: John & Wiley & Sons, 1998), pp.91–201 and Ch.9.

[57] See para.3.249.

Site-specific or quantified risk assessment leans heavily on professional **3.55**
judgment as to what is an acceptable level of risk, involving as it does
choices on what assumptions should be made on matters such as exposure
periods, reference data on toxicity or cancer potency, risk estimation
models, and site data. Modelling techniques are sometimes used, but have
their own difficulties in terms of reliability. Risk assessment of contaminated sites is primarily an art which depends on professional judgment and
cannot be reduced to standardised instructions or guidelines.[58]

The requirements of the Guidance that information, in order to be **3.56**
relevant to the determination process, must be scientifically based, authoritative and relevant does not answer these questions in itself. The use of
guideline values is addressed further in the context of the determination
process itself. Paragraph B.48 of the Guidance requires attention to be
paid to the assumptions underlying any numerical values, any conditions
relevant to their use, and any adjustments that need to be made to reflect
site-specific circumstances.

Pollution of controlled waters

Under s.78A(2)(b), as currently in force in England and Wales, if pollution **3.57**
of controlled waters is being caused or is likely to be caused by the
condition of land by reason of substances present in, on or under it, that
land is contaminated for the purposes of Pt IIA. The question then is
whether the water pollution is being caused by the condition of land, which
as pointed out above, is defined to include buildings or other structures.[59]
This raises some interesting issues as to the relationship with powers
under water pollution control legislation. For example, if a spill occurs in
the course of handling chemicals and water pollution results, this will not
be within the definition. Equally clearly, substances leaching from land into
controlled waters will be within the definition. But what of the situation
where the pollution, or risk of it, stems from defective bunding, drainage
systems or other fixed structures? It could be argued that such pollution is
caused by a combination of the substances present and the defective
condition of the land.

"Pollution of controlled waters" is defined simply as "the entry into **3.58**
controlled waters of any poisonous, noxious or polluting matter or any solid
waste matter".[60] The pollution need not be "significant" in this context.[61]
"Controlled waters" are defined in s.78A(9) as having the same meaning as
in Pt III of the Water Resources Act 1991.[62]

The two definitions are similar in that they both cover:

(a) territorial waters;

(b) coastal waters;

[58] See Ch.21.
[59] See paras 3.17 and 3.18 above.
[60] 1990 Act s.78A(9).
[61] Although the prospective amendment in the Water Act 2003 will remove this, see
para.3.66ff.
[62] 1990 Act s.78A(9).

(c) inland waters; and

(d) groundwaters.[63]

3.59   Under s.78A(8) controlled waters are "affected by contaminated land if (and only if) it appears to the enforcing authority that the contaminated land in question is, for the purposes of subs.78A(2), in such a condition, by reasons of substances in, on or under it, that pollution of those waters is being or is likely to be caused". In respect of these subsections it is helpful to look at s.78J which deals with restrictions on liability relating to the pollution of controlled waters.[64]

In considering pollution of controlled waters under s.78A(2)(b) there is currently no need to show "harm" or "significant harm". The question arises, therefore, whether any degree of pollution is enough. As stated above, pollution of controlled waters is defined simply by reference to the entry of certain things into the controlled waters. In one case it was held that the offence of causing polluting matter to enter controlled waters was not committed by stirring up silt that was already on the bed of a river, so as to cause the silt to enter the water.[65]

3.60   The question of whether pollution of controlled waters is being caused, or is likely to be caused, is to be determined in accordance with the statutory guidance—see subs.78A(5)(c). The current guidance is, however, extremely brief on this issue, simply stating that the authority should be satisfied that a substance is continuing to enter controlled waters or is likely to do so, and that "likely" in this context means more likely than not.[66]

3.61   The case law on the question of what constitutes "polluting matter" suggests that the term is referable to the potentially harmful nature of the matter in question, not whether it had any demonstrably harmful effect on the controlled waters. Thus in *National Rivers Authority v Eggar UK Ltd*[67] discolouration of water by a visible but transient brown stain was held sufficient to constitute the offence of causing or knowingly permitting poisonous, noxious, or polluting matter to enter controlled waters. Similarly, in *R. v Dovermoss Ltd* the Court of Appeal rejected a submission that pollution must involve harmful effects and adopted the *Oxford English Dictionary* definition of "to make physically impure, foul or dirty; to dirty, stain, taint, befoul".[68]

3.62   The possibility that relatively minor levels of water pollution could trigger the "contaminated land" definition was addressed by amendments to that definition by the Water Act 2003.[69] In the period prior to

---

[63] Although groundwaters does not include waters contained in underground strata but above the saturation zone, see Water Act 2003 s.86(1), (2)(f). See further para.3.17ff, below.

[64] See para.5.135ff.

[65] *National Rivers Authority v Biffa Waste Services Ltd* [1996] Env. L.R. 227.

[66] DEFRA Circular 01/2006, *Contaminated Land*, Annex 3 para.A.36. An alternative approach is to focus on the seriousness of the results that might occur if the risk materialised. If that risk is sufficiently serious, then "likely" might mean simply "a real risk, a risk that should not be ignored": see *In re M (Minors)* [1996] A.C. 563; *R. v Whitehouse, The Times*, December 10, 1999.

[67] Newcastle-upon-Tyne Crown Court, June 15–17, 1992, unreported.

[68] [1995] Env. L.R. 258.

[69] Water Act 2003 s.86(1). See further, para.3.66ff.

implementation of the amendment, the Guidance points out that if the contamination is only slight, then the remediation requirements ought to be correspondingly low.[70]

Likelihood of pollution of controlled waters

The Guidance on the definition of "contaminated land" does not deal with **3.63** what is meant by the likelihood of pollution of controlled waters being caused, beyond saying that it depends on the authority judging it more likely than not to occur. However, more detailed criteria are set out in Ch.B of the Guidance, dealing with the determination process. Essentially, however, the approach is one of source, pathway and target, involving the mobility of the pollutant, the geological or other pathways to controlled waters, and the existence of any suitable risk management arrangements.

Water pollution which has already occurred

There is a clear distinction between land and water in Pt IIA, in that it is **3.64** water which is affected by the presence of substances in the land.[71] The statutory Guidance reinforces this distinction by stating that land should not be designated as contaminated where a substance is already present in controlled waters, entry into the water has ceased and it is not likely that further entry will take place.[72] For this purpose, substances are to be regarded as having entered controlled waters where they are dissolved or suspended in them, or if they are immiscible with water and have direct contact with it on or beneath the surface of the land.[73] "Continuing to enter" means any additional entry to that which has already taken place.[74] Accordingly, any determination should be based on the existence of substances in, on or under land which are continuing to enter controlled waters, or are likely to do so in future. The requirement to consider not only the present position but also what is likely in the future may serve to avoid the anomalous results which could occur with the status of land as "contaminated" varying according to whether the water table happens to be high or low at a particular time.

The practical consequence is therefore that the contaminated land **3.65** provisions will not apply to land under which there is contaminated groundwater, unless the condition of the land is making, or is likely to make, that contamination worse, or unless the presence of the substances in the groundwater means that the "significant harm" part of the definition is applicable. This does not mean that there is no way of securing clean-up of the groundwater: the provisions of ss.161 and 161A–D of the

---

[70] DEFRA Circular 01/2006, *Contaminated Land*, Annex 2 para.6.31.
[71] 1990 Act s.78A(8)
[72] DEFRA Circular 01/2006, *Contaminated Land*, Annex 3 para.A.37. The definition of ground-waters in this context is limited to water in the saturation zone. For the implications of this see para.3.71ff.
[73] DEFRA Circular 01/2006, *Contaminated Land*, Annex 3 para.A.38.
[74] DEFRA Circular 01/2006, *Contaminated Land*, Annex 3 para.A.39.

Water Resources Act 1991 may apply to cases where polluting matter is already present in controlled waters but where entry of pollution from the land has ceased or there is no likelihood that further entry will take place.[75]

The amended definition in respect of water pollution

3.66 As indicated previously, the "water pollution" limb of the definition at s.78A(2)(b) was amended for England and Wales by s.86(1) of the Water Act 2003 so as to refer to "significant pollution of controlled waters" and to the "significant possibility" of such pollution being caused. The issue of whether such pollution and the possibility of pollution are "significant" will fall to be determined in accordance with Guidance under s.78A(5)(a) and (b), as also amended. These changes will come into force on a day to be appointed. DEFRA guidance notes CLAN 3/04 (February 2004) and CLAN 5/04 (October 2004) indicate that the process of implementation would be staged, involving first the power to issue guidance, then consultation on draft guidance. This is still awaited. One key issue referred to in CLAN 3/04 and 5/04 is the relationship between new guidance and implementation of the Water Framework Directive 2000/60.

Scotland

3.67 The change has however already been made for Scotland and took effect on April 1, 2006.[76] It may be noted that the legislation as it applies in Scotland now replaces references to "controlled waters" in s.78A(8) and (9) with references to "the water environment", which is given the same meaning as in s.3 of the Water Environment and Water Services (Scotland) Act 2003, i.e. all surface water, groundwater and wetlands. The concept of a "wetland" is new and means: "an area of ground the ecological, chemical and hydrological characteristics of which are attributable to frequent inundation or saturation and which is directly dependent, with regard to its water needs, on a body of groundwater or a body of surface water". This in turn reflects one of the purposes of the Water Framework Directive at Art.1(a), which is to protect and enhance the status of terrestrial eco-systems and wetlands which are directly dependent on aquatic ecosystems.

3.68 Guidance on "significance" in this context for Scotland may be found in edition 2 of the Scottish Executive Guidance (June 2006) Annex 3 paras A.45–A.46. It may give some indication of how the guidance for England and Wales could be framed in due course. Paragraph A.45 states that significant pollution is determined "by assessing the potential for impact/harm/damage associated with the substance in the water environment". The pollution needs to be attributable to the pollutant linkage on its own, or where it contributes to significant pollution in conjunction with other sources, the land in question must be a material contributor to the resultant pollution of the water environment.

---

[75] As to the relationship between Pt IIA and the Water Resources Act 1991 provisions, see further, Ch.7.
[76] SSI 2005/658.

Paragraph A.46 of the Scottish Guidance requires the authority to have **3.69** regard to two matters: measures of significant pollution and the scale of pollution. The stated measures of significance are:

- whether there is a breach of, or failure to meet, any statutory quality standard for the water environment at an appropriate pollution assessment point. In the absence of any suitable UK or EU standard, other international standards can be used where demonstrated to be appropriate;

- whether there is a breach of, or a failure to meet, any operational standard adopted by SEPA for the protection of the water environment;

- whether the pollution results in an increased level of treatment for an existing drinking water supply to ensure it is suitable for use, and to comply with the requirements of Council Directive 98/83 on the quality of water intended for human consumption. The potential for an increased level of treatment must also be considered for future use in drinking water protected areas as defined in ss.6 and 7 of the Water Environment and Water Services (Scotland) Act 2003;

- whether the pollution results in an increased level of pre-treatment of water abstracted for industrial purposes;

- whether the pollution results in:
  - ○ deterioration in the status of a water body or failure to meet good status objectives, as defined in the Water Framework Directive 2000/60; and/or
  - ○ the failure of a Protected Area to meet its objectives, as defined in the Water Framework Directive 2000/60;

- whether there is a significant and sustained upward trend in the concentration of pollutants in groundwater being affected by the land in question;

- whether there is a material and adverse impact on the economic, social and/or amenity use associated with a particular water environment.

In respect of the scale of significant pollution, "to assist in determining a **3.70** site specific minimum threshold to filter out lower priority cases, and to highlight the most serious and pressing problems first", the Scottish Guidance requires that failure of the relevant standards be determined with reference to the following factors:

- the extent and longevity of the resultant pollution;
- the area/volume of water impacted;
- whether the period of time for which the water will be affected will be very short (e.g. hours, days, weeks compared with months, years, decades); and

- the characteristics of the pollutants such as persistence, toxicity, potential for bioaccumulation; also carcinogenicity, mutagenicity and teratogenicity.

Groundwater above the saturation zone

3.71 One change which has been made for England and Wales is that the definition of "controlled waters" at s.78A(9) now excludes from the definition of ground waters "waters which are contained in underground strata but above the saturation zone".[77] CLAN 5/04 suggests that the purpose of the amendment is ". . . to ensure that the regime deals effectively with situations where contaminating substances have left the surface of the land, are contained in underground strata, but have not yet fully entered the saturation zone".

3.72 What this would appear to mean in practice is that where contaminants exist in the subsurface but have not yet penetrated down to the saturation zone, and are not likely to do so, the "pollution of controlled waters" limb will not be applicable to any other groundwater affected, i.e. water which is present in the ground but above the saturation zone. If such contaminants affect or are likely to affect surface waters, e.g. by being washed out into a watercourse, then the controlled waters limb will be applicable to that extent.

3.73 The legislation does not seek to define the "saturation zone", nor does the Guidance enlarge upon it. The saturation zone or "saturated zone" is however generally understood to equate to the water table, that is to say the surface in an underground water body at which the water pressure is equal to atmospheric pressure so that water below is under hydrostatic pressure, or the level at which water will stand in a well or borehole.[78] Above this will be the capillary fringe, i.e. the layer in which water is held in pore spaces by the action of capillarity. There may be extensive amounts of water present in this zone; indeed the rock may be more or less saturated and the thickness of the fringe will differ according to the type of rock. The saturation zone or water table is of course itself not fixed and will vary according to factors such as rates of abstraction and recharge. By contrast, an aquifer, as defined in the Water Framework Directive 2000/60 (Art.2(11)) is simply a subsurface layer of rock or other strata of sufficient porosity and permeability to allow either a significant flow of groundwater or the abstraction of significant quantities of groundwater, and so in principle could include the capillary fringe. However, the Directive itself defines "groundwater" and "body of groundwater" as being water "in the saturation zone".

Cumulative effect of sites

3.74 It is possible that a pollution problem may be the result of the cumulative impact of contamination from a number of sites, in circumstances where it could not be said that each individual site would itself have a sufficiently

---

[77] Water Act 2003 s.86(2)(f), brought into force in England on October 1, 2004 (SI 2004/2528, art.2(q)) and in Wales on November 11, 2004 (SI 2004/2916, art.2(e)).

[78] Michael Price, *Introducing Groundwater* (London, George Allen & Unwin, 1985), pp.22–25. See further, para.7.52.

significant effect. Perhaps the most obvious example is where a number of sites together contribute to a critical load of heavy metals or organic pollutants to water.

Section 78X(1) deals with this situation by providing that where it **3.75** appears to a local authority that two or more different sites, when considered together, are in such a condition as to satisfy the tests of significant harm or pollution of controlled waters, then Pt IIA shall apply in relation to each of them whether or not they would be "contaminated land" if considered alone. It does not seem to follow from the section that they have to be dealt with as if they were one site; indeed they may not necessarily be adjacent. Rather the provisions of Pt IIA apply "to each of them", implying they may be dealt with separately.

Matters excluded from the contaminated land regime

There are other types of problems which are excluded from the contami- **3.76** nated land regime, so that they are to be dealt with by the appropriate enforcing authority under other powers. These in particular relate to prescribed processes, licensed waste facilities, fly-tipped waste and consented discharges to controlled waters. The local authority should be mindful of these exclusions in exercising its duties of inspection and enforcement. The authority will also need to bear in mind the issue of overlap with other powers.

Contamination from industrial installations subject to the Pollution Prevention and Control regime

Special provision is made in respect of Contamination caused by any **3.77** activities carried out at installations which are subject to the Pollution Prevention and Control regime under the Pollution Prevention and Control Act 1999 and the Pollution Prevention and Control (England and Wales) Regulations 2000.[79] Part IIA does not apply at all, and thus land may not be identified as contaminated or a remediation notice served, where significant harm or pollution of controlled waters is attributable to the final disposal by deposit of controlled waste in or on land and enforcement action[80] may be taken under the PPC enforcement regime.[81] In cases where the final deposit of controlled waste is not involved, a remediation notice shall not be served if and to the extent that the significant harm or pollution may be taken in relation to the activity to which the harm or pollution were attributable.[82] The corollary of this is that the Pt IIA powers will be available where the harm or pollution of controlled waters is not attributable to the activities which are subject to the PPC permit or where there is no applicable enforcement action which can be taken under the

---

[79] For further discussion of the PPC regime see Ch.10.
[80] "Enforcement action" means either service of an enforcement notice or the exercise of powers of the regulations to remedy pollution (s.78YB(2C)).
[81] 1990 Act s.78YB(2A).
[82] 1990 Act s.78YB(2B).

PPC regime.[83] The prohibition under s.78YB(2B) relates only to serving a remediation notice, not to the initial duty to cause land to be inspected. PPC installation sites have no immunity in that respect and may be identified as contaminated save in respect of finally deposited waste to which s.78YB(2A) applies.

Contamination from prescribed processes

3.78 Somewhat similar provisions to those precluding the operation of Pt IIA for PPC activities also apply to prescribed processes falling within Pt I of the Environmental Protection Act 1990 (integrated pollution control), though those provisions become less relevant as PPC supercedes IPC. Thus where contamination results from an offence committed by the operator of a prescribed process,[84] and the Environment Agency may exercise enforcement powers under s.27 of the 1990 Act, an enforcing authority is precluded from serving a remediation notice.[85] In that respect, the Pt IIA powers may be regarded as something of a "long stop" where s.27 powers are not available (which of course they generally will not be in relation to historic contamination). Note, however, that land may still be identified as contaminated in all cases of contamination caused by IPC processes.[86]

Licensed waste sites

3.79 Part IIA is entirely disapplied by s.78YB(2) in relation to land in respect of which there is for the time being in force a waste site licence under Pt II of the 1990 Act. The expression "site licence" covers not only licences granted under Pt II, but also those originally granted under Pt I of the Control of Pollution Act 1974 which were statutorily converted into such licences.

3.80 Not only is the service of a remediation notice prevented in such cases, but also the statutory duty of inspection does not apply. The rationale is no doubt that any problems from licensed waste activities are best dealt with under waste licensing inspection and enforcement powers so long as the licence remains extant.[87] Section 39 of the 1990 Act will prevent surrender of the licence until the Agency is satisfied that environmental pollution or harm to human health are unlikely. However, the contaminated land regime will apply to the extent that the relevant harm or pollution are attributable to causes other than:

    (a) breach of the licence conditions; or

    (b) the carrying on of activities authorised by the licence in accordance with the conditions of the licence.[88]

---

[83] DEFRA Circular 01/2006, Contaminated Land, Annex 1 para.49.
[84] Under s.23(1)(a) or (c) of the EPA 1990.
[85] 1990 Act s.78YB(1).
[86] i.e. it is only the service of a remediation notice which is precluded.
[87] Waste licensing is discussed at Ch.8 but it may be noted that many waste management activities will now be controlled as PPC installations, for example large landfill sites.
[88] 1990 Act s.78YB(2)(a)(b)

The effect of this rather complex wording is therefore that the contami- **3.81** nated land regime will apply to certain problems affecting licensed waste sites, in particular contamination arising from pre-existing activities, or from other sources than the licensed waste activities.[89] Thus the local authority as enforcing authority under Pt IIA will not be obliged to inspect licensed waste sites to discover contamination caused by the licensed activities: it will, however, remain under a statutory duty to inspect for historic contamination or contamination from other causes. An example might be a licensed transfer station or waste treatment facility which is located on a previously contaminated site: such land will enjoy no protection from a remediation notice by reason of its current licensed use.

Unlawfully deposited (fly-tipped) waste

Where waste is deposited on land except under and in accordance with a **3.82** waste management licence and in consequence the land becomes contaminated, it may be possible to require its removal or other remedial action under s.59 of the 1990 Act ("Powers to require removal of waste unlawfully deposited"). Section 78YB(3) provides that to the extent it appears to the enforcing authority that such powers may be exercised by the appropriate Agency, a remediation notice may not be served. The intention of the Government in giving precedence to the s.59 powers was to preserve for the benefit of innocent occupiers the defence provided by s.59(3), i.e. that they neither caused nor knowingly permitted the deposit of waste. However, one problem is that the applicability and efficacy of s.59 powers in relation to contaminated land is itself by no means clear.[90] In particular, the occupier of land who was not involved in the initial deposit may have a complete defence to any notice served under these powers, and the original "depositor" may no longer exist or may not be capable of being traced. In such circumstances, an owner of the land can be served with a similar notice.

It is worth noting that the scope for action under s.59 is at least in one **3.83** respect wider than Pt IIA, in that by s.59(7) action need only be necessary to remove or prevent pollution of land, water or air, or harm to human health: the issue of "significant" harm does not figure in s.59.

In order to come within s.59, the relevant contamination must result **3.84** from controlled waste having been deposited in breach of s.33 of the 1990 Act.[91] If this is the case, a remediation notice is precluded if and to the extent that it appears that s.59 powers may be exercised. The question is whether they may be exercised, not whether they are likely to be exercised successfully, nor which regime would provide the more expedient remedy.

---

[89] DEFRA Circular 01/2006, *Contaminated Land*, Annex 1 para.52.
[90] See para.8.37 below.
[91] A key question may be whether this is to be read as also including waste deposited in breach of the previous legislation, the Control of Pollution Act 1974, and the Deposit of Poisonous Waste Act 1972. It is a somewhat curious position if s.59 must be used (and Pt IIA cannot) to deal with contamination which may have occurred after May 1, 1994 (when s.33 came into force), whereas the opposite would be the case for contamination which occurred before that date but which was also in breach of the waste legislation which applied at that time.

3.85   The wording of s.78YB(3) is in that respect problematic. The enforcing authority under Pt IIA must act reasonably in deciding whether it appears that the s.59 powers may be exercised, not whether they should be exercised. On whom is the burden of proof that the land was actually contaminated by fly-tipping? It will almost certainly be to the advantage of the owner or occupier to argue that s.78YB(3) is applicable: indeed, if the section is widely interpreted, it would open up a very large gap in the operation of the Pt IIA regime, leaving the problem to be dealt with at the public expense either under Pt IIA or under the powers of s.59(7) to remove the waste and remedy the consequences of its deposit.

3.86   For example, take the situation where the enforcing authority discovers asbestos buried in a field; it is not known who placed it there. Under Pt IIA where the original polluter cannot be found, the owner will be liable. The owner however suggests that the asbestos must have been dumped there before he acquired the land, either by the previous owner or by persons unknown—it is therefore controlled waste unlawfully deposited on land and as such within s.59. If the enforcing authority accepts that this is the case, then by s.78YB(3) they cannot serve a remediation notice. A notice requiring removal of the asbestos may be served on the occupier by s.59(1) but in the circumstances any notice is likely to be quashed under s.59(3)(a) on the basis that the occupier neither deposited it nor knowingly caused or permitted its deposit. The waste regulation or waste collection authority will then be thrown back on their power to deal with the situation themselves under s.59(7): the waste not only becomes their problem, it also becomes their property on removal by s.59(9).

3.87   Further, although s.59 is colloquially referred to as relating to "fly-tipping", it applies to all waste unlawfully deposited, and is not limited to fly-tipping as commonly understood. There is a further possible argument that any spillage of material could constitute the deposit of waste, since once spilt the material is no longer usable.[92]

Consented discharges to controlled waters

3.88   Two main issues arise in relation to water pollution. The first is the relationship between Pt IIA and other statutory powers specifically related to water pollution.[93] The second is the relevance of the existence of consents to discharge to controlled waters. By s.78YB(4), a restriction on the content of remediation notices applies so as to prevent any notice requiring anything which would impede or prevent the making of a discharge pursuant to a consent under the Water Resources Act 1991. If the effect of a consented discharge from contaminated land is to cause significant harm, then the appropriate course will lie with the Environment Agency to exercise its powers to revoke or vary that consent.

3.89   Consents which may be relevant to groundwater contamination can also be granted under the Groundwater Regulations 1998.[94] Under reg.18, the Agency may grant authorisation for the disposal or tipping of List I or List

---

[92] See discussion at para.8.39.
[93] See Ch.7.
[94] SI 1998/2746.

II substances[95] in circumstances which might lead to an indirect discharge to groundwater. Similarly, under reg.19, activities on or in the ground which may lead to such discharges to groundwater, may be the subject of a notice by the Agency authorising the activity subject to conditions. Such authorisations constitute a defence of authorised discharge to offences under the water pollution legislation.[96] The same principle as in s.78YB(4) should presumably therefore apply to such authorisations.

Radioactivity

When Pt IIA was enacted, it was seen in principle as providing a suitable **3.90** basis for dealing with radioactive contamination, but recognised that changes to the detail of the legislation might be required to cater for the possibility of different technical issues arising. The solution adopted was that by s.78YC, nothing in Pt IIA was to apply to harm or pollution so far as attributable to any radioactivity possessed by a substance, except as provided for by regulations. Contaminated land powers under Pt IIA could be exercised in relation to other harmful properties of radioactive substances, for example, toxicity. Regulations have now been made to apply the Pt IIA regime, with modifications, to radioactively contaminated land.[97] This regime is discussed separately below.[98]

Civil remedies

Part IIA is concerned with the clean up of contaminated land in the public **3.91** interest, in the context of statutory public law codes. The enforcing authority represents that public interest, supported by criminal sanctions and administrative powers. However, as with statutory nuisance, the common law remains in place to provide remedies as between the parties to a civil suit[99]; the public law liabilities under Pt IIA must therefore be considered in that context. The damage from contamination may only come about when stricter regulatory standards are applied: the liabilities under Pt IIA may therefore be a trigger for civil actions which would otherwise not have been brought.[100] The Act is concerned with actual or prospective physical harm or damage, whereas often the concern of a landowner affected by nearby contaminated land will be property blight or diminution in value. The common law remains the appropriate redress (to the extent that it recognises such losses) for these concerns.[101]

Relationship to the identification process

The approach taken in the Guidance, which in turn follows the structure of **3.92** Pt IIA, is to give separate guidance on the meaning of "contaminated land" (Ch.A) and on the process of identifying land as contaminated (Ch.B). The

---

[95] These are the substances listed in the Groundwater Directive 80/68 and specified in the Schedule to the Regulations.
[96] Groundwater Regulations reg.14(2).
[97] See for example, the Contaminated Land (England) Regulations 2006 (SI 2006/1380).
[98] See Ch.9.
[99] Common law liabilities and remedies are discussed at Ch.14.
[100] See para.14.93ff.
[101] See, e.g. *Blue Circle Industries Plc v Ministry of Defence* [1999] 2 Ch. 289 (CA).

distinction is not watertight, however, and some aspects of the substantive definition are amplified or glossed in the guidance on determination. The essential point, therefore, is that Chs A and B of the Guidance need to be read together.

PART 2: ENFORCING AUTHORITIES

The enforcing authority

3.93 The general principle is that the task of identifying contaminated land and serving remediation notices falls to local authorities, defined to mean[102]:

    (a) unitary authorities;

    (b) district councils; and

    (c) the Common Council of the City of London and the relevant officers of the Inner and Middle Temples.

However, a different approach applies to "special sites" in respect of which a special procedure for designation applies[103] and for which the Environment Agency (or in Scotland, SEPA) is the enforcing authority.[104]

Site specific guidance by the Environment Agency

3.94 It is open to the Environment Agency to issue guidance to any local authority with respect to the exercise of performance of that authority's powers or duties under the contaminated land provisions in relation to any particular contaminated land; where such guidance is issued it must be considered by the local authority concerned in performing their duties or exercising their powers.[105] However, the guidance should be consistent with any guidance issued by the Secretary of State, and insofar as it is not, it must be disregarded.[106] The Environment Agency also has power to require the local authority, by written request, to furnish such relevant information as the Agency may require for the purpose of enabling it to issue site-specific guidance.[107] The information covers not only that which the local authority may already have received in the exercise of its functions under Pt IIA, but also such information as it may be reasonably expected to obtain under those powers.[108]

3.95 It is presumed that such site specific guidance was envisaged as involving guidance of a technical nature, but it is not specifically limited in that way, and could on its face extend to guidance as to how liability is to be

[102] 1990 Act s.78A(9).
[103] See para.3.321ff.
[104] 1990 Act s.78A(9).
[105] 1990 Act s.78V(1).
[106] 1990 Act s.78V(2).
[107] 1990 Act s.78V(3).
[108] 1990 Act s.78V(4).

allocated or apportioned. It seems somewhat unlikely in practice that the Agency would wish to offer guidance of that type. However, the ability of the Agency to give such guidance does in principle present an additional way in which a landowner or other potentially liable party may seek to challenge demands of local authority which it regards as excessive.

Where the Agency has given guidance which is incorporated in a **3.96** remediation notice and is then subject to appeal, the Agency will no doubt wish to participate in the appeal process in order to justify its position.[109]

Relationship of central and local regulatory functions: Secretary of State's guidance

As already stated, with the exception of special sites, it is at the local level **3.97** that the legislation on contaminated land is enforced. However, local enforcing authorities do not enjoy a measure of discretion comparable with many other local authority regulatory functions. An important feature of Pt IIA of the 1990 Act is the provision of statutory guidance by the Secretary of State[109a]; the local enforcing authority or the Agency then is required to act in accordance with such guidance.[110] In normal circumstances under other codes, Government guidance is one factor to which local authorities must have regard; there is accordingly an inherent discretion in applying such guidance. With the prescriptive guidance under Pt IIA the position is different; the only discretion is any which is built into the Guidance itself. The procedure for issuing such Guidance reflects its unusual statutory status, in that the Guidance is not only required to be issued for consultation before issue, but must also be laid before Parliament in draft for 40 days, subject to a negative resolution by either House that it should not be issued.[111] The issues on which such Guidance is relevant are:

3.98

1. Whether land is contaminated within the statutory definition.[112]

2. Whether for that purpose harm or the possibility of harm are significant.[113]

3. The inspection function of local authorities.[114]

4. Which of the two of more persons who may be "appropriate persons" to bear the responsibility for remediation is to be treated as not being an "appropriate person", i.e. exclusion from liability.[115]

---

[109] Failure by the Agency to participate may present procedural problems that are considered in para.6.51ff.

[109a] In the case of Wales, the functions of the Secretary of State were transferred to the National Assembly for Wales by the National Assembly for Wales (Transfer of Functions) Order 1999 No. 672, Art.2, Sch.1.

[110] For a discussion on this novel legislative technique, see L. Etherington, *Mandatory Guidance for Dealing with Contaminated Land: Paradox or Paradigm?* [2002] S.L.R. 23 at 202–226.

[111] 1990 Act s.78YA.

[112] 1990 Act s.78A(2).

[113] 1990 Act s.78A(5).

[114] 1990 Act s.78B(2).

[115] 1990 Act s.78F(6).

5. Where two or more persons are "appropriate persons" to bear responsibility, in what proportions they are to bear the cost of remediation, i.e. apportionment of liability.[116]

6. The inspection and review of special sites and termination of designation as special sites.[117]

3.99 In addition to prescriptive guidance, there is the more familiar type of guidance to which enforcing authorities must have regard: such guidance must be subject to consultation, but does not require to be laid before Parliament.[118] It covers the following issues:

1. What is to be done by way of remediation, the standard of remediation required, and what is or is not to be regarded as reasonable by way of remediation.[119]

2. Whether to recover all or part of remediation costs incurred by the enforcing authority from the appropriate person.[120]

3. General guidance to the Agency with respect to the exercise or performance of its powers of duties.[121] This provision does not apply to local enforcing authorities.

The guidance and its structure

3.100 The final statutory guidance is contained in the DEFRA Circular, 01/2006,[122] Contaminated Land. It is Annex 3 of that Circular which contains the statutory guidance, Annexes 1 and 2 and 4–6 containing explanatory material and a glossary of terms. Annex 3 is divided into five Chapters, each Chapter dealing with one aspect of the guidance:

Chapter A—the definition of contaminated land.

Chapter B—identification of contaminated land.

Chapter C—remediation of contaminated land.

Chapter D—liability exclusion and apportionment.

Chapter E—recovery of costs for remediation.

Land falling outside a local authority's area

3.101 In general, a local enforcing authority's functions relate to contaminated land within its administrative area. However, contamination is no respecter of local government boundaries, and land situated outside a local

---

[116] 1990 Act s.78F(7).
[117] 1990 Act s.78Q(6).
[118] 1990 Act ss.78YA(1) and (2). Guidance given to the Agency under s.78Q(6) also seems to fall into this category, though it is prescriptive in effect.
[119] 1990 Act s.78E(5).
[120] 1990 Act s.78P(2).
[121] 1990 Act s.78W(1).
[122] Replacing the original DEFRA Circular 02/2000, but making few changes of any substance.

authority's boundaries may represent a threat of harm within its area. An example would be the migration of landfill gas across a boundary so as to affect residential property. Another possible example would be a river which flows through the area of a number of authorities, which is affected by pollutants leaching from contaminated land upstream.

To deal with such problems, s.78X(2) states that where it appears to a **3.102** local authority that land outside, but adjoining or adjacent to, its area is effectively within the definition of "contaminated land" and the significant harm or pollution of controlled waters is or will be caused within its area, then the authority may exercise its functions under Pt IIA as if the land were situated within its area. The provision is stated to be without prejudice to the functions of the local authority in whose area the land is actually situated.

The relevant land must be "adjoining or adjacent to" the authority's **3.103** area. If the use of the two terms together were not sufficient to indicate that the land can be adjacent to an authority's area without adjoining it, then case law confirms this. On the meaning of "adjacent" it was said in one case that it "is not a word to which a precise and uniform meaning is attached by ordinary usage. It is not confined to places adjoining, and it includes places close to or near. What degree of proximity would justify the application of the word is entirely a question of circumstances".[123] In construing the section it should be borne in mind that where pollution of surface or ground water is concerned, contaminants can be transported for considerable distances. Therefore if the authority can reasonably form the view that significant harm is being caused in its area, or there is a significant risk of such harm, there is a good argument that there is sufficient proximity to satisfy s.78X(2).

As stated above, the power of an affected authority to take action under **3.104** this section is without prejudice to the functions of the local authority in whose area that land is in fact located. That authority may itself be required to take enforcement action because of harm or pollution within its own area. Indeed, there seems to be nothing in the legislation to limit the consideration by the local authority to harm or pollution within its own area. Accordingly there must be the risk of an appropriate person being faced with possibly conflicting remediation requirements by two local authorities. It is suggested that to avoid this situation, any authority considering exercising its powers under s.78X(2) should as a matter of good practice consult the local authority in whose area the relevant land is located.

---

[123] *Wellington v Lower Hutt* [1904] A.C. 733, in which two New Zealand boroughs were held to be adjacent for the purpose of making statutory contributions to the cost of building a bridge, despite being nowhere closer to each other than six miles apart); see also *Stanward Corp v Denison Mines Ltd* 67 DLR (2d) 743, in which a similar approach was taken but two mining claims one and a quarter miles apart were held not to be adjacent. In Scotland, it has similarly been held that the word does not require actual contact: *Anderson v Lochgelly Iron & Coal Ltd* (1904) 7F.187, where an accident which took place on a private railway connecting a mine to the public railway some 800 yards from the mine was held (with the Lord Justice Clerk dissenting) to be "adjacent to the mine" in terms of the statutory definition in the Coal Mines Regulation Act 1887; see also *Dunbeath Estate Ltd v Henderson* 1989 SLT (Land Ct.) 99.

3.105 As a matter of practice it may be wise for local authorities in setting up their procedures under Pt IIA to arrange for the establishment of a cross-boundary joint liaison sub-committee with neighbouring authorities, in anticipation of this eventuality.[124] This may also present the possibility of the sharing of costs of investigation, thereby allowing financial savings.

Delegation of functions and contamination straddling boundaries

3.106 Delegation of an enforcing authority's functions under Pt IIA will be important in practice, and may arise in two main contexts:

1. delegation to officers or committees;

2. delegation to other authorities.

3.107 With regard to delegation to officers or committees, s.101 of the Local Government Act 1972 gives the power for a local authority to arrange for the discharge of its functions by a committee, sub-committee or officer, but not the chairman of a committee alone. Decisions such as whether to serve a remediation notice may therefore be delegated, as may functions such as inspecting land, serving a notice, or taking enforcement action. In relation to the powers of entry and investigation under s.108 of the Environment Act 1995, there must be specific authorisation in writing to a person who appears suitable, to exercise the relevant powers.[125]

3.108 In relation to administrative matters, such as the preparation and issue of a notice, it may be the case that formal delegation is not strictly necessary on the basis of *Provident Mutual Life Assurance Association v Derby CC*[126] and other cases.[127] However, it remains desirable for the avoidance of doubt that standing orders should address this issue. In particular, because the Guidance within which the authority must act is so detailed and prescriptive, a court may well be persuaded that formal prior delegation is necessary.[128]

3.109 Given the legal significance and likely costs involved in identifying land as contaminated it seems most unlikely in practice that the relevant decision-making functions will be delegated to an officer. However, arrangements may need to be made for sub-committees to meet to deal with urgent cases, for example, an urgent action sub-committee. The execution of a decision, once made, is a different matter entirely, and local authorities will probably in practice leave the execution of matters such as the detailed preparation and service of remediation notices to their officers and staff.

---

[124] See also the issue of delegation, explained in the next paragraph.

[125] 1995 Act s.108(1).

[126] (1981) 79 L.G.R. 297, HL.

[127] *Cheshire CC v Secretary of State for the Environment* [1988] J.P.L. 30; *R. v Southwark LBC, Ex p. Bannerman* (1989) 22 H.L.R. 459; *Fitzpatrick v Secretary of State for the Environment* (1990) 154 L.G. Rev. 72, CA.

[128] See *R. v Edmundsbury BC Ex p. Walton* [1999] Env. L.R. 879.

The second issue involves delegation of the enforcing authority's func- **3.110** tions to some other authority. By s.101 of the Local Government Act, arrangements may be made for another local authority to discharge the functions; effectively, though not necessarily accurately, as an "agency arrangement". This power may be useful, for example where a contaminated site straddles the boundary of two local authorities, and it is desired that one authority should take the lead in dealing with it. The alternative is either to constitute a formal joint committee for that purpose under s.102 of the Local Government Act 1972, or alternatively to set up a joint liaison committee, which has no power, usually, to pass binding resolutions. One authority may supply professional or technical services, or the use of plant, to another under the Local Authorities (Goods and Services) Act 1970.[129]

Use of external advisers

The technically difficult nature of some types of problems arising from **3.111** contaminated land may mean that some local authorities, who have not developed internal expertise in this field, may need to rely on environmental consultants in order to fulfil their statutory duties under Pt IIA.

Whilst there is no objection to a local authority seeking advice from **3.112** external sources in order to enable it to make the necessary decisions, there are dangers in relying too heavily on such advice. This is particularly so where the functions involve making decisions of a quasi-judicial nature as to which party should be liable,[130] and to what extent, for the clean-up of contamination.[131] The incidental powers of s.111 of the Local Government Act 1972 will allow an authority to employ consultants as agents or contractors to provide advice or, indeed, to exercise functions on the authority's behalf.[132] The authority will not be allowed to delegate the ultimate decision-making power on whether land is contaminated, whether a notice should be served and on whom, to external consultants: the best course will be to use the consultant to obtain and present factual data, scientific conclusions, judgments and predictions, and make recommendations to the appropriate committee of the enforcing authority to allow the committee to reach its own decision.

One practical question is the extent to which consultants should conduct **3.113** actual negotiations with the owner and other potentially liable persons: the authority will need to make the scope of the consultant's brief clear in this regard. There should, however, certainly be consultation between the local authority's consultants and the landowner[133]; exchange of reports and other material may be more problematic and should be a topic addressed in the contract appointing the consultant.

---

[129] See *R. v Yorkshire Purchasing Organisation Ex p. British Educational Supplies Association* (1997) 95 L.G.R. 727, 732.

[130] Often the decision will be a mixed one of fact, scientific judgment, conclusions, prediction, and law.

[131] See *R. v Chester CC Ex p. Quietlynn Ltd* (1984) 83 L.G.R. 308, CA.

[132] *Credit Suisse v Allerdale BC* [1997] Q.B. 306 at 346 and 359.

[133] See para.4.09ff on the issue of consultation before serving a remediation notice.

3.114   The authority may also turn to the Agency for advice. s.37(3) of the Environment Act 1995 allows the Agency to provide advice or assistance as respects any matter in which it has skill or experience. Where a "special site" is involved, the Agency has of course a more formal role. The Agency has power to delegate its own functions to members, officers, employees, committees or sub-committees under para.6 of Sch.1 to the 1995 Act.

PART 3: INSPECTION

Local authority inspection: the duty

3.115 Under s.78B(1) every local authority shall cause its area to be inspected from time to time for the purpose:

(a) of identifying contaminated land; and

(b) of enabling the authority to decide whether any such land is land which is required to be designated as a special site.

3.116   In performing its duty under this subsection by s.78B(2) it is mandatory that the authority acts in accordance with guidance issued for the purpose by the Secretary of State. The relevant Guidance is to be found at Ch.B of Annex 3 to the DEFRA Circular, 01/2006. Government policy is that the approach should be a flexible one, which is proportionate to the seriousness of any actual or potential threat. The difficulty is of course that the object of inspection is precisely that of establishing the significance of such harm or potential harm: thus inspection should be seen as an iterative process during which such significance will become clearer and which will constantly require re-appraisal at each stage of the process.

Guidance on the strategic approach

3.117 Local authorities are required to take a strategic approach to inspection: this approach is to be set out in a written strategy. The approach is intended to enable authorities to identify, in a rational, ordered and efficient manner, the land which merits detailed inspection, identifying the most pressing and serious problems first and concentrating resources on the area where contaminated land is most likely to be found.[134]

3.118   The Guidance states that in carrying out its inspection duty, the local authority should take a strategic approach which should[135]:

(a) be rational, ordered and efficient;

(b) be proportionate to the seriousness of actual or potential risk;

(c) seek to ensure that the most pressing and serious problems are located first;

[134] DEFRA Circular 01/2006, Contaminated Land, Annex 2 para.3.3.
[135] DEFRA Circular 01/2006, Contaminated Land, Annex 3 para.B.9.

(d) ensure that resources are concentrated on investigating in areas where the authority is most likely to identify contaminated land; and

(e) ensure that the local authority efficiently identifies requirements for the detailed inspection of particular areas of land.

The Guidance also stresses the necessity to reflect local circumstances **3.119** (para.8), in particular any available evidence that significant harm or significant pollution of controlled waters is actually being caused[136]; the extent to which any relevant receptor is likely to be found in different parts of the area and is likely to be exposed to a particular pollutant in view of geological or hydrogeological factors; the extent to which information is already available; past contaminative uses in the area and their nature and scale; the nature and timing of any past redevelopment; previous or likely future remedial action; and the extent to which other regulatory authorities are likely to be considering such harm).[137] The geology and groundwater vulnerability of the area are also relevant and in this respect consultation with the Environment Agency is vital. The authority must also consult other appropriate public bodies, such as the county council (if any), statutory regeneration bodies, Natural England and the Food Standards Agency.[138]

The key point here is that there is no established approach for every **3.120** local authority. It would be reasonable for an authority in a traditional area of heavy industry which has been subject to extensive residential development to have an entirely different approach to identifying contaminated land to that of an authority whose area is a sparsely populated rural one. That is not to say that the latter case will not have examples of serious contamination problems, simply that the approach may be different.

Written strategy

The Guidance requires the formal adoption and publication of a written **3.121** strategy setting out an ordered approach to the identification of contaminated land.[139] Once published the authority is obliged to send a copy to the Environment Agency. The Strategy is to be kept under periodic review.[140]

While the detailed content of strategies varies considerably between **3.122** authorities and between different parts of their areas, the strategy should include a lengthy list of issues[141]:

(a) a description of the particular characteristics of the area and how that influences its approach;

(b) the authority's particular aims, objectives, and priorities;

---

[136] DEFRA Circular 01/2006, Contaminated Land, Annex 3 para.B.10.
[137] DEFRA Circular 01/2006, Contaminated Land, Annex 3 para.B.10.
[138] DEFRA Circular 01/2006, Contaminated Land, Annex 3 para.B.11.
[139] DEFRA Circular 01/2006, Contaminated Land, Annex 3 para.B.12.
[140] DEFRA Circular 01/2006, Contaminated Land, Annex 3 para.B.13.
[141] DEFRA Circular 01/2006, Contaminated Land, Annex 3 para.B.15.

    (c) appropriate timescales for the inspection of different parts of its area (no doubt related to those priorities);

    (d) arrangements and procedures for:

        (i) considering land for which the authority may itself have responsibilities by virtue of its current or former ownership or occupation;

        (ii) obtaining and evaluating information on actual harm or pollution controlled waters;

        (iii) identifying receptors and assessing the risk to them;

        (iv) obtaining and evaluating existing information on the possible presence of contaminants and their effects;

        (v) liaison with, and response to information from, other statutory bodies, including the Environment Agency and Natural England;

        (vi) liaison with and response to information from the owners or occupiers of land and other relevant interested parties;

        (vii) responding to information or complaints from members of the public, businesses and voluntary organisations;

        (viii) planning and reviewing a programme for inspecting particular areas of land;

        (ix) carrying out the detailed inspection of particular areas of land;

        (x) reviewing and updating assumptions and information previously used to assess the need for detailed inspection of different areas, and managing new information; and

        (xi) managing information obtained and held in the course of carrying out its inspection duties.[142]

3.123 Any strategy should take into account the relevant development plan policies of the authority. Many development plans contain a chapter on pollution and contamination, and in some cases specific reference to Pt IIA.[143] While Pt IIA is not directly concerned with the clean-up of land for regeneration purposes, authorities should consider how the strategy relates to the wider agenda for urban renewal.

Information from other statutory bodies

3.124 Other regulatory authorities may be able to provide information relevant to the identification of contaminated land. In particular, these may include the Environment Agency in its water protection functions. Local authorities should consider making specific arrangements with such bodies to avoid duplication of effort.[144] The role of the local authority in this respect is to receive and consider the information: the authority cannot abdicate its ultimate responsibility for determining whether land is contaminated.

---

[142] See para.3.146ff.
[143] See Ch.16.
[144] DEFRA Circular 01/2006, *Contaminated Land*, Annex 3 para.B.16.

Technical advice

Given the importance of the inspection strategies it is somewhat surprising **3.125**
to note that there is little prescriptive advice on the process of producing
them and other than in outline what they should contain. The DETR (as it
then was) and the Environment Agency have produced technical guidance
on the production of strategies which sets out a procedure for the
formulation of inspection strategies. Unlike the guidance from the Secretary of State, it is not mandatory. *Contaminated Land Inspection Strategies—
Technical Advice for Local Authorities* provides advice on technical good
practice and checklists. Although the guidance is quite detailed it is
flexible and reiterates the statutory guidance. The Technical Advice on
drawing up the strategy is divided into seven main stages, namely:

(a) definition of roles, responsibilities and programme for
development;

(b) review of local authority position by reference to the statutory
guidance;

(c) definition of strategy, structure and objectives;

(d) collection, collation and evaluation of relevant information;

(e) production of draft strategy;

(f) consultation on strategy and revision if necessary;

(g) adoption and publication of strategy.

The Technical Advice also provides examples of detailed content which **3.126**
would meet the minimum requirements set out in the statutory guidance.

Experience with written strategies

In practice, the publication of written strategies was slow.[145] Of local **3.127**
authorities, 33 per cent missed the deadline for the publication of a
strategy to inspect and identify sites. By 2002, however, this defect had
been largely rectified with some 92 per cent of local authorities completing
their inspection strategies. By October 2006, all of the 353 Pt IIA local
authorities in England had formally adopted a strategy with the one
exception having published a draft.

The content of the strategies is varied, reflecting the need to take into **3.128**
account local circumstances. This flexibility has led to a great deal of
inconsistency in both the way in which strategies were drawn up and the
subsequent practical implementation of Pt IIA. This was predictable in the
light of the general nature of the statutory framework and the fact that

---

[145] Much of the factual information here is taken from R. Lee, "Local Authority Inspection
Strategies and Experience of Remediation Notices" (BRASS Centre unpublished Research
Paper).

what would be appropriate in an area with an industrial legacy may not necessarily be appropriate in a rural authority. However, the presence or absence of contamination is not only linked to known past heavy industrial uses, and so "rural" authorities cannot be complacent as to the potential risks.[146]

3.129 This inconsistency can be seen in different authorities' approach to risk assessment. There appears to be two broad approaches to the assessment of risks within different areas. The first, mainly adopted in authorities with a background of extensive industrial uses, is based upon potential sources of pollution. Varying methodologies have been used, from identifying specific known contaminative sites,[147] to generic classes such as IPPC sites within the authority area[148] or versions of the list of potentially contaminative uses produced in 1991 in connection with the registers of potentially contaminated land.[149] The alternative approach, used in the majority of rural authorities, is based upon potential receptors such as the location of sensitive drinking water sources, ecological sites and other "aesthetic" assets.

3.130 Many written strategies are available online although it is quite common to have some of the relevant information missing. Some are little more than a repetition of the statutory definitions and of the wording found in the statutory guidance. Others go much further by identifying lists of potential sites which require further investigation.

The process of inspection

3.131 Although there is a link between the process of inspection and the production of the written strategy there is also a clear distinction between the two. It is important to note that an authority is not exempt from its inspection duty while its strategy is in the course of preparation or review. The authority should not await publication of its strategy before commencing detailed inspection work on particular areas of land, where this appears necessary.[150]

3.132 What is required by the Act is an inspection of the local authority's area rather than simply an inspection of registers, documents, plans or other purely "desktop" matters; the inspection should be a physical one. However, such desktop matters will be relevant in the context of the local authority's strategy in informing and prioritising the process of inspection. The normal process of site investigation will involve a desktop study as the first stage. Secondly, it is clear that an inspection can be carried out other than by the authority itself, provided they cause it to be carried out. In this connection, the reputation and level of insurance cover of any consultants appointed to that task is obviously a material consideration.

---

[146] There are many examples of rural landfill sites or of town gasworks serving small market towns, which may well have resulted in contamination.

[147] e.g. Barking and Dagenham identified a former button factory.

[148] e.g. Halton BC.

[149] e.g. Richmond LBC.

[150] DEFRA Circular 01/2006, *Contaminated Land*, Annex 3 para.B.14.

Reasonable grounds approach to inspection

The trigger for inspection should be where there are "reasonable grounds" **3.133** for believing that land may be contaminated.[151] The only grounds which are covered in the Statutory Guidance deal with historic uses which could give rise to exposure to radiation above the specific limits.[152]

Physical inspection

The Guidance deals with the process of physical inspection at paras B.18– **3.134** B.25. The starting point is particular areas of land where a pollution linkage may exist. In other words, there may be present a pollutant which would be capable of affecting a recognised relevant receptor through an environmental pathway.[153] The authority should carry out detailed inspections of areas where it is possible that a pollutant linkage exists to obtain sufficient information to allow it to determine whether the land appears to be contaminated land and, if so, whether it is a special site.[154] The information which will be required to make a determination includes evidence of the actual presence of the pollutant[155]: intrusive investigation is the most reliable way through which such evidence can be obtained. However, it is not the only way, and will rarely be appropriate or admissible as the first step. As the Guidance states, detailed inspection may include all or any of the following[156]:

(a) the collation and assessment of documentary information or other information from other bodies (including the Environment Agency in respect of radioactivity);

(b) a visit to the site for visual inspection and limited sampling (for example, surface deposits); or

(c) intrusive investigation.

The Guidance also considers the use of statutory powers of entry[157] and **3.135** stresses that any intrusive investigations should be carried out in accordance with appropriate technical procedures and ensuring that all reasonable precautions are taken to avoid harm, water pollution or damage to natural resources that might be caused.[158] Authorities will almost certainly wish to take specialist technical advice on these issues.

It is of course possible that land may previously have been subject to **3.136** investigation, either by an authority or an owner or prospective purchaser, so that reports as to its condition already exist. If such available information provides an appropriate basis for the authority to make its determina-

---

[151] 1990 Act s.78B(1)
[152] DEFRA Circular 01/2006, *Contaminated Land*, Annex 3 para.B.17A-B and para.A.41.
[153] See further, Ch.21.
[154] DEFRA Circular 01/2006, *Contaminated Land*, Annex 3 para.B.18.
[155] DEFRA Circular 01/2006, *Contaminated Land*, Annex 3 para.B.19.
[156] DEFRA Circular 01/2006, *Contaminated Land*, Annex 3 para.B.20.
[157] See below.
[158] DEFRA Circular 01/2006, *Contaminated Land*, Annex 3 para.B.24.

tion as to whether the land is contaminated, then it should not press for further intrusive investigation—the same is true where an owner or occupier offers to provide such information themselves within a reasonable timescale.[159] In those circumstances, the duty of the authority becomes rather that of checking, or getting checked, the information or report provided by the landowner, before deciding if further action is required.

3.137　Having once embarked on contaminated land investigation, it can be difficult to know when to stop. The aim of intrusive investigation is not to produce a complete characterisation of the nature and extent of pollutants, pathways and receptors, going beyond what is necessary to make the statutory determination. The question is whether the authority has enough information to come to a reasoned conclusion. If, at any stage, on the basis of information obtained, the authority considers there is no longer a reasonable possibility that a particular pollutant linkage exists, it should no longer carry out any further detailed inspection for that linkage.[160]

Special sites

3.138　Land which is designated as a "special site" becomes the responsibility of the Environment Agency as enforcing authority.[161] The Guidance makes it clear that the Agency should have a formal role at the inspection stage for such land. Where it is clear from the information available before carrying out any detailed inspection that the land would be a special site, then the authority should in all cases seek to make arrangements with the Agency to carry out inspection on its behalf.[162] This may be the case, for example, where the land is known to have been put to a use which would bring it within the definition of a special site. The Guidance also requires the authority to seek to make arrangements for inspection by the Agency where there is a reasonable possibility that a particular type of pollutant linkage may be present, which would make the land a special site.[163] An example would be particular types of pollution of controlled waters. These circumstances could quite possibly only become apparent once the authority has already embarked on the investigation process. The guidance does not address this situation specifically, but it is submitted that the authority should involve the Agency as soon as possible, and should consider whether in the circumstances it is practicable for the Agency to take over the investigation process.

Powers of entry and investigation

3.139　The powers of local authorities to obtain access to land for the purpose of investigation are found in s.108 of the 1995 Act: a local authority acting in its capacity as enforcing authority for the purpose of Pt IIA is a "local enforcing authority" within that section.[164] Accordingly, the local authority

---

[159] DEFRA Circular 01/2006, *Contaminated Land*, Annex 3 para.B.23.
[160] DEFRA Circular 01/2006, *Contaminated Land*, Annex 3 para.B.25.
[161] See below at para.3.221ff on special sites.
[162] DEFRA Circular 01/2006, *Contaminated Land*, Annex 3 para.B.28.
[163] DEFRA Circular 01/2006, *Contaminated Land*, Annex 3 para.B.29.
[164] 1995 Act s.108(15).

may authorise in writing any person who appears suitable to exercise the powers conferred by s.108. That person need not be an employee or officer of the authority, so in the context of contaminated land investigations there is no reason why an authority should not authorise employees of a consultancy engaged by the authority. Similarly, in the case where the land in question is likely to be designated as a special site, the authorised person may be an officer of the appropriate Agency. The relevant powers include[165]:

(a) entry of premises;

(b) entry with other authorised persons and with equipment or materials;

(c) examination and investigation;

(d) direction that premises be left undisturbed;

(e) taking measurements, photographs and recordings;

(f) taking samples of air, water and land;

(g) subjecting articles or substances suspected of being polluting to tests;

(h) taking possession of and detaining such articles;

(i) requiring persons to answer questions;

(j) requiring production of records or the furnishing of extracts from computerised records;

(k) requiring necessary facilities or assistance to be afforded; and

(l) any other power conferred by Regulations.

These powers are broad, and in each case the detailed conditions as to **3.140** their exercise will need to be considered. An authority might, for example, require consultants who have been involved in the previous investigation of a site to answer questions. Failure, without reasonable excuse, to comply with requirements imposed under s.108, or obstructing the use of the powers, can be an offence.[166] The powers may not be used to compel the production of documents covered by legal professional privilege.[167]

The investigation of land by physical sampling may well require the use **3.141** of heavy equipment. In such cases at least seven days' notice is required, and the entry can only take place with the consent of the occupier, or under the authority of a warrant.[168] These requirements apply in all cases to residential property, whether heavy equipment is involved or not.[169] Subsections 108(5)(a) and (b) provides express power to carry out "experi-

---

[165] 1995 Act s.108(4).
[166] 1995 Act s.110(1).
[167] 1995 Act s.108(13).
[168] 1995 Act s.108(6).
[169] 1995 Act s.108(6).

mental borings" or other works and to install, keep or maintain monitoring or other apparatus on land. Both of these powers may be necessary in contaminated land investigations. However, the subsection states that they are exercisable for determining whether "pollution control enactments" have been complied with, whereas inspection by a local authority under Pt IIA is not to determine compliance with that legislation. The local authority will therefore need to rely on its more general powers under subss.108(4)(b) and (f) as to the taking onto land of equipment and the taking of samples.

3.142   Before using these statutory powers, the authority will also need to consider carefully the statutory guidance on the subject, which may restrict the circumstances in which those powers should be exercised. Before using its powers of entry, the authority should be satisfied that there is a reasonable possibility that a pollutant linkage site exists.[170] For intrusive inspection the test is more onerous, in that the authority must be satisfied on the basis of information already obtained that it is likely that the contaminant is actually present and that the receptor is actually present or likely to be present.[171] In other words, the authority cannot use its investigative powers for a pure "fishing exercise". Nor, as explained above, can it insist on using those powers where adequate information has already been provided, or will be within a reasonable timescale.

Securing information

3.143   One of the most important practical problems in relation to Pt IIA is the cost of investigation. The sampling and analysis costs of a large site can easily exceed £100,000. Once a remediation notice is served, the recipient may be required to carry out works to assess the condition of the land in question, controlled waters or adjoining or adjacent land.[172] However, the authority will itself have to bear the cost of such investigations as are necessary to reach the view that the land is contaminated land: mere suspicion as to the presence of contaminants or the existence of harm will not be sufficient for this purpose.[173] It seems inherently unlikely at first sight that a landowner will wish to volunteer to bear the cost of investigations which may ultimately result in the imposition of statutory clean-up liabilities, unless there is some valid commercial incentive for so doing, such as the need to obtain planning permission for the development of land, or to achieve a sale or other disposal of the site. However, larger companies may well have in place environmental policies which mandate a proactive and co-operative approach to potential contamination; there may therefore be cases where the authority is able to secure voluntary co-operation.

3.144   In the absence of such co-operation, a local authority may be attracted to the idea of using its statutory powers to obtain existing reports or data which demonstrate the land to be contaminated, as a cheaper course than

---

[170] DEFRA Circular 01/2006, *Contaminated Land*, Annex 3 para.B.22.

[171] DEFRA Circular 01/2006, *Contaminated Land*, Annex 3 para.B.22

[172] This follows from the definition of "remediation" at s.78A(7), which includes these matters.

[173] See the statement by Ministers in *Hansard*, HL Vol.562, col.175; House of Commons Standing Committee B, 11th sitting, col.341.

carrying out its own physical investigations. There may well be a number of reports in existence which have been commissioned by companies for internal management purposes or in the context of transactions or development proposals: these reports may indicate that the land is contaminated.

Assuming that the authority has at least some basis to believe the land **3.145** may be contaminated the question then might be whether the authority could compel disclosure of such data or findings as "records" under s.108(4)(k) of the 1995 Act, or even ask the persons involved in such investigations (whether as company employees or officers or as external consultants) to answer questions under s.108(4)(j). Such a course might be regarded as somewhat heavy-handed; it would also raise the question of whether such reports could be regarded as "records" falling within the statutory power, and of whether the relevant documents are protected from disclosure by legal privilege. On the first issue there is authority to suggest that the term "records" refers only to primary or original sources of information, and that reports which summarise or opine on such material are not "records".[174] On that basis, consultant's reports might not be available, but the underlying data might be. Documents covered by legal privilege cannot be compelled to be produced under s.108.[175] With the heightened awareness of environmental liability risks in recent years, many reports have been produced with the involvement of lawyers with a view to seeking privilege. Whether this will be successful in actually securing privilege is another matter; this will depend on whether the information was produced and has since remained on a confidential basis, and whether its purpose was to provide legal advice. Mere involvement of lawyers in the process is unlikely to be enough in itself.[176]

Handling information

One of the components of the authority's written strategy must include **3.146** procedures for the management of information obtained and held in the course of carrying out its inspection duties.[177] This is a somewhat different issue from the provision of information on the statutory registers required by s.78R. Those registers relate to the various notices and other procedural steps consequent upon determination that land is contaminated. However, the authority will also amass a potentially huge volume of information prior to, and in the process of making, that determination. Much of that information will be voluminous, indigestible and in a form which may be largely unintelligible to the general public, for example readings of borehole logs, and toxicological data. However, it may also have significant commercial implications in affecting the value of land, even if the ultimate

---

[174] See *R. v Tirado* (1974) 59 Cr.App.R. 50; *R. v Gwilliam* [1968] 1 W.L.R. 1839; *R. v Schering Chemicals Ltd* [1983] 1 W.L.R. 143; *Savings and Investment Bank v Gasco Investments (Netherlands) B.V.* [1984] 1. W.L.R. 271.

[175] 1995 Act s.108(13).

[176] See *Three Rivers DC v Governor and Company of the Bank of England* [2003] EWCA Civ 474; [2003] Q.B. 1556; *Collidge v Freeport Plc* [2007] EWHC 645, QB.

[177] DEFRA Circular 01/2006, *Contaminated Land*, Annex 3 para.B.15(d)(xi).

determination is that the land is not "contaminated" in the statutory sense. Moreover, it may be useful information for a plaintiff in any civil proceedings involving the land in question. As part of the local search process on property transactions, local authorities may be asked to provide information about land which has not yet been identified as contaminated land; for example, whether the authority has at any stage investigated that land and, if so, the details of the outcome of those investigations.

3.147   Care will be needed in the practical processes necessary for collating and managing this information, whether in electronic or paper form. One legal issue is whether such information is within the Environmental Information Regulations 2004[178] and as such must be provided to the public on request. It is certainly information relating to the environment (concerning as it does the state of water, soil or land, and possibly the state of human health and safety, as well as measures designed to protect these elements)[179] and is held by a public body. In particular, the authority will have to take a view on whether any of the information falls within any of the exceptions in reg.12. It could be argued for example that it is confidential as relating to land which may be the subject of legal proceedings,[180] i.e. service of a remediation notice and subsequent appeal or enforcement. If so, then under the 2004 Regulations it may be withheld but need not necessarily be. The authority will thus have to decide whether the information should be disclosed, bearing in mind the public interest in the state of land being known and the fact that reg.12(2) requires it to apply a presumption in favour of disclosure.

3.148   Other possibly relevant exceptions relate to material which is still in the course of completion, unfinished documents or incomplete data. These issues were considered in the case of *Maile v Wigan Metropolitan BC*[181] where the authority had commissioned a baseline study of potentially contaminated sites in its area from Nottingham Trent University. The exercise had been put "on hold" and no report had been released. The applicant sought access to a database compiled for the study, using the then current 1992 Regulations as the basis of his request. The authority argued that the information fell within reg.4(c) (information relating to the confidential deliberations of a public body) or 4(d) (information contained in a document or record still in the course of completion). It was accepted by the court that the information fell within these exempting provisions. The data was still incomplete and possibly inaccurate: disclosure of what was still a speculative database could cause unnecessary alarm to local citizens and landowners. However, in any such exercise there will come a point where information is complete and refusal to disclose it can no longer be justified on that basis.

---

[178] SI 2004/3391.

[179] 2004 Regulations reg.2(1)(a), (b), (c) and (f). A broad approach to the interpretation of this issue was taken in *R v British Coal Corp Ex p. Ibstock Building Products Ltd* [1995] Env. L.R. 227.

[180] 2004 Regulations reg.12(5)(d). But compare *R. v British Coal Corp* (above) where the possibility of an appeal being made was held not to constitute prospective legal proceedings.

[181] [2001] Env. L.R. 201.

Other possible exceptions from disclosure relate to adverse effects on **3.149** intellectual property rights, commercial confidentiality, or the interests of a person who has provided information voluntarily and could not have been put under any legal obligation to provide it.

If information falls within the Environmental Information Regulations **3.150** (whether or not an exception within those regulations allows it to be withheld) then it will be exempt information for the purpose of the Freedom of Information Act 2000.[182] Most information relating to investigations under Pt IIA seems likely to be "environmental information", but if it is not then the requirements under the 2000 Act to disclose such information, and any potentially applicable exemptions, would need to be considered.

Consideration must also be given to the provisions of Pt VA of the Local **3.151** Government Act 1972 on access to reports and background papers for meetings of committees and sub-committees of the authority. In *Maile v Wigan BC*[183] an attempt to secure disclosure of the baseline study under these provisions failed. The database of potentially contaminated sites had not been used for preparing the report which had gone to the authority and, accordingly, was not "background papers" falling within s.100D. It should also be noted that the categories of "exempt Information" under Schedule 12A to the Act include: "information which, if disclosed to the public, would reveal that the authority proposes . . . to give under any enactment a notice . . . by virtue of which requirements are imposed on a person."

It is certainly arguable that information which shows that land is in such **3.152** a condition that a remediation notice will be served falls within that category; however, at the stage of identifying land as contaminated, it may not be clear that a remediation notice will be served. Again, the authority will have to take a view on this in each case, in the light of individual circumstances.

There are arguments that the European Convention on Human Rights **3.153** requires, as aspects of the Art.2 right to life and the Article 8 right to respect for home and family life, the provision of information to enable the citizen to assess the risks which they and their family may be exposed to by virtue of living where they do.[184] The reality however is that in the vast majority of cases these rights will be satisfied by the administrative framework created by Pt IIA and by the duties of the authority to make available information as discussed above.

Resource implications

There can be few local authorities who will not be concerned about the **3.154** potentially major costs of instigating and maintaining a programme of inspection of its area for contaminated land. Although the language used

---

[182] FOIA 2000 s.39.
[183] [2001] Env. L.R. 201.
[184] See for example, *Guerra v Italy* (1998) 26 E.H.R.R. 357, para.60; *Öneryildiz v Turkey* (2005) 41 E.H.R.R. 20, paras 89, 90; *Giacomelli v Italy* [2006] ECHR 59909/00, para.83.

echoes the long-standing provisions on statutory nuisance by referring to inspection "from time to time", a very different approach is likely to be necessary for contaminated land. Whereas many types of statutory nuisance will be all too self-evident, the risks and problems of contaminated land may only be yielded up on detailed examination.

3.155 There is no requirement for review of land at specified intervals; during the passage of the 1995 Act, the Government rejected an amendment proposing a requirement for a five-yearly review, stating that local authorities should concentrate resources on areas where there were likely to be problems.[185]

3.156 It must be kept firmly in mind that the function of inspection is a duty, and as such a local authority which treats it as discretion, to be dispensed with on resource, economic or other grounds, will be vulnerable to judicial review.[186] On the other hand, it is a duty which is couched in broad terms, so that apart from extreme cases, it may be difficult to categorise a particular course of conduct as being in breach of the duty. The reality is that local authorities must act within a framework of limited resources and competing calls on those resources, and even a matter which is stated in terms of a duty may not necessarily be treated as absolute in its effect where this would lead to a result which it would be difficult to attribute to Parliament's intention.[187] The key to this dilemma may lie in the adoption by the authority of an acceptable strategy which accords with the Guidance. That Guidance itself recognises the need for prioritisation of resources.

3.157 On the other hand, where the legislation bases duties on objective criteria, the courts will often be reluctant to dilute the duty to a power by allowing the local authority to plead scarcity of resources: this would be to take into account irrelevant considerations, and the only proper course for the authority in such circumstances may be to divert resources from discretionary spending.[188]

3.158 This is where the Government's statutory guidance on inspection is important: provided a local authority can show that it has formulated a reasoned strategy on inspection which is consistent with that Guidance, the risk of a successful challenge may be relatively low. Different considerations may arise where the allegation is that the authority has failed to take action with respect to a specific site, and these are considered below. In any event, it is clear that more than a simply "paper" approach is needed; the authority must be able to show that it has put its "paper" strategy into effect and has kept it monitored, with regular reports to committee.

Enforcing local authority duties

3.159 The inspection, identification and ultimate remediation of contaminated land is an iterative process, beginning with general inspection of the area, and progressing through investigation of specific sites to the service of a

---

[185] See *Hansard*, HL Vol. 562, col.229.

[186] *R. v Carrick D Ex p. Shelley* [1996] Env. L.R. 273.

[187] *R. v Gloucestershire CC, Ex p. Barry* [1997] A.C. 584; *R. v Norfolk CC, Ex p. Thorpe* [1998] C.O.D. 208.

[188] *R. v East Sussex CC Ex p. Tandy* [1998] 2 W.L.R. 884, 891–2.

remediation notice and, if necessary, the taking of enforcement action. Decisions or inaction of a local authority may be susceptible to challenge at each of these stages, but it is probably at the later ones, with specific sites in mind, that the duties will bite hardest.

3.160 As is demonstrated by *R. v Carrick DC Ex p. Shelley*,[189] once it is apparent that land may well be contaminated within the meaning of the Act, either on the basis of complaints by third parties or on the local authority's own investigations, judicial review for failure to serve a remediation notice may become a real possibility. The normal rules on standing, delay and the exercise of judicial discretion will of course need to be carefully borne in mind by those considering such action.

3.161 There are also other courses which may be contemplated. Unlike statutory nuisance, the Pt IIA provisions do not provide a direct complaint procedure for persons aggrieved by the existence of contaminated land. However, the possibility exists of making representation to the appropriate Agency with a view to site-specific guidance being given to the local authority.[190] Another possibility is of course a complaint to the Local Government Ombudsman, or to apply indirect pressure to the local authority through local MPs.

Civil liability in relation to inspection functions

3.162 The existence of a statutory duty to cause land in its area to be inspected inevitably raises the issue of potential liability for failure to inspect or for alleged faulty inspection. Would the authority, for example, be liable to an adjoining landowner, or to an owner downstream of a plume of pollution, or to a subsequent owner of the contaminated land itself, for failure to identify land that should have been identified as contaminated? The statute makes no express provision as to liability in the event of breach of the statutory duty to cause the authority's area to be inspected from time to time. Whilst the duty of inspection is mandatory, rather than discretionary, it is not an absolute duty. The words "from time to time" imply a degree of discretion as to the timing and prioritisation of inspection, which clearly accords with the terms of the Guidance. Provided therefore that an authority adheres to that guidance in formulating its inspection strategy, it may, as explained in the previous section, be difficult to demonstrate any breach of duty which gives rise to liability.

3.163 Three main situations can be foreseen. The first is where a local authority has failed to inspect a particular site, and accordingly has not identified it as contaminated: essentially, what is complained of is an omission on the part of the authority. The second such situation is where an authority has inspected land (or has caused it to be inspected by a third party) but the inspection has allegedly been carried out negligently. The third situation is where the land has been identified as contaminated, but it is alleged that the authority has failed to take proper and effective enforcement action to remediate the relevant risks.

---

[189] [1996] Env. L.R. 273 (a case dealing with the use of statutory nuisance remedies in the context of beaches affected by litter from sewage outfalls).
[190] 1990 Act s.78V.

Failure to inspect

3.164 In the first type of case, that of failure to inspect or identify land as contaminated, the analysis of the majority of the House of Lords in *Stovin v Wise and Norfolk CC*[191] is relevant. The argument that the authority has a duty to act in any given situation depends on the public nature of its powers, duties and funding.[192] As mentioned above, the duty to inspect from time to time under s.78B does not appear to be absolute in nature. In order to challenge successfully a decision by a local authority not to inspect a particular site at a specific time, it would be necessary to show, on Wednesbury principles, that no authority, properly directed as to the facts and the law, and having before it all the information that this particular authority had, could possibly come to the decision they did. An example might be an authority which had failed to develop a strategy at all, or had failed to act in accordance with their own strategy without adequate reason, or had misconstrued the mandatory guidance or its legal duties.

3.165 Even in such a case, it would not follow that breach of the public law duty should necessarily give rise to a cause of action for damages at common law, either for breach of statutory duty or for negligence.[193] This will involve a question of statutory construction, bearing in mind the increased burden on public funds involved in giving a cause of action (which in the case of the contaminated land provisions could obviously be significant). As *Stovin v Wise* itself graphically demonstrates, it is possible for distinguished judges to have different views on this issue,[194] and doubtless any decision on s.78B would be coloured to a degree by the specific factual background to the case before the court.

3.166 The concept of general reliance, as discussed by Lord Hoffmann in *Stovin v Wise*, may help to provide some guidance, i.e. whether there could be said to be a general expectation as to the exercise of the duty by the authority, or a general reliance or dependence on its exercise.[195] If the strategy is well-drafted, and consulted on and published in draft, the "general expectation" in this respect cannot or should not exceed the terms of the strategy. The examples of general expectation given in *Stovin v Wise* include the control of air traffic, the safety inspection of aircraft and the fighting of fire. All of these issues would seem to have a greater degree of predictability and uniformity involved than the inspection function under s.78B. On the analysis of Lord Hoffmann,[196] it would also be relevant to consider the extent to which members of the public might reasonably be expected to protect themselves against the relevant risks by other means— which in this context might involve commissioning their own site investigation before acquiring land,[197] or by taking action themselves under civil law against the owners of contaminated land which affects their own interests.

---

[191] [1996] A.C. 923.
[192] [1996] A.C. 935–936, 946.
[193] [1996] A.C. 952.
[194] The decision was a 3/2 majority, Lord Slynn and Lord Nicholls of Birkenhead dissenting.
[195] [1996] A.C. 953 et seq.
[196] [1996] A.C. 954–955.
[197] They will of course have no statutory powers of access to do so.

Defective inspection

Somewhat different, but related, arguments would arise in a case where **3.167** the authority had inspected land but had negligently failed to identify it as contaminated. The question here, applying the principles of *Stovin v Wise and Norfolk CC*[198] and *Barrett v Enfield LBC*,[199] is whether the authority owes a common law duty to care to those who may be affected by failure to observe the appropriate standard of care, or whether any such duty may be enlarged by the statutory context to create a relationship of "proximity" which would not otherwise exist. Inspection of land for contamination is a significantly more complex exercise than, say, inspecting the adequacy of foundations. There are many ways in which inspection for contamination may be carried out, and there is no guarantee that any investigation will provide total certainty. There is therefore a degree of discretion as to how the inspection duty is carried out, and a court applying the analysis of Lord Hoffmann in *Stovin v Wise* might hesitate before imposing liability where a local authority for policy reasons had decided to carry out its duty in a certain way. Indeed, if the authority could be seen to have acted consistently with the relevant Guidance and its own strategy, it may be doubtful that there is negligence at all.

The issue of whether a duty of care exists will depend on the well- **3.168** established but unpredictable principles of foreseeability of harm, analogy with existing common law duties, policy, fairness and justice.[200] The existence and ambit of any duty of care is likely to be influenced by the statutory framework within which the authority is operating. The distinction between policy and operational matters, enunciated in *Anns v Merton LBC*,[201] is unlikely to be conclusive in this respect. While the inspection of land might be said to be an operational matter, as mentioned above, there is inevitably a discretion as to how the inspection is performed. A dimension which may be present in this type of case is that of specific reliance by an individual on the outcome of an inspection, as opposed to the general reliance of all members of the public referred to above. However, even specific reliance will not necessarily imply a duty of care if policy considerations dictate otherwise.

The allegation may of course be not that the authority has been remiss **3.169** in detecting contamination, but rather that it has been over-zealous in its enforcement functions to the detriment of the owner or occupier, perhaps resulting in disruption of business or the devaluation of the property. Again, there are serious obstacles in the way of a successful action in negligence in such cases. In particular, given that the purpose of the statutory functions under Pt IIA is to protect the public's safety and the public interest in protecting the environment, a court is likely to be reluctant to find that a duty of care is owed to the owner or occupier of the land by the local authority in carrying out those functions.[202] To impose

---

[198] [1996] A.C. 923.
[199] (1999) 1 L.G.L.R. 829.
[200] *Barrett v Enfield LBC* (n.61 above); *Caparo Industries Plc v Dickman* [1990] 2 A.C. 605; *Rice v Secretary of State for Trade and Industry* [2007] EWCA Civ 289; [2007] P.I.Q.R. P23
[201] [1978] A.C. 728.
[202] *Harris v Evans* [1998] 3 All E.R. 522, CA.

such a duty would be likely to result in excessive caution and reluctance to act on the part of the authorities.[203] The legislation by virtue of its inherent nature may have adverse effects on property values, and contains its own checks and safeguards against unreasonable action by enforcing authorities.[204]

Inadequate enforcement

3.170 A third possible liability situation is where it is alleged that the enforcing authority has failed to make proper use of its powers to secure the remediation of contaminated land, in consequence of which a third party has suffered loss or damage—perhaps because their health or their adjoining property has been affected by the contamination. A similar issue arose in relation to the use of planning and statutory nuisance powers in *R. v Lam and Brennan (t/a Namesakes of Torbay) and Torbay BC*.[205] In that case it was alleged that the local authority had (inter alia) failed to take enforcement action against a workshop which emitted fumes from chemicals and paint sprays. The owner of a nearby Chinese restaurant brought an action in negligence against the local authority for damage caused to his business and for health effects on his family. The alleged negligence lay in failure by officers to make proper recommendations to committee, and in failing to take enforcement proceedings.

3.171 The Court of Appeal, referring to the principles of *X (Minors) v Bedfordshire CC*,[206] and *Stovin v Wise*,[207] held that neither the planning legislation nor the provisions on statutory nuisance were such as to create a duty of care at common law with regard to the exercise or non-exercise of those powers. The provisions were regarded as being for the benefit of the public at large, and as not derogating from the right of affected individuals to take their own action in nuisance against the source of the problem.[208] Nor would it be said that this position was affected by arguments of "assumption of responsibility" going beyond the simple performance of the relevant statutory functions.[209]

3.172 These arguments could no doubt also be applied to the functions of local authorities under Pt IIA. The purpose of Pt IIA in dealing with contamination for the public good seems not to be particularly different from the purpose of the planning and statutory nuisance regimes. Yet it is not difficult to conceive of circumstances where such a result might be thought unjust. For example, contaminated land may present significant and alarming risks to local residents, whose health may be jeopardised. Pt IIA

---

[203] *X (Minors) v Bedfordshire CC* [1995] 2 A.C. 633, HL.

[204] Compare the position, however, where the legislative powers are used in an unlawful fashion to impose inappropriate action: *Welton v North Cornwall DC* [1997] 1 W.L.R. 570 (distinguished in *Harris v Evans*).

[205] [1998] P.L.C.R. 30.

[206] [1995] 1 A.C. 633.

[207] [1996] A.C. 923.

[208] [1998] P.L.C.R. 30, 48–49; see also *Sub.nom Chung Tak Lam v Borough of Torbay* [1997] P.I.Q.R. P488 and admissibility decision in European Court of Human Rights (App. 41671/98; July 5, 2001).

[209] [1998] P.L.C.R. 30, 50.

has provided a series of duties on the relevant authorities to deal with those risks; in reality the affected local residents (who may be a relatively small group) will be relying on the proper performance of those duties to safeguard their health, in a way which the generality of the public will not. Also, whereas it may be a reasonable argument in the case of an ongoing nuisance from fumes or noise that those affected can deal with the problem themselves by an action for private nuisance or by a complaint as a person aggrieved under s.82 of the 1990 Act, the same argument is not so strong in the case of a contaminated site. Securing effective redress under common law is likely to be much less straightforward, and Pt IIA contains no provision for direct enforcement action by citizens. There may also in some cases be the potential argument that the local authority has contributed to the risks, by giving planning permission for housing development which is now affected by contamination.[210]

The Human Rights Act 1998

In these circumstances, local residents may well feel rightly aggrieved if **3.173** the law offers them no remedy where the enforcing authority, through inertia or ineptitude, fails to protect them. Should the common law not provide a remedy in these circumstances (as in the current state of the authorities it may not) then it may be possible to rely on the relevant provisions of the European Convention on Human Rights as requiring effective action to protect the health and safety of individuals, and their homes. Under the Human Rights Act 1998, primary and subordinate legislation must be read and given effect to, so far as possible, in a way which is consistent with the Convention rights set out in Sch.1 to the Act. It is unlawful for public authorities to act in a way which is incompatible with convention rights, and the victim of such an unlawful act may bring proceedings against the authority.

Case law of the European Court of Human Rights suggests that the **3.174** rights to life under Art.2 and to the respect for home and private life under Art.8(2) may be capable of applying to situations where an authority fails to take effective action to protect individuals from harm caused by pollution, whether this arises from acts of the state itself or those of private entities.[211] It remains to be seen whether these authorities can be used in relation to contaminated land situations, but the possibility must exist.[212] A local authority which is aware that it has contaminated land in its area, yet for whatever reason fails to act effectively to avoid harm, could therefore potentially find itself faced with proceedings under the Human

---

[210] See *Kane v New Forest DC* [2002] 1 W.L.R. 312. *Stovin v Wise* is essentially about omissions, not acts: see *Thames Trains Ltd v HSE* [2003] EWCA Civ 720.

[211] See for example *Lopez Ostra v Spain* (1994) 20 E.H.R.R. 277; *Guerra v Italy* (1998) 26 E.H.R.R. 357; *Fadayeva v Russia* (2007) 45 E.H.R.R. 10. In *Cameron v Network Rail Infrastructure Ltd* [2006] EWHC 1133 (QB) it was accepted that the concept of "right to life" goes further than the mere preservation of life itself (See para.38, citing *R (Middleton) v West Somerset Coroner* [2004] 2 A.C. 182).

[212] The closest case to date may be *Öneryildiz v Turkey* (2005) 41 E.H.R.R. 20, which involved a methane explosion and landslip at a municipal tip which was in close proximity to slum dwellings.

Rights Act 1998 from a local resident who claims to be a "victim" of the contamination. What may be important in any claim is whether the authority acts in accordance with recognised scientific and technical guidelines.[212a]

Position of local authority consultants

3.175 It seems likely in practice that many local authorities will use the services of environmental consultants to investigate, assess and advise on the remediation of contaminated land. An authority is perfectly entitled to do so, but the question may then arise as to the position of those consultants if negligence is alleged by a landowner, local resident, or other person who claims to have suffered damage as a result of that negligence.

3.176 The question will be whether the consultant and the person affected were in a relationship of sufficient proximity, in legal terms, to give rise to a duty of care. This seems unlikely, since the consultant's duty of care is owed to the authority, and there is no duty to the person whose past activities or whose land are the subject of such advice, or to the general public who may be affected by decisions made on the basis of that advice.[213] Such a duty would only arise if it was clear on the facts that the consultant, as well as performing his duty to the authority, had assumed personal responsibility for the relevant individual owner, occupier, etc.[214] The problems faced by any claimant in such circumstances are illustrated by the decision of the House of Lords in *Sutradhar v National Environment Research Council*[215] in which it was held that a Bangladeshi suffering from arsenic poisoning had no reasonable prospect of success in an action against the NERC for negligence arising from a geological report that, according to him, had induced the health authorities in Bangladesh not to take steps that would have ensured that his drinking water was not contaminated by arsenic. The Court held that the fact that a person had expert knowledge did not in itself create a duty to the whole world to apply that knowledge in solving its problems, and moreover the fact that the consultant had chosen to run tests for some elements for the purposes for which the report was commissioned could not create a duty to test for other elements. Use of a consultant will not, of course, release the authority from its own legal responsibilities, such as they are; if the authority is sued, it may well join its consultant as a third party.

How should landowners react?

3.177 The practical question arises as to how a landowner who finds their land the subject of scrutiny by an enforcing authority under Pt IIA should react. The risk that land will be subject to investigation may appear from the

---

[212a] See *Hans Gaida v Germany* (Application No. 9355/03, July 3, 2007) (radiation from mobile phone base station).

[213] *Kapfunde v Abbey National Plc and Daniel* [1998] IRLR 583, CA (no duty owed by doctor examining prospective employees on behalf of company). See also the example given by Lord Browne-Wilkinson in *X (Minors) v Bedfordshire CC* [1995] 2 A.C. 633 at 752 of a doctor employed by an insurance company to examine an applicant for life insurance.

[214] See *Phelps v Hillingdon LBC* [1999] 1 W.L.R. 500; *Jarvis v Hampshire CC* [2000] ELR 36.

[215] [2006] UKHL 33; [2006] 4 All E.R. 490; [2007] Env. L.R. 10.

authority's draft or final strategy for inspection: either the strategy may identify particular areas of search, or it may prioritise types of contaminative use for early inspection.

To what extent should the owner co-operate with the authority? This will **3.178** depend on many factors, both environmental and commercial. The immediate response may be one of dismay or indignation that this particular site should be singled out for attention. A broader view is necessary however. There is little doubt that the authority has the legal powers—and probably the resources—to follow through the investigative process. Given that statutory duties are involved, this is a problem which is not likely simply to "go away". The question therefore is the extent to which the owner merely lets the authority get on with the investigation at their expense, or whether the owner seeks to pre-empt the process by commissioning their own investigations and actively co-operating at their own cost.

Two points should be borne in mind here. First, it is not a foregone **3.179** conclusion that land which is subject to investigation will ultimately be identified as contaminated within the statutory definition. For the landowner who becomes actively involved, at least there may be opportunities to influence that process. The owner will be more in control of the situation, and may also benefit from reassurance that the investigation work is being carried out to a satisfactory standard. The current and projected future use of the land may also be relevant factors here.

Secondly, nor is it a foregone conclusion that the owner will ultimately **3.180** be the person with financial responsibility for any clean-up. If there is an original polluter who is identifiable, the owner may wish to involve that person at this stage, since they will have an interest in whether the site is identified as contaminated, and may have greater resources to deploy in safeguarding their interests.

A number of other factors may also be relevant to the landowner. These **3.181** will include the desire to minimise disruption to operations on site; whether site investigation is already in hand or is proposed for other reasons (e.g. a prospective sale); the desire to maintain good relations with the authority; the desire to avoid bad publicity or to appear responsible; existing corporate environmental policies and management systems; and any contractual restrictions or freedom of action (for example, as to confidentiality, or the terms of any indemnities that may have been entered into).

The situation may also be complicated by transactions which are in **3.182** progress at the time the issue arises. Here careful attention will need to be paid to the respective interests and any contractual rights of the parties concerned. These are tactical issues which will need to be thought through carefully and discussed in each specific case. If the site is to be redeveloped, then as part of the development process the local planning authority will probably require full investigation at the landowner's expense, together with appropriate remediation measures imposed by conditions or by a s.106 obligation.[216]

---

[216] See Chs 16 and 17 on Development and Cleanup.

PART 4: IDENTIFYING LAND AS CONTAMINATED

Guidance on identification: generally

3.183 The determination that land is contaminated is to be made in accordance with the statutory Guidance. The Guidance at Annex 3 Ch.B Pt 4 deals separately with the six possible situations where that determination may be made, namely:

    (a) significant harm is being caused;

    (b) there is a significant possibility of significant harm being caused;

    (c) pollution of controlled waters is being caused;

    (d) pollution of controlled waters is likely to be caused;

    (e) harm so far as attributable to radioactivity is being caused; and

    (f) there is a significant possibility of harm so far as attributable to radioactivity being caused.

3.184 The Guidance also deals with the issues of the physical extent of land to be covered by the determination, consistency with the approach of other statutory bodies, the actual process of making the determination and the preparation of a written record of determination.

3.185 In dealing with these issues, the Guidance at the outset reminds the authority that whilst it may receive and rely on information or advice from other persons, such as the Environment Agency or an appointed consultant, the actual determination remains the sole responsibility of the authority and cannot be delegated other than in accordance with statutory powers of delegation.[217] This applies even where it appears that the land, if contaminated, would be a special site, so that inspection has been undertaken by the Agency.

Determining that significant harm is being caused

3.186 According to the Guidance, the authority should determine that land is contaminated land on the basis that significant harm is being caused where[218]:

    (a) it has carried out an appropriate scientific and technical assessment of all the relevant and available evidence; and

    (b) on the basis of that assessment, it is satisfied on the balance of probabilities that significant harm is being caused.

---

[217] See further para.3.106ff.

[218] DEFRA Circular 01/2006, *Contaminated Land*, Annex 3 para.B.44. Delegation powers arise under s.101 of the Local Government Act 1972 or s.56 of the Local Government (Scotland) Act 1973.

The key points of this guidance are the nature of the scientific and **3.187** technical assessment which is necessary (discussed below), and the fact that the test is based on the balance of probabilities. This is of course the standard of proof generally required in civil cases and involves the authority being able to say they think it more probable than not that the relevant circumstances exist; if the probabilities are equal, or it is not possible to say which is more likely, then this standard is not met.[219] Annex 2 of the Circular deals with the situation where there is uncertainty.[220] There may be situations either where the investigation yields insufficient information to make a determination that the land is or is not contaminated, or where on the "balance of probabilities" test it is not contaminated, but there remains the possibility that it might be. In such cases, the authority will need to consider if further investigation or analysis might assist: if not, then the authority will have to determine that the land is not contaminated.

Determining that there is a significant possibility of significant harm being caused

The Guidance on this issue states that the authority should determine that **3.188** land is contaminated land on the basis that there is a significant possibility of significant harm being caused where[221]:

(a) it has carried out a scientific and technical assessment of the risks arising from the pollutant linkage or linkages, according to appropriate, authoritative and scientifically based guidance on such risk assessments;

(b) the assessment shows that there is a significant possibility of significant harm being caused; and

(c) there are no suitable and sufficient risk management arrangements in place to prevent such harm.

Point (b) above will involve the authority referring to that part of the **3.189** Guidance which defines what is meant by "significant possibility" for the various types of harm.[222] Point (c) could be important in practice, in that there may be cases where a risk of harm is present, but the risk is controlled to acceptable levels. An example might be the presence of explosive landfill gases within range of occupied premises, but where those premises are fitted with appropriate gas detection and venting equipment. There is a source, a pathway and a target, and certainly the harm in question if it occurred would be "significant", but so long as the measures are properly maintained the risk should not be regarded as "significant".

---

[219] *Miller v Minister of Pensions* [1947] 2 All E.R. 372 at 373–4; *Hornal v Neuberger Products Ltd* [1957] 1 Q.B. 247.

[220] Annex 2 paras 3.23 and 3.24.

[221] DEFRA Circular 01/2006, *Contaminated Land*, Annex 3 para.B.45.

[222] See para.3.38ff.

The authority will have to form a view as to whether the measures are suitable and sufficient, which may in itself involve technical assessment. The measures must be "in place", i.e. present and operational. A promise to instal them at some point in the future will not be sufficient. Point (a) raises the most potentially difficult issues and is discussed in the next paragraph.

Assessment of risk and use of guidelines

3.190 The assessment of the significance of risk, following the words of the Guidance, must be "scientific and technical", according to "relevant, appropriate, authoritative and scientifically based guidance".[223] The authority will therefore have to be prepared to defend its decision-making process against those criteria, and will require appropriate technical support in this. In particular, if using any external guidance on risk, the authority must satisfy itself that such guidance is relevant to the actual circumstances in hand, and that appropriate allowances have been made for particular circumstances.[224]

3.191 The Guidance countenances the possibility that, in order to simplify the assessment process, the authority may use "authoritative and scientifically based" guideline values for assessing the acceptability of certain concentrations of substances; the test remains essentially the same where such guidelines are used.[225] There are potential problems with this generic approach of quantitative assessment which are described elsewhere.[226] The Guidance accepts that care is needed in using such values. In particular, the authority must satisfy itself of a number of matters when using guideline values.[227] These are:

(a) the relevance of the values to the circumstances in question and, in particular, to the judgment of whether the pollutant linkage in question constitutes a significant possibility of harm;

(b) the relevance to those circumstances of any assumption underlying the values[228];

(c) the observance of any conditions relevant to the use of the values[229];

(d) the making of any appropriate adjustments to allow for such differences in factual circumstances and underlying assumptions.

3.192 It is also stated that the authority should be prepared to reconsider any determination based on the use of such guideline values if it is demonstrated to the authority's satisfaction that under some other more appro-

---

[223] For more on risk assessment see, Ch.21.

[224] DEFRA Circular 01/2006, *Contaminated Land*, Annex 3 para.B.46.

[225] DEFRA Circular 01/2006, *Contaminated Land*, Annex 3 para.B.47.

[226] See Ch.21.

[227] DEFRA Circular 01/2006, *Contaminated Land*, Annex 3 para.B.48.

[228] For example, assumptions on soil conditions or land-use patterns, behaviour of contaminants or presence of pathways.

[229] For example, number of samples or methods of preparation and analysis.

priate method of assessing the risks the determination would not have been made.[230]

The way in which the Guidance is written clearly places the onus of **3.193** exploring the validity and applicability of any guideline values on the authority. It is not the case that the authority can simply rely on such values, leaving others to show why they are inappropriate. The overall impact is that an authority will not be able to rely exclusively or simplistically on such generic values, which will often reflect political or pragmatic choices as much as hard science.[231] As already indicated, it may however appoint consultants to use their own expertise to evaluate the risk within the framework of such generic values, and to report upon it.

Determining that pollution of controlled waters is being caused

The Guidance states that the authority should determine that land is **3.194** contaminated land on the basis that pollution of controlled waters is being caused where[232]:

(a) it has carried out an appropriate scientific and technical assessment of all the relevant and available evidence, having regard to any advice provided by the Environment Agency; and

(b) on the basis of that assessment, it is satisfied on the balance of probabilities that:
(i) a potential pollutant is present in, on or under the land in question, which constitutes poisonous, noxious or polluting matter, or which is solid waste matter; and
(ii) that potential pollutant is entering controlled waters by the pathway identified in the pollutant linkage.

As explained above, the entry of the pollutant into controlled waters **3.195** must be a present, not a past, phenomenon for this determination to be made.[233]

Determining that pollution of controlled waters is likely to be caused

The Guidance provides that the authority should determine that land is **3.196** contaminated on the basis that pollution of controlled waters is likely to be caused where[234]:

(a) it has carried out an appropriate scientific and technical assessment of all the relevant and available evidence, having regard to any advice provided by the Environment Agency;

---

[230] DEFRA Circular 01/2006, *Contaminated Land*, Annex 3 para.B.49.
[231] See Judith Petts, Tom Cairney and Mike Smith, *Risk Based Contaminated Land Investigation and Assessment* (Chichester: John Wiley & Sons, 1997).
[232] DEFRA Circular 01/2006, *Contaminated Land*, Annex 3 para.B.51.
[233] See para.3.64.
[234] DEFRA Circular 01/2006, *Contaminated Land*, Annex 3 para.B.51.

(b) on the basis of that assessment it is satisfied that, on the balance of probabilities, all of the following circumstances apply:

    (i) a potential pollutant is present in, on or under the land in question, which constitutes poisonous, noxious or polluting matter, or which is solid waste matter;

    (ii) the potential pollutant in question is in such a condition that it is capable of entering controlled waters;

    (iii) taking into account the geology and other circumstances of the land in question, there is a pathway by which the potential pollutant can enter controlled waters;

    (iv) the potential pollutant is more likely than not to enter the controlled waters and when it does so will be in a form that is poisonous, noxious or polluting, or solid waste matter; and

    (v) there are no suitable and sufficient risk management arrangements relevant to the pollution linkage in place to prevent such pollution.

3.197   These requirements follow closely the criteria for what constitutes likelihood of pollution of controlled waters earlier in the Guidance and reference should be made to that discussion. The Guidance on this issue creates a rather curious double standard of proof, namely that the authority must be satisfied on the balance of probabilities that entry of the pollutant into the waters is more likely than not. One of those elements might arguably be thought to be redundant. The concept of "suitable and sufficient risk management arrangements" is again potentially important, but should also be seen in the wider context of whether there is a pathway at all. For example, a cut-off ditch which prevents pollutants reaching a river might be said not only to constitute such arrangements but also, more fundamentally, to prevent there being any pathway at all.

The physical extent of the contaminated land

3.198 The determination that land is contaminated land will have to be made in relation to a specific area. This may have important consequences in terms of the subsequent service of any remediation notice, so the decision is critical and may in practical terms be one of the most difficult decisions for the authority.

3.199   The Guidance states that the primary consideration should be the extent of land which is contaminated.[235] This is at one level simply stating the obvious, but implies that the precise extent of the contaminants present will be known with some certainty. However, the degree of certainty will in fact depend on the conditions encountered and on the level of investigation. Clearly, it will not be possible to sample every square metre of an extensive site, for reasons both of cost and practicability. Some areas (for example buildings in use) may be inaccessible for intrusive survey purposes. A measure of pragmatism, informed by expert judgment, will be necessary here. The Guidance suggests that the authority may need to

---

[235] DEFRA Circular 01/2006, *Contaminated Land*, Annex 3 para.B.32.

begin by reviewing a wider area, subsequently refining it down to the "precise" areas which meet the statutory tests, and using these as the basis for its determination.[236]

Difficult issues have arisen in some cases where housing estates have **3.200** been built on contaminated land. An extreme example is the Thames View estate at Barking and Dagenham, where it was reported that some 900 houses and gardens were affected by deposits of power station ash.[237] Where the evidence suggests that any part of the estate may in principle be affected, investigation to identify specific gardens (or parts of gardens) affected might seem to be an impossible task and, moreover, "patchwork" remediation by simply dealing with those areas specifically identified may well not be an acceptable solution in terms of reducing future risks to an acceptable level. In practical terms, a comprehensive approach to identification may be desirable, provided this is underpinned by expert advice. In the last resort, the owner or tenant of any particular garden included within the determination will have their statutory right of appeal, on the grounds that their land is unreasonably identified as contaminated, should a remediation notice be served.

A somewhat different, but related, issue is the case where a large area is **3.201** identified as contaminated, but separate designations of different parts of it may lead to simplicity in the actions which will follow. The Guidance states that four factors must be taken into account by the authority in seeking to achieve simplicity of administration, namely[238]:

(a) the location of the pollutants;

(b) the nature of the remediation that might be required;

(c) the likely identity of those who may be appropriate persons to bear responsibility for the remediation (where this is reasonably clear at this stage: which of course it may well not be); and

(d) in the case of radioactive harm, the views of the Environment Agency on the desirability of a separate determination of part of the land.

The Guidance suggests that in practice this is likely to mean that the **3.202** land to be covered by a single determination is likely to be the smallest area covered by a single remediation action, which cannot sensibly be broken down into smaller actions. Subject to this the land will be the smaller of[239]:

(a) the plots which are separately recorded in the Land Register or are in separate ownership or occupation; and

(b) the area of land in which the presence of significant pollutants has been established.

---

[236] DEFRA Circular 01/2006, *Contaminated Land*, Annex 3 para.B.33.
[237] See ENDS Report 360, January 2005, pp.3–4.
[238] DEFRA Circular 01/2006, *Contaminated Land*, Annex 3 para.B.32.
[239] DEFRA Circular 01/2006, *Contaminated Land*, Annex 3 para.B.34.

3.203   This part of the Guidance is perhaps not as clearly worded as might be desirable, but essentially the premise is that subdivision into smaller areas is a good thing, so far as that is consistent with sensible remediation solutions. If a single comprehensive, remediation programme is required, for example, removing soil to a specific level from all gardens in a major housing estate and then reinstating to a given specification, it clearly will not make a great deal of sense to issue a separate determination for each garden.

3.204   The assumption that subdivision is preferable is in fact questionable. Determinations made separately in relation to a number of small plots may be helpful in avoiding the need to serve notices apportioning liability on a number of different owners or occupiers. But, equally, it may not be desirable to serve multiple notices on a single appropriate person in relation to small plots of land. Ownership may in fact not be relevant at all if the original polluter can be found. The problem is that the authority at the time of making the determination may well not have the information available to make sensible decisions on the matter.

3.205   The potential difficulties may be seen by considering the following simple case. Contamination by organic solvents is found to exist on part of a disused industrial site. It has spread to varying extents into the back gardens of adjoining residential properties. Should a single determination be made in relation to the entire area of contamination, or should separate determinations be made for the relevant parts of the industrial area and of each garden? Clearly the determination should not extend to a wider area than that where the contamination is physically present. However, whether the land can sensibly be subdivided into separate ownerships will depend to some extent on the nature of the proposed remediation actions. If what is required is (for example) simply to dig up and remove contaminated material, somewhat simplistically it could be said that it could practicably be carried out separately by each individual owner, though economies of scale might well make co-operation sensible. On the other hand, if the remediation consists of pumping and treating contaminated groundwater, or inserting some form of artificial barrier, it will be entirely impracticable or indeed impossible to treat each individual garden separately. The matter may not however be as simple as just digging out and removing soil. This may need to be done on a carefully controlled and uniform basis if it is to be effective. The authority will therefore need to have a reasonably clear idea of what the appropriate remediation will be in order to take sensible decisions on this issue.

3.206   Another factor which may have an important bearing on the issue is the likely identity of the appropriate person or persons to undertake the remediation. As we shall see later, a key issue is whether the original polluter can still be found. The statutory rules in s.78K on the escape or migration of contaminants will also be relevant, since the gardens were contaminated by substances escaping from elsewhere. If the application of those rules leads to the conclusion that a single former polluter is the appropriate person to clean up the entire area of contamination, it makes little sense to make separate determinations for smaller plots, based on current ownership. On the other hand, such a determination may be more appropriate where the original polluter cannot be found and where each separate owner or occupier will be potentially responsible. The authority may well not have sufficient information at the time of determining whether the land is contaminated land to make sensible decisions on this.

One possible solution to the problem is that there may be an element of **3.207** flexibility to subdivide the relevant area at the time of serving remediation notices. This issue is considered later.[240] On the basis that there is such flexibility it might be more sensible for the authority to concern itself with the practicalities of remediation rather than with land ownership at the time of making the determination, while retaining the flexibility to subdivide on the basis of liability or tenure at a later stage.

Consistency with other bodies

The Guidance requires the authority to adopt a consistent approach to **3.208** other relevant regulatory authorities. In practice, this means that in making any determination which relates to an ecological system effect the authority should consult Natural England.[241] Similarly, where the determination relates to the pollution of controlled waters the Environment Agency should be consulted and regard given to its comments.[242]

General points on making the determination

The Guidance also lays down some general requirements on the deter- **3.209** mination process:

1. A particular pollutant linkage or linkages must form the basis of the determination. All three elements of the linkage (pollutant, pathway and receptor) must be present.[243]

2. The authority should consider any evidence that additive or synergistic effects between potential pollutants (whether the same substance on different areas of land or between different substances) may result in a significant pollutant linkage.[244] This, if done thoroughly, will not necessarily be a straightforward or easy exercise.

3. The authority should also consider whether a significant pollutant linkage may result from a combination of several different pathways (inhalation, plus dermal contract, plus oral ingestion, for example.)[245]

4. The authority should address the issue of whether there is more than one significant pollutant linkage on any land; if so, then each

---

[240] See para.4.66ff.
[241] DEFRA Circular 01/2006, *Contaminated Land*, Annex 3 para.B.42.
[242] DEFRA Circular 01/2006, *Contaminated Land*, Annex 3 para.B.43.
[243] DEFRA Circular 01/2006, *Contaminated Land*, Annex 3 para.B.40.
[244] DEFRA Circular 01/2006, *Contaminated Land*, Annex 3 para.B.41(a).
[245] DEFRA Circular 01/2006, *Contaminated Land*, Annex 3 para.B.41(b).

linkage must be considered separately, since different people may be responsible for their remediation.[246]

3.210   This last point is particularly important. It stresses the foundational nature of the pollutant linkage concept, which though it appears nowhere in the legislation derives its statutory force from the prescriptive Guidance.

The legal process of determination

3.211 The identification of land as "contaminated land" is an important step which has significant legal consequences, triggering the duty under s.78E(1) to serve a remediation notice. As such it is likely that in practice the matter will go to a committee of the authority for decision, rather than being delegated to an officer to determine. The report to committee is likely to be a crucial document in this respect. The question which the decision-making body should ask itself is whether the statutory criteria for contaminated land are satisfied, not whether it is appropriate or expedient to take enforcement action.[247] The officer's report should make clear what the legal tests are, and how the facts relate to those tests and to the statutory guidance.[248] Failure in this respect to report the legal tests accurately may lead to the undermining of the authority's action at a later date.

3.212   If the authority forms the view that the land is not contaminated land, then the resolution should state the basis on which that decision is reached; whilst there may be other ways of addressing the problem than service of a remediation notice, that is not a correct basis for determining to take no action.[249] In short, the issue for the authority is not whether they feel it is or is not appropriate to serve a remediation notice (which may present all sorts of local, legal or financial problems) but simply whether or not the land in question is contaminated within the statute. There may be other factors that will preclude service of a remediation notice (for example, hardship, or the fact that remediation will be undertaken in any event), but consideration of these issues comes at a later stage.

Notice to the Environment Agency and others

3.213 Under s.78B(3) the local authority must give notice of the identification of any contaminated land in its area to:

(a) the Environment Agency;

(b) the owner of the land;

(c) any person who appears to the authority to be in occupation of the whole or any part of the land; and

---

[246] DEFRA Circular 01/2006, *Contaminated Land*, Annex 3 para.B.41(c).
[247] *R. v Carrick DC Ex p. Shelley* [1996] Env. L.R. 266.
[248] *R. v Carrick DC Ex p. Shelley* [1996] Env. L.R. 266, 280–281.
[249] *R. v Carrick DC Ex p. Shelley* [1996] Env. L.R. 266, 284.

(d) each person who appears to the authority to be an appropriate person.

The system of notification in s.78B(3) makes early dialogue between the **3.214** local authority and the present owners a prerequisite. Provisions for locating the owner and occupier might presumably have followed the procedure laid down in the Town and Country Planning Act prior to the service of enforcement notices, namely s.330, where a requisition for information as to interests in land may be served on the occupier and on any person in receipt of rent. There are, however, two non-specific powers which may assist. The first is the general power to require persons to answer questions under s.108(4)(j) of the Environment Act 1995. The second is the general power under s.16 of the Local Government Act (Miscellaneous Provisions) Act 1976 to serve notice on the occupier of the land, on any person having an interest in it or who receives rent for it, and on any manager or letting agent, a notice requiring information on his own interest and that of others interested in the land. This seems likely to be a widely used power in relation to Pt IIA.

The authority will also need to consider making use of the information **3.215** on current and past freehold ownership and on certain leasehold interests which is available from the Land Registry.

As to identifying an "appropriate person", the authority must for the **3.216** purposes of the notice determine the appropriate person in accordance with the statutory provisions, under s.78F. It follows that the process of identifying the "appropriate persons" should be carried out at an early stage. However, the authority may not at the initial stage of identifying contaminated land, be able to establish who falls into these categories.[250] The authority must proceed on an iterative basis on the best information it has at the relevant time. Special provision is accordingly made to deal with "latecomer" appropriate persons. Under s.78B(4) if the enforcing authority later discover that another person is an "appropriate person", then they must also serve notice on that person. Whereas the initial notice under s.78B(3) will in all cases be served by the local authority, the term "enforcing authority" in subs.78B(4) will embrace not only the local authority but also the Environment Agency in relation to special sites.

No provision is made for the situation where, having served a notice, the **3.217** authority concludes that the recipient is not in fact an appropriate person, though presumably it is open to the authority to withdraw the notice, without prejudice to the service of a second or subsequent one. Such a power to withdraw a notice in appropriate cases seems likely to be implied on the analogy with the power in Pt III of the 1990 Act, established by the Court of Appeal in *R. v Bristol CC Ex p. Everett*; in respect of statutory nuisance abatement notices.[251]

---

[250] DEFRA Circular 01/2006, *Contaminated Land*, Annex 2 para.4.2.
[251] [1999] Env. L.R. 587, 600.

Record of determination

3.218 The authority is required by Annex 3 para.B.52 of the Guidance to prepare a written record of any determination that land is contaminated land. The record should include (if necessary by means of reference to other documents):

  (a) a description of the particular significant pollutant linkage, identifying each of the three components of pollutant, pathway and receptor;

  (b) a summary of the evidence on which the determination is based;

  (c) a summary of the relevant assessment of this evidence; and

  (d) a summary of the way in which the authority considers that the relevant requirements of Chs A and B of the Guidance have been satisfied.

3.219 Because of the prescriptive nature of the Guidance, the record of determination has effectively a statutory status. In any challenge to the determination of the authority, whether on appeal or by judicial review, it is likely to be a key document. It must therefore be drafted carefully and precisely, with adequate and accurate cross reference to any supporting reports or other documents. If properly prepared, the officer's report to committee will provide the basis for much of the material in the record of determination.

3.220 The Guidance only requires a record to be prepared where land is determined to be "contaminated"; it does not cover the situation where the opposite result is reached. Information on the decision-making process may, in such cases, be available under freedom of information provisions.[252] This may be important since local residents or amenity groups may be very concerned to know why land has been determined not to be contaminated; as may persons whose land has been determined to be contaminated where neighbouring land has not.

PART 5: SPECIAL SITES

The concept of "special sites"

3.221 Whilst all contaminated land within the meaning of Pt IIA involves, of its nature, significant harm or risk, some types of contaminated land may present particular risks or technical problems making them more suitable to be dealt with by the Environment Agency, rather than local authorities. An example is land on which an IPPC installation has been or is situated or a IPPC prescribed process has been carried on, where the relevant

---

[252] See para.3.146ff.

expertise is likely to reside within the Agency. Drafts of the Environment Act proposed the creation of a special class of "closed landfills", so as to provide a "more tailored approach" to this type of site.[253] The distinction was ultimately dropped however, on the basis that other types of site could present equally serious problems.[254] In fact, landfill sites or other land used for waste activity are not as such designated as special sites, on the basis that the waste management provisions of the 1990 Act already contains wide powers for the Agency to tackle the problems presented by such sites.[255]

Special sites defined

Although the legislation contains a definition of a "special site" it brings us no nearer to what exactly the legislature has in mind for their designation. Section 78A(3) defines a special site as: **3.222**

> "any contaminated land—(a) which has been designated as such a site by virtue of sections 78C(7) or 78D(6) below; and (b) whose designation as such has not been terminated by the Environment Agency under s.78Q(4)."

It follows from this definition that a special site must be contaminated land within s.78A(2), that is, in such a condition by reason of substances in, on or under the land, that significant harm is being caused, or there is significant possibility of such harm being caused, or pollution of controlled waters is being caused or likely to be caused. The key to what constitutes a special site lies in the Regulations. By s.78C(8) land is required to be designated as a special site if, but only if, it is land of a description prescribed for that purpose. The Regulations may make different provision for different cases, circumstances, areas or localities, and may describe land by reference to its area or locality.[256] **3.223**

By s.78C(10), in prescribing descriptions of land as special sites, the Secretary of State may have regard to whether the harm or pollution involved are likely to be serious, and whether the Environment Agency is likely to have expertise in dealing with the kind of pollution in question. However, this is expressly stated to be without prejudice to the generality of the power to prescribe such descriptions of land. Annex 4 to the Circular indicates four main groups of cases where descriptions of land have been prescribed as special sites[257]: **3.224**

> (a) water pollution cases, in particular those where the Agency will have concerns under other legislation, on drinking water, surface water quality, and groundwater;

[253] *Hansard* HL Vol.560, col.1432.
[254] *Hansard* HL Vol.562, cols 156, 158, 160.
[255] DEFRA Circular 01/2006, *Contaminated Land*, Annex 4 para.14.
[256] 1990 Act s.78C(9).
[257] DEFRA Circular 01/2006, *Contaminated Land*, Annex 4 paras 9–13.

(b) industrial cases, where the land in question is being or has been used for specific types of activity that either pose special remediation problems or are subject to other statutory regimes, for example, oil refining, explosives, IPC sites, PPC installations and nuclear sites;

(c) defence cases, designed to ensure that the Agency deals with most cases where the land involves the Ministry of Defence Estate, on the basis that the Agency is best placed to ensure uniformity and appropriate liaison with the MoD across the country;

(d) radioactivity cases, where land is contaminated by virtue of radioactive substances.

The Regulations on special sites

3.225 The Regulations prescribe those descriptions of land which are required, if contaminated, to be designated as a special site. These are[258]:

(a) Land to which reg.3 applies (as to which, see below).

(b) Land which is contaminated by virtue of waste acid tars. These are defined as tars which contain sulphuric acid, which were produced as a result of the refining of benzole, used lubricants or petroleum, and which are or were stored on land used as a retention basin for the disposal of such tars.[259] The Guidance to the Regulations states that the retention basins (or lagoons) involved are typically those where waste arose from the use of concentrated sulphuric acid to produce lubricating oils or greases, or to reclaim base lubricants from mineral oil residues; the description is not intended to cover cases where the tars resulted from the manufacture of coal products, or where these tars were placed in pits or wells.[260]

(c) Land on which at any time there has been carried out either:

(i) the purification (including refining) of crude petroleum or of oil from petroleum, shale or any bituminous substance except coal; or

(ii) the manufacture or processing of explosives.

(d) Land on which an IPC-prescribed process (Pt A) has been or is being carried on under an authorisation under Pt I of the 1990 Act. It does not cover cases where the process comprises solely things being done that are required by way of remediation, that is where an authorisation has had to be obtained to carry out the remediation process itself. The Guidance points out that it also does not cover land where the activity was of the nature of a prescribed process, but ceased before the application of the IPC regime to it.[261]

---

[258] Reg.2.
[259] Reg.2(1)(b) and (2).
[260] DEFRA Circular 01/2006, *Contaminated Land*, Annex 4 para.11(a).
[261] DEFRA Circular 01/2006, *Contaminated Land*, Annex 4 para.11(d).

(e) Land on which an activity has been or is being carried out under a PPC permit in a PPC installation or by means of a PPC mobile plant (Pt A(1)). It does not cover cases where the activity comprises solely things being done that are required by way of remediation, that is where a permit has had to be obtained to carry out the remediation process itself. The Guidance points out that it also does not cover land where the activity was related to a prescribed installation, but ceased before the application of the PPC regime to it.[262]

(f) Land within a nuclear site, that is any site in respect of all or part of which a nuclear site licence under the Nuclear Installations Act 1965 is in force, or where the nuclear site licence has terminated, but where the licensee's period of responsibility under the 1965 Act still applies.[263]

(g) Land owned or occupied by or on behalf of the Secretary of State for Defence, by the Defence Council, or by the relevant bodies under the Visiting Armed Forces Act 1952 or the International Headquarters and Defence Organisations Act 1964, being land used for naval, military or defence purposes. Land used for residential purposes or by the NAAFI is to be treated as such land only if it forms part of a base occupied for naval, military or air force purposes.[264] This category covers only land in current military use, and will not extend to land which has been disposed of to civil ownership or occupation; nor does it cover training areas or ranges which are not owned by the MoD but are subject to occasional military use.[265]

(h) Land on which the manufacture of certain military weapons has been carried on at any time. These are: chemical weapons, biological agents or toxins and associated weapons or delivery systems.[266] The current ownership or occupation is irrelevant in this case.

(i) Land designated under the Atomic Weapons Establishment Act 1991.

(j) Land held for the benefit of Greenwich Hospital to which s.30 of the Armed Forces Act 1996 applies.

(k) Land which is contaminated by virtue of radioactive substances.

(l) Land which is adjoining or adjacent to land falling within categories (b)–(k) above, and which is contaminated land by virtue of substances which appear to have escaped from land within those categories. The intention here is that the Agency will be the enforcing authority for both sites, thereby avoiding the splitting of regulatory control.[267]

---

[262] DEFRA Circular 01/2006, *Contaminated Land*, Annex 4 para.11(e).
[263] Reg.2(5).
[264] Reg.2(7).
[265] DEFRA Circular 01/2006, *Contaminated Land*, Annex 4 para.12.
[266] See further the Biological Weapons Act 1974 and the Chemical Weapons Act 1996.
[267] DEFRA Circular 01/2006, *Contaminated Land*, Annex 3 para.14.

3.226   Regulation 3 deals with special sites which relate to water pollution and covers the following categories of land:

(a) Where controlled waters used or intended to be used for the supply of drinking water for human consumption are being affected by the land, and as a result require treatment or additional treatment before use in order to be regarded as "wholesome" under the Water Industry Act 1991 Pt III. The category therefore relates essentially to where the contamination impacts on the standards of wholesomeness set out in the Water Supply (Water Quality) Regulations 2000 (SI 2000/3184) as amended, or the Private Water Supplies Regulations 1991 (SI/2790). The Guidance suggests that an intention to use water for drinking purposes would be demonstrated by the existence of an abstraction licence for that purpose, or an application for such a licence.[268]

(b) Where controlled waters are being affected so that they do not meet or are not likely to meet the criteria for water quality classification for waters of their relevant description. Again, it is standards set under other legislation which are critical: in this case, the Surface Waters (Dangerous Substances) (Classification) Regulations (SI 1989/2286, SI 1992/337, SI 1997/2560, SI 1998/389) which apply classification criteria for inland freshwaters with a view to reducing the pollution of such waters by listed dangerous substances, reflecting in turn the requirements of Directive 76/464 on Dangerous Substances discharged into the aquatic environment.

(c) This category covers impacts on major aquifers. It applies where controlled waters are being affected by substances falling within a number of families or groups listed in Sch.1 to the Regulations, and the waters or any part of them are contained within underground strata comprising or including rock formations listed in Sch.1. The substances involved include organohalogens, mercury, cadmium, mineral oils and hydrocarbons, cyanides, and those possessing carcinogenic, mutagenic or teratogenic properties in the aquatic environment. The list corresponds to List I of the Groundwater Directive 80/86/EEC. The formations of rock include various chalk, sandstone and limestone formations, and are essentially the major aquifers. The fact that the land lies over one of these aquifers does not of itself make it a special site: pollution of the controlled waters within the relevant strata by the relevant substances must be occurring or likely to occur.[269]

Investigation and designation of special sites

3.227 Normally the procedure under Pt IIA involves simply identification of land as contaminated, following which the remediation provisions apply. However, for special sites, the process is identification, followed by

---

[268] DEFRA Circular 01/2006, *Contaminated Land*, para.9(a).
[269] DEFRA Circular 01/2006, *Contaminated Land*, para.10.

designation, then remediation. Identification can be by either the local authority (s.78C(1)) or by the Secretary of State (s.78D(5)) or can be initiated by the Environment Agency (s.78C(4)).

The question of whether a site falls within one of the special site **3.228** categories must be considered before any inspection is authorised or takes place, since if it appears that the land would be a special site, or this is a reasonable probability, the authority should seek to make arrangements with the Environment Agency for the Agency to carry out the inspection on behalf of the authority.[270]

Where contaminated land has been identified by the local authority, a **3.229** decision has to be taken as to whether or not the land is required to be designated as a special site, by reference to the Regulations and in accordance with any statutory guidance.[271] This may be a committee decision or one delegated under proper procedures to an officer. Before making the decision, the local authority must request the advice of the Environment Agency, and have regard to it.[272] Having taken the advice of the Agency, either for or against designation as a special site, the local authority has a discretion not to follow it, provided it has regard to it. Where it is decided that land is required to be designated as a special site then notice must be given to those persons set out in s.78C(2).[273] For the purposes of s.78C the relevant persons are[274]:

(a) the Environment Agency;

(b) the owner of the land;

(c) any person who appears to the local authority concerned to be in occupation of the whole or any part of the land; and

(d) each person who appears to that authority to be an appropriate person.

Where the Environment Agency disagrees with a decision that land **3.230** should be designated a special site, it may, by giving a counter-notice and a statement of reasons before the expiry of 21 days from the statutory notice being given, require the authority to refer the matter to the Secretary of State.[275]

Agency notice as to special site designation

In parallel with the procedure set out above where the local authority **3.231** identifies and designates a special site, the Environment Agency can also give notice to the local authority in whose area the land is situated that it considers contaminated land should be designated as a special site.[276] The

---

[270] See para.3.138.
[271] 1990 Act ss.78C(8) and 78B(2).
[272] 1990 Act s.78C(3).
[273] 1990 Act s.78C(1)(b).
[274] 1990 Act s.78C(2).
[275] 1990 Act s.78D(1).
[276] 1990 Act s.78C(4).

local authority are then obliged to consider the Agency's notice and decide whether the land is required to be designated as a special site or otherwise, and having made their decision shall give notice to the Agency accordingly and to all the other relevant persons.[277] In other words, it is still the local authority which designates the site; the role of the Agency is to initiate the procedure which may lead to designation.

3.232 So what happens if the local authority disagrees with the Agency in this instance? Under s.78D, if a local authority gives notice of its decision to the Environment Agency that the land is not to be designated as a special site, then before the expiry of the period of 21 days beginning on the day the notice was given, the Agency may serve a counter-notice that it disagrees with the decision, together with a statement of its reasons for disagreeing; The local authority must then refer the decision to the Secretary of State and send to him a statement of its reasons for the decision it has reached.[278] At the same time that the Environment Agency gives the local authority notice that it disagrees with its decision, it must also send to the Secretary of State a copy of the notice of disagreement, together with a statement of reasons why it disagrees with the local authority.[279]

3.233 Where a local authority refers the decision to the Secretary of State under these provisions, it must give notice of the fact to the relevant persons.[280]

Disagreement between local authority and Environment Agency: Secretary of State's decision

3.234 There are two ways in which disputes between the local authority and Agency may be referred to the Secretary of State. First where the authority decides that a site is a special site and the Agency disagrees; secondly, where the Agency gives notice that it considers the site to be a special site and the local authority disagrees.

3.235 Where a dispute has arisen between the local authority and the Environment Agency as to whether a site should or should not be designated, then the Secretary of State, by s.78D(4), on reference to him by the authority, in accordance with the procedure in the previous paragraph:

(a) may confirm or reverse the decision of the local authority in respect of the whole or any part of the land to which it relates; and

(b) shall give notice of his decision on the referral:

(i) to the relevant persons; and
(ii) to the local authority.

3.236 No procedure is laid down for how the Secretary of State is to arrive at his decision, and it seems to be envisaged that he will deal with the matter on the basis of the statement of reasons given by each party under s.78D(1)

---

[277] 1990 Act s.78C(5).
[278] 1990 Act s.78D(1).
[279] 1990 Act s.78D(2).
[280] 1990 Act s.78D(3).

and (2). No doubt the Secretary of State may request further information if he so chooses, and may consider representations submitted by third parties and other Government departments and agencies. The Secretary of State's decision here seems essentially an administrative rather than a judicial one; accordingly it may be subject to challenge by a party with sufficient interest on ordinary administrative law principles.

Notice of decision: when designation as special site takes effect

There are a number of somewhat complex statutory provisions as to when **3.237** a decision that a site shall be designated as a special site takes effect. A distinction is drawn between the decision that a site is required to be designated and the effective date of designation. Generally, where a local authority makes a decision of its own volition that land shall be designated a special site,[281] or accepts the decision of the Environment Agency to that effect,[282] the decision takes effect on the day after whichever of the following events first occurs[283]:

(a) the expiry of 21 days beginning with the date on which notice of the local authority's decision is given to the Environment Agency; or

(b) if the Agency gives notice that it agrees with the decision of the local authority, the giving of that notice.

Where the decision takes effect as above, the local authority must give notice of that fact to the relevant persons.[284] The point of the 21-day period at (a) above is that under s.78D(1) the Agency may within that period give notice that it disagrees with the decision, thereby triggering a reference to the Secretary of State.

There is a distinction between the time when a decision that a site is **3.238** required to be designated as "special" takes effect, as set out above, and the time when the designation itself shall take effect. It is the notice of the decision given to the relevant persons which has effect as the designation, and it does so as from the time the decision takes effect.[285] However, where a decision of a local authority is referred to the Secretary of State because of a disagreement with the Environment Agency under s.78D, the decision does not take effect until the day after that on which the Secretary of State gives notice of his decision: it then takes effect as confirmed or reversed by him.[286] Where this is the case the notice given by the Secretary of State of his decision to the local authority and to the relevant persons takes effect as a designation as from the same time as the decision takes effect.[287]

---

[281] 1990 Act s.78C(1)(b).
[282] 1990 Act s.78C(5)(a).
[283] 1990 Act s.78C(6).
[284] 1990 Act s.78C(6)
[285] 1990 Act s.78C(7).
[286] 1990 Act s.78D(5).
[287] 1990 Act s.78D(5).

3.239 These provisions need to be read in conjunction with the restrictions on serving a remediation notice until a three month period has expired, as set out in s.78H(3). This period runs from the date on which the notices of decision are given to the "relevant persons", including the owner of the land, any apparent occupiers, and each apparent appropriate person.[288] There are therefore no less than three relevant dates envisaged by the legislation for special sites:

1. the date that the decision takes effect;

2. the effective date of designation; and

3. the date of service of notices on relevant persons (from which the three month period is calculated).

Special sites: adoption by the Environment Agency of remediation notice

3.240 We have already seen that one of the factors in framing the Regulations on special sites turns on the relative ability of local authorities and the Environment Agency to deal with the problem in question, and in particular which of them has the necessary expertise.[289] It is therefore not surprising to find provisions under which the Environment Agency may adopt a remediation notice where it later becomes apparent that the land in question should be treated as a special site.[290] If it does so, it must give notice of that decision to the appropriate person and to the local authority,[291] and the remediation notice then takes effect henceforth as a remediation notice given by that Agency.[292] It is provided that this process shall not affect the validity of the original remediation notice.[293] The effect of adoption is that the local authority ceases to have jurisdiction as the enforcing authority, this passing to the Agency. However, where the local authority has already begun to act under s.78N to carry out remediation itself, the authority may continue with that action, and will still be able to use s.78P to seek to recover its costs.[294] This ability extends only to the "thing, or series of things", which the local authority has begun to do prior to adoption of the notice by the Agency; it does not extend to the remediation process in its entirety.

Special sites: termination of designation

3.241 If it appears to the Environment Agency that a special site is no longer land which is required to be designated as such, they may give notice to the Secretary of State and to the local authority concerned terminating the

---

[288] See Ch.5.
[289] 1990 Act s.78C(10)(b).
[290] 1990 Act s.78Q(1).
[291] 1990 Act s.78Q(1)(a).
[292] 1990 Act s.78Q(1)(b).
[293] 1990 Act s.78Q(1)(c).
[294] 1990 Act s.78Q(2).

designation as from the date specified in the notice.[295] If such a notice is given, this does not prevent all or any part of the land being designated as a special site on a subsequent occasion.[296] The Agency is required in exercising this function to act in accordance with any guidance for the purpose given by the Secretary of State.[297] Unlike the original designation of a special site, no procedure is provided for resolving disputes between the Agency and local authority, which may not necessarily want to see the designation terminated. The Agency's action under s.78Q(4) is presumably subject to judicial review on the normal grounds, but the local authority may also seek to persuade the Secretary of State to give site-specific guidance under s.78W to the Agency on the issue.

Special sites: review

If and so long as any land is a special site, the Environment Agency may **3.242** from time to time inspect that land for the purpose of keeping its condition under review.[298] The purpose of this provision is not entirely clear; the review might lead either to further remediation requirements, or to possible withdrawal of special site status. The function is expressed in terms of a power rather than a duty. However, in exercising this function the Environment Agency must act in accordance with government guidance.[299]

PART 6: PROGRESS ON IDENTIFYING CONTAMINATED LAND

In general terms it is fair to say that progress in identifying land as **3.243** contaminated since the inception of the Pt IIA regime in 2000 has been slow. That is not to underestimate the real difficulties faced by local authorities in respect of their new responsibilities. By March 2002 it was reported that only some 33 sites, 11 of them special sites, had been identified.[300] In June 2003, DEFRA sent a questionnaire to all English local authorities, the responses to which[301] suggested that relatively few had got to the stage of correlating areas of potential contamination with known vulnerable receptors, or establishing a prioritised programme of detailed inspections. Figures published in May 2007 indicated that since 2000 there had been 659 determination notices issued in England and Wales, but only six in Scotland. Of that number, many were multiple notices served on separate owners in respect of the same site, and it has ben estimated that the figure corresponds to about 100 cases,[302] which is a very small number relative to the scale of contamination in the UK.

---

[295] 1990 Act s.78Q(4).
[296] 1990 Act s.78Q(5).
[297] 1990 Act s.78Q(6).
[298] 1990 Act s.78Q(3).
[299] 1990 Act s.78Q(6).
[300] ENDS Report 362, March 2002, pp.8–9.
[301] Published by DEFRA as CLAN 2/04 (December 2005). In fact only about 47% of the 354 Pt IIA English authorities responded at all.
[302] ENDS Report 388, May 2004, p.14.

3.244   The reasons for what might be seen as disappointing progress are varied but probably come down the the following[303]:

1. limited financial resources;

2. initial limited technical expertise and experience;

3. late publication of, and confusion over, technical guidance; and

4. a general attitude of conservatism or caution by local authorities, due in part to the technical and legal complexities of the regime and in part to concerns as to the possibility of blight, stigma and anxiety which might affect local communities.

Funding

3.245 So far as financial resources are concerned, there have been a number of developments since the introduction of Pt IIA. At the time of introducing the regime, the then Conservative Government expressed the view that it simply reflected existing responsibilities under provisions such as statutory nuisance, and that substantial additional funding would not be required for its implementation.[304] Funding for local authorities was through the supplementary credit approval (SCA) scheme, which allowed bids for specific projects (including intrusive investigations to determine if land was contaminated) to be submitted on an annual basis to central government for approval. This scheme was limited in extent, in that to be eligible the authority had to show that it was liable to undertake remediation as an owner or occupier of contaminated land, or was responsible for the contamination, or had other statutory or contractual obligations to remediate.[305] It was not available for work needed to facilitate the development, redevelopment or sale of such land.[306] The effect of SCA approval was to sanction the borrowing of money by the local authority to undertake the work, the cost of servicing the loan then being addressed under revenue support grant calculations. This was not necessarily an attractive option for debt-free councils. In addition, following an announcement in July 1998 of the provision of £50 million additional funding to local authorities to assist in implementation of Pt IIA, some £36 million was added to the "Environmental Protection and Cultural Services" components of the total expenditure figure for local authorities over three years. However, this was not ring-fenced and could be spent on other services.

3.246   The major change to funding occurred in April 2004, when SCAs were abolished and replaced by the Contaminated Land Capital Projects Programme, by which Pt IIA local authorities could apply for supported capital

---

[303] See Dr Bill Baker, "Barriers to the Effective Implementation of the Pt IIA Contaminated Land Regime and Recommendations for Progress" in *Contaminated Land—Achievements and Aspirations* (proceedings of a conference of the Society for Chemistry and Industry and Royal Society for Chemistry) (EPP Publications Ltd, 2004), p.19.

[304] See para.2.16ff and the Ministerial statement of Earl Ferrers at *Hansard*, HL Vol.565, col.1501 (July 11, 1995).

[305] See DEFRA Circular 01/2006, *Contaminated Land*, Annex 2 para.16.12; DEFRA *Contaminated Land Supplementary Credit Approvals: A guide for English Local Authorities* (December, 2002)

[306] See further, Ch.17 on redevelopment finding.

expenditure (revenue) (SCE(R)).[307] The main difference to the SCA system was that whereas under SCA borrowing limits were set for local authorities, under SCE(R) the local authority was free to make its own decisions on borrowing, so that capital expenditure which is not financed by borrowing was also eligible for support. The authority would then set its prudential expenditure limits for the coming year taking that support into account.

In 2006, the system again changed. Instead of the SCE(R) approach of **3.247** feeding amounts into Revenue Support Grant, CLAN 1/06 introduced a system of direct grants (the Contaminated Land Capital Projects Programme or CLCPP) under which authorities simply bid for support in accordance with the guidance on a "first come, first served" basis. Revenue support is provided through the Environmental Protection and Cultural Services Component of Rate Support Grant. Applications under the CLCPP are assessed by the Environment Agency as DEFRA's advisers. Reference should be made to CLAN 1/06 in terms of eligibility criteria and the type of projects which are covered. Funding may therefore be applied for in respect of intrusive investigations and remediation under Pt IIA; in addition it can be used for works under s.59 of the Environmental Protection Act 1990 to remove illegal deposits of controlled waste, where the occupier cannot be held liable, provided these are more than just removing surface deposits of waste.[308] Limited works to reinstate a site upon completion of remediation may also be eligible (e.g. re-fencing or re-turfing). Desk studies and other work short of intrusive investigation are regarded as revenue costs and are dealt with under revenue support grant.

Authorities are expected to use to the full their Pt IIA powers of cost **3.248** recovery where appropriate. However, CLCPP support may be available where cost recovery is both uncertain and likely to be slow, or where costs have been waived or reduced under the Guidance. Appendix A to CLAN 1/06 contains guidance on prioritisation of projects. The CLAN covers the year 2006/2007 and at the time of writing it is not known what the approach will be thereafter.

Technical guidance

There is a plethora of technical guidance provided on Pt IIA, including **3.249** Technical Advice produced by DEFRA under CLR (Contaminated Land Reports) series—for example CLR 11 *Model Procedures for the Management of Land Contamination* (2004).[309] However, a significant source of confusion and delay has been soil guideline values (SGVs) as to the risks presented by the presence of particular substances. For many years the ICRCL Guidance Notes provided important guidance on the hazards of different types of contamination: in particular ICRCL 59/83, revised in July 1987, set out Trigger Values (threshold and action concentrations) for a number of metal and other substances present in soil.

[307] See DEFRA, CLAN 1/04 *Contaminated Land Capital Projects Programme* (February, 2004).
[308] See DEFRA CLAN 1/106, para.2.19.
[309] Discussed further in Ch.21.

3.250   However in March 2002, DEFRA and the Environment Agency published a series of reports based on the Contaminated Land Exposure Assessment Model (CLEA) as CLRs 7, 8, 9 and 10. The CLEA models seek to estimate the amount of substances an individual would take in as a result of exposure to soil under specific conditions. This led to the withdrawal of ICRCL 59/83 by CLAN 3/02 (December 2002). A number of Toxicological (TOX) and SGV reports for specific substances were published, based on Health Criteria Values (HCVs or benchmarks of human toxicity) and on the CLEA methodology, but concerns both as to the limited number of SGVs and their use led to the creation in 2004 of the Cabinet Office Soil Guideline Value Task Force. Actual or potential misunderstanding of how SGVs should be used led to DEFRA issuing CLAN 2/05 (September 2005).

3.251   This stated that there was a "wide body of opinion" within the Task Force that concentrations of substances in soil equivalent to the SGV would not necessarily satisfy the legal test of "significant possibility of significant harm" in Pt IIA or would represent an unacceptable intake or direct contact. Accordingly, basing a determination that land was contaminated simply on applying the SGV would be legally vulnerable. Further work has since been undertaken, leading to the issue of a major report by DEFRA, *Assessing Risks from Land Contamination—A Proportionate Approach* (November 2006) seeking a way forward for the development and use of SGVs.

3.252   These technical issues are discussed further below, but the history of the development of the guidance has not instilled confidence in local authorities which might in any event have been diffident about how to approach very difficult issues of risk assessment in this context.

Best value indicators

3.253   In April 2005 the Government introduced two new indicators as part of its "Best Value" initiative: BV216A on "identifying contaminated land" and BV216B on "information on contaminated land". The effect of this is that local authorities are required to supply data, which is collated by the Audit Commission and published by the Department for Communities and Local Government, on first which "sites of potential concern" have been identified and secondly for which of these sites the authority has sufficiently detailed information to decide whether or not remediation is needed.[310] The idea is that this will allow progress to be compared in a consistent way. Information, rather than remediation, is seen as the critical factor, since progress in remediation may be influenced by factors outside the authority's control, whereas collating information is a truer indicator of performance. There is of course a risk that authorities may focus on satisfying the BV indicators rather than their formal Pt IIA duties, but the Government is clear that it is the statutory requirement of a strategic approach to inspection that should remain paramount, rather than switching resources or skewing effort towards cases which would more easily get

---

[310] DEFRA, CLAN 2/06, *Advice Note on Best Value Performance Indicators: Contaminated Land* (February 2006).

a good result in terms of BV or any related local targets.[311] There are numerous potential problems of interpretation, for example the possibility of artificial subdivision of sites in order to increase numbers, which are to varying degrees addressed in the CLAN guidance.

Well-being powers

One interesting and potentially important question is whether apart from **3.254** Pt IIA a local authority may use its power under s.2 of the Local Government Act 2000 to do anything which it considers is likely to achieve the promotion or improvement of the environmental well-being of its area. It is possible to conceive of cases where a contaminated site may be remediated at relatively modest expense, whereas the technical and legal costs to the authority of pursuing Pt IIA procedures could far exceed that cost. The authority will of course seek voluntary remediation if it can; but if it cannot, the ability to do the necessary work, or to offer to contribute to it in part, may save very considerable sums of money overall. Section 2 is a broad power; it cannot be used, however, where the authority is unable to carry out the desired action by virtue of any statutory prohibition, limitation or restriction on their powers (s.3(1)). However, the courts have interpreted this as only preventing the use of s.2(1) where there is an express, or at least clearly implied prohibition, limitation or restriction.[311a] Accordingly, therefore, the fact that the local authority's powers to act under Pt IIA (for example, under s.78N) are subject to constraints and limitations does not rule out the authority proceeding under s.2(1) if, having regard to its community strategy (s.2(3)) action by the authority entirely or partly at its own expense is considered likely to promote or improve the environmental well-being of its area. It is suggested that it is appropriate for the authority to weight the costs against the ability to deal with the problem expeditiously and to avoid potential huge legal costs of an appeal under Pt IIA.

Voluntary progress

The foregoing may seem a somewhat pessimistic approach. However, the **3.255** effect of Pt IIA in bringing about voluntary remediation of land, often through the planning system, without recourse to formal procedures on identification and remediation, should not be underestimated.[312]

---

[311] See DEFRA, CLAN 2/06, para.14

[311a] *R(J) v Enfield LBC* [2002] EWHC 432 (Admin); [2002] 2 FLR 1; *R (Theophilus) v Lewisham LBC* [2002] EWHC 1371 (Admin); [2003] LGR 98; *R(W) v Lambeth LBC* [2002] EWCA Civ 613; [2002] FLR 327; *R(K) v Lambeth LBC* [2003] EWCA Civ 1150; [2004] 1 W.L.R. 272.

[312] See paras 1.11 and 1.12.

Chapter 4

REMEDIATION NOTICES

PART 1: INTRODUCTION AND BASIC CONCEPTS

The basic scheme

4.01 The essential idea behind the Guidance is that the significant harm (or pollution of controlled waters) must be cleaned up or otherwise dealt with by those responsible for it. Because different present or past owners or occupiers, or indeed third-party perpetrators, may be responsible for substances in or under the land during a site's history, the principle is that they should only be responsible for the significant harm (or pollution of controlled waters) that those substances caused. The way in which the Guidance seeks to achieve this result is to make use of the same pollutant linkage concept as is central to the identification of contaminated land; that is, a harmful relationship between a contaminant, a pathway, and a receptor (or target).

4.02 A remediation notice will contain a "remediation action", which is the action to be taken by way of remediation, or a "remediation package"; that is a set or sequence of remediation actions, perhaps with associated timescales. "A liability group", that is a group of "appropriate persons" who are responsible for the linkage in question, bear responsibility to carry out the remediation action or package required to remediate that problem. Each member of the group gets effectively the same notice, save that the apportionment of liability may differ as between them.

It can also be the case, where a number of distinct pollutant linkages exist on the same site, that separate remediation notices will be served, on different liability groups.

Duty to serve remediation notice

4.03 By s.78E(1) where land has been identified as contaminated land or designated as a special site, the enforcing authority shall serve on each person who is an "appropriate person" a notice (known as a remediation notice) specifying what that person is to do by way of remediation and the periods within which he is required to do each of the specified things.

"Pollutant linkage"

4.04 The term "pollutant linkage", though it appears nowhere in Pt IIA itself, is an important concept in the guidance dealing with the definition of contaminated land.[1] The term refers to the relationship between the

[1] See para.3.07ff.

contaminant, a pathway which it can take, and a receptor which is susceptible to damage by the contaminant. The concept is also relevant for the purposes of the Guidance on who should be the appropriate person, and on how the remediation requirements should be framed, as will be seen from the next paragraph.

"Remediation" and associated terminology

Remediation is a defined term by s.78A(7), meaning: **4.05**

    (a) the doing of anything for the purpose of assessing the condition of:

        (i)   the contaminated land in question;

        (ii) any controlled waters affected by that land; or

       (iii) any land adjoining or adjacent to that land;

    (b) the doing of any works, the carrying out of any operations or the taking of any steps in relation to any such land or waters for the purpose:

        (i)   of preventing or minimising, or remedying or mitigating the effects of, any significant harm, or any pollution of controlled waters, by reason of which the contaminated land is such land; or

        (ii) of restoring the land or waters to their former state; or

    (c) the making of subsequent inspections from time to time for the purpose of keeping under review the condition of the land or waters.

It will be seen therefore that the concept of remediation extends through **4.06** the assessment of land which is found to be contaminated (but not the original assessment as to whether it is contaminated) to the carrying out of preventive, remedial or restorative measures, and to subsequent inspection and review.[2] The term therefore encompasses the whole spectrum of clean-up techniques for contaminated land, from basic removal of contaminated material, to encapsulation or in-situ remediation, or the treatment of contaminated groundwater. The definition is not inherently limited to practicable or reasonable measures; rather the protection against unreasonable requirements is to be found in the provisions relating to the content and procedures for remediation notices, discussed below.

The Guidance contains its own terminology on remediation, using the **4.07** following definitions[3]:

    (a) "remediation action": any individual thing which is being, or is to be done by way of remediation (for example, excavating and removing material, installing a gas control system, etc.);

---

[2] In that sense it is wider than the meaning sometimes associated with remediation of just the clean-up stage: see DEFRA Circular 01/2006, *Contaminated Land*, Annex 3 para.C.7.

[3] DEFRA Circular 01/2006, *Contaminated Land*, Annex 3 para.C.8.

(b) "remediation package": the full set or sequence of remediation actions, within a remediation scheme, which are referable to a particular significant pollutant linkage (i.e. the totality of actions relating to a pollutant linkage);

(c) "remediation scheme": the complete set or sequence of remediation actions (referable to one or more significant pollutant linkages) to be carried out with respect to the relevant land or waters (i.e. the totality of actions relating to the land as a whole);

(d) "relevant land or waters": the contaminated land in question, any controlled waters affected by that land, and any land adjoining or adjacent to the contaminated land on which remediation might be required as a consequence of the contamination. This clearly therefore goes potentially much wider than the contaminated land itself[4];

(e) "assessment action": an action falling within s.78A(7)(a) (i.e. anything for assessing the condition of the land or controlled waters);

(f) "remedial treatment action": an action falling within s.78A(7)(b) (i.e. works or operations for preventing, remedying or mitigating harm or pollution);

(g) "monitoring action": an action within s.78A(7)(c) (i.e. the making of subsequent inspections for keeping the condition of the land or waters under review).

"Appropriate person"

4.08 Remediation notices are to be served on the "appropriate person" or, if more than one exists, on each of them. "Appropriate person" is defined by s.78A(9) to mean any person who is an appropriate person, determined in accordance with s.78F, to bear responsibility for any thing which is to be done by way of remediation in any particular case. The crucial words are therefore the reference to s.78F; it is this section which is decisive in allocating or channelling liability for remediation.

PART 2: CONSULTATION BEFORE SERVICE OF REMEDIATION NOTICE

4.09 By s.78H(1), before serving a remediation notice, the enforcing authority must reasonably endeavour to consult:

(a) the person on whom the notice is to be served;

---

[4] See the definition at s.78G(7), which is similarly broad, in the different context of rights of entry and compensation.

(b) the owner of any land to which the notice relates;

(c) any person who appears to be in occupation of the whole or any part of the land; and

(d) any person of any such other description as may be prescribed.

4.10 The consultation should concern what is to be done by way of remediation. The question of which additional persons need to be consulted, and the steps to be taken for the purpose of consultation, may be provided for by the Regulations—see s.78H(2). In fact, the Regulations for England do not deal with this issue.

4.11 In relation to remediation notices (s.78H(1)) the requirements of consultation are, as a minimum, that the recipient should be consulted about the details of what he is being required to do, and the time within which he must do it.[5] In addition, it is suggested that the enforcing authority is likely to find a wider process of discussion and consultation useful, which could cover:

(a) whether the land should, in fact, be identified as contaminated land (where, for example, the owner or appropriate person may have additional sampling information);

(b) what would need to be achieved by the remediation, in terms of the reduction of the possibility of harm or pollution; and

(c) what particular remediation actions would achieve that remediation.[6]

4.12 It is suggested that this wider process of discussion may also help to identify opportunities for agreed remediation to be carried out without the service of a remediation notice,[7] and where a remediation notice is served, to resolve as many disagreements as possible before the service of the notice, thus limiting the scope of any appeal against it.[8]

4.13 The enforcing authority is also required by the statutory guidance to make reasonable endeavours to consult those who may be affected by any exclusion or apportionment,[9] which might also involve a wider discussion of the identification of other appropriate persons.[10]

Consultation relating to possible grant of rights

4.14 Section 78G relates to the grant of rights which may be necessary to allow the recipient of a remediation notice to carry out the works concerned, whether on the land subject to the notice, or on adjacent or adjoining land.

[5] DEFRA Circular 01/2006, *Contaminated Land*, Annex 2 para.6.11.
[6] DEFRA Circular 01/2006, *Contaminated Land*, Annex 2 para.6.12.
[7] See para.4.55ff.
[8] DEFRA Circular 01/2006, *Contaminated Land*, Annex 2 para.6.13.
[9] DEFRA Circular 01/2006, *Contaminated Land*, Annex 3 para.D.36.
[10] DEFRA Circular 01/2006, *Contaminated Land*, Annex 2 para.6.17.

The relevant consent is required to be given by s.78G(2), and compensation may be claimed for the grant of such rights under s.78G(5).

4.15 Under s.78G(3) an entirely separate consultation requirement arises before serving a remediation notice. The enforcing authority must reasonably endeavour to consult every person who appears to the authority:

(a) to be the owner or occupier of any of the relevant land or waters; and

(b) to be a person who might be required under s.78G(2) to grant, or join in granting, the necessary rights.

4.16 Here the consultation should concern the rights which the relevant person may be required to grant. A couple of examples may help to illustrate how these provisions will work and how they relate to the consultation requirements under s.78H.

Example 1

4.17 The contaminated land in question comprises a gassing landfill site. The remedial measures involved will include the provision of extraction and monitoring boreholes on adjacent land. As well as consulting the appropriate person, owner, occupier, etc. in relation to the landfill site, the authority would need to consult under s.78G the adjacent landowners on whose property the boreholes would need to be placed, concerning the rights they would be required to grant.

Example 2

4.18 The contaminated land question is an old industrial site which used to be operated by X Co Ltd, which is still in existence. The site is now owned by Y Plc. X Co Ltd is a potential appropriate person to be made responsible for clean-up and as such would have to be consulted as to what is to be done by way of remediation under s.78H. Y Plc would have to be consulted in two capacities:

(1) under s.78H as the current owner of the site concerning what is to be done by way of remediation; and

(2) under s.78G as someone who may well be required to give rights to entry to the site to X Co Ltd in order to carry out the works, concerning the rights it would be required to grant.

The three-month period

4.19 Section 78H(3) provides that no remediation notice is to be served within a period of at least three months beginning and ending on the dates specified in subss.78H(3) (a)–(c). Two points need to be kept in mind with regard to this provision. First, it is subject to being overridden in cases of imminent danger of serious harm (see below). Secondly, whilst the intention may well be to allow time for the consultation processes required by ss.78G(3) and 78H(1) to take place, the period is not expressly a consultation period as such. The period is not linked to when consultation commences, and applies even if consultation is concluded satisfactorily within that period. In practice, in many cases the consultation process is likely to require a longer period than three months, in order to reach a satisfactory conclusion, or at least to offer reasonable prospects of such a conclusion.

When does the "moratorium" period begin and end?

Section 78H(3) contemplates three distinct situations: **4.20**

(a) Where the land is not a special site and is simply identified by the local authority. Here the period begins with the date on which the land is identified as contaminated, and ends with the expiration of the period of three months beginning with the day on which notice was given as required by ss.78B(3)(d) or (4) to each person who appears to the authority to be an "appropriate person".

(b) Where the land is determined by the local authority to be a special site, the period begins with the making of that decision and ends with the expiration of the period of three months, in the case where no reference is made to the Secretary of State under s.78D, beginning with the day on which notice of the decision taking effect was given under s.78C(6) to the relevant persons. Alternatively, if the decision has been referred to the Secretary of State to resolve, the three-month period begins with the day on which the Secretary of State gave notice of his decision under s.78D(4)(b) to the relevant persons and to the local authority.

(c) Where the land is considered by the Agency to be a special site and notice has accordingly been given by the Agency to the local authority under s.78C(4), then the period begins with the day on which that notice was given and ends with the expiration of the period of three months beginning with:

(i) where the local authority decides the land is indeed a special site, the date on which the authority gives notice under s.78C(6) to the relevant persons of the decision taking effect;

(ii) where the local authority decides the land is not a special site, and the Agency does not give notice within the prescribed 21–day period that it disagrees, the day following the expiration of the 21–day period. In other words, the three-month period does not begin running until the period for possible dispute of special site status has passed;

(iii) where the local authority decides the land is not a special site, the Agency disagrees within the 21–day period, and the decision is then referred to the Secretary of State, the day on which the Secretary of State gives notice of his decision under s.78D(4)(b) to relevant persons and to the local authority.

4.21   As will be appreciated, the period will in total usually be more than three months—the principle is that the three months does not begin to elapse until:

(a) it is clear that no dispute exists as to whether the site is a special site, or if there is a dispute, it is settled; and

(b) the statutory notices of the decision have been given.

Calculating the period

4.22 In calculating the end date for the period, after which a remediation notice can be served, the starting point is to ascertain the correct day on which time begins to run under s.78H(3). The period ends with the expiry of three months beginning with that date.

4.23   The starting point will in many cases be the date on which the statutory notice was "given". This will probably be treated as being the date on which the notice reached its relevant destination[11] rather than the date on which it actually came to the attention of the intended recipient.[12] This will usually be the date on which the notice was personally delivered,[13] or was received through the post. If posted, the notice will be presumed to have been delivered in the ordinary course of the post, but this may be rebutted by proof of late delivery, or no delivery at all.[14] It should also be possible to give the notice by fax, but the legal uncertainties involved mean that service personally or by post will be the safest means to use.[15]

4.24   The next question is what is meant by "three months". "Month" here means calendar month,[16] and the courts will presumably follow the "corresponding date rule" so that the period will expire on the same number day in the month as the start date.[17] Thus if the statutory notice was given on, say, February 13, the period would end on May 13. If there is no corresponding day in the end month, because it is a short month, then the period will end on the last day of the month. So if notice was given on November 30, the period would end on February 28 (or 29 if a leap year).

---

[11] See s.160 of the 1990 Act.

[12] *Papillon v Brunton* (1860) 5 H. & N. 518; *Price v West London Investment Building Society* [1964] 1 W.L.R. 616; *Lord Newborough v Jones* [1975] Ch. 90; *Sun Alliance and London Insurance Co Ltd v Hayman* [1975] 1 W.L.R. 177, at 183, 185; *Re: 88 Berkeley Road, NW9* [1971] Ch. 648. If a notice is served at an incorrect address but subsequently discovered by the intended recipient, the date of discovery will be the date on which service is effected (see *Butland v Powys CC* [2007] EWHC (Admin) 734.

[13] Putting it through the letter box of the relevant premises may be sufficient: *Lambeth LBC v Mullings* [1990] R.V.R. 259.

[14] Interpretation Act 1978 s.7; *R. v London Quarter Sessions Appeal Committee Ex p. Rossi* [1956] 1 Q.B. 682; *Beer v Davies* [1958] 2 Q.B. 187; *Hewitt v Leicester CC* [1969] 1 W.L.R. 855.

[15] The fax must be shown to have reached its destination in a legible form: see *Ralux NV/SA v Spencer Mason, The Times*, May 18, 1989; *Hastie and Jenkerson v McMahon* [1990] 1 W.L.R. 1575; *Pearshouse v Birmingham CC* [1999] E.H.L.R. 140; and *PNC Telecom Plc v Thomas* [2002] EWHC 2848 (Ch).

[16] See ss.5 & 22(1) of and Sch.1 to the Interpretation Act 1978.

[17] *Dodds v Walker* [1981] 1 W.L.R. 1027.

The consequences of inadequate notification on the period

As mentioned above, the three month embargo on service of a remediation **4.25** notice is calculated by reference to the date on which the notices required by statute were given under ss.78B(3)(d), 78B(4), 78C(1)(b), 78C(6) or 78D(4)(b) as the case may be.

In relation to the simplest cases of ss.78B(3)(d) or 78B(4), where there is **4.26** no question of the land being a special site, the notices are required to be given simply to each person who appears to the authority to be an appropriate person. In the other cases, where the issue arises as to whether the land may be a special site, the notices must be given to "the relevant persons", defined as[18]:

(a) the Environment Agency;

(b) the owner of the land;

(c) any person appearing to the local authority to be in occupation of the whole or part of the land; and

(d) each person who appears to the authority to be an appropriate person.

There is no obvious reason why s.78H(3)(a)–(c) should distinguish between **4.27** putative "appropriate persons" and "relevant persons" in this way.

In any event, failure to give the necessary notices to all those who should **4.28** receive them could have serious consequences; until the notices have been given, the three-month moratorium period cannot begin to run, and until it expires "no remediation notice shall be served on any person" in relation to the contaminated land. This is therefore a matter that goes to the vires of the authority to serve a notice, and it seems is an issue that could be raised by a person on whom notice had in fact been served, if he can show that there are others to whom notice should have been given, irrespective of whether he himself was prejudiced.[19] Also the prohibition is on serving any notice in relation to the land identified as contaminated, not in relation to the particular pollutant linkage[20]; this means that the authority will have to consider who the appropriate persons for all significant pollutant linkages are and serve notices accordingly if the problem is to be avoided. On the other hand, the requirement to give notice relates to those persons who appear to the authority to be appropriate persons—a subjective test based on knowledge at the relevant time, rather than hindsight. Should other appropriate persons come to the attention of the local authority subsequently, then a further notice can be given under s.78B(4), and the three months will be calculated from that later notice.[21]

---

[18] 1990 Act ss.78C(2) and 78D(7).

[19] Contrast *O'Brien v Croydon LBC* [1999] J.P.L. 47 at 52.

[20] This is not surprising, since the pollutant linkage concept is found only in the Guidance and appears nowhere in the legislation.

[21] Curiously, there is no similar provision in relation to the notices required to be given in relation to Special Sites under ss.78C and 78D.

Cases of imminent serious harm

4.29 Neither the duty to consult under s.78G(3) and s.78H(1), nor the three-month moratorium under s.78H(3), preclude the service of a remediation notice in any case where it appears to the enforcing authority that the contaminated land in question is in such a condition, by reason of substances in, on or under the land, that there is imminent danger of serious harm, or serious pollution of controlled waters, being caused—see ss.78G(4) and 78H(4). The use of the words "imminent danger" and "serious harm" obviously indicate a situation going beyond the criteria of "significant harm" and "significant possibility" of such harm, which are the test for contaminated land.

Failure to consult

4.30 The imposition of an express duty to consult avoids the difficulties that might otherwise arise in deciding whether any duty would arise on grounds of fairness or natural justice, and the scope and content of any such duty.[22] The fact that the statute expressly indicates who is to be consulted probably precludes success by others in arguing that they should have been consulted.[23]

4.31 The case law on consultation requirements is extensive, but it can be anticipated that the context of the consultation will be relevant, and that the courts are likely to view seriously any failure to comply with the statutory requirements here, given the serious consequences of a remediation notice. Whereas the consultation requirements in relation to works notices for water pollution state specifically that failure to comply with the requirement to consult will not render the notice invalid, or invalidly served,[24] there is no such provision for remediation notices. On the other hand, the requirement is to "reasonably endeavour" to consult, and as such is not an absolute requirement. It will be a question of fact whether reasonable endeavours have been made.

4.32 A court will no doubt be concerned to see that the consultation followed a fair process, involving[25]:

(a) consultation while the proposals for the notice are still formative;

(b) the provision of adequate information on which a response can be based (including disclosure of any technical data)[26];

---

[22] For example, in *R. v Falmouth and Truro Port Health Authority Ex p. South West Water Ltd* [2000] Env. L.R. 658 it was held that there was no duty to consult the prospective recipient of an abatement notice, this being a matter of discretion. See also *R. v Birmingham CC Ex p. Ferrero* [1993] 1 All E.R. 530.

[23] See *Bates v Lord Hailsham* [1972] 2 W.L.R. 1373; *R v Secretary of State for Education and Employment Ex p. Morris*, The Times, December 15, 1995.

[24] Water Resources Act 1991 s.161A(6); Control of Pollution Act 1974 s.46A(6).

[25] For example, see *R. v Warwickshire CC Ex p. Bailey* [1991] C.O.D. 284; *R. v Gwent CC and Secretary of State for Wales Ex p. Bryant* [1988] C.O.D. 19; *R. v Brent LBC Ex p. Gunning* (1986) 84 L.G.R. 168; *R. v North and East Devon Health Authority Ex p. Coughlan* [2000] L.G.L.R. 1, 38; *R. v Wrexham BC Ex p. Wall and Berry* [2000] J.P.L. 32, 50; *R. (Greenpeace Ltd) v Secretary of State for Trade and Industry* [2007] EWHC 311.

[26] This may involve making available internal reports prepared for authority if these are material to the decision: see *R. (Edwards) v Environment Agency* [2007] Env. L.R. 9; [2006] EWCA Civ. 877.

(c) allowing adequate time in which to respond, bearing in mind the complexity of the matters concerned; and

(d) conscientious and open-minded consideration of the response.

One other factor also needs to be borne in mind given the nature of the **4.33** matters being consulted on here: the parties consulted may have very different interests in whether, and on what terms, a remediation notice is served. The authority may therefore well find itself in receipt of conflicting representations. The key principle to follow would seem to be that of fairness. Clearly the authority should not act so as to favour one consultee over another. The issue will also arise as to whether the authority should give parties the chance to comment on representations made by other consultees.[27] Provided the authority treats all parties fairly in this respect, it might be argued that the best course would be to allow that opportunity, subject to the time constraints imposed by the legislative guidance.

However, it ought not to be overlooked that the authority's functions are **4.34** being exercised in the public interest to remedy or avoid harm or pollution. It is possible to envisage circumstances where allowing each party to comment on the other's representation might impact adversely on the effective discharge of those public functions. One solution which may be helpful is to convene a meeting (rather like a "time and place" meeting in planning law) which consultees and their experts could attend. Such a meeting would have the elements of an informal hearing, i.e. the chair could identify issues from the representations made and invite comment and discussion. The practicalities of the consultation exercise are discussed in the following paragraph.

The practicalities of consultation

The starting point for considering how consultation prior to serving a **4.35** remediation notice is to be conducted are the words of ss.78G and 78H themselves, together with any Regulations made under s.78H(2). Issues to be considered are:

1. How to initiate consultation.

2. How much time to allow.

3. How to draw up the list of consultees.

4. Whether to consult on a proposed remediation notice in draft, or on some other basis.

5. Whether to make the process public, and if so, to what extent?

6. How to deal with those who do not wish to cooperate.

7. Whether to invite further comment on responses received.

[27] For cases suggesting there is generally no duty to consult further unless the proposal changes radically, see *R. v Islington LBC Ex p. East* [1996] I.L.R. 74; *R. v Secretary of State for Wales Ex p. Williams* [1996] C.O.D. 127.

8. How and when to draw the process to a conclusion.

9. Whether to invite all consultees to a meeting.

4.36 The difficulty of some of these issues, and the serious likelihood of challenge in the event that the process is defective, indicate the importance of establishing a considered and clear set of ground rules for consultation in advance of the process. The local authority's written strategy may be the right place for such ground rules.

4.37 In particular, whilst the interests of transparency might suggest that a draft remediation notice should form part of the consultation process, this may create potential problems for the authority. Information may be incomplete at the time of consultation, and the use of a draft notice may invite comparison with the final version on appeal, with the authority either being required to justify changes, or to explain why changes have not been made. If the draft does not change substantially, the argument may arise that the authority has effectively pre-judged the issue by producing a draft notice. It is suggested that it will be preferable therefore to consult on the basis of a general document covering:

1. The condition of the land which is regarded as rendering it contaminated.

2. The reasons why harm or the possibility of harm are regarded as significant.

3. The range of remediation measures which at this juncture appear appropriate.

4. Whether there is the prospect of voluntary remediation.

5. Who appears to be the appropriate persons to take responsibility for the various aspects of remediation, and whether there are circumstances which would bring the case within one of the exclusion tests in the Guidance.

4.38 This approach also has the advantage of being consistent with the non-prescriptive guidance as to the type of discussion and consultation which the authority may find helpful.[28]

PART 3: RESTRICTIONS ON SERVING REMEDIATION NOTICES AND PROCEDURE WHERE A NOTICE CANNOT BE SERVED

Cases where no remediation notice may be served

4.39 Under s.78H(5) the enforcing authority shall not serve a remediation notice if one or more of the conditions set out in that section apply:

[28] DEFRA Circular 01/2006, *Contaminated Land*, Annex 2 paras 6.10–6.17.

(a) The authority is satisfied there is nothing by way of remediation they could specify in a notice, taking into account s.78E(4) and (5). These subsections deal with the only things that may be contained in a remediation notice, namely those that are reasonable having regard to the costs involved, the seriousness of the harm or of the pollution of controlled waters, etc. and having regard to Government guidance. In other words, this situation will arise where nothing could be required to deal with the contamination which would not involve unreasonable expense—a somewhat unlikely situation.[29]

(b) The authority is satisfied that appropriate things are being or will be done by way of remediation without the service of a notice. This is a very important provision in practice because it enables those who would be the appropriate persons to receive a remediation notice to give undertakings to carry out remediation as part of the consultation process preceding service of a notice. Anybody likely to be served with a remediation notice may well be wise to consider offering a programme which they can afford, over a given time-span, if the alternative is to become embroiled in proceedings. They may also point to redevelopment proposed for the land and a s.106 obligation requiring clean up as part of the redevelopment.

(c) It appears to the authority that the person on whom the notice would be served is the authority itself. This is another extremely important provision and is discussed separately below.[30]

(d) The authority is satisfied that it can exercise the powers conferred on it by s.78N to do what is appropriate by way of remediation. The cross reference to s.78N is awkward drafting and does little to aid intelligibility. However, it will cover, for example, cases where action is necessary to prevent serious harm or pollution of which there is imminent danger[31]; or where the appropriate person has entered into a written agreement with the authority for the authority to carry out works at his expense[32]; or where after reasonable inquiry, no person has been found on whom responsibility for a particular remediation action can be fixed.[33] Perhaps most importantly, it will also cover those cases where the authority considers that if it were to carry out remediation itself, it would not seek to recover all of its costs on grounds of hardship.[34] It will also cover the situation where the special provisions of s.78J on water pollution or s.78K on escapes of contamination prevent some particular remediation requirement.[35]

---

[29] It should be remembered that at the very least the notice may require further investigation, or monitoring so as to keep the condition of the site under review.

[30] paras 4.47 and 4.48.

[31] 1990 Act s.78N(3)(a).

[32] 1990 Act s.78N(3)(b).

[33] 1990 Act s.78N(3)(f).

[34] 1990 Act s.78N(3)(e).

[35] 1990 Act s.78N(3)(d).

Remediation declarations

4.40 Under s.78H(6), where s.78E(4) or (5) apply, so that service of a notice is precluded by the unreasonableness of the costs that would be involved, the authority must serve a remediation declaration stating why they consider themselves precluded from specifying the relevant things in the remediation notice. This declaration must record the reasons why the authority would have specified those things, and the grounds on which it is satisfied it is precluded from doing so. The possible reasons for preclusion are that the proposed requirements are not considered to be reasonable, having regard to the likely cost involved and to the seriousness of the harm in question, or that the proposed requirements are contrary to guidance issued by the Secretary of State. The declaration must be prepared and published by the authority. Presumably, this means published in the local press by way of advertisement. The declaration must also be placed on the public register under s.78R(1)(c).[36]

4.41 For the owner of land, the remediation declaration is something of a two-edged sword; on the one hand the polluter or owner may welcome the public recognition that the authority cannot require a particular type of remediation. On the other hand, the notice will make it clear that but for considerations of cost or Government guidance, such action would be required. A prospective purchaser may be understandably nervous that the circumstances which led the authority to be satisfied that the action cannot be required may change. The seriousness of the risk of harm may increase, possibly due to factors outside the owner's control; the cost of remedial techniques may fall, or cheaper techniques may become available; or Government guidance may change. Such factors, and others, may lead the authority to reconsider its decision under s.78E(4) or (5).

4.42 Where an owner does not consider that the land should be the subject of a remediation declaration (e.g. because it is not within the definition of contaminated land at all) there is no statutory mechanism for appeal, though the declaration could no doubt be challenged by way of judicial review.

Remediation statements

4.43 Remediation statements represent a practical and important alternative to service of a remediation notice. They are issued under s.78H(7) in circumstances where there is something that can be done by way of remediation but as a matter of law, a remediation notice cannot be served. Those circumstances, as indicated above, are where:

> (a) The authority is satisfied that the appropriate things are being or will be done by way of remediation by a person served with a remediation notice; this might be because of assurances that the works will be carried out voluntarily, or because, for example, a

---

[36] For the details of requirements for the public register, see para.6.113ff.

works notice under the Water Resources Act 1991 has been served requiring the appropriate action, or because such works are required by planning obligations.

(b) It appears to the authority that the person on whom a remediation notice should be served is the authority itself, i.e. because the authority is itself the appropriate person.

(c) The authority is satisfied that the powers conferred on it by s.78N (that is powers enabling them to remediate the contaminated land concerned) are exercisable.

4.44 Whereas a remediation declaration is prepared and published by the enforcing authority, it is the "responsible person" who must prepare and publish the remediation statement. This term is defined by s.78H(8). In situation (a) above, it is the person who is responsible for carrying out the relevant works. In cases (b) and (c) it is the authority. The sanction for failure to prepare and publish the statement within a reasonable time in case (a) is that under s.78H(9) the authority may do so itself and recover its reasonable costs. The statement must be placed on the public register under s.78R(1)(c).

4.45 The remediation statement shall include:

(a) the things which are being, have been, or are expected to be done by way of remediation;

(b) the name and address of the person who is doing, or has done, or is expected to do the things in question; and

(c) the period or periods within which these things are being or are expected to be done.

4.46 Where there are a number of persons who have agreed to carry out remediation jointly, then it appears that they will jointly be responsible for preparing and publishing the statement. The question arises as to what happens when the responsible person fails to prepare a remediation statement, or fails to comply with a remediation statement they have prepared. As mentioned above, failure to publish a remediation statement at all within a reasonable time means that the authority itself may prepare and publish the statement and recover its reasonable costs of so doing—see s.78H(9). This begs the question of what then happens if the responsible person, having produced a statement, fails to comply with it. The answer appears to lie in s.78H(10). If the authority was precluded from serving a remediation notice because it believed assurances that the relevant works would be carried out without a remediation notice being served, then if it appears that those assurances will not in fact be honoured, a remediation notice must be served under subs.78H(10). This raises the question of why an authority would wish to follow the procedure of s.78H(9). Indeed, where there is a failure to publish the remediation statement, there seems no reason why the authority could not proceed to serve a remediation notice on the basis that it is not now satisfied that the appropriate things will be done.

Where the local authority is itself the appropriate person

4.47 In practice, s.78H(5)(c) is a very important provision. Here it is the authority itself which is responsible for the contamination as original polluter or as current owner or occupier. In these circumstances the authority does not have to serve a remediation notice on itself. The question arises, and it may well be a frequent one, of what next is to happen in circumstances where the neighbouring landowners would expect the authority to serve notice upon itself but for subs.78H(5)(c). The answer is that the authority is required by s.78H(7) to publish a remediation statement and should then take the appropriate steps to comply with it. The legislation presumes that the authority will act responsibly, and no doubt failure to do so could be the subject of judicial review proceedings.

4.48 Another difficulty relates to the situation where there are a number of appropriate persons, of whom the authority is one. The language of s.78H(5)(c) refers to the authority as "the person" (not "a person") on whom the notice would be served, and therefore does not expressly contemplate the position where the authority is one among a number of appropriate persons. In such circumstances, by virtue of s.78H(5)(c) the local authority would not serve a remediation notice on itself; instead it would prepare and publish a remediation statement. However, in respect of the others who are responsible it would serve a remediation notice. The situation will raise important issues of fairness and possible bias in terms of allocation and apportionment of liability. These are considered at para.5.264ff., below.

Remediation notice where circumstances change

4.49 The circumstances under s.78H(5) where a remediation notice should not be served apply "if and so long as any one or more of the following conditions is for the time being satisfied in the particular case". It will be recalled that those conditions include the cases where there is nothing by way of remediation that can be specified in a notice, or the authority is satisfied that the appropriate things are being done, or the authority itself is the person on whom a notice should be served, or they have the power to carry out the works themselves. However, there may come a time when the "if and so long as" proviso ceases to apply. Where those circumstances were the only reason why a notice could not be served then, if those circumstances change, the authority is required by s.78H(10) to serve a remediation notice. Section 78H(10) expressly provides that such notice may be served without any further endeavours to consult the relevant persons, if and to the extent they have already been consulted pursuant to s.78H(1) concerning the things to be specified in the notice.

4.50 Even if the remediation actions described in the remediation statement are being carried out as planned, the enforcing authority may consider that further remediation is necessary, for example, where the action is phased, and a further phase can now be seen to be necessary, or where further significant pollutant linkages have been identified. In this situation, the authority will need to repeat the consultation procedures, and revisit the question of whether those additional measures will be carried out without a remediation notice being served.[37]

PART 4: AVOIDING SERVICE OF A REMEDIATION NOTICE

Using the consultation period

4.51 As indicated earlier, the owner, occupier or other "appropriate person" in relation to contaminated land is entitled to be consulted prior to the service of a remediation notice. Such a person will certainly have been informed of the fact that the land has been identified as contaminated under s.78B(3). However, in practice, it is likely that the fact that land is under consideration as potentially contaminated land will have been known some months previously, and indeed representations may have been put to the committee of the authority making the determination.

4.52 The period of consultation represents a valuable opportunity for those who are likely to be faced with service of a remediation notice. Once a notice has been served, an adversarial position will have been created which may then make further constructive dialogue more difficult. It may be possible to avoid that situation arising by providing the authority with relevant information, or by putting forward acceptable proposals for remediation.

4.53 The formal consultation process which is required by s.78H(1) relates only to "what is to be done by way of remediation". This will be an important focus for discussion, but the owner, occupier or other appropriate person may well wish to put to the authority other points, as discussed below.

Points for consideration

4.54 The owner, occupier or other appropriate person ("the consultee") may wish to raise with the authority a number of points which may preclude service of a notice, or the inclusion of certain requirements within it, or which may suggest that some other person would be the appropriate recipient of the notice:

(a) Arguments that the land is not "contaminated land" at all. The consultee may wish to put forward their own data, reports or risk assessments to suggest that the land does not in fact meet the statutory criteria for identification as contaminated, or for designation as a special site.

(b) Arguments that the consultee is not an appropriate person to receive a remediation notice at all, or is only an appropriate person with regard to certain aspects of the contamination, or

---

[37] DEFRA Circular 01/2006, *Contaminated Land*, Annex 2 para.8.28.

should benefit from one of the exclusion tests contained in the statutory guidance. This will involve bringing to the attention of the authority relevant factual circumstances, and quite possibly the terms of past transactions or commercial agreements that may have a bearing on the allocation of responsibility.

(c) Information relevant as to how responsibility for a particular remediation action should be apportioned between the consultee and other appropriate persons. This may involve both the disclosure of past events and agreements, and also any current agreements reached as to how liability should be shared.

(d) Representations concerning the proposed remediation requirements of the authority, in particular, whether those requirements are reasonable having regard to the statutory criteria of s.78E(4) and to the Guidance. This may involve the consultee putting forward an alternative scheme, which meets the relevant criteria but at a lower cost. Clearly if more than one consultee is involved, such proposals are likely to carry more weight if they are put forward on a united basis.

(e) Facts relevant to whether the service and enforcement of a remediation notice would entail hardship to the person from whom the cost would be recoverable. Again, the guidance will be relevant to the discussion on this issue—see s.78P(2).

(f) Any circumstances which may restrict the requirements of a remediation notice under s.78J where water pollution is involved.

(g) Any circumstances relating to the origin and mobility of the substances where they have been subject to migration, which may affect the allocation of liability under s.78K.

(h) The timescale for any proposed remediation will be relevant if remediation can be achieved over a reasonable period of time, integrated into current use of the land so as to avoid, for example, loss of income, or so that the scheme is tax effective, which may be a major consideration.

(i) Any proposed immediate action which will alleviate the most serious consequences and give time for longer term solutions to be evaluated. An example might be the creation of a temporary barrier or layer to prevent immediate exposure to pollutants.

Proposals for voluntary clean-up

4.55 By s.78H(5)(b), no remediation notice can be served so long as the enforcing authority remains satisfied that appropriate things are being done, or will be done, by way of remediation without the service of a notice.[38] The consultee wishing to avoid service of a remediation notice on this basis will need to satisfy the authority:

[38] See DEFRA Circular 01/2006, *Contaminated Land*, Annex 2 paras 8.3–8.8 on voluntary clean-up.

(a) that what is proposed is appropriate to address the harm, pollution or risk arising from the contamination; and

(b) that those measures either are already in progress, or will take place, and (presumably, though not expressly stated) that they will be satisfactorily completed on an acceptable timescale.

The first of these issues is essentially a technical one, where clearly views **4.56** may differ as to the preferred solution. Here it is important to note that the test is whether the measures are "appropriate", not whether they are the optimal measures or constitute the best practicable environmental option, or use the best available technology, or some similar test. The consultee may well have in mind a relatively cheap solution, such as excavation and consignment to landfill, to which the authority may have objections on environmental grounds; however, provided the course proposed is appropriate to deal with the threat presented by the contaminated land, such objections ought not to be relevant.

Other questions may arise where what is proposed is a new or **4.57** experimental technique, which may be relatively untried. The authority will have to consider here whether doubts as to its ultimate effectiveness mean that it is not an appropriate technique in the context in which it is to be used: this may involve a risk assessment as to what would be the consequences of the technique not working. It will be relevant to take into account here those aspects of the Guidance dealing with the content of remediation notices, which bear on similar issues.

The second issue is a factual one, namely whether the authority can be **4.58** satisfied that the remediation will be carried out without the need to serve a remediation notice. The following issues may require consideration in that respect:

(a) Have the works already commenced, and if so at what stage are they? Do they appear to have been carried out satisfactorily so far, and what is the timescale for their conclusion?

(b) If the works have not yet been commenced, is there a clear scheme, designed by reputable consultants? Have engineers or contractors been appointed or have tenders been invited?

(c) Are all necessary permits or licences for the scheme (e.g. planning permission, waste management licences) in place or have they been applied for, and if so are they likely to be granted? Where there is a planning application for development which may be objectionable in itself on grounds of planning policy, a view will have to be taken of the likelihood of its being successful. The outcome of the application, or any ensuing appeal, may be uncertain, and the owner may argue that clean-up under Pt IIA should not be enforced until it is known whether the larger scheme will proceed: in those circumstances, it will no doubt be relevant to consider the urgency for remediation, and how that relates to the likely period of uncertainty, as well as the costs involved and possible hardship issues.

(d) Is the scheme adequately financed, or are there otherwise clear commercial incentives for its completion within a reasonable timescale, e.g. the completion of proposed development?

(e) What are the risks associated with a partly-implemented scheme which, for one reason or another, is not completed?

(f) Are the grant of rights or the permission of third parties necessary for the implementation of the scheme? If so, have those rights been obtained or appropriate arrangements made? If not, service of a remediation notice may be necessary in order to serve the grant of such rights under s.78G.

(g) Where a number of potential appropriate persons is involved, is there sufficient agreement between them as to what is to be done, by whom and at whose cost, to ensure implementation of the scheme?

(h) The authority may well wish to see a draft remediation statement, recording these matters.

4.59   It will be appreciated that there may well be difficult issues of judgment as to what degree of assurance the enforcing authority will need on these matters. The consultees might point to the fact that the authority can always keep the situation under review and serve a remediation notice if it becomes apparent that matters are not progressing as they should. On the other hand, the authority will no doubt be mindful that a partly remediated site may leave just as great a problem (if not a greater one) than the site in its original condition.

Written agreement with appropriate person

4.60 Section 78N(2)(b) provides for the situation where an appropriate person has entered into a written agreement for the enforcing authority to undertake the necessary remediation at the expense of the appropriate person. In such circumstances, s.78N applies and accordingly by s.78H(5)(d) no remediation notice may be served. It seems debatable whether most local authorities would wish to enter into such arrangements, with the scope for potential contractual liability if things go wrong, unless they are themselves partly responsible for remediation. However, there may be attractions in the authority undertaking the work where other statutory powers might be useful, for example, if the matter involves highway works or highway closure. The other key attraction is perhaps simply that the authority gets the job done as it would like. Clearly if the authority does undertake such works it will need to be insured for contractors' liability and will probably enter into an engineering works contract through its environmental services department. The authority will also have to comply with applicable rules on procurement and with its statutory "best value" duties in relation to any contract for the works. To avoid disputes at later cost-recovery stage, more than one estimate should be obtained and put to the appropriate person for his consideration.

The agreement can only relate to those works which the appropriate **4.61** person would have been obliged or is obliged to carry out; it cannot bind a third party. Accordingly, such agreements are perhaps more likely where there is a single appropriate person and a clearly defined set of remediation actions in contemplation. Clearly, the appropriate person will be concerned to have some control over the total costs for which they are responsible. The contract between the appropriate person and the authority will therefore probably contain provisions for the appropriate person to be consulted over any proposed variations in the works or in the price during the course of remediation.

PART 5: DRAFTING AND SERVING REMEDIATION NOTICES

Duty to serve notice

When land has been identified as contaminated land or designated as a **4.62** special site then the local authority or (as the case may be) the Environment Agency or SEPA is under a duty to serve a remediation notice on each person who is an appropriate person.[39] Identification and designation are in this sense formal legal processes. "Identification" is not in this context to be equated with mere suspicion that land may be contaminated. The duty to serve a notice is one that may be enforced by judicial review proceedings: it is not a matter for the general discretion of the authority.

The nature of remediation notices

The key purpose of a remediation notice is to specify what the recipient is **4.63** to do by way of remediation and the periods within which he is to do each of the things specified. The vital point to note is that a remediation notice is personal in nature—it does not describe what is to be done in general with regard to a contaminated site, but rather what the individual recipient is to do. This is where the principle of referability arises.[40] Only certain remedial actions may be properly referable to an individual appropriate person, and accordingly the requirements of an individual remediation notice may be narrower than the works needed on the site as a whole.

The drafting of remediation notices presents many potential difficulties, **4.64** some of which are addressed in this chapter and some in the chapter dealing with the identification of the "appropriate person" or persons to receive notices. It is conceivable that the words of Harman L. J. in *Britt v Buckinghamshire CC*[41] may come to be applied to remediation notices:

> "Local authorities . . . have had practically to employ conveyancing counsel to settle these notices which they serve . . . instead of

[39] 1990 Act s.78E(1).
[40] See 1990 Act s.78F(3).
[41] [1964] 1 Q.B. 77 at 87.

trying to make this thing simple, lawyers succeeded day by day in making it more difficult and less comprehensible until it has reached a stage where it is very much like the state of the land which their plaintiff has brought about by his operations—an eyesore, a wilderness and a scandal."

Jurisdiction

4.65 The enforcing authority will need to be satisfied that it has jurisdiction to serve a remediation notice. In the case of the Environment Agency or SEPA, the land will need to have been designated as a special site under ss.78C(7) or 78D(6).[42] In the case of a local authority, the land must have been formally identified as contaminated, and must be in the authority's area,[43] except where the authority relies on s.78X(2) to serve notice in respect of land outside its area. The authority must also be satisfied that it is not precluded from serving a notice by s.78H.

Land covered by remediation notice

4.66 The notice must make clear to which land it relates. The primary legislation is silent on the issue, simply stating at s.78E that where land is identified as contaminated, a remediation notice shall be served on every appropriate person. However, the Regulations on form and content of remediation notices state that the notice must specify the location and extent of the contaminated land, in sufficient detail to enable it to be identified.[44] This issue is both important and potentially difficult.

4.67 The area covered by an individual remediation notice will not necessarily be the same area as the whole of the land identified as contaminated: this potential difference stems from the fact that it is the presence of substances which determines the extent of the land to be identified as contaminated, whereas it is the involvement of the individual appropriate person that determines the land to be included within the remediation notice served on them. It is also possible that remediation notices requiring the doing of different things may be served in respect of the same land, if different pollution linkages arise on that land. This is clear from s.78(E)(2), which provides for the situation where different remediation actions are necessary to deal with the presence of different substances. The authority will have had to take a decision as to the extent of the land to be identified as contaminated at the earlier stage of identification; a further decision will be required when drafting the individual notice or notices. The extent of the notice clearly cannot be wider than the extent of the land identified as contaminated.

---

[42] 1990 Act s.78E(1)(a).

[43] 1990 Act s.78E(1)(b).

[44] Contaminated Land (England) Regulations 2006 (SI 2006/1380) reg.4(1)(b). The 2006 Regulations made a slight amendment to this provision, the phrase used (on a number of occasions) in the 2000 Regulations being "sufficient to enable it to be identified". This would appear to be designed to clarify the scope of what "sufficient" may require.

Whilst the Regulations do not state that a plan must be annexed to the **4.68** notice showing the boundaries of the land covered by the notice, in many cases this will be advisable. The requirement of reg.4(1)(b) is that the land can be identified, "whether by reference to a plan or otherwise". The question is whether it is possible to specify the location and extent of the land, in sufficient detail to enable it to be identified without a plan. In this respect, the requirements for remediation notices may be compared with those applying to planning enforcement notices under s.172 of the Town and Country Planning Act 1990. Here the notice must specify "the precise boundaries of the land to which the notice relates, whether by reference to a plan or otherwise"[45]: even this more exacting requirement has been held to be capable of being satisfied by giving an address.[46]

It is also possible to argue by extrapolation from planning enforcement **4.69** cases that there should be a degree of discretion as to the area covered by the notice: the concept of the "planning unit"[47] may perhaps be translated in this connection into the "pollutant linkage unit".

Multiple remediation notices

The legislation envisages the possibility of several remediation notices **4.70** requiring different works; they may well be served on different persons because they relate to different substances for which the persons in question are responsible.[48] This situation needs to be distinguished from the position where more than one person is responsible for the same works in respect of the same substance. Here the notice is served on each appropriate person, but must state the proportion of the cost, determined under s.78F(7), which each of them is to bear.[49]

In practical terms, the use of multiple remediation notices would seem **4.71** to be fraught with difficulty. Where one site with a range of inter-linked pollution problems is involved the remediation works will also often in practice be inter-linked. The problem with multiple notices is that it may be difficult to determine appeals against such notices on an individual, isolated basis: any appeal hearing may well need to be on a joint basis to operate satisfactorily.

Consecutive remediation notices

It is clear that the remediation of contaminated land may involve a phased **4.72** approach, and there is nothing to prevent this being reflected in a series of consecutive remediation notices which might require sampling, trials and

---

[45] Town and Country Planning (Enforcement Notices and Appeals) (England) Regulations 2002 (SI 2002/2682) reg.4(c).
[46] *Wiesenfeld v Secretary of State for the Environment* [1992] 1 P.L.R. 32.
[47] See, e.g. *Gregory v Secretary of State for the Environment* [1990] 1 P.L.R. 100; *Richmond upon Thames LBC v Secretary of State for the Environment* [1988] J.P.L. 396; *Ralls v Secretary of State for the Environment* [1998] J.P.L. 444.
[48] 1990 Act s.78E(2).
[49] 1990 Act s.78E(3).

feasibility studies prior to actual remediation, and operational monitoring thereafter. If after one remediation notice has been served the land continues to be "contaminated" then another notice should be served. This might occur if, for example, an authority determined that land was contaminated, but required monitoring or sampling to establish what should be done by way of remediation. Similarly, if it transpires that remediation has been inadequate or ineffective, and the land remains contaminated, another notice will have to be served.

4.73   The Guidance refers to the fact that a phased approach may be necessary, with different actions being carried out in sequence.[50] For example, the land may have been identified as contaminated, but further assessment may be necessary to determine what type of remedial action is appropriate. The authority will have to consider what phasing is appropriate in the individual circumstances of each case: the first stage of remediation actions may, for example, yield information which indicates that assessment is desirable before any further phase of remediation is commenced.[51] It may not be possible in such phased cases to include all the requirements in a single notice, so that further notices will be served (assuming of course that the land still meets the definition of "contaminated land").[52]

Restrictions on requirements of remediation notice: reasonableness

4.74 Section 78E(4) and (5) provide restrictions on what may be required by a remediation notice. Under s.78E(4) the authority may not require more than it considers reasonable having regard to:

(a) the costs likely to be involved; and

(b) the seriousness of the harm or pollution involved.

4.75   Clearly, this issue is likely to be a major focus of discussion between the authority and potential recipients of a notice. The issue is not dissimilar to that arising under s.39 of the Environment Act 1995 in relation to action by the Agency, in the sense of balancing costs and benefits of the exercise or non-exercise of powers. As the seriousness of the harm to be averted increases so does the justification for increased costs. However, given that land will not be "contaminated" at all unless the harm or risk involved is significant, the issue will perhaps most often be one of incremental benefit, i.e. comparing different techniques which will have different costs and which may offer different marginal benefits.

4.76   The second restriction is that by s.78E(5), in determining (a) what is to be done by way of remediation, (b) to what standard, and (c) what should or should not be regarded as reasonable in terms of cost versus harm, the

---

[50] DEFRA Circular 01/2006, *Contaminated Land*, Annex 3 para.C.12.
[51] DEFRA Circular 01/2006, *Contaminated Land*, Annex 3 paras C.12 and C.13.
[52] DEFRA Circular 01/2006, *Contaminated Land*, Annex 3 paras C.14 and C.15.

authority must have regard to the Guidance issued by the Secretary of State. These issues are discussed in the following paragraphs.

Identifying a remediation scheme

The procedural description of Pt IIA in Annex 2 of the Circular[53] outlines **4.77** the approach to identifying a remediation scheme. This involves identifying the remedial treatment action or actions which will ensure the relevant land or waters are remediated to the appropriate standard (see below). Where assessment is necessary before decisions can be taken on the remedial treatment aspect of the scheme, then the first step will be to identify the appropriate assessment actions. At all stages, the authority should review whether urgent action is necessary. In the most straightforward cases there will be only one significant pollutant linkage involved. However, where there is more than one, then the authority should be aware that to consider each linkage in isolation may result in conflicting or overlapping requirements. A remediation scheme should therefore deal with the relevant land or waters as a whole, which may involve subsuming what would otherwise have been separate remediation actions within a "remediation package". In other words, in considering what might be the appropriate remediation action for a particular pollutant linkage, the authority cannot ignore any practical limitations which are imposed by other problems on the same site.

Guidance on the standard of remediation

A specific issue on which guidance is provided is the standard to which **4.78** remediation should be required—see s.78E(5)(b). The authority is required to have regard to this Guidance, but not necessarily to act in accordance with it. Chapter C Pt 4 of the Guidance deals with this issue.

Just as the "suitable for use" concept underlies the issue of what **4.79** constitutes "contaminated land", the intention of remediation is that the land should be brought into such a condition that, in its current use, it is no longer "contaminated land".[54] The standard should be established by considering separately each significant pollutant linkage: the appropriate standard is "that which would be achieved by the use of a remediation package which forms the best practicable techniques of remediation" for[55]:

(a) ensuring that the linkage is no longer a significant pollutant linkage, by removing or treating the source, breaking or removing the pathway, or protecting or removing the receptor; and

(b) remedying the effect of any significant harm or pollution of controlled waters which is resulting, or has already resulted from, the pollutant linkage.

---

[53] See DEFRA Circular 01/2006, *Contaminated Land*, paras 6.18–6.32.
[54] DEFRA Circular 01/2006, *Contaminated Land*, Annex 2 para.C.17.
[55] DEFRA Circular 02/2006, *Contaminated Land*, Annex 2 para.C.18.

4.80   The issue is therefore to consider what means might be employed to address the pollutant linkage, whether by source, pathway or receptor and to determine what measure or combination of measures would constitute the "best practicable techniques". The use of the word "practicable" implies that considerations of cost and convenience will be involved, and that the exercise will involve striking a balance. The Guidance addresses the question of what represents the best practicable technique by stating that the authority should look for the method of achieving the desired result which, in the light of the nature and volume of the pollutant concerned, and the timescale for remediation is[56]:

   (a) reasonable taking account of Guidance on that issue; and

   (b) represents the best combination of the following qualities:

      (i) practicability, both in general and in the specific circumstances of the case;

      (ii) effectiveness in achieving the aims above; and

      (iii) durability in maintaining that effectiveness over the timescale within which the significant harm or pollution of controlled waters may occur.

4.81   The balancing exercise involved is both crucial and potentially highly controversial, with possibly large discrepancies between the cost of different solutions. Robustness, certainty of outcome and durability will often come at a heavy price. Different solutions may also have different impacts in terms of disruption on those caught up in the problem: a solution which benefits the person responsible for clean-up by lower costs may be highly inconvenient for the occupier of the land affected. The Guidance states that in considering these questions, the authority should work on the basis of authoritative scientific and technical advice, considering what comparable techniques have recently been carried out successfully on other land, and also any technological advances or changes in scientific knowledge and understanding.[57]

4.82   Where there is "established good practice" for the remediation of a particular type of linkage, this should in general be assumed to represent the best practicable technique,[58] though the Guidance does not indicate the criteria for judging whether something is established good practice. In any event, the authority should satisfy itself that the practice is appropriate to the circumstances in hand, and that the costs would be reasonable, having regard to the seriousness of the relevant harm.

4.83   The Guidance also acknowledges the limitations of the remediation measures which may be available, in that they may not be able fully to ensure termination of the pollutant linkage. In such cases, the required standard is that which comes as close as practicable to that objective, and which remedies the adverse consequences of the harm or pollution caused and puts in place arrangements to remedy such future effects which may be caused by the continuing existence of the pollutant linkage.[59] Similarly,

---

[56] DEFRA Circular 02/2006, *Contaminated Land*, Annex 2 para.C.19.
[57] DEFRA Circular 01/2006, *Contaminated Land*, Annex 2 para.C.21.
[58] DEFRA Circular 01/2006, *Contaminated Land*, Annex 2 para.C.22.
[59] DEFRA Circular 01/2006, *Contaminated Land*, Annex 2 para.C.23.

total rectification of the effects of past harm or pollution may not be possible, in which case the requirement is to mitigate such harm or pollution so far as is practicable.[60]

In all cases, remediation should be implemented in accordance with best **4.84** practice, including any precautions necessary to prevent damage to the environment and any other appropriate quality assurance procedures.[61] This aspect of the Guidance will itself however be subject to the test of reasonableness in terms of cost, since quality assurance procedures may themselves constitute a significant component of the cost of some schemes.

Multiple pollutant linkages

The position where there are multiple pollutant linkages on a given piece **4.85** of land has been mentioned briefly above. The statutory Guidance states that it may be possible to arrive at the necessary overall standard of remediation for the land by considering what would constitute the best practicable techniques for each linkage in isolation, and implementing each separately.[62] However, the authority must also consider whether there is an alternative scheme which, by dealing with the linkages together, would be cheaper or more practicable to implement: such a scheme should be preferred if it can be identified.[63]

Practicability, effectiveness and durability

As mentioned above, the practicability, effectiveness and durability of **4.86** possible remediation schemes are factors which are required to be consid- ered. Chapter C Pt 6 deals with those issues. The Guidance acknowledges that in some cases there may be little to go on in assessing particular remediation actions or packages.[64] Field-scale testing may not have been carried out. Here the authority will have to consider the issues on the basis of the information which it has at the relevant time. This may involve allowing a person who wishes to use innovative techniques to do so, and requiring further remediation if they prove ineffective.[65] The authority should not however, force an unwilling person to use innovative techniques for the purpose of establishing their effectiveness in general.[66]

Practicability

The key question for practicability, according to the Guidance, is whether **4.87** the remediation can be carried out in the circumstances of the land and waters under consideration.[67] Relevant factors should include[68]:

[60] DEFRA Circular 01/2006, *Contaminated Land*, Annex 2 para.C.24.
[61] DEFRA Circular 01/2006, *Contaminated Land*, Annex 2 para.C.25.
[62] DEFRA Circular 01/2006, *Contaminated Land*, Annex 3 para.C.26.
[63] DEFRA Circular 01/2006, *Contaminated Land*, Annex 3 para.C.27.
[64] DEFRA Circular 01/2006, *Contaminated Land*, Annex 3 para.C.45.
[65] DEFRA Circular 01/2006, *Contaminated Land*, Annex 3 para.C.46. The use of alternative or innovative technologies is promoted by Contaminated Land: Applications in Real Environ- ments (CL:AIRE), a not-for-profit organisaition. See online at *http://www.claire.co.uk*.
[66] DEFRA Circular 01/2006, *Contaminated Land*, Annex 3 para.C.47.
[67] DEFRA Circular 01/2006, *Contaminated Land*, Annex 3 para.C.48.
[68] DEFRA Circular 01/2006, *Contaminated Land*, Annex 3 para.C.49.

(a) Technical constraints, such as the commercial availability of the relevant technologies on the scale required, and constraint or problems imposed by the inter-relationship with other remedial action required.

(b) Site constraints, such as access, the presence of buidings or other structures, and the condition of the land and water concerned.

(c) Time constraints, bearing in mind the need to obtain any necessary regulatory permits, and to design and implement the relevant actions.

(d) Regulatory constraints, such as statutory requirements on health and safety, whether any necessary permits are likely to be forthcoming, whether the conditions likely to be attached to such permits would affect practicability. The authority should also consider the possibility of any adverse environmental impacts in this context (discussed below).

Adverse impacts of remediation

4.88 This aspect is considered at paras C.51–C.57 of the Guidance. The process of remediation may itself create adverse environmental impacts, for example, dust, noise, odours, the possibility of water pollution, and movements of heavy vehicles. In some instances, the process of remediation may require a permit, for example, for a prescribed process under Pt I of the 1990 Act, or a PPC permit, or a Pt II waste management licence, or a discharge consent or abstraction licence under the Water Resources Act 1991. In such cases the authority should assume that the conditions attached will provide adequate levels of environmental protection. However, where no such permit is needed, the authority should consider whether the proposed remediation package can be carried out without damaging the environment, and in particular without:

(a) risk to water, air, soil, plants and animals;

(b) causing a nuisance through noise or odours;

(c) adversely affecting the countryside or places of special interest; and

(d) affecting buildings of special architectural or historic interest.

4.89 These criteria correspond (though the Guidance does not expressly say so) to the objectives of the EC Waste Framework Directive 91/156/, and the intention is clearly to ensure that remediation which could arguably be said to involve the disposal of waste does not fall foul of the Directive. Where the authority considers that there is such risk involved, it should address the question of whether the risk is sufficiently great to tip the balance of advantage towards a different remediation scheme, even though this might be less effective when judged against the test of effectiveness; it should also consider whether it may be possible to reduce that risk by incorporating particular precautions into the remediation scheme.[69] This

---

[69] DEFRA Circular 01/2006, *Contaminated Land*, Annex 3 para.C.55.

requirement is in some respects akin to considering what constitutes the best practicable environmental option in terms of risk. For example, a site may be surrounded by housing, which would mean that some types of remediation measures may be particularly harmful in terms of nuisance. The impacts of remediation on groundwater will also need careful consideration and consultation with the Environment Agency.[70] The concept of attaching what may effectively be requirements akin to waste licensing conditions to a remediation notice is an intriguing one, which merits careful consideration. There will be no equivalent detailed enforcement procedures for such requirements, akin to those found in Pt II of the 1990 Act. It may well be preferable to deal with such matters by planning conditions or s.106 agreements, where the nature of the remediation is such that planning permission is needed.

Effectiveness

Effectiveness is to be considered in the sense not only of how far the relevant objectives would be achieved, but also in terms of timescale before the remediation becomes effective.[71] Hence the authority will need to balance the speed of reaching a particular result against the longer timescales which may be involved in obtaining a higher level of effectiveness. **4.90**

Durability

On durability, the authority will have to consider how long the remediation package will need to remain effective in order to control and resolve the problem, taking into account normal maintenance and repair.[72] For example, if a site is producing gases or leachates which need to be managed, for how long is that production likely to continue? If development is in prospect within a short timescale, which may resolve the problem, then this should be taken into account so as to justify a shorter period being considered.[73] **4.91**

Should it not be possible to ensure that the remediation measures will remain effective during the whole period of the problem, then the authority should require such measures as will be effective for as long as is practicable.[74] Additional monitoring may be required, and when the measures cease to be effective it may be necessary to consider whether another remediation notice should be served, since new methods of remediation may by then have emerged. If the remediation method chosen requires on-going maintenance and management, then this should be specified in the remediation notice; additional monitoring actions may also be required.[75] **4.92**

---

[70] DEFRA Circular 01/2006, *Contaminated Land*, Annex 3 paras C.56 and C.57.
[71] DEFRA Circular 01/2006, *Contaminated Land*, Annex 3 paras C.58 and C.59.
[72] DEFRA Circular 01/2006, *Contaminated Land*, Annex 3, para.C.61.
[73] DEFRA Circular 01/2006, *Contaminated Land*, Annex 3 para.C.61.
[74] DEFRA Circular 01/2006, *Contaminated Land*, Annex 3 para.C.62.
[75] DEFRA Circular 01/2006, *Contaminated Land*, Annex 3 para.C.63.

Reasonableness criteria

4.93 Reasonableness of the remediation action, having regard to cost, is a factor in its own right under s.78E(4), and Ch.C Pt 5 provides the Guidance on this. The status of this Guidance under s.78E(5)(c) is again that the authority must have regard to it. The key issue is whether the anticipated benefits justify the likely costs.[76] The authority should therefore prepare an estimate of the costs of the proposed course and a statement of the benefits (which need not necessarily have financial values ascribed).[77] By "benefits" the Guidance means the benefits of reducing the seriousness of the harm or pollution involved.[78] In carrying out the assessment the authority should make allowance for timing issues, of which three examples are given[79]:

(a) Expenditure at a later date will have a lesser impact on the person liable than immediate expenditure than would an equivalent cash sum to be spent immediately.

(b) The gain from achieving earlier remediation should be set against any such higher costs from immediate expenditure. Allowance should also be made for the fact that natural processes may have a beneficial effect over that longer timescale.

(c) The same benefits may be achievable in future at a significantly lower cost, possibly through the development of new techniques or as part of a wider redevelopment scheme.

4.94 What is not relevant to the issue of reasonableness of costs is the identity or financial standing of the person responsible for remediation.[80] This may however be relevant at the stage of considering hardship.

Remediation costs

4.95 The authority in considering the cost of the proposed remediation package should take into account[81]:

(a) all initial costs (including tax) of the actions, including feasibility studies, design, specification, management, and making good;

(b) ongoing management and maintenance costs;

(c) any "disruption costs", that is depreciation in the value of land, or other loss or damage likely to result from carrying out the remediation. Specific guidance is given that the enforcing authority should assess these costs as their estimate of the amount of

---

[76] DEFRA Circular 01/2006, *Contaminated Land*, Annex 3 para.C.30.
[77] DEFRA Circular 01/2006, *Contaminated Land*, Annex 3 para.C.30.
[78] DEFRA Circular 01/2006, *Contaminated Land*, Annex 3 para.C.31.
[79] DEFRA Circular 01/2006, *Contaminated Land*, Annex 3 para.C.32.
[80] DEFRA Circular 01/2006, *Contaminated Land*, Annex 3 para.C.33.
[81] DEFRA Circular 01/2006, *Contaminated Land*, Annex 3 para.C.34.

compensation which would be payable if the owner of the land or interest had granted rights under s.78G(2) to permit the action to be carried out, and had made a claim for compensation.[82] However, it appears that this category could include other forms of consequential loss, such as loss of rental income, disruption to business, or relocation costs.

For the purpose of assessing these costs, it is irrelevant whether they are **4.96** carried out by contractors, or "in-house".[83] The evaluation of the cost in this sense is not affected either by the identity of the person carrying out the work, or the internal resources available to them. Evaluation is therefore an objective exercise, which may result in valuing costs at greater than their actual cost in the specific circumstances.

In looking at the costs of a proposed remediation action or package, an **4.97** overriding test of reasonableness is whether there is any alternative that would achieve the same purpose, to the same standard, for a lower cost.[84] This may be particularly important when considering how to deal overall with a number of pollutant linkages.[85]

Assessment of seriousness of harm

Assessment of the benefits of the remediation action will involve looking at **4.98** the seriousness of the significant harm which needs to be addressed. This involves the following factors[86]:

(a) whether it is already being caused;

(b) the degree of the possibility of it being caused;

(c) the nature of the harm with respect to the type and importance of the receptor, the extent and type of effects, the number of receptors and whether the effects would be irreversible; and

(d) the context in which the effects might occur, in particular whether the receptor has already been damaged by other means and, if so, whether further effects from the contaminated land would materially affect its condition. Secondly, this element involves considering the relative risk associated with the harm or pollution in the context of wider environmental risks. This issue of "context" might in practice be an important moderating factor, in areas of widespread environmental degradation, but authorities are unlikely to accept the argument when pushed to extremes, that harm from a badly contaminated site ought to be discounted because it is an already polluted area.

Separate and essentially similar advice is given in relation to water **4.99** pollution.[87] The consideration of effects on water quality will involve advice from the Environment Agency,[88] and where harm to ecological systems are

---

[82] DEFRA Circular 01/2006, *Contaminated Land*, Annex 3 para.C.35.
[83] DEFRA Circular 01/2006, *Contaminated Land*, Annex 3 para.C.36.
[84] DEFRA Circular 01/2006, *Contaminated Land*, Annex 3 para.C.38.
[85] DEFRA Circular 01/2006, *Contaminated Land*, Annex 3 para.C.37.
[86] DEFRA Circular 01/2006, *Contaminated Land*, Annex 3 para.C.39.
[87] DEFRA Circular 01/2006, *Contaminated Land*, Annex 3 para.C.41.
[88] DEFRA Circular 01/2006, *Contaminated Land*, Annex 3 para.C.42.

involved, advice from the relevant nature conservation body will be needed.[89]

What is to be done by way of remediation

4.100 To complete the picture, the Guidance also covers "what is to be done by way of remediation" (s.78E(5)(a)). This is dealt with at Ch.C Pt 7. This covers the three aspects of assessment, remedial treatment and monitoring. Assessment should only be required where it falls within one of three purposes and constitutes a reasonable means of achieving them[90]:

    (a) characterising the pollutant linkage which has already been identified for the purpose of establishing the appropriate remedial action;

    (b) enabling the technical design or specifications of treatment to be established; and

    (c) evaluating the ongoing condition of land which remains contaminated after remedial treatment, to support future decisions on whether further remediation might be required.

4.101 The main point of this aspect of the Guidance is to make it clear, or to reinforce the point, that a remediation notice cannot be used for the purpose of assessing whether the land should be identified as contaminated.

4.102 For remedial treatment actions, the test is whether the action is necessary to achieve the standard of remediation required by the Guidance, but no more.[91] Such action can include complementary assessment or monitoring measures to evaluate its implementation, effectiveness and durability. It should include appropriate verification measures to provide assurance that the treatment has been properly carried out.

4.103 Monitoring should be limited to providing information on changes to aspects of an already identified pollutant linkage, where the authority needs to consider whether any further remediation should be required in consequence of such changes.[92] It should not be used as a means of gathering general information to satisfy the authority's duty of inspecting its area.[93]

4.104 Finally, perhaps from an abundance of caution, para.C.70 emphasises that remediation may not be required for dealing with matters that do not in themselves form part of a significant pollutant linkage, or to make the land suitable for any use going beyond its current use. These wider objectives are a matter for voluntary remediation.

Summary and checklist on remediation requirements

4.105 It will be appreciated from the previous paragraphs that the Guidance involves a complex and sophisticated exercise in determining what remediation should be required. It may therefore be helpful to summarise

---

[89] DEFRA Circular 01/2006, *Contaminated Land*, Annex 3 para.C.40.
[90] DEFRA Circular 01/2006, *Contaminated Land*, Annex 3 para.C.66.
[91] DEFRA Circular 01/2006, *Contaminated Land*, Annex 3, para.C.67.
[92] DEFRA Circular 01/2006, *Contaminated Land*, Annex 3 para.C.68.
[93] DEFRA Circular 01/2006, *Contaminated Land*, Annex 3 para.C.69.

the elements involved in that exercise (references are to Parts and paragraph numbers in Ch.C of the Guidance).

1. Has each significant pollutant linkage been identified? (para.C.18).

2. What standard would be achieved for each significant linkage by use of a package forming the best practicable remediation techniques? (para.C.18). Consider here:
   (a) reasonableness (Pt 5, see point 5 below);
   (b) practicability, including any adverse environmental impacts (Pt 6; paras C.48–C.57);
   (c) effectiveness (Pt 6; paras C.58–C.60);
   (d) durability (Pt 6; paras C.61–C.63);
   (e) striking a balance between these factors (para.C.20).

3. Also take into account Guidance on what is the best practicable technique (Pt 4):
   (a) nature and volume of pollutants (para.C.19);
   (b) timescale needed for remediation (para.C.19);
   (c) comparable techniques that have been successful (para.C.21);
   (d) technological advances and changes in knowledge (para.C.21);
   (e) appropriate and authoritative technical advice (para.C.21);
   (f) established good practice (para.C.22).

4. For multiple pollutant linkages, consider whether practicability favours addressing each pollutant linkage separately or as an overall scheme (paras C.26–C.27).

5. On the issue of reasonableness (see 2 above) consider:
   (a) costs involved (Pt 5; paras C.34–C.38); and
   (b) seriousness of harm or pollution (Pt 5; paras C.39–C.43).

6. Keep in mind the general tests on what can and cannot be required by way of remediation for:
   (a) assessment (Pt 7; paras C.65–C.66);
   (b) remedial treatment (Pt 7; para.C.67);
   (c) monitoring (Pt 7; paras C.68 and C.69).

Restrictions on requirements of remediation notice: pollution of controlled waters

Where land is identified as contaminated by virtue of its effects in polluting **4.106** controlled waters, consideration must also be given by the enforcing authority to the restrictions on what a remediation notice may require which are imposed by s.78J. This section is discussed below.

Remediation notices and certainty

The issue may well arise as to whether a remediation notice is defective for **4.107** failing to specify the remediation actions to be carried out sufficiently clearly. This has been a frequent argument in relation to abatement notices in the case of statutory nuisance and enforcement notices in relation to planning, and might also be expected to arise in the context of Pt IIA, though the more recent case law in the area of statutory nuisance may restrict this (see below).

4.108   The wording of s.78E(1) itself, referring to "each of the things so specified", is indicative that some degree of precision is required. On the other hand, in debates the Government indicated their intention that remediation notices "should generally be phrased in terms of objectives to be achieved rather than specific works which have to be undertaken".[94] The Regulations on remediation notices do not add any extra requirements with regard to the remediation actions to be specified in the notice. The overall intention is, however, that the notice be clear and self-contained; and that it gives a clear indication of what is to be done to whom, where and by when.[95]

4.109   The problem with specifying works as opposed to objectives is where to stop in terms of detail, given that the success or otherwise of a remediation scheme may well lie in the detail of how the scheme is executed. In the context of planning and waste management licensing conditions, one possible solution to this type of problem is to require a detailed scheme to be prepared, and submitted to the authority for approval: the question is whether this approach, which might be eminently sensible, is sanctioned by s.78E(1). Given the need for the recipient of the notice to know what they must do, and the short timetable allowed for appeals against notices, it seems unlikely that such an approach would be acceptable.

4.110   It also needs to be remembered, however, that a remediation notice should have been preceded by a period of consultation as to its requirements with the recipients, during which time the authority's requirements may have been explained and clarified. In practice, the authority should seek to agree the works if possible before serving the notice. The debate may in some cases centre on the cost of the works rather than their nature.

4.111   The problem of clarity has arisen frequently in cases relating to abatement notices for statutory nuisance, where the issue has been whether a local authority is required to specify the steps required in order to abate such a nuisance in a notice served under s.80 of the 1990 Act. A line of cases suggested that an abatement notice must inform the recipient of what he did wrong, and must also ensure that he knows what he has to do to abate the nuisance, but identifying two classes of cases.[96] One class was where what is to be done by way of abatement is clear, so that it is sufficient simply to require the nuisance to be abated,[97] but in many cases it was thought necessary to state the works to be carried out.[98] However, the issue of specification has been clarified by the Court of Appeal in *R v Falmouth & Truro Port Health Authority Ex p. South West Water Ltd*,[99] which

---

[94] *Hansard*, HL Vol.562, col.1047.

[95] See DEFRA Circular 01/2006, *Contaminated Land*, Annex 4 para.18.

[96] *Kirklees MC v Field* [1998] Env. L.R. 337; see also *R. v Wheatley* [1885] 16 Q.B.D. 34; *Millard v Wastall* [1898] 1 Q.B. 342.

[97] For example, cases of noise from barking dogs (*Myatt v Teignbridge DC* [1995] Env. L.R. 78; *Budd v Colchester BC* [1999] J.P.L. 739) or amplified music (*SFI Group Plc v Gosport BC* [1999] Env. L.R. 750).

[98] *Network Housing Association v Birmingham CC* [1996] Env. L.R. 121.

[99] [2001] Q.B. 445; [2000] Env. L.R. 658.

found that an enforcing authority is free to leave the choice of means of abatement to the perpetrator in all cases, if it so desired. It is only where a particular means of abatement is required by the authority that the works or steps to be undertaken have to be specified.[100]

Quite clearly, remediation notices are likely to fall into the latter of the **4.112** two classes of cases originally identified in relation to abatement notices, in that it will not be at all obvious simply from the fact that the land is contaminated as to what type and degree of work will be necessary to satisfy the authority.

Although there are some analogies with the abatement notice scheme, **4.113** that scheme is different to Pt IIA. Perhaps most importantly, s.80 gives the local authority the option of requiring the abatement (etc.) of a statutory nuisance under para.(a) of subs.(1), and/or requiring the execution of works, or taking of other steps under para.(b), with actions only required to be specified with sufficient particularity where particular works or steps are so specified. Section 78E(1), on the other hand, makes it clear that the remediation notice must specify what is to be done by way of remediation.

Where the nature of the work required is specified by the authority the **4.114** temptation to qualify this by adding words such as "or other equivalent work", "other equally effective work" or similar phrases, should be resisted. This may have the effect of vitiating the notice by referring to other, unspecified measures.[101]

Form and content of remediation notices: Regulations

Section 78E allows Regulations to make provision for or in connection with **4.115** the form or content of remediation notices and with procedural steps in connection with service. Regulation 4(1) of the Regulations sets out the matters which a remediation notice must specify (in addition to those required by s.78E(1) and (3)):

(a) the name and address of the person on whom the notice is served;

(b) the location and extent of the land, in sufficient detail to enable it to be identified, whether by reference to a plan or otherwise;

(c) the date of any notice under s.78B identifying the land as contaminated;

(d) whether the authority considers the person on whom the notice is served to be an appropriate person because they are a causer or knowing permitter or because they are owner or occupier of the land;

(e) particulars of the significant harm or pollution by reason of which the land is contaminated land;

(f) the substances by reason of which the land is contaminated and, if they have escaped from other land, the location of that land;

---

[100] [2000] Env. L.R. 658 at 686.
[101] *Perry v Garner* [1953] 1 All E.R. 285.

    (g) brief particulars of the reasons for the remediation action required, showing how the Guidance has been applied;

    (h) where there are two or more persons in relation to the contaminated land:

        (i) a statement that this is the case;

        (ii) their names and addresses; and

        (iii) the thing by way of remediation for which each is responsible.

    (i) where the authority has applied the tests in the Guidance to exclude an appropriate person from liability, the reasons for the authority's determination and how the Guidance has been applied;

    (j) where the notice involves apportionment of responsibility, the reasons for the apportionment, and how the Guidance on that issue has been applied;

    (k) where known to the authority, the name and address of the owner and of any person who appears to be in occupation of the whole or any part of the land;

    (l) where known, the name and address of any person whose consent is required under s.78G before anything required by the notice may be done;

    (m) where appropriate, that it appears the land is in a condition of imminent danger of serious harm or serious pollution to controlled waters;

    (n) a statement that a person on whom such a notice is served may be guilty of an offence for failure, without reasonable excuse, to comply with any of the requirements of the notice;

    (o) for such an offence the penalties which may be applied on conviction;

    (p) the name and address of the enforcing authority serving the notice; and

    (q) the date of the notice.

4.116   The notice must also inform the recipient of the right of appeal under s.78L and of how, where, within what period and on what grounds such appeals may be made, and that the notice will be suspended, where an appeal is duly made, while an appeal is pending until final determination or abandonment of the appeal.[102] The actual form (as opposed to the content) of remediation notices is not prescribed.[103]

Apportionment of costs for the same remediation works

4.117 Where the situation is that two or more persons are responsible for the same remediation works, then, although subs.78E(3) does not expressly say so, each is presumably liable to secure compliance with the notice; but as

---

[102] Contaminated Land (England) Regulations 2006 (SI 2006/1380) reg.4(2).

[103] Initial indications that the Government and the Environment Agency intended to produce a model form of remediation notice have not been followed up.

to cost, the notices in question must specify that proportion of the cost of remediation that each of them has to bear separately. It is the cost of the works, not the works themselves, which are apportioned. It follows that it would be a defence to the non-completion of the works in question that the other party served with the notice is unable to, or has otherwise failed to, fulfil his part of the obligation and that it was therefore impossible from a practical point of view to start with remediation, the party in question being unable to bear the whole of the costs.

This is effectively the statutory position under s.78M(2), which provides **4.118** a defence that the only reason that the defendant has not complied with the notice is that one or more of the other persons who are liable to bear a proportion of the cost refused or was not able to comply with the requirement. In such circumstances, it is presumed that the local authority would do the works itself and charge the parties according to the proportions already determined and stated in the notices concerned. As to how precisely the apportionment is to be done, s.78F(7) requires the authority to act in accordance with Government guidance.

Giving reasons for notices

As will be appreciated many of the decisions on which a remediation notice **4.119** is based may well be controversial; in particular, what is required, who is determined to be an appropriate person, and how the costs are apportioned where there are a number of appropriate persons. Service of the notice may well have been preceded by dialogue on these issues, and may well be followed by an appeal or other legal challenge. The question therefore arises as to whether the enforcing authority, when serving the notice, is under any obligation to explain the reasoning behind its decisions.

As mentioned above, the Regulations on form and content of notices **4.120** require reasons to be given as to the remediation action required, the allocation of liability and the apportionment of costs (if any). This is clearly a mandatory requirement.

The question is whether general legal principles require any further **4.121** reasons. The current principles relating to the giving of reasons for decisions were distilled and summarised by the Divisional Court in *R. v Ministry of Defence Ex p. Murray*[104] as follows:

(a) The law does not at present recognise a general duty to give reasons.

(b) Where a statute has confirmed the power to make decisions concerning individuals, the court will not only require the statutory procedure to be followed, but will readily imply as much (and no more) to be introduced by way of additional procedural standards as will ensure fairness.

(c) In the absence of a requirement to give reasons, the person seeking to argue that reasons should have been given must show that the procedure adopted of not giving reasons is unfair.

---

[104] [1998] C.O.D. 134; see also *R. v Civil Service Appeal Board Ex p. Cunningham*; [1991] 4 All E.R. 310; *R. v Secretary of State for the Home Department Ex p. Doody*; [1994] 1 A.C. 531; *R. v Higher Education Funding Council Ex p. Institute of Dental Surgery* [1994] 1 W.L.R. 241.

(d) There is a perceptible trend towards an insistence on greater openness or transparency in the making of administrative decisions.

(e) In deciding whether fairness requires reasons, regard will be had to the nature of any further remedy. The absence of a right of appeal strengthens the need for reasons, and if the remedy is judicial review, then reasons may be necessary in order to detect the type of error which may justify intervention.

(f) The fact that a tribunal is carrying out a judicial function (which the local authority is not) is a consideration in favour of requiring reasons, particularly where personal liberty is concerned.

(g) If the giving of a decision without reasons is insufficient to achieve justice, then reasons should be required.

(h) Giving of reasons is helpful in concentrating the decision-maker's mind on the right questions and in demonstrating to the recipient that this was so.

(i) Against giving reasons is the fact that it may place an undue burden on decision makers; demand an appearance of unanimity where there is diversity; call for articulation of sometimes inexpressible value judgments; and offer an invitation to nit-pick the reasons to discover grounds of challenge.

4.122   Clearly, some of these criteria are more relevant than others to remediation notices. However, based on them, a respectable case can be mounted that, irrespective of the Regulations, remediation notices should be accompanied by reasons. Such notices will have considerable financial and legal consequences for those in receipt of them; they also have penal consequences. Although they can be subject to appeal, no recipient is going to embark on a potentially lengthy and expensive legal process lightly, and in the absence of reasons it may be difficult or impossible to gauge the likelihood of such a challenge being successful. Particularly compelling is the fact that the decisions in question are such as ought to be taken on a rational basis, rather than "value judgments". The matters will have been the subject of a reasoned report by officers, often after discussion with potential recipients, and debate in committee: the formulation of reasons should therefore not constitute an undue administrative burden.

4.123   However, there is also the issue of the standard and detail of the reasons required. Some aspects of the process are more susceptible to detailed reasons than others: matters based on scientific considerations may well be capable of being supported by detailed reasons. The same is less true of decisions on apportionment or relief on hardship grounds, which involve value judgments. Whilst reasons will be required in both cases, the reasons involving scientific facts may need to be given in greater depth than those involving value judgments.

4.124   At heart, the question is one of fairness. Parliament has seen fit to provide a formal consultation process for potential recipients of notices to express their views and it may be seen as unfair for those who have such rights to have an inadequate indication as to the thought processes of the authority or to find their representations rejected out of hand, without reasons. There may also be arguments in favour of reasons based on the right to an effective remedy under Art.6 or Art.13 of the European Convention on Human Rights.[105]

Delegation of the service of notices

Normal principles of local government law will apply to the internal **4.125** procedures for authorising service of remediation notices. By s.101 of the Local Government Act 1972 the function of authorising the issue of a notice may be delegated to a committee, sub-committee or officer; similarly the function of preparing and serving the notice may be delegated in this way. On the basis of *Albon v Railtrack Plc*,[106] there seems to be nothing to prevent a senior officer who is empowered to serve a notice authorising a member of his or her staff to do so.[107] However, to reduce so far as possible the risk of challenge to the notice, the authority should ensure that the arrangements for delegation are clearly evidenced by specific authority or by standing orders.[108] Whilst it may be possible for a decision to serve a notice to be subsequently ratified, no sensible authority would wish to enter such uncharted waters.[109]

Signature of notices

On general principles, the notice must be properly authenticated to be **4.126** valid.[110] Neither the Act nor Regulations requires a remediation notice to be signed on behalf of the authority. Given the absence of any statutory requirement of signature, the notice probably does not require to be signed: the essential point is that it should be possible for the recipient to see where it emanated from and verify its authenticity.[111] Reference to the name of the officer with primary authority to issue the notice should be sufficient for this.

However, by s.234 of the Local Government Act 1972 a remediation **4.127** notice (being a document which the local authority are required to issue) may be signed on behalf of the authority by the proper officer; that is, an

---

[105] Incorporated into UK law by the Human Rights Act 1998. Compare *R. v Secretary of State for the Environment, Transport and the Regions and Parcelforce Ex p. Marson* [1998] J.P.L. 869 where the applicant was held to have a "fundamental right" to reasons as to why an environmental assessment was not required. The reasoning in that case does not appear particularly apt to the situation discussed above. See also the comments of Laws J. at *Chesterfield Properties Plc v Secretary of State for the Environment* [1998] J.P.L. 568–579 on the importance of justifying interference with fundamental or constitutional rights.

[106] [1998] E.H.L.R. 83 (a case on the Prevention of Damage by Pests Act 1949).

[107] In that case, authorisation was by the Assistant Chief Environmental Health Officer to a Principal Environmental Health Officer. See also *Fitzpatrick v Secretary of State for the Environment* [1990] P.L.R. 8.

[108] See *Cheshire CC v Secretary of State for the Environment* [1988] J.P.L. 300.

[109] *Co-operative Retail Services v. Taff-Ely BC* (1981) 42 P. & C.R. 1, HL. By s.100G(2) of the 1972 Act, a list of powers delegated to officers must be kept open for public inspection.

[110] See Carter, Pengelly and Saunders, *Local Authority Notices* (London: Sweet & Maxwell, 1999), pp.54–55.

[111] *Albon v Railtrack Plc* [1998] E.H.L.R. 83 (*sub nom. Basildon DC v Railtrack Plc*); *Pamplin v Gorman* [1980] R.T.R. 54.

officer appointed for that purpose by the authority.[112] The "signature" may be a facsimile of the signature, though it is questionable whether remediation notices will be issued in such numbers as to make this necessary.[113] The benefit of signature under this provision is that the notice is deemed by s.234(2) to have been duly issued, unless the contrary is proved.[114]

Copies of notices

4.128 Under the Regulations, when serving a remediation notice the authority must send a copy of it to[115]:

(a) any person who was required to be consulted under s.78G(3) (being a person whose consent would be needed for the remediation actions to be carried out);

(b) any person who was required to be consulted under s.78H(1) before serving the notice;

(c) where the local authority is the enforcing authority, the Environment Agency; and

(d) where the Environment Agency is the enforcing authority, the local authority in whose area the land is situated.

4.129 It will be good practice to notify such persons of the capacity in which they are being sent a copy of the notice.[116] Where there is imminent danger of serious harm or pollution, the authority must send copies of the notice to those persons as soon as practicable after service of the notice[117]; in other words the requirements for sending copies should not delay service in urgent cases. What constitutes a "copy" of a notice was considered in *Ralls v Secretary of State for the Environment*.[118] The addition to the copy of the name and address of the person on whom the copy is being served may give rise to confusion and is probably best avoided. The Courts could possibly construe the requirement to serve copies of notices as directory only, so that failure to do so will not necessarily be fatal to the original notice, provided that no-one is prejudiced by the breach.[119]

Service of notices

4.130 By s.78E(6)(b), Regulations may be made with regard to procedures in connection with, or in consequence of, service of a remediation notice. In fact, the Regulations do not make such provision, other than that in relation to copies of notices.

---

[112] Local Government Act 1972 s.234(1).

[113] *FitzPatrick v Secretary of State for the Environment* [1990] P.L.R. 8.

[114] Section 234 will probably be treated as an enabling rather than a mandatory provision in this respect: *Tennant v London CC* [1957] 121 J.P. 428; *Albon v Railtrack Plc* (n.111, above). These are cases on s.284 of the Public Health Act 1936.

[115] Contaminated Land (England) Regulations 2006 (SI 2006/1380) reg.5(1).

[116] DEFRA Circular 01/2006, *Contaminated Land*, Annex 4 para.20.

[117] Contaminated Land (England) Regulations 2006 (SI 2006/1380) reg.5(2).

[118] [1998] J.P.L. 444.

[119] See *O'Brien v London Borough of Croydon* [1999] J.P.L. 47 at 52; *Nahlis, Dickey and Morris v Secretary of State for the Environment* (1996) 71 P. & C.R. 553.

Since the remediation notice is one required to be served under the 1990 **4.131**
Act, s.160 of that Act will apply to it. This provides that the notice may be
served by delivering it to the intended person, or by leaving it at his proper
address, or by sending it by post to him at that address.[120]

Special provision is made for companies and partnerships.[121] In the case **4.132**
of a company or other body corporate, the notice may be served on or given
to the secretary or clerk; in the case of a partnership, it may be served on a
person having the control or management of the partnership business.[122]

As to the time of service, by s.7 of the Interpretation Act 1978, where **4.133**
service is effected by post, then it will be deemed to be effected by properly
addressing, prepaying and posting a letter containing the notice, and
unless the contrary is proved, shall be deemed to have been effected at the
time when the letter would be delivered in the ordinary course of post.

A key question is therefore what constitutes the "proper address" for **4.134**
service. This can be the address specified by the person to be served as one
at which he or some other person will accept notices of that description.[123]
Otherwise, it is the last known address of the person, except that[124]:

(a) in the case of a body corporate or its secretary or clerk, it shall be
the address of the registered or principal office of that body; and

(b) in the case of a partnership or person having control or management of the business, it shall be the principal office of the
partnership.

For this purpose, the principal office of a non-UK registered company or **4.135**
of a partnership carrying on business outside the UK shall be their
principal office within the UK.[125] Given that the end result of a remediation notice may be criminal proceedings, the courts can be expected to take
a relatively unforgiving approach to errors in service.[126] So, getting the
name of a company wrong, or specifying the wrong company within a group
of companies, might give rise to serious difficulties.[127]

---

[120] 1990 Act s.160(2).

[121] 1990 Act s.160(3).

[122] In *Leeds v London Borough of Islington* [1998] Env. L.R. 655, it was held by the Divisional
Court that s.160(3) is mandatory as to the person to whom the notice must be addressed.
There a notice addressed to "the Senior Estate Manager" was held not sufficient. Compare
the more relaxed approach taken in *Pearshouse v. Birmingham CC* [1999] L.G.R. 169; and
Hall v Kingston-upon-Hull CC [1999] L.G.R. 184 (but on the basis of procedures intended to
be operated by private individuals).

[123] Section 160(5). The question is whether they have accepted service for that particular
purpose—accepting service for general property notices may not be sufficient—see *Leeds v
London Borough of Islington* [1998] Env. L.R. 655 at 661. Specification of an address for all
future correspondence does not include an abatement notice, as such a notice is not a
communication by letter and so does not come within the meaning of the word
"correspondence" (*Butland v Powys CC* [2007] EWHC 734 (Admin)). Also the person who
specifies the address for service need not be the secretary or clerk—see *Hall v Kingston-
upon-Hull CC* [1999] L.G.R. 184.

[124] 1990 Act s.160(4).

[125] 1990 Act s.160(4).

[126] *Leeds v Islington LBC* [1998] Env. L.R. 655 at 661.

[127] See *Amec Building Ltd v Camden LBC* [1997] Env. L.R. 330; but compare *Malkins Bank Estates
Ltd v Kirkham* (1966) 64 L.G.R. 361.

4.136 For a company, its registered office will be ascertainable, in that every company must have a registered office,[128] to which as a matter of company law communications, notices and proceedings can be addressed.[129] That address must be shown on the company's business letters[130] and service will be valid for a 14-day transitional period at the old office where a change of office is registered.[131] The authority will be entitled to proceed on the basis of the registered office as disclosed by the official file.[132] Thus the registered office will be the safest address for service.

4.137 The "principal office" of a company is the place at which the business of the company is controlled and managed.[133] "Principal" in this sense means chief, or most important.[134] There is a question of statutory construction arising from s.160(4) as to whether the "principal office" is an alternative address for service in all cases, or whether it is only relevant for companies registered in Scotland or outside the UK. The better view seems to be that the "principal office" is a true alternative address for service in all cases and this has been the approach taken by the High Court in relation to statutory nuisance notices served by "persons aggrieved".[135] The concept of a principal office is clearly distinct from the registered office as a matter of company law.[136] References to service on companies at their principal office go back to the Public Health Act 1936,[137] by which time the separate concept of a registered office had emerged,[138] and Parliament may be assumed to have been aware of the difference between the two terms. Nor does the language of s.160(4) justify confining "principal office" to the more limited circumstances mentioned there of companies registered outside the UK.

4.138 Be that as it may, there may well be uncertainties as to what is a company's principal office, and as mentioned above, for practical purposes the safest course will be service at the registered office, addressed to the company secretary.[139]

---

[128] Companies Act 1985 s.287(1).

[129] Companies Act 1985 s.725(1).

[130] Companies Act 1985 s.351(1).

[131] Companies Act 1985 s.287(4).

[132] *Ross v Invergordon Distillers Ltd* 1961 S.L.T. 358.

[133] *Palmer v Caledonian Railway Co* [1892] 1 Q.B. 823, 827–8.

[134] *The Rewia* [1991] 2 Lloyd's Rep. 325. A company can have more than one place of business (*Davies v British Geon Ltd* [1956] All E.R. 389) but only one principal place.

[135] See *Hewlings v McLean Homes East Anglia Ltd* [2001] Env. L.R. 17, where s.160 was considered to be "permissive" rather than "mandatory" in that context.

[136] *Palmer's Company Law* (London: Sweet & Maxwell), para.2.504.

[137] The Public Health Act 1936 s.285 refers to service at the registered office or principal office. Earlier public health legislation (e.g. the Public Health Act 1875) referred to notices being serviced at the residence of the recipient.

[138] The Companies Act 1929 s.370 stated that service may be effected by leaving notices at the registered office. Section 62 of the Companies (Consolidation) Act 1908 required every company to have a registered office to which all communications and notices could be addressed, as did s.39 of the Companies & c. Act 1862. The concept of principal office goes back further: the Companies Clauses Consolidation Act 1845 s.135 (and associated railways legislation) provided for service at the principal office of the company, and the Companies Act 1844 s.7, required the certificate of registration to include the principal or only place for carrying on business, and any branch office.

[139] *Leeds v Islington LBC* [1998] Env. L.R. 655.

In the case of service of notices on an owner or occupier of land, if that **4.139** person cannot after reasonable inquiry be ascertained, the notice may be served either by leaving it in the hands of a person who is or appears to be resident or employed on the land or by leaving it conspicuously affixed to some building or object on the land.[140] The authority can, and should, before doing so, consider whether it could gain that information by use of its statutory powers to obtain particulars of persons interested in land under s.16 of the Local Government (Miscellaneous Provisions) Act 1976, or whether it can obtain the necessary information direct from the Land Registry.

Withdrawal of notices

Neither Pt IIA nor the Regulations makes express provision for withdrawal **4.140** of a remediation notice; unlike planning enforcement notices, where s.173A of the Town and Country Planning Act 1990 states that they may be withdrawn whether or not they have taken effect. Nonetheless, there may well be circumstances where the appropriate course is to withdraw a remediation notice. Examples might include:

1. Cases where the authority is now satisfied that the land is no longer "contaminated land" (for example, because it has been cleaned up voluntarily).

2. Cases where the authority is satisfied that things will now be done within an appropriate timescale, which although not in compliance with the terms of the notice, will in fact effect satisfactory remediation.

3. Cases where the authority has now concluded that the notice was served on the wrong person, or stated the wrong apportionment of liability.

4. Cases where the authority simply "got it wrong" so that the notice is defective or is open to challenge, and the authority wants to start again with a clean slate.

Notwithstanding any express statutory power, the authority almost **4.141** certainly has inherent powers to withdraw a notice it has served by analogy with *R. v Bristol CC Ex p. Everett*,[141] on statutory nuisance. It would be sensible to give notice of withdrawal to every person who should have originally been notified. Alternatively, the authority may simply decide to take no further action on the notice, i.e. not to enforce it. Again, notice of that decision should be given to all the relevant parties.

The authority should also bear in mind that it is under a duty to serve a **4.142** remediation notice or notices where contaminated land has been identified. Clearly, therefore, withdrawing a notice without sound reasons for doing

---

[140] Local Government Act 1972 s.233(7).

[141] [1999] 1 W.L.R. 1170, applying the first instance decision at [1999] 1 W.L.R. 92. See also *Woods v Sevenoaks DC* [2005] Env. L.R. 11.

so, and without replacing it with a further notice, may be subject to challenge by third parties by way of judicial review; as may a decision to take no further action on a notice.

4.143 Unlike planning enforcement notices, remediation notices do not have to state a period after which they take effect; the ability to withdraw a notice is not therefore a question as to whether the notice has taken effect. It may well be advisable to obtain the consent of the appropriate person to withdrawal of the notice. Apart from anything else, unilateral withdrawal where the recipient has expended money on compliance or on legal or other advice may result in a claim for losses incurred in tort, or a complaint to the local government ombudsman for alleged maladministration.

Chapter 5

LIABILITY

PART 1: OVERVIEW

Part IIA provides a complex (arguably over-complex) set of rules for the **5.01**
allocation of liability for the remediation or cost of remediation of
contaminated land. It does so by a combination of the statutory provisions
which define who is an "appropriate person" to bear this liability, and
statutory guidance which applies where there are a number of appropriate
persons. This guidance dictates how and in what proportions that liability
is to be allocated. In a sense the complexity of the regime is not surprising,
since land may historically have been contaminated by a number of persons
over a potentially lengthy period of time. In addition, there may be other
parties than the original polluter who bear responsibility for the harm or
risk of harm presented—for example by having failed to take steps which
were within their power as owner or occupier to deal with a known
problem, or by having made the situation worse by building houses or other
structures on the land. Liability does not depend on fault in the sense of
negligence or intentional harm, but issues of fault do nevertheless underlie
the guidance in a number of respects.

A remediation notice must be served on each "appropriate person", i.e. **5.02**
any person who should bear responsibility for any thing which is to be done
by way of remediation in relation to the land in question. Who is an
appropriate person is to be determined in accordance with s.78F, which
contemplates two main categories of appropriate persons. The first category (described in the Guidance as "Class A") comprises the persons who
have caused or knowingly permitted the relevant contaminated substances
to be in, on or under the land. The second category ("Class B") consists of
the current owners and occupiers; this category is only responsible where
no person falling within Class A can be found.

Special provisions apply to water pollution and to the escape of contami- **5.03**
nants. It will frequently be the case that contamination present in the soil
or groundwater undergoes chemical or other transformations over time, or
in some cases spreads to other land or groundwater. Provisions of Pt IIA
deal with these specific eventualities, and will require careful application to
the facts where such migration or transformation has occurred. Section 78J
places certain restrictions on the possible requirements of remediation
notices in cases where the contaminated land in question has been
identified as such wholly or partly as a result of water pollution. There is
one restriction of a general nature (s.78J(2)), and one relating specifically
to water from abandoned mines (s.78J(3)).

5.04   Certain commercial situations may give rise to particular concerns under Pt IIA as to who is an appropriate person. In particular, there is the position of banks, insolvency practitioners, trustees, and parent companies. Other issues of concern are the position on the dissolution of companies and the death of individuals, and the position of the Crown. These issues may require consideration of other areas of law, such as company law, insolvency, and succession.

5.05   Once the appropriate persons have been ascertained then, if there is more than one such person, the enforcing authority will have to apply the rules on exclusion of persons from liability and on apportionment. Where two or more persons are appropriate persons to be served with a remediation notice in relation to the same remediation action, s.78F(6) requires the enforcing authority to determine, in accordance with statutory guidance, whether any of them should be treated as not being an appropriate person in relation to that thing. The Guidance provides six tests for this purpose for Group A persons and a single test for Group B persons.

5.06   Where two or more persons are appropriate persons in relation to any particular remediation action, they shall be liable to bear the cost of doing that thing in proportions determined by the enforcing authority (and stated in the remediation notice) in accordance with statutory guidance. The Guidance deals with three separate issues: apportionment within a Class A liability group; apportionment within a Class B liability group; and attribution of responsibility between different liability groups.

5.07   A local authority may well find itself in the position of an appropriate person, either in relation to land which it has itself contaminated in the past (for example as a municipal waste disposal facility or transport depot) or as the current owner or occupier of land. Particular care is needed in such cases in relation to the legal framework, and in managing situations of potential bias or conflict of interest which may arise where the authority is also the enforcing authority for the purpose of Pt IIA.

5.08   There may be sites in respect of which the necessary remediation works, in whole or in part, cannot be attributed to any appropriate person, thereby leaving remediation in the hands of the enforcing authority. The Guidance uses the term "orphan linkage" to describe the situation where either no owner or occupier can be found for some land, or where those who would otherwise be liable are exempted by one of the statutory provisions.

PART 2: THE "APPROPRIATE PERSON"

Definition of the "appropriate person"

5.09 The term "appropriate person" in Pt IIA is defined by s.78(A)(9) as the person "who is the appropriate person to bear responsibility for any thing which is to be done by way of remediation in any particular case". This question naturally lies at the heart of the statutory regime. Who is an appropriate person is to be determined in accordance with s.78F, but it may be noted from the definition that the crucial issue is the relationship between the person and the particular thing which is to be done by way of remediation.

In relation to s.78F, government guidance plays a central role in **5.10** channelling and apportioning liability in the situation where two or more persons are potentially appropriate persons. However, the starting point is subss.78F(2), (3) and (4), all of which deal with the primary question of who are appropriate persons. Essentially, there are two ranks, tiers, or groups of appropriate persons: the first defined in subss.78F(2) and (3) and the second in subs.78F(4). The Guidance refers to these respectively as "Class A" and "Class B". Class B only comes into play where no person in Class A can be found. This effectively continues a system of liability for statutory nuisances which goes back at least as far as the Nuisances Removal Act 1855[1] in channelling liability first to the perpetrator or person responsible and only secondarily to the owner or occupier.

By Sch.1 to the Interpretation Act 1978, the word "person" includes a **5.11** body of persons, corporate or unincorporated. It could therefore include an association, club or partnership. As a matter of general law, the term "person" denotes an entity which is the subject of rights and duties,[2] and has been held to include, for example, a fund,[3] and a Hindu Temple.[4] It would clearly include a local government body, statutory body, or corporation. The Crown has been held to be a "person".[5]

The first rank of appropriate persons: "Class A"

The ambit of Class A is defined by s.78F(2) and (3) as "any person, or any **5.12** of the persons, who caused or knowingly permitted the substances, or any of the substances, by reason of which the contaminated land in question is such land to be in, on or under that land is an appropriate person". This approach is qualified by the concept of referability, discussed in the next paragraph.

It is important to note that the terminology is in the past tense, which **5.13** might arguably suggest that s.78F(2) and (3) are directed toward the original contaminator who either introduced the substances in question into the land or who caused them to be introduced by instructing servants, agents or independent contractors to put them there, or who stood by and watched them being introduced into the land. Although the use of the term "knowingly permitted" indicates that passive conduct can be sufficient, nevertheless it might on that construction denote only passive conduct in respect of the past event or events giving rise to the original contamination. On this construction it would be wrong to suggest that the terminology would catch someone who merely came to the land, who knew or ought to have known of the existence of contamination caused by a predecessor in title, and nevertheless did nothing about it. It could be said that if the

---

[1] Statutes 18 & 19 Vict. C. 121, s.12.
[2] See L.S. Sealy, *Cases & Materials in Company Law*, 6th edn (London: Butterworths, 1996), p.37.
[3] *Arab Monetary Fund v.Hashim (No. 3)* [1991] 2 A.C. 114.
[4] *Bumper Development Corp Ltd v Metropolitan Police Commissioner* [1991] 4 All E.R. 638.
[5] *Boarland v Madras Electrical Supply Co Ltd* [1954] 1 W.L.R. 87.

legislation was intended to catch him, then the word would be in the present tense, namely "permits".

5.14 However, "knowingly permitted" might also plausibly be read as denoting not only those concerned with the original introduction of the substances to the land, but also those who were subsequently in control of the land so as to be in a position to remove or render harmless the substances, but who, knowing of its presence, did not take steps within their power to do so: on that reading they knowingly permitted the presence of the substance during their period of control. This difficulty is discussed below in the context of subsequent owners and occupiers.

The referability exclusion

5.15 Subsection 78F(3) is conceptually complicated. Instead of saying that a person shall only be responsible for contamination arising from substances for which he is responsible the subsection says a person shall only be an appropriate person within Class A in relation to things which are to be done by way of remediation which are to any extent referable to the substances which he caused or knowingly permitted to be present. This is a very important provision because of what follows. The effect of subs.78F(3) is to take certain persons out of the category of "appropriate persons" altogether and thus there could in certain circumstances be no "appropriate person" in the first rank in Class A. If the remediation works are not referable to substances which he caused or knowingly permitted to be present in, on or under the contaminated land, then he is not an appropriate person at all. The enforcing authority is then entitled, in such circumstances, to look to the second rank of Class B.

5.16 The effect of this referability exclusion is to negative what would otherwise be the wide words of s.78F(2), referring as they do to "any of the substances", and the effect of joint and several liability which those words would otherwise potentially create. If a number of substances are causing land to be contaminated, it will be necessary to establish to which of them the remediation action is referable. The range of people who may be held responsible for those requirements will be limited accordingly.

5.17 However, it is equally important to note some limitations on the referability exclusion. First, a person may be liable if there is referability "to any extent" (s.78F(3)). This implies that the referability need not be total, i.e. not all of the measures in question need to be referable to the contamination for which the person is responsible. Secondly, the position on referability may be affected by specific provisions on chemical reactions between substances (s.78F(9)) and on escapes of substances between different sites (s.78K). Finally, s.78F(10) provides that a thing to be done by way of remediation may be regarded as referable to the presence of a substance notwithstanding that it would not have to be done in consequence of the presence of that substance alone, or in consequence of the presence of the quantity for which the person was responsible. This makes it clear that where a number of people have contributed the same substance or different substances so as to result in contamination which requires remediation, it will not be open to any of them to argue that their contribution alone would not justify such remediation measures. In such cases, were it not for the requirement under s.78E(7) that the remediation notice must apportion liability for the costs of remediation, the end result would be joint and several liability.

5.18 Essentially, referability will be a question of fact and of science. It stresses the critical importance of a causal link between the substances in respect of which the person is responsible and the remedial action necessary to deal with the harm or risk which makes the land "contaminated".

Caused

5.19 One way to be a first tier appropriate person is to have caused the contaminating substances to be present in, on or under the land. This will generally be a question of fact, and by its nature the concept of causation seems most naturally to relate to the entry of the substances in question on to or into the land. Case law in the field of water pollution offences suggests that the courts are likely to approach the issue in a robust, common sense way, without knowledge, fault or negligence needing to be shown.

5.20 There have of course been many recent cases interpreting the word "caused" in the context of water pollution offences.[6] The leading authority is the decision of the House of Lords in *Environment Agency v Empress Car Co. (Abertillery) Ltd*.[7] Lord Hoffman there laid down a series of principles to be considered in cases on causing pollution. Many of these will be equally relevant to the contaminated land regime and s.78F(2) in particular:

1. What is it that the defendant did to cause pollution? This is equally valid as a starting point under s.78F: what is the action or activity which forms the basis of a person having caused the presence of contaminating substances?

2. That thing need not have been the immediate cause of the pollution. Maintaining tanks, lagoons or storage systems containing polluting substances is "doing something" for this purpose, even if the immediate cause of the pollution was lack of maintenance, a natural event, or the act of a third party. This point seems highly relevant to many contaminated land situations.

3. Did that thing cause the pollution? This is not the same as asking whether it was the sole cause, or whether something else was also a cause. The fact that something else (e.g. vandalism or natural events) was also a cause does not mean that the defendant's conduct was not a cause. Again, this has relevance to contamination of land.

4. Where a third party act or natural event was involved in the escape of the pollution, it should be considered whether that act or event was a normal fact of life, or something extraordinary.

---

[6] See for example *Attorney General's Reference No. 1 of 1994* [1995] Env. L.R. 356 setting out general principles.
[7] [1999] 2 A.C. 22; [1998] 2 W.L.R. 350.

Ordinary occurrences will not negate the causal effect of the defendant's conduct, even if the intervention was not foreseeable at all or in the form in which it occurred. This distinction is one of fact and degree, to which common sense and knowledge of what happens in the locality should be applied. In that case, vandalism was regarded as an ordinary normal fact of life, whereas an act of terrorism might well not be. In a subsequent case the failure of a seal on a pipe, though unforeseeable, was held to be an ordinary rather than extraordinary event.[8]

5.21   These principles would appear to constitute a sound basis for decisions on whether a person or company be present within s.78F(2). Contamination will often come about because pipes leak, tanks corrode, vandals open taps, etc. In such circumstances, responsibility seems likely to follow. In particular, earlier cases which suggested that some positive act was required, have been disapproved as too restrictive.[9] This approach seems to accord with the Government's view that the test of "causing" will require that the person concerned was involved in some active operation, or series of operations, to which the presence of the pollutant is attributable, and that such involvement may also take the form of a failure to act in certain circumstances.[10] It is possible that such failure might involve, for example, the omission to undertake, or act upon, a proper risk assessment when potentially polluting activities are to be undertaken.[11]

5.22   There is, however, a note of caution in the application of water pollution case law to the contaminated land regime. That case law has been developed in the context of criminal proceedings where a significant point of distinction is the ability of the court to mitigate the harshness of taking a strict approach to concepts such as "causing" (and "knowingly permit") through sentencing, where perceived blameworthiness can be accounted for.[12] The operation of the exclusionary tests, apportionment and hardship provisions may alleviate some of the more inequitable results, though this may rely upon the good fortune of having more than one person liable for remediation, for example.

Causing and consignment to landfill

5.23   In some cases, the contaminated land in question may comprise a former tip, landfill or similar facility to which many companies (or for that matter local authorities) may have consigned material over the years. The person

---

[8] *Environment Agency v Brock Plc* [1998] J.P.L. 968. See also *CPC (U.K.) Ltd v National Rivers Authority* [1995] Env. L.R. 131 (pollution arising from a latent defect in pipework at the defendant's factory held to be caused by defendant).

[9] *Price v Cromack* [1975] 1 W.L.R. 988; and *Wychavon DC v National Rivers Authority* [1993] 1 W.L.R. 125, disapproved in *Environment Agency v Empress Car Co (Abertillery) Ltd.*

[10] DEFRA Circular 01/2006, *Contaminated Land*, Annex 2 para.9.9. Compare *Environment Agency v Biffa Waste Services and Eurotech Environmental Ltd* [2006] EWHC 1102 (Admin) where the departure of a contractor from site and his failure to continue taking waste away were regarded as correctly classified as an omission and not as "causing" pollution.

[11] See by way of analogy, *Express Ltd v Environment Agency* [2004] EWHR 1710 (Admin); [2005] Env L.R. 6.

[12] In *CPC (UK) Ltd v National Rivers Authority* [1995] Env. L.R. 131, for example, the defendant was given an absolute discharge (albeit with costs awarded of many thousands of pounds).

or company which operated the site may long ago have ceased to exist, but some or all of those whose waste was sent there may still be in existence. In such circumstances it is important to decide whether or not the consignors of the waste may be regarded as having "caused" the material to be present. The exact circumstances of the deposit may now be lost in the mists of history—for example, it may not be clear whether the consignor's own employees transported and tipped the waste themselves, or whether the material was collected by the operator of the tip or by a carrier (who, likewise, may or may not still be in existence and, if so, may be a candidate to be regarded as an appropriate person).

Ideally, the primary legislation would have made the law clear on what is, essentially an issue of policy.[13] In the event, it is left to the Guidance to deal with this issue. This is an important matter not least for the current owner and occupier of the site, who if the waste consignors are not regarded as falling within Class A, may well find themselves held responsible for the cost of remediation. Applying authority on the meaning of "caused", the starting point would appear to be to identify what it is said the consignor of the waste did that could constitute causing the contaminants to be present in the land. Obviously if the consignor's own employees or agents carried out the tipping there is such an act. But what of the situation where the consignee simply had the waste collected? In the days before the duty of care on waste producers under s.34 of the Environmental Protection Act 1990, a waste consignor may well not have known what the destination of the waste would be; though good practice would suggest even at that time that he should have enquired. **5.24**

The issue was one which arose in debate on the Environment Bill. The Government expressly indicated that it did not intend the words "caused or knowingly permitted" to be construed as including persons "merely on the grounds that they had consigned materials to an authorised waste stream".[14] The Government believed that this was already the effect of the relevant words without the need for any amendment. However, comments were also made at the Commons Standing Committee Stage indicating that the Government was not necessarily as sympathetic to those transporting waste to sites: **5.25**

> "When individual lorry drivers or companies deliver material, they bear some responsibility for the quality of the material."[15]

This would appear to reinforce the distinction, suggested above, between those who actively participated in bringing material on to the land in question, and those whose involvement was less direct. In any event, the position is clarified in practice by the Guidance on exclusion discussed below.[16] These issues may be put to the test in the case of Brofiscin **5.26**

---

[13] The liability of waste producers is a key feature and complicating factor in the US "Superfund" legislation. See for further discussion, D. Lawrence and R. Lee "Talking 'bout my generation: The Remediation Liability of Waste Producers" [2006] Env. L.R. 93.

[14] *Hansard*, HL Vol.562, col.182.

[15] *Hansard*, HC Standing Committee B, May 23, 1995, col.341.

[16] See para.5.189ff.

Landfill, Groes Faen, South Wales. This former limestone quarry was used from 1965 to 1970 for the disposal of drummed waste, including liquid wastes from a number of industrial companies. The site was identified as contaminated in 2005 and is being progressed by the Environment Agency as a special site.

Knowingly permitted

5.27 The other basis for a person falling within the first tier of appropriate persons is having knowingly permitted the contaminating substances to be in, on or under the land. In *Alphacell Ltd v Woodward*,[17] knowingly permitting was said to involve a failure to prevent the relevant situation accompanied by knowledge. The caution to be exercised when considering the application of water pollution case law in the contaminated land context is noted above. In relation to "knowingly permitting" there is a further issue in that the provision under the Water Resources Act relates to knowingly permitting the "entry" of matters, rather than the presence of substances. If *Alphacell* is followed, however, under Pt IIA, the test of "knowingly permitting" would require both knowledge that the substances in question were in, on or under the land and the possession of a power to prevent their presence there.[18]

5.28 Whilst it is difficult to see how someone could be said to have permitted something they were unaware of, in that knowledge is already inherent within the concept of permitting, it is helpful for the purposes of analysis to consider the two issues separately. The following paragraphs attempt such analysis.

5.29 A preliminary and vital question is, however, what precisely "knowingly permitted" relates to. As mentioned above, it could be interpreted as relating to the original entry of the contaminants to the land, i.e. a specific event or series of events; or to the continued presence of the substances in the land, i.e. a state of affairs. The question obviously has fundamental implications for subsequent owners, amongst others.[19]

5.30 Comments during the passage of the Environment Bill suggest that the Government intended the words to have the latter, wider, effect. In particular, references were made to the responsibility of those having control over the sites where pre-existing contaminants remain[20]:

> "We believe that it would be reasonable for somebody who has had active control over contaminants on a site, for example, when redeveloping it, to become responsible for any harm to health or the environment that may result, even if he did not originally cause or knowingly permit the site to become contaminated."

5.31 Another indication of Parliamentary intention arises when at one point an amendment was proposed to replace the words in s.78F(2) "be in, on or under the land" with "come into, onto or under the land".[21] This

---

[17] [1972] A.C. 824.
[18] See also DEFRA Circular 01/2006, *Contaminated Land*, Annex 2 para.9.10 to similar effect.
[19] See generally D. Lawrence and R. Lee, "Permitting Uncertainty: Owners, Occupiers and Responsibility for Remediation" [2003] M.L.R. 261.
[20] *Hansard*, HL Vol.560, col.1461.
[21] *Hansard*, HL Vol.562, col.189.

amendment, which would obviously have excluded subsequent owners, was rejected by the Government on the basis that it would ignore the responsibility of those who ". . . genuinely and actively permit the continued presence of contaminating substances in land".[22]

It therefore seems clear from these statements, and the retention of the **5.32** word "be" in s.78F(2), that the concept of permitting can refer to the continued presence of the contaminants. Whilst the Government's subsequent guidance cannot be conclusive as to the intention behind the statute, it seems apparent from various of the exclusion tests that the Government envisages that subsequent owners may fall within the first tier of appropriate persons.

Knowingly permitted: what knowledge?

The issue of what must be known in order to be said to knowingly permit **5.33** may be a difficult one; it raises the question of whether there must be knowledge simply of the entry or presence of the substances, or also of their contaminating nature or potential. The only interpretation which would make the Act workable would appear to be the former. If the enforcing authority had to demonstrate knowledge of the contaminating effect of substances—perhaps in relation to activities many years ago—this would be a difficult task, indeed impossible in many cases. A decision which supports the former interpretation is *Shanks & McEwan (Teeside) Ltd v Environment Agency*[23] where it was held that in the context of a waste licensing offence, the word "knowingly" related only to the fact of the deposit, and not to the other elements of the offence. This approach has now been endorsed in relation to Pt IIA in the case of *Circular Facilities (London) Ltd v Sevenoaks DC*.[24] Here, Newman J. found that knowledge is only required as to the presence of substances, and not knowledge as to their harmful potential.[25] This finding was made by reference to knowledge as to the potential for reaction with other substances or change through biological processes, provided for in s.78F(9) but applies equally to s.78F(2).

Another issue relates to knowledge which is supplied by the enforcing **5.34** authority itself: a subsequent owner may not know of the actual presence of contaminating substances until he is informed by the authority that they have been discovered. The question is whether, by virtue of that knowledge, he then becomes a knowing permitter if he fails to take appropriate action. The difficulty with treating such a person as a knowing permitter is that it would potentially result in the statutory distinction drawn between knowing permitters in Class A and current owners or occupiers in Class B being almost entirely eroded. For this reason the Government's view in the Guidance is that knowledge resulting from notification under s.78B or consultation under s.78H is not sufficient to trigger the "knowingly permit" test.[26] However, this in turn involves

---

[22] *Hansard*, HL Vol.562, col.189.
[23] [1997] J.P.L. 824; see also *Ashcroft v Cambro Ltd* [1981] 1 W.L.R. 1349.
[24] [2005] EWHC 865; [2005] Env. L.R. 35.
[25] [2005] EWHC 865; [2005] Env. L.R. 35 at 765.
[26] DEFRA Circular 01/2006, *Contaminated Land*, Annex 2 paras 9.12–9.14.

drawing a distinction between knowledge deriving from notification and from other sources; a distinction which does not appear in the Act itself. Also, it might be argued that if Parliament had intended to draw such a distinction then it could have done so expressly, by providing that only knowledge prior to the notification of contaminated land being identified was relevant, or that knowledge arising from notification should be disregarded. In any event, it is quite likely in practice that formal notification under s.78B may be preceded by a period of dialogue between the authority and owner, during which the owner may well acquire the relevant knowledge. The owners of residential properties which are affected by soil contamination in their gardens may be aware for many months, or indeed years that contamination is present prior to the land being identified as contaminated under Pt IIA: leaving aside considerations of hardship wich may arise, it is hard to see how they are not to be said to be knowingly permitting its continued presence during that period.

5.35 Another issue is whether actual knowledge is required, or whether constructive knowledge may suffice. There is authority to suggest that a person may be held to know that which in all the circumstances they could reasonably be expected to have known. Shutting one's eyes to the obvious may therefore not assist.[27] Such cases may be relevant where, for example, the person or company in question was aware of circumstances which might well have resulted in the land being contaminated (for example, a spill, a defective pipe, or a contaminative previous use), yet refrained from making any further enquiries. This type of blindness or "turning a blind eye" to known facts is likely to be regarded as more blameworthy, and more likely to amount to knowledge than simple negligence in making enquiries which perhaps a reasonable man would have made.[28]

5.36 The main consideration to date as to the type of knowledge required under Pt IIA was in *Circular Facilities (London) Ltd v Sevenoaks DC*.[29] Here Newman J. took a restrictive view as to the types of knowledge which could form the basis for liability under s.78F. The suggestion that the availability to the developer of a report on the planning register containing information as to the presence of substances in the land could provide the requisite knowledge was clearly rejected.[30] Whilst the case is more concerned with the lack of clarity in the findings by the magistrates' court, it does suggest that there is a requirement for an appropriate person to have actual knowledge of the presence of substances, rather than knowledge which is purely constructive or implied, though this could be imputed in some circumstances. The particular factual circumstances were that the "controlling mind" of the company served with a remediation notice had not had personal knowledge of the presence of organic matter and other contaminants, though there was reference to this in a report at the time of

[27] See *Westminster CC v Croyalgrange* [1986] 2 All E.R. 353; *Schulmans Incorporated v National Rivers Authority* [1993] Env. L.R. DI; *Roper v Taylor's Central Garages (Exeter) Ltd* [1951] 2 T.L.R. 294; *Vehicle Inspectorate v Nuttall* [1999] 1 W.L.R. 629; *Kent CC v Beaney* [1993] Env L.R. 225

[28] See *The Eurysthenes* [1976] 2 Lloyd's Rep. 171; *Roper v Taylor's Central Garages (Exeter) Ltd* [1952] 2 T.L.R. 294.

[29] [2005] EWHC 65; [2005] Env. L.R. 35.

[30] *Kent CC v Beaney* [1993] Env. L.R. 225 at 764.

the development and an individual who was in an "informal partnership" with the company and probably acted as its agent may have had actual knowledge of substances at the time. Newman J. referred to the possibility of imputing the individual's knowledge to the company on the basis of an agency relationship, but the evidential difficulties, including the individual now being deceased, provide an example of the practical problems with establishing knowledge in such cases. This restrictive approach to interpretation of the "knowledge" requirement has been criticised by some, given the policy underlying the statute and the evidential difficulties.[31]

5.37 The other leading Pt IIA case to date, *R. (National Grid Gas Plc, formerly Transco Plc) v Environment Agency*[32] does not consider the issue directly. It does, however, identify how the Environment Agency had included property developers within an initial group of potential Class A appropriate persons and Lord Scott considered that it seemed likely that these "persons would have been aware of the presence of the coal tar under the ground of the site" and that it would have been arguable that they had "knowingly permitted" the coal tar to remain there.[33]

Knowingly permitting: knowledge by companies

5.38 Where it is a company which is said to have knowingly permitted the presence of contaminants, the question arises as to what knowledge is to be attributed by the company. This will be determined on ordinary principles of corporate law, which were discussed by the Privy Council in *Meridian Global Funds Management Asia Ltd v Securities Commission*.[34] In that case, Lord Hoffman indicated that it will first be necessary to look at the rules of attribution of knowledge (if any) contained in the company's constitution and in general company law. These would seem unlikely to provide much help in the specific case here. A second line of approach is to look at the general rules of attribution contained in the principles of agency, i.e. the extent to which the knowledge of a servant or agent is to be attributed to the company as employer or principal. The question is then essentially one of construction as to whether s.78F(2) intends that such knowledge shall be attributed. This is a question of the language, content and policy of the statute, and given the very serious consequences inherent in being held to have knowingly permitted under s.78F(2) it seems somewhat unlikely that the draftsman intended knowledge by every employee or agent to be attributed. It seems clear from the Circular Facilities case that some knowledge may be imputed from agents, though the basis of such an approach will need to established very clearly.[35]

5.39 Lord Hoffman in the *Meridian* case went on to suggest that if applying these primary and secondary rules of attribution did not produce a satisfactory result, then the court "must fashion a special rule of attribution for the particular substantive rule". This will be a matter of statutory

---

[31] See V. Fogleman, [2005] J.P.L. 1269.
[32] [2007] UKHL 30.
[33] [2007] UKHL 30, para.19.
[34] [1995] 3 W.L.R. 413.
[35] See para.5.36 above and also the discussion of *Shanks & McEwan (Teeside) Ltd v Environment Agency* (para.5.41 below).

157

interpretation, bearing in mind the purpose, content and policy of the relevant provision. The answer will not necessarily be confined to knowledge by persons who could be described as representing the "directing mind and will" of the company.[36] In the context of the securities legislation under consideration in the Meridian case, it was held that the relevant knowledge was that of the person who had the authority of the company to acquire the relevant interest. In a different context, in *R. v Rozeik*,[37] the relevant knowledge was held to be that of an employee who had authority to draw a cheque and sign it, but not those whose job was simply to type it out.

5.40 It may therefore be that in the context of contaminated land, knowledge by someone who was not a director, yet who had authority to take decisions involving the presence of contaminants, might well be attributed to a company. Such persons might include the environmental manager or safety officer, for example.

5.41 The question of the level at which there must be knowledge within a company arose in the environmental context in *Shanks & McEwan (Teeside) Ltd v Environment Agency*.[38] The issue was whether the company could be said to have knowingly permitted the deposit of waste at one of its sites in breach of a licence condition. It was held that if knowledge by senior management was required for the offence, then it was sufficient that the management knew that the site was generally used for receiving waste of the relevant type. This approach may be appropriate for some, but not all, types of contaminated land situations. The Court also suggested, without deciding, that a wide rule of attribution might be appropriate for that purpose under s.33 of the Environmental Protection Act 1990:

> "where the company would be treated through its employees at the site as knowingly causing or knowingly permitting the deposit of any controlled waste in respect of which instructions or authorisation for off-loading onto the site were given by such employees".[39]

5.42 However, whereas in the context of s.33 the strictness of such an approach is tempered by the availability of a defence of all reasonable precautions and all due diligence, such a defence would not be available in the context of s.78F.

5.43 The position here is somewhat different to that of the "wilful blindness" described earlier: it is rather the situation where a company had within its organisation the knowledge of facts relevant to the condition of the land as contaminated, yet that information never reached the senior management of the company. Bearing in mind that the condition of the land must be significant in terms of harm before Pt IIA can apply at all, a court may not be sympathetic to a company which claims not to have had the relevant knowledge because of the absence or inadequacy of its own internal

---

[36] See *Bank of India v Morris* [2005] EWCA Civ 693 considering the possibly relevant factors.
[37] [1996] 2 All E.R. 281.
[38] [1997] J.P.L. 824.
[39] [1997] J.P.L. 824, 833.

management systems, or a company which had in place "paper systems" but did not implement them adequately.

Knowingly permitting: what constitutes permitting?

"Permitted" is a difficult word to pin down to a single precise meaning.[40] It **5.44** could mean giving permission, leave or licence for something to be done. In this sense it relates most aptly to permitting the original entry of contaminants into or onto the land and in this context might include, for example, the owner of land who grants a licence for waste to be tipped on it. It could also in this sense be taken to cover someone who has the power to prevent the entry of the contaminants, yet knowing of their entry fails to exercise that power. It is this interpretation which is potentially of concern to parties such as landlords and lenders. The safeguard for such persons lies in the test provided in the statutory guidance, which has the effect of excluding a range of persons such as landlords, lenders, insurers and statutory permitting authorities, who fall within Group A only by reason of the capacity in which they stand in relation to the polluter. This test is discussed in more detail below, but it should be noted that the inclusion of a particular description of persons within the test does not imply that they will necessarily fall within Group A. This must be correct, since clearly the subsequent guidance cannot alter the effect of, or place a gloss on, the words used by Parliament.

The second aspect of "permitting" relates to the permitting of a state of **5.45** affairs, i.e. the continued presence of the contaminants in the land. Whether "permit" is used in the broader sense will depend on the context and the objective of the legislation.[41] As discussed above, it appears to be the case that Parliament intended this aspect to be covered by s.78F(2). If this is correct, the question will then turn on what the relevant person could have done, at the relevant time, in relation to the presence of the relevant substances. It cannot be said that a person permitted something that they did not have knowledge of,[42] or could not control or prevent.[43] Moreover a person does not permit something by failing to take steps which it would be unreasonable to expect them to take.[44] This would therefore seem to involve consideration of what opportunity the person had to remove the contaminants and whether it was reasonable to expect them to take advantage of that opportunity. Clearly, a freehold owner who is developing land and knows of the presence of contaminants will have the opportunity to remove them: whether it was reasonable to expect him to do so may depend on many factors, including the use for which the land is being developed. On the other hand, a tenant of property may not have the opportunity to carry out works to remove contaminants; it would not generally be reasonable to expect a tenant of, say, an office building to excavate the subsoil of the building to remove contaminants which are present. Indeed, he may be barred from so doing under the terms of the lease.

[40] *Vehicle Inspectorate v Nuttall* [1999] 1 W.L.R. 629.
[41] *Vehicle Inspectorate v Nuttall* [1999] 1 W.L.R. 629.
[42] *Vehicle Inspectorate v Blakers Chilled Distribution Ltd* [2002] EWHC Admin 208.
[43] *Earl of Sefton v Tophams Ltd (No.2)* [1967] A.C. 50.
[44] *Bromsgrove DC v Carthy* (1975) 30 P. & C.R. 34.

Substances: in, on or under the land

5.46 A substance may be present on land before it makes its way into or under the land. An example would be chemicals which are stored in a surface installation at an industrial plant, but then are accidentally released and contaminate the subsurface: the chemicals were originally "on" the land, but are now "in" or "under" the land. The person (A) who caused or knowingly permitted the chemicals to be placed originally on the land may be a different person to the person (B) who caused or knowingly permitted them to escape and thus to be in or under the land. Since the chemical which was in the tank on the surface is the same substance by reason of which the land is now contaminated, a strict and literal reading of s.78F(2) would indicate that A, as well as B, is an "appropriate person". Such a result could obviously be unjust to A, and might well be avoided by construing the subsection so that the presence of the substance in, on or under the land is read as referable only to the point at which the land is in such a condition that harm or pollution of controlled waters (or the possibility or likelihood thereof) occur. On that basis, the presence of the substances on land in a proper storage installation would not be relevant so as to fix A with liability. Such a reading is not easy to reconcile with the wording of the subsection however, and in any event would not benefit A if he had placed the chemicals in a defective storage installation which presented the significant possibility of a harmful escape. In that case, A would have caused the substances to be on land and the land thereby to come within the definition of contaminated land in s.78A. The issue may therefore be essentially one of apportionment as between A and B.

5.47 The point was not addressed directly in debate, though at one point an amendment was proposed to replace the words "be in, on or under land" with "come into, onto or under land" as defining more accurately the polluter: such an amendment would also have limited the scope for subsequent owners to be liable, and as pointed out above was rejected by the Government.[45]

5.48 One practical implication of the storage installation, example given above, is that a seller of land on which potentially contaminative substances are stored should consider emptying such installations on sale or seeking indemnities from any purchaser whose activities or failure to maintain such installations might result in the escape of substances originally brought on to the land by the seller.

The second rank of appropriate persons: "Class B"

5.49 Subsection 78F(4) provides that if no person has, after reasonable enquiry, been found who is under subs.78F(2) an appropriate person to bear responsibility for the things which are to be done by way of remediation, then the owner or occupier for the time being of the contaminated land in question is an appropriate person. The subsection is not readily intelligible, and raises a number of questions which are considered in the following

---

[45] See also paras 5.13–5.14, above.

paragraphs. In particular, does it mean that the person concerned has not been "found" physically, or does it mean "identified"?[46]

The question has a bearing on individuals who are known, but who have **5.50** died, and on companies or other corporate entities which have ceased to exist. The previous Government's view, expressed in debates, was that the circumstances where a polluter cannot be found would include cases where the company concerned had gone into liquidation.[47] On that basis, the "reasonable enquiry" will be not only into whether the person who caused or knowingly permitted the contaminating event or events can be identified, but also whether they still exist as a person or legal entity.

What does "reasonable enquiry" mean in this context? It is an important **5.51** question because the enforcing authority cannot refer to the second group of appropriate persons until they have satisfied themselves as to the absence of anyone in the first rank. How long, for example, does this "reasonable enquiry" have to go on?[48] The authority which seeks to fix liability on a Class B party may well find itself faced with the argument either that it should have looked harder for a Class A party, or possibly that it should have pursued the estate of a deceased Class A party.

The problem does not end there. Section 78F(4) contemplates not just a **5.52** reasonable inquiry into whether there is a person who is an "appropriate person"; it refers to an "appropriate person to bear responsibility for the things which are to be done by way of remediation". Those additional words might be thought to cause a further difficulty in suggesting that even where a person within s.78F(2) is found, they may not be appropriate to bear responsibility, for example, because they lack the funds. However, similar words appear in the definition of "appropriate person" itself in s.78A(9). Thus analysed, the words add nothing and accordingly the subsection does not mean that the appropriate person in the front rank (the actual contaminator) would have to be solvent and financially capable of complying with the notice in order to be an appropriate person. To hold otherwise would be to encourage those with contaminated land to divest themselves of adequate funding.

One other issue is what happens if a person or company within Class A **5.53** has been found, but dies or ceases to exist before a remediation notice is served, for example during the statutory period of consultation. It is submitted that in such circumstances the party has been "found" and accordingly s.78F(4) cannot then operate to make the current owner or occupier liable. The consequence is that remediation will then be at the cost of the authority. The situation where the person dies or ceases to exist after the remediation notice has been served is considered below.[49]

When is no Class A person found?

As stated above, the meaning and construction of the word "found" in **5.54** s.78F(4) is crucial to the operation of Pt IIA and will in particular in many cases determine whether or not the current owner or occupier can be held

---

[46] See 5.54 for further discussion.
[47] *Hansard*, HL Vol.562, col.209.
[48] See 5.58 for further discussion.
[49] See para.5.125.

responsible for remediation. As indicated above,[50] the view of the Conservative Government which promoted Pt IIA was that a company which no
longer exists could not be said to be "found". This approach is followed by
the Guidance, which suggests that a person who is no longer in existence
cannot meet the description of "found".[51] Earlier versions of the Guidance
referred to the *Oxford English Dictionary* definition of the word "found" as
meaning "discovered, met with, ascertained, etc.". Unfortunately, this
definition actually serves only to highlight the possible ambiguity of the
word. Clearly, a person or company which is no longer in existence cannot
be "met with", but their identity can be ascertained. Reference in the *OED*
to the verb "find" demonstrates the richness of meanings attributable to
the word, some of which imply a physical encounter or determination of
the whereabouts of a person or object; but others of which could certainly
be applied to the process of discovering the identity of a person who no
longer exists.[52]

5.55   There are authorities which have construed "found" as denoting physical
presence, but it may be difficult to extrapolate from these as they relate to
matters such as the offence of being "found" drunk in a public place,[53] or
being "found within the jurisdiction" for enforcement purposes.[54] Nor does
such case law as exists on similar wording under earlier public health
legislation help greatly.[55] In construing the provisions under trust legislation as to powers when a trustee cannot be "found", there are two cases
which suggest that a company which has been dissolved cannot be
"found".[56] However, there is also a case to the opposite effect, that where a
trustee company is known to have been dissolved, it is not correct to say it
"cannot be found": ". . . I am not ignorant where it is, I know that it is not
anywhere; it does not exist".[57]

5.56   The best way of approaching the matter may be to look at the structure
and purpose of Pt IIA as a whole. The point of s.78F is to set out a scheme
with the object of getting contaminated land cleaned up in the public
interest.[58] If someone is an "appropriate person", then the expectation is
that they will be served with a remediation notice and legal sanctions and
consequences will follow if they do not comply. If there is no-one against
whom such action can be taken then the statutory scheme is that the
owner and occupier are responsible. To hold that a person or company
which no longer exists can be "found" would mean that the legislation
would be ineffective in those circumstances, and would thereby leave a
potentially large gap in the scheme of channelled liability envisaged by
s.78F. Coupled with the *Hansard* statement of intention referred to above,
this gives robust support to the view that "found" implies physical
existence of the person in question.

---

[50] See para.5.50.
[51] DEFRA Circular 01/2006, *Contaminated Land*, Annex 2 para.9.17.
[52] For example, "to discover, come to the knowledge of"; "to discover or attain by search or
efforts".
[53] *Palmer-Brown v Police* [1985] 1 N.Z.L.R. 365, 369.
[54] *R. v Lopez, R. v Sattler*, 27 L.J.M.C. 48.
[55] *The Conservators of the River Thames v The Port Sanitary Authority of London* [1894] 1 Q.B. 647.
[56] *Re General Accident Assurance Co Ltd* [1904] 1 Ch. 147; *Re Richard Mills & Co (Brierley Hill) Ltd*
[1905] W.N. 36.
[57] *Re Taylors Investment Trusts* [1904] 2 Ch. 737 at 739, Buckley J.
[58] Compare *Rhymney Iron Co v Gelligaer DC* [1917] 1 K.B. 589 at 594, Ridley J.

Whilst the issue may still be capable of argument the other way, the **5.57** Administrative Court has accepted in the *Transco* case that dissolved companies whose assets have been sold or distributed to other persons cannot be "found" for the purposes of s.78F.[59] Although the House of Lords overruled Forbes J. comprehensively on the substantive issues in the case, there is nothing in their Lordships' judgments which suggest a contrary view on this specific point.[60]

"After reasonable enquiry"

The question is not simply whether a Class A person can be found, but **5.58** whether such person can be found "after reasonable enquiry". In *Rhymney Iron Co. v Gelligaer DC*,[61] the question arose of what steps a local authority had to take under the Public Health Act 1875 s.94, to establish the cause of a blocked sewer before serving notice on the owner of the house in question. It was stressed by the Court that the aim and purpose of the 1875 Act in protecting the public had to be kept in mind, and any duty on the local authority to carry out what might be a lengthy or difficult inspection process was rejected. As Ridley J. put it, the object of s.94 was[62]:

> ". . . not to put upon the local authority the duty of finding out who in the ultimate result is the person responsible for the nuisance; the object is, as it appears to me, that they should by all means possible procure that such a nuisance should be abated."

However, given the express pre-condition of reasonable enquiry in Pt IIA **5.59** and the magnitude of the potential liabilities that may fall on the owner or occupier if persons in Class A cannot be found, the courts seem likely to take a more rigorous approach to what constitutes reasonable inquiry under s.78F(4). At the same time, the enforcing authority is fulfilling a public function in which it needs to balance the cost and delay of possibly fruitless inquiries against the public interest in getting the land cleaned up.

What is critical is that the authority should be able to demonstrate that **5.60** it has approached its task of inquiry logically and consistently. The relevant steps are likely to include the following:

1. Careful review of data collected on the initial investigation of the land to establish how far this helps to identify a relevant person or persons.

2. Further enquiries as necessary as to ownership and occupation of the land during the relevant period, including appropriate Land Registry searches and enquiries.

---

[59] *R. (on the application of National Grid Gas Plc, formerly Transco Plc) v Environment Agency* [2006] EWHC (Admin) 1083 [2006] Env. L.R. 49, para.65.
[60] [2007] UKHL 30.
[61] [1917] 1 K.B. 589.
[62] [1917] 1 K.B. 589, 595.

3. Enquiries as to the nature of activities and substances used on the site during that period. These may possibly be by way of reviewing local sources of information, by direct enquiries of those involved, or former employees, or neighbours. It is possible that the authority may wish to use consultants or enquiry agents to undertake some or all of this work.

4. Searches at the Companies Register, or other sources of information on companies, to establish the current status of any companies involved, and the identities of their directors and senior officers.

5. Service of a requisition for information on all relevant parties, using where necessary its statutory powers to obtain information under s.16 of the Local Government (Miscellaneous Provisions) Act 1976.

5.61   This aspect of local authority and Agency duties under Pt IIA is likely to be one of the more difficult in practice. Whilst there is considerable technical experience of tracing those responsible for recent pollution incidents—often successfully—the attribution of responsibility for contamination of soil or groundwater which may have occurred many decades ago, and over the course of many years, is a different matter entirely. The nature of the inquiry will differ depending on the circumstances, and will, for example, be very different if the contamination is the result of a single, recent and identifiable incident.

5.62   The problem is that if an owner or occupier receives a remediation notice in circumstances where a Class A person cannot be found, they will be able to argue that if reasonable enquiry has not been made by the local authority, and thus the precondition for the notice being served on them has not been fulfilled, the notice would in fact be ultra vires.[63] This problem may arise in many cases. The owner or occupier may argue either that the original polluter is or should be traceable; or where they are themselves in Class A as a knowing permitter, that the original polluter is traceable and should be in Class A as well.

Companies in liquidation

5.63   It follows from the discussion above that if a company is in liquidation, which may either be voluntary or compulsory, then such a company could be an appropriate person. A company in liquidation still exists for the time being, and there is nothing in subss.78E(4) or 78H(5) which suggests that insolvency, receivership or liquidation necessarily bars the service of a remediation notice.[64] However, if a company has been struck off the Companies Register it ceases to exist as a legal entity, and a dissolved company cannot be "found" for the purposes of s.78F.[65] In any liquidation

---

[63] This of course brings us back to the question of whether the owner/occupier can be said to be a "knowing permitter" and so within Class A themselves.

[64] The issue is discussed more fully in para.5.121ff.

[65] *R. (on the application of National Grid Gas Plc, formerly Transco Plc) v Environment Agency* [2006] EWHC Admin 1083; [2006] Env. L.R. 49, para.65 (see below).

situation, recovery of the costs of clean-up would be tenuous. The enforcing authority carrying out the works themselves under s.78N would not be a preferred creditor. Any charging notice served under s.78P is registrable as a charge but may not necessarily take priority.[66] The enforcing authority has the same powers and remedies under the Law of Property Act 1925 as if it were a mortgagee by deed having power of sale and lease.[67]

Privatised utilities and reorganised local authorities

Class A appropriate persons may well include utility companies such as **5.64** gas, electricity and water undertakers, which may have gone through a series of transitions, possibly from private to nationalised companies, then privatisation. In the course of this process the entity which caused or knowingly permitted the relevant contamination may have ceased to exist, to be replaced by a successor. The same may well be true of local authorities which have been subject to reorganisation, and of NHS trusts. The question is whether the successor can be regarded as the Class A appropriate person. On a strict application of the rules of corporate personality, the two are separate entities and there is no reason why, for example, Network Rail Ltd should be treated as the appropriate person in respect of contamination caused by Railtrack Plc, British Railways or, for that matter, Great Western Railways before it. One additional factor is, however, that in many of these situations, there will have been a statutory transfer scheme passing assets, rights and liabilities. The question is whether such a scheme could have the effect of bringing the successor company or authority within Class A; the difficulty with this argument being that at the time of the transfer the liability in question would not have existed (indeed, the legislation creating that liability would not have existed). Ordinarily it would be difficult to see how a transfer scheme could properly be said to have the effect claimed in such circumstances. The counter arguments to this approach are that adherence to strict rules on corporate identity in cases of statutory succession could frustrate the purposes of the legislation and undermine Parliamentary intention. The House of Lords in the *Transco* case was unconvinced by these counter arguments, finding that in cases of statutory succession Pt IIA clearly did not have the effect of overriding the specific provisions of a transfer scheme.

The Transco case

The first serious examination of the Pt IIA regime was in the *Transco* (or **5.65** *"Bawtry"*) case.[68] The case concerned housing development in the 1960s on a former gasworks site where coal tar residues buried in tanks were later discovered and required remedial works. The claimant, National Grid Gas

---

[66] This issue is discussed at para.6.44ff.
[67] 1990 Act s.78P(11).
[68] *R. (on the application of National Grid Gas Plc, formerly Transco Plc) v Environment Agency* [2007] UKHL 30.

Plc, was a company which had been established as part of the corporate reorganisation of British Gas Plc a few years after the privatisation of the gas industry. British Gas had been the statutory successor to the British Gas Corp under a transfer scheme in 1986. The British Gas Corp had itself been the subject of a statutory transfer from organisations including the East Midlands Gas Board ("EMGB"), which was one of the original polluters of the site. In identifying the Class A liability group for those works, the Environment Agency included the claimant on the basis that one or more of its statutory predecessors had caused or knowingly permitted the presence of the relevant substances through operating the gasworks. Other potentially appropriate persons in the form of dissolved companies had been considered not to be "found" for the purposes of the regime. The claimant sought judicial review of the Agency's determination that it was an "appropriate person". The claimant based this on three grounds:

1. that it had not itself caused or knowingly permitted the presence of the substances, and so did not fall within s.78F(2);

2. that at the time of the various transfers of liability through the "chain" of statutory succession, no relevant liabilities had existed in law, or arisen in fact (there being no evidence of a statutory nuisance, for example); and

3. even if there had been liability under any of the then applicable liability regimes, the transfers could only have been effective as to those liabilities and not that under Pt IIA which had not been in force at the time of any of the transfers.

5.66   The Administrative Court rejected these arguments, and considered that the provisions of Pt IIA should be given a purposive construction. Forbes J. found that Parliament's intention had been clearly to place primary responsibility for the remediation of contaminated land on the original polluters in the form of causers and knowing permitters, rather than "innocent" owners or the public purse, referring to the parliamentary record on the basis that legislative intent in s.78F(2) was ambiguous or obscure. The only way of giving effect to the intent expressed in the record was to construe the term "person" so as to include statutory successors as well as the original polluter, so that liability passed to successors in title.[69]

5.67   The House of Lords took the opposite view,[70] finding the statutory language plain and unambiguous, so that *Pepper v Hart* provided no authority for recourse to the parliamentary record, and that there was little if anything to support the imposition of liability in *Hansard* in any event. The critical issue was considered to be the phrase "immediately before" used in transferring liabilities under the relevant statutory transfer schemes. These provided that the successor would take over the liabilities of the predecessor "immediately before" the transfer date. The unanimous view of their Lordships was that as liability under Pt IIA had not been

---

[69] [2006] Env. L.R. 49 at para.65.
[70] [2007] UKHL 30.

created until many years after the transfer dates, that liability had not existed (even as a contingent) "immediately before" the transfers, and so could not have passed as part of the succession. Although Pt IIA was retrospective in the sense of creating potential present liability for past acts, it did not create a deemed past liability for those acts. The claimant had not caused or knowingly permitted the presence of the substances and the language used in s.78F could not be construed so as to incorporate them within this definition.

Implications of the Transco Case

The first point which might be made regarding the House of Lords decision **5.68** is that it focuses upon the specific provisions of the statutory transfer scheme in question, albeit that such schemes are widespread, having been commonly used since post-war nationalisation of industry and the privatisations of the 1980s and subsequently. The precise wording used in such provisions varies and has tended to become more detailed and elaborate over time. Thus, as was identified in the case, different wording might have a different outcome,[71] as should cases where transfers were post-enactment of Pt IIA, or its coming into force. It seems that the particular circumstances of the case, whereby the Government sold shares to the public in a newly created privatised company, and then introduced legislation providing for potentially retrospective liability affecting that company (amongst others), were influential. Their Lordships were clearly hostile to a perceived undermining of the value of investments purchased by the public from the Government, and this is reflected in some unusually forceful passages in their speeches. For property developers, the implications are that they may have to bear the burden of Class A liability in cases of statutory succession of polluters. The implications of this approach for owners and occupiers as potential Class B appropriate persons are also significant. It was only the Environment Agency's application of the hardship provisions within Pt IIA which precluded the costs of remediation from falling on the householders. In different circumstances, it may well be that the burden has to be borne by such "innocent" parties.

Moving from the specific context of privatisation transfers, the logic of **5.69** the approach suggests that local authorities may similarly be found not to be responsible for the acts of their statutory predecessors, depending upon the precise terms of any transfer provisions. The distinction in such cases would, of course, be that the costs would potentially be borne by the innocent landowners, rather than the public purse. Whether this factor could justify a departure from "clear and unambiguous" provisions seems highly doubtful.

Whilst the *Transco* case does not concern liability for corporate succes- **5.70** sion, the approach taken to the issue of statutory succession and discussion of some points within the speeches do raise some issues. The essential

---

[71] The example given was that of schemes under the Water Act 1989, where provision was made (in Sch.2 para.2(3)) for transfers to include future liabilities not existing at the date of transfer.

question is whether a person who has caused or knowingly permitted the presence of contaminants can be "found". In the corporate context, this should mean that the usual distinction between share sales and asset or business sales would be the primary factor. Where a company's shares are purchased, therefore, that purchase includes contingent and future liabilities attached to the company. Where a company's assets or business are purchased, but not the shares themselves, liabilities not attached to the specific assets purchased remain with the company. Where assets, such as land, have liabilities attached to them, these will pass with the asset.[72] In the case of Pt IIA, this will be on the basis of knowingly permitting, with liability also remaining with the original causers and other knowing permitters. Whilst on one view the comments made in *Transco* as to the retrospective falsification of the basis upon which shares were acquired could be applied to the general corporate context, it would seem that the general principles of corporate personality should apply so that the original polluting company still exists and can be found, albeit that the ownership of its shares (and usually the assets owned or controlled by the company) have changed, and so may be within Class A. Lord Neuberger's judgment includes an obiter discussion regarding the sale and purchase of "assets" and the "business" or part of the "business" of a polluting company, but without clear distinction between asset, business and share transactions.[73] The key consideration for the House of Lords appears to have been a lack of connection between the successor company and the contaminated land, so that the claimant company could be considered to have neither knowingly permitted nor caused the presence of substances.

Groups of companies

5.71 Another practical issue which may frequently arise is identifying which one of a group of companies actually operated a site or process so as to be the appropriate person within Class A. It may well be common knowledge that a particular contaminated site was for many years operated by "X Co" which may have comprised a group of several companies, all of which are still in existence. In the absence of cooperation from X Co the authority may not be able to identify with certainty on which company in the group a notice should be served.

A practical first step is possibly for the local authority to serve a requisition for information on the companies. If this does not elicit any helpful response, then one possible pragmatic solution may be to serve the holding company and each of the subsidiaries with a remediation notice, stating that some of the notices may be withdrawn when liability is clarified. The authority will however have to attempt to apportion liability between the companies, which may be far from straightforward.

Foreign companies

5.72 Another potential problem may occur where the company, which is the Class A appropriate person, is now outside the jurisdiction: it may for example be a foreign company registered outside the UK, which had

---

[72] See the discussion of corporate transactions at Ch.20.
[73] [2007] UKHL 30, paras 29–34.

operated for a time in the UK. The company may have been registered in the Channel Isles or elsewhere, and may have operated in the UK direct, or through a subsidiary. If such a company can be found, there would seem to be no mandate in s.78F(4) for turning to the persons in Group B, simply because it would be complex, costly and difficult to seek to enforce against it.

Directors of companies

One other important issue is whether officers of a company can be **5.73** responsible as Class A appropriate persons in their own right. There seems no reason why not in principle, if the director can be said to have caused the contamination, or knowingly permitted it through decisions which they took or the way in which they ran the company. At a practical level, the smaller the company, the easier it will probably be to find such circumstances.

The issue has practical significance, not only the obvious concern for the **5.74** individuals involved, but also for the current owners and occupiers. If the company which caused contamination has ceased to exist, its directors may still be alive and as such potential Class A persons. This in turn may mean that the current owner or occupier will not be liable.

At one level, there seems no reason why a director should not be held **5.75** responsible in this way. A director who undertakes wrongful trading prior to a liquidation may be liable personally under statutory provisions, so why not a director who knowingly operates a contaminating process, then winds up the company? It should be noted, however, that the practical consequence may be that although liability will fall on the director, he or she may be able to argue hardship. In that case, the authority will not be able to turn to the owner and occupier as Class B persons, so the clean-up may have to be in whole or in part at the public expense.

"Owner"

As discussed above, the second group of appropriate persons only comes **5.76** into contention when no appropriate person from the first rank has been found. The second group comprises the owner or occupier for the time being of the contaminated land. There is a definition of "owner" in s.78A(9), namely:

> "a person (other than a mortgagee not in possession) who, whether in his own right or as a trustee for any other person, is entitled to receive the rack rent of the land, or, where the land is not let at a rack rent, would be so entitled if it were so let."

Taking the long leaseholder at a ground rent as an example, he may well **5.77** have sub-let and will not therefore be an occupier. He will not be the freeholder either, but he will fall within the definition of "owner", as one entitled to the "rack rent". The freeholder will not, if the leaseholder is paying only a ground rent, be the "owner".

5.78 A person who holds an option or other contractual interest in the land (for example, a contract to purchase) would not appear to fall within the definition of "owner". Other cases, such as trustees and managing agents, are discussed below.[74]

Proving ownership

5.79 Ownership can be a difficult issue to prove conclusively in some cases. It seems likely that the courts will not require an enforcing authority to prove the exact nature of the legal interest held by the appropriate person, and that evidence such as letters or applications for certificates of lawful use and the like may be sufficient. This was the position in *Walton v Sedgefield BC*[75] where it was said that what is sufficient to establish ownership depends on the circumstances of the particular case. It was also accepted in that decision that if ownership is proven at a particular date, there will be a presumption of its continuance.

Going behind sham ownership

5.80 Since ownership of land may carry with it serious liabilities under Pt IIA, there may be incentives for owners wishing to evade such liabilities to transfer land to a company which is a separate legal entity. This is a sensitive area, since there may well be legitimate reasons why land should be held by a single purpose company. The difficulties inherent in this area for enforcing authorities are illustrated by a case in the planning contect, *Buckinghamshire CC v Briar*.[76] In that case Buckinghamshire CC sought to make Mr and Mrs Briar liable for the clean up costs of land at Iver, under s.178(1) of the Town and Country Planning Act 1990. This provides that where any steps are required by an enforcement notice and are not taken within the stated period for compliance, the planning authority may enter the land, take the steps, and recover its reasonable expenses from the person who is then owner of the land.

5.81 The facts were that in 1988 Mr Briar bought for about £80,000 a small patch of open land abutting an industrial estate, within the green belt. It was registered with Mr and Mrs Briar as owners. Mr Briar engaged a company to raise the surface of the land by unauthorised tipping of waste, the land being raised by tipping by some 3–4 metres. In 1990 enforcement proceedings were taken for the removal of the waste. Despite those proceedings and an injunction obtained by the council, tipping continued.

5.82 At this time, various transfers of ownership of the land were taking place. In June 1997 Mr and Mrs Briar transferred the land for £86,000 to LJB Electronics Ltd (Mr Briar's business company). In July 1997 LJB Electronics transferred it to a company called Deli Bar Ltd for £1. Deli Bar was formed in March 1997, with a Mr Charnjit Singh and Surjit Singh

---

[74] See paras 5.105 and 5.106.
[75] [1999] J.P.L. 541.
[76] [2002] EWHC 2821 (Ch).

(neither of whom could be traced subsequently) as the officers. The council alleged that these were in fact pseudonyms of Mr and Mrs Briar.

5.83 The cost of clean up was estimated at £1,270,000 to remove some 47,000 cubic metres of waste. The land had a value of about £50,000. The council sought a declaration that Mr and Mrs Briar were in fact the owners within the meaning of s.36(1) of the 1990 Act; an order that the land be vested in them; and an injunction restraining them from transferring it until the enforcement notice had been complied with. Essentially this was based on arguments that the transfer to Deli Bar was a fiction and that the company held the land on constructive trust for Mr and Mrs Briar, or that the Land Register should be rectified to make the Briars the proprietors, or that the transfer should be set aside as a transaction at an undervalue under ss.423–425 of the Insolvency Act 1986.

5.84 Lawrence Collins J. held that the register should be rectified under s.82(1)(d) of the Land Registration Act 1952, which allows rectification where the court is satisfied that any entry in the register has been obtained by fraud. The officials at the Register were found to have been deceived by false documents; furthermore the falsely back-dated transfer to LJB Electronics was found to be a fraudulent sham as there never was any intention to sell the land to the company, but merely to distance Mr and Mrs Briar from Deli Bar and to further the overall fraudulent design.

5.85 However, the council was not successful on its other two arguments. Section 336(1) of the Planning Act defines "owner" as the person entitled to receive the rack rent of the land, or who would be if the land were let. In *East Lindsey DC v Thompson*[77] Brooke L.J. had stressed the importance of equating the register proprietor with the owner for the purposes of the section, though Lawrence Collins J. thought the case did not altogether preclude the beneficial owner being held to be the owner. Having considered cases on constructive trusts and piercing the corporate veil[78] the judge was satisfied that there was a sham and that the criteria for piercing the corporate veil were met. The company was a façade or sham and in truth no more than the nominee of the Briars.

5.86 However, the problem was that there was a statutory definition of owner. The judge's provisional view was that despite the merits of the council's case, under that statutory definition the Briars could not be liable. If correct, this is obviously a potentially serious problem in areas such as contaminated land, where essentially the same definition applies.

5.87 Finally, the council were also unsuccessful in their arguments that the transfer should be set aside under s.423 of the Insolvency Act 1986. The problem here was that the provision is worded to apply to transactions entered into at an undervalue. Here, although the land was transferred for only £1, given the liabilities attached, this was in fact a sale at an *overvalue*, as the land had a negative value of over £1.2 million. It therefore according to the judge simply did not fit in with the scheme of the provision.

5.88 Therefore, whilst the council was successful on a point which was heavily dependent on the fraudulent nature of the dealings with the Land Registry, the points on which it was unsuccessful are in fact much more worrying for

---

[77] [2001] EWHC Admin 81 at 25–6.
[78] *Paragon Finance v DB Thakerar & Co* [1999] All E.R. 400; and *Trustor AV v Smallbone (No.2)* [2001] 1 W.L.R. 1177.

regulators seeking to combat schemes for avoiding environmental liabilities, in that it may be difficult to go behind the statutory definition of "owner" where land with negative value has been transferred.

"Occupier"

5.89 The term "occupier" is not defined in Pt IIA and the question of whether a person is in occupation will have to be determined on the facts of each case. The test is that of the degree of control exercised over the land rather than exclusively of rights of occupation: a licence entitling a person to possession may make someone an "occupier".[79] Similarly, it appears that a statutory tenant is an "occupier"[80] but there is authority to suggest that a person who entered premises forcibly and unlawfully is not.[81] In the context of the Wildlife and Countryside Act 1981, it has been held that a contractor coming onto land on a transient basis to carry out work is not an "occupier".[82]

5.90 In Scotland, it has been established that receivers may become occupiers.[83] Thus, those receivers acting in a management capacity may conceivably find themselves regarded as occupiers for the purposes of contaminated land provisions, although the specific statutory protection afforded to them should be noted.[84]

Liability of owner and occupier: generally

5.91 Government policy is that the owner and occupier of land, even if "innocent" in relation to the presence of the contaminating substances, should in some cases bear responsibility for the condition of their land. Lord Northbourne, in debate, put forward extreme examples of cases where it would be unjust to regard an innocent owner as liable: for example, an owner whose land was contaminated by a crashed tanker, or by migrating dust or particles.[85] The Government's response was that it was not justifiable to relieve owners of liabilities which they might already incur under existing legislation, and that it was reasonable for owners to bear responsibility for their property and its effects on others and the wider environment in cases where no original polluter can be found.[86]

5.92 As originally drafted, there were three circumstances where the current owner or occupier would be the appropriate person to bear responsibility for remediation. Two of these circumstances were dropped in the course of the passage of the Bill; namely cases where the owner/occupier refused consent for remediation works to be carried out on their land, and cases

---

[79] *Stevens v Bromley LBC* [1972] 1 All E.R. 712, CA.
[80] *Brown v Minister of Housing and Local Government* [1953] 2 All E.R. 1385.
[81] *Woodcock v South West Electricity Board* [1975] 2 All E.R. 545.
[82] *Southern Water Authority v Nature Conservancy Council* [1992] 3 All E.R. 481, HL.
[83] *Lord Advocate v Aero Technologies (in receivership)* 1991 S.L.T. 134.
[84] See further, Ch.25.
[85] *Hansard*, HL Vol.562, Col.1052.
[86] *Hansard*, HL Vol.562, Col.1052.

where the liability of the original "polluter" had been directly or indirectly transferred. The original provisions on transfer of liability were particularly difficult to understand, though they were basically prompted by the Government's wish to respect contractual provisions.[87] On looking at the matter more closely, however, the Government concluded that it would be more practical to leave the question to be dealt with through the normal contractual means of guarantees and indemnities rather than detailed statutory provisions.[88]

Two circumstances now remain where the owner or occupier is liable **5.93** under this provision; namely where after "reasonable enquiry" no appropriate person has been found under subs.(2), or where something to be done by way of remediation cannot be regarded as "referable" to anyone under subs.(3).

Liability of owner or occupier where original polluter still in existence

What happens if there are still in existence original contaminators but **5.94** they are not appropriate persons because what is to be done by way of remediation is not referable to the substances which they caused or knowingly permitted to be present, etc. in the land in question? This is dealt with by subs.78F(5). In those circumstances it is the owner or occupier for the time being who is the appropriate person. Thus there could be a situation where a number of remedial actions are required as a result of land having been contaminated in various ways. It may be possible to find Group A appropriate persons to whom some but not all of the remedial actions are referable. The owner and occupier will in such circumstances be appropriate persons with respect to those things which are not referable to the Class A appropriate persons. The general concept of referability is discussed above.[89]

Protection of owner and occupier

Persons liable under subss.(4) and (5) are in a better position than persons **5.95** liable under subs.(2) in one respect. This relates to the situation where the contamination results or is likely to result in pollution of controlled waters.[90]

The innocent fly-tipped owner

One situation for which the Government did have evident sympathy was **5.96** the plight of the owner or occupier who suffers from fly-tipping on their land. Imposing liability for clean-up of such contamination on the owner or

[87] *Hansard*, HL Vol.562, cols.1048–1051.
[88] *Hansard*, HL Vol.562, col.1498.
[89] See para.5.15ff.
[90] See para.5.135ff.

occupier on the basis that the fly-tipper could not be found would have resulted in significantly harsher liabilities than under s.59 of the 1990 Act which deals with the removal of unlawfully deposited waste. The Government's view was that the best way of dealing with the problem was to disapply Pt IIA in cases where s.59 could be used.[91] This was achieved by an amendment at third reading stage in the House of Lords. Full responsibility for dealing with unlawfully deposited waste would thereby be placed with the Environment Agency as the waste regulation authority (or the local authority as waste collection authority) and the exemption for innocent victims of fly-tipping was retained.[92] Certainly in relation to contamination occurring after controls over waste deposits on land were introduced, the availability of s.59 as a remedy might turn out to be a significant restriction on the use of Pt IIA powers. However, it must be remembered that s.59 is a very limited remedy compared with Pt IIA. It only deals with removal of the waste, not the consequences of the deposit of the waste. Also, it applies only to controlled waste, that is to say "household, industrial and commercial waste or any such waste".[93] Not every type of contaminant dumped on land will necessarily fall within the relevant definitions.[93a]

The role of guidance

5.97 This chapter has concentrated on the statutory provisions of s.78F, which as will be appreciated, are complex enough in their own right. They are, however, not the whole story.

5.98 Section 78F(6) applies where there are two or more appropriate persons in relation to any particular remediation action. Here the enforcing authority must determine in accordance with guidance from the Secretary of State, whether any of them is to be treated as not being an appropriate person. In other words, an appropriate person may be entitled to be excluded from the liability group if the guidance so dictates.

5.99 Secondly, by s.78F(7), where two or more persons are appropriate persons in relation to a particular remediation action, they shall be liable to bear the cost of that action in proportions determined in accordance with guidance issued by the Secretary of State. Again the guidance is mandatory in effect.

PART 3: LIABILITY—PARTICULAR CASES

Banks and other lenders

5.100 The question of the potential liability of lenders under the new provisions aroused considerable interest in debate. The Government did not regard it as likely that the act of lending money to a polluter would of itself

[91] *Hansard*, HL Vol.562, col.182.
[92] *Hansard*, HL Vol.562, cols.1048–1051.
[93] Environmental Protection Act 1990 s.75(4).
[93a] Environmental Protection Act 1990 s.75(4).

constitute causing or knowingly permitting contamination.[94] This view is reflected and supported in the statutory guidance on the exclusion of lenders from liability.[95] Lending money in itself is, however, not really the issue: what is more important for most lenders is the security for the loan provided by the land.

The definition of "owner" adopted in the Act expressly excludes a **5.101** mortgagee not in possession.[96] The Government expressed the view that banks should not be treated as "deep pockets", that the simple act of lending should not result in liability, and that the lender should retain the right to walk away from security without taking possession if the costs of remediation appeared to exceed its ultimate value.[97] However, the banks and other institutions such as the Council of Mortgage Lenders were still concerned that a lender might find itself in possession by default where a borrower simply abandoned the property.[98] Although it agreed to look into the issue, the Government concluded that no changes were necessary to protect the lenders in this situation; they were already exposed to similar liabilities under existing legislation on public health, highways and building standards.[99] Similarly, the Government was not sympathetic to the argument that special provision was needed to protect lenders who took possession to a limited extent to secure property or deal with obvious hazards.[100]

Insolvency practitioners and similar persons

Persons acting in certain capacities in relation to insolvency enjoy specific **5.102** protection by virtue of s.78X(3) and (4). Subsection (3) is intended to protect persons acting in various capacities (specified in subs.(4)) in insolvency situations. The provisions cover liquidators, administrators, administrative receivers, supervisors of voluntary arrangements, trustees in bankruptcy, the official receiver, and any person acting as a receiver under an enactment (e.g. the Law of Property Act 1925) or appointed as such by a court, or by any instrument. The protection is twofold:

(a) the person is not liable in a personal capacity for remediation costs unless the remediation requirement is referable (see s.78F(10) for the meaning of this) to substances whose presence in, on or under the land is a result of any act done or omission made by him, which was unreasonable for a person acting in his capacity; and

(b) he shall not be guilty of an offence of failing to comply with a remediation notice unless the relevant requirement relates to a thing for which he is personally responsible under (a).

---

[94] Hansard, HL Vol.565, col.1497; see also DEFRA Circular 01/2006, *Contaminated Land*, Annex 2 para.9.11.
[95] See para.5.189ff.
[96] 1990 Act s.78A(9).
[97] *Hansard*, HL Vol.560, col.1448.
[98] *Hansard*, HL Vol.560, col.1445; Vol.562, col.1040.
[99] *Hansard*, HL Vol.562, cols.1042–1053.
[100] *Hansard*, HL Vol.562, cols.1042–1053.

5.103   This wording is potentially difficult. It seems unlikely that the presence of contamination is likely to be the result of the positive act of an insolvency practitioner or similar person, but its presence might well be said to result from an omission on his part, i.e. failure to remove it, or failure to take steps which would have prevented it occurring. An obvious example might be the case where a receiver is appointed and becomes aware that leaking drums of chemicals are being stored on the property, in such conditions that soil contamination is continuing to occur.

5.104   The concept of an unreasonable omission is a difficult one, raising issues of what it is or is not reasonable to expect an insolvency practitioner to do as regards land which is, might be, or might become contaminated. Where there is an obvious problem such as corroded drums, it might well be said to be unreasonable to take no action to prevent further contamination occurring, for example by arranging for disposal by a specialist contractor. In less obvious cases, however, it might be questioned to what extent an insolvency practitioner should investigate for possible contamination, or should expend money on remedial or preventive measures, in order to avoid being held to have acted (or failed to act) unreasonably. In this respect, the case of *John Willment (Ashford) Ltd*[101] may be relevant, in that it was suggested there that a receiver could not exercise his discretion in such a way as to lead the company to act unlawfully. It will also be relevant to consider the terms of appointment or the debenture under which appointment takes place, to establish exactly what powers the receiver has. A receiver can hardly be said to be acting unreasonably in failing to do what he has no powers to do.

Managing agents

5.105 The definition of "owner" in s.78A(9) includes a person receiving the rack rent of the land, whether in their own capacity or as a trustee for another person. This means that a professional managing agent could find them-selves falling within the category of Class B appropriate persons.[102] The agent in such circumstances will not have the benefit of the statutory protection accorded to insolvency practitioners, as outlined above.

Trustees

5.106 The definitions of owner at s.78A(9) include a trustee. The possible hardship of the provisions applying to trustees was drawn to the attention of the Government in debate.[103] The response was that to provide an exemption for trustees would be to open up an easy route for evasion.[104] Therefore there is no provision in the legislation to protect trustees as such, for example by reference to reasonableness of conduct (as in the case

---

[101] [1979] 2 All E.R. 615.
[102] See *London Borough of Camden v Gunby* [2000] 1 W.L.R. 465 (a case on statutory nuisance); also see *Midland Bank Ltd v Conway Corp* [1965] 1 W.L.R. 1165.
[103] *Hansard*, HL Vol.562, col.163.
[104] *Hansard*, HL Vol.562, col.165; Vol.560, col.1448.

of insolvency practitioners) or by limiting liability to the extent of assets held. The trustee will however have a lien over the trust funds to be indemnified for work and expenses properly incurred in relation to liabilities under Pt IIA.[105]

Unincorporated associations

Where property belongs to a club or unincorporated association, it will be a **5.107** question of fact who is the owner or occupier.[106] Where the property is held by trustees, then they will be the owner.[107] Otherwise, consideration will have to be given as to whether liability rests with the members as a whole or with a committee which exercises control over the use of the property.[108]

Parent companies

Part IIA does not deal expressly with the issue of parent and subsidiary **5.108** companies, but it is undoubtedly an issue which will arise in practice, particularly in cases where a subsidiary which caused or knowingly permitted contamination either no longer exists or has insufficient assets to meet its remediation obligations.

The question here is whether it may ever (and if so, in what circum- **5.109** stances) be appropriate for an enforcing authority to treat the parent company as an appropriate person. It is submitted that this raises three distinct questions, as follows, which are considered in subsequent paragraphs:

1. Did the parent company itself cause or knowingly permit the contamination, i.e. is there some direct relationship between the parent and the contamination?

2. Did the parent company cause or knowingly permit the contamination indirectly, through the activities of the subsidiary, for example by funding the contaminating activity, or by failing to exercise control or supervision so as to prevent it?

3. Are there broader policy reasons for attributing the act of a subsidiary to its parent, for example to prevent evasion of the liability scheme of the Act?

At a practical level, local government or Environment Agency officers **5.110** may have no wish to become embroiled in complex issues of corporate personality and control. If during the period of consultation prior to service of a notice neither the parent or subsidiary has accepted responsibility, the

---

[105] See *X v A* [2000] Env. L.R. 104.
[106] *Bolton v Stone* [1951] A.C. 850, 858.
[107] *Verrall v Hackney LBC* [1983] Q.B. 445.
[108] See *Evans v Waitmeta District Pony Club, East Coast Bays Branch* [1972] N.Z.L.R. 773; affirmed [1974] 1 N.Z.L.R. 28.

pragmatic answer may be to serve notice on both companies, and leave it to them as to how they respond in terms of compliance or any appeal.

Direct activity by parent

5.111 Each case here will depend on its own facts, and close attention will need to be paid to which company actually carried out the activities in question which gave rise to contamination: who provided the employees, engaged the contractors, gave the instructions, owned the relevant assets? On the basis of the case law on "cause" it will not necessarily be a matter of choosing whether one or other company caused the contamination: it may well be possible for both to be said to have caused it.[109] It may, depending on the circumstances, be possible to find that a relationship of agency existed between a company and one of its members, or between companies in the same group, so that (for example) one company might have been acting as another's agent in carrying on the business ostensibly carried on by the principal company.[110]

5.112 One potentially important issue will be whether the parent's own directors took an active management role at the facility, or if there were common directors, whether they were acting on behalf of the parent or the subsidiary. The identity of the directors should be readily ascertainable from the Register of Companies, but the capacity in which they acted will require examination of the facts. Here, norms of corporate behaviour may well be relevant in deciding what conduct might normally be expected in the parent/subsidiary relationship.[111]

Indirect activity by parent

5.113 Here the issue is not whether the parent itself directly caused the contamination, but whether it might be said to have caused or knowingly permitted it by reference to the relationship between parent and subsidiary. This might take the form of active facilitation (for example, the parent providing resources to a subsidiary which is carrying on a contaminating activity) or failure to prevent (for example, knowing that a subsidiary is causing contamination and failing to prevent it). Another possible scenario would be the situation where a parent exercises strict financial control over a subsidiary, so that the subsidiary is denied the resources to deal with contamination that is known to be present.

5.114 Again, each set of circumstances will require careful consideration. The nature and degree of control of the parent over the subsidiary will be relevant. Certain cases have considered, in the context of company law, whether one company can be a "shadow director" of another by exerting

---

[109] See para.5.20.

[110] *Smith Stone & Knight Ltd v Birmingham Corp* [1939] 4 All E.R. 116; *Re FG (Films) Ltd* [1953] 1 W.L.R. 483; *Firestone Tyre and Rubber Co Ltd v Lewellin* [1957] 1 W.L.R. 464. Compare however, *William Cory & Son Ltd v Dorman Long & Co* [1936] 2 All E.R. 386.

[111] See the decision of the US Supreme Court in *United States v Bestfoods* [1998] U.S. Lexis 3733; 118 S. Ct. 1876.

management, strategic or financial control.[112] However, it is questionable whether the concept of shadow director adds very much to the environmental law tools of causing and knowingly permitting.

A parent company may have all sorts of reserve powers over a subsidiary. **5.115** These may not necessarily be exercised, but their existence may be relevant to the question of whether the parent could have prevented a particular course of action and thus may be held to have knowingly permitted it.[113]

Attributing liability to parent on policy grounds

On ordinary principles of corporate personality a subsidiary company is a **5.116** separate legal entity, with rights and liabilities distinct from those of its parent or other shareholders.[114] It is common for these rules to be utilised, often for entirely legitimate reasons, so as to isolate potential liabilities within particular companies in a group structure.

The provisions of Pt IIA are silent on the issue of liabilities of parent **5.117** companies, though it would have been possible to insert provisions making the position clear. In the context of the US "Superfund" legislation, the Supreme Court held in *United States v Bestfoods*[115] that the relevant US statute does not affect the fundamental principle of corporate law that a parent is not liable for the acts of its subsidiaries simply by being a parent. The same position is likely to apply under UK law; namely that in view of the reasoning behind the principle of separate corporate personality, and its long-standing recognition, any parliamentary intention to pierce the corporate veil would need to be expressed in clear and unequivocal language.[116]

Nonetheless, under UK law there is certainly authority to suggest that a **5.118** court may look beyond corporate structures which are a device to circumvent legal restrictions,[117] to perpetuate fraud,[118] to conceal the true facts,[119] or to avoid liability to another.[120] Such principles may apply to property transactions.[121] However, the use of a company as a single purpose vehicle may be an entirely legitimate approach which is more than a "mere

---

[112] The concept is found in s.741 of the Companies Act 1985 and see now s.251 of The Companies Act 2006. See *Re Unisoft Group Ltd (No. 2)* [1994] B.C.L.C. 766; *Re Hydrodam (Corby) Ltd* [1994] 2 B.C.L.C. 180; *R. v Secretary of State for Trade and Industry Ex p. Laing* [1996] 2 B.C.L.C. 324; *Standard Chartered Bank of Australia v Antico* [1995] 13 A.C. L.C. 1381.

[113] See *Unilever Plc v Gillette (UK) Ltd* [1989] R.P.C. 583, CA (reserve powers of US parent over UK subsidiary were relevant to application for patent action against subsidiary).

[114] *Salomon v A Salomon & Co Ltd* [1897] A.C. 22.

[115] [1998] US Lexis 3733; 118 S. Ct. 1876.

[116] *Dimbleby & Sons Ltd v National Union of Journalists* [1984] 1 W.L.R. 427, HL, at 435.

[117] *Merchandise Transport Ltd v British Transport Commission* [1962] 2 Q.B. 173, 206–207; *Adams v Cape Industries Plc* [1990] Ch. 433; compare *Ord v Belhaven Cut Ltd* [1998] N.L.J. 938.

[118] *Aveling Barford Ltd v Perion Ltd* [1989] B.C.L.C. 626; *Re H* [1996] 2 All E.R. 391; *Re Darby Ex p. Brougham* [1911] 1 K.B. 95.

[119] *Woolfson v Strathclyde RC* (1978) 38 P. & C.R. 521; *Re FG (Films) Ltd* [1953] 1 W.L.R. 483.

[120] *Creasey v Beachwood Motors Ltd* [1993] B.C.L.C. 480; *Gilford Motor Co Ltd v Horne* [1933] Ch. 935; *Yukong Line Ltd of Korea v Rendsburg Investments Corp of Liberia (No. 2)* [1988] 4 All E.R. 82.

[121] *Gisborne v Burton* [1989] 1 Q.B. 390; *MacFarlane v Salfield Investments Ltd* [1997] S.C.L.R.

facade"; nor is a court free to disregard the principle of separate corporate personality merely because it considers that justice so requires.[122] Nor should the closeness of economic and commercial relationships between companies in a group justify, in general, treating them as a single entity.[123]

5.119 Particular problems may arise in relation to loose inter-company arrangements where one company in a group occupies property belonging to another on an informal basis, which confers no rights of exclusive occupation. This may fall short of giving rights of occupation which are recognised as having legal consequences for the purposes of Pt IIA.[124] The question is perhaps most likely to arise where a subsidiary company is liable as owner of a contaminated site and has insufficient assets to carry out the necessary remediation. Much will no doubt depend on particular circumstances[125]: a court may view very differently a parent which has conducted a particular aspect of its business through a trading subsidiary for many years, from a company which, knowing it is to be faced with a remediation notice for a site of which it is owner, transfers that site to a subsidiary company with no assets, created for that purpose. There is much to be said for retaining some flexibility in this area, provided the courts are aware of the dangers of too readily upsetting matters of property or contract.[126] In the circumstances where a parent transfers a site knowing of its contaminated condition, there may well be an argument that the parent is responsible in its own right for knowingly permitting. Those exclusion tests described below which relate to transfers of property will also require consideration in this context.[127]

Dissolution of companies and restoration to the register

5.120 Liability of a company under Pt IIA may arise from its past acts as a causer or knowing permitter of contamination, or from its ownership or occupation of contaminated land. Both situations need to be considered in the situation where a company is dissolved. Once the company is dissolved it ceases to exist as a legal entity and, it is submitted, can no longer be "found" for the purposes of s.78F.[128] It may however be possible for an application to be made for the dissolution to be declared void, or for the company to be restored to the register.[129] The enforcing authority would need to consider carefully whether any purpose would be served by such an application if the company has no assets remaining. If some other person

---

[122] *Re Polly Peck International Plc* (in administration) [1996] 2 All E.R. 433, 447–8.

[123] *Lonrho Ltd v Shell Petroleum Co Ltd* [1980] Q.B. 358; affirmed [1980] 1 W.L.R. 627, HL; *The Albazero* [1977] A.C. 774 at 807; *Bank of Tokyo Ltd v Karoon* [1987] A.C. 45n at 64.

[124] *Butcher Robinson & Staples v London Regional Transport* [1999] 36 E.G. 165. Compare the more liberal approach taken in *DHN Food Distributors Ltd v Tower Hamlets LBC* [1976] Q.B. 852.

[125] Sealy points out that commentators have failed to discern any set pattern in the decided cases: ". . . indeed, in many instances they seem to contradict each other in the most baffling way". (L.S. Sealy, *Cases and Materials in Company Law*, 6th edn, 1996, p.56.)

[126] L.S. Sealy, *Cases and Materials in Company Law*, 6th edn, 1996, p.56.

[127] See para.5.194ff.

[128] See 5.54ff.

[129] Companies Act 1985 ss.651 and 653(2B) (to be replaced from a date to be appointed by s.1029 of the companies Act 2006).

or company is liable in their own right, revival of the dissolved company will not be necessary to enable that party to be pursued. However, the power to have a company restored to the register may bear further reflection in some cases. By s.653(2B) (inserted by the Deregulation and Contracting Out Act 1994, Sch. 5, para. 3) a "notifiable person" may apply for the company to be restored to the register on the ground that the duties as to notifying them were not complied with, or that it is for some other reason just to do so. "Notifiable person" includes any "contingent or prospective creditor".[129a] When the Companies Act 2006 is in force, this will also include "any person with a potential legal claim against the company" (s.1029(2)(f)). The basis of a claim for restoration may be that the applicant wishes to have the company restored in order to make a claim against a third party.[129b] The restoration of a company which was a Class A party, so that it can now be "found" may have a significant impact upon how liability under Pt IIA is allocated and appointed. Accordingly, other appropriate persons may consider carefully whether there is any basis for arguing that it is "just" to restore the dissolved company.

Winding-up and dissolution of companies: effect on property

One of the assets of the company being wound up may be contaminated **5.121** land. The issue may arise in two ways: first, on disclaimer by the liquidator during winding up, and, secondly, the effect of dissolution of the company if by that time the property has neither been disclaimed nor disposed of.

By s.178 of the Insolvency Act 1986, where a company is being wound up in England or Wales the liquidator may disclaim onerous property, even if he has already taken possession, attempted to sell, or otherwise exercised rights of ownership.[130] The definition of "onerous property" under s.178(3) includes property which may give rise to an obligation to pay money or perform an onerous act or which may well not be saleable readily or at all. Contaminated land may well fall within this definition, whether or not a remediation notice has yet been served.[131]

The effect of disclaimer under s.178(4) is to determine, as from the date **5.122** of disclaimer, the rights, interests and liabilities of the company "in or in respect of the property disclaimed". However, the subsection expressly provides that it does not affect the rights or liabilities of any other person

---

[129a] See ss.652B(6) and 652D(8).

[129b] *City of Westminster Assurance co Ltd v Registrar of Companies* [1997] BCC 960, *Re Harvest Lane Motor Bodies Ltd* [1969] 1 Ch.457.

[130] The liquidator will need to follow the appropriate procedures of s.178(2) by giving the prescribed notice.

[131] For the application of s.178 to a waste management licence as onerous property, see *Official Receiver (as liquidator of Celtic Extraction Ltd and Bluestone Chemicals Ltd) v Environment Agency* [2000] Env. L.R. 86. In *Environment Agency v Hillridge Ltd* [2003] EWHC 3023 (Ch); [2004] Env. L.R. 32, the effect of a disclaimer of a waste management licence was to deprive both the insolvent company and the Environment Agency of recourse to a trust fund set up for remedial works and aftercare of the waste site, as works could only be undertaken in accordance with the trust deed whilst a licence was in force. The result was that the trust funds passed to the Crown as *bona vacantia*.

except insofar as is necessary for the purpose of releasing the company from liability. It is not totally clear how this provision will apply to the situation where the company may be subject to liabilities either in its capacity as the original perpetrator of contamination, or in its capacity as continuing owner or occupier. Where the company's liability depends on its continuing ownership of the property, then disclaimer will terminate that liability. In respect of liability for past acts as a perpetrator of the contamination, the question is perhaps whether this type of liability constitutes liability "in respect of the property disclaimed". Whilst it could be argued that the liability stems from the past actions of the company rather than its current ownership or occupation of the property, and so is not affected by s.178(4), the case law on the section and its predecessors does not address this specific issue.[132]

Position of parties affected by disclaimer

5.123 By s.178(6) any person who has sustained loss or damage in consequence of disclaimer is deemed to be a creditor of the company to the extent of their loss or damage, and can prove for it in the winding up as ordinary creditors. This would potentially apply to an enforcing authority, which claims to have suffered loss in having to take responsibility for dealing with disclaimed property. This course may have its own problems for the enforcing authority.[133] However the specific statutory procedures for charging notices[134] will in general make this unnecessary. Section 178(6) might also potentially apply to another appropriate person who claims that their share of liability has been increased by the effect of disclaimer in extinguishing the liability otherwise attributable to the company. Such a third party is unlikely to be able to argue that their own share is extinguished by the effect of the disclaimer, in view of the proviso to s.178(4) that disclaimer should not in general affect the liabilities of other persons.

Effect of dissolution on property: bona vacantia

5.124 By s.654 of the Companies Act 1985[134a] the effect of dissolution of a company is that all property and rights vested in the company (excluding those held on trust for others) are deemed to be *bona vacantia* and to belong to and vest in the Crown, the Duchy of Lancaster or the Duke of Cornwall, as appropriate.[135] It is possible for the Crown's title to be disclaimed within 12 months by notice under s.656, signed by the Treasury Solicitor or by the Queen's and Lord Treasurer's Remembrancer as representative of the

---

[132] See especially *Stacey v Hill* [1901] 1 K.B. 660; *Warnford Investments Ltd v Duckworth* [1979] 1 Ch. 127.

[133] See the discussion in *Re. Mineral Resources Ltd* [1999] 1 All E.R. 756.

[134] See para.6.44ff.

[134a] To be replaced from a date to be appointed by s.1012 of the Companies Act 2006.

[135] For consideration of s.654 in the different context of a waste management licence, see *Wilmott Trading Co. Ltd (No. 2)* [2000] Env. L.R. 54.

Crown. By s.657 of the 1985 Act the effect of such disclaimer is that the property is deemed not to have vested in the Crown, so determining the relevant interests, rights and liabilities in the same way as disclaimer by a liquidator. However, this may be a pointless exercise, since in such circumstances the property will revert to the Crown on general principles of escheat, as the owner of the ultimate reversion in the property (assuming there is no mesne lord).[136]

Effect of death of individual

In the same way as for a company, an individual may incur liability for **5.125** their own acts or omissions with regard to contamination, irrespective of ownership or occupation of land. Death of the individual will mean that they can no longer be "found",[137] and the question will be whether there is any right to proceed against their estate. The following paragraphs consider the principles of testate and intestate succession.

Effect on property of individual dying testate

Where the estate of a deceased person includes contaminated land, **5.126** consideration will need to be given to the effect of the rules of testate and intestate succession.

As a trustee, an executor can incur personal liability in their capacity as **5.127** owner of the land.[138] The executor may quite understandably in those circumstances wish to consider renouncing probate, the effect of which under s.5 of the Administration of Estates Act 1925 will be that his rights will cease and that the administration of the estate will devolve as if he had not been appointed. Renunciation is equally an option open to trust corporations, normally by an instrument under seal or by an official duly appointed for that purpose. Similarly, it is a course open to a person appointed by an order of the Court of Protection or an attorney acting under an enduring power or attorney, on behalf of the incapable person. What is vital is that the executor should not have intermeddled in the estate of the deceased.

A distinction needs to be drawn between the liabilities of the deceased, **5.128** and the ongoing liabilities which as it were pass with the land. To the extent that the deceased had liabilities as an "appropriate person" under Pt IIA, his real and personal estate will constitute assets to meet these liabilities, by s.32 of the Administration of Estates Act 1925. If there was a subsisting cause of action against the deceased before his death then this will survive against his estate by s.1(1) of the Law Reform (Miscellaneous Provisions) Act 1934. Since the section refers to all causes of action "whether in contract or in tort or otherwise", it appears wide enough to

---

[136] See Ing, *bona vacantia* (London: Butterworths, 1971), p.5; Enever, *Bona Vacantia* (HMSO, 1927), p.15.

[137] See para.5.54ff.

[138] See para.5.106.

cover statutory liabilities under Pt IIA. Whilst the personal representatives should pay such liabilities with due diligence having regard to all the circumstances of the case, they should also consider whether any defence is available, and rely on it if appropriate.[139]

5.129 Where the land remains in a contaminated condition, liability as knowing permitter or owner could obviously pass to the beneficiary as the next owner. He may elect not to take under the will, or disclaim the legacy. As it was colourfully put in one case: a man "cannot have an estate put into him in spite of his teeth".[140]

Effect on property of individual dying intestate

5.130 By s.6 of the Administration of Estates Act 1925 the estate of an intestate person vests in the President of the Family Division of the High Court as the Probate Judge until an administrator of the estate is appointed. By s.21 of the 1925 Act the administrator will be liable in the same manner as an executor. The administrator may, in the same way as an executor, renounce his right to grant of letters of administration.

5.131 The distinction between the liabilities of the deceased for previous actions and those liabilities which follow the ownership or occupation land needs to be borne in mind. With respect to the first type of liability the principles set out above will apply with respect to claims against the estate. In relation to the second type of liability which passes with the land, the view of commentators is that a beneficiary in an intestacy can disclaim his entitlement.[141]

5.132 Subject to the possibility of such disclaimer, the property will pass according to the rules of succession contained in s.46 of the 1925 Act, and by s.46(1)(vi) in default of any person being entitled to take an absolute interest, the residuary estate will belong to the Crown, Duchy of Lancaster or Duke of Cornwall as bona vacantia, and in lieu of any right to escheat.[142] It is the practice of the Treasury Solicitor not to administer an estate which is prima facie insolvent, or the solvency of which is doubtful, but to leave it to the creditor to do so: this is on the basis that in such cases there is no bona vacantia to collect.[143] This may be a relevant principle where the estate includes contaminated land or associated liabilities. To what extent the Crown can be liable (bearing in mind that bona vacantia was originally an aspect of the Royal Prerogative)[144] is doubtful and is considered below.

Crown land and Crown liability

5.133 The Crown may be an appropriate person to be liable under Pt IIA either because its own activities (e.g. those of the armed forces) have caused the contamination, or in its capacity as an owner or occupier of land. Such

---

[139] *Re Rownson* (1885) 29 Ch. D. 358.
[140] *Townson v Tickell* (1819) B. & Ald 31 at 37.
[141] Sherrin & Bonehill, *The Law and Practice of Intestate Succession* (London: Sweet & Maxwell, 1994), pp.104, 358. But compare Williams, Mortimer & Sunnucks, *Executors, Administrators and Probate* (London: Sweet & Maxwell, 1993), p.940.
[142] As to procedural issues, see Ing, *Bona Vacantia* (London: Butterworths, 1971), Pt II.
[143] Ing, *Bona Vacantia* (London: Butterworths, 1971), Pt II, p.36.
[144] Enever, *Bona Vacantia* (HMSO, 1927), pp.13, 87.

ownership may arise in respect of operational land, or land which devolves on the Crown under the principles of bona vacantia, as described above. It is therefore necessary to consider s.159 of the Environmental Protection Act 1990, which deals with its application to the Crown.

By s.159(1) the 1990 Act and regulations under it bind the Crown, but by **5.134** s.159(5) do not affect Her Majesty in her private capacity. The Crown can therefore be an appropriate person under Class A or B in the same way as any other person. But by s.159(2) the Crown cannot be made criminally liable for non-compliance with a remediation notice. However, it will be possible to obtain a declaration from the High Court or Court of Session that the Crown is acting unlawfully in failing to respond to a remediation notice, if that be the case.

PART 4: RESTRICTIONS ON LIABILITY RELATING TO WATER POLLUTION

When section 78J applies

The section is stated to apply where any land is contaminated land by **5.135** virtue of s.78A(2)(b) of the Act, whether or not the land is also contaminated by virtue of para.(a) of that subsection. In other words, if the condition of the land is such that pollution of controlled waters is being caused, or is likely to be caused, then s.78J applies. It does not matter that significant harm, or the significant possibility of such harm, are also involved.

The general restriction

Section 78J(2) provides that no remediation notice shall require a person **5.136** who is an appropriate person by virtue by s.78F(4) or (5) (i.e. a Class B owner or occupier where a causer or knowing permitter cannot be found) to do anything by way of remediation which he could not have been required to do if the water pollution limb of the definition of "contaminated land" in s.78A(2) did not exist. In other words, the remediation required may relate only to the "significant harm" limb of the definition, that is, harm to the health of living organisms, interference with ecological systems, or harm to property. The restriction relates not only to the remediation required on the contaminated land itself, but also to remediation of other land or of any waters.

The object behind this somewhat convoluted wording is to avoid any **5.137** additional liability accruing to an owner or occupier of land beyond that which could accrue under the provisions of the Water Resources Act 1991, dealing with the clean-up of polluted waters or the prevention of such pollution. These provisions (including the "works notice" procedures introduced by the Environment Act 1995) are based on liability for causing or knowingly permitting, hence the restriction of the s.78J protection to owners and occupiers.

5.138   Two points may be made on this restriction. First, its effectiveness as a means of protection for owners and occupiers will depend on the interpretation given to "knowingly permitting".[145] If an owner or occupier who knows of the presence of contamination can be regarded as knowingly permitting its continued presence, then they will fall into the first tier of appropriate persons and will not be able to take advantage of s.78J(2). They will be an appropriate person by virtue of s.78F(2) rather than s.78F(4) or (5).

5.139   Secondly, pollution of controlled waters may well involve one of the forms of "significant harm" under s.78A(4), allowing remediation requirements to be imposed on that basis. Examples would be harm to fish or plant life, and possibly, in the case of groundwater contamination, rendering the water unfit for the purpose for which it is abstracted.[146] Where remediation cannot be required in consequence of s.78J(2) the authority may still use its own clean-up powers under s.78N, but will not be able to recover its costs under s.78P.[147]

Pollution from abandoned mines

5.140   Sections 78J(3)–(6) provide a further restriction on the requirements of remediation notices, relating to water pollution from abandoned mines. As with s.78J(2), the notice may not go further than could be required were the contamination related only to significant harm or the significant risk of such harm. The provision was introduced to prevent the potential problem that the Pt IIA provisions might be used to impose liability in the three-year period of grace given by Parliament under the Environment Act 1995 before the withdrawal at the end of 1999 of the defence in relation to water pollution from abandoned mines.[148] In the event, the provisions of Pt IIA were not introduced during that period.

5.141   The provision applies to any person who permits, has permitted, or might permit water from an abandoned mine or part of such a mine to enter controlled waters, or to reach a place from which it is or was likely to enter controlled waters. The effect is to mirror the position as to liability for pollution from abandoned mines contained in the Water Resources Act 1991, as amended by the Environment Act 1995. As with those provisions, by s.78J(4) the restriction does not apply to owners or former operators of mines which become abandoned after December 31, 1999. The restriction only applies to those permitting (as opposed to causing) such pollution or potential pollution.

5.142   The question of what is a "mine" is dealt with by s.78J(8) which applies the definition contained in s.180 of the Mines and Quarries Act 1954. This refers to:

---

[145] See para.5.27ff.

[146] This could arguably constitute damage to property, in the sense that abstraction is a natural right incidental to the ownership of land.

[147] 1990 Act s.78J(7).

[148] See *Hansard*, HL Vol.562, cols 144–5; *Hansard*, HL Vol.562, col.151. For detailed explanation of the statutory regime relating to abandoned mines; see Stephen Tromans and Mark Ponstie, *Environemental Protection Legislation 1990–2002* (London: Sweet & Maxwell, 2003), p.569.

". . . an excavation or system of excavations, including all such excavations to which a common system of ventilation is provided, made for the purpose of, or in connection with, the getting, wholly or substantially by means involving the employment of persons below ground, of minerals (whether in their natural state or suspension) or products of minerals."

This definition relates to the original purpose of the excavations in question. In some cases, mine workings may have been used for the disposal of waste, but would still appear to fall within the definition, given their original purpose. An opencast mine or quarry is an "excavation", but would not fall within the definition since the getting of opencast minerals does not involve the employment of persons below ground (as opposed to below the pre-existing ground level). The 1954 Act draws a distinction between mines and quarries, and opencast working will be a quarry rather than a mine. The point is one of some practical significance, since many open excavations will subsequently have been used for waste tipping or landfill. **5.143**

The vital question of when abandonment occurs is dealt with by s.78J(5) and (6). "Abandonment" is not defined by s.78J, but receives a detailed definition as to what it does and does not include by ss.91A(1) of the Water Resources Act 1991, inserted by s.58 of the 1995 Act. **5.144**

The question arises as to what should happen when water pollution is occurring from a mine abandoned before the relevant date, but is not causing significant harm or a significant risk of such harm. By s.78F(7) the enforcing authority can still carry out remediation itself under s.78N, but will be precluded from recovering its expenses under s.78P in relation to any thing which it could not have included in a remediation notice. **5.145**

Section 91B(7) of the Water Resources Act provides a link between the new requirements on abandonment and the contaminated land provisions. Where the Environment Agency receives notice of abandonment from the operator, or otherwise learns of proposed abandonment, if it considers that any land (including land beyond the mine) has or is likely to become "contaminated land" in consequence of the abandonment, then it must inform the local authority for the area. It is therefore clear that the local authority is intended to use its contaminated land powers where appropriate in relation to mines abandoned after December 31, 1999. **5.146**

Part 5: Migration Of Contamination And Chemical Changes

Chemical reactions or biological process

Where as a result of chemical or biological changes a substance which a person caused or knowingly permitted to be in the ground becomes or generates a contaminant, which it may not have been initially, the person **5.147** who caused or knowingly permitted the original substance to be present bears responsibility for the resulting contamination.[149] This is so whether or not he knew or ought to have known that the reaction or process was likely to happen.[150] The provision will thus cover substances which degrade so as to produce more toxic or harmful products, or substances which react together to create harmful synergistic effects.

Escape of contaminating substances to other land

5.148 Section 78K deals with liability in respect of contaminating substances which escape to other land. Who is the "appropriate person" in such circumstances? A number of different situations can arise—s.78K distinguishes four, which are considered separately below.

Liability of contaminator for escapes to other land

5.149 The original contaminator, i.e. the person who caused or knowingly permitted the substances to be in, on or under the land, is taken, by s.78K(1), to have caused or, as the case may be, knowingly permitted, the substances to be in, on or under any other land to which they appear to have escaped.

5.150 "Appear" here means appears to the local authority; determining where contaminants may have originated from can be a highly complex technical issue. The word "appear" indicates that the authority must have some factual basis for its view, but that 100 per cent certainty is not necessary.[151] It will of course be open the "appropriate person" to adduce evidence to the contrary on appeal.

5.151 Responsibility therefore follows the event of the escape, making the contaminator a first tier appropriate person in relation to that other land. There is no requirement that the escape should have been foreseeable, or that it must have been caused by the original contaminator. The original contaminator stands in the same position to the escaped substances as he does in relation to their original presence on the land from which they escaped: this will have relevance for the purposes of exclusion and apportionment tests.

Persons onto whose land substances escape

5.152 Section 78K(3) applies where it appears to the enforcing authority that substances are present in, on, or under land as a result of their escape, directly or indirectly, from other land where some person caused or

---

[149] 1990 Act s.78F(9).

[150] See *Circular Facilities (London) Ltd v Sevenoaks DC* [2005] EWHC 865; [2005] Env. L.R. 35 at 765. See also, however, the exclusion test relating to changes to substances, explained at para.5.208.

[151] See *Ferris v Secretary of State for the Environment* [1988] J.P.L. 777 in the context of planning enforcement.

knowingly permitted them to be. Its effect is to prevent any remediation notice requiring the owner or occupier of the land to which the substances have escaped to carry out remediation to any land or waters other than that of which he is the owner or occupier. By inference, the owner or occupier can be required to carry out remediation to his own land, although provided the original contaminator of the land from which the escape occurred can be found, they ought to be a first tier appropriate person under s.78K(1).

The section applies only to innocent owners, in that it excludes those **5.153** who caused or knowingly permitted the substance to be in, on, or under their land. In that respect, there appears to be no difference between A, who knows his predecessor X dumped chemicals on the property, and B who knows his neighbour Y dumped chemicals which have migrated onto his land.

The net effect is therefore that someone onto whose land contaminants **5.154** have escaped and who is not a knowing permitter should only be liable in respect of his own land, and then only if the original contaminator cannot be found. The potential flaw in this logical scheme lies in the use of the words "knowingly permitted" at s.78K(3)(b). If the person to whose land the substances have escaped knows of their presence and fails to take action, can they be regarded as knowingly permitting their presence? If so, they will lose any protection conferred by s.78K(3).

As a matter of policy, it could be asked whether there is any logical **5.155** distinction between a person who comes to a site, discovers it is contaminated, and does nothing, as against a person whom comes to a site which has been contaminated by substances which have escaped from elsewhere, and does nothing.

Escapes to further land

Section 78K(4) complements and reinforces (arguably, duplicates) **5.156** s.78K(3). It refers to the situation where contaminants escape from their original location where some person caused or knowingly permitted them to be, to land A, and then escape to further land, (land B). This situation may occur where, for example, a plume of contamination passes through land which is in a number of ownerships. The effect of s.78K(4) is that the owner or occupier of land A—provided he cannot be said to have caused or knowingly permitted the substances to be in, on or under land A—will not be responsible for the remediation of land B unless he is also the owner or occupier of that land. In such circumstances, the enforcing authority should be able to pursue the original contaminator under s.78K(1), or if he cannot be found, the owner or occupier of land B.

Subsequent owners or occupiers of the land from which escape takes place

The situation can obviously arise where a person A contaminates land and **5.157** the contamination escapes to adjoining land; person B at some stage becomes the owner or occupier of the land from which the escape took place. Is B liable to receive a remediation notice? Section 78K(5) states that no remediation notice may require B to remediate the other land to which the substances escaped, except where he himself caused or knowingly permitted the escape. The wording of s.78K(5) is somewhat curious, stating that B should not be required to do anything in consequence of the apparent acts or omissions of A. But there is no reason in any event why B should be held liable for A's acts or omissions, unless he himself is an appropriate person on the basis of causing or knowingly permitting.

5.158   The subsection could potentially apply in two cases. First, where the escape took place entirely before B became owner or occupier. In that situation it seems difficult to see on what possible basis B could be liable, unless he had some prior separate connection with the escape (e.g. as a contractor); in which case his liability would not arise as owner or occupier in any event.

5.159   The second situation is where the escape occurs or continues after B becomes the owner or occupier. Here, B may be liable as occupier or owner of the land from which the escape took place, if he caused or knowingly permitted the escape. It is not the presence of contamination on his land which makes him liable to receive a remediation notice, but rather causing or allowing the escape, which may have happened some time later. B could still be responsible for remediation of the land he acquired, to clean up contaminants remaining there, or to prevent future escapes. He will not be responsible however for past escapes, save to the extent he caused or knowingly permitted them.

5.160   There is a possible conflict between the specific drafting of s.78K(5) and the general principle at s.8K(1), which could apply where person B knowingly permitted the continuing presence of the substances in his land, but did not knowingly permit their escape. It appears fairly clear that the more specific wording of s.78K(5) should prevail in this respect.

Use of authority's own clean-up powers in case of escapes

5.161 Nothing in subss.(3), (4) or (5) of s.78K prevents the enforcing authority from carrying out remediation itself under s.78N, but the authority will not be entitled under s.78P to recover from any person any part of the cost incurred by the local authority in carrying out the remediation in circumstances where it is precluded from requiring the person concerned to carry out the remediation himself—see s.78K(6). In other words, the use of the cost recovery powers in s.78P cannot circumvent the scheme of liability created by s.78K.

Example of provisions on escape

5.162 A is the original contaminator of land X. Land X is sold to B. An escape of contaminants to land Y (owned by C) occurred both before and after this sale. The contaminants also escaped from land Y to land Z (owned by D). The position under s.78K is as follows (leaving aside the ensuing application of rules on exclusion and apportionment):

1. A is an appropriate person (Group A) for land X, land Y and land Z (s.78K(1)).

2. B can be an appropriate person (Group A or B depending on the knowingly permitting issue) in relation to land X.

3. B will not be an appropriate person in relation to land Y and Z for substances which escaped prior to his acquiring the land (s.78K(5)).

4. B may be an appropriate person (Group A) in relation to land Y and Z to the extent only that he caused or knowingly permitted the escape from land X (s.78K(5)).

5. C may be an appropriate person (Group B or possibly Group A) in relation to his own land Y (s.78K(3).

6. C will not be an appropriate person in relation to land Z (s.78K(4)) unless he caused or knowingly permitted the escape from land Y to land Z (s.78K(5)).

7. D will be an appropriate person (Group B or possibly Group A) in relation to land Z (s.78K(3)).

Relevance of Guidance

These provisions also need to be read in conjunction with the Guidance on **5.163** exclusion from liability. In particular, Test 4 deals with "Changes to substances" and Test 5 deals with "Escaped substances". Both may have the effect of excluding from liability some of the parties involved where substances have interacted or escaped.

PART 6: EXCLUSION OF PARTIES FROM LIABILITY

The general approach to exclusion

Before considering in detail the content of the Guidance on the exclusion **5.164** of appropriate persons from liability, a number of general points should be restated:

1. The starting point is in fact not the Guidance, but the words of s.78F and the related ss.78J and 78K. The first step is to establish who, under those sections, are the appropriate persons in relation to each relevant remediation action[152] ("the liability group", which may be a "Class A" or a "Class B" group).[153]

2. The Guidance on exclusion is only relevant where there are two or more appropriate persons.[154] It therefore cannot help a person

---

[152] DEFRA Circular 01/2006, Contaminated Land, Annex 3 paras D.7–D.10.
[153] DEFRA Circular 01/2006, Contaminated Land, Annex 3 paras D.11–D.14.
[154] DEFRA Circular 01/2006, Contaminated Land, Annex 3 para.D.28.

who is the only appropriate person in relation to a particular remediation action.

3. By the same token, if there is a group of appropriate persons, not all of them can be excluded. If the application of an exclusion test would exclude all of the (remaining) members of a liability group, that test is not to be applied and those members will not be able to claim exclusion.[155]

Terminology

5.165 Chapter D of the statutory Guidance, dealing with exclusion from and apportionment of liability, creates its own inner world of terminology, in addition to the statutory definitions of Pt IIA. This is set out at para.D.5:

(a) appropriate persons who caused or knowingly permitted are "Class A persons";

(b) appropriate persons who are unfortunate enough to be the current owner or occupier where no Class A person can be found are "Class B persons";

(c) appropriate persons in relation to a particular pollutant linkage form a "Class A liability group" or "Class B liability group", as the case may be;

(d) determination that a person is not to be treated as an appropriate person under s.78F(6) is "exclusion";

(e) determination under s.78F(7) dividing the cost between appropriate persons is "apportionment". The process of dividing the cost between liability groups is "attribution";

(f) each individual thing to be done as remediation is a "remediation action";

(g) all the remediation actions referable to a particular pollutant linkage is a "remediation package"; and

(h) the complete set or sequence of remediation actions to be carried out on the land in question is a "remediation scheme".

The procedure by stages

5.166 Part 3 of Ch.D deals with the discrete stages involved in the procedure for determining liabilities, and as such sets the exclusion process in context. Not all stages will necessarily be relevant in each case.

Stage 1—identifying appropriate persons and liability groups

5.167 Paragraphs D.9–D.19—The starting point is the pollutant linkage or linkages by virtue of which the land is contaminated land. The authority should first make reasonable enquiries to find all Class A persons to whose

---

[155] DEFRA Circular 01/2006, Contaminated Land, Annex 3 para.D.41(c).

activities the linkage is referable. If no Class A persons can be found, and the linkage relates solely to water pollution, then by s.78J there can be no liability on Class B persons, and the linkage will be an "orphan linkage".[156] In other cases, the authority seeks to identify all Class B persons for the land in question. This process is repeated for each pollutant linkage until all liability groups have been identified, bearing in mind that a person may be a member of more than one liability group for different linkages. The authority should then consider whether any member of a group can benefit from the statutory exemptions of ss.78J, 78K or 78X(4), it should be noted that hardship does not enter into the exercise at this point.

Stage 2—characterising remediation actions

Paragraphs D.20–D.23—This stage is only relevant where there is more **5.168** than one significant pollutant linkage on the land involved. The authority should establish whether each remediation action is referable to a single linkage or to more than one linkage, in which case it is termed a "shared action", such shared actions may be either "common actions" or "collective actions". This issue is of primary relevance to the apportionment exercise, and is discussed in Pt 7 of this Chapter.

Stage 3—attributing responsibility between groups

Paragraphs D.24–D.27—Again this stage is only relevant where there are **5.169** multiple pollutant linkages. The exercise may result in a Class B group not having to bear any liability. Again, it is discussed in Pt 7 of this Chapter.

Stage 4—excluding members of a group

Paragraph D.28—This involves applying the Guidance on exclusion, which **5.170** forms the substance of this Part.

Stage 5—apportioning liability between members of a group

Paragraphs D.29–D.31—This is covered in Pt 7. **5.171**

General guidance and information for appropriate persons

Part 4 of Ch.D contains guidance on some general considerations applying **5.172** to the exclusion, and apportionment processes. It requires that enforcing authorities should ensure that any person who might benefit from an exclusion, apportionment or attribution rule is aware of the Guidance, so that they may make appropriate representations to the authority. This raises some interesting questions of how far the authority must go to comply with this aspect of the Guidance. At the very least, the authority should presumably tell the person that there are rules which may benefit them, and that those rules may be found in the Guidance. Many appropri-

---

[156] See para.5.277ff.

ate persons will no doubt have access to sophisticated legal advice, and nothing more than this will be needed. Other appropriate persons may find it difficult to understand the Guidance and how it may apply to their particular circumstances. All parties involved in the more complex multiple linkage cases will find it difficult to take sensible decisions until they know how the authority is proposing to analyse the situation in terms of the remediation package. The authority will need to be careful not to leave itself open to the accusation of unfairness by giving one party more help than another. Authorities may wish to consider producing a standard form letter which summarises the main points, and directs the reader to the relevant parts of the Guidance for the definitive position. Clearly the person must be given an adequate time to take legal advice and make representations. Authorities faced with complex multi-linkage situations might also need to consider adopting an iterative process, whereby further representations are invited at particular stages, so that the impact of decisions taken at the earlier stages can be assessed.

Financial circumstances

5.173 Another general factor is financial circumstances. The Guidance states that, in relation to exclusion, apportionment and attribution, the financial circumstances of individual members of the liability group should have no bearing on the application of the tests and procedures involved.[157] In particular, it should be irrelevant:

> (a) whether the person would benefit from any limitation on the recovery of costs under the hardship provisions of s.78P(2) or the guidance on cost recovery; or
>
> (b) whether they would benefit from any insurance or other means of transferring their responsibilities to any other person, for example, an indemnity.

5.174 The intention behind this aspect of the Guidance is clearly to avoid a "deep pocket" approach of making those with substantial resources responsible for a proportionately greater responsibility for remediation.

Information available and decisions

5.175 The application of the principles of exclusion and apportionment may require much information about past activities and current circumstances which may be impossible or very difficult to obtain. The authority may also be faced with conflicting accounts of such activities or circumstances. The Guidance recognises the difficulties which may arise, by stating that the authority should seek to obtain only such information as it is reasonable to seek, having regard to[158]:

---

[157] DEFRA Circular 01/2006, *Contaminated Land*, Annex 3 para.D.35.
[158] DEFRA Circular 01/2006, *Contaminated Land*, Annex 3 para.D.36.

(a) how the information might be obtained;

(b) the cost of obtaining the information for all parties involved; and

(c) the potential significance of the information for any decision.

The authority should however at least make reasonable endeavours to consult those who may be affected by any exclusion or apportionment.[159] **5.176**

The authority can only make judgments on the information available to it at a particular time, and should do so on the basis of the balance of probabilities.[160] The burden of providing additional information relevant to an exclusion or apportionment rests with the person wishing to benefit from it.[161] Where such information is provided, any other person who may be affected by decisions based on that information should be given a reasonable chance to comment on it before the decision is made.[162] **5.177**

One can readily see how all too easily an authority could become embroiled in a dispute between a number of potentially liable parties, each seeking to refute or comment on information provided by the others. There will have to come a point where the authority draws such exchanges to a conclusion and makes its determination. It will be for the authority to judge when that point has been reached. However, it is important that the authority seeks to establish a clear framework or set of ground rules for this process, so that those affected know where they stand. Otherwise, arguments of procedural unfairness may well arise. **5.178**

Agreement on liabilities

Where two or more parties are or may be responsible for remediation it is quite conceivable that they may reach agreement as to the basis on which they wish to share or to allocate the costs. Such an approach may be a sensible alternative to lengthy litigation and in those circumstances it would be a waste of time and effort for the authority to form its own view on exclusion or apportionment. There may be legitimate tax advantages arising from one company rather than another funding the work. The Guidance therefore provides that in such cases, where a copy of the agreement is provided to the authority, and none of the parties has informed the authority that it challenges the application of the agreement,[163] then the authority should generally make such determinations on exclusion or apportionment as are needed to give effect to the agreement.[164] This principle can naturally only apply as between the parties to the agreement, and the normal rules on exclusion or apportionment should still be applied as between those parties and any other appropriate persons who are not parties to the agreement.[165] **5.179**

---

[159] DEFRA Circular 01/2006, *Contaminated Land*, Annex 3 para.D.36.

[160] DEFRA Circular 01/2006, *Contaminated Land*, Annex 3 para.D.37.

[161] DEFRA Circular 01/2006, *Contaminated Land*, Annex 3 para.D.37.

[162] DEFRA Circular 01/2006, *Contaminated Land*, Annex 3 para.D.37.

[163] The challenge might relate to the existence, enforceability or terms of the agreement. The agreement will need to be sufficiently precise as to the intended outcome if the authority is to be able to give effect to it.

[164] DEFRA Circular 01/2006, *Contaminated Land*, Annex 3 para.D.38.

[165] DEFRA Circular 01/2006, *Contaminated Land*, Annex 3 para.D.38.

5.180   An important exception to this aspect of the Guidance is that such agreements should not be allowed to be used for the purpose of evading liabilities. So, where giving effect to such an agreement would increase the share of the costs by a person who would be able to claim the benefit of the hardship provisions of the Act and Guidance, the authority should disregard the agreement.[166] It is therefore not possible to agree to pass liability to a "man of straw". It should be noted, however, that this provision of the Guidance does not apply only to agreements entered into with that purpose in mind, but to any agreement which would in practice have that effect. The authority may, therefore, be obliged to disregard a bona fide agreement, where one party has later become insolvent or otherwise subject to hardship factors. Parties entering into such agreements should bear this in mind.

Exclusion of members of Class A groups

5.181 Part 5 of the Guidance lays down some six tests which can have the effect of excluding one or more persons from a Class A liability group (i.e. those who are responsible for causing or knowingly permitting). The tests are stated to be based on the notion of fairness[167] and are subject to specific "overriding guidance"[168]:

>   (a)   The exclusions are to be applied to each specific pollutant linkage separately. Accordingly, it is perfectly possible for a person to be excluded with respect to one pollutant linkage, but not another.

>   (b)   The tests are to be applied in the order in which they are set out. This is important since clearly different members of the group may be able to benefit from different tests—the order of application may therefore be critical. The Guidance does not explain the reasoning behind the order in which the tests are set out, but presumably this is again a reflection of what the Government regards as fair.

>   (c)   No test should be applied if it would result in the exclusion of all the remaining members of the group. In other words, there must always be at least one member of the group left to bear responsibility for each pollutant linkage.

Effect of applying tests

5.182 Paragraphs D.42 and D.43 draw an important distinction between the effect of applying different tests. For Tests 1, 4, 5 and 6, the effect is that the relevant person is completely excluded. It is as if he had never been a member of the liability group at all, and any further exclusion or

---

[166] DEFRA Circular 01/2006, *Contaminated Land*, Annex 3 para.D.39.
[167] DEFRA Circular 01/2006, *Contaminated Land*, Annex 3 para.D.40.
[168] DEFRA Circular 01/2006, *Contaminated Land*, Annex 3 para.D.41.

apportionment process proceeds accordingly. For Tests 2 and 3 (respectively, "payments made for remediation" and "sold with information") the position is different. The point about these Tests is that they are based on an inferred transactional transfer of responsibility for contamination. Accordingly the person who it is inferred accepted responsibility (either for payment or through buying with knowledge) should bear the responsibility of the notional transferee of responsibility as well as his own. Accordingly, the authority is required to assume that the person excluded under these Tests remains part of the liability group for the purposes of applying further Tests and apportioning liability. The notional or hypothetical share of the excluded person, determined on this basis, is then allocated to the recipient of the payment or the buyer, as the case may be. This is so irrespective of whether the recipient or buyer would be excluded in respect of their own acts by another exclusion test.

To give an example of how the Guidance might work in this regard, **5.183** assume there are three Class A appropriate persons, X, Y and Z. X sold to Y with a payment for remediation. X is excluded from liability, but is assumed still to be a member of the group for apportionment, which is determined to be in equal shares. The final result is that Y bears two-thirds and Z one-third. Taking the same parties, now assume X sold to Y with information, and Z introduced a later pathway or receptor (Test 6). X is excluded by Test 3, but is assumed to remain a member of the group for applying Test 6. If the application of Test 6 is to exclude both X and Y, then X has no ultimate share for Y to bear. But if for some reason that Test did not apply to X, but only to Y, then Y would assume X's residual share.

"Related companies"

The Guidance also considers exclusion tests by reference to the situation **5.184** where "related companies" are involved. Where the application of an exclusion test involves the relationship between, or relative positions of, "related companies", the authority should not apply a Test so as to exclude any of the related companies.[169] The objective of the Guidance in this respect is probably to prevent group companies evading their proper liabilities by structuring themselves to place liability on a subsidiary without resources.[170] Whilst this may be the intention, the same result will apply whether the relevant structure was created for such reasons, or for entirely legitimate fiscal, business or other reasons.

The question is whether at the "relevant date" the companies are or **5.185** were "related" for the purposes of the Guidance. The "relevant date" is the date on which the authority first served on anyone a notice under s.78B(3) identifying the land as contaminated land.[171] The critical date is, therefore, service of the notice identifying the land as contaminated. If the

---

[169] DEFRA Circular 01/2006, *Contaminated Land*, Annex 3 paras D.45–D.46.
[170] The terms "holding" and "subsidiary" companies have the same meaning as in s.736 of the Companies Act 1985: see para.D.46.
[171] DEFRA Circular 01/2006, *Contaminated Land*, Annex 3 para.D.46.

companies were "related" at that date, their position before and after is irrelevant. Once a notice has been received, it is therefore too late to try to create a non-group relationship.

5.186 The rule is predicated on both companies being members of the same liability group for the pollutant linkage in question. It does not allow (for example) liability to be attributed to a parent company if that parent is not a member of the liability group into which its subsidiary falls. The circumstances in which a parent company may be held liable is a different question, discussed elsewhere.[172]

5.187 It may be noted that the approach required by the Guidance is simply to preclude the operation of exclusion in relation to any related company by virtue of transactions or relative circumstances within the group. Earlier drafts of the Guidance applied a different approach of requiring the authority to treat the companies as a single person. This would have created a number of uncertainties and, it is submitted, has wisely not been pursued as an approach in the final Guidance.

5.188 Finally it may be noted that the "related company" provision in the Guidance refers to the exclusion tests, but not to the provisions on Agreements on Liabilities.[173] Hence it is possible for related companies to enter into Agreements on Liabilities under paras D.38 and D.39 of the Guidance.

Test 1—Excluded activities

5.189 This is a complex test, set out at paras D.47–D.50, the general purpose of which is to exclude those who have been identified as having caused or knowingly permitted contamination solely through having carried out certain activities, which are such as to carry limited responsibility, in the Government's view.[174] It is by no means certain that any of the listed activities would amount to "causing or knowingly permitting" in the first place and the Guidance does not imply that this would be the case.[175]

5.190 The test operates by listing a number of activities. Where the person in question is within the liability group solely by reason of those activities (not including any associated activity falling outside the descriptions), the person should be excluded from the Group. The list of activities is detailed, and subject to detailed qualifications in some cases. As well as the commentary below, reference should accordingly be made to the actual wording of the Test. The activities are:

(a) Providing (or withholding) financial assistance to another person (whether or not a member of the liability group) in one or more of the following ways:

(i) making a grant;

---

[172] See para.5.108ff.
[173] See para.5.179.
[174] DEFRA Circular 01/2006, *Contaminated Land*, Annex 3 para.D.47.
[175] DEFRA Circular 01/2006, *Contaminated Land*, Annex 3 para.D.47.

    (ii) making a loan or providing credit in any other form, including leasing arrangements and mortgages[176];

    (iii) guaranteeing the performance of a person's obligations;

    (iv) indemnifying a person against loss, liability or damage;

    (v) investing in a company by acquiring share or loan capital, but without acquiring control[177]; or

    (vi) providing any other financial benefit, including the remission in whole or in part of any financial liability or obligation.

(b) Underwriting an insurance policy under which another person was insured in respect of matters by reason of which that person has been held to have caused or knowingly permitted contamination.[178] It is irrelevant whether or not that person can now be found.

(c) Carrying out any action for the purpose of deciding whether to provide such financial assistance or underwrite such an insurance policy.[179]

(d) Consigning the substance to another person as waste under a contract[180] whereby he knowingly took over responsibility for its proper disposal or other management on a site not under control of the person seeking exclusion. The thinking behind this category appears to be to exclude from liability waste producers who contracted for others to dispose of or otherwise manage their wastes.[181] It would appear to be irrelevant whether the waste producer in so doing complied with their statutory responsibilities under the "duty of care" provisions of s.34 of the Environmental Protection Act 1990. It is irrelevant whether or not the person to whom the waste was consigned can now be found.

(e) Creating at any time a tenancy over the land in question in favour of another person who subsequently caused or knowingly permitted contamination (whether or not they can now be found). This category protects a landlord who finds their tenant has contami-

---

[176] In respect of remediation of St Leonard's Court, St Albans, built on the site of a former chemical works, the Agency determined that the lender to the development, Woolwich Homes Ltd, was not an appropriate person despite the fact that under the off-balance sheet financing arrangements in the 1980s, Woolwich took ownership of the site during development. The Agency accepted that this was simply a form of lending and that the reference to "providing credit in any form" was broad enough to cover the arrangements. A notice was served on the original polluter and on the developer.

[177] "Control" is by reference to the test of s.736 of the Companies Act 1985 as to whether a holding company has control over a subsidiary.

[178] Underwriting a policy for this purpose includes imposing any conditions on the insured, for example relating to the manner in which he carries out the insured activity.

[179] The exclusion will not however include any intrusive investigation in respect of the land for the purposes of indemnity, where the investigation itself is a cause of the existence, nature or continuance of the pollutant linkage and the person who applied for the financial assistance or insurance is not a member of the liability group.

[180] The contract need not be in writing. It is quite conceivable that, in the past and prior to modern legislation, waste may have been collected for disposal without any written contract.

[181] See the discussion at para.5.23.

nated the land, provided their presence in the group of category A persons is due simply to their identity as landlord. The test may not assist where they are implicated in the contamination in other ways than having granted the lease (e.g. by failing to take steps within their power to prevent contamination).

(f) As owner, granting a licence to occupy to another person who has subsequently caused or knowingly permitted contamination (whether or not they can now be found). Importantly, this does not include a case where the person granting the licence operated the land as a site for waste disposal or storage at the time of the grant of the licence. The wording is slightly curious. The exclusion does not apply if the licensor was already operating the site for waste disposal prior to the licence, but would apply if the licence related, as it were, to a greenfield site to be used for waste disposal.

(g) Issuing any statutory permission, licence or consent required for any action or omission by which some other person causes or knowingly permits contamination, whether or not that person can now be found. The Test does not apply to statutory undertakers who grant permission to contractors to carry out work.

(h) Taking, or not taking, any statutory enforcement action with respect to the land, or against some person who has caused or knowingly permitted contamination, whether or not that person can now be found. This potentially avoids arguments either that some enforcement authority such as the Environment Agency has failed to take steps to prevent land becoming contaminated (for example, by failing to exercise its waste regulation functions), or that a planning authority has failed to enforce against some unlawful contaminative use and as such in either case has knowingly permitted contamination (provided, as always, that there are others in the liability group so that the test can be applied).

(i) Providing legal, financial engineering scientific or technical advice[182] to a client:

  (i) in relation to an action or omission by reason of which the client causes or knowingly permits the presence of the pollutant; or

  (ii) for the purpose of assessing the condition of the land; or

  (iii) for the purpose of establishing what might be done to the land by way of remediation.[183]

(j) Carrying out any intrusive investigation in respect of the land as a person providing advice or providing services within (i) above except where:

---

[182] This includes other design, contract management or works management services.

[183] The purpose is presumably to ensure that knowledge gained by a consultant or other advisor is not treated as constituting "knowingly permitting". But in any event, even with such knowledge, it is difficult to see how such an advisor would have the power autonomously to deal with the contamination so as to be said to permit its continued presence.

(i) the investigation is itself a cause of the existence, nature or continuance of the pollutant linkage; and

(ii) the client is not himself a member of the liability group.[184]

(k) Performing any contract (whether of employment or for the provision of goods or services) where the contract is made with another member of the liability group, whether the service is provided on a direct subcontracting basis. The exclusion does not apply if the activity falls within another part of Test 1, or if the act or omission in question was not in accordance with the terms of the contract, or in a situation where the contractual service was provided to a company by a director or similar officer, and the actions or omissions resulting in the company being liable were carried out with the consent or connivance of the officer, or were attributable to any neglect on his part.[185] This Test can operate at different levels. For example, a company which supplies vehicles or equipment to another company, which then uses them to commit acts causing contamination, would be excluded from any liability they might thereby have. The same would apply to a company which supplies fuel or chemicals which its customer spills, or which installs tanks or pipework from which contaminants escape. The contractor's acts must however be in accordance with the contract—so, for example, a supplier of defective pipework which causes a contaminating release would not be excluded. Employees who act in accordance with their conditions of employment will also be able to rely on this Test; but not senior corporate officers whose consent, connivance or neglect is involved. The wording of the Test on this latter point is a somewhat strange mix of the principles of criminal liability for senior managers contained in provisions such as s.157 of the 1990 Act; the essential idea is that senior officers should not escape personal liability where they were personally implicated. So, for example, a director of a company who was aware, or ought to have been aware, that the company was allowing seepage of contaminants from its equipment to occur, yet did nothing, could not rely on the fact that he was acting under a service contract with the company to obtain exclusion from liability as a causer or knowing permitter.

As will be appreciated, the application of Test 1 may vary in complexity **5.191** in that some of the categories are quite straightforward (and are clearly intended to allay concerns of commercial sectors such as banks, insurers

---

[184] The exception here relates to the situation where in carrying out intrusive investigation, the consultant might be said to have caused a pollutant linkage. The consultant will not be excluded from liability if the investigation is itself the cause of the problem and the client cannot be held liable. Where the client is liable he may of course have a cause of action against the consultant.

[185] "Consent" implies that a director or officer is aware of an activity and agrees to it, "connivance" that there is such awareness but acquiescence, or tacit (rather than active) encouragement, and "neglect" implies a failure to perform a duty which the person knows, or ought to have known, of (see *Huckerby v Elliott* [1970] 1 All E.R. 189; and *Wotherspoon v H.M.Advocate* 1978 J.C. 74).

and consultants) whereas others are much more complex and will involve detailed consideration of the relevant circumstances. The following paragraph contains some further thoughts on the application of Test 1.

Test 1: Further remarks

5.192 Before passing on to Test 2, it is worth highlighting the somewhat uneasy relationship between the excluded activities and the concept of "causing or knowingly permitting". If the person did not cause or knowingly permit they will not be in category A at all, and the exclusion test will be irrelevant. The excluded activities focus for the most part on the status of the person concerned: a lender should not be liable just because they provided credit, an insurer because they wrote a policy, a landlord because they granted a lease, a planning authority just because they gave permission, etc. But this leaves open the possibility of liability stemming from later activities associated with the main activity.

5.193 Indeed, the Guidance is explicit on this point; para.D.48 removes from the exclusion "any associated activity outside these descriptions". So a landlord, who having granted a lease, then acts as a landlord in such a way as to knowingly permit contamination may not be able to rely on the exclusion test. Indeed, if all he had done was to grant a lease, it is difficult to see how he could be within Group A at all. Test 1, therefore, for all its length and complexity, may remain in reality something of a "belt and braces" exercise.

Test 2—Payments made for remediation

5.194 The purpose behind this Test (paras D.51—D.56) is to exclude from liability those who have already effectively met their clean-up responsibilities by having made a payment, sufficient to provide for remediation, to some other member of the liability group.[186] For past transactions this avoids the unjust enrichment which might otherwise occur, and for future transactions it offers a way of managing risk.

5.195 The Guidance requires the authority to consider whether all of the following circumstances exist:

(a) one member of the Group has made a payment to another member for the purpose of carrying out particular remediation on the land in question. In this respect, only certain types of payments are to be considered (see below);

(b) the payment would have been sufficient at the date when it was made to pay for the remediation;

(c) had that remediation been carried out effectively, the land would not now be regarded as "contaminated land"; and

(d) the remediation in question was not carried out or was not carried out effectively.

---

[186] DEFRA Circular 01/2006, *Contaminated Land*, Annex 3 para.D.51.

It will be appreciated that the key to this test is payment made to cover **5.196** a particular remediation action: an assessment then has to be made as to whether that action would have been sufficient to deal with the problem if it had been carried out effectively. This may prove to be a difficult technical question. The test precludes payments made simply to reflect the fact that the land is or may be contaminated, with no particular plan of remediation in mind.

Only three types of payment[187] may be taken into account for the **5.197** purpose of this test. These are[188]:

    (a) payments made in response to a claim for the cost of particular remediation, whether voluntarily or to meet a contractual obligation;

    (b) payments made in the course of civil proceedings, arbitration, mediation or other dispute resolution procedures, whether paid as part of an out of court settlement, or under the terms of a court order; or

    (c) payments as part of a contract[189] for the transfer of ownership of the land, which is either specifically provided for in the contract to meet the relevant cost or which consists of a reduction in purchase price explicitly stated to be for that purpose.

One important qualification is that the benefit of the test will be lost **5.198** where the person making the payment retained any subsequent control over the condition of the land in question.[190] Holding interests, such as easements, restrictive covenants, reversions expectant on long leases, similar statutory agreements (such as s.106 agreements) or statutory undertakers' rights to install equipment, is not "control" for this purpose. Nor is "holding contractual rights to ensure the proper carrying out of the remediation for which the payment was made". The application of this principle may be a trap for those who make such payments yet wish to assure themselves that the money has been properly spent. Requiring proof of remediation activity ought not to be a problem, nor should imposing a contractual obligation to carry out the works; but when the person making the payment reserves rights of direct supervision or intervention over the remediation activity, that may be another matter.

Another possible trap lies within the test for innocent parties whose land **5.199** is contaminated by migration or escape of substances from elsewhere. If the original polluter agrees to fund clean-up measures which are properly carried out but then turn out to be ineffective, the application of the test effectively places the risk in those circumstances on the person receiving the payment. This should be borne in mind by that person's professional advisors.

The end result of applying Test 2 is that where the conditions are met, **5.200** the authority will exclude the person who made the payment in respect of the remediation action in question. Subsequent tests on exclusion and

---

[187] "Payments" includes consideration of any form: see para.D.54.
[188] DEFRA Circular 01/2006, *Contaminated Land*, Annex 3 para.D.53
[189] This includes "a group of interlinked contracts".
[190] DEFRA Circular 01/2006, *Contaminated Land*, Annex 3 para.D.55.

apportionment should however be made as if the exclusion had not occurred and the person in receipt of the payment ultimately bears that excluded person's share.[191]

Test 3—"Sold with information"

5.201   The purpose of this important test (paras D.57–D.61) is to exclude from liability those who sell or grant long leases of land, and who in doing so ensure that the purchaser or tenant had sufficient information as to the presence of the pollutant and thus (inferentially) the opportunity so take that into account in agreeing the price. The test will only operate at all where both vendor and purchaser are within Group A, and the test does not presuppose that the purchaser will be a "knowing permitter" simply by having such information: this will require consideration of all the circumstances.

5.202   The authority is required to consider whether all the following circumstances exist[192]:

(a) one of the members of the liability group has sold the land to a person who is another member of the group;

(b) the sale took place at arm's length, (that is, on terms which could be expected in a sale on the open market between a willing seller and a willing purchaser);

(c) before the sale became binding, the purchaser had information[193] that would reasonably allow that particular person[194] to be aware of the presence of the relevant pollutant "and the broad measure of that presence"[195]; and the seller has done nothing material to misrepresent the implications of that presence to the purchaser[196]; and

(d) after the date of the sale the seller retained no interest in the land or any rights to use or occupy the land.[197]

5.203   The test applies in the equivalent circumstances in relation to the grant or assignment of a long lease as well as a sale of the freehold.[198] For these purposes, a long lease is a lease or sublease granted for a period of more than 21 years under which the lessee satisfies the definition of "owner" in s.78A.[199]

---

[191] See paras 5.182 and 5.183.

[192] DEFRA Circular 01/2006, *Contaminated Land*, Annex 3 para.D.58.

[193] Such information may be generated by the purchaser's own investigations, or by the provision of reports or data by the seller.

[194] The test is thus a subjective one, depending on the buyer's characteristics.

[195] The meaning of this phrase is not totally clear, but presumably it refers to the physical extent of contamination.

[196] In this respect the purchaser will presumably be taken to know the legal position and the consequent risks of liability.

[197] Easements, rights of statutory undertakers, reversions expectant on long leases and restrictive covenants are disregarded for this purpose.

[198] DEFRA Circular 01/2006, *Contaminated Land*, Annex 3 para.D.59(a).

[199] See para.5.76.

Where the Test applies the seller or lessor is to be excluded. As with **5.204**
Test 2 however, they are treated as remaining liable for the purposes of
future exclusion and apportionment, the buyer then becomes responsible
for their share.[200]

Test 3: in practice and commercial transactions

Test 3 seems likely to be one of the most difficult to operate in practice, **5.205**
because of the uncertainty inherent in deciding whether sufficient information was given to activate it—particularly where the transaction may have
taken place some years ago. As indicated above, the question is whether
"the buyer had information that would reasonably allow that particular
buyer to be aware of the presence on the land of the pollutant identified in
the significant pollutant linkage in question, and the broad measure of that
presence". Thus it would appear that reports which simply give a gener-
alised indication of potential contamination (for example, a desk survey
relating to past uses) will not of themselves suffice, in that they will not
provide details of the actual substances involved.

Another possibility is that the buyers obtain the information for them- **5.206**
selves, rather than having it provided by the seller. In this context it has
become more common for buyers in commercial transactions to carry out
their own intrusive investigations. The Guidance recognises this by formulating a rule (at para.D.59(d)) that in transactions since January 1, 1990
where the buyer is (here it presumably means to say "was") a "large
commercial organisation" or public body, permission from the seller to
carry out investigations on the condition of the land should "normally" be
taken as a sufficient indication that the buyer had the requisite information to activate the Test. This is problematic Guidance in certain respects.
What constitutes a "large commercial organisation" is not defined, and will
have to be decided by the authority or the appellate tribunal. Also, what
may constitute permission to carry out investigations "of the condition of
the land" is far from clear. The standard reply to preliminary enquiries,
"the purchaser should rely on his own investigations" would not of itself
seem to amount to such permission, though the point is arguable. Would
access to carry out a normal structural survey constitute permission to
investigate the condition of the land for this purpose? Such permission
would clearly not extend to sinking boreholes or taking soil or groundwater
samples. Unless there is specific evidence of an offer of access for this
purpose being made, the matter may effectively come down to the seller
saying, "If you had asked me for access for investigations, I would have
given it". This, however, is not the same as giving permission. If permission
was given, but the investigations were inadequate to discover the contamination, the seller will be excluded, and the buyer will need to consider
action against his consultants.

Finally, para.D.59(c) states that where there is a group of transactions or **5.207**
wider agreement (such as the sale of a business) which includes a sale of
land, the sale should be taken to have been at arm's length where the
person relying on the test can show the net effect of the overall deal was a

---

[200] See paras 5.182 and 5.183 above.

sale at arm's length. The classic example is probably the situation where assets are transferred within a group of companies, to place them in a corporate vehicle (often "Newco") which is then sold. The transfer to Newco may not, seen in isolation, be at arm's length; but the transaction as a whole is. Therefore, if the other relevant criteria of Test 3 are met, the transfer of land to Newco may have the effect of excluding from liability the company within the seller's group which transferred it.[201] It does not follow from this that the purchaser of the shares in Newco will become liable, since at that point there is no sale of land.

Test 4—"Changes to substances"

5.208 The purpose of this test (paras D.62–D.64) is to protect by exclusion those who find themselves within a liability group having caused or knowingly permitted the presence of a substance which in itself would not have resulted in a pollutant linkage, but has only done so because of the later actions of others in adding another substance which has interacted with the earlier substance; or otherwise causing a change to that substance.[202]

5.209 In applying the Test, the authority must consider whether all these circumstances set out at para.D.63 exist:

(a) the substance in question is only present, or is only a significant pollutant, because of a chemical, biological or other change (called "the intervening change") involving both a substance previously present which would not have given rise to a pollutant linkage in itself ("the earlier substance") and a "later substance" (which might or might not have given rise to a pollutant linkage of itself);

(b) the intervening change would not have occurred in the absence of the later substance;

(c) a person (A) is a Class A member of the liability group in relation to the earlier substance, but not the later;

(d) one or more persons are Class A members of the liability group in relation to the second substance;

(e) before the date when the later substances were introduced, A either:

(i) could not reasonably have foreseen their introduction; or
(ii) could not reasonably have foreseen the intervening change; or
(iii took what were at the time reasonabie precautions to prevent these consequences; and

---

[201] There is a potential trap, however, in para.D.45 if the transferee and Newco are related companies, in which case the exclusion test would not apply. There is potentially a similar issue, where a company is to be sold pre-divests itself of a contaminated site by transferring it to another company; the first company is then sold as a "clean company". However, the two companies are related, the transferee will not be able to rely on the exclusion tests, so may not in fact be "clean".
[202] DEFRA Circular 01/2006, *Contaminated Land*, Annex 3 para.D.62.

(f) after that date, A did not cause or knowingly permit any further earlier substances to be introduced, or do anything to contribute to the conditions that brought about the intervening change, or fail to do something that he could reasonably be expected to do to prevent the intervening change happening.

If conditions (a)–(f) are satisfied, person A is excluded. The require- **5.210** ments at (f), effectively to mitigate and minimise the harm after the intervening change has commenced, could be onerous—at least where person A retains control of the land and has the power to act.

Test 5—"Escaped substances"

Escapes and migration of contaminants from one piece of land to another **5.211** is a complex issue in its own right. The purpose of Test 5 (paras D.65–D.67) is to exclude those who would otherwise be liable for contamination caused by the escape of substances from other land, where it can be shown that another Class A person was responsible for their escape.[203]

Given the statutory rules on escapes, it is conceivable that a liability **5.212** group might comprise the original polluter, those onto whose land the contamination has escaped, and the person who caused the escape of the pollutant. In applying this test, the authority is required to consider whether all the following circumstances exist:

(a) a significant pollutant is present on the land wholly or partly as a result of its escape from other land;

(b) a member of the liability group (person A) caused or knowingly permitted the pollutant to be present in the land from which it escaped and is liable only for that reason; and

(c) one or more other members of the group caused or knowingly permitted the pollutant to escape from that land and the escape would not have occurred but for their acts or omissions.

In these circumstances, person A is excluded. Unlike Test 4, there is no **5.213** qualification as to the foreseeability of the escape or as to the precautions taken by B to prevent it. The Test might be applicable where trespassers or vandals cause the escape of substances from A's land. Provided the vandals can be found (and as such are members of the liability group) it seems that A could rely on the Test. In this respect it is perhaps curious that A would not need to show that his precautions to prevent vandalism had been reasonable.

Test 6—Introduction of pathways or receptors

The purpose of this Test (paras D.68–D.72) is to exclude from liability **5.214** those who would otherwise be liable solely because of the subsequent introduction by others of the relevant pathways or receptors.[204]

---

[203] DEFRA Circular 01/2006, *Contaminated Land*, Annex 3 para.D.65.
[204] DEFRA Circular 01/2006, *Contaminated Land*, Annex 3 para.D.68.

5.215   The Test uses the terms "relevant action" and "relevant omission". A relevant action is the carrying out at any time of building, engineering, mining or other operations in, on, over or under the land in question, or the making of any material change in use for which a specific application for planning permission was required at the time the change was made (as opposed to permission granted by a general development order, simplified planning zone, enterprise zone or the like).[205] A relevant omission is failing to take a step in the course of carrying out a relevant action which would have ensured that the pollutant linkage did not come into being; or unreasonably failing to maintain or operate a system installed for the purpose of reducing or managing a risk associated with the contamination (for example, gas venting systems).[206]

5.216   The authority must consider whether all the following circumstances exist:

(a) one or more members of the liability group have carried out a relevant action or made a relevant omission ("the later actions") either as part of a series of actions or omissions which resulted in them being Class A persons in relation to the pollutant linkage, or in addition to that series of actions or omissions;

(b) the effect of the later actions was to introduce the pathway or the receptor forming part of the pollutant linkage;

(c) if those later actions had not occurred, there would not have been a significant pollutant linkage; and

(d) person A is a member of the liability group solely by reason of other earlier actions or omissions which were completed before the later actions were carried out.

5.217   In these circumstances, any person meeting the description of person A is excluded from liability. In legal terms, it is as if the later action which introduced the pathway or receptor broke the chain of causation from the original polluter. However, the Test has its limitations: it can only apply where the person carrying out the later action is himself a Class A person; that is, he caused or knowingly permitted the contamination to be present. Introducing a pathway or receptor in itself does not make someone a causer or knowing permitter of the presence of the contamination. One consequence of this is that the Test can only apply in respect to developments on the contaminated land itself—it does not apply where the relevant acts or omissions take place on other land, even if their effect is to introduce a receptor.[207] This is because the person carrying out development on neighbouring land cannot be said to be knowingly permitting the presence of contamination on the land which presents the threat—unless that is, he also owns the contaminated land (an issue which the Guidance does not address).

---

[205] DEFRA Circular 01/2006, *Contaminated Land*, Annex 3 para.D.70(a).
[206] DEFRA Circular 01/2006, *Contaminated Land*, Annex 3 para.D.70(b).
[207] DEFRA Circular 01/2006, *Contaminated Land*, Annex 3 para.D.71.

It is not immediately apparent why the introduction of a pathway or **5.218** receptor under this test is limited by the definition of "relevant action" effectively to development which would require planning permission. The making of a material change of use does not constitute a relevant action where specific planning permission is not required because of an enterprise zone or simplified planning zone scheme. This could potentially exclude much development carried out during the 1980s and 1990s in the traditional heavy industrial areas. However, such development will in practice have involved building operations, and so will be caught by the other limb of "relevant action", covering all operational development. The concept of "relevant omission" is, by its nature, more likely to give rise to a pollution pathway than a receptor.

Exclusion of members of Class B liability group

Compared with the rules for exclusion from Class A, set out in Pt 7 of the **5.219** Guidance,[208] those from Class B are simple. This is because the members of Class B will simply be the owner and occupier of the land in question.

The purpose of the single test for Class B is to exclude from liability **5.220** those who do not have a capital interest in the land.[209] There are various precedents for what is perceived to be the justice of allocating responsibility to the person whose interest carries with it the actual or potential right to receive the rack rent.[210]

Where Class B comprises two or more people, the authority should **5.221** exclude any of those persons who[211]:

(a) occupies the land under a licence or other agreement of a kind which has no marketable value or which he cannot legally assign or transfer to another person[212]; or

(b) is liable to pay a rent equivalent to the rack rent and who holds no beneficial interest in the land other than any tenancy to which such rack rent relates.[213]

The effect is therefore in general to channel liability from those with **5.222** only personal interests or full market-rent leaseholds to the "owner", who may be either the freeholder or the holder of a long lease. The position of a tenant who is, for whatever reason, paying a rent less than the full market rent is problematic in that he may well be unable to rely on the exclusion test. What is the market rent due, however, needs to be considered in the context of all the terms of the lease, as a matter of valuation.

---

[208] DEFRA Circular 01/2006, *Contaminated Land*, Annex 3 paras D.87—D.90.

[209] DEFRA Circular 01/2006, *Contaminated Land*, Annex 3 para.D.87.

[210] See *Pollway Nominees Ltd v Croydon LBC* [1986] 2 All E.R. 849, HL, at 853.

[211] DEFRA Circular 01/2006, *Contaminated Land*, Annex 3 para.D.89.

[212] For these purposes, the fact that a licence may not actually attract a buyer in the market, or its actual marketable value, are irrelevant.

[213] Thus a tenant with an option to purchase the freehold might not be able to rely on this exclusion. Where the rent is subject to periodic review, it should be considered to be the rack rent if, at the latest review, it was set at the current full market rent.

PART 7: APPORTIONMENT OF LIABILITY

The general approach to apportionment

5.223 As with exclusion, discussed in the previous chapter, it is important to keep in mind the statutory basis for apportionment before attempting to apply the Guidance. The starting point, again, is to establish who, under the primary legislation, the appropriate persons are with regard to each remediation action. The general principle of ss.78E and 78F is one of joint and several liability, modified by the principle of referability in relation to Group A appropriate persons,[214] and by the requirement of apportionment.[215] Having established who are the appropriate persons for each liability group and how, if necessary, responsibility is to be attributed between the groups as a whole, it should then be considered whether any of them should be treated under s.78F(6) as not being appropriate. Only then, if there are two or more left, will the principles of apportionment under s.78F(7) come into play.[216]

5.224 In practical terms, the authority may well begin by looking at the circumstances of the case in a "common sense" way, and applying the Guidance in the context of that initial evaluation. The rules are really no more than a sophisticated attempt to formulate principles of fairness.

Different types of apportionment

5.225 As the Guidance points out, apportionment operates at two levels. The first is apportionment between members of the liability group for the pollutant linkage in question. The Guidance considers this issue at Pts 6 and 8 of Ch.D, dealing with Class A and Class B groups separately. However, there is also the possibility that there may be more than one significant pollutant linkage, and therefore more than one liability group for a given area of land. In that case, it may be necessary for the costs of some remediation actions to be allocated between the various liability groups, and Ch.D Pt 9 deals with this issue, which it terms "attribution".

Class A apportionment: general principles

5.226 Given that the history and circumstances of any piece of contaminated land may vary widely, as may the nature of the responsibility of different persons, the Guidance does not attempt to prescribe detailed rules for apportionment which would be "fair" in every case.[217]

5.227 Instead, the authority is required to follow the general principle that liability should be apportioned to reflect the relative responsibility of each member of the Class A group for creating or continuing the relevant

---

[214] 1990 Act s.78F(3).
[215] 1990 Act ss.78E(3) and 78F(7).
[216] See the process at Pt 3 of Ch.D of the Guidance.
[217] DEFRA Circular 01/2006, *Contaminated Land*, Annex 3 para.D.74.

risk.[218] This general principle is subject however to guidance on a number of "specific approaches", discussed below.

If appropriate information is not available and cannot reasonably be **5.228** obtained to allow an apportionment based on individual responsibility to be made, then liability should be apportioned in equal shares, subject to a special rule for companies and their officers which is explained in the next paragraph.[219]

Companies and officers

Where a Class A liability group, after the application of all relevant **5.229** exclusion tests, includes a company and one or more of its officers,[220] then the authority should by para.D.85:

(a) treat the company and its officers as a single unit for the purpose of applying the general principles of relative responsibility and apportionment in equal shares; and

(b) having thus determined the aggregate share of responsibility for the company and its officers together, that share should then be apportioned between them on a basis which takes into account the degree of personal responsibility of those directors and the relative levels of resources which may be available to them and the company to meet the liability.

Effectively, (b) means that hardship considerations for individual dir- **5.230** ectors will apply at this stage (rather than at enforcement) so potentially increasing the share of liability of the company; this constitutes a specific exception to the normal principle of not targeting the "deep pocket". Of course, the principle could work the other way in the case of the wealthy director of an impecunious company.

When considering the relative responsibility of a company and its **5.231** officers, as against that of the other members of the group, the company and the officers, under the principle at (a), should be treated as a single unit. In practice, this will mean that knowledge and fault amongst a number of directors can be aggregated with that of the company. Also it will avoid the risk of the company being disadvantaged by any element of "double-counting" of responsibility in the apportionment exercise.

Class A groups—specific approaches for apportionment

In applying the general principle of relative responsibility, the authority **5.232** should apply a number of specific approaches where these are relevant. Effectively, they are attempts to refine the general principles of fairness and relative responsibility.

---

[218] DEFRA Circular 01/2006, *Contaminated Land*, Annex 3 para.D.75.
[219] DEFRA Circular 01/2006, *Contaminated Land*, Annex 3 para.D.76.
[220] "Relevant officers", by DEFRA Circular, Annex 3 para.D.86, means any director, manager, secretary or similar officer, or any other person purporting to act in any such capacity.

Partial applicability of an exclusion test

5.233 If, for any member of the liability Group the circumstances set out in one or more of the exclusion tests applies to some extent, but not sufficiently to allow the test to apply, the authority should assess the person's degree of responsibility as being reduced to the extent which is appropriate in the light of all the circumstances, and the purpose of the test in question. The example is given where a payment made for remediation was "sufficient to pay for only half of the necessary remediation".[221] In that case translating the shortfall into numerical terms is not difficult, but in other cases it may be less easy to quantify the extent to which the test has not been met; for example, in relation to the "sold with information" test or the test on the introduction of pathways and receptors. In such cases, a broad, equitable approach will be needed, involving judgments of reasonableness.

Original contamination versus continued presence

5.234 Situations may well arise where a Class A liability group comprises a person (X) who caused or knowingly permitted the initial entry of a contaminating substance onto land, and one or more others (Y) who knowingly permitted its continued presence. Paragraph D.78 requires the authority, when assessing their relative responsibility, to consider the extent to which Y "had the means and a reasonable opportunity to deal with the presence of the pollutant in question or to reduce the seriousness of the implications of that presence". The assessment should then be on the following basis:

(a) if Y had the necessary means and opportunity, he should bear the same responsibility as X;

(b) if Y did not have the necessary means and opportunity, his responsibility relative to that of X should be "substantially reduced"; and

(c) if Y had some, but insufficient, means or opportunity, his relative responsibility should be reduced "to an appropriate extent".

5.235 As originally drafted, this guidance contained the added complication of the foreseeability of harm on the part of Y. This aspect has been dropped, but even without it the Guidance may still pose problems for enforcing authorities. It is not clear what is meant by the phrase "means and opportunity", but this could in principle embrace considerations such as the length of time that Y has had to deal with the problem since becoming aware of it; the technical feasibility of dealing with the problem; and the financial and other resources at Y's disposal. The concept of "knowingly permitting" itself inherently requires some opportunity or ability to deal with the problem. The responsibility of Y should, it appears, never be

---

[221] DEFRA Circular 01/2006, *Contaminated Land*, Annex 3 para.D.77.

greater than that of X, but it can be reduced to an appropriate extent where there was less than full opportunity, and "substantially" where there was no opportunity. In this last case, the Guidance appears to contemplate something less than complete exoneration, or reduction to nil; presumably if there really was no opportunity at all to remove or deal with the contamination, Y would not be a knowing permitter within the liability group in the first place.

Original polluters

The specific Guidance also deals with the situation where within the **5.236** liability group are a number of persons who all caused or knowingly permitted the entry of the pollutant into the land. This could be because they operated similar processes on the land at different times, or because they operated processes on different sites, each of which contributed to the contamination of soil or, perhaps more likely, groundwater.

The starting point, set out at para.D.80, is to consider whether the **5.237** nature of the remediation action required points clearly to different members being responsible for particular circumstances. The example given in the Guidance is where different persons were in control of different areas of land, with no interrelationship between those areas. In that case, the authority should regard the persons in control of the different areas as being "separately responsible for the events which make necessary the remediation actions or part of actions referable to those areas of land". The wording of the Guidance is rather opaque on this issue and, in particular, it is not clear why in such circumstances it would not be possible to identify distinct pollutant linkages in relation to the different areas requiring remediation.

If the circumstances in para.D.80 do not apply, but the quantity of the **5.238** pollutant is a major influence on the cost of remediation, then by para.D.81 the authority should regard the relative amounts of the pollutant involved as an appropriate basis for apportionment. An example might be the amount of oil or solvent in groundwater, which determines the length of time that pumping and treatment has to occur. The first step is to consider whether there is direct evidence of the relevant quantities involved—unless there are clear records of spillages or losses in known quantities this seems unlikely. "Surrogate measures" will then have to be used, which may include the relative periods during which broadly equivalent operations were carried out, the relative scale of such operations (which may be indicated by the quantities of a product manufactured), the relative areas of land on which operations were carried out and combinations of these factors.[222] The area of land may be a very rough factor, since the intensity of operations may vary widely.

If none of the above circumstances apply, then the authority should by **5.239** para.D.83 consider the nature of the activities involved. If they are "broadly equivalent", then responsibility should be apportioned on the basis of the relative periods of time that the different persons were in

---

[222] DEFRA Circular 01/2006, *Contaminated Land*, Annex 3 para.D.82.

control. This should be adjusted where the activities were not broadly equivalent, for example where they were on a different scale.

Knowing permitters

5.240 Paragraph D.84 deals with apportionment between persons who have knowingly permitted the continued presence of a contaminant over a period of time. Here the apportionment should be in proportion to the length of time each controlled the land, the area that they controlled, the extent to which each had the means and a reasonable opportunity to deal with the problem and combinations of these factors.

5.241 Applying these principles seems unlikely to be a straightforward or simple exercise, and will involve the assimilation of potentially complex and uncertain facts coupled with the exercise of judgment. In reality, once the authority leaves the relative certainty of apportionment in equal shares, the Guidance cannot provide the answer: it can simply list the factors to be taken into account. Except in relation to the issue of "means and opportunity" for knowing permitters to deal with continuing pollution, the Guidance does not refer to what might be termed "behavioural factors". Such factors might include whether the pollution was foreseeable, the precautions actually taken by the appropriate person, contemporary standards and best practice at the relevant time, and so on. These matters might be thought to be relevant to the general test of "relative responsibility". However, their absence from the Guidance on specific issues might be taken to preclude their consideration: against this, it could be said that the overriding test is that of "relative responsibility" at para.D.75, and that these are material considerations in that determination.

Class A apportionment: examples

5.242 It may be helpful to give a few examples of how the principles of apportionment within a Class A liability group may apply; though given the complexity of the issues, they are offered with some trepidation. Of necessity the examples are simpler and clearer than the likely cases which will arise in practice. However, they do illustrate that the exercise may well prove contentious. They assume that Pt IIA is fully applicable and is not ousted by waste, PPC or some other regime.

Example 1

5.243 S, a company which has operated on the same site for 60 years, sold in 1989 a small portion of its site to B, a management buy-out company. B's site is now found to be contaminated both by organic chemicals released before its acquisition, but also by such chemicals spilled since 1989. When selling the site to B, a certain amount of information on contamination was provided by S, but this gave only a partial picture, insufficient to trigger the "sold with information" test.

The authority will have to consider the following issues as between S and B:

1. Assuming the organic substances are of the same nature and the amount of those substances is a determinative factor of the cost of remediation, can the relative contributions of S and B be quantified? Their respective periods of occupation are known, but the scale of operations may have been very different, as may the respective precautionary measures taken, so that time in itself may not necessarily be helpful as a guide.

2. As well as bearing responsibility for its own contamination, does B bear any responsibility for the contamination already present when it acquired the land, having knowingly permitted its continued presence? If B had the means and opportunity to prevent or reduce the risks then the Guidance suggests that B may bear equal responsibility with S.

3. To what extent should the responsibility which S would otherwise bear be reduced to reflect the fact that some information was provided?

Example 2

On the facts of Example 1, now assume that it is the whole of S's present **5.244** and former site (including what is now B's land) which requires comprehensive remediation for a single pollutant linkage:

1. An initial issue is whether it is possible to draw a clear distinction in terms of allocating responsibility between the land of S and that of B and to distinguish clearly between the costs attributable to each area.

2. If so, then S would be wholly responsible for the costs relating to the S land, and the costs relating to the B land would be apportioned as in Example 1 above.

3. Otherwise, if the S and B land have to be treated as a whole, can the respective contributions of the polluting organic solvents by S and B be quantified or assessed? Such assessment may be by a combination of the areas controlled and length of control. However, that in itself would not attribute any responsibility to B as a knowing permitter, only as a causer.

4. An alternative approach would be to look at the respective areas as between the S land and the B land, to apportion the appropriate proportion of the total reflecting the area of the S land to S, then to apportion separately the portion attributable to the B land in accordance with the principles at Example 1 above.

Example 3

S, an industrial company, occupied the same site for 30 years, having **5.245** acquired it from P (another industrial company) which had occupied it for 50 years before that. The land is now divided into light industrial units, which in 1985 were sold by S to X and Y. X still occupies its unit, whereas Y sold its unit to Z in 1993. The sale to Z was not "with information". The whole area is contaminated by heavy metals and requires clean-up:

1. Assuming there is a single pollutant linkage which must be dealt with together, there are five Class A parties: P (causer), S (causer and knowing permitter), X (knowing permitter), Y (knowing permitter) and Z (knowing permitter).

2. Assuming X, Y and Z all had knowledge of the harm in question and the means and opportunity to do something about it, the Guidance might suggest that they should all bear equal responsibility with the original causers, P and S. But does that mean each of the five bears 20 per cent, or that P and S together bear 50 per cent and X, Y and Z together bear 50 per cent?

3. Whichever is the case, if any of X, Y or Z did not have a reasonable opportunity to correct the problem, to what extent does that reduce their responsibility, and if so which of the other parties picks up that share?

4. The issue of apportionment as between P and S as causers will involve consideration of their respective contributions to the contamination, which may relate to periods of occupation, modified by the intensity of operations.

5. The issue of apportionment as between the knowing permitters (X, Y and Z) will depend on their respective areas of occupation and length of occupation, which ought in principle to be a straight-forward mathematical exercise. However, if there are differences in opportunity which they had to deal with the problem, this will also have to be factored in.

6. However, what of the position of S, who has "dual capacity" both as a causer, and as a long term "knowing permitter"? Is S effectively apportioned two shares, one as a causer for 30 years and the other as a knowing permitter of previous contamination over the same period? The Guidance does not expressly address that issue, yet it will have an important bearing on the ultimate outcome. If S is simply regarded as a causer, this will increase the responsibility of P, but not that of X, Y and Z. Regarding S as both causer and knowing permitter will result in S bearing a proportionately heavier burden than P, and will greatly dilute the responsibilities of X, Y and Z, given the fact that S occupied the whole site for 30 years compared with their shorter occupations of different parts of the site.

5.246 These examples, brief and imperfect as they are, should illustrate how difficult it is in fact to adopt a totally prescriptive approach to the apportionment issue. What is perhaps most important in practice is that the authority should be able to explain the process by which it reached its decision. This may, however, be easier said than done, given the complexity and subjective nature of some of the tests. In practice, the authority may have received various conflicting representations from the parties, and it may be easier to state why a submission from a particular party is accepted or rejected rather than starting from scratch.

Apportionment within Class B

Part 8 of Ch.D deals with apportionment between members of a Class B **5.247** liability group. The Guidance states that where the whole or part of a remediation action for which a Class B liability group is responsible clearly relates to a particular area of land within the larger area of that pollutant linkage, then liability for that remediation action (or the relevant part of it) should be apportioned among those owning or occupying that area of land.[223] This is the first question to be considered, and the key words are "clearly relates to a particular area within the land".

The authority is therefore directed to consider the relationship between **5.248** the remediation action and the area of land.[224] It is submitted that this must mean something more than simply the action being physically carried out on that land. Take the example of a large area of land affected by mobile contaminants with a sensitive river down-gradient. The remediation consists of inserting a cut-off wall at the site boundary to form a barrier and protect the river. It would clearly be inequitable if the whole cost fell on the person who happened to own that part of the site where the wall was constructed.

It is submitted that what is required is a relationship between the need **5.249** for the remediation action and the land, not the action itself and the land. This would mean, for example, that where a contaminated site contains isolated "hotspots" which require additional remediation measures, the cost of those measures will fall to the owner or occupier of that specific area or areas.

In any event, where these circumstances do not apply (and in many cases **5.250** they will not) the authority should apportion liability for all the actions relating to the significant pollutant linkage amongst all members of the liability group.[225] The Guidance goes on to state that in so doing it should do so in proportion to capital values, including those of buildings and structures on the land.[226]

Where different areas of the land are in different occupation or **5.251** ownership the apportionment is on the basis of the respective capital values of the various areas relative to the aggregate of all such values.[227] Where different interests exist in the same area of land, the apportionment should be based on the respective capital values of those interests relative to the aggregate of all such values.[228] Where both ownership or

---

[223] DEFRA Circular 01/2006, *Contaminated Land*, Annex 3 para.D.92.
[224] The fact that apportionment is required reflects the fact that it is not possible to characterise that area as giving rise to a separate pollutant linkage.
[225] DEFRA Circular 01/2006, *Contaminated Land*, Annex 3 para.D.93.
[226] DEFRA Circular 01/2006, *Contaminated Land*, Annex 3 para.D.94.
[227] DEFRA Circular 01/2006, *Contaminated Land*, Annex 3 para.D.94(a).
[228] DEFRA Circular 01/2006, *Contaminated Land*, Annex 3 para.D94(b). It should be recalled, in this respect, that the effect of the relevant exclusion test should be to channel liability from the rack-rented tenant to the owner.

occupation of different areas and the holding of different interests are involved, the overall liability should first be apportioned between the different areas, then between the interests in each area.[229]

5.252 The capital values used for this purpose should be estimated by the authority on the basis of the available information and disregarding the existence of any contamination.[230] The date for valuation is the date immediately before the notice of identification of the land as being contaminated was served under s.78B.[231] Where the land in question is "reasonably uniform in nature and amenity", it can be "an acceptable approximation" to apportion on the basis of the area occupied by each.[232] If appropriate information is not available to enable an assessment of relative capital values, and such information cannot reasonably be obtained, then the authority is directed to apportion liability in equal shares.[233]

5.253 The Guidance also deals with the situation where no owner or occupier can be found for part of the land. Here the authority should deduct from the overall costs a sum reflecting the apportioned share for that land, based on its relative capital value, before apportioning between those owners or occupiers who can be found.[234] This is effectively an "orphan share" situation.

Attribution between liability groups

5.254 Part 9 of Ch.D deals with apportionment in the situation where one remediation action is referable to two or more significant pollutant linkages. Such a remediation action is referred to as a "shared action".[235] This situation can arise either where both linkages require the same action, or where a particular action is part of the best combined remediation scheme for two or more linkages. This process of apportionment between the liability groups is termed "attribution of responsibility".

5.255 The authority will have to consider whether the remediation action in question is referable solely to the significant pollutant in a single pollutant linkage ("a single-linkage action"), or is referable to the significant pollutant in more than one pollutant linkage ("a shared action").[236] Apportionment applies only in the case of shared actions. An example of a shared action might be the installation of a cut-off barrier to prevent mobile pollutants from more than one source reaching a watercourse. The analysis of whether a remediation action is a shared or single action should be carried out for each separate remediation action rather than the package as a whole.

5.256 The Guidance also requires the authority to consider whether the shared action is "a common action" or "a collective action". A common action is one which addresses together all of the relevant pollution linkages, and

---

[229] DEFRA Circular 01/2006, *Contaminated Land*, Annex 3 para.D.94(c).
[230] DEFRA Circular 01/2006, *Contaminated Land*, Annex 3 para.D.95.
[231] Thus the effect on value of the notice itself is also disregarded.
[232] DEFRA Circular 01/2006, *Contaminated Land*, Annex 3 para.D.95.
[233] DEFRA Circular 01/2006, *Contaminated Land*, Annex 3 para.D.97.
[234] DEFRA Circular 01/2006, *Contaminated Land*, Annex 3 para.D.96.
[235] DEFRA Circular 01/2006, *Contaminated Land*, Annex 3 para.D.98.
[236] DEFRA Circular 01/2006, *Contaminated Land*, Annex 3 para.D.21.

would still have been part of the remediation package for each of those linkages if each had been addressed separately.[237] A collective action is one which addresses together all of the relevant pollutant linkages, but which would not have been part of the remediation package for each of them if they had been addressed separately.[238] This might be because some different solution would have been more appropriate for each linkage in isolation, or because the action would not have been needed to the same extent for one or more of the linkages, or because the action is adopted as a more economical way of dealing with the linkages than requiring separate solutions for each linkage.

Taking the example of the remedial cut-off barrier given above, the **5.257** authority is thus required to ask, effectively, "Is this the solution we would have adopted for each of the pollution linkages had we been considering each alone?" The answer will of course depend on the exact circumstances.

Common actions

For common actions, the apportionment between the liability groups **5.258** should be on the following basis[239]:

(a) If there is a single Class A group, then the full cost of the common action falls to that group, with no cost falling to any Class B group or groups.

(b) If there are two or more Class A groups, then an equal share of the cost of the common action should be apportioned to each of those groups, and no cost should be attributed to any Class B group.

(c) If there is no Class A group and there are two or more Class B groups, the cost of the common action should be apportioned among the members of the Class B groups as if they were members of a single group, that is, on the basis of the value of their interests.

Effectively therefore, the approach is one of preferential liability for **5.259** Class A groups over Class B, otherwise equal shares to reflect the fact that each linkage would have needed that remediation action in its own right. Liability for Class A rather than Class B reflects both the "polluter pays" principle and the general liability scheme of Pt IIA.

Collective actions

For collective actions the process of apportionment is the same as for **5.260** common actions, except that where the cost falls to be divided among a number of Class A groups, then rather than being divided equally, they should be divided on the following basis[240]:

[237] DEFRA Circular 01/2006, *Contaminated Land*, Annex 3 para.D.22(a).
[238] DEFRA Circular 01/2006, *Contaminated Land*, Annex 3 para.D.22(b).
[239] DEFRA Circular 01/2006, *Contaminated Land*, Annex 3, para.D.99.
[240] DEFRA Circular 01/2006, *Contaminated Land*, Annex 3 para.D.100.

(a) The authority should estimate the cost of the collective action, and the hypothetical costs of the actions which would have been necessary for each pollutant linkage considered separately: these are termed the "hypothetical estimates".

(b) The authority should then apportion the cost of the collective action among the liability groups in proportion to the hypothetical estimate for that group relative to the aggregated hypothetical estimates for all groups.

5.261 This attempts to reflect the fact that the collective action solution may be quite different to the common actions relative to each linkage and seeks to achieve fairness.

5.262 The Guidance also allows for any appropriate person to demonstrate that the result of an attribution on the above basis would be that his liability group bears a disproportionate burden, taking into account the overall relative responsibilities for the condition of the land of the person or persons concerned, so that the result as a whole would be unjust.[241] The authority should then reconsider the attribution, consulting the appropriate persons, and adjust it if necessary so as to make it fair in the light of all the circumstances. Such an adjustment, according to the Guidance, should be necessary only in very exceptional circumstances.[242] One possible case is where the same group of persons forms the liability groups in respect of several pollution linkages, which though numerous, are of relatively low significance compared with one or more of the other linkages. The risk is that the larger number of the less serious linkages might result in those responsible bearing a disproportionate share.

Orphan linkages and attribution

5.263 As discussed elsewhere[243] an orphan linkage may arise either where no owner or occupier can be found, or where those who would otherwise be liable are exempted by one of the relevant statutory provisions. The Guidance considers the attribution process in four separate situations here:

(a) If a shared action is referable to an orphan linkage and to one Class A group, then the entire cost should be attributed to the Class A group.[244] Thus, the polluter pays, rather than the public purse.

(b) Similarly, if the shared action is referable to the orphan linkage and to a number of Class A groups, the entire cost is attributed between the Class A groups, ignoring the orphan linkage.[245]

(c) If a common action is referable to an orphan linkage and a Class B group, then the entire cost should be attributed to the Class B

[241] DEFRA Circular 01/2006, *Contaminated Land*, Annex 3 para.D.101.
[242] DEFRA Circular 01/2006, *Contaminated Land*, Annex 3 para.D.102.
[243] See para.5.277, below.
[244] DEFRA Circular 01/2006, *Contaminated Land*, Annex 3 para.D.107.
[245] DEFRA Circular 01/2006, *Contaminated Land*, Annex 3 para.D.108.

group.[246] This reflects the fact that the common action would have been necessary for the Class B linkage in any event.

(d) If a collective action is referable to an orphan linkage and a Class B group, then the attribution to the Class B group should not exceed the hypothetical cost of dealing with the Class B group's pollution linkage in isolation.[247] To the extent that the collective action involves a more expensive solution, the excess will fall to the public purse.

PART 8: WHEN THE LOCAL AUTHORITY IS ITSELF AN APPROPRIATE PERSON

Local authorities as "appropriate persons"

There is no reason in principle why a local authority cannot be an **5.264** "appropriate person", either as an original contaminator or as a current owner or occupier of land. An authority's regulatory role in issuing planning permission or other licences should not of itself lead to liability, and if it did, the authority will be able to rely on exclusion Test 1 in the statutory guidance in this regard, provided that it is not the sole member of a Class A liability group.[248] However, local authorities may well have operated facilities, such as highways maintenance depots, waste transfer stations or landfill sites, which may have caused contamination. Attention will need to be given here to whether liability has passed from an earlier authority to the current one where local authority reorganisation has occurred, where the terms of the relevant orders and of any related agreements may vary in this respect and may need to be considered carefully.[249]

The legal framework

As is discussed elsewhere, s.78H(5)(c) provides that if it appears to the **5.265** enforcing authority that the person on whom a remediation notice would be served is the authority itself, it should not serve the notice. Rather, by s.78H(7), the authority as the "responsible person" should prepare and publish a remediation statement, indicating what it will do and within what timescale.

This will be the position where the authority is the only appropriate **5.266** person with regard to a particular remediation action. In circumstances where the authority is one among a number of appropriate persons, the

---

[246] DEFRA Circular 01/2006, *Contaminated Land*, Annex 3 para.D.109(a).

[247] DEFRA Circular 01/2006, *Contaminated Land*, Annex 3 para.D.109(b).

[248] DEFRA Circular 01/2006, *Contaminated Land*, Annex 3 para.D.48(g).

[249] Compare, for example, the Local Government Reorganisation (Property) Order 1986 (SI 1986/148), made under the Local Government Act 1985 and the Local Government Area Changes Regulations 1976 (SI 1976/246), made under the Local Government Act 1972. See the discussion of the *Transco* case at paras 5.65ff, above.

authority will serve remediation notices on the other appropriate persons, stating the appropriate remediation action, and will publish a remediation statement with regard to its own responsibility. Naturally, depending on the circumstances, the authority may wish to take the lead in securing remediation, and one way forward may be for the authority and other parties involved to enter into an agreement under s.78N(3)(b) for the authority to carry out the work under powers in that section. In that case the authority will not need to serve a remediation notice on the other parties (indeed, it will be precluded from doing so by s.78H(5)(d)).

5.267   If remediation notices are to be served, the authority will have to apply the statutory guidance to determine the proportions of the cost which it and the other parties should bear, and state those proportions in the notices—see s.78E(3). Such notices may be subject to appeal by one or more of the recipients, which may in turn lead to the remediation declaration requiring reconsideration.

5.268   This represents the bare statutory framework under which local authorities will operate in such cases. However, there are other issues which must also be considered, which are canvassed below.

Bias

5.269 The problem is that where the enforcing authority is itself an actual or potential appropriate person, there is a danger that the authority may favour itself (or be perceived to do so) in the decisions which it takes as enforcing authority. There are a number of stages where this problem might potentially arise:

1. Considering whether the relevant land is "contaminated" at all.
2. Considering what should be the remediation requirements.
3. Applying the statutory provisions to determine who are appropriate persons.
4. Applying the tests on whether any appropriate persons should be excluded.
5. Applying the Guidance on apportionment as between appropriate persons.

5.270   It is not necessarily the case that any authority would consciously set out to apply these rules in such a way as to favour itself. However, any owner or other person served with a remediation notice is almost certainly going to be aggrieved if he feels either that the authority has taken a more lenient approach with regard to comparable local authority land, or has been the very body applying the rules which determine who is liable for what, in a way that could be seen as being to its own advantage.

Relevant legal principles

5.271 The legal principles of administrative law on bias are concerned not only with actual bias but also with the appearance or risk of bias: "Justice should not only be done, but should manifestly and undoubtedly be seen to be done".[250] The fact that the authority is involved in taking decisions which will be to its own financial benefit or detriment might be thought to raise a reasonable suspicion of bias in itself.

However, it is hardly possible to treat the local authority as disqualified **5.272** from fulfilling statutory duties expressly assigned to it by Parliament. The statute makes no provision for any other body to become the enforcing authority simply because the local authority is an "appropriate person": though, of course, in cases where the land is a special site this function will fall to the Environment Agency. Accordingly, the focus seems likely to rest not so much on the fact that the authority is in a situation of potential bias, but in how it behaves in that situation and in particular whether there is any suggestion that it acted unfairly. Whilst there is a statutory safeguard open to aggrieved parties by the statutory appeal process against remediation notices, this does not in any sense absolve the authority from the overriding duty to act fairly.

Potential conflicts of interest where a local authority is fulfilling a **5.273** statutory function are not new; for example, they can occur in the planning law context. The important point is that the authority should preserve its impartiality by keeping an open mind,[251] take account of all proper considerations, exclude all improper ones, and reach its decision fairly.[252]

Practical measures

The authority can best guard itself against allegations of bias by ensuring **5.274** that it follows scrupulously the legal requirements on matters such as statutory consultation, that it takes great care in applying the statutory Guidance on exclusion and apportionment, and that it is in a position to give clear reasons for its decisions. It should ensure that it takes so far as possible a consistent approach as between its own sites and those of others, and that it is in a position to explain and justify any differences of approach. Where in doubt on technical issues, it might well consider seeking site specific guidance from the Environment Agency under s.78V.

The main problems are likely to arise where the authority is itself one of **5.275** a group of appropriate persons. The authority will still have to carry out an apportionment exercise, but clearly they could be wise to call in an independent consultant to advise on the issue, whose report could be made public. Another possibility might be to separate out the role of dealing with enforcement from that of dealing with the authority's own liabilities and to allocate these responsibilities to different people.

Funding

Where the authority is liable for clean-up as an appropriate person, the **5.276** question of funding will arise. This is discussed below in the context of "orphan sites".

---

[250] *R. v Sussex Justices Ex p. McCarthy* [1924] 1 K.B. 256, 259 (Lord Hewart C.J.); see also *R. v Bow Street Magistrates Ex p. Pinochet* [1999] 2 W.L.R. 272, 284 (Lord Browne-Wilkinson).

[251] *Lower Hutt CC v Bank* [1974] 1 N.Z.L.R. 545, 550.

[252] *R. v St. Edmundsbury BC Ex p. Investors in Industry Commercial Properties Ltd* [1985] 3 All E.R. 234, 256.

PART 9: "ORPHAN SITES" AND "ORPHAN LINKAGES"

Can there be orphan sites?

5.277 The basic scheme of the legislation would suggest that orphan site situations should not readily arise. If the original contaminator (the causer or knowingly permitter) cannot be found under s.78F(2), then the authority may turn to the owner or occupier. In most cases there will be both, and in all cases there should be an owner, even if it is the Crown as a matter of escheat.[253] Even in cases where contamination has migrated from one piece of land to another, in general under s.78K each owner or occupier will at least be responsible, in the last resort, for cleaning up their own land.

5.278 The real possibility of an orphan site therefore rises not from the inability to find someone who is an appropriate person within the scheme of Pt IIA, but rather from the fact that the authority may be precluded from serving a remediation notice on that person under s.78J because the remediation relates solely to water pollution or to water pollution from abandoned mines; or under s.78H(5)(d) because of hardship considerations; or in respect of persons acting as insolvency practitioners or some other relevant capacity under s.78X(4).

5.279 One particularly important situation in practice may be where a Class A appropriate person has been found, but they can successfully argue on hardship grounds that a remediation notice may not be served on them. Here an appropriate person under s.78F(2) has actually been found (albeit that service of a notice on them is precluded) and on that basis it is not possible to look to those in Group B under s.78F(5). In that case, the site is effectively an orphan site. Interestingly, the Guidance, in discussing orphan linkages at para.D.103, does not refer to the hardship scenario, but does refer to s.78K on escapes.

Can there be orphan actions?

5.280 Another possibility is that a series of different remediation actions, relating to different types of contamination or pollution linkages, may be required for a site. Some of those actions may not be referable to a Class A appropriate person under s.78F(3). However, those actions would then naturally fall to the owner and occupier as Class B appropriate persons under s.78F(5).

5.281 The same question will then arise as described above, namely whether the authority is precluded from serving notice on those persons. If so, then the relevant actions will effectively be orphan actions. The Guidance generally treats the situation of orphan sites and orphan actions together, within the concept of "orphan linkages".[254]

---

[253] See para.5.124.
[254] See DEFRA Circular 01/2006, *Contaminated Land*, Annex 3 paras D.12, D.14, D.17 and D.103.

Can there be orphan shares?

The situation that may potentially arise here is where a number of **5.282** appropriate persons are found to be responsible for the same remediation action, the cost of which has been apportioned between them by the authority. The issue may be one of hardship, in that one or more of the recipients may be able to resist service of a notice on them on grounds of hardship with regard to their share. In that situation, it is the share of such persons which is, effectively, an orphan share. The problem then is that other appropriate persons may seek to argue a defence under s.78M(2) that others involved refused, or were unable, to bear their share.[255] However, the answer to such an argument is that the person on whom the remediation notice could not be served is not a "person liable to bear a proportion of that cost": hence s.78M(2) will not apply.

Dealing with orphan sites

This is the most straightforward case, where there is no pollutant linkage **5.283** other than an orphan linkage; in other words, there is no-one whom the authority could proceed against in relation to the whole site. The Guidance at para.D.104 states that in such circumstances the enforcing authority should itself bear the cost of any remediation which is carried out. The question is then whether the authority uses its s.78N powers to carry out remediation at its own cost. Doing nothing may be politically, and possibly legally, unacceptable. The issue of funding work in such circumstances is considered below.

Dealing with orphan actions

This situation is more complex. A site may be subject to a number of **5.284** pollutant linkages involving different substances and different factual backgrounds. One or more of these linkages may be orphan linkages, on the principles described above. The authority will then need to consider each remediation action separately.[256] If the action in question is referable only to the orphan linkage, and no other, then the authority will itself have to bear the cost of carrying out that action.[257] In those circumstances the authority's decisions as to how and when it uses its powers to carry out work under s.78N will need to take into account the other remediation works being carried out on the same site.

However, where the action is referable to both the orphan linkage and to **5.285** one or more other linkages in respect of which there are liability groups, then the cost of the shared action may fall on those liability groups. If the persons involved are Class A causers or knowing permitters, then the authority should attribute the entire cost to them, apportioning it if

---

[255] See para.6.04.
[256] DEFRA Circular 01/2006, *Contaminated Land*, Annex 3 para.D.105.
[257] DEFRA Circular 01/2006, *Contaminated Land*, Annex 3 para.D.106.

necessary between the separate liability groups, if there are more than one, as if the orphan linkage did not exist.[258] In other words, it is the polluters, rather than the public purse, which bear the cost of that part of the shared action attributable to the orphan linkage. Class B owners and occupiers are treated somewhat more favourably in this respect. Such groups will only be exposed to bearing the cost of action attributable to an orphan linkage where there is a shared action which cannot be referred to a pollutant linkage involving a Class A group.[259] In such cases, the authority's approach will have to vary depending on whether the shared action involved is a common action or a collective action. For common actions (that is, those which would have been required if each pollutant linkage was considered individually) the entire cost should be attributed to the Class B Group.[260] For collective actions (those that would not have been part of the remediation package for individual linkages) the attribution of cost to the Class B liability group should not exceed the estimated hypothetical cost of dealing with their pollutant linkage separately.[261]

Dealing with orphan shares

5.286 The Guidance does not deal explicitly with the orphan share situation where within the relevant liability group there are one or more individuals on whom the authority cannot serve a remediation notice, for example under s.78J or s.78X, or for hardship reasons. The point to keep in mind is that such persons are not excluded from the liability group (unless, of course, they can rely on one of the exclusion tests). Rather, they are exempted from having a notice served on them. So long as there remains one or more persons in the group who do not benefit from such exemptions, the linkage will not be an orphan linkage.[262] The exempted persons must still be apportioned an appropriate share of the cost, and for this purpose it is irrelevant whether or to what extent they would benefit from the hardship provisions.[263] To the extent that the authority cannot recover the cost from them, it will be an "orphan share" falling to the authority.

Fairness

5.287 As will be appreciated, the way in which orphan linkages are treated may be highly controversial, since it may involve on the one hand substantial calls on the public purse, and on the other persons having to bear the cost of dealing with actions for which they do not feel fairly responsible. It is therefore vital that the authority acts fairly and transparently in applying the Guidance and in making the relevant decisions.

Funding

5.288 Substantial expenditure could be necessary to deal with actions for which the authority has to bear the cost, either as an orphan share or linkage, or as an appropriate person in its own right. On general principles of local govern-

---

[258] DEFRA Circular 01/2006, *Contaminated Land*, Annex 3 paras D.107 and D.108.
[259] DEFRA Circular 01/2006, *Contaminated Land*, Annex 3 paras D.108 and D.109.
[260] DEFRA Circular 01/2006, *Contaminated Land*, Annex 3 para.D.109(a).
[261] DEFRA Circular 01/2006, *Contaminated Land* Annex 3 para.D.109(b).
[262] DEFRA Circular 01/2006, *Contaminated Land*, Annex 3 para.D.17.
[263] DEFRA Circular 01/2006, *Contaminated Land*, Annex 3 para.D.35.

ment finance such expenditure is not subject to capital controls if funded from revenue or from reserves. However, if it is funded from borrowing, credit provisions or capital receipts, then until 2004 central government approval was necessary. The original system of Supplementary Credit Approval (SCAs) was administered under Pt IV of the Local Government and Housing Act 1989. A new "prudential" Capital Finance System was introduced on April 1, 2004 under Pt 1 of the Local Government Act 2003, which completely replaced the system under Pt IV of the 1989 Act. SCAs were abolished and local authorities allowed to make borrowing decisions on the basis of what they can afford.

DEFRA runs a programme of support for capital costs incurred by local **5.289** authorities in dealing with contaminated land where the authority is a responsible person, or has powers to carry out remediation under s.78N. The programme covers both investigation and remediation of contaminated land. Eligible authorities are invited annually to bid for support for particular schemes, which are assessed against environmental criteria and prioritised. This support is not available where work is needed solely to facilitate development, redevelopment, or sale of land.[264] The current programme is the Contaminated Land Capital Projects Programme (CLLP), and is now delivered by way of direct grants, rather than Supported Capital Expenditure (Revenue). Central government funding for dealing with contaminated land is also provided through the "Environmental Protection and Cultural Services" component of the Revenue Support Grant (though this is not ring-fenced for those purposes).

Where clean-up is related to economic regeneration, funding may be **5.290** available from Regional Development Agencies under the Regional Development Agencies Act 1998 or under the Single Regeneration Budget operated under Pt IV of the Housing Grants, Construction and Regeneration Act 1996 or under the European Regional Development Fund in designated areas. "State Aid Rules" approval for these schemes has been obtained from the European Commission.[265]

Other sources of financial support for dealing with Contaminated Land **5.291** include exemptions from Landfill Tax for qualifying activities,[266] and enhanced Corporation Tax relief for expenditure on remediation of contaminated land.[267]

The Environment Agency has general statutory powers to carry out such **5.292** engineering operations as it considers appropriate as facilitating, or conducive or incidental to, the carrying out of its functions.[268] In principle, the funding for such work as is necessary could come from Government

---

[264] DEFRA Circular 01/2006, *Contaminated Land*, Annex 3 paras 16.12–16.14.
[265] State Aid Rules relating to Environmental aid are under review. See further at Ch.17, below.
[266] See HM Revenue & Customs Notice LFT2—Reclamation of contaminated land (April 2003).
[267] Introduced under the Finance Act 2001. See further at Ch.17, below.
[268] Environment Act 1995 s.37(1)(b).

grants,[269] borrowing,[270] or from Government loans,[271] including financial support from DEFRA.[272]

PART 10: ACCESS FOR REMEDIATION AND COMPENSATION

The need for access or other rights

5.293 By s.78G(1) an enforcing authority is expressly permitted to include in a remediation notice things which the recipient is not entitled to do. These could include, for example, carrying out engineering works or conducting monitoring on adjacent land, obtaining access across the land of a third party or, in the case of an original contaminator, returning to a site which he no longer owns in order to carry out remediation.

Obligation to grant rights

5.294 By s.78G(2) any person whose consent is needed before the thing required by the remediation notice can be done is required to grant, or join in granting, such rights in relation to the "relevant land or waters" as will enable the appropriate person to comply with the requirements of the remediation notice. Although the word used in s.78G(2) is "granting", it does not follow that this need necessarily involve a grant by deed of legal rights. In most cases, a contractual licence may be all that is necessary. Where more permanent works are in prospect (for example the laying of pipework across land) then more formal rights may be appropriate. The rights to be granted relate to "relevant land or waters", defined by s.78G(7) to mean:

(a) the contaminated land in question;

(b) any controlled waters affected by that land; or

(c) any land adjoining or adjacent to that land or those waters.

5.295 It will be appreciated from this definition that the relevant land may be some considerable distance from the site of contamination in cases where controlled waters have been affected. The obligation under s.78G(2) might, for example, involve granting rights to pump and treat groundwater many kilometres downstream, or providing access to remove contaminated silt from the downstream bed of a river where it has been carried by the current.

5.296 The grant of the relevant rights may involve cost, disruption and inconvenience. The Act itself contains no sanction for failure to grant such rights, nor any mechanism by which the local authority or appropriate

---

[269] Environment Act 1995 s.47.

[270] Environment Act 1995, s.48.

[271] Environment Act 1995 s.49.

[272] DEFRA Circular 01/2006, *Contaminated Land,* Annex 2, para.16.15 (including works in relation to radioactivity).

person may compel the grant of rights; nor is there any express dispute resolution mechanism, where the third party claims that the rights sought are unreasonable. It would appear therefore that the onus is on the appropriate person to take civil proceedings to secure the grant of the rights where necessary. The court would in those circumstances have to determine whether the rights were in fact needed to comply with the relevant requirement of the notice.

Consultation

Where the terms of a proposed remediation notice will involve the grant of **5.297** rights under s.78G, the enforcing authority must reasonably endeavour to consult the relevant owners or occupiers—see s.78G(3). This requirement does not however preclude service of a notice where it appears there is imminent danger of serious harm or serious pollution being caused.[273]

Compensation

A person who grants, or joins in granting, rights under s.78G is entitled to **5.298** make an application for compensation.[274]

Regulations may prescribe:

1. the time within which such applications shall be made;

2. the manner in which applications are made;

3. to whom they are made; and

4. how the amount of compensation is to be determined.

Regulation 6 of, and Sch.2 to, the Regulations deal with these issues. **5.299**

How Applications for Compensation are Made

Any application for compensation under s.78G must be made within the **5.300** prescribed period beginning with the date of the grant of the rights in question and ending on the expiry o whichever is the latest of the following periods[275]:

(a) 12 months after the date of the grant;

(b) where operation of the remediation notice is suspended by an appeal, 12 months after the date of its final determination or abandonment; or

(c) six months after the date on which the rights were first exercised.

---

[273] 1990 Act s.78G(4).
[274] 1990 Act s.78G(5).
[275] The Contaminated Land (England) Regulations 2006 (SI 2006/1380) Sch.2 para.2.

5.301   It must be made to the appropriate person to whom the right was granted and must be in writing and delivered at or sent by pre-paid post to the last known address for correspondence of the appropriate person.[276] It must contain, or be accompanied by, the following particulars[277]:

(a) a copy of the grant of right in respect of which the grantor is applying for compensation and of any plans attached to such grant;

(b) a description of the exact nature of any interest in land in respect of which compensation is applied for; and

(c) a statement of the amount of compensation applied for, distinguishing the amounts under the various prescribed headings, and showing how the amount applied for under each heading of compensatable loss or damage has been calculated.

Types of loss and damage which are compensated

5.302   Compensation is payable for five descriptions of loss and damage.[278] The five categories distinguish between effects on "relevant interests" (that is, those interests out of which the rights in question were granted) and other interests in land (which may include land other than that over which the rights were granted). They also distinguish between depreciation in the value of the interest and other loss or damage, disturbance or "injurious affection" (adopting the terminology of land compensation legislation). Finally, there is a distinction drawn between those effects stemming from the grant of the right in question, and those resulting from the exercise of the rights. It is not entirely straightforward to understand how those categories relate to each other, and there would appear to be some potential for overlap between them. The five categories of compensation are as follows:

(a) Depreciation in the value of any relevant interest to which the grantor is entitled which results from the grant of the rights. The "relevant interest" is defined by para.1 of the Schedule to mean an interest out of which rights have been granted, and so will be that interest which enables the grantor to grant the rights in question. It may accordingly be freehold or leasehold. "Grantor" in this context is defined to include any person joining in the granting of rights. It should be noted that the depreciation in question for this category is that resulting from the grant of the right, not its exercise.

(b) Depreciation in the value of any other interest in land to which the grantor is entitled which results from the exercise of the rights. It therefore does not cover relevant interests falling within paragraph

---

[276] The Contaminated Land (England) Regulations 2006 (SI 2006/1380) Sch.2 para.3(1).
[277] The Contaminated Land (England) Regulations 2006 (SI 2006/1380) Sch.2 para.3(2).
[278] The Contaminated Land (England) Regulations 2006 (SI 2006/1380) Sch.2 para.4.

(a) above, and relates to depreciation caused by the exercise of the right rather than its grant. An example might be the situation where it can be shown that the exercise of the rights affects the value of neighbouring land owned by the grantor.

(c) Loss or damage in relation to any relevant interest to which the grantor is entitled, which is attributable either to the grant of the right or its exercise, but which does not consist of depreciation in its value, and is loss or damage of a kind in respect of which compensation for disturbance, or any other matter not directly based on the value of that interest, is payable on a compulsory acquisition. The important point here is that the loss or damage in question must not be too remote, and must be a natural and probable consequence of the grant or exercise of the right, as the case may be.[279] Subject to this, as the Circular suggests, compensation might be payable where the land or things on it are damaged, or where there is a loss of income or profits on the part of the grantor.[280] This may be particularly relevant where remediation disrupts the ongoing business operations of the current owner or occupier.

(d) Damage to, or injurious affection of, any interest in land to which the grantor is entitled which is not a relevant interest, and which results from the grant of the rights or their exercise. Though the wording of the Regulations does not make this explicit, the Circular gives the example of works on the contaminated land involved having "some permanent adverse effect" on adjoining land.[281] Again the analogy is with compulsory purchase law, and on that basis the damage or adverse effects must not be too remote.[282] The reference to "permanent adverse effect" in the Circular is potentially confusing, however, since by definition the effects of the remediation works are unlikely to be permanent and, although what is being compensated is damage to an interest in land, not nuisance generally, temporary damage can form the basis of a claim under compulsory purchase legislation in some circumstances.[283] In any event, this head of compensation can only be helpful to those who have granted or joined in granting rights; those who are simply affected as neighbours will have to rely on their normal common law remedies in nuisance.

(e) Loss in respect of work carried out by or on behalf of the grantor which is rendered abortive by the grant of the rights or their exercise. The example given by the Circular is of a newly erected

---

[279] *Horn v Sunderland Corp* [1941] 2 K.B. 26; *Harvey v Crawley Development Corp* [1957] 1 Q.B. 485, 494.

[280] DEFRA Circular 01/2006, *Contaminated Land*, Annex 4 para.26(b).

[281] DEFRA Circular 01/2006, *Contaminated Land*, Annex 4 para.26(c).

[282] See *Metropolitan Board of Works v McCarthy* (1874) L.R. 7 H.L. 243.

[283] See *Wildtree Hotels Ltd v Harrow LBC* [2001] 2 AC 1, where temporary damage in the form of noise, dust and vibration from road works was found to be capable of substantiating a claim under s.10 of the Compulsory Purchase Act 1965, where the claimant could prove that the letting value of his land had been reduced.

building which can no longer be accessed and used after the grant of the rights.[284] Less dramatic examples can be contemplated, for example, an access road or drainage system, the route of which needs to be altered.

Basis of assessing compenstation

5.303 Schedule 2, para.5 sets out a number of rules or principles for the assessment of compensation under s.78G. For the purposes of assessing valuations of land, the rules set out in s.5 of the Land Compensation Act 1961 have effect, so far as applicable and subject to any necessary modifications.[285] This involves valuation on the basis of sale in the open market by a willing seller. Where the interest in land is subject to a mortgage, the compensation is to be assessed as if it were not so subject, and no compensation is payable in respect of the interest of the mortgagee.[286]

Expenditure by grantor

5.304 In assessing compensation, no account is to be taken of expenditure which enhances the value of the land in question by carrying out works, improvements or erecting buildings, where that work was not reasonably necessary and was carried out with a view to obtaining enhanced compensation.[287] Where genuine abortive expenditure has been incurred on the land, this will be recoverable under (e) above, and can include expenditure on plans or similar preparatory matters,[288] such as obtaining planning permission or building approval.

Professional expenses

5.305 Compensation can include reasonable legal and valuation expenses.[289]

Mortgages

5.306 The position of any mortgagee will need careful consideration in relation to compensation. Since, as mentioned above the "grantor" for the purposes of compensation includes a person who joins in granting the relevant rights, this could include a mortgagee whose consent is required to the grant of an easement or similar right. Also, a mortgagee in possession might be required to grant rights of access. A mortgagee can therefore obtain compensation in

---

[284] DEFRA Circular 01/2006, *Contaminated Land*, Annex 4 para.26(d).

[285] The five rules contained in s.5 of the 1961 Act are discussed in S. Tromans and R. Turrall-Clarke, *Planning Law, Practice and Precedents* (Sweet and Maxwell, 1991, Looseleaf) paras 10.07 et seq.

[286] Contaminated Land (England) Regulations 2006 (SI 2006/1380) Sch.2 para.5(5).

[287] Contaminated Land (England) Regulations 2006 (SI 2006/1380) Sch.2 para.5(3).

[288] Contaminated Land (England) Regulations 2006 (SI 2006/1380) Sch.2 para.5(4).

[289] Contaminated Land (England) Regulations 2006 (SI 2006/1380) Sch.2 para.5(6).

his own right. However, by Sch.2 para.5(5) where the interest in which compensation is assessed is subject to a mortgage, then the mortgage is ignored for the purpose of assessing the compensation, and no compensation is payable separately in respect of the mortgagee's interest. This avoids the risk of double compensation being payable. The compensation in such circumstances must by Sch.2 para.6(1) be paid to the mortgagee, or to the first mortgagee if there is more than one; it must then be applied as if it were proceeds of sale. It is questionable how well thought out these provisions are: the intention, according to the Circular, is to ensure that the mortgagee and any subsequent mortgagee "will get any appropriate share".[290] However, it is possible to foresee disputes arising between the mortgagor and mortgagee, in particular where the compensation relates to matters such as disturbance to the mortgagor's business or to abortive expenditure by the mortgagor.

Dispute resolution

By Sch.2 para.6(3) disputes on compensation are to be referred to the Lands **5.307** Tribunal for determination. The provisions in the Land Compensation Act 1961 are applicable as to the procedure and costs of such references.[291] As the Circular points out, under its own Rules, the Lands Tribunal may deal with the matter on the basis of written representations (r.27), or by a simplified procedure, if appropriate (r.28). One issue which may in practice lead to disputes, it is anticipated, is the relationship between the different categories of compensation, which do not appear to be entirely mutually exclusive. Care will be needed to ensure that the claimant is not compensated twice over in respect of what is essentially the same loss.

Date for payment and interest

Compensation is payable in accordance with the date or dates agreed **5.308** between the parties, either in a single payment or in instalments; otherwise it is payable, subject to any direction of the Tribunal or Court, as soon as reasonably practicable after the amount is determined.[292] The provisions for interest under the Planning and Compensation Act 1991 are applicable to compensation under s.78G.[293] Claims may be substantial in some cases, and may take some time to settle (particularly as novel points may arise). The question of interest may accordingly be an important one.

The authority's role

The enforcing authority is not involved directly in the question of compensa- **5.309** tion under s.78G, other than its obligation to consult grantors under s.78G(3) before serving a remediation notice and the requirement that it

---

[290] DEFRA Circular 01/2006, *Contaminated Land*, Annex 4 para.31.
[291] Contaminated Land (England) Regulations 2006 (SI 2006/1380) Sch.2 para.6(3) and (4).
[292] Contaminated Land (England) Regulations 2006 (SI 2006/1380) Sch.2 para.6(2).
[293] See the Planning and Compensation Act 1991 (Amendment of Schedule 18) (England) Order 2002 (SI 2002/116), which amended Sch.18 and provides the dates from which interest is to be payable.

serve a copy of the notice on them. However, the Circular suggests that it is good practice for authorities to inform those they have consulted in this way of the final outcome of any appeal against the notice, so that they are alerted to the need to be ready to apply for compensation.[294] This raises the interesting question of whether an authority may be liable for failure to comply with this "good practice" if in consequence of not being notified, the grantor of rights misses the deadline for applying for compensation.

---

[294] DEFRA Circular 01/2006, *Contaminated Land*, para.38.

Chapter 6

ENFORCEMENT, APPEALS AND REGISTERS

PART 1: ENFORCEMENT

Offence of non-compliance with remediation notice

Section 78M(1) provides that a person on whom an enforcing authority **6.01** serves a remediation notice who fails, without reasonable excuse, to comply with any of its requirements, shall be guilty of an offence. It should be kept in mind that a remediation notice may, and often will, be served on a number of persons.

These prosecution provisions seem weak in some respects. Under s.78M **6.02** there is a general qualification, namely that only a person who fails to comply with any of the requirements of a remediation notice "without reasonable excuse" is guilty of an offence. This would appear to provide a great deal of latitude for debate whether or not an offence has been committed in the first place. Whilst lack of funds will not generally be a reasonable excuse,[1] the physical inability to carry out works, for example for lack of access, may be relevant. However, it would be difficult to rely on lack of access without first seeking to exercise the statutory rights of access given by s.78G. Care must be taken to distinguish between matters which constitute reasonable excuse, and those which go only to the issue of mitigation.[2] Nonetheless, it is not possible to provide an exhaustive and comprehensive definition of what may be a reasonable excuse, and reasons of personal hardship (e.g. illness) may be relevant.[3]

Like statutory nuisances, the question arises whether the prosecution **6.03** have to produce evidence of the lack of a reasonable excuse. As with the provisions on statutory nuisance, the requirement of "without reasonable excuse" is an inherent part of the offence rather than a defence that has to be specifically raised as such. That being so, it is probably sufficient for the defendant to simply adduce some evidence of an excuse, and it will then be for the prosecution to satisfy the court, on the criminal standard of beyond reasonable doubt, that there was no reasonable excuse.[4]

Secondly, by s.78M(2) where the notice states that only a proportion of **6.04** the cost is chargeable against the recipient, it is a defence for him to prove that the only reason why he has not complied with the requirements of the

---

[1] *Saddleworth UDC v Aggregate and Sand* (1970) 114 S.J. 931; *Kent CC v Brockman* [1996] 1 P.L.R. 1.

[2] *Wellingborough BC v Gordon* [1993] Env. L.R. 218.

[3] *Hope Butuyayu v London Borough of Hammersmith and Fulham* [1997] Env. L.R. D13.

[4] *Polychronakis v Richards and Jerrom Ltd* [1998] J.P.L. 588, following *R. v Clarke* [1969] 1 W.L.R. 1109. Compare the position where a defence is actually involved—see s.101 of the Magistrates' Courts Act 1980 and *R. v Hunt* [1997] A.C. 392.

notice is that one or more other persons liable to pay a proportion of the cost have refused, or were not able, to comply with the requirement. If one of the other appropriate persons is in liquidation or bankrupt, insolvent or merely impecunious, the remediation works may well not have been carried out, since a responsible party will not wish to be committed contractually to the engineering or other costs involved if he is not satisfied that a contribution is likely to be forthcoming from the others responsible. The defence will be available to someone who can prove that this is the only reason for his non-compliance. The onus of proving the defence rests with the defendant, on the balance of probabilities.[5] It would therefore be prudent for the person seeking to rely on the defence to demonstrate that tenders have been obtained, that attempts have been made to invite the others involved to contribute, and that generally the defendant is willing and able to do his part.

6.05 The statutory provisions do not create an offence triable in the Crown Court, or either way, that is in either magistrates' or Crown Court at the election of the defendant. Section 78M(3) is concerned only with "summary conviction". This in itself seems extraordinary given that, by definition, the harm or risk of harm relating to the land will be of a serious nature. The "summary conviction only" nature of the offence has the consequence that any prosecution must be brought within six months from the time when the offence was committed.[6] By analogy with *Hodgetts v Chiltern DC*,[7] failure to comply with a remediation notice probably constitutes an offence which is complete once and for all when the period for compliance with the notice expires. The six-month period will therefore run from that date.[8]

6.06 The normal penalty is set at a maximum of level 5 on the standard scale, i.e. £5,000. For each day on which failure to comply continues, until such time as the authority exercises its s.78N powers a further fine of one-tenth of that sum applies.[9]

6.07 In respect of an offence committed in circumstances where the contaminated land to which the remediation notice relates is industrial, trade or business premises the fine on summary conviction has an upper limit of £20,000 unless the Secretary of State by Order increases it.[10] The daily penalty is one-tenth of that sum (i.e. £2,000). "Industrial trade or business premises" are defined by s.78M(6) to mean premises used for any industrial, trade or business purposes, or premises not so used on which matter is burnt in connection with such premises; it specifically includes premises used for industrial purposes of any treatment or process as well as for manufacturing. The term, as so defined, refers at subs.78M(4) to

---

[5] *Islington BC v Panico* [1973] E.R. 485; *Neish v Stevenson* 1969 S.L.T. 229. See also *R. v Hunt* [1997] A.C. 392.

[6] Magistrates' Court Act 1980 s.127.

[7] [1983] A.C. 120. Like remediation notices, the case was concerned with a "do" notice, requiring positive steps.

[8] Compare *Camden LBC v Marshall* [1996] 1 W.L.R. 1345, where there was an express statutory provision (s.376(2) of the Housing Act 1985) that the obligation to carry out the works continued despite the expiry of the period. Part IIA contains no such provision.

[9] 1990 Act s.78M(3). This does not mean that the daily fine must be that figure. The general discretion under s.34 of the Magistrates' Courts Act 1980 allows a lesser figure to be imposed—see *Canterbury CC v Ferris* [1997] Env. L.R. D14.

[10] 1990 Act s.78M(4).

cases "where the contaminated land to which the remediation notice relates is" such premises. Where the contaminated land was once industrial, but has since been changed to residential use, subs.(4) will not apply.

Practical issues in prosecution

Prosecution for failure to comply with a remediation notice is, like other **6.08** aspects of criminal enforcement, a discretionary matter. Where the Environment Agency is the enforcing authority, it will need to have regard to its own published prosecution policy. However, having said that, prosecution will normally follow the situation where the recipient of a notice fails to comply with it. Issues of discretion may arise where the recipient of the notice—perhaps now taking the situation seriously for the first time—seeks additional time to comply, or partially complies with the notice. On the issue of time, the authority should be mindful of the fact that failure to comply with the notice is an offence triable only summarily, so that the six-month rule for bringing prosecutions applies. The authority should therefore be careful not to prejudice its position by delay in proceeding. If the six-month period is missed, it will have to serve a new notice and start again.[11] Unless all the requirements of the notice are complied with by the time stated, an offence is committed; the authority may however wish to consider the practical extent of compliance in such circumstances, and whether prosecution would serve any useful purpose.

Another issue in prosecuting is whether there is sufficient evidence of **6.09** non-compliance to sustain a conviction. Again, by analogy with statutory nuisance, the magistrates will only require proof that the notice has not been complied with, if the land remains harmful or potentially harmful so as to constitute "contaminated land".[12]

Finally, there is the situation where a number of parties are required to **6.10** contribute to the cost of carrying out the same remediation action. One or more of them may conceivably have a defence under s.78M(2) as outlined in the previous paragraph. The question is whether the enforcing authority should prosecute the whole group by a joint charge, or lay separate informations against each. As a matter of principle, each remediation notice is separate, and non-compliance with each notice is a separate offence. Each information can relate to one offence only, but a single document can contain a number of informations.[13] The best course is to charge separate offences, but to seek a joint trial on the basis that the facts are so interconnected that the interests of justice would be best served by a single hearing.[14]

Use of civil remedies

If the enforcing authority is of the opinion that proceedings for an offence **6.11** under s.78M(1) would be an ineffectual remedy for non-compliance with the notice by s.78M(5) then they may take proceedings in the High Court

---

[11] See *Camden LBC v Marshall* [1996] 1 W.L.R. 1345 at 1350 (Henry L.J.).
[12] *AMEC Building Ltd and Squibb & Davies Ltd v London Borough of Camden* [1997] Env. L.R. 330.
[13] Magistrates' Courts Rules 1981 r.12.
[14] *Chief Constable of Norfolk v Clayton* [1983] 2 A.C. 473; *R. v Assim* [1996] 2 Q.B. 249.

for the purpose of securing compliance with the remediation notice. This should, however, be viewed as a consequential step to serving a remediation notice. The use of an injunction should probably only be viewed as a "last resort".[15] The question which the authority must ask is whether prosecution would be effectual against the person in default: the attitude, past conduct and resources of that person will therefore be relevant. On the basis of the decision in *Vale of White Horse DC v Allen & Partners*,[16] the power under s.78M to seek an injunction will probably be regarded as a self contained code, so that s.222(1) of the Local Government Act 1972 may not be used as a separate means of obtaining an injunction. Accordingly, the authority must have formed the opinion required by s.78M(5); it is not enough simply that injunctive proceedings are seen as more convenient or appropriate.[17]

6.12   Given that a remediation notice will normally impose positive requirements, the appropriate remedy will be a mandatory injunction. The wording of s.78M(5) would certainly seem wide enough to allow for a mandatory injunction to be sought.[18] There are precedents for the use of such injunctions in the environmental context, even where it is alleged that the defendant is impecunious.[19] The injunction will need to be as specific as possible, though the courts have accepted that where enforcement of public law is involved, if adequate protection cannot be given in any other way then an injunction may be granted in extensive terms.[20]

Remediation carried out by enforcing authority

6.13   By s.78N there are a number of situations in which the enforcing authority itself has power to carry out remediation works to the relevant land or waters. Those works will not always have been set out in a remediation notice because in some of the cases concerned no remediation notice will have been served, or if one has been served, it may not necessarily have included the works concerned. However, the structure of s.78P is such that the right to recover the costs is based on the person concerned being an "appropriate person" who could be required to do the works concerned in a remediation notice. Bearing in mind the Government's stated commitment that local authorities should not be involved in additional costs in implementing the legislation, it is perhaps curious to find them in a position where in certain cases they may have to carry out works without any legal right to reclaim the costs from any person. However, it should be remembered that s.78N confers a power to act, not a duty.

6.14   The situations where the enforcing authority may carry out remediation works are the following[21]:

15 *The Barns (NE) Ltd v Newcastle Upon Tyne CC* [2006] Env L.R. 25.
16 [1997] Env. L.R. 212 at 223–4.
17 [1997] Env. L.R. 212 at 224.
18 See, in the context of listed buildings, *South Hams DC v Halsey* [1996] J.P.L. 761, CA (injunction given although prosecution for breach of notice had failed in Crown Court because of a wrong decision on the law). See also *Runnymede BC v Harwood* [1994] 1 P.L.R. 22, CA.
19 *Warrington BC v Hall* [1999] Env. L.R. 869, CA (mandatory injunction requiring £2 million expenditure).
20 See *Kettering BC v Perkins* [1999] J.P.L. 166, 173.
21 1990 Act s.78N(3).

(a) where the authority considers the works to be necessary for the purposes of preventing the occurrence of any serious harm, or serious pollution of controlled waters, of which there is imminent danger[22];

(b) where an appropriate person has entered into a written agreement with the enforcing authority for the authority to do the works that otherwise he would have to do[23];

(c) where a person on whom a remediation notice has been served fails to comply with any of its requirements;

(d) where the enforcing authority is precluded under ss.78J or 78K from including something by way of remediation in a remediation notice which nevertheless is required to be done[24];

(e) where the enforcing authority considers that if it did carry out works itself, it would decide not to seek to recover the costs of the work or to recover only a proportion of them under s.78P (this situation relates to hardship); and

(f) where no person after reasonable enquiry has been found to be an appropriate person.[25]

Only in case (c) does it follow that a remediation notice will have been **6.15** served. Quite clearly, no notice will have been served in cases (d), (e) and (f).

By subs.78N(2) the authority does not have power to do anything in **6.16** circumstances where the contaminated land regime is excluded by s.78YB where the relevant statutory regimes apply.[26]

Serious harm or serious pollution

There is no indication of what constitutes serious harm or serious pollution **6.17** as the term is used in s.78N. It is therefore a matter of the judgment of the enforcing authority, and that judgment could not be challenged unless it was unreasonable in the *Wednesbury* sense. Further, there is no requirement to publish a decision that serious harm or serious pollution had or was likely to arise. Nevertheless, there would need to be a committee decision that the enforcing authority should carry out the works itself, or a decision to that effect by a responsible officer if the delegation agreement of the authority conferred delegated power to make that decision on him. In any event, the danger has to be "imminent". Bearing in mind that land is not contaminated at all for the purposes of the legislation unless and until

---

[22] "Serious harm" or "serious pollution" are not defined in s.78(P) nor, it would appear, does the Secretary of State have powers to issue guidance or make regulations in respect of that aspect.

[23] See para.4.60.

[24] See paras 5.135 and 5.147ff.

[25] See the discussion at para.5.54ff as to what is meant by "found".

[26] See para.3.76ff.

"significant harm" is being caused, or there is a significant possibility of such harm being caused, the term "serious" in the present context would appear quite different from "significant". Clearly, harm could be "significant" without being "serious"; it could never be "serious" without also being "significant".

Failure to comply with notice

6.18 There are a number of practical points which are important in respect of an enforcing authority's decision to carry out works upon failure of the recipient to comply with a notice. First, it is prudent for notice to be given to the appropriate person that this procedure is to be adopted and any such notice should contain a time limit. Secondly, the matter will have to go to committee, or a duly delegated officer, with estimates of the cost of the work, having in mind that full recovery may not be possible, even where legally permitted. Some experience of good practice in this field has been gained by local planning authorities carrying out works under s.178 of the Town and Country Planning Act 1990.[27] In particular, good practice may involve supplying the appropriate person with copies of a number of estimates for the cost of the works, giving an opportunity for comment.

6.19 There is not only the question of the nature of works that need to be done to remediate the harm (which may be the subject of an appeal against the notice) but the way in which those works shall be done. By s.78N(4)(c) the authority may do only those things which the recipient of the remediation notice was required to do. The terms of the notice therefore need to be considered carefully, since the authority's powers to act (and of cost recovery) may be jeopardised by departing from, or going beyond, what the remediation notice requires. In any event, the authority clearly should not exercise its powers before the statutory period for appeal has expired.

Works which cannot be included in a remediation notice

6.20 An enforcing authority is precluded by ss.78J and 78K, from including certain things in a remediation notice which nevertheless ought to be done.[28] Where that situation arises the enforcing authority can carry out the works, but it will not be able to recover the reasonable cost. This is because the power of cost recovery under s.78P(1) does not apply to the s.78N(3)(d) power to carry out remediation works in those circumstances; a position confirmed by ss.78J(7) and 78K(6).

What is the authority allowed to do?

6.21 Section 78N(1) allows the authority "to do what is appropriate by way of remediation to the relevant land or waters". The phrase "relevant land or waters" is defined to mean:

---

[27] See, Tromans and Turrall-Clarke, *Planning Law Practice & Precedents*, (London: Sweet & Maxwell, 1991), paras 9.133 et seq.

[28] See paras 5.135 and 5.147ff.

(a) the contaminated land in question;

(b) any controlled waters affecting that land; or

(c) any land adjoining or adjacent to those waters.

Thus the remediation may involve land some distance from the source of **6.22** the contamination if controlled waters have been affected; for example, the construction of barriers or extraction wells.

The power is not, however, as wide as this wording might indicate. The **6.23** things which are "appropriate" are defined by s.78N(4) by reference to each of the grounds on which the action is based. The authority will need to refer carefully to paras (a)—(e) of s.78N(4) in that regard, as some paragraphs are much wider than others. In relation to paras (b) and (c) in particular, reference will have to be made to the terms of the agreement or of the remediation notice, as appropriate.

Recovery of costs

By s.78P(1) the enforcing authority which exercises its powers of remedia- **6.24** tion under s.78N is entitled in some but not all cases to recover the reasonable costs incurred in carrying out the remediation from the appropriate person or persons. Where there is more than one such person, the costs are recoverable in the proportions determined under s.78F(7). Those cases where costs may be recovered are paras (a), (c), (e) or (f) of s.78N(3), namely:

(a) action to prevent serious harm or pollution where there is imminent danger;

(c) where a recipient of a remediation notice has failed to comply;

(e) hardship cases (where part of the costs may be recoverable);

(f) where no appropriate person has been found after reasonable enquiry.

In cases (c) and (e) it should be reasonably clear who is the appropriate **6.25** person, but in cases under (a) urgent action may have been taken before any remediation notice was served, or before the identity of the appropriate person was established. In such cases, the phrase "appropriate person" must mean the person determined to be appropriate under s.78F, and the authority will have to make that determination before it can seek to recover its costs.

With regard to case (f), it might seem somewhat curious to give the **6.26** power to the enforcing authority to recover its costs from an appropriate person in cases where no appropriate person can be found. However, there is presumably the possibility that the authority might, having made enquiry and failed to find an appropriate person, commence the works under s.78N, then later find that an appropriate person exists.

As to cases not falling within s.78P, in situations falling within **6.27** s.78N(3)(b) (where there is a written agreement for the authority to carry out the work) the authority will be able to recover its costs by virtue of the agreement. The real situation where "orphan sites" or "orphan shares" may arise seems to be under s.78N(3)(d) (i.e. where the authority finds itself precluded from serving notice under ss.78J or 78K), which is discussed above.

Hardship and discretion

6.28 Recovery of costs is not an automatic process. The enforcing authority has a discretion to be exercised in accordance with s.78P(2) which requires the authority to have regard to:

(a) any hardship which the recovery may cause to the person from whom the costs are recoverable; and

(b) any guidance issued by the Secretary of State.

6.29 In considering these issues, it should be remembered that, in the first place, the only things which the enforcing authority may require to be done by way of remediation are things which it considers reasonable having regard to the cost involved.[29] Also, the Courts will no doubt be concerned to ensure that impecuniosity should not be too readily accepted simply on the basis of the assertions of the appropriate person, or by the production of a bank statement showing an overdraft.[30] The *Oxford English Dictionary* definition of "hardship" refers to "hardness of fate or circumstance; severe suffering or privation". As the Circular points out, there is a certain amount of case law on the expression.[31] The cases suggest that a wide meaning will be given to the word, to cover any matter of appreciable detriment, whether financial, personal or otherwise.[32] The term would thus seem to embrace the hardship inherent in facing worrying legal proceedings in appropriate cases or possibly personal circumstances such as serious illness. Also, the test seems likely to be an objective one, based on what the reasonable person would view as hardship[33]: "The rich gourmet who because of financial stringency has to drink vin ordinaire with his grouse may well think that he is suffering a hardship; but sensible people would say he was not".

6.30 Whilst the authority can only judge these issues at the time before serving the notice, it may be that subsequent changes of circumstance in terms of hardship would be taken into account on any appeal.[34]

Guidance on hardship

6.31 In deciding whether and to what extent to seek to recover costs, the authority must have regard to guidance of the Secretary of State.[35] Part 3 of Ch.E of Annex 3 of the Guidance deals with cost recovery decisions. It

---

[29] 1990 Act s.78E(4).

[30] *Kent CC v Brockman* [1996] 1 P.L.R. 1.

[31] DEFRA Circular 01/2006, *Contaminated Land*, Annex 2 paras 10.8–10.10.

[32] See *Purser v Bailey* [1967] 2 Q.B. 500; *F G O'Brief v Elliott* [1965] N.S.W.R. 1473; *Director-General of Education v Morrison* (1985) 2 N.Z.L.R. 431; *Re Kabulan* (1993) 113 A.L.R. 330.

[33] *Rukat v Rukat* [1975] 1 All E.R. 343 at 351 (Lawton L.J.).

[34] *Leslie Maurice & Co Ltd v Willesden Corp* [1953] 2 Q.B. 1.

[35] 1990 Act s.78P(2).

sets out a number of general principles. It should be kept in mind that this is "traditional" guidance to which the authority must have regard, not prescriptive advice which it must follow. The approach is to set out "principles and approaches, rather than detailed rules".[36] In particular, the authority should aim for an overall result which is as just, fair and equitable as possible to all those who have to meet the costs of remediation, including local and national taxpayers.[37] It should also have regard to the "polluter pays" principle, which will involve considering the nature and degree of responsibility of the persons concerned.[38] In general, this means that the authority's starting point is that it should seek to recover all its costs, subject to the considerations outlined below.[39]

Deferred recovery

As a general point, the authority should consider whether it could **6.32** maximise recovery by deferring receipt and securing the costs with a charge on the land under s.78P.[40] In such a case costs may be recovered either in instalments or when the land is sold. This may mean that less hardship will be involved than would be the case if immediate recovery were demanded.

Information on hardship

As hardship is essentially a personal issue for the appropriate person **6.33** concerned, it is to be expected that they rather than the authority will have access to the information to support any such claim. As such, the onus is on the person seeking a reduction in cost recovery on hardship grounds to present any information needed to support that request.[41] The authority should of course consider such information, but should also give thought to the possibility of obtaining relevant information itself where it is reasonable to do so, give the practicalities of how the information is to be obtained, the cost of doing so, and the potential significance of the information.[42] To take a practical example, where an authority is faced with an individual owner who is clearly of limited resources, the authority must ask itself what real purpose would be served in devoting time and money to investigating the issue of hardship further. On the other hand, where the remediation actions required involve very substantial cost, and the authority is met with a claim by a polluter who is a major company that they should pay only a small proportion of that cost, or indeed nothing at all, on hardship grounds, then the authority may well be justified in making its own enquiries into the matter, and taking professional advice as to the

---

[36] DEFRA Circular 01/2006, *Contaminated Land*, Annex 3 paraE.10.
[37] DEFRA Circular 01/2006, *Contaminated Land*, Annex 3 para.E.11(a).
[38] DEFRA Circular 01/2006, *Contaminated Land*, Annex 3 para.E.11(b)
[39] DEFRA Circular 01/2006, *Contaminated Land*, Annex 3 para.E.12.
[40] DEFRA Circular 01/2006, *Contaminated Land*, Annex 3 para.E.13.
[41] DEFRA Circular 01/2006, *Contaminated Land*, Annex 3 para.E.14.
[42] DEFRA Circular 01/2006, *Contaminated Land*, Annex 3 para.E.15.

validity of the company's hardship case. If it did not, the authority could properly be criticised for failing to take proper steps to safeguard the public purse, which would otherwise have to bear the cost of remediation.

Cost recovery policies

6.34 The Guidance suggests the possibility that local authorities may wish to prepare and adopt public policy statements about the general approach to be adopted in making cost recovery decisions.[43] This, the Guidance suggests, would promote transparency, fairness and consistency, by outlining circumstances in which the authority would waive or reduce cost recovery, having had regard to hardship and the statutory guidance. It is questionable, however, how advisable such a policy really would be. An authority cannot fetter its statutory role of considering the circumstances of every case, and the application of the guidance to those circumstances. It is difficult to see what the authority could sensibly say about its general approach without simply paraphrasing the Guidance. An adopted policy on cost recovery might simply turn out to be a hostage to fortune, as the basis for arguments that a remediation notice should not have been served at all in any given case. It is also suggested in the Guidance that any cost recovery policy should be taken into account by the Environment Agency, when acting as enforcing authority in relation to a special site in the area; this of course means that the Agency may be faced with inconsistent or at least different policies when acting in relation to sites in different local authority areas.

General considerations on cost recovery

6.35 The Guidance sets out a number of general considerations on cost recovery which apply to both Class A and Class B persons. These are:

> (a) General parity of approach for all commercial enterprises, whether public corporations, limited companies, partnerships or sole traders.[44]

> (b) In the case of small and medium-sized enterprises (defined by reference to EC State aid guidelines relating to numbers of employees, turnover or annual balance sheet), the authority should consider whether the imposition of full cost recovery would mean that the enterprise is likely to become insolvent and cease to exist. If so, then where the cost to the local economy of closure would exceed the cost to the authority of having to clean up the land itself, the authority should consider waiving or reducing its costs to the extent necessary to avoid insolvency.[45]

> (c) However, the authority should not waive or reduce cost recovery where it is clear that the enterprise has deliberately arranged

---

[43] DEFRA Circular 01/2006, *Contaminated Land*, Annex 3 para.E.17.

[44] DEFRA Circular 01/2006, *Contaminated Land*, Annex 3 para.E.20

[45] DEFRA Circular 01/2006, *Contaminated Land*, Annex 3 paras E.21, E.22, E.24

matters to avoid liability, or where insolvency appears likely irrespective of the costs of remediation, or where the enterprise could remain in, or be returned to, business under different ownership.[46]

(d) Where the enforcing authority is a local authority, it may wish to take into account any policies it may have for assisting enterprise or promoting economic development, for example, for granting financial assistance under s.2(1)(a) of the Local Government Act 2000 including any strategy which the authority has published under s.4 of the 2000 Act.[47]

(e) Where the Environment Agency is the enforcing authority, it should seek to be consistent with the approach of the local authority in whose area the land is situated, should consult that authority and take its views into consideration.[48] The Agency's perspective may naturally be wider than the local one, since the threat posed by the contaminated land may be to resources of regional or even national importance—for example, where a major aquifer is involved.

(f) Where trustees are appropriate persons, the authority should assume that they will exercise all the powers they have or may reasonably obtain to make funds available from the trust, or from borrowing on behalf of the trust, to pay for remediation. The authority should consider waiving the recovery of costs to the extent that such costs exceed the amount that could be made available from these sources.[49] However, the authority should not waive or reduce cost recovery where it is clear that the trust was formed for the purpose of avoiding payment for remediation, or to the extent that the trustees have personally benefited from, or will benefit from, the trust. The focus of this Guidance is on the effect of cost recovery on the trustees of the trust, rather than the beneficiaries. However, there appears to be nothing to prevent those beneficiaries seeking to raise general arguments of hardship flowing from depletion or exhaustion of trust funds.

(g) Since charities are intended to operate for the benefit of the community in the broad sense, the authority should consider the extent to which cost recovery might jeopardise the charity's ability to continue to provide a benefit or amenity which is in the public interest. If this is the case, the authority should consider waiving or reducing its cost recovery accordingly.[50]

(h) Similarly, the authority should consider waiving or reducing cost recovery in relation to bodies such as housing associations eligible for registration as social housing landlords under s.2 of the

---

[46] DEFRA Circular 01/2006, *Contaminated Land*, Annex 3 para.E.23.
[47] DEFRA Circular 01/2006, *Contaminated Land*, Annex 3 para.E.25.
[48] DEFRA Circular 01/2006, *Contaminated Land*, Annex 3 para.E.26
[49] DEFRA Circular 01/2006, *Contaminated Land*, Annex 3 para.E.27
[50] DEFRA Circular 01/2006, *Contaminated Land*, Annex 3 para.E.29.

Housing Act 1996, where the liability relates to land used for social housing, and where full recovery would lead to financial difficulties, such that provision or upkeep of the social housing might be jeopardised.[51]

6.36 With the exception of the guidance on trustees (at (f) above), these aspects of the Guidance involve a utilitarian balancing exercise of considering the consequences of remediation falling on the public purse as against the adverse social consequences which would ensue from pursuing full cost recovery. It is a different issue from that of personal hardship on the part of the appropriate person. Determining which is the lesser of the two evils may not be an easy matter, and could be one which requires expert advice, for example, in relation to the likelihood of corporate insolvency, and the quantification of the wider economic consequences of such insolvency. In these circumstances, authorities may well see a charging order, with deferred cost recovery, or recovery by instalments, as a relatively attractive option.

Cost recovery against Class A persons

6.37 Part 5 of Ch.E on cost recovery deals with the specific issues on cost recovery relating to Class A appropriate persons. Essentially there are two principles. The first is that in general the authority should be less willing to waive or reduce costs where the Class A person caused or knowingly permitted the contamination in the course of carrying on a business, on the basis that he is likely to have earned profits from the activity in question (para.E.35).[52] In practice, naturally, most if not all contamination will have been caused by those carrying on a business.

6.38 The other point made in the Guidance on Class A persons related to the position where one Class A person (X) can be found, but there are others who also caused or knowingly permitted who cannot now be found, for example, because they were a company which has now been dissolved. In that case, the authority should consider waiving or reducing cost recovery if X can demonstrate to its satisfaction that if the other Class A person could in fact be found, then the tests in the Guidance on exclusion or apportionment would have operated to exclude X from liability altogether, or to reduce significantly its proportion of the cost. Firm evidence will be needed from X as to the actual identity of the other Class A person or persons involved.[53] This aspect of the Guidance is therefore essentially based on fairness to a Class A party who has acted in ways recognised as exculpatory by the Guidance, but who cannot rely on those circumstances because he is now the only Class A party who can be found.

Cost recovery against Class B persons

6.39 The Guidance on cost recovery against Class B appropriate persons at Pt 6 of Ch.E is potentially important in practice. It needs to be recalled that such parties are liable not because of their past actions, but because of

---

[51] DEFRA Circular 01/2006, *Contaminated Land*, Annex 3 paras E.30 and E.31.
[52] DEFRA Circular 01/2006, *Contaminated Land*, Annex 3 para.E.35.
[53] DEFRA Circular 01/2006, *Contaminated Land*, Annex 3 para.E.36.

their present ownership or occupation of land. There are three main categories of situation envisaged here.

The first situation is where the costs of remediation exceed the value of **6.40** the land in its current use after remediation: here the authority should consider waiving or reducing cost recovery if the appropriate person can show this is the case.[54] The value to be considered is that of the land on the open market, post clean-up, but disregarding any possible residual diminution in value from blight. In general, the authority should seek to ensure that the costs of remediation which it recovers do not exceed the value of the land. It may, however, take into account whether remediation would result in an increase in the value of other land that the relevant person owns. As will be appreciated, this principle could in some cases represent a very significant restriction on the ability to recover costs, or from the other side of the coin, protection for the appropriate person concerned. It emphasises the importance of two factors discussed in earlier chapters: first, determining whether a given person falls within Class A or Class B and, secondly, determining exactly what land should be included within the remediation notice.

Another issue canvassed in the Guidance is that of the precautions taken **6.41** by the Class B person before acquiring the land to determine whether it was contaminated. The issue of due diligence is not relevant for the purposes of the primary legislation, and in terms of the prescriptive Guidance on exclusion is relevant primarily to Test 3 ("Sold with information") as between Class A persons. However, on cost recovery, the authority should consider reducing the costs recovered against a Class B person who can show that he took such steps as were reasonable at the time before acquiring his interest to check for the presence of contaminants, that despite those precautions he was not aware of the contamination and could not reasonably have been expected to be so aware, and that taking into account the interests of national and local taxpayers it is reasonable that he should not bear the entire cost of remediation.[55] The authority should bear in mind that what constitutes reasonable precautions will differ as between different types of transactions and as between buyers of different types. The Guidance here appears to contemplate the reduction of costs, rather than complete waiver. There may be very considerable variations in practice as to the discount given for due diligence, as well as the inherent uncertainty as to what could reasonably have been expected at some point in time, by way of investigation on the specific transaction and by the specific purchaser. It is possible that authorities who are under financial pressure may not be particularly sympathetic to arguments that they should bear the partial cost of clean-up where there is a solvent landowner, notwithstanding the adequacy of the investigations undertaken by that person. Where there were investigations which failed to detect contamination, the question may arise as to why the landowner should not seek to recover the costs from the consultants who failed to detect the contamination, or their insurers.

The third category concerns Class B persons who own or occupy **6.42** dwellings. It is suggested that where such a person did not know of the contamination at the time of purchase, and could not reasonably be

---

[54] DEFRA Circular 01/2006, *Contaminated Land*, Annex 3 para.E.39.
[55] DEFRA Circular 01/2006, *Contaminated Land*, Annex 3 para.E.42(a).

expected to have known of it, then there should be waiver or reduction of costs to the extent necessary to ensure he bears no more than is reasonable, having regard to his income, capital and outgoings.[56] This approach is intended to be applied only to the dwelling and its curtilage, not to any more extensive land which the person in question owns. Again, this is a highly subjective issue, but the Guidance suggests the possibility of applying a means-test approach analogous to that used for applications for housing renovation grants (HRG) under the Housing Renewal Grants Regulations 1996,[57] which consider income, capital, outgoings and allowance for any special needs.[58] How practical a suggestion this will be remains to be seen, but this is of course an area where the local authority and indeed the Environment Agency will need to have regard to the political acceptability of being seen to recover substantial sums from private individuals who have the misfortune to have bought a property sited on contaminated land.

Reasons for decisions

6.43 In all cases, the enforcing authority, whether the local authority or Agency, should inform the appropriate person of any cost recovery decisions taken, and explain the reasons for those decisions (para.E.16). This constitutes a demanding requirement to give reasons for what will in many cases ultimately be value judgments as to what is fair and reasonable in the circumstances. The authority will have to pay close attention to the Guidance, and explain how it has been taken into account and applied, or not as the case may be.

Recovery of costs: charging notices

6.44 Sections 78P(3)–(14) deal with charging notices for the recovery of costs by enforcing authorities under s.78P(1) where the authority has carried out the work itself. The powers only apply where the relevant costs are recoverable from a person who is the owner of any premises which consists of or includes the contaminated land in question and who caused or knowingly permitted the substance or any of the substances to be in the land concerned.[59] Thus the scope of recovery is relatively narrow. A notice cannot be served on an occupier, or on an original polluter who is no longer owner. The procedure is initiated by serving a charging notice, which must specify the amount of costs claimed and state the effect of subss.(4), (7) and (8).[60] On the same date, a copy must be served on every other person who, to the knowledge of the authority, has an interest in the premises capable of being affected by the charge.[61]

---

[56] DEFRA Circular 01/2006, *Contaminated Land*, Annex 3 paras E.44 and E.45.
[57] SI 1996/2890.
[58] DEFRA Circular 01/2006, *Contaminated Land*, Annex 3 paras E.47–E.49.
[59] 1990 Act s.78P(3).
[60] 1990 Act s.78P(5).
[61] 1990 Act s.78P(6).

The cost specified in the charging notice carries interest at such **6.45** reasonable rate as the enforcing authority may determine from the date of service of the notice until the whole amount is paid.[62] More problematic from the chargee's point of view is that the costs and accrued interest are charged on the premises.[63] Such charge takes effect at the end of a period of 21 days from service of the notice, unless an appeal is made.[64] Where any cost is a charge on premises under the section, the enforcing authority may by order declare the costs to be payable with interest by instalments within the specified period until the whole amount is paid.[65] The enforcing authority has the same powers and remedies under the Law of Property Act 1925, and otherwise, as if it were a mortgagee by deed, having power of sale and lease, of accepting surrenders of leases and of appointing a receiver.[66]

A person served with a charging notice or a copy of a charging notice **6.46** may appeal against the notice to a County Court within a period of 21 days beginning with the date of service.[67] Regulations will provide the grounds on which such an appeal may be made and the procedure for dealing with appeals of this sort.[68]

Appeals against charging notices

As mentioned above, a right of appeal lies against a charging notice under **6.47** s.78P(8), within the period of 21 days beginning with the date of service. The right of appeal extends to the person served with the notice and to anyone served with a copy pursuant to s.78P(6) who has an interest in the premises capable of being affected by the charge, for example, a mortgagee or tenant-in-common. Appeal is to the County Court. On appeal, the Court may confirm the notice without modification, substitute a different amount, or order that the notice is to be of no effect.[69] The grounds for appeal and procedures for appeal are to be dealt with by Regulations.[70]

Scope and priority of charge

As mentioned above, a statutory charge under s.78P may be enforced by **6.48** the powers and remedies of sale, lease and receivership available to a mortgagee by deed under the Law of Property Act 1925.[71] The statutory charge is a charge on "the premises" (subs.(6)) "consisting of or including" (subs.(3)(a)(i)) the contaminated land. This raises the question of what constitutes "the premises" where these may be greater in extent than the

---

[62] 1990 Act s.78P(4)(a)
[63] 1990 Act s.78P(4)(b).
[64] 1990 Act s.78P(7).
[65] 1990 Act s.78P(12).
[66] 1990 Act s.78P(11).
[67] 1990 Act s.78P(8).
[68] 1990 Act s.78(P)10.
[69] 1990 Act s.78P(9).
[70] 1990 Act s.78P(10). At the date of writing no such Regulations have been made.
[71] 1990 Act s.78P(11).

contaminated area—a possibility which subs.(3)(a)(i) acknowledges. Where a charging notice may be served, there appears to be nothing to prevent the enforcing authority service a notice charging the whole of any premises in the ownership of the same person, provided that those premises include the previously contaminated land. Such premises may be far more valuable than the part of it which is contaminated; this is therefore an important protection for the enforcing authority, as well as a possible major concern for mortgagees.

6.49   The second question is how the statutory charge rates in terms of priority with existing mortgages. If the wording were a charge "on the land," then on the authority of *Westminster CC v Haymarket Publishing Ltd*[72] it could be said that the charge is on all the estates and interests in the land, including prior mortgages. The wording here is "premises", but in fact this phraseology was used in earlier statutes and was held to have the effect of charging all proprietary interests in a series of cases followed in the *Westminster CC* case.[73] On this basis, there seems a strong argument that the statutory charge will affect, and take priority over, all existing mortgages, charges, options and other legal or equitable estates or interests in land; another serious concern for mortgagees. The mortgagee will at least have the comfort that the works will have improved the condition of the property. In practice, the mortgagee would probably have had to carry out those works at its own expense in any event in order to be able to exercise its power of sale.

"Signing off"

6.50   One practical aspect of enforcement is how the authority signifies its view that the remediation notice has been properly and adequately complied with. The statute itself does not provide for this, but the procedural description of the system in Annex 2 of the Circular suggests a possible procedure. This involves the authority writing to the person concerned, stating that it currently sees no grounds, on the basis of available information, for further enforcement action (or where remediation has been carried out prior to the service of any notice, no grounds for serving such a notice). The limitations of such a system in practice are obvious: should it transpire that in fact the land remains contaminated, so that further action is necessary, any such letter (which is likely to have been heavily qualified in any event) could not bind the authority not to comply with its statutory duties or estop it from doing so (at least so far as the current owner is concerned). Nonetheless, it may be anticipated that owners of land will seek such letters in practice, if only on the basis that some reassurance is better than none. There might also arise the question of a person who acquires the land on the basis of any such letter by the authority, and whether such a party might claim any cause of action for negligent mis-statement, or perhaps argue some form of estoppel against

---

[72] [1981] 2 All E.R. 555.
[73] See *Birmingham Corp v Baker* (1881) 17 Ch.D. 782, *Tendering Union Guardians v Dowton* [1891] 3 Ch. 265; *Paddington BC v Finucane* [1928] Ch.567.

the authority in relation to its cost recovery powers (having changed his position in reliance on the information). These considerations mean that any authority which is minded to "sign off" under the Circular should consider very carefully the wording of the letter.

PART 2: APPEALS AGAINST REMEDIATION NOTICES

The right of appeal

By s.78L(1) there is a right of appeal against a remediation notice within **6.51** the period of 21 days beginning with the day on which the notice is served. This appears to be a short period, but it has to be recalled that there is a period for prior consultation under s.78H between the authority and the person on whom the notice is to be served. The recipient is therefore unlikely to be taken entirely unawares, and in any event at least three months will normally have passed since the contaminated land was identified.

Originally, there was a division between appeals against remediation **6.52** notices served by local authorities, which were heard by the local Magistrates' Court and those served by the Environment Agency which were heard by the Secretary of State. The justification for such a distinction was obscure and the procedure was amended in the Clean Neighbourhoods and Environment Act 2005. All appeals now lie to the Secretary of State or in Wales to the National Assembly.[74] The only exception is in the case of residual appeals against remediation notices served by local authorities before August 4, 2006 which will continue to be heard by the local Magistrates' Court.[75]

Appeals regulations

Regulations may deal with a considerable number of matters in relation to **6.53** appeals,[76] including the grounds on which appeals may be made and the relevant procedure. No express mention is made in this context of grounds on which an appeal may be made against a decision of the Secretary of State, and it is therefore assumed that, there being nothing in the primary legislation, judicial review will lie against such decisions.

The Regulations may also deal with the circumstances in which the **6.54** remediation notice is to be suspended until the appeal has been decided.[77] The obvious problem is that of significant harm already being caused,

---

[74] In Scotland, if the remediation notice was served by a local authority, appeal is still to the sheriff by way of summary application, and the standard rules governing such applications will apply: see Scottish Guidance (Edn 2, June 2006) Annex 4 para.42. If the notice was served by SEPA, or is subsequently adopted by SEPA, appeal lies to the Scottish Ministers (ibid. para.44).

[75] See Clean Neighbourhoods and Environment Act 2005, s.104.

[76] 1990 Act s.78L(4).

[77] 1990 Act s.78L(5)(b).

which may continue or even worsen during any suspension period. Logically the enforcing authority should use its own powers under s.78N to deal with this problem, to the extent necessary, and seek recovery of its costs from liable persons.

6.55 There is also provision for the Regulations to prescribe cases in which the decision on appeal may in some respects be less favourable to the appellant than the original remediation notice.[78] The Regulations may also prescribe cases in which the appellant can claim that a remediation notice should have been served on some other person and the procedure to be followed in those cases.[79]

6.56 The Regulations made under the above powers for England are the Contaminated Land (England) Regulations 2006.[80] The relevant provisions are regs 7–12.

Grounds of appeal

6.57 The grounds on which a person on whom a remediation notice is served may appeal under s.78L(1) are set out at reg.7 of the Regulations and are:

    (a) That in determining whether any land to which the notice relates appears to be contaminated land, the authority either:

        (i) failed to act in accordance with the Guidance; or

        (ii) unreasonably identified all or any of the land as contaminated, whether by reason of such a failure or otherwise. This ground will be relevant where there is a dispute as to the proper extent of the contaminated land, or as to the harm, risk or pollution presented by the land, or where it is suggested that the authority otherwise made a wrong decision (for example, by incorrect analysis or identification of contaminants). It should be noted however that, in cases otherwise than where failure to act in accordance with the Guidance is alleged (sub-ground (i)), the ground is not that the authority "wrongly" identified the land as contaminated, but that they "unreasonably" did so. What is contemplated may be therefore something narrower than a completely open review on the merits, but at the same time not a ground as narrow as *Wednesbury* unreasonableness.

    (b) That, in determining a requirement of the notice, the authority either:

        (i) failed to have regard to the Guidance; or

        (ii) whether by reason of such a failure or otherwise, unreasonably required the appellant to do anything by way of remediation. This is the appropriate ground where there is

---

[78] 1990 Act s.78L(5)(c).
[79] 1990 Act s.78L(5)(d).
[80] SI 2006/1380.

dispute as to the remediation action or package specified in the notice, though the Guidance here has advisory rather than prescriptive status.

(c) That the authority unreasonably determined that the appellant was the appropriate person to bear responsibility for remediation. This ground may apply where there are factual disputes as to the involvement of the appellant, or legal dispute as to the proper interpretation of the legislation on who is an appropriate person. However, again it should be noted that the test is whether the determination was unreasonable, not whether it was wrong; presumably any determination based on a wrong interpretation of the law must inevitably be unreasonable.

(d) That the authority unreasonably failed to determine that some person in addition to the appellant was an appropriate person. This covers the situation where the authority failed to find some other appropriate person who was in existence. It is qualified by reg.7(2), which limits its application to cases where the appellant claims to have found some other appropriate person within the appropriate liability class. It cannot therefore assist the appropriate person who simply alleges generally that there must have been some other appropriate person, but who cannot identify them.

(e) That the authority failed to act in accordance with the Guidance on exclusion of appropriate persons under s.78F(6). This is simply an issue of whether the authority understood the Guidance correctly and applied it to the facts. It does not explicitly address the situation where it is alleged that the authority got the facts wrong; in those circumstances the appeal may have to lie under ground (c).

(f) That the authority, where two or more appropriate persons were involved, either:

(i) failed to act in accordance with the Guidance on apportionment under s.78F(7); or

(ii) by reason of that failure or otherwise, unreasonably determined the proportion of the cost to be borne by the appellant. Apportionment disputes seem likely to be fertile sources of appeals.

(g) That service of the notice contravened the requirements of s.78H(1)–(3) for the three-month moratorium, and for consultation before service.

(h) In cases where the authority served notice without consultation and within the three-month moratorium, that the authority could not reasonably have taken the view that there was imminent danger of serious harm or pollution falling within s.78H(4). The way in which this ground is worded looks more like a *Wednesbury* test—which may well be appropriate, given that the authority will have had to act urgently, balancing the interests of proper consultation against the public interest in the face of serious risk.

(i) That the authority has unreasonably failed to be satisfied, in accordance with s.78H(5)(b), that reasonable things are being or will be done by way of remediation, without any notice being served. This will be relevant where the appellant has put forward a proposed scheme which has been rejected as inadequate by the authority.

(j) That anything required by the notice was in contravention of the restrictions on liability applying in cases of water pollution under s.78J.

(k) That anything required by the notice was in contravention of the provisions of s.78K dealing with the escapes of substances between land.

(l) That the enforcing authority itself has power under s.78N(3)(b) to do what is appropriate. This applies where the appropriate person has entered into an agreement with the authority for it to carry out the work at his expense.

(m) That the authority has power under s.78N(3)(e) to carry out the work itself. This covers cases where it is alleged that a notice ought not to have been served on hardship grounds.

(n) That in considering hardship and cost recovery issues, the authority either:
   (i) failed to have regard to hardship, or to Guidance; or
   (ii) whether by reason of that failure or otherwise, unreasonably determined that it would seek to recover all its costs.

(o) That the authority failed to have regard to any guidance issued by the Environment Agency under s.78V.

(p) That any period specified in the notice for doing anything is not reasonably sufficient.

(q) That the notice imposes requirements on an insolvency practitioner in his personal capacity, contrary to s.78X(3)(a).

(r) That service of the notice contravened the provisions of s.78YB, dealing with the interaction of Pt IIA and other regimes, and where appropriate it ought reasonably to have appeared to the authority that the relevant other powers might be exercised.

(s) That there has been some informality, defect or error in, or in connection with the notice, in respect of which there is no other ground of appeal. By reg.7(3) where an appeal is made on the basis of informality, defect or error in, or in connection with, the notice, the appeal must be dismissed if the appellate authority is satisfied that the informality, defect or error was not material.

6.58   As will be appreciated the number and diversity of the grounds of appeal reflect the complexity of the Pt IIA regime itself, with its restrictions on service of notices, exclusion and apportionment provisions. The grounds of appeal will need to be considered carefully in each case against the detailed facts to determine which of them may be applicable. The question of whether a remediation notice can be a nullity, in which case there is nothing to appeal against, is discussed below.[81] However, the comprehensive nature of the grounds, especially the "catch-all", means that the scope for judicial review of notice is likely to be limited in practice.

Who can appeal?

By s.78L(1), an appeal can be brought only by a person on whom the **6.59** remediation notice is served. A person on whom a copy of the notice was served has no statutory right of appeal. An example of such a person would be the current owner or occupier of the land, where the notice has been served on the original polluter. The current owner or occupier, if they are aggrieved by the land being subject to a remediation notice, or by its terms, and do not wish to leave conduct of any appeal exclusively in the hands of the original polluter, will have to rely on challenging the notice by way of judicial review.

Appeal to Secretary of State

By reg.8 of the Regulations, an appeal in respect of a special site made to **6.60** the Secretary of State must be made by notice of appeal, which shall state[82]:

(a) the name and address of the appellant;

(b) the grounds on which the appeal is made; and

(c) whether the appellant wishes the appeal to be in the form of a hearing or to be decided on the basis of written representations.

The appellant must serve a copy of the notice of appeal on the Secretary **6.61** of State, the enforcing authority and on relevant third parties, including any person named in the remediation notice and the owner/occupier of the land in question.[83] Additionally, the appellant must include with the notice of appeal a statement of the names and addresses of all persons (other than the Agency) on whom he is serving a copy of the notice and must serve a copy of the remediation notice on the Secretary of State and on any person named in the appeal as an appropriate person who is not named in the remediation notice.[84]

The Regulations make provision for abandonment of appeals to the **6.62** Secretary of State.[85] Notification to that effect is to be given to the Secretary of State. The appeal is then treated as abandoned on the date

---

[81] See para.6.98ff.
[82] 2006 Regulations reg.8(1).
[83] 2006 Regulations reg.8(2).
[84] 2006 Regulations reg.8(2)(b)(c).
[85] 2006 Regulations reg.8(3).

the Secretary of State receives the notification. Where the appeal is abandoned, the Secretary of State shall give notice to any person on whom the notice of appeal was required to be served.[86] However, the Secretary of State may refuse to allow abandonment of the appeal where he has already notified the appellant of a proposed modification to the notice.[87]

Suspension of notices pending appeal

6.63 Where an appeal is duly made against a remediation notice the notice is of no effect pending the final determination or abandonment of the appeal.[88] The effect is therefore that no offence is committed by failing to comply with the suspended notice, nor can the authority take other enforcement action. In order to have this effect, the appeal must be "duly made"; that is to say it must comply with the appropriate procedural requirements.[89] Perhaps, surprisingly, there is no exception to this rule in cases where it appears there is imminent danger of serious harm or pollution, and the notice recites those facts.

Procedure for joining third parties

6.64 One of the potential shortcomings of the appeals procedures is the lack of any clear mechanism for involving third parties. Obviously, if the appellant is arguing that someone else other than the appellant is the appropriate person to be responsible for remediation, or that the appellant is entitled to benefit from some exclusion of liability to the detriment of another, or that the appellant's apportioned share should be less and some other person's commensurately greater, then the other person or persons involved have a direct interest in the outcome of the appeal. It would be contrary to natural justice, and quite probably the Human Rights Act 1998, for the issues to be determined without giving them adequate notice, time to prepare, the opportunity to submit evidence, cross-examine and present a case.

6.65 As explained above, the Regulations at least contain procedures whereby such persons are notified that an appeal has been made, and of the grounds of the appeal.[90] For appeals to the Secretary of State there is a right for such persons to be heard at a hearing[91] (and presumably to make written representations).

6.66 Beyond this there are no clear procedural rules governing the involvement of such third parties, either at the preliminary stages of the appeals process, or at the appeal hearing itself. In practice, therefore, this will be a matter for the magistrates, the sheriff, the inspector or reporter (as appropriate) to determine as part of the procedure of the relevant tribunal.

---

[86] 2006 Regulations reg.8(5).
[87] 2006 Regulations reg.8(4).
[88] 2006 Regulations reg.12(1).
[89] 2006 Regulations reg.12(2).
[90] 2006 Regulations reg.8(2).
[91] 2006 Regulations reg.9(3).

In principle, the procedures should be capable of accommodating such third parties though complex issues may well arise as to how to structure the appeal. Structurally, there may be a situation where there are two or more appeals which are heard jointly, or where there is a single appeal in which a third party participates.

Joined appeals

Where a number of persons have been served with remediation notices in **6.67** respect of the same land, they may well all wish to appeal on the same ground, for example that the land was not contaminated land at all, or that the requirements of the notice were excessive. Although the Regulations do not make any express provision for appeals being joined and determined together, this must in many cases be the sensible course, and there seems no reason why it cannot be done.

Powers of appellate authority

By s.78L(2) on any appeal against a remediation notice the appellate **6.68** authority is required to quash the notice, if satisfied that there is a material defect in it; but subject to that duty, has a discretion to confirm the notice, with or without modification, or to quash it. Where the notice is confirmed, the appellate authority may extend the period for complying with the notice.[92]

Before modifying the notice in any way which would be less favourable to **6.69** the appellant or any other person on whom the notice was served, the appellate authority must:

(a) notify the appellant and other persons involved in the proposed modification;

(b) permit those notified to make representations; and

(c) permit the appellant or any other person on whom the notice was served to be heard if they so request.[93] The enforcing authority is also entitled to be heard in such circumstances.[94]

In so for as an appeal against a remediation notice is based on the **6.70** ground of some informality, defect or error in the notice, or in connection with it, the appellate authority shall dismiss the appeal if satisfied that the informality, error or defect was not a material one.[95] The reference to material defects is similar language to that used in planning legislation prior to 1981 in relation to enforcement notices.[96] Applying case law on

---

[92] 1990 Act s.78L(3).
[93] 2006 Regulations reg.11(1).
[94] 2006 Regulations reg.11(2).
[95] 2006 Regulations reg.7(3).
[96] See S. Tromans and R. Turrall-Clarke, *Planning Law, Practice and Precedents* (Sweet and Maxwell, 1991), para.9.30.

that wording, the issue may well be whether the defect is such as to result in injustice.[97]

Appeals procedure

6.71 Appeals to the Secretary of State are by s.78L(6) subject to the provisions of s.114 of the Environment Act 1995.[98] This allows the Secretary of State to appoint any person to exercise the appellate functions on his behalf. Appeals may therefore be referred to the Planning Inspectorate, either for report to the Secretary of State, or to determine the appeal. Schedule 20 to the 1995 Act applies to such appeals.[99] Schedule 20 deals with the appointment process (which must be in writing),[100] the powers of appointed persons,[101] the holding of local inquiries and hearings,[102] and evidence and costs.[103]

6.72 The Guidance on the Regulations contained at Annex 4 to the Circular indicates[104] that most cases will be delegated to inspectors, but that "some cases" may be recovered by the Secretary of State or in Scotland, "recalled" by the Scottish Ministers.[105] Cases which involve sites of major importance, or which have more than local significance, which raise significant local controversy, or give rise to difficult legal points or major, novel issues, will be the categories most likely to be recovered.[106]

6.73 The options for determining an appeal under the Schedule are therefore to determine it on written representations only, to hold a hearing, or to hold a public local inquiry. Either party can require a hearing[107]; if no such preference is expressed it is expected that appeals will be decided on the basis of written representations[108] unless the Secretary of State decides that it is desirable to hold a hearing or public local inquiry.[109]

6.74 Where a local inquiry or hearing is held, an assessor may be appointed by the Secretary of State to sit with the inspector or reporter in an advisory capacity.[110] This is likely to be a useful procedure for technically complex appeals, which may raise highly specialist issues.

6.75 Under regs 8–9 of the Regulations, the following procedures apply to appeals:

>   1. Before determining the appeal, the Secretary of State may if he thinks fit:

---

[97] *Miller-Mead v Minister for Housing and Local Government* [1963] 2 Q.B. 196; considered in *Simms v Secretary of State for the Environment and Broxtowe BC* [1998] P.L.C.R. 24.

[98] 1995 Act s.114(2)(iii)

[99] 1995 Act s.114(4).

[100] 1995 Act Sch.20, para.2.

[101] 1995 Act paras 3 and 7.

[102] 1995 Act para.4.

[103] 1995 Act para.5.

[104] Circular, Annex 4 paras 52–55

[105] See Scottish Guidance, Annex 4 para.53.

[106] Scottish Guidance, Annex 4 para.54.

[107] 1995 Act Sch.20 para.4(1) and see DEFRA Circular 01/2006, *Contaminated Land*, Annex 4 para.56.

[108] DEFRA Circular 01/2006, *Contaminated Land*, Annex 4 para.56

[109] 1995 Act Sch.20 para.4(2).

[110] 1995 Act Sch.20 para.4(4).

(a) cause the appeal to take or continue in the form of a hearing (which may be held wholly or partly in private); or

(b) cause a public local inquiry to be held.[111]

2. The Secretary of State shall act as mentioned in (a) or (b) above if a request is made to be heard by either party to the appeal.

3. The persons entitled to be heard are the appellant, the Environment Agency and any person on whom the appellant was required to serve a copy of the notice of appeal.[112] Others may be permitted to be heard by the inspector, and such permission shall not be unreasonably withheld.[113]

4. After the conclusion of a hearing, the person appointed to conduct it shall (unless appointed to determine the appeal) make a report in writing to the Secretary of State, which shall include his conclusions and his recommendations or his reasons for not making any recommendations.[114]

5. The Secretary of State must notify the appellant of his decision and provide a copy of the inspector's report.[115]

6. At the same time, the Secretary of State shall send a copy of the determination and report to the appropriate Agency and to any other person on whom the appellant served a copy of his notice of appeal.[116]

It will be appreciated that these rules provide only the bare bones of **6.76** procedure. The three possible forms of determination—written representation, informal hearing and public local inquiry—correspond to those applicable in planning appeals, and the detailed procedures for each largely mirror the procedures adopted there. All appeals are to be submitted to the Planning Inspectorate.[117] Within 14 days of receiving the notice of appeal, the enforcing authority has to send a copy of the appeal to all relevant parties to the appeal to make them aware of the right to make written representations to the Secretary of State within 21 days and that all those who make such representations will be informed of any public hearing.[118] Accordingly, it is important that all such representations are dated.[119]

The detailed procedure for written representations appeals and hearings **6.77** are to be held in the "spirit" of the relevant regulations in the planning system.[120] In the less formal context of informal hearings, it needs to be

---

[111] 2006 Regulations reg.9(1).
[112] 2006 Regulations reg.9(3).
[113] 2006 Regulations reg.9(4).
[114] 2006 Regulations reg.9(5).
[115] 2006 Regulations reg.10(1).
[116] 2006 Regulations reg.10(2).
[117] DEFRA Circular 01/2006, *Contaminated Land*, Annex 4 para.49
[118] DEFRA Circular 01/2006, *Contaminated Land*, Annex 4 para.50
[119] DEFRA Circular 01/2006, *Contaminated Land*, Annex 4 para.51
[120] See Town & Country Planning (Appeals)(Written Representations Procedure)(England) Regulations 2000 and the Town & Country Planning (Hearings Procedure)(England) Rules 2000 and further guidance in DETR Circular 05/2000, *Planning Appeals: Procedures (Including into Called-in Planning Applications)*, Annexes 1 and 2.

remembered that the rules of natural justice remain paramount, and that the use of such procedure places an onus on the inspector to adopt a fair, thorough and inquisitorial approach.[121] Indeed, given the disputed issues of fact and of expert evidence which may arise on Pt IIA appeals, it is questionable whether any procedure other than formal cross-examination is likely to provide sufficient rigour, other than in relatively straightforward cases. Similarly, if written representations are used, considerations of fairness and natural justice will be relevant,[122] though the courts are more likely to look to the substance of whether the relevant parties have been given a fair opportunity to consider the relevant material and to comment upon it.[123]

6.78   By their nature, public inquiries are more formal and will involve complex arguments or locally controversial arguments. In such cases, the procedure will be dictated by the "spirit" of the Town & Country Planning Appeals (Determination by Inspectors) (Inquiries Procedure) (England) Rules 2000 for inquiries determined by an Inspector or the Town & Country Planning (Inquiries Procedure) for appeals which have been recovered by the Secretary of State. In the case of such inquiries a pre-inquiry timetable will make provision for the submission and exchange of evidence and a pre-inquiry meeting may be held.[124]

Alternative dispute resolution and appeals

6.79 Appeals under s.78L are likely in many cases to be lengthy, complex and expensive. The novelty of the legislation and the absence of full procedural rules for appeals means that there is potential for time being wasted in arriving at appropriate procedures, agreeing facts and identifying the key issues. Given the low number of appeals, planning inspectors are likely to lack experience in determining some of the issues likely to arise; this may make the outcome of the appeals process unpredictable.

6.80   All of these factors mean that the professional advisers to the parties to an appeal would do well to consider whether alternative dispute resolution (ADR) techniques may have a role to play in the appeal process. Whilst any attempt at ADR will have to be without prejudice to the formal appeal process, it may at the very least assist in clarifying the issues and the relative positions of the parties. Issues of what exactly is required by way of remediation and issues of apportionment of liability as between appropriate persons may be examples of matters which would be particularly susceptible to the use of ADR. However, it has to be remembered that one of the parties is a public body, acting in the public interest; the role that ADR can play will ultimately be limited accordingly.

6.81   It should also be remembered that a dispute on appeal will not necessarily simply lie between the appellant and the enforcing authority: the dispute may be between a number of potential appropriate persons as

---

[121] *Dyason v Secretary of State for the Environment* [1998] J.P.L. 778.

[122] See *Geha v Secretary of State for the Environment* [1994] J.P.L. 717.

[123] *Stockton on Tees BC v Secretary of State for the Environment* [1988] J.P.L. 834; *Parkin v Secretary of State for the Environment and East Devon DC* [1993] J.P.L. 141.

[124] DEFRA Circular 01/2006, *Contaminated Land*, Annex 4 para.62.

to which of them should bear responsibility, or in what proportions such responsibility should be shared. There may be advantages in those parties engaging in ADR in parallel with any formal appeal, and thus reaching their own solution rather than having one imposed by the Secretary of State. The Guidance itself recognises the ability of appropriate persons to agree the allocation of costs between themselves.

Evidence in appeals

Appeals to the Secretary of State are administrative proceedings. Hearsay **6.82** evidence and documentary evidence will therefore be admissible, though the issue will arise of what weight is to be attached to it.[125]

The inspector will be entitled to bring to bear his experience and such **6.83** technical knowledge as he possesses.[126] However, this must be based on evidence, and issues of natural justice will arise if the parties are not given the opportunity to comment on the relevant issues.[127] The issue of consultation with other Government departments or agencies will also be important, as their views may carry considerable weight.

The same principles govern the role of expert witnesses as in civil **6.84** proceedings—that is to say, the role of the expert is to draw the attention of the inspector to material considerations, not to argue his own client's case.[128] Legal advisers should be mindful of this when working with the experts on their evidence.

Costs

No provision is made for costs in the case of an appeal determined on the **6.85** basis of written representations. By Sch.20 para.5(1) the provisions on costs of ss.250(2)–(5) of the Local Government Act 1972 apply to local inquiries or hearings. Section 250(5) of the 1972 Act allows orders to be made as to the costs of the parties and as to the parties by whom such costs are to be paid. Subject to those provisions, the costs of any local inquiry are to be defrayed by the Secretary of State.

The same principles as apply to awards of costs on planning appeals are **6.86** likely to apply to costs on appeals to the Secretary of State under Pt IIA.[129] Cost awards will therefore be based on unreasonable behaviour by one or other party and will not follow the event.[130] A specific application for an award of costs will probably relate to the conduct of the appeal; for

---

[125] *Knights Motors v Secretary of State for the Environment and Leicester CC* [1984] J.P.L. 584.

[126] *Westminster Renslade Ltd v Secretary of State for the Environment* [1983] J.P.L. 454; *Homebase Ltd v Secretary of State for the Environment* [1993] J.P.L. B54.

[127] *Archer and Thompson v Secretary of State for the Environment* [1991] J.P.L. 1027; *Relayshine Ltd v Secretary of State for the Environment* [1994] E.G.C.S. 12. See also *Wordie Property Co Ltd v Secretary of State for Scotland* 1984 S.L.T. 345.

[128] *Burroughs Day v Bristol CC* [1996] N.P.C. 3.

[129] See Circular 8/93, *Costs Awards in Planning Appeals*. For Scotland, see the Scottish Office Circular 6/1990, *Awards of Expenses in Appeals and Other Planning Proceedings and in Compulsory Purchase Order Inquiries*.

[130] Circular 8/93, *Costs Awards in Planning Appeals*, Annex 1 para.1; Circular 6/1990, para.4.

example, putting forward material at a late stage, lack of co-operation in the appeals process, refusal to discuss data in advance, or late withdrawal of an appeal or of specific grounds of appeal. The power to award costs relates to costs of and in connection with the inquiry or hearing into the appeal: thus the behaviour of the parties before submission of the appeal is not a matter to be taken into account.[131]

Reasons for appeal decisions

6.87 Where the appeal is determined by an inspector it is to be expected that reasons will be given. While reasons need not cover in detail every argument raised, it is to be expected that they will be intelligible and will deal with the substantial issues, so as to enable the parties to know on what grounds the appeal has been decided. Paragraph 65 of Annex 4 of Circular 01/2006 indicates that details of decision letters will be placed on the register and where decisions do not involve confidential information, copies will be available from the Planning Inspectorate for a small charge.

Appeals from decisions of Secretary of State

6.88 No provision is made in the Act or Regulations for appealing against decisions of the Secretary of State. It is therefore a matter of challenge on ordinary principles of judicial review. Given that the rules applying to the Secretary of State require reasons to be given, challenges may be based on deficiencies in reasoning. However, the courts will most likely be wary of setting too high a standard for the reasoning required, or of setting aside decisions on the basis of unclear or defective reasoning where there is no real or substantial prejudice arising.[132] Ultimately, the question is whether the decision enables the parties to understand on what grounds the appeal was decided and is in sufficient detail to enable them to know what conclusions were reached on the main substantive issues.[133]

Consequence of appeal decision

6.89 By s.78L(2) the outcome of the appeal will be that the notice is quashed, confirmed or modified. Circular 01/2006, Annex 2 para.12.7, raises one potential practical difficulty, which is that if a number of appropriate persons are involved, and separate notices have been served on each, then if an appeal on one notice against the stated apportionment is successful, that will inevitably mean that the other apportionments are affected. If those other notices have not been appealed, there is no power to vary the apportionment, short of issuing fresh notices. The practical answer sug-

---

[131] [1983] J.P.L. 333 (Appeal Decision).

[132] See especially *Save Britain's Heritage v Secretary of State for the Environment* [1991] 2 All E.R. 10; *Bolton Metropolitan DC v Secretary of State for the Environment* (1995) 71 P. & C.R. 309.

[133] *Edinburgh Council v Secretary of State for Scotland* [1998] J.P.L. 224, approving *Hope v Secretary of State for the Environment* [1975] 31 P. & C.R. 120 at 123.

gested in the Circular is to serve at the outset a single notice on all the persons involved, allowing the appellate authority to adjust the apportionment in the single notice. Annex 4 para.70 also points out that in order to give effect to the appeal decision, it may be necessary for the enforcing authority to serve a new notice or notices on another person (for example, where there is a successful appeal that another person should have been served). Such notices will themselves be fully subject to the requirements of the Act, including rights of appeal.

Abandonment of appeals

The appellant can seek to abandon their appeal by notifying the Secretary **6.90** of State under reg.8(3). The request may be refused if by that time the appellant has been notified under reg.11(1) of unfavourable proposed modifications by the appellate authority. This effectively prevents the appellant authority "cutting his losses" in such circumstances: he will be stuck with the proposed modification, subject to this rights under reg.11 to make representations or to be heard.

PART 3: CHALLENGING REMEDIATION NOTICES OTHERWISE THAN BY APPEAL

Judicial Review

A remediation notice is in principle capable of challenge in judicial review **6.91** proceedings on the normal grounds—namely that the issue of the notice was ultra vires; or some procedural defect has affected the issue and service of the notice or the requisite prior procedures, such as consultation; or that service of the notice was motivated by irrelevant considerations or failed to take relevant considerations into account; or that no reasonable authority could have served such a notice. The applicant for judicial review in such circumstances will no doubt seek an order to quash the notice. Any such proceedings will be subject to the normal rules of judicial review in terms of the requirement of leave, promptness and delay, and the grant of relief will be discretionary. The existence of a defect will therefore not necessarily result in the notice being quashed.

Issues for which a judicial review is not appropriate

The inherent limitations on the scope of judicial review mean that it will **6.92** not be an appropriate means of challenging remediation notices on some of the most common grounds likely to occur in practice—except perhaps in the most extreme cases. Arguments of a technical nature that the land is not contaminated as a matter of fact, or that the requirements of the notice are unreasonably onerous, or legal arguments that it has not been served on the appropriate person, are much more suited to the statutory appeal process, involving as they do the detailed examination of issues of fact. Judicial review will be most effective where there has been a clear breach of the requirements of the legislation. An example might be where the notice has been served before the end of the moratorium period,[134] or where the authority has acted in some way which is patently contrary to the mandatory Guidance, where it has made a relevant mistake of law, or has acted ultra vires or unfairly.

Possible exclusion of judicial review

6.93 The provisions of Pt IIA do not seek explicitly to exclude the remedy of judicial review. However, the argument may well arise that judicial review is not available where the applicant has the possibility of a statutory appeal against the notice. The courts are likely to be reluctant to find that the possibility of judicial review is ousted entirely.[135] A relevant issue here may be whether the grounds of appeal conferred by the Regulations include judicial review grounds.[136] The existence of an alternative remedy is however not in itself a ground for refusing judicial review relief. The question may in such cases be whether the existence of the statutory right of appeal is a reason for refusing to allow judicial review as a matter of discretion, judicial review being regarded in this respect as a "long stop" or remedy of last resort.[137] Where the appeal process is a legally more convenient or appropriate remedy, exceptional circumstances may be needed to convince the court to entertain judicial review.[138] Thus, the closer the grounds of judicial review are to the grounds for a statutory appeal, the more likely the courts are to decline jurisdiction.[139] The courts are also likely to be mindful, where the applicant for judicial review is seeking to raise what are effectively procedural defects in a notice, that such defects might well be capable of being remedied as part of the appeal process. The adequacy, speed and convenience of the alternative remedy will also be relevant.[140] Where it appears that there are grounds for judicial review, the discretion to refuse relief will not be lightly exercised,[141] and it may be possible to argue that a statutory appeal to the magistrates, thence to the Divisional or High Court on a point of law, may be a less convenient way of dealing with the matter; as always much will depend on the exact facts and circumstances.

---

[134] See para.4.19ff.
[135] *Pyx Granite Co. Ltd v Ministry of Housing and Local Government* [1960] A.C. 260 at 304, 286; *Leech v Deputy Governor of Parkhurst Prison* [1988] A.C. 533, 580–581.
[136] *R. v Dacorum DC Ex p. Cannon* [1996] 2 P.L.R. 45.
[137] *R. v Panel on Take-Overs and Mergers Ex p. Guinness Plc* [1990] 1 Q.B. 146, 177–178; *R. v Hammersmith and Fulham Ex p Burkett* [2001] Env L.R. 684.
[138] *Harley Development Inc v Commissioner of Inland Revenue* [1996] 1 W.L.R. 727; *R. v Inland Revenue Commissioners Ex p. Preston* [1985] A.C. 835, 852; *R. v Secretary of State for the Home Department Ex p. Swati* [1986] 1 W.L.R. 477, 485.
[139] *R. v IRC Ex p. Bishopp* [1999] C.O.D. 354.
[140] *Ex p Waldron* [1986] Q.B. 824 at 852.
[141] See *R. v Lincolnshire CC and Wealden DC Ex p. Atkinson, Wales and Stratford* (1996) 8 Admin. L.R. 529, 550.

Collateral challenge in criminal proceedings

Another possibility is that the recipient of a remediation notice who **6.94** believes the notice to be invalid may not comply with the notice and, if prosecuted for non-compliance, may seek to raise the invalidity by way of a defence in the criminal proceedings. The law on this issue is difficult and is largely derived from the cases on planning enforcement and on prosecution for breach of bye-laws discussed which are in the following paragraphs. However, this is an area where close regard must be paid to the specific statutory provisions and the overall scheme in which they operate, and it is dangerous to seek to derive general principles from the case law under other legislation.

It is clear from the decision of the House of Lords in *R. v Wicks*[142] that **6.95** the correct approach in cases of collateral challenge is now to consider the interpretation of the provision under which the offence is charged. In *Wicks*, the prosecution was for failure to comply with an enforcement notice under s.179(1) of the Town and Country Planning Act 1990. The question according to the House of Lords was whether "enforcement notice" in this section meant:

(a) a notice which was not liable to be quashed on standard public law grounds (in that case it was alleged that the service of the notice was ultra vires because it had been motivated by bad faith and improper reasons); or

(b) a notice which complies with the formal requirements of the 1990 Act and which has not actually been quashed on appeal or judicial review.[143]

The correct approach was to be found by examining the scheme of the **6.96** legislation, and having considered Pt VII of the 1990 Act, dealing with enforcement, the conclusion was that "enforcement notice" meant a notice issued by the planning authority which was formally valid and which had not been quashed. It should not, however, be concluded from Wicks that the same interpretation should necessarily be applied to notices under analogous legislation. A different conclusion was drawn by the Divisional Court in *Dilieto v Ealing LBC*[144] in relation to a breach of condition notice served under a different section of the same Part of the 1990 Act. When prosecuted for failure to comply, the recipient argued (a) that the notice had been served out of time, and (b) that the relevant condition of the notice was so vague and imprecise as to be a nullity. It was held to be too simplistic an approach to follow *Wicks* simply because the relevant provisions were in the same Part of the same Act. In particular, whereas elaborate provision exists for challenging enforcement notice notices on appeal, no such provision is made in the case of breach of condition notices.[145] It was unlikely that Parliament intended an owner or occupier to

---

[142] [1998] A.C. 92; and *Palacegate Properties Ltd and Camden LBC* [2004] P.L.R. 59.
[143] *Palacegate Properties Ltd and Camden LBC* [2004] P.L.R. 59 at p.119.
[144] [1998] 3 W.L.R. 1403.
[145] [1998] 3 W.L.R. 1403 at 1416.

have no means of challenging a breach of condition notice on the basis that it was out of time. Nor was it appropriate to require such a challenge to be made only by judicial review, as was argued by the prosecuting authority: the question would involve detailed examination of oral and written evidence—a function which was better fulfilled by magistrates in the context of a prosecution rather than by the High Court in judicial review proceedings.[146]

6.97 The general approach to the issue of statutory construction, according to the decision of the House of Lords in *Boddington v British Transport Police*,[147] should begin from the premise that Parliament ought not to be taken to have removed the right of individuals to challenge the relevant administrative measures unless the intention to do so is clear. Such an intention may be more readily found where, as in *R. v Wicks*, the statutory scheme in question is concerned with administrative acts specifically directed at the defendant, and where there is clear and ample opportunity under the legislation for the defendant to challenge the legality of those acts, before being charged with an offence.[148]

Nullity and invalidity

6.98 The distinction between a notice which is so defective as to be a nullity and one which may be affected by invalidity has often been drawn in the context of planning enforcement notices. The traditional approach is that an enforcement notice will be a nullity where it is bad upon its face, so that it is legally ineffective: in such circumstances no prosecution can lie for non-compliance with it, nor can any appeal against it be entertained.

6.99 Matters which can mean that a notice is a nullity include where it is "hopelessly ambiguous and uncertain",[149] for example by failing to state what is required to comply with it[150] or by inadequate identification of the land to which the notice relates.[151] Both of these fundamental defects clearly could occur in relation to remediation notices. In one case reference was made to notices:

> ". . . so utterly extravagant in their terms that anyone acquainted with the property or any other relevant fact would say unhesitatingly that there must be some mistake somewhere,"

---

[146] [1998] 3 W.L.R. 1403 at 1417. To like effect, see *R. v Wicks* [1998] A.C. 92 at 106; and *R. v Jenner* [1983] 1 W.L.R. 873 at 877, CA. Compare *R. v Eterick Trout Co Ltd* [1994] Env. L.R. 165, CA, where it was regarded as inappropriate and an abuse of process to allow arguments as to the validity of a discharge consent condition to be raised before a jury by way of collateral challenge.

[147] [1999] 2 A.C. 143.

[148] [1999] 2 A.C. 143 at 216.

[149] *Miller-Mead v Ministry of Housing and Local Government* [1963] 2 Q.B. 196.

[150] *Dudley Bowers Amusements Enterprises Ltd v Secretary of State for the Environment* [1986] J.P.L. 689.

[151] However, lack of clarity may not be fatal if in the circumstances the recipient was aware what was required or to which premises the notice related: *Coventry Scaffolding Company (London) Ltd v Parker* [1987] J.P.L. 127; *Pitman v Secretary of State for the Environment* [1989] J.P.L. 831.

in which case the recipient may, "if of sufficiently strong nerve, simply disregard them".[152] Issues of bad faith on the part of the authority in serving the notice might also raise the possibility of nullity. By contrast, a notice which is invalid (as opposed to a nullity) is effective until such time as it is set aside, and there may also be the possibility of the defect being rectified as part of the appeal process.

It seems clear on the basis of *R. v Wicks*[153] and *Boddington v British Transport Police*[154] that the distinction between nullity and invalidity is neither conclusive nor critical in the context of collateral challenge. In *Bugg v DPP, DPP v Percy*[155] Woolf L.J. had differentiated between byelaws or subordinate legislation affected by procedural defects (which were valid until such time as set aside by a court) and laws which were "substantially invalid": **6.100**

> "No citizen is required to comply with a law which is bad on its face. If the citizen is satisfied that is the situation, he is entitled to ignore the law".[156]

However, that distinction was rejected by the House of Lords in *R. v Wicks* for the purpose of deciding whether there was a defence to a criminal charge.[157] The Court of Appeal in *R. v Wicks*[158] by contrast had based its judgment on that distinction; a result which can be heavily criticised for perpetrating a flawed legal distinction and for denying the ability to raise matters of invalidity as a defence as of right, rather than as a matter of the court's discretion in judicial review proceedings.[159] In *Boddington*, the House of Lords went further, overruling *Bugg*, and rejecting any distinction between substantive (patent) and procedural (latent) invalidity.[160] The application of these principles to remediation notices is considered in the next paragraph. **6.101**

Application of nullity and collateral challenge principles to remediation notices

How do the principles outlined in the preceding paragraphs apply to remediation notices? As required by *R. v Wicks*, the starting point must be to consider the words of the offence provision at s.78M(1) of the 1990 Act, which states that a person on whom an enforcing authority serves a remediation notice who fails, without reasonable excuse, to comply with any of the requirements of the notice, shall be guilty of an offence. The question is therefore whether a "remediation notice" has been served on **6.102**

---

[152] *Graddage v London Borough of Haringey* [1975] 1 All E.R. 224 at 231.
[153] [1998] A.C. 92.
[154] [1999] 2 A.C. 143.
[155] [1993] Q.B. 473.
[156] [1993] Q.B. 473 at 500.
[157] [1998] A.C. 92 at 108–9, 116–7.
[158] [1996] J.P.L. 743.
[159] Barry Hough, "Collateral Challenge and Enforcement Notices" [1997] J.P.L. 111.
[160] [1999] 2 A.C. 143, 157G, 158E, 164H, 172E.

that person, and what is meant by a "remediation notice" in that context. Looking at the cases on the issue, especially *R. v Wicks*,[161] *Dilieto v Ealing LBC*,[162] and *Boddington v British Transport Police*[163] the following factors will be relevant:

1. *Boddington* suggests that the courts should be reluctant to prevent a defendant raising issues of validity as a defence to criminal proceedings: it is unjust to require magistrates to convict for an offence based on an invalid order or notice.[164]

2. However, Pt IIA provides a statutory scheme for appealing on various grounds against remediation notices: this gives support to the view that those matters which may be grounds of appeal under the statutory system ought not to be allowed to be raised by way of defence in criminal proceedings. Parliament has chosen to confer the right to appeal subject to specific procedures, and different procedures would apply if the matter were raised in the context of a criminal prosecution.

3. It is also relevant to consider whether refusing to hear arguments based on collateral challenge would result in unfairness to the defendant. It is difficult to see how it would be unfair to require the defendant to follow the statutory appeal procedures where these are available.

4. Where the defendant's challenge to the remediation notice is based on grounds other than those falling within the statutory appeal procedure, the issue is whether the matter should be challenged by judicial review rather than by raising a defence in the criminal courts. The courts here will have regard to the issue of fairness to the defendant (in the sense that he may be prejudiced by having to rely on the discretionary remedy of judicial review and by having to take lengthy and expensive judicial review proceedings in respect of a defective notice) and also the issue of good administration of justice (in that judicial review proceedings may be better or worse suited to dealing with different issues and may result in long delay before any prosecution can be brought).

5. On those principles, where the notice is quite obviously bad—for example, in failing to identify the land or to state what is required by way of remediation and who is responsible for it—there are grounds for arguing that the notice is not a "remediation notice" at all, and that the defendant is entitled to ignore it.[165] If the issue however is one of the procedures behind the notice—for example, defective consultation—then the courts may say that these are

---

[161] [1998] A.C. 92.
[162] [1998] 3 W.L.R. 1403.
[163] [1999] 2 A.C. 143.
[164] [1999] 2 A.C. 143, at 162E-G, 164D, 173B and G.
[165] As it was put by Lord Radcliffe in *Smith v East Elloe Rural DC* [1956] A.C. 736, 769–770, does the notice bear a "brand of invalidity upon its forehead?".

issues better suited for determination by judicial review. In that sense, the old and discredited distinction between patent and latent defects may be relevant, even though it is not conclusive. However, various dicta in *Boddington* suggest that the difficulties of dealing with complex legal issues in magistrates' courts should not be exaggerated.[166]

6. The offence under s.78(M)(1) is failure to comply with the notice "without reasonable excuse". It may be argued that an honest belief that the notice is void is a "reasonable excuse." Such an argument seems most unlikely to succeed however, as no mens rea is involved in the offence of not complying with a notice and so the state of mind of the defendant (and in particular, any mistake as to the legal effect of the notice) is not relevant.[167]

It is clearly the intention behind Pt IIA that the issues arising under a **6.103** remediation notice as to what should be done and who should do it, or contribute to its cost, will be dealt with under the statutory appeal process. A party who fails to protect their position by participating in that appeal process does so at their own risk. There may be substantial problems if that appeal process, which may have been lengthy, could be later "unpicked" by collateral challenge. Nevertheless, it is impossible to rule out entirely the possible success of such challenges, in particular in the case of defective notices; and particularly if that defect might have misled the recipient into not exercising their statutory right of appeal.

Challenge in cost recovery proceedings

As described above, the enforcing authority has the power, in specified **6.104** circumstances, to carry out remediation itself.[168] In particular, the power can be used where it is considered necessary to avoid the occurrence of serious harm or pollution in cases of imminent danger, or where the recipient of an enforcement notice fails to comply with any of its requirements.[169] In either case, the authority has power to recover its reasonable costs from the appropriate person or persons,[170] and in some cases to serve a charging notice making the costs and accrued interest a charge on the premises.[171]

If a charging notice is served, then there is a statutory right of appeal **6.105** against it within 21 days to the county court, which may confirm the notice, substitute a different amount, or order that the notice shall be of no effect.[172] However, no appeal procedure is provided in cases where no charging notice is served, and the appropriate person may wish to defend

---

[166] [1999] 2 A.C. 143 at 162E-G, 164D, 173B and G.
[167] See *DPP v Morgan* [1976] A.C. 182; *R. v Bradish* [1990] 1 Q.B. 981.
[168] 1990 Act s.78N.
[169] 1990 Act ss.78N(3)(a) and (c).
[170] 1990 Act s.78P(1).
[171] 1990 Act s.78P(7).
[172] 1990 Act ss.78P(8) and (9).

the civil proceedings for cost recovery by the authority on a number of possible bases:

    (a) that the original remediation notice was a nullity;

    (b) that the circumstances allowing the authority to carry out remediation itself were not in fact applicable;

    (c) that the works carried out by the authority were not "appropriate by way of remediation"[173];

    (d) that the costs were unreasonable[174];

    (e) that the authority failed to have regard to hardship and to the statutory guidance on that issue[175]; or

    (f) that the authority has apportioned too great a share of the cost to the defendant.[176]

6.106   The issue is whether the defendant will be allowed to raise these issues by way of defence in civil proceedings. This involves the question of procedural exclusivity; namely whether matter is such that can be raised as part of the civil proceedings, or whether judicial review is the only appropriate route of challenge to what is essentially an exercise of public law powers.[177]

6.107   In response to the exclusivity argument, if raised by the plaintiff enforcing authority, the defendant will no doubt seek to rely on the line of cases following *Wandsworth LBC v Winder*,[178] which emphasise the right of a defendant to put forward whatever defences are available. It could be said that, as in *Winder*, the defendant is simply defending the action on the ground that he is not liable for the whole sum claimed by the plaintiff.[179]

6.108   On the other hand, there have been cases where the court has refused to allow challenges to action by public authorities by way of defence to civil proceedings, on the basis that it was not a true defence on the merits but rather a challenge on a public law basis to the decision of the authority to initiate the action or proceedings.[180] In such cases the appropriate course will be to consider granting a stay of the proceedings to allow leave for judicial review proceedings to be sought.

6.109   The courts' approach to this issue is inherently a flexible and somewhat unpredictable one, but is at its heart a question of whether the defence constitutes an abuse of the process of the court[181]; the onus resting with the plaintiff enforcing authority to show that the defence is such an abuse.

---

[173] 1990 Act s.78N(1).

[174] 1990 Act s.78P(1).

[175] 1990 Act s.78P(2).

[176] 1990 Act ss.78P(1) and 78F(7).

[177] *O'Reilly v Mackman* [1983] 2 A.C. 237; *Cocks v Thanet DC* [1983] 2 A.C. 286.

[178] [1985] A.C. 461.

[179] See also *R. v Inland Revenue Commissioners Ex p. T.C. Coombs & Co* [1991] 2 A.C. 283 at 304; *British Steel Plc v Commissioners of Customs and Excise* [1996] 1 All E.R. 1002 at 1013; *Credit Suisse v Allerdale BC* [1996] 3 W.L.R. 894 at 926, 937; *Warwick DC v Freeman* (1995) 27 H.L.R. 616.

[180] *Waverley DC v Hilden* [1988] 1 W.L.R. 246; *Avon CC v Buscott* [1988] Q.B. 656.

[181] See *Mercury Communications Ltd v Director General of Telecommunications* [1996] 1 W.L.R. 48 at 57 (Lord Slynn).

Some of the arguments indicated at (a)–(f) above by way of illustration **6.110** would clearly be genuine issues to raise in the context of civil cost recovery proceedings—for example that the costs involved are unreasonable, or that the authority did not apply the criteria on hardship correctly. There would appear to be no abuse inherent in raising those matters in answer to the authority's claim. The position may however be different where the challenge is based on matters which could have been challenged at the time of the original remediation notice: for example, the contaminated condition of the land, the works required to be undertaken, or the share of cost apportioned to the defendant. All of these would be matters which the defendant could have raised at a much earlier stage, either by appealing against the remediation notice or by challenging it in judicial review proceedings—which in either case would have been subject to stringent time limits. Here the authority will have a strong argument that to allow the recipient of a notice to sit back without objection and wait until the authority has expended considerable sums before raising any challenge would be to permit not only an abuse of the process of the court, but also would be contrary to the public interest in securing the clean-up of contaminated land. This argument would of course have less force in cases of urgency under s.78N(3)(a) where no remediation notice has been served and where there may have been no adequate opportunity to challenge or question the authority's chosen course of action (though even there it may have been possible to obtain competitive estimates for the work).

There may naturally be grey areas falling between the examples **6.111** discussed above, but the overarching concept of abuse of process does appear to offer a more satisfactory framework for considering the issues, rather than seeking esoteric distinctions between public and private law. In general, the clearer the authority makes its intentions before exercising its s.78N powers, the more arguments it will have in its favour should its decision be attacked at the later cost—recovery stage.

What is the situation where a remediation notice is served, no appeal is **6.112** made, but at the later stage of cost recovery the defendant asserts that the notice was a nullity? If the notice was a nullity then the authority will have acted ultra vires in acting under s.78N and consequently its costs will not be recoverable. Failure to appeal will not prevent the nullity argument being raised later in civil proceedings, though on the principles stated above, it probably will debar the defendant from objecting to matters which could have been the subject of a statutory appeal.[182]

---

[182] See *West Ham Corp v Charles Benabo and Sons* [1934] 2 K.B. 253 at 264; *Graddage v London Borough of Haringey* [1975] 1 All E.R. 224 at 227, 231.

PART 4: REGISTERS

Registers

6.113 By s.78R(1), subject to exclusions relating to information affecting national security[183] and commercially confidential information,[184] every enforcing authority is required to maintain a register containing prescribed particulars of a number of matters as set out below. The form and descriptions of information contained in the register are to be prescribed by the Secretary of State.[185] The matters to be contained on the register and listed at s.78R(1)are:

(a) remediation notices served by the enforcing authority;

(b) appeals against remediation notices;

(c) remediation statements or remediation declarations under s.78H;

(d) appeals against charging notices;

(e) notices by the local authority effecting designation of land as a special site;

(f) notices of the Secretary of State effecting designation as a special site;

(g) notices terminating the designation of land as a special site;

(h) notifications of what has been done by way of remediation by a person served with a remediation notice or who is required to publish a remediation statement;

(j) notification given by owners or occupiers of what has been done on land by way of remediation;

(k) convictions for prescribed offences; and

(l) any other matters relating to contaminated land prescribed by the Secretary of State.

6.114 It will be appreciated from this list that the register is not intended to be a register of sites which are, or may be, contaminated as such. Rather, it is a register of what is effectively the enforcement history of a site once a remediation notice has been served (or in the case of special sites, their prior designation). As indicated below, those seeking information of a more special nature, such as the outcome of inspections of land carried out by local authorities, will need to consider other provisions.

6.115 Where any particular is entered on a register by the Environment Agency, the Agency must send a copy of those particulars to the local

---

[183] 1990 Act s.78S.
[184] 1990 Act s.78T.
[185] 1990 Act s.78R(2).

authority in whose area the land in question is situated. Information received in this way is entered by the local authority on its own register.[186]

Enforcing authorities must secure that the registers are available at all **6.116** reasonable times for inspection by the public free of charge, and there must be facilities for members of the public to obtain copies of entries on payment of reasonable charges.[187] The Secretary of State may prescribe the places where such registers or facilities are to be made available, and the prescribed places are the principal office of the local authority or (if the enforcing authority is the Agency) its office for the area in which the contaminated land is situated.[188] The registers may be kept in any form.[189]

Other prescribed particulars

The particulars to be contained on the registers are prescribed pursuant to **6.117** s.78R by the Contaminated Land (England) Regulations 2006 reg.13(1) and (2) and Sch.3. A number of matters, with prescribed particulars for each, are listed as follows. Schedule 3 to the Regulations refers to "full particulars" in this respect. This indicates that a summary or précis of the relevant information will not suffice.

Remediation notices

The required particulars in relation to remediation notices served are: **6.118**

(a) the name and address of the person on whom served;

(b) the location and extent of the contaminated land in question sufficient to enable it to be identified, whether by reference to a plan or otherwise;

(c) the relevant significant harm or pollution of controlled waters;

(d) the contaminating substances, and the location of any land from which they have escaped, if that is the case;

(e) the current use of the contaminated land;

(f) what each appropriate person is to do by way of remediation and within what period each of the things is to be done; and

(g) the date of the notice.

Appeals

The particulars for appeals against remediation notices are: **6.119**

---

[186] 1990 Act ss.78R(4) and (6).
[187] 1990 Act s.78R(8).
[188] The Contaminated Land (England) Regulations 2006 reg.13(3).
[189] 1990 Act s.78R(9).

(a) the appeal itself ("full particulars" would indicate that at least the date, the details of the appellant and the grounds of appeal would need to be given);

(b) any decision on the appeal.

Remediation declarations

6.120 In relation to remediation declarations published by the authority under s.78H(6) by the authority where it cannot include particular actions in a remediation notice, the particulars are:

(a) the declaration itself (which must record the things the authority would have required in the notice, the reasons why they would have required them, and the grounds on which they are satisfied they cannot include them);

(b) the location and extent of the contaminated land, sufficient to enable it to be identified; and

(c) the particulars referred to at (c), (d) and (e) above in relation to remediation notices.

Remediation statements

6.121 In relation to statements under s.78H(7) by the person responsible, or under s.78H(9) by the enforcing authority in default, the relevant matters are as for remediation declarations, namely:

(a) full particulars of the statement (which must contain the past, present or future remediation actions, the person carrying them out and the date by which they are expected to be carried out);

(b) the location and extent of the contaminated land; and

(c) the same particulars (c), (d) and (e) as remediation notices.

Appeals against charging notices

6.122

(a) any appeal against a charging notice served by the enforcing authority under s.78P; and

(b) any decision on the appeal.

Special sites

6.123 The Environment Agency must register particulars of:

(a) any notice given by the local authority of the Secretary of State which has effect as the designation of a special site;

(b) the relevant provision of the Regulations by dint of which the land is a special site;

(c) any notice given by the Agency under s.78Q of its intention to adopt a remediation notice already served; and

(d) any notice given under s.78Q terminating the designation of land as a special site.

Notification of claimed remediation

Full particulars of any notification given to the authority under s.78R(1)(h) **6.124** or (j) of remediation claimed to have been carried out. This is discussed further below.

Convictions

Any convictions for offences under s.78M for failure to comply with a **6.125** remediation notice, including:

(a) the name of the offender;

(b) the date of conviction;

(c) the penalty imposed; and

(d) the name of the court.

Agency guidance

In relation to site-specific guidance issued by the Agency to a local **6.126** authority under s.78V(1), the date of the guidance must be placed on the register. It appears that the substance of the guidance, curiously, need not be.

Other controls

This category covers the situations where the enforcing authority is **6.127** precluded from serving a remediation notice because of the application of other statutory controls. The particulars in this case are:

(a) the location and extent of the contaminated land;

(b) the matters covered by particulars (c), (d) and (e) in the case of remediation notices;

(c) any steps carried out by means of enforcement action under the Pollution Prevention and Control regime towards remedying the relevant harm or pollution;

(d) any steps of which the authority has knowledge, carried out under s.27 of the 1990 Act towards remedying the relevant harm or pollution;

(e) any steps of which the authority has knowledge, carried out under s.59 of the 1990 Act in relation to unlawfully deposited waste or the consequences of its deposit, including the name of the waste collection authority involved, if any; and

(f) any water discharge consent the existence of which precludes the enforcing authority from specifying a particular thing in a remediation notice.

Registers: notifications by owners, occupiers and other appropriate persons

6.128 Most of the matters listed as requiring to be included within the register are obvious and require no explanation. However, ss.8R(1)(h) and (j) are somewhat different. They require the enforcing authority to place on the register notifications by persons served with a remediation notice, or owners or occupiers, of what they claim has been done by way of remediation. This is the only statutory reference to such notifications contained in Pt IIA.

6.129 The Regulations state that such notifications must contain[190]:

(a) the location and extent of the land sufficient to enable it to be identified;

(b) the name and address of the person who it is claimed has done each thing;

(c) a description of any thing it is claimed has been done; and

(d) the period within which it is claimed each such thing was done.

6.130 The statutory reference to such notifications provides a means by which an appropriate person, owner or occupier can record in a public form what has been done to comply with a remediation notice or remediation statement. In this way some of the blight which might otherwise affect the land may be alleviated. However, it is important to note subs.(3), which negatives any implied representation by the authority that what is stated on the register as having been done has in fact been done, or has been done adequately. The authority's role is therefore simply one of a "postbox", recording notification which it receives; as it was put in debate, it is not the responsibility of the enforcing authority to indicate that the land has "a clean bill of health".[191] The owner of the land might well ask, in those circumstances, how the land is to get a "clean bill of health" and how the blighting effects of the service of a notice are to be removed where all that the notice required has been done.

Exclusions from the register: national security

6.131 By s.78S(1) no information may be included on the register if in the opinion of the Secretary of State its inclusion could be contrary to the interests of national security. It is for the Secretary of State to issue a

---

[190] 2006 Regulation reg.13(2).
[191] *Hansard*, HL Vol.562, col.1047.

direction under s.78S(2) relating to information which in his view affects national security. That direction may either be specific or general, that is related to information of a particular description. It may also require certain descriptions of information to be referred to the Secretary of State for his determination: such information must not be included on the register in the interim. The enforcing authority is required by s.78S(3) to notify the Secretary of State of any information which it excludes from the register in pursuance of such directions.

Section 78S(4) provides a procedure whereby any person who feels that **6.132** information may be such as to fall within s.78S(1) can give a notice to the Secretary of State specifying the information and indicating its apparent nature. The enforcing authority must at the same time be notified and the relevant information may then not be included on the register until the Secretary of State determines that it should be included.

Commercially confidential information: procedures

By s.78T(1) no information relating to the affairs of an individual or **6.133** business shall be included on the register without the consent of the individual or, unless pursuant to a direction from the Secretary of State, where that information is commercially confidential. Information is only commercially confidential for this purpose where it is determined to be so by the enforcing authority or by the Secretary of State on appeal, pursuant to the following procedures:

1. Where it appears to the enforcing authority that information might be commercially confidential, it must give notice to the person or business to whom the information relates, effectively warning them that the information will be placed on the register unless excluded under the section.[192]

2. The authority must give the person or business a reasonable opportunity of objecting to its inclusion and of making representations to justify that objection.[193]

3. The authority must determine, taking into account any representations made, whether the information is or is not commercially confidential.[194]

4. Where the determination is that the information is not commercially confidential, a period of 21 days from the date on which the decision is notified to the person concerned must be allowed to elapse before the information is entered on the register.[195]

5. The person concerned may appeal to the Secretary of State within that period, and if an appeal is brought the information shall not

---

[192] 1990 Act s.78T(2)(a).
[193] 1990 Act s.78T(2)(b).
[194] 1990 Act s.78T(2).
[195] 1990 Act s.78T(3)(a).

be entered until seven days after the appeal is finally determined or is withdrawn.[196]

6. Appeal shall be by way of private hearing if either party requests it or if the Secretary of State so directs.[197]

7. Appeals are subject to s.15(10) of the 1990 Act[198] and to s.114 of the 1995 Act, which allows the Secretary of State to delegate determination of the appeal to an appointed person.[199] Schedule 20 of the 1995 Act has effect with regard to such delegated appeals, in respect of which the appointed person has the same powers as the Secretary of State.[200] No local inquiry may be held in relation to appeals under s.78T.[201] The provisions of the Local Government Act 1972 ss.250(2)–(5) on evidence and costs will apply to hearings under Sch.20.[202]

8. The Secretary of State may give directions to enforcing activities as to specified information, or descriptions of information, which are required in the public interest to be included in registers notwithstanding that the information may be commercially confidential.[203]

9. Information which is excluded on commercial confidentiality grounds ceases to be treated as confidential after four years from the date of the relevant determination.[204] The onus rests with the person who furnished it to apply to the authority for it to remain excluded. There is no obligation on the authority to give any warning or notice that this period is about to elapse. The same procedures for determination and appeals as above will then apply. There is an oddity in the drafting of subs.78T(8), which refers to "the person who furnished the information". This may not by now be the same person as the person whose commercial interests are affected: indeed the two persons may never have been the same. The subsection should presumably have read: ". . . the person to whom or to whose business it then relates may apply, . . . etc.".

Meaning of "commercially confidential"

6.134 By s.78T(10) information is commercially confidential for the purpose of making a determination under the section if its inclusion on the register would prejudice to an unreasonable degree the commercial interests of the relevant person or business.

[196] 1990 Act s.78T(3).
[197] 1990 Act s.78T(4).
[198] 1990 Act s.78T(5).
[199] 1990 Act s.78T(6).
[200] 1995 Act Sch.20 para.3.
[201] 1995 Act Sch.20 para.4(3).
[202] 1995 Act Sch.20 para.5.
[203] 1990 Act s.78T(7).
[204] 1990 Act s.78T(8).

The main concern of an owner of contaminated land is likely to be the **6.135** blighting effect on value, resulting from public knowledge that the land is contaminated or is subject to enforcement action. However, s.78T(11) expressly states that any prejudice relating to the value of the contaminated land in question, or otherwise to its occupation or ownership, is to be disregarded in making the determination. As the Circular makes clear, this means that information cannot be excluded from the register solely on the basis that its inclusion might affect its saleability or sale price.[205]

Reports by the Environment Agency on contaminated land

Under s.78U, so that the public may be reassured that action is being **6.136** taken in respect of contaminated land, the Environment Agency is required from time to time to prepare and publish a report on the state of contaminated land. Such reports are to be published "from time to time", or at any time requested by the Secretary of State.[206] For that purpose a local authority must respond to a written request to furnish the Agency with the relevant information, namely such information as the local authority may have, or may reasonably be expected to obtain, with respect to the condition of contaminated land in its area, acquired in the exercise of its functions under Pt IIA.[207]

Handling information outside the statutory registers

As indicated above, the registers under s.78R provide only a partial picture. **6.137** They are focused on the enforcement history of the site and do not relate to actions or information preceding the service of a remediation notice (or if the site is a special site, its designation as such). It is the process of inspecting land and determining whether it is contaminated which may in practice prove more controversial and which may have serious effects on value and marketability well before any notice is served. The question of how authorities handle such information is therefore important. Local authorities will need to consider the Environmental Information Regulations 2004, the provisions of the Local Government Act 1972 and general issues of confidentiality and data protection legislation.[208]

---

[205] DEFRA Circular 01/2006, *Contaminated Land*, Annex 2 para.17.11.
[206] 1990 Act s.78U(1).
[207] 1990 Act ss.78U(2) and (3).
[208] See para.3.146ff.

SECTION 3
OTHER REGIMES

Chapter 7

WATER

Contaminated land may have an adverse effect on the water environment **7.01** in a number of ways. Contaminants present in soil or shallow groundwater may run off, leach or be washed out of the soil so as to cause pollution of surface waters. They may enter underground drains, culverts or other conduits which discharge into such waters. Further, contaminants may be transported vertically down into deeper groundwater, where they may compromise important water supply resources in the form of aquifers.

The contaminated land regime in Pt IIA itself recognises these risks in **7.02** that pollution of controlled waters is one of the two main limbs of the definition of "contaminated land".[1] However there is also of course a regime for the control of pollution of water resources, which is contained in Pt III of the Water Resources Act 1991. Apart from the reference at s.78YB(4) to the fact that a remediation notice should not require anything which would impede or prevent the making of a discharge in pursuance of a consent given under the Water Resources Act,[2] Pt IIA is not explicit on how the relationship between these two sets of provisions is to operate. Nor is the guidance provided in the current version of the DEFRA Circular helpful in this respect.

This chapter seeks to provide a basic description of how the water **7.03** pollution provisions operate in the context of contaminated land. It is not the intention to provide a detailed exposition of water pollution law generally, for which reference may be made to the specialist texts on that subject.[3]

Water pollution offences

Section 85 of the Water Resources Act 1991 creates the principal offences **7.04** in relation to pollution of controlled waters. Some of these offences may be of relevance in the case of surface waters or groundwater polluted by the ingress of substances from contaminated land:

1. Causing or knowingly permitting any poisonous, noxious or polluting matter or any solid waste matter to enter controlled waters. Clearly, this offence may be applicable to a contaminated land situation.

---

[1] See para.3.57ff.
[2] See para.3.88.
[3] See, e.g. J.H. Bates, *Water and Drainage Law* (London: Sweet & Maxwell, looseleaf); W. Howarth and D. McGillivray, *Water Pollution and Water Quality Law* (Shaw & Sons Limited, 2001).

2. Causing or knowingly permitting any matter, other than trade effluent or sewage effluent, to enter controlled waters by being discharged from a drain or sewer in contravention of a prohibition imposed under s.86 of the Act. This offence, being dependent on the matter in question being discharged through a drain or sewer, is perhaps unlikely to be relevant in the majority of contaminated land situations, unless there has been ingress of contaminants from the soil into a drainage system.

3. Causing or knowingly permitting any trade effluent or sewage effluent to be discharged:

   (a) into any controlled waters; or
   (b) from land in England and Wales, through a pipe into the sea outside the seaward limits of controlled waters.

   The second limb of the offence is not relevant here, but, to the extent that the material which enters controlled waters from contaminated land is regarded as trade effluent or sewage effluent, the first limb may be of relevance.

4. Causing or knowingly permitting trade effluent or sewage effluent to be discharged, in contravention of a s.86 prohibition, from a building or from fixed plant:

   (a) on to or into any land; or
   (b) into waters of a lake or pond which are not inland freshwaters.

   This offence is only committed if the discharge contravenes a prohibition imposed under s.86 by notice served by the Environment Agency on the discharger or by virtue of regulations prescribing either substances or processes for this purpose.[4] The implication of this is that in the absence of such a prohibition, trade and sewage effluent may be discharged in the ways mentioned in the subsection without any discharge consent. For example, therefore, trade effluent may be discharged (subject to any requirement for a waste management licence) onto land or into a pit, or into a pond or lagoon, provided that it does not itself discharge into a river or watercourse or into another lake or pond which so discharges. The provision only applies, and consequently an offence can only be committed, where the discharge is from a building or from fixed plant. Thus the removal of trade effluent from open land (e.g. leachate from a landfill site) by road tanker to a settlement lagoon would not be within the subsection, whereas conveyance of the same material by a system of pipework would. The provision is therefore unlikely to be of relevance in normal contaminated land situations.

5. The entry of matter into land freshwaters so as to impede the flow, thereby aggravating pollution. Its relevance to most contaminated land situations would appear to be limited.

---

[4] Water Resources Act 1981 s.86(1) and (2).

6. The contravention of the conditions of any discharge consent. In practice most discharges from contaminated land are of their nature likely to be unconsented.[5]

"Controlled waters"

The offences referred to above are in the main related to the pollution of **7.05** controlled waters. The definition of this term is provided by s.104 of the Water Resources Act and encompasses:

1. territorial waters extending seaward for three miles from the territorial sea baselines;

2. coastal waters, i.e. those within the territorial sea baseline as far as the high tide level or fresh water limits and including any enclosed dock adjoining such waters;

3. waters of relevant lakes or ponds, i.e. any lake or pond (whether natural or artificial or above or below ground) which discharges into a relevant river or watercourse (see below) or into another lake or pond which is itself a relevant lake or pond[6];

4. waters of relevant rivers or watercourses above the fresh water limit.[7] This term includes underground and artificial rivers or watercourses but excludes public sewers and sewers or drains which run into public sewers. It may include canals,[8] which is of practical relevance, given that many canal systems are within areas of historically heavily contaminated land and are increasingly used for recreational purposes for which water quality is important;

5. groundwaters, i.e. "any waters contained in underground strata".[9]

Some of these provisions are subject to the power of the Secretary of **7.06** State to make an order providing how waters are to be treated in terms of these definitions.[10]

The "poisonous, noxious or polluting matter" offence

As stated above, the offence relating to the entry of poisonous, noxious or **7.07** polluting matter into controlled waters is of relevance to contaminated land. The Act provides no definition of the phrase "poisonous, noxious or polluting"; but there is now some judicial authority on the point.

---

[5] On the collateral challenge to consent conditions by way of defence to prosecution, see *R. v Ettrick Trout Co Ltd and William Baxter* [1994] Env. L.R. 165.

[6] Together, relevant lakes or ponds and relevant rivers or watercourses are known as "inland freshwaters"; See s.104(1)(c).

[7] ibid.

[8] See also *Environment Agency v Brock Plc* [1998] Env. L.R. 607 (DC) where a man-made ditch was included within the definition.

[9] *cf.* the definition in Pt IIA (see para.3.71ff).

[10] Water Resources Act 1981 s.104(4).

7.08   In *National Rivers Authority v Egger UK Ltd*[11] a ruling was given in the context of a submission relating to the meaning of the term "polluting" in s.85. The defence argued that the word can only be understood in the context of what the matter in question affects, harms or worsens; in other words that some form of demonstrable effect was a prerequisite. The prosecution argued that all that was necessary was that the matter discharged was, of its nature, capable of causing harm. The judge accepted the prosecution's argument and suggested that the correct test was to look at the nature of the discharge and ask:

> "Is that discharge capable of causing harm to a river, in the sense of causing damage to uses to which a river might be put; damage to animal, vegetable or other—if there is such other life which might live in a river, or damaging that river aesthetically? ... One looks at that test in relation, it seems to me, to a natural, unpolluted river, and if the discharge is capable of causing such harm, then the offence is made out; the material amounts to polluting matter... It is, in my view, wholly unnecessary to prove that damage was, in fact, caused."

7.09   "Polluting" is in this context a wider term than poisonous or noxious: in *R v Dovermoss*[12] it was held that the word "pollute" and its derivations should be given their ordinary *Oxford English Dictionary* definition: "to make physically impure, foul or filthy; to dirty, stain, taint or befoul" and that polluting matter does not need to be either poisonous or noxious. What is relevant is not necessarily actual harm but the potential for such harm.[13]

7.10   The issue is a very important one since unlike incidents of surface water pollution, water pollution resulting from contaminated land may take years to present any signs of harmful effects. Even then, the harm is unlikely to present itself in any obvious form such as dead fish; but may, rather, have aesthetic effects such as discolouration from leaching or may present a threat to public or private abstraction sources. If the argument is accepted that capability to cause harm is sufficient and that "harm" is determined by effect on legitimate uses of surface and groundwater, then the task of bringing prosecutions under s.85 for pollution from contaminated sites will be eased considerably. The suggestion in *Egger* that the test is to be applied in relation to "a natural, unpolluted river" will also make the prosecution's task easier by avoiding, for example, arguments by the defence that their contribution to the state of an already less than pristine aquifer or watercourse could not be regarded as "polluting".

Pollution from abandoned mines

7.11   By s.89(3) of the 1991 Act, a person was not guilty of the offence by reason only of permitting water from an abandoned mine to enter controlled waters. The issue of the polluting effects of such mine water gave rise to

---

[11] Newcastle upon Tyne Crown Court, June 15–17, 1992; [1992] Water Law 169.
[12] [1995] Env. L.R. 258.
[13] *Express Ltd v Environment Agency* [2005] EWHC Admin 1710; [2005] 1 W.L.R. 223; [2005] Env. L.R. 7.

much public controversy, particularly as former mines were being closed in increasing numbers during the 1990s.[14] The Environment Act has removed the defence in relation to mines (or parts of mines) abandoned after December 31, 1999.[15] The difficulty however will remain of showing that the acts or omissions of the operator (as opposed to natural forces) were causative of the pollution.[16] The removal of the defence was coupled with the introduction of a new regime in Ch.IIA of Pt III to the 1991 Act dealing with procedures for abandonment, including the requirement for the operator to give the Agency at least six months' notice of proposed abandonment.[17]

Responsibility for investigating and dealing with polluting discharges **7.12** from coal mines rests with the Coal Authority, which was established following the privatisation of British Coal in 1994. Under the Coal Industry Act, as amended by the Water Act 2003, the Coal Authority has power to prevent, mitigate or otherwise remediate discharge of water from abandoned or other coal mines vested in the Authority, including powers of entry and of compulsory purchase where significant pollution or serious harm to human health are involved.[18] The Authority has a memorandum of understanding with the Environment Agency. The closure and aftercare of mining facilities will be affected by the requirements of the Mining Waste Directive 2006/21, which is due to be transposed into law by May 1, 2008, and which will require the compilation of an inventory of closed and abandoned facilities that cause serious negative environmental impact, or which may potentially do so in the short and medium term, by May 1, 2012.

The "trade effluent" or "sewage effluent" offences

By s.85(3), the discharge of trade effluent or sewage effluent into any **7.13** controlled waters may result in an offence. If trade or sewage effluent is discharged then it does not matter whether the material is poisonous, noxious or polluting: it is the origin of the effluent which is crucial, not its characteristics.[19] "Sewage effluent" is defined by s.221(1) as including any effluent from the sewage disposal or sewage treatment works of a sewage undertaker. "Trade effluent" includes, by s.221(1), any effluent which is discharged from premises used for carrying on any trade or industry, other

---

[14] For example pollution from the Wheal Jane tin mine in Cornwall and the Dalquharran Colliery in Ayrshire; see generally M. Poustie, "The Demise of Coal and Causing Water Pollution" [1994] 6 E.L.M. 96 and also the consultation paper, *Paying for Our Past* (DoE, March 1994).

[15] See ss.89(3A)–(3C).

[16] Shown in the failure of the private prosecution of British Coal by the Anglers' Co-operative Association in 1993: Cardiff Crown Court, December 2, 1993; ENDS Report 44, 1997, p.44.

[17] 1991 Act ss.91A and 91B, and see the Mines (Notice of Abandonment) Regulations 1998 (SI 1998/892). "Abandonment" is defined broadly and includes the discontinuance of operations for the removal of water from the mine.

[18] Coal Industry Act 1994 ss.4A, 4B and 4C, inserted by Water Act 2003 s.85, in force April 1, 2004 (SI 2004/641).

[19] Trade effluent or sewage effluent can also of course be poisonous, noxious or polluting matter: *National Rivers Authority v Yorkshire Water Services Ltd* [1995] 1 A.C. 444 (sewage effluent containing iso-octanol).

than surface water or domestic sewage. The application of this definition to contaminated land situations is problematic, though it is certainly possible to envisage situations where the offence could be relevant. Leachate from a still operational landfill site (possibly one which has ceased to receive waste but is being actively managed) can be regarded as trade effluent; as can waste oils or solvents leaking from tanks or drums on an industrial site, or material which escapes from defective drainage systems.

7.14   It should be noted, however, that the language of s.85(3) is materially different to that of s.85(1): whereas the latter refers to an entry of matter into controlled waters, s.85(3) refers to the discharge from premises used for trade or industry. It does not necessarily follow that every entry of matter from such premises into controlled waters can be aptly described as a "discharge".[20]

Causing and knowingly permitting

7.15 The offences in relation to controlled waters may be committed either by causing or by knowingly permitting. The concepts of "causing" and "knowingly permitting" have been adopted in Pt IIA to define who are the primary "appropriate persons" to bear liability for remediation of contaminated land.

7.16   In the case of water pollution from contaminated land the offence of "causing" under s.87 will normally be committed by the person who initially caused the contamination. Causation in this respect will be approached in an everyday common sense way and does not imply any requirement of intention, negligence or foreseeability.[21] Thus an accidental spillage which has the consequence of contaminating land and subsequently surface water or groundwater may constitute the offence. The storage or handling of material can be sufficient to establish causation in that sense.[22]

7.17   However, it remains the case that a charge of "causing" will require some specific act that caused the pollution to be identified, and thus causing may not be appropriate as a charge where the defendant's role is a completely passive one, for example where contaminated material leaches onto the defendant's property from another site and thence into controlled waters, or where the defendant owns historically contaminated land within which contaminants are entering an aquifer. Here a charge of "knowingly permitting" may be the appropriate course: permitting is a looser and vaguer concept than causing[23] and may have various shades of meaning

---

[20] This argument appears to have been accepted by magistrates in the unsuccessful prosecution of Coal Products Limited by the NRA (Chesterfield Magistrates Court, 1994). The magistrates held that tar deposits from a closed coal carbonisation site which had seeped into the River Rother had not been "discharged", that term implying release via a pipe or similar connection. Accordingly there was no case to answer under s.85(3).

[21] *Alphacell Ltd v Woodward* [1972] A.C. 824, HL; *Wrothwell v Yorkshire Water Authority* [1984] Crim. L.R. 43.

[22] *Environment Agency v Empress Car Co (Abertillery) Ltd* [1999] 2 A.C. 22 (pollution arising from vandalism on defendant's site); *Environment Agency v Brock Plc* [1998] Env. L.R. 607 (escape of leachate where seal in new pipe failed unexpectedly).

[23] *McLeod v Buchanan* [1940] 2 All E.R. 179; *James & Son Ltd v Smee* [1955] 1 Q.B. 78.

ranging from giving permission, or giving control, through to failing to prevent.

Therefore, in cases of historic contamination, where the owner or **7.18** occupier of land was not the cause, criminal liability will turn on the issue of "knowingly permitting", There are two elements to this offence: the failure to prevent pollution, and knowledge on the part of the defendant.[24] Clearly, a landowner who does not know that his land is contaminated and is polluting controlled waters cannot be guilty of the offence. However, the crucial question is exactly what knowledge is necessary for the offence and whether such knowledge may in any circumstances be inferred. There is authority to suggest that as well as knowledge that land is contaminated, there must also be knowledge that contaminants are entering controlled waters and that such contaminants are of their nature poisonous, noxious or polluting.[25] However, there is also authority to suggest that it may be possible to infer such knowledge in the absence of evidence from the defence that there was no knowledge; and also that deliberately shutting one's eyes to the obvious may constitute constructive knowledge.[26] As Lord Bridge stated in *Westminster CCl v Croyalgrange Ltd*[27]:

> ". . . it is always open to the tribunal of fact, when knowledge on the part of the defendant is to be proved, to base a finding of knowledge on evidence that the defendant has deliberately shut his eyes to the obvious or refrained from inquiring because he suspected the truth but did not want to have his suspicions confirmed."

Once the landowner is aware of the situation, he becomes vulnerable to **7.19** the argument that, by failing to prevent the continuation of the pollution, he is knowingly permitting it. In such cases the crucial question is likely to be what steps the defendant could have taken to prevent the pollution: a man cannot be taken to permit that which he cannot control.[28] In some statutory contexts the word "permit" connotes giving permission, leave or licence for some thing to be done.[29] However, it can also mean abstention from taking reasonable steps to prevent something, where it is within a man's power to prevent it.[30] The difficulty then may lie in what constitutes

---

[24] *Alphacell Ltd v Woodward* [1972] A.C. 824, per Lord Wilberforce.

[25] *R. v Hallam* [1957] 1 Q.B. 569, 573; *Schulmans Incorporated Ltd v NRA* (Queens Bench Division, unreported, December 3, 1991); summarised at [1993] Water Law 25 in an article by David Wilkinson.

[26] *Westminster CC v Croyalgrange Ltd* [1986] 1 W.L.R. 674; *Schulmans Incorporated* case and article cited at fn.25 above.

[27] [1986] 1 W.L.R. 674, p.684.

[28] "One cannot permit that which one does not control:" *Tophams Ltd v Earl of Sefton* [1967] A.C. 50, at 65 (Lord Hodson). See also, on different statutory wording, *R. v Staines Local Board* (1888) 60 L.T. 261, at 264: "A man cannot be said to suffer another person to do a thing which he has no right to prevent."; *Yorkshire West Riding Council v Holmfirth Urban Sanitary Authority* [1894] 2 Q.B. 842; *Rochford Rural Council v Port of London Authority* [1914] 2 K.B. 916.

[29] *Lomas v Peek* [1947] 2 All E.R. 574; *Shave v Rosner* [1954] 2 Q.B. 113; *Kent CC v Beaney* [1993] Env. L.R. 225.

[30] *Berton v Alliance Economic Investment Co* [1922] 1 K.B. at 759; *Bromsgrove DC v Carthy* (1975) P. & C.R. 34; *Tophams Ltd v Earl of Sefton* [1967] A.C. 50 at 62, 64–5, 68, 75, 83, 85.

reasonable steps: this may not necessarily equate to any steps which may be scientifically demonstrated to have a remedial or mitigating effect.[31] Such steps may include, for example, the exercise of contractual rights to exert legitimate pressure on another party to cease polluting activity.[32]

Contamination of water sources

7.20 By s.72 of the Water Industry Act 1991 a person commits an offence if he is guilty of any act or neglect whereby the water in any waterworks which is used or likely to be used:

    (a) for human consumption or domestic purposes; or

    (b) for manufacturing food or drink for human consumption,

is polluted or likely to be polluted.

"Waterworks" includes for the purposes of the section:

    (a) any spring, well, adit, borehole, service, reservoir or tank; and

    (b) any main or other pipe or conduit of a water undertaker;[33] and

    (c) any pipe or conduit of a licensed water supplier.[34]

7.21 The offence may therefore involve either public or private water supplies. Two exclusions apply: one relating to the cultivation of land in accordance with the principles of good husbandry, the other to the reasonable use of oil or tar on public highways.[35]

7.22 The offence is punishable on summary conviction by a fine not exceeding the statutory maximum and, in the case of a continuing offence, to a further fine not exceeding £50 for each day the offence is continued; on indictment the penalty is an unlimited fine and/or up to two years' imprisonment.[36] In 1994 it was reported that Severn Trent Water was considering bringing a prosecution (presumably under this provision) against a Telford company which polluted the River Severn with industrial solvent, causing serious disruption to domestic supplies in the Worcester area.[37]

Penalties for water pollution offences

7.23 The offences under s.85 are subject to imprisonment for a term not exceeding three months and/or to a fine not exceeding £20,000 on summary conviction. On conviction on indictment, imprisonment may be for a term up to two years and the fine is unlimited.[38]

---

[31] See *Mayor and Corpn of High Wycombe v The Conservators of the River Thames* (1898) 78 L.T. 463, at 465.

[32] *London Borough of Tower Hamlets v London Docklands Development Corp* (Knightsbridge Crown Court, April 13, 1992).

[33] Water Industry Act 1991 s.72 subs.(5).

[34] Added by Water Act 2003 s.101 and Sch.8, para.21.

[35] Water Industry Act 1991 s.72 subss.(2) and (3).

[36] Water Industry Act 1991 s.72 subs.(4).

[37] *The Times*, June 15, 1994.

[38] Water Resources Act 1991 s.85(6).

There is the usual provision whereby criminal liability may be imposed **7.24** on directors, managers, secretaries and similar officers where the company's offence was committed with the consent or connivance or was attributable to any neglect on their part.[39]

Most prosecutions under these provisions involve straightforward pollu- **7.25** tion incidents affecting surface waters. However, there have been a number of notable prosecutions where soil contamination and groundwater have been involved (many emanating from underground storage tanks):

1. In November 1989, Mid-Sussex Water Company were fined £20,000 and ordered to pay £5,000 costs when 1,000 gallons of diesel oil leaked from a corroded pipe into a borehole at Poverty Bottom, near Seaford, Sussex.

2. In 1992, knitwear manufacturer Pringle of Scotland was prosecuted successfully by the NRA for polluting an unconfined sandstone aquifer with chlorinated solvents discharged from a soakaway forming part of the company's effluent disposal system. The company was fined £5,000 and ordered to pay costs of £21,908 (including the NRA's extensive investigations) and compensation of £1,890.[40]

3. In 1993 a metal plating company, Deniet & Son of Mildenhall, Suffolk was fined £5,000 for pollution of groundwater by a leak of effluent containing cyanide from a sump on its site.[41]

4. In 1995, Shell UK became the first petrol retailer to be prosecuted for pollution from an underground storage tank at a filling station near Lytham St Annes. It received a £2,500 fine.[42]

5. In 1998, ICI was fined £300,000 at Warrington Crown Court under water pollution and other offences after a major choloform spill into groundwater from a pipeline at its Runcorn site.[43]

6. In 1999, British Energy was fined £70,000 when a drinking water aquifer was contaminated with oil from its Dungeness power station, involving a £1.5 million clean-up.[44]

7. In 2000, Railtrack Plc and Silverlink Trains were each fined £125,000 by Aylesbury Crown Court for polluting groundwater with 200,000 litres of oil after a nine-month underground leak at Bletchley, involving a £1 million clean up.[45]

8. In 2000 and 2002, Total Fina was fined £66,000 and £54,000 in respect of separate leaks from underground tanks at filling stations in Hertfordshire, Essex and Hampshire.[46]

[39] Water Resources Act 1991 s.217(1).
[40] ENDS Report No.211 (August 1992) p.37.
[41] ENDS Report No.224 (September 1993).
[42] ENDS Report No.247 (August 1995).
[43] ENDS Report No.278 (March 1998).
[44] ENDS Report No.289 (February 1999).
[45] ENDS Report No.301 (February 2000).
[46] ENDS Report Nos 305 (June 2000) and 328 (May 2002).

9. In 2001 waste company Southern Refining Services was fined £76,000 in total for various offences when it was found to be discharging solvents into an offsite drain, polluting soil and groundwater. Its managing director was personally fined £10,000.[47]

10. In 2002, BP was fined £60,000 following a leak of petrol from an underground storage tank at a service station close to the water abstraction point for Luton.[48]

11. In 2003 chemical company Rhoda was fined £19,000 for three offences in respect of a leak of 22 tonnes of polyphosphoric acid involving groundwater pollution.[49]

12. In 2007, BP was again prosecuted and fined for groundwater contamination from a filling station. The contamination was discovered in the context of a ground condition survey. BP was fined £8,000 by Luton magistrates. Clean up costs were some £320,000.[50]

Costs and compensation orders

7.26 In cases where a prosecution is brought for water pollution arising from contaminated land, the Agency as enforcing authority may have incurred very considerable expenses both in investigating the offence and possibly in dealing with its consequences.

7.27 Section 18 of the Prosecution of Offences Act 1985 provides for the court to make an order for the convicted person to pay such costs as are just and reasonable to the prosecutor. This sum may properly include not only the actual costs of prosecution but also the investigation costs.[51] In principle, whilst there is no necessary relationship between the fine imposed and the costs, it has been said that the two should not be grossly disproportionate[52]; the reality however is that in many environmental cases, especially those heard in magistrates' courts, the sums sought and recovered by the prosecution for the costs of investigating the incident will far exceed the fine imposed.

7.28 Under s.130 of the Powers of Criminal Courts (Sentencing) Act 2000 a court by or before which a person is convicted of an offence, instead of or in addition to dealing with him in any other way, may, on application or otherwise make a compensation order requiring him to pay compensation for any personal injury, loss or damage resulting from that offence or any other offence taken into consideration by the court in determining sentence; the court must give reasons if it does not make an order in cases where it is empowered to do so.[53] A monetary limit of £5,000 applies to the

---

[47] ENDS Report No.323 (December 2001).
[48] ENDS Report No.333 (October 2002).
[49] ENDS Report No.345 (October 2003).
[50] ENDS Report No.386 (March 2007).
[51] See *R v Associated Octel Ltd* [1997] 1 Cr. App. R. (S) 435, CA.
[52] *R v Northallerton Magistrates' Court Ex p. Dove* [2000] 1 Cr. App. R. (S) 136, DC.
[53] Powers of Criminal Courts (Sentencing) Act 2000 s.131.

powers of magistrates' courts to make such orders. Compensation shall be of such amount as the court considers appropriate, having regard to any evidence and to any representations made on behalf of the accused or the prosecution.[54] Where the court considers that it would be appropriate to impose a fine and make a compensation order, but the offender has insufficient means to satisfy both, then preference shall be given to compensation.[55] It is possible to include an amount in respect of interest, particularly when the amount is large and the period a long one, provided the amount can be calculated without difficulty.[56] Appeal against compensation orders lies to the Court of Appeal, which may annul or vary the order irrespective of whether the conviction is quashed.[57]

The courts' powers under the section are dependant upon the accused **7.29** having been convicted of an offence.[58] In theory therefore the various offences referred to above in relation to water pollution may give rise to a compensation order: the power is not confined to cases where there is civil liability.[59] Hence, in principle, clean-up costs incurred by the enforcing authority could be recoverable, as might costs incurred by a third party, such as a water supply undertaker or private owner of an affected borehole. Any sum claimed must be properly substantiated by evidence.[60] However, the procedure is intended for cases where the issues are clear and simple and where generally no complex examination is required.[61] It is preferable for substantial claims to be dealt with in civil proceedings and the absence of any civil remedy of damages is a factor to be taken into account by the court.[62] This will tend to restrict the use of compensation orders in the majority of contaminated land cases where the issues of liability for remedial works will of their nature be legally, evidentially and technically complex in anything other than very clear-cut cases.

Prosecution policy

A decision whether to prosecute or take other enforcement action in **7.30** relation to contaminated land problems is, like all other similar decisions, a matter of policy for the Environment Agency. The Agency's Guidance on prosecution and enforcement policy is used by its staff to indicate the most appropriate enforcement response.[63] The public interest factors to be considered will be the environmental effect of the incident, the nature of the offence (i.e. whether it undermines the efficacy of a regulatory regime),

---

[54] Powers of Criminal Courts (Sentencing) Act 2000 s.130(4).
[55] Powers of Criminal Courts (Sentencing) Act 2000 s.130(12).
[56] *R v Schofield* [1978] 2 All E.R. 705; 67 Cr. App. Rep. 282, CA.
[57] Powers of Criminal Courts (Sentencing) Act 2000 s.132(3).
[58] *Herbert v Lambeth LBC* (1992) 13 Cr. App. Rep. (5) 489 DC.
[59] *R v Chappel* [1984] Crim.L.R. 574.
[60] *R v Horsham Justices Ex p. Richards* [1985] 1 W.L.R. 986; 82 Cr. App. Rep. 254, DC; *R v Watson* 12 Cr. App. Rep. (S.) 508.
[61] *R v White* [1996] 2 Cr. App. Rep. (S.) 58; *Davenport v Walsall MBC* [1997] Env. L.R. 24, QB (statutory nuisance case on unfit housing).
[62] *Herbert v Lambeth LBC* (1992) 13 Cr. App. Rep. (S.) 489, DC.
[63] The current version, available on the Agency's website, is Version 15, issued June 26, 2007. The policy is regularly reviewed and reference should be made to the updated version.

whether the offence was financially motivated or resulted in the defendant gaining financially, whether the offence detrimentally affected legitimate business or activities, the deterrent effect of prosecution, whether the offence was committed deliberately, recklessly or negligently, the previous history of the defendant, the attitude of the defendant generally, the defendant's personal circumstances, and whether the circumstances leading to the offence could reasonably have been foreseen and avoided or prevented.

7.31   Incidents are categorised according to the Agency's Common Incident Classification System (CICS) depending upon the seriousness of their consequences. In addition it may be appropriate to apply the Agency's Compliance Classification Scheme (CCS). This may result in a higher classification, for example where non-compliance could give rise to more serious environmental consequences than occurred in fact. The Agency has produced Guidance on applying the CCS to particular situations, for example groundwater quality. A prosecution may be expected to follow major incidents: in the context of groundwater pollution which entailed closure of potable, industrial or agricultural abstraction sources would certainly be likely to lead to prosecution, as would an incident making extensive remedial measures necessary, or which had the potential for any extensive and serious effect on water quality, the use of water resources, or aquatic life. Soil contamination may also result in pollution of surface water, in which case issues such as effect on amenity, fish kill, harm to aquatic life and risk to abstraction sources will also be relevant.

7.32   As a matter of practice, any enforcing agency will have regard to its likely prospects of securing a successful outcome before initiating a prosecution: this will be particularly relevant in contaminated land cases where issues of proof and causation may be extremely difficult—obvious recent spillages aside.

Section 161 cost recovery

7.33   Section 161 of the Water Resources Act 1991 contains powers to prevent, remedy and mitigate pollution which may be of some (though now, for reasons explained below, limited) relevance in contaminated land situations. The power applies where it appears to the Environment Agency that any poisonous, noxious or polluting matter[64] or any solid waste matter is:

(a) likely to enter any controlled waters; or

(b) likely to be present in any controlled waters; or

(c) likely to have been present in any controlled water.[65]

7.34   In such cases the Agency is entitled to carry out works and operations to prevent the matter entering controlled waters[66]; in the contaminated land context this could include, for example, excavating and removing the

---

[64] For the meaning of "poisonous, noxious or polluting" see paras 7.07–7.10.

[65] For "controlled waters," see subs.(6) and para.2.45; the definition includes surface water and groundwater.

[66] Water Resources Act 1991 s.161(1)(a).

matter or constructing some impervious barrier between it and the controlled waters. Where the matter has already reached the controlled waters then the works may include removing and disposing of the matter, remedying or mitigating any pollution which has been caused, and restoring the water and dependent flora and fauna to their previous condition.[67] In the case of polluted groundwater this may involve solutions such as pumping and treatment. As amended,[68] s.161 also allows the Agency to carry out investigations for the purpose of establishing the source of the polluting matter and the identity of the relevant person who caused or knowingly permitted its presence.

Subsection (3) provides: **7.35**

> "Where the Agency carries out any such works, operations or investigations as are mentioned in subs.(1) above, it shall, subject to subs.(4) below,[69] be entitled to recover the expenses[70] reasonably incurred in doing so from any person who as the case may be:

> (a) caused or knowingly permitted the matter in question to be present at the place from which it was likely, in the opinion of the Agency, to enter any controlled waters; or
>
> (b) caused or knowingly permitted the matter in question to be present in any controlled water."

The wording imposing liability here is similar to the offences relating to **7.36** water pollution in s.85 of the Act in that they extend not only to the original polluter but also to a subsequent owner or occupier of land who knowingly permits the entry of polluting matter to continue. It should also be noted that permitting potentially polluting matter to remain in place may also result in liability if in the Authority's opinion it may migrate into controlled waters in future.

Despite the potentially wide powers conferred by s.161, in one important **7.37** sense the power is an unattractive one for the Agency in that potentially heavy costs must be incurred before steps can be taken to recover them, with no certain prospect of recovery. This is particularly the case where groundwater contamination is widespread and involves many potential sources, or where the source of the contamination is unclear.

Arguments may also arise after the costs have been incurred as to **7.38** whether the works or operations were reasonable. The power was little-used in the contaminated land context by the Agency, or the NRA before it.[71] In practice, it may be that the powers of s.161 were most effective as a threat to compel landowners or polluters to co-operate "voluntarily" in

---

[67] Water Resources Act 1991 s.161(1)(b).

[68] By s.60 of the Environment Act 1995.

[69] Water Resources Act 1991 s.161 subs.(4) provides that expenses are not recoverable in respect of works or operations relating to water from abandoned mines.

[70] "Expenses" includes costs: s.161(6) inserted by the Environment Act 1995 s.60.

[71] Indeed, the only reported case on its use generally is the proceedings in the Cambridge County Court in *NRA v Clarke* (July 23, 1993) following a major pollution incident affecting the River Sapiston and Little Ouse, when 3 million gallons of slurry were released after the collapse of a retaining bank at a lagoon, when the NRA recovered some £90,000 in total: see [1994] Water Law 145 and [1995] Water Law 20.

clean-up schemes and the section appears to have been used as a lever by the NRA in agreeing a remediation plan with Eastern Counties Leather, the defendant in the *Cambridge Water Company* case,[72] for a treatment strategy to contain pollution and treat groundwater at the company's site.[73]

7.39 These inadequacies led to the provision of stronger powers under the "works notice" provisions of ss.161A–D of the Water Resources Act, described below. Section 161 has been amended by the insertion of subs.161(1A) which provides that, without prejudice to the Agency's power to carry out investigations under s.161(1), the power to carry out works and investigations is only exercisable in a case where:

(a) the Agency considers it necessary to carry out works or operations forthwith; or

(b) it appears to the Agency, after reasonable inquiry, that no person can be found on whom to serve a works notice under s.161A.

7.40 The position is therefore that s.161 can be used by the Agency to investigate cases where pollution is affecting or is likely to affect controlled waters, to establish the source of the problem and the person or persons responsible. However, when it comes to carrying out works or operations, the Agency can only act itself under s.161 if matters are sufficiently urgent to justify this, or where investigation has failed to produce a person who may be served with a works notice requiring them to carry out the works. To that extent, s.161 remains a potentially valuable fall-back power.

Works notices

7.41 The deficiencies in s.161 powers, described above, were recognised and rectified by the new powers contained in ss.161A–D of the Water Resources Act 1991[74] and, for Scotland, ss.46A–D of the Control of Pollution Act 1974.[75] These provisions create a new type of notice, the "works notice", which may be served where it appears to the Environment Agency that any poisonous, noxious or polluting matter, or any solid waste matter, is likely to enter, or to be or have been present in, any controlled waters. The notice is to be served on any person who, as the case may be:

(a) caused or knowingly permitted the matter in question to be present at the place from which it is likely, in the opinion of the Agency to enter controlled waters; or

(b) caused or knowingly permitted the matter in question to be present in any controlled waters.

7.42 A works notice may require the carrying out of specified works or operations for the purpose of preventing the polluting matter entering controlled waters, or where this has already happened, removing the

[72] See para.14.54.
[73] ENDS Report No.233 (June 2004).
[74] Inserted by the Environment Act 1995 Sch.22 para.162.
[75] Inserted by the Environment Act 1995 Sch.22 para.29(22).

matter, remedying or mitigating the pollution, and restoring the waters and any dependent flora or fauna, so far as is reasonably practicable.[76]

The more detailed requirements of works notices are provided for in **7.43** s.161A and in Regulations made thereunder.[77] These include a requirement reasonably to endeavour to consult with the intended recipient of a works notice before serving it.[78] However, failure to consult in this way is not of itself a ground for regarding a works notice as invalid.[79] Other sections deal with the grant of rights of entry necessary to comply with a works notice,[80] appeals against notices,[81] and the consequences of not complying with a works notice.[82]

Works notices and remediation notices compared

There may be situations where it is clear that a remediation notice cannot **7.44** be served, for example, where all contamination has already passed from the soil to controlled waters, but in many cases the circumstances which require the service of a remediation notice will also be those which would allow service of a works notice. The provisions on works notices in the 1991 Act and the accompanying regulations are terse when compared with those on remediation notices, and do not contain anything equivalent to the sophisticated provisions on allocation and apportionment of liability of the latter; nor is there any provision for detailed Government guidance, though there is a general power of direction by the Secretary of State. Service of a works notice could therefore in principle be a more attractive option in terms of administrative simplicity to the regulator. However, while the works notice provisions do not contain provisions on apportionment of liability, there is an inherent apportionment in that a liable party can only be required to carry out works or operations in respect of the polluting "matter" which they caused or knowingly permitted to be present. This may lead to problems for the enforcing authority where a series of persons, some of which no longer exist, have contributed to contamination. In the Part IIA situation, the remaining polluter would, by contrast, be responsible for the entire remediation, subject to the discretion of the enforcing authority to waive or reduce recovery of full costs.

Relationship of contaminated land and water protection provisions

As explained in the previous paragraph, there may be cases where **7.45** although land is not to be regarded as "contaminated", there may still be the possibility of clean-up requirements being imposed in relation to water

[76] Water Resources Act 1991 s.161A(2); Control of Pollution Act 1974 s.46A(2).
[77] Water Resources Act 1991 s.161A(3), (5), (7)–(9); Control of Pollution Act 1974 s.46A(3), (5), (7)–(9). See the Anti-Pollution Works Regulations 1999 (SI 1999/1006).
[78] Water Resources Act 1991 s.161A(4); Control of Pollution Act 1974 s.46A(4).
[79] Water Resources Act 1991 s.161A(6); Control of Pollution Act 1974 s.46A(6).
[80] Water Resources Act 1991 s.161B; Control of Pollution Act 1974 s.46B.
[81] Water Resources Act 1991 s.161C; Control of Pollution Act 1974 s.46C.
[82] Water Resources Act 1991 s.161D; Control of Pollution Act 1974 s.46D.

pollution under ss.161 or 161A–D of the Water Resources Act 1991. Also, there may be cases where the two regimes overlap, raising the question as to which one should be used to deal with a specific problem. Situations can be foreseen where a chicken and egg situation could arise, with subsequent uncertainty for enforcing authorities and potentially liable parties alike.

In particular in this regard, attention needs to be given to the discrepancy between the definition of "controlled waters" for the purposes of the Pt IIA and works notice regimes. The definition for works notices is the same as that generally applying to Pt III of the Water Resources Act, i.e. any waters contained in underground strata.[83] Under Pt IIA, as amended, groundwaters do not, for England and Wales, include waters contained in underground strata above the saturation zone.[84] If all the contaminants have passed into the saturated zone, so that there is no longer any continuing ingress to groundwaters as defined in Pt IIA, the only option would seem to be a works notice. However, there could be a situation where contaminants are present in groundwater in the unsaturated zone so that they are likely to enter the saturated zone, even though there is no source of contamination (e.g. leaking drums) still present on the land. In that case, in principle action could be taken under either regime.

7.46 Once the amendments for England and Wales are brought into force which require a threshold of significance for pollution of controlled waters,[85] there will be a potentially greater discrepancy, in that the works notice provisions simply refer to the entry of polluting matter to controlled waters,

7.47 The issue is addressed at Annex 1 of Circular 01/2006, paras 59–63, which simply points out that there is obvious potential for overlap and that the decision as to which regime is used may have important implications. It goes on to state that the works notice powers may be particularly useful in cases of historic pollution of groundwater but where Pt IIA does not apply. It is suggested this might occur where the pollutants are entirely contained within the relevant body of groundwater, or where the "source site cannot be identified". However, if it not possible to identify a "source" site, it is difficult to see how a works notice could be served on a specific person in any event.

7.48 The Environment Agency has published a policy statement on the relationship between Pt IIA and works notice powers, which has been agreed with DEFRA.[86] This indicates that regulatory action will generally be taken under Pt IIA where both regimes are applicable, and experience suggests that this is the way in which the Agency has proceeded to date. The effect of this policy, taken together with the legislation, can be summarised as follows:

(a) the local authority should consult the Agency before determining that land is contaminated under Pt IIA;

---

[83] Water Resources Act 1991 ss.104(1)(d) and 161A(13).
[84] 1990 Act s.78A(9). See further para.3.71ff.
[85] See para.3.66ff.
[86] Environment Agency Policy and Guidance on the Use of Anti-Pollution Works Notices (1999).

(b) where the authority has identified contaminated land that appears to be affecting controlled waters, it is required by the Guidance to consult the Agency, and to take into account any comments of the Agency with regard to remediation requirements. This allows the Agency to indicate the type of measures it would require in any works notice if such notice were served;

(c) where the Agency identifies any land which is affected by contamination and is causing actual or potential water pollution, it will notify the local authority, to enable the authority to identify the land as contaminated under Pt IIA (if it is appropriate to do so); and

(d) in any case where contaminated land is identified under Pt IIA, the Pt IIA remediation notice procedure should normally be used rather than the works notice procedures. This follows from the fact that Pt IIA involves a duty to serve a remediation notice, whereas service of a works notice is discretionary.

There may be a situation where the Environment Agency is already **7.49** taking enforcement action under the Water Resources Act 1991 before the local authority becomes involved. If such action is in progress, then the authority should consider what standard of remediation would be achieved by it. If the authority is satisfied that the standard would be such as to deal with all the relevant pollutant linkages, then subs.78H(5)(b) will preclude service of a remediation notice, and the person who is carrying out, or will carry out, the action is required to prepare and publish a remediation statement.

The overall situation can therefore be summarised as follows: **7.50**

1. If the Agency is already using its works notice powers, the local authority should not serve a remediation notice if satisfied that all the problems which arise from the land being contaminated will thereby be resolved.

2. If the local authority is using the contaminated land provisions, there is nothing as a matter of law to prevent the Agency using its works notice powers. However, its own policy should preclude the duplication of regulatory effort, and therefore it is likely to confine itself to giving site specific guidance to the local authority.

3. If the problem relates to controlled waters which are not subject to further contamination from the land in question, then the only remedy for such historic pollution will be through the works notice powers.

4. Difficulties could arise in the "chicken and egg" type of situation where neither the Agency nor the local authority has yet taken action. Here it will be relevant that the local authority is under a duty to act, whereas the Agency only has power to act. The Agency's own guidance suggests that Pt IIA should be used in such cases.

Powers of water undertakers to deal with contamination

7.51 Section 162 of the Water Industry Act 1991 confers on water undertakers certain powers to deal with contamination. By s.162(1) street works[87] may be carried out to secure that water in a relevant waterworks[88] is not polluted or contaminated; such works may include opening up the street, tunnelling or boring, opening up any sewer or drain and moving or removing earth and other materials. Perhaps more importantly, subs.(2) enables works to be carried out on any land other than a street for securing that water in any relevant waterworks is not polluted or otherwise contaminated.[89] By subs.(3) in relation to land which the undertaker owns or over which it has the necessary rights, the works may extend to the construction of "drains, sewers, watercourses, catchpits and other works" for the purpose of intercepting foul water or otherwise preventing the pollution of reservoirs and abstraction sources of strata. Whilst these powers are undeniably useful, they include no statutory power to recoup the cost of such measures from any person.

Groundwater: generally

7.52 Almost all types of rock in the Earth's upper crust contain openings called pores or voids.[90] This property is known as porosity: rocks containing a high proportion of such void space are known as "porous" or "highly porous". To a greater or lesser extent these pores may be filled with water. The situation where all the pores are entirely filled with water is known as saturation: it is the complete filling with water which distinguished the "saturated zone" from the "unsaturated zone"—where part only of the void space contains water. Where a well or borehole is sunk, this will fill with water until the water reaches a constant level, known as the "water table": this will generally correspond to the upper level of the saturated zone. The depth of the water table will vary from the surface level to 100 metres or more. All water which occurs naturally below the Earth's surface is called sub-surface water, whether it occurs in the saturated or unsaturated zone; water in the saturated zone is called groundwater.

7.53 The extent to which groundwater is useable varies, depending on factors such as depth, salinity and quality. The other crucial factor as to the exploitability of groundwater resources is the ease with which water can flow through the relevant strata, known as permeability. Layers of rock which are sufficiently porous to store water and permeable enough to allow water to flow through them in economic quantities are known as aquifers. An aquifer may be "confined" in the sense of being surrounded above and

---

[87] "Street" has the same meaning as in the New Roads and Street Works Act 1991 s.219(1).

[88] "Relevant waterworks" means any waterworks containing water which is or may be used by a water undertaker for providing a supply of water to any premises; "waterworks" includes water mains, resource mains, service pipes, discharge pipes, springs, wells, adits, boreholes, service reservoirs or tanks: subs.(8).

[89] The provisions of s.159 as to notice to the owner and occupier of the land apply to the exercise of this power: subs.(2).

[90] See generally M. Price, *Introducing Groundwater* (London: George Allen & Unwin, 1985).

below by impervious strata through which water cannot readily pass, e.g. clays or shales. In such circumstances the water in the aquifer will be under pressure so that the water will naturally rise if a borehole is sunk. The final factor which is crucial to the amount of groundwater available is the degree of replenishment from rainfall or from adjacent aquifers: this involves consideration of the water balance of the area.

The UK has a varied and interesting geology.[91] Much of Scotland, Wales **7.54** and Northern Ireland is formed of older rocks with low permeabilities, so that these areas have little in the way of useful aquifers. The main aquifers in England and Wales consist of consolidated sedimentary rocks— principally chalk and sandstones: these are found generally in the south-eastern part of the British Isles. The porosity of the chalk will vary and in fact much of the groundwater movement within the chalk occurs in cracks or fissures. In the sandstone aquifers permeability is more dependent upon pore size and whether the sandstone is of a fine or coarse-grained nature.

The Environment Agency sets out its framework for the protection of **7.55** groundwater in Groundwater Protection: Policy and Practice (GP3).[92] Part 1 sets out its general core policy, Pt 2 sets out a technical framework, Pt 3 introduces the tools used for analysis and assessment of groundwater risks, and Pt 4 (issued for consultation in 2007) sets out detailed policies and position statements for different activities. It has been estimated that about one-half of water abstracted in England and Wales for public supply comes from groundwater resources, rising to more than 70 per cent in the south-east, and in rural areas groundwater may be the only source of supply for isolated properties.[93] A much wider variety of risk screening and risk management tools have been developed since the original groundwater vulnerability maps which underlay the earlier Policy on groundwater protection,[94] and the Agency is developing new and more sophisticated approaches to groundwater vulnerability based on geographical information systems (GIS), in order to implement the Water Framework Directive.[95] The concept of water source protection zones for groundwater abstractions continues to be important.[96]

The Groundwater Directive

The EC legislation currently dealing with groundwater is Directive 80/68 **7.56** on the protection of groundwater against pollution caused by certain dangerous substances.[97] The preamble to the Directive refers to the urgent

---

[91] M. Price, *Introducing Groundwater* (London: George Allen & Unwin, 1985), p.79.

[92] This replaces the Policy and Practice for the Protection of Groundwater, first published in 1992 and reissued in 1998.

[93] Environment Agency, Groundwater Protection: Policy and Practice Part 1, para.4.1.

[94] GP3, Pt 3 refers to maps (e.g. vulnerability and source protection zone maps), screening tools to determine which risks require further assessment, analytical tools such as ConSim (used to assess the risk to groundwater from contaminated sites) and detailed individual numerical models.

[95] See GP3, Pt 2 para.5.3.3.

[96] See GP3, Pt 2 para.5.4.

[97] The Directive will be repealed on December 22, 2013 by the Water Framework Directive 2000/60; Art.17 provides for a new daughter directive to prevent and reduce groundwater pollution.

need for action to protect the groundwater of the Community from pollution. Particularly pollution caused by certain toxic, persistent and bioaccumulable substances. The scheme of the Directive is to place families and groups of certain substances into two lists, I and II; List II being those substances which could have a harmful effect on groundwaters and List I being those substances which are considered to present more serious risks. Both Lists contain some very broad generic categories. For example, List I refers to "substances which possess carcinogenic, mutagenic or teratogenic properties in or via the aquatic environment" whilst List II includes "substances which have a deleterious effect on the taste and/or odour of groundwater and compounds liable to cause the formation of such substances in such water as to render it unfit for human consumption".

7.57 Member States are required to prevent the introduction of List I substances into groundwater by prohibiting all direct discharges and by subjecting to prior investigation any disposal or tipping for the purpose of disposal of those substances which might lead to indirect discharge. Such tipping must either be prohibited or authorised on the proviso that all the technical precautions necessary to prevent indirect discharge are observed.[98] Appropriate measures must also be taken to prevent any indirect discharge of List I substances due to activities other than tipping or disposal. The main exception to these requirements is where investigations reveal that the groundwater in question is "permanently unsuitable for other uses, especially domestic or agricultural": here the discharge may be authorised provided the presence of List I substance does not impede exploitation of ground resources (e.g. minerals) and if all technical precautions have been taken to ensure that the substances cannot reach other aquatic systems or harm other ecosystems.[99]

7.58 In relation to List II substances Member States must limit their introduction into groundwater so as to avoid pollution: this requires direct discharges and tipping for disposal which might lead to indirect discharges to be subject to investigation.[100] In the light of that investigation, authorisation may be granted, provided that all the technical precautions for preventing groundwater pollution are observed. Further, Member States shall take the appropriate measures they deem necessary to limit all indirect discharges of List II substances due to other activities in or on the ground.[101]

7.59 Despite the fact that the European Court has made clear that the Directive was intended to create clear and absolute obligations for the benefit of individuals,[102] the Government's implementation of the Groundwater Directive was originally unsatisfactory. In its formal compliance letter to the European Commission relating to the Groundwater Directive the Government referred to the waste licensing and waste pollution provisions of the Control of Pollution Act 1974 as the means of

[98] Directive 80/68 Arts 3(a) and 4.1.
[99] Directive 80/68 Art.4.2.
[100] Directive 80/68 Art.5.1.
[101] Directive 80/68 Art.5.2.
[102] Case C-131/88 *Commission v Germany* [1991] E.C.R. I–825.

implementation—despite the fact that not all of the relevant provisions were by then in force.[103] The Directive was explained in DoE Circular 4/82, issued on March 1, 1982. This Circular put forward a somewhat relaxed interpretation of the Directive, relating it essentially to whether the discharge in question would "force a change in the use of the aquifer or would make necessary a significant difference in the treatment of its water before use".[104] Also, the Circular suggested that pollution of groundwater occurring as the result of historical activities should not require action under the terms of the directive once those activities had ceased, unless it constituted a breach of continuing and enforceable conditions on the original consent.[105] Misfortune befell the UK Government when a complaint was made to the Commission concerning a "dilute and disperse" landfill at Pakefield in Suffolk, from which pesticide residues were said to be leaching into groundwater. Infringement proceedings resulted in the issue of Circular 20/90 which contained firmer advice. It indicated the Government's agreement with the Commission that the three pesticides in question were to be regarded as List I substances, suggested that waste disposal authorities should seek the advice of the NRA at sites involving the disposal of List I substances, and that site licences should be reviewed where discharges were liable to affect groundwater adversely, other than that which was permanently unuseable. However, it was not until the Waste Management Licensing Regulations 1994 that express statutory provisions transposed the requirements of the Directive, and then only with respect to sites subject to a waste management licence.

The Groundwater Regulations

The Groundwater Regulations 1998[106] came into force on April 1, 1999 and **7.60** complete the transposition into UK law of the EC Groundwater Directive.[107] The Regulations do not apply to activities for which a waste management licence is required.[108] One of the aspects of the Regulations is the need to prevent or control the disposal or tipping of List I or List II substances[109] in circumstances which might lead to an indirect discharge of those substances to groundwater, as well as other activities which might lead to such discharges. The Regulations deal with this issue as follows:

1. Causing or knowingly permitting such disposal or tipping without authorisation is treated as an offence under s.85 of the Water Resources Act 1991 or s.30F of the Control of Pollution Act 1974.[110]

---

[103] See M. Pallemaerts and N. Haigh (eds), *Manual of Environmental Policy: The EC and Britain* (Marvey Publishing, Leads, 1992), p.4.7–3.
[104] Directive 80/68 para.8.
[105] Directive 80/68 para.14.
[106] SI 1998/2746.
[107] [1980] O.J. L20, 80/68. Draft Guidance on the 1998 Regulations was issued for consultation in November 1999.
[108] Groundwater Regulations 1998 reg.2(1)(d).
[109] See the Schedule to the Regulations as to these substances, which include many organics, metals and pesticides.
[110] Groundwater Regulations 1998 reg.14(1)(a).

2. Authorisation for these purposes may be granted by the appropriate Agency and may be subject to conditions.[111] Contravention of the conditions of such authorisation is an offence.[112]

3. Where a person is carrying on, or is proposing to carry on, any activity in or on the ground which might lead to an indirect discharge to groundwater of a List I substance, or to pollution of groundwater, by a List II substance, the appropriate Agency may by notice in writing either prohibit the carrying on of that activity, or may authorise it subject to conditions.[113] Contravention of any such authorisation is an offence.[114]

7.61 The Groundwater Regulations may obviously apply to situations where contaminated land is involved, including situations where it is being remediated or investigated. However, the main thrust of the Regulations is the prevention of groundwater pollution rather than its clean-up. Accordingly, they should be seen as complementing rather than supplementing the procedures of Pt IIA. So, where for example, a remediation notice requires the excavation of contaminated material, and this activity might lead to listed substances being disturbed and so contaminating groundwater, the Agency may wish to impose conditions on the carrying out of those works by way of notice under the Regulations. To that extent, the requirements of the Regulations are no different from any other of the permits or consents which may be needed to carry out the remedial works.

7.62 A different situation might arise where listed substances are continuing to leach into groundwater, perhaps from a number of sources. Because the pollution is ongoing, this may lead to service of a Pt IIA remediation notice, or to a works notice under s.161A. The Groundwater Regulations only allow control to be exercised over the tipping or disposal of Listed substances, or other activities in or on land. They cannot therefore be used to prohibit or control passive discharges, where the activities in question have ceased. This limits their applicability in contaminated land situations, arguably contrary to the requirements of the Groundwater Directive to take the necessary steps to prevent the introduction into groundwater of List I substances and to limit the introduction of List II substances.

The new Groundwater Directive

7.63 It may well be that the approach to pollution of groundwater by diffuse contaminants will require reconsideration with implementation of the Water Framework Directive 2000/60, which is intended to prevent further deterioration and enhance the status of the aquatic environment, including groundwater.[115] Programmes will have to be put in place for the monitoring

---

[111] Groundwater Regulations 1998 reg.18.
[112] Groundwater Regulations 1998 reg.14(1)(b).
[113] Groundwater Regulations 1998 reg.19.
[114] Groundwater Regulations 1998 reg.14(1)(b).
[115] Directive 2000/60 Art.1(a); groundwater is defined as "all water which is below the surface of the ground in the saturation zone and in direct contact with the ground or subsoil" (Art.2.2).

of the chemical status (Art.8). Article 17 requires the adoption of specific EC measures to prevent and control groundwater pollution, based on the objective of achieving good groundwater chemical status, in accordance with the criteria in Annex 5 of the Directive.

The new Groundwater Directive 2006/118 was adopted in December **7.64** 2006. It sets out criteria for assessing groundwater chemical status, which must use the quality standards for substances referred to in Annex I (nitrates and active substances in pesticides) and threshold values to be established by Member States for pollutants identified as contributing to the characterisation of groundwater bodies as being at risk, taking into account the minimum list at Pt B of Annex II, which includes arsenic, cadmium, lead, mercury, ammonium, chloride, sulphate, tricholoroethylene and tetrachloroethylene. These threshold values are to be initially estab-lished by December 22, 2008. By Art.6, Member States must ensure that the programme of measures established under Art.15 of the Water Framework Directive includes all measures necessary to prevent inputs into groundwater of any hazardous substances, to be identified by Member States taking into account the substances referred to in Annex VIII of the Framework Directive. Article 15.2 requires inputs of pollutants from diffuse sources having an impact on the groundwater chemical status to be taken into account wherever possible. The laws, regulations and admin-istrative provisions necessary to comply with the Directive are to be brought into force by January 16, 2009.

Chapter 8

WASTE

8.01 Control over where waste is deposited, how and by whom, is a fundamental component of preventing the contamination of land with all its attendant problems. The issue of contaminated land formed part of the enquiry by the House of Commons Environment Committee which led to its report, "Toxic Waste"[1]: the report scathingly condemned the minimalist and laissez-faire attitudes surrounding the issue of waste disposal in the UK and concluded with the recommendation that what was then the Department of Environment should pay more attention to the problem of contaminated land, particularly with regard to environmental protection, public health and safety.[2] The report is by no means the only one to have been critical of waste disposal policy and practice in the period before the introduction of Pt IIA.[3] Practice on refuse disposal varied widely between local authorities, but was consistently underfunded (many authorities were very small) and standards were poor. Some authorities, especially in the North-east, relied on dumping waste at sea. Many operated municipal incinerators ("destructors"). Others relied on "controlled tipping" on land, a practice which was encouraged by the Ministry of Health which in 1922 published "Suggested Precautions for the Controlled Tipping of Waste". By 1939, tipping was the most-favoured solution, not only for rural authorities but also for a number of urban ones (such as Carlisle, Exeter, Gloucester, Reading, Walsall and West Ham). Direct incorporation of refuse into farmland was also used, especially in Scotland.[3a]

8.02 It is not the intention of this chapter to provide a comprehensive analysis of waste management law, which would be far beyond its scope—reference can be made to other works for this. However, an awareness of the way in which waste disposal law has historically evolved in the UK is essential to the understanding of contaminated land problems. Whilst there was some

---

[1] Session 1988–89, 2nd Report, HC 22–I, II and III.
[2] Session 1988–89, 2nd Report, HC 22–I, II and III, para.273.
[3] See also: House of Lords Select Committee on Science and Technology, *First Report on Hazardous Waste Disposal*, Session 1980–81 HL 273–I and II (July 1981); Royal Commission on Environmental Pollution, *11th Report on Managing Waste: The Duty of Care* (Cmnd. 9675, December 1985); Department of Environment, DoE (Northern Ireland), Welsh Office and Scottish Office, Hazardous Waste Inspectorate Reports 1–3: *1st Report on Hazardous Waste Management: an Overview* (June 1985); *2nd Report on Hazardous Waste Management: Ramshackle and Antediluvian?* (July 1986); 3rd Report (June 1988); House of Commons Environment Committee, Session 1990–91, *7th Report of the Environment Committee on The EC Draft Directive on the Landfill of Waste*, HC 263 I and II (July 1991).
[3a] See L. Herbert 7, *The History of the Institute of Wastes Management 1898–1998* (1998).

early local legislation which regulated waste disposal,[4] national legislation truly began with the Deposit of Poisonous Waste Act 1972. The legislative history since then falls into three stages:

1. the Deposit of Poisonous Waste Act 1972;

2. the more comprehensive system of waste disposal licensing introduced by Pt I of the Control of Pollution Act 1974 (the 1974 Act); and

3. the system of waste management licensing under the Environmental Protection Act 1990 (the 1990 Act), Pt II. Within this stage there can be seen the growing influence of Community law in relation to improving the standards of facilities such as landfill sites and vehicle dismantling yards which have historically been serious sources of past contamination.[4a]

The Deposit of Poisonous Waste Act 1972

Prior to the enactment of this legislation, there was no general control over **8.03** the deposit of poisonous, noxious or potentially polluting waste. Control over new sites could be achieved through the planning system to an extent, though many sites enjoyed the benefit of lawful or established use rights. The question of what wastes were suitable for disposal on a site, whether they should be segregated from other wastes, and what (if any) special precautions should be taken in their disposal were matters for the best judgment of the site operator. The result of such lack of control was the existence of open dumps, such as the notorious Malkins Bank in Cheshire, used from the 19th century until 1932 as a salt and chemical works, and after that date for the indiscriminate tipping of toxic waste from a variety of industries covering some 15 hectares up to depths of 15 metres.[5]

However, what caught the attention of the public was the well-publicised **8.04** discovery of cyanide waste dumped on open land in Nuneaton which presented a gross and obvious threat to local children. Within a matter of months, the Deposit of Poisonous Waste Act 1972 received Royal Assent on March 30, 1972. The Act was of an emergency nature, never intended to be more than a stop-gap, and was replaced by the 1974 Act and the Special Waste Regulations 1980 made under that Act.

Section 1 of the Act, which came into force on March 30, 1972, made it **8.05** an offence to deposit waste on land, or to cause or permit waste to be deposited, where the waste was "of a kind which is poisonous, noxious or

---

[4] The Essex County Council (Canvey Island Approaches, etc.) Act 1967 contained the requirement (s.46) for prior written consent to be obtained from the county council and the local authority before refuse was deposited. This was a response to concern about the huge quantities of London waste being disposed of by tipping in the Essex marshes.

[4a] The next, prospective, stage is replacement of the waste licensing regime and the PPC regime with a system of Environmental Permitting, which will (it is hoped) streamline the permitting process. Draft Regulations were published in October 2007, and are intended to come into force on April 1, 2008.

[5] The site is graphically described by Professor Kenneth Mellanby in *Waste and Pollution: The Problem for Britain* (1992), pp.56–7.

polluting and its presence on land is liable to give rise to an environmental hazard." By subs.(3):

> "The presence of waste on any land is to be treated as giving rise to an environmental hazard if the waste has been deposited in such a manner, or in such quantity (whether that quantity by itself or cumulatively with other deposits of the same or different substances) as to subject persons or animals to material risk of death, injury or impairment of health, or as to threaten the pollution or contamination (whether on the surface or underground) of any water supply; and where waste is deposited in containers, this shall not of itself be taken to exclude any risk which might be expected to arise if the waste were not in containers."

8.06 The degree of risk relevant for this purpose was to be assessed with particular regard to the measures, if any, taken by the depositor of the waste, or by the owner or occupier of the land, or by others for minimising the risk; and the likelihood of the waste or its container being tampered with by children or others.

8.07 By subs.(7) nothing done in accordance with the terms of any consent, licence or approval granted under an enactment was to be taken to be a breach of s.1; but planning permission was expressly stated not to be sufficient authority for this purpose.

8.08 Section 3, which came into force on August 3, 1972, instituted a system of notification, requiring notices specifying various particulars to be given to the relevant authorities[6] before waste was removed from any premises with a view to being deposited elsewhere or before waste was deposited on land. The requirement applied to waste of any description (the word was not defined) whether solid, semi-solid or liquid, other than that specified in regulations by the Secretary of State as not being so poisonous, noxious or polluting that it need not be subject to the section.[7] The Deposit of Poisonous Waste (Notification of Removal or Deposit) Regulations 1972[8] provided two categories of exemption from the notification requirements: an unqualified exemption for certain specified types of waste[9] and a qualified exemption for waste of a prescribed description and deposited pursuant to certain types of statutory authority.[10] This "exclusive list" approach was criticised by the House of Lords Select Committee on Science and Technology in its 1981 Report on hazardous waste disposal as "being too wide ranging and sometimes imprecise".[11]

8.09 This policy of providing authorities with information as to the nature, quantities and location of hazardous waste deposits was continued by s.4 of the Act, which applied to the commercial operators of refuse tips and

---

[6] The local authority and river authority or river purification board: ss.3(5) and 7.

[7] Deposit of Poisonous Waste Act 1972 s.3 subs.3(4).

[8] Deposit of Poisonous Waste (Notification of Removal or Deposit) Regulations 1972 (SI 1972/1017).

[9] Deposit of Poisonous Waste (Notification of Removal or Deposit) Regulations 1972 (SI 1972/1017) reg. 3 and Sch.

[10] SI 1972/1017 reg.4.

[11] House of Lords Select Committee on Science and Technology, *First Report on Hazardous Waste Disposal*, Session 1980–81 HL 273–I and II (July 1981) para.13.

required the provision of information as to the location of the tip, the nature and chemical composition of the waste, the quantity deposited, and the name of the person who brought the waste to the tip and of their employer. Local authorities operating tips themselves were required to give notice of similar particulars to the river authority or river purification board.[12]

Whilst the Act was a considerable step forward, its scope was limited: its **8.10** approach in recognising the significance of environmental hazards— especially groundwater pollution—as well as harm to human health was basically sound, but the definitional provisions were imprecise and were interpreted inconsistently by different authorities.[13]

The Control of Pollution Act 1974

Part I of the 1974 Act replaced the Deposit of Poisonous Waste Act 1972 by **8.11** providing a more comprehensive system of controls over the disposal of "controlled waste." In particular, it was made an offence to deposit controlled waste on land, or to use any plant or equipment for the purpose of disposing of controlled waste or of dealing in a prescribed manner[14] with controlled waste, unless the relevant land was occupied by the holder of a waste disposal licence and the deposit or use was in accordance with the licence conditions.[15] Section 5 of the Act provided for the grant of waste disposal licences: in particular, where an application was received for a disposal licence for a use of land, plant or equipment for which planning permission was in force, the waste disposal authority was under a duty not to reject the application unless the authority was satisfied that its rejection was necessary "for the purpose of preventing pollution of water or danger to public health".

By s.6 the licence could include such conditions as the authority thought **8.12** fit to specify: these could relate to such matters as:

(a) the duration of the licence;

(b) supervision of activities by the licence-holder;

(c) the kinds and quantities of the waste allowed, the methods of dealing with them and the recording of information relating to them;

(d) the precautions to be taken on land to which the licence relates;

(e) the steps to be taken with a view to facilitating compliance with the conditions of the relevant planning permission;

(f) hours; and

(g) the works to be carried out, in connection with the land, plant or equipment, before the activities authorised were begun or while they were continuing.

[12] Deposit of Poisonous Waste Act 1972 s.5(3).
[13] House of Lords Select Committee on Science and Technology, *First Report on Hazardous Waste Disposal*, Session 1980–81 HL 273–I and II (July 1981), para.10.
[14] See the Collection and Disposal of Waste Regulations 1988 (SI 1988/819) reg.8 and Sch.5.
[15] Control of Pollution Act 1974 s.3(1).

8.13 By s.9, the authority was under a duty to take the steps needed:

    (a) for the purpose of ensuring that the activities to which the licence relates do not cause pollution of water or damage to the public health or become seriously detrimental to the amenities of the locality affected by the activities; and

    (b) for the purposes of ensuring that the conditions specified in the licence are complied with.

8.14 During the 20 years or so following enactment of the 1974 Act, the risks presented by landfill without strict control of gas and leachate became more fully perceived. This was reflected in the increased comprehensiveness and complexity of licence conditions. In 1977, for example, a licence relating to a landfill site for putrescible waste might typically have run to three or four pages with perhaps 25 conditions the majority of which would have been intended primarily to address local short-term problems of amenity,[16] such as mud on roads, the cover of obnoxious materials, prohibitions on burning, and control of vermin. By the 1990s the licence for a corresponding site would often exceed 70 pages in length with hundreds of conditions and sub-conditions, and with detailed requirements as to a working plan, monitoring leachate and gas, leachate and gas control measures, water balance records, and containment. The requirements as to containment will frequently be highly technical, dealing with phasing, cell construction, the use of clays and synthetic liners, capping, and materials testing (both before and after emplacement).

Shortcomings of the Control of Pollution Act 1974

8.15 The system of waste licensing instituted by the 1974 Act suffered from a number of problems in preventing land becoming contaminated.[17]
Chief among these were the following:

    (a) the inability to exercise long term control over aftercare and monitoring, in that a licence could be surrendered unilaterally by the operator and conditions could not relate to activities after the deposit of waste had ceased.[18] This problem could only partially be overcome by the practice of seeking to impose planning conditions or planning agreements as to long term precautions[19];

    (b) case law established that there were difficulties in enforcing breaches of condition which were not related directly to a deposit of waste[20];

---

[16] In *Attorney General's Reference (No. 2 of 1988)* [1990] Q.B. 77, it was held that a condition prohibiting the creation of public nuisances of all kinds could not lawfully be imposed under s.6(2).

[17] See *Nicola Atkinson* [1991] 3 J.E.L. 256.

[18] See s.6(2).

[19] See e.g. Waste Management Paper No.4, *The Licensing of Waste Facilities*, paras 3.7, 3.8, 3.10.

[20] *Leigh Land Reclamation Ltd v Walsall MBC* [1991] 1 Env. L.R. 16; [1991] 3 J.E.L. 281. Section (3), which provides a power to specify conditions the breach of which would be of itself an offence, was never used by the Government for that purpose.

(c) the controls and powers centred around the protection of public health, amenity and the protection of water resources,[21] rather than the protection of the environment generally or the prevention of contaminated land; and

(d) most seriously of all, waste disposal authorities were able to operate their own sites under a special procedure provided by s.11 by which the authority specified the conditions in a resolution, which it then monitored and "policed" itself. Whilst the strict terms of s.11 provided broadly equivalent controls to sites in private hands, in practice double standards applied in many cases, with lax procedures and controls being applied at many local authority sites: some of which were to present great problems in future years.

These problems were coupled with a prevalent philosophy during the **8.16** 1970s and much of the 1980s that "dilute and disperse" or "attenuate and disperse" was an acceptable means of utilising the environment's putative capacity to degrade and disperse waste. The result has been, in some cases, serious problems of contaminated soil and groundwater, uncontrolled leachate, and persistent problems of gas generation. These problems are frequently of a long term nature, arising only after closure of sites: the House of Lords Select Committee on Science and Technology in its 1981 Report on hazardous waste disposal referred to landfill as follows[22]:

> "Well-executed landfill is acceptable. But it is a low technology process which relies on natural degradation and attenuation, and the only way of proving its safety, or rather proving that the level of risk is tolerable since there can be no absolute guarantee of safety, is by constant vigilance, to check that no pollution has happened. At the same time the scope for abuse is considerable, whether through ignorance, negligence, willful short-cuts or accidents."

The Environmental Protection Act 1990 Part II

The Environmental Protection Act introduced a new scheme of waste **8.17** management licensing intended to remedy some of the perceived deficiencies of the site licensing system under the 1974 Act. Part II of the 1990 Act creates a system of waste management licensing: as with the COPA system this refers to the concept of "controlled waste", but has introduced the concept of "directive waste" with important changes to the approach to defining waste. Also there are important differences in detail as to the scope of the two systems:

1. the 1990 Act applied not only to the deposit and disposal of controlled waste, but also to its treatment and keeping;

[21] Control of Pollution Act 1974 s.5(3), 9(1).
[22] House of Lords Select Committee on Science and Technology, *First Report on Hazardous Waste Disposal*, Session 1980–81 HL 273–I and II (July 1981), para.129.

2. the 1990 Act contains an important additional restriction on treating, keeping or disposing of controlled waste in a manner likely to cause pollution of the environment or harm to human health[23]—this applies irrespective of whether a site licence is in force;

3. the old distinction between controlled waste and controlled waste liable to give rise to an environmental hazard was discontinued, though offences relating to what was special waste (now hazardous waste) carry a higher tariff of penalties[24];

4. waste disposal authorities were replaced by waste regulation authorities and waste disposal authorities, each with different responsibilities[25]; thus ending the "poacher and gamekeeper" problem—waste disposal authorities could in any event no longer operate active disposal sites themselves but were required do so either by way of contract with a private sector contractor or through the medium of an arm's length company[26];

5. the criteria for site licensing were widened to include the prevention of pollution of the environment and harm to human health[27];

6. conditions on this licence could extend to activities to be carried out after the deposit of waste or other authorised activities have ceased[28];

7. such conditions were capable of enforcement per se, it being a separate offence to contravene a condition[29];

8. a new requirement was imposed that the holder of the licence be a "fit and proper person"[30]; and

9. more stringent requirements are imposed as to the surrender of licences.[31]

8.18 The implementation of Pt II of the 1990 Act was dogged by delay and frustration on the part of both regulatory authorities and the waste industry. Originally scheduled to take effect on April 1, 1993, implementation was subject to first a short delay, then indefinite postponement apparently on the basis of the need to achieve consistency with EC law. The provisions were ultimately implemented on May 1, 1994, subject to certain transitional exceptions.[32]

---

[23] 1990 Act s.33(1)(c): the concepts of harm to the environment and to health are extremely widely defined at s.29(1).
[24] 1990 Act s.33(9).
[25] 1990 Act ss.30, 51.
[26] 1990 Act ss.32 and 51 Sch.2.
[27] 1990 Act s.35(3).
[28] 1990 Act s.35(3).
[29] 1990 Act s.33(6).
[30] 1990 Act ss.36(3) and 74.
[31] 1990 Act s.39.
[32] The Environmental Protection Act 1990 (Commencement No. 15) Order 1994 (SI 1994/1096).

Non-controlled waste

Various waste streams were historically excluded from the definition of **8.19** controlled waste and hence from licensing control, for example radioactive waste, explosives, waste from mines and quarries and waste from premises used from agriculture,[33] some of which may have significant potential to cause pollution. Such waste have only very recently (for example, agricultural waste) been brought within the ambit of waste licensing.[33a] Before such comprehensive control, a partial means of controlling the deposit of such waste was provided by s.18(2) of the 1974 Act. This subsection provided that a person was guilty of an offence if they deposited waste other than controlled waste on land[34] (or caused or knowingly permitted such deposit) in a case where, if the waste were controlled waste and any disposal licence were not in force, an offence would be committed under s.3(3) of the Act. The effect of the provision was to prohibit the deposit of non-controlled waste which satisfied the criteria of s.3(3) of the Act, i.e. it was poisonous, noxious or polluting, and its presence was likely to give rise to an environmental hazard and it was deposited in such circumstances that it may reasonably be assumed to have been abandoned or disposed of as waste. No offence was committed if the act was done in pursuance of and in accordance with the terms of any consent, licence, approval or authority granted under any enactment, excluding planning permission.[35]

Thus the effect of s.18(2) was quite intelligible: unfortunately the same **8.20** could not be said of its successor, s.63(2) of the Environmental Protection Act 1990, which suffered from infelicitous draftsmanship. Section 63(2) created an offence of depositing on land waste other than controlled waste (or knowingly causing or knowingly permitting such deposit) in a case where if the waste were special waste (the precursor of hazardous waste) and any waste management licence were not in force an offence would be committed under s.33. The problem stems from the fact that the old wording of s.3(3) of COPA, which referred to the nature of the waste (poisonous, noxious or polluting) and the manner of its deposit (so as to create an environmental hazard) was a test which could equally well be applied to non-controlled as to controlled waste. Section 3(3) was replaced in the EPA by s.33(9) which created enhanced penalties for offences which related to special waste. By definition, waste which is not controlled waste could not be special waste: the assumption required by s.63(2) could not therefore logically follow. This defective drafting was cured by a new s.63(2), substituted by the Environment Act 1995, which referred to waste which is not controlled waste, but if it were would be special waste because of its hazardous properties. The provision has now in any event been repealed in respect of England and Wales,[36] but the essential point to

---

[33] Control of Pollution Act 1974 s.30; Environmental Protection Act 1990 s.75.

[33a] The deposit of waste on agricultural land may have other implications: see *R (Davies) v Agricultural Land Tribunal* [2007] EWHC 1395 (certificate of bad husbandry; judge agreed with Tribunal that deposit of farm was "extremely bad husbandry".

[34] "Land" for this purpose included water covering land above the low water mark which is not water in a stream: subss.18(2) and 4(4).

[35] See s.62(1).

[36] SI 2005/894 reg.73.

remember is that non-controlled waste may not have been the subject of effective control over its deposit and hence may have resulted in contaminated land.

Licence conditions

8.21 The key to ongoing control of waste disposal activities is through the imposition and enforcement of conditions. A waste management licence shall be granted on such terms and conditions as appear to the waste regulation authority to be appropriate and the conditions may relate not only to the activities which the licence authorises but also to precautions to be taken and works to be carried out in relation to those activities[37]: e.g. the installation of gas venting, impervious caps and liners, etc. Requirements imposed by way of condition can relate to preparatory precautions or works before waste disposal commences, or to such matters after waste disposal ceases.[38] Such conditions must be related to the general purpose of waste management licensing which is to prevent harm to human health, pollution of the environment, or serious detriment to local amenity[39]; these grounds are significantly wider than those stated in the 1974 Act. Licence conditions may be modified during the term of the licence by notice served on the holder to any extent which in the opinion of the authority is desirable and is unlikely to require unreasonable expense on the part of the licence holder.[40] Additionally, the Agency is under a duty to modify licence conditions to the extent necessary to ensure that the activities authorised do not cause pollution of the environment, harm to human health or become seriously detrimental to the amenities of the locality.[41]

8.22 In recent years, the conditions imposed on facilities for the management of waste have increasingly been driven by the requirements of EC law and include elaborate precautions to ensure that contamination of soil or groundwater does not result from the activity. Notably these include the Landfill (England and Wales) Regulations 2002,[42] the Waste Incineration (England and Wales) Regulations 2002,[43] the Hazardous Waste (England and Wales) Regulations 2005,[44] the Sludge (Use in Agriculture) Regulations 1989,[45] the Animal By-Products Regulations 2006,[46] the End of Life Vehicles Regulations 2003,[47] and the Waste Electrical and Electronic Equipment (Waste Management Licensing) (England and Wales) Regulations 2006.[48]

---

[37] 1990 Act s.35(3).
[38] 1990 Act s.35(3).
[39] See s.36(3).
[40] 1990 Act s.37(1).
[41] 1990 Act s.37(2).
[42] Landfill (England and Wales) Regulations 2002 (SI 2002/1559).
[43] Waste Incineration (England and Wales) Regulations 2002 (SI 2002/2980).
[44] Hazardous Waste (England and Wales) Regulations 2005 (SI 2005/894).
[45] Sludge (Use in Agriculture) Regulations 1989 (SI 1989/1263).
[46] Animal By-Products Regulations 2006 (SI 2006/2347).
[47] End of Life Vehicles Regulations 2003 (SI 2003/2635).
[48] Waste Electrical and Electronic Equipment (Waste Management Licensing) (England and Wales) Regulations 2006 (SI 2006/3315).

In practice, therefore, the risks of future contaminated land from such **8.23** activities should be significantly reduced, though they can never of course be entirely obviated. As indicated previously,[49] the provisions of Pt IIA do not apply to land in respect of which there is a waste site licence under Pt IIA in force, unless the contamination is attributable to other causes than the licensed activities.

Surrender of waste site licences

Under s.37(2) of the 1990 Act, the waste regulation authority must modify **8.24** the conditions of existing licences to the extent required to ensure the authorised activities do not cause pollution of the environment, harm to human health, or serious detriment to the amenities of the locality. This duty of variation allows both for problems to be addressed as they come to light, and also, to an extent, for licence conditions to keep pace with changing standards of environmental protection.[50]

A major problem with licences under the 1974 Act was the ease with **8.25** which they could be cancelled by the holder when no longer required.[51] This is no longer the case under the 1990 Act. A site licence may be surrendered only if the Agency accepts the surrender.[52] The application to surrender must be accompanied by prescribed information and evidence,[53] the Agency must inspect the land,[54] and must determine whether it is likely or unlikely that the condition of the land, so far as that condition is the result of the use of the land for the treatment, keeping or disposal of waste (whether or not in pursuance of the licence) will cause pollution of the environment or harm to human health.[55] If satisfied that the condition of the land is unlikely to have those effects, the Agency shall accept the surrender.[56] Surrender is effected by the Agency issuing a certificate of completion, on which the licence shall cease to have effect.[57] If the authority is not satisfied that the condition of the land is unlikely to have the specified adverse effects it shall refuse to accept the surrender.[58]

---

[49] Para.3.79.

[50] This flows from the extremely wide and flexible definitions given to "harm to the environment" and "harm to human health" by s.29(1).

[51] 1974 Act s.8(4) simply required the holder to deliver the licence to the issuing authority and to give notice he longer required it.

[52] 1990 Act s.39(1).

[53] 1990 Act s.39(3); the information required is prescribed in the Waste Management Licensing Regulations 1994 Sch.1 and includes details of engineering works carried out in the case of landfills or lagoons, the presence of contaminants and geological, hydrological and hydrogeological information.

[54] 1990 Act s.39(4).

[55] 1990 Act s.39(5).

[56] 1990 Act s.39(6). The Agency must refer the proposal to the local planning authority and consider any representations it may make during a three month period, before accepting surrender: s.39(7).

[57] 1990 Act s.39(9).

[58] 1990 Act s.39(6). Appeal lies to the Secretary of State against refusal or deemed refusal (s.39(10) under s.43(1)(f)). Guidance to operators and waste authorities is to be provided in *Waste Management Paper 26A, Landfill Completion* which includes guidance on assessing completion, relevant criteria as to leachate and gas, and the completion report.

8.26   The effect of these provisions is therefore that the holder of a site licence will remain responsible for the aftercare of the site until surrender is accepted: conditions can be tightened up as mentioned above, and can relate to post-closure activities and precautions.[59]

8.27   The same applies to licences granted under the 1974 Act in existence on the relevant appointed day, which are then treated as site licences granted under the new provisions.[60] The impending stringency of the new provisions undoubtedly led to a number of licence holders taking steps to surrender licences unilaterally while this was still possible under COPA.[61]

Closed landfill

8.28   Of particular current concern is the increasing number of old landfill sites which are being identified as the source of potential problems, principally gas generation or water pollution. Many such sites date from the 1940s and were completed in the 1970s and 1980s, if not earlier, when the prevalent policy approved by the then Department of Environment was "dilute and disperse" or "attenuate and disperse" and before the problems of methane and other landfill gas generation came to be widely appreciated. Typically, such sites will have received either domestic putrescible wastes, or liquid industrial wastes, or both; as a practical matter industry and society at large enjoyed the benefits of low waste disposal costs at such sites. The price for such practices has effectively arisen later in terms of actual or potential pollution, in some cases putting at risk public or private potable water supplies, affecting surface water quality, and potentially infringing the EC Groundwater Directive 80/68.[62] In a number of cases such sites have attracted the attention of local planning authorities, district environmental health departments and the Agency: however, until the advent of Pt IIA, the previous powers under water protection and statutory nuisance provisions were ill-adapted to deal with such complex and historical problems. The Government's initial intention was that s.39 would be complemented by the provisions on "closed landfills" at s.61 of the 1990 Act. The effect of the two provisions read together would have been that the waste regulation authority would be under a duty to take steps to remediate closed sites presenting a risk of harm to the environment or to human health by virtue of noxious gases or liquids: but, if the authority had previously granted a certificate of completion in respect of the land there would be no ability to recover its costs from the owner for the time being. Thus, acceptance of surrender would effectively shift the risk in

---

[59] 1990 Act s.35(3). For cases considering the relationship between surrender, corporate insolvency and financial provision for aftercare costs, see *Official Receiver (Celtic Extraction Ltd and Bluestone Chemicals Ltd) v Environment Agency* [2000] Env. L.R. 86 (Court of Appeal, reviewing previous authorities); and *Environment Agency v Hillridge Ltd* [2003] EHWC 3023.

[60] 1990 Act s.77(2).

[61] A survey by Friends of the Earth published in May 1993 revealed that one in four of the landfill site licences extant in England at the beginning of 1993 had since been surrendered: see ENDS Report 220, May 1993, p.9. These included the licence for at least one site (Helpston, Peterborough) which presented a significant threat to underlying aquifer resources: see *The Independent*, June 17, 1993.

[62] See para.7.56ff.

relation to future problems from the owner to the authority. However, the Government never implemented s.61, which was repealed by the Environment Act 1995.[63] The relationship between closed and active landfills, in the sense of "piggy-backing" new waste deposits over existing fill was addressed in *R (Anti-Waste Ltd) v Environment Agency*.[63a]

Unlawful waste deposits: section 59 of the Environmental Protection Act

As well as the obvious example of domestic or industrial refuse disposed of **8.29** by final deposit in a landfall site, the following situations which may involve the deposit of waste on or in land also need to be considered:

1. storage of waste materials, such as scrap metal or drums of chemicals, on the surface of land where contamination may result from leakage or leaching;

2. "made ground"—where usable ground has been created for industrial or other purposes by the deposit of materials such as rubble, slag, foundry sand or other potentially contaminative materials;

3. general soil contamination from the handling of waste materials, for example the accumulation of particulate matter such as asbestos from demolition, ship-breaking or railway-carriage breaking;

4. the deposition on soil of airborne particulate waste matter, such as lead, emitted from industrial premises or from vehicles;

5. industrial slag heaps and effluent lagoons or ponds;

6. deposits on land of water-borne waste matter, such as oil;

7. contaminated dredgings from canals or docks; and

8. general spillages of liquids or powders in the course of industrial activity—though the substance may originally have been product or raw material, it may become waste as a result of the spill, having become contaminated or otherwise unusable.

In respect of problems such as these, s.59 of the Environmental **8.30** Protection Act 1990 may be relevant. Section 59 contains powers for waste regulation authorities (i.e. the Agency) or waste collection authorities (district councils or unitary authorities) to require the removal of waste deposited on land in contravention of s.33(1). The power is exercisable by notice served on the occupier of the land requiring him to do either or both of the following:

(a) remove the waste from the land within a specified period not less than 21 days beginning with the service of the notice;

---

[63] 1990 Act Sch.22, para.79.
[63a] [2007] EWHC 717 (Admin); [2007] Env. L.R.28.

(b) take within such a period specified steps with a view to eliminating or reducing the consequences of the deposit of the waste.

8.31 The recipient of the notice may appeal against it within the 21–day period to the magistrates' court or to the sheriff in Scotland, who must quash the requirement of the notice if satisfied that:

(a) the appellant neither deposited the waste nor knowingly caused nor knowingly permitted its deposit; or

(b) there is a material defect in the notice.[64]

8.32 If the notice is not quashed, its requirements may be modified by the magistrates, for example by extending its period for compliance.[65] The notice is of no effect pending determination of the appeal.[66]

8.33 Failure to comply with the requirements of a s.59 notice without reasonable excuse is punishable by a fine on summary conviction of up to £5,000 and to a further fine of up to £500 for each day that the failure continues after conviction.[67] Additionally, the authority may itself do what was required by the notice and recover its expenses reasonably incurred from the defaulter.[68]

Section 59: summary power

8.34 A separate summary power is given to the waste authorities by subs.(7). This is a power to remove waste which appears to have been deposited on land in contravention of s.33(1) and to take other steps to eliminate or reduce the consequences of the deposit. It is exercisable where:

(a) it is necessary to remove the waste forthwith or take other steps in order to remove or prevent pollution of land, water or air or harm to human health[69]; or

(b) there is no occupier of the land; or

(c) the occupier neither made nor knowingly permitted the deposit of the waste.

8.35 Where these powers are exercised the authority may recover its costs (including ultimate disposal of waste removed) from either[70]:

(a) the occupier in a case falling within (a) above unless he proves his innocence in relation to the deposit; or

---

[64] 1990 Act s.59 subss.(2) and (3).
[65] 1990 Act s.59 subss.(3) and (4).
[66] 1990 Act s.59 subs.(4).
[67] 1990 Act s.59 subs.(5).
[68] 1990 Act s.59 subs.(6).
[69] See definitions at subss.29(1) and (5).
[70] 1990 Act s.59 subs.59(8).

(b) in any of cases (a)—(c) any person who deposited or knowingly caused or knowingly permitted the deposit of *any of*[71] the waste.

The occupier or other person may escape liability by demonstrating that **8.36** costs were incurred unneccessarily.

Problems with section 59

Section 59 seems ostensibly very straightforward, but is perhaps more **8.37** difficult in practice. Certainly many waste authorities encountered difficulties in using its precursor, s.16 of the 1974 Act. Some of the main problems would appear to be as follows:

1. The deposit of waste giving rise to the problems may have predated in whole or in part the controls exercised by s.33(1), or indeed control under s.3 of the 1974 Act. If it pre-dated s.33, which came into force on May 1, 1994, there is an argument as to whether s.59 applies to deposits made in breach of the predecessor s.3 of COPA. If the deposit pre-dated COPA, it seems clear that s.59 cannot on any basis apply.

2. The occupier of the land may not have been involved with the deposit, in which case he will have a complete defence to the requirements of any notice. In such a case the authority will have to rely on its summary powers under subs.(7) the cost of which will be irrecoverable if the original "depositor" cannot be traced or is no longer existence.

3. The summary power under subs.(7) involves the authority in potentially heavy expenditure with no certain prospect of cost recovery.

4. It may be extremely difficult to frame the requirements of the notice with sufficient precision in a case involving contamination of land as well as waste deposits, so as to avoid a successful challenge to the notice on appeal.[72]

5. The burden of proving all the elements necessary to succeed in a prosecution for non-compliance with a notice under s.59 rests with the prosecution and is the high criminal burden.[73]

Whilst there are features in s.59 which do lend themselves to contami- **8.38** nated land problems, overall the section appears better adapted to dealing with incidents such as fly-tipping and unlicensed temporary deposits of

---

[71] The italicised words are significant, effectively creating joint and several liability in the case of commixed deposits.

[72] *Berridge Incinerators v Nottinghamshire CC*, Nottingham Crown Court, June 12, 1992, unreported (conviction quashed on basis that notice was unreasonable). See however *R v Metropolitan Stipendiary Magistrate Ex p. LWRA*; *Berkshire CC v Scott* [1993] 1 All E.R. 113 (validity of notice under s.16 COPA upheld despite an argument that the description of the waste to be removed was too vague).

[73] *Berridge Incinerators v Nottinghamshire CC*, June 12, 1992, unreported.

waste, such as at transfer stations. Were it the case that s.59 was simply an optional power to be exercised on a discretionary basis, that would not be problematic. The difficulty however is that s.78YB(3) requires consideration of whether the contaminated land in question falls within the scope of s.59(1) or (7), i.e. whether the contamination is due to controlled waste having been deposited in or on the relevant land in contravention of s.33, and if so then a remediation notice cannot be served based on that waste or the consequences of its deposit, if and to the extent that it appears that the powers under s.59(1) or (7) may be exercised.

8.39 The problematic aspects of these provisions are discussed in the context of Pt IIA,[74] but they have been compounded by the decision of the European Court in Case C-1/03 *Van de Walle v Texaco Belgium SA*.[75] The case related to a service station in Belgium owned by Texaco, which was operated by another party under a contract with Texaco. When hydrocarbons were found to have leaked from the underground tanks and to have contaminated the soil under the station and infiltrated an adjacent building, the Belgian authorities used a strict liability law on abandonment of waste to require clean up. Belgian does not have its own contaminated land regime and, accordingly, the prosecuting authority needed to establish that the contaminated soils were waste in order for its waste abandonment law to apply. The case was referred to the ECJ by the Belgian court for clarification.

8.40 The ECJ's judgment establishes that the definition of "waste" in the Waste Framework Directive 75/442 (as amended) does extend to spilled or escaped products, even where the discarding of the contaminant was accidental (see para.50). Equally, the soil or groundwater contaminated by the spilled product would also be waste (para.52). There then arises an obligation on the Member State to ensure that the "holder" of the contaminated soils either has them handled by a waste contractor or recovers/disposes of them himself (Art.8 of the Directive). In addition, responsibility for the recovery or disposal of the waste must be borne by the holder and/or the previous holders or the producer of the product from which the waste came (Art.15). The ECJ held that the service station manager, being the possessor and producer of the waste, should be considered to be the "holder" (para.59). However, the possibility was mooted that if the poor condition of the tanks and the consequent leak could be attributed to the disregard of contractual obligations by the petrol supplier and owner of the station, its activities could be seen as having produced the waste, making it the holder. Accordingly, the ECJ left it to the Belgian court to look at Texaco's contractual obligations with the petrol station manager and determine whether it was in fact the waste holder for the purposes of waste regulation.

8.41 The case has aroused speculation as to its implications in national law.[75a] It has been suggested that it creates a new regime providing for "strict, retroactive, joint and several liability of operators, land owners, and

[74] See para.3.82.
[75] [2005] Env. L.R. 24.
[75a] It was followed in a different context in Case C-252/05, *R (Thames Water Utilities) v South East London Division, Bromley Magistrates' Court* in respect of sewerage which escaped from the sewage system.

product manufacturers for the costs of spill cleanup and soil and groundwater remediation".[76] More immediately, the issue is how the ruling impacts on the UK's own contaminated land and waste regimes and their interrelationship. In particular, absent any changes to the exemptions regime for waste management licensing, it will need to be considered whether the occupier of contaminated land may be said to be criminally liable for "keeping" controlled waste without a licence,[77] and if so what form the licence would take. The problem is of course that if the site is presenting risks, for example to groundwater, what licence would or could be granted?

There also arises the problem of the interrelationship with Pt IIA, in **8.42** view of the restrictions of using the Pt IIA regime in ss.78YB(2) and (3) where waste is involved. The problem is essentially that in Belgium, the contaminated land regime operated through a 1991 Order of the Brussels-Capital Region, Implementing the Waste Framework Directive and which depends on the material in question being classified as waste. The UK regime is essentially predicated on separate legislation to secure the clean-up of contaminated soil and groundwater, which is based on principles of risk assessment absent from the simply classification of material as "waste".

The key focus should perhaps be on what the Waste Framework **8.43** Directive itself may require. It may be noted that the ruling of the ECJ was foreseeable in that the list of wastes at Annex I of the Directive includes at item Q4, "Materials spilled, lost or having undergone any other mishap, *including any materials, equipment, etc, contaminated as a result of the mishap*" (indeed the previous edition of this work had suggested exactly that). However, it may also be noted that the key articles of the Directive—in particular Arts 4, 7–10 and 15—bite on the "disposal" or "recovery" of waste and it is not clear how contaminated material which simply remains without any interference in soil or groundwater can be said to be the subject of disposal or recovery operations as listed in the Directive— whether it *should* be recovered or disposed of by way of remediation is a different matter.

In practice, the full implications of the case appear to have been **8.44** studiously ignored by government and regulatory authorities in the UK. It may be that this was the best course, since the proposed revised Waste Framework Directive published by the Commission in 2005 has proposed excluding from the Directive "unexcavated contaminated soil", as regards its specific aspects "which are already covered by other Community legislation".[78]

Waste: the duty of care

One of the refinements introduced by the Environmental Protection Act **8.45** 1990 was the duty of care as respects waste: this is discussed elsewhere in the context of preventing contamination.[79] The question arises as to the

[76] *Prof Lucas Bergkamp* [2004] 4 Env. Liab. 171.
[77] See para.8.17 and also para.8.46 on "Keeping".
[78] COM 2005/667 Final (21/12/05). This formulation however begs the question of what "other Community legislation" would be in play, and to what extent.
[79] Environmental Protection Act 1990 s.34.

extent to which the requirements of the duty of care may bite upon the occupier of land contaminated by waste: if the duty does apply then failure to prevent escape of the waste from control (e.g. by dispersal into groundwater) may result in criminal liability unless all measures applicable to the occupier to prevent the escape have been taken. The operative words of the section in this respect would appear to be[80]: ". . . the duty of any person who . . . keeps . . . controlled waste . . .".

8.46 Is the occupier of land in which waste has been deposited a person who "keeps" the waste? Waste stored on a land in a readily recoverable form, in drums or some other container or repository, may be said to be "kept", and it could be asked whether that waste would cease to be "kept" if it were covered with a layer of topsoil. On the other hand, it seems much less apt to speak of waste being "kept" where it comprises material infilled or used to provide "made ground": still less apt where liquid waste has been spilt or disposed of into land so as to be physically irrecoverable in its original form. "Keep" is not defined in the Act, but in ordinary usage would appear to involve retaining the waste with at least a limited degree of continuity.[81] It must be questionable, to say the least, that the occupier of a closed landfill site is "keeping" the waste in that sense: in the context of s.33 of the 1990 Act such an interpretation would have the curious result of requiring a waste management licence to be retained for the site in perpetuity.

8.47 Thus, whilst it cannot be said that s.34 can never apply to historically contaminated land, it appears that it is unlikely to be of widespread application.

---

[80] Leaving aside cases where the defendant is the producer, carrier, treater or disposer of the waste.
[81] See *Blue v Pearl Assurance Co* [1940] 3 W.W.R. 13 at 19–20.

Chapter 9

RADIOACTIVITY

Generally

Although radioactive substances have been used for a wide variety of **9.01** purposes since the start of the 20th century, most have only been subject to regulation since 1963 when the Radioactive Substances Act 1963 came into force,[1] so that unregulated use was undertaken for a substantial period of time. Examples of industrial activities which have involved the use of materials containing radioactivity include those where radioactive materials have been employed for their radioactive properties (such as luminising works); where radioactive properties are incidental in materials that are used for their non-radioactive properties (such as gas mantle production); the use of phosphatic substances and rare earths in certain industrial processes; and where radioactive materials have been inadvertently handled, or escaped accidentally (such as lead mining).[2] Little information is available on the scale of radioactive contamination outside of nuclear licensed sites, but a study for the Government put the likely number of sites in England and Wales where activities took place capable of giving rise to radioactive contamination (if a pollutant linkage was in place) in the range of 100–1,000, and most likely to be in the range of 150–250.[3]

Nuclear sites

As well as the general use of radioactive materials, the UK has a history **9.02** since the 1940s of the development of both nuclear weapons and the civil nuclear industry, which has left a legacy of contaminated sites and of radioactive waste. Operational nuclear sites are controlled by way of site licences granted under the Nuclear Installations Act 1965. Such licences will require the implementation of decommissioning programmes during the "period of responsibility" of the operator.[4]

Part 1 of the Energy Act 2004 deals with the civil nuclear industry and **9.03** established the Nuclear Decommissioning Authority to manage the clean-up of sites previously managed by British Nuclear Fuels Limited and the

---

[1] Some degree of control had existed previously under the Radioactive Substances Act 1948. Many types of potentially contaminating radioactive substances have historically been exempt from control by exemption order made under the Acts, e.g. thorium, rare earths, electronic valves, etc.

[2] DEFRA Circular 01/2006, *Contaminated Land*, Annex 1 para.68. An Industry Profile setting out Industrial Activities Which Have Used Materials Containing Radioactivity, is available from *http://www.defra.gov.uk/environment/radioactivity/conland/pdf/industryprofile.pdf*.

[3] DEFRA Circular 01/2006, *Contaminated Land*, Annex 1 para.69.

[4] Nuclear Installations Act 1965 s.5(3).

UK Atomic Energy Authority (basically the facilities developed by BNFL and the UKAEA between the 1940s and 1960s, and the Magnox nuclear reactors designed and built in the 1960s and 1970s). These liabilities have been estimated as likely to cost £1 billion a year for the decade 2004–2014 and about £48 billion (undiscounted) over the next century. Consideration of that topic, and of the disposal of radioactive waste generally, is beyond the scope of this work and is not considered further.[5] Operators of nuclear sites are subject to a specific regime of statutory liability to third parties for harm or damage, which is dealt with below so far as it interacts with the contaminated land regime.[6]

Extension of Part IIA to radioactive contamination

9.04 Part IIA has been extended to apply, in a modified form,[7] to land which is contaminated by way of harm so far as this is attributable to radioactivity possessed by any substance.[8] This reflects the particular scientific problems involved, including consideration of how to apply established concepts and principles of radiological protection to contaminated land,[9] and the need to integrate with other regulatory schemes, which implement obligations under European and International Law.[10]

9.05 These specific and potentially difficult issues meant that such land was originally excluded from the scope of Pt IIA,[11] though the Government always viewed Pt IIA, with changes to some detailed aspects, as providing a suitable basis for dealing with radioactive contamination on old industrial sites.[12] The result has been the modification of Pt IIA so far as it applies to such properties of substances through regulations[13] and amendments to the Statutory Guidance and Departmental Circular.[14] Modification of the main

[5] For further commentary see The Energy Act 2004 (Current Law Statutes).

[6] See para.9.09 and 15.14ff.

[7] From August 4, 2006 in England.

[8] Rather than other harmful properties which a radioactive substance may have, such as toxicity, which fall within the scope of the general Pt IIA regime.

[9] See the National Radiological Protection Board publication *Radiological Protection Objectives for Land Contaminated with Radionuclides* (Documents of NRPB, Vol.9, No.2, 1998).

[10] Such as the Basic Safety Standards Directive (96/29/EURATOM) and the 1960 Paris Convention on Third Party Liability in the Field of Nuclear Energy.

[11] Under s.78YC.

[12] The first consultation paper discussing the proposed extension of the regime *Control and Remediation of Radioactively Contaminated Land* was published by the DETR on February 28, 1998.

[13] The Radioactive Contaminated Land (Enabling Powers) (England) Regulations 2005 (SI 2005/3467), which enabled the laying before Parliament of draft Guidance and Regulations, and the Radioactive Contaminated Land (Modification of Enactments) (England) Regulations 2006 (SI 2006/1379) ("Modification Regulations"), which provide for an extended and modified regime in relation to such properties of substances in England, both made under s.78YC, and the Contaminated Land (England) Regulations 2006 (SI 2006/1380), which make provision for an additional special site description. See also outside England, the Radioactive Contaminated Land (Scotland) Regulations 2007 (SSI 2007/179), the Radioactive Contaminated Land (Modification of Enactments) (Wales) Regulations 2006 (SI 2006/2988, W. 277) and the Radioactive Contaminated Land Regulations (Northern Ireland) 2006 (NI SI 2006/345).

[14] DEFRA Circular 01/2006 *Contaminated Land*, which was revised mainly in order to set out the amended Guidance and explain how the modified regime is expected to work (see para.4 of the introduction).

regime is effected through regulations setting out modified versions of sections of the 1990 Act, with reg.3 applying those amended provisions in relation to harm so far as attributable to any radioactivity possessed by any substance.

The modified regime implements obligations under Arts 48 and 53 of the **9.06** Basic Safety Standards Directive 96/29, which require, and set out the requirements of, "intervention in cases of radiological emergencies or in cases of lasting exposure resulting from the after-effects of a radiological emergency or a past or old practice or work activity" (Art.48).

The main ways in which the normal regime is modified are: **9.07**

1. the definition of "contaminated land";

2. the inspection duty on local authorities;

3. special sites and enforcing authorities; and

4. establishing remediation requirements.

Relationship of Part IIA and Nuclear Installations Act liabilities

The scope of the modified Pt IIA is restricted in a number of respects. As **9.08** well as limiting the scope through modifying the definition of "contaminated land", specific exclusions are set out in s.78YB(5) (as inserted by reg.17(4)). These provide that nothing in Pt IIA applies to land which is contaminated by reason of the presence in, on or under the land of any substances, in so far as by reason of such presence damage to any property occurs, being:

(a) damage caused in breach of any duty imposed by ss.7–10 of the Nuclear Installations Act 1965 or which it is deemed to be so caused by s.12(2) (i.e. because it is not reasonably separable from injury or damage so caused);

(b) damage which would have been so caused if in s.7 the words "other than the licensee" had not been enacted, i.e. damage which occurs to the licensee's own property; or

(c) damage in respect of which any relevant foreign operator or other person is liable under any relevant foreign law, or for which he would be so liable but for any exclusion or limitation of liability applying under that foreign law made for purposes corresponding to specified provisions of the 1965 on matters such as time limits and financial limits.

9.09   The effect of these provisions can only be understood by reference to the regime governing liability for "nuclear occurrences" under the Nuclear Installations Act 1965. Detailed consideration of that regime is outside the scope of this work,[15] but essentially the Act implements the UK's obligations under the OECD Paris Convention of 1960 on third party liability in the field of nuclear energy. Sections 7–10 impose duties on licensees of nuclear sites and on specified other persons (i.e. the UK Atomic Energy Authority and the Crown in relation to certain sites and "foreign operators" who operate installations in other territories). Those duties are to secure that no specified type of occurrence involving nuclear matter (essentially the emission of ionising radiation from the site or from waste discharged from the site) causes injury to any person or damage to the property of any person other than the licensee. Where such injury or damage is caused in breach of the duty, then compensation is payable wherever the injury or damage is caused (s.12(1)(a)) but no other liability shall be incurred by any person in respect of the injury or damage (s.12(1)(b)). This liability to pay compensation is limited in certain respects, in particular by a time limit for claims (s.15) and an aggregate limit on liability in respect of any one occurrence (s.16).

9.10   "Damage to property" can include the contamination of land by radioactive material.[16] The effect of s.78YB(5) is therefore that Pt IIA will not apply to land which has been contaminated where the contamination which constitutes the "harm" for the purposes of Pt IIA as modified also amounts to damage to property and where it occurred in breach of a duty under the 1965 Act. In those circumstances the person who suffered the damage will have a claim against the nuclear operator in question to be compensated. Examples might be where radioactive material or waste escapes from a site and contaminates nearby land, or where airborne fallout from an accident at a nuclear plant in the UK, or indeed overseas, contaminates land. Since for these purposes it has to be assumed that the duties apply in respect of the property of the licensee and operator, Pt IIA will also not apply where a nuclear occurrence contaminates and damages property on the licensed site itself. In such circumstances in any event it seems likely that the necessary remedial measures would be required and enforced by the Nuclear Installations Inspectorate using its powers under the site licence and under the Nuclear Installations Act. if there is no "damage to property" for whatever reason, then Pt IIA will be applicable if, as explained below there is "harm" in the special sense of lasting exposure to any person or the significant possibility of such harm.

9.11   The reasoning behind these somewhat opaque provisions is to avoid conflict with the international law on nuclear liability which underlies the 1965 Act and which requires liability to be channelled to the operator and made subject to limitations. The Pt IIA provisions, if applicable, could undermine that regime. The point appears to have been overlooked when the initial Enabling Powers Regulations were made in December 2005.

---

[15] See S. Tromans and J. Fitzgerald, *The Law of Nuclear Installations and Radioactive Substances* (London: Sweet & Maxwell, 1997), p.99 et seq.

[16] For cases on this question see *Merlin v British Nuclear Fuels Ltd* [1990] 2 Q.B. 557; *Blue Circle Industries Plc v Ministry of Defence* [1999] 2 W.L.R. 295; [1999] Env. L.R. 22; *Magnohard v UK Atomic Energy Authority* [2004] Env. L.R. 19. See also para.15.14ff.

Definition of radioactive contaminated land

Section 78A(2) (as modified) defines contaminated land as: **9.12**

> ". . . any land which appears to the local authority in whose area
> it is situated to be in such a condition, by reason of substances
> in, on or under the land, that —
>
> (a) harm is being caused; or
> (b) there is a significant possibility of harm being caused".[17]

By s.78A(4) (as modified), "harm" is defined as "lasting exposure to any **9.13**
person resulting from the after-effects of a radiological emergency, past
practice or past work activity".[18] Determination of whether any land
appears to be such land, whether harm is being caused, and whether the
possibility of such harm being caused is serious, is required to be in
accordance with the Statutory Guidance.[19]

A number of consequences flow from this modified definition of contami- **9.14**
nated land. First, the potential "receptors" in any "pollutant linkage"[20] are
restricted to humans, and so non-human receptors, such as animals or
crops, are excluded from the scope of the modified regime. Similarly,
pollution of controlled waters is excluded so far as such waters constitute
the receptors (though they could still potentially be a human exposure
pathway). The corollary of this narrower definition is that provisions within
the main regime which relate to pollution of controlled waters only (such
as s.78J) are disapplied in the modified regime.

Secondly, the definition is limited to exposure which results from **9.15**
specified occurrences: radiological emergencies, past practices or past work
activities. The terms derive from those in the Basic Safety Standards
Directive and the relevant definitions are reproduced in the Schedule to
the Modification Regulations. A "radiological emergency" is "a situation
that requires urgent action in order to protect workers, members of the
public or the population either partially or as a whole". A "practice" is "a
human activity that can increase the exposure of individuals to radiation
from an artificial source, or from a natural radiation source where natural
radionuclides are processed for their radioactive, fissile or fertile properties, except in the case of an emergency exposure". The terminology
precludes the application of the modified regime in relation to current, as
opposed to past, "practices". In relation to such current practices, the
keeping, use and disposal of radioactive substances and wastes is regulated
under the Radioactive Substances Act 1993.

Thirdly, the definition excludes natural background radiation, e.g from **9.16**
radon. The definition by reference to "harm" rather than "significant
harm" also means that a number of consequential changes are made in
relation to the modified regime.

---

[17] Modification Regulations reg.5.
[18] Modification Regulations reg.5.
[19] Modification Regulations reg.5.
[20] See para.3.07.

The modified definition of "substance" at s.78A(9) refers to:

> ". . . whether in solid or liquid form or in the form of a gas or vapour, any substance which contains radionuclides which have resulted from the after-effects of a radiological emergency or which are or have been processed as part of a past practice or past work activity, but shall not include radon gas or the following radionuclides . . .".[21]

9.17   In relation to liability for changes to substances, modified s.79F(9) includes substances present as a result of "radioactive decay" (as well as from chemical reaction or biological process).[22]

9.18   This limitation of scope is largely a result of the approach and definitions found in the Basic Safety Standards Directive, with transposition and implementation of obligations being a primary concern. The focus on harm to human receptors only is being kept under review, though the Environment Agency considers that there is no evidence of widespread risk to protected ecosystems or of pollution from past activities impacting animals or crops.[23] Water can still be a "pathway" in a pollutant linkage, the possibility of including "significant" pollution of controlled waters through radioactive properties within the scope of the modified regime is an issue which may be revisited in the future.[24]

Guidance on "harm"

9.19 The criteria for the determination of whether or not "harm" is occurring are based on levels of effective or equivalent dose at which it is appropriate for a site to be investigated, remedial options considered, and where subsequent action is likely to be justified.[25] "Harm" should be regarded as being caused where lasting exposure gives rise to radiation doses which exceed one or more of prescribed values set out in the Guidance (Pt 5 of Annex 3):

1. an effective dose of 3 millisieverts per annum;

2. an equivalent dose to the lens of the eye of 15 millisieverts per annum; or

3. an equivalent dose to the skin of 50 millisieverts per annum.[26]

---

[21] Po-218, Pb-214, At-218, Bi-214, Rn-218, Po-214 and Tl-210. Radon gas and its short-lived decay products are excluded because they are only a matter of concern within buildings and other policy exists in respect of them (DEFRA Circular 01/2006, *Contaminated Land*, Annex 1 para.75).

[22] Modification Regulations reg.9 which is followed up by the Statutory Guidance on Test 4 of the Exclusionary tests (DEFRA Circular 01/2006, *Contaminated Land*, Annex 3 D.63).

[23] DEFRA Circular 01/2006, *Contaminated Land*, Annex 1 para.73.

[24] DEFRA Circular 01/2006, *Contaminated Land*, Annex 1 para.74, with the Government wishing to assess the implications of the Water Framework Directive (2000/60), DEFRA Circular 01/2006, *Contaminated Land*, Annex 2 para.2.3.

[25] DEFRA Circular 01/2006, *Contaminated Land*, Annex 1 para.89.

[26] DEFRA Circular 01/2006, *Contaminated Land*, Annex 3 A.41.

"Lasting exposure" is not defined in the Basic Safety Standards Directive **9.20** but the Government considers it to be exposure that could take place over a protracted period as a result of the nature of the contamination and the use to which land is put.[27] Any human receptors which are not likely to be present, given the "current use" of the land or other land which might be affected, are to be disregarded for this purpose.[28] "Current use" means any use which is currently being made, or is likely to be made, which is lawful under town and country planning legislation, and includes: any temporary (permitted) use to which the land is, or is likely to be, put from time to time; future uses or developments which do not require a new, or amended, grant of planning permission (though note the requirements with regard to the possibility of significant harm, below). The current use should also be taken to include any likely informal recreational use of the land, whether authorised by the owners or occupiers or not, such as children playing on the land (giving due attention to measures taken to prevent or restrict access to the land) in deciding the likelihood of such informal use).[29]

Significant possibility of harm being caused

The evaluation of whether the possibility of harm being caused is "signifi- **9.21** cant" is approached in a much more detailed and technical manner in the modified regime for radioactivity than under the general regime.[30] "Possibility of harm" is to be taken as referring to a measure of the probability, or frequency, of the occurrence of circumstances which would lead to lasting exposure being caused.[31]

Where (a) the potential annual effective dose[32] is below or equal to 50 **9.22** millisieverts per annum, and (b) the potential annual dose equivalents to the lens of the eye and to the skin are below or equal to 15 millisieverts and 50 millisieverts respectively, the local authority should regard the possibility of harm as "significant" if, having regard to any uncertainties, the potential annual effective dose from any lasting exposure multiplied by the probability of the dose being received is greater than 3 millisieverts.[33] In other circumstances, the local authority should consider whether the possibility of harm being caused is significant on a case by case basis, taking into account relevant information[34] concerning[35]:

1. the potential annual effective dose;

---

[27] DEFRA Circular 01/2006, *Contaminated Land*, Annex 1 para.76(a).
[28] DEFRA Circular 01/2006, *Contaminated Land*, Annex 3 A.42.
[29] DEFRA Circular 01/2006, *Contaminated Land*, Annex 3 A.43.
[30] See para.3.38ff.
[31] DEFRA Circular 01/2006, *Contaminated Land*, Annex 3 A.44.
[32] "Potential annual effective dose" and "potential annual equivalent dose", refer to doses that are not certain to occur; DEFRA Circular 01/2006, *Contaminated Land*, Annex 3 A.44.
[33] DEFRA Circular 01/2006, *Contaminated Land*, Annex 3 A.45. These dose levels have been selected in accordance with advice from the Health Protection Agency DEFRA Circular 01/2006, *Contaminated Land*, Annex 1 para.90).
[34] "Relevant information" means information which is appropriate, scientifically-based and authoritative; DEFRA Circular 01/2006, *Contaminated Land*, Annex 3 A.47.
[35] DEFRA Circular 01/2006, *Contaminated Land*, Annex 3 A.46.

2. any non-linearity in the dose-effect relationship for stochastic effects;[36]

3. the potential annual equivalent dose to the skin and to the lens of the eye;

4. the nature and degree of any deterministic effects[37] associated with the potential annual dose;

5. the probability of the dose being received;

6. the duration of the exposure and timescale within which the harm might occur; and

7. any uncertainties associated with those factors.

9.23 In considering the duration of harm, the local authority should take into account any evidence that the "current use" of the land will cease in the foreseeable future.[38]

9.24 There are some specific requirements with regard to the consideration of the possibility of harm being caused by future changes of use. When considering such possibility as a result of any change of use of any land to one which is not a "current use" of that land is not to be regarded as a significant possibility of harm.[39] When considering such possibility in relation to any future use or development which falls within the description of a "current use", the local authority should assume that if the future use is introduced, or the development carried out, this will be done in accordance with any existing planning permission for that use or development. In particular, the local authority should assume that any remediation which is the subject of a condition attached to that planning permission or of any planning obligation, will be carried out in accordance with that permission or obligation, and that where such conditions require steps to be taken to prevent problems which might be caused by contamination, approved by the local planning authority, that the local planning authority will ensure that those steps include adequate remediation.[40]

9.25 The recommended approach for the exposure assessment of a site is the Radioactively Contaminated Land Exposure Assessment (RCLEA) methodology, comprising the technical guidance and software for assessing exposure on sites contaminated by radioactivity.[41]

---

[36] "Stochastic effects" means the type of health effect (the principal one being radiation induced cancer) where the likelihood of radiation-induced health effects which may be assumed to be linearly proportional to the radiation dose over a wide range of doses and where the severity of the health effect is not dependent on the level of the dose: DEFRA Circular 01/2006, *Contaminated Land*, Annex 3 A.47.

[37] "Deterministic effects" means the type of health effect (such as a radiation-induced cataract of the eye, or a burn) which occur following a dose of radiation above a certain level, with the severity of the health effect dependent on the level of the dose: DEFRA Circular 01/2006, *Contaminated Land*, Annex 3 A.47.

[38] DEFRA Circular 01/2006, *Contaminated Land*, Annex 3 A.48.

[39] DEFRA Circular 01/2006, *Contaminated Land*, Annex 3 A.49.

[40] DEFRA Circular 01/2006, *Contaminated Land*, Annex 3 A.50.

[41] CLAN 5/06 revised edition (July 2006).

Radioactive "pollutant linkage"

As well as the restriction of receptors to humans (see above), the modified **9.26** definition of "substance" in relation to radioactivity needs to be considered when assessing whether there is a contaminant present, as part of the "contaminant-pathway-receptor" pollutant linkage. A substance must contain one or more radionuclides and for the purposes of determining whether a pollutant linkage exists, the local authority may treat two or more substances containing radionuclides as being a single substance.[42] This reflects the fact that a number of radionuclides may contribute to the effective dose and to the equivalent dose to the lens of the eye and to the skin which need to be assessed in determining whether harm is being caused.[43]

Inspection of radioactive contaminated land

The modified regime imposes a more limited inspection duty on local **9.27** authorities, with s.78B(1) requiring any land to be inspected for the purpose of identifying whether it is contaminated land, and to enable the authority to decide whether the land is required to be designated as a special site, *only* where the authority considers that there are reasonable grounds for believing it may be contaminated[44] (by substances with radioactive properties). The fact that substances have been, or are, present on the land is not of itself to be taken to be such "reasonable grounds".[45] The local authority will have such reasonable grounds where it has knowledge of relevant information relating to either a former historical land use, past practice, past work activity or radiological emergency, or levels of contamination present on the land arising from past practices, etc. capable of causing lasting exposure giving rise to the radiation doses set out in the Guidance on "harm".[46] "Relevant information" means information that is appropriate and authoritative and may include information held by the local authority, including information already gathered as part of its inspection strategy for the general regime of Pt IIA, or as part of the town and country planning process, or information received from a regulatory body, such as the Environment Agency or the Health and Safety Executive.[47] These grounds mean that the local authority needs to be aware of land use which could be capable of giving rise to the dose criteria, or that it has been presented with evidence of a contamination level capable of giving rise to the dose criteria before it considers undertaking detailed individual inspection. In the Government's view "knowledge of relevant information" will not require the local authority to review actively its records compiled before the modified regime came into force.[48]

---

[42] DEFRA Circular 01/2006, *Contaminated Land*, Annex 3 A.18A.
[43] DEFRA Circular 01/2006, *Contaminated Land*, Annex 2 para.2.15.
[44] Modification Regulations reg.6.
[45] Modified s.78B(1A).
[46] DEFRA Circular 01/2006, *Contaminated Land*, Annex 3 B.17A.
[47] DEFRA Circular 01/2006, *Contaminated Land*, Annex 3 B.17B.
[48] DEFRA Circular 01/2006, *Contaminated Land*, Annex 2 para.3.4A.

9.28   Where satisfied that such reasonable grounds exist for believing that land may be contaminated in relation to radioactivity, the local authority should carry out a detailed inspection of the land, to obtain sufficient information for it to make the determinations as to whether it is contaminated land, and whether it is a special site.[49] In the first instance, the local authority should aim to identify that there is a reasonable possibility both of the presence of a receptor and that this receptor could be exposed to a contaminant.[50] As with the general regime, such inspection might include collation and assessment of documentary information or other information from other bodies, might include a site visit for visual inspection and limited sampling (where a survey might use hand-held radiation meters), and/or the carrying out of intrusive investigations. In carrying out the detailed inspection, the local authority should have regard to any advice from the Environment Agency on the manner of carrying this out, and should always seek to make arrangements for the Agency to carry out any intrusive investigations.[51] The power of local authorities to authorise others to exercise specific powers of entry under s.108 of the 1990 Act is extended to the Agency for these purposes.[52]

Determination that land is "radioactive contaminated land"

9.29 The local authority should determine that land is contaminated land on the basis that harm is being caused which is attributable to radioactivity where:

1. it has carried out a scientific and technical assessment of the dose arising from the pollutant linkage, according to relevant, appropriate, authoritative and scientifically based guidance on such assessments, having regard to any advice provided by the Environment Agency, and taking into account the requirements as to "effective dose" and "equivalent dose" (see below);

2. that assessment shows that such harm is being caused; and

3. there are no suitable and sufficient risk management arrangements in place to prevent such harm.[53]

9.30   In following any such guidance on the assessment of dose, the local authority should satisfy itself that it is relevant to the circumstances of the pollutant linkage and land in question, and that any appropriate

---

[49] DEFRA Circular 01/2006, *Contaminated Land*, Annex 3 B.18A.
[50] DEFRA Circular 01/2006, *Contaminated Land*, Annex 3 B.19A. It was reported in 2006 that SEPA was seeking funding to investigate radioactive contamination on a beach at Dalgety Bay on the Firth of Forth for radioactive particles, possibly deriving radium 220 from instrument dials on WWII aircraft burnt and broken up at Donibristle Airbase from 1945–59 (See ENDS Report 376, May 2006, p.17).
[51] DEFRA Circular 01/2006, *Contaminated Land*, Annex 3 B.20.
[52] Through reg.18 of the Modification Regulations.
[53] DEFRA Circular 01/2006, *Contaminated Land*, Annex 3 B.51A.

allowances have been made for particular circumstances.[54] To simplify such an assessment of dose, the local authority is permitted to use authoritative and scientifically-based guideline values for concentrations of the potential pollutants in, on or under the land in pollutant linkages of the type concerned. If it does so, the local authority should be satisfied that: an adequate scientific and technical assessment of the information on the potential pollutant, using those based guideline values, shows that requirements 2 and 3 (above) are met.[55] In using any guideline values, the local authority should be satisfied that:

(a) the guideline values are relevant to the judgment of whether the effects of the pollutant linkage in question constitute harm attributable to radioactivity;

(b) the assumptions underlying the derivation of any numerical values in the guideline values (such as assumptions regarding soil conditions, the behaviour of potential pollutants, the existence of pathways, the land-use patterns, and the presence of human beings) are relevant to the circumstances of the pollutant linkage in question;

(c) any other conditions relevant to the use of the guideline values have been observed (such as the number, and methods of preparation and analysis, of samples taken);

(d) appropriate adjustments have been made to allow for the differences between the circumstances of the land in question and any assumptions or other factors relating to the guideline values; and

(e) the basis of derivation of the guideline values has taken into account the requirements as to "effective dose" and "equivalent dose" (see below).[56]

The possibility of differing views as to the most appropriate method of **9.31** risk assessments is implicitly recognised in the Guidance, and local authorities are required to be prepared to reconsider any determination based on such use of guideline values where it is demonstrated to the authority's satisfaction that under some other more appropriate method of assessing the risks it would not have determined that the land appeared to be contaminated land.[57]

The estimation of an effective dose and an equivalent dose is subject to **9.32** two specific requirements. First, the estimation should be undertaken in accordance with Arts 15 and 16 of the Basic Safety Standards Directive. Secondly, the estimation should not include the local background level of radiation from the natural environment.[58]

---

[54] DEFRA Circular 01/2006, *Contaminated Land*, Annex 3 B.51B.
[55] DEFRA Circular 01/2006, *Contaminated Land*, Annex 3 B.51C.
[56] DEFRA Circular 01/2006, *Contaminated Land*, Annex 3 B.51D.
[57] DEFRA Circular 01/2006, *Contaminated Land*, Annex 3 B.51E.
[58] DEFRA Circular 01/2006, *Contaminated Land*, Annex 3 B.51F.

9.33   The local authority should determine that land is contaminated land on the basis that there is a significant possibility of harm being caused which is attributable to radioactivity where it has carried out a scientific and technical assessment of the *potential* dose arising from the pollutant linkage,[59] which shows that there is a significant possibility of such harm being caused; and there are no suitable and sufficient risk management arrangements in place to prevent such harm.[60] In following any guidance on assessment of the potential dose, the local authority should be satisfied that it is relevant to the circumstances of the pollutant linkage and land in question, and that any appropriate allowances have been made for particular circumstances.[61]

9.34   In making its determination as to harm so far as attributable to radioactivity, the local authority is required to consult the Environment Agency, providing it with a draft record of the determination, and have regard to the Agency's advice on the basis for, and extent of land covered by, the determination.[62] In deciding whether separate designations of a larger area of contaminated land might simplify the administration of the consequential actions, the views of the Environment Agency should be taken into account concerning the desirability of a separate determination so far as harm is attributable to radioactivity.[63] In preparing the written record of any determination the local authority needs to take account of the Environment Agency's comments on the draft record of determination.[64]

Enforcing authority for radioactive contaminated land

9.35 Where land is contaminated land by virtue of any radioactivity possessed by any substances, the Environment Agency is the enforcing authority, having expertise available in relation to radioactive substances. Under reg.2(1)(k) of the Contaminated Land (England) Regulations 2006, land which is contaminated land "wholly or partly by virtue of any radioactivity possessed by any substance in, on or under that land" is required to be designated as a special site.[65]

Remediation of radioactive contaminated land: "practices" and "interventions"

9.36 The most distinct aspect of the modified regime is the determination of remediation requirements in relation to land contaminated in relation to radioactivity. In part this stems from the requirements of the Basic Safety

---

[59] Meeting the same requirements as to guidance, advice, etc. as those imposed in relation to determinations that harm is being caused (see above).
[60] DEFRA Circular 01/2006, *Contaminated Land*, Annex 3 B.51G.
[61] DEFRA Circular 01/2006, *Contaminated Land*, Annex 3 B.51H.
[62] DEFRA Circular 01/2006, *Contaminated Land*, Annex 3 B.43A.
[63] DEFRA Circular 01/2006, *Contaminated Land*, Annex 3 B.32(d).
[64] DEFRA Circular 01/2006, *Contaminated Land*, Annex 2 para.3.35.
[65] The Modification Regulations amending the scope of the Secretary of State's powers to prescribed descriptions of land for this purpose (reg.7).

Standards Directive which form the basis of radiological protection in the UK.[66] This distinguishes between "practices", where radiation exposures can be introduced in a controlled manner, and "interventions", dealing with situations where the exposures are already present and where the only type of action available is an intervention to reduce them. An example of a "practices" scenario is the redevelopment of land contaminated with radioactivity, where the Environment Agency would advise the local planning authority on the optimal remediation option to ensure that the land is made suitable for any new permitted use.[67] Thus practices are not regulated under the modified regime, but are instead subject to other regimes.[68]

An intervention is defined in the Basic Safety Standards Directive as "a **9.37** human activity that prevents or decreases the exposure of individuals to radiation from sources which are not part of a practice or which are out of control, by acting on sources, transmission pathways and individuals themselves",[69] and so may comprise a remedial treatment action to ensure that land is suitable for its current use.

"Reasonableness", "justification" and "optimisation"

Interventions are subject to two principles which do not apply to remedia- **9.38** tion under the general regime (and which apply only in relation to harm so far as it is attributable to radioactivity). First, as interventions may themselves cause adverse effects, they are only to be undertaken where they will do more overall good than harm (the principle of Justification). Secondly, where an intervention is undertaken it should seek to maximise its net benefit (the principle of Optimisation).[70] When deciding what is reasonable where remediation includes an intervention to deal with harm attributable to radioactivity the enforcing authority may only require things which it considers reasonable, having regard to the cost which is likely to be involved, and the seriousness of the harm in question.[71] When evaluating the seriousness of any harm attributable to radioactivity for the purposes of assessing the reasonableness of any remediation, the enforcing authority should consider:

1. whether the harm is already being caused;

2. the degree of the possibility of the harm being caused;

3. the nature of the harm with respect, in particular, to:

   (a) the extent and type of effects that may arise,
   (b) the number of people who might be affected, and

---

[66] Based upon the recommendations of the International Commission on Radiological Protection (ICRP) (DEFRA Circular 01/2006, *Contaminated Land*, Annex 1 para.77).

[67] DEFRA Circular 01/2006, *Contaminated Land*, Annex 1 paras 82–86.

[68] Such as Town and Country Planning and Building Regulations. See Chs 16 and 17.

[69] Basic safety Directive Art.1 (see also the Schedule to the Modification Regulations).

[70] DEFRA Circular 01/2006, *Contaminated Land*, Annex 1 para.79.

[71] Modified s.78E(4).

      (c) whether the effects would be irreversible; and

    4. the context in which the effects might occur, in particular the relative risk associated with the harm in the context of wider exposure risks.[72]

9.39   In addition, that part of the remediation which consists of an intervention may only be considered reasonable where[73]:

    1. the reduction in detriment due to radiation is sufficient to justify any adverse effects and costs, including social costs, of the intervention (Justification); and

    2. where the form, scale and duration of the intervention is optimised—to be taken to be optimised if the benefit of the reduction in health detriment less the detriment associated with the intervention is maximised (Optimisation).[74]

9.40   The Guidance states that "detriment" principally means a health detriment, but may also include other detriments such as those associated with blight.[75] The requirements as to justification and optimisation apply even where the enforcing authority does not need to consider whether a proposed remediation scheme would be "reasonable" as it is proposed by the appropriate person.[76] For an intervention to be optimised on land affected by both radioactive and non-radioactive significant pollutant linkages, the optimisation should also have regard to the effect of any remedial actions addressing the non-radioactive significant pollutant linkage.[77] The assessment of whether a potential intervention is justified and optimised should include the preparation of: an estimate of the financial costs of the intervention (as with the general scheme); a statement of the social costs and adverse effects associated with the intervention; and a statement of the benefits (such as the reduction in radiation exposure) likely to result from the intervention.[78]

9.41   Guidance is given on the methodology for assessment of whether the intervention is justified or optimised, with the enforcing authority directed to:

    (a) consult publications of international bodies, including the International Atomic Energy Agency;

    (b) apply the approaches of multi-attribute analysis in assessing the balance between the various factors that need to be taken into consideration and the weightings which may be appropriate to assign to the various attributes;

---

[72] DEFRA Circular 01/2006, *Contaminated Land*, Annex 3 C.43A.
[73] Modified s.78E(4A).
[74] Modified s.78E(4B).
[75] DEFRA Circular 01/2006, *Contaminated Land*, Annex 3 C.8(j).
[76] DEFRA Circular 01/2006, *Contaminated Land*, Annex 2 para.6.34A.
[77] DEFRA Circular 01/2006, *Contaminated Land*, Annex 3 C.43E.
[78] DEFRA Circular 01/2006, *Contaminated Land*, Annex 3 C.43F.

(c) consult with relevant stakeholder groups so as to understand their perceptions of the relative importance of different attributes; and

(d) consider quantitative and qualitative methods as a decision-aid in helping to reveal the key issues and assumptions and allowing an analysis of the sensitivity to various assumptions.[79]

As well as following the general Guidance on risk assessment for adverse **9.42** environmental impacts,[80] in assessing benefits and costs, the enforcing authority should consider both the seriousness of impacts of any social costs and also the likely duration of any impact.[81] The types of social costs and adverse effects to be considered as arising from an intervention may include[82]: social disruption (such as vacating or limiting use of property); doses to remediation workers; heavy traffic from vehicles associated with the intervention; risks to water, air, soil and plants and animals; risks of noise or odour nuisance; risks to the countryside or places of special interest, or to buildings of special architectural or historic interest[83]; the generation of waste and, where relevant, the transport and disposal of such waste.

The requirement that any intervention must meet the requirements of **9.43** justification and optimisation means that if there is more than one significant pollutant linkage attributable to radioactivity then these should be considered separately and then together, ensuring any proposed intervention to deal with one or more such linkages is justified and optimised before consideration is given to any possible wider remediation scheme also dealing with linkages not attributable to radioactivity. Once the wider remediation scheme has been identified, the enforcing authority must check that any intervention is still justified and optimised for any linkages attributable to radioactivity.[84]

What is to be done by way of remediation

Under the modified regime as well as defining "remediation" to exclude **9.44** pollution of controlled waters, and by reference to "harm", rather than "significant harm",[85] modified s.78A(7A) further provides that:

> "For the purpose of para.(b) of subs.(7) above, "the doing of any works, the carrying out of any operations or the taking of any steps in relation to any such land" shall include ensuring that—

(a) any such area is demarcated;

[79] DEFRA Circular 01/2006, *Contaminated Land*, Annex 3 C.43G.
[80] DEFRA Circular 01/2006, *Contaminated Land*, Annex 3 C.55–57 (see Annex 3 C.43H).
[81] DEFRA Circular 01/2006, *Contaminated Land*, Annex 3 C.43J.
[82] DEFRA Circular 01/2006, *Contaminated Land*, Annex 3 C.43I.
[83] A building listed under town and country planning legislation or a building in a designated Conservation Area, or a site of archaeological interest (as defined in Art.1(2) of the Town and Country Planning (General Permitted Development) Order 1995).
[84] DEFRA Circular 01/2006, *Contaminated Land*, Annex 2 para.6.29A.
[85] Modified s.78A(7) (see reg.5 of the Modification Regulations).

(b) arrangements for the monitoring of harm are made;

(c) any appropriate intervention is implemented; and

(d) access to or use of land or buildings situated in the demarcated area is regulated."

9.45 The accumulation or disposal of radioactive waste resulting from remediation actions will require an authorisation under the Radioactive Substances Act 1993, unless covered by an Exemption Order.

Enforcing Authorities' Powers to Carry Out Remediation

9.46 A highly significant amendment to the general regime is made under the modified regime in relation to the enforcing authorities' powers to carry out remediation themselves under s.78N. Where either:

1. the person on whom a remediation notice is served fails to comply with any requirements under it (s.78N(3)(c));

2. the enforcing authority is precluded from serving a remediation notice in the context of escape of substances to other land (s.78N(3)(d));

3. the costs recovery and hardship provisions (under s.78P) are applicable (s.78N(3)(e)); or

4. no appropriate person has been "found" (s.78N(3)(f)), the enforcing authority is under a *duty* to exercise its remediation action powers.[86]

9.47 Complementing this duty, however, is a provision allowing the Secretary of State the discretion to make monies available to the enforcing authority in relation to the exercise of the duty.[87] DEFRA provides financial support to the Environment Agency, including works in respect of radioactivity.[88]

---

[86] Modified s.78N(1A) reg.14 of the Modification Regulations.
[87] Modified s.78N(1B).
[88] DEFRA Circular 01/2006, *Contaminated Land*, Annex 2 para.16.15.

Chapter 10

POLLUTION PREVENTION AND CONTROL

PPC Generally

The regime of Pollution Prevention and Control (PPC) is in large measure **10.01** intended to implement the Integrated Pollution Prevention and Control Directive 96/61. The Pollution Prevention and Control Regulations 2000[1] as amended, which came into force on April 1, 2000, apply to the types of "installations" and mobile plant listed in Sch.1. A permit from the Environment Agency is required to operate such an installation or plant (reg.9). Most conceivable types of major types of industrial activity are covered, many of which may have high potential for soil contamination.[2] The intention is to create a comprehensive system of control over all activities within such installations which may give rise to pollution, that is to say emissions due to human activity which may be harmful to human health or the quality of the environment, cause offence to human senses, result in damage to material property, or impair or interfere with amenities or other legitimate uses of the environment (reg.2(1)).

Prior to the introduction of PPC, the system of Integrated Pollution **10.02** Control (IPC) had been introduced by Pt I of the Environmental Protection Act 1990, again applying to specified "prescribed processes" and (whilst less sophisticated and comprehensive than PPC) applying an approach which focused on the effects on the environment as a whole as opposed to air, water or land in isolation. IPC is being replaced on a phased basis by PPC.

As has already been explained, provisions in subss.78YB(1) and (2B) **10.03** mean that it may not be possible to serve a remediation notice where the harm or pollution by reason of which the land is contaminated are attributable to an process or activity regulated under IPC or PPC and where the Agency may take enforcement action under those regimes.[3]

In addition, if the activity in question was the final disposal by deposit in **10.04** or on land of controlled waste, and enforcement action may be taken under the PPC regime, Pt IIA will not apply at all (subs.78YB(2A)). An obvious

---

[1] The Pollution Prevention and Control Regulations 2000 (SI 2000/1973). PPC (together with waste licensing) will be the subject of regulatory reform from April 1, 2008 (so it is currently intended) with new regulations on Environmental Permitting. At the time of writing, these Regulations have just been published in draft and are not in final form; accordingly, this Chapter confines itself to the current system.

[2] For example, production and processing of metals, including coating and surface treatment, the chemical industry, many forms of waste recovery, tanning, and intensive livestock farming. Large landfill sites are also covered; and see the Landfill (England and Wales) Regulations 2002 (SI 2002/1559) which provide a special regime within PPC for such installations.

[3] See paras 3.77 and 3.78.

example is the deposit of waste in a landfill site regulated as a PPC installation, but it could also apply to on-site waste disposal sites at industrial installations.

10.05   It is not the intention to provide a detailed or full analysis of the IPC or PPC regimes. Rather this chapter will seek to relate those regimes to the remediation of contaminated land.

IPC

10.06 Authorisations for the carrying on of a prescribed process must contain such conditions as the enforcing authority considers appropriate for achieving a number of objectives specified at s.7(2) of the 1990 Act. These include:

(a)   the use of best available techniques not entailing excessive cost (BATNEEC) for preventing the release of substances prescribed for any environmental medium into that medium or, where that is not practicable by such means, for reducing the release of such substances to a minimum and for rendering harmless any such substances which are so released;

(b)   the use of BATNEEC for rendering harmless any other substances which might cause harm if released to any environmental medium[4];

(c)   compliance with any prescribed statutory limits, requirements, quality standards or quality objectives; and

(d)   where the process is likely to involve the release of substances into more than one environmental medium, the use of BATNEEC for minimising the pollution which may be caused to the environment taken as a whole by the releases, having regard to the best practicable environmental option available in respect of the substances which may be realeased.[5]

10.07   In addition to such specific conditions, there is implied into every authorisation by virtue of s.7(4) a general condition requiring the use of BATNEEC:

(a)   for preventing the release of prescribed substances to the relevant environmental medium or, where that is not practicable by such means, for reducing the release of such substances to a minimum and for rendering harmless any such substances which are so released; and

(b)   for rendering harmless any other substances which might cause harm if released into any environmental medium.

---

[4] "Harm" is defined by s.1(4) to mean harm to the health of living organisms or other interference with the ecological systems of which they form part and, in the case of man, is to include offence caused to any of his senses or harm to his property.

[5] 1990 Act s.7(7).

Since IPC is concerned with minimising pollution to the environment as **10.08** a whole, it is certainly a relevant means of seeking to control and minimise the contamination of soil which may be caused by prescribed processes. What it cannot do is to regulate the final disposal of controlled waste by deposit in or on land,[6] which is dealt with by Pt II of the Environmental Protection Act. Subject to that constraint, IPC will be concerned with releases to land or groundwater of any potentially harmful substances, and particularly with prescribed substances. In relation to land, "release" includes any deposit, keeping or disposal of the substance in or on land,[7] In relation to water, it includes any entry into water[8] and any release into groundwater is such a release.[9] "Groundwater" is defined widely to mean any waters contained in any underground strata or in a well, adit or borehole sunk into underground strata.[10]

IPC can therefore be used to ensure that wastes for disposal to land are **10.09** produced in such a form as to minimise the likely polluting effects. Further, the general concept of "good housekeeping" inherent in the use of BATNEEC means that steps should be taken to avoid and minimise the consequences of spills; a number of the Chief Inspector's process guidance notes refer to issues such as the loading and unloading of vehicles in designated areas, contingency plans, site design and validated emergency procedures to cover spillages or leakages on site.

A good example of the relevance of the IPC regime to soil contamination **10.10** is provided by the IPC authorisation which was granted to Rechem International Limited in respect of their high-temperature incinerator at Pontypool, Gwent.[11] Conditions on this authorisation included the following:

1. By a given date (September 1, 1993) the operator shall have begun an ongoing environmental monitoring programme, acceptable to the Chief Inspector, for the assessment of the impact of the Company's operations on levels of PCBs, PCDDs/PCDFs and heavy metals in local soils and herbage.

2. By a given date (October 1, 1993) the operator shall have produced a detailed report of PCBs and PCDDs/PCDFs contamination of all site soil areas, to include proposals acceptable to the Chief Inspector for the treatment of areas of the site to minimise migration of PCBs and PCDDs/PCDFs to air or to controlled waters.

3. Operational requirements relating to bunding, impermeable site surfaces, drainage channels routed to a sump or holding tank, and treatment or incineration of contaminated surface water.

It should, however, be remembered that conditions on IPC authorisa- **10.11** tions were subject to two important limitations. First, they were concerned with preventing or rendering harmless emissions from the prescribed

[6] 1990 Act s.28(1).
[7] 1990 Act s.1(10)(c).
[8] 1990 Act s.1(10)(b).
[9] 1990 Act s.1(11)(a)(iii).
[10] 1990 Act s.1(12).
[11] Ref. No.AG7946, July 16, 1993.

process: they could not therefore be used to require clean-up of historic contamination caused by unrelated processes. Secondly, the conditions were linked to the "carrying on" of the process both in their imposition[12] and enforcement.[13] It was not therefore possible to use IPC conditions as a means of imposing clean up requirements when a prescribed process had ceased to operate. As will be seen, these defects have been addressed in the PPC regime.

10.12 The main remedial power under IPC is s.27 of the 1990 Act, which provides that where the commission of an offence under s.23(1)(a) (carrying on a prescribed process without an authorisation or without complying with the conditions of the authorisation) or s.23(1)(c) (failing to comply with an enforcement or prohibition notice) had caused harm which it was possible to remedy, then the Agency could arrange for reasonable steps to be taken towards remedying the harm and recover the costs from the person convicted. However, by subs.27(2) the powers could not be exercised by the Agency without the approval in writing of the Secretary of State. In addition, the power could only be used to deal with harm that had occurred and not to prevent harm that was likely to occur. The power could therefore in principle be used where unauthorised activity or a breach of condition had led to soil or groundwater contamination, but only if this amounted to "harm" according to the definition in s.1(4) (i.e. harm to the health of living organisms or other interference with the ecological systems of which they form part, offence to man's senses or harm to his property).

PPC

10.13 The PPC regime requires the regulator in setting conditions, to take account of the general principles that the installation should be operated in such a way that (a) all the appropriate measures are taken against pollution, in particular through the application of the best available techniques[14]; and (b) no significant pollution is caused (reg.11(1) and (2)). The contamination of soil or groundwater could clearly fall within the definition of "pollution" in potentially affecting human health or the quality of the environment.

10.14 In the case of Pt A installations, i.e. those listed in Pt A of Sch.1, account must be taken of a further general principle:

> ". . . that, upon the definitive cessation of activities, the necessary measures should be taken to avoid any pollution risk and to return the site of the installation or mobile plant to a satisfactory state."

10.15 What is meant by a "satisfactory state" is not defined by either the PPC Regulations or the Directive, and in particular whether a similar risk based approach to Pt IIA is appropriate, or whether a more stringent standard of

---

[12] 1990 Act ss.7(2)(a) and 7(4).
[13] 1990 Act ss.6(1), 13(1) and 14(1).
[14] Best available techniques is given a wide definition by reg.3.

restoration is required whereby the soil simply has to be returned to its previous condition.[15] The DEFRA Practical Guide to IPPC[16] indicates clearly that PPC may require a standard of remediation that is significantly stricter than Pt IIA,[17] though also accepting that the requirement must be applied in a proportionate manner.[18] The starting point is that the aim is to restore a site to its condition before the permit was granted, so far as is practicable.[19] It should be noted that a different regime applies to large landfill sites within the PPC system, where closure and aftercare is governed by specific provisions under the Landfill Regulations.

The Agency's IPPC Guidance on Site Surrender Reports[20] takes this **10.16** somewhat further. Appendix A deals with Assessing Changes in the Condition of the Site and begins with the presumption that the operator will return the site to the condition it was in before the permit was granted. However, it goes on to say that the obligation on the operator will be approached in a proportionate and reasonable manner. Nevertheless the onus is on the operator to produce a robust scientific case and cost benefit analysis to justify the proposition that it is not just and proportionate to remediate to the pre-permit condition. The guidance indicates the factors that will be relevant in this decision, which include:

(a) the nature and degree of the hazard presented by the contamination, i.e. its toxicity, persistence, and other hazardous properties;

(b) the amount of contamination relative to what was already present;

(c) its location and accessibility;

(d) the site setting and vulnerable receptors;

(e) feasibility of remediation, timescale and consequent impacts;

(f) costs and benefits generally.

The permit must also include conditions ensuring appropriate protection **10.17** of the soil and groundwater and setting out the steps to be taken "after the definitive cessation of operations" (reg.12(9)(b) and (d)). This would require for example, the removal of pollution risks such as tanks full of chemicals, but also in principle gives the power to require more extensive remedial operations.

Application site report

The provisions on applications for permits require provision of a site report **10.18** describing the condition of the site of the installation or mobile plant, which must in particular identify any substance in, on or under the land

---

[15] See D. Lawrence, "IPPC Site Condition Reports—Is Risk Relevant?" [2001] Env. Liab. 161, arguing that references to risk and harm in the Directive and Regulations mean that a risk based approach is appropriate.

[16] DEFRA, *Integrated Pollution Prevention and Control: A Practical Guide* (4th edn), June 2005.

[17] See DEFRA, *Integrated Pollution Prevention and Control: A Practical Guide* (4th edn), paras 14.27 and 14.40.

[18] See DEFRA, *Integrated Pollution Prevention and Control: A Practical Guide* (4th edn), para 14.30.

[19] See DEFRA, *Integrated Pollution Prevention and Control: A Practical Guide* (4th edn), para 14.26.

[20] IPPC H8 (June 2004, draft).

which may constitute a pollution risk.[21] These provisions tie in with reg.19 which provides the procedure for surrender of permits. The Agency has provided guidance on Application Site Reports (ASRs) in a technical guidance note.[22] This indicates what the Agency expects from an ASR. Whereas the regulations indicate that the report should identify any substance present in, on or under the land which may present a pollution risk,[23] the Agency does not require a report based on intrusive investigations: rather it envisages a desk-based study which identifies the site's setting, substances that may have been used and may in future be used, and a conceptual site model based on source-pathway-target methodology. What the Agency requires is a Site Protection and Management Plan (SPMP) based on the conceptual site model an aimed at avoiding pollution risk. The Agency may or may not, depending on the ASR, require the further provision of reference data based on soil or groundwater sampling. Appendix C to the guidance deals with investigating and remedying pollution which is identified in the course of the SPMP. The basic approach is that the operator will be required to identify the source and remediate to reference data levels. The starting point is the assumption that the source is the current activities on site.

Site surrender report

10.19 The application for surrender of a permit under reg.19 must include a site report describing the conditions of the site and identifying any changes in the condition of the site as described in the original site report, together with a description of any steps taken to avoid any pollution risk in the site report which results from the operation of the installation or mobile plant, or to return the site to a satisfactory state.[24]

10.20 Regulation 19 then goes on to provide a procedure for the Agency either to accept the surrender or refuse the application; by reg.19(4) the Agency may only accept surrender if satisfied that the appropriate steps have been taken. However, in deciding whether a pollution risk results from the operation of the installation, the Agency may only take account of risks resulting from the operation of the installation after the date on which the permit was granted,[25] or in the case of a specified waste management activity, risks resulting from carrying out that activity after "the relevant date".[26]

10.21 The Agency's technical guidance on SSRs[27] indicates that the SSR must provide a robust account of the condition of the site and how it is protected, monitored, investigated, remediated, and decommissioned to

---

[21] Sch.4 para.1(d) and 2.

[22] IPPC H7 Application Site Report and Site Protection and Management Programme (August 2003).

[23] Sch.2 para.1(2); see also DEFRA, *Integrated Pollution Prevention and Control: A Practical Guide* (4th edn), paras 14.4 and 14.5.

[24] reg.19(3)(c) and (d).

[25] i.e. it could not take account of risks created when the site was operated under an IPC authorisation, or possibly even before that under the Alkali, etc Works Regulation Act 1906.

[26] reg.19(11). The "relevant date", where the activity was carried out on the site of the installation under a waste management licence which ceased to have effect by s.35(11A) when superseded by the PPC permit, is the date on which the waste management licence was granted.

[27] IPPC H8 (June 2004, draft).

achieve a satisfactory state and remove pollution risks. It should include the ASR, relevant records on inspection of the site, plant and equipment such as tanks, reference data, details of any pollution incidents, a site closure plan and any investigative or remediation reports prepared in the course of decommissioning. Appendix A: Assessing Changes in the Condition of the Site deals with the standard of remediation required. Box A2 in that Appendix suggests that the operator should be deemed to have caused the presence of any new contaminant not identified in the ASR. This accords with the approach in the DEFRA Practical Guide, which says that additional pollution, not previously identified, should normally be attributed to the operator, who should be held responsible for it unless the Agency is convinced that the operator cannot reasonably be held responsible.[28]

Accordingly, the PPC Regulations in principle should offer a clear way in **10.22** which the pre-permit and end-of-permit conditions of the site can be compared and appropriate remedial action required where contamination has occurred, the system being potentially more stringent than the Pt IIA regime in terms of the standard of remediation required to return the site to a satisfactory state. However, this approach is predicated on an ASR which acts as a reasonably reliable reference point.[29] If, as may be the case under the Agency's guidance, the ASR does not offer any clear indication of actual baseline conditions, the risk is that contamination which was present but not identified is likely to be regarded as the operator's responsibility at the stage of surrender, or possibly sooner if identified in the course of the SPMP, unless there is some very obvious reason why the operator could not have been the source of that particular substance. The operator might therefore wish to consider whether producing a more comprehensive report than required under the Agency's guidance would be desirable as a precaution to avoid facing a possibly uphill evidential struggle in convincing the Agency at some later date that the relevant contamination pre-dated the permit. However, even where there is an investigation there is no guarantee that it will uncover every significant area of contamination. Techniques of investigation improve over time and not all areas of the site may be accessible for investigation until decommissioning occurs.

Further difficult issues may arise where the permit has been transferred **10.23** during the operation of the site under reg.18. The transferee may find that they are fixed with having to remediate soil contamination caused by the transferor when the time comes to surrender the permit, and this needs to be considered in the transactional context when the sale takes place.

Enforcement

The Agency has a range of enforcement tools at its disposal to ensure that **10.24** the site is restored: these are enforcement notices under reg.24 requiring compliance with the relevant conditions and the power under reg.26(2),

---

[28] DEFRA, *Integrated Pollution Prevention and Control: A Practical Guide* (4th edn), paras 14.11 and 14.12.
[29] DEFRA, *Integrated Pollution Prevention and Control: A Practical Guide* (4th edn), para 14.5.

where the commission of an offence under reg.32(1)(a), (b) or (d) causes pollution, to arrange for steps to be taken towards remedying the effects of pollution and to recover its costs under reg.26(4). This cost recovery power could apply where contamination has occurred because of breach of conditions, e.g. inadequate bunding, or where an enforcement notice has been served and not complied with. However, reg.26(2) is worded in such a way as to apply where pollution has occurred, not where there is a risk of pollution. There is a separate power under reg.26(1) where the Agency is of the opinion that the operation of the installation, or its operation in a particular manner, involves an imminent risk of serious pollution to arrange for steps to be taken to remove that risk and recover its costs. The way in which the provision is worded however seems to contemplate an ongoing risk from current operation, rather than a risk which has come into being from past operations.

Relevance of site reports to Part IIA

10.25 The site information generated in the course of these PPC procedures is likely to be disclosed to the local authority and may be relevant information so far as inspection under Pt IIA is concerned. Where the contamination does not relate to final deposits of controlled waste, there is nothing to prevent the site being identified as contaminated land. If the land is the site of a Pt A PPC process regulated by the Agency, whether the process is being carried on now or previously, the land will be a special site, so the Agency will be regulator and enforcing authority under both regimes. It is only when it is now longer possible to take enforcement action under the PPC regime that it will be possible to serve a remediation notice.[30]

---

[30] DEFRA, *Integrated Pollution Prevention and Control: A Practical Guide* (4th edn), para.14.40.

Chapter 11

COMAH

Generally

The DEFRA Circular on Pt IIA refers briefly to the subject of major **11.01** accident hazards. The Control of Major Accident Hazards Regulations 1999[1] (COMAH) require operators of establishments handling prescribed dangerous substances to prepare on-site emergency plans and local authorities to prepare off-site emergency plans. The objectives of these plans include providing for the restoration and clean-up of the environment following a major accident.[2]

The COMAH Regulations

The Regulations came into force on April 1, 1999.[3] They implement the **11.02** requirements of Directive 96/82 on the control of major accident hazards involving dangerous substances (the Seveso II Directive).[4] The competent authority is the Health and Safety Executive (HSE) and the Environment Agency (or SEPA) acting jointly.

The Regulations apply to an establishment, defined[5] as the whole area **11.03** under the control of the same person where dangerous substances are present in one or more installations[6] where a listed dangerous substance is present in more than a stated quantity.[7] For this purpose the presence of a substance includes both the anticipated presence of a substance and the presence of those substances which it is reasonable to believe may be generated during the loss of control of an industrial chemical process.[8] The dangerous substances and the relevant quantities are set out at Sch.1 and include both named substances and categories of substances having

---

[1] SI 1999/743 as amended by The Control of Major Accident Hazards (Amendment) Regulations 2005 (SI 2005/1088). For general guidance see HSE L111: *Guide to COMAH Regulations 1999*.

[2] DEFRA Circular 01/2006, *Contaminated Land*, Annex 1 para.64(d).

[3] Replacing the Control of Major Industrial Accident Hazards Regulations 1984 (CIMAH).

[4] As amended by Directive 2003/105.

[5] COMAH reg.2(1).

[6] An installation is defined as a unit in which dangerous substances present are, or are intended to be, produced, handled, used or stored, and includes equipment, structures, pipework, railway sidings, docks and quays, and jetties, warehouses and similar structures: reg.2(1).

[7] COMAH reg.3(1).

[8] COMAH reg.3(4).

properties such as toxicity, flammability, or dangerous to the environment.[9] The Regulations do not apply to:

(a) defence establishments;

(b) nuclear licensed sites;

(c) the exploration, extraction and processing of minerals in mines, quarries or boreholes (but do apply to chemical and thermal processing operations and to storage relating to such operations); and

(d) waste landfill sites (but do apply to tailing ponds or dams and other operational tailings disposal facilities containing dangerous substances, especially when used in connection with chemical and thermal processing of minerals).[10]

In the main the COMAH Regulations will apply to chemical plants, but they also have important application to facilities for the bulk storage of petrol and other hazardous liquids.

11.04 The operator of a COMAH site (essentially, the person who is in control of an establishment or installation[11]) is under a general duty, so far as the establishment or installation which he controls is concerned, to take all measures necessary to prevent major accidents and limit their consequences to persons and the environment.[12] The operator must prepare and keep a document setting out his policy on major accident prevention and must implement that policy.[13] The operator must also provide the competent authority with a safety report showing how the policy has been implemented and the safety management systems and other arrangements in place; this must be reviewed at least every five years or earlier if there are changes to the systems that could have significant repercussions or where necessary to take account of new facts or new technical knowledge.[14] The safety report must include a detailed description of major accident scenarios and their probability or conditions under which they could occur, and an assessment of the extent and severity of the consequence of identified major accidents, including maps, images or equivalent descriptions showing areas liable to be affected by such accidents.[15]

Emergency plans

11.05 Part 4 of the Regulations deal with emergency plans. Regulation 9 requires the operator to prepare an on-site emergency plan in consultation with employees, the Agency, emergency services, the local authority and health

[9] Substances are classified according to reg.4 of the Chemicals (Hazard Information and Packaging for Supply) Regulations 2002 (SI 2002/1689).

[10] COMAH reg.3(3), as amended.

[11] COMAH reg.3(2).

[12] COMAH reg.4.

[13] COMAH reg.5. See Sch.2 for the principles to be taken into account in preparing the document.

[14] COMAH reg.7 and Sch.4.

[15] COMAH Sch.4 Pt 2 para.4 as amended by SI 2005/1088 reg.17. See HSG 190: *Preparing Safety Reports*. See also *Guidance on Environmental Risk Assessment of COMAH Safety Report* (HSE/Environment Agency, December 1999).

authorities. The plan must be reviewed at suitable intervals not exceeding three years, such review to take into account changes and new knowledge in the interim.[16] Regulation 12 places the operator under a duty to take reasonable steps to put it into effect without delay when either a major accident occurs, or an uncontrolled event occurs which could reasonably be expected to lead to a major accident. A "major accident" is an occurrence (including in particular a major emission, fire or explosion) resulting from uncontrolled developments in the course of the operation of the establishment and leading to serious danger to human health or the environment, immediate or delayed, inside or outside the establishment, and involving one or more dangerous substances.[17]

The on-site emergency plan must contain the information listed in Sch.5 **11.06** Pt 2, and must be adequate for securing the following objectives listed in Sch.5 Pt 1:

1. containing and controlling incidents so as to minimize the effects and limit damage to persons, property and the environment;

2. implementing the measures necessary to protect persons and the environment from the effects of major accidents;

3. communicating the necessary information to the public, emergency services and authorities concerned; and

4. providing for the restoration and clean-up of the environment following a major accident.

Enforcement of the Regulations is through the general powers of the **11.07** Health and Safety at Work, etc Act 1974; in addition the Environment Agency's powers of entry and inspection under s.108 of the Environment Act 1995 are applicable.[18]

If there is a major accident at a COMAH plant the consequences in **11.08** terms of soil and groundwater contamination, both onsite and offsite, may be considerable. It is the COMAH regime rather than Pt IIA which is likely to provide the driver for remedial action. Such major accidents have not been uncommon: examples include Laporte Chemicals at Warrington in 1984, Allied Colloids at Bradford in 1992, Hickson and Welch at Castleford in 1992, Associated Octel at Ellesmere Port in 1994 and Conoco Phillips at the Humber in 2001.[19] Most recently, on December 11, 2005, explosions occurred at the Buncefield Oil Storage Depot, Hemel Hempstead, involving a number of large fuel storage tanks. This was of environmental concern as the site is over a chalk aquifer providing regional water supplies and within the catchment of groundwater abstraction. Groundwater and surface water were sampled up to 9km offsite for fuels and fire-fighting foams, including

---

[16] COMAH reg.11. See HSG 191: *Emergency Plans*.

[17] COMAH reg.2(1).

[18] COMAH reg.20.

[19] See *Review of High Cost Chemical/Petrochemical Accidents since Flixborough 1974* (IchemE Loss Prevention Bulletin, April 1998 No.140, available on HSE website: *http://www.hse.gov.uk*) and HSE: *Public Report of Fire and Explosion at Conoco Phillips Humber Refinery 16 April 2001*.

fluoro-surfactants such as perfluorooctane sulphonate (PFOS).[20] The Drinking Water Inspectorate made a recommendation that PFOS should not be present in drinking water supplies at a concentration above $3\mu g/l$; in June 2006 the Inspectorate announced that independent tests showed no evidence of drinking water having been contaminated. The incident has highlighted concerns as to the bulk storage of hazardous liquids at COMAH sites: many such facilities were built 40 years ago and are not designed to current standards of containment. The HSE and Environment Agency have published recommendations on such standards, but it is estimated that it may take between 10–20 years for sites to complete the necessary upgrading.[21]

---

[20] Buncefield Major Accident Investigation Board, *Initial Report to Health and Safety Commission and the Environment Agency* (July 2006). See *http://www.buncefieldinvestigation.co.uk*.

[21] *Policy on Containment of Bulk Hazardous Liquids at COMAH Establishments* (HSE, Environment Agency, SEPA, consultation draft, June 2007) The published response of the Buncefield Investigation Board is that a 20–year implementation period "is likely to be open to criticism".

Chapter 12

HEALTH AND SAFETY

The law relating to health and safety at work is a major area, the detailed **12.01**
treatment of which falls outside the scope of this book. However, health
and safety law does have a bearing on the management of risks relating to
contaminated land, and specifically the issue of asbestos contamination
requires an understanding of the special regime which applies to asbestos.
This chapter aims to identify the main areas of health and safety
legislation that are relevant.

General duties under Health and Safety Law

Early in the 19th century it was realised that the common law could not **12.02**
adequately deal with the scale of injury and disease arising in post-
industrial society. Early legislation regulated factory activity and was the
paradigm for later codes on mines and quarries, agriculture, offices, shops
and railway premises. The legislation took an essentially piecemeal and
reactive approach, often in response to some industrial disaster. Many
workers were not covered by any legislation, and also there were criticisms
of the Factory Inspectorate for lack of effective enforcement, in some case
involving wider environmental contamination.[1] In 1972 the Report of the
Robens Committee (Cmnd.5034) on safety and health described the then
current system as "haphazard . . . a mass of ill assorted and intricate
detail". The Committee suggested that the sheer mass of law was
counterproductive and that a clear central framework of control for all
workplaces was required, with the aim of creating conditions conducive to
self-regulation, and with the legislation to be "constructive" rather than
"prohibiting". These recommendations were embodied in the Health and
Safety at Work, etc Act 1974, which sets out "basic and overriding
responsibilities of employers and employees". The general statutory duties
contained in the 1974 Act can be summarised as follows.

Section 2 of the 1974 Act provides that it shall be the duty of every **12.03**
employer to ensure, so far as is reasonably practicable, the health, safety
and welfare at work of all his employees. By subs.(2) that duty extends,
without prejudice to its generality, to the provision and maintenance of
safe plant and systems of work, safety in respect of the use, handling,

---

[1] For example the site of Central Asbestos, Bermondsey (closed 1969). In *Central Asbestos Co Ltd v Dodd* [1972] 2 All E.R. 1135, Lord Salmon described HM Factory Inspectorate as "supine". Another example was the Rio Tinto-Zinc Imperial lead smelter, Avonmouth, where many workers became ill from lead poisoning and there was widespread pollution: see Report of a Committee under the Chairmanship of Sir Brian Windeyer to Inquire into Lead Poisonings at the RTZ Smelter at Avonmouth (Cmnd. 5042, 1971).

storage and transport of articles and substances, the provision of information, instruction, training and supervision, the maintenance of any place of work under the employer's control in a safe condition without risks to health, and the provision and maintenance of a safe working environment without risks to health.

12.04   The term "so far as is reasonably practicable" is important in mitigating what would otherwise be strict duties and providing the courts with a flexible tool to apply to varying circumstances. The fact that a precaution is physically possible does not mean that it is reasonably practicable.[2] It involves the weighing of risk against the time, trouble and money involved in averting the risk.[3] As put by Lord Goff in *Austin Rover v HM Inspector of Factories*[4]:

> " .. the risk of accident has to be weighed against the measures necessary to eliminate the risk, including the cost involved. If, for example, the defendant establishes that the risk is small, but that the measures necessary to eliminate it are great, he may be held to be exonerated from taking steps to eliminate the risk on the ground that it was not reasonably practicable to do so."

12.05   Section 3 of the 1974 Act imposes a duty on every employer to conduct his undertaking in such a way as to ensure, so far as is reasonably practicable, that persons not in his employment who may be affected thereby are not exposed to risks to their health and safety. By subs.(2) this duty extends to self-employed persons in respect of their own safety and that of other persons not being their employees.

12.06   This provision has potentially important ramifications for employers whose activities result in contaminated land or increase the risks from already contaminated land. The purpose of these provisions is to protect all relevant persons, including the general public,[5] and for example, it could include passers-by endangered by escaping fumes.[6] The section is concerned with risk—it is not necessary to prove harm or causation of harm.[7] Subject to the "so far as is reasonably practicable" qualification, the offence is absolute in nature and has again been interpreted widely, in part to reflect the breadth of the term "undertaking". It is non-delegable and can apply to risks caused by independent contractors.[8] Moreover it may apply to risks arising from the premises that have been closed down.[9]

12.07   Section 4 of the 1974 Act imposes duties on persons having control of premises in connection with the carrying on of a trade, business or other undertaking in relation to those who are not their employees but who use

---

[2] *West Bromwich Building Society v Townsend* [1983] I.C.R. 257. In *Case C-127/05 Commission v UK* (June 14, 2007), the European Court held that restricting the employer's duty to what is reasonably practicable did not contravene the EC requirement of Art.5 of the Directive 89/391/EEC that the employer shall have a duty to ensure the safety and health of workers, which was not intended to require the imposition of a strict liability scheme.

[3] *Edwards v NCB* [1949] 1 K.B. 704.

[4] [1989] 3 W.L.R. 520.

[5] *R v Lightwater Valley* (1990) 12 Cr. App. Rep. (S.) 328.

[6] *Sterling-Winthrop Group Ltd v Allan* 1987 S.C.C.R. 25.

[7] *R v Board of Trustees of the Science Museum* [1993] 1 W.L.R. 1171.

[8] *R v Mersey Docks and Harbour Co* (1995) 16 Cr. App. Rep. (S.) 806; *R v Associated Octel Co Ltd* [1996] 4 All E.R. 846.

[9] *R v Mara* [1987] 1 All E.R. 478.

non-domestic premises made available to them as a place of work or as a place where they may use plant or substances provided for their use there. The duty is to take such measures as it is reasonable for a person in that position to take to ensure, so far as is reasonably practicable, that the premises, together with means of access and any plant or equipment in the premises, are safe and without risks to health. The duty under the section is of an absolute nature, subject to the limited qualification "so far as is reasonable practicable"; it does not require the occupier to take precautions against unknown and unexpected events.[10] The section is not confined to a single person—more than one person may be in control of premises.[11]

In a number of cases the basic duties are amplified by way of specific **12.08** regulations dealing with problems such as asbestos and lead (see further below). Any approved codes of practice issued by the Health and Safety Commission will also be relevant and failure to comply with such codes of practice will be admissible evidence in criminal proceedings for contravention of the relevant duty.[12] In other words, if the defendant cannot show some other means of compliance, breach of the ACOP becomes good and complete evidence of the offence.[13]

Failure to discharge the duties referred to above is an offence under **12.09** s.73(1) of the 1974 Act subject to a fine not exceeding £20,000 on summary conviction and an unlimited fine on conviction on indictment.[14] In any proceedings alleging failure to comply with a duty involving a requirement to do something so far as is practicable or reasonably practicable (as is the case with the duties mentioned above) s.40 provides that:

> ". . . it shall be for the accused to prove (as the case may be) that it was not practicable or not reasonably practicable to do more than was in fact done to satisfy the duty or requirement, or that there was no better practicable means than was in fact used to satisfy the duty or requirement."

In other words the prosecution need only show that there is a prima **12.10** facie case that the defendant has failed to ensure safety, and does not have to prove that it was reasonably practicable to comply. The onus is on the defence and is on the basis of probability.[15]

Importantly, the "so far as is reasonably practicable" provision acts not **12.11** as a defence but as a qualification to what would otherwise be an absolute offence. It is this distinction that prevents reg.21 of the Management of

---

[10] *Mailer v Austin Rover Group Ltd* [1989] 2 All E.R. 1087, HL.

[11] *Austin Rover Group Ltd v Inspector of Factories* [1990] 1 A.C. 619; *Westminster City Council v Select Management Ltd* [1985] 1 W.L.R. 576.

[12] 1974 Act s.17(2).

[13] *West Cumberland By-Products Ltd v DPP* [1988] R.T.R. 391. *Compare Tudhope v City of Glasgow DC* 1986 S.C.C.R. 168 where the ACOP was not followed but no breach of duty was found, since on the facts there had been an emergency situation and the employers had acted on specialist advice.

[14] 1974 Act s.33(1A).

[15] *R v Carr-Briant* [1943] 2 All E.R. 156. See also *Janway Davies v HSE* (2003) I.C.R. 586; [2002] EWCA Crim 2949 holding that the imposition of this burden on the defendant was compatible with the Human Rights Act.

Health and Safety at Work Regulations 1999 from having the effect that was probably intended. That regulation provides that it is no defence to health and safety criminal proceedings for an employer to show that the alleged contravention came about by reason of an act or default of an employee of his. Given that "reasonable practicability" simply qualifies the duty as opposed to providing a defence, it remains open to an employer to argue that he has taken all reasonable steps to train and instruct his employees and that the alleged breach was due to the default of an employee in failing to put such training and instruction into effect.[15a]

Risk assessment

12.12 The general duties referred to above are supplemented by additional requirements contained in the Management of Health and Safety at Work Regulations 1999.[16] Under these Regulations every employer must make a suitable and sufficient assessment of:

(a) the risks to the health and safety of his employees to which they are exposed while they are at work; and

(b) the risks to the health and safety of persons not in his employment arising out of or in connection with the conduct by him of his undertaking.

For the purpose of identifying the measures he needs to take to comply with the requirements or prohibitions imposed on him by or under the relevant statutory provisions.[17] Similar requirements apply to self-employed persons.

12.13 The Regulations impose general requirements as to arrangements for the effective planning, organisation, control, monitoring and review of protection and preventive measures[18]; also there is an obligation to provide appropriate health surveillance of employees, having regard to the risks identified in the risk assessment.[19] Regulation 8(1)(c) may be important in the context of contaminated land—this requires an employer to ensure that none of his employees has access to any area occupied by him to which it is necessary to restrict access on grounds of health and safety unless the employee concerned has received adequate health and safety instruction.[20] There is no statutory definition of a suitable and sufficient assessment but the relevant Approved Code of Practice makes it clear that the level of sophistication should be related to level of risk involved. It should include all those potentially at risk, not just employees. Where construction works, which will include civil engineering works, site investigation, clearance and demolition works, are involved, the Construction (Design and Management) Regulations 2007[21] must also be considered.

[15a] See R v HTM Ltd [2007] All E.R. 665.
[16] Management of Health and Safety at Work Regulations 1999 (SI 1999/3242). 2051.
[17] Management of Health and Safety at Work Regulations 1999 reg.3(1).
[18] Management of Health and Safety at Work Regulations 1999 reg.4.
[19] Management of Health and Safety at Work Regulations 1999 reg.6.
[20] Management of Health and Safety at Work Regulations 1999 reg.7(1)(c).
[21] SI 2007/320.

Construction and reclamation works on contaminated land may present **12.14** risks to those working on the site. The Health and Safety Executive has produced guidance on the subject, HS(G) 66: *Protection of Workers and the General Public during the Development of Contaminated Land*.[22] This guidance summarises the types of risk which may be associated with contaminated land, which include skin absorption of dusts, tars or other substances, ingestion, inhalation of dusts, vapours or fumes, asphyxiation or gassing, and fire or explosion. The Guidance suggests that in all cases before work begins developers should always consider the possibility of the ground and associated buildings being contaminated and should assess the risks to health and the precautions required[23]:

> "All derelict land, whether or not previously used for the industrial processes already described, may be regarded as potentially suspect. A full site investigation including analysis of soil and water samples and a geotechnical survey should be carried out. Initially the responsibility lies with the client for carrying out such works. However, the main contractor must ensure that this has been done."

Control of substances hazardous to health

Work carried out on a contaminated site may involve potential exposure to **12.15** substances which may be hazardous to health and consequently the Control of Substances Hazardous to Health Regulations 2002[24] (COSHH) are of fundamental importance. They must be read in combination with other regulations dealing with specific substances or situations.[25] Hazardous substances are defined by reg.2(1) so as to include substances classified as very toxic, toxic, corrosive, harmful or irritant under CHIP, substances for which the Health and Safety Commission has approved a Maximum Exposure Limit (MEL) or Occupational Exposure Standard (OES), biological agents (micro-organisms, etc. which may cause infection, allergy, toxicity or other hazard), any dust present at specified concentrations in air and a catch-all category of any other substance creating a risk to health because of its chemical or toxicological properties and the way it is used or is present in the workplace.

Duties under COSHH extend both to employees and (so far as is **12.16** reasonably practicable) to other persons, whether at work or not, who may be affected by the work carried on, i.e. contractors, visitors, customers, or

---

[22] HS(G) 66, HMSO, 1991. See also R132: *A Guide for Safe Working on Contaminated Sites* (CIRIA, 1996).

[23] COHH para.29.

[24] SI 2002/2677 (amended by SI 2003/ 978). See also the Approved Code of Practice on Control of Substances Hazardous to Health.

[25] For example the Chemicals (Hazard Information and Packaging for Supply) (CHIP) Regulations 2002 (SI 2002/1689); the Control of Asbestos at Work Regulations 2006 (SI 2006/2739) (below); the Control of Lead at Work Regulations 2002 (SI2002/2676); the Dangerous Substances (Notification and Marking of Sites) Regulations 1990 (SI 1990/304); and the Ionising Radiations Regulations 1999 (SI 1999/3232).

members of the public).[26] By reg.6 of the COSHH Regulations, an employer shall not carry on any work which is liable to expose any employees to any substance hazardous to health unless he has made a suitable and sufficient assessment of the risk created by that work to the health of the employees and of steps needed to meet the requirements of the Regulations and has implemented those steps. By reg.7 the employer is under a duty to ensure that exposure to substances hazardous to health is prevented, or where this is not reasonably practicable, adequately controlled. Other provisions of the Regulations relate to the application of control measures, the monitoring of exposure, health surveillance, information, instruction and training. HS (G) 66 states that in order to comply with the requirements of these Regulations the client and person in control of the site should ensure that sufficient information is provided on the nature, extent and level of the contamination so that the firms involved can then assess the risks to which they or their employees are likely to be exposed; however, each contractor must decide what precautions are necessary and take steps to ensure that these precautions are taken. Those in control of sites should satisfy themselves that the various contractors have carried out an assessment which is sufficient and suitable and that the specified control measures are provided and are in fact used; in most cases this assessment should be in writing.

12.17   The COSHH Regulations will be most obviously relevant in the context of contaminated land where development or remediation works are being undertaken which may expose workers or others to hazardous substances. In the context of proceedings for breach of statutory duty where injury has occurred it has been held that the relevant duties are not qualified by state of knowledge or foreseeability of risk.[27]

Asbestos

12.18 Asbestos comprises a group of minerals of a fibrous nature, which have many useful applications. There are essentially three types: chrysotile (white) which is the most commonly used and is made up of flexible fibres which can be woven, crocidolite (blue) consisting of brittle fibres with high tensile strength, and amosite (brown) which has good insulation properties. All three types are dangerous, though blue is regarded as the most dangerous.

12.19   Manufacture of asbestos products began in 1870s with companies such as Turner & Newall. It was widely used in the 20th century, especially in the 1960s and 1970s for applications such as thermal insulation, roof sheets and electrical insulation. Unfortunately, exposure to asbestos may result in various serious diseases: the main ones being mesothelioma (cancer of the lining of the lungs), asbestosis (scarring or fibrosis of the lungs), lung cancer, pleural thickening and pleural plaques (small areas of thickening

---

[26] COSHH reg.3(2).
[27] *Williams v Farne Trout and Salmon Ltd* 1998 SLT 1329 (OH); *Dugmore v Swansea NHS Trust and Morriston NHS Trust* [2002] EWCA Civ 1689; [2003] ICR 574; *Naylor v Volex Group Plc* [2003] EWCA Civ. 222.

on the wall of the lung) which do not themselves lead to other asbestos induced conditions, but whose presence may indicate a cumulative level of asbestos exposure at which there is an increased risk of mesothelioma or other asbestos-related disorders.[28] The world's first recorded case of asbestosis was in 1924—Nellie Kershaw, a spinner at Turner Bros Asbestos, Rochdale. The first recorded case of mesothelioma was in 1936— William Pennington, also employed by Turner Bros Asbestos. There were various reports which proved to be important landmarks in the recognition of the risks of asbestos exposure, in particular the 1930 Report by Merewether & Price on *Effects of Asbestos Dust on the Lungs and Dust Suppression in the Asbestos Industry* and the 1955 study of lung cancer mortality by Doll, published in the American Journal of Medicine. Accordingly, the risks of exposure to substantial quantities of asbestos dust were known by the 1950s.[28a] It was, however, not until the 1960s that it became apparent that that even limited exposure to asbestos could give rise to asbestos-related disease. A South African paper written by Wagner et al in 1960 demonstrated the link between asbestos and mesothelioma and showed that the disease can result from far shorter exposure to asbestos than is the case with asbestosis. An epidemiological study by Newhouse and Thompson, published in 1965, looked at neighbourhood exposure to asbestos in East London and showed that persons only casually or non-occupationally exposed to asbestos, including dockers' families, were at risk from mesothelioma. The study attracted media attention including the *Sunday Times* (October 31, 1965) which ran a front-page story on the topic under the headline, "Scientists track down a killer dust disease". That date has become a watershed in terms of setting upon a period in time whereafter an employer is fixed with constructive, if not actual, knowledge of the risk of exposing employees to small amounts of asbestos dust. That is not to say that the employer should not have been aware of the more general dangers of asbestos dust before that date.[28b]

12.20 To give one example of the sheer scale of the problem, in August 1957 Turner Bros Asbestos applied to the Factory Inspectorate for exemption from certain requirements under the Asbestos Industry Regulations 1931 and stated:

> "At present 2,200 people are employed in the Rochdale factory, of whom 1,390 work in 'scheduled areas' . . . The total weight of dust recovered in the filter rooms weekly is about 15,000 lbs, all of which is dumped to waste."[29]

12.21 Until the 1960s, when, as indicated above, the link was made between mesothelioma and limited exposure to asbestos dust, only partial controls were applied to such activities.[30] It is therefore not surprising that asbestos

---

[28] See Dr Robin Rudd, *Occupational Disorders of the Lung* (2002).

[28a] See *O'Toole v Irish Rail* (QBD February 19, 1999) holding that while this was the position in the UK, Ireland was over 40 years behind the UK and that the danger would not have been so obvious to Irish Rail.

[28b] See *Shell Tankers UK Ltd v Jeromson* [2001] EWCA Civ 101; [2001] P.I.Q.R. p.265.

[29] See further, G. Tweedale, *Magic Mineral to Killer Dust: Turner & Newall and the Asbestos Hazard* (Oxford University Press, 2000).

[30] For example, the Asbestos Industry Regulations 1931, the Factories Acts 1937 and 1961 and the Shipbuilding and Ship Repairing Regulations 1960.

contamination may be found on many sites.[31] In some cases it may be found below ground, for example on former waste disposal sites where asbestos containing materials such as asbestos, cement or woven cloth may have been buried as a convenient means of disposal. At other sites it may be found above ground, for instance where it has been used for heat insulation, fire control or in the construction of roofs. The main risk presented by disturbance of the asbestos is that of the release of fibres or dust into the atmosphere; this risk will be dependent upon the nature of the asbestos, its concentrations, the extent to which the asbestos fibres are linked in a matrix (e.g. asbestos cement as in asbestos roofing) and ambient conditions such as whether the site is wet.

12.22   The main controls are now imposed by the Control of Asbestos at Work Regulations 2006.[32] In particular reg.4 imposes an obligation on the "dutyholder" to manage risk from asbestos in non-domestic premises, to ensure a suitable and sufficient assessment is carried out of whether asbestos is or is liable to be present. This assessment must take account of building plans, the age of the premises, and involves inspection of reasonably accessible parts.[33] It applies to all non-domestic premises, including common parts of flats. If asbestos containing materials are present, the duty holder must determine the risk and prepare written plans identifying those parts of the premises concerned and specifying measures to be taken for monitoring, maintenance, or removal of the asbestos. The "dutyholder" is (a) every person who has an obligation of maintenance or repair under a contract or tenancy in relation to non-domestic premises; and (b) if there is no such contract or tenancy, any person who has control to any extent of the relevant part of the premises. Where there is more than one such dutyholder, the relative contribution to be made by each such person in complying with the requirements of the regulation will be determined by the nature and extent of the maintenance and repair obligation owed by that person. It will therefore be important to establish the position under any lease as to the extent of the demise and responsibility for common parts. Third parties are under a duty to co-operate, for example in providing information or allowing access.

12.23   The Regulations will be of particular relevance where asbestos has been incorporated into buildings, for example for insulation or fireproofing. However, "premises" as defined by s.53(1) of the 1974 Act includes any place, any vehicle, vessel or aircraft, any installation on land or offshore, and any movable structure. In *Geotechnics Ltd v Robbins*,[34] it was held that an open area of bogland where a geographical surveying company was checking soil samples fell within the meaning of "any place" and therefore

[31] Including, perhaps not surprisingly, the site of the former Turner Bros factory at Spodden Valley, Rochdale, where a highly controversial residential development is proposed.
[32] SI 2006/2739.
[33] HSE MDHS 100: *Survey, Sampling and Assessment of Asbestos-Containing Materials* deals with the types of survey, which are: Type 1 (location and assessment without sampling, assuming if materials may reasonably be expected to contain asbestos, they are presumed to do so); Type 2 (standard sampling and identification, taking representative samples); Type 3 (full access survey and identification, to allow a method statement for removal to be prepared where demolition or major refurbishment is envisaged).
[34] May 2, 1995 (QBD) Unreported.

amounted to "premises". Accordingly, the area was found to constitute "non-domestic premises" for the purposes of s.4 of the 1974 Act. Hence reg.4 may be capable of applying to land where asbestos is present, though its terms would perhaps suggest that the draftsman had buildings in mind. The HSE website[35] indicates that such premises include all industrial, commercial or public buildings such as factories, warehouses, offices, shops, hospitals and schools and that non-domestic premises also include those "common" areas of certain domestic premises such as purpose-built flats or houses converted into flats. The common areas of such domestic premises might include foyers, corridors, lifts and lift shafts, staircases, roof spaces, gardens, yards, outhouses and garages—but would not include the flat itself. The HSE also suggests that such common areas would not include rooms within a private residence that are shared by more than one household such as bathrooms, kitchens, etc. in shared houses and communal dining rooms and lounges in sheltered accommodation.

12.24 Under reg.5 an employer shall not undertake work in demolition, maintenance, or any other work which exposes or is liable to expose his employees to asbestos in respect of any premises unless either (a) he has carried out a suitable and sufficient assessment as to whether asbestos, what type of asbestos, contained in what material and in what condition is present or is liable to be present in those premises; or (b) if there is doubt as to whether asbestos is present in those premises he assumes that asbestos is present, and that it is not chrysotile asbestos alone, and that he observes the applicable provisions of these Regulations. The Regulations also deal with the assessment of risks before work is undertaken, the licensing of work involving asbestos, and the prevention and reduction of exposure.

12.25 There is also a general duty on employers by reg.16 to prevent or, where this is not reasonably practicable, reduce to the lowest level reasonably practicable, the spread of asbestos from any place where work under his control is carried out.

---

[35] *http://www.hse.gov.uk.*

Chapter 13

EC DEVELOPMENTS

13.01 The issue of contaminated land (as opposed to groundwater or landfill sites) has not been a prominent part of EC environmental law. This is despite the fact that there are numerous suspected contaminated sites throughout Europe. The European Environment Agency in 1998 estimated the number of contaminated sites in the then nine Member States as about 1.3 million[1]; it may be anticipated that with the accession of new East European members of the Community that number will have increased significantly.[2] The Commission has expressed the view that the identification and remediation of contaminated sites is principally a matter for Member States.[3]

13.02 The role of the Community to date has largely been in relation to the important areas of technical co-operation and data collation. In 1996 the Concerted Action on Risk Assessment for Contaminated Soil (CARACAS) was set up, a DGXII funded programme, based in Vienna, which focuses on the co-ordination of research in order to achieve an improved state of scientific knowledge on environmental risk from contaminated sites to support the development of consistent risk assessment methodologies, and to strengthen the collaboration between the EU Member States in this area. Another similar organisation is the Network for Industrial Contaminated land in Western Europe, also set up in 1996. The European Environment Agency (EEA) was created by Council Regulation 1210/90, which provides that the State of Soil and Land Use and Natural Resources are two topic areas. It created a European Topic Center on Soil (ETC/S) in September 1996; from 2001 that area of work passed to the new European Topic Centre on the Terrestrial Environment (ETC/TE). The EEA has produced some significant publications on soil contamination, including a major comparative review on the management of sites across Europe.[4] It also set up the European Environmental Information and Observation Network (EIONET) which has organised collaboration between national experts on soil contamination.[5]

13.03 There are however two areas where EC developments are likely to impinge on national contaminated land regimes. These are the Directive on the prevention and remedying of environmental damage 2004/35 (the

---

[1] *EEA: Europe's Environment, the second assessment* (1998, Aarhus).
[2] A figure of 3.5 million sites is given in the 2006 Thematic Strategy on Soil Protection: see para.13.48.
[3] Waste Strategy Review COM(96)399 (30/7/96).
[4] Management of Contaminated Sites in Western Europe (EEA, Topic Report 13/1999, June 2000).
[5] European Soil Monitoring and Assessment Framework (EEA, Technical Report 67, Report of EIONET workshop, 2001).

Environmental Liability Directive) and the proposal for a Directive establishing a framework for the protection of soil (the Soil Protection Directive). These are considered below.

PART 1: THE ENVIRONMENTAL LIABILITY DIRECTIVE

History of the Directive

The Environmental Liability Directive (ELD) has a troubled history, dating **13.04** back to the 1980s, when provisions on strict liability for environmental damage were proposed for inclusion in early drafts of the Transfrontier Shipment of Hazardous Waste Directive 84/631. These were deleted on the basis that the Commission would produce proposals for a separate directive on environmental liability, which it did in its 1989 proposal for a Directive on civil liability for damage caused by waste.[6] The proposal referred to the possible adverse effects of disparities among laws of Member States concerning such liability and to the principle established in Art.130R of the EC treaty that the polluter should pay; "the strict liability of the producer constitutes the best solution to the problem". In its amended form of June 1991, the proposed Directive provided that: "the producer of waste shall be liable under civil law for the damage and impairment of the environment caused by waste, irrespective of fault on his part".[7] One notable feature of the proposal was the imposition of liability for not only personal injury and damage to property, but also "impairment of the environment", defined as any significant physical, chemical or biological deterioration. However, this proposal became effectively shelved.

In March 1993 the Commission adopted a communication on repairing **13.05** damage to the environment.[8] This so-called "Green Paper", which was issued as a consultative document, considered various issues relating to the different forms of liability and their shortcomings, how environmental damage is defined and the mechanisms by which such damage may be made good. The Commission's work reflected not only experience within Member States, but also the Council of Europe's Lugano convention on civil liability.[9] Effectively, what was envisaged was an integrated pro-

---

[6] COM(89)282. See also the House of Lords Select Committee on the European Communities *Paying for Pollution*, Session 1989–90, 25th Report, HL Paper 84–1.

[7] COM(91)219, Art.3.1.

[8] COM(93)47.

[9] *Convention on Civil Liability for Damage Resulting from Activities Dangerous to the Environment*, CETS No: 150, June 1993. The general aim of the Convention is to ensure that "adequate compensation for damage resulting from activities dangerous to the environment" and also provides for means of prevention and reinstatement. "Damage" is defined by Art.2.7 so as to include not only loss of life or personal injury and damage to property but also impairment of the environment and the costs of preventive measures. The Convention also includes some relatively sophisticated provisions of a transitional nature dealing with retrospective liability and in particular with closed waste disposal sites. See [1994] Env. Liab.11 (M.J. Bowman) for a further summary. The Convention was signed in 1993 by Finland, Greece, Italy, Luxembourg, and The Netherlands, and by Portugal in 1997. No State has yet ratified it. The Convention requires three ratifications to enter into force.

gramme, using no fault civil liability where damage may be linked to a particular party's actions and, where damage is not so attributable, using compensation systems to spread the cost of restoration action among economic sectors. The paper raised a common issue to be addressed in all Member States of how to define and treat impairment of the environment which falls outside accepted categories of physical injury, damage to tangible property and interference with third party rights; in particular at what point impairment becomes sufficiently serious to impose liability. The issue is essentially one of policy as to who decides what is an acceptable level of environmental damage: attitudes on this issue can vary geographically and on a cultural basis, and can change over time in the light of new scientific information or hypothesis.

13.06 The Green Paper gave rise to vigorous and heated debate, including two major studies undertaken for the Commission on the legal and economic implications (1994–96) and a strongly rejected suggestion that the EU should accede to the Lugano Convention. It was not until February 2000 that a White Paper, based on an amended version of the 1999 text, was approved.[10] This generally followed the Lugano model of a civil law approach of compensatory actions for damage, and covering both "environmental damage" and traditional forms of personal injury and property damage.

13.07 In 2001, following a change of Commissioner at DGXI, there was an important shift in direction away from civil liability and towards an approach based entirely on public law remedies, with a markedly different proposal being approved by the Commission in January 2002.[11] Proceedings on the proposal in the European Parliament were highly contentious, with sharp political dispute over many aspects, and with the Environment and Legal Affairs Committees taking different lines. Ultimately, no significant amendments to the Commission's proposal resulted from the Parliament's readings, or the conciliation process between Parliament and Council.

13.08 The ELD was ultimately approved, came into force on April 30, 2004, and required Member States to bring the necessary laws into force by April 30, 2007.

Overview of the ELD and contaminated land

13.09 The recitals to the ELD point to the number of contaminated sites in the Community posing significant health risks and a dramatic acceleration in loss of biodiversity.[12] The ELD's objective is to establish a common framework for the prevention and remedying of environmental damage at a reasonable cost to society.[13] It covers "environmental damage", comprising three elements, of which "land damage" is one, but with the potential for all three to result from land contamination. Before considering the provisions of the ELD in more detail, it is worth making some preliminary points:

[10] COM(2000) 66.
[11] COM (2002)17.
[12] ELD Recital (1).
[13] ELD Recital (3).

1. the ELD requires the Member States to implement provisions relating to the prevention and remediation of damage—it does not cover compensation for damage between private parties;

2. its application is restricted to "environmental damage" as defined, which is limited in scope and provides some discretion allowing Member States to take a narrow view of that definition[14];

3. there are a number of exceptions, or restrictions, to responsibility for remediation, some of which are "optional";

4. the temporal scope of the provisions is limited in that it does not apply to "damage caused by an emission, event or incident" that took place before April 30, 2007 or which took place subsequent to that date, when it derived from a specific activity that took place and finished before that date[15]; and

5. the ELD requires minimum rather than complete harmonisation, so that the Member States are required to provide the minimum rights, obligations and other provisions but are free to maintain or adopt more stringent domestic provisions,[16] including, for example, more strict forms of liability, or the extension or exclusion of limitation periods.

13.10 The restriction on temporal scope is important as it means that the primary means of implementation should be through the prospective control methods for potentially contaminating activities, such as the Pollution Prevention and Control and Waste Licensing regimes. Whilst the specific system of contaminated land regulation found in Pt IIA of the Environmental Protection Act 1990 will comprise one means of implementation, the primary focus of that regime is on dealing with historic contamination and so would only come into play where prospective controls have failed to prevent environmental damage, and have not secured clean up where such damage has occurred.

Scope of "damage"

13.11 The scope of the ELD is restricted to three types of environmental damage:

1. damage to protected species and natural habitats;

2. water damage; and

3. land damage.

13.12 "Damage" is defined as "a measurable adverse change in a natural resource or measurable impairment of a natural resource service which may occur directly or indirectly".[17]

---

[14] Notably the scope of the "protected species and natural habitats" within Art.2.1(c).

[15] ELD Art.17. Whether the burying of a drum of chemicals is classed a "specific activity", so that damage caused by a subsequent leak from it after the said date, for example, is not entirely clear.

[16] ELD Art.16.1.

[17] ELD Art.2.2.

13.13   "Biodiversity damage" consists of significant adverse effects on the favourable conservation status of specified species and habitats, with the significance of such adverse effects to be assessed by reference to specified criteria.[18] The scope includes[19] species and habitats protected under Art.4.2 or listed in Annex I to the Birds Directive[20] and in Annexes I, II and IV of the Habitats Directive.[21] One of the significant areas of discretion for the Member States is the permission in Art.2.3(c) to determine further (nationally protected) sites or species for inclusion.

13.14   "Water damage" comprises[22] any damage that significantly adversely affects the ecological, chemical and/or quantitative status and/or ecological potential, as defined in the Water Framework Directive,[23] of the waters covered by that Directive.

13.15   "Land damage" is defined as "any land contamination that creates a significant risk of human health being adversely affected as a result of the direct or indirect introduction, in, on or under land, of substances, preparations, organisms or micro-organisms".[24]

13.16   The scope of the ELD is further limited by exceptions and exclusions under which environmental damage is not covered, or is limited, in a number of specified circumstances. These include armed conflict, civil war, etc. and exceptional natural phenomena,[25] damage arising from incidents covered by specified international liability regimes[26] and activities whose main purpose is national defence, international security, or protection from natural disasters.[27] There is a further exception with regard to diffuse pollution, with damage only covered "where it is possible to establish a causal link between the damage and the activities of individual operators".[28]

Scope and nature of liability

13.17   The "fundamental principle" of the ELD is that operators whose activity has caused environmental damage or the imminent threat of this are to be held financially liable, in order to provide incentives to minimise such risks.[29] Liability is based upon the "occupational activities"[30] which cause

---

[18] Set out in Annex I.

[19] ELD Art.2.3.

[20] Directive 79/409.

[21] Directive 92/43.

[22] ELD Art.2.1(b).

[23] Directive 2000/60.

[24] ELD Art.2.1.

[25] ELD Art.4.1.

[26] Damage falling within the scope of international oil pollution liability, nuclear radiation liability, and other listed Conventions, where in force in the Member State where damage occurs (see Art.4 and Annexes IV and V). Thus listed Conventions which are not in force in the UK, such as those of 1989 on Civil Liability for Damage Caused during Carriage of Dangerous Goods by Road, Rail and Inland Navigation Vessels and of 2001 on Civil Liability for Bunker Oil Pollution Damage, would not act to exclude liability from the ELD.

[27] ELD Art.4.6.

[28] ELD Art.4.5.

[29] ELD Recital (2).

[30] Defined in Art.2.7.

environmental damage (or the imminent threat of this), with obligations placed upon those operating or controlling such activities ("operators") to prevent or remedy such damage.[31] An important distinction is made between those activities which are listed in Annex III to the Directive[32] and other activities. In relation to Annex III activities, the ELD applies to all types of "environmental damage", but for other activities, only applies to "biodiversity" damage.[33] Liability is further limited by the mandatory and optional defences discussed below. For Annex III activities, liability is strict, with only causation required, whereas for other activities, the ELD applies only where the operator has been at fault or negligent.[34] This does not mean that the Member States cannot introduce or maintain more stringent or wide-ranging liability, but that it is not required under the ELD.

In cases of multiple-party causation, the Member States are free to **13.18** choose their preferred method of "cost allocation".[35] The effect of this is that joint and several liability may be imposed so that each party is potentially liable for the costs of the whole remedial works, or proportionate liability so that each party is only required to bear the costs of their own "share" of these.

There is an effective limitation period of 30 years from the date of the emission, event or incident giving rise to damage[36] and a limitation period of five years for recovery of costs by competent authorities.[37]

Obligations on operators and responsibilities of competent authorities

The main obligations imposed upon operators are to: **13.19**

1. take action, without delay, to prevent imminent threat of damage[38];

2. notify the competent authority if preventive measures fail[39];

3. notify the competent authority in the event of significant environmental damage[40];

4. take immediate action to control, contain, remove or manage any potential causes of damage[41];

---

[31] Under Arts 5 and 6.

[32] Essentially activities which are potentially particularly damaging to the environment and subject to control under European environmental law, such as waste management operations, IPPC installations, groundwater discharges, GMOs, and plant protection products. Certain sewage sludge spreading operations may be excluded from Annex III at the Member State's discretion.

[33] ELD Art.3.1.

[34] ELD Art.3.1(b). Whether the competent authority or operator is required to (dis)prove fault is not clear, but the onus is likely to be on the operator.

[35] ELD Art.9.

[36] ELD Art.17.

[37] ELD Art.10.

[38] ELD Art.5.1.

[39] ELD Art.5.2.

[40] ELD Art.6.1.

[41] ELD Art.6.1(a).

5. propose potential remedial measures and submit to the competent authority for approval[42];

6. undertake remedial measures as agreed by the competent authority[43]; and

7. pay the competent authority's assessment and other administrative costs.[44]

13.20   In cases of imminent threats the competent authority can:

1. require the operator to provide information on any imminent threat of environmental damage or in suspected cases of such a threat;

2. require the operator to take, and give the operator instructions on, the necessary preventive measures; and

3. take the necessary measures itself.[45]

13.21   In cases of environmental damage the competent authority:

1. may require the operator to provide supplementary information on any damage[46];

2. may take, require the operator to take, or give instructions to the operator to take all practical steps for the immediate control, containment, removal, or management of the relevant potential causes of damage, and/or regarding the necessary remedial measures[47];

3. must decide which remedial measures, from among the options presented by the operator, are to be taken[48];

4. in cases where several instances of environmental damage have occurred which cannot all be addressed simultaneously, can decide the priority for remedial measures[49];

5. must require the operator to take the necessary remedial measures[50]; and

6. may take the remedial measures itself, as a means of last resort.[51]

13.22   For both imminent threats and environmental damage, the competent authority must recover its costs from the operator, although it may decide not to do so if the costs of such action would exceed the amount to be

[42] ELD Art.7.1.
[43] ELD Art.6.1(b).
[44] "Costs" including administrative, legal and enforcement costs (Art.2.16).
[45] ELD Art.5.3.
[46] ELD Art.6.2(a).
[47] ELD Art.6.2.(b)–(d).
[48] ELD Art.7.2.
[49] ELD Art.7.3.
[50] ELD Art.6.3.
[51] ELD Art.6.3.

recovered or the operator cannot be identified. It must also consider requests for action by parties, including NGOs, and respond to such requests as soon as possible, giving reasons for its decision.[52] These persons must be provided with access to a court or other independent and impartial public body competent to review the procedural and substantive legality of the decisions, acts or failure to act of the competent authority.[53] As operators are included within this class of persons, an effective right of appeal is provided against decisions by competent authorities. Substantive grounds for an appeal would be based upon denial of liability, including:

(a) that there is no "environmental damage";

(b) that damage was not caused by the operator's occupational activity; and

(c) that temporal or other exceptions to liability apply.

The mandatory nature of many of these provisions regarding competent **13.23** authorities can be compared with those under Pt IIA, and contrasted with the discretionary powers under many other relevant regimes, such as the Water Resources Act works notices.[54]

Remediation requirements

As is apparent from these obligations, the primary objective of the ELD is **13.24** for preventative action to be taken where possible. Where "environmental damage" does occur and so requires remediation, the initial requirements are aimed at managing contaminants and minimising their effects. For longer term remedial works, the standard varies according to the type of damage.[55] Article 7 sets out how operators' proposed remedial measures are to be approved by the competent authorities. The proposals are to be identified, and the competent authority's decision as to which are to be implemented is to be taken, in accordance with Annex II. This sets out a common framework to be followed in order to choose the most appropriate measures to ensure the remedying of damage. For biodiversity and water damage[56] the objectives are to restore damaged resources and services to, or towards, the condition at the time of the damage of the natural resources and services that would have existed had the environmental damage not occurred (the "baseline condition"). A remedial measure which returns the damaged resources or services to or towards baseline condition is referred to as "primary remediation". As it will generally take some time for such restoration (particularly where some degree of natural

---

[52] ELD Art.12. Under Art.12.5, the Member States have a discretion not to apply these provisions in cases of imminent threat of damage.

[53] ELD Art.13.1.

[54] See para.74ff.

[55] For a detailed discussion of remediation requirements under the ELD (and of the ELD in general), see G. Betlem and E. Brans (eds), and *Environmental Liability in the EU* (Cameron May, 2006).

[56] See para.1 of Annex II.

recovery is considered appropriate), "interim losses" should be assessed in such cases and "compensatory" remediation is to be undertaken in the form of additional improvements to protected natural habitats and species, or water, at either the damaged site itself or at an alternative site. This does not consist of financial compensation to members of the public. Where full primary restoration is not possible, some form of permanent compensatory measures are required, referred to as "complementary remediation". Where such measures take place at an alternative site, this should be geographically linked to the damaged site, where appropriate and possible, taking into account the interests of the affected population. Further detail is provided in Annex II as to the identification of appropriate measures, including the preference for resource-to-resource and service-to-service equivalence for complementary and compensatory measures. Criteria for evaluating remedial options are set out, including: effects on public health and safety; cost; likelihood of success; prevention of future damage and avoidance of collateral damage; social, economic and cultural concerns; length of time; and restoration of the site damaged. Competent authorities are entitled to determine that no further remedial measures should be taken if:

(a) the remedial measures already taken secure that there is no longer any significant risk of adversely affecting human health, water or protected species and natural habitats; and

(b) the cost of the remedial measures that should be taken to reach baseline condition or similar level would be disproportionate to the environmental benefits to be obtained.

13.25   The remediation requirements for land damage are quite different.[57] Necessary measures are to be taken to ensure, as a minimum, that the relevant contaminants are removed, controlled, contained or diminished so that the contaminated land (taking account of its current use or approved future use at the time of the damage) no longer poses any significant risk of adversely affecting human health. Natural recovery options, where no direct human intervention in the recovery process would be taken, are to be considered.

13.26   Risk-assessment procedures taking into account the characteristic and function of the soil, the type and concentration of the harmful substances, preparations, organisms or micro-organisms, their risk and the possibility of their dispersion will identify the presence of such risks. Use is to be ascertained on the basis of the land use (or other relevant) regulations in force when the damage occurred. If the use of the land is changed, all necessary measures are to be taken to prevent any adverse effects on human health.[58]

"Defences" to liability

13.27   Four classes of situations are provided for which are often referred to as "defences", though the nature of their operation suggests that they might not be classified as such in a technical sense. The situations are where the operator:

[57] See para.2 of Annex II.
[58] Whether by the operator or developer, and at whose cost, is not specified.

1. can prove that the environmental damage or imminent threat of such damage was caused by a third party and occurred despite the fact that appropriate safety measures were in place[59];

2. can prove that the environmental damage or imminent threat resulted from compliance with a compulsory order or instruction emanating from a public authority, other than an order or instruction consequent upon an emission or incident caused by the operator's own activities[60];

3. demonstrates that he was not at fault or negligent and that the environmental damage was caused by an emission or event expressly authorised by, and fully in accordance with the conditions of, an authorisation granted in relation to Annex III regimes[61]; or

4. was not at fault or negligent and the environmental damage was caused by use of a product in the course of an activity which the operator demonstrates was not considered likely to cause environmental damage according to the state of scientific and technical knowledge at the time when the emission was released or the activity took place.[62]

The first two of these provisions are required to be provided by the **13.28** Member States which are to take appropriate measures to enable the operator to recover costs incurred in such cases. (3) and (4), however, are optional "defences" where the Member States may allow the operator not to bear the costs of remedial actions, so that there is a discretion to narrow the scope of the ELD within individual Member States.

Costs recovery and liability of third parties

Whilst the main provisions of the ELD do not explicitly set out the liability **13.29** of third parties, the operation of the costs recovery and related provisions make it clear that such inclusion of liability comprises part of the obligations on the Member States. Competent authorities are to require preventive actions and remedial actions to be taken by the operator,[63] other than where the operator cannot be identified or is not required to bear such costs under other provisions of the ELD, when the competent authority may take such measures itself. Article 8 further provides that the operator is to bear the costs for preventive and remedial actions and, subject to the four "defences" outlined above, the competent authority is required to recover costs it has incurred from the operator, through security over property or other appropriate guarantees.[64] In the case of the

---

[59] ELD Art.8.3(a).
[60] ELD Art.8.3(b).
[61] ELD Art.8.4(a).
[62] ELD Art.8.4(b).
[63] ELD Arts 5.4 and 6.3.
[64] ELD Art.8.2, other than where the costs of such recovery would be greater than the recoverable sum, or the operator cannot be identified.

first two (compulsory) defences, the ELD states that the operator is to be enabled "to recover the costs incurred",[65] which suggests that the operator will carry out works and then seek to recover its costs from either a third party or public authority as the case may be. What the position is where such costs cannot be recovered because third parties cannot be identified or have insufficient funds is unclear, which is the basis for questioning the classification of these provisions as "defences". The same provisions state that operators shall not be required to bear the cost of actions in such circumstances, but the means for ensuring this, such as recovery from the competent authority or others, are not specified. The UK Government takes the view that the public purse should not fill this gap, as it would introduce Member State subsidiary liability which is not part of the ELD. Instead it has proposed that the "defence" should be considered before remedial measures are actually undertaken, though how workable this will be in practice remains to be seen, and it is questionable whether this approach accords with the wording of the ELD's provisions. The ELD also provides that competent authorities shall be entitled to initiate cost recovery proceedings against operators, or against third parties if appropriate.[66] This might help to avoid some problems of cost recovery, though not regarding unidentifiable or insolvent third parties. Whilst Art.11.3 requires Member States to ensure that competent authorities may empower or require "third parties" to carry out preventive or remedial such measures, it is not clear whether this is limited to agents carrying out works on their behalf, or extends to other third parties, such as those who have caused damage.

Other provisions

13.30 The co-operation provisions in Art.15 include a Member State's ability to seek costs recovery for damage caused within its territory with a cause outside. Member States are allowed to prevent double recovery under the operation of the ELD and private law claims.[67]

13.31 Given the scale of potential liability, Art.14 requires measures to be taken to encourage the development of financial security instruments and markets in order to enable operators to use insurance or other guarantees to cover their responsibilities. This represents a watering down of initial proposals which would have made such guarantees compulsory. The Commission is required to report on the effectiveness of the operation of the ELD and the availability of insurance, etc. including consideration of whether there should be a move towards some form of mandatory financial security.

---

[65] ELD Art.8.3.
[66] ELD Art.10.
[67] ELD Art.16.2.

Domestic implementation

Although the deadline date for putting in place national legislation was **13.32**
April 30 2007, transposition in the United Kingdom was still at the first
stage of consultation in the middle of 2007,[68] with a second round
scheduled for Autumn 2007. The latter will set out the specific measures
for implementing the ELD, including draft legislation. It is likely that this
will identify those existing measures which cover part of the scope of the
ELD, together with general provisions to complete implementation where
there are "gaps".[69] The two main areas of debate concern the Government's desire to avoid "gold-plating" transposition through a presumption
of minimal implementation,[70] with consequent inclusion of the optional
"defences" and exclusion of national biodiversity sites and species, for
example,[71] and the difficulties of "dovetailing" transposition with existing
domestic provisions, such as the Water Resources Act 1991, the Pollution
Prevention and Control Regulations 2000, the proposed Environmental
Permitting Programme, and Pt IIA of the Environmental Protection Act
1990.

The House of Commons Environment, Food and Rural Affairs Com- **13.33**
mittee has been highly critical of the Government's approach in this
regard.[72] Noting the amount of time and effort expended by both DEFRA
and respondents with regard to the consultation process on implementing
the Directive, and the discretion afforded under the Directive to the
Member States in a number of respects, the Report states that ". . . the
Government's attitude to implementing the Directive, set out in the
consultation document, appears to have made all this effort practically
worthless", because of the policy of minimal transposition. "[T]his has
meant that the Government proposes not to go beyond the minimum
requirements even when its own analysis found that there would be an
overall societal and economic benefit from doing so."

The Committee considered that the Government must provide a proper **13.34**
justification of its policy choices, rather than simply relying upon the
avoidance of "gold-plating", for example Government's unwillingness to
extend the Directive to nationally-protected biodiversity.[472]

As indicated above, the preventive and prospective focus of the ELD **13.35**
suggests that ongoing permitting regimes should provide the primary
means of implementation. In most cases, this will be through the permit-

---

[68] See *Consultation on options for implementing the Environmental Liability Directive*, at http://
www.defra.gov.uk/corporate/consult/env-liability. The United Kingdom Environmental Law Association has produced a number of detailed papers commenting on the ELD and the
implementation proposals set out in the first consultation paper available at http://
www.ukela.org. uk. (accessed October 2007).

[69] Such an approach was adopted for elements of the final stage of transposition of the
Groundwater Directive (80/68) in the Groundwater Regulations 1998 (SI 1998/2746), for
example.

[70] One example where this is not proposed is the "natural phenomena" exclusion, which is to
be subject to demonstration that all reasonable steps to minimise damage were taken.

[71] This has been the subject of criticism by the House of Commons Environment, Food and
Rural Affairs Committee: *Implementation of the Environmental Liability Directive*, Sixth Report
of Session 2006–7 (HC 694) as discussed below.

[72] *UK's Implementation of the Environmental Liability Directive* (Sixth Report of Session 2006–07;
HC 694).

[472] See also the Government Response to the Committees Report (HC 1058, October 2007).

ting regimes which are required for control of Annex III activities. Thus existing provisions such as powers to require the remedying of the effects of pollution caused by PPC permit breaches, on or off site, site restoration conditions and liability for illegal waste deposits will play roles in securing preventive action and remedial works. The liability provisions in the PPC and Waste Management Licensing regimes will be combined in the proposed Environmental Permitting Programme, which includes provisions relating to the prevention and remediation of environmental damage, with powers to serve enforcement notices, revoke permits, and for regulators to require operators to prevent or remedy pollution. For non-Annex III activities, general provisions will provide the means of implementation in some cases, with gaps filled by the new legislative measures. Liability under the works notices provisions of the Water Resources Act 1991 will implement many aspects of the ELD where contaminated land causes water damage. Part IIA will cover some cases where there is environmental damage from incidents which took place on or after April 30, 2007, but have not been, or cannot be, remedied under ongoing permits. As well as differences such as thresholds for damage (discussed below), Pt IIA includes provisions such as those on "hardship"[73] to mitigate the harshness of strict liability, which the ELD does not, and the ELD provisions for recovery of costs via security[74] are more extensive than those under Pt IIA.

13.36   Clearly all three types of "environmental damage" might result from contaminated land and one of the issues faced in transposition of the ELD is the potential complexity of different types of damage resulting from different activities. In reality, single remedial actions might often relate to both water and biodiversity damage, for example, with potential differences as to the strictness of liability. This complexity is exacerbated when seeking to integrate the ELD with existing provisions, which include both proportionate and joint and several, as well as strict and fault-based, liability. A further level of complexity arises from devolved powers, for example, the Welsh Assembly's disapplication of the permit "defence" for GMO-related activities. One way in which this potential complexity has been mitigated is by the Government applying the minimal transposition principle only to the extent that it would increase liabilities over and above the existing situation. Thus existing measures which exceed the minimum requirements under the ELD are retained. In some ways the ELD is more extensive than existing provisions, such as the requirement for complementary and compensatory remedial works where appropriate. In other respects, existing measures are more extensive as they apply to a wider range of activities, or impose strict liability more widely, for example.

Thresholds for "damage"

13.37 One major source of potential difficulty in integrating the ELD obligations within domestic law is the matching of thresholds for "damage" and methods for assessment. In the case of land damage, defined by reference

---

[73] See para.6.28ff.
[74] In Art.8.2.

to risks of adverse effects on human health, the Government proposes to use the same threshold as for Pt IIA, whilst acknowledging that this does not include harm arising from organisms and GMOs. The new measures will, therefore, need to cover such organisms, to at least the minimum standards of liability required by the ELD. Whether the two thresholds are the same is debatable. In particular, the threshold under Pt IIA requires "significant harm" to be caused, or a significant possibility of significant harm, whilst the ELD requires only a "significant risk of human health being adversely affected", so that in the case of Pt IIA there is a threshold both for harm and the risk of harm (the threshold being significant in both cases), whereas under the ELD there is a single threshold of significant risk. Whether this is a real or semantic difference only is a moot point. The Government has stated that even if there are differences between these thresholds, it would be very difficult to manage that difference in practice and that to follow the same approach to risk assessment is the only workable option.

13.38 The threshold for water damage is to be based upon criteria giving practical effect to the ELD, drawing upon the Water Framework Directive standards, and will need to be compared with existing standards, such as that of "poisonous, noxious or polluting matter or any solid waste matter".

13.39 The options under consideration for the biodiversity damage threshold are either to assess by reference to the integrity of an individual site, or the effect on favourable conservation status more generally (which would be a higher threshold). The ELD threshold is close to those under Pt IIA for "European" sites and species, as set out in 'Table A': "harm which is incompatible with the favourable conservation status of natural habitats at that location or species typically found there".

13.40 A further issue is how to identify and apportion liability where a number of sequential activities cumulatively result in a breach of a damage threshold.

Notification and "self-executing" duties

13.41 The notification requirements and so called "self-executing duties"[75] represent important points of departure in the ELD from most of the existing regimes. Part IIA and most other regimes do not require the notification of damage or threat of damage and remedial action is generally only required after some form of regulatory action (usually the serving of a notice). The PPC Regulations do, however, provide that conditions are to be set in permits "requiring the operator to supply the regulator regularly with the results of the monitoring of emissions and to inform the regulator, without delay, of any incident or accident which is causing or may cause significant pollution".[76] This provides something of a precedent for notification duties, at least. The proposed Environmental Permitting Programme includes two important elements which will assist

---

[75] See V. Fogleman, "Enforcing the Environmental Liability Directive: Duties, Powers and Self-Executing Provisions" [2006] Env. Liab.127.
[76] SI 2000/1973 reg.12(9)(f).

in implementation of the ELD: first, powers to impose conditions which require notification to regulators of significant non-compliance; and secondly, requirements as to complementary and compensatory remediation for environmental damage caused by a regulated activity.

Enforcement

13.42 The competent authorities for the purposes of the ELD are likely to be the Environment Agency for land damage and water damage and Natural England for biodiversity damage in England, with equivalents in Wales and elsewhere in the UK. Despite the possible overlap with Pt IIA, local authorities are not included because of their number, the multi-media nature of much damage and the historic focus of Pt IIA. In addition, many Annex III activities are already regulated by the Environment Agency. Appeals will be made to the Secretary of State in England, and to the National Assembly in Wales.

13.43   Whilst there are no obligations as to sanctions for non-compliance in the ELD itself, Member States are assumed to apply appropriate sanctions in line with national legislation as part of their implementation. Penalties for non-compliance will be provided in the new measures, to supplement those in the existing regimes which are to form part of the implementation. Likely criminal offences include: the failure to take the necessary preventive measures where there is an imminent threat of environmental damage occurring; failure to notify competent authorities of such threats or the occurrence of such damage; failure to comply with preventive or remedial measures required by the competent authority; and failure to identify and submit potential remedial measures.

Practical issues

13.44 Although the ELD does not in itself require prior assessment or routine monitoring, and so does not require operators to take actions which incur costs unless environmental damage is caused or imminently threatened, concern to avoid the costs of preventive and remedial works may make such measures practically important. Generally, operators will need to ensure that they have plans to prevent environmental damage and to take immediate action if this is threatened or occurs, whether required under existing regulatory regimes or not. In particular, the pro-active notification obligations on operators will require internal reporting systems to be in place. Operators may also find it expedient to undertake baseline condition assessments, to avoid pre-existing damage wrongly being attributed to their activities. As part of due diligence, investigations might be made as to the existence of internal reporting and response plans. Due diligence itself could trigger reporting obligations, by unearthing a failure to notify of threats or damage, or to respond adequately to such threats or damage.

13.45   The thresholds for damage under the ELD are problematic in that they require a scientific assessment in order to identify clearly whether damage has been caused or is threatened. This is in conflict with the need for preventive measures to be taken without delay, and practical steps to manage contaminants, etc. immediately. National criteria for reporting and taking such emergency steps, established by reference to substances and quantities released, would provide a more practical trigger for such actions. Similarly, there is a potential conflict between the desire to encourage timely preventive and remedial action in cases where an operator may benefit from one of the "defences" and so be concerned about its ability to recover the costs of works subsequently.

The rights to request action and access to justice provisions which are **13.46** applicable to NGOs and others raise questions as to whether existing judicial review remedies will fulfil the obligations under Arts 12 and 13.[77] Such rights may also be used to instigate investigations and subsequent remedial works in a number of cases where there is "environmental damage" within the meaning and scope of the ELD.

PART 2: SOIL PROTECTION

Generally

Soil itself has not previously been a subject of specific protection at EU **13.47** level, but has been identified as a serious problem in Europe, the main processes of degradation being erosion, decline in organic matter, contamination, salinisation, compaction, decline in biodiversity, and general loss to development. Impact analysis carried out in line with Commission guidelines, using available data, suggests that soil degradation could cost up to €38 billion a year. Accordingly the Commission now accepts that co-ordinated action at Community level is needed, given the risk of distortions of the internal market which may be involved in remedying contaminated sites, the potential for cross-border impacts, and the international dimension of the problem. This has led to the publication in September 2006 of a Thematic Strategy for Soil Protection and a proposed Directive.

Thematic Strategy

The EU's Sixth Environmental Action Programme in 2002[78] called for the **13.48** development of a Thematic Strategy on Soil Protection. An initial Communication on the subject was published in 2002.[79] The Thematic Strategy published in 2006[80] presents a gloomy picture of the prognosis for European soil and in particular estimates the number of potentially contaminated sites in the 25 Member States as 3.5 million.[81] Existing EU

---

[77] Although Art.13.2 includes the provision that this without prejudice to national provisions regulating access to justice, there is a question as to whether recourse to review of the substantive merits of decisions is required, rather than procedural lawfulness under judicial review.

[78] Decision 1600/2002.

[79] COM (2002) 179.

[80] COM (2006) 231.

[81] COM (2006) 231 para.2.1.

policies contribute to soil protection, but not in a comprehensive way. The following guiding principles underlie the Strategy[82]:

1. preventing further soil degradation and preserving its functions;

2. action on soil use and management;

3. action to be take at source where soil acts as a sink or receptor for human activities or environmental phenomena; and

4. restoring degraded soils to "a level of functionality consistent at least with current and intended use, thus also considering the cost implications of the restoration of soil".

13.49   The main plank of the Strategy is a new Framework Directive, aimed at ensuring a comprehensive approach to soil protection while respecting Member State subsidiarity. Member States will be required to take specific measures to address soil threats, but the Directive will leave them "ample freedom" on how to implement this requirement, in that risk acceptability, the level of ambition regarding targets to be achieved and the choice of measures to achieve those targets would be left to Member States.[83] For contaminated sites, it is proposed that on the basis of a common definition of contaminated sites (sites which pose significant risk to human health or the environment) and a common list of potentially polluting activities, Member States will be required to identify the contaminated sites on their territory and establish a national remediation strategy, based on sound and transparent prioritisation of the sites to be remediated, including a mechanism for the remediation of orphan sites. This would be complemented by "the obligation for a seller or a prospective buyer to provide to the administration and to the other party in the transaction a soil status report for sites where a potentially contaminating activity has taken or is taking place".[84] The Soil Protection Strategy is complementary to the Thematic Strategy on the Urban Environment,[85] which sets out co-operation measures and guidelines aimed at Member States and local authorities to enable them to improve urban management in Europe; this includes the issue of industrial wastelands and derelict land.

Proposed Directive

13.50 The proposal for a Directive establishing a framework for the protection of soil was published in September 2006.[86] Its main features can be summarised as follows:

---

[82] COM (2006) 231 para.3.1.

[83] para.4.1. For an article providing a comprehensive discussion of the merits of developing voluntary environmental quality standards for soil, see Birgitte Egelund Olsen, *Voluntary Standards as an Instrument in Environmental Regulations: The Problem of Contaminated Soil* [2001] 2 Env Liability 53.

[84] para.4.1.2

[85] COM (2004) 60 and COM (2005) 718.

[86] COM (2006) 232.

1. It applies to soil forming the top layer of the Earth's crust, between the bedrock and the surface, and excluding groundwater as defined in the Water Framework Directive.[87]

2. Member States shall ensure that any land user whose actions affect the soil in a way that can reasonably be expected to hamper significantly the soil's functions is obliged to take precautions to prevent or minimise such effects.[88]

3. Appropriate measures are to be taken to limit "sealing" (the permanent covering of the soil with impermeable material) or to mitigate its effects.[89]

4. Within five years from transposition, Member States shall identify the areas in their national territory, at the appropriate level, where there is decisive evidence, or legitimate grounds for suspicion, that one or more of a number of soil degradation processes has occurred or is likely to occur in the near future ("the risk areas"). The processes are erosion, organic matter decline, compaction, salinisation and landslides.[90]

5. Within seven years of transposition, Member States shall, in respect of the risk areas, draw up, at the appropriate level, a programme of measures including at least risk reduction targets, the appropriate measures for reaching those targets, a timetable for the implementation of those measures and an estimate of the allocation of private or public means for the funding of those measures, giving due consideration to the social and economic impacts of the measures envisaged.[91]

6. Member States shall take appropriate and proportionate measures to limit the intentional or unintentional introduction of dangerous substances on or in the soil, excluding those due to air deposition and those due to a natural phenomenon of exceptional, inevitable and irresistible character, in order to avoid accumulation that would hamper soil functions or give rise to significant risks to human health or the environment.[92]

7. Member States shall identify the sites in their national territory where there is a confirmed presence, caused by man, of dangerous substances of such a level that Member States consider they pose a significant risk to human health or the environment ("contaminated sites"). That risk shall be evaluated taking into account current and approved future use of the land. Each Member State shall designate a competent authority to be responsible for the identification of contaminated sites.[93]

[87] ELD Art.1.2.
[88] ELD Art.4.
[89] ELD Art.5.
[90] ELD Art.6.
[91] ELD Art.8.
[92] ELD Art.9.
[93] ELD Arts 10.1 and 11.1.

8. Member States shall establish a national inventory of contaminated sites, hereinafter "the inventory". The inventory shall be made public and reviewed at least every five years.[94]

9. A detailed timetable is proposed for the identification process. Within five years from transposition the competent authorities shall have identified the location of at least the sites where the potentially soil-polluting activities referred to in Annex II are taking place or have taken place in the past.[95]

10. The competent authorities shall measure the concentration levels of dangerous substances in the identified sites, and where the levels are such that there may be sufficient reasons to believe that they pose a significant risk to human health or the environment, an on-site risk assessment shall be carried out in relation to those sites. The timetable for such work is within five years from transposition for at least 10 per cent of the sites, 15 years for at least 60 per cent of the sites and 25 years for the remaining sites.[96]

11. Where a site is to be sold on which a potentially polluting activity listed in Annex II is taking place, or for which the official records, such as national registers, show that it has taken place, Member States shall ensure that the owner of that site or the prospective buyer makes a soil status report available to the competent authority and to the other party in the transaction. The soil status report shall be issued by an authorised body or person appointed by the Member State and shall include at least the following details:

   (a) the background history of the site, as available from official records;

   (b) a chemical analysis determining the concentration levels of the dangerous substances in the soil, limited to those substances that are linked to the potentially polluting activity on the site; and

   (c) the concentration levels (to be determined under a methodology established by the Member State) at which there are sufficient reasons to believe that the dangerous substances concerned pose a significant risk to human health or to the environment.[97]

   The information contained in the soil status report shall be used by the competent authorities for the purposes of identifying contaminated sites.

[94] ELD Art.11.2.

[95] ELD Art.11.2. These activities include sites where dangerous substances are or were present falling within the Seveso Directive (see Ch.11), activities listed in the IPPC Directive (disregarding the thresholds in that Directive except for the activities carried out by micro-enterprises, as defined in point 3 of Art.2 in the Annex to Commission Recommendation 2003/361, and those relative to the rearing of livestock), airports, ports, former military sites, petrol and filling stations, dry cleaners, mining installations, landfills, waste water treatment installations, and pipelines for the transport of dangerous substances.

[96] ELD Art.11.3.

[97] ELD Art.12.

12. Member States shall ensure that the contaminated sites listed in their inventories are remediated. Remediation shall consist of actions on the soil aimed at the removal, control, containment or reduction of contaminants so that the contaminated site, taking account of its current use and approved future use, no longer poses any significant risk to human health or the environment.[98]

13. Member States shall set up appropriate mechanisms to fund the remediation of the contaminated sites for which, subject to the polluter pays principle, the person responsible for the pollution cannot be identified or cannot be held liable under Community or national legislation or may not be made to bear the costs of remediation.[99]

14. Member States shall, on the basis of the inventory and within seven years from transposition, draw up a National Remediation Strategy, including at least remediation targets, a prioritisation starting with those sites which pose a significant risk to human health, a timetable for implementation, and the funds allocated by the authorities responsible for budgetary decisions in the Member States in accordance with their national procedures. Where containment or natural recovery are applied, the evolution of the risk to human health or the environment shall be monitored. The National Remediation Strategy shall be applicable and be made public no later than eight years after transposition date and shall be reviewed at least every five years.[100]

15. The ELD would be amended. Whereas Art.6.3 of the ELD currently provides that if an operator cannot be identified or cannot be made liable for remedial measures, the competent authority may take the measures itself, as a matter of last resort. This will be amended to make it subject to the obligation in Art.13 of the Soil Protection Directive to ensured that contaminated sites listed on national inventories are remediated.[101]

Implications for UK practice

The final form of the Directive and how it will be implemented in the UK **13.51** are not clear at present. However, in principle Pt IIA could provide an appropriate means by which the obligations of the Directive could be fulfilled. The Environment Agency could be given the responsibility of compiling the national inventory, and the approach to evaluating sites in terms of risk would appear to be at least broadly compatible with that of Pt IIA. The main challenges seem likely to be in the strict timetable for investigating sites to measure concentration levels of dangerous substances and in the production of a transparent and prioritised strategy at national

[98] ELD Arts 13.1 and 13.2.
[99] ELD Art.13.3.
[100] ELD Art.14.
[101] ELD Art.23.

(as opposed to local authority) level for remediation of sites. The approach to remediation techniques and standards also seems compatible with that of Pt IIA. However, there will need to be clearer and more comprehensive mechanisms than exist at present for funding the remediation of orphan sites.[102]

13.52   The other main innovation is the requirement for a soil status report for the sale of sites on which a potentially polluting activity listed in Annex II is taking place, or which is shown by national registers or other official records to have taken place. This would be a potentially onerous exercise, since it would require an intrusive survey to determine the presence and concentrations of dangerous substances linked to the potentially polluting activity, together with an assessment of the concentration levels at which there are sufficient reasons to believe that the substances concerned pose a significant risk.[103] It would apply equally to sales of domestic properties as to commercial transactions. The scope of the requirement is critically dependent on the interpretation applied to Annex II activities. In some cases these are defined by reference to EC legislation, i.e. the Seveso, IPPC and Landfill Directives. However, the reference is to the descriptions of the activities concerned, not to whether they were actually regulated under those measures. Thus, to give an example, where there are records to show that a site was used as a gasworks (an activity falling within the IPPC Directive as coal gasification) or a landfill (defined by the Landfill Directive as a waste disposal site for the deposit of the waste onto or into land)[104] then it would appear that the requirement for a status report will apply, whether or not the sites were ever regulated pursuant to those measures, or whether they predated them. In any event a number of the other Annex II categories are very broad in nature, such as "former military sites", "petrol and filling stations" and "dry cleaners". The draft Directive refers, perhaps curiously, to evidence of the past activity solely by reference to "official records, such as national registers", but there are of course numerous other means, such as old maps, by which the use of the site for the former activity could be reliably established.

---

[102] See para.5.277ff See the DEFRA Consultation Paper on the Proposed Dirctive, July 2007.

[103] ELD Art.12.2.

[104] As to the breadth of that definition see *Blackland Park Exploration Limited v Environment Agency* [2003] EWCA Civ 1795; [2004] Env. L.R. 33.

SECTION 4
LIABILITY IN PRIVATE LAW

Chapter 14

COMMON LAW

PART 1: CIVIL LIABILITY GENERALLY

Any attempt to extract clear principles from the common law relating to **14.01** environmental problems is an exercise certain to lead to frustration.[1] The basic ingredients of the common law of tort are well known:

(a) nuisance;

(b) negligence;

(c) trespass; and

(d) the rule in *Rylands v Fletcher*.

To these may be added, in appropriate cases (which are discussed in the **14.02** next chapter) statutory causes of action, whether expressly provided by the statute or by way of action for breach of statutory duty. What is not always clear is how these various components interrelate and to what extent their requirements differ. Such confusion is reflected in the cases. Actions are usually brought relying on a number of different legal bases, pleaded in the alternative, and it may be unpredictable which issues will be fastened on by the court. In the Irish case of *Hanrahan v Merck Sharp & Dohme (Ireland) Ltd*[2] an action against a pharmaceutical plant in respect of allegedly harmful emissions was based on negligence, nuisance and *Rylands v Fletcher*; the Supreme Court concurred with the trial judge who treated the claim solely as one in nuisance.

In the case of *Cambridge Water Company v Eastern Counties Leather Plc*[3] a **14.03** claim for pollution of a supply borehole by chlorinated solvents from two tanneries was brought in negligence, nuisance and *Rylands v Fletcher*. The trial judge considered all three heads, devoting most attention to *Rylands v Fletcher* and ultimately dismissing the claim on all three grounds. The Court of Appeal focused instead on the nuisance aspect and held one of the two tanneries liable, making only brief (and obscure) reference to the main arguments put to them on the *Rylands v Fletcher* issue.[4] On appeal to the House of Lords, *Rylands v Fletcher* again became a dominant issue.[5]

[1] For a detailed treatment, see J. Lowry and R. Edmonds (eds), *Environmental Protection and the Common Law* (Oxford: Hart Publishing, 2000).
[2] [1988] I.L.R.M. 629.
[3] [1992] Env. L.R. 116.
[4] [1994] 2 W.L.R. 53; [1993] Env. L.R. 287.
[5] [1994] 2 A.C. 264.

14.04 It is beyond the scope of this chapter to provide a detailed summary of the various components of the law of tort, in respect of which reference should be made to the standard texts. However, the main strengths and weaknesses of each area in relation to typical contaminated land issues will be referred to, together with those areas where the law is still developing and remains inherently uncertain.

PART 2: TRESPASS

Direct or immediate damage: trespass

14.05 Trespass is of potential application to environmental actions, though in practice its use in contaminated land situations is likely to be limited. Such limitation stems from the historic roots of the tort: in its original form the tort was one for which the writ of trespass—"that fertile mother of actions"—would lie.[6] The writ was the remedy for all forcible and direct injuries, whether to persons or to property and in that sense was the antithesis of the action of trespass on the case (or simply "case") which dealt with injuries which were consequential as opposed to forcible and direct. The test was whether the injury followed so immediately upon the act of the defendant as to be a direct part of the act as opposed to a consequence of it. In the *Prior of Southwark's* case[7] the prior complained because the defendant, a glover, had made a lime pit for calf-skins so close to a stream as to pollute it (possibly one of the earliest reported cases on contaminated land). It was held that if the glover had dug the lime pit in the prior's soil the action ought to be in trespass; but if it was made in the glover's soil it should be an action on the case (now nuisance or negligence).

14.06 In practice this means that trespass will be of limited application to the typical contaminated land situation. As well as its more obvious manifestations, the tort includes the placing or projecting of any object or substance on to the plaintiff's land: this has been held in one Canadian case to include the accidental discharge of carbon monoxide gas from a vehicle exhaust into a dwelling.[8] Thus the placing of waste or some noxious substance on the claimant's land without their consent would be trespass,[9] as would placing it on the boundary so that it falls onto or comes into contact with the claimant's land.[10] In that respect trespass is not limited to incursions on the surface, and trespass may be committed to underlying strata.[11] Thus, for example, trespass might be committed where an occupier of land or contractor, in carrying out engineering works, breaches

---

[6] Salmond and Heuston, *The Law of Torts* (20th edn, 1992), p.5.

[7] (1498) YB 13 Hen. 7, f.26, pl.4; summarised by Denning L.J. in *Southport Corp v Esso Petroleum Co Ltd* [1954] 2 Q.B. 182 at 195.

[8] *McDonald v Associated Fuels* (1954) 3 D.L.R. 775.

[9] Salmond and Heuston, *The Law of Torts* (20th edn, 1992), p.48.

[10] *Simpson v Weber* (1925) 41 T.L.R. 302; *Westripp v Baldock* [1939] 1 All E.R. 279.

[11] *Corbett v Hill* (1870) L.R. 9 Eq. 671, 673.

some form of containment which results in the immediate ingress of contaminated material on to the plaintiff's land. The discharge of water, whether contaminated or not, onto another's land will be a trespass.[12] There must be some voluntary, i.e. intentional or negligent, act on the part of the defendant.[13]

More typically however, pollutants will leach or migrate over a period of **14.07** months or years as the result of gravity, groundwater flow, or gas generation. Such incursions will be consequential rather than direct, and so arguably trespass will not be an appropriate remedy.[14] As was said in the Irish case of *Hanrahan v Merck, Sharp & Dohme (Ireland) Ltd*[15]:

> "the claim based on trespass has not been proceeded with, presumably because it could not readily be said that any of the loss or damage complied of was a direct or immediate result of the acts complained of. The loss or damage could more properly be said to be an consequential on the conduct complained of."

The discharge of oil into a navigable river is not a trespass, but rather a **14.08** matter for an action by nuisance by riparian owners.[16] However, there is at least one decision which suggests that matter deposited on the plaintiff's land by the back washes and undercurrents of a tidal river constitutes a trespass.[17]

A further restriction is that trespass will be actionable only by the person **14.09** in possession of the land, e.g. entitled to immediate and exclusive possession. However, if the difficulties of direct injury and title to sue can be surmounted, trespass is a powerful remedy since it is actionable irrespective of fault and without proof of actual damage.[18] Where damage is caused, the measure of damages will be the resulting loss to the plaintiff: whether this is the diminution in value of the land or the cost of reinstatement will depend on the circumstances.[19]

---

[12] *Menzies v Earl Breadalbane* (1828) 3 Bli NS 414 (HL); *Brine v Great Western Railway* (1862) 2 B&S 402; *Whalley v Lancashire & Yorkshire Railway* (1884) 13 Q.B.D. 131, CA.

[13] *League Against Cruel Sports v Scott* [1986] 1 Q.B. 240.

[14] *Tenant v Goldwin* (1704) 2 Ld. Ray. 1089; *Price's Patent Candle Co v LCC* [1908] 2 Ch. 526. The availability of trespass as a remedy has also been doubled where oil is discharged in navigable waters and is carried by the flow: see *Southport Corp v Esso Petroleum Co* [1954] 2 Q.B. 182 at 195; [1956] A.C. 218 at 242 and 244; but *cf.* the same case at [1953] 3 W.L.R. 773 at 776 and [1954] 2 Q.B. 182 at 204.

[15] [1988] I.L.R.M. 629 at 632.

[16] *British Waterways Board v Severn Trent Water Ltd* [2002] Ch.25, CA.

[17] *Jones v Llanrwst Urban DC* [1911] 1 Ch.393. It appears from the report at (1911) 27 T.L.R. 133 that the deposit was not made directly on to the plaintiff's land; however the case might equally well have been decided on nuisance or *Rylands v Fletcher*.

[18] The distinction will of course be academic if actual damage has occurred: *Home Brewery Plc v William Davis & Co (Loughborough) Ltd* [1987] 1 All E.R. 637.

[19] The cost of reinstatement may, for example, exceed the diminution in value of the land—not an unlikely circumstance in some contamination cases: see *Nalder v Ilford Corp* [1951] 1 K.B. 822, 830.

PART 3: RYLANDS V FLETCHER

Rylands v Fletcher: liability for escapes

14.10 The classic formulation of the *Rylands v Fletcher* doctrine is stated by Blackburn J. in the judgment of the Exchequer Chamber in that case[20]:

> "We think that the true rule of law is, that the person who for his own purposes brings onto his lands and collects and keeps there anything likely to do mischief if it escapes, must keep it in at his peril, and, if he does not do so, is prima facie answerable for all the damage which is the natural consequence of its escape . . . it seems but reasonable and just that the neighbour, who has brought something on his own property which was not naturally there, harmless to others so long as it is confined to his own property, but which he knows to be mischievous if it gets onto his neighbour's, should be obliged to make good the damage which ensues if he does not succeed in confining it to his own property. But for his act in bringing it there no mischief could have accrued, and it seems but just that he should at his peril keep it there so that no mischief may accrue, or answer for the natural and anticipated consequences. And upon authority, this we think is established to be the law whether the things so brought be beasts, or water, or filth, or stenches."

14.11 Thus the essential requirements for liability under the tort may be seen to be as follows:

(a) the defendant must bring, collect and keep something on his land for his own purposes;

(b) the thing must be not naturally there;

(c) the thing must be known to be likely to do harm if it escapes;

(d) the thing must escape; and then

(e) the defendant is liable for the natural and anticipated consequences of the escape. The House of Lords decision in *Cambridge Water Co v Eastern Counties Leather Plc* established that foreseeability of damage of the relevant type is a prerequisite for recovery.[21]

14.12 These various requirements are considered below. The rule in *Rylands v Fletcher* has many attractions for the plaintiff. It is a rule of strict liability with no requirement to show fault on the part of the defendant and no

---

[20] *Rylands v Fletcher* (1866) 1 Exch. 265 at 280: approved by Lord Cairns at (1868) 3 App. Cas. 330, 339.
[21] [1994] 2 A.C. 264.

defence of due diligence or the equivalent. It may apply to cases where the damage complained of is not sufficiently repeated or continuous as to constitute a nuisance.[22] It is however a branch or special form of the tort of nuisance and therefore a tort against land, so that damages for personal injury are not recoverable.[23]

There have proved to be many difficulties in applying the rule to modern **14.13** industrial society, and until the House of Lords decision in *Cambridge Water Co v Eastern Counties Leather Plc* one of the main difficulties lay in the requirement that the use of land in question be "non-natural". It remains to be seen whether, after that decision, the rule will prove to be powerful tool in the context of environmental liability under modern law.[24] It has not in general proved to be a viable independent cause of action in most cases in recent years.

Rylands v Fletcher: bringing and accumulation on land

In some contaminated land cases this aspect of the rule may present no **14.14** difficulty whatever: quite clearly a manufacturing company which pur-chases and stores solvent on its land is doing so for its own purposes; as is a waste management company which receives waste for deposit in one of its landfill sites. However, in some cases the potentially harmful material is not actually brought onto the land by the defendant but is in fact generated there—examples would be waste generated and stored within a chemical plant or methane gas generated by the decomposition of waste within a landfill site. It should make no difference to the issue of liability whether the defendant acquired the harmful material or generated it himself on site; indeed the formulation of the rule by Blackburn J. with its reference to "fumes and vapours" and "stenches" is clearly confirmatory of that position. Certainly the rule has been held in a Canadian case to apply to methane gas escaping from a municipal landfill site.[25]

However, this aspect of the rule will probably present difficulties in the **14.15** case of subsequent owners or occupiers of land, who cannot be said to have accumulated on land noxious materials which were already in place when they acquired the property; nor could contaminants which have already been spilled or dispersed into soil by a previous occupier be said to be held for their own purposes. Any remedy in such circumstances would appear to lie in the tort of nuisance or possibly negligence.

Rylands v Fletcher: things "not naturally there"

The original statement in the formulation of the *Rylands v Fletcher* doctrine **14.16** that it applies to things not naturally on the defendant's land has subsequently become equated to the issue of whether the defendant's use

---

[22] *Hanrahan v Merck, Sharp & Dohme (Ireland) Ltd* [1988] I.L.R.M. 629 at 633; see also *McKenna v British Alcan Aluminium Ltd* [2002] Env. L.R. 30.
[23] See *Cambridge Water Co v Eastern Counties Leather Plc* [1994] 2 A.C. 264; *Transco Plc v Stockport MBC* [2003] UKHL 61; [2004] 2 A.C. 1, para.35 per Lord Hoffmann.
[24] See further, para.14.30.
[25] *Gertsen v Municipality of Metropolitan Toronto* (1973) 41 D.L.R. (3d) 646.

of land was natural or non-natural[26] and as such the requirement has proved to be one of the most important and controversial limitations on the rule.[27]

14.17   Thus whether a use of land—be it the storage and use of solvents, the deposit of waste, or general manufacturing—is categorised as natural or non-natural will be decisive as to liability under *Rylands v Fletcher*. In *Gertsen v Municipality of Metropolitan Toronto*[28] the Ontario High Court held decisively that the filling of a small ravine in a highly populated area with putrescible refuse was a non-natural use; the court had regard to the unsuitable geology and geography, the known problems of gas-generation and that the primary purpose of filling the ravine was "selfish and self-seeking" rather than for the benefit of the immediate local community.

14.18   Similar arguments have fared much less well in the English courts. In *British Celanese Ltd v AH Hunt (Capacitors) Ltd*[29] the manufacture of electrical and electronic components in 1964 on an industrial trading estate was held not to be a non-natural use:

> ". . . nor can the bringing and storage on the premises of metal foil be a special use in itself. The way the metal foil was stored may have been a negligent one; but the use of the premises for storing such foil did not, by itself, create special risks. The metal foil was there for use in the manufacture of goods of a common type which at all material times were needed for the general benefit of the community."[30]

14.19   Of even more relevance to typical contaminated land issues is the decision in *Cambridge Water Co v Eastern Counties Leather Plc*. There Ian Kennedy J. at first instance[31] had to consider whether the storage of organochlorine solvents in drums at a tannery in a village with various current and historical industrial uses was natural or non-natural. The brief passage from his judgment dealing with this decisive issue refers to two elements:

(a) whether the storage created risks for adjacent occupiers; and

(b) whether the activity was for the general benefit of the community.

He regarded the magnitude of the storage and its geographical location as inevitable considerations and referred to the creation of employment as being clearly for the benefit of the local community.

14.20   On that basis the storage was held to be a natural use of the land[32]:

---

[26] (1868) 3 App. Cas. 330 at 339; *Rickards v Lothian* [1913] A.C. 263; *Read v Lyons & Co Ltd* [1947] A.C. 156.

[27] *Newark, Non-Natural user and Rylands v Fletcher* (1961) 24 M.L.R. 557.

[28] (1973) 41 D.L.R. (3d) 646 at 666. See also *Chu v District of North Vancouver* (1982) 139 D.L.R. (3rd) 201 (fill material used to extend garden at edge of ravine; material slumped after heavy rain, demolishing homes below it; held to be a non-natural use).

[29] [1969] 1 W.L.R. 959.

[30] [1969] 1 W.L.R. 959, 963 (Lawton J.).

[31] [1992] Env. L.R. 116.

[32] [1992] Env. L.R. 116 at 139.

"In reaching this decision I reflect on the innumerable small works that one sees up and down the country with drums stored in their yards . . . Inevitably that storage presents some hazard, but in a manufacturing and outside a primitive and pastoral society such hazards are part of the life of every citizen."

However, the House of Lords[33] took a somewhat different approach to **14.21** the question of natural use, having already decided that the rule in *Rylands v Fletcher* was confined by the requirement of foreseeability of harm.[34] Lord Goff referred to the way in which the principle had become more complex since the simple notion of "natural use" was first introduced. He took at his starting point the formulation of Lord Moulton in *Rickards v Lothian*[35]:

"It is not every use to which land is put that brings into play that principle. It must be some special use bringing with it increased danger to others, and must not merely be the ordinary use of the land or such a use as is proper for the general benefit of the community."

In particular, Lord Goff felt that if the closing words "such a use as is **14.22** proper for the general benefit of the community" were interpreted widely, it was difficult to see how the exception could be kept within reasonable bounds. Lord Goff did not feel able to accept that the creation of employment as such, even in a small industrial complex, was sufficient to constitute a use as being a natural use; nor could the mere fact that solvents were commonly used in the tanning industry have that effect. He therefore held that the storage of substantial quantities of chemicals on industrial premises should be regarded as almost a classic case of non-natural use and found it difficult to see how the imposition of strict liability for their escape could be thought to be objectionable: this is potentially an extremely important finding in terms of future development of the rule. Lord Goff expressed the view that, following recognition that foreseeability of harm of the relevant type is a pre-requisite of liability under the rule, the courts might feel less pressured to extend the scope of the concept of natural use, which he saw as a principle akin to that of reasonable user in the tort of nuisance, serving the same function of limiting the ambit of these strict liability torts.[36]

In *Transco Plc v Stockport MBC*[37] Lord Bingham of Cornhill regarded **14.23** ordinary user as a preferable test to natural user or reasonable user, to make it clear that the rule is engaged only when the user is shown to be extraordinary and unusual at the time and in the location in question; a user may be quite out of the ordinary but not unreasonable, as in *Cambridge Water*.[38]

[33] The issue did not arise in the judgment of the Court of Appeal.
[34] [1994] 2 A.C. 264.
[35] [1913] A.C. 263, 280.
[36] [1994] 2 A.C. 264, 299–300. For further discussion, see G. Cross, "Does Only the Careless Polluter Pay?" (1995) 111 L.Q.R. 445.
[37] [2003] UKHL 61; [2004] 2 A.C. 1 (see para.14.29).
[38] para.11. See also *LMS International Ltd v Styrene Packaging and Insulation Ltd* [2005] EWHC 2065 (TCC) (hot wire cutting of flammable polystyrene material held to be non-natural use).

Rylands v Fletcher: harmful propensities

14.24 The *Rylands v Fletcher* doctrine applies only to things likely to do mischief if they escape.[39] What is relevant here has been said to be not the knowledge of the defendant or any other particular witness, but "the common experience of mankind in general"[40]: it must be doubtful, however, whether this can apply to complex chemicals, whose harmful properties may be a subject for the expert. In the *Cambridge Water* case[41] at first instance it was held that the onus lies with the defendant to establish the harmless nature of the substances in question, and also that what is to be considered is the consequences of an escape of the entire quantity of the substance rather than the amount which actually did escape.[42]

14.25   It is possible to see how difficulties may arise in future with this aspect of the rule. Arguments may be raised as to how far the surrounding of the site are relevant: for example, methane gas generated from a landfill site in open countryside will vent into the atmosphere—but once a housing estate is constructed nearby the considerations are entirely different. In *Transco Plc v Stockport MBC*[43] the House of Lords were of the view that bearing in mind the historical origin of the rule and also that its effect is to impose liability in the absence of negligence for an isolated occurrence, the mischief or danger test should not be easily satisfied[44]:

> "It must be shown that the defendant has done something which he recognised, or judged by the standards appropriate at the relevant place and time, he ought reasonably to have recognised, as giving rise to an exceptionally high risk of danger or mischief if there should be an escape, however unlikely an escape may have been thought to be."

Rylands v Fletcher: escape

14.26 There must be an escape from the defendant's land in order to establish liability under *Rylands v Fletcher*.[45] More precisely, there must be an escape "from a place where the defendant has occupation or control over land to a place which is outside his occupation or control".[46] What is relevant is control or occupation as opposed to legal title.[47] Therefore where harmful

---

[39] For example, it has been applied to sewage (*Smeaton v Ilford Corp* [1954] Ch.450); oily smuts containing sulphate (*Halsey v Esso Petroleum Co Ltd* [1961] 1 W.L.R. 683, 692 and 701); and colliery spoil tipped on a hillside which slipped, causing damage (*Att-Gen v Cory Bros* [1921] 1 A.C. 521).

[40] *West v Bristol Tramways Co* [1907] 2 K.B. 14, at 21.

[41] [1992] Env. L.R. 116.

[42] [1992] Env. L.R. 116 at 133.

[43] [2003] UKHL 61; [2004] 2 A.C. 1 (see para 14.32).

[44] para.10. See also Lord Hoffmann at para.46, suggesting that a useful guide is to ask whether the damage which eventuated was something against which the claimant could have reasonably been expected to insure himself.

[45] (See para.14.32 below).

[46] *Read v J. Lyons & Co Ltd* [1947] A.C. 156. Re-affirmed by the House of Lords in *Transco Plc Stockport MBC* [2003] UKHL 61; [2004] 2 A.C. 1 at 168.

[47] *Benning v Wong* (1969) 122 C.L.R. 249 at 294.

consequences such as a methane gas explosion occur within the defendant's own land the rule will have no application. It appears that the thing which escapes need not be the thing which was accumulated so as to give rise to application of the rule: for example, if explosives accidentally cause rocks to be thrown from the land the rule will apply to damage caused by the rocks.[48] This will be important where, for example, refuse on land generates gas which escapes. It appears that the "escape" need not be accidental. In *Crown River Cruises Ltd v Kimbolton Fireworks Ltd*[49] the rule was applied to hot debris falling from a firework display which seriously damaged the claimant's vessels.

Where contaminated land is resulting in a continuing escape of contaminating substances, following the *Cambridge Water* case,[50] it may be argued that there is no liability where the contaminants in question have passed out of the control of the defendant by becoming "irretrievably lost" in the ground. This difficult issue is considered below.[51] **14.27**

Rylands v Fletcher: liability for natural and anticipated consequences and the relevance of foreseeability

It was not clear until the House of Lords decision in *Cambridge Water Co v Eastern Counties Leather Plc*[52] how far concepts of remoteness of damage based upon foreseeability were applicable to the strict liability principles of *Rylands v Fletcher*. The House of Lords in that case held that, given the historical connection between the rule in *Rylands v Fletcher* and the tort of nuisance, it would be logical to extend the rules on foreseeability which apply to nuisance to *Rylands v Fletcher*. Thus not only must the thing which escapes be of such a nature as to be likely to cause harm if it does escape, but also the kind of harm which occurs must be reasonably foreseeable if damages are to be awarded; otherwise the damage will be too remote.[53] The introduction of foreseeability in this sense does not affect the strict nature of liability under the rule; fault remains irrelevant. **14.28**

Relationship to statutory regulation

In *Transco Plc v Stockport MBC*[54] Lord Hoffmann referred to the issue of statutory authority as a restriction on the rule, in the principle that it is excluded in respect of works constructed or conducted under statutory authority.[55] Lord Hoffmann later stated that the rule will not apply to works or activities authorised by statute and hence "will usually have no **14.29**

---

[48] *Miles v Forest Rock Granite Co* (1918) 34 T.L.R. 500.
[49] [1996] 2 Lloyds' Rep. 533.
[50] [1994] 2 A.C. 264.
[51] See para.14.62ff.
[52] [1994] 2 A.C. 264.
[53] See *Hamilton v Papakura DC* [2002] UKPC 9 (damage to tomatoes from hormone herbicides present in water supply not reasonably foreseeable).
[54] [2003] UKHL 61; [2004] 2 A.C. 1.
[55] paras 30–31, citing *Green v Chelsea Waterworks Co* (1894) 70 L.T. 547; *Dunne v North Western Gas Board* [1964] 2 Q.B. 806.

application to really high risk activities".[56] Certainly the rule will not apply to activities which the statute expressly authorises, according to the authorities. However, it is of course not the case that modern high risk activities will normally be the subject of statutory authority in the sense of a statute authorising the construction and operation of the facility[57]—most such activities are now carried on under statutory regulatory regimes such as PPC, COMAH, etc. That the activity is regulated under statute should not, it is submitted, disapply the rule: the fact that Parliament has subjected the hazardous activity to regulation does not imply that the person affected by that activity should suffer a private loss for the public benefit.[58] However, it is arguable that where the statute regulating the activity provides for liability, then that amounts to "an exhaustive code of liability for a particular form of escape" which excludes the rule.[59]

Rylands v Fletcher: the future

14.30 As a principle of liability, *Rylands v Fletcher* has been both diminished and enhanced by the decision in *Cambridge Water Co v Eastern Counties Leather Plc*.[60] It has been diminished in the sense that it was regarded as essentially an application of the principles of nuisance to isolated escapes and accordingly subject to the same requirement that the kind of harm which occurred was reasonably foreseeable. On the other hand, the element of uncertainty which hung over the rule following some obscure remarks by the Court of Appeal which might have confined it to passive escapes[61] has been removed. Also, the courts are less likely in future to come to strained conclusions as to what constitutes a natural use of land. The rule therefore seems set to continue to fulfil a useful role in environmental cases; indeed the Lords' decision overall may well have enhanced that role.

14.31 However, the decision also places a brake on any attempts to develop *Rylands v Fletcher* into a "general rule of strict liability for damage caused by ultra-hazardous operations", as in the USA.[62] The decision in *Read v J. Lyons & Co Ltd*[63] was regarded as having foreclosed that particular development. Additionally, the House of Lords expressed the view that the imposition of strict liability in relation to operations of high risk was a matter for Parliament, rather than the courts, since statute could lay down more precisely than the common law the precise scope and criteria of such liability. The rapid development of international, EC and domestic law on the subject of environmental protection was seen as another reason why

---

[56] para.39.
[57] See, e.g. *Allen v Gulf Oil Refining Ltd* [1981] A.C. 1001, 1011 per Lord Wilberforce.
[58] Put a different way, there is no presumption, as there would be for an activity expressly authorised by statute, that it cannot be characterised as an unreasonable use of land with which those affected by side effects must put up provided it is carried on with due care: see para.89 per Lord Scott of Foscote.
[59] para.45, referring to s.209 of the Water Industry Act 1991, s.73(6) of the Environmental Protection Act 1990 and s.7 of the Nuclear Installations Act 1965 by way of examples.
[60] [1994] 2 AC 264.
[61] [1993] Env. L.R. 287, 296.
[62] Restatement of Torts (2nd edn, Vol.3, 1977), para.519.
[63] [1947] A.C. 156.

the courts should be reluctant to venture into the area, though it may be noted that the EC has not pursued initiatives on strict private law liability for environmental harm which were being mooted during the early 1990s, nor has the Lugano Convention of the Council of Europe on that subject come into effect.[64]

In *Transco Plc v Stockport MBC*[65] the House of Lords considered the rule in **14.32** the context of leakage of a large quantity of water from a pipe serving a block of flats owned by the Borough Council, which caused the collapse of a nearby disused embankment (also owned by the Council), which in turn exposed a high pressure gas main requiring work to prevent it fracturing, and also caused serious damage to the premises of a golf club. The House of Lords undertook an extensive review of the rule's scope and application in modern conditions. Whilst recognising that few if any claimants have in recent years succeeded in reliance on the rule in *Rylands v Fletcher* alone, the House of Lords declined to discard the rule or treat it as subsumed by negligence. There remained a category of cases, even if it was small, in which it would be just to impose liability regardless of fault. *Cambridge Water* was regarded as one such case. Equally however, as in *Cambridge Water*, it was not regarded as appropriate to apply the rule widely, so as to extend the scope of strict liability. The way forward was felt to be to retain the rule, but to insist on its essential nature and purpose, and to restate it so as to achieve as much clarity as possible.[66] In that respect the rule was seen as a sub-species of nuisance, so that there must be interference between neighbouring land-holdings, i.e. an escape from land in one occupation to another. In other respects such as what constitutes non-natural user, it was also to be narrowly confined.

Rylands v Fletcher: Scotland

Ryland v Fletcher is not part of Scots law and the suggestion that it may be **14.33** "is a heresy which ought to be extirpated".[67] Thus fault or negligence (culpa) will need to be proven in an action for damages, though not where interdict is the remedy sought.[68] Nonetheless, it has been suggested that there may be little difference between the rule of strict liability and an approach based in culpa (which may take many forms) where the facts raise a presumption of negligence so compelling as to be practically incapable of being displaced.[69] Thus Scots law by a different route can arrive at a situation bearing a strong resemblance to strict liability for hazardous activities: the escape of a dangerous substance or thing, or the creation of some other danger that would not have been there but for the

---

[64] See paras 13.05–13.07.
[65] [2003] UKHL 61; [2004] 2 A.C. 1; [2004] Env. L.R. 24. See also *Arscott v Coal Authority* [2005] Env. L.R. 6.
[66] See para.8, per Lord Bingham of Cornhill. See also paras 43–44 per Lord Hoffmann, para.52 per Lord Hobhouse of Woodborough.
[67] *RHM Bakeries (Scotland) Ltd v Strathclyde RC* 1985 S.L.T. 214 at 217 per Lord Fraser.
[68] *Logan v Wang (UK) Ltd* 1991 S.L.T. 580 (Outer House) is authority that it is not necessary to plead fault or negligence for an award of interdict.
[69] *McLaughlan v Craig* 1948 S.C. 599.

act of the defender, will give rise to a strong presumption of fault or negligence.[70] Liability in these circumstances lies for the original act of placing on his land materials of a dangerous nature in respect of which no reasonable precautions could avoid injury.[71]

PART 4: NUISANCE

Nuisance generally

14.34 Nuisance is the traditional environmental tort and as such might be expected to play a large role in relation to problems emanating from contaminated land. However, the very breadth and flexibility of the tort give rise to a number of uncertainties. Its essence lies in some activity or condition which unduly interferes with the beneficial occupation, use or enjoyment of land.[72] The fact that it can apply both to activities and to conditions is crucial to an understanding of its application. The operation of a landfill site may constitute a nuisance, but, equally, so can the condition of that site once completed. It must also be appreciated that the interference which constitutes the tort of nuisance can take a multiplicity of forms, amongst them:

(i) physical harm, such as damage to crops from percolating gas, or migrating chemicals which have an aggressive effect on foundations or service conduits;

(ii) interference with the enjoyment of land, for example restrictions on growing crops or on allowing children to play in contaminated soil;

(iii) interference with an easement or other interest in land, or with a natural right such as the abstraction of water.

14.35 Finally, nuisance may be concerned with some on-going activity where the primary objective of the plaintiff is to secure an injunction to restrain its continuance; equally, however, it can take the form of a concluded interference in which case the action is for damages. The two situations may raise very different considerations in regard to the issue of fore-

---

[70] *Kerr v Earl of Orkney* (1857) 20 D. 298. The principle is in many senses akin to *Rylands v Fletcher* in that it applies where the defendant voluntarily brings onto or creates on his land some *novum opus*, creating a danger not naturally there. The distinction is that there must be a finding of fault, though that finding is lightly inferred from an especially heavy duty of care in the absence of any exculpating explanation from the defendant: "... A dam that gives way in a night's rain is not such as the maker was bound to erect. The fact that it gives way is a proof that his obligation was not fulfilled, and that the protection was not afforded which he was bound to provide" (1857) 20 D. 298 at 302. See also *Tennent v Earl of Glasgow* (1864) 2 M. (HL) 22, 26; *Caledonian Railway v Greenock Corp* 1917 SC (HL) 56, 60, 63, 65; *Campbell v Kennedy* (1864) 3 M 121.

[71] *Chalmers v Dixon* (1876) 3R 461 at 464.

[72] *Hunter v Canary Wharf Ltd* [1997] A.C. 655.

seeability and both situations may be relevant in the case of contaminated land.

Nuisance: who can sue?

The House of Lords held in *Hunter v Canary Wharf Ltd and London Docklands* **14.36** *Development Corp*[73] that it is necessary to have a proprietary interest in land in order to bring an action in nuisance. The Court of Appeal had held that whilst a substantial link between the person enjoying the use of property and the land on which he or she was enjoying it was necessary, the occupation of property as a home would be sufficient in this regard, given the general trend in the law to give additional protection to occupiers. The House of Lords rejected this approach as inconsistent with the basis of nuisance as a tort protecting rights in property, rather than effects on individuals. Accordingly an action in nuisance will normally only lie with the person who has the right to exclusive possession. A mere licensee does not have standing.[74] In the case of interference with other proprietary rights in land (e.g. riparian rights) the claimant will be the person entitled to the rights.[75] Where injury to land has been inflicted over successive ownerships, it will be possible to recover in respect of damage caused before the plaintiff became owner, provided that it is a loss which he as current owner has suffered.[76]

Nature of nuisance: location

Where nuisance involves injury to property or interference with an **14.37** easement the locality of the activity is not relevant.[77] Where interference with physical comfort is involved, locality will be relevant and whether the interference constitutes a nuisance is an issue of degree.[78] In many cases the ingress of contaminants into the plaintiff's land will constitute physical injury rather than interference with comfort. However it is possible to envisage cases where the effect is manifested principally in non-physical damage, such as a diminution in the value of property: whether this falls within the category of "material injury to property" may be regarded as open to serious doubts.

Nuisance: liability of originator

The person who created a nuisance will be liable for it, irrespective of **14.38** whether he is the occupier of land. In certain circumstances, there can be liability for nuisances created by an independent contractor: in particular

---

[73] [1997] A.C. 655.
[74] *Khorasandjian v Bush* [1993] Q.B. 727 was overruled in that respect.
[75] *Tate & Lyle Industries Ltd v Greater London Council* [1983] 2 A.C. 509.
[76] *Masters v Brent LBC* [1978] Q.B. 841.
[77] *St Helen's Smelting Co v Tipping* (1865) 11 H.L.C. 642; *Halsey v Esso Petroleum Co Ltd* [1961] 2 All E.R. 145; *Horton's Estate Ltd v James Beattie Ltd* [1927] 1 Ch. 75.
[78] See JE Penner, "Nuisance and the Character of the Neighbourhood" (1995) 5 J.E.L. 1.

where it is reasonably foreseeable that the works to be carried out are likely to result in a nuisance unless preventive means are employed.[79] Thus the waste contractor who operates and fills a landfill site will be liable if that site results in a nuisance; and will continue to be liable irrespective of whether or not he ever held any right or interest in the site.[80] Similarly where a company, delivering oil, spills the cargo onto land in the course of unloading it, the company will be responsible for any ensuing nuisance. Whether a contractor who negligently installs a pipe which some time later fails, causing contamination, is liable for the nuisance is rather more debatable.

Nuisance: liability of owner or occupier

14.39 As explained above, nuisance may arise from either an activity or from a condition. Contaminated land, by its state and condition, may constitute a nuisance. This leads to the disturbing conclusion that liability may attach to an owner or occupier of land for contamination which they did not create, either because a third party created it during their ownership, or because it already existed when they acquired the land.

14.40   There are cases which indicate that an owner of land may be liable for a nuisance created by a predecessor in title, provided that he knew, or ought to have known of its existence by the exercise of reasonable diligence[81]: failure to make proper investigations means that it was his fault "to contract for an interest in land in which there was a nuisance".[82] Knowledge for this purpose includes not only actual knowledge of the nuisance, but also cases where ignorance is due to failure to use reasonable care to ascertain the relevant facts.[83] What constitutes reasonable investigation in relation to possible contamination of land has undoubtedly changed over the years and will continue to do so. Whilst the position is not entirely clear, it seems likely that liability in such circumstances will only arise where the defendant not only was aware of the nuisance but was in a position to take steps to prevent it.[84]

14.41   The other main line of cases of relevance in this area deals with nuisances naturally occurring on land or resulting from the act of a trespasser. The position here is that the occupier will be liable if knowing of the nuisance (or where he should have known of it by the exercise of reasonable diligence) he fails to take prompt and effective steps to prevent it.[85] The authorities were reviewed at length in the decision of the Court of Appeal in *Leakey v National Trust*[86] where in relation to a naturally-occurring nuisance it was held that failure to abate the nuisance may result in liability: however, the duty is limited in scope to doing what is reasonable

[79] *Bower v Peate* (1876) 1 QBD 321.
[80] *Gertsen v Metropolitan Municipality of Toronto* (1973) 41 D.L.R. (3rd) 647, pp. 669–671.
[81] *Broder v Saillard* (1876) 3 Ch.D. 692; *Wilkins v Leighton* [1932] 2 Ch.106.
[82] *Rosewell v Prior* (1701) 12 Mod. 635.
[83] *Brew Bros Ltd v Snax (Ross) Ltd* [1970] 1 Q.B. 612 at p.636 per Sachs L.J.
[84] *Smeaton v Ilford Corp* [1954] Ch.450 at 462.
[85] *Sedleigh-Denfield v O'Callaghan* [1940] A.C. 880; *Goldman v Hargrave* [1967] 1 A.C. 645.
[86] [1980] Q.B. 485. See also *Holbeck Hall Hotel Ltd v Scarborough BC* [2000] Q.B. 836 (CA).

in all the circumstances to prevent or minimise the known risk of damage or injury. This will involve consideration of the likely extent of the damage, the practicability of action and its difficulty and cost, the resources of the defendant and the plaintiff's resources and ability to protect himself from damage.

What is not clear, but is of great importance, is to what extent these **14.42** limiting factors, which apply in the case of naturally-occurring nuisances, would also apply where a nuisance has arisen artificially by the activities of a predecessor in title either by deliberate action in depositing waste on land or by negligence or accident in spilling materials on land. Both natural and artificial nuisances may be capable of discovery by the exericse of diligence and there would seem to be little basis in policy or logic for distinguishing between them: neither results directly from the fault of the defendant. In *Cambridge Water Co v Eastern Counties Leather Plc*[87] the House of Lords clearly thought that the principles of *Leakey v National Trust* and similar cases might apply to land contaminated by previous spillages of chemical solvents; however the point remains to be fully tested. The position is further complicated by remarks of the House of Lords concerning the situation where contaminating substances have become "irretrievably lost"; these remarks are considered below.[88]

Nuisance: disposal of property

The originator of a nuisance cannot escape his liability by disposing of **14.43** property: he will remain liable even though he can no longer take steps to abate the nuisance.[89] The position is different where the owner of property who did not create the nuisance sells it; here, though there is little authority, he will on principle cease to be liable. In many cases the contamination, or at least the potential for contamination, will have been identified in the course of the transaction. The position may be different if the vendor has undertaken a continuing contractual responsibility to take remedial action.

Where property is disposed of by way of granting a lease, the position **14.44** becomes more complex. If the owner knew, or ought to have known, of the nuisance before letting he will remain liable irrespective of whether the tenant has covenanted to repair.[90] If the nuisance arises after the tenancy commenced, the landlord may still be liable if he has either the duty to repair the property (by covenant) or a power to do so (by right of entry). It has been said that where the nuisance arises after the lease was granted, the test of an owner's duty to his neighbour depends on "the degree of control exercised by the owner in law or in fact for the purpose of repairs".[91] The cases establishing these propositions in general relate to

---

[87] [1994] 2 A.C. 264.

[88] See para.14.62.

[89] *Thompson v Gibson* (1841) 7 M. & W. 456; *Rosewell v Prior* (1701) 12 Mod. 635.

[90] *Brew Bros Ltd v Snax (Ross) Ltd* [1970] 1 Q.B. 612; *Sampson v Hodson-Pressinger* [1981] 3 All E.R. 710.

[91] See *Brew Bros Ltd v Snax (Ross) Ltd* [1970] 1 Q.B. 612 at 638 per Sachs L.J. citing *Mint v Good* [1951] 1 K.B. 517 at 528. Compare, however, the suggestion by Phillimore L.J. at 644 that a lease with a full repairing covenant to a responsible tenant must represent "reasonable care" by the landlord.

the physical condition of the buildings or other structures on the demised premises and it may be open to argue that contaminated soil raises different issues. In any event, the position between the landlord and tenant will be governed by the terms of the lease and the landlord may well have a right of redress against the tenant. The fact that the landlord may be liable for nuisance under these principles will in no way relieve the tenant from liability, either as the originator of the nuisance or as the occupier of premises: nor will the fact that under the lease the landlord may have covenanted to repair relieve the tenant.[92]

Possible defences

14.45 The following arguments may be raised (though not necessarily successfully) by way of defence to a nuisance action.

1. Exercise of care and skill or "reasonable user"

14.46 Since nuisance focuses on the effect on the plaintiff rather than the conduct of the defendant, negligence will not usually be an issue: liability is in this sense strict.[93] Whether the nuisance was inevitable notwithstanding the exercise of all due care and skill may, however, be an issue in the defence of statutory authority.[94] In *Cambridge Water*, Lord Goff referred to the way in which strict liability for nuisance had been "kept under control", namely by the principle of reasonable user: if the user is reasonable the defendant will not be liable for harm to his neighbour's enjoyment of his land; but if the user is not reasonable he will be liable, even though he exercised reasonable skill and care to avoid the harm.[95] What is clear is that "reasonable user" is not equated to the degree of care and skill exercised in the use of land, but rather to the whole complex of factors in the sense of locality, degree and duration of interference, etc.[96] What is a reasonable user is judged not according to the user's point of view, but according to the governing principle of good neighbourliness.[97] The fact that the defendant conducted their activities by modern methods and in accordance with good practice and applicable regulatory regimes will not be a defence.[98]

2. Public benefit

14.47 It may be argued that the activity in question is in the public interest, though it may be difficult to see how this could readily be applied to an activity which causes harmful contamination of nearby property. The

---

[92] *Wilchick v Marks and Silverstone* [1934] 2 K.B. 56; *St Anne's Well Brewery Co v Roberts* (1929) 140 L.T. 1.

[93] *Cambridge Water Company v Eastern Counties Leather Plc* [1994] A.C. 264.

[94] *Vaughan v Taff Vale Railway Co* (1880) 5 H. & N. 679; *Manchester Corporation v Farnworth* [1930] A.C. 171.

[95] [1994] 2 A.C. 264, 299–300.

[96] See *Blackburn v ARC Ltd* [1998] Env. L.R. 469, Q.B., 526–7 (use of land as a rubbish tip creating smells and gas not a reasonable use).

[97] *Southwark LBC v Tanner* [2001] A.C. 1, HL.

[98] See *Bamford v Turnley* (1860) 3 B&S 62.

correct approach is not to say that the public interest in the continuance of the activity means that there is no nuisance, but rather by having regard to the public interest in terms of remedies, so that the activity is allowed to continue, but with damages being paid to individuals affected.[99]

3. Act of trespasser

The defendant will not generally be liable for the acts of a trespasser **14.48** unless, possibly, the defendant is regarded as having some positive duty to control them. There may, as explained above,[100] be a duty to take reasonable steps to abate the nuisance caused by the trespasser once the defendant is aware of it.

4. Coming to the nuisance

It is not a defence that the plaintiff came to the nuisance. So, for example, **14.49** development near a landfill site may result in a nuisance to the occupants of the houses and the fact that the landfill was there first will provide no defence. However, it may be that a defence based on contributory negligence could be raised if reasonable investigations prior to the development would have revealed the problem.[101]

5. Regulatory authority

The existence of planning permission or other regulatory licence for an **14.50** activity (such as a waste management licence or PPC permit) will not in general prevent actions in nuisance.[102] The limited possible exception is confined to instances where the development is so major in scale as to alter the character of the locality.[103] Authorisation by statute is a different matter and may give rise to a defence where the activity is conducted with proper care.[104]

6. Comprehensive statutory scheme

In *Marcic v Thames Water Utilities Ltd*,[105] the House of Lords held that the **14.51** existence of a cause of action in nuisance for flooding from overloaded sewers was inconsistent with the scheme of the Water Industry Act 1991, under which the sewerage undertaker could not control the volume of

---

[99] *Dennis v Ministry of Defence* [2003] EWHC 793 (QB); [2003] Env. L.R. 34. See also S. Tromans, "Nuisance: Prevention or Payment?" [1982] CLJ 87.
[100] para.14.41.
[101] The Law Reform (Contributory Negligence) Act 1945 applies to nuisance: *Caswell v Powell Duffryn Associated Collieries Ltd* [1940] A.C. 152; *Trevett v Lee* [1955] 1 W.L.R. 113.
[102] *Wheeler v J.J. Saunders Ltd* [1995] 3 W.L.R. 466; [1995] Env. L.R. 286. See also *Blackburn v ARC Ltd* [1998] Env. L.R. 469, 526.
[103] *Gillingham BC v Medway (Chatham) Dock Co Ltd* [1993] 1 Q.B. 343.
[104] *Allen v Gulf Oil Refining Ltd* [1981] A.C. 1001.
[105] [2003] UKHL 66; [2004] 2 A.C. 42; [2004] Env. L.R. 25. See also *Hanifa Dobson v Thames Water Utilities Ltd* [2007] EWHC 2021 (TCC), where the same principle was held applicable to the management of sewage within the works, so as to preclude actions for odour nuisance where these would conflict with the statutory scheme of the Water Industry Act 1991.

sewage and water entering its system and was under a statutory system of powers and duties as to the provision of adequate sewerage systems which included enforcement mechanisms. The parallel existence of a cause of action in nuisance would supplant the statutory scheme. The regime on sewage functions is probably unique in this respect, in that there is not a similar regime dealing with, for example, the management and disposal of municipal or other waste.

Pollution of surface waters

14.52 Contaminated land may disperse pollutants into surface waters, either directly or through groundwater. Alteration to the natural quality of the stream will be actionable as a nuisance by the riparian owner.[106] On general principles of nuisance as discussed above, liability may extend to the originator of the nuisance and to the occupier in respect of the condition of his land once he has actual or constructive notice of it. Interference with a legal profit a prendre of fishing (e.g. by killing fish) will also be actionable, and indeed is actionable by analogy to trespass without proof of pecuniary loss.[107]

Pollution of groundwater

14.53 Unlike surface waters in a defined channel, no person has proprietary rights in percolating underground waters.[108] However, subject to the statutory requirements as to abstraction licences or any statutory limitations on volume, every landowner has the right to abstract as much percolating water as they wish from the strata underlying their property: and, by pumping, to draw water from beneath the land of others.[109]

14.54 In *Cambridge Water Co v Eastern Counties Leather Plc*[110] the plaintiff's borehole was contaminated by chlorinated solvents spilt on the defendant's site. At first instance a claim based on nuisance failed because it was held that the type of harm which had occurred was not foreseeable. However, the Court of Appeal came to a different conclusion based on interference with the right of an owner to have such of the water as he abstracts come to him in an uncontaminated condition. The Court of Appeal also relied upon the case of *Ballard v Tomlinson*[111] in which the defendant, by disposing

---

[106] *Young v Bankier Distillery* [1893] A.C. 691.

[107] *Nicholls v Ely Sugar Beet Factory Ltd* [1936] 1 Ch.343; *Fitzgerald v Firbank* [1897] 2 Ch.96; *Broderick v Gale and Ainslie Ltd* [1993] Water Law 127.

[108] *Bradford Corporation v Ferrand* [1902] 2 Ch.655.

[109] *Acton v Blundell* (1843) 12 M. & W. 324; *Chasemore v Richards* (1859) H.L.C. 349.

[110] [1992] Env. L.R. 116; [1993] Env. L.R. 287; [1994] 2 A.C. 264.

[111] (1885) 29 Ch.D. 115. See also *Hubbs v Prince Edward County*; *Boyd and Boyd v Prince Edward County and Preston* (1957) 8 D.L.R. (2nd) 394 (not cited) a case where the defendant, knowing of the presence of drinking wells on the plaintiff's land, placed a massive pile of sand mixed with calcium chloride and sodium chloride on bare limestone some 100–120 feet away. The defendants were liable for the ensuing contamination of the wells in nuisance and negligence. The report contains the evocative sentence: "Just before Christmas 1955 Mrs. Boyd noticed that the blooms dropped off her Christmas cactus, that cream curdled when placed in tea and that water from both wells has a most unpleasant and salty taste . . .".

of sewage and refuse into a disused well on his property, contaminated the nearby abstraction source of a brewery. It was held that this case was not distinguishable and that it was sufficient that the defendant's act, whether deliberate, negligent or non-negligent, caused the contamination. The House of Lords, however, did not regard *Ballard v Tomlinson* as determinative. The main focus there was the argument that the plaintiff had no property in percolating water and therefore no cause of action for its pollution.[112] The concept of natural rights was held to equate to those rights which are protected by the law of tort. However, whether liability attaches to any particular act depends on the relevant rules of tort (nuisance and *Rylands v Fletcher*) and those rules include foreseeability of damage. Thus *Ballard v Tomlinson* was essentially concerned with the plaintiff's title to sue rather than the criteria for a successful action, and did not confer any special status on the protection of groundwater abstraction rights.

Nuisance: the foreseeability issue

14.55 The Court of Appeal decision in the *Cambridge Water* case left the issue of foreseeability in relation to environmental harm (at least so far as interference with natural rights of abstraction is concerned) in a state of some doubt. Prior to that decision the tendency had been to assimilate nuisance with negligence to the extent that damages were only recoverable in respect of reasonably foreseeable harm.[113] Certainly that was the approach adopted Ian Kennedy J. at first instance. The House of Lords, in a passage which was strictly obiter, considered the issue of foreseeability of damage in nuisance. The Lords emphasised that although liability for nuisances created by the defendant (or those for whom he was responsible) is strict, it does not follow that the defendant should be held liable for a type of damage which he could not reasonably foresee. It was seen as reasonable to equate the rules on remoteness in nuisance with those in negligence; this was supported by the Privy Council's decision in *The Wagon Mound (No. 2)*.[114]

14.56 Therefore in cases of nuisance caused by contaminated land it will be necessary to consider to what extent the damage caused was reasonably foreseeable. It is not necessary that the precise type of damage be foreseeable, but rather the kind of damage in general. Foreseeability of "harm" in the abstract is not sufficient: in the *Cambridge Water* case it was held that the reasonable supervisor of ECL's premises prior to 1976 would not have foreseen the groundwater pollution which resulted from repeated spillages of small amounts of solvent, although it could have been foreseen

---

[112] This is clearer from the fuller report at 54 L.J. Ch. 404.

[113] *Overseas Tankship (UK) Ltd v Miller Steamship Co Pty (The Wagon Mound (No. 2))* [1967] 1 A.C. 617; *Solloway v Hampshire CC* (1981) 79 L.G.R. 449; *Home Brewery v Davis (W) Ltd* [1987] Q.B. 339; *Swan Fisheries v Holberton* QB December 14, 1987, unreported (a case on riparian rights); *Anglian Water Services Ltd v H.G. Thurston & Co Ltd* [1993] E.G.C.S. 162 (CA—tipping of large quantities of spoil on land damaged sewage pipes beneath the surface; the existence of the sewer was not known and damage was not foreseeable).

[114] [1967] 1 A.C. 617.

that if a significant quantity were spilled someone might be overcome by fumes.

14.57   It remains to be seen how the concept of foreseeability will be worked out in practice in the contaminated land context. Clearly there have been major advances in the awareness of effects on the environment by chemical substances since 1976, and in relation to spillages of solvent occurring during the 1990s it would not be difficult to demonstrate a general awareness in the industrial community of the risks of pollution. Clearly, also, the courts will be concerned not with what the defendant actually foresaw but what he could have been reasonably expected to have foreseen. The degree of foresight to be imputed to a back street garage may be different from that to be imputed to a major chemical company.

14.58   The issue of foreseeability of harm in the context of emissions of asbestos dust from the Turner & Newall factory in Armley, Leeds, during the 1930s, 1940s and 1950s was considered in *Margereson and Hancock v J.W. Roberts Ltd.*[115] Foreseeability was regarded as being the key issue to the claims in negligence, nuisance and *Rylands v Fletcher*. It was held that the duty of care owed by the operators of the factory was not confined to their employees, since persons outside could be exposed to equivalent hazards from dust. The finding that a duty of care existed related to specific conditions at houses near to the factory and to locations near the curtilage of the factory where children played, and where dust conditions were as bad as inside the factory; there was no general duty found based on ambient environmental conditions. However, exposure in *Margereson* had occurred up to and during the 1950s at a time when the connection had not been made between asbestos exposure and mesothelioma. With such knowledge having been in the public domain from October 1965 onwards (see para.12.19, above) it is not difficult to foresee the risk of injury arising from low levels of asbestos dust in the atmosphere. A Spanish study has concluded that there may be an increased risk of mesothelioma for those living up to 2km from a source of airborne asbestos fibres.[115a]

14.59   The issue of foreseeability was also considered in *Savage v Fairclough*,[116] where it was held that a farmer was not liable for damage caused by contamination of a water supply by nitrates from animal wastes, on the basis that at the relevant time this consequence was not reasonably foreseeable. The test was said to be whether an appropriate notional person, fit to run the business, would have foreseen the pollution at the relevant time. Whilst it was generally known by the mid-1980s that nitrates could pollute water, it was held that a good farmer would not have known by 1991 (the date the enterprise ceased) of associated changes in agricultural good practice; prima facie it was reasonable for farmers to rely on good practice at the time.

14.60   The foreseeability issue will extend not only to the harmful characteristics of the substance in question but also to its properties and means of transport in the environment. Arguments may therefore arise as to whether the defendant ought reasonably to have been aware of the possible migration of contaminants off-site by groundwater flow or other means. On the other

---

[115] [1996] Env. L.R. 304. See also para.12.19ff.
[115a] Agudo et al, *British Journal of Cancer* (2000) 83(1), 104–111.
[116] [2000] Env. L.R. 183.

hand it would probably not be necessary that the defendant could have foreseen precisely where the substance would go; in the *Cambridge Water* case Lord Goff summarised the position of the "reasonable supervisor" at ECL as follows:

> "Even if he had foreseen that solvent might enter the aquifer, he would not have foreseen that such quantities would produce any sensible effect upon water down-catchment, or would otherwise be material or deserve the description of pollution."

The closing words of that extract impliedly introduce another dimension **14.61** of foreseeability: that of the material effect of the contamination. The real harm to Cambridge Water Co's interests was caused by the combination of small quantities of solvent in the aquifer and introduction (four years after the spillages ceased) of EC legislation prohibiting the presence of those quantities in water for human consumption.[117] It is possible to see how such arguments might arise in future in relation to new or more stringent legislation on soil quality standards or the presence of certain substances in the environment. A defendant might foresee that spillages on his land could migrate to his neighbour's but without any material adverse effects; if however soil clean up legislation is introduced in future years which requires the neighbour to remove or neutralise those contaminants present on his land, the contamination will hence become material. One answer might be that the reasonable industrial undertaking operating now would be aware of the possibility of more stringent legislative developments in the area of soil contamination, and that the future materiality of the contamination was therefore foreseeable.

Nuisance: continuing pollution and foreseeability

Consequent upon the House of Lord's ruling on foreseeability in the **14.62** *Cambridge Water Co* case, another issue arose. It was asserted during the course of argument that pools of neat solvent were still in existence at the base of the chalk aquifer beneath ECL's premises and that the escape of solvent was continuing; it was argued that since the adverse effects of that escape were now foreseeable, ECL were liable under nuisance and *Rylands v Fletcher* for that continuing escape. The House of Lords rejected that argument.[118] It was said that "long before the relevant (EC) legislation came into force, the PCE had become irretrievably lost in the ground below"; it had "passed beyond the control of ECL". In such circumstances, it was held, ECL should not be under any greater liability that that imposed for negligence, or for naturally occurring nuisances under the line of cases including *Leakey v National Trust*.[119]

What this appears to suggest is two possible stages of liability for the **14.63** original pollution. The first stage is that of the spillage or other incident causing pollution. Here liability is strict, through the damage will be too

---

[117] This has been described as "a singular feature" of the case: see A. Ogus, [1994] J.E.L. 151, 155.
[118] [1994] 2 A.C. 264.
[119] [1980] Q.B. 485.

remote if it was not reasonably foreseeable. This stage extends until such time as the contamination has passed beyond the control of the polluter by passing irretrievably into the relevant environmental medium. At that point there is a second stage of potential liability where liability is based on negligence, or at least on notions of reasonableness. This leaves the question of when exactly the transition occurs. Some forms of contamination, such as waste contained in a landfill site, may not be irretrievable in that they could be excavated and removed; the same goes for contaminants such as heavy metals which are fixed in soil. Even contaminated groundwater may not be totally beyond control, given modern remediation methods.

14.64 If contaminants have passed beyond control, it must be questionable whether it can ever be correct to impose liability on the basis of negligence or under the principles of *Leakey v National Trust*, since these are based upon the reasonableness of measures which could be taken. Conceivably, contamination might be said to have passed beyond control at a certain date but at a later date—given improvements in remedial technologies perhaps combined with a worsening environmental impact—it might become reasonable to expect the polluter (or future owner) to do something about it.[120]

Public nuisance

14.65 If contamination is such as to endanger the life, health or property of a sufficient number of citizens, or to interfere with their reasonable comfort, then it may constitute a public nuisance.[121] As such it is a crime as well as a tort and any individual wishing to take action will need to show particular damage beyond that suffered by the general public. The House of Lords critically examined the scope and rationale for the crime of public nuisance in *R v Rimmington*; *R v Goldstein*[122] in 2005 and concluded that it should be retained as a common law offence, being sufficiently well-defined and based on rational, discernable principles, so as to be consistent with Art.7 of the European Convention on Human Rights. There must be a common injury to the community as a whole, or a significant section of it, not just injury to an individual or even a large number of individuals in separate incident.[123]

14.66 Historically, public nuisances have frequently involved environmental problems.[124] It is conceivable that a public nuisance could be constituted, for example, by land contaminated with harmful particulate matter which is blown over a wide area, or by land generating methane gas in such quantities to threaten the safety of a large number of dwellings, or possibly by contamination which affects a major aquifer so as to present a health risk

---

[120] Indeed, the NRA subsequently took steps, with the co-operation of the defendant in the *Cambridge Water* case, to secure treatment of the contaminated groundwater, though these appear not to have been particularly successful: see paras 7.33 and 20.61.

[121] See J.R. Spencer, *Public Nuisance—a Critical Examination* [1989] C.L.J. 55.

[122] [2005] UKHL 63; [2006] 1 A.C. 459.

[123] [2005] UKHL 63; [2006] 1 A.C. 459, para.37 (Lord Bingham of Cornhill).

[124] For example, "using a shop in a public market as a slaughterhouse, erecting a manufactory for hartshorn, erecting a privy near the highway, placing putrid carrion near the highway": see *R v Rimmington*; *R v Goldstein* [2005] UKHL 63; [2006] 1 A.C. 459, para.9, per Lord Bingham of Cornhill, citing the first edition of *Archbold* (1822).

to consumers of the water.[125] The words of Lindley L.J. in *Att.-Gen. v Tod Heatley*[126] are relevant in this respect:

> "Now is it, or is it not, a common law duty of the owner of a vacant piece of land to prevent that land from being a public nuisance? It appears to be that it is . . . If the owner of a piece of land does permit it to be in such a state, e.g. smothered or covered with filth, that is a public nuisance, he commits an indictable offence. It is no defence to say 'I did not put the filth on but somebody else did.' He must provide against this if he can. His business is to prevent his land from becoming a public nuisance."

Another example might be contaminated land which is producing offen- **14.67** sive odours which affect a sufficiently large section of the local community.[127] It should be noted however that in *R v Rimmington*; *R v Goldstein* the House of Lords were of the view that there was force in the argument that where the activity constituting the public nuisance was covered by express statutory provisions, then so far as the criminal law was concerned it should be charged under those provisions and not as a public nuisance.[128] However, the statutory nuisance regime is disapplied as regards nuisances caused by "land in a contaminated state" and hence it may not be possible to deal with, for example, serious odour nuisance from such land other than under the common law.

It is not necessary to show that a landowner had actual knowledge of a **14.68** public nuisance on their land but merely that he was responsible for a nuisance which he knew or ought to have known would be the consequences of activities carried out on his land.[129] Knowledge of risk, or the means of knowledge, may thus suffice.

PART 5: NEGLIGENCE

Generally

The tort of negligence may of course be of relevance to environmental **14.69** litigation, but the case law has tended instead to focus attention on the torts of nuisance and *Rylands v Fletcher*. The need to establish a duty of care owed to the plaintiff and failure to exercise the relevant standard of care are difficulties which do not have to be overcome in relation to the other environmental torts. Detailed consideration of the rules of negligence is

---

[125] *Gibbons v South West Water Services Ltd* [1993] Env. L.R. 266, CA.

[126] [1897] 1 Ch.560, 566.

[127] See *R v White and Ward* (1753) 1 Burr 333 ("noisome and offensive stinks and smells" affecting passing highway users).

[128] [2005] UKHL 63; [2006] 1 A.C. 459, para.29, per Lord Bingham of Cornhill, referring to provisions on statutory nuisance and the dumping of waste in particular.

[129] *R v Rimmington*; *R v Goldstein* [2005] UKHL 63; [2006] 1 A.C. 459, para.39, approving *R. v Shorrock* [1994] Q.B. 279, CA.

beyond the scope of this chapter, but the tort's potential application to issues of contaminated land can be appreciated from the following paragraphs. The starting point will be establishing that a duty of care was owed. This will depend on all the circumstances, but in essence the relevant factors will be the foreseeability of the harm which occurred, whether there was justified reliance by the claimant on the defendant exercising reasonable care, and generally whether it is fair, just and reasonable to impose a duty. These may give rise to difficult issues in cases where the defendant's past actions have given rise to damage potentially some considerable time later.

Standard of care

14.70 Various factors will be relevant in determining the standard of care where a duty of care is found to exist in environmental cases. Useful parallels may be found in the case law relating to employers' liability. The test there is the conduct of the reasonable and prudent employer, taking positive thought for the safety of his employees in the light of what he knows or ought to know, following recognised practices where these exist (unless in the light of common sense or later knowledge such practices are clearly bad), keeping reasonably abreast of developing knowledge, and taking account of whether he has in fact greater than average knowledge of the relevant risks.[130] It involves the weighing up of the risks in the terms of the likelihood of injury occurring and the consequences if it does, and against this the probable effectiveness of the relevant precautions and their cost and practicability.

14.71 There seems no reason why such factors should not be equally applicable in principle to the issue of the environmental risks arising from the activities of an operator, though there may be practical differences as to how the tests will operate. In the employment context, where a common practice has been followed for many years without mishap in similar circumstances, a reasonably prudent man might potentially rely on that in not taking further precautions.[131] However in the environmental context, there may be examples of common practices (such as dilute and disperse landfill) which were followed for many years before their consequences were realised; simply having followed such a practice will not necessarily amount to fulfillment of a duty of care (assuming one to exist).

14.72 Relevant factors may include the requirements of any relevant statutory provisions on the prevention of harm or management of risk,[132] or possibly the requirements of any waste management licence, PPC permit, or other authorisation. These will be relevant factors, but not necessarily conclusive, and attention must be paid to the nature and function of the provision in question, bearing in mind that some environmental provisions may be intended to protect the environment in general rather than persons or their property.[133] A provision which creates an absolute duty will not be a reliable

---

[130] *Stokes v Guest Keen and Nettlefold Ltd* [1968] 1 W.L.R. 1776 (QB), approved in *Thompson v Smith's Ship Repairers Ltd* [1984] 1 Q.B. 405 (QB). On the duty to keep in touch with current improvements, see *Brown v Rolls Royce Ltd* [1960] 1 All E.R. 577.

[131] *Morris v West Hartlepool Steam Navigation Company* [1956] A.C. 552, 574 (Lord Reid).

[132] See, e.g. *LMS International Ltd v Styrene Packaging and Insulation Limited* [2005] EWHC 2065 (TCC) (Fire Precautions (Workplace) Regulations 1997).

[133] See *Franklin v Gramophone Company Ltd* [1948] 1 K.B. 542; *Tan Chye Coo v Chong Kew Moi* [1970] 1 All E.R. 272.

guide as to a standard of care based on negligence.[134] Compliance with applicable statutory requirements will be evidence, but not conclusive evidence, that the common law duty has been complied with.[135] It has been held that the absence of any documentary evidence confirming compliance with the relevant requirements does not necessarily indicate that there was non-compliance.[136] The Code of Practice on the duty of care as regards waste will be admissible in evidence and any relevant provisions are to be taken into account.[137] It will not be appropriate to set or measure the duty of care simply by reference to the perspective of a government agency which has carried out research and offers advice[138]; for example the numerous guidance documents produced by the Environment Agency.

By s.1 of the Compensation Act 2006, a court considering a claim in **14.73** negligence or for breach of statutory duty many, in determining whether the defendant should have taken particular steps to meet a standard of care (whether by taking precautions against a risk or otherwise) have regard to whether a requirement to take those steps might:

(a) prevent a desirable activity being undertaken at all, to a particular extent, or in a particular way; and

(b) discourage persons from undertaking functions in connection with a desirable activity.

By s.2 of the 2006 Act, an apology, offer of treatment or other redress **14.74** shall not of itself amount to an admission of negligence or breach of statutory duty.

Professional skill

Standards of professional skill may be relevant in deciding whether any duty **14.75** owed has been breached. A professional is expected to meet the standard of the ordinary skilled man exercising and professing to have the special skill in question.[139] If there are two schools of thought on an issue (as well there may be in matters involving contaminated land) and both are respected by their professional peers, then it is not negligent to choose to follow one course rather than the other.[140] But if it can be shown that one such school of thought is not capable of withstanding logical analysis, a judge is entitled to hold that the body of opinion that supports it is neither reasonable nor

---

[134] *Excel Logistics Ltd v Curran* [2004] EWCA Civ 1249 (CA) at para.25.

[135] *Gray v Stead* (July 20, 1999, CA) Otton L.J. citing Somervell L.J. in *England v NCB* [1953] 1 Q.B. 724 at 732: "the reasonable employer is entitled to assume prima facie, that the damages which occur to a reasonable man have occurred to Parliament or the framers of the regulations".

[136] See *Brett v Reading University* [2007] EWCA Civ 88 (CA) (Asbestos Regulations 1969).

[137] Environmental Protection Act 1990 s.34(10). See further para.17.40.

[138] *Gray v Stead* (July 20, 1999, CA) (views of Sea Fish Industry Authority on wearing of life jackets).

[139] *Bolam v Friern Hospital Management Committee* [1957] 2 All E.R. 118 at 121.

[140] *De Freitas v O'Brien* [1995] 6 Med. L.R. 108 (CA); *Maynard v West Midlands Regional HA* [1985] 1 All E.R. 635.

responsible.[140a] The extent of a professional's duty to warn of risk is to be assessed by reference to the standards and public guidelines of his profession.[141] The issue of standards of care of consultants in relation to contaminated land specifically is considered further below.[142]

Liability for spillages

14.76 Where damage arises from spillage of substances such as solvents the essential issue will be what damage was reasonably foreseeable at the time: failure to exercise proper care or good housekeeping is not sufficient of itself to ground liability.[143] In the *Cambridge Water* case small spillages of solvent were found to have occurred over a period of years prior to 1976. Ian Kennedy J. emphasised the need for some relationship at least between that type of harm which could have been foreseen and that which actually occurred[144]: to say simply that "pollution" could have been foreseen and did in fact occur was too wide a category.[145] Some types of harm could have been foreseen from spillages (for example, danger from fumes), but the type of harm which occurred was different. Nor could it have been foreseen that small regular spills would have the same effect as one major spill. The reasonable plant manager would not have expected the spills to get into the aquifer or, if they did, to cause appreciable harm.[146]

14.77 Standards of awareness of course change over time, and it is submitted that it would be very difficult to argue that the relevant damage would not have been reasonably foreseeable had the spills occurred during the late 1980s or 1990s: the effect of industrial solvents on groundwater is now a matter of widespread concern. The exact point at which such awareness came to be accepted as a reasonable component of plant management is of course open to argument; one issue which may be relevant are the standards expected by regulatory authorities, though this may certainly not be the decisive issue. The existence of official advice or guidance may be a relevant, though not conclusive, factor,[147] though a distinction may need to be drawn between what was known in specialist circles and what was general knowledge in the relevant industry or sector.[148] In any event, the courts are likely to be very wary of imputing foreseeability with the benefit of hindsight, however sympathetic they may be to the plaintiff.[149]

[140a] *Bolitho v City and Hackney Health Authority* [1997] 3 W.L.R. 1151.

[141] *Blyth v Bloomsbury HA* [1993] 3 Med. L.R. 151, CA; *Sidaway v Board of Governors Royal Hospital and Maudsley Hospital* [1985] A.C. 871.

[142] See para.18.18.

[143] *Cambridge Water Co v Eastern Counties Leather Plc* [1992] Env. L.R. 116 at 139, 145.

[144] See *Hughes v Lord Advocate* [1963] A.C. 837.

[145] [1992] Env. L.R. 116 at 142.

[146] *Salvin v North Brancepath Coal Co* (1874) 9 Ch. App. 705 at 708.

[147] See *Roe v Minister of Health* [1954] 2 Q.B. 66; *Gunn v Wallsend Slipway and Engineering Co Ltd*, *The Times*, January 23, 1989; *Tutton v A.D. Walter Ltd* [1986] 1 Q.B. 61.

[148] *Cartwright v GKN Sankey Ltd* (1973) 14 K.I.R. 349. See also para.14.72 above.

[149] *Thompson v Smiths Ship Repairers (North Shields) Ltd* [1984] Q.B. 405. See also *Maguire v Harland & Wolff Plc* [2005] EWCA Civ 1; [2005] P.I.Q.R. P21, CA (no duty owed to spouse affected by washing overalls contaminated with asbestos dust).

Liability for landfill gas

The most detailed reported judicial discussion of liability on negligence for **14.78** the escape of landfill gas occurs in the Canadian case of *Gertsen v Municipality of Metropolitan Toronto*.[150] The defendants, the municipal waste disposal authority and the local borough authority were found to be negligent in respect of the disposal of household garbage mixed with earth into a ravine in a residential area. The landfilling was carried out between 1958–59, under an agreement between the authorities on land owned by the borough. In 1963 the gas generated by the site had caused a flash fire in a garage on nearby property, seriously injuring the owner. The plaintiff purchased the property in 1967 and in 1969 suffered serious injury when an explosion occurred in the same garage.

It was held that both defendants knew or ought to have known of the **14.79** generation of methane gas as a potential danger. Even if unaware of it before 1965 they were certainly aware of it thereafter. Their negligence lay not only in burying the waste but in failing to take proper steps thereafter to prevent the migration of gas or disperse it safely, to inspect the effectiveness of such steps as had been taken, to warn adjoining owners of the dangers, and (in the case of the borough) in granting permits for the construction of garages and outbuildings on the adjoining land.

Natural methane

Liability for failure to foresee the possible presence of methane as a natural **14.80** phenomenon and to take appropriate measures to alleviate the risks from it was considered in the action following the disastrous explosion at the Abbeystead Pumping Station in Lancashire in 1984.[151] Factors which were regarded as relevant in that case included:

(i) the magnitude of the risk and the difficulty of the measures needed to eliminate it; the distinction between transient "stress methane" and long term "reservoir methane" was relevant in this context;

(ii) British Standards Association documents and general scientific literature current at the relevant time;

(iii) the professional man should command the corpus of knowledge which forms part of the professional equipment of the ordinary member of his profession. He should not lag behind other ordinarily assiduous and intelligent members of his profession in knowledge of new advances, discoveries and developments in his field; but "the law does not require of a professional man that he be a paragon, combining the qualities of polymath and prophet";

(iv) the first instance judge found the defendant engineers "to some slight degree negligent in not keeping abreast with, passing on to

---

[150] (1973) 41 D.L.R. (3rd) 646.
[151] *Eckersley v Binnie & Partners* [1998] 18 Con. L.R. 78, CA.

[their clients] and considering, in relation to design, developing knowledge about methane between handover and 1984". The Court of Appeal regarded this suggestion as placing "startlingly onerous responsibilities" upon professionals and suggested that if any such duty were to be imposed then its nature, scope and limits would need to be very carefully and cautiously defined.

Negligence: potential relevance

14.81 Despite the difficulties discussed above, negligence is a possible cause of action in relation to contaminated land and may be particularly apt in cases where:

(i) the defendant's conduct caused the contamination; or

(ii) the defendant, being aware of the dangers from contamination, failed to take steps to prevent or to warn[152]; or

(iii) the defendant's actions resulted in pre-existing contaminants being released.

Negligence and public bodies

14.82 Where problems arise with contaminated land, involvement by the local authority or the Environment Agency can in principle take various forms, and may in some cases raise issues of potential liability on the part of the authority where problems subsequently occur. Advice offered by officers of an authority, whether formally or informally, may potentially result in liability under standard *Hedley Byrne* duty of care principles.[153] The same is true of the provision of information which gives an impression of accuracy that is not justified on the facts.[154] The onus is therefore on the authority, in offering advice, to ensure that an appropriate disclaimer of liability is made. Other considerations will arise where the authority is exerting pressure for a particular course to be followed rather than just offering advice. In *Harris v Evans*[155] the Court of Appeal qualified the general principle that an enforcing authority should not be liable in tort for loss resulting from its enforcement functions, saying that if a requirement of the authority introduced a new risk or danger which materialised, resulting in physical damage and economic loss, then it should not be ruled out that such loss might be recoverable in negligence. Where an authority decides to offer physical assistance in dealing with urgent problems, it will do so at its own risk should its intervention actually make matters worse. This depends on ordinary principles of negligence, and is the case even if the authority was under no legal duty to assist or intervene.[156]

---

[152] Effectively this may impose liability for an omission; but such liability certainly seems capable of arising in a similar basis in nuisance. See para.14.41.

[153] See, e.g. *Lambert v West Devon BC* [1997] 1 W.L.R. 570.

[154] *Mason v Coal Authority* (QBD, March 15, 2001) (statement that "the property is clear of disused mine shafts" was inaccurate and misleading).

[155] [1998] 1 W.L.R. 1285.

[156] See *Capital and Counties Plc v Hampshire CC* [1997] 2 All E.R. 865; [1997] 3 W.L.R. 331; *Rigby v Chief Constable of Northamptonshire* [1985] 1 W.L.R. 1242; *Knightley v Johns* [1982] 1 W.L.R. 349.

In *Welton v North Cornwall DC*[157] the Court of Appeal held that a local **14.83** authority could have a duty of care in negligence in respect of inspection functions of its officers. The circumstances where such a duty could arise were the imposition by the officer, outside the legislative powers, of detailed (and misconceived) requirements backed by the threat of closure. Where the officers are simply carrying out "straight" enforcement functions, or are offering advice, the courts will be aware that imposing liability might tend to discourage performance of the statutory functions. *Welton* was, however, confined to its own facts in another Court of Appeal decision, *Harris v Evans*[158] where it was held that enforcement powers inevitably involved striking a balance in the public interest. It was implicit that the exercise of such powers might give rise to economic loss or damage, and the Act itself provided remedies against excessive or erroneous enforcement action. No duty of care in tort was owed to the operator save in exceptional circumstances.

The leading case on liability for failure by local authorities to act is the **14.84** House of Lords decision in *Stovin v Wise*.[159] A statutory duty will not necessarily give rise to a duty of care in tort. The majority view, expressed by Lord Hoffmann, was that civil liability should only follow if there were grounds for holding that the policy of the statutory duty was to require compensation to be paid to persons suffering loss because of inaction. The issue will be whether there was a relationship of proximity and whether imposition of a duty of care would be fair, just and reasonable; this will involve considering the facts of the case and the background to the statutory scheme in question.[160] Where statutory powers are involved, there is also the question of whether failure to exercise the power could be regarded as irrational in public law terms.[161]

PART 6: GENERAL ISSUES

Causation and proof

One of the first general problems to be faced in any action involving soil **14.85** contamination is that of proof. It may be extremely difficult to demonstrate a causal link between the acts or omissions of the defendant, or the state of the defendant's land, and the harm which is alleged to have resulted from it.[162] On normal principles it is for the plaintiff to prove (save where there are admissions) all the necessary ingredients of the tort; as such it is not necessary for the defendant to disprove anything.[163] The difficulties of

---

[157] [1997] 1 W.L.R. 570.
[158] [1998] 1 W.L.R. 1285.
[159] [1996] A.C. 923.
[160] See *Rice v Secretary of State for Trade and Industry* [2007] EWCA Civ 289; [2007] P.I.Q.R. P23 (duty of National Dock Labour Board to protect its employees from exposure to asbestos).
[161] The issue is discussed further in the context of Part IIA at para.3.159ff.
[162] For a helpful practical discussion, see C. Pugh and M. Day, *Toxic Torts* (London: Cameron May 1992), Ch.6.
[163] *McGhee v National Coal Board* [1973] 1 W.L.R. 1; *Hotson v East Berkshire Area HA* [1987] A.C. 750; *Wilshire v Essex Area HA* [1988] A.C. 1074.

establishing causation in environmental cases is emphasised by the decision in *Graham v Re-Chem International Ltd*,[164] which related to the alleged contamination of the plaintiffs' farmland by aerial transmission and deposition of toxic chemicals emitted from the defendants' incinerator. The hearing took some 198 court days, spread over 14 months, covering numerous factual issues, many of great scientific complexity. There was no doubt that from mid-July 1983 onwards the plaintiffs' main dairy herd was beset by serious problems leading eventually to the cessation of dairy farming at the holding. However, the main physical problem, that the animals were over-fat, was held not to be attributable to toxic emissions, but to "fat cow syndrome" caused by excessive feeding on concentrate and lush grass.

14.86 In some cases, by contrast, this burden of proof may be capable of discharge reasonably easily: in particular where a given site is the only possible source of the particular contaminants in the relevant area of search. However in many cases there may be a number of possible sources of the problem or the contaminant in question, such as industrial triazines, may be ubiquitous. Dislosure may of course assist the plaintiff,[165] as may the use of public sources of information and liaison with relevant public agencies. Public registers of waste disposal licences and prescribed processes may be particularly useful, as may information held by public authorities: this may include, for example, monitoring data held by the authorities.[166]

14.87 Expert evidence is likely to be crucial in such actions and may well involve a number of fields and disciplines depending on the nature of the case. These may include: process engineering, hydrology, geology, hydrogeology, chemistry, toxicology, ecology, biology, biochemistry, civil engineering, geotechnical engineering, materials science, waste management and even industrial archaeology. An expert witness should make it clear to the court when an issue or question falls outside his or her area of specialism or expertise and should be aware of the stringent duties owed by an expert to the court.[167] The expert should be wary of over-dramatising problems.[168]

14.88 In the *Cambridge Water* case[169] detailed inquiries were carried out before any litigation to identify the source of the contaminants: these included the sinking of various boreholes by the Anglian Water Authority and further work by the British Geological Survey. This resulted in a considerable amount of data, calculations and deductions, none of which was admitted by the judge, who based his findings on the expert evidence before him. This evidence concerned both the general structure and behaviour of chalk aquifers and of the specific aquifer in question. It is notable that the trial

[164] [1996] Env. L.R. 158.
[165] For example, it may reveal damaging surveys or consultants' reports commissioned by the defendant before litigation was in contemplation.
[166] See further, Ch.22.
[167] *National Justice Compania Naviera SA v Prudential Assurance Company Ltd (Ikarian Reefer)* [1993] 2 Lloyd's Rep. 58 (Creswell J.), approved in *Stevens v Gullis* [2000] 1 All E.R. 527, CA; and see CPR 35PD on Experts and Assessors. It should be noted that in *R v Balfour Beatty Civil Eng Ltd and Geoconsult GES* (Central Criminal Court, February 15, 1999) Creswell J. ruled that similar principles also apply to criminal case.
[168] See, e.g. *Foliejohn Establishment v Gain SA*, July 7, 1993 (Chancery Division), para.19.37ff below.
[169] [1992] 116 (first instance); [1993] Env. L.R. 287, C.A.: [1994] 2 A.C. 264, HL.

judge generally preferred the evidence of a civil engineer who had subsequently specialised in hydrology and hydrogeology and that of a qualified geologist and hydrogeologist to that of an equally senior civil engineer who had practised in geotechnical engineering; his chosen specialism involved consideration of ground loadings and this required an understanding of groundwater influences, but his knowledge of the particular subject was "considerably less detailed".[170]

Concurrent causes

Problems can arise in that harm which is related to pollution may have come **14.89** about from one or more of a number of sources between which it may be impossible to allocate responsibility. Two situations must be distinguished. The first is where it is clear that one source has made a material contribution to the damage, but its extent is not clear. The inability to allocate contributions precisely will not be a bar to recovery,[171] though it may raise issues of joint and several liability. The second situation is where it is clear that only one exposure among a number could have caused the problem. This has given rise to controversy in the context of claims for asbestos-related diseases.[172] In *Holtby v Brigham & Cowan (Hull) Ltd*[173] the Court of Appeal distinguished between divisible injury, which was dose related and where damages were to be apportioned by the court and indivisible injury—for example mesothelioma cases—where the defendant who caused the injury was liable in full. This distinction was addressed by the House of Lords in *Fairchild v Glenhaven Funeral Services Ltd*,[174] a mesothelioma case where the claimant had been subject to potential exposure over several periods of employment. The Court of Appeal had held the claimant could not recover as he could not prove which employer had been responsible for the fibre which caused the disease and creating an exposure to risk was not sufficient as a basic for liability. The House of Lords disagreed, holding that the usual "but for" test of causation should be relaxed in mesothelioma cases, where a material increase in risk was sufficient to establish liability, so that each successive employer was liable despite the inability to say which of them had actually caused the injury.

The Lords held that this relaxed causation test was to be applied with **14.90** restraint to cases where science could not currently prove who caused the injury, the breach of duty materially increased risk and was capable of having caused the injury, and the agent arising from the breach (the asbestos fibre) was the cause of injury and not just one of number of potential causes. In *Barker v Corus (UK) Plc*[175] the House of Lords held that the principle in *Fairchild* was limited to cases where the impossibility of

---

[170] [1992] Env. L.R. 116 at 121–122. See also the helpful summary of Stuart-Smith L.J. as to evaluation of expert evidence in *Loveday v Renton & Wellcome Foundation Ltd* [1990] 1 Med. L.R. 117.
[171] *Bonnington Castings v Wardlaw* [1956] A.C. 613.
[172] See generally para.12.18ff.
[173] [2000] 3 All E.R. 421, CA.
[174] [2002] UKHL 22; [2002] 3 W.L.R. 89.
[175] [2006] UKHL 20; [2006] A.C. 572.

proving causation arose from the fact that there was another possible causative agent which operated in the same way. Further, since the basis of the principle was the creation of risk, liability should be attributed between those who had created risk on the basis of their proportionate contribution to the overall risk. This latter aspect of the decision has now been reversed by s.3 of the Compensation Act 2006, but only so far as mesothelioma is concerned: the section provides for joint and several liability in respect of the whole of the damage.[176] Whether there is liability at all will depend on whether factually there was a contribution to the risk and whether this involved legal fault, i.e. negligence or breach of statutory duty.[177]

Remedies: damages

14.91 Two distinct questions arise in relation to the issue of damages: first, whether damage is a pre-requisite of actionability and, secondly, the type of damage which may be recovered. Some torts are actionable without proof of damage, such as trespass and interference with easements or profits. Others, such as negligence and *Rylands v Fletcher*, clearly require material damage in order to be actionable (save in *Hedley Byrne* type case and the like[177a]) and unless there is such damage pure economic loss will be irrecoverable. With nuisance, the position appears to depend upon the type of nuisance in question: some nuisances involve an encroachment upon land and are actionable without proving actual financial or physical damage.[178] In other cases, where the nuisance involves physical damage to land, it is necessary here to show actual, as opposed to prospective, damage.[179] Where the nuisance is of the type involving interference with the use and enjoyment of land, no actual financial loss or interference with health need be proved.[180]

Bodily injury

14.92 Contaminated land may cause physical damage to property, personal injury, or even death. However, there are cases where there may be a dispute as to whether actionable damage has occurred. In the context of physical injury,

---

[176] The Explanatory Notes to the Act summarise the decision in *Barker* and the effect of s.3 as follows: "That decision did not impose a limit on the damages which could be recovered from those responsible for the exposure to asbestos. But it did mean that the risk of any of them being insolvent and unable to pay the appropriate share would fall on the claimant, and that in practice the claimant would have to trace all relevant defendants, as far as this was possible, before liability could be apportioned and full compensation paid, or alternatively to issue multiple claims to recover damages on a piecemeal basis. The practical effects of this decision (which their Lordships were not asked to consider) were that claims could take much longer to be concluded, and would be much more difficult and time-consuming for claimants in circumstances where they and their families are already under considerable pain and stress. The Act reverses the effects of the Barker judgment to enable claimants, or their estate or dependants, to recover full compensation from any liable person. It will then be open to the person who has paid the compensation to seek a contribution from other negligent persons".

[177] *Brett v Reading University* [2007] EWCA Civ 88 (CA).

[177a] See e.g. para.14.82 on negligence and public bodies.

[178] *Fay v Prentice* (1845) 1 C.B. 828; in one case, it has been reported that a substantial settlement has been reached for alleged contamination of farmland by dioxin, involving restrictions in sale of produce and consequent economic loss: see "Coalite Dioxin Settlement" [1993] E.L.R. December 5, 1993.

[179] *Sedleigh Denfield v O'Callaghan* [1940] A.C. 880, 919.

[180] *Crump v Lambert* (1867) L.R. 3 Eq. 409.

exposure to contaminants may result in possible predisposition to future illness, e.g. cancer, or may give rise to serious anxiety or depression and related physical effects. The term "worried well" has gained popular currency. Where there is some physical change which causes symptoms, such as pleural plaques or bronchitis, then this may be regarded as bodily injury.[181] However, simple anxiety from awareness of having been exposed to risk will to be too remote to be recoverable,[182] unless there are specific circumstances such as involvement in an incident such as an explosion or other emergency,[183] or there is a real risk of serious harm.[184] This follows from the recognised need for the law to set limits upon the extent of admissible claims where numerous people may claim to have suffered stress and anxiety over some incident.[185] The principle was re-emphasised by the House of Lords in Johnston v NEI International Combustion Ltd[185a] in relation to pleural plaques caused by exposure to asbestos which (save in the most exceptional cases) would not cause future symptoms or increase susceptibility to disease or shorten life expectancy. In the absence of any compensatable injury, the risk of future disease or anxiety by the person exposed will not give a cause of action.

Damage to land

Contamination of land or groundwater by migrating pollutants may be a **14.93** gradual, even imperceptible, process, and thus the issue arises of the point at which material damage occurs. The real harm may lie in the fact that the development potential of the land is affected. It is therefore an important question as to what constitutes damage. In the context of cases under the compensation provisions of the Nuclear Installations Act 1965, which apply to "damage to any property",[186] the contamination of land by radioactive material mixed with mud,[187] and the presence on a beach of "a peculiarly unpleasant type of physical contamination which cannot easily be cured"[188] have been held to be such damage.[189] Similarly, the presence of dust in

---

[181] See also *British Coal Respiratory Disease Litigation* (QBD, 1998) (bronchial symptoms).

[182] *Coleman v British Gas Services Ltd* (2002, QBD) (exposure to carbon monoxide from faulty gas fire); *Owen v Esso Exploration & Production UK Ltd* (2007, CC Liverpool) (thickening of lung lining but medical evidence suggested unlikely to affect health; simple anxiety not enough).

[183] *Page v Smith* [1996] A.C. 310. Distinguished on the facts in *Johnston v NEI International Combustion Ltd* [2007] UKHL 39.

[184] See *Aston v Imperial Chemical Industries Plc* (QBD, 1992) (depressive illness of employee who was told of risk that he would die from liver cancer as a result of exposure to fumes from vinyl chloride monoma).

[185] *McLoughlin v O'Brien* [1983] 1 A.C. 410; *White v Chief Constable of South Yorkshire Police* [1999] 2 A.C. 455, 494, 497, 511; *Magnohard Limited v UK Atomic Energy Authority* [2004] Env. L.R. 19 (Court of Session, Outer House) paras 149–150.

[185a] [2007] UKHL 39.

[186] See para.15.14.

[187] *Blue Circle Industries Plc v Ministry of Defence* [1999] 2 Ch.289, CA.

[188] *Magnohard Limited v UK Atomic Energy Authority* [2004] Env. L.R. 19 (Court of Session, Outer House) para.156.

[189] Compare *Merlin v British Nuclear Fuels Plc* [1990] 2 Q.B. 557 where levels of radioactivity were found in dust vacuumed from the claimant's house, but the reduction in the value of the house was held to be pure economic loss.

quantities which affects the use and value of carpets, requiring the cost of professional cleaning, has been regarded by the Court of Appeal as damage and not simply financial loss.[190] It therefore seems likely that the Courts will regard the presence of contaminants on land as damage, at least where these bring about some physical or chemical change, or require substantial remediation.

14.94   The damage from contamination may only come about when it is discovered, or when increasingly strict regulatory standards apply,[191] or when a regulatory body takes action, or when proposals for development are adversely affected, or when a transaction is aborted. In this respect, each case will depend on its own facts. Once such damage is shown, then in principle the quantum of damages will be the sum required to put the plaintiff back into the position he would have been in had the tort not been committed: in general, this may be either the cost of remedial measures or the diminution in the value of the land.[192] Where stigma will result in continued loss of value even after remediation, this may be recoverable.[193] It has been held that where land is contaminated, the reasonable costs of investigation to establish whether there is a long term problem can be recovered.[194]

14.95   The *Cambridge Water Co* case gives some indication of possible approaches to damages in aquifer pollution cases.[195] The plaintiffs in that case first tried pumping the contaminated water to waste. When it was apparent that this was not removing the contaminants, the course adopted was to move up catchment and tap the aquifer above the source of pollution; this involved research, the acquisition of land, construction of a new pumping station and the laying of new mains. The possible alternative solutions of blending with uncontaminated water and constructing an air-stripping plant were both rejected. It was held contrary to the arguments of the defendants, that it was reasonable not to adopt the air-stripping solution, which could have given rise to other environmental problems. The quantum of damage was thus effectively the cost of the new source of supply, less any element of betterment to reflect over-design of the new pumping station. The defendants argued unsuccessfully that the correct approach was to take the value of the polluted borehole and treat that as redundant, applying an inflation correction.

---

[190] *Hunter v Canary Wharf Ltd* [1996] 2 W.L.R. 348; [1996] Env. L.R. 138 (reversed by HL on other grounds: [1997] A.C. 685. See also *Losinjska Plovidba v Transco Overseas Ltd (The Orjula)* [1995] 2 Lloyd's Rep. 395, QB (contamination of vessel by cargo).

[191] [1992] Env. L.R. 116, 144.

[192] For cases considering loss of value, see *Blackburn v ARC Ltd* [1998] Env. L.R. 469, Q.B.; *Dennis v MoD* [2003] Env. L.R. 34, Q.B.

[193] *Blue Circle Industries Plc v Ministry of Defence* [1999] Ch.289; [1999] Env. L.R. 22, CA (considering also issues such as interest, loss of a chance of sale).

[194] *Jan de Nul (UK) Ltd v Axa Royale Belge SA* [2002] 1 Lloyd's Rep. 583, CA (nature reserve potentially affected by negligent deposit of silt from dredging).

[195] [1992] Env. L.R. 116, 147. For a discussion on the quantum of damages for reinstatement of a damaged asset, see *Aerospace Publishing v Thames Water Utilities Ltd* [2007] EWCA Civ 3 (CA).

The courts will be wary of awarding damages in lieu of an injunction in **14.96** the case of a continuing nuisance, because there will be nothing to prevent the plaintiff pocketing the damages, selling his property, and leaving the defendant exposed to further actions by the purchaser.[196]

Remedies: exemplary damages

The case of *AB v South West Water Services Ltd*[197] raised, in a very stark way, **14.97** the potential applicability of exemplary damages to pollution cases. The action arose from the contamination of public water supplies at Camelford, Cornwall by the accidental introduction of some 20 tonnes of aluminium sulphate. Consumers of the water brought actions for damages under negligence, nuisance, public nuisance, contact, breach of statutory duty and the rule in *Rylands v Fletcher*. Those claims included aggravated and exemplary damages on the basis of alleged arrogant and high-handed responses to the problem by the water undertaker. Liability for breach of statutory duty was in fact admitted by the defendant, who had already been prosecuted for and convicted of public nuisance. The Court of Appeal held following *Rookes v Barnard*[198] that there was binding House of Lords authority that awards of exemplary damages should be restricted to torts recognised in 1964 as being capable of grounding such a claim. On that basis it does not appear that, in the absence of further House of Lords authority to the contrary, exemplary damages can be awarded for negligence or for breach of statutory duty (unless the statute itself expressly creates such a remedy). Nor, the Court of Appeal held, could exemplary damages be awarded for public nuisance. On the other hand, there was (at least arguably) authority in favour of private nuisance as a cause of action for which exemplary damages could be awarded.[199] However, it appears from the decision that such awards should be confined to those cases of private nuisance where there is deliberate and wilful interference with the plaintiff's rights of enjoyment of land and the defendant has calculated that the profit or benefit for him will exceed the damages he may have to pay.[200] The Court of Appeal held that the defendant's conduct did not fall within that description, nor was the privatised water company to be regarded as an agency of Government which might have brought it within the other category of cases where exemplary damages might be awarded.[201] Therefore the potential applicability of exemplary damages to contamination cases, whilst not to be ignored, is relatively limited.

Remedies: injunctive relief

Where ongoing activity is causing contamination of land which is resulting in **14.98** a nuisance (for example by contaminating an aquifer) an injunction restraining the continuation of that action may be an appropriate and

---

[196] *Bar-Gur v Squire* [1993] E.G.C.S. 151.
[197] [1993] Q.B. 507; [1993] Env. L.R. 266, CA.
[198] [1964] A.C. 1129, read in conjunction with *Cassell & Co Ltd v Broome* [1972] A.C. 1027.
[199] *Bell v Midland Rly Co* (1861) 10 CBNS 287; *Guppys (Bridport) Ltd v Brookling* (1983) 14 H.L.R. 1.
[200] See *Rookes v Barnard* [1964] A.C. 1129 at 1225 per Lord Devlin.
[201] *Rookes v Barnard* [1964] A.C. 1129 at 1225 per Lord Devlin.

effective remedy. In the *Cambridge Water Co* case at first instance Ian Kennedy J. had no doubt that if there were continuing spillages, there should be an injunction to restrain their continuance, indeed in appropriate circumstances a quia timet injunction.[202] However, where the spillage or other contamination has already happened, any injunctive relief is likely to be essentially mandatory in form, requiring the defendant to remove or neutralise contaminants, or at least to keep them within his own boundary. Any such remedy would be at the discretion of the court and would need to follow the principles laid down in *Morris v Redland Bricks Ltd*[203]:

(a) the jurisdiction should be used cautiously and only in cases where extreme or at least very serious damage would be likely to ensure were the injunction withheld;

(b) the damage which would follow refusal of the injunction must be such that any damages awarded in respect of it would be an inadequate remedy;

(c) the defendant must be able to comply legally;

(d the cost to the defendant must be taken into account relative to the risk of damage; and

(e) the defendant must know exactly what he has to do to comply, so that he may give precise instructions to his contractors. This last principle is particularly important and would preclude the grant of any injunction in general terms such as "to remove contaminants to safe levels" or "to take all necessary steps to ensure containment of contaminants within the defendant's land".

A mandatory injunction will be refused where the defendant has himself carried out sufficiently effective works.[204]

Remedies: abatement

14.99 Whilst in theory the self-help remedy of abatement may be available in contaminated land cases, it is one which will need to be considered and exercised with extreme caution. It has been said that a man may enter a neighbour's land "and remove an accumulation of filth and offal which interferes with the use and enjoyment of his own property".[205] Entry on a neighbour's land to carry out extensive remedial works in relation to contaminated land is, however, a different matter altogether, and not one to be undertaken lightly. In particular, it will need to be a case where the plaintiff would be likely to be able to obtain a mandatory injunction; as little damage as possible should be caused to the wrongdoer and other third parties; entry must be peaceable; and in most cases prior notice will need to

---

[202] [1992] Env. L.R. 116 at 144.
[203] [1970] A.C. 652 at 665–6.
[204] *Leakey v National Trust* [1978] Q.B. 849, affirmed on other grounds at [1980] Q.B. 485.
[205] *Jones v Williams* (1843) 11 M. & W. 176.

be given. In practice therefore to avoid risks to the plaintiff, the nature of the works will need to be agreed in most significant details with the defendant: the remedy is unlikely to be employed in any but the most straightforward and urgent cases. Clearly it will in general be preferable for such matters to be dealt with under the statutory regime of Pt IIA, which includes powers of entry for regulatory bodies and those required to comply with remediation notices.

Works of abatement carried out on one's own land raise different **14.100** considerations. Such action is not risk free. In *Midland Bank Plc v Bardgrove Property Services Ltd and John Willmott (GB) Ltd*[206] the plaintiffs carried out sheet piling work on their own land at a cost of £230,000 to counteract the probability of future subsidence resulting from excavations on adjoining land; no opportunity was given to the defendants to do the work themselves. It was held that no cause of action arose until there was actual physical damage; accordingly there was no right to recover money spent to prevent anticipated future instability.

Where contamination migrates by means of transport in water, whether **14.101** surface or groundwater, the decision in *Home Brewery Co Ltd v William Davis & Co (Leicester) Ltd*[207] may be relevant. It was held in that case that:

(a) an occupier of land has no cause of action against the occupier of higher adjacent land for permitting the passage of natural, unchannelled water onto the lower land;

(b) however, nor is the lower occupier under any obligation to accept such water and as such is entitled to take steps consistent with his reasonable user of land to prevent it entering, even if that causes damage to the higher land;

(c) if those steps by the lower owner are unreasonable and the damage to the higher land is reasonably foreseeable, the occupier of the higher land will have an action in nuisance; and

(d) general works of construction or infilling which "squeeze out" water from the lower to the higher land resulting in reasonably foreseeable damage will also be actionable.

Joint and several liability

Contaminated land cases may raise issues of joint and several liability in **14.102** various ways. Two or more parties may be joint tortfeasors in the strict sense of having together committed a tort (as in the case of a landowner and a waste contractor who enter into a tipping licence which results in a tort); alternatively they may both be liable in respect of the same tort (for example the former landowner who is responsible for having caused a nuisance and his successor in title who is responsible in respect of its continuance).

Other than these cases, there are situations where two or more parties **14.103** have contributed in some way to damage suffered by the plaintiff. This may be the case where the actions of the parties have created a single source of

---

[206] [1992] N.P.C. 83; see also *Midland Bank v Bardgrove Property Services Ltd* (1992) 60 B.L.R. 1.
[207] [1987] 1 Q.B. 339; see also *Palmer v Bowman* [2000] 1 W.L.R. 842, CA.

pollution, for example where a number or companies have independently disposed of wastes at the same site. Alternatively, the parties may have created separate sources of pollution, which have then contaminated the same property; as where a number of industrial companies all contribute to the contamination of an aquifer.

14.104   In such cases the essential, though often difficult, distinction to be drawn is between those cases where the actions of the defendants cause different damage to the plaintiff and those cases where they cause the plaintiff to suffer a single injury. In the first case the causes of action against each tortfeasor are distinct and the plaintiff may recover from each only that part of the damage for which they were responsible.[208] In the second case the plaintiff may recover the entirety of his loss against all or any of the tortfeasors, irrespective of the extent of their individual participation.[209] Statutory rights of contribution between the joint tortfeasors exist in these circumstances.[210]

14.105   The distinction outlined above may be difficult to draw, but by way of illustration, where a number of parties create a single source of pollution which then migrates onto the plaintiff's land their liability would appear to be joint and several; the same would seem to be the case where, from independent sources, the parties contaminate the plaintiff's land with the same or similar substances in such a way that the separate pollution cannot be distinguished. If by contrast one party had contaminated the plaintiff's land with migrating heavy metals and another with organic compounds, so that the two types of contamination could be distinguished, it would seem arguable that liability should not be joint and several, there being no reason why either party should be held liable for injury which they clearly did not cause.

14.106   The situation was considered in the *Cambridge Water* case at first instance[211] where there were two potential sources of the contaminant solvents affecting the plaintiff's borehole; both were tanneries. It was concluded that the vast majority of the contamination came from the premises of Eastern Counties Leather Plc and that on the evidence it was not possible to find that the second defendants, Hutchings and Harding Ltd, had produced any measurable effect on the water of the borehole. Ian Kennedy J. said[212]:

> "I cannot think it right that a contributor whose addition is insignificant must be held liable because his mite is associated with a clear case of pollution by another. I suspect there can be no rule to meet every case and that each case must be seen on its own."

As such Hutchings and Harding Ltd were not jointly liable, nor indeed liable at all. The position might well have been different had their contribution to

[208] *Performance Cars Ltd v Abraham* [1962] 1 Q.B. 33.
[209] *Dougherty v Chandler* (1946) 46 S.R. (NSW) 370, 375. See also the discussion on concurrent causes at para.14.89, above.
[210] Civil Liability (Contribution) Act 1978.
[211] [1992] Env. L.R. 116.
[212] 1992] Env. L.R. 116 at 146.

the pollution been "sensible", albeit not as substantial as that of Eastern Counties Leather.[213]

Limitation of actions: the Limitation Act 1980

Under the Limitation Act 1980 s.2 an action founded on tort shall not be **14.107** brought after the expiration of six years from the date on which the cause of action accrued. This general provision does not apply to actions for negligence, nuisance or breach of duty where the damages claimed include damages in respect of personal injuries to the plaintiff or any other person: in such cases by s.11 the limitation period is three years from:

(a) the date on which the cause of action accrued; or

(b) the date of knowledge (if later) of the injured person.[214]

Limitation is potentially an extremely important and difficult issue in **14.108** contaminated land cases, given the long timescales which can be involved before harm occurs or before harm, having occurred, is detected. It may be very difficult to pinpoint the time at which any cause of action accrued.

In many cases involving contaminated land there may be a continuing **14.109** wrong as contaminated groundwater or gas migrates over time onto the plaintiff's property: here it can be said that fresh causes of action continue to accrue and that action can be brought in respect of whatever portion of the continuing wrong lies within the limitation period. This is easy to state but much more difficult to apply. Similarly, where groundwater is polluted, it is arguable that damage continues to occur for so long as the pollutants remain in the groundwater, regardless of how long it has been since the defendant's acts or omissions which caused the pollution.[215] Certainly, limitation appears not to have been a problem for the plaintiff in the *Cambridge Water* case, even though it was some seven years from the date when spillages were found to have ceased to the date when the plaintiff's well was closed down.

Where damage is an essential ingredient of the tort, the rule is that there **14.110** is no cause of action and the limitation period does not begin to run until the damage occurs. In some cases involving contaminated land it may be obvious when the damage occurred (for example a methane explosion); in other cases it may be obscure (for example contamination of a water supply source or aggressive effect on foundations or services). The difficulty for a plaintiff is that in general the time runs from the date the damage occurred, not the date on which it was discovered or reasonably could have been discovered.[216] In claims involving personal injury the difficulty is alleviated by s.11 of the Limitation Act[217]: in other cases the only argument open to the plaintiff may

---

[213] *Pride of Derby & Derbyshire Angling Association Ltd v British Celanese Ltd* [1952] 1 All E.R. 1326 at 1342; [1953] 1 Ch. 149, 152–153.

[214] See s.14; on the issue of knowledge see *Nash v Eli Lilly & Co* [1993] 4 All E.R. 383.

[215] An analogy can be drawn with *Darley Main Colliery v Mitchell* (1886) 11 H.L. Cas. 127 which holds that a fresh action or withdrawal of support for land will lie for each separate incident of subsidence, however long since the defendant ceased acting.

[216] *Pirelli General Cable Works Ltd v Oscar Faber and Partners* [1983] 2 A.C. 1.

[217] Also by the discretionary power of the court to disapply the time limits of s.11 and s.33.

be that some fact relevant to the plaintiff's right of action has been deliberately concealed from him by the defendant.[218]

14.111   It should be noted that the general time limit for actions based on tort does not apply to claims for injunctions or other equitable remedies, except in so far as the court may apply those time limits by analogy.[219]

Limitation of actions: latent damage

14.112   Sections 14A and 14B of the Limitation Act 1980, inserted by the Latent Damage Act 1986, deal with actions in respect of latent damage other than those involving personal injuries (to which s.11 applies). By subs.(4) the limitation period is either:

(a) six years from the date on which the cause of action accrued; or

(b) three years from the "starting date" if that period expires later than the six-year period mentioned at (a).

14.113   The "starting date" is the earliest date on which the plaintiff or any person in whom the cause of action was vested before him had both the knowledge required for bringing an action and a right to bring it.[220] Knowledge in this sense means knowledge of the material facts about the damage[221] and other facts such as causation and the identity of the defendant.[222] It includes knowledge which the plaintiff might reasonably have been expected to acquire from facts observable or ascertainable by him or from facts ascertainable with the help of appropriate expert advice which it is reasonable for him to seek.[223]

14.114   By s.14B an overriding time limit is applied to actions for negligence not involving personal injuries: this is a period of 15 years from the date (or, if more than one, the last of the dates) on which there occurred any act or omission:

(a) which is alleged to constitute negligence; and

(b) to which the damage in respect of which damages are claimed is alleged to be attributable (in whole or in part).

The effect of this "long-stop" provision is to bar any cause of action to which the section applies even if the cause of action has not yet accrued and even if the starting date for reckoning the period under s.14A has not yet occurred.[224]

---

[218] Limitation Act 1980 s.32(1)(b).

[219] Limitation Act 1980 s.36(1).

[220] Limitation Act 1980 s.14A(5).

[221] Limitation Act 1980 s.14A(6)(a) and (7).

[222] Limitation Act 1980 s.14A(6)(b) and (8).

[223] Limitation Act 1980 s.14A(A)(10). The issue is not the date at which the claimant knew or was told they might have a claim, but the date on which claimant first had enough knowledge to justify investigating whether they might have a claim: see *Haward v Fawcetts Ltd* [2006] UKHL 9; [2006] 1 W.L.R. 682, HL.

[224] Limitation Act 1980 s.14B(2).

14.115 The potential significance of these provisions in relation to contaminated land situations depends to a large extent on the meaning given to the term "negligence" in ss. 14A and 14B. If it is the case that the word covers only the tort of negligence per se and not, for example, the tort of nuisance, at least where negligence is not involved, this is a potentially significant difference between negligence and the other torts, since it could frequently be argued in contaminated land cases that the ordinary six-year period should be extended in accordance with the provisions of s.14A to allow, for example, expert evidence to be taken to establish the source of groundwater contamination.

14.116 Conversely, the overriding time limit of s.14B could be important in the context of, say, a landfill site completed more than 15 years ago. If it is alleged that the site was operated or engineered negligently, then the 15–year period would run from the completion of the site at the latest: though it might be argued that failure to monitor or to take remedial action constitute further acts or omissions so as to defer the commencement of the period. The issue is the latest date on which negligent conduct occurred,[225] and it should be borne in mind that conduct may only become negligent part way through the activity in question if it goes on for some time.[226] If it is correct that s.14B does not apply to nuisance or *Rylands v Fletcher*, time in respect of those torts would run from the time the cause of action accrued, which might well allow an action to be brought after the expiry of the 15–year period under the section.

Coverage

14.117 The date as to when damage was caused by the negligence can be highly relevant for the purposes of ascertaining whether and, if so, with whom a defendant was insured.[227] Whereas the question of whether an employers' liability insurer is on risk is usually determined by whether the negligent act or omission causative of the injury occurred during the period of insurance, the question of whether a public liability insurer is on risk is usually determined by whether the injury occurred during the period of insurance. The latter gives rise to the question in disease cases as to when it was that injury occurred. The Courts have rejected the notion that actionable injury occurs simply when there is some insult to the body, such as occurs when an asbestos fibre is inhaled. In mesothelioma cases, actionable injury occurs some 30 or 40 years later when a malignant tumour is first created, or even some 10 years later still when identifiable symptoms first occur.[228]

---

[225] See *Pearson Education Ltd v Charter Partnership Ltd* [2007] EWCA Civ 130; [2007] 21 E.G. 132.
[226] *Brookes v South Yorkshire Passenger Transport Executive* [2005] EWCA Civ 452 (CA).
[227] See further the discussion at para.23.21 ff.
[228] See *Bolton MBC v MMI Ltd* [2006] EWCA Civ 50, para.18 (Auld LJ).

Chapter 15

STATUTORY CAUSES OF ACTION

Introduction

15.01 In addition to the common law liabilities discussed in the previous chapter, it is important in the context of contaminated land to be aware of the possibility of those suffering injury or damage to be able to rely on statutory causes of action. Essentially there are three types of situation to be considered:

1. general principles of liability for breach of statutory duty;

2. cases where statute creates a specific cause of action; and

3. the provisions on liability for occupiers of land.

Breach of statutory duty

15.02 As protection of the environment and human health becomes increasingly regulated by statute, so it is arguable that the role of the tort of breach of statutory duty should become correspondingly more significant. However, this does not necessarily appear to be the case in practice. In most instances statutes are silent on the issue of civil liability and in recent years the courts have been wary of inferring that statutory requirements may give rise to a civil cause of action.

15.03 In particular, there will be the need in general to demonstrate either that the statutory obligation or prohibition was imposed for the benefit of a particular class of persons or (more obscurely) that the statute created a public right, interference with which caused the plaintiff to suffer special damage peculiar to himself.[1] In actions for breach of statutory duty outside the principles of negligence the principles are as stated in *Cutler v Wandsworth Stadium Ltd*,[2] i.e. whether on its true construction the statute imposes a duty for the protection of a limited class and whether that class is intended to have a private remedy. Unlike health and safety, consumer or factories legislation, which clearly have in mind a class of individuals (albeit potentially very large) as the object of protection, environmental legislation is generally intended to protect society at large, or indeed the environment at large as opposed to persons. Indeed, the tendency in some recent environmental legislation is to provide explicit restrictions on that

---

[1] *Lonhro Ltd v Shell Petroleum Co Ltd (No. 2)* [1982] A.C. 173, at 185–6.
[2] [1949] A.C. 398.

legislation being used to protect the health and safety of persons at work in its own right.[3] Therefore in the absence of any express provision giving a civil remedy for breach of statutory duty, the arguments for imposing such a duty in relation to environmental offences, whilst not impossible, would appear difficult.[4]

Such difficulty is illustrated by the decision of the Court of Appeal in *Issa* **15.04** *v Hackney LBC*.[5] It was claimed that tenants of a local authority had a statutory cause of action for damages where a nuisance abatement order had been made in respect of housing which was of such poor condition as to be a statutory nuisance.[6] The Court of Appeal rejected that submission, partly on the basis that it would, if correct, give to all who suffered loss or damage as a result of the potentially very wide categories of statutory nuisances, where in most cases such persons would have a common law cause of action. It was regarded as unlikely that Parliament intended to create a new cause of action. There are clear parallels with the Pt IIA regime for contaminated land, which like Pt III is a self-contained regime, not restricted to criminal sanctions, and in respect of which those affected by contaminated land may well have a common law remedy in negligence, nuisance or under *Rylands v Fletcher*. Also, it is difficult to speak of Pt IIA as creating "duties" as such with regard to contaminated land, other than the public law duties of local authorities to inspect land and of enforcing authorities to serve remediation notices.[7] Someone who is responsible for contaminated land as an "appropriate person" is under no duty until such time as a remediation notice is served and takes effect.

So far as Pt II of the Environmental Protection Act 1990 dealing with the **15.05** management of waste is concerned, the existence of a specific cause of action under s.73(6) would suggest strongly that no other or wider civil cause of action was intended to be created. In *C v Imperial Design*[8] a boy was injured when setting light to a can containing solvent which was among rubbish left outside the defendant's premises. The trial judge found liability established in negligence and also found that a breach of the s.34 duty of care had been established. The decision of the Court of Appeal is unenlightening on the relationship between negligence, the s.34 duty of care, and the statutory cause of action under s.73(6) (which does not mention s.34).[9] However, the relevance of s.34 would seem to lie in establishing negligence on the part of the defendant.

For the Water Resources Act 1991 s.100 provides that nothing in Pt III, **15.06** dealing with control of pollution of water resources, confers a right of action in civil proceedings in respect of any contravention of any provision of Pt III, or of any subordinate legislation, or of any consent issued under Pt III.[10]

---

[3] See Environmental Protection Act 1990 s.7(1).

[4] Compare the express provisions on liability of water undertakers for escapes of water: Water Industry Act 1991 s.209.

[5] [1997] 1 W.L.R. 156; [1997] Env. L.R. 157, CA.

[6] At that point, under s.94 of the Public Health Act 1936, now Pt III of the Environmental Protection Act 1990.

[7] The possibility of liability in negligence in relation to those duties is discussed at para.3.162ff.

[8] [2001] Env. L.R. 33, CA.

[9] See para.15.11.

[10] See to similar effect s.105(2) of the Control of Pollution Act 1974.

15.07 A more fruitful source of liability in practice will probably be regulations made under the Health and Safety at Work, etc Act 1974. The 1974 Act itself does not confer a right of action in civil proceedings in respect of any failure to comply with the general duties under ss.2–7 with regard to exposure of employees and others to risks to their health and safety.[11] However, breach of a duty imposed by health and safety regulations shall, insofar as it causes damage, be actionable except insofar as the regulations provide otherwise.[12] "Damage" is confined to bodily injury, i.e. death or personal injury, including disease and any impairment of a person's physical or mental condition.[13] Moreover, any term of an agreement purporting to exclude or restrict the operation of that provision, or of any liability arising under it, is void except insofar as health and safety regulations provide otherwise.[14] In some cases health and safety regulations may be relevant to contaminated land, and may impose duties which benefit persons other than employees: for example, the duties under the Control of Asbestos Regulations 2006[15] apply to other persons, whether employees or not, who may be affected by the work activities being carried out.[16] However, careful attention must be given to whether the regulations in question expressly exclude civil liability in whole or in part. For example, the Management of Health and Safety at Work Regulations 2007, which contain some potentially very broad-ranging duties with regard to the management of risk, expressly do not confer a right of action in civil proceedings, with the very limited exception of duties relating to the employment of young persons.[17] Similarly, breach of the Construction (Design and Management) Regulations 2007, which could be relevant where works of demolition, site clearance, excavation or construction are being carried out on contaminated land, does not (subject to various exceptions) confer a right of action in civil proceedings.[18] Where exposure to harm has occurred in the past it may be necessary to consider the legislation in force at that time.[19]

---

[11] Health and Safety at Work, etc. Act 1974 s.47(1).

[12] Health and Safety at Work, etc. Act 1974 s.47(2).

[13] Health and Safety at Work, etc. Act 1974 s.47(6).

[14] Health and Safety at Work, etc. Act 1974 s.47(5).

[15] SI 2002/2739.

[16] Control of Asbestos Regulations 2006 reg.3(1). See also the Control of Substances Hazardous to Health Regulations 2002/2677 reg.3(4) and note also the extended meaning given to the term "work" by reg.19.

[17] SI 1999/3242 reg.22(1). See *Cross v Highlands & Islands Enterprises* [2001] I.R.L.R. 336 (Court of Session, Outer House) (held that exclusion not in breach of EC Framework Directive). These Regulations may however be relevant in that non-compliance may provide evidence of breach of a common law duty of care: see *Poppleton v Trustees of Portsmouth Youth Activities Committee* [2007] EWHC 1567 (QB).

[18] SI 2007/320, reg.45. Those exceptions (which could have practical relevance) are the duty on the client to ensure suitable arrangements for managing the project (reg.9(1)(a)), the duty on the contractor not to begin work until reasonable steps have been taken to prevent access by unauthorised persons (reg.13(6)), to take reasonable steps to prevent access by unauthorised persons to the site (reg.22(1)(l)) and a significant number of specific duties relating to management of aspects of risk on the site (regs 26–44).

[19] See for example, *Fairchild v Glenhaven Funeral Services Ltd* [2001] EWCA Civ 1881; [2002] 1 W.L.R. 1052, CA, paras 111–112, where a breach was admitted on one occasion in respect of s.63(1) of the Factories Act 1961 (then in force) which provided that in every factory in

Section 1 of the Compensation Act 2006 provides that, in determining **15.08** whether the defendant should have taken particular steps to meet a standard of care (whether by taking precautions against a risk or otherwise), a court considering a claim for breach of statutory duty may have regard to whether a requirement to take those steps might either prevent a desirable activity being undertaken at all, to a particular extent, or in a particular way, or discourage persons from undertaking functions in connection with a desirable activity. By s.2 of the 2006 Act, an apology, offer of treatment or other redress shall not of itself amount to an admission of negligence or breach of statutory duty.

Specific statutory causes of action

The main statutory causes of action, leaving aside occupiers' liability, **15.09** which may be relevant to contaminated land are:

1. harm from unlawfully deposited waste;

2. harm from occurrences involving nuclear matter.

Other provisions which are of less relevance and which are not consid- **15.10** ered further are those relating to damage by contamination resulting from oil pollution caused by tankers under the Merchant Shipping Act 1995 s.153,[20] and to civil liability for loss or damage caused by escapes of water from pipes vested in water undertakers under s.209(1) of the Water Industry Act 1991.

Unlawful waste deposits

Section 73(6) of the Environmental Protection Act 1990 is one of the few **15.11** environmental provisions which does provide an express civil cause of action. Under the subsection where any damage is caused by waste which has been deposited on land so as to commit an offence under s.33(1) (controlled waste) or s.63(2) (other waste) then the person who deposited it, or who knowingly caused or knowingly permitted the deposit so as to commit an offence, is liable for the damage. This liability is subject to possible defences under subs.73(6) and (7). In *C v Imperial Design*[21] the provision was considered in relation to injuries to a 13-year-old boy who set fire to solvent in a can left lying on an area of ground near the defendant's factory. The Court of Appeal reduced the contributory negligence attribu-

which, in connection with any process carried on, there is given off any dust or fume or other impurity, all practicable measures shall be taken to protect the persons employed against inhalation and to prevent it accumulating in any workroom.

[20] See *Landcatch Ltd v International Oil Pollution Compensation Fund* [1999] 2 Lloyd's Rep. 316 (Court of Session, Inner House); *P&O Scottish Ferries Ltd v Braer Corporation* [1999] 2 Lloyd's Rep. 535 (Court of Session, Inner House); *Alegrete Shipping Company, Inc v International Oil Pollution Compensation Fund 1971 (The Sea Empress)* [2003] 1 Lloyd's Rep 327; [2003] Env. L.R. 191 (CA) (considering issue of recoverability of economic loss).

[21] [2001] Env. L.R. 33.

table to the claimant from 70 to 50 per cent,[22] though the decision is inconclusive as to the real scope of s.73(6). Potter L.J., while not deciding the point, found "some force" in the submission for the defendant that the Act was aimed at damage directly caused by the deposit of waste, not at cases where waste was removed and used by the claimant in such a way as to cause himself injury. Arden L.J. proceeded on the basis that a claim under s.73(6) had not been made out, but observed that the section could not be regarded as simply for the protection of the environment, but was also to protect those who might suffer personal injury.

15.12   It should be noted that liability is not confined to cases where waste is deposited on land without a licence; it may also arise where waste is deposited on a licensed site in a manner likely to cause pollution of the environment or harm to human health.[23] However, the offence of breach of site licence conditions will not give rise to liability under this provision.[24]

15.13   Similar provision for liability was made by the Deposit of Poisonous Waste Act 1972 s.2 and by the Control of Pollution Act 1974 s.88. Any possible application of these provisions to historical unlawful deposits of waste remains to be tested.

Liability for nuclear "occurrences"

15.14 Section 7(1)(a) of the Nuclear Installations Act 1965 imposes a duty on the licensee of a nuclear installation not to permit an occurrence involving nuclear matter[25] to cause injury to any person or damage to property of any person other than the licensee, arising out of or resulting from the radioactive properties, or a combination of those and any toxic, explosive or other hazardous properties of that nuclear matter. Under s.7(1)(b) there is a further duty not to cause injury or damage from the emission of ionising radiation from anything caused or suffered to be on a nuclear installation that is not nuclear matter, or any waste discharged on or from the installation.[26] By s.12 there is a statutory right to compensation, up to the maximum limit established under s.16, in respect of injury or damage caused in breach of these duties. This is the only remedy, as s.12(1)(b) excludes any other liability on the part of the licensee or any other person.

15.15   These provisions will be relevant where land is contaminated by nuclear matter which escapes from a nuclear licensed site, or where waste discharged from such a site contaminates land, or where nuclear matter escapes which being carried.[27] Indeed they will be the only remedy so far as

---

[22] Essentially on the basis that the trial judge had misapprehended the relevance of the extent to which a 13-year-old should have been aware of the explosive risks presented by the mixture of combustible solvent and air in the can.

[23] 1990 Act s.33(1)(c).

[24] The offence here is under s.33(6), not s.33(1).

[25] "Nuclear matter" is defined by s.26. The occurrences in question are broadly those which occur on the licensed site during the licensee's period of responsibility, those involving nuclear matter being carried and those involving matter which has been on the licensed site or in the course of carriage on behalf of the licensee, until such time as responsibility has passed to some other person in accordance with the provisions of the Act.

[26] Similar duties apply by ss.8 and 9 in relation to UK Atomic Energy Authority and Crown sites and by s.11 to nuclear matter in the course of carriage.

[27] As to the relationship between the 1965 Act and the provisions of Pt IIA as applied to radioactive contamination, see para.9.08ff.

injury or damage caused in breach of the relevant duties is concerned. Any injury or damage which, though not caused in breach of such duties, is not reasonably separable from injury or damage so caused, is deemed to have been so caused.[28] The injury or damage do not have to arise solely from the radioactive properties of the nuclear matter, but can also arise from a combination of those properties and other hazardous properties, such as toxicity.[29]

"Injury" in this context means personal injury and includes loss of life,[30] **15.16** and may include disabilities caused to children as a result of exposure of their parents to radioactivity, or the inability to have normal, healthy children caused by such exposure.[31] It has been held that the risk of future injury by the presence of radioactive particles in the human airways, digestive tracts or bloodstream do not of themselves amount to injury.[32]

Damage to property is a concept which has given rise to uncertainty in **15.17** the case law, and where the facts as to the nature and degree of the contamination of land will be important.[33]

Occupiers' liability: lawful visitors

An occupier of premises owes the same duty, the "common duty of care", **15.18** to all his visitors, except insofar as he is free to and does extend, modify or exclude his duty by agreement or otherwise.[34] The duty is to take such care as in all the circumstances of the case is reasonable to see that the visitor will be reasonably safe in using the premises for the purpose for which he is invited or permitted by the occupier to be there.[35] These duties regulate the position in place of the common law.[36]

Risks to visitors may arise either from the condition of premises or from **15.19** activities carried out on the premises. In *Fairchild v Glenhaven Funeral Services*[37] some claims related in part to occupiers' liability, where the defendant had employed contractors to carry out work involving asbestos materials at their premises. The issue arose as to whether the occupier of the premises was liable in cases where that exposure was after the introduction of the 1957 Act. The Court of Appeal (this point not being addressed in the House of Lords) held that the exposure did not arise from the static state of the premises but from the way in which the contractors carried out the relevant work. The occupier's duty did not extend to risks

---

[28] 1990 Act s.12(2).

[29] See s.7(1)(a).

[30] 1990 Act s.26(1).

[31] Congenital Disabilities (Civil Liability) Act 1976 s.3. See *Reay v British Nuclear Fuels*; *Hope v British Nuclear Fuels* [1994] P.I.Q.R. P71; [1994] Env. L.R. 320, Q.B.

[32] *Merlin v British Nuclear Fuels plc* [1990] Q.B. 557 at 571, QB; approved in *Magnohard Ltd v UK Atomic Energy Authority* [2004] Env. L.R. 19, para.148 (Court of Session, Outer House).

[33] See *Blue Circle Industries plc v Ministry of Defence* [1999] Ch. 289, CA and other cases referred to at para14.93.

[34] Occupier's Liability Act 1957 s.2(1).

[35] Occupier's Liability Act 1957 s.2(2).

[36] Occupier's Liability Act 1957 s.1(1).

[37] [2001] EWCA Civ 1881; [2002] 1 W.L.R. 1052, CA; [2002] 3 W.L.R.89 (HL). As to that case on the issue of causation, see para.14.89.

arising from those activities. Under the pre-1957 common law, the duties of an occupier distinguished between "occupancy duties" (the dangerous static state of premises) and "activity duties".[38] The Occupiers' Liability Act 1957 was similarly concerned with the state of premises and with occupancy liability. It was held not to be correct to impose what amounted to an employer's duty of care in relation to someone else's employees. Whilst an occupier can be liable in respect of the "activity duty" for activities which they encourage or permit, this will be in negligence rather than the 1957 Act.[39]

15.20 In contaminated land cases it will therefore be necessary to distinguish between instances where liability relates to the state of the land, as opposed to the activity of contractors on the land releasing or spreading contaminants so as to expose visitors to risk. Factually this may not always be an easy distinction to draw. Where no activity is involved, the 1957 Act duty will be applicable if land is contaminated in such a way as to present risks to visitors in relation to the purposes for which they are on the premises.[40] It will be irrelevant that the occupier was not responsible for creating the contamination; in that sense the Act may require the taking of positive remedial steps to ensure safety.

15.21 The test of who is the "occupier" is based upon the degree of control over the premises rather than ownership or exclusive rights of occupation.[41] It is not necessary to have full or exclusive control; the question is whether there was sufficient control as lessor, lessee, sublessee, as the case may be, that such person ought to realise that failure of care on their part could result in injury to a lawful visitor.[42] The terms of any lease will be relevant in this regard, and it appears that what is relevant is not simply what degree of control a landlord exercised in fact, but what powers they had under the lease to exercise control.[43] Where the state of the premises results from the acts of a tenant or licensee, the owner (if an occupier) may be found to have discharged their duty of care if they have taken reasonable steps through urging or warning to require the licensee or tenant to address the risk.[44]

15.22 The Act does not impose strict liability. The key test will be what is reasonable by way of the steps to be taken in each case. This will involve consideration of what action by a visitor was reasonably foreseeable, and whether the situation created a foreseeable risk of injury.[45] Such cases will be fact-sensitive, but the duty may involve a requirement to put in place an

---

[38] See *Indermauer v Dames* (1866) L.R. 1 C.P. 274.

[39] See *Bottomley v Tormorden Cricket Club* [2003] EWCA Civ 1575 (CA) (cricket club allowed dangerous pyrotechnic display by stunt team with no public liability insurance or written safety plan); *Ferguson v Welsh* [1987] 1553 W.L.R. (HL) considered. Existence of insurance was regarded as relevant to the test of competence of a contractor in *Gwilliam v West Hertfordshire Hopital NHS Trust* [2002] EWCA Civ 1041; [2002] 3 W.L.R. 1425, CA.

[40] For this purpose it does not matter whether or not there is a contract between the occupier and visitor: *Maguire v Sefton MBC* [2006] EWCA Civ 316 (CA).

[41] *Wheat v E. Lacon & Co Ltd* [1966] A.C. 552.

[42] *Wheat v E. Lacon & Co Ltd* [1966] A.C. 552.

[43] See *Ribee v Norrie* [2001] P.I.Q.R. P128, CA.

[44] *Piccolo v Larkstock Ltd (t/a Chiltern Flowers)* (July 17, 2007, QBD) (owners of station concourse not in breach of duty in respect of slippery floor caused by florist's stall).

[45] *Christian Lewis v Six Continents Plc* [2005] EWCA Civ 1805 (CA).

effective system of risk management measures which is not simply reactive to situations which have already occurred.[46] The duty will not necessarily require the occupier to improve premises which were built in accordance with contemporary standards, to bring them up to modern standards of safety.[47] Whether appropriately qualified experts were retained will be a relevant consideration.[48] In many cases involving contaminated land the most practical way of discharging the duty may be by means of warning signs or notices and barriers[49]; however, a warning will not be treated without more as absolving the occupier from liability, unless in all the circumstances it was enough to allow the visitor to be reasonably safe.[50]

Duty to trespassers

An occupier of premises owes a duty to persons other than his visitors in respect of any risk of their suffering injury on the premises by reason of any danger due to the state of the premises[51] or to things done or omitted to be done on them.[52] The duty only comes into being if: **15.23**

(a) the occupier is aware of the danger or has reasonable grounds to believe that it exists;

(b) the occupier knows or has reasonable grounds to believe that the other person is in the vicinity of the danger concerned or that he may come into its vicinity; and

(c) the risk is one against which, in all the circumstances of the case, he may reasonably be expected to offer the other some protection.[53]

The facts and circumstances which are relevant are those which were known at the time of the accident or injury, not those which only became known later.[54] Where the source of danger is not apparent to the occupier, they must have awareness of it, or reasonable grounds for awareness, to pass the threshold test for liability; there is no duty to inspect for unseen hazards where there is no reasonable ground to suspect their existence.[55] **15.24**

---

[46] *Piccolo v Larkstock Ltd (t/a Chiltern Flowers)* (July 17, 2007, QBD); *Ward v Tesco Stores* [1976] 1 W.L.R. 810, CA *Cole v Davies-Gilbert* [2007] EWCA Civ 396 (CA) (hole on village green for maypole filled in but then re-excavated, probably by children).

[47] *McGivney v Golderslea Ltd* (CA, November 6, 1997).

[48] *Maguire v Sefton MBC* [2006] EWCA Civ 316; [2006] 1 W.L.R. 2550, CA (inspection of gym equipment).

[49] See *Rae v Mars (UK) Ltd* [1990] 3 EG 80 (no warning sign or fencing of deep pit, close to unlit entrance to shed).

[50] 1957 Act s.(4)(a).

[51] There must be a defect in the state of the premises. There is no liability if a child falls off a fire escape which is in perfect condition: *Keown v Coventry Healthcare NHS Trust* [2006] EWCA Civ 39; [2006] 1 W.L.R. 953; *Tomlinson v Congleton BC* [2004] 1 A.C. 46.

[52] Occupier's Liability Act 1984 s.1(1).

[53] Occupier's Liability Act 1984 s.1(3).

[54] *Donoghue v Folkestone Properties Ltd* [2003] EWCA Civ 231; [2003] 2 W.L.R. 1138; *Maloney v Torfaen County BC* [2005] EWCA Civ 1762; [2006] P.I.Q.R. P21, CA.

[55] *Rhind v Astbury Water Park Ltd* [2004] EWCA Civ 756 (CA) (underwater hazard at lake).

Thus an occupier will not fall under the duty if he is not or has no reason to be aware that the site is contaminated so as to present a danger; nor if he could not reasonably anticipate the presence of trespassers. However, many contaminated sites are of the very type to attract trespassing children, or adults, gypsies or travelers. Such circumstances can, in practical terms, present very real difficulties for the occupier of the site, given that they may quite naturally be reluctant to advertise to the whole world by warning signs the fact that the site may be dangerously contaminated.

15.25   The occupier will first need to consider whether the risk is one in respect of which he may reasonably be expected to offer protection: this will depend principally on the nature of the risk, site conditions and on the nature of the likely trespass. The occupier must be prepared for children to be less careful than adults.[56] Interesting items such as drums containing toxic or flammable materials may be a "trap" or "allurement" for a child.[57] Obviously, more will be expected of the occupier where small children are trespassing on bare toxic soil than where adults are trespassing; since it may be anticipated that children are more likely to come into bodily contact with, or even ingest, soil. On the other hand in some cases the risks to adults and children may be identical—for example the risk of exposure to radioactive materials. Also, the risk that a trespasser may disturb contaminants, for example by digging or scavenging, should be considered. What matters is the broad nature of the injury foreseeable, not the precise means by which it occurs.[58]

15.26   Special attention now needs to be given to land over which the public has a "right to roam" for open air recreation under Pt I of the Countryside and Rights of Way Act 2000. This right applies to land shown as "open country" on maps prepared by Natural England. The Act originally was capable of applying to mountain land, moorland, heathland and downland, but there is a power to extend it also to coastal land. Such land may well be subject to contamination to varying degrees. By s.13 of the 2000 Act, a person entering land in exercise of these rights is not a visitor within the Occupiers' Liability Act 1957, but will rather be subject to the Occupiers' Liability Act 1984, as if they were a trespasser. Also, the duty under the 1984 Act is itself modified so that no duty is owed in respect of a "risk resulting from the existence of a natural feature of the landscape, or any river, stream, ditch or pond whether or not a natural feature".[59] It seems doubtful that risk resulting from the presence of man-made contamination would fall within that exclusion.

15.27   Assuming it is reasonable to expect some steps to be taken, the duty is to take such care as is reasonable in all the circumstances.[60] In appropriate cases the risk may be discharged by taking reasonable steps to give warning of the danger or to discourage persons from incurring the risk[61];

---

[56] s.2(3)(a).
[57] See *Jolley v London Borough of Sutton* [2000] 1 W.L.R. 1082, HL (rotten boat abandoned on land).
[58] *Jolley v London Borough of Sutton* [2000] 1 W.L.R. 1082, HL
[59] s.1(6A), inserted by s.13(2) of the 2004 Act.
[60] s.1(4).
[61] s.1(5).

further, no duty is owed in respect of risks voluntarily accepted.[62] In many cases the nature of contamination will not be such as to present an obvious indication of risk: in practical terms the options will lie between the use of warning signs or the construction of physical barriers. However, a warning sign may not of itself be sufficient if trespass by small children or even young adults may be anticipated and in such cases the only safe solution may be steps physical to prevent access.[63] It has not been settled whether the occupier's own financial resources are to be taken into account in determining what steps may be reasonably required[64] though this may be a very important practical issue in relation to a derelict and contaminated site. Since the duty is to take such care as is reasonable in all the circumstances of the case, there seems no reason in principle why the question of financial resources should not be relevant. In the case of risks to persons exercising the "right to roam" over open country,[65] it is provided that in determining what duty is owed under the 1984 Act, regard must be had to the fact that the existence of the right to roam ought not to place an unfair burden (whether financial or otherwise) on the occupier.[66] It may be noted that in cases where dangerous material is fly-tipped on land, the powers of a local authority to secure its removal, for example under s.59 of the Environmental Protection Act 1990, may be relevant.[67]

---

[62] s.1(6).

[63] Any barriers used will need to be properly maintained: see *Adams v Southern Electricity Board*, *The Times*, October 21, 1993.

[64] Compare *British Railways Board v Herrington* [1972] A.C. 877.

[65] See para.15.26.

[66] 1984 Act s.1A, inserted by s.13(3) of the 2004 Act.

[67] See *Jolley v London Borough of Sutton* [2000] 1 W.L.R. 1082, HL where it was noted that a rotten cabin cruiser left abandoned on the defendant local authority's land for a considerable time could have been removed by it under the Refuse Disposal (Amenity) Act 1978.

SECTION 5
DEVELOPMENT

Chapter 16

PLANNING PERMISSION

Introduction

The planning system has for some years been an important way in which **16.01**
contaminated land issues may be addressed by local authorities in the
context of applications for planning permission to develop land. Part of the
"suitable for use approach" which underlies the operation of Pt IIA is
ensuring that land is made suitable for any new use, as planning
permission is given for that use, and that land is remediated before a new
use commences where this is necessary to avoid unacceptable risks to
human health or the environment.[1] The approach is seen as the best
means of reconciling the various environmental, social and economic needs
in relation to contaminated land. Land contamination, or the possibility of
it, is a material consideration for the purposes of town and country
planning, both in formulating plans and in considering individual planning
applications. Thus, where development is taking place, the enforcement of
remediation requirements will normally be through the planning and
building control systems, rather than through a remediation notice under
Pt IIA.[2] Indeed, the successful remediation of many contaminated sites in
the course of development may go at least some way to explain the
relatively low numbers of such sites identified under Pt IIA in the early
years of that regime.

Thus planning law presents one way in which problems of contaminated **16.02**
land can be addressed, but only if the development of land is in prospect. In
such circumstances planning conditions or s.106 obligations can provide
legally-binding mechanisms to ensure that risks from contamination are
effectively addressed at the expense of the landowner or developer
applicant. The situation may arise where contamination comes to the
attention of the district council as enforcing authority when development is
in prospect—perhaps as a result of information supplied as part of a
planning application. The fact that planning powers may be able to secure
decontamination will not of itself discharge the enforcing authority's duty
to serve a remediation notice. The appropriate course is rather to consider
whether the appropriate things will in any event be done by way of
remediation without service of a notice—if so then by s.78H(5)(b) service
of a remediation notice will be precluded.[3] The authority should however
bear in mind that whilst planning powers may be able to secure remedia-

[1] DEFRA Circular 01/2006, *Contaminated Land*, Annex 1 para.10(b).
[2] DEFRA Circular 01/2006, *Contaminated Land*, Annex 1 paras 41–44.
[3] See para.4.39ff. See also advice at PPS 23, Annex 2: *Development on Land Affected by
Contamination*, paras 2.12–2.16.

tion in the event that development goes forward, the fact that planning permission will be implemented is not a foregone conclusion. This is a situation that may therefore need to be kept under review on a regular basis. Local planning authorities may need to resist the temptation to elide the two regimes, which have different purposes. Planning law is concerned with ensuring that the risks consequent on developing and changing the use of contaminated land are properly identified and addressed. Part IIA is concerned with ensuring that unacceptable risks arising from the land in its current use are removed and allocating and apportioning the liability for the costs of doing so. To try to deal with complex liability issues in the context of a planning application or s.106 agreement risks going beyond the proper bounds of land use planning. It may also result in an adverse costs award against the authority, as in one case involving an application for 80 dwellings on an old gasworks site in Leamington Spa, where the planning authority tried to impose detailed arrangements for long-term liability on the developer and its consultants.[4]

Policy guidance: generally

16.03 Planning guidance on contaminated land can be traced back to Circular 21/87 and in essence has changed little over the years. The 1987 Circular stressed the desirability of recycling and re-use of previously developed land, and the importance of taking potential contamination into account as a material consideration at all stages of the development control process, and as early as possible. Local planning authorities should take account of contamination, actual or potential, in preparing policies for future land use and development will be set out, together with actual allocations. It is fundamental to the system that planning permission will only be granted if the applicant can secure a clean-up of the site to an acceptable standard which will turn on the proposed use. That remains the position under the current guidance, which is to be found in PPS 23: *Planning and Pollution Control*, which came into effect on November 3, 2004. Annex 1 of PPS23 deals with pollution control, air and water quality in the context of development control. Annex 1 should be read alongside PPS23 with which it has equal weight in development control matters. Annex 2 gives detailed guidance about development of land affected by contamination. It deals amongst other things with the following:

1. The Contaminated Land Regime.

2. Radioactively contaminated land.

3. Relationship between planning control and the Contaminated Land Regime.

4. Responsibilities of the parties in the development process.

5. Planning control.

[4] *Warwick DC v Tom Pettifer Homes Ltd* (1995) 10 P.A.D. 665.

6. Development Plans.

7. Development control.

As to the relationship between planning control and the Contaminated **16.04**
Land Regime, para.2.16 of Annex 2, importantly states:

> "Where contaminated land is identified and determined as such
> under Part IIA [of the Contaminated Land Regime] but the
> enforcing authority (the local authority or the Environment
> Agency in the case of special sites) is satisfied that appropriate
> actions are being or will be undertaken by way of remediation
> without the service of a remediation notice, it cannot serve such
> a notice. Instead a remediation statement can be agreed and
> placed in the public register and kept under review."

A guide to the relevant paragraphs in PPS23 is set out in tabular form
below.

Subject Matter	PPS23 reference
Government policy (planning and pollution control)	Paras 8–12
Development plans (pollution)	Para.13 App.A and Annex 1 paras 1.25–1.28
Pre-application discussions (pollution)	Para.14 and Annex 1 para.1.3
Development control (pollution)	Para.15 and Annex 1 paras 1.29–1.32
Applications for permission	Annex 1 paras 1.34–1.35
Water pollution	Annex 1 paras 1.21–1.23
Outline planning permission	Annex 1 paras 1.36–37
Environmental Impact Assessment	Annex 1 paras 1.38–1.41
Consultation	Annex 1 paras 1.42–1.46
Planning conditions	Annex 1 paras 1.47–1.49
Planning obligations	Annex 1 para.1.50
Need and alternative sites	Annex 1 paras 1.54–1.55
Assessment of risk	Annex 1 paras 1.56–1.59
Pollution control responsibilities	App.1A paras 1A.1—1A.10.

Subject Matter	PPS23 reference
Contamination	
Government policy on land contamination	Paras 16–20
Development plan (contamination)	Para.21 and see paras 2.28–2.32 of Annex 2
Pre-application discussions (contamination)	Para.22 and see para.2.34 Annex 2
Development control (contamination)	Paras 23–25 and see para.2.33 PPS23
Examples of potentially contaminating uses	Table 2.1 Annex 2
Examples of pathways and effects	Table 2.2 Annex 2
Determining applications	Paras 2.49–2.54 PPS23
Outline planning applications	Para.2.55 Annex 2
Consultation	Paras 2.56–2.58 Annex 2
Planning conditions	Paras 2.61–2.65 Annex 2 and see examples in App.2B
Planning obligations	Para.2.66 Annex 2

Relationship to other planning policy areas

16.05 Other policy guidance, such as that on housing, stresses that the priority for development should be "previously developed land", in particular vacant and derelict sites and buildings.[5] "Previously developed land" is defined in this context to mean land which is or was occupied by a permanent structure, including the curtilage of the developed land and associated fixed surface infrastructure, but excluding restored mineral extraction or landfill sites and land where the remains of the structures have blended into the landscape over time, so as to be reasonably considered part of the natural surroundings.[6] The relationship between policies on contaminated land and green belt was considered in *Dowmunt-Iwaszkiewicz v First Secretary of State*[7] where there was a planning application to develop an old mushroom farm in the Nottingham Green Belt for housing. The derelict buildings on site contained approximately 3,000 cubic metres of asbestos, and the applicant could not afford to deal with this unless the land could be developed for housing. The inspector on appeal

---

[5] See, para.36.
[6] PPS 3 Housing, Annex B.
[7] [2004] EWHC 2537 (Admin); [2005] Env. L.R. 19, Q.B.

concluded that while it was in the general public interest to deal with the risk associated with the asbestos, citing the then current Circular 02/2000 on Contaminated Land, the presence of the contamination did not amount to very special circumstances sufficient to set aside the presumption against inappropriate development in the green belt. The court held that the inspector had not misinterpreted the guidance; the fact that contamination on a site was causing unacceptable risks was not itself justification for undertaking development that was unsuitable in the green belt. However, the inspector's decision was quashed for failing to give adequate reasons for arriving at his conclusion as to why the public interest in this case did not amount to very special circumstances. In other words, the need to address contamination can be a material consideration to weigh against other countervailing considerations, but is not an automatic "trump card".

The need for planning permission

Many schemes for the clean-up of contaminated land arise within the **16.06** framework of wider proposals for the physical development and possibly the change of use of a site. In such cases, the issue of contaminated land is likely to be addressed as part of the application for that ultimate development and the planning permission for the new development will include proposals for any necessary clean-up operation. However, even where clean-up operations are undertaken on land with no immediate view to further development, for example in order to reduce the risk of liability or under compulsion or pressure from a regulatory authority, those operations may well of themselves constitute development requiring planning permission.

Development is defined by s.55(1) of the Town and Country Planning **16.07** Act 1990 to mean "the carrying out of building, engineering, mining or other operations in, on, over on under or the making of any material change in the use of any buildings or other land". Whilst a reclamation scheme of itself may not involve building operations, which are defined by s.55(1A) of the 1990 Act to include demolition of buildings, rebuilding, structural alterations of or additions to buildings, and other operations normally undertaken by a person carrying on business as a builder, it may well fall within the category of "engineering operations" or "other operations". Such operations are not exhaustively defined in s.336 of the 1990 Act and in view of the statutory definition of "building operations" it is perhaps a reasonable presumption that they are operations normally undertaken by a person carrying on business as an engineer or ground contractor. As such, they could well include the earth moving operations which will inevitably form part of most clean-up schemes. Such an approach would be consistent with the decision of Deputy Judge David Widdicombe Q.C. in *Fayrewood Fishfarms Limited v Secretary of State for the Environment and Hampshire C.C.*.[8] In that case, the Deputy Judge referred to engineering operations as being those of a type usually undertaken by, or

[8] [1984] J.P.L. 267.

calling for the skills of an engineer. It was not necessary that the engineer should actually be engaged on the project, not that any specific branch of the engineering profession (such as civil engineering) should be involved; nor is it necessary for there to be detailed plans of the proposed works, though the existence of such plans might constitute important evidence indicating operational development.

16.08 Section 336 of the 1990 Act defines "engineering operations" as including "the formation or laying out of means of access to highways," and therefore might apply to a reclamation scheme which has in mind the creation of such an access, particularly where highly contaminated areas of the site are to be used for hard covered areas.

16.09 In any event, consideration should be given in each case whether the operations in question are such as to benefit from any of the categories of permitted development under the Town and Country Planning (General Permitted Development) Order 1995, as amended.[9] Likewise, special considerations will apply in relation to schemes within enterprise zones and simplified planning zones; reference should be made to standard works on planning law for the position here.

Environmental assessment

16.10 European Council Directive 85/337 of July 5, 1985 introduced a requirement of the assessment of the environmental effects of certain public and private projects. The Directive has been implemented by the Town and Country Planning (Environmental Impact Assessment) Regulations 1999 as amended.[10] In broad terms the Directive distinguishes between Annex I projects where assessment is required in all cases, and Annex II projects where a decision on the significance of the likely effects has to be made on a case-by-case basis. Under the Environmental Impact Assessment Regulations the division is between Sch.1 and Sch.2 applications. As para.12 of PPS23 indicates:

> "The consideration of an Environmental Statement prepared as part of an Environmental Impact Assessment (EIA) is usually the most convenient way of ensuring the environmental impacts of a significant development proposal are comprehensibly considered."

16.11 The matter was put more strongly by Richards J. in *Gillespie v First Secretary of State*[11]:

> "There are legitimate public concerns about the risks of development on contaminated land and, although that is not in itself a reason for requiring an EIA, the EIA procedure should ensure

[9] SI 1995/418 (as amended).
[10] SI 1999/293.
[11] [2003] EWHC 8 (Admin); [2003] 1 P. & C.R. 745, para.80; upheld by Court of Appeal [2003] EWCA Civ 400; [2003] Env. L.R. 30.

that the public is fully informed of, and given a full opportunity to comment on, the extent of those risks and the measures proposed to meet them."

The scope of the Directive and Regulations is broad, and includes **16.12** general infrastructure projects within Sch.2: these may include, for example, significant residential, retail or other commercial development on land which may be contaminated.[12] Schedule 2 applications are only classed as "EIA development" if they are likely to have significant effects by virtue of factors such as its nature, size or location (reg.2(1)). In practice the first step is to determine whether the development proposed falls within Sch.2 at all; if it does so then a "screening process" must be applied to determine whether an EIA is required. How contamination is addressed and treated is clearly one of the potentially significant effects of the development, and as such is information which may need to be included within the environmental statement. One potential problem is that at the time of seeking planning permission (particularly outline permission) only limited information may be available on the exact nature and extent of the contamination and on the proposed treatment methods. This will have implications for any screening process (if there is an issue as to whether or not development within Sch.2 requires EIA) and for the adequacy of the environmental statement (if one is provided).

Screening

As to screening, the case law is clear that the question of whether a **16.13** development is likely to have significant effects on the environment is a matter for the judgment of the local planning authority, but there is a logically prior question for the authority of whether it has sufficient information to allow it to form a sensible judgment on that question.[13] These decisions will only be challengeable on *Wednesbury* unreasonableness grounds.[14] Where a multi-stage project is being approached by way of separate applications, whether it falls within Sch.1 or Sch.2 is to be decided by reference to the application itself. If there is a Sch.2 project, then, in deciding whether significant effects are likely so as to require EIA, the authority must consider the wider cumulative implications, if any.[15]

Thus the first question for the planning authority, where Sch.2 develop- **16.14** ment is proposed on a potentially contaminated site, is what information it has on the condition of the site and whether the gaps in information make it possible to undertake a screening process. The fact that further investigations will take place at a later stage to provide fuller information does not necessarily mean that the information presently available is inadequate for this purpose.[16] One possible approach where there are gaps

[12] See, e.g. Sch.2 paras 10(a) and (b).
[13] See for example *R (Malster) v Ipswich BC* [2001] EWHC 711 (Admin).
[14] *R (Jones) v Mansfield DC* [2003] EWCA Civ 1408; [2004] Env. L.R. 21, CA; *R (Noble Organisation) v Thanet DC* [2005] EWCA Civ 782; [2006] Env. L.R. 8.
[15] *R (Candlish) v Hastings BC* [2005] EWHC 1539 (Admin); [2006] Env. L.R. 13.
[16] *R (Jones) v Mansfield DC* [2003] EWCA Civ 1408; [2004] Env. L.R. 21, CA; *R (PPG11 Ltd) v Dorset CC* [2004] Env. L.R. 5, Q.B.

in the information is to assume the worst case, i.e. that contamination is present, and to consider whether the effects are likely to be significant on that basis. The second question is whether significant effects are likely. Clearly development of contaminated land is capable in principle of having such effects, though of course in practice whether such effects are likely will depend on how the development is carried out, the precautions taken, and the remedial measures carried out. An important question here is how far the authority should take into account the remedial measures proposed by the developer in deciding whether significant effects are likely.

16.15   This question was addressed by the Court of Appeal in *Gillespie v First Secretary of State*,[17] where the redevelopment of a former gas works site was proposed, in close proximity to dense residential development and a school. A full picture of the contamination could not be obtained until the site structures were removed. The Secretary of State was of the view that significant effects were not likely because of a condition requiring further investigation and remediation. The Court held that the Secretary of State had applied the wrong test in assuming that this meant that significant effects were unlikely. A case-specific consideration of the nature of the proposed measures, any uncertainties and contingencies, and whether their effectiveness could be reliably established. Otherwise, simply relying on an assumption of effectiveness would pre-empt the very form of enquiry contemplated by the Directive and Regulations.[18] It may be noted in that case that the potential contamination covered a large part of the site, and might reasonably have been expected to affect the form and layout of the development, as well as presenting hazards to local residents in its excavation and treatment. The issue was considered further by the Court of Appeal in *R (Catt) v Brighton and Hove CC*,[19] where it was held that in deciding whether EIA was required, it was necessary to examine the actual characteristics of any given project. Unless the project could on the basis of proper assessment be regarded as being not likely to have significant effects, then EIA was required.[20] This approach did not lend itself to easy rules of thumb on whether remedial measures might be taken into account, or the extent to which their likely effect might be predicted, and there is no rule that conditions providing for ameliorative or remedial measures must be ignored. Much the same approach will apply to controls exercised over the development under other legislative regime (for example waste management licensing). The local authority is not entitled, in relation to a particular area of potential impact, to take the view that, simply because subsequent consent from some other responsible body would be required, no further consideration need be given as to whether there are likely to be significant effects in that area, what those would be, or what mitigation measures were needed. However, a local authority is entitled to reach the conclusion, on the basis of such information as it has and in the light of the need for subsequent consent from the other responsible body, that the effects are unlikely to be significant.[21]

[17] [2003] EWCA Civ 400; [2003] Env. L.R. 30.
[18] [2003] EWCA Civ 400; [2003] Env. L.R. 30 para.46 per Laws L.J.
[19] [2007] EWCA Civ 298.
[20] Applying Case C-435/97 *World Wildlife Fund (WWF) v Autonome Provinz Bozen* [1999] E.C.R. I–5613.
[21] *Atkinson v Secretary of State for Transport* [2006] EWHC 995 (Admin) (issue of disposal of excavated spoil from proposed tunnel).

Screening is therefore an area where a local planning authority will need **16.16** to tread carefully where development is proposed on contaminated land. Certainly, if contamination is an aspect of the development which is plainly relevant and is not considered as part of the screening process there is a risk that the planning permission will be quashed.[21a] From the developer's perspective, the safest course may often be simply to submit an environmental statement and avoid possible argument or legal challenge. This is particularly so in view of the approach to outline planning permission and reserved matters in the *Barker* litigation.[22] The effect of the decisions of the European Court and House of Lords in these cases is that outline planning permission and the approval of reserved matters constitute a multi-stage development consent process for EIA purposes. European law requires EIA to be undertaken at the earliest possible stage. However, there may be cases where the authority is required to carry out an EIA after outline permission has been granted. Examples are where the need for an EIA was overlooked at the outline stage, or where the increased level of detail at reserved matters stage reveals that the development may have significant effects that were not anticipated earlier, or where new matters come to light in the interim period. In that event account will have to be taken of "all the aspects of the project that which have not yet been assessed or which have been identified for the first time as requiring assessment".[23] If it is likely that there will be significant effects on the environment which have not previously been identified, an EIA must be carried out at the reserved matters stage before consent is given for the development[24]; it is no longer the case that if significant adverse impacts on the environment are identified at the reserved matters stage and it is then realised that mitigation measures will be inadequate, the local authority is powerless to prevent the development proceeding. Thus, where outline planning permission is sought for development of contaminated land, it will be sensible for the developer to undertake as thorough an EIA as is possible at that stage, and for the planning authority to ensure that the ultimate form of the development is tied as closely as possible to the basis on which that assessment was undertaken, by way of conditions or s.106 obligations. But even then, if further contamination problems come to light before application for approval of reserved matters, which have not been the subject of adequate assessment previously, the need for further formal EIA may arise.

Adequacy of EIA

An environmental statement is required to contain such of the information **16.17** referred to in Pt I of Sch.4 to the EIA Regulations as is reasonably required to assess the environmental effects of the development and which the

---

[21a] See e.g. *R (Mortell) v Oldham MBC* [2007] EWHC 1526 (Admin) paras 42–46.

[22] See Case C-290/03 *R (Barker) v London Borough of Bromley* [2006] Q.B. 764 [2007] Env. L.R. 2; Case C-508/04 *Commission v UK* [2006] Q.B. 764; [2007] Env. L.R. 1; *R (Barker) v Bromley LBC* [2006] UKHL 52; [2007] 1 A.C. 470; [2007] Env. L.R. 20. See also *R (Anderson) v City of Bradford MDC* [2006] EWHC 3344 (Admin) (a case decided before the HL decision in *Barker*).

[23] See [2007] 1 A.C. 470; [2007] Env. L.R. 20, para.24, per Lord Hope of Craighead.

[24] [2007] 1 A.C. 470; [2007] Env. L.R. 20, para.29, per Lord Hope of Craighead.

applicant can, having regard to current knowledge and methods of assessment, reasonably be expected to compile; this must include at least the information referred to in Pt II of Sch.4.[25] In the contaminated land context, such information might for example include effects arising from the remediation process, the risks presented by soil contamination to the development and its future users, the measures envisaged to prevent or reduce adverse effects, any alternatives considered in that regard, and an indication of the areas of uncertainty (e.g. areas of the site which are not accessible for investigation). The environmental statement will however only consider the effects of the development, which will not necessarily be the same as the effects of the contaminated land. For example, a proposal to cover a site with inert material so as to allow development to proceed, would not necessarily have significant environmental effects, whereas the ongoing ingress of contaminants beneath the surface into groundwater will not be covered by the environmental statement, but may result in the land being identified under Pt IIA, which could be a material planning consideration.[26]

16.18   The adequacy or inadequacy of the statement in these respects will be a matter primarily for the local planning authority exercising planning judgment, not the courts.[27] It is not every effect which needs to be assessed; the regulations refer to likely significant effects and main effects.[28] Detailed scrutiny of an environmental statement leading to challenge on the basis of perceived omissions from the effects considered is rarely likely to be a fruitful exercise.[29] Difficulty may however arise where at the time of the environmental statement, investigations of contamination have not yet been completed. If it is the case that the presence of contamination would be an inescapable significant effect, but the presence has neither been established nor ruled out, then the authority will not be in a position to know whether it has the information required by the Regulations; in such a case the only course may be to await the results of the investigations.[30] However, this is again an issue for the judgment of the planning authority, and the fact that contamination may be present does not necessarily dictate a conclusion that full information is necessary. In *Kilmartin Properties v Tunbridge Wells BC*[31] an existing hospital and associated buildings, which had previously been a workhouse, were being redeveloped for a new district hospital. The environmental statement contained seven pages dealing with the subject of ground contamination. Although no chemical site investigation had been carried out, desk-based research and a walkover survey indicated the potential for contamination from bulk storage of fuels and chemicals and the disposal of clinical waste, with potential risk to a minor

---

[25] EIA Regulations reg.2(1).
[26] See PPS 23, Annex 2 para.2.48.
[27] See, e.g. *R v Rochdale MBC Ex p Milne* [2001] Env. L.R. 406, QB, paras 106–110.
[28] *Atkinson v Secretary of State for Transport* [2006] EWHC 995 (Admin) (consideration of disposal of possibly contaminated spoil from tunnelling).
[29] See e.g. *R (Bedford and Clare) v London Borough of Islington* [2002] EWHC 2044 (Admin); [2003] Env. L.R. 22, paras 204–232 (including contaminated land issues); *R (Burkett) v LB of Hammersmith and Fulham* [2003] EWHC 1031 (Admin); [2004] Env. L.R. 3, para.36 (contamination of former gas works site; risks to local residents).
[30] See *R v Cornwall CC Ex p. Hardy* [2001] Env. L.R. 473.
[31] [2003] EWHC 3137 (Admin); [2004] Env. L.R. 36, Q.B.

aquifer from groundworks and piling. The planning permission was subject to a condition requiring submission of a detailed report and approval of detailed proposals for decontamination before development was commenced. There was unchallenged evidence for the local planning authority that the potential for ground contamination was not of a nature or scope so as to be one of the likely "main effects" of the development on the environment, and that the suggested remedial measures in the environmental statement were modest in scope, easily achievable and uncontroversial in their effectiveness. On that basis it was held that as a matter of fact and degree there was no basis for a challenge to the statement as falling short of the statutory requirements; it contained a good deal of information about potential ground contamination and proposed remedial measures.[32]

Policy guidance on planning and pollution control

The relationship between development control and specialised systems of control of pollution and contamination is a comparatively complex matter which from time to time comes before the courts. PPS23: *Planning and Pollution Control*[33] sets out the Government's policy generally in relation to planning, pollution and contamination control. Waste management is now dealt with in PPS10. Importantly, the Precautionary Principle applies in this area.[34] The planning and pollution control systems are separate but complementary. The planning system plays an important part in determining the location of development which may give rise to pollution or contamination so as to ensure as far as possible that other developments already in existence, be they residential or commercial, are either not affected, or any effect is controlled so as to be acceptable. This will require close co-operation with the Environment Agency and the relevant departments of the local authority responsible for pollution control, as well as other relevant bodies such as Natural England, drainage authorities and water and sewerage undertakers. **16.19**

Water protection issues

Issues of water protection are dealt with comprehensively from the point of view of policy in PPS23 as set out below. **16.20**

---

[32] [2003] EWHC 3137 (Admin); [2004] Env. L.R. 36, Q.B., para.57.
[33] See para.16.03 above.
[34] PPS 23, para.6.

Subject Matter	PPS23
Preparing Local Plans; adverse impact on water quality etc.	App.A PPS23
Water quality	Paras 1.17–1.20 Annex 1 PPS23
Control of water pollution	Paras 1.21–1.23 Annex 1
Water policy	App.1D Annex 1 PPS23

Development control

16.21 PPS23 deals with development control in paras 15–18 and 23–26. In considering individual planning applications, the potential for there to be contamination or pollution on the site in question has to be considered together with any contamination which the proposed use itself may produce. The local planning authority has to satisfy itself that the development proposals incorporate any necessary remediation and subsequent management measures to deal with unacceptable risks. Pre-application discussions are encouraged with all those likely to have an interest in the application, whether as consultees or otherwise. Paragraph 22 again emphasises the importance of pre-application discussions with the relevant persons and bodies. The local planning authority should satisfy itself that the potential for contamination and any risks arising are properly assessed and that the development incorporates any necessary remediation and subsequent management pressures to deal with unacceptable risks. In certain cases consideration will be given to a continuing monitoring programme. Intending developers must be able to assure the local planning authority that their consultants have the necessary expertise and experience to make such an assessment. Pre-application discussions with the planning authority and other relevant regulators are advised.[35] As to the role of the owner/developer, this is explained in paras 2.17 and 2.18 of Annex 2 to PPS 23; the role of the local authority and regional planning bodies is explained in paras 2.19–2.22 and that of the Environment Agency in paras 2.23 and 2.24.

16.22 Paragraphs 2.25–2.27 of Annex 2 emphasise that, on a precautionary basis, the possibility of contamination should be assumed when considering both development plans and individual planning applications in relation to all land subject to or adjacent to previous industrial use, examples of which are found in Table 2.1. Not surprisingly this Table includes gasworks, power stations, oil refineries, rubber industry premises, munitions and textile industry, food catering, laboratories, abattoirs and scrap yards. The Table indicates that there are other uses which can give rise to contamination, such as radioactive substances found in luminising paint works, and agricultural land using pesticides, herbicides, etc. and that some land may have naturally occurring radioactivity, including radon. As indicated in

---

[35] PPS 23, Annex 2 para.2.34.

448

para.2.33, an assessment of contaminative and historical uses of land is likely to be one of the supporting documents which would accompany any assessment of risk in appropriate cases. It must also be borne in mind that contamination may exist on sites which have not been put to such uses, for example because of the migration of contaminants, or the use of unsuitable fill for made ground.[36] The general approach is one of source-pathway-target, as for Pt IIA.[37] Some uses are particularly sensitive (for example, schools, nurseries, residential gardens and allotments, and the possibility of contamination should be considered in all such cases, regardless of whether there is evidence of past contaminative uses.[38] Paragraphs 2.42–2.45 deal with the information that should be required from the applicant in cases where contamination is known suspected, or an especially vulnerable use is proposed: the minimum required should be a desk study report and site reconnaissance (walk-over). The issue is whether this is sufficient to enable an adequate conceptual model of the site to be developed, enabling risks to be assessed and remedial options appraised, or whether further investigation is required.

Planning authorities are expressly cautioned against granting outline **16.23** planning permission unless the authority is satisfied that it understands the contaminated condition of the site and that the proposed development is appropriate as means of remediating it.[39] More information is therefore likely to be required than might be the case for an outline application on non-contaminated land; indeed it may not be advisable to proceed by way of the outline procedure at all.

The issue for the planning authority in determining an application is **16.24** whether it is satisfied that the development does not create or allow the continuation of unacceptable risk arising from the condition of the land in question.[40] It should be satisfied that existing significant pollutant linkages will be broken and that the development will not create new pollutant linkages. The scope of unacceptable risk is potentially wider under the planning system than under the "significant harm" guidance of Pt IIA.[41] Paragraph 2.51 states:

> "The standard for remediation to be achieved through the grant of planning permission for new development (including permission for land remediation activities) is the removal of unacceptable risk and making the site suitable for its new use, including the removal of existing pollutant linkages. All receptors relevant to the site should be protected to an appropriate standard. As a minimum, after carrying out the development and commencement of its use, the land should not be capable of being determined as contaminated land under Pt IIA of the EPA 1990."

[36] Para.2.36.
[37] Para 2.39. Table 2.2 gives examples of pathways and adverse effects.
[38] Para.2.40.
[39] See Annex 2 para.2.55.
[40] Annex 2 para.2.49.
[41] Annex 2 paras 2.49 and 2.50.

16.25   The Government is of course able to lay down what policy it chooses on the standard of remediation, but this wording presents serious problems. A "minimum" standard that there should be clean-up to the extent that the land should not be capable of being determined as contaminated at some future date sets a very high requirement if applied literally. Further, in many cases it must be questionable whether some contamination risks are properly related to the development. The obvious example is land where there is ongoing groundwater contamination. The proposed development will neither make that contamination better or worse and the contamination will not render the site unsuitable for the proposed use. It must be questioned whether it is an appropriate use of planning powers to require remediation of that problem as a condition of permitting the development, or to refuse permission if there is no adequate solution. It could be argued that if the groundwater pollution problem is to be addressed, this should be through the proper procedures of Pt IIA or works notice powers. The practical reasons why it is so attractive to require remediation as part of the planning process are that of course this offers significant leverage on the developer and the grant of planning permission may generate the land values to facilitate expenditure on clean-up. These however are practical, rather than sound legal or planning, reasons.

Planning conditions and obligations

16.26 PPS 23 offers guidance at Annex 2 paras 2.61–2.66 on the use of planning conditions and planning obligations. Where the planning authority is satisfied that the risks are sufficiently well known that there is a viable remediation option, it may be appropriate to use a three-stage condition that:

1. provides for further investigation to confirm the nature and extent of the contamination and allow more refined risk assessment and appraisal of options;

2. requires submission and approval of a remediation scheme to ensure the removal of unacceptable risks to make the site suitable for use; and

3. requires submission and approval of a validation report that demonstrates the effectiveness of the remediation carried out, preferably before building begins and certainly before the site is occupied by future users.

16.27 Examples of the wording of conditions are given at App.2B to Annex 2. The guidance also advocates conditions which require the reporting of contamination discovered during the course of development and submission of a scheme to deal with its risks, as well as linking conditions where practicable to phases of the development, so that the authority is aware of what is happening at each stage. In some cases it may also be appropriate to require ongoing monitoring to check the continuing effectiveness of any remediation scheme, and to require necessary contingency action. Any such condition must comply with the normal criteria applied as to validity as reflected in case law and in the six-fold test provided by Circular 11/95. On that basis, the condition must be:

(a) necessary;

(b) relevant to planning;

(c) relevant to the development to be permitted;

(d) enforceable;

(e) precise; and

(f) reasonable in all other respects.[42]

Planning obligations are regarded as potentially useful in ensuring **16.28** necessary off-site works, such as gas-migration barriers or water treatment, are put in place, or in restricting the future use of land to non-vulnerable uses, or requiring payments to the authority to cover the costs of future monitoring or make financial provision for future contingencies.

Overall advantage issues

As mentioned earlier, Government policy favours the bringing of derelict **16.29** land back into beneficial use, both as a means of improving the local environment and as a way of reducing pressure for development in the green belt, urban fringe and rural areas. This is the case, for example, with proposals for the development of redundant and cleared Thames-side sites in central London and along the East Thames corridor. The development of land may well provide the funds which would otherwise be lacking for problems of contamination on the site to be thoroughly addressed. It is therefore possible to envisage circumstances where an argument could be put forward in favour of granting planning permission for a more intensive or high value use of land than might otherwise be the case, if that is the only means by which the money can be made available for the site to be cleaned up and where clean-up is a necessary pre-condition of the site being brought back into beneficial use.

It seems clear from the case law, in particular *R v Westminster CC Ex p.* **16.30** *Monahan*[43] that such financial considerations may legitimately be taken into account as material by the planning authority. The Court of Appeal held in that case that it was legitimate for a planning authority to balance against the objections to the proposed inclusion of high value office elements within a scheme of development, that the provision of such offices, by way of departure from the development plan, was necessary to fund and achieve much-needed improvements to The Royal Opera House, Covent Garden. In that case, Kerr L.J. stated that[44]:

---

[42] See also *Newbury District Council v Secretary of State for the Environment*; *Same v International Synthetic Rubber Co* [1981] A.C. 578; [1980] J.P.L. 325.

[43] [1989] 3 W.L.R. 408, CA; [1989] J.P.L. 107.

[44] [1989] 3 W.L.R. 408, CA; [1989] J.P.L. 107, 425; see also 434 and 435.

"financial constraints on the economic viability of a desirable planning development are unavoidable facts of life in an imperfect world. It would be unreal and contrary to common sense to insist that they must be excluded from the range of considerations which may probably be regarded as material in determining planning applications . . . virtually all planning decisions involve some kind of balancing exercise."

16.31 Nicholls L.J. in his judgment amplified this point with a specific reference to contamination problems[45]:

"For example, take a run-down site, littered with derelict buildings. The soil is contaminated from previous industrial use. Preparation of the site for development will be expensive. The planning authority is anxious that such an eyesore shall be removed, and housing is the preferred use. An application is submitted for development with high-density housing. In my view it is clear that in considering this application the planning authority is entitled to take into account, first, that a lower density of housing will not be commercially viable, having regard to the heavy cost of site clearance, so that, secondly, the probable consequence of refusing to permit the development south will be the absence of any development for the foreseeable future, in which event the eyesore will remain."

16.32 In practice, the crucial question will be whether the benefits to be achieved from remedial works are such as to overcome planning objections to the development or additional density and whether the authority or inspector is satisfied that development in the form proposed is the only likely means of serving those benefits. Thus the issue will depend to a large extent on how serious the consequences would be of failing to remedy the contamination. The proposed scheme may be out of scale to the risks posed by the site in its current condition and thus may go further than is necessary to address any perceived problem. On the other hand where those risks are severe, for example buried chemicals contaminating groundwater with toxic and persistent compounds, the benefits of reclamation may be sufficiently great to overcome even greenbelt policy objections.[46]

Relevant appeal decisions

16.33 The following relevant appeal decisions illustrate the types and variety of issues which can arise in relation to proposals for the development of contaminated sites and the involving approach of the Secretary of State and his inspectors.[47]

---

[45] [1989] 3 W.L.R. 408, CA; [1989] J.P.L. 107, 433.
[46] See para.16.05 above.
[47] Some of the following appeal decisions were provided by Development Control Services Ltd (Compass); others appear in the Planning Appeals Digest (PAD).

Decision	Comments
(1) Ref: APP/M0655/ A/02/1082333, Decision Letter dated September 13, 2002, reported in [2003] P.A.D. 29.	Important example involving EIA Regulations 1999 and Pollution Prevention and Control Regulations 2000 (SI 2000/1973). Site unoccupied, in derelict condition with disused and dilapidated buildings, accumulations of scrap metal, decommissioned machinery and furnaces, areas of contaminated land on which stored bags of aluminum dross, tannery waste and oil drums. Site used for aluminum smelting, reclamation of scrap metal, vehicle dismantling, etc. Appellant offered unilateral undertaking under s.106 supported by clean-up bond. Planning permission allowed with conditions including "Development shall not begin until a scheme to deal with contamination of the site has been submitted to and approved in writing by the local planning authority. The site shall include an investigation and assessment to identify the extent of contamination and the measures to be taken to avoid risk to the public and the environment when the site is developed. Development shall not commence until the measures approved in the scheme have been implemented".
(2) Ref APP/J0350/A/062014310 of March 6, 2007.	Past landfill site in Green Belt proposed for contaminated soil treatment facility (bio remediation). Environmental Statement inadequate but local authority had powers to require further information. Appeal allowed.

Decision	Comments
(3) Ref APP/K0805/ A/06/2018355 of January 30, 2007.	Former care home, outline application for single dwelling-house. Previous mining activity in area but risk of land contamination from arsenic or chromium requiring more detailed investigation. Appeal dismissed.
(4) Ref APP/F1230/A/06/2009079 of December 4, 2006.	Former scrap yard to be developed for houses and offices. Environmental benefit of remediation to prevent further ground water contamination. Appeal allowed.
(5) Ref PP/U1430/A/05/1189278 of November 9, 2006—important case.	Area formerly used for solvent recovery, oil refining, tar distillation and disposal of gas works waste. The Inspector was apprehensive of agreeing to grant permission subject to conditions because significant evidence of contamination and complex technical problems related to the migration of hydo-carbons and other pollutants. Detailed assessment required to address foundation design, drainage and vapour protection. Insufficient evidence for Inspector to conclude that a viable remedial scheme could be provided. Appeal dismissed.
(6) Ref APP/C4235/ A/04/1141466 of October 12, 2006.	Application for 163 flats on 4.7 hectares of land formerly used for tipping. Council confirmed that it supported the scheme subject to appropriate conditions relating to the control of methane and other gasses. Deputy Prime Minister reconsidered Inspector's conclusion that permission could be allowed.

Decision	Comments
(7) Ref APP/M2270/ A/05/1189307 of May 23, 2006.	Former gas works site. Two schemes for seven dwellings and four maisonettes. Inspector held that present contamination would not warrant dismissal. Appeal allowed in part.
(8) Ref APP/T/0355/ A/05/1173468 of May 11, 2006.	Landfill waste site with hospital and asbestos, etc. waste present. Proposal for decontamination works. Permission granted subject to conditions.
(9) Ref APP/Z4718/A/04/1167421 of February 14, 2006.	Former tipped clay quarry. Residential development proposed. Unacceptable hazard due to contamination by volatile organic compounds (methane). Inspector concluded that the problem could not be overcome by conditions.
(10) Ref APP/C1570/ A/04/1167268 of January 25, 2006.	Former scrap yard to be redeveloped for dwellings. The Inspector dismissed the appeal noting that this contaminated site required an initial PPS23 desk study and at the current stage conditions would be inadequate. Appeal dismissed.
(11) Ref APP/K2420/ A/04/1168055 of January 20, 2006.	Former industrial buildings. Residential proposal that reuse for employment not fully investigated. Lack of detailed assessment of contamination issues. Appeal dismissed.
(12) APP/R2520/C/05/2002096 of November 24, 2005.	Former coal yard used as unauthorised gypsy caravan site. Inspector held that site unsuitable for residential use due to uncertain levels of ground contamination. Appeal dismissed.

Decision	Comments
(13) APP/X1165/A/04/1163711 of November 3rd, 2005.	Former gas works proposed for public open space. No detailed investigation to identify location and degree of contamination nor the type of contaminants and no assessment of risks to public human health. Appeal dismissed.
(14) APP/B3030/A/05/1174909 of September 13, 2005.	A potential contaminated land problem arose not from the previous use but from the proposal for a 10,000 bird free-range egg production unit posing a potential risk to ground and surface water contamination from discarded waste. Appeal allowed.
(15) APP/C3430/V/04/1151055 of June 30, 2005.	Application called in. Proposal for dwellings on former vehicle repair site. Inspector satisfied with the desk study report in relation to contaminated land but application dismissed on grounds of sustainability.
(16) APP/E2734/A/00/1054521 of June 20, 2005.	Contaminated site proposed for affordable housing, residential, retail warehouse and bulky goods retail. Inspector accepted that a high value development was required to produce a viable scheme because of the high costs of developing this site and dealing with contamination.
(17) APP/PPC/04/03 of April 5, 2005.	Sand and gravel extraction site proposed for inert landfill site with recycling plant and soil processing plant. Appeal dismissed because of serious concerns by Environment Agency about the risk of contamination of ground water. Inspector concluded that there was no latitude under the Landfill Directive to overcome the concerns of the Environment Agency.

Decision	Comments
(18) APP/K0805/A/04/1149628 of October 8, 2004.	Former mining activities, high levels of arsenic and cadmium in the top soil risking harm to health of future occupiers of proposed residential development. Inspector concluded that suitable remediation was possible and allowed the appeal accordingly.
(19) APP/B125/A/03/1128885 of October 5, 2004.	Burial cemetery in Green Belt proposed. Inspector noted that Environment Agency content that the quality of controlled waters would be adequately protected by the development. Appeal allowed.
(20) APP/A3655/A/03/1123572 of March 12, 2004.	Redevelopment of industrial premises by proposal for 12 flats. Inspector satisfied that conditions relating to clean-up of contamination would be adequate to protect the public interest. Appeal allowed.
(21) APP/X0630/A/02/1093573 of March 7, 2004.	Application for variation of expiry date of planning permission for burial ground. Inspector noted that graves dug to depth of two metres and water table within four metres of the surface leaving insufficient buffers between graves and water table. Pathogens could enter the water undermining public health. Permission not to be renewed. Appeal dismissed.
(22) APP/V2825/A/02/1087416 of October 15, 2002.	Former contaminated site proposed for retail development. Appeal against conditions. Inspector considered that land contamination conditions should have been imposed at the outline stage and not subsequently. Appeal allowed.

Decision	Comments
(23) APP/V4305/A/99/1021565 of September 9, 2002.	Local planning authority not satisfied about adequacy of remediation scheme. Inspector concluded, and Secretary of State agreed, that this aspect of the case would be more appropriately considered by the Environment Agency under the Pollution Prevention Control Regulations 2000. Appeal allowed in part.
(24) APP/H0520/A/01/1080367 of May 27, 2002.	Application for the retention of a conservatory extension to a dwelling. Gas (methane and carbon dioxide) contamination revealed. The dwelling and other dwellings had suitable measures to reduce gas omissions including low gas permeable gas proof membranes and cavity trays but extension was not built to the same standard of construction. Appeal dismissed.
(25) APP/E2734/A/01/1076386 of May 27, 2002.	Former landfill site proposed for housing. Inspector concluded that concentration of landfill gas was low and little risk of harm to existing or proposed houses. Some risk that ammonium from the land could reach nearby SSSI but risk not sufficient to justify granting permission on the basis of prevention. Appeal dismissed.
(26) APP/A1015/A/00/1054151 of January 3, 2001.	Proposal for food store on contaminated site. Appellant maintained that the development was necessary in order to create a viable scheme including a large proportion of B1 development because of costs of clean-up and potential land instability. Inspector decided that a more comprehensive scheme for a wider area in need of regeneration was required. Appeal dismissed.

Regional policy

Government policy is set out in PPS23.[48] Regional policy is referred to in **16.34** relation to contamination in Annex 2 of PPS23 at paras 2.19–2.22.

Development plan policies

A number of paragraphs in PPS23 deal with the preparation of Develop- **16.35** ment Plan Documents, including Regional Spatial Strategies. Paragraphs 13 and 21 of PPS23 refer to Development Plans. Matters relating to pollution and contamination will be referred to in any general strategy for dealing with such matters found in Regional Spatial Strategies. Local Development Documents (LDD) should set out the criteria against which applications for potentially polluting developments will be considered. Local Development Documents should include appropriate policies and proposals for dealing with the potential for contamination and the remediation of land taking account of Annex 1. As para.21 points out, one of the most effective ways that planning control can achieve the clean-up of contaminated sites is by steering development onto appropriate previously-developed land, some of which may be contaminated.

Annex 2 paras 2.19–2.22 and 2.28–2.32 deal with the responsibilities of Regional Planning Bodies in relation to Regional Spatial Strategies and of local authorities in relation to Local Development Documents insofar as they concern contaminated land.

Examples of policies

As a result of the requirements set out in PPS23 and in particular Annex 2, **16.36** contaminated land will be dealt with in policies found in Regional Spatial Strategies and Local Development Documents. A number of examples are set out below in the Appendix which concludes this chapter.

---

[48] See para.8.03.

Appendix

EXAMPLES OF POLICIES DEALING WITH CONTAMINATED LAND

CONTENTS

MIDDLESBOROUGH CORE STRATEGY SUBMISSION DRAFT MAY 2007

Policy DC1 General Development

In the determination of planning applications, unless there is a specific and acceptable reason for an exception to be made, all development proposals will be required to take account of, or satisfy, as a minimum the following principles:

(a) there is sufficient information supplied to enable the Council to determine the application;

(b) the visual appearance and layout of the development and its relationship with the surrounding area in terms of scale, design and materials will be of a high quality;

(c) the effect upon the surrounding environment and amenities of occupiers of nearby properties will be minimal both during and after completion;

(d) there is limited impact upon the capacity of existing and proposed transportation infrastructure both during and after completion, with no impact on highway safety being evident at all throughout the development process.

(e) the effect on protected open space within the urban areas, Green Wedges, the countryside beyond the limit to development, and the best and most versatile agricultural land is limited both during and after completion.

(f) the effect on levels of air, water, land or noise pollution of the environment is limited both during and after completion; and

(g) emphasis is placed upon the use of sustainable construction methods and environmentally sound resources and materials.

PLYMOUTH CITY COUNCIL, CORE STRATEGY, ADOPTED APRIL 2007

Policy CS22 Pollution

To protect people and the environment from unsafe, unhealthy and polluted environments through:

1. Ensuring development proposals will be refused which cause unacceptable noise, nuisance or light pollution.

2. Ensuring development causes no unacceptable impact on water or air quality.

The control and prevention of pollution is given high priority due to the negative impact it can have on human health, quality of life and the natural environment. This policy aims to protect our environment from the introduction of polluting activities or developments. Pollution could take the form of radiation, fumes, smoke, dust, ash, grit litter, noise, vibration, light, heat, odour and liquid discharges. There are currently two Air Quality Management Areas (AQMA) designated in the city, one is at Mutley Plain and one at Exeter Street, both of which result from traffic pollution. These are issues which are also will be tackled through the city Local Transport Plan. The East End AAP will need to address the impact of development and road schemes on traffic pollution with the objective of reducing air pollution. Transport and development proposals in the Site Allocations DPD will need to have regard to the same objectives in Mutley Plain.

The policy will be implemented in the following ways:

— Control of development

— Promotion of Environment Agencies Pollution Prevention Guidelines

— Designated and potential AQMA's to addressed in relevant AAPs and DPD's.

LONDON BOROUGH OF HAVERING—CORE STRATEGY AND DEVELOPMENT CONTROL POLICIES SUBMISSION DPD NOVEMBER 2006

DC-54—Contaminated Land

Planning permission for development will only be granted where both of the following criteria are met:

— where the development is on or near a site where contamination is known, or expected to exist, a full technical assessment of the site's physical stability, contamination and/or production of land-fill gas must be undertaken. Where the assessment identifies unacceptable risk to human health, flora or fauna or the water environment, the applicant will be required to agree acceptable long term remediation measures before any planning permission is granted to ensure there is no future harm with regard to the future use of the site. Where feasible, on-site remediation, especially bio-remediation, is encouraged.

— the development does not lead to future contamination of the land in and around the site.

Reasoned Justification

Havering Council is receiving an increasing number of planning applications for development on previously used land. In many cases, these sites are affected by the presence of contamination due to historic industrial or waste disposal processes. Contamination can affect the health of people, flora, and fauna as well as affecting the development potential of the site, however, development presents and opportunity to remediate this.

Implementation

The Havering Council leaflet entitled "Land Contamination and the Planning Process" provides information on what the Council requires in order to assess of a development is suitable for the proposed use on land which is potentially affected by contamination. This is available on the Council's website.

Where these is a proposal to develop land which may be contaminated, it is advisable to contact the Environmental Health Service (EHS) to discuss potential land contamination issues before submitting a planning application. This will determine whether a Phase I Preliminary Risk Assessment Report and Checklist is required as part of the planning application. The document also provides contact details for the Council's Environmental Health Service.

For details on Bioremediation applicants should refer to the Environment Agency's Remedial Action Datasheets which are available on its website. Applicants should also consider Model Procedures for Management of Land Contamination, CLR 11 from the Environment Agency, which have been developed to provide the technical framework for applying a risk management process when dealing with land affected by contamination.

CAMDEN UNITARY DEVELOPMENT PLAN ADOPTED JUNE 2006

Hazards
SD10—Hazards

A—Hazardous Substances

The Council will not grant planning permission for the siting of hazardous substances or for development in close proximity to sites used to store hazardous substances, unless it considers there will be no harm to the environment or to the health, safety and well-being of local residents, workers and visitors to the Borough.

B—Contaminated Land and Uses

The Council will only grant permission for development on sites that it knows or suspects to be contaminated if the applicant has investigated the hazards and proposed remedial measures to the Council's satisfaction. Where a development includes any potentially contaminating uses, the Council will expect proposals to be submitted for preventing future contamination and may impose conditions to that effect.

C—Unstable Land

The Council will only grant planning permission for development in locations where it considers there is geological instability if it can be satisfied that any actual or potential instability can be overcome and that there is no risk to adjoining land and local amenities.

In order to bring land back into beneficial use, it is important that hazards are removed or minimised. Land is an important resource in a densely built up borough and hazards that potentially make development unsafe or unhealthy have to be identified and dealt with.

Hazardous Substances

The Planning (Hazardous Substances) Act 1990 and the Hazardous Substances Regulations 1992, require Hazardous Substance Consent for the presence on site of specified quantities of defined substances. The Control of Major Accident Hazards Regulations 1999 (COMAH) requires certain sites where large quantities of fuels, chemicals or gases are stored or handled to be operated with a licence from the Environment Agency and Health and Safety Executive.

The Council places a high priority on protecting the local environment and the health and well-being of local residents, workers and visitors. It will therefore undertake careful assessment of any proposals for the siting of hazardous substances or of developments in close proximity to such sites. Before granting consent, the Council will need to be satisfied that adequate provision is made to contain such substances and that there are adequate and safe security arrangements which effectively restrict access by unauthorised personnel to areas where substances are stored or used. Further information on hazardous substances is included in supplementary guidance.

Contaminated Land and Uses

In line with government targets to reuse brownfield sites and in order to maximise scarce land resources, contaminated land should be brought back into beneficial use in a state suitable for its proposed use. Land used for contaminative industrial processes can remain idle for years, creating a health hazard and affecting amenity. Contamination of ground and underground water can affect human health causing harm to the natural environment and damage buildings and underground services.

Where a development includes any potentially contaminating land uses, for example vehicle repairs or a petrol station, the Council will expect proposals to be submitted for preventing future contamination of land or groundwater and may impose conditions to that effect. Where a contaminated site may have biodiversity value, applications will also be judged against policy N5–Biodiversity.

Planning Policy Guidance 23—Planning and Pollution Control states that when determining a planning application consideration should be given to whether the proposal takes proper account of contamination. Planning conditions may be used to prevent development until any necessary tests and a decontamination programme have been agreed and carried out. The Council has a Contaminated Land Strategy, which sets out how it will deal with contaminated land, make information available to the publish and how it will implement the requirements of the Environment Act 1990. Developers should liaise with the Council's Environmental Health team, which has a database of potentially contaminated land. Further guidance on contaminated land is contained within supplementary guidance.

Unstable Land

Planning Policy Guidance 14—Development on Unstable Land emphasises the need for instability to be taken into account in the planning process. Land instability can result from natural factors or through human intervention. Where land is potentially unstable, development or intensification of existing land uses can trigger instability. Geological conditions, such as unstable slopes, made-up ground, landfills or excavations can create problems of instability.

Responsibility for determining the extent and effects of geologically unstable land remain with the developer. In order to prevent risks to property, infrastructure and the public, the physical constraints of the land should be taken into account at the early planning stages so that remedial measures can be fully explored. It is the function of the Building Regulations to determine whether the detailed design of the buildings and their foundations will allow the buildings to be constructed and used safely.

WOLVERHAMPTON CITY COUNCIL, UDP ADOPTED JUNE 2006

Policy EP11: Development on Contaminated or Unstable Land

For all sites where:

- There is reason to suspect contamination or unstable land (for example, land formerly used for industrial purposes or landfill waste disposal or falling within a Lower Limestone or British Coal Consideration zone); and

- The possibility of contamination/instability has the potential to materially affect the development or use for which planning permission is being sought or neighbouring users/occupiers (for example, housing, community services or open space uses)

the developer will be required to carry out a desk study of readily available records assessing the previous uses of the site and their potential for contamination/instability in relation to the proposed development

If the desk study establishes that contamination/instability is likely but does not provide sufficient information to establish its exact extent or nature, the developer will be required to carry out a site investigation and risk assessment to determine the standard of remediation required to make the site suitable for its intended use.

Where remediation measures are deemed necessary, conditions or obligations may be used to ensure that the development does not take place until such measures are completed to the satisfaction of the Council.

Due to Wolverhampton's industrial heritage, industrial processes have affected ground conditions in much of the City. There are former mineshafts and workings on many sites, including those related to abandoned limestone mines. Some sites are contaminated as a result of tipping of domestic, commercial and industrial wastes in landfill sites, resulting in varying degrees of ground pollution. Development on or near contaminated or unstable land can prejudice health and safety and cause harm to the environment, both on the site itself and in neighbouring areas. For example, methane gas produced by some landfill sites can cause explosions if it is allowed to accumulate and mixed with air. Toxic chemicals can leach into watercourses and groundwater, harming local wildlife and water quality. The stability of structures built on mineworkings may be compromised due to the risk of collapses.

However, modern methods now allow on-site pollution to be treated or removed and mine workings to be made stable. In the pursuit of more efficient use of land, the Council will encourage the regeneration of potentially contaminated and unstable sites. Where development is proposed on or near such sites, including areas within 250 metres of a landfill site, the Council will consult the Environment Agency about the risks involved and may require desk studies and/or site investigations to be undertaken and any necessary treatment completed before development can take place. PPG14: Development on Unstable Land, Circular 02/2000: Contaminated Land and Technical Advice on Development of Land Affected by Contamination provide more detailed guidance on contamination and instability issues affecting development proposals. the preference will be for treatment and disposal of contaminants on-site, where appropriate, rather than simply transporting untreated contaminants elsewhere.

Plans showing known former landfill sites and the Lower Limestone and British Coal Consideration Zones are available for public inspection at Council Offices, However, the Council does not hold exhaustive information about contaminated and unstable land and it remains the responsibility of the developer to determine the extent and effects of such constraints.

The Council is currently implementing a Contaminated Land Strategy, which describes how it will identify and investigate contaminated land which has been given a statutory definition in the Environmental Protection Act 1990. This definition is restricted to a small number of sites where significant harm is being or may be caused to people, on such sites is proven to pose unacceptable risks, given the actual or intended use of the site, Part IIA of the Environmental Protection Act 1990 requires the person responsible for the contamination to clean up the site.

Policy EP12: Reclamation of Derelict Land

The Council will seek to reclaim, and support others to reclaim, derelict land and bring it back into productive use, in accordance with regeneration priorities, historic environment and nature conservation policies and where resources allow.

Given the lack of land for new development in Wolverhampton, one of the key objectives of the Plan is to make effective use of brownfield (previously developed) land. Many of the brownfield sites allocated in the Plan for development are derelict, that is they have been so damaged by a previous use that some form of reclamation or remedial action will be required before development or environmental improvements can take place. The Council keeps an up-to-date record of all derelict land and buildings in Wolverhampton which forms part of the National Land Use Database. The Council will work with relevant bodies, such as the Regional Development Agency, and the private sector to enable these sites to be brought back into productive use, including the creation of open space.

Priorities for reclamation of derelict land will be determined by wider regeneration strategies. The Council will explore mechanisms to enable the reclamation of derelict land, including securing external funding and serving compulsory purchase orders, where necessary. The Council also has powers under section 215 of the Town and Country Planning Act 1990 to require the clean up of unsightly land for reasons of visual amenity.

Long term dereliction and neglect of sites can result in natural regeneration, producing valuable natural habitats of a type which are scarce in Wolverhampton and provide refuges for rare plant and animal species. Before reclamation takes place, such sites should be surveyed, in accordance with Policies in Nature Conservation Chapter, the Historic Environment Chapter, and the forthcoming Supplementary Planning Document on Nature Conservation, and any proposals for reclamation and development should take full account of the nature conservation value of the site, either by preserving the important elements of the habitat or by providing equivalent replacement habitat nearby, as appropriate. Reclamation of derelict sites may also offer opportunities to create new wildlife habitat, for example wetland features or woodlands, at a low cost.

Peterborough Local Plan (First Replacement) Adopted July 2005

Contaminated Land

Where planning permission is sought for development on or adjacent to land which is known or is suspected, to be contaminated to an extent that may adversely affect the proposed development, the City Council will require an investigation by the developer to identify toe remedial measures required to deal with any such hazard.

Planning permission will only be granted for development if the City Council is satisfied that the land is remediated, or (if not already remediated) can be remediated by the imposition of planning conditions, or by entering into a planning obligation, to the extent necessary to ensure that:

a) the land (once remediated) would not cause any risk to the health or safety of people living on, working on, or visiting the development site; and

b) any proposed structures would not be at risk of damage from contamination; and

c) the proposed development of the land would not cause significant harm, or a significant possibility of harm, to controlled waters or to air.

The Government wishes to encourage full and effective use of land and the re-use of sites which have previously been developed. Recycling of land helps to revitalise most areas and reduces the need to use new sites outside built-up areas, thus assisting the safeguarding of the countryside. The re-use of contaminated land can contribute towards these objectives, but it is necessary to balance the aim of bringing it back into beneficial use with the need to protect the health and safety of occupiers, visitors and the construction work force both during and after redevelopment.

Where the previous history of a site suggests that contamination may have occurred, an investigation to assess the condition of the site and identify any particular problems or hazards will normally need to be undertaken by the prospective developer prior to the determination of a planning application. The possibility of contamination is a material factor which the City Council will take into account in the determination of planning applications, and if the information provided is insufficient to enable the Council to determine any application, the applicant may be asked or directed to provide further information. The assessment of the significance of contamination requires careful professional judgement and the City Council will obtain specialist advice, as appropriate, when considering applications to develop contaminated or potentially contaminated site.

If there is a need to erect a building or undertake other development as part of the remediation works, planning permission will normally be granted, even if the site lies in the open countryside, where policy LNE1 applies, or in a green wedge, where policy LNE2 applies. However, such permission will be restricted to proposals where the need is proven and conditions will be imposed to secure the removal of the development once the need no longer exists.

In cases where planning permission is granted for development of a site on which the presence of contamination is known or suspected, the Council will notify the applicant that the responsibility for safe development and secure occupancy of the site rests with the developer; and that the authority has determined the application on the basis of the information available to it, but that the authority could not be held liable if that information is subsequently proved to be inaccurate of inadequate.

Halton Unitary Development Plan Adopted April 7, 2005

PR14 Contaminated Land

1. Before determining any planning applications for development on or adjacent to land which is known or suspected to be contaminated, the applicant will be required to satisfy all of the following:

    a) Submit details to assess the nature and degree of contamination (type, degree and extent of contamination).

    b) Identify remedial measures required to deal with any hazard to safeguard future development and neighbouring uses.

    c) Submit details of a programme of implementation for the roll out and completion of mitigation measures to be agreed with the Council.

2. The requirement to undertake the above work will be controlled by either planning conditions or, when necessary, by planning obligations.

Justification

3. Many sites in the Borough are known to be contaminated e.g. historical chemical work/tips, former landfill sites. Therefore, discussion prior to the submission of any planning application should be carried out with the appropriate bodies, including the Borough Council.

4. Development on or near to contaminated land can cause the release of contaminants which may result in significant harm to the local environment, and population. It is therefore necessary to assess any risks and identify appropriate remediation measures necessary to make the land developable or to reduce harm to the existing environment, and so that new receptors and pathways are not introduced. It is advisable to liaise and discuss proposals as early as possible with the Council and other appropriate agencies so that a clear understanding of the implications and requirements of the agreed mitigation measures is known.

5. The Council will require that the implementation of mitigation measures are enforceable through either planning conditions or by other forms of planning obligations.

CITY OF DURHAM LOCAL PLAN ADOPTED MAY 19, 2004

Development on Contaminated Land

Development on sites which have known to be, or suspected of being contaminated will only be permitted provided that:

1. The nature and extent of contamination is first established;

2. The development will not add to the level of contamination;

3. Proposals for development include remedial measures which address the actual or potential hazard of contaminance identified;

4. There is no detrimental affect on the environment as a result of the disturbance of contaminates during and after development.

Justification: Contamination may result from land previously used by industries employing hazardous substances. Alternatively contaminated land may include completed domestic and industrial landfill sites where combustion might be induced, settlement is occurring, leachates are being generated or gas emissions are happening. The hazard to which this may give rise can put at risk people working on the site, the occupiers and users of building and land, the buildings themselves and water services. Unless precautions are taken, contaminants may escape to cause air and water pollution, while emissions of landfill gases may lead to concentrations in which explosions or asphyxiation may occur.

Within the context of securing sustainable development by the full and effective use of land within settlements the redevelopment of contaminated sites may generally by desirable. The former Cape Universal site at Bowburn is a prime example.

Before development takes place on such sites, however, it is important that the nature and extent of contamination is fully understood. As a result measures must be incorporated into any proposals to ensure the protection of buildings, services and other infrastructure against possible harmful effects of the substances involved, and to prevent the exposure of personnel to material which may be prejudicial to their health and safety.

Development near Contaminated Land

Development will only be permitted adjacent to, or in the vicinity of, contaminated sites where it can be shown that:

1. Measures can be undertaken on the periphery or within the site of the proposed development which would be sufficient to stop contaminates, leachate or gases penetrating the site and accumulating in buildings and structures in quantities which could prove harmful; or

2. Ground conditions around the contaminated site are such as to prevent gases from migrating into surrounding land.

Justification

The threat from contaminants may not be confined to the site itself. Landfill gases and leachates have the ability to migrate over wide distances depending upon ground conditions. If the floor of a landfill site has not been properly sealed with impermeable layer or the sub-soil and ground conditions are of friable or fractured materials, the potential exists for gases to spread underground away from the site until such time as an obstruction is met or a way to the surface reached. The foundations of a building, drains and pipelines may provide such an escape route.

In order that considerable areas around such sites are not needlessly sterilised against development, the Council will expect potential developers of sites nearby to demonstrate that ground conditions and topography are such that underground migration of contaminates to their site will not occur. Where this cannot be shown, it will be open to developers to introduce measures which protect their sites against penetration by gas.

Royal Borough of Kensington and Chelsea Unitary Development Plan Adopted May 25, 2002

Identification

The Council will be conducting survey work to identify the most serious areas of contamination in the Borough and any other sites where available information suggests that contamination is likely. The history of use will usually give an indication of whether a site is likely to be contaminated or not. Land uses renowned for leaving contamination including gas works, ex-railway land, riverside wharves and related processes, sewage installations, areas of landfill, scrap yards and certain types of industry. The responsibility for assessing whether or not land is suitable for a particular purpose, including whether it is contaminated, rests primarily with the developer. Where contamination is confirmed, the developer is also obliged to prepare a comprehensive remediation plan, with objectives which are appropriate for the proposed end-use.

Development of Contaminated Land

Contamination is subject to controls under pollution control legislation but it is a material consideration in dealing with development of contaminated land. When dealing with proposals for development which could be affected by contaminated land, consultation with the Environmental Health Department and the Environment Agency at the earliest possible stage will be necessary. Where a development site might be contaminated, the Council will expect developers to provide information on the severity of contamination and the steps they intend to take to make the land safe for the type of development proposed. The extent of decontamination measures appropriate will depend on the level of contamination, the proposed use of the site and the use of the adjoining land. Developers should also specify any mechanisms programmed for dealing with problems that may arise after a development has been completed. The agreed measures to deal with contamination must be carried out in association with the development and the Council will imposed conditions and where appropriate, will seek Planning Obligations to secure this.

Policy

To require development to submit information in association with development proposals on land that is or might be contaminated.

(a) to set out a full assessment of the condition of the land;

(b) to specify adequate measures to negate or minimise the effects of the contamination on the proposed development and adjacent land.

471

Policy

To require that development of contaminated land include appropriate measures to protect future users or occupiers of the land, the public, new structures and services, wildlife, vegetation, groundwater and surface water.

ST HELENS UNITARY DEVELOPMENT PLAN ADOPTED JULY 2, 1998

Contaminated Land Policy

On contaminated sites or sites suspected of being either contaminated or affected by contamination, the Council will require developers to carry out investigations to assess the nature and extent of contamination and to prepare programmes or schemes of works to treat or minimise the problems. Planning permission will normally only be granted subject to conditions requiring appropriate remedial works to be undertaken.

Justification

Contaminated land is a significant problem in St Helens as a result of its industrial past. The problems include heavy metal contamination, alkali waste from the chemicals industry and methane gas from landfill sites. The Environment Agency has notified the Council of 60 sites where it requires to be consulted on any development within 250 metres, under the terms of Article 10 of the General Development Procedure Order 1995. Approximately 16% of the Borough's land area may be affected by landfill gas within these consultation zones.

Circular 21/87 advises local planning authorities to set out in their Development Plans policies for the use of contaminated land and criteria which will be applied in determining planning applications.

Development or disturbance of contaminated land may mobilise contaminants and introduce them into the water environment. Schemes for developing contaminated land must include measures to avoid pollution of groundwater and surface water.

BRISTOL LOCAL PLAN ADOPTED DECEMBER 1997

Contaminated Land Policy

Development on land which is contaminated will only be permitted if appropriate remedial measures are included in any planning proposal submitted to the Council to ensure that the site is suitable for the proposed use and that there is no unacceptable risk of pollution within the site and in the surrounding area.

Implementation

Through the use of planning conditions and planning obligations. For all sites which are contaminated or suspected of being contaminated the city council will normally require developers to carry out a detailed site survey to determine the nature, extent and level of contaminants present both in the soil and underlying geology before the application is determined. The city council will expect to be appraised of the scope of the study and the sampling measures used. In cases where contamination is shown to exist a detailed scheme showing appropriate remedial measures required will need to be agreed before planning permission is granted. The city council will consult closely with the relevant pollution control authorities when deciding what measures are needed. Close liaison with the Directorate of Health and Environmental Services will also be sought in identifying sites which are or are suspected of being contaminated.

Supporting text

Land contamination is a serious cause of pollution. Land may be contaminated with toxic or hazardous substances as a result of previous activity. The nature and extent of the contamination will depend on the particular contaminative substances which are present. Potentially contaminated sites include former sewage and gas works, former tannery sites, landfill sites and derelict industrial sites. If appropriate precautions are not taken during redevelopment contaminants may be released into the environment resulting in risk to public health and safety and to local wildlife. The risk is not always confined to the site itself. Toxic gases from landfill sites for example can travel to surrounding land. Liquid pollution may also leach through soil and underlying geology and contaminate groundwater supplies. However, the re-use of contaminated land is treated appropriately, can contribute towards the revitalisation of urban areas, providing development and employment opportunities, and will regarded as a community benefit to be taken into account in the determination of planning proposals. The city council will encourage the decontamination of such sites and will have regard to the costs and difficulties involved in this work when determining planning applications for new uses.

Chapter 17

OTHER RELEVANT LEGISLATION

Introduction

17.01 As well as the planning system discussed in the previous Chapter, there are other legal regimes which may be relevant to the development and clean-up of contaminated land. Detailed consideration of them all is beyond the scope of this work, but the following issues are discussed in broad outline:

1. Building Regulations

2. Waste controls

3. Tax

4. Regeneration

PART 1: BUILDING CONTROL

The Building Regulations 2000

17.02 Section 1 of the Building Act 1984 gives the Secretary of State power to make regulations with respect to the design and construction of buildings and the provisions of services, fittings and equipment. These powers are for the purposes of, among other things, securing the health, safety, welfare and convenience of people in and around buildings; they have been extended by the Sustainable and Secure Buildings Act 2004 to include also the protection and enhancement of the environment, and facilitating sustainable development. Certain types of premises are exempt from the Act, for example those of statutory undertakers.[1] Contravention of building requirements is an offence under s.35 of the Building Act and, in addition, the local authority may itself take steps to remedy the defect and recover the cost from the person contravening the Building Regulations; alternatively, notice may be served requiring the owner or occupier to take the relevant action. Building Regulations may require plans to be deposited with the local authority for approval. These should be passed unless they are defective or show that the proposed work would contravene the

---

[1] Energy Act 2004 s.4. See *Manchester CC v Railtrack Plc* [2002] EWHC 2719 (Admin) (retail development at station premises).

Building Regulations.[2] Breach of a duty imposed by Building Regulations will give rise to a civil action if damage results.[3]

The current Building Regulations under the 1984 Act are the Building **17.03** Regulations 2000.[4] The Regulations impose requirements with respect to the carrying out of "building work" which will include the erection of extension or extension of a building and material alterations.[5] Building work must be carried out so that it complies with the relevant functional requirements contained in Sch.1 to the Regulations and so that the building after the work is completed so complies.[6] Requirements are also applicable where there is a material change of use of a building, e.g. to residential use.[7] The developer is required to give a building notice and deposit full plans with the local authority, and to give notice of commencement of works.[8] The local authority may provide a completion certificate, which is evidence, though not conclusive evidence, that the requirements specified in the certificate have been complied with.[9] It is important to note that the power to withhold a certificate will only be exercisable on the basis of the objects of the Building Act and Regulations, i.e. the health, safety and welfare of occupants of the building and those around the building (e.g. visitors), not any wider environmental issues relating to the presence of contamination (which might include, for example, occupiers of nearby property).[10]

There are appeal procedures in respect of decisions taken by local **17.04** authorities—these are determinations relating to questions of compliance of plans with the Regulations, and appeals, dealing with refusal by local authorities of applications to relax or dispense with requirements. Details of determinations and appeal decisions are provided on the Department for Communities and Local Government website, but none to date appear to have related to contaminated land.

The functional requirements of Sch.1 to the Regulations fall into some **17.05** fourteen Parts, dealing with matters such as structure, fire safety, sound resistance, ventilation, etc. Part C of Sch.1 contains the requirements relating to Site Preparation and Resistance to Moisture. Of particular relevance in relation to site contamination is Section C1: *Preparation of Site and Resistance to Contaminants which require is that*:

1. The ground to be covered by the building shall be reasonably free from any material that might damage the building or affect is

[2] Building Act 1984 s.16.
[3] Building Act 1984 s.38(1). "Damage" includes death of or injury to any person (including disease and any impairment of physical or mental condition).
[4] SI 2000/2531. See also the Building (Approved Inspectors) Regulations 2000 (SI 2000/2532). Amendments to the Regulations are detailed in various Departmental Circulars: see DETR Circular 07/2000 and ODPM Circulars 03/2002, 04/2004, 05/2004, 08/2004, 05/2005. The Regulations are currently under review: see DCLG, *The Future of Building Control* (March 2007); *Housing Green Paper: Homes for the Future* (July 2007); Building Regulations Advisory Committee, Annual Report 2006 (July 2007).
[5] Building Regulations 2000 reg.3(1)(a).
[6] Building Regulations 2000 reg.4(1) and (2).
[7] Building Regulations 2000 reg.6.
[8] Building Regulations 2000 regs 12, 14, 15.
[9] Building Regulations 2000 reg.17(4).
[10] See *Northamptonshire County Fire Officer v City Logistics Ltd* [2001] EWCA Civ 1216; [2002] 1 W.L.R. 1124, CA (fire certificate).

stability, including vegetable matter, topsoil and pre-existing foundations.

2. Reasonable precautions shall be taken to avoid danger to health and safety caused by substances on or in the ground covered or to be covered by the building and any land associated with the building.

3. Adequate subsoil drainage shall be provided if it is needed to avoid damage to the building including damage through the transport of water-borne contaminants to the foundations.

17.06   For the purposes of these requirements "contaminants" means:

"Any substance which is or may become harmful to persons or buildings, including substances which are corrosive, explosive, flammable, radioactive or toxic."

17.07   The Regulations themselves contain no technical detail on these requirements: this is to be found in the relevant Approved Documents.[11] Approved Document C on *Site Preparation and Resistance to Moisture* (2004 edn) deals with contamination. In the Secretary of State's view the requirements of C1 will be met by making reasonable provision to secure the health and safety of persons in and about the building and by safeguarding them and the building against adverse effects of unsuitable matter and contaminants on or in the ground covered or to be covered, by the building and any land associated with the building.[12] Thus contaminants present in garden areas will need to be addressed. The Approved Document points out that Pt IIA may impose additional requirements. Generally, the synergies between the planning system and building control are highlighted in this respect, and it is suggested that investigations used in the planning process can be further developed for building control purposes.[13] Section 1 deals with clearance or treatment of unsuitable material, stressing the importance of well-defined site investigation and referring to guidance in British Standard BS 5930:1999 (*Code of Practice for Site Investigations*) and various Building Research Establishment (BRE) Digests on matters such as procurement, desk studies, walk-over surveys, trial pits, and direct investigation. Section 2 deals with resistance to contaminants, both man-made and natural. Table 2 provides a list of examples of sites likely to contain contaminants, drawn from the former DoE "Industry Profile" guides. Risk assessment should follow the familiar "source-pathway-target" approach, and so is consistent with that under both Pt IIA and planning law. Hazards to the building, building materials and services need to be considered since these are also receptors; the hazards to consider are aggressive substances such as acids, alkalis, solvents, sulphates and chlorides; combustible fill such as colliery spoil or plastics; expansive slags, such as blast furnace slags, which may expand if exposed to water; and floodwater affected by sewage or

---

[11] Available on the Planning Portal website.
[12] Para.C1.0.1.
[13] Para.C1.0.10.

other contaminants. Further advice is provided on methane and other ground gases and on radon. The guidance on remedial measures is non-prescriptive in nature as regards treatment, containment, removal or control; this may be contrasted with earlier versions of the Approved Document which provided for specified relevant actions in response to particular types of contaminants.[14]

PART 2: WASTE CONTROLS

Generally

It is widely accepted that clean-up operations and physical development of **17.08** contaminated land can be problematic in that they may affect the concentrations of contaminated material and may increase the mobility of contaminants, either by physical dispersion or by altering ground conditions. It is therefore important to be aware of the general environmental controls which apply to such works, and similarly to the waste management and other legislation dealing with removal of contaminated material off-site.[14a]

There is a great variety of possible clean-up measures which may be **17.09** applicable either in-situ or ex-situ. Broadly, if the contaminated soil or fill is excavated it can be:

(a) removed from the site and deposited elsewhere in a controlled manner; or

(b) re-deposited on-site in a controlled manner; or

(c) treated (either on-site or elsewhere) to remove or destroy the contaminants or reduce their mobility or availability to the environment.

If the soil is left in place it may be contained or encapsulated or treated **17.10** to remove or destroy the contaminants or reduce their mobility or availability to the environment. The treatment options may broadly be categorised as chemical, physical, thermal, microbial and solidification/stabilisation.

Historically the most common procedure for dealing with contaminated **17.11** sites has been to excavate contaminated material for disposal at a licensed landfill site, followed by replacement by imported clean material where necessary. This can be a fast and effective method of dealing with isolated pockets of highly contaminated soils. The main disadvantage of this

---

[14] See Approved Document C (1992) s.C2 Table 2.

[14a] Consideration is being given to making site management plans (SWMPs) a legal requirement for construction and demolition projects in England and Wales: see DEFRA *Consultation on Site Waste Management Plans for the Construction Industry* (April 2007). Such plans which will require an assessment of the waste to be produced on the site and how it will be managed are likely to become a legal requirement as from April 2008.

method is that the contamination is merely transferred from one place to another, but also the process can be highly disruptive on-site and in relation to the traffic movements generated. The main constraint was an increasing shortage of landfill capacity, particularly in the South-East.[15] However, such offsite disposal is no longer such a viable or financially attractive route after the introduction of the Landfill Directive (Directive 99/31). Article 6 of the Directive requires pre-treatment of waste before being sent to landfill and the segregation of different types of waste (hazardous, non-hazardous and inert) between differently classified land-fills. Only hazardous waste which fulfils criteria set out in accordance with Annex II of the Directive may be consigned to landfill; such criteria and procedures require the composition, leachability, long-term behaviour and general properties of a waste scheduled for landfill to be known as clearly as possible. These requirements have been brought into force by the Landfill (England and Wales) Regulations 2002,[16] and have been fully in force so far as waste acceptance procedures are concerned since July 16, 2004. The effect has been that some more severely contaminated soils may not be suitable for landfill at all, whereas others are no longer able to be disposed of at normal municipal or non-hazardous landfills.[17] Together with the increased costs of landfill, and the imposition of Landfill Tax, this has meant that other methodologies have had to be applied, in particular soil treatment on-site or off-site.[18]

Waste management licensing

17.12 The regulation of waste hinges on the concepts of "controlled waste" and "directive waste". It is necessary to consider whether excavated soil or other material arising from groundworks is or is not waste falling within these concepts: if so, then unless any of the exemptions from waste management licensing apply, the keeping, treatment, recovery or disposal of the material will require a waste management licence under Pt II of the Environmental Protection Act 1990.[19] If the material in question is "directive waste" then it will be regarded as industrial waste, and therfore controlled waste. The category of industrial waste includes:

(a) waste arising from works of construction or demolition, including waste arising from work preparatory thereto;

---

[15] The general position across Europe was that soil remediation techniques were strongly determined by price and that the most common approach was disposal of contaminated soil in landfill: see Project Terra Nova Report (EC Commission, 2002).

[16] SI 2002/1559.

[17] See Sch.1 of the Regulations for waste acceptance criteria.

[18] For a European-wide review, see M. Doak, "The Future for Excavated Contaminated/ Brownfield Site Materials: New Policy and Practice across the EU" (2004) 12 Land Contamination and Reclamation 39. See also House of Commons Environment, Food and Rural Affairs Committee, *4th Report on Waste Policy and the Landfill Directive* (Session 2004– 2005, HC 102).

[19] The Agency operates a "low risk waste regulation" initiative, under which certain activities which do not benefit from an exemption are identified on the basis of their low risk nature as not justifying enforcement. An up-to-date list of such identified activities may be consulted on the Agency's website.

(b) waste arising from tunneling any other excavation; and

(c) waste removed from land on which it had previously been deposited and any soil with which such waste had been in contact.[20]

The crucial issue is therefore whether the material is directive waste, i.e. **17.13** any substance or object set out within the categories as Pt II of Sch.4 to the 1994 Regulations which the producer or the person in possession of it discards or intends or is required to discard.

The relevant categories include "Contaminated materials, substances or **17.14** products resulting from remedial action with respect to land" (Category 16). However, this does not necessarily mean that the material is waste: the question is whether the relevant person discards it or intends to discard it. Detailed consideration of the voluminous but somewhat inconclusive case law on the concept of waste is beyond the scope of this chapter, and reference should be made to standard general works on this issue. Within the context of a reclamation scheme it will in most cases be clear that excavated material is being discarded, or disposed of as waste. For example, those materials which are so contaminated as to present a substantial hazard to man or the environment may be placed within a specially engineered repository on site. This activity will be subject to the stringent requirements of the Landfill Regulations in the same way as much the same way as an off-site landfill. On the other hand there are general site works whereby the less contaminated earth is moved around the site by way of spreading, mixing, grading, covering, contouring and landscaping. There may be arguments to be made[20a] that excavated material which is used in this way is not waste on the basis that its holder intends at all times that it shall be put to beneficial use. However, the Environment Agency may well regard the material as waste,[20b] and the issue will be whether an exemption is applicable. Other issues will arise where excavated material has been treated to produce a material that may legitimately be regarded as a non-waste product, e.g. an aggregate conforming to CEN European standards for aggregates.[21]

Environment Agency policy generally on remediation is found in a **17.15** number of Remediation Position Statements, accessible on the Agency's website.[22] These distinguish between disposal and recovery operations for contaminated soil and groundwater. The following are relevant:

[20] See the Controlled Waste Regulations 1992 (SI 1992/588) reg.5(1) and (2)(a) and Sch.3 paras 6 and 11.

[20a] See e.g. *Case C-9/00 Palin Granit Oy* [2002] 1 WLR 2644; *Case C-416/02 Commission v Spain.*

[20b] See Environment Agency, *The Definition of Waste: Developing Greenfield and Brownfield Sites* (2006) which now accepts in principle that contaminated excavated material which is used without further treatment and is suitable for such use (e.g. regrading and capping) may not necessarily be regarded as waste.

[21] Further information is available on the Waste and Resources Action Programme (WRAP) website.

[22] See Environment Agency, *Review and Summary of Existing Environment Agency Guidance on the Regulation of the Remediation of Contaminated Soils* (Entec UK Ltd, final report, December 2005).

17.16 *Remediation Position Statement No. 3: excavation, segregation of material, storage of waste and use of treated waste.* Excavation itself is not regarded as a licensable treatment process, but the subsequent storage, treatment and use of material will be.

17.17 *Remediation Position Statement No. 3A: removal of groundwater for disposal or recovery.* Removal of contaminated groundwater for the purpose of remedial action is not regarded as licensable treatment, but the removal of 20 cubic metres or more per day will require an abstraction licence under the Water Resources Act 1991. Treatment of the abstracted water will require a mobile treatment licence (see below), waste management licence or PPC permit, as applicable. Discharge back into the ground will be subject to a discharge consent under the Water Resources Act.

17.18 *Remediation Position Statement No. 4: monitored natural attenuation.* Although natural attenuation is seen by the Agency as effecting the treatment of waste, there is no human intervention other than monitoring and therefore no permitting implications.

17.19 *Remediation Position Statement No. 5: ex-situ bioremediation.* Bioremediation processes using natural agents such as microbes or fungi in soil treatment beds are regarded as recovery operations, for which there are no applicable exemptions, and hence will require a licence or permit.

17.20 *Remediation Position Statement No. 6: in-situ bioremediation.* Such processes aid the natural degradation properties by adding nutrients, oxygen or microbes to the soil, or where undertaken at depth, by installing water recirculation systems. These activities are regarded as licensable recovery operations.

17.21 *Remediation Position Statement No. 7: bioventing.* Active aeration of the soil by injection of air is regarded as a recovery operation.

17.22 *Remediation Position Statement No. 8: soil flushing.* Use of aqueous solutions to dissolve and recover contaminants will generally be regarded as a recovery operation.

17.23 *Remediation Position Statement No. 9: solvent extraction.* This is normally an ex-situ process where excavated soil is mixed with solvent in a reaction vessel, to separate out the contaminants. These will generally be waste recovery operations. The re-use of the resulting cleaned soil may benefit from an exemption, or otherwise the Agency will make a risk-based decision on whether to require a waste management licence for such re-use (this assumes of course that the cleaned material still is waste).

17.24 *Remediation Position Statement No. 10: transformation by chemical treatment.* Processes of oxidation, reduction, hydrolysis or precipitation may be undertaken either on site or ex-situ. They will be regarded generally as waste recovery operations.

Remediation Position Statement No. 11: soil vapour extraction. This involves **17.25** the injection of air, causing volatile contaminants present in the soil to volatilise. They are extracted and treated by granulated active carbon filters or catalytic oxidation. These will be regarded as waste recovery operations.

Remediation Position Statement No. 12: soil washing. This is generally an ex- **17.26** situ process whereby contaminated soil physically processed by various means to separate out contaminant particles. This will be a waste recovery operation. The re-use of the washed soil may benefit from an exemption, or otherwise the Agency will make a risk-based decision on whether to require a waste management licence for such re-use (this assumes of course that the soil remains waste after processing).

Remediation Position Statement No. 13: permeable reactive barriers. These are **17.27** engineered treatment zones of reactive material within the saturated zone, which are intended to allow the flow of groundwater, but attenuate the contaminants. This will be regarded as a waste recovery operation. A risk-based decision will be taken on whether to require a waste management licence to be obtained.

Remediation Position Statement No. 14: solidification and stabilisation. These **17.28** are processes used to reduce the mobility of contaminants, by changing the nature of the soil or contaminants, often using cements, fly ash, lime, clays or asphalt. The processes may be undertaken by direct injection into the soil, or ex-situ. They will be regarded as waste recovery.

Remediation Position Statement No. 15: thermal desorption. This is an ex-situ **17.29** process involving the low temperature heating of soils to desorb volatile contaminants. It is viewed as a waste recovery operation, but is not considered an incineration process which is subject to the Waste Incineration Directive's requirements.[23]

It will also in some cases be relevant to consider the Agency's Position **17.30** Statements 1.1 on trials and small scale remediation schemes, and 1.2 on trials of new techniques.

Waste licensing exemptions

The Waste Management Licensing Regulations 1994[24] confer a number **17.31** of exemptions from the requirement for a waste management licence.[25] Some of these exemptions are of potential relevance to land reclamation and remediation activities and are considered below. However, a number of points should be noted in relation to such exemptions:

---

[23] Directive 2000/76; see DEFRA *Guidance on the incineration of waste* (2nd edn) s.2.4.3.
[24] SI 1994/1056, as amended.
[25] Waste Management Licensing Regulations 1994 reg.17 and Sch.3.

1. Exemption is only in relation to the need for a waste management licence: the prohibition on disposing of waste in an environmentally harmful manner under s.33(1)(c) still applies.

2. Certain of the exemptions only apply if the exempt activity is carried on by or with the consent of the occupier of the relevant land or where the person carrying on the activity is otherwise entitled to do so on the land.

3. In general the exemptions do no apply insofar as the activity involves hazardous waste.

4. In order to comply with the requirements of Directive 91/156, where waste is disposed of or recovered by an establishment or undertaking, the exemptions only apply if the type and quantity of waste, and the method of disposal and recovery, are consistent with the need to attain the objectives of Sch.4 of the Regulations: not to endanger human health, and without using processes or methods which could harm the environment, and in particular without risk to water, air, soil, plants or animals, causing nuisance through noise or odours, or adversely affecting the countryside or places of special interest.

17.32 As the Waste Management Licensing Regulations have been amended over the years, a distinction has been drawn between what are termed "simple" and "complex" exemptions. All exempt activities require registration with the Agency under reg.18, which is a simple process involving only the name of the operator, the category of activity, and the place where it is carried on. But certain "notifiable" exempt activities are subject to a more onerous regime under reg.18AA, under which additional particulars must be provided, annual renewal is required, and records of the activities and the quantities of waste involved must be kept. The information required in support of such an exemption, to satisfy the Agency that the activity will meet the terms of the exemption and will not be contrary to the objectives of the Directive, may be considerable and may require specialist technical input; for most such exemptions the Agency requires a period of 35 days to consider the notification.

17.33 An example of a "simple" exemption which may apply to land reclamation is para.13(2), which covers the manufacture from waste arising from construction or demolition work or excavations, or from waste ash, slag or clinker, of soil or soil substitutes, if carried out at the place either where the waste is produced or the manufactured product is to be applied to land, and the total amount manufactured on any day does not exceed 500 tonnes.[26] This exemption, at para.13(3) and (4), also covers the treatment of waste soil or rock which when treated is to be spread on land under paras 7A or 9A exemptions (subject to a maximum daily amount of 100 tonnes) and the storage of waste which is to be submitted to such treatment (at the place where the treatment is to be carried on, and

---

[26] As with other exemptions, the terms are only summarised selectively here, and reference should be made to the full wording in the Regulations, as amended.

subject to a maximum total quantity stored of 20,000 tonnes). Another "simple" exemption, though worded in such vague terms that caution needs to be exercised in relying on it, is at para.15: the beneficial use of waste if it is put to that use without further treatment, and that use does not involve its disposal. This exemption is unlikely to be of much use in contaminated land situations, as it does not apply where the waste activity is within the ambit of the more specifically applicable exemptions, or would be but for a limitation or condition attached to the exemption[27]; there are also the problems that excavated contaminated soil is unlikely in most cases to be capable of being put to beneficial use without some treatment, and that there may be arguments as to whether such use amounts in reality to its disposal.

17.34 Paragaph 9A is the "complex" exemption with most obvious applicability to land reclamation. It allows the spreading of wastes of specified kinds from specified sources on land, for the purposes of reclamation, restoration or improvement of land which has been subject to industrial or other man-made development, and where the use to which the land could be put would be improved by the spreading. The waste must be spread in accordance with any applicable requirement under planning law, to a depth not exceeding the lesser of two metres or that shown on submitted cross-sections, and no more than 20,000 cubic metres must be spread per hectare. The types of waste that can be used under this exemption include excavated soil from contaminated sites and solid wastes from soil remediation (other than those containing dangerous substances). The secure storage of such waste for up to six months, at the place where it is to be spread, is also within the exemption (para.9A(3)). If more than 2,500 tonnes of waste is used, records of the quantity, nature, origin and (if relevant) treatment of the waste must be kept and reatiend for at least two years.

17.35 Another possibly relevant "complex" exemption is at para.19A, which relates to the storage and use of specified kinds of waste, where these are suitable for "relevant work" to be carried out on land where the waste is stored. The kinds of waste include waste crushed rocks, sands and clays, ashes and slags, bricks, tiles and ceramics, concrete and excavated soils. "Relevant" work means work for the construction, maintenance or improvement of a building, highway, railway, airport, dock or other transport facility, recreational facilities or drainage, but not including work involving land reclamation. The exclusion of land reclamation means that the exemption is likely to be more relevant for off-site use of wastes excavated from land reclamation schemes. There are limitations in that not more than 50,000 tonnes of waste may be stored at any one time, for a maximum period of six months, and the waste must be used to a depth not exceeding that shown on the plans submitted to the Agency.

[27] Para.15(3).

Controls over on-site remediation

17.36 Use of mobile plant to treat waste on a contaminated site will require a waste management licence.[28] The definition of plant which is to be treated as mobile plant, if designed to move or be moved from place to place, or if not so designed, readily capable of moving or being so moved, includes plant for the treatment of waste soil and plant for the treatment of contaminated material, substances or products, for the purposes of remedial action with respect to land or controlled waters.[29] The Environment Agency has developed an approach which it hopes will facilitate the use of mobile plant to redevelop brownfield land. This involves a single mobile treatment licence (MTL) allowing operators to use several pieces of mobile plant, either singly or in combination, at the same time on different sites.[30] This involves a "deployment form" allowing the operator to identify all the relevant information for each site in question. The single MTL allows the operator to operate at as many operating sites as there are agreed deployment forms, over the time period specified in the form. The technologies for which this system can be used include air sparging, bioremediation, chemical treatment, soil vapour extraction, soil flushing, soil washing, solidification, solvent extraction and soil stabilisation. Other technologies will require a bespoke MTL. The approach is risk-based and requires preparation of a site conceptual model and risk assessment. "Fit and proper person" status must be shown through absence of relevant convictions, detailing a technically competent person to manage the plant, and showing that the applicant is in a position to make adequate financial provision through credit checks or overdraft facilities.[31]

17.37 There may also be cases where remediation activities require a PPC permit, if the activity is undertaken in a facility which constitutes fixed plant, and involves the disposal of hazardous waste in a facility with a capacity of more than 10 tonnes per day, or of non-hazardous waste in a facility with a capacity of more than 50 tonnes per day, which uses biological or physico-chemical treatment and results in final compounds or mixtures which are then discarded by disposal.[32] Applying a purposive approach to the legislation, the requirement for a permit will apply to the plant where the physico-chemical treatment takes place, whether the discarding of the compounds produced takes place on that site or elsewhere.[33]

---

[28] See Agency Position Statements at para.17.15ff, above for the various forms of treatment currently used.

[29] Waste Management Licensing Regulations 1994 (as amended) (SI 1994/1056) reg.12(1)(d) and (h).

[30] See Mobile Treatment Licence: Guidance on Licensing and Supervision Processes (available on Agency website).

[31] Mobile Treatment Licence: Guidance on Licensing and Supervision Processes, paras 6.7 and 6.8.

[32] Pollution Prevention and Control (England and Wales) Regulations (SI 2000/1973) Sch.1 Pt I s.5.3 (a) and (c).

[33] See *United Utilities Plc v Environment Agency* [2007] UKHL 41.

The duty of care

17.38 As already described, work on a contaminated site may well involve the production, treatment, handling or disposal of controlled waste. Whether such waste is disposed of on-site, or is removed for disposal elsewhere, the duty of care created by s.34 of the Environmental Protection Act 1990 will be relevant. The duty applies to any person who imports, produces, carries, keeps, treats or disposes of controlled waste or who, as a broker, has control of such waste.[34] No definition of "producer" is provided by the Act, but the view of the relevant Government Department is that in the case of contracting, the producer of waste may be regarded as the person undertaking the works which give rise to the waste, not the person who issues instructions or lets contracts which give rise to the waste.[35] Where there are several contractors or sub-contractors on site, the Government suggests, the producer of a particular waste is the particular contractor or sub-contractor who (or whose employees) takes an action which creates waste, or who begins to treat something as if it were waste.[36] However, the client or contractor who makes arrangements for the carriage or disposal of waste, for example by letting a disposal sub-contract to a haulier, may thereby assume responsibility as a "broker".[37]

17.39 The duty imposed by s.34 as amended requires the person under the duty to take all such measures applicable to him in the relevant capacity (producer, importer, carrier, etc.) as are reasonable in the circumstances[38]:

(a) to prevent any contravention by any other person of s.33 (prohibition on unauthorised or harmful deposit, treatment or disposal, etc. of waste) or of the permitting requirements of the PPC regime under regs 9 and 10 of the Pollution Prevention and Control (England and Wales) Regulations 2000;

(b) to prevent the escape of the waste from his control or that of any other person; and

(c) on transfer of the waste, to secure:

(i) that the transfer is only to an authorised person or to a person for authorised transport purposes; and

(ii) that there is transferred with the waste such a written description of the waste as will enable other persons to avoid

---

[34] 1990 Act subs.34(1).

[35] DETR Circular 19/91 (Welsh Office 63/91) (Scottish Office 25/91) *Environmental Protection Act 1990 Section 34 The Duty of Care*, para.17.

[36] DETR Circular 19/91 (Welsh Office 63/91) (Scottish Office 25/91) *Environmental Protection Act 1990 Section 34 The Duty of Care*, para.17.

[37] DETR Circular 19/91 (Welsh Office 63/91) (Scottish Office 25/91) *Environmental Protection Act 1990 Section 34 The Duty of Care*, para.17.

[38] It appears from the decision of the House of Lords in *Seaboard Offshore Ltd v Secretary of State for Transport ("The Safe Carrier")* [1994] 2 All E.R. 99 that in order to be liable the producer, etc. of waste must fail personally in the duty in order to be criminally liable, and that where the producer has taken all reasonable steps they will not be liable for the acts or omissions of subordinate employees. See also *Shanks & McEwan (Southern Waste Services) Ltd v Environment Agency* [1999] Env. L.R. 138 (duty not solely "forward-looking" and may also relate to those further back down the chain).

a contravention of s.33, or the PPC Regulations, and to comply with their own duty under s.34 as respects preventing escape of the waste.

17.40 Subsection 34(3) lists the persons who are authorised persons for the purpose of requirement (c)(i) above. In most cases where waste is being removed as part of a reclamation scheme the relevant categories of authorised person will be the holder of a waste disposal or waste management licence, or a registered carrier. However, it should also be noted that waste may be carried for "authorised transport purposes" between different places within the same premises[39]: a registered carrier therefore is not necessary in order to move waste around within the reclamation site. Various persons are exempted from the requirement to register as a carrier[40]: these include in particular the producer of the waste in question "except where it is building or demolition waste".[41] Some (but not necessarily all) waste arising from site reclamation or remediation works may be regarded as resulting from building or demolition works and thus the producer of the waste cannot lawfully carry it off-site without being registered. Section 34 makes provision for a code of practice providing practical guidance on how to discharge the duty of care[42]: such a code has been issued[43] and is admissible in evidence or any proceedings as to breach of the duty.[44] In practical terms, therefore, all those involved with site reclamation activities will need to consider the applicability of the duty of care to their activities: this is so whether waste is disposed of on-site or whether it is removed for disposal. This will involve assessing the problems presented by the waste and may often require expert assistance by way of analysis and advice on handling methods.

The duty of care—transfer documentation

17.41 By subs.34(5) the Secretary of State may make regulations imposing requirements on any person who is subject to the duty of care as respects the making and retention of documents and the furnishing of documents or copies of documents. The Environmental Protection (Duty of Care) Regulations 1991[45] have been made under this subsection. The Regulations require the transferor and transferee of waste, at the same time as the waste is transferred, to ensure that a "transfer note" is completed and signed on their behalf.[46] The transfer note must identify the waste and give details of its quality, form of containment (if any) and the time and place

---

[39] 1990 Act s.34(4)(a).
[40] The Controlled Waste (Registration of Carriers and Seizure of Vehicles) Regulations 1991 (SI 1991/1624) reg.2.
[41] The Controlled Waste (Registration of Carriers and Seizure of Vehicles) Regulations 1991 (SI 1991/1624) reg.2(1)(b).
[42] 1990 Act subs.(7).
[43] Issued 1991, revised 1996.
[44] 1990 Act subs.(10).
[45] SI 1991/2839.
[46] Environmental Protection (Duty of Care) Regulations 1991 reg.2(1).

of its transfer.[47] It must also give details of the transferor and transferee, each of whom must keep the written description and transfer note for a period of two years.[48] It is not necessary, according to Departmental guidance[49] for each individual transfer to be documented, and multiple consignments, where the nature of the waste and the parties remain the same, may be covered by a single note for a period of up to a year. This procedure may be particularly suitable where large quantities of excavated contaminated soil are being removed in lorry loads for disposal to landfill, where it would be impracticable or onerous for a separate note to be completed for each trip. Section 34(4A) (as inserted by the Deregulation and Contracting Out Act 1994) provides that for these purposes a transfer of waste in stages shall be treated as taking place when the first stage of the transfer takes place, and that a series of transfers between the same parties of waste of the same description shall be treated as a single transfer taking place when the first transfer takes place. Where the waste in question is hazardous waste, compliance with the duty of care does not discharge the need for compliance with the Hazardous Waste (England and Wales) Regulations 2005.[50]

Waste carrier registration

The Control of Pollution (Amendment) Act 1989 instituted a new system **17.42** for the registration of waste carriers. By s.1 of the Act, it is an offence for any person who is not a registered carrier, in the course of any business of his or otherwise with a view to profit, to transport any controlled waste to or from any place in Great Britain. Exemptions to this requirement are provided by s.1(2), including the transport of waste within the same premises between different places in those premises; other exemptions are given by regulations,[51] including waste carried by the person who produces it, except if it is building or demolition waste.[52] Provision is made by regulations[53] as to applications for registration, certificates of registration, the keeping of registers, duration and revocation of registration, and appeals. Of particular importance is the power to refuse registration or to revoke registration where the applicant or holder, or another "relevant person",[54] has been convicted of a prescribed offence[55] and in the opinion of the authority it is undesirable that they be authorised to transport

---

[47] Environmental Protection (Duty of Care) Regulations 1991 reg.2(2). The transfer note can also be used to comply with the duty at s.34(1)(c)(ii) to provide an adequate written description of the waste: see Circular 19/91, para.20. Amendments made by the Landfill (England and Wales) Regulations 2002 reg.19, require that the waste must now be identified by reference to the appropriate codes in the European Waste Catalogue.

[48] Environmental Protection (Duty of Care) Regulations 1991 reg.3.

[49] DETR Circular 19/91 (Welsh Office 63/91) (Scottish Office 25/91) *Environmental Protection Act 1990 Section 34: The Duty of Care*, para.21.

[50] See para.17.45 below.

[51] The Controlled Waste (Registration of Carriers and Seizure of Vehicles) Regulations 1991 (SI 1991/1624) reg.3.

[52] SI 1991/1624 reg.2(1)(b).

[53] SI 1991/1624.

[54] As to "relevant person" see s.2(5).

[55] The offences are prescribed by SI 1991/1624 reg.1(2) and Sch.1.

controlled waste.[56] Also important are the powers provided by the Act and the Regulations to seize and dispose of vehicles used for illegal waste disposal—effectively a means of inducing those with knowledge as to the identity of the person using the vehicle to come forward in order to reclaim the vehicle.[57]

Registration of waste brokers and dealers

17.43 The Waste Management Licensing Regulations 1994[58] make provision for registration of waste brokers and dealers: it is an offence for an establishment or undertaking after December 31, 1994 to arrange (as dealer or broker) for the recovery of controlled waste on behalf of another person unless it is a registered broker of controlled waste.[59] The requirement to register as a broker does not apply to persons who are to carry out disposal or recovery of the waste in question and who are duly licensed or otherwise authorised to do so, or who are to transport the controlled waste as part of the arrangement and who are registered as waste carriers. As under the duty of care, there may be some doubt as to who is a "broker". Circular 11/94, Annex 8, suggests that an establishment or undertaking which acts as a broker has control of waste in the sense that it arranges for the disposal or recovery on behalf of another and is outside the chain of people who handle waste (i.e. the producer, holder, carrier, recovery operator, or disposal operator).[60] An environmental consultant who contracts to arrange for the disposal of a producer's waste is instanced as an example of a broker.[61] However, the guidance distinguishes those who on a building site (such as a main contractor, architect or engineer) arrange for disposal of controlled waste to an appropriate facility: it is suggested that they are acting as holders of the waste rather than brokers.[62] Similarly, managing agents, janitors and development companies providing common services (including waste management) will not normally be acting as brokers, because they are producers of the waste concerned.[63] Despite this advice, which in some respects is debatable, the final decision as to whether an establishment or undertaking is acting as a broker will be a matter for the courts. Schedule 5 to the 1994 Regulations contains detailed provisions on registration, including the form for applications for registration and renewal. Registration or renewal may be refused (or registration revoked) where the applicant, or registered broker, or other "relevant person" has been convicted of a relevant offence and in the view of the authority it is

---

[56] 1990 Act s.3(1) and (2); reg.5(1) and 10(1).

[57] 1990 Act s.6 and regs 20–25.

[58] SI 1994/1056.

[59] SI 1994/1056 reg.20.

[60] DETR Circular 11/94 *Environmental Protection Act 1990: Part II, Waste Management Licensing, The Framework Directive on Waste*, Annex 8 para 84.

[61] DETR Circular 11/94 *Environmental Protection Act 1990: Part II, Waste Management Licensing, The Framework Directive on Waste*, Annex 8 Para.8.5

[62] DETR Circular 11/94 *Environmental Protection Act 1990: Part II, Waste Management Licensing, The Framework Directive on Waste*, Annex 8 Para.8.5

[63] Circular 11/94 *Environmental Protection Act 1990: Part II, Waste Management Licensing, The Framework Directive on Waste*, Annex 8 Para.8.5

undesirable that the applicant be authorised to arrange (as dealer or broker) for the disposal or recovery of controlled waste on behalf of other persons.[64]

Hazardous waste

The Environmental Protection Act 1990[65] allows special provision to be **17.44** made by regulations for controlled waste which is, or may be, particularly dangerous or difficult to dispose of, as did the Control of Pollution Act 1974 before it.[66] The regulations previously dealing with such waste were the Control of Pollution (Special Waste) Regulations 1980[67] and the Special Waste Regulations 1996.[68] These Regulations imposed a means of control based upon documentary tracking of special waste from the point of removal from the premises at which it was produced to the point of ultimate disposal: the system is known as "the consignment note system". They also required any person making a deposit of special waste on land to record the location of each such deposit, on the basis of a site plan, either with a grid or with translucent overlays showing deposits in relation to the contours of the site,[69] and to keep such records until his disposal licence was surrendered or revoked—at which time the records were to be sent to the disposal authority for retention. Where such records still exist, they may provide a useful source of information on contaminated sites, for Pt IIA or other purposes.

Hazardous waste is now regulated under the Hazardous Waste (England **17.45** and Wales) Regulations 2005, which came into force on April 16, 2005.[70] The definition of hazardous wastes is a complex matter, which will often require specialist technical advice. According to reg.6 waste is hazardous if it is listed as a hazardous waste in the List of Wastes set out in the Lists of Wastes (England) Regulations 2005 having relevant hazardous properties,[71] or if a specific batch of waste is determined to be hazardous pursuant to reg.49. This List is based on Commission Decision 2000/532, as amended, often referred to as the European Waste Catalogue. Whether material arising from a contaminated site is hazardous waste will involve detailed consideration of these provisions, and in particular Category 17 which deals with construction and demolition wastes, including excavated soil from contaminated sites.[72]

---

[64] 1990 Act Sch.5 paras 3(13) and 5(1).

[65] 1990 Act s.62.

[66] 1990 Act s.17.

[67] SI 1980/1709, as amended by SI 1988/1790. These Regulations came into force on March 16, 1981, replacing the Deposit of Poisonous Waste Act 1972.

[68] SI 1996/ 972, which came into force on September 1, 1996.

[69] In the case of liquid wastes discharged without containers into underground strata or disused workings the record had only to comprise a written record of the quantity and composition of the waste so discharged.

[70] SI 2005/894.

[71] SI 2005/895. See Schs 1–3 to the Hazardous Waste (England and Wales) Regulations 2005, dealing with types of wastes, constituents of wastes and properties of wastes which may render them hazardous.

[72] Relevant materials may include coal tar and other bituminous mixtures, soil or mixed construction or demolition wastes containing dangerous substances, and materials containing asbestos.

17.46   Part 4 of the Regulations deals with mixing hazardous waste with other categories of hazardous waste, or with non-hazardous waste, or with another material; this is generally prohibited unless conducted in accordance with a waste permit, or under a registered exemption.[73] Part 5 imposes requirements to notify to the Agency premises at which hazardous waste is produced, or from which it is removed; these requirements could apply to a contaminated site which is being remediated. Part 6 deals with the movement of hazardous waste, and requires a unique consignment code to be assigned to hazardous waste before it is moved from premises, together with the completion of the appropriate documentation. Part 7 requires site records to be kept of tipped (discharged) hazardous waste and retained for three years after deposit or until any relevant waste permit is surrendered or revoked.[74] Records must also be kept of hazardous waste disposed of or recovered by other means.[75] Consignees must make quarterly returns to the Agency, covering both accepted and rejected consignments.[76] In cases of emergency or grave danger involving hazardous waste, the holder is under a duty to take all reasonable steps to avert the emergency or grave danger, or where this is not reasonably practicable, to mitigate it.[77]

Radioactive substances

17.47 Control over radioactive materials and wastes is provided by the Radioactive Substances Act 1993 which consolidates the Radioactive Substances Act 1960 and subsequent amendments. Broadly, no person may keep or use radioactive materials on premises used for the purposes of an undertaking carried on by him unless he is registered under the Act or can claim the benefit of an exemption.[78] Further, ss.13 and 14 of the Act require an authorisation to be obtained for, respectively, (a) the disposal of radioactive waste[79] on or from premises used for the purposes of an undertaking carried on by him; and (b) the accumulation of radioactive waste on such premises with a view to its subsequent disposal. These requirements are backed up by criminal offences and penalties. By s.20 of the 1993 Act the chief inspector may by notice impose requirements in relation to site and disposal records. These requirements may deal with the retention of copies of records for a specified period after the authorised activities have ceased and the provision of copies to the chief inspector if registration is cancelled, authorisation revoked, or the relevant activities cease.[80] Such

---

[73] SI 2005/895 reg.19.

[74] SI 2005/895 reg.47.

[75] SI 2005/895 reg.48.

[76] SI 2005/895 reg.53.

[77] SI 2005/895 regs 61 and 62. Emergency or grave danger means for this purpose a present or threatened situation constituting a threat to the population or the environment in a particular place.

[78] See further, Ch. 9.

[79] Defined by s.2(4). The definition covers waste material which has been contaminated by contact with or proximity to radioactive waste: it may therefore include, for example, irradiated soil.

[80] Radioactive Substances Act 1993 s.20(2).

disposal records, in particular, may be useful in identifying the location of recently disposed of radioactive wastes.

Some contaminated sites may contain or comprise radioactive waste, or **17.48** soil or other material which has been irradiated by contact with such waste, so as to be classified as radioactive waste itself. In that case, the requirements of the Radioactive Substances Act 1993 will need to be observed in relation both to the disposal of waste from the premises[81] and its accumulation with a view to subsequent disposal.[82] The requirement for authorisation for these activities applies to the person using "any premises for the purposes of an undertaking carried on by him". The term "premises" includes any land, whether covered by buildings or not, and "undertaking" is defined as including[83]:

> ". . . any trade, business or profession and, in relation to a public or local authority, includes any of the powers or duties of that authority, and, in relation to any other body or persons, whether corporate or unincorporate, includes any of the activities of that body."

These requirements could therefore potentially apply to consultants, **17.48.1** contractors and sub-contractors on site, as well as the developer. The person to whom authorisation is granted must arrange for copies of the certificate to be posted on the premises concerned where they can conveniently be read by persons having duties on the premises which might be affected by the matters set out in the certificate".[84]

Since radioactive waste is outside the scope of the definition of Directive **17.49** Waste (being excluded by Art.2 of the Waste Framework Directive) it will not in general be hazardous waste for the purposes of control under the Hazardous Waste (England and Wales) Regulations 2005.[85] However, if the radioactive waste is exempt from ss.13 or 14 of the Radioactive Substances Act 1993, and has one or more hazardous properties arising other than from its radioactive nature, it is to be treated as hazardous waste to which the Regulations apply.[86]

PART 3: TAX

Two issues are relevant in respect to tax: the Landfill Tax regime and **17.50** capital expenditure relief. Both are considered only in outline and further reference should be made to specialist tax works if necessary.

Landfill tax

Landfill tax was introduced by the Finance Act 1996 and was the UK's first **17.51** major environmental tax. It applies to specified landfill disposals of waste made after October 1, 1996. By s.40(2), a disposal is taxable if:

[81] Radioactive Substances Act 1993 s.13.
[82] Radioactive Substances Act 1993 s.14.
[83] Radioactive Substances Act 1993 s.47.
[84] Radioactive Substances Act 1993 s.19.
[85] See reg.2(1)(b)(ii).
[86] SI 2005/895 reg.15.

(a) it is a disposal of material as waste;

(b) it is made by way of landfill; and

(c) it is made at a landfill site.

17.52   For this purpose it is made at a landfill site if the land on or under which it is made constitutes or falls within the land which is a landfill site at the time of the disposal (s.40(3)). The term "disposal" is not defined and bears its ordinary meaning; it has been held not to include the deposit of material by way of recycling, e.g. using waste which is used for engineering works at a landfill site; what is critical is the intention of the person utilising the material, not its original producer.[87] The disposal of material is disposal of it as waste if the person making the disposal does so with the intention of discarding the material (s.64(1)). There is a disposal by way of landfill if material is deposited on the surface or land or in a structure set into the surface, or is deposited under the surface of land; whether it is covered with soil or other material is irrelevant (s.65). A site is a landfill site if a waste site licence or PPC permit is in force which authorises disposals in or on the land (s.66).

17.53   The person liable to pay the tax is the landfill operator, who will of course pass it back to the consignor in the rates charged. There are differential rates per tonne for normal material, and a much reduced rate for "qualifying material", which is specified in Regulations.[88] The main implication for remediation of contaminated sites is therefore to increase landfill disposal costs, or the costs of disposal in an on-site landfill repository. However, this effect is mitigated by s.43A which provides an exemption whereby a disposal is not taxable if it is of material removed from land in respect of which a certificate under s.43B was in force at the time of removal, unless it was removed in order to comply with a remediation notice under Pt IIA, or works notice, or under other specified enforcement requirements (see s.43A(4)).[89]

17.54   Removal qualifies for a certificate of exemption under s.43B(7) where the reclamation in question is either to be carried out either (a) with the object of facilitating development, conservation, provision of a public park or other amenity, or the use of land for agriculture or forestry; or (b) with the object of reducing or removing the potential of contaminants to do harm.

17.55   The exemption applies only to material removed during the "qualifying period", which in the case of the development limb lasts until construction work commences, or otherwise until the contaminants have been cleared to the extent that they no longer prevent the desired object being fulfilled, or in the case of the "harm" limb, until pollutants have been cleared to the

---

[87] *Parkwood Landfill v Commissioners for Customs and Excise* [2002] EWCA Civ 1707; [2003] 1 W.L.R. 697; [2003] Env. L.R. 19; *HG Bendall Ltd v Commissioners for Customs and Excise* (February 28, 2003) (V&D Tr (London)).

[88] See s.42 and the Landfill Tax (Qualifying Material) Order 1996 (SI 1996/1528).

[89] The exemption is not however disapplied where removal of the material is carried out by or on behalf of a local authority, development corporation, the Environment Agency, English Partnerships, or the Welsh Development Agency (s.43A(5)).

extent that the potential for harm has been removed.[90] It is a condition of the exemption that "relevant activities" have ceased, or have ceased to give rise to contaminants in relation to the land: relevant activities are those which were carried out by the applicant for exemption or any person connected with him, or by any person on the land in question, which has at any time resulted in the presence of pollutants in, on or under the land (other than without the consent of the occupier of the land at the time, or by being carried by air or water).[91] This is a useful exemption which will benefit many land reclamation or remediation schemes, provided the work is being done voluntarily rather than under compulsion of a remediation or works notice, and provided the contaminating activity is no longer being carried out. This may provide a significant incentive to proceed with remediation before a notice under Pt IIA is served.

There is another exemption under s.43C of "qualifying material" which **17.56** is used to restore a landfill site (other than by capping waste) after the cessation of waste disposal operations, if required by a planning permission, waste management licence or PPC permit.[92]

Capital expenditure relief

Enhanced relief against corporation tax for capital expenditure in respect **17.57** of contaminated land was introduced by Sch.22 to the Finance Act 2001. The deduction, which is designed to encourage the remediation of contaminated land,[93] applies at the election of the company. The relief takes the form of a deduction equal to 150 per cent of the cost incurred. Where however, a company cannot obtain immediate benefit for this tax relief because it is not in a taxpaying position, it can choose to surrender losses to the Inland Revenue. The company will then receive a cash payment equal to 16 per cent of the losses it has surrendered to the Inland Revenue. The conditions of the relief are:

(a) land in the United Kingdom is, or has been, acquired by a company for the purposes of a trade carried on by the company;

(b) at the time of acquisition all or part of the land is or was in a contaminated state; and

(c) the company incurs capital expenditure which is qualifying land remediation expenditure in respect of the land.

"Qualifying land remediation expenditure" means expenditure of the company that meets the following conditions:

---

[90] Finance Act 1996 s.43A(3). This can be applied to parts of land where a site is reclaimed in phases, so the fact that the qualifying period has expired on one phase does not prevent other parts qualifying.

[91] Finance Act 1996 ss.43B(9)–(11).

[92] Added by the Landfill Tax (Site Restoration and Quarries) Order 1999 (SI 1999/2075). See *Ebbcliff Ltd v Commissioners of Customs and Excise* [2004] EWCA Civ 1071; [2004] S.T.C. 1496; [2005] Env. L.R. 8, CA. See also *Harley v Commissioners of Customs and Excise* (V & D Tr (London)) November 2, 2001. (waste deposited in an uncompleted landfill with a view to agricultural improvement by raising land was not within the exemption).

[93] See HMRC Rev. BN22. Further detail on the relief is available on the HMRC website. .

1. it is expenditure on land all or part of which is in a contaminated state;

2. the expenditure is expenditure on relevant land remediation directly undertaken by the company or on its behalf[94];

3. the expenditure is incurred on employee costs[95] or on materials,[96] or is qualifying expenditure on sub-contracted land remediation[97];

4. the expenditure would not have been incurred had the land not been in a contaminated state; and

5. the expenditure is not subsidised.[98]

17.58 The definition of "contaminated state" is in structure the same as for Pt IIA, i.e. land is in a contaminated state if, and only if, it is in such a condition, by reason of substances in, on or under the land, that:

(a) harm is being caused or there is a possibility of harm being caused; or

(b) pollution of controlled waters is being, or is likely to be, caused.

However, there is no threshold of significance of harm or the possibility of harm as there is for Pt IIA.

17.59 A company is not entitled to a deduction in respect of expenditure if the land is in the contaminated state wholly or partly as a result of anything done or omitted to be done at any time by the company or a person with a relevant connection to the company. The words "wholly or partly" suggest that if any part of the contamination, however small, was attributable to the company seeking relief, then no relief at all will be available. This could be an issue, for example if the company has failed to take action after acquisition of the land which has resulted in incremental contamination. The rule of "relevant connection" may have implications for the structure of transactions. If the land had been contaminated by a company, it appears that relief would not be available to a purchaser of the shares of the company, but would be available to a buyer of the assets (including the contaminated land) from the company.

17.60 If a company is not able to use relief to reduce tax payable because it has insufficient taxable profits and cannot surrender the loss as group relief or consortium relief, then it can surrender losses to the Revenue in exchange for a cash payment (referred to as a land remediation tax credit) equal to 16 per cent of the losses surrendered.

---

[94] See para.4.
[95] See para.5.
[96] See para.6.
[97] See para.9.
[98] See para.8.

PART 4: REGENERATION

Background

Reclamation of contaminated land necessarily involves considerable expen- **17.61** diture in the form of site clearance, consultants' and analysts' fees, removal or treatment of contaminated soil or groundwater, and gas control or other remedial measures. The high cost of such work will often act as a considerable barrier to investment in those areas which need it most: hence the various schemes which exist for financial assistance.

Currently, in England, there are two main forms of agency involved in **17.62** facilitating redevelopment of land: these are English Partnerships and the Regional Development Agencies (RDAs). The role of each is considered further below. Useful information may be found on the English Partnerships website and those of each RDA, as well as on that of the Department for Communities and Local Government.

In Wales, from 1976–2006 regeneration was primarily the responsibility **17.63** of the Welsh Development Agency (WDA), which was established by the Welsh Development Agency Act 1985. On April 1, 2006 the WDA ceased to exist, and regeneration is now part of the functions of the Welsh Assembly, working with Welsh local authorities.[99] In Scotland, regeneration is facilitated by Scottish Enterprise and its 12 local enterprise companies, funded by the Scottish Executive.

English Partnerships

English Partnerships in its current form came into being in May 1999. It is **17.64** in fact two organisations, the Commission for the New Towns and the Urban Regeneration Agency, which carry out their activities under the name English Partnerships. The Commission for New Towns was created under Pt II of the New Towns Act 1959, and operates under the provisions of the New Towns Act 1981 Pt II, as amended by the New Towns and Urban Development Corporations Act 1985. In March 1998 the then remaining Urban Development Corporations, which had largely been established during the 1980s under the Local Government, Planning and Land Act 1980, were dissolved and their assets and functions transferred to the Commission. It has also taken over the property and functions of some Housing Action Trusts created under the Housing Act 1988. The purposes of the Commission are to take over and, with a view to ultimate disposal, manage, the property transferred to it, and to dispose of such property as soon as it considers it expedient to do so.[100] It is required to have regard to the convenience and welfare of persons, residing, working or carrying on

---

[99] An example of such work is the remediation and redevelopment of the 185–acre Ebbw Vale Steelworks site, at a cost of £300m. The site was acquired by the Welsh Assembly Government and Blaenau Gwent County Borough Council and planning permission for the scheme was given in 2007.

[100] New Towns Act 1981 s.36.

business in the area, and to the maintenance and enhancement of the value of the land held.

17.64.1   The Urban Regeneration Agency was constituted by s.58 of the Leasehold Reform, Housing and Urban Development Act 1993. The Agency is a body corporate and is not a servant or agent of the Crown.[101] The main object of the Agency is to secure the regeneration of land in England which falls within one or more of a number of specified categories and which the Agency determines to be suitable for regeneration.[102] The relevant categories include land which is vacant or unused; land which is contaminated, derelict, neglected or unsightly; and land which is likely to become derelict, neglected or unsightly by reason of actual or apprehended collapse of the surface as a result of the carrying out of relevant operations, e.g. coal mining, which have ceased to be carried out. The objects of the Agency are to be achieved in particular by various means (or by such of them as seem to the Agency to be appropriate in any particular case), which include[103]: securing that land and buildings are brought into effective use; developing, or encouraging the development of, existing and new industry and commerce; and by facilitating the provision of housing and providing, or facilitating the provision of, social and recreational facilities. The Agency's powers include[104]:

(a)   acquisition of land;

(b)   carrying out the development or redevelopment of land;

(c)   provision of means of access, services or other facilities for land;

(d)   acting with other persons, whether in partnership or otherwise; giving financial assistance to other persons; and

(e)   generally doing anything necessary or expedient for the purposes of its objects or for purposes incidental to those purposes.

17.65   These powers therefore include the reclamation and remediation of contaminated land; whilst the investigation and appraisal of land for possible contamination is not expressly mentioned, s.163 gives powers to enter and survey land for the purpose of ascertaining the nature of the subsoil.

17.66   Currently, English Partnerships is the national regeneration agency for England, with the object of delivering high quality, sustainable, growth, through developing a portfolio of strategic projects and acting as the Government's advisor on brownfield land. It is also a major owner of contaminated land, with perhaps the largest portfolio in Europe, as a result of transfers of land from the former urban development corporations, British Coal and the NHS. It has a strategic role in the assembly of land to meet the Government's Sustainable Communities Plan. In January 2007 it

---

[101] Leasehold Reform, Housing and Urban Development Act 1993 subs.158(3). See also Schs 17 and 18.
[102] Leasehold Reform, Housing and Urban Development Act 1993 subs.159(1).
[103] Leasehold Reform, Housing and Urban Development Act 1993 subs.159(4).
[104] Leasehold Reform, Housing and Urban Development Act 1993 s.160.

was announced that the Government intended to create a new agency, Communities England, bringing together the work of English Partnerships, the Housing Corporation, and relevant parts of the Department for Communities and Local Government. Until the creation of that unified agency, the work of English Partnerships will continue as normal. The main components of that work are:

National Brownfield Strategy

English Partnerships published in November 2003 a document, *Towards a* **17.67** *National Brownfields Strategy*, which was the most comprehensive study then published on England's brownfield land supply. It showed that as much as one-third of the 66,000 hectares of such land on the National Land Use Database could be readily available for redevelopment. Twelve pilot brownfield projects were set up in 2005, covering a mix of urban and rural areas, with "local development partnerships" being established in each area. Further recommendations were submitted to the Government in June 2007, intended to initiate a National Strategy to ensure an adequate supply of land and its effective and efficient re-use. This would involve a number of overarching principles, including the need for developers to take account of full environmental impacts when redeveloping sites, and the compilation of local brownfield strategies in areas of most need. The recommendations also seek to address the fact that four out of the five English regions with the most deprived areas, according to the 2004 Index of Deprivation, also have the highest level of derelict or vacant land.

Housing Gap Funding

Grants may be given to private developers and housing associations by **17.68** English Partnerships and the RDAs to support housing-led regeneration. The Partnership Investment Programme (PIP), launched in 1995, used gap funding to bridge the gap between development costs of derelict land and forecast end value, to enable the projects to proceed which would otherwise have been commercially non-viable. However, in December 1999, the European Commission announced a decision that the PIP contravened Community State Aid rules,[105] and the scheme was closed. This meant that regeneration activity previously facilitated by gap funding could only happen through direct development by English Partnerships or the RDAs, which was far less cost-effective than the PIP approach, the up-front costs of land acquisition, reclamation and redevelopment being some three times greater than gap funding. The House of Commons Environment Select Committee regarded the Commission decision as having "disastrous" consequences and as undermining urban regeneration in England "at a stroke", as well as being "perverse and bizarre" and the work of "Commissioner Monti, an academic with renewed zeal and determination to search for breaches of the State Aid rules".[106] The Commission's view was that

---

[105] See N656/99 and N447/A/99. The concern of the Commission was partly prompted by the fact that some beneficiaries of the scheme were companies with derelict landholdings, such as the automotive sector, which were engaged in intra-Community trade.

[106] See House of Commons, Environment, Transport and Regional Affairs Committee (Session 1999–2000, 16th Report, HC 714) paras 43–46.

gap funding could continue in economically disadvantaged European "Assisted Areas" on a reduced basis, as an exception to the State aid rules. In 2002, the Commission approved as compatible with State aid a scheme of Partnership Support for Regeneration.[107] The basis of approval was in part that the funding was the minimum necessary to make the scheme viable, and hence the benefits were largely directed to the end-users of the housing, rather than the developer. This scheme is administered by English Partnerships and the RDAs, on the basis that it is available selectively and strategically against clear criteria.[108] There is no national fund.

National Coalfields Programme

17.69 This programme, which began in 1997, assists former coalfield communities. English Partnerships currently manages some 107 sites; over 2,000 hectares of non-operational British Coal property were transferred to English Partnerships in December 1996. In its first 10 years, the programme has reclaimed some 1,900 hectares of brownfield land, sometimes using innovative techniques. Projects have included the former Avenue Coking Works near Chesterfield (which has been referred to as "Europe's most contaminated site") through a joint venture with the East Midlands Development Agency and private sector contractors, and with Government funding of £104.5 million. Other projects are the former Hawthorn Colliery and Cokeworks at Murton, County Durham.

Hospital Sites Programme

17.70 Under a £320 million transaction in 2005, some 96 sites of surplus NHS hospitals will be transferred from the Department of Health to English Partnerships, which it is believed may deliver up to 14,000 new homes nationally.

Pathfinder Housing Renewal

17.71 The Pathfinder market renewal areas for housing form part of the 2003 Sustainable Communities Plan, and is a major programme of action for housing renewal over 15–20 years, in the nine current areas (Birmingham and Sandwell, East Lancashire, Humberside, Manchester and Salford, Merseyside, Newcastle and Gateshead, North Staffordshire, Oldham and Rochdale, and South Yorkshire). This programme can include the provision of new housing on former industrial land, for example derelict mills in Rochdale.

Land Restoration Trust

17.72 English Partnerships is part of a partnership which also includes Groundwork, the Forestry Commission and the Environment Agency. This Trust acquires land that is not considered to have any economic value (which

---

[107] N239/02 (24/5/02).

[108] Full details and the relevant application forms, appraisal guidance and template legal agreements are available on the English Partnerships website.

may include contaminated and derelict land) and works with local community interests to provide open space and other "green amenities".

Urban Regeneration Companies

URCs are independent companies established by local authorities and **17.73** RDAs, which work alongside English Partnerships, with the aim of engaging the private sector in regeneration, working within a strategic regeneration framework or masterplan. Their establishment followed a recommendation by Lord Rogers' Urban Task Force in 1999, and there are currently 20 URCs in England, including towns and cities such as Blackpool, Bradford, Derby, Gloucester, Hull, Southend, Swindon, Sunderland, the Tees Valley, and Walsall. The sums available may be significant: for example the Sandwell URC in the West Midlands is expected to make available £1.6 billion over the next 10–15 years.

English Cities Fund

This Fund was established by English Partnerships with two private sector **17.74** partners, to invest in mixed use projects in towns and city centres, including on derelict land. Projects include Canning Town in London, Westgate Wakefield, and Gateshead Town Centre.

Regional Development Agencies

The Regional Development Agencies for England were created under the **17.75** Regional Development Agencies Act 1998. This provides for the creation of nine RDAs for areas nominated in Sch.1 as the East Midlands, Eastern, London, North East, North West, South East, South West, West Midlands, and Yorkshire and the Humber. The purposes of the RDAs under s.4(1) include furthering the economic development and the regeneration of their area, as well as promoting business efficiency and employment and contributing to sustainable development. The powers of the RDAs in achieving these purposes are broad, and will include giving financial assistance and disposing of land for less than the best consideration reasonably obtainable, in each case with the consent of the Secretary of State (s.5). They are funded by grants made by the Secretary of State under s.10, or by use of borrowing powers under s.11. The Secretary of State may vest land previously owned by local authorities or other public bodies in an RDA (s.19) and RDAs have their own powers to acquire land by agreement, or compulsorily (s.20).

The names of the nine RDAs are: **17.76**

Advantage West Midlands

East of England

East Midlands

One North East

North West

South East

South West

Yorkshire Forward

London

17.77   Further information on the specific initiatives of each RDA in the area of land reclamation and regeneration can be found on their respective websites. A significant proportion of RDA budgets is focused on land development.

Single Regeneration Budget

17.78 The Single Regeneration Budget (SRB), which began in 1994, brought together a number of programmes from several Government Departments with the aim of simplifying and streamlining the assistance available for regeneration. Part IV of the Housing Grants, Construction and Regeneration Act 1996 deals with grants for regeneration, development and relocation and provided a legislative basis for the SRB. The Secretary of State may, with the consent of the Treasury, give financial assistance to any person in respect of expenditure incurred in connection with activities which contribute to the regeneration or development of an area (s.126). Activities which are regarded as so contributing include securing that land and buildings and brought into effective use and also creating a safe and attractive environment: both could include the treatment of contaminated land. Such assistance may, by s.127, be given by grants, loans, guarantees or by incurring expenditure for the person benefited.

17.79   The SRB is administered at regional level by the Regional Development Agencies and, in London, by the London Development Agency. It provides resources to support regeneration initiatives in England carried out by local regeneration partnerships The priority is to enhance the quality of life of local people in areas of need by reducing the gap between deprived and other areas. It supports initiatives that build on best practice and represent good value for money. The types of bid supported will differ according to local circumstances. To obtain funding, organisations have to demonstrate that their bid meets one or more of the eligible objectives, for example: improving the employment prospects, education and skills of local people; addressing social exclusion and improving opportunities for the disadvantaged; and promoting sustainable regeneration, improving and protecting the environment and infrastructure, including housing. Schemes aimed at tackling the problems faced by communities in the most deprived neighbourhoods are also normally expected to include the following four key objectives:

(a) tackling worklessness;

(b) reducing crime;

(c) improving health; and

(d) raising educational achievements.

SRB partnerships are expected to involve a diverse range of local **17.80** organisations in the management of their scheme, including local businesses, the voluntary sector and the local community.

New Urban Development Corporations

The first generation of Urban Development Corporations created under **17.81** the Conservative Government in the 1980s and early 1990s under the Local Government, Planning and Land Act 1980 were wound up in 1998 and their assets transferred to English Partnerships. However, under the 2003 Sustainable Communities Plan, new UDCs have been established, still under the 1980 Act, to promote development in certain areas. These are the Thurrock Thames Gateway UDC (established 2003), the London Thames Gateway UDC (2004) and the West Northamptonshire UDC (2004). Thames Gateway spans 16 local authority areas and is one of the largest regeneration areas in Europe, with over 4,000 hectares of re-usable brownfield land, including two of the largest brownfield sites in the South-East: Greenwich Peninsula and Barking Riverside.

The new UDCs have a term of 7–10 years and broadly the same **17.82** functions and powers as their 1980s predecessors, i.e. the objective of regenerating its designated area, in furtherance of which the UDC seeks to bring land and buildings into effective use, to encourage the development of industry and commerce, to create an attractive environment, and to ensure housing and social facilities are available to encourage people to live and work in its area.

UDCs have powers of to acquire, hold, manage, reclaim and dispose of **17.83** land. They have development control functions for strategic planning applications only (unlike the previous UDCs). Particular emphasis is placed upon reclaiming and servicing land, renovating and re-using buildings, and providing adequate infrastructure; the overall objective is to encourage the development of land by the private sector, joint venture arrangements being actively encouraged. Government is by a small board of around 12 people, with guaranteed local authority representation.

European funding

The basis of European funding programmes are the relevant provisions of **17.84** the EC Treaty: Art.34(3) dealing with agricultural funds, Art.159 on the Regional Development Fund, Art.161 on the Cohesion Fund, and Art.146 on the Social Fund. As has been pointed out by Krämer, no general environmental fund has been created.[109] The main source of EU funding relevant to land regeneration is the European Regional Development Fund

---

[109] See L. Krämer, *EC Environmental Law* (6th edn) para.4–19 (Sweet and Maxwell London, 2007). There is also, since 2002 an EU Solidarity Fund, for "major disasters, mainly natural disasters" (Regulation 2012/2002).

(ERDF).[110] The Fund operates under Council Regulation 1080/2006, within the overall framework of Regulation 1260/1999 on the Structural Funds. The objective of the ERDF is to help reinforce economic and social cohesion by redressing regional imbalances. This is achieved by supporting the development and structural adjustment of regional economies, including the conversion of declining industrial regions. The ERDF focuses its assistance on a number of thematic priorities reflecting the general objectives of "Convergence", "Regional Competitiveness and Employment" and "European Territorial Cooperation". In particular, it contributes towards the financing of investment which contributes to creating sustainable jobs; investment in infrastructure; and measures which support regional and local development, including support and services for businesses, in particular small and medium-sized enterprises (SMEs).

17.85   These programmes may in some cases be an important source of funding for land reclamation and decontamination schemes; for example EU Structural Funds contributed £5.8 million to Wolverhampton's regeneration programme between 1993 and 1998. The main purpose of intervention is angled towards the general economic development of regions. However, there is scope for environmental regeneration as a priority. Article 4 of the Regulation, dealing with the Convergence objective, refers to a number of priorities, such as research and technical development, information society, tourism and health and social infrastructure, leaving the precise mix for Member States. Among the environmental priorities are rehabilitation of the physical environment, including contaminated sites and land and brownfield redevelopment. Also, within the Regional Competitiveness and Employment objective, Art.5 mentions "stimulating investment for the rehabilitation of the physical environment, including contaminated . . . and brownfield sites and land". This is however only one among a list of environmental priorities, including biodiversity, renewable energy, the natural and cultural heritage, and green transport.

17.86   The 2006 Regulation, which governs the period 2007–2013, aims to provides a somewhat simpler framework than Regulation 1783/1999, which it replaced. Structural Funding under the Convergence objective corresponds to what was previously known as Objective 1, and applies only to the identified poorest regions. Commission Decision 2006/595 of August 4, 2006 draws up the list of regions eligible for funding from the Structural Funds under the Convergence objective for the period 2007–2013. This includes West Wales and the Valleys, and Cornwall and the Isles of Scilly. Previously, Merseyside and West Yorkshire had benefited from Objective 1 status, but this is no longer the case.[111] All other areas are eligible under the Regional Competitiveness and Employment objective (formerly Objectives 2 and 3). The UK has been allocated €9.4 billion from the ERDF for the period 2007–2013, €2.6 billion of which is earmarked for the Convergence objective. Under Regulation 1080/2006 there is a new require-

---

[110] Also of relevance is the European Social Fund.

[111] Proposals by the UK government for classification of areas under regional selective assistance programmes are matters of national economic policy and as such are subject to an extremely high threshold of "unreasonableness" in any challenge: see *R v Secretary of State for Trade and Industry, Ex p. Isle of Wight Council* [2000] COD 245 (unsuccessful challenge to failure to include Isle of Wight).

ment for Member States to produce a national strategic framework, establishing priorities for allocation of the funds. The UK's National Strategic Reference Framework for the EU Structural Fund Programmes 2007–2013 was published by the Regional European Funds Directorate of the Department of Trade and Industry in October 2006, but makes no particular reference to land regeneration and clean up. The competent authority for the purpose of the ERDF in England is the Department for Communities and Local Government, and the funds are managed by its regional offices.

SECTION 6
TRANSACTIONS

Chapter 18

USE OF CONSULTANTS

Introduction

The investigation, assessment and remediation of contaminated land **18.01** involve a range of expertise. The necessary skills include accessing, compiling and interpreting maps and other information concerning historical and current site uses, and geological and hydrogeological records; designing strategies and methodologies for site investigations, including consideration of optimal locations for trial pits and boreholes and the collection of soil and groundwater samples; selecting and using appropriate equipment and methodologies for assessing sub-surface features and collection of soil, gas and groundwater samples, including use of appropriate equipment and methodologies for the installation of boreholes; safeguarding and documenting the chain of custody of samples; ensuring that appropriate quality control/assurance procedures are followed; interpreting chemical analytical data and its significance; soil science; hydrogeology; environmental chemistry; environmental toxicology; assessment of contaminant transport mechanisms and exposure pathways and quantitative risk assessment; and designing and implementing remediation technologies. Given the wide range of expertise required it is important to obtain professional advice from consultants who are experienced in the assessment and remediation of contaminated land. Consultancy services may be required as part of a transaction, such as an asset or share acquisition, or in the context of a scheme for clean-up or redevelopment of land. Many different specialist areas of knowledge and experience may be relevant depending on the nature of the contamination, the use for which the land is intended to be used and the risks to relevant receptors, but the main areas are geology, geo-chemistry, engineering, chemical engineering, hydrogeology, groundwater hydrology, soil science and mechanics, and toxicology. Added to these areas, various specialisms may be relevant in certain cases, e.g. ecology, mining engineering, industrial archaeology, meteorology, landfill engineering, landscape engineering, asbestos contracting, radiochemistry, explosives and ordnance, gas control, land reclamation, quantitative risk assessment, and cost/benefit (economic) analysis. This chapter provides guidance as to the issues which can arise when commissioning consultants and other experts to carry out contaminated land investigations, appraisals and remediation works.

Selection of consultant

Numerous companies, firms and individuals offer "environmental consul- **18.02** tancy" services. Many factors are relevant to the choice of consultant apart from the obvious question of price. In some cases it may be clear that a particular specialist expertise is required, for example in dealing with a site contaminated by radioactive material or asbestos. Other potential relevant factors include:

1. The consultant's expertise—whether the relevant technical areas are adequately represented.

2. The extent of the consultant's experience. Consultants tend to specialise and some have more experience than others in certain areas. Some consultants may be expert in characterising problems but have little experience of advising on or implementing remediation technologies; others may have a particularly strong track record in dealing with certain types of site, such as landfill. In contentious matters the consultant's experience in giving expert evidence may be critical.

3. Interpersonal skills—in some cases the ability of a particular person will be crucial, for example the ability to communicate technical issues clearly, or to negotiate effectively in the context of a commercial transaction or with regulatory authorities.

4. Capability and resources—the ability to field a large team where multi-site and/or multi-jurisdictional transactions are involved or there is a tight time-scale for carrying out and reporting on investigations.

5. National or international reputation—while there are some excellent sole practitioners and small consultancies, it may be that market perception or confidence in the outcome is so crucial as to require the retention of a "big name".

6. Analytical support—some consultancies have in-house analytical facilities, but the majority make use of outside laboratories. Sound and defensible sampling and analysis techniques are essential and support by an accredited laboratory is important.

7. Whether the work involved is such as to require a contractor who holds a particular licence. Examples would be the requirement for a licence for work with asbestos under reg.8 of the Control of Asbestos Regulations 2006,[1] or where remediation requires a mobile plant licence operated by a technically competent person under the Waste Management Licensing regime.[2]

8. Terms of engagement—these vary and some may be materially more disadvantageous to the client than others.

9. Professional indemnity and public liability insurance—it is important that these are adequate for the nature of the work to be undertaken by the consultant.[3]

18.03   When inviting consultants to submit their proposals for work, it is important to indicate clearly the scope of their brief, the level of insurance regarded as acceptable, the extent to which reliance on their work and

[1] See para.12.22.
[2] See para.17.36.
[3] See Ch.23.

reports will need to extend to third parties, any conditions of engagement which will not be acceptable, the timescale for performing their work and delivering reports, and so forth. Caution needs to be employed when comparing prices, as some fees quoted may be exclusive of matters such as hire of plant and equipment, and analysis charges (which can be as expensive as the investigation fees, if not more so). It also needs to be borne in mind that initial investigations may result in a need for additional investigations and monitoring to be carried out, so it can be advantageous for a degree of flexibility as to further instructions regarding scope to be allowed in the appointment document.

Sources of information on consultants

There are a number of sources of information as to environmental **18.04** consultants and their various strengths. The most immediately relevant is the Specialist in Land Condition (SiLC) scheme. This is a register of accredited specialists, which was created in response to the report of the Government's Urban Task Force, in 1999, which recommended the formulation of a standard format land condition report, which would provide factual information, and would be produced by an accredited specialist. The scheme provides a unifying qualification for the assessment and remediation of brownfield sites. The participating institutions and organisations in the SiLC scheme are the Institute of Environmental Management and Assessment (IEMA) (which provides the secretariat), the Association of Geotechnical Specialists, the Chartered Institution of Water and Environmental Management, the Institution of Civil Engineers, The Chartered Institution of Environmental Health, the Royal Institution of Chartered Surveyors, the Royal Society of Chemistry and the Geological Society. The scheme has a website,[4] which provides a register and details of those accredited. Other relevant institutions and their details are listed in the Appendix to this chapter.

The consultant's brief

It is of the utmost importance to agree a clear and adequate brief for the **18.05** consultant's investigations and report. Prior to commencing work, the consultant should be asked to set out in writing a proposal for the scope of his investigations, the components of that work, and the end product to be expected by way of reports. This basically needs to define what the consultant is being asked to do and the timeframe for doing it. Any divergence from the agreed scope of work should be agreed only in writing. The purpose of the exercise is to protect the position of both client and consultant, to expedite the production of draft and final reports (by avoiding disputes as to scope when the work is part-completed), to enable competitive tenders from consultants to be adequately compared, and to give certainty to the issue of the services included within any agreed fee or

---

[4] *http://www.silc.org.uk.*

"not to exceed" estimate. In the context of a transaction, potential purchasers (particularly in an auction situation) will want to understand the scope of the works undertaken in order to plan their own due diligence. Also, if the report is to be produced to and relied on by a purchaser (or subsequent purchaser), tenants or persons providing finance they will, if properly advised, wish to see a copy of the initial letter of appointment which led to the work and obtain a suitable reliance agreement or collateral warranty. Ensuring that the scope of work is clear and adequate is an exercise requiring care and skill. The initial instructions to the consultant should give a clear indication of what is expected and within what timescale, together with any special considerations such as restrictions on site access, confidentiality, details of previous work and reports, etc. It is also important to clarify from the outset whether the client has any other objectives above and beyond legal compliance in mind. For example, the client may be a developer who wishes to allay public concerns about contamination, so the minimum level of information or remediation required to comply with the law may not suffice for the purposes of its public relations.

18.06   From the brief the consultant can prepare a detailed draft scope of work for the client's consideration. Reference can usefully be made to any relevant published sources of guidance on investigation, in particular guidance on the investigation of potentially contaminated sites or other appropriate technical guidance on investigating matters such as landfill gas or spillages of petroleum, where these problems are known or suspected.[5] Obtaining appropriate confidentiality undertakings from the consultant may be important, where a commercially-sensitive transaction is involved. Issues of privilege over the consultant's reports and correspondence may also need to be considered, as where the consultant's work will be undertaken in connection with a contentious matter (for example, in connection with contemplated litigation involving an adjoining landowner who alleges damage caused by migration of contamination its land). In addition, the consultant should always be asked to confirm (and in some cases warrant) that it has no conflict of interest in acting for the client in relation to the site or sites in question.

The solicitor's role

18.07 A solicitor may well become involved, at the client's request, in appointing a consultant and agreeing his brief and terms of work; or indeed advising on the need for consultants in the context of due diligence. The same may be true of other professions, particularly architects and surveyors. A measure of caution is advisable here. The solicitor, architect or surveyor will owe a duty to exercise proper care and skill in advising on or appointing a consultant[6] and also as to whether the consultant's terms of

---

[5] See Ch.21 on technical issues.

[6] *Collard v Saunders* [1971] C.L.Y. 116. An architect can also be liable for failure to make proper enquiries before advising on contractors: *Pratt v George J. Hill Associates (a firm)* (1987) 38 B.L.R. 25.

engagement are acceptable from the client's point of view. He or she may or may not be experienced enough to discharge that duty adequately; if they are not competent to advise then they should tell the client so.[7] Involvement in agreeing the detailed technical scope of work may be even more dangerous, especially given the exclusions in professional indemnity insurance cover which may apply to environmentally related claims. If the agreed scope of work was inadequate, so that a person relying on it suffers loss or damage, the consultant who undertook the work in accordance with the defective scope (or their insurers) could repudiate liability, leaving the person who relied on the work with a potential claim against the solicitor or other advisor who agreed the scope on the client's behalf. For this reason, the solicitor should ensure either that the client itself agrees the scope with the consultant, or at least that the client approves the scope before it is finalised.

Another problematic area for solicitors arises where consultants provide **18.08** advice in their reports on compliance or liability issues, for example by offering views on whether or not the client is in breach of law or a remediation liability arises for the client—perhaps basing recommendations for remedial actions on such views. This can present difficulties where the view offered by the consultant on a legal compliance or liability conflicts with that arrived at by the solicitor. It also raises the issue for the solicitor of the extent to which the solicitor is expected to review and advise on the legal implications arising from the consultant's factual findings and report. Again, solicitors who lack the specialist expertise to advise the client on such matters should inform the client accordingly.

Sometimes the client may be inclined to keep costs to the minimum by **18.09** limiting the numbers of sampling points, trial pits, etc. The solicitor should be wary of being seen to suggest that what will inevitably be a compromise between economy and confidence is going to protect the client to any greater degree than will actually be the case.[8] Obviously the consultant should be asked to confirm expressly that the agreed scope is in their professional opinion adequate, but many may be understandably reluctant to do this where the scope has been subject to client-imposed cost constraints.

Terms of contract

Most consultants have standard conditions of engagement or terms of **18.10** work. These will vary from consultant to consultant and in many cases it will be necessary to negotiate variations to those standard terms in order to protect the client's interests. The standard terms and conditions of some consultants contain indemnities in the consultant's favour which may be unacceptable from the client's point of view, such as an indemnity to

---

[7] *Buckland v Mackesy* (1968) 208 E.G. 969; *Neushul v Mellish & Harkavy* (1967) 111 S.J. 399; *cf. Carradine Properties Ltd v D.J. Freeman & Co* (1982) 126 S.J. 157 which suggests that the client's own experience and sophistication will also be relevant.

[8] Where work is "designed down" to a low price, the same quality as for a higher price cannot be expected, but there will still be a minimum standard to be expected in terms of care and skill: *Brown v Gilbert-Scott and Payne* (1993, Official Referees' Business, unreported).

protect the consultant against losses incurred by the consultant arising from claims brought by third parties against the consultant (e.g. for negligence) in excess of the contractual limit on liability as between the client and consultant. Some firms of solicitors have developed their own standard forms of appointment with particular consultants with whom they often work which are designed to be more advantageous to the client than the consultants' standard forms and also to save time by not having to engage in detailed negotiations on the terms and conditions of appointment for each new instruction. The following points will need to be considered.

Exclusion or limitation of liability

18.11 Standard terms typically seek to limit the consultant's liability to a given sum (or in some cases the amount of the fee or a multiple of it) in respect of any one incident or series of incidents arising out of the same event. A total exclusion of liability for consequential loss or damage will often not be acceptable; nor will a limitation to the amount of the consultant's fees. An exclusion clause will be subject to the Unfair Contract Terms Act 1977; amongst the factors to be taken into account in considering whether the exclusion was reasonable will be the bargaining power of the parties, whether it would have been practicable to obtain the advice elsewhere, the difficulty of the professional task being undertaken, and the practical consequences of upholding or striking down the exclusion.[9] This last consideration will bring in the issues of insurance and relative hardship. Exclusion of negligence will not automatically be unreasonable—as was said in one case[10]:

> "Sometimes breathtaking sums of money may turn on professional advice against which it would be impossible for the adviser to obtain adequate insurance cover. . . . In these circumstances it may indeed be reasonable to give the advice on a basis of no liability or possibly of liability limited to the extent of the adviser's insurance cover."

Given the complex and dynamic state of the insurance market in respect of environmental risk this may be an extremely important point.[11]

Sub-contractors

18.12 It should be clear to what extent the agreed work, or any aspect of it (e.g. analytical testing) may be subcontracted. Some standard terms seek to restrict the client's ability to make claims against sub-contractors: gener-

---

[9] *Smith v Eric S. Bush* [1990] 1 A.C. 831 858 per Lord Griffiths.

[10] *Smith v Eric S. Bush* [1990] 1 A.C. 831 at 859; see also *Photo Production Limited v Securicor* [1980] A.C. 827 in which the House of Lords held that Securicor were entitled to rely upon a total exclusion clause and escape liability when one of its employees set fire to the property he was guarding: "In commercial matters generally when the parties are not of unequal bargaining power and when risks are normally borne by insurance, not only is the case for judicial intervention undemonstrated but there is everything to be said . . . for leaving the parties free to apportion the risks as they think fit and for respecting their decisions".

[11] See paras 18.40 and 23.61ff.

ally this will not be acceptable. It may be appropriate to provide that the consultant is not to subcontract to any person without the prior written agreement of the client, and for the subcontracting party to be bound by the same terms and conditions as the consultant, and also to provide expressly that the duty of care of the consultant under the contract extends to selection and supervision of any sub-contractor.

Indemnity

Intrusive site investigations may cause damage, for example by cutting into **18.13** services or mobilising contaminants. A high proportion of consultants' standard terms seek to place such risks on the client, providing that the client shall indemnify the consultant against any losses, damages or claims arising.[12] Again, such a provision will generally not be acceptable, save where the problem arises from the client's own negligence. There is a general presumption of law that an indemnity will not readily be granted to a party against loss caused by their own negligence.[13]

Site conditions and safety

It will be reasonable for the consultant to require the client to notify any **18.14** special site conditions, such as cables and drains, and any necessary safe operating procedures. Similarly, it is reasonable for the consultant to be required to comply with site safety and access requirements. Careful attention must be paid to the requirements of the Construction (Design and Management) Regulations 2007, which may well apply to investigations and remediation works.[14] These require those appointing contractors to make sure that the person engaged is competent (reg.4) and for all concerned in a project to co-operate in ensuring performance of the duties under the Regulations and to co-ordinate their activities to ensure, so far as is reasonably practicable, the health and safety of persons carrying out the construction work and those affected by it (regs. 5 and 6).

Confidentiality

In some cases, disclosure of the proposed corporate transaction in connec- **18.15** tion with which the consultant is being asked to advise could prejudice the commercial positions of the parties or constitute price-sensitive information, the use or misuse of which may be subject to insider trading and market abuse legislation. The consultant should undertake not to divulge or disclose to any third party any information of a confidential nature in connection with the project. Often this obligation will be restricted to any information which is expressly designated as confidential by the client. It may also be appropriate to restrict the consultant from approaching

---

[12] Even if a client is aware of the risks of damage if work is not done properly, he will be entitled to assume that a competent consultant has taken all precautions necessary to assume that damage will not occur, and this may provide a defence to a negligence action against the client: see *Anglian Water Services Ltd v H.G. Thurston & Co Ltd* [1993] E.G.C.S. 162 (tipping of spoil to raise surface caused sewer fracture).

[13] See *Brown v Drake International Ltd* [2004] EWCA Civ 1629 (CA).

[14] See para.12.13.

regulatory authorities concerning any aspect of the work without the prior written consent of the client.

Third parties

18.16 In many situations, the client will want to be able to allow another party to rely on the consultant's report without assigning away its own rights. For example, if the site is to be refinanced, the bank will almost certainly want to place reliance on the consultant's work. The consultant on the other hand will wish to limit the number and range of parties and possibly impose a total aggregate limit on liabilities, and this issue will need to be negotiated with the consultant, bearing in mind the client's needs. The issue of third party reliance should be addressed at the outset: otherwise any such extension will need to be negotiated after the work is completed, for which the consultant may require an additional fee. It should be made clear exactly to whom the report should be extended, and how this should be done—whether by reissuing the report in their name, by written agreement, or by formal collateral warranty in the form of a deed. A reliance agreement will generally give the third party the right to rely on the consultant's report and is enforceable for six years, whereas a collateral warranty will normally contain a warranty as to the duty of the consultant to exercise skill, care and diligence in performing the works and entitle the beneficiary to sue up to 12 years from the breach of that duty. It should also be clarified whether, or on what terms, the client can assign the benefit of its rights under the contract, though it needs to be remembered that if the rights are assigned then the assigning entity loses them.

Insurance

18.17 Insurance is a difficult issue in relation to contaminated land generally and is considered separately in Ch.23. The agreement with the consultant should make clear which types of insurance the consultant should hold (third party, public liability and professional indemnity), the amount of cover required and the period for which that cover is to be maintained.[15]

Standard of care and implied terms

18.18 The consultant will not normally be guaranteeing a given result and his or her obligation will be limited to the exercise of reasonable professional care and skill, as judged by experts in the field in question.[16] Failure to achieve the desired result (for example missing a pocket of contamination, or the failure of a particular method of clean-up) will not normally of itself be evidence of negligence.[17] Reported cases dealing with the standard of care to be expected of environmental consultants as such are relatively rare. One case that did consider the issue was *Urban Regeneration Agency/*

---

[15] See further, para.18.40 below.

[16] *Bolam v Friern Hospital Management Committee* [1957] 2 All E.R. 118. See further para.18.40 below.

[17] *Greaves & Co v Baynham Meikle* [1975] 1 W.L.R. 1095; *Thake v Maurice* [1986] Q.B. 644.

English Partnerships v Mott Macdonald,[18] the facts of which involved the claimants having employed the defendant to investigate a major development site, regarding the extent to which it was contaminated, and to advise on the extent of remediation required. The defendant significantly underestimated the extent of the remediation that was necessary, and was subsequently ordered by the court to compensate the claimant for its losses incurred in connection with undertaking additional remediation works. It was held to be relevant to the defendant's standard of care that its client was inexperienced in contaminated land matters, even though it was otherwise a sophisticated purchaser of commercial property. The court also saw fit to comment on the defendant's internal communications and management as having contributed to the loss by being below the appropriate standard.

Since there is little specific guidance at hand, and because of the **18.19** multitude of different tasks undertaken by environmental consultants, it is worth considering the general test for "reasonable professional care and skill" in more detail. Where there is a choice of different courses of action, of which more than one is potentially appropriate, the principle in *Bolam* applies.[19] This principle is still basically as stated by Lord Scarman in *Sidaway v Bethlem Royal Hospital Governors*.[20] The *Bolam* principle may be formulated as a rule that a professional (in the *Bolam* case itself, a doctor) is not negligent if he acts in accordance with a practice accepted at the time by a responsible body of expert opinion even though other experts adopt a different practice. In short, the law imposes a duty of care but the standard of care is a matter of expert judgment. This means that in practice, unless comprehensive professional codes are developed for environmental consultants, they need only stay within accepted practices, carried out with a degree of care and skill ordinarily exercised by reasonably competent members of their profession,[21] in order to comply with the requisite standard of care. There may be a duty to follow up on factors that ought to put the consultant on notice of an issue even if it is outside the remit of their limited task.[22] Consideration must be given to the role of the consultant within the team as a whole. If a particular matter is the responsibility of a specialist consultant, then other members of the team may not be negligent for failing to spot defects which fall within that specialist area.[22a] Equally, a member of the team with a limited remit may be entitled to rely on assumptions as to ground conditions.[22b]

Site investigation

Care will need to be taken in advising on the appropriate method of site **18.20** investigation: for example, trial pits may be useless for investigating certain forms of contamination or ground conditions, and boreholes may be

---

[18] (2000) 12 Envtl. L. & Mgt. 24.

[19] *Bolam v Friern Hospital Management Committee* [1957] 2 All E.R. 118 *JD Williams & Co Ltd v Michael Hyde & Associates* [2001] B.L.R. 99, CA

[20] [1985] 1 All E.R. 643 at 649. See also para.14.75 above.

[21] See *Hammersmith Hospitals NHS Trust v Troup Bywaters & Anders* [2000] Env. L.R. 343 (advice on best way to dispose of clinical wastes).

[22] *Roberts v J. Hampson & Co* [1990] 1 W.L.R. 94.

[22a] *J Sainsbury Plc v Broadway Malyan* (1998) 61 Con. LR 31; [1999] PNLR 286.

[22b] *Richard Reed (Transport) Ltd v Barpro Group Plc* (QB, TCC, July 18, 2000, unreported) (designer of floor slab).

the only reliable method.[23] There will be a duty on the engineer on site to draw attention to adverse ground conditions discovered during the works and to take appropriate steps to warn of their consequences.[23a]

Codes of practice

18.21 Departure from accepted codes of practice may involve a considerable risk of being found negligent in the absence of sound reasons for doing so.[24] Published guidance on the investigation of potentially contaminated sites will therefore be very important. Further discussion of technical guidance and standards on the management of contamination is given at Ch.21.

Legal issues

18.22 Whilst a consultant will not be expected to be a legal expert, he will be expected to have a working knowledge or familiarity with the law so far as it is relevant to his work. The consultant who liaises with the relevant regulatory authorities can probably in most cases assume that they are acting legally and correctly, even where he has some doubts about the attitude they are taking.[25] Multi-jurisdictional contaminated land investigations can pose particular challenges owing to the different approaches in the law and enforcement from one jurisdiction to the next.

Specialist advice

18.23 The consultant must be aware of his own limitations and where necessary advise the client to retain specialist advice, either from within his own firm or externally. Given the multiplicity of disciplines which can be relevant to contaminated land, this can be a very real issue: an obvious example is the geotechnical expert who may not be qualified to advise on chemical contamination. Where the consultant participates in the selection of such specialist advisers, he will be under a duty to exercise reasonable care and skill in so doing. Once the specialist has been appointed, the consultant's duties are likely to be confined to directing and co-ordinating the specialist's work, though the consultant cannot rely blindly on the specialist and may well be under a duty to warn the client of any danger or problem which arises of which a consultant of ordinary competence ought to be aware.[26]

Design

18.24 Consultants may become involved in the design of remedial works, such as the installation of barriers, venting equipment or earthworks. The consultant's duty of care will not be discharged simply by relying on the views of

---

[23] See *Investors in Industry Ltd v South Bedfordshire DC* [1986] 1 All E.R. 787,808.

[23a] *Hart Investments Ltd v Fidler* [2007] EWHC 1058 (TCC); [2007] 112 Con. LR 33.

[24] *John Maryon International Ltd v New Brunswick Telephone Co Ltd* (1982) 141 D.L.R. (3d) 193; *London Borough of Newham v Taylor Woodrow (Anglian) Ltd* (1980) 19 B.L.R. 99; *Bevan Investments Ltd v Blackhall & Struthers (No. 2)* [1973] 2 N.Z.L.R. 45.

[25] *B.L. Holdings v Robert J. Wood & Partners* (1979) 12 B.L.R. 1.

[26] *Investors in Industry Ltd v South Bedfordshire DC* [1986] 1 All E.R. 787, 808. See also para.18.19 above.

others, for example planning or other regulatory authorities,[27] or manufacturers in relation to the suitability of materials or equipment.[28] The issue will be different where certain aspects of design are properly delegated to a specialist. Special care will be needed when applying novel or relatively untried remedial techniques to think through and anticipate potential problems, such as specific site conditions.[29] The client should also be warned of the uncertainties inherent in new techniques.[30]

Estimating cost

An important function of the consultant will often be to estimate the likely **18.25** costs of remediation for an identified problem. Not surprisingly, many consultants are reluctant to commit themselves on this issue; often with good reason, since cost can vary enormously between different remedial techniques and problems of contamination can often be seen as greater when remediation is commenced than they might at first sight have appeared. Absolute accuracy is not required of a professional exercising such judgment, but certainly a serious under-estimate could give rise to liability.[31] The consultant may also be under a duty to monitor continuing costs and to warn if these appear to be getting out of hand.[32] It will also be relevant to consider the implied terms of care and skill under the Supply of Goods and Services Act 1982, in particular the implied term of s.13 that the supplier of the service will carry out the service with reasonable care and skill.

Reliance on report: client

The consultant's potential liability lies in contract and tort as regards the **18.26** appointing party. However, in the light of the decision of the Privy Council in *Tai Hing Cotton Mill Ltd v Liu Chong Hing Bank Ltd*[33] the contractual duties will be the relevant ones:[34] "Their Lordships do not believe that there is anything to the advantage of the law's development in searching for a liability in tort where the parties are in a contractual relationship. This is particularly so in a commercial relationship."

On ordinary principles of contract, the client who suffers loss or damage **18.27** as a result of the consultant's breach will be able to recover as damages all losses (whether physical or purely financial), subject to any valid limitation of liability, so long as they arise naturally, according to the usual course of

---

[27] *B.L. Holdings Ltd v Robert J. Wood & Partners* (1978) 10 B.L.R. 48; *Eames London Estates v North Hertfordshire DC* (1980) 259 E.G. 491.

[28] *Sealand of the Pacific Ltd v Robert C. McHaffie Ltd* (1974) 51 DLR (3d) 702.

[29] *Urban Regeneration Agency/English Partnerships v Mott Macdonald* [2000] 12 Envtl L & Mgt. 24, in which the defendant significantly underestimated the costs of remediation measures and was ordered to pay £18.5 million in compensation to the claimant; *IBA v EMI and BICC* (1980) 14 B.L.R. 1.

[30] *Victoria University of Manchester v Wilson* (1984) 2 Con. L.R. 45.

[31] *Columbus Co v Clowes* [1903] 1 K.B. 244.

[32] *J. & J.C. Abrams Ltd v Ancliffe* [1978] 2 N.Z.L.R. 420.

[33] [1986] 1 A.C. 80.

[34] [1986] 1 A.C. 80, at 107 per Lord Scarman.

things, from the breach of contract or alternatively were in the contemplation of the parties when the contract was made.[35] If the client makes it clear to the consultant that one objective of the investigation is to guard against the inadvertent assumption of liabilities flowing from the condition of the site, then such liabilities may well be recoverable losses. Where the liability is of a criminal nature, for example a prosecution for pollution of controlled waters or in respect of statutory nuisance, it will be relevant to remember that as a general rule of public policy fines should be paid by the convicted party. However, it may still be possible to recover the fine as damages, at least where it was the advice of the consultant which led to the client committing the offence.[36]

18.28   It is conceivable, indeed in many cases likely, that the client may at some future stage dispose of the property which was the subject of the investigation or remedial work. Various questions can then arise, in particular whether the client can validly assign his contractual rights to the purchaser[36a] and whether the client, having disposed of the property, can still assert contractual rights against the consultant. These issues were considered in detail in the context of construction contracts by the House of Lords in *Linden Gardens Trust Ltd. v Lenesta Sludge Disposals Ltd*[37] The decision suggests the following:

1. The assignment of the benefit of a contract may be prohibited by the terms of the contract. The wording of cl.17(1) of the JCT form, which provides that "the Employer shall not without the written consent of the Contractor assign this Contract", was held, though "unhappily drafted" to have that effect.

2. Likewise, the assignment of benefits arising under a contract, e.g., to enforce accrued rights of action, may be prohibited. Clause 17(1) was held to have this effect.

3. Such restrictions on assignment are not void as contrary to public policy.

4. A purported assignment in breach of such prohibitions will not be effective to vest the benefit of the contract or the cause of action in the assignee.

5. Where the client sells the property with an obligation to indemnify the purchaser against defects, loss flowing from that obligation may well be too remote to be reasonable under the criteria in *Hadley v Baxendale*.

6. In general, lack of a proprietary interest by the plaintiff in the property at the date of the breach will preclude any claim for substantial damage.[38]

---

[35] *Hadley v Baxendale* (1854) 9 Exch. 341.

[36] *Osman v J. Ralph Moss Ltd* [1970] 1 Lloyd's Rep. 313, CA.

[36a] Where rights are assigned, the assignee acquires the course of action of the assignee and any remedies the assignor would have had. The fact that the assignor suffers no loss themselves does not preclude a claim by the assignee who suffers loss: *Technotrade Ltd v Larkstore Ltd* [2006] EWCA Civ (CA); [2006] 1 W.L.R. 2926.

[37] [1993] 3 All E.R. 417.

[38] *The Albazero* [1977] A.C. 774; cf. the more liberal approach of Lord Griffiths at [1993] 3 All E.R. 417 at 421–2.

7. However, there are exceptions to this general rule which may avoid the situation where "the claim to damages would disappear . . . into some legal black hole, so that the wrongdoer escaped scot-free".[39] The importance of avoiding this "legal black hole" has since been emphasised.[40] In *Offer-Hoar v Larkshore*,[41] it was stated that the principle allowing the assignee to recover no more than the assignor was not intended to enable the contract breaker or debtor to escape liability by relying on the fact of assignment. Thus, the claimant could recover for damage that had occurred after it had purchased the property in question, but before the right to damages had been assigned.

8. Amongst those exceptions[42] is the case where to the knowledge of both parties the property is going to be occupied, and possibly purchased, by third parties and where it could be foreseen that damage caused by breach would cause loss to a later owner and not merely to the original contracting party. In such a case it appears proper to treat the parties as having entered into the contract on the footing that the client would be entitled to enforce contractual rights for the benefit of those who suffered from defective performance but who under the terms of the contract could not acquire any rights. If the Contracts (Rights of Third Parties Act) 1999 applies and has not been excluded, it could now be used by the third party to enforce the terms of the contract on the basis that those terms purport to confer a benefit on them. If the ultimate purchaser is given a direct cause of action against the contractor (for example by a collateral warranty) then the exception referred to above has no application and the original client will not be entitled to recover damages for loss suffered by others who can themselves sue for such loss.[43]

Reliance on report: third party

A consultant's report may be produced to third parties such as a purchaser, **18.29** its financiers, a tenant or a mortgagee, who may in some cases act in reliance upon it. In any event it will be a question of judgment as to whether it is prudent to rely upon the substantive content of the report, which may have been produced some time ago, and for different purposes. There are also substantial legal difficulties in any third party relying on the report. The starting point is that the third party will not have a contractual relationship with the consultant. In the absence of a contractual arrangement, any action will therefore lie either in tort or under the Contracts (Rights of Third Parties) Act 1999. More recent years have seen a drawing back from some of the innovative decisions of the 1970s and 1980s and in

---

[39] *GUS Property Management Ltd v Littlewoods Mail Order Stores Ltd* 1982 S.C. (HL) 157 at 177.
[40] *Darlington BC v Wiltshier Northern Ltd* [1995] 3 All E.R. 895.
[41] [2006] EWCA Civ 1079.
[42] See also *Dunlop v Lambert* (1839) 6 C.L. & F. 600.
[43] See *Alfred McAlpine Construction v Panatown Ltd* [2001] EWCA Civ 485.

particular from the recovery of purely economic loss in tort.[44] Recovery for purely economic loss has not generally been allowed, however foreseeable it may have been. Essentially, courts will only allow recovery for pure economic loss where it can be said that the defendant has assumed a responsibility to the claimant and that the imposition of such a duty would be fair, just and reasonable.

18.30   The main potential basis for liability to a third party in tort is that line of authority which stems from the decision in *Hedley Byrne & Co. Ltd v Heller & Partners Ltd*.[45] This involves liability for advice or opinion given in a professional capacity or in some special relationship, where it is reasonable to expect that the recipient of the information will rely on it: in such circumstances even purely economic loss can be recovered. Whether such a duty of care is owed will depend on whether the professional adviser, at the time of giving his advice, was or ought to have been aware that his advice or information would in fact be made available to and would be relied on by a particular person or class of persons for the purpose of a particular transaction or type of transaction, and so assumed responsibility to the ultimate recipient.[46] It has been said that the precise limits regarding the concept of assumption of responsibility are in a state of development, with no comprehensive list of guiding principles; hence the courts must look at all the circumstances and at analogous situations in which a duty of care has been previously found to exist.[47] The consultant should also be aware that he can become liable even in rather informal circumstances, since responsibility towards the recipient of any advice can potentially arise by holding himself out as having special expertise. This can become an issue if an informal discussion with a prospective client amounts to advice.[48] Where a statement put into general circulation might be relied on by a variety of third parties for a variety of purposes there will not be the requisite relationship of proximity to give rise to a duty of care.[49] There must be a sufficiently clear idea on the part of the defendant as to the purpose to which it may be put.[50] There is no reason of public policy why an expert advising a local authority (or for that matter any other developer) as to soil conditions should be liable to a subsequent purchaser who has not relied on the expert's report and who, at the time of the negligent act cannot be identified other than as a member of a class of potential purchasers.[51]

18.31   It is therefore certainly arguable that a consultant who prepares a report knowing that the client requires it in connection with an imminent forthcoming sale or refinancing could be liable to the purchaser or bank,

---

[44] See *D. & F. Estates Ltd v Church Commissioners for England* [1989] A.C. 177; *Department of the Environment v Thomas Bates & Son* [1991] 1 A.C. 499; *Murphy v Brentwood DC* [1991] 1 A.C. 398.

[45] [1964] A.C. 465.

[46] *Cann v Willson* (1888) 39 Ch.D. 39; *J.E.B. Fasteners Ltd v Marks Bloom & Co* [1981] 3 All E.R. 289; *Caparo Industries Plc v Dickman* [1990] 2 A.C. 605.

[47] *Precis (521) Plc v William M Mercer Ltd* [2005] EWCA Civ 114.

[48] See *Lidl Properties v Clarke Bond Partnership* [1998] Env. L.R. 662, where gratuitous advice on remediation measures was given over the telephone and relied upon—when damage occurred as a result, it was held that the defendant owed Lidl Properties a duty of care.

[49] *Caparo Industries Plc v Dickman* [1990] 2 A.C. 605. See also the "masterly analysis" of Denning L.J. in *Candler v Crane Christmas & Co* [1951] 2 K.B. 164 at 179–184, approved by Lord Bridge in *Caparo Industries*.

[50] *Precis (521) Plc v William M Mercer Ltd* [2005] EWCA Civ 114.

[51] *Preston v Torfaen BC*, *The Independent*, September 24, 1993.

even though their precise identity may not be known at the date of the report. At the other extreme, in the case where the client makes available the report to a local authority, who may then be statutorily obliged to disclose the information contained in it to the general public, it seems most unlikely that any relationship of proximity would exist with those who might come upon and rely on that information; the same would apply to those who may be affected by action or inaction by the public body on the basis of the report. Between those two extremes there is obviously considerable room for debate and uncertainty. Careful attention will be needed to what the consultant is being asked to do; the fact that a person has expert knowledge does not impose a duty on them to apply that knowledge in resolving every problem they encounter in carrying out their work.[52]

It should be noted that the *Hedley Byrne* type of duty will extend only to **18.32** professional relationships and to persons such as consulting engineers, architects or structural engineers.[53] It seems likely that environmental consultants will fall into this category. The duty will not apply to specialist manufacturers of equipment, even though they may give advice.[54]

It is also important to note that it is open to the consultant to attempt to **18.33** negate any duty to third parties by way of express disclaimer, such as a statement on the face of the report that it is not intended to be relied on by any third party. Any such disclaimer may well be regarded as a notice which excludes liability for negligence which would have arisen but for the notice.[55] As such it may be subject to the test of reasonableness under the Unfair Contract Terms Act 1977.[56] However, the counter argument (unsuccessful on different facts in *Smith v Eric S. Bush)* is that the disclaimer is an important evidential consideration in determining whether a special relationship of reliance existed at all under the rule in *Hedley Byrne v Heller*. Where the exclusion is not a disclaimer on the face of the report but forms part of the private terms of engagement between the consultant and their employer, it can have no effect on whether liability is assumed as a matter of tort.[57]

Pursuant to the Contracts (Rights of Third Parties) Act 1999 (which **18.34** applies, unless expressly excluded by the parties, to contracts entering into force on or after May 11, 2000) a third party can enforce a term of a contract in his own right if that contract either expressly provides that he may, or a term purports to confer a benefit on him. The third party must be expressly identified in the contract by name, as a member of a class or as answering a particular description, but need not be in existence when the contract is entered into. In general, however, the Act tends to be excluded by contract parties. The consultant would be anxious not to

---

[52] See *Sutradhar v Natural Environment Research Council* [2006] UKHL 33; [2006] 4 All E.R. 490; [2007] Env. L.R. 10 (no duty owed by consultants testing groundwater for irrigation project to public later affected by arsenic in drinking water).
[53] *Pirelli General Cable Works Ltd v Oscar Faber & Partners* [1983] 2 A.C. 1.
[54] *Nitrigin Eireann Teoranta v Inco Alloys Ltd* [1992] 1 All E.R. 854.
[55] See Unfair Contract Terms Act 1977 s.11(3).
[56] *Smith v Eric S. Bush; Harris v. Wyre Forest DC* [1990] 1 A.C. 831, especially per Lord Griffiths at 856–7.
[57] *Precis (521) Plc v William M Mercer Ltd* [2005] EWCA Civ 114.

increase their potential liability by unknown amounts, and the client and third parties would probably not be comfortable relying merely on an implied conferral of benefit. A "third party memorandum", expressly stating the rights of a third party in an appointment contract, can be used to the same effect as a collateral warranty, together with an express exclusion of Act in respect of other third parties.

Extension of duty to third parties

18.35 In view of the inherently uncertain position as to the ability of third parties to rely on a consultant's report, the issue is frequently addressed by creating a direct contractual relationship between the consultant and third party. This may involve the report being re-issued in the name of the third party, or by a formal collateral warranty or third party memorandum under the Contracts (Rights of Third Parties) Act 1999. These matters should ideally be addressed at the time of the consultant's initial appointment. The consultant will want to be clear as to whom he may be required to extend his duty of care and understandably may be unwilling to go beyond the first purchaser or tenant. No consultant is likely to relish the idea of extending the duty to a large number of tenants in a case where the development is to be let. From the client's point of view, where the intention is to use the report in financing a project, the possibility of a number of financial institutions being involved will need to be catered for.

18.36 From the third party's point of view, the desired objective is a clear contractual relationship with the consultant. The preferred option will thus probably be a collateral warranty agreement by way of deed, which will avoid any arguments as to consideration and will provide a 12–year limitation period. Alternatively, and perhaps now more commonly, there will be a "reliance letter", indicating that the third party may rely on the report.The essence of the agreement will be a warranty by the consultant that it has exercised all reasonable care, skill and diligence in the production of the report and the work leading up to it. Depending on the terms of their professional indemnity insurance, consultants are unlikely to be prepared to increase their liability by warranting achievement of any higher standard of care than in the original appointment document. Difficulties are most likely to arise where the draftsman attempts to impose on the consultant more onerous liabilities than were owed under the original contract and the consultant will wish to see any limitations or exclusions from the main contract carried over into the collateral warranty. The consultant will also wish to see a suitable "other parties" clause to ensure that it is not held solely liable where the negligence of other professionals is also involved.

Sub-contractors

18.37 The consultant may in practice make use of sub-contractors in the course of his work: the obvious example is the sub-contracting of the analysis of soil samples to a laboratory. Sub-contractors may also be used for drilling boreholes and undertaking excavations in connection with investigations or remediation. This situation may give rise to a number of potential difficulties. The first issue is whether the consultant is entitled to delegate performance of the agreed work. In *Moresk Cleaners Ltd. v Hick*[58] it was held that an architect is not entitled to delegate the design of a building to a sub-contractor; however it is arguable that this principle is limited to the function of design, where the client may reasonably expect that the architect he has chosen will actually do the work.[59]

18.38 Secondly, whilst a professional person is free to sub-contract the actual performance of certain aspects of their work to another, they are not under common law principles allowed to delegate responsibility: regardless of the care which they took themselves in selection and supervision, they will be liable for the negligence of the sub-contractor. Thirdly, the position will naturally be otherwise where the consultant's role is to recommend to the client the appointment of independent specialists: here the consultant's responsibility is limited to care in recommendation and supervision. Finally, where the consultant employs the laboratory or other sub-contractor, the client will of course have no direct contractual relationship with the sub-contractor. Any attempts to construct or spell out a contractual relationship are likely to be fraught with difficulty[60] so the client will have to fall back on arguing the existence of a duty of care in tort. This may be easier said than done in the case where a laboratory is simply analysing a batch of samples with no knowledge of the context or the reliance to be placed on the results.

18.39 From the point of view of all concerned it is therefore important to be clear as to the relationship between the parties. The consultant could be explicitly made responsible to the client for lack of care on the part of the laboratory, or (and perhaps preferably from the consultant's point of view) there could be a separate contract for analysis between the client and laboratory. The best solution however from the client's point of view is to require that a collateral warranty be given by the sub-contractor in the client's favour. In fact, the client would be well-advised to include a requirement for collateral warranties in respect of any sub-contractors when they appoint the consultant, in order to avoid delay and price negotiations at a later date. Preferably, in order to stay in control of information, the client should also include a clause in the main contract requiring the consultant to obtain the client's consent before sub-contracting. A separate contractual relationship does not however solve all the client's problems, since it may not be straightforward to establish whether the fault lay with the consultant or the laboratory; on the other hand, major laboratories may be more substantial than some small consultancies.

---

[58] [1966] 2 Lloyd's Rep. 338.
[59] *Investors in Industry Ltd v South Bedfordshire DC* [1986] 1 All E.R. 787, 807.
[60] See, e.g. *Scuttons Ltd v Midlands Silicones Ltd* [1962] A.C. 446; *Morris v C.W. Martin & Sons Ltd* [1966] 1 Q.B. 716; *New Zealand Shipping Co Ltd v. A.M. Satterthwaite & Co Ltd The Eurymedon* [1975] A.C. 154; *Salmond and Spraggon (Australia) Pty Ltd v Port Jackson Stevedores Pty Ltd, The New York Star* [1979] 1 Lloyd's Rep. 298.

Insurance

18.40 The general difficulties relating to insurance of environmental risks are discussed elsewhere.[61] However, in dealing with consultants it is important to be aware of the difficulties which they face in relation to professional indemnity insurance. On the one hand, the insurance market as a whole has hardened in recent years, to the effect that premiums have risen but coverage generally has become less favourable for the insured. On the other hand, a fear of big claims in the environmental sector has not so far been realised, shifting the balance in favour of the insured. The result of these developments is that the ability of environmental consultants to obtain professional indemnity insurance has in general stayed broadly the same in recent years. However, insurance contracts are commonly negotiated individually, and also depend to a large extent on the underwriter, so there is likely to be a good deal of variation between the different consultants' policy terms. Most risks can be insured for an appropriate premium, but many consultancies do not have the capital base to maintain comprehensive cover.[62]

18.41 Both insurers and reinsurers remain "risk averse" to possible claims involving environmental damage and this has been reflected in the general withdrawal of cover or exclusion of liability for pollution or contamination, with the exception of sudden, unintended and unexpected happenings. It appears that insurers now also generally exclude cover for any loss arising from claims for bodily injury or property damage directly caused by the insured arising out of the actual, alleged or threatened discharge, dispersal, release or escape of pollutants. Even more sweeping exclusions may apply in relation to claims in respect of US jurisdiction. Such exclusions are potentially very serious for consultants engaged in environmental work, and for their clients and others who may seek to rely on their work.

18.42 Whereas in the past cover was generally written on an each and every claims basis with an upper limit applicable to each claim but not to the aggregate of claims, coverage may now only be available with an upper aggregate limit. Smaller environmental consultancies may find it difficult to pay large premiums for the higher levels of cover, and can also be reluctant to commit a major proportion of their yearly cover to a particular project. Clients and their lawyers will therefore need to take a realistic approach to what can be demanded in terms of insurance cover. The fact that professional indemnity insurance is written on a "claims made" basis and needs to be renewed annually means that it is very difficult for the consultant to guarantee that any specific level of cover will be maintained year-on-year, given the vagaries of the market, for periods such as six or twelve years. The underwriting will depend on the nature of the services provided, the claims history and the fee income of the business. The answer may be a warranty to use best endeavours to obtain cover, provided it is available in the market at reasonable rates. In any event it must be questionable how an absolute obligation to maintain insurance would

---

[61] See Ch.23.
[62] For a case on construction of a policy dealing with "civil and environmental engineering", see *Encia Remediation Ltd v Canopius Managing Agents Ltd* [2007] EWHC 916 (Comm).

ultimately protect the client if the consultant did fall into breach of it. Clients are likely to be prepared to accept realistic caps on financial liability in the appointment contract, linking any cap to the professional indemnity insurance cover of the consultant, where they are confident that the liability caps offered by the consultant are an accurate reflection of the level of professional indemnity cover actually available to the consultant in the market. Arguably, the degree of certainty achieved this way is preferable to imposing liabilities that are highly unlikely to result in recoverable payments.[63] Finally, the insurance aspects will be important in relation to collateral warranties, since most policies will exclude any claim arising out of a specific liability assumed under contract which increases the insured's standard of care or measure of liability above that normally assumed. Mindful of that exclusion, many consultants will wish to obtain their insurer's approval to the terms of any proposed warranty.

Many of these problems will also apply to analytical laboratories and to **18.43** remediation contractors, probably a smaller proportion of which will be insured for professional negligence. Where a contractor is carrying out remediation activities, it should be remembered that unless a specific environmental impairment liability policy has been obtained, the general public liability policy of the contractor will generally not cover gradual pollution. Where data or samples are to be transferred to an off-site laboratory or offices by third parties, it is recommended that the consultants obtain extra insurance cover for these trips: these items will generally be deemed by the transporters to have no commercial value, and so their own insurance cover would not provide adequate compensation.

---

[63] *A Client's Guide to Professional Indemnity Insurance* (January 2007), The Association of Geotechnical and Geoenvironmental Specialists, at *http://www.ags.org.uk*.

Appendix

SOURCES OF INFORMATION ON CONSULTANTS AND SPECIALISTS

Specialists in Land Contamination Scheme (SiLC)
c/o IEMA (see below)
http://www.silc.org.uk

Institute of Environmental Management and Assessment (IEMA)
St Nicholas House,
70 Newport,
Lincoln, LN1 3DP,
Tel: 0790 763613
http://www.iema.net
Detailed database of consultants.

EIC Environmental Consultancies Group (ECG)
45 Weymouth Street,
London, W1G 8ND
Tel: 0207 935 1675
http://www.eic-uk.co.uk/envcons/
A specialist working group operating under the auspices of the Environmental Industries Commission (EIC). The website contains a list of ECG members together with contact details.

Environmental Data Services (ENDS)
11–17 Wolverton Gardens,
Hammersmith,
London, W6 7DY
Tel: 020 8267 8123
http://www.endsdirectory.com
ENDS produces a directory of UK and international consultancies, which can be searched by specialist service, consultancy characteristics or alphabetical index. It also provides information on the consultancies' experience and accreditations

Association of Consulting Engineers (ACE)
Alliance House,
12 Caxton Street,
Westminster,
London, SW1H 0Ql
Tel: 020 7222 6557
http://www.acenet.co.uk

The Association represents the business interests of the consultancy and engineering industry in the UK. It holds a database of consulting engineer members of various specialisms, including contaminated land. The Association does not give out any information members as a matter of policy; its members participate in SiLC.

Institution of Chemical Engineers (ICE)
Davis Building,
165–171 Railway Terrace,
Rugby,
Warwickshire, CV21 3HO
0788 78214
http://cms.icheme.org/
The professional body for chemical and process engineers, with international membership. The website has consultants search option, with the ability to search by name, international experience, technical expertise or key word.

Royal Society of Chemistry (RSC)
Thomas Graham House
Science Park
Milton Road
Cambridge, CB4 4WF
01223 420066
http://www.rsc.org/Chemsoc
The website contains a directory of consulting practices, which can be searched under various headings.

Chartered Institution of Water and Environmental Management (CIWEM)
15 John Street,
London, WC1N 2EB
0207 831 3110]
http://www.ciwem.org
CIWEM website contains a professionals' directory which includes listings for consultancies with experience of advising on contaminated land.

Association of Geotechnical and Geoenvironmental Specialists (AGS)
Forum Court
83 Copers Court Road
Beckenham
Kent, BR3 1NR
0208 6588212
http://www.ags.org.uk
The website contains a directory of members, which can be searched for environmental consultants and shows the type of consultancy/contracting undertaken.

Geological Society,
Burlington House,
Piccadilly,
London, W1V 0BN
0207 4349944.
http://www.thegeologistsdirectory.co.uk
The website contains the "geologist's directory online", which includes companies and the products serving the geoscience industry in the UK and Ireland. It does not however keep a list of members with relevant expertise.

United Kingdom Accreditation Service (UKAS)
21–47 High Street
Feltham
Middlesex
TW13 4UN
0208 9178400
http://www.ukas.org
Lists accredited laboratories.

Chapter 19

PROPERTY TRANSACTIONS

Introduction

Whilst the contaminated land regime of Pt IIA may not have yet lived up to **19.01** initial expectations in terms of the numbers of sites identified as contaminated,[1] it is fair to say that it has had a significant impact on the way property transactions are conducted since its implementation in 2000. It is now commonplace for some form of contaminative land survey to be undertaken, whether the transaction involves domestic or commercial property, although this is usually confined to the commissioning of desktop surveys with their obvious limitations. The possibility or reality of land being contaminated, whether or not Pt IIA applies, may impact upon property transactions in various ways. The fitness of the land for its current or intended purpose may be affected, requiring expenditure to rectify the problem: how much expenditure depends on the applicable remediation standards for its current or proposed use at the time remediation is to be carried out.[2] In the absence of regulatory intervention under Pt IIA or any contractual provision to the contrary, such a problem will lie where it falls, with the current owner. Contaminated land may also involve actual or contingent liabilities. Whilst a transfer of the ownership or occupation of contaminated land will not rid the transferor of any liability which he has already accrued, for example in respect of water pollution, the transferee may find himself liable for the future as owner or occupier.[3] Part IIA adds another layer of complexity; the transferor may avoid liability for the cost of remediation depending on whether both he and the transferee are deemed to be within Class A and he is able to rely on one of the exclusions set out in Ch.D of Annex 3 of the Guidance or if no Class A party is found to exist (in which case liability will fall entirely on the transferee as the Class B owner or occupier).[4] Finally, the potential problems of fitness for purpose and liability may be subject to market perception in such a way as to have a serious blighting effect on the property and its value, irrespective of the actual scale of the risks.

These issues may be considered in the context of three main types of **19.02** transaction, each of which raises its own particular problems:

    (a) sale;

---

[1] See para.3.243ff.

[2] Although further expenditure cannot be altogether ruled out should the works undertaken not involve complete eradication of the problem and remediation standards subsequently become more stringent

[3] For example, for an ongoing common law or statutory nuisance.

[4] See further para.5.49.

(b) lease; and

(c) mortgage or charge.

Essentially, there are two main concerns:

(i) the provision or acquisition of information; and

(ii) the contractual allocation of risk between the parties.

19.03   In this regard it is worth noting that environmental insurance products are now available to support contaminated land transactions but the market is still developing, the premiums are high and policies are usually subject to a number of pre-conditions.[5] Perhaps not surprisingly the reported levels of uptake for these products is low, although increasing. There are also a number of innovative insurance-backed environmental risk transfer products coming onto the UK market broadly based on tried and tested US models. For example, some environmental consultants now offer perpetual indemnities against a range of environmental risks on a site-specific or portfolio basis in return for lucrative and exclusive remediation contracts.

Purchaser considerations

19.04 The purchaser of land should be concerned to ensure that it is not subject to such contamination as may:

(a) affect its fitness for the intended purpose;

(b) diminish its value unacceptably; or

(c) carry with it hidden liabilities; and

(d) increasingly, companies and funds are concerned with reputational risk which may flow from contaminated assets or any perceived shortcomings in due diligence.

Ways of guarding against these risks are essentially:

(a) the obtaining of information about the land's conditions; and

(b) contractual provisions shifting the risk from the purchaser to the seller.

So far as information is concerned this may be obtained from three sources:

(i) the purchaser's own investigations;

(ii) regulatory and local authorities; and

(iii) the seller.

---

[5] On insurance, see Ch.23.

Contractual provisions can take a wide variety of forms: some, such as **19.05** indemnities, may be apt mainly to address the risks of liabilities, whereas others—for example a reduction or retention in price—may be best suited to deal with issues such as fitness for purpose and diminution in value.

Information: generally

The issues of information and investigation are considered at Chs.21 and **19.06** 22, which should be read in conjunction with this chapter. Two specific information issues are considered in this chapter, in that they arise particularly within the context of property transactions. These are:

(a) local authority enquiries; and

(b) pre-contract enquiries of the seller.

The exercise of obtaining information, particularly where professional **19.07** assistance is involved, has implications in terms of cost and time, particularly for smaller value transactions. There may therefore be difficult practical issues to be faced in deciding how far to go in seeking information. The problem can be particularly acute in the case of domestic property, where even the costs of a basic investigation may be regarded as prohibitive, yet the subsequent discovery of contaminative problems may have disastrous personal consequences for the purchaser.

Solicitor's duty of care to client

It is arguable to what extent a solicitor owes a duty of care to the client to **19.08** warn of the risks of contamination and to offer advice as to investigations in that regard. The Law Society's Contaminated Land Warning Card (often known as the Green Card) indicates that as a matter of best practice solicitors must consider whether contamination is an issue in every property transaction. In relation to purchases, mortgages and leases, the Green Card indicates that solicitors should:

(i) advise clients of potential liabilities associated with contaminated land;

(ii) make enquiries of the seller and statutory and regulatory bodies;

(iii) undertake a desktop study by way of independent site history investigation and in commercial cases, if there is a likelihood of contamination;

(iv) advise an independent full site investigation by appropriate environmental consultants; and

(v) consider the use of contractual protection and the use of the Pt IIA exclusion tests.

For unresolved problems the possibility of advising withdrawal from the **19.09** transaction or obtaining insurance is suggested. The Green Card makes it clear that the advice is not a professional requirement for solicitors but clearly it is likely to have a bearing in any action brought by a client against a solicitor relating to negligent advice concerning contaminated land liabilities.

19.10 The general standard expected is that of the ordinary competent solicitor, having regard to the standards normally adopted by the profession.[6] Where the solicitor practices in environmental law as a specialist, then the standard is that appropriate to a firm of solicitors with a specialist environmental department.[7] This does not imply however that the solicitor undertakes to achieve a specific result for the client. Specialist solicitors may legitimately rely on advice from the Bar, in the same way as generalists, but must bring their own skill and experience to bear and exercise independent judgment, rejecting counsel's advice which is obviously wrong.[8] The solicitor duty is defined by the terms of his retainer; he is not obliged to spend time and effort on issues outside the scope of that retainer. However, if in the course of that work he becomes aware of issues of concern which present a risk or potential risk to the client, he is under a duty to inform the client.[9] This principle may have a bearing on contaminated land; even if the solicitor's retainer expressly excludes investigating contamination, if as part of the title investigations the solicitor has information which presents a warning of potential contamination (for example, old title deeds or leases indicating waste disposal has occurred at the site) the client should be warned of the possible risks. The solicitor is under a duty to follow up on matters which are of importance where satisfactory replies to preliminary inquiries are not forthcoming; the absence of a satisfactory reply does not cause the duty to evaporate.[9a] The precise scope of the solicitor's duty to advise in this respect may vary according to the knowledge, experience and sophistication of the client.[10]

19.11 So far as solicitors acting for mortgagees are concerned, the detailed standard form instructions produced by mortgagees will be relevant, and there may be little room for implying additional duties outside these specific requirements, particularly since most mortgagees are experienced and powerful institutions.[11] In *Mortgage Express v Bowerman*[12] it was held that a solicitor's primary duty to the mortgagee is to investigate and perfect title; beyond that, the solicitor is under a duty to pass on information which comes into his possession in the course of work done for the mortgagee or mortgagor. Bingham M.R. in that case suggested the test of "information which a reasonable solicitor would realise might have a material bearing on the valuation of the mortgagee's security or on some other ingredient of

---

[6] *Midland Bank Trust Co Ltd v Hett Stubbs & Kemp* [1979] Ch. 384, 402–403.

[7] *Matrix-Securities Ltd v Theodore Goddard* [1997] 147 N.L.J. 1847.

[8] *Matrix-Securities Ltd v Theodore Goddard* (above), applying *Davy-Chiesman v Davy-Chiesman* [1984] 1 All E.R. 321; and *Locke v Camberwell HA* [1991] 2 Med.L.R. 249. See also *Bond v Royal & Sun Alliance Insurance Plc* [2001] F.N.L.R. 30.

[9] *Credit Lyonnais SA v Russell Jones & Walker* [2003] 1 L.L.l.R. (PN) 7 (Laddie J.), approved in *Stone Heritage Developments Ltd v Davis Blank Furness* [2007] EWCA Civ 765, paras 34–36 (CA).

[9a] See *Cottingham v Attey Bower & Jones* [2000] P.N.L.R. 557 (Failure to pursue request for copy of Building Regulations approval).

[10] *Stone Heritage Developments Ltd v Davis Blank Furniss* [2007] EWCA Civ 765, paras 37 (CA).

[11] *National Home Loans Corp Plc v Giffen Couch & Archer* [1998] 1 W.L.R. 207; [1998] P.N.L.R. 111, CA. See further, para.19.85 below.

[12] [1996] 2 All E.R. 836.

the lending decision".[13] Quite clearly, information indicating potentially serious contamination could materially effect valuation and might, by virtue of the risks of lender liability, influence the decision whether to lend.

Local authority enquiries

Enquiry 3.12 of Part I of the standard form of Enquiries of Local **19.12** Authorities (form CON 29 (2002 Edition)) relates specifically to Pt IIA and whether the property has been entered on the contaminated land register required to be kept by local authorities pursuant to s.78R(1) of the Environmental Protection Act 1990, or whether a notice identifying the land as contaminated has been, or has been resolved to be, served. Care should, however, be exercised in analysing the local authority's response to this enquiry given the problems many local authorities have faced in finalising their contaminated land strategies, let alone in undertaking the required surveys to determine if land is contaminated for the purposes of the regime. Assuming the strategy is not available on the relevant local authority's website, then enquiries should be made of the appropriate officer in the Environmental Health Department to ascertain progress on this and any concerns that he may be aware of concerning potential contamination of the property. Contamination may still be in issue even if the provisions of Pt IIA are not triggered, yet few of the other enquiries in either Pt I or II of CON 29 are of great assistance in attempting to flush this out. Enquiry 1 deals with entries in the Register of planning applications and permissions, which may be of assistance in determining if remediation may have been undertaken as a consequence of compliance with the requirements of a planning condition in the course of implementation of the planning permission.[14] Enquiry 18, in the optional Pt II section of the form, asks for details of entries on the Register relating to hazardous substance consents maintained under s.28 of the Planning (Hazardous Substances) Act 1990: this will indicate whether land has been used for the bulk storage of certain specified quantities of a number of hazardous substances, though this will not help in relation to the normal incidental industrial storage of substances such as solvents or oil.

However, it is possible to raise supplementary questions of the authority **19.13** if it is thought appropriate to make enquiries not contained in the printed form: conventionally this is done by way of questions typed in duplicate on separate sheets and attached to form CON 29.[15] An authority is under no statutory obligation to answer such enquiries, whether on the standard form or otherwise, and given the potential liability involved for negligent answers many authorities may be reluctant to respond. However, so far as regards environmental information in its possession an authority may have no option but to respond in view of public rights of access to certain

[13] *Mortgage Express v Bowerman* has been followed in a number of cases including *Nationwide Building Society v Balmer Radmore* (1999) P.N.L.R. 606, Ch.D; and *Maes Finance Ltd and Mac No. 1 Ltd v Sharp and Partners* (1999) 69 Con. L.R. 46, QBD.
[14] See further Ch.16.
[15] Silverman and Hewitson, *Conveyancing Searches and Enquiries* (3rd edn, 2006) p.90.

information.[16] It may, in responding, attempt—subject to the provisions of the Unfair Contract Terms Act 1977—to exclude or limit its liability. The authority may be placed in a particularly difficult dilemma where the information in its possession is essentially of a speculative nature, for example where the authority is still in the course of investigating or inspecting a site, or is monitoring it, and is asked to disclose whether they are carrying out any such activities. A positive response may be extremely damaging to the owner, whereas failure to disclose the position may be seen as quite wrong from the point of view of the prospective purchaser: either way it is conceivable that litigation could arise. Despite the introduction of Pt IIA and the information gathering requirements that necessarily attach to local authorities as a consequence of this, providing an accurate picture of the position regarding a particular site may not be easy: the relevant information may be uncollated and may be spread between a number of departments of the authority. Some authorities may be understandably reluctant to disclose potentially damaging information.

19.14 Ultimately, the safest course for an authority is probably to follow as closely as possible the Environmental Information Regulations 2004,[17] to exercise restraint in disclosing information outside the ambit of the Regulations and extreme caution in cases where one of the exemptions to the Regulations may apply.

Enquiries of other bodies

19.15 In addition to searches and inspections of the various public registers, and enquiries of local authorities, it may be necessary to try and elicit information from other bodies, who may have knowledge of material facts in relation to contamination. These include:

(a) Natural England, Scottish Natural Heritage and the Countryside Council for Wales to establish whether there are any sites of special scientific interest in the vicinity which might be affected by contaminants migrating off-site;

(b) where the site is in proximity to a canal, British Waterways or other owner (e.g. the Manchester Ship Canal Company) to establish whether there have been any problems with contamination from the site;

(c) the Health and Safety Executive to establish whether they have been consulted or have exercised any of their statutory powers in relation to contamination;

(d) in certain areas, mining searches may be appropriate as a matter of good conveyancing practice: these include coal mining enquiries of the Coal Authority, tin and arsenic mining searches in Cornwall and South-West Devon, searches with the Mining Records

---

[16] See para.3.146ff.
[17] See para.3.146ff.

Office for abandoned mines, and limestone mining enquiries in areas of the West Midlands.[18] Such searches and enquiries are mainly for the purpose of detecting possible problems of land instability but it should be remembered that abandoned mines can also present serious problems of environmental contamination, either from polluted water or hazardous gases, and that it was not an uncommon practice in the past for old mineshafts to be filled with industrial waste;

(e) the Ministry of Defence in relation to former military land which may be contaminated with munitions or explosives;

(f) the Department of Environment, Food and Rural Affairs (and also local environmental health departments) as to the location of diseased animal carcasses;

(g) Network Rail in relation to operational or former railway land;

(h) the Environment Agency in relation to pollution of ground and surface water and the location of licensed sources of abstraction, amongst other matters; local environmental health departments for data on private wells.

19.16 Such enquiries may be made by way of letter, or by personal telephone enquiry. In practice, the helpfulness of organisations and individuals may vary widely; there may, however, in some cases be an obligation to disclose information in the case of a body with public responsibilities for the environment.[19] The purchaser's solicitors should in all cases bear in mind the possible sensitivity of such contact with regulatory or other interested parties so far as the seller is concerned.

Disclosure of information by the seller

19.17 The general principle is that a seller is under no obligation to the purchaser to disclose information as to the physical condition of the property, even in the case of defects which are not readily apparent, yet are known to the seller. It is for the purchaser, if he does not protect himself by an express warranty, to ". . . satisfy himself that the premises are fit for the purposes for which he wants to use them, whether that fitness depends on the state of their structure or the state of the law or any other relevant circumstances".[20] This general principle can be qualified in certain circumstances, and with the advent of Pt IIA and its "sold with information" exclusion test there are in event potential commercial advantages to disclosing information on site condition.

---

[18] Silverman and Hewitson, *Conveyancing Searches and Enquiries* (3rd edn, 2006) pp.287–289.

[19] The Coal Authority is under duties to facilitate the provision of information under the Coal Industry Act 1994.

[20] *Edler v Auerbach* [1950] 1 K.B. 359, 374; *Hill v Harris* [1965] 2 Q.B. 601. See also *Turner v Green* [1895] 2 Ch. 205; *Greenhalgh v Brindley* [1901] 2 Ch. 324.

Defective premises

19.18 The seller who is also the builder of a house may have liability at common law and under the Defective Premises Act 1972 in relation to some defects of a physical nature.[21]

Misleading statements

19.19 Whilst there may be no obligation to disclose a physical defect, failure to do so may make what is stated about the property false or misleading so as to constitute misrepresentation.[22] Such statements if made in the course of an estate agency business or property management business, can also constitute a criminal offence under the Property Misdescriptions Act 1991. The Act applies to statements about the fitness for purpose of the land itself and the historical use of the land.[23] The term "statement" is given a very wide meaning for the purpose of this legislation, including the spoken and written word and non-verbal means of communicating information, such as pictures. There is, however, a statutory defence that "all reasonable steps" and "all due diligence" were exercised to avoid committing the offence.

Concealment of defects

19.20 Deliberate concealment of a physical defect (for example, in one case[24] the covering up of dry rot) can be equated to fraudulent misrepresentation. This could apply for example, where a seller takes steps to conceal signs of contamination, such as covering up discoloured soil.

Negligent works by seller

19.21 A seller may potentially be under a duty of care to the purchaser in relation to defective improvements or other works carried out to the property.[25] Conceivably, this principle could apply where a seller carries out defective reclamation or remediation works which present a hazard to future occupiers or users of the property.

Misdescription

19.22 Where a misdescription of the property, though not fraudulent, is such that it affects the subject-matter of the contract so that the purchaser can reasonably be said to be not getting what he contracted for then the

---

[21] *Hancock v Brazier (Anerley) Ltd* [1966] 1 All E.R. 901. Under the Defective Premises Act, and the standard NHBC agreement, the question would probably be whether the house had not been built in a workmanlike manner and was not fit for human habitation: the wording is not entirely apt to cover problems with contaminated land. However, *Hancock v Brazier* was in fact a case involving the adverse effects of a chemical on the structural integrity of foundations. The position on common law applies equally to a council selling to a tenant under right to buy legislation: see *Blake v Barking and Dagenham LBC* [1997] 30 HLR 963, approved in *Payne v Barnes LBC* [1997] 30 HLR 295 (no duty when stating value of property; but see also para.19.22A below).

[22] *Nottinghamshire Patent Brick and Tile Co v Butler* (1886) 16 Q.B.D. 778 (statement that the seller is not aware of restrictive covenants was literally true, but misleading because no check had been made on the relevant documents).

[23] The Property Misdescription (Specified Matters) Order 1992 (SI 1992/2834) Sch. paras 8 and 13.

[24] *Gordon v Selico Ltd* [1986] 1 E.G.L.R. 71.

[25] *Hone v Benson* (1978) 248 E.G. 1013 (defective heating system).

contract may be avoided.[26] It is possible that a serious physical defect in the property could fall within this principle, as in one case where property described as "valuable prospective building element" and "suitable for development" was seriously affected by an underground culvert.[27] The potential application of such cases to soil contamination remains to be explored.

Right to buy sales

Where a council house is sold to a protected tenant under the "right to **19.22.1** buy" legislation in Pt V of the Housing Act 1985, by s.125(4A) the council must serve a notice which contains (inter alia) "a description of any structural defect known to the landlord affecting the dwelling house or the building in which it is situated or any other building over which the tenant will have rights under the conveyance". In *Rushton v Worcester CC*,[27a] it was held that where there is a breach of this requirement the remedy is for breach of statutory duty and not for misrepresentation. The statement of value was held to carry the implication that the council knows of no structural defect which would render the statement of value substantially inaccurate.[27b]

However, contamination will not necessarily, or even normally, be a "structural defect".

Notices and disputes

There is some authority to suggest that substantial undisclosed liabilities **19.23** arising from disputes with third parties or from the exercise of statutory powers may be matters affecting the title to property and hence give rise to the remedy of recission.[28]

Joint ventures and Non-disclosure

Where the transfer of title or the granting of other interests in land form **19.24** part of a wider commercial relationship such arrangements may constitute a partnership. Where this is the case, the presumed basis is one of mutual trust and confidence, giving rise to a requirement of good faith.[29] In cases falling short of a partnership, a joint venture may be seen to be fiduciary as to some or all of its aspects, such duties arising from the agreement between the parties. In *Noranda Australia Ltd v Lachlan Resources NL*[30] Bryson J. categorised this area as being ". . . the limit of the activities as to which

---

[26] *Flight v Booth* (1834) 1 Bing. N.C. 370.
[27] *Re Puckett and Smith's Contract* [1902] 2 Ch. 258.
[27a] [2201] EWCA Civ 367; [2002] HLR (CA).
[27b] ibid, para.50.
[28] *Re Englefield Holdings Ltd and Sinclair's Contract* [1962] 1 W.L.R. 1119 (certificate of disrepair); *Carlish v Salt* [1906] 1 Ch. 335 (party wall award); *Beyfus v Lodge* [1925] 1 Ch. 350 (tenants' notices requiring repairs); *Citytowns Ltd v Bohemian Properties Ltd* [1986] 2 E.G.L.R. 258 (local authority dangerous structure notice).
[29] *Floydd v Cheney* [1970] Ch. 602; and *Thompson (Trustee in Bankruptcy) v Heaton* [1974] 1 All E.R. 1239.
[30] [1988] 14 N.S.W.L.R. 1.

the parties have mutual trust and confidence in each other". It has also been held that fiduciary obligations may arise where a prospective joint venture or partnership is being negotiated, before its express definition by any formal agreement.[31]

19.25   It is possible therefore to envisage circumstances where failure to disclose land contamination, which could affect the viability of the proposed project, may constitute a breach of such fiduciary duties. However, the starting point is that keeping silent on a point which the other party may regard as important will not give rise to a cause of action, however morally questionable this may be, unless on the facts there has been a voluntary assumption of responsibility by the defendant and reliance by the claimant.[31a]

Pre-contract enquiries

19.26 As a result of the coming into force of Pt IIA, it is now usual for all published standard form preliminary enquiries to include a section dealing with environmental matters, including enquiries relating to possible contamination of the property. The enquiries tend to be broad brush in an attempt to elicit useful information and in some cases additional enquiries may need to be raised. The key questions which the purchaser should address are as follows, although more specific questions may be useful in relation to particular kinds of property, e.g. those subject to environmental permitting under the waste management or integrated pollution prevention and control regimes:

1.   Has the seller himself carried out any investigations as to potential contamination, or does the seller hold any such reports commissioned by a third party, or is he aware of the existence of such reports? If so, sight of such reports should be requested.

2.   Is the seller aware of any previous or current uses on the property which are such as to present a risk of contamination?

3.   Is the seller aware, either during his current ownership or during any previous ownership, of incidents such as leaks or spills on the site which may have led to soil contamination? This is not an enquiry necessarily to be confined to commercial or industrial property; it has been known for serious soil contamination to occur in the case of domestic properties from the storage of oil for domestic heating.

4.   Where the property is one on which potentially contaminative materials are or have been kept, have all proper precautions (so far as the seller is aware) been observed against soil contamination? This is an issue where to some extent the purchaser can rely upon his own observations when inspecting the site; such observa-

---

[31] *United Dominions Corp Ltd v Brian Proprietary Ltd* [1985] 157 C.L.R. 1.
[31a] See *Hamilton v Allied Domecq Plc* [2007] UKHL 33, considering *Banque Keyser Allmann SA v Skandia (UK) Insurance Co Ltd* [1989] 3 W.L.R. 25.

tions cannot, however, identify past defective storage practices which have subsequently been rectified.

5. In a similar vein, is the seller aware of the current or past presence of underground storage tanks or pipework under the property? This is again a matter which will not readily be ascertainable by physical inspection, but which may be within the seller's knowledge. A positive answer will merit further investigation.

6. Has any notice, claim or other communication been received from a public or regulatory authority, or any third party, concerning actual or possible contamination?

7. Is the seller aware of any other circumstances which would indicate the presence of potentially harmful materials within the property, or on adjacent or nearby land such as to present a threat to the property? The seller is of course likely to be wary of giving any meaningful answer to this question, but there may well be matters within the seller's knowledge (such as the presence of an old waste site near the property) which the purchaser might legitimately expect to be informed of.

Care should be taken in placing over-reliance on loosely-worded answers **19.27** to enquiries. Whilst the question asked (and the answers to other questions) can be used as an aid to interpreting the answers,[32] careful analysis may indicate that their scope is somewhat narrower than the purchaser might wish to suggest. In one case[33] answers given in relation to questions specifically on contamination and the disposal of effluent and waste were expressly warranted to be correct. It was held that none of the answers could be taken to be a warranty that the site (a former laboratory) was free from contamination, nor as a warranty that the laboratory or its drainage system had been decontaminated.

In relation to questions on possible contamination or contaminative uses, **19.28** the seller's solicitor should be wary of giving the response "Not so far as the seller is aware" or words to similar effect. It has been held that such a statement implies that the seller has taken reasonable steps to ascertain whether such matters as are referred to in the inquiry do in fact exist.[34] This is particularly the case where the seller is in a better position than the purchaser to ascertain the true facts.[35] This may represent a heavy onus on the seller to check for the existence of possible contamination.[36]

---

[32] *Foliejon Establishment v Gain S.A.* (Ch.D., July 7, 1993),unreported.

[33] *Foliejon Establishment v Gain S.A.* (Ch.D., July 7, 1993),unreported.

[34] *William Sindall Plc v Cambridgeshire CC*, [1994] 1 W.L.R. 1016; citing *Heywood v Mallalieu* [1883] 25 Ch.D. 357; and *Brown v Raphael* [1958] Ch. 636.

[35] *Smith v Land and House Property Corp Ltd* [1884] 28 Ch.D. 7 at 15.

[36] In the *Sindall* case the seller was held to have acted correctly by checking deeds and files, inspecting the property, and checking public records. *Sindall* was followed in *Clinicare Limited v Orchard Homes and Developments Ltd* [2004] EWHC 1694 (QB) where the defendant property owner was held to be liable to take reasonable steps to see whether dry rot existed where it had given a written indication during negotiations for a lease that it was unaware of the presence of dry rot. This was despite the fact that a subsequent verbal statement by it alluded to the historic existence of dry rot. This did not correct the implied representation that the owner had performed reasonable investigations.

Home Information Packs

19.29 In the context of residential conveyancing, under the Home Information Pack Regulations 2007,[37] the "search report" required to be provided by the seller[38] as part of a Home Information Pack (HIP) must contain the answers to specified enquiries, which include matters not entered on the appropriate local land charges register relating to the property transacted and also land adjacent to, or adjoining, that property. Those enquiries include whether any of the following "apply":

 (a) a "contaminated land notice" given under s.78B(3) of the Environmental Protection Act 1990;

 (b) a decision to make an entry, or an entry, on a register maintained under s.78R; or

 (c) consultation with the owner or occupier of the property conducted under s.78G(3) before service of a remediation notice.[39]

19.30 This information is similar, though not identical, to that indicated on the standard form Local Authority Enquiry 3.12 (discussed above). The Regulations do not require the provision of contaminated land or general environmental reports, though HIPs may include information as to actual or potential environmental hazards, including the risks of flooding or contamination from radon gas or any other substance.[40]

Standard contract provisions

19.31 The standard form contracts of sale all adopt, by and large, the philosophy of caveat emptor and are not helpful in providing the purchaser of contaminated land with any redress. In relation to the condition of the property, condition 3.2.1 of the Standard Conditions of Sale[41] provides that:

> "The buyer accepts the property in the physical state it is in at the date of the contract, unless the seller is building or converting it."

19.32 This provision should be read in conjunction with Standard Condition 3.2 which provides that the property is sold free from encumbrances other than those:

---

[37] The Home Information Pack (No. 2) Regulations 2007 (SI 2007/1667). The regulations have been introduced in phases, with the first of these applying to homes with four or more bedrooms from August 1, 2007.

[38] Home Information Pack (No. 2) Regulations 2007 reg.8(k).

[39] Home Information Pack (No. 2) Regulations 2007 Sch.7 Pt 2 para.17. The Regulations were made under Pt 5 of the Housing Act 2004, which in turn reflected the 1999 Report. *The Key to Easier Home Buying: Procedural Guidance on the HIP Regulations* is provided on the Department for Communities and Local Government website.

[40] SI 2007/1667 reg.9(m)(5).

[41] 4th edn, which now incorporate the National Conditions of Sale and the Law Society Conditions of Sale.

(a) specified in the contract;

(b) discoverable by inspection of the property;

(c) those the seller does not and could not reasonably know about;

(d) entries made in any public register before the date of the contract; and

(e) public requirements.

Contamination may involve a liability affecting the property, and hence **19.33** an encumbrance, though it may be a difficult question as to whether the seller ought reasonably to know about it or whether it would be discoverable on inspection on the property. Consequently, where contamination is, or may be, in issue, it will be necessary to tailor the property documentation to accord with the agreed position of the parties.

Warranties and indemnities

A purchaser may wish to seek comfort in relation to potential contamina- **19.34** tion by way of express warranties from the seller as to the condition of the property, absence of hazardous substances, compliance with environmental legislation, etc. Needless to say, the seller will usually resist giving such warranties: nonetheless there may be matters exclusively within the seller's knowledge and on which the purchaser is relying where it is, legitimate to expect a formal warranty. Warranties are in fact more commonly encountered as a component of corporate transactions and the relevant legal and drafting considerations are discussed below in that context.[42]

There may also be circumstances where it will be appropriate for the **19.35** parties to a property transfer to seek indemnities against actions, claims and costs arising from contamination on the property. In the absence of an indemnity, the loss will lie where it falls: the seller will retain any liability as the original cause of contamination, but the purchaser will assume ongoing liability as the occupier and owner of the property. The purchaser's argument will be that they should not be liable for conditions originating before completion and that they should be indemnified in respect of such liabilities. The seller, on the other hand, may argue that all liabilities in relation to the property should be assumed by the purchaser, whenever the condition giving rise to the liability originated, and may indeed seek an indemnity from the purchaser in respect of any liability that arises after completion. One effect of Pt IIA is that it is increasingly common for there to be liability transfer in some form from the seller to the buyer, particularly in the context of sales by institutions or funds.

There is no ready answer to this clash of views and, as always, the **19.36** ultimate result will be determined by commercial considerations. These include the commercial context of the transaction, the perceived risks

[42] See Ch.20.

presented by the property, the relationship of price to risk, and the extent, if any, by which the price is being discounted to reflect risk, the respective knowledge of the parties about site conditions, the proposed future use of the site and the general approach of the parties and their advisers. Where the site has been subject to a contamination survey, the discussion is likely to be more focused, since the results of the survey can be used as a baseline and it may be possible to confine the indemnity to specific substances or specific parts of the site which are perceived as presenting particular risks. Issues regarding the unwillingness of the indemnifying party to give unlimited indemnities and the possibility that it may not have the funds to satisfy the indemnity at some point in the future also come into play. The problems and detailed points which arise in the drafting of indemnities are discussed below.[43]

Construction of warranties

19.37 The construction of warranties relating to environmental matters in the context of the sale of land was considered in the case of *Foliejon Establishment v Gain S.A.*[44] The defendants Gain, a company incorporated in Switzerland, owned an estate including a substantial manor house bordering Windsor Great Park, the house being used in part as a residence and in part as offices. A stable block and outbuildings were used as laboratories by a company in the defendant's group, carrying on highly specialised research in the development of high purity metal alloys. Contracts were exchanged for the sale of the estate to Foliejon Establishment S.A., a company incorporated in Liechtenstein. The contract included what was described as "an unusual provision" introduced by the purchaser at the meeting for exchange of contracts, which read as follows:

"Contamination

(A) The Vendor hereby warrants that the replies attached hereto given by its solicitors to the Enquiries attached hereto are accurate as at the date hereof and hereby undertakes that nothing shall be done on the property between the date hereof and the date of actual completion which will render such replies materially inaccurate. The Purchaser shall have the right to enter the Property prior to the Completion Date with Specialist Contractors for the purpose of carrying out an environmental audit or inspection of the property and the Vendor will if requested by the Purchaser provide details of all chemicals and similar substances which to its knowledge have been used or stored in the laboratories on the Property."

19.38 Subsequently the purchaser instructed consulting engineers to carry out a survey of the property; their report indicated that part of the laboratories, the drainage system and surrounding land, and an adjacent stream

---

[43] See para.20.42ff. et seq.
[44] *Foliejon Establishment v Gain SA* (Ch.D., July 7, 1993, unreported).

running through the estate were seriously contaminated by radicals and a variety of heavy metals. It was alleged by the purchaser that the warranted replies to preliminary enquiries were not accurate. Following the break-down of negotiations as to a deduction from the purchase price, the seller's solicitors served notice to complete. The response of the purchaser's solicitors was to require a substantial retention fund, to be released against a certificate as to completion of remedial works. The purchasers then issued a writ claiming specific performance with an abatement in the price or in the alternative damages for breach of warranty; injunctive relief was also sought by way of a Mareva injunction restraining the sellers from remitting the whole of the proceeds of sale to Switzerland. Such an injunction was granted in October 1992, following which the sellers instructed their own expert and in July 1993 applied to discharge the injunction. It was clear, however, that there were serious deficiencies in the initial report produced by the purchaser's expert and that the problems of contamination were much less serious than was alleged by that initial report.

Several of the preliminary enquiries were directed to the state of the **19.39** property and potential contamination, but a number of these were either not answered or were answered in such terms as not to constitute warranties. However, one specific enquiry asked how trade effluent was disposed of from the property and the answer given was effectively that acid waste was neutralised and thereafter disposed of through the ordinary drainage system. It was suggested by counsel for the purchasers that this amounted to a warranty that nothing went down the drain except acid waste which was then neutralised. This interpretation was rejected, on the basis that it would lead to absurd results which could not have been intended: clearly some non-acid material would have been put down the drain. It was held that the correct interpretation of the warranty was that waste which could be safely discharged down the normal drainage system was so discharged, any acid content being neutralised. It was accepted that it could be implicit in such a warranty that the normal waste outlets were properly designed and were properly maintained.

Two further enquiries related to the disposal of industrial waste; it was **19.40** held that the answers to these effectively amounted to a warranty that non-trade effluent waste, whether solid or liquid, was disposed of outside the property while the laboratory was in use and that when the laboratory ceased to be used, any remaining waste was removed and disposed of outside the property. It was held on the facts that there was no breach of these warranties. In particular, selective sampling in the laboratory had detected small isolated beads of metal or chemical debris: it was argued for the purchasers that this indicated the laboratories had not been properly "decommissioned" and that the warranties had been broken: proper decommissioning, it was said, would involve steam cleaning, stripping out of potentially contaminated sheeting, partitions or wall coverings. In the court's view it was impossible to spell out of the warranties given any warranty that the laboratories had been decommissioned in this sense: at most, the warranty was to the effect that solid waste and toxic effluent not flushed down the drain were regularly and carefully removed. There was no clear evidence that such a warranty had been broken. Similarly, the finding of contamination in various parts of the drainage system did not constitute breach of any warranty, no warranty having been given that the drainage system had been decommissioned in the sense of being cleansed of every trace of chemicals, metals or solid deposits. At most, there was a warranty that during the operation of the laboratories there had been an adequate system of disposing of effluent and waste and that it was properly maintained.

19.41 Finally, it was alleged that there was serious contamination of a filter bed forming part of the draining system, together with the bed of a nearby stream. It was found that the levels of contamination identified would not present a realistic threat to human health or plant uptake; nor was there any evidence that the stream itself was contaminated to any significant extent by substances which could be identified as possibly emanating from the processes carried on in the laboratory. The risk to human health from contamination of the irrigation or filter bed was therefore held to be remote, and there was no evidence that any regulatory body would insist that any corrective action need be taken. In summary therefore, the claim that the sellers warranted that the laboratories and drainage system had been decommissioned—"that every particle of waste product had been removed and that every contaminated piece of absorbent material had been ripped out and taken away"—was misconceived.

19.42 A claim emerged at a late stage that there was a warranty that the system for removing waste was adequate if properly maintained to ensure that no contaminants entered the filter bed or the stream; this was held to be speculative on the basis of evidence adduced. Whilst it could not be said that it was so unarguable that it ought to be struck out, the damages recoverable if there was a breach of it were unquantified and, if quantified, were likely on the evidence to be comparatively small: the purchaser's expert had suggested that corrective action would involve the removal of a top layer of soil, but had not addressed the issue of whether much cheaper corrective action involving fixation of chemicals and covering would be sufficient. In those circumstances, the court held that the right course was to discharge the injunction.

Agreements as to liability

19.43 The parties may make an agreement as to who should be responsible. This solution suffers from the same potential problems as the equivalent method referred to below under the heading of "Seller considerations", namely that its statutory effect is limited to the Pt IIA regime and, in any event, the seller may cease to exist, (though in property transactions it is commonly the buyer who takes liability) or the enforcing authority may take the view that it should not give effect to the agreement.

Price adjustment

19.44 The price may be adjusted downwards to reflect the risk of future liability to the buyer. This is a different situation to where the payment is made to be used for remediation of land, and the buyer should ensure this is explicitly reflected in the agreement, to avoid any argument that the test of "payments made for remediation" should apply in the seller's favour should Pt IIA later be found to apply.

Clean up

The contamination may be cleaned up, thereby removing (hopefully) the **19.45** risk of future liability. Either the contamination may be cleaned up by the seller before completion, or alternatively the price may be reduced by a sum appropriate to allow the buyer to carry out clean-up. The question here is partly one of who bears the risk that the remediation proves ineffective. Under Pt IIA, if the remediation is to be carried out by the buyer, then potentially the test of "payments made for remediation" may be applied to impose the risk solely on the buyer, and thus exclude the seller from further liability. Where the remediation is carried out by the seller, he may well retain residual liability if remediation proves ineffective, but this will not necessarily release the buyer from also being liable. If Pt IIA does not apply, and the contamination is historic, i.e. pre-dates the seller, liability is likely to fall solely on the buyer assuming he is the current owner when the contamination manifests itself; if the contamination is caused by the seller then both he and the current owner may attract liability. In all cases, the risks to the buyer may be reduced by an indemnity given by the seller and/or by collateral warranties given by the engineers carrying out the remedial work.

Contamination surveys

If there is to be a contamination survey then the question will arise as to **19.46** which party should carry it out. The survey may be commissioned by the seller, perhaps preparatory to marketing the property; or the prospective purchaser may carry it out; or it may be commissioned jointly by both parties. Each of these possible sources has potential benefits and drawbacks. There may be advantages from a seller's point of view in taking the initiative, particularly if it is known that the site is likely to be sensitive in environmental terms: the work will be under the seller's control and time may be saved in marketing and achieving a sale. On the other hand, any purchaser will be unwise to rely on the survey without the benefit of a collateral warranty from the consultants, or the entering into of a reliance agreement, commonly provided in letter form. The mere reissue of the report addressed to the purchaser is not a satisfactory way of dealing with this issue from the purchaser's point of view, since no contractual agreement as to the level of care exercised by the consultant in carrying out the report or indemnity in favour of the purchaser where a want of care may have occurred is created. These issues will need to be discussed with the consultants at the time of their appointment.[45]

It is still more usual in practice for the purchaser to commission their **19.47** own survey, or for the purchaser's consultant to peer-review previous work, not least because this is now commonly a requirement of a funder if a loan

---

[45] See para.18.16.

to finance the purchase is required. This has the benefit of avoiding doubt as to whether the purchaser can rely on it, though there is the risk of wasted fees if the transaction does not proceed. The co-operation of the seller will be necessary and there may well be practical and operational constraints, for example as to the location of boreholes, as well as potential problems of confidentiality. Allowing access for such a survey will present the seller with risks. The seller may have to live with those risks as the price for the purchaser proceeding, but a written agreement may be used to minimise the risks as far as possible, covering the following matters:

1. prior approval by the seller of the consultant/contractor. Details to be provided of their third party liability insurance;

2. prior approval by the seller of the proposed scheme of investigation, including location of boreholes and (if permitted) trial pits;

3. an indemnity from the purchaser in respect of liability or damage arising from the investigation;

4. access by the seller to the results of the survey (which will be a vital negotiating tool) plus the ability to verify the results of any analysis;

5. a restriction on contact with regulatory authorities (and possibly others, such as employees) without the seller's prior consent; and

6. obligations as to confidentiality in respect of the results, with an obligation to deliver up all copies of the report to the seller forthwith in the event that the purchase does not proceed.[46]

19.48   A solution which may be well worth considering in some cases (though it remains rare in practice) is for an agreed consultant to be commissioned jointly by the parties to conduct the survey. This may avoid any feeling by one party of lack of objectivity where a consultant is retained by the other. Problems can of course arise if one or other party argues with the results of the joint report, and this eventuality should be addressed at the outset, either by agreeing that the report will be accepted as conclusive, or that either party will have the right to ask the consultant to reconsider certain points, or to obtain a "second opinion".

The use of conditional contracts

19.49 Where it is not possible, for whatever reason, to conduct a full contamination survey prior to exchange of contracts, the parties may consider entering into a conditional contract. Such a solution, whilst ostensibly attractive, should be treated with caution. The difficulty lies in drafting a

---

[46] This issue may take on an additional dimension once the Environmental Liability Directive is implemented in the UK. If post implementation, new (as opposed to historic) contamination is found to have occurred it may trigger a requirement to notify the relevant enforcement authority and the preventative and remediation requirements that apply pursuant to the regime. See further para.13.41.

condition which is sufficiently precise to be effective. Simply providing that the contract is "subject to a contamination survey" will almost certainly be too vague to constitute a valid condition.[47] The same may be the case if the condition refers to a survey "satisfactory to the purchaser".[48] Contamination surveys can take many forms and different methodologics will produce results of differing degrees of statistical confidence; it is common for a report to conclude by highlighting areas of uncertainty and recommending further monitoring activity. Even if the results are agreed, views can differ as to how those results should be interpreted and whether there is indeed any serious risk of liability. There may well be doubts as to whether a purchaser is acting reasonably in regarding results as unsatisfactory and, if there are unresolved questions, whether a purchaser is under an obligation to seek to clear them up by commissioning further (and possibly costly) work.[49] For these reasons, such conditional contracts are best avoided.[50]

Retentions

In some cases where land is sold on the basis that contamination may be **19.50** present, but time or circumstances (such as the seller's presence) do not admit of a full site investigation, it may be agreed that part of the purchase price will be retained on completion, that a survey will be undertaken within a given period, and that the contingency sum will be released if the survey is satisfactory. Obviously such arrangements may give rise to disputes if the sum is significant, and will need to be drafted carefully as to the conditions on which the retained sum is and is not to be released.[51] There is also the obvious difficulty of valuing a contingent liability.

Seller considerations

The seller is likely to be keen to ensure that any actual or contingent **19.51** liability is avoided and that he achieves a "clean exit" by passing any liability onto the purchaser. If, for example, liability under Pt IIA is subsequently triggered, if the seller himself caused the land to be contaminated or if prior to the sale he was aware of the presence of contamination, there is a risk he may remain liable following completion if the provisions of the Guidance relating to exclusion of Class A members are found not to apply. The possible ways of seeking to protect against such risk are as follows.

---

[47] *Marks v Board* (1930) 46 T.L.R. 424; *Astra Trust v Adams and Williams* [1969] 1 Lloyd's Rep. 81.

[48] See *Lee-Parker v Izzet (No. 2)* [1972] 1 W.L.R. 775; and cf. *Janmohamed v Hassam, The Times*, June 10, 1976.

[49] See *Re Longland's Farm, Alford v Superior Developments* [1968] 3 All E.R. 552; *Hargreaves Transport Ltd v Lynch* [1969] 1 W.L.R. 215; *Richard West and Partners (Inverness) v Dick* [1969] 2 Ch. 424; *Smallman v Smallman* [1972] Fam. 25.

[50] The case of *Foliejon Establishment v Gain S.A.* (see para.19.37) above provides a salutary warning of the difficulties which can flow from carrying out a contamination survey after a contract has been entered into.

[51] For a case considering such a provision, see *BBS Fashion Merchandising Ltd v Urban Regeneration Agency* [2006] EWHC 2754 (Ch).

Indemnities

19.52 For the converse of the reasons given above, the purchaser may well be unwilling to give the seller an indemnity, or may only be prepared to do so on limited terms; and in any event the value of such indemnity will depend upon the worth of the party giving it. At best, therefore, an indemnity should be seen as a method of reducing rather than removing risk.

Agreements as liabilities

19.53 The seller and the purchaser may agree that the buyer will be responsible for the cost of any future remediation. Assuming Pt IIA is triggered and (as, depending on the facts, arguably may become the case) that the buyer's state of knowledge and capacity to act will make it a "knowing permitter", then according to paras D.38 and D.39 of the Guidance the enforcing authority should make such determinations on exclusion and apportionment as are needed to give effect to any such agreement, and should not apply the remainder of the Guidance between the parties to the agreement.[52] However, where Pt IIA is not triggered there is no alternative statutory basis for recognising such an agreement by the relevant authority. Accordingly, the authority may be unwilling to give effect to the agreement, although if it is backed up by an indemnity this can assist in alleviating any liability that is determined to lie at the seller's door. In any event, such an agreement will only apply as between the seller and the buyer, and would not affect the position of any subsequent purchaser or, indeed, any other appropriate person who is not a party to the agreement. Another risk is that should the buyer cease to exist before any notice is served, then he would not be in the liability group at all, and accordingly the authority would not be able to give effect to the agreement.

19.54 The Guidance contains its own limitations as to the effect of such agreements. A copy of the agreement must be provided to the authority, and none of the parties must inform the authority that it challenges the application of the agreement. Secondly, the authority should disregard the agreement where the party whose share of costs would be increased under it would benefit from the "hardship" limitation on cost recovery. Accordingly, an adverse change in the financial circumstances of one party after the agreement may prejudice the other.

Payments to cover clean-up

19.55 If the extent of the contamination is known, and a clean-up method can be agreed and costed, then the seller may make a payment to the buyer to cover that remediation, either by way of a direct payment or by an express deduction from the purchase price. Where Pt IIA applies, provided that the payment is adequate, then in the event that the remediation is not carried out, or is not carried out effectively, the seller should be excluded by Test 2 at paras D.51—D.56 from future liability under the Pt IA regime (although not necessarily under the other statutory sources of liability). In order to

---

[52] See further para.5.179.

ensure the seller's protection, the position should be stated explicitly in the contracts.

To satisfy this test, the seller must not retain any further control over **19.56** the condition of the land in question. The seller can, however, safely retain contractual rights to ensure that the work is carried out properly. This route will not be suitable for all circumstances, and is best suited to cases where land is sold either for development or with a clear idea as to the remedial measures required, or where there is a specific and clearly identified contamination problem which is capable of being addressed by specific measures.

"Sold with information"

The seller may seek to apply the "sold with information" test (Test 3, set **19.57** out at paras D.57—D.61 of the Guidance) in relation to liability under Pt IIA. This can be triggered either by the seller acquiring information as to the presence of contamination itself, and providing that information to the buyer, or alternatively by the seller allowing the buyer to carry out its own investigation, so that the buyer thereby generates the information. The information must be sufficient to allow the buyer to be aware of the relevant pollutant and the "broad measure of its presence". The information must be available before the sale becomes binding, and therefore either the investigation must be carried out before exchange of contracts, or exchange must be on a conditional basis to allow subsequent investigations to take place. The problem with the conditional contract approach is the difficulty of framing the conditions so as to achieve sufficient certainty as to the circumstances in which the contract does become binding. Also, the price may need to be left flexible (or some mechanism agreed for adjusting the price) following the completion of the investigations. Clearly, the preferable course would be to obtain the information prior to exchange.

Knowledge of contamination may be deemed to exist where the buyer is **19.58** a "large commercial organisation" or a public body, and permission has been given to the buyer to carry out its own investigations. The Guidance, however, only suggests that this should "normally be taken as sufficient indication" that the purchaser had the necessary information. Obviously, it would be as well to make it clear in writing that the opportunity had been given (and the scope of that opportunity), either in correspondence or in the contract itself.

Restriction of future uses

The seller may seek to restrict the future uses or development of the land **19.59** so as to minimise the risk that the contamination will migrate or otherwise be exacerbated, thereby triggering enforcement action. Buyers can in many cases, however, be expected to resist attempts to encroach in this way upon their autonomous use of the land.

Future access by the seller

Where there is a possibility (for example, under the contaminated land or **19.60** works notice provisions) that the seller may require access to the land following the sale, in order to comply with statutory clean-up requirements, the seller could seek to secure the necessary rights of access in the sale contract. This would in particular prevent the buyer from claiming statutory compensation for the disturbance and other costs associated with compliance, pursuant to s.78G of the Environmental Protection Act 1990, s.161B of the Water Resources Act 1991 or (in Scotland) s.46B of the Control of Pollution Act 1974. The seller who will be seeking to rely on Test 2 or 3 (payments for remediation or sale with information) should be aware that the retention of such rights may prejudice his ability to rely on those tests, as constituting retention of control under Test 2 or retention of rights to use and occupy under Test 3.

19.61 In the light of this risk, rather than reserving rights of access, it may be preferable simply for the seller to seek the inclusion of an acknowledgement from the buyer that it will not apply for statutory compensation in relation to access by the seller (if necessary) to carry out such works.

Leases

19.62 The grant of a lease raises rather different considerations from a sale of the freehold. Whereas on a sale the risk essentially lies with the purchaser in the absence of contractual stipulations to the contrary, in the case of a lease there are risks on both sides. The tenant will be at risk of liability as occupier in relation to pre-existing contamination[53]: the landlord may well have concurrent liability as owner or under Pt IIA as a causer[54] or knowing permitter[55] and could be prejudicially affected either during the lease or after it expires by contamination caused by the tenant.[56]

19.63 The approach taken to these risks may well depend on how the contamination was caused. A well advised tenant would be unlikely to accept liability for contamination which the landlord had caused, or of which the landlord was aware prior to the grant of the lease but had failed to draw to the attention of the tenant. Equally a well-advised landlord is unlikely to accept liability for contamination which the tenant itself causes during the term of the lease. With regard to unknown contamination which has been caused by a third party, this essentially comes down to an issue of allocation of risk between landlord and tenant, and in some respects is akin to the risk of inherent defects in buildings. The distinction may be drawn between long leases (more than 21 years) where the situation can be

---

[53] If Pt IIA applies then where pre-existing contamination was caused by some third party who has ceased to exist, both the landlord and tenant may potentially attract Class B liability in their capacity as owner and occupier. In cases where the tenant is paying a rack rent, the exclusion test under the Guidance at para.D.89 will result in the tenant being excluded from liability, leaving the landlord solely responsible.

[54] If the landlord himself caused the contamination he may attract Class A liability as a result.

[55] If the landlord was aware of the contamination prior to the grant of the lease he may have responsibility for having knowingly permitted its continued presence.

[56] This may arise, for example, where the landlord is deemed to have sufficient knowledge of and control over the tenant's activities or where the lease comes to an end and the landlord, having regained possession and having become aware of contamination, knowingly permits its continued presence. However, it is clear from the first exclusion test that simply creating a tenancy would not of itself constitute such a level of control: see further para.5.189ff.

regarded as akin to that of seller and buyer of land, as outlined above. With regard to shorter leases, the landlord should work on the assumption that it will retain responsibility (and indeed may be solely responsible) for pre-existing contamination unless the lease expressly provides otherwise.[57] The issue therefore comes down ultimately to the drafting of the leasehold covenants.

Selection of tenant

Some types of tenant may present a greater risk than others in terms of **19.64** contamination: the landlord would be well-advised to obtain information prior to the grant of the lease in order to be able to assess that risk.

Drafting and construing leases

Even the lengthiest and most comprehensive of leases granted before the **19.65** 1990s is unlikely to contain any provisions drafted with contamination specifically in mind. Various covenants and other provisions may, however, have a bearing on the issue.

Repairing covenants

Whether a repairing covenant can impose an obligation to rectify a **19.66** problem caused by contamination will, fundamentally, depend on the nature of the problem and the wording of the covenant. The general view is that a repairing covenant is unlikely to be held to apply to remediation of contamination of a property on the basis that decided cases as to the meaning of such covenants always involve a consideration of the actual buildings or other structures on the premises demised, rather than the ground beneath them. There can be no liability under a covenant to repair unless the property is in disrepair[58]; unless, that is, the covenant has been extended to cover all defects whether or not manifesting themselves in physical damage. Thus contamination may have serious effects—for example, gas generation—but not yet have had any adverse impact on the structure of the property. Conversely, contamination may result in disrepair of the demised building itself, for example by attacking services or foundations. The fact that the contamination was pre-existing, or indeed that the services or foundations were already affected prior to the grant of the lease, will not of itself provide an excuse from the obligation to repair.[59]

---

[57] Note that under Pt IIA, the tenant may attract potential liabilities for pre-existing contamination of which he becomes aware and which he may be said to have knowingly permitted to remain present or alternatively for pre-existing contamination where no Class A causer or knowing permitter can be found, and where the tenant may be responsible in his capacity as occupier (although the effect of the Class B exclusion test is to exclude tenants liable to pay a rack rent).

[58] *Post Office v Aquarius Properties Ltd* [1987] 1 All E.R. 1055; *Quick v Taff Ely BC* [1986] Q.B. 809, although also see *London and North East Railway Company v Berryman* [1946] A.C. 278 where the court held that a covenant to repair includes the taking of preventative measures to avoid damage occurring.

[59] *Lurcott v Wakely and Wheeler* [1911] 1 K.B. 905; *Proudfoot v Hart* (1890) 25 Q.B.D. 42; *Brew Bros Ltd v Snax (Ross) Ltd* [1970] 1 Q.B. 612.

Moreover, it is arguable that work may be required going beyond simply the immediate works necessary to bring the structure into repair—for example the removal of contaminated soil or the insertion of impervious membranes—if the immediate works of repair would otherwise be rendered abortive.[60] However, where the works required are extensive and would render the premises a different thing from that demised, counter-arguments are possible.[61] It is possible for a covenant to be drafted so as to require the doing of works that go beyond repair but even so, such obligations will generally presuppose some physical damage or deterioration such that work is necessary having regard to what would be reasonably acceptable to a reasonable-minded tenant likely to take a lease of the premises.[61a] Where the repairing covenant relates to the "structure" of the building this may well cover contamination beneath the structure or outside the footprint of the building.[61b]

Service charges

19.67 Whether work required to rectify problems caused by contamination can be recovered under a service charge will be a question of construction, akin to that referred to above in relation to repairing obligations.[62] It is not inconceivable that problems of this type will arise in future, as many developments of contaminated sites for commercial purposes have been carried out on a "footprint specific" basis, with areas where contamination is worst or where contaminants are left in situ being designated as common areas such as access roads and car parks.

Tenant-like use

19.68 All tenants have an implied obligation to use the premises in a tenant-like manner, including abstention from acts of wilful or negligent damage.[63] Egregious acts of contamination could well constitute a breach of this obligation: so also might failure to take obvious precautionary measures such as draining disused underground tanks.

Waste

19.69 Intentional or careless acts by the tenant which result in the property becoming contaminated might well fall within the tort of waste.[64]

---

[60] *Smedley v Chumley & Hawke Ltd* (1981) 44 P. & C.R. 50; See also *Gibson Investment Ltd v Chesterton* [2002] EWHC 19 (Ch).

[61] *Ravenseft Properties Ltd v Davstone Holdings Ltd* [1980] Q.B. 12; *Wates v Rowland* [1952] 2 Q.B. 12.

[61a] *Fluor Daniel Properties Ltd v Shortlands Investments Ltd* (Ch D, January 12, 2001) [2001] EGCS 8.

[61b] For a case on "structure", see *Fincar SRL v Mount Street Management Co Ltd* [1998] EGCS 173 (CA).

[62] *Rapid Results College Ltd v Angell* [1986] 1 E.G.L.R. 53; *Mullaney v Maybourne Grange (Croydon) Management Co Ltd* [1986] 1 E.G.L.R. 70.

[63] *Warren v Keen* [1954] 1 Q.B. 15.

[64] *Mancetter Developments Ltd v Garmanston Ltd* [1986] 2 W.L.R. 871 (a case where directors of the tenant company were also personally liable); *West Ham Central Charity Board v East London Waterworks Co* [1900] 1 Ch. 624 (raising height of marsh land by 10 feet by dumping demolition and household rubbish on it held to be waste by changing nature of property, regardless of whether or not the material was offensive).

Keep premises clean and tidy

It is common for leases to contain a provision requiring the tenant to keep **19.70** and yield up the premises "in a clean and tidy condition" (or words to that effect). Whilst on general principles the extent of the demise may include the sub-surface[65] it would appear extremely unlikely that such a covenant could be used to compel the tenant to clean up contaminated soil. The purpose behind such provisions is to ensure that surface buildings and structures are properly maintained.

Compliance with statutory requirements

Modern leases will contain a covenant by the tenant to comply with all **19.71** statutes, regulations and notices affecting the property, sometimes even where the notice is served on the landlord. Such a covenant may well oblige the tenant to comply with a notice served as a result of contamination: for example, a statutory nuisance abatement notice or a remediation notice under Pt IIA. It may also require the tenant to take steps to avoid contravening statutory obligations; for example, to prevent unconsented polluting matter entering controlled waters. The potential breadth of such obligations may well widen as the Environmental Liability Directive, and possibly the requirements of any future Soil Protection Directive, are implemented.[66] However, in some cases there may be no specific obligation imposed by law on the tenant: rather the statutory authorities will themselves take steps to clean-up and then seek to recover their costs. It is far less clear that the covenant relating to statutory requirements would apply in these circumstances, and instead the landlord may seek to rely on the other usual covenants as to payment of rates and other impositions and outgoings. There is a large and confusing body of case law on such covenants and the tenant may contend with some force that capital expenditure to remedy contamination conditions is not covered.[67] Where works are required under a notice by a statutory authority, there may be express power for the court to apportion those costs between the owner and occupier. For example, the Statutory Nuisance (Appeals) Regulations 1995[68] give such a power and require the court in exercising that power to have regard to the terms and conditions of any tenancy and the nature of works required.[69] Apart from such express guidance, there is mixed authority as to whether the court has power to overthrow the terms of the bargain embodied in the lease.[70]

---

[65] *Grigsby v Melville* [1974] 1 W.L.R. 80.

[66] See para.Ch.13.

[67] *Wilkinson v Collyer* (1884) 13 Q.B.D. 1; *Farlow v Stevenson* [1900] 1 Ch. 128; *Villenex Co Ltd v Courtney Hotel Ltd* (1969) 20 P. & C.R. 575.

[68] SI 1995/2644.

[69] SI 1995/2644 reg.2(7)(a).

[70] *Monk v Arnold* [1902] 1 K.B. 761; *Munro v Lord Burghclere* [1918] 1 K.B. 291; *Horner v Franklin* [1905] 1 K.B. 479.

Nuisance

19.72 There may be a covenant not to do anything on the demised premises so as to constitute a nuisance: this could be relevant in some cases. Acts by the landlord or tenant which constitute a common law nuisance as against the other will be actionable in any event irrespective of the lease.[71]

Protecting the landlord

19.73 The landlord's position can to some extent be protected by careful drafting, but equally important will be the exercise of vigilance during and at the expiry of the lease. A number of provisions, specifically angled towards the problems of contamination, could be inserted in the lease, particularly if the tenant's intended use presents risks:

1. A covenant as to compliance with statutory requirements as to the storage, keeping use and disposal of contaminative substances: including the obtaining, renewal and maintenance in force of all necessary licenses required under environmental law.[72] This might be extended to require compliance with good industrial practice.

2. A covenant not to dispose of waste substances within the demised premises.

3. A covenant to inform the landlord immediately of any spills or other potentially contaminative incidents on the property, to remedy the results of such incidents to the landlord's satisfaction and to indemnify the landlord against losses, costs, claims or demands resulting from any such incident.

4. A covenant to leave the demised premises, including the sub-surface, not contaminated to any greater extent than was the case at the commencement of the term.

5. Rights of entry and inspection, including soil sampling and analysis, during the lease to determine the tenant's compliance with the covenants, and at the expiry or sooner determination of the term to determine compliance with the covenant suggested at point 4 above.

6. Provisions ensuring that the liability of the tenant for contamination of the property will not cease on termination of the lease;

7. A covenant to notify the landlord of any proceedings brought against the tenant relating to environmental matters.

19.74 The covenants should be subject in the normal way to a proviso as to re-entry. In the light of the powers of courts to apportion certain clean-up liabilities as between landlord and tenant, referred to above,[73] it would also

---

[71] *Manatia v National Provincial Bank* [1936] 2 All E.R. 633; *Meadows and Morley v Homor Properties Ltd* (QBD, February 25, 1993, unreported).

[72] This should include an obligation to renew the licence where necessary, as failure to do so may have serious consequences for the value of the property: see *Davy Ltd v Guy Salmon (Service) Ltd*, June 9, 1993, reported *Chartered Surveyor Weekly*, July 23, 1992; a case involving a petroleum spirit licence.

[73] See para.19.71.

be sensible to insert a proviso to make it absolutely clear that the tenant is to bear the entire cost of remedying contamination caused by the tenant. It is possible that the type of covenants referred to above, whilst they may involve physical remedial works, will not be subject to the requirements of the Leasehold Property (Repairs) Act 1938 in relation to enforcement by the landlord or to the restriction on damages under s.18 of the Landlord and Tenant Act 1927. In *Starrokate Ltd v Burry*[74] it was held that the 1938 Act did not apply to a covenant to cleanse the demised premises. The landlord may also wish to exercise control over disposition by assignment or underletting from the point of view of the contamination potential of the assignee or underlessee.

Fitness for purpose

From the tenant's point of view, pre-existing contamination may render **19.75** the premises unsuitable for the purpose for which they were demised. In the case of leases there is no implied term as to fitness or suitability for purpose, though the position may be different in the case of a licence.[75] In *Sutton v Temple*[76] a lease of pasture was granted; unfortunately the land was contaminated by poisonous flakes of paint which had been mixed into a manure heap. A number of cattle died and the tenant refused to pay a second instalment of rent which was due. It was held that the agreement was for the letting of a specified area and that nothing was agreed as to its fitness for a particular purpose: the tenant was obliged to pay the rent "whether the land answer the purpose for which he took it or not."

The prospective tenant, particularly in the case of a long-term lease, **19.76** would therefore be well advised to investigate whether the premises are subject to such contamination as might affect their use; or indeed, as might give rise to potential liability. In some circumstances it might be appropriate to ask the landlord for an express warranty to that effect, for example where the landlord has constructed the premises; though most landlords are unlikely to accede to such requests without considerable argument. In an extreme case, for example failure of gas control systems, the tenant may wish to have an option to terminate the lease.[77]

The possibility or reality of contamination may have an effect on rent **19.77** review valuations, though no cases appear to have been reported on the issue. The tenant should be particularly wary of the usual clause requiring the exclusion from the normal disregard of improvements, those carried out by the tenant pursuant to an obligation to the landlord[78]: this could potentially have the effect of the rent being increased where works required by statutory notice have been carried out at the tenant's cost.[79]

---

[74] (1983) 265 E.G. 871.
[75] *Wettern Electric Ltd v Welsh Development Agency* [1983] 1 Q.B. 796; *cf. Morris-Thomas v Petticoat Lane Rentals Ltd, The Times,* June 17, 1986.
[76] (1843) 12 M. & W. 52; [1986] Conv. 70.
[77] A precedent for such a clause is given in the Precedent section.
[78] See, e.g. s.34 of the Landlord and Tenant Act 1954, often incorporated by reference.
[79] *Forte & Co Ltd v General Accident Life Assurance Ltd* [1986] 2 E.G.L.R. 115.

Safeguarding the tenant

19.78 Whilst as a matter of principle it may be difficult for the tenant to argue against having to shoulder responsibility for contamination caused during the term, it is less obvious that the tenant should assume liability for pre-existing contamination, particularly where the lease term is for less than 21 years. On the general principle of caveat lessee, the tenant will be deemed to take the property in its actual condition, defects and all. This seems likely to include pre-existing contamination and the main risk of liability lies for contamination which the lease provides is the tenant's liability to rectify, or pay for the cost of rectifying, as a result of inadvertently wide drafting of the "normal" leasehold covenants, for example those requiring compliance by the tenant with statutory requirements. Furthermore, where Pt IIA applies, the covenants contained in the lease may be regarded as an agreement between the parties as to which of them shall be responsible, in which case the enforcing authority would be required under the Guidance to seek to give effect to that agreement in applying the exclusion and apportionment tests. The tenant's advisers should therefore ensure, so far as possible, that the covenants in the lease impose liability for pre-existing contamination on the landlord rather than the tenant and in doing so need to be particularly alive to the risk that if a Class A liability as a causer or knowing permitter for the purposes of Pt IIA is triggered (potentially a real risk if the tenant is or becomes aware of the existence of contamination) then the only way in which the tenant can completely guard against liability to remediate is by providing expressly in the lease that the landlord is responsible for pre-existing contamination, a position which may or may not be acceptable to the landlord.

19.79 One way of ensuring that the tenant is not fixed with responsibility for contamination pre-dating the lease is for a survey to be undertaken initially, and for the contaminative equivalent of a schedule of dilapidations to be prepared; this may then be compared with the results of any investigation carried out by the landlord during the lease or upon its termination. Obviously, whether the cost of the exercise can be justified within the commercial context is another matter. The tenant should also be wary of the possibility of being held liable for contamination found on the demised premises during or at the end of the lease which has migrated there from other premises; any drafting should at least retain the ability for the tenant to demonstrate that the pollution arose from external sources outside the tenant's control, and thereby avoid liability.

19.80 Where it is known that the demised premises have been constructed on or near problematic land, it will be prudent from the tenant's point of view to make provision for the eventuality that the remedial or precautionary measures taken in developing the site may prove to have been inadequate. The tenant may wish, for example, to reserve a break clause in the event that the premises become incapable of beneficial use or occupation. Such a provision may also deal with suspension of rent in that event and make it clear that the tenant is under no obligation to rectify, or contribute to the cost of rectifying, such defects. The terms may be extended, as appropriate, beyond contaminative effects to problems of ground conditions generally, such as slip, subsidence or heave.

Mortgages and financing

The concerns of a secured lender in a sense combine those of the purchaser **19.81** with those of the landlord: the lender's position may be prejudiced by the state of the property at the time the mortgage is granted but, equally, it may be worsened by the use or abuse of the property by the borrower. Essentially the concerns are threefold[80]:

1. the effect of liability for contamination and its consequences on the ability of the borrower to service the loan;

2. the effect of contamination on the value of security; and

3. the possibility of primary liability on the part of the lender.

The first two problems speak for themselves; the third requires some **19.82** further explanation. So long as the lender takes no steps to enforce the security, the risks are relatively slight.[81] However, once the mortgagee seeks to exercise its security, whether by foreclosure, or possession,[82] or by exerting influence over the actions of borrower, the risks inevitably increase. In particular, there is the risk that a lender could be liable by virtue of the degree of control which it exerts, or by being regarded as "owner". Even in the absence of occupation or control, it is arguable that receipt of rent, or the right to receive rent, may give rise to liability as owner.[83] For this reason, taking an assignment of rents, or reserving the right to do so, may be prejudicial. Being a "mere conduit" for the transmission of rental income is not, however, of itself enough.[84]

The provisions of Pt IIA also reflect the general position; the definition **19.83** of "owner" provided by s.78A of the Environmental Protection Act makes it clear that liability does not extend to a mortgagee who is not in possession of the land. The mortgagee who wishes to enforce his security can therefore take an informed decision as to potential risks of liability under Pt IIA before doing so. The position may be different if "involuntary possession" occurs, where for example the borrower simply returns the keys of the property to the lender. The Guidance also makes clear that even if the mortgagee is deemed to fall within the Class A liability group as a result of enforcing its security, the act of providing a loan or other form of credit should not of itself result in liability. A more direct form of

---

[80] See generally, S. Tromans, "The Relevance of Environmental Law for Banks" [1990] 11 J.T.B.L. 433; Jarvis and Fordham, *Lender Liability: Environmental Risk and Debt* (Cameron May, London, 1993).

[81] See para.5.189ff on the exclusion test for providers of finance.

[82] For example, the International Banking and Financial Law [1995] Vol.14, No.1 reported that Midland Bank were involved in clean-up liabilities for a residential site in Dartmoor, where some 13,000 used tyres, many contaminated by oil, were deposited in an old mill leat. The problem became apparent after the bank went into possession and action requiring removal of the tyres was taken by Devon CC as waste regulation authority under s.59 of the Environmental Protection Act 1990.

[83] *Maguire v Leigh-on-Sea Urban DC* (1906) 95 L.T. 319; *Solomons v Gerzenstein* [1954] 2 Q.B. 243; *Midland Bank Ltd v Conway Corp* [1965] 1 W.L.R. 1165.

[84] *Midland Bank Ltd v Conway Corp* [1965] 1 W.L.R. 1165.

control is necessary. The dilemma here for mortgagees perhaps lies mainly in the wish to take steps to protect the value of their security, without going so far as to exercise control over contamination prevention or remediation measures. This is the balance which needs to be struck in drafting the contractual arrangements, and in the practical measures put in place to ensure compliance. The documentation could, for example, make it clear that whilst the borrower must report to the lender any matters which may affect the value of the property, and must take steps to address those matters, the responsibility for the nature of the steps to be taken and their adequacy, rest with the borrower.

19.84 It is obviously helpful that, where a receiver is appointed under the Law of Property Act 1925, the receiver will be regarded as the agent of the mortgagor rather than the mortgagee. However, excessive practical control by the mortgagee over the actions of the receiver may result in the loss of this protection.[85] Moreover, in most cases the mortgagee will have given an indemnity to the receiver; this, combined with the receiver's personal exposure, presents real risks for the mortgagee.[86]

Lending policy

19.85 It is now commonplace for lenders to require investigation of contamination issue as part of the due diligence procedure to be conducted by the purchaser or lessee as a pre-condition of leading on the property. Despite this, enormous variations of awareness and sophistication as between financial institution as to environmental risk remain. The Council of Mortgage Lenders requires solicitors to advise the lender of any contaminated land entries revealed in the local authority search, with individual lenders specifying if they want to receive environmental or contaminated land reports.[87] The Law Society's Green Card[88] also suggests that solicitors should advise lenders if enquiries reveal potential for, or existence of, contamination, and seek instructions.

19.86 Any checklist for a lender is likely to combine the investigations of the site and its history appropriate to a purchaser with the scrutiny of a landlord as to the likely and ongoing activities of the borrower. Reference should therefore be made to the preceding sections. Vigilance is required not only before granting the loan but also during the period of the loan and, critically, before taking steps to exercise security: at which point it may be sensible to require the completion of a further checklist or questionnaire.

---

[85] See *Standard Chartered Bank v Walker* [1982] 1 W.L.R. 1411.

[86] See para.20.78ff on receivers.

[87] *The CML Lenders' Handbook for England and Wales* (June 1, 2007) para.5.2.4. The instructions of individual lenders can be found on the CML website (*http://www.cml.org.uk/handbook*) and in fact vary widely. Some (such as C&G) say they never want to receive reports; others (such as Couts & Co) say they always do; others (such as HSBC) ask to be consulted; others (such as Bradford & Bingley) ask the solicitor to send a copy of the report if the solicitor believes it may affect the security.

[88] See para.19.08.

Mortgage documentation

As with standard leases, traditional mortgage documents make little **19.87** specific provision as to contamination problems, though general provisions on repair, inspection, and care of the property may well be relevant. It is suggested that the following types of provision could be of benefit to a lender:

1. an obligation on the borrower to disclose the existence of contamination, however arising, affecting the property;

2. reservation of the right to inspect and monitor the site during the term of the mortgage, including the right to production of relevant authorisations, licences, notices, etc.;

3. reservation of the right to limit uses, types of equipment and substances on the property, particularly in relation to sites with very sensitive neighbouring uses and potential pathways of pollution;

4. a general covenant not to use the site so as to contaminate it or to give rise to liability arising from the condition of the property, including the sub-surface;

5. a requirement of notification in the event of any spills or other incidents which might give rise to contamination, changes in operations such as to increase the risk of contamination, complaints, claims, investigations and prosecutions;

6. an obligation on the mortgagor to supply such information, or to carry out such monitoring, as the mortgagee may require—including an obligation to complete regular questionnaires on request;

7. an obligation to remedy, to the lender's satisfaction, contamination conditions affecting the property, however arising;

8. an indemnity against any liability, costs, claims or demands affecting the lender, preferably supported by directors' or parent company guarantees;

9. a requirement to maintain insurance in respect of own-site clean-up and contamination-related liabilities, to the extent such cover is available from time to time on the market; and

10. provisions giving adequate flexibility in the appointment of receivers; for example allowing certain property to be excluded if the mortgagee so wishes.

At the more general level, rates of interest may be set so as to reflect the **19.88** lender's perception of environmental risk; the training of credit officers should also be considered, so that they are alert to identify and respond to environmental warning signs, both at the time of the credit application and subsequently during the term of the loan.

Chapter 20

CORPORATE TRANSACTIONS AND INSOLVENCY

Corporate transactions: general issues

20.01 The issue of contaminated land poses challenges in the context of corporate transactions. This is due to a variety of factors, including the inherent uncertainties which are often involved in determining whether land is contaminated (for example, where no or insufficient intrusive investigations have been carried out prior to the transaction), assessing the likelihood or extent of remedial requirements that may arise in future and quantifying the amount of remediation costs that may need to be incurred to address the contamination. Contamination can potentially have a serious impact on the value of the real estate assets of a business that is being sold as a going concern (or a company whose shares are being sold), for example by limiting the ability of a purchaser to make optimum use of the assets acquired. There may also be actual or contingent liabilities associated with land contaminated by past activities of a company whose shares are being sold, including liabilities arising under agreements relating to the previous acquisition or disposal of such land.

20.02 Contaminated land is but one of a number of environment-related compliance and other issues which should be investigated in the context of a corporate transaction. Its importance relative to other potential environmental problems will depend upon the nature of the target company or assets, but in many cases it is likely to be amongst the most significant and problematical issues.

20.03 Consideration needs to be given from the outset as to the nature of the transaction that is being proposed, in particular whether it involves a merger or acquisition transaction (involving the sale of shares or assets), an initial public offering (IPO) of shares or some other type of financing transaction. The distinction between sales of shares and asset sales in the context of merger and acquisition transactions deserves particular attention because of the significant scope for actual and potential liabilities associated with contaminated land to be effectively transferred to the purchaser in such transactions.

20.04 Environmental liabilities associated with contaminated land can be broadly categorised into three types:

Liability as the original polluter

20.05 Where shares in a company are being sold, the company will remain liable as the person who caused or knowingly permitted the presence of the substances by reason of which the land is contaminated. Such liability may relate not only to currently operational sites and assets of the company, but also to property no longer owned or occupied by the company. In the case of a sale of assets such liabilities will not automatically pass, though effectively the purchaser may be at risk where that liability results from the condition of the assets being transferred and that condition is of an ongoing nature: in such circumstances the purchaser may very soon themselves become liable for continuing the pollution. With reference to the Pt IIA regime, so far as a seller of land is concerned, the basic position is that if the seller himself caused the land to be contaminated, he will remain potentially liable as a Class A "causer" following completion. If prior to the sale, the seller was aware of the presence of contamination, there is also a risk that the seller may remain liable following completion on the basis that he had knowingly permitted the contamination to remain present during his period of ownership. This point is open to argument but there must at least be a risk of such responsibility. The key commercial question for the seller is whether he wishes to avoid retaining such risks following completion. The possible ways of seeking to achieve this are discussed later in this Chapter.

Liability as occupier

This category of liability (or contingent liability) will pass in relation to the **20.06** assets being transferred, whether in relation to asset sales or the assets belonging to the company whose shares are acquired. The additional consideration where the shares in a company are being acquired is that there may be actual or contingent liabilities of the company in relation to premises it has previously disposed of (e.g. where the company caused or permitted the contamination of such premises while in occupation), whereas there could be no question of these liabilities passing in the case of a sale of assets, save by a contractual allocation mechanism. So far as the Pt IIA contaminated land regime is concerned, the purchaser may become responsible as a second tier appropriate person in his capacity as occupier, if it is the case that no person can be found who caused or knowingly permitted the contaminants to be present. Unlike the first kind of liability, this risk lasts only for so long as the purchaser continues to occupy the land.

Liability as the owner of property

For this category of liability the position is effectively the same as in **20.07** relation to liability as occupier above: under a transfer of assets the purchaser will step into the position of owner and, in the case of a sale of the shares in a company, any liabilities which accrued during the company's ownership of former assets will remain with the company. Thus, with reference to the Pt IIA regime, the purchaser may become responsible as an owner if no person can be found who caused or knowingly permitted the contaminants to be present. Again, this risk lasts only for so long as the purchaser continues to own the land.

To summarise, two significant types of risk will apply to the purchaser in **20.08** the case of a company share sale which will not apply in the case of an assets transaction. These are, first, liability of the company as the person who caused or knowingly permitted the presence of contamination in, on or under the land that is owned or occupied by the company at completion of the transaction and, secondly, continuing liability of the company (whether as polluter or contractually) in relation to properties previously disposed of and therefore not forming part of the "transaction. Liability should not be considered exclusively as liability to regulatory authorities or other third parties: contamination may also give rise to losses in the sense of voluntary remediation costs and diminution in value.

20.09   The additional risks inherent in a company share sale can to a large extent be safeguarded against by the device (which may be expedient in any event for tax or other reasons) of transferring the target assets into a new and "clean" company,[1] which is then sold to the purchaser (though it would not be appropriate for such a transfer of assets to be used as a device to evade the original company's *existing* obligations)[2] Other methods are use of single purpose vehicles (SPVs) or structures distinguishing between property owning and operating companies ("Propco" and "Opco").

20.10   In the case of IPOs and other finance transactions involving public offerings of equity securities, the issue of focusing on actual and contingent contaminated land liabilities is important in the context of the due diligence that is intended to protect the sponsor and the company against the risk that the prospectus or listing particulars[3] may prove to be inaccurate or incomplete in terms of information provided to potential investors.

Investigations and information

20.11   As with property transactions, which are considered in the previous chapter, it will be important to make appropriate investigations as to potential contamination and associated liabilities. Like property transactions the sources of information are essentially threefold: public sources, the seller, and the purchaser's own enquiries. The seller as well may wish to conduct investigations into potential contamination, particularly in view of the "sold with information" liability exclusion test which can operate in favour of the seller. Reference should be made to other chapters for further details on such investigations.[4]

---

[1] See further, para.20.27ff.

[2] See *Sithole v Thor Chemical Holdings* (Court of Appeal, September 28, 2000) in which the Court was critical of a demerger process by Thor Chemical Holdings in which subsidiary companies and assets were transferred to a new parent after the company faced claims from workers and families of deceased employees who were employed at a mercury reprocessing plant operated by a subsidiary in South Africa. The Court took the view that the 1997 demerger could have been motivated by a desire to put assets beyond the reach of future claimants and that the holding company was "deliberately isolated from the resources of the majority of companies within the group" (para.62 of judgment). See Halina Ward, *Corporate Accountability in Search of a Treaty? Some insights from foreign direct liability* (Royal Institute of International Affairs, Briefing Paper, May 2002, No.4: *http://www.chathamhouse.org.uk/publications/papers/view/-/id/56/*).

[3] A prospectus is required where the issuer is applying for listing and its shares are to be offered to the public for the first time; otherwise listing particulars are required.

[4] See Chs 19 and 22.

In the context of share and asset purchase transactions the equivalent of **20.12** pre-contract enquiries is the usual information request forwarded to the seller. This may be used to elicit information as to environmental matters. The practice of seeking warranties from the seller is another, indirect, means of eliciting information, in that the seller will have an incentive to disclose against the warranties any matters which would otherwise result in a breach of the warranties. The issue of warranties is further considered below.[5] Also, in auction situations, the practice of using data rooms (also considered below) is important.

Solutions to identified problems

Assuming that problems are identified in the course of investigations, **20.13** various possible solutions are open, including:

1. warranties (though these will offer little comfort where the relevant contamination has been disclosed);

2. indemnities;

3. restructuring of the deal, for example as an assets rather than a company sale, or by excluding certain "problem" assets;

4. price adjustment, though this can be risky even when problems are known, given the uncertainty which often surrounds the quantification of clean-up costs;

5. a retention in price or amount held in escrow against the cost of rectifying identified problems;

6. postponement of completion to allow further investigations to proceed, or perhaps making completion conditional on problems being rectified;

7. agreeing on a programme of post-completion investigations with the seller being obliged to fund remediation; or

8. some form of "put" option, by which the purchaser can require the seller to buy back problematic assets.

Of these, the issue of warranties and indemnities require further explanation.

Risk allocation

Even though investigations have been carried out in relation to a property, **20.14** or some remedial works have been undertaken, there will always be an element of risk. The investigations carried out may not have identified all problems, which may become apparent later; sometimes many years later.

---

[5] See para.20.31ff.

The seller may wish to sell the company or assets without retaining liabilities going forward; equally, the purchaser may wish the seller to retain responsibility for rectifying contamination that existed prior to completion of the transaction. The issue of risk allocation between seller and purchaser therefore needs to be addressed. Various factors will influence the negotiations on risk allocation, though ultimately the most important will usually be bargaining power and relative risk-sensitivity of the respective parties. It is by no means always the case that the seller will accept all the risk for historic contamination. Some financial sellers, such as private equity houses, may not be willing to offer purchasers any meaningful contractual protection when selling businesses or assets they purchased with a view to realising returns on short term investments. There may well be cases where the purchaser will have to accept a significant measure of risk or indeed the entire risk. One example of such a situation is where the purchaser knows of the risks and is taking the asset "as seen"—for example in a management buy-out or where the purchaser has conducted a thorough pre-acquisition audit (though it is unusual in practice for prospective purchasers to be allowed to carry out pre-completion intrusive investigations). A purchaser who is acquiring assets for development may also in practice be prepared to accept a measure of environmental risk, as one of the general risk factors involving development.

Particular risk allocation considerations under Part IIA

20.15 The Pt IIA liability exclusion and apportionment mechanisms need to be considered because they have brought an increased focus in corporate transactions involving UK assets on the contractual allocation of risks associated with contaminated land. To some extent the principles remain much as they were prior to the introduction of Pt IIA in terms of the general allocation of risks discusssed above; however, the increased sophistication of the Pt IIA liability allocation mechanisms requires certain adjustments to previous practices. It will be appreciated that contractual provisions designed to take advantage of the provisions for channelling liability under the contaminated land regime are strictly speaking relevant only to that regime. However, to the extent that a regulator (for example, the Environment Agency or SEPA under the s.161A–D of the Water Resources Act 1991 works notice provisions in relation to water pollution) has a discretion as to how to target enforcement action, and has sympathy with the policy rationale for the contaminated land exclusion and apportionment provisions, then the person whom such agreements are designed to protect might also seek to use their existence to influence the regulator's exercise of discretion.

20.16 It is also needs to be recognised that certain of the liability exclusion mechanisms discussed below (in particular, the "payments made for remediation" and "sold with information" mechanisms) would not apply in circumstances where the members of the liability group in question are "related companies", i.e. companies which are, or were at the date on which the enforcing authority first served a notice identifying the land as contaminated land, members of a group of companies consisting of a "holding company" and its "subsidiaries" (with those two terms having the same meaning as in s.736 of the Companies Act 1985). This could, for example, be relevant in the case of corporate reorganisations, where real estate assets are being moved from one group company to another.[6]

Part IIA—agreements on liability

It needs to be borne in mind (particularly in the context of transactions **20.17** involving the sale of assets) that the Pt IIA regime makes express allowance for the seller and the purchaser to agree that the purchaser will be responsible for the cost of any future remediation. Assuming (as, depending on the facts, arguably may become the case) that the purchaser's state of knowledge and capacity to act will make it a "knowing permitter" at some point following the transaction, then according to paras D.38 and D.39 of the Guidance the enforcing authority should make such determinations on exclusion and apportionment as are needed to give effect to any such agreement, and should not apply the remainder of the Guidance between the parties to the agreement. However, only Pt IIA (as opposed to the other potential sources of liability) contains a mechanism for such an agreement to determine on whom the regulator serves a notice. In any event, such an agreement will only apply as between the seller and the purchaser, and would not affect the position of any subsequent purchaser or, indeed, any other appropriate person who is not a party to the agreement. Any such agreement would need to be notified in writing to the relevant authority. Another risk is that should the purchaser cease to exist before any notice is served, then he would not be in the liability group at all, and accordingly the authority would not be able to give effect to the agreement. Also, if the purchaser seeks to sell rapidly on, then the purchaser with whom the seller entered into the agreement on liabilities may not constitute an appropriate person under Pt IIA at the time the issue of liability arises (e.g. where the purchaser in question did not itself cause or knowingly permit the relevant contamination). Also, the Guidance contains its own limitations as to the effect of such agreements. A copy of the agreement must be provided to the authority, and none of the parties must inform the authority that it challenges the application of the agreement. Secondly, the authority should disregard the agreement where the party whose share of costs would be increased under it would benefit from the "hardship" limitation on cost recovery. Accordingly, an adverse change in the financial circumstances of one party after the agreement may prejudice the other.[7]

Part IIA—payments made for remediation

If the extent of the contamination is known, and a clean-up method can be **20.18** agreed and costed, then the seller may make a payment to the purchaser to cover that remediation, either by way of a direct payment or by an express

---

[6] See also para.5.184.
[7] See further, para.5.179ff.

deduction from the purchase price. Provided that the payment is adequate, then in the event that the remediation is not carried out, or is not carried out effectively, the seller should be excluded by Test 2 at paras D.51—D.56 from future liability under the contaminated land regime (although not necessarily under the other statutory sources of liability discussed above). In order to ensure the seller's protection, the position should be stated explicitly in the contracts. To satisfy this test, the seller must not retain any further control over the condition of the land in question. The seller can, however, safely retain contractual rights to ensure that the work is carried out properly. As mentioned above, this test will not be suitable for all circumstances, and may well be confined in practice to cases where land is sold either for development or with a clear idea as to the remedial measures required, or where there is a specific and clearly identified contamination problem which is capable of being addressed by specific measures. In those circumstances Test 2 may be particularly useful.

20.19   The "payments made for remediation" test is most likely to become relevant where the parties have applied their minds to the costs of cleaning up particular contamination problems, in which case either the contamination may be cleaned up by the seller before completion, or alternatively the price may be reduced by a sum appropriate to allow the purchaser to carry out clean-up. The question here is partly one of who bears the risk that the remediation proves ineffective. If the remediation is to be carried out by the purchaser of the land, then potentially the test of "payments made for remediation" may be applied to impose the risk solely on the purchaser, and thus exclude the seller from further liability under the contaminated land regime. Where the remediation is carried out by the seller, he may well retain residual liability if remediation proves ineffective, but this will not necessarily release the purchaser from also being liable. The risks to the purchaser may be reduced by an indemnity (see below) given by the seller and/or by collateral warranties given by the engineers carrying out the remedial work. It is conceivable that the transaction could be structured in such a way that the purchaser could be regarded as making a payment to the seller in order to carry out the remediation, but this would require careful structuring and drafting, and would not remove the risk that the seller might in future cease to exist, leaving the purchaser as the sole member of the liability group.

Part IIA—"sold with information"

20.20   The seller may seek to apply the "sold with information" test (Test 3, set out at paras D.57–D.61 of the Guidance) in relation to liability under the contaminated land regime.[8] This can be triggered either by the seller acquiring information as to the presence of contamination itself, and providing that information to the purchaser, or alternatively by the seller allowing the purchaser to carry out its own investigation, so that the purchaser thereby generates the information. The information must be sufficient to allow the purchaser to be aware of the relevant pollutant and

[8] See further para.5.201.

the "broad measure of its presence". The information must be available before the sale becomes binding, and therefore either the investigation must be carried out before exchange of contracts, or exchange must be on a conditional basis to allow subsequent investigations to take place. The problem with the conditional contract approach is the difficulty of framing the conditions so as to achieve sufficient certainty as to the circumstances in which the contract does become binding.[9] Also, the price may need to be left flexible (or some mechanism agreed for adjusting the price) following the completion of the investigations. Clearly, the preferable course would be to obtain the information prior to exchange.

Knowledge of contamination may be deemed to exist where the pur- **20.21** chaser is a "large commercial organisation" or a public body, and permission has been given to the purchaser to carry out its own investigations. The Guidance, however, only suggests that this should "normally be taken as sufficient indication" that the purchaser had the necessary information. Obviously, it would be as well to make it clear in writing that the opportunity had been given (and the scope of that opportunity), either in correspondence or in the contract itself. There may be issues about the extent of investigations that would have been needed to arrive at a detailed understanding of the contamination, its measure and whether, in fact, the seller had afforded the buyer with an adequate opportunity for such investigations to be carried out. This is especially problematic since the term "investigations" is not defined. Similarly, with Test 3 generally there may be issues concerning the quality or adequacy of information about the presence of contamination that is given to prospective purchasers at the time of the land transfer. Issues may also arise as to whether the seller did anything to misrepresent the implications of the presence.[10]

The other situation is where the purchaser does not know for sure that **20.22** the land is contaminated, but is aware of the risk that it might be. Awareness of this risk would not in itself be enough to trigger the "sold with information" test. However, if the purchaser is a large commercial organisation or public body there is a risk that it might be deemed to have knowledge of the contamination by virtue of having had permission to carry out an investigation, but having failed to do so. Effectively, this puts the onus on sophisticated purchasers of land to take professional advice as to the investigations which they should carry out, and to assess the risks accordingly. From the purchaser's point of view, that risk may be reflected either in an indemnity from the seller or by a reduction in the purchase price to reflect that risk.

Part IIA—sellers of company shares

As discussed above, a company carries with it the full spectrum of potential **20.23** responsibilities for the company's past, present or future contamination. Any residual risk would relate to whether the main party selling the shares

---

[9] See para.19.49.
[10] A material misrepresentation by the seller would disallow the application of the test—see para.D.59(c).

could be said, through his past control over the company, to have caused or knowingly permitted the contamination. Under Exclusion Test 1, investing in a company, acquiring shares or loan capital should not of itself result in liability under the contaminated land regime, unless the level of control is equivalent to that of a holding company over its subsidiary under s.736 of the Companies Act 1985. Holding companies who are disposing of subsidiaries should therefore be aware that they may not be able to rely upon that exclusion test. However, it must be emphasised that being in a position of holding company will not necessarily be equated to having caused or knowingly permitted contamination. This would depend on the facts, and in particular the degree of knowledge and the level of control exercised by the holding company over the relevant acts of the subsidiary.[11]

20.24   Whether an indemnity is required from the seller of the shares is a matter for negotiation between the parties. In circumstances where a holding company considers that it may have exercised sufficient control to have a residual liability, this will also need to be considered carefully, since if it is the intention that the holding company should divest itself of all liability, it will need to reflect this in the agreement either by way of an indemnity from the purchaser, or by express agreement to that effect which can be notified to the regulatory authority as envisaged under the Guidance.

Part IIA—purchasers of company shares

20.25   So far as sites which are owned by the company being sold are concerned, the position, in terms of risk to the purchaser of the company, is effectively the same as for a purchaser of land. However, there is the further dimension that the company will also carry with it any liabilities it may have by virtue of previous actions or omissions, and in particular these will include:

1. Liability for contamination which the company may have caused or knowingly permitted during its general business activities. The risk here will no doubt depend upon the nature of those activities. For example, in the case of a construction company which may have been involved in many contaminated sites over the years, the risk could be significant. Similarly, for a company which has been involved in the transport and distribution of contaminative substances such as oil, again the risk could be significant.

2. Liability relating to sites which the company has owned in the past, either where it caused contamination on its own site, or where it was aware of the presence of contamination on the site which it knowingly permitted to remain.

20.26   Both of these are difficult matters to deal with. A company may only have limited knowledge of contamination which it has caused in the past. There may only be incomplete or inadequate information as to sites which

[11] See para.5.108ff.

have been previously owned or occupied, and even where these are known investigation may be impossible. The matter can therefore either be dealt with by structuring the transaction in terms of an assets purchase in order to confine the risks to those assets currently owned by the company, or alternatively by way of indemnification. Assets "hive down" arrangements also need some careful thought in the light of the Pt IIA regime and are considered below.

Part IIA—assets "hive down" and similar arrangements

A common practice is to package or "hive down" assets of a company into a **20.27** new corporate vehicle ("Newco"), the shares of which are then sold. Even where a "Newco" is not involved, there may be some re-arrangement of assets within a group to be carried out before a company is sold. The possible operation of the regime of Pt IIA will need thinking through carefully in the circumstances of such cases. Take, for example, the situation where the assets hived down from the seller to Newco include a site which is known to be contaminated. If the disposal to Newco was at arm's length, it might well be argued that Test 3 would apply so as to exclude the seller from future liability. However, if at the time the seller and Newco are related companies, then under para.D.46 of the Guidance, the seller will not be excluded from liability by Test 3. The subsequent sale of the shares of Newco to the purchaser will not change that position.

Similar considerations could apply where a company to be sold, "Tar- **20.28** getco", disposes of sites which are known to be contaminated prior to the sale, so that they are excluded from the sale to the purchaser of Targetco. If Targetco disposes of those assets to a company within the same group, Test 3 will not operate to rid Targetco of any residual liability it may have in respect of those sites and, consequently, this will pass with Targetco to the purchaser.

In both examples above, the end result may not necessarily be in **20.29** accordance with the intention of the parties. In the first example, the seller might have thought it was selling the site in a known contaminated condition and that the purchaser would be taking over all liabilities. In the second example, the purchaser might have thought it was acquiring Targetco free of liability for the site which had previously been divested.

Test 3 is in fact qualified by para.D.59(c), which states that where a **20.30** group of transactions or a wider agreement includes a sale of land, the sale of land should be taken to be at arm's length where the person seeking to be excluded can show that the net effect of the group of transactions or the agreement as a whole was a sale at arm's length. In the first example above, the seller might seek to argue that, looked at overall, the land was being sold to the purchaser, via Newco, at arm's length, and that accordingly Test 3 should operate on the disposal to Newco. This is probably not an argument that would be open to the purchaser in the second example. In any event, para.D.59(c) is not precisely worded, and it would be inadvisable for either side to make assumptions as to whether or not it would apply to their circumstances. The important thing is, therefore, to think through carefully how the Guidance might apply to the arrangements proposed (which may be driven by tax or other non-environmental considerations) and whether this accords with what is intended in terms of allocation of environmental risk. The contractual allocation of environmental risks is considered generally below both in relation to the drafting of warranties and indemnities.

Warranties

20.31 The practice of seeking warranties on an acquisition of a company is a response to the fundamental principle of *caveat emptor*, which applies with all its force in relation to such transactions.[12] However, sellers ought to be wary of over-reliance on the caveat emptor rule as protection. The Law Commission (*Caveat Emptor in Sales of Land—Consultation Paper from the Conveyancing Standing Committee of the Law Commission* (1988)) described caveat emptor as "an unjustifiably ramshackle principle" the foundation of which "may be regarded as suffering from the legal equivalent of subsidence". The following are exceptions to the application of the rule which may have some relevance to sales of potentially contaminated land: where the parties are in a relationship of *uberrimae fidei*, there will be an overriding duty of disclosure; where there is a fiduciary relationship between the parties; where a positive representation is distorted by later non-disclosure[13]; where there is a misrepresentation by the seller including a false representation by conduct[14]; where there is a defect as to the title of the property which the seller failed to disclose such that the seller could not sell free from encumbrances of which the purchaser could have no knowledge[15]; where there is negligence on the part of an owner who has undertaken work upon the land[16]; and where conduct by the owner might constitute the tort of deceit. Also, the traditional immunity of the seller under the caveat emptor rule may be lost on account of the dangerous state of the premises following "work of construction, repair, maintenance or demolition or other work done" in accordance with s.3(1) of the Defective Premises Act 1972. In addition, the Property Misdescriptions Act 1991 renders it a criminal offence to: "make a false or misleading statement about a prescribed matter in the course of an estate agency business or a property development business. . .".[17]

---

[12] W. J. L. Knight, *The Acquisition of Private Companies* (6th edn, 1993), p.99; Neil Sinclair, *Warranties and Indemnities on Share Sales* (3rd edn, 1992). The Financial Services Act 1986 s.47 provides that it is a criminal offence for any person to induce or attempt to induce another to enter into an agreement for the acquisition of securities by dishonest concealment of material facts; however it does not appear that any civil remedy based on the section has yet been awarded by the courts; *Securities and Investment Board v Danfell SA* [1991] 4 All E.R. 883, 887.

[13] See *Laurence v LexCourt Holdings Ltd* [1978] 1 W.L.R. 1128.

[14] See *Gordon and Texeira v Selica Ltd* (1986) 11 H.L.R. 219.

[15] See *City Towns Ltd v Bohemian Properties* [1986] 2 E.G.L.R. 258—"a liability of uncertain amount at some future time" may constitute "a latent defect which goes to the title of the property" (at 261).

[16] See for example: *Hone v Benson* (1978) 248 E.G. 1013.

[17] A property development business is one concerned "wholly or substantially with the development of land" and a statement can be caught where it is made with a view to disposing of an interest in land. The prescribed matters are sufficiently widely drawn to include most physical attributes of the land including "condition" and "environment".

There has been further erosion of the caveat emptor principle by the **20.32** exclusionary tests under Pt IIA of the EPA 1990, which not only allow risk transfer between potentially appropriate persons under the liability regime but also, because of the strict and retroactive nature of Pt IIA, make it possible for a seller to transfer land while retaining historic liabilities.

For a successful claim for breach of warranty to be made the purchaser **20.33** needs to prove loss flowing from the breach. The loss must fall within one of the two following categories: (1) loss which flows naturally from the breach, a natural consequence of the breach, the type and extent of which a reasonable person would expect in the circumstances; or (2) loss which was fairly and reasonably in the contemplation of both parties, at the time they entered into the contract, as the probable result of the breach. The damages aim to put the purchaser in the position he would have been in had the contract not been breached, subject to the duty to mitigate. This may be difficult to quantify, and may depend on what basis the target has been valued by the purchaser. In the case of a share sale and subsequent breach of warranty, the purchaser's loss is the difference between the value of the shares if the warranty had been true, and their actual value; therefore the basis used for the valuation of the shares will be relevant in assessing the loss.

Warranties are an important mechanism for forcing a seller to disclose **20.34** relevant information, and the use and breadth of warranties in typical acquisition agreements has expanded over the years, with environmental matters simply one factor which needs to be reflected in the range of such warranties. The purpose of warranties in connection with a share or asset sale is twofold. First, they elicit disclosure of information, which otherwise might not be forthcoming from the seller, concerning matters which are likely to be of concern to the purchaser. Focusing on the disclosure of information within the scope of the warranties enables both parties' minds to be concentrated on the relevant issues so that an informed negotiation on key value issues can take place. Secondly, environmental warranties are used to allocate risk as between the warrantor and the beneficiary of the warranties, essentially by defining who takes responsibility for problems of the kind referred to in the warranties.

It is unusual to give warranties in two cases: first, cases where the **20.35** purchase consideration is satisfied wholly or partly by the allotment of shares in the purchaser and, secondly, bids for listed companies.[18] Various commentators[19] have pointed out that there is no practical logic in this distinction drawn between private and listed companies, or any compelling logical reason why the purchaser of a listed company should be prepared to accept the risk of undisclosed liabilities which the purchaser would not be prepared to countenance if purchasing a private company. Nonetheless, the distinction is well accepted in practice. A possible justification for the distinction is that publicly listed companies have certain disclosure obligations under listing rules and all shareholders should be entitled to the same information on which to base their decisions to invest in such companies.

[18] Neil Sinclair, *Warranties and Indemnities on Share Sales* (3rd edn, 1992) p.2.
[19] Neil Sinclair, *Warranties and Indemnities on Share Sales* (3rd edn, 1992).

20.36   Careful consideration needs to be given to the drafting of warranties relating to contamination and other environmental matters. A number of the issues arising are common to other types of warranty—for example clear procedures for notification of claims and tax treatment of payments. Other issues relate specifically to the nature of environmental liabilities, and to the effects of standard drafting in the context of such liabilities. Detailed issues of drafting are considered below.

20.37   It is standard practice to disclose various matters against warranties in the context of a disclosure letter written by or on behalf of the party who is giving the warranties. The principal purpose of the disclosure letter is to qualify the warranties given. Whilst as discussed above a function of a warranty may be to allocate some or all of the risk in relation to the existence or extent of a particular liability from the beneficiary to the warrantor, the effect of a disclosure is to pass that risk back to the beneficiary in respect of the matter disclosed. Both general and specific disclosures are typically made. For example, the warrantor may seek to make general disclosure of all matters contained in the documentation in the data room and all matters that can be gleaned from publicly available documents and enquiries. Where environmental reports are prepared, for a safe, it is common to have general disclosure of those reports. Speaking of the disclosure process generally, in the Scottish case of *Edward Prentice v Scottish Power Plc*[20] it was said:

> "It is difficult to avoid the impression that disclosure has become a tactical exercise, with vendors' representations seeking to off-load responsibilities by the delivery of indigestible documents in quantity to purchasers' representatives who are put under pressure to investigate the material with inadequate time and facilities, and in turn resort to equally meaningless qualified acceptance if they are permitted to do so."

20.38   In practical terms the digitisation of information has increased this problem for solicitors, with the emergence of "virtual data rooms", accessible electronically. The use of such methods of disclosure means that large amounts of information may be added during the course of the potential purchaser's investigations, and often late in the process either because such information has recently come to light, or (more cynically) for strategic reasons. The sheer volume of information—mainly worthless—which can be made available in this way increases the possibility that some really important item of disclosure may be overlooked and raises problems for solicitors. Such virtual data rooms are often used in "auction" or competitive bid situations, where time for investigation is limited, and where the bidders are given simultaneous access to the data.

20.39   Obviously, when acting for a purchaser the general disclosures need to be scrutinised with particular care and may need to be resisted (though such resistance may be futile in the case of some transactions). Specific disclosures are made with reference to particular warranties and describe

[20] *The Times*, October 28, 1996.

facts or circumstances which would, but for the disclosure, constitute breaches of the relevant warranties. A purchaser needs to be wary of accepting specific disclosures in some cases, as where the information disclosed may be general or vague or insufficiently detailed to give a fair understanding of the risk. Often the sale and purchase agreement will dictate that the warranties are qualified by any disclosures "fairly made" by the seller. Where the sale and purchase agreement is silent as to the standard of disclosure, the question arises as to exactly what detail must be disclosed in order to constitute effective disclosure.[21] In the past courts have tended to apply a fairness standard such that "mere reference to a source of information. . . will not satisfy the requirements of a clause providing for fair disclosure with sufficient details to identify the nature and scope of the matter disclosed".[22] This would seem to imply some necessary steps to draw important matters to the attention of the party seeking the benefit of the warranties. However, as between commercial parties, the Court of Appeal has indicated that a significant factor is the precise language used by the parties in the sale and purchase agreement and disclosure letter.[23] Particular care should be taken where there is disclosure of environmental investigation reports, as the requirement of disclosure may be satisfied in relation to such matters as might fairly be expected to come to the knowledge of the purchaser's advisers from examination of the documents supplied.[24] Where a purchaser has actual knowledge of facts relating to what would otherwise constitute a breach of warranty, he may not be permitted to rely on the fact that such breach had not been formally disclosed.[25] Disclosure can be appropriate where a specific breach of legislation, incident, or regulatory problem can be identified. Often, however, disclosure will pose more questions than it answers. Also, a disclosed "one-off" problem may be symptomatic of more widespread difficulties.

20.40 A seller may wish the disclosure terms to state that each disclosure should be treated as a disclosure in respect of all of the warranties (or, at least, those warranties to which the disclosure may reasonably be regarded as being relevant) and not just in respect of the warranty to which it most obviously relates. On the other hand, a purchaser who has accepted that the environmental warranties should be "boxed" may insist that the disclosures are also boxed.

Misrepresentation

20.41 Contaminated land liabilities in the context of a sale and purchase transaction may also potentially arise for misrepresentation. A misrepresentation is a false statement of fact made by one party to the contract to

---

[21] See *Levison v Farin* [1978] 2 All E.R. 1149.

[22] Per *Lord Penrose* in *New Hearts Ltd v Cosmopolitan Investments Ltd* [1997] 2 B.C.L.C. 249 at 258–9.

[23] See *Infiniteland Ltd v Artisan Contracting Ltd* [2005] EWCA 758, which involved examination of a company's accounts by a purchaser's accountants in the course of due diligence involving a sale and purchase transaction.

[24] *Infiniteland Ltd v Artisan Contracting Ltd* [2005] EWCA 758.

[25] See *Eurocopy v Teesdale* [1992] B.C.L.C. 1067.

the other, which induces the other party to enter into the contract. If a purchaser can prove that he has relied on a representation to enter the contract, which turns out to the false, he will prima facie have a claim for misrepresentation. The remedies for misrepresentation include recission, which is an equitable remedy that aims to put the parties back into their pre-contractual positions,[26] and damages, which are measured on a tortious basis, aiming to put the innocent party in the position he would have been in if the tort had not been committed. It is common for sale and purchase agreements to incorporate an acknowledgement by the purchaser that he has not relied on any representations which are not contained in the contract, and that the contract sets out the entire agreement and understanding between the parties. However, any such entire agreement clause can only exclude liability for misrepresentation if it is reasonable.[27] Moreover, it has been held by the courts that in order to exclude liability for pre-contractual misrepresentation a clause has to do so expressly, and an entire agreement clause cannot exclude liability for *fraudulent* misprepresentation—if it purports to do so the whole clause will be unreasonable.[28]

Indemnities

20.42 In sale and purchase agreements governed by English law liability for breach of warranty is to be distinguished from liability under an indemnity; in the latter case liability arises not because of breach of any obligation but because the parties have stipulated that one shall save another from loss in specified circumstances.[29] An indemnity allows the purchaser to recover amounts on a "pound for pound" basis (subject to any financial limitations which have been agreed between the parties). Also, whereas a warranty is essentially an issue between the seller and purchaser, an indemnity may be given by the seller in favour of the target company. It has become common drafting practice in recent years for certain types of environmental liabilities to be dealt with by way of indemnity, sometimes rather than or in addition to warranty. From the point of view of the beneficiary, there are significant advantages of an indemnity over a warranty. The relevant circumstances in which a claim under an indemnity may arise are normally strictly construed and liability under them will not go beyond that expressly stipulated. Enforcement is far simpler, with no arguments as to whether the warranty was breached. With an indemnity the amount of the claim will equal the exact amount of the liability incurred, avoiding complex arguments which could arise over the measure of damages for breach of warranty, i.e. whether the cost of cure is recoverable or whether damages are limited to the difference in value of the assets between their actual value as warranted.[30] This may not necessarily equate with the

---

[26] Though a court can award damages instead of recission for innocent misrepresentation—see s.2(2) of the Misrepresentation Act 1967.

[27] S.8. Unfair Contract Terms Act 1977.

[28] *Thomas Witter v TBP Industries* [1996] 2 All E.R. 573; upheld in *South West Water Services Limited v International Computers Ltd* [1999] B.L.R. 420; [1999] 1 T.C.L.R. 439, Q.B. TCC.

[29] W. J. L. Knight, *The Acquisition of Private Companies* (6th edn, 1993), p.134.

[30] *Tito v Waddell (No. 2)* [1977] Ch. 106.

direct cost of cure or out of pocket expenses which could be recovered under an indemnity.

Since the warranty is essentially a representation by the seller that a **20.43** particular state of affairs does or does not exist, warranties are typically used where the purchaser has carried out no investigation, or where investigations have been carried out in respect of matters remaining within the exclusive knowledge of the seller, or where the purchaser simply wishes to ensure that the seller is obliged to disclose all relevant information. Indemnities may be appropriate, on the other hand, where investigation has been carried out and has revealed specific problems in respect of which the seller has agreed to take the risk. An indemnity may also be appropriate where potential liabilities have been disclosed against the warranties, or where investigations have not been carried out or disclosed by the seller but the nature of the target sites/business is such that the purchaser considers there is a risk of liability that needs to be covered by indemnity.

There is no settled rule as to the circumstances in which warranties and **20.44** indemnities respectively should be used, but it will be important, where both warranties and indemnities are given, to consider the extent to which they may conflict. For example, specific environmental indemnities that are given by a seller may to an extent overlap with matters covered in general warranties. There may be valid tax reasons why the seller would prefer a claim to be made under a warranty rather than the indemnity, and appropriate provision should be made to as to the precedence of claims.[31] Particular care would be needed where an indemnity, for example, contains a different limitation period or maximum limit on liability from the warranties. Where there is both, an indemnity and a warranty that may cover the same ground, the normal practice is that a claim may only be made under the indemnity. The contractual allocation of environmental risks is considered below both in relation to the drafting of indemnities and warranties.

A common approach in sale and purchase agreements governed by US **20.45** law is for an indemnity to be given in relation to a breach of warranty. In the UK it is not clear what the precise legal effect of such a provision would be. It may confirm only that damages are recoverable for breach of the warranty or operate as a true indemnity. Also it is unclear whether such a provision would have the effect of removing the usual limitations on contractual damages: causation, foreseeability and the duty to mitigate. If a target is valued on the basis of the net asset value, and there is a breach of warranty, claiming damages would involve proving breach, causation and that the duty to mitigate has been discharged. However, claiming under an indemnity for breach of warranty would theoretically mean that the damages awarded would not be subject to such limitations.

Common drafting issues

Warranties and indemnities on environmental issues present a number of **20.46** common drafting issues.

---

[31] Neil Sinclair, *Warranties and Indemnities on Share Sales* (3rd edn, 1992), pp. 4, 24.

Relationship with general provisions

20.47   Standard sale and purchase documentation will contain warranties which, although general in scope, may cover certain environmental matters such as compliance with all laws, the absence of disputes or litigation and the condition of assets. Such warranties may be argued to be preferable to those specifically angled at environmental issues, in that their generality means that they should catch the widest possible range of problems. However, warranties which are more specifically aimed at particular environmental issues have considerable advantages over general warranties. First, they leave less room for argument as to whether the parties intended a specific circumstance to be covered. Secondly, warranties of a general nature will not necessarily draw the seller's attention to particular environmental matters of potential concern to a purchaser; therefore the seller may inadvertently not disclose the matter to the purchaser. In any event, general warranty provisions are no substitute for a specifically agreed and precisely-drafted allocation of risk. Where specific environmental warranty provisions are negotiated, care should be taken to ensure that the general warranty provisions do not alter the specific allocation of environmental risk which has been agreed, and it may be necessary to exclude or "box" the specific environmental warranties from these other general warranty provisions.

20.48   Also, asset sale and purchase agreements normally contain cross indemnity provisions given by the seller and purchaser, respectively, which operate in respect of certain classes of liabilities retained by the seller (e.g. in respect of pre-completion acts or omissions) and other liabilities which are expressly assumed under the agreement by the purchaser. Such indemnities can have the effect of allocating liabilities for contaminated land, even though they normally make no specific reference to soil or groundwater contamination.

Retrospective legislation

20.49   A warranty is usually inserted to the effect that the seller (in relation to the business/assets being sold) and the target companies have complied with all environmental laws. Indemnities are also sometimes sought in respect of losses arising from pre-completion non-compliance with environmental laws. Environmental laws in these contexts are normally widely defined to include primary and subordinate legislation, requirements of public authorities and, frequently, any European Community legislation. Following the introduction of the Pt IIA regime, the definition of environmental laws is often extended to include statutory guidance and circulars, such as DEFRA Circular 01/2006. Warranties are typically given at the signing of the transaction agreement and repeated at completion, so the definition of environmental laws in the context of a compliance warranty rarely needs to extend in practice to future laws—only to laws that are in force and binding at signing/completion. However, the same cannot be said for the definition of environmental laws in the context of indemnities, particularly those which are intended to be triggered by future enforcement action that is referable to historic (pre-completion) contamination. In this case it may be important from a purchaser's perspective to seek that the definition of environmental laws not only extends to current laws, but also future legislation and especially to that applying retrospectively. It is usual to find a definition provision to the general effect that references to enactments are to be construed as a reference to the enactment as amended or re-enacted or as modified by other provisions. Care is needed here on the part of the warrantor or indemnifying party, since the effect of such general provisions could be to throw onto them the risk of liability arising from future retrospective legislation. This would be inconsistent with the normal principle that, as from the exchange of contracts or at least from completion, the business of the target company is conducted at the risk of the purchaser.[32] The risk for the warrantor may be reduced by providing that legislative modifications after the date of completion are excluded or, alternatively, by excluding any amendment or modification enacted after completion which would materially extend or increase the liability of the warrantor. Another facet of this problem relates to the legislative practice of enacting provisions which may remain on the statute book for a considerable time before being brought into force (if ever) by a commencement order. It should be made clear which party is to bear the risk in this case: at least the nature of the liability can be appreciated at the outset, although it is not certain as to when that liability may become a reality.[33]

Presence of "hazardous substances"

In the US environmental warranties and indemnities commonly refer to **20.50** the presence of "hazardous substances" on relevant land. This is a reflection of the scheme of liability under relevant US legislation.[34] It is not uncommon for the term "hazardous substances" to be used in the context of UK sale and purchase agreements and defined so as to include a broad range of substances which are capable of causing pollution, contamination, harm or damage to the environment. Of course, any substance may be "hazardous" in this sense if present at the wrong place in the wrong quantities at the wrong time; indeed, many warranties relating to "hazardous substances" could be taken as requiring disclosure of the presence of innocuous substances such as milk, fruit juice or common cleaning fluids. The warrantor or indemnifier may wish to seek to have the definition limited to an appropriate range of specified substances, if there is genuine concern as to the presence of those substances on the company's property.

Problems not caused by the seller

Contamination may be due to causes other than the seller's own activities. **20.51** The seller may not be inclined to accept the risk of liability for historical contamination or the migration of contamination from other land. From

---

[32] Neil Sinclair, *Warranties and Indemnities on Share Sales* (3rd edn, 1992), p.28.

[33] In some cases, however, the extent of the risk or liability may not be apparent from the face of primary legislation; an example is Pt IIA of the Environmental Protection Act 1990 which made provision for various important liability attribution and allocation mechanisms to be elaborated in statutory guidance (now contained in DEFRA Circular 01/2006).

[34] See Ch.27.

the purchaser's point of view, the origin of the contamination may be seen as irrelevant to the risks it poses; also it can be argued that the seller as owner of the land is currently subject to those risks, as much as to the risks of contamination arising from the conduct of the seller's business. Ultimately the issue of responsibility for such contamination will be determined by negotiation and the bargaining power of the respective parties rather than strict logic.

Seller's knowledge

20.52 It is common for sellers when giving warranties to seek to qualify certain warranties (e.g. compliance with environmental laws and presence of contamination) to the extent of the knowledge and belief of the warrantor. Without such qualifications the warranties would be effective to allocate the risks of unknown problems to the warrantor. This is particular relevant in the context of contaminated land because environmental law typically imposes strict liability for causing pollution. However, since contamination problems may not be readily apparent without intrusive investigations it would be easy for the warrantor to avoid liability simply by not looking for problems. It is therefore particularly important that, where the warranties are so limited, there is the usual provision that the warrantor has made full (or at least reasonable) enquiry into the subject-matter. Similar issues can arise where it is sought to limit an indemnity to matters known to the indemnifying party. In transactions involving large (perhaps multi-site) businesses the issue of warrantor's knowledge can sometimes be further complicated by provisions in the sale and purchase agreement to the effect that only the actual knowledge of a small class of persons (perhaps at senior management level) is relevant, in which case the purchaser may wish to see additional wording incorporated requiring such persons to have made due and careful enquiry of lower-level management who are responsible for environmental matters at individual site level .

Time limitations

20.53 It is usual for limitations to be placed upon the time periods for notifying claims under environmental indemnities and for breach of warranties. An appropriate limitation period for some (non-environment related) warranty provisions may not necessarily be appropriate in the case of environmental liabilities, which of their nature may not become apparent for many years, though sometimes it is suggested that time limits for environmental provisions be aligned with those for tax liabilities. Consideration therefore needs to be given as to whether different limitation periods should be negotiated in relation to bringing warranty or indemnity claims in respect of environmental liabilities. From the purchaser's point of view, too short a period can present difficult problems in that it may be necessary to investigate immediately to establish whether there are any problems giving rise to possible grounds for claim, which could result in liabilities crystallising sooner than would otherwise be the case. Negotiation of an unreasonably short period may therefore be something of a mixed blessing for the seller. It is not unusual for environmental indemnities covering soil and groundwater contamination to contain "hard" triggers, requiring for example unprovoked regulatory action in order for claims to be triggered under the indemnity; such indemnities may also include restrictions on the purchaser's ability to claim where the claim arises as a result of post-completion investigations, other than where required under environmental law or by a regulatory authority exercising its enforcement powers. It may be reasonable in such circumstances for the purchaser to insist upon a longer time period for notifying claims, given the need to wait for third party action to trigger an indemnity claim. The issue of time limitations is closely linked to that of the conditions to be satisfied for a claim, considered below.

Caps and thresholds

Sellers will almost invariably seek a "cap" on their liabilities under **20.54** warranties and indemnities: often with reference to a percentage of the amount of consideration paid for the target company or assets. Environmental liabilities do not necessarily bear any relation to the amount of consideration paid for the "asset" which gives rise to the liability; however, a justification that is usually given for limiting liabilities to the amount of consideration paid is that, if substantial liabilities do become apparent, then the purchaser (in the case of a share acquisition) may avoid further liability by allowing the target company to be placed in solvent liquidation. This, however, is not necessarily a sound argument, since there may be very good reasons why a purchaser would not wish to abandon the target in this way.[35] It is also common for liability to be subject to thresholds, below which no claim can be made.[36] Sometimes environmental indemnities are negotiated on the basis that different caps and other financial limitations (such as de minimis and aggregate thresholds) apply to specified categories of indemnified losses—perhaps also distinguishing between known and unknown issues—as a mechanism for further limiting a seller's liability with reference to particular sites or contamination problems.

Effect of post-completion events

The underlying contamination problems that can result in environmental **20.55** liabilities may be of an on-going nature spanning both the period before and after completion. Whilst warrantors and indemnifiers may be willing to accept limited risks in relation to liabilities that arise after completion as the result of pre-existing contamination, they are not generally inclined to assume liabilities caused by the purchaser's or target company's activities after completion. This will be particularly important where a business is being sold as a going concern or where a site forming part of the assets is to be the subject of a change of use or other development which could materially increase the risk of a remediation requirement arising. Environmental warranty and indemnity provisions are therefore often limited so as to provide that the warrantor or indemnifier shall not be liable for any

---

[35] Neil Sinclair, *Warranties and Indemnities on Share Sales* (3rd edn, 1992), p.23.; W. J. L. Knight, *The Acquisition of Private Companies* (6th edn, 1993), p.132.
[36] For a case construing a threshold provision, see *RWE Nukem Ltd v AEA Technology Plc* [2005] EWCA Civ 1192 (CA).

claim which would not have arisen but for an act, event, omission or default occurring after completion. Care needs to be taken in considering how this type of standard limitation provision might apply in the context of a contaminated site. For example, simple and unqualified use of the words "omission or default" could imply that a purchaser would not be able to claim under a warranty where the purchaser has failed to take action to rectify some pre-existing state of contamination.[37] Other typical provisions may operate to limit the seller's liability where the claim arises or is increased as a result of post-completion acts of the purchaser, such as intrusive investigative works (other than where required by law); disclosure of information to the regulatory authorities (again, other than where required by law); closure, decommissioning, demolition or sale of the relevant site; admissions of liability to third party claimants; and failure to act as a reasonable and prudent operator.

Indemnities and negligence

20.56 A important point related to post-completion events is that of negligence by the indemnified party. On ordinary principles an indemnity will be construed against the person in whose favour it is given and will not cover loss due to a person's own negligence or that of his servants unless adequate and clear words were used, or unless the indemnity could have no reasonable meaning unless so applied.[38] In particular, where the loss in question arises concurrently from breach of statutory duty and negligence the indemnity may be construed as not extending to the negligence.[39] These principles could potentially be very difficult to apply in cases where it is alleged that the post completion actions (or inaction) of the purchaser have exacerbated a pre-existing problem, or have turned a possible liability into an actual one.

Counter-indemnities

20.57 It is important to achieve as complete and unambiguous an allocation of risk as possible. For example, where a seller agrees to indemnify a purchaser in respect of environmental liabilities up to a maximum of £15,000,000, does this imply that the purchaser is accepting all other risks? There may also have been provisions in the sale and purchase agreement designed to effect an express transfer of such liabilities to the purchaser, subject to limited contractual indemnities agreed in favour of the purchaser. Bearing in mind that in an asset sale the seller retains the residual risk as original polluter, logically the purchaser should provide a counter-indemnity to the seller against all liability in excess of that figure. The availability of the Pt IIA risk transfer mechanisms (such as the "sold with information" exclusion test under paras D.57—D.61 of DEFRA Circular 01/2006) may provide some comfort to sellers in circumstances where their purchasers are (as may often be the case) unwilling or unable to provide such counter-indemnities.

---

[37] Neil Sinclair, *Warranties and Indemnities on Share Sales* (3rd edn, 1992), p. 31.

[38] *Canada Steam Ship Lines Ltd v The King* [1952] A.C. 192; *Walters v Whessoe* (1960) 6 B.L.R. 35.

[39] *E. E. Caledonia Ltd v Orbit Valve Company Europe QBD*, May 28, 1993; *cf. Smith v South Wales Switchgear* [1978] 1 W.L.R. 165.

Conditions of claims

20.58 Clear conditions and procedures need to be laid down in respect of claims for breach of warranties or under indemnities. Conditions which are excessively onerous can substantially negate or diminish the protection of such provisions. Elaborate claims provisions are commonly employed in the context of environmental indemnities, including various trigger conditions or combinations of conditions requiring certain criteria to be satisfied in order for indemnity claims to be made, for example:

(a) the existence of relevant contamination;

(b) the existence of actual claims by third parties or regulatory authorities; or

(c) expenditure being incurred on clean-up.

20.59 A seller will not wish liability to be triggered simply by the discovery of contamination. Many sites are contaminated and may continue in that condition without resulting in the imposition of any liabilities or costs on the owner. On the other hand, a purchaser may not wish the ability to claim to be restricted to situations where a third party sues or a regulatory authority seeks clean-up: for one thing the purchaser may wish to put the problems right before that happens, and for another delays in a third party or regulatory authority discovering the problem and deciding to take action may take the claims outside any agreed time limit for the indemnity. Out of pocket expenditure by the purchaser on clean-up could be used as the trigger for a claim, but the seller will need protection against costs being incurred unnecessarily or against unreasonable expenditure. It may be possible to limit such circumstances to cases where contamination would or could result in liability or have a material adverse effect on the conduct of the business by the purchaser. However, both of these formulations involve a degree of subjective judgment and inherent uncertainties for the parties, which increases the potential for disputes between them.

20.60 What amounts to a trigger for a claim is of significant importance, as is shown by the few reported cases on environmental indemnities. The construction of a complex set of environmental indemnity provisions was considered in *BAL 1996 Ltd v British Alcan Aluminium Plc*,[40] where there had been the sale of a business which included land on which industrial waste had been deposited since the 1930s and which continued in use as the site for disposal of the business's waste under a waste management licence. There was concern as to the presence of ammonia from the site in the groundwater. After completion, there were discussions between the Environment Agency and the purchaser, which culminated in a letter from the Agency complaining of a breach of a licence condition relating to site restoration and referred to the powers available to the Agency to enforce the condition. The indemnity provision required there to have been a serious threat of proceedings received in writing. In the context of an application by the seller to have the buyer's claim under the indemnity

---

[40] [2006] Env. L.R. 26, QB TCC.

struck out, it was held that the clause on its true construction did not require an express threat of proceedings and that it could not be said that the buyer's claim had no reasonable prospect of success. Further, it was held that action already taken by the buyer which had incurred expenditure was not to be categorised as "voluntary action" which was excluded from the indemnity.[41]

20.61   Similarly, in *Eastern Counties Leather Plc v Eastern Counties Leather Group Ltd*[42] an indemnity was given in respect of "demands, claims, actions or proceedings" commenced by the Environment Agency arising out of an incident in which chemicals used at a tannery had contaminated a groundwater supply source.[43] The Agency wrote to the indemnified party asking for it to prepare proposals for remedial works, failing which it would serve a works notice under s.161A of the Water Resources Act. It was held at first instance that on a proper construction of that letter, the Agency had made a "claim" for the purposes of the indemnity; it was not necessary that an actual works should have been served. Importantly, the court also rejected an argument by the indemnifying party that a term should be implied that the indemnified party should not do anything to incite or encourage the Agency to make a claim; accordingly if a seller wishes such a restriction to be imposed on the indemnified buyer it should expressly stipulate this. The case was appealed on a limited point relating to what works the indemnified party had undertaken to carry out, but the more generally important first instance rulings were not appealed.[44]

20.62   The negotiation of financial limitations such as de minimis and aggregate thresholds for claims may operate to reduce the risks to the seller of claims being brought under the relevant warranties or indemnities, by placing responsibility on the purchaser for costs up to the levels of the thresholds. Another mechanism is the use of costs sharing provisions, which typically operate on a sliding scale under which the proportion of costs borne by the seller under an indemnity diminishes over time, depending on when the claim is made (e.g. if the claim is made in the first year of the indemnity period the seller might bear 100 per cent, whereas if made in the third year the seller's liability might be limited to 70 per cent of the costs incurred, with the purchaser bearing the other 30 per cent). From the point of view of a company's finance director, the risks of claims arising under environmental warranties and indemnities is a question of the size of any provision to be made in reserves on the balance sheet, the date at which payments may have to be made and the spread of such payments; any tax consequences may also be important.

20.63   It will also have to be established whether costs of investigating possible contamination or actual or potential claims is covered within any indemnity: such costs can of course be very considerable.

---

[41] The case contains detailed examination of other aspects of the drafting, and repays reading in full.

[42] [2002] EWHC 494 (Ch); [2002] Env. L.R. 34.

[43] The common law claim arising from the incident is discussed at paras 14.19 *et seq.*.

[44] [2002] EWCA Civ 1636; [2003] Env. L.R. 13.

Mechanics of claims

20.64 Clear procedures should exist for the making of claims and the conduct of claims. Where the indemnity is against third party liability or regulatory claims, the indemnifying party may wish to have the right to take over the conduct of the action or response to the claim. There should be provisions for mutual co-operation, assistance and exchange of information in relation to any claims, and the ability of one party to settle or compromise the claim without the consent of the other may need to be restricted.

Date of application of warranties or indemnities

20.65 Provision should be made in relation to any interval between exchange of contracts for purchase of the target company and the date of completion. Where the sellers are continuing to run the target company in that interim period, the purchaser may wish to make provision as to the way in which the business should be run so as to lessen the risk of contamination occurring during that interim period. Additionally, the purchaser will wish the warranties to apply both to the date of exchange of contracts and at completion, and for any relevant events in the interim period (such as spills or the discovery of contamination) to be disclosed.

Loss of profits

20.66 The first priority of an indemnity will probably be to cover third party liabilities and the direct costs of on-site clean-up or statutory claims relating to such clean-up. It is more unusual for indemnities to address expressly the indirect costs of such operations, such as loss of profit, production or business, or internal costs.[45] Yet such costs may in fact present a considerable burden. In some cases, elaborate formulae have been devised, for example limiting the indemnity in relation to loss of profits by reference to earlier profits, and avoiding any obligation to indemnify in respect of unusual profits or lost contracts.

Practical problems with warranties and indemnities

20.67 Aside from the drafting problems mentioned above, both warranties and indemnities share the common problem that they are only as good as the financial strength of the warrantor or covenantor, respectively. Additionally, claims under indemnities and warranties in relation to pollution problems can be costly, protracted and difficult to make out: for example, it may be very difficult (or at least very expensive, even with modern forensic techniques) to establish whether or not pollution or contamination (or damage thereby caused) took place before or after completion, or both.

Many sellers (and purchasers) will stop short of carrying out intrusive investigations in the context of a sale and purchase transaction owing to

---

[45] The inclusion of internal costs would be intended to cover the situation where large organisations devolve financial management responsibilites to a number of cost centres. It is common in these situations for a range of expenses to be incurred initially in a given cost centre and then subsequently distributed on a user pays basis throughout the organisation.

the prospect of opening a Pandora's Box[46] of problems, in circumstances where (for the seller) there is no certainty the purchaser will proceed with the transaction or (for the purchaser) the discovery of significant contamination could increase the prospects of prematurely crystallising liabilities for the business. The problematic nature of acquiring knowledge of contamination is evident from the "knowingly permitted" limb of liability under Pt IIA and also under ss. 161A–D of the Water Resources Act 1991. It also will assume more importance in future as a result of the implementation of the EU environmental liability directive, which requires operators to take preventative action to avoid environmental damage occurring; to own up to regulators to having caused environmental damage should it occur; and to make and agree proposals to remediate any environmental damage caused.[47]

20.68 Notwithstanding the problems associated with having knowledge of contamination, it is generally preferable in practice to discover as much as possible about the assets before completion to enable the risks to be reflected in the purchase price. Even where the liability risks have been factored into the price, warranties and indemnities must still have an important role, in that there will still be residual risk which needs to be allocated (for example, in relation to unknown contamination). The existence of data about the contaminative state of the property will in that event be useful to provide a "baseline" as at the date of exchange or completion, thereby reducing uncertainty as to where the risk falls under the contractual provisions.

Finance transactions

20.69 As discussed earlier in this chapter and elsewhere in this book, the persons who may incur liabilities in relation to contaminated land include the polluter (as the person who caused or knowingly permitted the pollution) or, where the polluter cannot be traced, the owner or occupier of the property. An owner or occupier of a property may accordingly have liability as such for so long as it owns the relevant property or occupies it. Causing pollution involves strict liability in the sense that it is not necessary to establish fault or negligence—all that is needed is to establish that a person was responsible for an event or chain of events which leads to pollution. To have knowingly permitted pollution requires the power to do something about the set of circumstances, even if the nature of that power is not clear. This general point is confirmed by the position of lenders under Pt IIA, as explained by Earl Ferrers when the Environment Bill was making its way through Parliament in 1994/95. In particular he stated that he was:

"... advised that there is no judicial decision which supports the contention that a lender, by virtue of the act of lending the

---

[46] A reference from Greek legend to the box given by Jupiter to Pandora for her to present upon her marriage to Epimetheus, who upon opening the box released all the evils which have ever since continued to afflict the world.

[47] See Ch.14.

money only, could be said to have 'knowingly permitted' the substances to be in, on or under the land such that it is contaminated land. This would be the case if for no other reason than that the lender, irrespective of any covenants it may have required from the polluter as to its environmental behaviour, would have no permissive rights over the land in question to prevent contamination occurring or continuing."[48]

20.70 This suggests the position would be different in circumstances where such permissive rights (or other analogous rights, such as the right of a lender to enforce the covenants under a finance agreement) were retained by a lender. Indeed the legislation implies that a mortgagee who takes possession of land could incur liabilities as a knowing permitter, without expressly saying that a lender will necessarily become such as a result of taking such possession. Elsewhere, there is an available exclusion for lenders where their actions might be construed as knowingly permitting by reason of the provision or withdrawal of financial assistance. However, this does little to indicate what form of control over the borrower might be necessary to place a lender in this position.

20.71 It seems unlikely that a decision to advance funds pursuant to a loan or facilities agreement would lead to a lender incurring liability for causing pollution at a secured property since this is, arguably, not sufficiently positive or proximate conduct to constitute causation in the context of strict liability. But might such a decision result in a lender incurring liability for having knowingly permitted the presence of the pollution? To have knowingly permitted pollution requires (i) knowledge (actual, implied or constructive) or a deliberate disregard of circumstances; and (ii) power to prevent the pollution or the continuance of pollution. The permission to pollute may be granted verbally or in writing or inferred from conduct, such as a deliberate disregard of information. Knowledge in itself is not sufficient to attract liability. It must be linked to permitting pollution. In the absence of knowledge, it is not possible to have knowingly permitted pollution. Much then would depend on the circumstances and, importantly, how the covenants are structured in the relevant loan finance agreement. For example, there may be no obligation on the borrower to inform the lender of any potentially polluting activity, save where such activity would, essentially, have a material adverse effect or constitute a loan event of default. In the absence of knowledge, it is not possible to knowingly permit pollution. Similarly, there may be no express powers reserved in the finance agreement whereby the lender could prevent pollution by the relevant borrower. Even if the lender had knowledge of a potentially polluting activity by a borrower, the monies under the relevant finance agreement may already have been advanced and the lender may have no right to demand repayment of the monies for that reason (unless the same constitutes a loan event of default). Moreover, it might be argued that any potentially polluting activity of which the lender may have knowledge is likely to be regarded as unrelated to the purpose of the finance agreement and the application of the proceeds of the monies by the borrower.

[48] HL Vol.560 col.1497 incorporated into Annex 2 of the Circular at para.9.11.

20.72   Part IIA defines "owner" in relation to any land in England and Wales as "a person (other than a mortgagee not in possession) who, whether in his own right or as trustee for any other person, is entitled to receive the rack rent of the land, or, where the land is not let at a rack rent, would be so entitled if it were so let".[49] A lender will not become the "owner" of a secured property for the purposes of Pt IIA merely by virtue of being a beneficiary of the security to be granted under a debenture. A lender would only become "owner" for this purpose if it were to become a mortgagee in possession of the relevant mortgaged property upon enforcement of the debenture. However, alternative remedies are normally available to the lender on the enforcement of such security, such as the appointment of administrators, or of a receiver appointed under the Law of Property Act 1925. Until the relevant borrower goes into liquidation, the receiver would be an agent of the relevant borrower, and its appointment would not, therefore, result in the lender becoming a mortgagee in possession of the relevant mortgaged property unless the lender unduly directed or interfered with and influenced the receiver's actions.[50] Following a borrower going into liquidation, the agency of the receiver would cease and the receiver would either act as principal or act as agent of the lender. If the receiver is deemed to be principal, the lender would only become a mortgagee in possession of the relevant mortgaged property if it unduly directed or interfered with and influenced the receiver's actions.[51] If the lender were to be deemed principal, it would become a mortgagee in possession.

Company accounts and listing particulars

20.73 Liabilities arising from contaminated land may be sufficiently serious to require reference in listing particulars or company accounts. In relation to company accounts (and, where applicable, group accounts) prepared under the Companies Act 1985, the key principles are that the company accounts must present a true and fair view and that only material amounts need be shown or disclosed.[52] The Companies Act 1985 Sch.4, requires provision to be made for liabilities or loss which are either likely to be incurred or certain to be incurred but are uncertain as to amount or as to the date on which they will arise. In the case of a contingent liability not provided for in the accounts, the amount or estimated amount of that liability must be disclosed, together with its legal nature and whether any valuable security has been given by the company in connection with the liability.[53] "True and

---

[49] s.78A(9) EPA 1990.

[50] See *Noyes v Pollock* (1886) 32 Ch.D.53 and *Mexborough UDC v Harrison* [1964] 2 All E.R. 109).

[51] See *American Express International Banking Corp v Hurley* [1985] 3 All E.R. 564, where it was stated that "if the receiver continues to act, he does not automatically become the agent of the mortgagee but he may become so if the mortgage treats him as such".

[52] Jenny Bough, *Company Accounts* (1987), p.4. As a consequence of the International Accounting Standards Regulation (Regulation 1606/2002), the Companies Act 1985 was amended to recognise that companies subject to the Regulation must prepare their accounts in accordance with the Regulation's requirements.

[53] Companies Act 1985 Sch.4 para.50. Regulations to be made under s.396 of the Companies Act 2006 will replace these requirements from a date to be appointed.

fair view", though referred to in statute,[54] is not defined and ultimately can only be authoritatively interpreted by a court, which would doubtlessly look for guidance to the ordinary practices of professional accountants.[55] Whilst the meaning of "true and fair" remains the same, the content given to the concept can change over time[56]: this is important to bear in mind in the context of contaminated land, which may now have an impact on the valuation of assets and liabilities far greater than could have been foreseen when many standards of accounting practice were developed.

Also, s.417 of the Companies Act 2006 provides that in their Business **20.74** Reviews—which are to inform members of the company and help them assess how the directors have performed—quoted companies must, to the extent necessary for an understanding of the development, performance or position of the company's business, include (among other things) information about environmental matters.

The issue of what should be disclosed can also arise in relation to listing **20.75** particulars or prospectuses prepared by companies in connection with the admission of securities to the Official List of the Financial Services Authority (FSA) and to trading on the London Stock Exchange. Under the general duty of disclosure contained in s.80 of the Financial Services and Markets Act 2000 prospectuses must contain all such information as investors and their professional advisors would reasonably require, and reasonably expect to find there, for the purpose of making an informed assessment of:

(a) the assets and liabilities, financial position, profits and losses, and prospects of the issuer of the securities; and

(b) the rights attaching to those securities.

It should be noted that under s.80(2) of the Financial Services and **20.76** Markets Act 2000 the information required to be included in prospectuses under the general duty of disclosure is not limited to information that is within the knowledge of the persons responsible for the prospectus, but also includes information which it would be reasonable for such persons to obtain by making enquiries. Prospectuses must also contain the prescribed information set out in the FSA's prospectus rules. In particular, prospectuses must contain information relating to any actual, pending or threatened governmental, legal or arbitration proceedings which may have or

---

[54] Companies Act 1985, s.226A (Companies Act individual accounts) and s.227A (Companies Act group accounts). As from a date to be appointed, these sections will be repealed and replaced by s.396 and s.404 of the Companies Act 2006.

[55] See the joint opinion of Leonard Hoffman Q.C. and Mary Arden (as they then were), quoted at Jenny Bough, *Company Accounts* (1987), p.197, and the subsequent opinion by Mary Arden Q.C. (taking into account the changes made by the Companies Act 1989) which was issued as an Appendix to the Foreword of Accounting Standards—Statements of Standard Accounting Practice of the Accounting Standards Board. See also the legal opinion published in June 2005 by The Financial Reporting Review Panel on the effect of the IAS Regulation on the requirement for accounts to give a true and fair view.

[56] See the joint opinion of Leonard Hoffman Q.C. and Mary Arden (as they then were), quoted at Jenny Bough, *Company Accounts* (1987), p.197, and the subsequent opinion by Mary Arden Q.C. (taking into account the changes made by the Companies Act 1989).

have recently had significant effects on an issuer's (and/or its group's) financial position or profitability.

20.77 In practice the general disclosure duty and the more detailed prospectus rules may be very important because a high proportion of companies will have land assets, which may well have been subject to one or more contaminative uses. Actual or contingent liabilities or proceedings associated with contaminated land or the impact of contamination on the value of assets may be of such a magnitude as to require disclosure either under the general duty of disclosure or under the Prospectus Rules.

Corporate Insolvency

Receivership

20.78 A receiver may be appointed out of court either under an express power contained in the security document, or alternatively by a mortgagee under the statutory powers of the Law of Property Act 1925. Commonly in practice a debenture holder will appoint under an express power contained in the mortgage deed, and a mortgagee will appoint under the statutory powers contained in the Law of Property Act.

20.79 In relation to the first category of receiver, the Insolvency Act 1986 confers special powers and status upon a receiver or manager of the whole or substantially the whole of the company's property (an administrative receiver). As a result of the Enterprise Act 2002, except in a number of limited circumstances,[57] it is not possible to appoint an administrative receiver under a debenture or charge entered into subsequent to September 15, 2003. Rights of a debenture/charge holder are preserved however by way of an ability to appoint an administrator if the debenture/charge amounts to a "qualifying floating charge".[58] This distinction between a receiver and an administrative receiver is capable of presenting a difficulty in a case where part of the company's assets are subject to potential environmental liabilities: the lender may wish to exclude the problematic property from the receivership, but doing so may result in the receiver failing to be appointed as an administrative receiver, and consequently not having the special powers of Sch.1 to the Insolvency Act 1986. The problem is perhaps in practice theoretical rather than real, since nowadays most debentures and fixed charges will contain extensive powers removing the need for reliance on Sch.1.

20.80 There are a number of pertinent points to note about the position of an administrative receiver, or receiver and manager, in relation to contaminated land and environmental liability. First, and perhaps most importantly, a receiver will be regarded as an agent of the company, rather than of the lender, either by virtue of express provisions commonly included in the debenture, or (in relation to administrative receivers only) under the statutory presumption of agency by s.44(1)(a) of the Insolvency Act 1986. The effect of this agency is to insulate the debenture holder from the

---

[57] See ss.72A–H of the Insolvency Act 1986.
[58] See 14–21A Sch.B1 the Insolvency Act 1986 para.20.87 below.

consequences of wrongful acts committed by the receiver.[59] It follows from this that actions of the receiver may have adverse consequences for the company and it has been suggested in one case that a receiver may not exercise his discretion so as to lead to the commission of an offence by the company.[60] This may have important implications in the case where property is subject to a statutory notice or other requirement, failure to comply with which constitutes an offence.

Secondly, in relation to a receiver appointed under a debenture, the **20.81** receiver will have the power to carry on the day to day process of realisation and management of the company's property without interference from the board of directors.[61] Although the receiver is therefore the sole person in charge of the company's operations, the corporate structure of the company (including the statutory duties of the directors) however remains in place. This power may entail responsibility under environmental legislation or common law on the part of the receiver. Interference with the rights of third parties, however innocent, may be actionable in tort[62]; the extent to which a receiver may be responsible for the acts of employees of the company probably depends on his degree of personal conduct and culpability in the same way as a director of the company, since the employees are not employees of the receiver himself.[63]

As mentioned below, the position may change dramatically if the **20.82** company should go into liquidation. One Canadian case[64] suggests that where certain properties managed by the receiver are subject to environmental liabilities under statute, an administrative order may be addressed to the receiver rather than the company and indeed that this may involve application of proceeds or profits from other, non-problematic, assets managed by the receiver. It was suggested that the receiver cannot pick and choose between assets so as to walk away from liability on problematic assets, saying simply that remedial action would diminish distribution to secured creditors.

Thirdly, the receiver, whether appointed under a debenture or under the **20.83** Law of Property Act 1925, may potentially be liable in his capacity as occupier for breaches of legislative requirements. In *Lord Advocate v Aero Technologies (in receivership)*[65] injunctive relief was obtained against a receiver

[59] *Re Simms* [1934] Ch.1. It does not apply where the receiver is appointed by the court, in which case he acts as principal, subject to an implied right of indemnity in respect of liabilities properly incurred.

[60] *Re John Willment (Ashford) Ltd* [1979] 2 All E.R. 615.

[61] *Gomba Holdings Limited v Homan* [1986] 1 W.L.R. 1301 at 1306.

[62] See *Kerr on Receivers and Administrators* (18th edn, 2005), p.488 (together with amendments contained in the first supplement to the 18th edn).

[63] See *Kerr on Receivers and Administrators* (18th edn, 2005), p.488 (together with amendments contained in the first supplement to the 18th edn).

[64] *Panamericana de Bienes y Servicios, SA v Northern Badger Oil and Gas Ltd* (1991) 81 D.L.R. (4d) 280. See also the earlier Ontario Court of Appeal decision in *Canada Trust Co v Bulora Corp Ltd* (1980) 34 C.B.R. (NS) 145; affirmed 39 C.B.R. (N.S.) 152. But compare *A.G. (Ontario) v Tyre King Tyre Recycling Ltd* (1992) 8 C.E.L.R. (NS) 202 and *Re Lamford Forest Products Ltd* (1992) 86 D.L.R. (4th) 434; also the 1992 Bankruptcy and Insolvency Act which makes it clear that trustees have no personal liability in respect of environmental conditions arising before their appointment, save where the condition arose as a result of due diligence on their part: [1993] Env. Liab. 86.

[65] 1991 S.L.T. 134 (Outer House).

to prevent explosive materials being left in an insecure condition, in breach of the Explosives Act 1875, which applies to the occupier of a factory. In another case, *Meigh v Wickenden*[66] a receiver was held liable for contravention of Factories Act requirements as the occupier; the receiver in question had no practical or technical expertise in running a factory, and left these matters in the hands of the directors. Nonetheless, it was held, the receiver "was complete master of the affairs of the company" and "had absolute and complete power to manage the property of which he took possession".[67] The argument that he was agent of the company did not alter this: nonetheless, certainly for rating purposes a receiver will not be regarded as displacing the company as occupier, his occupation being treated as that of the company.[68]

20.84 Fourthly, the fact that the receiver may be in receipt of rents from the property, or would be entitled to be in receipt of such rents were any payable, may result in the receiver being regarded as "owner" of the property and consequently liable under any environmental legislation which bites upon the owner.[69] The question is in what capacity the receiver is receiving the rents; on general principles, so long as the receiver is acting as the agent of the company, he ought not to be regarded as receiving rents in his own right.

20.85 It should also be remembered that the appointment of a receiver is no bar to the company being wound up, and the effect of winding-up will be that the receiver will no longer be agent of the company, now in liquidation. He will either need the approval of the debenture holders to act as their agent, or he will be acting as principal. Thus the receiver's position is fundamentally different before and after liquidation. The power of a receiver to carry out a clean-up operation in relation to the property will depend upon the terms of the debenture or mortgage, and upon any statutory powers. It seems likely that the extent of statutory powers applying to administrative receivers under Sch.1 to the Insolvency Act 1986 could be sufficient to allow such clean-up costs to be incurred; it is much less likely that more limited powers of a Law of Property Act receiver under s.109 of the Law of Property Act 1925 would be wide enough for this purpose. One potential difficulty could be whether powers which are related to the carrying on of the company's business would necessarily apply to all clean-up costs.

20.86 Unlike a liquidator, a receiver has no power to disclaim onerous property, and therefore will need to persuade the lender to release problematic properties from the receivership or, as a matter of last resort, the receiver can resign. It will be appreciated that any receiver of a property which turns out to be contaminated may be in an exposed position; this risk being made all the worse by the speed with which a receiver is required to accept appointment.[70] Limited protection is afforded

---

[66] [1942] 2 K.B. 160.

[67] [1942] 2 K.B. 160 at 168.

[68] Ratford v Northavon DC [1987] Q.B. 357.

[69] See *Bacup Corp v Smith* [1890] 44 Ch. D. 395; *Solomons v Gertzensten Ltd* [1954] 2 Q.B. 243; *Midland Bank v Conway Corp* [1965] 1 W.L.R. 1165.

[70] Before the end of the next business day after receiving the letter of appointment: Insolvency Act 1986 s.33. In practice however, the receiver will previously have investigated the situation on behalf of the lender.

by s.78X(3) of Pt IIA, which provides that a person acting in a "relevant capacity"[71] shall not thereby be personally liable under Pt IIA to bear the whole or any part of the cost of doing any thing by way of remediation, unless that thing is to any extent referable to substances whose presence in, on or under the contaminated land in question is a result of any act done or omission made by him which it was unreasonable for a person acting in that capacity to do or make. Nevertheless, it is for the receiver to protect his or her own position by obtaining an appropriate indemnity from the lender as a condition of appointment. Save in the case of the clearing banks such an indemnity is standard practice: but the receiver should be wary that the indemnity (whether express or implied by common law) may not extend to negligence or unlawful or improper conduct on his part. The right to an indemnity against tort damages or fines may therefore depend on whether the receiver acted properly and with due care.[72] The common law indemnity will be limited to the assets[73] whereas environmental liabilities may be of such a scale as to exceed the value of those assets, particularly if those assets comprise contaminated land.

Insolvency Act administrators

The Enterprise Act 2002 introduced (save in relation to certain excep- **20.87** tions[74]) a new administration regime set out in Sch.B1 to the Insolvency Act 1986. Under the new regime an administrator is appointed judicially by the court on an administration application, or extra-judicially by the holder of a "qualifying floating charge", or by the company or by its directors.[75] An administrator under the Insolvency Act 1986 is in essence a receiver and manager of the company, appointed in order to facilitate one of the statutory purposes set out at para.3 of Sch.B1 to the Insolvency Act 1986.[76] The administrator has the power to do anything necessary or expedient for the management of the affairs, business and property of the company and has also all the powers statutorily conferred upon an administrative receiver.[77] Also, like a receiver, the administrator is deemed to act as the company's agent.[78] However, unlike a receiver, who may ask the lender to

---

[71] Subs.(4) of s.78X defines a person acting in a relevant capacity as including a person acting as an insolvency practitioner, within the meaning of s.388 of the Insolvency Act 1986.

[72] The standard of care required is probably that of a reasonably prudent man of business: *Speight v Gaunt* (1883) 9 App. Cas. 1 at 19.

[73] See *Boehm v Goodall* [1911] 1 Ch. 155; *Johnston v Courtney* [1920] 2 W.W.R. 459.

[74] s.249 Enterprise Act 2002 the previous administration regime remains in place in relation to certain specified public-utility companies and building societies. It also subsists where a petition for an administration order was presented to the court prior to September 15, 2003 (SI 2003/2093 art.3(2)).

[75] *Kerr on Receivers and Administrators* (18th edn 2005), p.274 (together with amendments contained in the first supplement to the 18th edn).

[76] Para.3 sets out three possible objectives for the administrator: (i) rescuing the company as a going concern; (ii) achieving a better result for the company's creditors as a whole than would be likely if the company were wound up (without first being in administration); or (iii) realising property in order to make a distribution to one or more secured or preferential creditors. The administrator may only consider objectives (ii) and (iii) if it is not possible to achieve objectives (i) or (ii) respectively.

[77] Insolvency Act 1986 Sch.B1 paras 59–63.

[78] Insolvency Act 1986 Sch.B1 para.69.

release properties from the receivership, the administrator has no obvious means of getting rid of environmentally problematic properties; nor is it common for an administrator to seek an indemnity (where relevant) from the party who appointed them. In contrast to an administrative receiver however,[79] an administrator is not deemed by statute to be personally liable on contracts entered into by him.

Liquidators

20.88 There are significant differences between the position of a liquidator and that of a receiver or an administrator. The powers of liquidators are more rigidly confined within the framework of the Insolvency Act 1986: there is no obvious power to conduct remedial or clean up operations in relation to contaminated property, though this may well be implied within the statutory power under Sch.4 to the Insolvency Act to do all things as may be necessary for the winding up of the company's affairs and distribution of its assets.

20.89   The basic duty of the liquidator on a compulsory liquidation under s.143 of the Insolvency Act is to secure the assets of the company and get in, realise and distribute them to the company's creditors and, if there is a surplus, to the persons entitled to it; thus the obligation is to realise the assets as efficiently as possible and to satisfy the liabilities in so far as the realised assets permit. Generally, there would appear less scope for personal liability on the part of a liquidator in relation to environmental problems, though this possibility cannot be precluded. Certainly in practice a liquidator is less likely than a receiver or administrator to run a business on an ongoing basis.

20.90   The liquidator is not an agent of the company in liquidation, and therefore the arguments which apply in the case of receivers and administrators as to the exercise of powers so as to avoid the company committing an offence may be of less force in relation to a liquidator faced with a statutory notice requiring remedial measures. Indeed to prefer such a notice to claims of other creditors, in the absence of any statutory preference or priority given to the notice, would appear to run counter to the liquidator's general duties. However, whilst it is true that a liquidator is not an agent of the company, his status is in practice similar, as the company can only act through him. For example, the liquidator might procure that certain assets of the company are put up for sale. To the extent that the liquidator incurs liability in realising those assets, or needs to expend money in realising them, then this will be a proper expense of the liquidation which he may quite properly pay out in preference to the claims of ordinary creditors. The crucial question in relation to contaminated land will usually be what liabilities and costs were reasonably and necessarily incurred to achieve proper realisation of the asset.

---

[79] Although an agent is not normally personally liable on a contract that it enters into on behalf of its principal, s.44(1)(b) of the Insolvency Act 1986 provides that administrative receivers will be so liable. Administrative receivers are however also entitled to be indemnified in respect of that liability out of the assets of the company (s.44(1)(c) of the Insolvency Act 1986).

Another significant point of difference is the liquidator's express power **20.91**
to disclaim onerous property under ss.178–182 of the Insolvency Act 1986.
Under s.178(2) the liquidator may, by giving prescribed notice, disclaim
any onerous property notwithstanding that he has taken possession of it,
endeavoured to sell it, or otherwise exercised rights of ownership over it.
The property which may be disclaimed includes property which is not
readily sellable, or is such that it may give rise to a liability to pay money
or perform any other onerous act: this would appear to be clearly
applicable to property which is found to be contaminated and subject to
liabilities at common law or under statutory provisions. It has been held
that the s.178 power of disclaimer extends to a waste management licence
as "property" or an interest incidental to property[80]; the same reasoning
would seem applicable to a PPC permit which may impose obligations to
remediate a site contaminated by the company in liquidation. The effect of
disclaimer under s.178(4) is to terminate the rights and liabilities of the
company in the property disclaimed—it does not beyond this affect the
rights and liabilities of any other person.

However, it should be noted that under the Insolvency Act s.178(6): "Any **20.92**
person sustaining loss or damage in consequence of the operation of a
disclaimer under this section is deemed a creditor of the company to the
extent of the loss or damage and accordingly may prove for the loss or the
damage in the winding up". Thus the cost of environmental clean-up
measures at one of the company's properties, even if disclaimed so as not
to be recoverable as a liquidation expense, could ultimately increase the
company's liabilities, possibly to a significant extent.

---

[80] *Official Receiver as liquidator of (1) Celtic Extraction Ltd; (2) Bluestone Chemicals Limited v
Environment Agency* [2001] Ch 475; [2000] Env. L.R. 86, CA.

SECTION 7
TECHNICAL AND RELATED ISSUES

Chapter 21

TECHNICAL ISSUES

Technical guidance generally

The aim of this chapter is not to provide detailed definitive guidance on the **21.01** investigation, appraisal and management to contaminated land, which would be an impossible task in this context, but rather to highlight for lawyers the key issues to assist in understanding how the technical knowledge in this area is developing and how it may be relevant to transactions and other matters bearing on contaminated land.[1] These issues are part of the broader context of environmental due diligence, which is an evolving subject and encompasses a wide range of issues (such as health and safety, waste management, carbon dioxide emissions and corporate social responsibility generally) of which contaminated land is only one.[1a]

Since the publication of the first edition of this book in 1994, a great deal **21.02** of technical guidance has been produced by central Government and other bodies on how contaminated land should be addressed. The Department for Environment, Food and Rural Affairs (DEFRA) and the Environment Agency (EA) have been the primary sources of such guidance, although useful documents have also been published by the Office of the Deputy Prime Minister (ODPM), English Partnerships (EP), the Welsh Development Agency (WDA) and Scotland and Northern Ireland Forum for Environmental Research (SNIFFER).

The sheer volume of the technical guidance available, and its constantly- **21.03** changing nature, makes it impracticable and potentially misleading to produce a full list. However, reference can be made to a number of internet sources for up-to-date lists of what is available. Apart from the DEFRA and Environment Agency websites, among the most useful sources follow.

The Chartered Institute of Environmental Health (CIEH)   The Institute has a **21.04** Standing Conference on Contaminated Land, with its own website, to provide a forum and resource for local authority regulators. It publishes the Local Authority Guide to the Application of Pt 2A, extended to cover radioactively contaminated land (2007) which includes a table, setting out the key publications, as well as a newsletter.

http://www.cieh.org/

---

[1] The authors are indebted to Mr Peter Leonard, Principal, SLR Consulting Ltd and Mr Mike Quint, Associate Director, ARUP, for having contributed most of this chapter.

[1a] See e.g. the standards of the American Society of Testing and Materials (ASTM) 1527 and ISO 14015.

21.05 *The Construction Industry Research and Information Association (CIRIA)* The Association operates a Portal for contaminated land information in the UK which includes comprehensive summaries of all available guidance on good practice in the UK, and selected overseas guidance which is widely used in the UK. The database is searchable by text and by keyword.
http://www.contaminated-land.org

21.06 *Nottingham University, School of the Built Environment* The School publishes a detailed bibliography which includes website links to other sources and academic and practitioner articles.
http://www.nottingham.ac.uk/sbe/planbiblios/bibs/vacant/04.html.

The Guidance available can be broadly categorised as follows:

21.07 (1)*DEFRA/Environment Agency, Model Procedures* for the management of contaminated land (CLR 11), providing an overview and primary procedures on good technical practice. Other relevant guidance in the CLR series includes CLR 2 (1994) on preliminary site inspection, CLR 3 (1994) on documentary research, CLR 4 (1994) on sampling strategies, and CLR 6 (1995) on prioritisation procedures for further action. A number of these deal with methodologies underlying the derivation of soil guideline values: CLR 9 deals with the issues of human toxicology and intake data, CLR 9 TOX 1–10 with toxicology in relation to specific substances, and CLR 10 with the CLEA exposure model used to derive these values. CLR 10 GV 1–10 set out actual substance specific guideline values for a range of substances including arsenic, cadmium, chromium, inorganic cyanides, lead, inorganic mercury, nickel, phenol, benzo(a)pyrene and selenium.[2]

21.08 (2)*DoE Industry Profiles* providing guidance on individual contaminative processes, e.g. airports, asbestos manufacture, various types of chemical works, dockyards, engineering works, gasworks, various forms of metal manufacturing, power stations, railway land, road vehicle fuelling, service and repair, textile and dye works, and timber treatment. Older DoE guidance may still be relevant on some issues, for example Methane and Other Gases from Disused Mines (1996).

21.09 (3)*Environment Agency Technical Guidance* on types of special sites, e.g. MOD Land (P5–042/TR/01), Acid Tar Lagoons (P5–042/TR/04) and Prescribed Processes (PPC) (P5–042/TR/07).

21.10 (4)*Other technical reports and model procedures published by the Environment Agency in its R&D series*, for example on the development of soil sampling strategies (P5–066/TR, 2001), on site investigation (P5–065/TR, 2001), on the derivation of remedial targets for soil and groundwater to protect water resources (R&D Publication 20, 1999), on monitored natural attenuation of contaminants (R&D Publication 95, 2000) and on the vapour transfer of soil contaminants (R&D Technical Report P309). A useful guide to communicating understanding of contaminated land risks is produced by SNIFFER and the Agency (SR97(11)F, 1999).

21.11 (5)*CIRIA's 12–volume guidance on remedial treatment for contaminated land* (1995) covering issues such as decommissioning and demolition, site investigation and assessment, excavation and disposal, containment and

---

[2] See further discussion below, para.21.32.

hydraulic measures, ex-situ and in-situ methods of remediation, and planning and management. CIRIA publishes other guidance on specific issues, for example methane and other ground gas hazards. In some cases the CIRIA Guidance may provide the most up-to-date and authoritative guidance on a particular topic, e.g. monitoring, assessing and measuring the risks posed by ground gases in buildings (CIRIA Guidance C659).

(6)*ICRCL Guidance Notes* on specific topics, e.g. *The Development and After-* **21.12** *use of Landfill Sites* (17/78, 8th edn, 1990), *The Redevelopment of Gasworks Sites* (18/79, 5th edn, 1986), *The Redevelopment of Scrap Yards* (42/80, 2nd edn, 1983), *The Fire Hazards of Contaminated Land* (61/84, 2nd edn, 1986). Much of this advice is now somewhat dated, but the information contained is still relevant to some situations. ICRCL 59/83 on *Assessment and Redevelopment of Contaminated Land* (2nd edn, 1987) was for over 20 years the key source of technical advice used in the UK. It set threshold and trigger action levels for a selection of substances and proposed redevelopment uses. The new UK guidelines for contaminants in soil will supersede these values as they become available. ICRCL Guidelines may still be used, for example, to assess phytotoxic risks.

(7)*Building Research Establishment (BRE) guidance* on matters such as the **21.13** effect of contaminated land on building materials (BR255, 1994) and concrete in aggressive ground (BRE Special Digest 1, 2005) and on some engineering-based remediation methods, e.g. slurry trench cut-off walls (Digest 395, 1994).

Principles

Perhaps the most important principle underpinning all of the guidance is **21.14** that, for regulatory purposes, the presence of contamination itself does not normally automatically result in remediation having to take place. This is because the legislation and guidance relating to contaminated land is, mainly, risk-based, in that action only needs to be taken if the contamination is causing, or has the potential to cause, significant harm to human health or the environment. For such harm to occur, or have the potential to occur, contamination has to be present (a source), along with actual or potential pathways via which contaminants can reach actual or potential receptors in sufficient quantity to pose an unacceptable risk. The precise meaning of these terms is dealt with elsewhere, with the source-pathway-receptor philosophy being referred to as the pollutant linkage concept.[3]

As a consequence of the risk-based approach, there are no legally **21.15** enforceable standards, in the form of contaminant levels in soil, which delineate what is or is not acceptable. This must be assessed on a site-specific basis using the pollutant linkage concept and in line with the risk-based methodology described below.

Recognising the primacy of the risk-based approach, the Environment **21.16** Agency produced, in 2004, an over-arching document which describes how land contamination should be addressed in a risk-based manner. This document is referred to as CLR11 or the Model Procedures[4] and it ties

---

[3] See para.3.07.
[4] Contaminated Land Report 11, *Model Procedures for the Management of Land Contamination*, 2004.

together and signposts multiple sources of other guidance to form a coherent land contamination management methodology. Due to its importance in relation to the current state of practice regarding the technical assessment of land contamination, the methodology outlined in the Model Procedures forms the basis of the remainder of this chapter.[5] An exception to the risk-based approach arises under the Pollution Prevention and Control (England and Wales) Regulations 2000, which may require sites to be returned to their original baseline condition when a permit is surrendered, regardless of risk. In addition, under non-regulatory requirements, such as leasehold covenants and the common law, a similarly non-risk-based approach may also be necessary. In such instances, the data collection activities outlined in the Model Procedures would still be relevant, although the interpretation of the results would need to take place outside of the risk-based paradigm.

Overview of the Model Procedures

21.17 The introductory paragraph to the Model Procedures states the following:

> "The Model Procedures for the Management of Land Contamination are intended to provide the technical framework for structured decision-making about land contamination. The basic process can be adapted to apply in a range of regulatory and management contexts, subject to any specific constraints arising from these contexts. The Model Procedures are intended to assist all those involved in 'managing' the land—in particular landowners, developers, industry, professional advisers, financial service providers, planners and regulators."

21.18 The Model Procedures are divided into three parts. The first part presents the overall risk-based approach to managing land contamination and has many useful flow-charts and decision trees to that end (a useful glossary of terms is also provided and is repeated at the end of this section). The second part provides important supporting information in the form of inputs, tools, criteria and outputs, all of which relate to specific activities flagged in the first part. The third part presents an "information map", in the form of comprehensive listings of key sources of further information relevant to particular activities. In the document's own words:

> "Part 1 of the Model Procedures focuses on clearly defining the decision-making process, and the key principles that underpin it, rather than providing detailed information on particular technical activities or legal requirements. Readers should refer to Parts 2 and 3 of the Model Procedures for further technical detail, and to other sources of information and guidance, such as the websites of government departments and regulatory bodies, for information on legal requirements.

[5] A glossary of the terms used in the Model Procedures is given at para.21.101.

600

Part 2 contains detailed supporting information to the procedures contained in Part 1, presented in the form of information boxes. These contain examples of the inputs, tools, criteria and outputs used or generated throughout the process of risk management. To facilitate the use of the information boxes, each is 'badged' using a coloured page banner, flow chart reference that links the information box to a particular process stage, and a symbol that indicates the type of information being presented.

"The Information Map (Part 3) contains details of over 80 individual or sets of key publications that give more detailed technical guidance on particular aspects of the risk management process. All the documents have been issued by authoritative bodies, such as Defra and its predecessor departments, the Environment Agency and predecessors, the British Standards Institution and others."

Throughout the document, it is emphasised that the methods and techniques applicable to the risk-based management of land contamination are constantly changing and that users should familiarise themselves with relevant updates. While it is envisaged that the overall framework of the Model Procedures will remain in place for some time, the specific details of how it is applied will necessarily develop from the 2004 publication date.[6] The sections that follow summarise the risk-based methodology outlined in the Model Procedures. They are principally concerned with Pt 1 of the document, which describes the approaches to be taken for managing contaminated land under the broad terms of *risk assessment options appraisal* and the *implementation of the remediation strategy*. **21.19**

Risk Assessment

Introduction

The Model Procedures classify the entire process of assessing the contamination status of a site, and therefore establishing whether there is a need for remediation, as risk assessment. Many activities must be undertaken within the over-arching process of risk assessment, to identify the need, if any, for remediation. These activities consist of information gathering and data interpretation and they rely on myriad skills, techniques and data sources. The Model Procedures advocate a tiered approach to risk assessment, whereby simple, low-cost approaches are used initially, followed by more time-consuming, complex approaches later on. With successive tiers, the data requirements and the sophistication of the analysis increase, but the confidence in the predicted impact also increases, thereby potentially allowing a relaxation of the remediation requirements, **21.20**

---

[6] For current developments, see para.21.36ff.

if the risk assessment is favourable. In accordance with international best practice, the tiered approach enables low-risk sites to be rapidly screened out and attention to be focused on those sites where the risks, and in consequence the information needs, are greatest. It should be noted that a variety of substances can be present on contaminated sites, including naturally occurring chemicals, man-made chemicals and radionuclides. There can also be multiple exposure pathways and potential receptors of contamination. The risk-based approach requires that practitioners methodically address the possibility of unacceptable risks to all feasible receptors, via all potential pathways and from all contaminants present.

Preliminary risk assessment

Objective

21.21 The first tier of risk assessment is referred to as a preliminary risk assessment (PRA). The objective of a PRA is to gather as much information as possible about a site so that a *conceptual model* can be developed. A conceptual model is a representation of the characteristics of the site in diagrammatic or written form that shows the possible relationships between contaminants, pathways and receptors. On the basis of the initial conceptual model, any need for further assessment is then identified or a remedial strategy is developed. This stage of the assessment process has historically been referred to as a "Phase 1 study" or, in the absence of a site visit, a Desk Study. Desk Studies and Phase 1 reports can often be obtained for minimal expense, although it should be noted that their quality can vary greatly. Users of such studies should be aware that important decisions are based on them and extreme care should therefore be taken in accepting any report which is incomplete.

Data needs

21.22 The following are required for a PRA, at a minimum:

1. site visit/reconnaissance, whereby the site is inspected for obvious signs of actual or potential contamination (soil staining, fuel storage tanks, waste management activities, etc.);

2. information on site drainage;

3. site history, focusing on possible historic contaminative uses of the site;

4. location of the site in relation to nearby receptors such as houses, schools, surface water bodies, protected habitats, etc.;

5. planning requirements (i.e., whether the site is to be redeveloped and, if so, the nature of the redevelopment in terms of use, building design, etc.);

6. underlying and local geology and hydrogeology;

7. responses to local authority and EA enquiries;

8. nature of activities carried out on nearby sites (which may cause contamination to migrate onsite);

9. environmental permits and licences both for the site itself and within the vicinity, particularly those relating to waste management (e.g. landfills);

10. details of any site investigation or risk assessment activities that have already been carried out and any remedial measures that have been taken; and

11. local climate characteristics.

Some of the above information is available from commercial vendors. **21.23** Information sources on the other categories are signposted in the Model Procedures.[7]

Data interpretation

The interpretation of the data outlined above is central to a PRA. It takes **21.24** the form of the development of an outline conceptual model and requires the assimilation of the data along with expert professional judgment. As mentioned above, the primary focus of an outline conceptual model is to elucidate the existence and location of potential contaminants, pathways and receptors (pollutant linkages). This then forms the basis for decisions regarding the next steps.

Outcome of the PRA

The outcome of the PRA is an initial conceptual model of the site and a **21.25** judgment as to whether or not pollutant linkages could exist, either now or in the future. In the event that they could, then the assessment must proceed to the next stage to see if the linkages are significant, or alternatively remediation is undertaken, should it be cost-effective to do so without further assessment. In the event that no potential pollutant linkages are identified, then no further action is required. It should be noted that considerable supporting information is likely to be required if a judgment is made that no further action is required on the basis of a PRA. This is because the judgment will be based primarily on qualitative information and in many cases there could be others who might have different or opposing views, such as regulators or prospective purchasers. The conceptual model is key to such an exercise and it cannot be emphasised too strongly how important it is that this model is correct.

Generic quantitative risk assessment

Objective

In the event that the PRA indicates the existence of potential pollutant **21.26** linkages and remediation is not planned, a second tier of risk assessment is carried out, referred to as a generic quantitative risk assessment (GQRA).

---

[7] See also Ch. 22 on information generally.

The objective of a GQRA is to prove or disprove the existence of potential pollutant linkages using site-derived data and assess whether such linkages are potentially significant. It may also involve a revision of the site's initial conceptual model, on the basis of additional information that comes to light.

Data needs

21.27 An important focus of a GQRA is the intrusive investigation of the site using various techniques to obtain and analyse samples of soil and other media (e.g. groundwater). A great deal of guidance exists on site investigation techniques and it is signposted in the Model Procedures. Key considerations to be aware of are as follows:

1. Careful consideration must be given to how many locations are sampled, at what depth and from which media. Reference should be made to the conceptual model for this as well as the detailed guidance on sampling patterns signposted in the Model Procedures.

2. Site investigation activities must comply with all relevant health and safety legislation, including, if appropriate, the Construction (Design and Management) Regulations 2007.[8]

3. Logs of boreholes and trial pits should be as descriptive as possible, with any staining or odours accurately noted. The depth at which any groundwater occurs should also be identified.

4. The suite of chemicals analysed for in the samples should include all those chemicals that could occur at the site on the basis of its past or present contaminative use.

5. If the site overlies a potential aquifer, groundwater samples must normally be taken. These should be collected from suitably installed monitoring wells, the drilling and construction of which should be performed correctly.

6. As well as chemical data, additional information should be collected on site characteristics which are relevant to data interpretation, such as soil and aquifer properties.

7. Consideration should be given to whether the testing laboratory is suitably accredited. For example, for Pt IIA work, laboratory data needs to be Monitoring Certification Scheme (MCERTS) accredited.

21.28 Overall, the process of investigating a potentially contaminated site in accordance with current guidance can be extremely complex and should be performed by suitably qualified consultants. Poor site investigation can result in erroneous conclusions regarding a site's contamination status, leading to potentially significant unrecognised liabilities and/or an increase in the time and expense required to manage a site.

[8] See para.12.13.

Data interpretation

Following the completion of the intrusive investigation, the resulting **21.29**
chemical test data should be interpreted with reference to generic
guidelines and standards. As mentioned previously, there are no legally
enforceable soil standards defining contaminated land in the UK, with the
emphasis instead being on site-specific assessment. To assist with such an
assessment, the Model Procedures signpost the following:

1. Soil Guideline Values (SGVs),[9] which are chemical levels in soil
   which present a minimal risk to human health under specified
   conditions of land use and exposure;

2. the Remedial Targets Methodology, which describes how to assess
   the potential impacts of soil and groundwater contamination on
   controlled waters, using various mathematical tools and
   approaches[10];

3. a methodology for assessing potential impacts on ecological receptors[11]; and

4. guidance on the assessment of risks to property from the effects of
   hazardous chemicals.[12]

A key question regarding the interpretation of site-specific chemical test **21.30**
data is how it should be interpreted with respect to generic guidelines such
as SGVs. Guidance is available for this process, including the use of
statistical methods, as described in the Model Procedures.

Outcome of the GQRA

The outcome of the GQRA is a revised conceptual model of the site and a **21.31**
judgment as to whether or not the potential pollutant linkages identified in
the PRA actually do exist, backed up with site-specific monitoring data. A
judgment is also made as to whether the identified linkages are likely to be
significant, as required under Pt IIA, or whether further work is needed to
assess this, via a detailed quantitative risk assessment (DQRA). In the
event that generic criteria are not available for specific contaminants,
pathways or receptors, a DQRA will also be required. If the linkages are
judged to be significant on the basis of a GQRA, then the process proceeds
to options appraisal. In the event that no significant potential linkages are
identified, then no further action is required.

SGVs and the CLEA Model

The Contaminated Land Exposure Assessment (CLEA) model was released **21.32**
in 2002 and can be downloaded, along with related documents, from the
internet. Its release followed almost 10 years of development by a team

[9] See para.21.32.
[10] Discussed further at para.21.40ff.
[11] Discussed further at para.21.92.
[12] Discussed further at para.21.99.

from Nottingham Trent University and it represented an important element within the Government's Pt IIA implementation process. The CLEA model was initially designed to produce successors to the Inter-Departmental Committee on the Redevelopment of Contaminated Land (ICRCL) levels. These levels were published in the mid-1980s to aid decision-making in relation to contaminated land although, since they are not explicitly risk-based, they were deemed inappropriate for use under Pt IIA. The use of quantitative tools is important under Pt IIA since it allows the significance of "pollutant linkages" to be judged.

21.33   Using standard risk modelling techniques, CLEA produces detailed simulations of human health risk from soil contamination to produce "Soil Guideline Values" (SGVs). To date, SGVs have been produced for nine contaminants, with further values being planned for release in due course. It should be noted that CLEA is only relevant to the assessment of chronic human health risks and that other receptors, such as controlled waters, buildings and ecosystems, as well as acute human health risks, cannot be assessed using CLEA or the SGVs it generates. In terms of its technical attributes, the CLEA model is characterised by the following:

1. It produces SGVs for three land uses: residential (with and without gardens), allotments, and commercial/industrial.

2. It uses Monte Carlo techniques to develop probability density functions of SGVs, from which the 95 percentile value is taken as the final figure.

3. It can only handle one chemical at a time.

4. Eighteen age classes of individuals, with different assumed body weights, etc. are considered.

5. Ten exposure pathways are considered, including direct contact ingestion/dermal), vapour/dust inhalation (indoors/outdoors), vegetable ingestion, and ingestion of soil clinging to vegetables.

6. For certain chemicals, it provides SGVs which may vary with pH, soil type, and other soil characteristics.

21.34   As with all exposure models, CLEA operates in conjunction with toxicological information to produce SGVs. Such information takes the form of "Tolerable Daily Soil Intake" (TDSI) or "Index Dose" (ID) values, the former being calculated by subtracting background exposure, or Mean Daily Intake (MDI) values, from Tolerable Daily Intake (TDI) values, while the latter are doses of carcinogens deemed to be insignificant from the perspective of cancer causation. TDIs and IDs (and/or their base data) are obtained from reputable sources such as the UK Department of Health and the World Health Organisation. As well as being used by the Government to provide SGVs, CLEA can be run in site-specific mode to provide more tailored estimates of acceptable contaminant levels (known as "site-specific assessment criteria"—SSACs). Users can specify variations in certain parameters such that deviations from the generic assumptions incorporated into the SGV-generation process can be accommodated. This is consistent with the "tiered" approach to site assessment described in the Model Procedures.

The limitation of the SGV approach is that values have only been **21.35** developed for a limited number of substances. There are numerous substances and compounds which may be encountered in contaminated land which do not have values. To assess their significance there is a need to generate health based standards using quantitative human health risk assessment models, and no fully-compatible UK risk assessment model is currently available. There are commercial models, such as the US RBCA (risk-based corrective action) model, but the different regulatory contexts in which such models were produced need to be borne in mind.[13] The Scottish and Northern Ireland Forum for Environmental Research (SNIFFER) has developed a risk-assessment model which is intended to be compatible with Pt IIA. This however has two current limitations: it does not consider the contribution of dermal uptake which may be significant for some contaminants; and there are some unresolved issues on the estimation of the indoor air inhalation pathway. Accordingly, while it may be the preferred methodology, it may need to be supplemented by others. In any event, the use of any such models are dependent on the availability of physico-chemical or toxicity data for the substance or compound in question. In the latter half of 2006, Land Quality Management (LQM), in conjunction with the Chartered Institute of Environmental Health (CIEH), utilised the CLEA model to produce generic assessment criteria (GACs) for 19 chemicals or groups of chemicals which did not have SGVs. The results were published in a document which outlined the methodology and provided the input physical/chemical and toxicological parameters for each substance. While not officially endorsed by government, these criteria are likely to be of considerable use to practitioners, as is the compilation of input parameters.

The SGV Task Force and DEFRA's "Way Forward" document

Primarily in response to widespread concerns regarding the slow speed of **21.36** delivery of SGVs, the Cabinet Office convened a Task Force to look into this issue in 2004. The SGV Task Force (SGVTF), as it became known, was made up of representatives of government departments, industry bodies and individual experts. By 2005 it became clear that there were wider issues relating to the relationship of the SGVs with the Pt IIA legislation, and whether they really helped in the assessment of "significant possibility of significant harm" (SPOSH). The SGVTF then focused on this issue, resulting in important clarifications of government policy in this area.

At the heart of the SGV issue were concerns that the values were too low **21.37** and that, if used as the basis for Pt IIA determinations (which in some cases they had been), they would render a great deal of the country's soil

---

[13] RBCA refers specifically to the standard entitled *Guide For Risk-Based Corrective Action Applied at Petroleum Release Sites* [E-1739–95] that was published by the American Society for Testing and Materials (ASTM) Subcommittee on Storage Tanks.

(including many natural soils) contaminated in a statutory sense, and therefore potentially in need of remediation. This was recognised as having the potential to cause widespread anxiety and blight, as well as possibly requiring vast sums of money to be spent on clean-up. Many experts argued that SPOSH must occur at levels much higher than the SGVs—the question then was how much higher? DEFRA's initial response to this was to issue a policy note: CLAN 2/05 *Soil Guideline Values and the Determination of Land as Contaminated Land under Part IIA* (2005) which stated explicitly that local authorities needed to exercise extreme caution when using SGVs in connection with Pt IIA determinations. It also promised further guidance on what constituted SPOSH.

21.38   The SGVTF began the process of trying to establish what should be done by way of further guidance but was unable to complete the task before the SGVTF was disbanded in 2006 and the issue was taken "in-house" by DEFRA. This was followed by the production of a further policy statement: CLAN 6/06 *Assessing Risks from Land Contamination—A Proportionate Approach, Soil Guideline Values: The Way Forward*. This document was published for consultation in November 2006, the consultation period ending in February 2007. The results of the consultation are not as at the time of writing, available from DEFRA. The *Way Forward* document is specifically focused on identifying how SPOSH should be determined on potentially contaminated sites. It builds on existing policy and guidance in this area and recommends many modifications to the underlying risk assessment methodology, the principal amongst these are as follows:

1. changes to the presentation of toxicological data for contaminants, so that there is a more explicit presentation of risk levels for genotoxic carcinogens along with the identification of Lowest Observed Adverse Effect Levels (LOAELs) and No Observed Adverse Effect Levels (NOAELs) for threshold substances.

2. changes to the CLEA model, focusing on exposure assumptions, plant uptake modelling and the underlying SGV calculation methodology (it is proposed to make CLEA deterministic rather than probabilistic).

3. changes to the approach for lead and an undertaking to produce guidance for asbestos.

4. new guidance on what constitutes "unacceptable intake", for both threshold and non-threshold substances.

5. undertakings to produce more guidance on DQRA, including the use of bioavailability/bioaccessibility data and site-specific adjustments to CLEA.

6. undertakings to produce more guidance on the statistical interpretation of site data, building on that in CLR7.[14]

7. undertakings to update many of the documents in the CLR series, to reflect the modifications to the approach.

---

[14] Defra/EA, CLR7, *Overview of the Development of Guideline Values and Related Research* (2002).

DEFRA also states that the same criteria used under Pt IIA should be **21.39** used under the planning system. In other words, there are no proposals for developing SGVs for any other level of risk. The overall impact of these suggested changes, if implemented, will likely be an increase in many of the SGVs to reflect more accurately where SPOSH occurs. It will also result in more sophisticated statistical analysis of site data at both the GQRA and DQRA stage, along with clearer guidance on the process of DQRA. DEFRA has set itself an ambitious programme for delivering the proposals recommended in the *Way Forward*. It remains to be seen if this programme will be met.

The remedial targets methodology

The remedial targets methodology[15] was published in 1999 as the Environ- **21.40** ment Agency's preferred approach to the assessment of soil and groundwater contamination, from the perspective of the protection of controlled waters. It advocates a tiered approach, and incorporates the pollutant linkage concept described previously. At each tier a remedial target is derived, and in most cases the target becomes less onerous as the tiers are progressed. This is because additional environmental processes (such as dilution and attenuation) that affect a contaminant's concentration along its pathway to the receptor are taken into account. The procedure for determining site-specific remedial targets is as follows:

1. Determine a target concentration at the receptor or compliance point in relation to its use (e.g. drinking water standard, environmental quality standard).

2. Undertake the tier assessment to determine whether the contaminant source would result in the target concentration being exceeded at the receptor or compliance point. At each tier, a remedial target is determined.

3. If the contaminant concentrations on-site exceed the remedial target, then the decision whether it is appropriate to upgrade the tier analysis is based on timescale, what additional information is required and can be obtained and cost-benefit analysis (i.e. the cost of tier upgrade in relation to the potential reduction in the cost of the remedial solution).

Four assessment tiers are proposed for the assessment of contaminated **21.41** soil to protect controlled waters:

1. Tier 1 considers whether contaminant concentrations in "pore water" in contaminated soil are sufficient to impact the receptor, ignoring dilution, dispersion and attenuation along the pathway.

2. Tier 2 considers dilution by the receiving groundwater or surface water body and whether this is sufficient to reduce contaminant

---

[15] EA, *Methodology for the Derivation of Remedial Targets for Soil and Groundwater to Protect Groundwater Resources*, 1999, R&D Publication 20.

concentrations to acceptable levels. The remedial target is defined as the target concentration, multiplied by a dilution factor.

3. Tiers 3 and 4 consider whether natural attenuation (including dispersion, retardation and degradation) of the contaminant as it moves through the unsaturated and saturated zones to the receptor are sufficient to reduce contaminant concentrations to acceptable levels. The remedial target is defined as the target concentration multiplied by the dilution factor and attenuation factor. In Tier 3 simple analytical models are used to calculate the significance of attenuation, whereas in Tier 4 more sophisticated numerical models are used.

21.42   For contaminated groundwater the assessment commences at Tier 2, as the contaminants have already moved through the soil zone, so that the only processes of significance are attenuation, dispersion and further dilution. In contrast to the approach for human health, the RTM does not provide generic assessment criteria akin to SGVs for the protection of controlled waters. As a result, a judgment needs to be made as to which assessment tiers from the RTM belong in a GQRA and which belong in a DQRA. In normal circumstances it is appropriate to include Tiers 1–3 within a GQRA while Tier 4 should take place as part of a DQRA.

21.43   The Remedial Targets Methodology was later updated by the Agency. The reasons for its update included the release of CLR11, *The Water Framework Directive*,[16] the new Groundwater Directive[17] and some functional issues that needed ironing out. The biggest charge is that there are now four "levels", not "tiers", and they operate somewhat differently from previously. Levels are based on looking at receptors further and further along the contaminant transport pathway, whereas the former "tiers" were based on increasing amounts of data collection and computing. New Level 2 now incorporates attenuation in the soil and unsaturated zone, and dilution in groundwater beneath the site. So theoretically, one can take account of retardation, degradation and volatilisation along this pathway. However, the manual and the spreadsheet only incorporate the ground-water dilution term, as before. New Level 4 now looks at the impact on a receiving watercourse or abstraction. This could use a simple dilution factor, as in the old Tier 2. But the point is that it now must be shown, prior to using Level 4, that any impact on groundwater quality (i.e. a Level 3 result) does not jeopardise future use of the groundwater resource, and the cost of remediation is disproportionate in relation to the improvement of groundwater or surface water quality. The end result is that the old concept of Tier 4 has disappeared, and has been incorporated into all the above levels, leaving it up to the assessor to use the best modelling technique that is justified by the amount of data available.

---

[16] Directive 2000/60.

[17] Directive 2006/118 on the protection of groundwater against pollution and deterioration.

Detailed quantitative risk assessment

Objective

The objective of a detailed quantitative risk assessment (DQRA) is to **21.44** analyse further the pollutant linkages identified in the PRA and GQRA as being of potential concern, using more site-specific data or more sophisticated risk modeling approaches. It may also involve a further revision of the site's conceptual model.

Data needs

The data needs for a DQRA are very site-specific, with each situation **21.45** requiring different activities to support different risk modeling approaches. The following are some of the main ones, with further details being available in the Model Procedures:

1. additional intrusive investigations to better delineate the nature and extent of potential contamination;
2. the collection of additional site-specific data relating to soil, groundwater and possibly vapour/gas characteristics;
3. the collection of site-specific data relating to human exposure patterns and land, via population monitoring, questionnaires, etc.;
4. bioavailability and bioaccessibility testing;
5. collection of physical/chemical and toxicological data on chemicals which lack generic criteria;
6. measurement of soil and groundwater processes such as degradation;
7. collection of additional hydrogeological data;

As with the GQRA, these activities can be complex and require **21.46** considerable technical expertise. As a result, they should only be performed by suitably qualified practitioners and they should be linked specifically with the requirements of the data interpretation.

Data interpretation

Following the collection of data, further risk-based modelling approaches **21.47** can be used to revise the findings of the GQRA. In addition, the site conceptual model may need to be revised. As with the GQRA stage, a key question relates to the interpretation of site-specific chemical test data and how it should be compared with site-specific assessment criteria (SSACs) derived via a DQRA. Guidance is available for this process, including the use of statistical methods, as described in the Model Procedures.

Outcome of the DQRA

The outcome of the DQRA is a final decision regarding which, if any, of the **21.48** potential pollutant linkages identified in the PRA and GQRA are significant. If any or all of them are, then the process proceeds to options appraisal. In the event that no significant pollutant linkages are identified, then no further action is required.

Options Appraisal

Overview

21.49 Remedial options appraisal is generally required where a generic or detailed risk assessment has identified an unacceptable risk. The options appraisal examines the ways to break the contaminant-pathway-target linkages which have been judged to be harmful or polluting—these are termed relevant pollutant linkages (RPL). The remedy, or method to reduce or control the unacceptable risk, may take many forms. The site-specific options appraisal weighs up the advantages and limitations of each option to select the method or methods which offer the best overall approach to remediation of the site. The planning does not stop once a remediation strategy has been agreed; detailed implementation plans need to be prepared alongside a method by which the remediation can be shown to be effective. The Model Procedures identify three main stages of options appraisal, their purpose and the key decisions at each stage of the appraisal.

Stage 1—Identifying feasible remediation options for each relevant pollutant linkage

21.50 *Purpose*: to identify a shortlist of feasible remediation options for each relevant pollutant linkage, taking all the circumstances of the site into account.

This stage needs to determine:

- What site-specific remediation and other objectives should apply to options appraisal.

- Which remediation options should be taken forward for more detailed evaluation.

Stage 2—Carrying out a detailed evaluation of feasible remediation options to identify the most appropriate option for any particular linkage

21.51 *Purpose*: to decide, for each relevant pollutant linkage, which of the feasible remediation options is the most appropriate given the specific circumstances of the site.

This stage needs to determine:

— Which remediation option(s) is most appropriate for each relevant pollutant linkage.

— Which options, (if any) need to be combined.

Stage 3—Producing a remediation strategy that addresses all relevant pollutant linkages, where appropriate by combining remediation options

Purpose: to develop a remediation strategy capable of practical implementa- **21.52** tion on the site and to describe in broad terms the characteristics of that strategy.

This stage needs to determine:

— How, in broad terms, the remediation strategy is to be implemented.

— Whether the remediation strategy will meet all site-specific objectives.

It should be noted that each stage has specific outputs and that the steps **21.53** above can be used to produce a remediation strategy for simple and complex sites. Depending on the circumstances the process could take anything from hours to months.

The Model Procedures are supported by a large number of technical **21.54** documents prepared by the EA, CIRIA, CL:AIRE and the BRE.[18] These provide details of the methods and merits of the technologies available. Notwithstanding the available guidance, the selection of the most appropriate remedial option for a particular site can be a challenging exercise, as views from various stakeholders (e.g. owners, developers, regulators and neighbours plus financial, legal and technical advisors) need to be taken into account. Those carrying out the appraisal need a good understanding of all aspects but are often driven towards solutions geared to achieve regulatory approval or solutions which can be implemented within a particular timeframe at the least cost. As an example, those developers looking to make fast returns often avoid soil treatment processes in favour of more traditional solutions which, although costly, enable relatively rapid discharge or satisfaction of planning conditions or obligations and enable development to proceed.

The model procedures advise that assessors should specify a series of **21.55** objectives at the outset of the options appraisal, objectives which will aim to ensure that the final remediation strategy achieves approval with most if not all of the people involved. Typical objectives are listed in the model procedures and include the: "degree of risk reduction; time; practicability, etc". Where options for the remediation of contaminated residential gardens under Pt IIA are being appraised the health effects, including stress experienced by owners or occupiers, should be considered.

The options appraisal process recycles a great deal of the site specific **21.56** information gathered during the preceding risk assessments stage, details which are crucial when considering the advantages and limitations of remedial option—in Stages 1 and 2. The main items are of course the details of the relevant pollutant linkages and it is important that one group

---

[18] CIRIA—Construction Industry Research and Information Association, CL:AIRE—Contaminated Land: Applications in Real Environments and BRE—Building Research Establishment. See para.21.07 above.

of objectives should relate directly to breaking those linkages—these are termed Remediation Objectives. The most common objectives act on the contaminant (by decreasing its mass, concentration, mobility or toxicity) but objectives can also target the pathway or receptor. As an example, one remediation objective for a garden soil containing harmful concentrations of hydrocarbons could be to reduce concentrations to acceptable levels. Allied to this would be a site-specific remediation criteria, in this case the criteria might be to remediate (e.g. perform soil treatment, soil removal, etc.) to a point where residual concentrations are consistently below the acceptable concentration determined in the preceding health risk assessment. The key point is that remediation criteria should provide a measure against which compliance with remediation objectives can be measured. Hence the options appraisal process considers the likely success of the remedial works in meeting their objectives, in an attempt to avoid costly mistakes, and sets criteria which post-remediation allows certification that the works have achieved their objectives. Certification is important to many of the stakeholders involved. The sections that follow discuss the three stages involved in the remediation Options Appraisal.

Identification of feasible remediation options

21.57 The purpose of this stage is to identify a shortlist of feasible remediation options for each relevant pollutant linkage, taking all the circumstances of the site into account. At the end of this stage the appraiser will be able to produce a document setting out the site-specific objectives and feasible options and how these were derived. In order to get to that point the appraiser will have reviewed the outputs of the various risk assessment stages, focused on the pollutant linkages that require remediation and identified site specific remediation objective for each linkage. Then, by considering the remedial objectives alongside the overall objectives of the stakeholders and the site conditions and constraints, the appraiser will form an opinion as to the feasible options. This requires a knowledge of applicability of the various remedial options available and in some cases additional site information may be needed to test the feasibility of particular techniques.

21.58 This stage is important as it lays the foundation for the activities which will eventually lead to an acceptable or more useful/marketable site, actions which are likely to be costly in comparison to the preceding risk assessment. Good communication is essential here as the technical work requires the specialist input of risk assessors and those with a robust knowledge of remedial work, and interaction of those technicians with the other stakeholders involved.

21.59 The basic approach to selection of feasible options concentrates on altering or breaking the relevant pollutant linkages. Various documents identify that unacceptable risks can be reduced or controlled by:

1. removing or treating the contamination or source of pollutant(s);

2. removing or modifying the pathway(s); and

3. removing or modifying the behaviour of receptor(s).

There are likely to be different technical options within each of these **21.60** categories. Most will involve actively applying a remedial technique or making a change in the characteristics of the land or land use, but the potential for the degradation and attenuation of pollutants under natural circumstances may be accepted as a feasible option if monitoring and modelling suggest the process would meet the remedial criteria within an acceptable time limits.

The number of options available depends on the site and techniques **21.61** available. Site-specific factors include: the area available (for site cabins and stockpiles, etc.), the neighboring land uses, distance to landfill and sources of acceptable fill, etc. Whilst the remedial options on sale have tended to be influenced by legislation (especially provisions concerning waste) and taxation, the large contaminated sites tackled in the last decade of the 20th century provided the opportunity for several ex-situ remedial techniques to enter the UK market, providing competition for the more tradition "dig and dump" solution. However, although the use of treatments, such as bioremediation, have more than doubled since the turn of the century, their uptake has been constrained by a lack of reliable track record in the UK and the perception that they are not feasible for the smaller urban sites which are commonly targeted by developers. When ex-situ treatments are pitted against landfill disposal, developers have tended to compare treatment costs and timescales and factor in long-term liabilities before choosing landfill, but perhaps in future they will choose techniques which can remediate the contamination whilst the foundations and walls are progressed.

There may well be a number of feasible remedial activities for each **21.62** relevant pollutant linkage. Those carrying out a feasibility appraisal are given a great deal of support by information presented within the Model Procedure, which provides a detailed remediation option applicability matrix which considers all methods available in the UK. The document also contains:

1. a list of factors that might affect the selection of feasible remediation options;
2. examples of remediation objectives;
3. examples of management and "other" technical objectives;
4. directions to sources of information on remediation options;
5. criteria for deciding whether sufficient information is available to select feasible remediation options;
6. examples of summary information on relevant pollutant linkages at the start of options appraisal; and
7. guidance explaining how to report the identification of feasible remediation options.

Detailed evaluation of options

The purpose of this stage is to decide, for each relevant pollutant linkage, **21.63** which of the feasible remediation options is the most appropriate given the specific circumstances of the site. At the end of this stage the appraiser will be able to produce a document setting out the basis on which particular options have been accepted and rejected and a description of the most appropriate remediation option for each relevant pollutant linkage and which, if any, options may need to be combined. In order to get to that point the appraiser will have:

1. developed formal evaluation criteria;

2. collected more information on the strengths and weaknesses of the shortlisted remediation options; and

3. re-examined the nature of pollutant linkages and the characteristics of the site before completing an analysis of the technical attributes of each option against the evaluation criteria and cost estimates.

21.64   The most appropriate remedial options come to the fore at the end of this stage and, where multiple remedial activities are favoured, the options appraisal must look at the feasibility of zoning the site or phasing the works so that the package of options can be implemented without delay or error. Examples of a treatment train or integrated solution might be excavation or containment of grossly contaminated soils combined with in-situ treatment of peripheral zones with moderately contaminated soils and groundwater; or separation of various material streams followed by re-use of acceptable fractions and the application of various chemical, physical or biological treatments to the remaining materials. Those carrying out a detailed evaluation of options are given a great deal of support by information presented within the Model Procedure. The document contains:

1. a list of factors to be considered when selecting site-specific evaluation criteria;

2. a list of the types of information required to enable proper evaluation of remedial options;

3. a list of the cost information required to produce ball park estimates for each remedial option;

4. advice about the development of weighted scoring systems which can be used when evaluating the technical attributes of remediation options;

5. advice about estimating remediation costs;

6. an example which demonstrates how to select an appropriate remediation option from the feasible options;

7. an examples which demonstrates how remediation options may be combined;

8. a list of questions which help decide whether sufficient information is available to proceed with detailed;

9. evaluation;

10. guidance explaining how to report the detailed evaluation of remediation options.

The list of questions given in the Model Procedure is most useful as it **21.65** acts as a checklist to ensure that all remediation, management and other technical objectives are satisfied. If these questions cannot be answered then further research, site investigation or perhaps laboratory or field-scale test data will be required.

Developing the remediation strategy

The purpose of this stage is to develop a remediation strategy capable of **21.66** practical implementation on the site and to describe in broad terms the characteristics of that strategy. At the end of this stage the appraiser will be able to explain how the remediation strategy was developed and set out the strategy and how it meets the objectives for both the individual pollutant linkages and the site as a whole. This stage, which concerns the application of the most appropriate remedial or techniques to the site, focuses on practical issues and the installation of efficiencies. Stakeholders, by having involvement in and by digesting the outputs of this stage, should gain a clear knowledge of:

1. the enabling works required (demolition, access creation, etc.);

2. an understanding of the site, with any zonation proposed; and

3. knowledge of the overall programme including any phasing of the remedial works.

The programme and costing should provide for all tasks, including any **21.67** long term monitoring or maintenance and those associated with the production of validation documents. The level of detail reached should allow revised cost estimates and a more meaningful cost-benefit analysis. Within this stage, stakeholders, especially funders, should work to introduce efficiencies to enable potential cost savings. This could be facilitated by some early contractor involvement and advice relating to the most appropriate form of contract. The supporting information within the Model Procedures for this stage is limited to:

1. a list of the practical issues that might arise out of the combination of remediation options;

2. examples of possible preparatory requirements; and

3. a list of the information required when reporting the development of the remediation strategy which includes details of the contents expected in a Decision Record.

The Decision Record is a document which includes a description of the **21.68** proposed remediation strategy.

IMPLEMENTATION OF THE REMEDIATION STRATEGY

Overview

21.69 The remedial options appraisal will have produced a remediation strategy which will offer the best overall approach to remediation of the site. The strategy will, however, need development before physical remediation and other site works can begin. When discussing implementation of the remediation strategy, the Model Procedures describe the actions by which the strategy is turned into a fully specified and programmed design package. That package aims to deliver a safe, practical and economical remediation project integrated with any other work (e.g. development activities) needed, and to deliver it to the satisfaction of all stakeholders including regulators. The Model Procedures identify three main stages within the implementation of the remediation strategy, their purpose, key decisions and outputs.

Stage 1—Preparing the Implementation Plan

21.70 *Purpose*: to prepare the Implementation Plan such that the remediation strategy can be put into place in an effective and orderly manner. The Implementation Plan describes the remediation works, but anticipates the detailed design work to follow and the later addition of other documents such as monitoring plans, etc.

Stage 2—Design, implementation and verification of the remediation

21.71 *Purpose*:

— to prepare a sufficiently detailed design to allow the contract to be let, awarded and carried out in a safe and effective manner which integrates with any other activities on site; and

— to verify that the completed remediation is in accordance with the design and any subsequent amendments whilst ensuring that the works meet with the approval of all stakeholders.

Stage 3—Long term monitoring and maintenance

21.72 *Purpose*: to monitor the effectiveness of remediation and to maintain the remedial works to ensure that they continue to function effectively and as designed. At the end of this stage, if the monitoring has proven that the remedial activities have rendered the site conditions acceptable, the stakeholders should agree that no further action is required.

21.73 It should be noted that: each stage has specific outputs; that the procedures can be used for simple and complex sites; and that Stage 3 is not always appropriate. On completion of the implementation stages the landowner and any other relevant parties should hold copies of the:

1. Implementation Plan;

2. Contract Documents, as-built drawings and specifications;

3. Verification Plan;

4. Monitoring and Maintenance Plan;

5. Verification Report;

6. Monitoring and Maintenance Reports, if any;

7. Health and Safety file under the Construction (Design and Management) Regulations 2007.

These documents will form the lasting record of the remediation, and of **21.74** the final quality of the land. Although remediation works are carried out for a multitude or reasons, the importance of these documents, especially the Verification Report, should not be underestimated. They are the documents which will prove that the site is fit for its current or intended use, which should increase or restore the value of the land, may be the key to allowing redevelopment or reoccupation, and may even prevent regulatory prosecution. The importance of the Validation Report is discussed further below. The sections that follow discuss the three stages involved in the Implementation of the Remediation Strategy.

Preparing the implementation plan

The purpose of this stage is to prepare the implementation plan such that **21.75** the remediation strategy can be put into place in an effective and orderly manner. By the end of this stage an implementation manager will have been identified and that person or organisation will have consulted with all relevant parties to produce an Implementation Plan. The Implementation Plan is the key reference document for those involved in the remedial works and later in the process is augmented by the addition of verification, monitoring and maintenance plans. The Implementation Manager has the task of identifying:

1. the remediation strategy for the relevant pollutant linkages;

2. individuals or organisations to undertake the main remedial tasks and other integral tasks including;

3. verification, monitoring, maintenance, health and safety and environmental protection;

4. the regulatory permits or licences needed;

5. the form of contract to be drafted; and

6. a programme for the entire project

Importantly, the Manager will have also given some thought to the **21.76** health and safety requirements of the scheme.

The scale of the Implementation Plan will reflect the complexity of the **21.77** project and number of relevant parties consulted. The Model Procedures suggest that the relevant parties could include:

1. professionals working on the project—for example ecologists;

2. the land occupier/owner or client and their legal advisors;

3. planners, environmental health or regeneration officers within the local authority;

4. regulators within the Environment Agency and other bodies such as the Health and Safety Executive (HSE), Natural England, etc.;

5. statutory undertakers;

6. prospective purchasers;

7. prospective insurers and funders;

8. neighbours to the site; and

9. local interest groups.

21.78   The Model Procedures provide several useful items of supporting information to those involved in this stage. The document contains:

1. A table listing the type of organisation capable of producing implementation plans for projects dealing with remedial works and projects where remedial works only form part of a package of works;

2. General advice about the procurement options available (traditional, design and build, partnering and management contracting) and their features;

3. A list of typical information gaps that may exist at this stage and the actions that may be needed; and

4. A list of potential consultees, including a set of questions that each consultee is likely to ask.

21.79   The typical consultee questions included are very useful as they highlight the requirements and likely aspirations of the stakeholders—and the need for good communication. Effective communication and the management of information is crucial to projects involving contamination, especially where private individuals and vulnerable groups (e.g. residents) are involved. The Model Procedures refer to the guidance documents produced by SNIFFER, the EA and CIRIA in this regard:

1. SNIFFER/EA, *Communicating Understanding of Contaminated Land Risks*, 1999, SR97(11)F;

2. CIRIA, *Community Stakeholder Involvement*, SAFEGROUNDS Learning Network, 2002; and

3. EA, *Participatory Risk Assessment: Involving Lay Audiences in Decisions on Environmental Risk*, 2004, E2–043.

21.80   Recent years have seen a small number of companies offering specialist communications services, these being predominantly aimed at large regeneration schemes, projects where residential land is being inspected or where neighbours are expected to be adversely impacted.

Design, implementation and verification

This is arguably the most important stage within the management of **21.81** contaminated land, as it sees completion of the detailed remedial design, implementation of the site works and actions to verify that these works have achieved their objectives. This stage has several objectives of its own, as the various parties involved aim to prepare a sufficiently detailed design to allow the contract to let, awarded and carried out in a safe and effective manner which integrates with any other activities on site such a building works. They also need to prove or verify that the completed remediation is in accordance with the design and any subsequent site-generated amendments, and ensure that the works meet with the approval of all stakeholders including regulators, insurers and funders.

This is a very busy time in the project and the Implementation Manager **21.82** will be involved with the procurement and instruction of the design, supervision and verification team alongside health and safety professionals and the main contractor and sub-contractors. As well as contracts, drawings and specifications, the manager will have to ensure that all the right paperwork is in place, including the appropriate licenses, permits and consents. In certain circumstances the manager will also have to ensure that HM Revenue & Customs have granted landfill tax exemptions.[19] There will also be progress meetings and quite possibly public relations events.

Those involved in the detailed design, implementation and verification of **21.83** the remedial works are given a great deal of support by information presented within the Model Procedures. The document contains:

1. a list of issues to be considered by the designer if there are site works, e.g. redevelopment works, alongside the remediation;

2. brief details of the standard forms of contract that may be used for remediation works;

3. a list of objectives for the overall design;

4. lists of the information needed for design purposes, including site information and details of contaminants and remedial techniques;

5. a list of verification and health and safety issues to be considered at the design stage;

6. an introduction to the difference between method based and performance based specifications;

7. a list of factors to be considered when appointing a remediation designer, planning supervisor and contractor.

8. a list of permits, licenses and consents which might be required; and

9. guidance regarding the typical content of; a verification plan; a monitoring and maintenance plan; a remedial works progress report; and a verification report.

---

[19] See para.17.49ff.

21.84   The production of a written Validation Document, independent report or certificate is a standard requirement where regulatory approval linked to discharge of planning conditions is involved. As with other building or construction activities it is often a requirement that the contractor or consultant certifies or even warrants that the work and/or workmanship has met the contract specification. For a remedial earthworks contract the contractor or consultant might warrant that all soil on site now contains Contaminant X at concentrations below the specified remediation criteria, or that the cover system installed meets its thickness and permeability criteria. The ultimate aim of such an approach is to ensure that remedial activities are carried out as designed and should reassure regulators, bodies such as the National House-Building Council (NHBC), and those lending funds, buying, working or living on land which has been subject to remedial works.

21.85   Other useful guidance on this stage has been prepared by the Institution of Civil Engineers (ICE), CIRIA and Environment Agency:

1. ICE, *Design and Practice Guide—Contaminated Land: Investigation, Assessment and Remediation*, 1994;

2. CIRIA, *Remedial Treatment for Contaminated Land*, 1995, SP 111, Volume xi, Planning and Management; and

3. Environment Agency, *DRAFT Verification of Remediation of Land Contamination*, 2007.

Long term monitoring and maintenance

21.86   Following completion of the Verification Report there may be a need for long term monitoring and maintenance of the remedial scheme. Obviously this only applies where significant opportunity exists for site characteristics to change over time—one example is the occasional checking of an engineered cap for damage or erosion and any minor repair work that may be required, another might be groundwater monitoring following cessation of active groundwater treatment. The Model Procedures state that the "purpose of this stage is to monitor the effectiveness of remediation, to confirm predicted behaviour as an early warning of adverse trends, and to maintain remediation to ensure continued functioning and effectiveness in accordance with the original design philosophy".

21.87   At the end of this stage, if the monitoring has shown that the remedial activities have rendered the site conditions acceptable, the stakeholders should agree that no further action is required.

21.88   The Monitoring and Maintenance Plan which describes the actions within this stage will have been developed across previous stages and laid out in the Implementation Plan. Before arranging any monitoring or maintenance the Implementation Manager is required to check that the actions described in those documents are reasonable given that the remedial scheme may have changed slightly during the implementation phase. Once the plans are finalised, the manager needs to arrange the monitoring and maintenance, ensure reports are submitted as agreed and keep the programme under review, perhaps making adjustments following comparison of the monitoring results and criteria.

Importantly, there should also be a system to investigate unexpected **21.89** events and implement corrective action. Such unexpected events could include vandalism, flooding, etc.

Documents to support those managing this stage of work are presented **21.90** within the Model Procedures. The document contains a list of:

1. issues which should be considered before finalising the monitoring and maintenance plans;

2. checks and items to consider when monitoring criteria are not met and—checks to be carried out before making the decision to modify the existing remediation so as to improve its effectiveness; and

3. the typical contents of a maintenance report and a monitoring report.

SPECIFIC ISSUES

This section describes key developments relating to contaminated land **21.91** technical guidance dealing with certain more specific issues, such as ecological risk assessment and radioactive contamination.

Ecological risk assessment

In 2002 the Environment Agency published a document entitled *Assessing* **21.92** *Risks to Ecosystems from Land Contamination*.[20] This document was the outcome of a study designed to examine and review a number of international decision-making and risk assessment methodologies and outline a simple ecological risk assessment framework. The Environment Agency study reviewed ecological risk assessment frameworks from the USA, Australia, Canada and the Netherlands. In addition, it provided examples of guideline values (GVs) that are used in these countries. The outcome of the study is a suggested ecological risk assessment framework, based on a three-tier system, and incorporating the use of GVs. This framework is described in more detail below.

The first tier of assessment recommended in the Agency's research **21.93** involves the characterisation of the site and the elucidation of a conceptual model of potential contaminants, pathways and ecological receptors. Soil samples are then taken and analysed for the presence of relevant contaminants, following which numerical hazard indices (HIs) or PEC/PNEC ratios are derived (PECs are "Predicted Environmental Concentrations" and PNECs are "Predicted No Effect Concentrations"). PEC/PNEC ratios are

---

[20] EA, *Assessing Risks to Ecosystems from Land Contamination*, 2002, R&D Technical Report P299.

obtained by simply dividing the measured chemical concentrations by suitable GVs, while HIs are the sums of such ratios for a number of chemicals where the mode of their toxic action is similar. In both cases, numbers greater than unity are suggested as being indicative of a need to proceed to Tier 2, or undertake risk management, while numbers of less than unity indicate that no further action is required. In the event that the PEC/PNEC ratio or HI is one, or close to one, then monitoring is suggested.

21.94   The second tier of assessment involves further site characterisation and the direct toxicity testing of soil samples. In terms of the latter, the following ex-situ tests are recommended for consideration, depending on the site-specific assessment needs, for example an acute earthworm test, an acute arthropod test, a root growth test with a species such as barley or cress, and a microbial test. There is also an option to perform biomonitoring, in the form of testing tissue samples for contaminants. As described previously, this can be used to confirm the existence of suspected pollutant linkages. No details are given on which tests should be performed during Tier 2 and there is no framework for their application at specific sites. Methods for interpreting the results are described in general terms, however, particularly in relation to their extrapolation to population, community and ecosystem effects, although again the details are only sketchy. Clearly this is an important consideration in the light of the requirements of the guidance. It is also suggested that site-specific PEC/PNEC ratios are derived, and that probabilistic uncertainty analyses are performed. Again, methods for doing so are not described in any detail, however.

21.95   In the event that Tier 2 indicates that the ecological risk is significant, the assessment either proceeds to Tier 3, or risk management is undertaken. In the event that the risk is shown to be insignificant, no further action is required. As at Tier 1, monitoring is suggested for a borderline situation. Tier 3 provides the opportunity for further, more detailed analysis of site-specific ecological risk. This may involve the use of similar tools to those used in Tier 2, or it may require the application of more comprehensive methods. Such methods include individual-based population models, the biological testing of a wider variety of species than at Tier 2 and chronic, sub-chronic or mesocosm toxicity tests. If, following such an assessment, ecological risks appear to be sufficient for the site to be identified as contaminated land, then remediation is required. Conversely, the demonstration of an absence of such risk will result in no further action being necessary. A borderline situation will be met with a requirement for monitoring.

Radioactively Contaminated Land Exposure Assessment (RCLEA)

21.96 Radioactively Contaminated Land Exposure Assessment (RCLEA) is DEFRA's recommended approach for the exposure assessment of a potentially radioactively contaminated site under the extended Pt IIA regime for managing contaminated land. It complements the Contaminated Land

Exposure Assessment (CLEA) approach for non-radioactive contamination. RCLEA is designed to support decision making under the extended regime; it may have wider applications, but care is needed if the methodology is applied in other circumstances. The methodology is based on a set of mathematical models and data that calculate radiation doses from radionuclides in soil. These have been implemented as a software application published by DEFRA as CLR 15, which is accompanied by a detailed technical report (CLR 14), and a more general summary and user guide (CLR 13).[21]

Using measured concentrations of radionuclides, RCLEA calculates **21.97** potential doses to human receptors for comparison with regulatory criteria. It can also be used to calculate "Guideline Values" in terms of radionuclide concentrations if reliable measurements are not yet available. In addition to specifying radionuclides present (and concentrations, if known), initial generic calculations simply provide the user with four basic options to select from:

1. reference land uses (consistent with CLEA), including residential (with or without home-grown vegetables), allotments and commercial/industrial use;

2. building type (timber framed or brick);

3. age (adult, infant or child); and

4. sex (male or female).

The user can select from any of the available options—if no preference is **21.98** specified, the worst-case assumptions will be adopted. The user can specify a greater level of detail if required by undertaking a "site-specific" calculation. This allows the user to define a new land use and adjust specific parameter values, such as the time spent on the contaminated site, so they better represent the situation. The dose calculated with RCLEA can be compared with the criteria which apply for radioactivity under the extended Pt IIA regime (provided the scenarios and assumptions are appropriate), and appropriate decisions made. Where results remain inconclusive, further assessment is likely to be needed, perhaps involving more detailed modelling.

Assessing risks to property

In 2001 the Environment Agency published a document entitled *Risks of* **21.99** *Contaminated Land to Buildings, Building Materials and Services.*[22] The objective of the report was to produce a practical, authoritative and useable guidance document on how risks to buildings, building materials and services (BBM&S) should be assessed. In addition, it covered the subse-

---

[21] DEFRA, DRAFT, *Using RCLEA—The Radioactively Contaminated Land Exposure Methodology*, 2006, CLR13.

[22] EA, *Risks of Contaminated Land to Buildings, Building Materials and Services—A Literature Review*, 2000, Technical Report P331.

quent selection and implementation of appropriate risk management action which is required to manage the identified risks when considering land contamination. The report focuses on the assessment of risks to existing and new buildings from four principal hazards: aggressive soils, expansive slag, combustible fill and unstable fill. It is based on available technical information in the literature and as well as providing essential source of reference papers for further reading.

21.100 The document guides assessors of contaminated land through a process for assessment and management of risks to BBM&S. It contains technical details on issues specific to BBM&S, whilst recognising that assessment and management will often be included within general contaminated land risk assessment and management.

Glossary (from the Model Procedures)

21.101 **Appraiser** A person who carries out the process of options appraisal.

Assessor A person who carries out the process of risk assessment.

Conceptual model A representation of the characteristics of the site in diagrammatic or written form that shows the possible relationships between contaminants, pathways and receptors.

Decision record A written account of the key decisions made at each stage of the risk management process.

Desk study Interpretation of historical, archival and current information to establish where previous activities were located, and where areas or zones that contain distinct and different types of contamination may be expected to occur, and to understand the environmental setting of the site in terms of pathways and receptors.

Detailed quantitative risk assessment Risk assessment carried out using detailed site-specific information to estimate risk or to develop site-specific assessment criteria.

Detailed site investigation Main stage of intrusive site investigation, which involves the collection and analysis of soil, surface water, groundwater, soil gas and other media as a means of further informing the conceptual model and the risk assessment. This investigation may be undertaken in a single or a number of successive stages.

Durability The extent to which a remediation treatment is likely to be effective in reducing or controlling unacceptable risks to a defined level over a period of time.

Effectiveness The extent to which a remediation treatment successfully reduces or controls unacceptable risks to a defined level.

Evaluation criteria (risk assessment) Parameters used to judge whether or not particular harm or pollution is unacceptable.

Evaluation criteria (options appraisal) Formal attributes or factors against which the ability of different remediation options to meet site-specific objectives are measured.

Ex-situ Where contaminated material is removed from the ground prior to above-ground treatment or encapsulation and/or disposal on or off site.

Generic assessment criteria Criteria derived using generic assumptions about the characteristics and behaviour of sources, pathways and receptors. These assumptions will be protective in a range of defined conditions.

Generic quantitative assessment Risk assessment carried out using generic assumptions to estimate risk or to develop generic assessment criteria.

Hazard A property or situation that in particular circumstances could lead to harm or pollution.

Health criteria value Benchmark criteria that represent an assessment of levels of exposure that pose a risk to human health. For example, tolerable daily intake (TDI) and index dose.

Implementation manager A person who is responsible for the implementation of the remediation strategy.

Implementation plan A plan that sets out all aspects of design, preparation, implementation, verification, long-term maintenance and monitoring of the remediation.

In-situ Where contaminated material is treated without prior excavation (of solids) or abstraction (of liquids) from the ground.

Land affected by contamination Land that might have contamination present which may, or may not, meet the statutory definition of contaminated land.

Lines of evidence Collection of data sets for key parameters that support agreed remediation criteria to demonstrate the performance of remediation.

Maintenance Activities carried out to ensure that remediation performs as required over a specified design life.

Management objectives Site-specific objectives defined by stakeholders that relate to regulatory, financial and commercial matters and the desired outcome of remediation.

MCERTS The Monitoring Certification Scheme is a quality assurance scheme for providers of monitoring services, equipment and systems, that is administered by the Environment Agency and accredited by UKAS.

Monitoring A continuous or regular periodic check to determine the ongoing nature and performance of remediation, which includes measurements undertaken for compliance purposes and those undertaken to assess performance.

Monitoring criteria Measures (usually, but not necessarily, expressed in quantitative terms) against which compliance with monitoring objectives will be assessed.

Monitoring objectives Site-specific objectives that define the monitoring programme needed to demonstrate the short and long-term performance of remediation or to track contaminant behaviour and movement.

Pathway A route or means by which a receptor could be, or is exposed to, or affected by a contaminant.

Pollutant linkage The relationship between a contaminant, pathway and receptor.

Practicability The extent to which it is possible to implement and operate a remediation option or strategy given practical constraints, such as treatment area, access, availability of support services, etc.

Preliminary risk assessment First tier of risk assessment that develops the initial conceptual model of the site and establishes whether or not there are any potentially unacceptable risks.

Quality criteria Measures of the sufficiency, relevance, reliability and transparency of the information and data used for risk management purposes.

Quality management The systematic planning, organisation, control and documentation of projects.

Receptor In general terms, something that could be adversely affected by a contaminant, such as people, an ecological system, property or a water body.

Remediation Action taken to prevent or minimise, or remedy or mitigate the effects of any identified unacceptable risks.

Remediation objective A site-specific objective that relates solely to the reduction or control of the risks associated with one or more pollutant linkages.

Remediation criteria Measures (usually, but not necessarily, expressed in quantitative terms) against which compliance with remediation objectives will be assessed.

Remediation option A means of reducing or controlling the risks associated with a particular pollutant linkage to a defined level.

Remediation strategy A plan that involves one or more remediation options to reduce or control the risks from all the relevant pollutant linkages associated with the site.

Risk A combination of the probability, or frequency of occurrence of a defined hazard and the magnitude of the consequences of the occurrence.

Risk assessment The formal process of identifying, assessing and evaluating the health and environmental risks that may be associated with a hazard.

Risk estimation Predicting the magnitude and probability of the possible consequences that may arise as a result of a hazard.

Risk evaluation Deciding whether a risk is unacceptable.

Risk management The processes involved in identifying, assessing and determining risks, and the implementation of actions to mitigate the consequences or probabilities of occurrence.

Site reconnaissance A walk-over survey of the site.

Site-specific assessment criteria Values for concentrations of contaminants that have been derived using detailed site-specific information on the characteristics and behaviour of contaminants, pathways and receptors and that correspond to relevant criteria in relation to harm or pollution for deciding whether there is an unacceptable risk.

Stakeholders Individuals or organisations with an interest in the scope, conduct and outcome of a risk management project.

Treatability studies Laboratory or field-scale trials that provide a means of determining the practicability and likely effectiveness of remediation, and estimating the timescales required to achieve the remediation objectives.

Treatment train A sequence of remediation treatments necessary to achieve the standard of remediation when treating contaminated material.

Uncertainty A lack of knowledge about specific factors in a risk or exposure assessment including parameter uncertainty, model uncertainty and scenario uncertainty.

Verification The process of demonstrating that the risk has been reduced to meet remediation criteria and objectives based on a quantitative assessment of remediation performance.

Verification plan A plan that sets out the requirements for gathering data to demonstrate that remediation meets the remediation objectives and criteria.

Verification report Provides a complete record of all remediation activities on site and the data collected as identified in the verification plan to support compliance with agreed remediation objectives and criteria.

Chapter 22

INFORMATION SOURCES AND ENVIRONMENTAL REPORTS

Environmental searches and desktop reports[1]

22.01   As a result of the introduction of the contaminated land regime, the Law Society produced a Contaminated Land Warning Card in June 2001. The Contaminated Land Warning Card is intended to help solicitors carry out the proper checks and enable them to give the necessary advice to their clients when acting on a range of transactions, including property purchases. Although solicitors are not bound by the advice contained in the Contaminated Land Warning Card, at the time of publication the advice contained in the Card was considered by the Law Society to conform to best practice.

22.02   The Contaminated Land Warning Card advises that there are three steps that lawyers should take in order to obtain information about the risk of contamination affecting a property:

1. raise specific enquiries of the seller;

2. make enquiries of public bodies; and

3. carry out an independent site history investigation, and in commercial cases if there is a likelihood that the site is contaminated, advise the client as to whether to carry out a full site investigation.

22.03   These steps are discussed in more detail below.[2] Significant improvements in the quality of environmental information, together with technological advances in mapping and the digitisation of information since the first edition of this book in 1994, mean that consultants are now able to provide comprehensive desktop reports quickly and cost effectively. These searches, combined with thorough enquiries of the vendor, local authority (Con 29) and (where necessary) the Environment Agency can provide a degree of protection both to solicitors (against a claim for negligence) and their clients (in respect of environmental liabilities). This chapter aims to provide an overview of the current enquiries, potential information sources and types of reports available on the market.

---

[1] This chapter is based on an article written by Simon Boyle and Chris Taylor of Argyll Environmental Ltd for PLC Environment, with the kind permission of the publishers (see *http://www.environment.practicallaw.com/main.jsp*).
[2] See further Ch.19 on Property Transactions.

Enquiries of the seller

There has recently been a move towards standardisation of pre-contract **22.04**
enquiries through the adoption by many firms of the Commercial Property
Standard Enquiries (CPSE) that were developed by the London Property
Support Lawyers Group (LPSLG) of information and know-how lawyers
within London firms. These will be sufficient for the purposes of an
acquisition of most commercial properties, although additional questions
may be necessary for industrial sites. The environment-related enquiries
contained in the LPSLG CPSEs[3] include (among others) an enquiry as to
the past and present uses of the Property and of activities carried out
there.[4] There is also an enquiry concerning the existence of any hazardous
substances or contaminative or potentially contaminative material in, on or
under the property, including asbestos-containing materials, any known
deposits of waste, existing or past storage areas for hazardous or radioactive substances, existing or former storage tanks (whether below or above
ground) and any parts of the property that are or were landfill.[5] In addition
there are enquiries requesting details of any notices, correspondence, legal
proceedings, disputes or complaints under environmental law or otherwise
relating to real or perceived environmental problems that affect the
property, or which have affected the property within the last ten years,
including any communications relating to the actual or possible presence of
contamination at or near the property[6]; and of any actual, alleged or
potential breaches of environmental law or licences or authorisations and
any other environmental problems (including actual or suspected contamination) relating to the property; or land in the vicinity of the property
that may adversely affect the property, its use or enjoyment or give rise to
any material liability or expenditure on the part of the owner or occupier
of the property.[7] Another enquiry requests a copy of all environmental
reports that have been prepared in relation to the property,[8] and a further
enquiry requests copies of any insurance policies that specifically provide
cover in relation to contamination or other environmental problems
affecting the property.[9]

The lawyer acting for the prospective purchaser cannot be criticised for **22.05**
raising such enquiries, but detailed and truly informative responses may
not be given by or on behalf of the seller. It is customary to carry out
enquiries of relevant public bodies in addition to raising enquiries of the
seller.

Enquiries of regulatory bodies

Although there are a number of regulatory bodies that could be contacted, **22.06**
in practice, for a normal transaction, these are usually restricted to
enquiries addressed to the local authority and to the Environment Agency.

[3] CPSE.1 (version 2.5) General pre-contract enquiries for all commercial property
transactions.
[4] Enquiry 15.4(a).
[5] Enquiry 15.4(b).
[6] Enquiry 15.5.
[7] Enquiry 15.7.
[8] Enquiry 15.1.
[9] Enquiry 15.8.

Local authority searches

22.07 The local authority search, CON 29, is divided into two parts, both of which contain enquiries relevant to environmental matters.

22.08 Part I of CON 29 contains a set of standard enquiries, including questions about planning consents and contamination (for example, whether an entry relating to the land appears on the local authority's contaminated land register). In particular, enquiry 3.12 of CON 29 asks whether any of the following apply (including any in relation to land adjacent to or adjoining the property which has been identified as contaminated land because it is in such a condition that harm or pollution of controlled waters might be caused on the property):

(a) a contaminated land notice[10]; or

(b) in relation to a register maintained under s.78R of the Environmental Protection Act 1990 (i) a decision to make an entry,[11] or (ii) an entry in such a register; or

(c) consultation has been conducted under s.78G(3) of the Environmental Protection Act 1990 with the owner or occupier of the property before the service of a remediation notice.[12]

22.09 Enquiry 3.7 of CON 29 asks whether any statutory notices that relate to (among other things) the environment, health and safety or public health subsist in relation to the property. Part II of CON 29 contains optional enquiries, including questions about hazardous substance consents[13] and environmental notices.[14] It is also possible to submit additional enquiries, although a reply is not guaranteed. A single fee is payable for the entire set of standard local authority enquiries, with a separate (further) charge for each optional and additional enquiry. There is no standard fee for dealing with any of these optional/additional enquiries; the cost varies between local authorities.

22.10 It should be noted that a negative reply to the contaminated land questions in Pt I of CON 29 does not necessarily mean that the land is not contaminated. It could mean instead that the land has not been inspected

---

[10] This is not defined in CON 29 but is presumed to mean a notice of determination that the land is contaminated land, as defined in Pt IIA of the EPA 1990.

[11] e.g. an entry that a remediation notice has been served.

[12] In particular, s.78G(3) provides that, before serving a remediation notice, the enforcing authority shall reasonably endeavour to consult every person who appears to the authority (a) to be the owner or occupier of any of the relevant land or waters, and (b) to be a person who might be required by s.78G(2) to grant or join in granting, any rights concerning the rights which that person may be so required to grant. Subsection (2) refers to situations where persons whose consent is required before any thing required by a remediation notice may be done, to grant or join in granting such rights in relation to the relevant land or waters as will enable the appropriate person to comply with any requirements imposed by the remediation notice.

[13] CON 29—enquiry 18.

[14] CON 29—enquiry 19—although this enquiry, which concerns (other) outstanding statutory or informal notices that may have been issued by the local authority under the Environmental Protection Act 1990 or the Control of Pollution Act 1974, is expressed not to cover notices under Pt IIA or Pt III of the EPA, to which the CON 29 enquiries 3.12 or 3.7 apply.

for contamination or that contamination is present on the land but is not (at the time) considered sufficiently serious to fall within the statutory definition of contaminated land. Only a relatively modest number of properties have so far been designated by local authorities as being contaminated to an extent that falls within the statutory definition; however, most potentially contaminated sites have still to be inspected in any detail by the relevant local authorities.[15]

Environment Agency searches

The Environment Agency formerly offered property search reports to the **22.11** public on payment of a fee; however, these have been discontinued by the Environment Agency, which continues to provide the information to a number of authorised resellers who offer a range of reports covering both residential and commercial property that contain the relevant Environment Agency data. It is possible to raise additional questions directly of the Environment Agency.[16] As a public body, they will need to respond in accordance with the Environmental Information Regulations 2004. It is likely that some of the questions will need to be referred to the relevant regional office so a delay in receiving a reply should be expected. The Environmental Information Regulations stipulate that the response should generally be given within 28 days. Where an environmental desktop report is carried out (see below), raising separate enquiries of the Environment Agency may not, however, be necessary.

It may also be noted that in 2002 the Agency published a detailed **22.12** technical report reviewing sources of information on contaminated land, including on background concentrations of contaminants.[17] The main objective of the study was to identify data sets that can be used to help assess land contamination in England. There are related reports for Scotland, Wales and Northern Ireland. The report includes a review of existing knowledge on "background" levels of contaminants in English soils. The research identified a wide range of land quality information, including soil survey data, environmental monitoring data, research studies and land use information. However, the emphasis was on identifying data sets representative of land quality at regional to national scales, rather than collating site specific and local scale information. The nature of the contamination considered in the review included chemical and radiological contaminants (both background and enhanced levels, present as a result of natural or anthropogenic processes); pathogens and munitions; saline soils; made ground and mine shafts; and closed or active landfill sites. Chapter 3 of the report summarised the content of various national and local data sets which were then available in the public domain for the contaminants under consideration.

---

[15] See para.3.243.

[16] This might be appropriate, for example, where a site was known to have been designated a "special site" for which the Environment Agency has jurisdiction, in order to ascertain the progress of any remediation works.

[17] B. Smith et al, *Information on Land Quality in England: Sources of Information* (R&D Technical Report P291, 2002).

Environmental reports

Types of environmental reports

22.13 Having regard to the Law Society's Contaminated Land Warning Card, lawyers advising in connection with a property transaction should at least consider obtaining information about the historic uses to which the relevant land may have been put, with a view to assessing whether there is a risk that it may be contaminated. Some care needs to be exercised when deciding whether to commission an independent site history investigation report and, if so, the extent (and detail) of information that is being sought. Broadly speaking, there are three types of report that can be commissioned, all of which should include information about historic uses:

1. Desktop (only) reports—which involve a review of publicly available material, such as public registers and current and historical maps and some privately owned databases.

2. Phase I report—which involves the same as a desktop report but includes a site visit and, in some cases, an interview with relevant site employees.

3. Phase II report—which involves the same as a Phase I report but includes sampling (such as soil, gas and/or water sampling).

22.14 The choice will vary depending of the nature of the transaction, and, particularly in the case of whether to commission Phase II reports, the extent to which there is a known contamination risk associated with a site. Usually, a desktop report is commissioned first and if this raises any issues of concern a Phase I Report might then be commissioned. However, this is not a hard-and-fast rule and in some cases (particularly if time is of the essence) it may be more appropriate to proceed directly to a Phase I, or even Phase II, report.

22.15 Environmental desktop reports in particular have caused confusion amongst lawyers and their clients, largely because of the number of different types of desktop reports available in the market, often with similar names. These reports are produced through the assessment of electronic data and maps (both historic and current) from which an initial risk-screening assessment can be made of the potential for contaminative uses to have been carried out at a site. Environmental desktop reports can be broadly divided into two types, depending on the amount of data reviewed: environmental desktop reports and commercial risk screening reports.

Environmental desktop reports

22.16 The main companies in the UK that specialise in providing environmental desktop reports to the legal market are, currently, Argyll Environmental, Groundsure and Landmark. The desktop reports produced by these providers are manually assessed by environmental consultants and involve a review of high-detail historic maps.

Commercial risk screening reports

Commercial risk screening reports are based on simpler assessments, **22.17** which generally do not involve a review of high-detail maps and, in some cases, are based partly on computer models. Computer models are often useful for screening out risks but may highlight false positives.

Factors affecting quality and price of environmental reports

The following is a summary of the main factors that will determine the **22.18** quality and price of an environmental desktop report.

Method of assessment

As noted above, there are drawbacks to those reports that are wholly or **22.19** partly computer-generated without involving a review of historic maps. The more expensive reports involve a manual assessment of the data and maps by qualified environmental consultants who then write the reports.

Mapping scales

There are two main scales of mapping: 1:10,000 and 1:2,500. The 1:2,500 is **22.20** clearly of a more detailed scale and consequently contains significantly more information. This means it takes the consultant longer to review the maps, but that a more detailed report can be provided. It is important that the report includes a schedule of the actual maps reviewed. It may be necessary to make additional enquiries if there are significant gaps in the mapping history.

Point- or polygon-based searches

Point-based searches involve defining the area to be searched with refer- **22.21** ence to a set radius around a point on a map located within the site boundary. Polygon-based searches involve defining the area to be searched by reference to the approximate outline of the site boundary. Point-based searches are simpler but less accurate than polygon-based searches. Polygon-based searches provide a more precise measurement from the boundary of a site, as opposed to an arbitrary central point somewhere within the site boundary. These types of searches therefore provide a more accurate assessment of potential contaminative sources within the boundary of the subject property. Most commercial environmental desktop searches are now polygon-based (that is, based on the site boundary).

Search radius

When reviewing a site, the consultant will need to draw a balance between **22.22** reviewing sufficient data to assess accurately the potential environmental liabilities and purchasing excessive data, resulting in increased reviewing costs. As a general rule, search radii for residential environmental desktop reports are more limited than those for a commercial search. For commercial properties, the distance searched will depend on the data being assessed. For example, while a consultant may wish to search landfill databases up to 1km from a site, a search radius of 250 metres is likely to be sufficient when searching datasets for small scale current industrial facilities. It is important to note that more data is not always best, as unnecessarily large search radii can provide a more cumbersome amount of information for the consultant to review, potentially reducing the clarity of the search and increasing the price of the report.

Datasets

22.23 Most commercial environmental desktop reports will use a similar range of datasets, but it is worth checking a report in detail to make sure that important datasets (such as those for landfills and other waste sites) are provided. In addition, it is vital to know the accuracy of the data used in the search and how often it is updated, as older and less accurate datasets may provide misleading and inaccurate search results. An example is the Environment Agency pollution incident register dataset, which is no longer available in many new desktop reports, due to problems with its accuracy. This database has been replaced by the more accurate Substantiated Pollution Incident database.

Other factors

22.24 Other factors that may affect the quality and price of an environmental desktop report which should be considered when selecting a desktop report provider include:

1. ease of use (that is, how easy is a report to understand and how often are problems highlighted);

2. the ability to follow through with further enquiries or obtain further consultancy services (such as a Phase I or Phase II report) at reasonable cost;

3. the speed of delivery and whether an expedited report can be produced (say inside a working day) and whether there is an additional cost for this;

4. the contractual terms, including the limit of liability and level of the consultancy's professional indemnity cover[18]; and

5. whether insurance for risks relating to contaminated land can be provided on the basis of the findings of the report (and without the need for insurers to require any further surveys).

22.25 These variables can be tested by inviting possible suppliers to provide a brief presentation, by direct enquiry or through a questionnaire, or by asking for some test sites to be assessed. This is important since inex-

---

[18] See further, Ch.18 on use of consultants.

perienced consultants may tend to err on the side of caution, which may result in an otherwise acceptable site being the subject of unnecessary further contractual negotiations aimed at allocating risk.

Sources of data in environmental desktop reports

All Environmental Desktop and Commercial Risk Screening Reports **22.26** involve the collation of data from a number of different sources. These will typically include the following:

Environment Agency	Abstraction licences
	Water discharge consents (plus Red List)
	Groundwater vulnerability
	Licensed landfill, waste transfer and treatment sites
	Historic landfill sites
	Main rivers
	Prosecutions and enforcement actions
	Integrated Pollution Control and Integrated Pollution Prevention and Control (IPPC) permits
	River quality information
	Registered radioactive substances
	Source Protection Zones
	Substantiated Pollution Incident Register
Local Authorities	Air Pollution Control/IPPC permits
	Air Pollution Control/IPPC enforcement actions
	Local authority recorded landfills
	Planning Hazardous Substance Consents
	Planning Hazardous Substance enforcement actions
British Geological Society	BGS Landfills
	Compressible ground subsidence hazards
	Ground dissolution subsidence hazards
	Gulls and cambering subsidence hazards
	Landslip subsidence hazards
	Shallow mining hazards
	Swelling clay subsidence hazards
Catalist	Fuel stations
PointX Industrial Dataset Thomson	Contemporary Trade Directories
Health and Safety Executive	Control of Major Accident Hazard sites
	Notification of Installations Handling Hazardous Substances
	Explosive Sites
Coal Authority	Coal Mining Areas

Health Protection Agency	Radon Affected Areas
	Radon Protective Measures
Historic maps	Potentially contaminative historic land use
	Potentially Infilled Land
Current OS maps	Base Mapping
Ove Arup	Mining instability
Peter Brett Associates	Natural and mining cavities
Natural England	Environmentally Sensitive Areas
(formerly English Nature	Local Nature Reserves
and the Countryside	Marine Nature Reserves
Agency)	National Nature Reserves
	Nearest surface water feature
	Ramsar Sites
	Sites of Special Scientific Interest
	Source Protection Zones
	Special Protection Areas
	Special Areas of Conservation
	Areas of Outstanding Natural Beauty
	National Parks
	National Scenic Areas
The Forestry Commission	Forest Parks

22.27   The solicitor will need to consider whether it is necessary to raise any further enquiries of the Environment Agency in light of any specific information they may have on the site in addition to the information provided by the Environment Agency in the environment search report that has been commissioned. For this reason it is important for the solicitor to be aware of exactly what Environment Agency information will be provided by the search provider that has been chosen.

22.28   In addition, as mentioned above, there are a number of privately held databases that are only made available for certain environmental desktop reports. For example Landmark Information Group holds detailed databases on historic landfill sites, which involves a detailed assessment of local authority and Environment Agency data. This assessment has taken ten years to complete and is still ongoing. These databases are currently only used in the Landmark and Argyll Environmental reports.

Chapter 23

INSURANCE

Introduction

Insurance is available for liabilities arising from contaminated land. It is **23.01** not possible, however, to ensure adequate protection for such liabilities by relying solely on public liability and other general liability policies. Whereas public liability policies generally provide cover for tort claims for bodily injury arising from sudden and accidental pollution incidents (though some underwriters will exclude pollution absolutely if there is a high risk potential), the extent of cover provided by them for other environmental liabilities is not clear. This chapter discusses cover for liabilities arising from contaminated land in general liability policies. The policies which are discussed are:

1. public liability policies;

2. property policies;

3. employers' liability policies;

4. directors' and officers' policies; and

5. professional indemnity policies.

The chapter then deals with insurance policies which are specially **23.02** designed to cover liabilities arising from contaminated land. Finally, the chapter discusses the issue of finite risk programmes for the remediation of contaminated land.

Public liability policies

In order to set the discussion of cover provided by public liability policies **23.03** for contaminated land in context, the following is a brief description of the interpretation of public liability policies and their general format.

Rules of construction

Public liability policies, like any other insurance policies for UK risks, do **23.04** not follow a standard form. Application of the rules of construction under English law means, therefore, that a word or phrase in one policy may have a different meaning from the same word or phrase in another policy. This is because, although a word or phrase in a contract is generally given its ordinary or plain meaning, it must be read in the context of the clause in which it appears and the entire policy wording.[1] In addition, the policy, like any other contract, must be interpreted against the background—or factual matrix—in which it is set. A contract is thus interpreted by ascertaining "the meaning which the document would convey to a reasonable person having all the background knowledge which would reasonably have been available to the parties in the situation in which they were at the time of the contract".[2] In respect of insurance policies in particular[3]:

> "The general principle is that the proper construction is to be determined by the ordinary and natural meaning of the words used in the contractual and commercial setting in which the words appear. The niceties of language may have to give way to a commercial construction which is more likely to give effect to the intention of the parties."

Format

23.05 Public liability and other insurance policies for UK risks tend to have the same general format. A schedule to the policy sets out information such as the named insured, any additional insureds, the limit, and any sub-limits, of indemnity, the amount of deductibles or self-insured retention, the policy period and the premium. The policy wording includes a coverage clause (also known as an insuring agreement), definitions of specified words and phrases, exclusions and conditions. The policy may contain endorsements which add, delete or otherwise revise the schedule and/or the policy wording. The limit of indemnity in a primary public liability policy generally includes the cost of defending the insured against third-party claims. If the insured has purchased an excess policy, that policy provides an indemnity above the limit of the primary policy and any other excess policies on lower layers.

23.06 The coverage clause of a primary public liability policy generally provides that the insurer agrees to indemnify the insured for all sums which the insured shall become legally liable to pay as damages (and/or compensation or a civil claim) for accidental bodily injury or death or loss of or damage to property which occurs during the policy period in connection with the insured's business. Depending on the wording, the policy may include cover in respect of a nuisance or trespass by the insured as well as other specified risks. Public liability policies are occurrence-based, that is, they provide cover for an "occurrence" of bodily injury or property damage. Excess policies, meanwhile, generally provide cover for an "event" or a "happening". Unless the policy wording indicates otherwise, courts tend to conclude that the three words have the same meaning.[4]

23.07 The insured bears the burden of showing, on a balance of probabilities, that the policy provides cover for the claim which has been made against the insured.[5] In respect of a public liability policy, the insured must show that:

---

[1] *Charter Reinsurance Company Ltd v Fagan* [1997] A.C. 313, HL.

[2] *Investors Compensation Scheme v West Bromwich Building Society* [1998] 1 W.L.R. 896, HL.

[3] *Tioxide Europe Limited v CGU International Insurance Plc* [2005] Lloyd's Rep. I.R. 114, QBD.

[4] See *Schiffshypothekenbank Zu Luebeck AG v Compton (The Alexion Hope)* [1988] 1 Lloyd's Rep. 311, CA; *Mann v Lexington Insurance Co* [2001] 1 All E.R. (Comm) 28 [2001] Lloyd's Rep. 1 CA; *American Centennial Insurance Co v Insco Ltd* [1996] Lloyd's Rep. L.R. 407, QBD.

[5] See *Regina Fur Co v Bossom* [1958] 2 Lloyd's Rep. 426, CA.

1. the occurrence which it is alleging was accidental;

2. it is "legally liable" to pay damages to the claimant;

3. a claim has been made against it;

4. its legal liability is for "damages" or "compensation" (or another term as specified in the policy); and

5. the alleged bodily injury or property damage occurred during the policy period.

In most claims against public liability policies, none of the above elements will be contentious. In claims arising from contaminated land, however, an issue may arise in connection with one or more of these elements for the reasons discussed below.

Accidental bodily injury and property damage

Insurance policies provide cover for fortuities, not certainties. Accordingly, **23.08** an insured must show that it did not intend or expect the bodily injury or property damage for which the claim against it has been made. A court determines whether an accident has occurred from the viewpoint of the insured rather than the person who has claimed against the insured.[6] An insured may be able to show that its policy provides cover for a claim arising from land which it contaminated, even though the insured intentionally disposed of chemicals on the land. For example, a company may have disposed of liquid hazardous waste from its operations into a clay-lined pit on its land for many years. If the liquid waste breached the clay liner and seeped to an aquifer beneath the land so that harm occurred to a person using abstracted groundwater, then even though the insured company's disposal of the waste was intentional, the company could contend that the property damage is accidental because it considered that the pit was a secure container for the waste and, therefore, it did not expect or intend to pollute the groundwater which led to the injury.

Knowledge that its past operations had caused harm does not mean that **23.09** an insured company necessarily expected or intended harm from subsequent operations. An Australian court concluded that an insured company's regular releases of chlorine gas, which reactivated an employee's asthma, were accidental because the company had investigated its prior releases and taken measures to prevent future releases. The court concluded that the subsequent releases were caused by the company operating in a different manner.[7]

---

[6] See *Gray v Barr* [1971] 2 Q.B. 554, CA (death of man during struggle with insured was not accidental because insured should reasonably have intended neighbour's death due to his unlawful and reckless act in going to neighbour's house—who he suspected of having an affair with his wife—with a shotgun); *Forney v Dominium Insurance Co Ltd* [1969] 1 W.L.R. 928, QBD (term "in respect of any one claim or number of claims arising out of the same occurrence" means from standpoint of insured because term contemplates several claims arising out of one occurrence).

[7] *Australian Paper Manufacturers Ltd v American International Underwriters (Australia) Pty Ltd* [1994] 1 V.R. 685 (Victoria S Ct).

641

Legally liable

23.10 In addition to showing that it did not expect or intend bodily injury or property damage, the insured must show that it is "legally liable" to pay sums in respect of the injury or damage. The term "legally liable" has a well-established meaning in English law. An insured company's liability arises when an accident due to the company's act or omission has occurred and a person has suffered harm resulting from the accident. Legal liability arises when the insured company and the claimant have agreed to a settlement or there is a judgment or an arbitral award.[8] Depending on the policy wording, it may be difficult for an insured to show that it is legally liable to pay costs to remediate contaminated land due to the nature of Pt IIA. A person who has received a notification of contaminated land may make a commercial decision to remediate the contamination rather than declining to do so and risk being served with a remediation notice. As provided by Pt IIA, that person then prepares a remediation statement indicating what is to be done and on what timescale. The terms and conditions of a remediation statement are not, however, legally enforceable. Thus, if the insured claims cover for the costs of the remedial works against its public liability policy, the insurer may well decline the claim on the basis that the insured was not legally liable and has carried out the remedial works voluntarily.[9] In such a situation, the insured may contend that its agreement with the enforcing authority to remediate the contamination is the functional equivalent of a settlement. However, the question is then whether the subject of the settlement is covered by the policy. The issue as to whether a settlement for property damage was covered by a public liability policy arose in *Yorkshire Water Services Ltd v Sun Alliance and London Insurance Plc (No.2)*.[10] A sewage sludge tip which was owned and operated by Yorkshire Water Services Ltd (Yorkshire Water) had collapsed into the River Colne in West Yorkshire, resulting in flood damage to various properties located by the river. Yorkshire Water claimed that its policy covered a settlement which it had entered into with ICI, the owner of one of the properties which had suffered flood damage. ICI had claimed that Yorkshire Water was liable in nuisance, negligence and the rule in *Rylands v Fletcher*. Humphrey Lloyd Q.C. of the Official Referee's Court concluded that ICI did not have a valid claim against Yorkshire Water. He therefore ruled that the settlement was not covered by the insured's policies.

Claim

23.11 A similar issue to whether an insured is legally liable to remediate contaminated land in the absence of a remediation notice under Pt IIA (or a works or other enforcement notice under other environmental legisla-

---

[8] *Bradley v Eagle Star Insurance Co Ltd* [1989] 1 A.C. 957, HL; see *Post Office v Norwich Union Fire Insurance Society Ltd* [1967] 2 Q.B. 363, CA (explaining difference between "liable" and "legally liable").

[9] *cf. Smit Tak Offshore Services Ltd v Youell* [1992] 1 Lloyd's Rep. 154, CA (letter from Ruler of Dubai which instructed insured to remove wreck did not impose legal liability; although Ruler threatened to withdraw insured's licence to operate in Dubai waters, letter was not enforceable by law).

[10] [1998] Env. L.R. 204, QBD.

tion) is whether a claim has been made against the insured. In such a situation, the insured could contend that if it had not carried out the works, the enforcing authority would have served a notice requiring it to carry them out and the policy would have covered such a claim. This issue arose in *Yorkshire Water Services Ltd v Sun Alliance and London Insurance plc (No.1)*[11] as to whether public liability policies purchased by the insured covered costs incurred by the insured in carrying out works on its land to minimise the risk of further flooding following the collapse of a sewage sludge tip. More precisely, the court was called on to determine whether "an insured under a public liability policy [can] recover the cost of measures taken in order to avoid or mitigate a loss which the insurers would or might have to meet". The coverage clause of Yorkshire Water's primary public liability policy provided that:

> "The Company will provide indemnity . . . against legal liability for damages in respect of accidental . . . loss of or damage to material property . . . happening during any Period of Insurance in connection with the Business."

The policy had a limit of indemnity of £1 million "in respect of any one **23.12** Event (meaning one occurrence or all occurrences of a series consequent on or attributable to one source or original cause)". The coverage clause of the excess policy, which had a limit of indemnity of £9 million excess £1 million, provided that:

> "The Company will indemnify the Insured against all sums which the Insured shall become legally liable to pay as damages or compensation in respect of . . . loss of or damage to property . . . happening in connection with the Business and occurring during the Period of Insurance."

The excess policy defined the word "occurrence" to mean "a series of **23.13** occurrences arising out of the original cause however many claims may arise therefrom". The Court of Appeal concluded that costs incurred by Yorkshire Water to minimise the risk of further flooding were not covered by the policy because they were neither an "event" nor an "occurrence". Stuart-Smith L.J. stated that Yorkshire Water had failed to show that: it had paid "sums" (i.e., "sums paid or payable to to third party claimants"); or it was "legally liable to pay" such sums; or the sums were payable as "damages" because they were owed due to a breach of duty or obligation; or that the sums were paid for "loss or damage to [a third party's] property". In so holding he referred to a further clause of the policy which provided that:

> "The Insured at his own expense shall . . . take reasonable precautions to prevent any circumstances or to cease any activity which may give rise to liability under this Policy."

---

[11] [1997] 2 Lloyd's Rep. 21, CA.

He held that this clause required Yorkshire Water to carry out measures, at its own expense, to prevent damage before and after the entry of the sewage sludge tip into the river.

Damages

23.14 Public liability policies provide cover for an insured's legal liability for "damages" and/or "compensation" or a similar term in respect of a claim for bodily injury, property damage or other risks covered by the policy. Claims for bodily injury are generally, but not necessarily, tort claims, the remedy for which is a judicial award of compensatory damages. In the context of contaminated land, a claimant may bring a bodily injury claim against the insured in negligence for harm suffered by the claimant due to exposure to a pollutant whose presence is caused by the insured. A public liability policy generally provides cover for such a claim, subject to other terms and conditions of the policy, in particular an exclusion for gradual pollution in post-1990 policies. Indeed, public liability policies have traditionally provided cover for "liability to the public at large for claims in tort or for the type of damage which [is] protected by the law of tort". Coverage of tortious liability may mean that claims based on losses which tort would not cover, e.g. pure economic loss, are not within the policy.[12]

23.15 It is not clear, however, whether a public liability policy provides cover in respect of an action by a governmental authority against an insured for the cost of remediating contamination. The crucial issue in this respect is the meaning of the word "damages" or "compensation". The issue as to whether the word "damages" in an insuring agreement provides cover for remediating pollution was determined in *Bartoline Ltd v Royal & Sun Alliance Insurance Plc*,[13] a claim which arose from a huge fire at a factory in East Yorkshire at which adhesives and hydrocarbons were stored. The fire resulted in chemicals and fire-fighting foam and water polluting two watercourses. The Environment Agency removed contaminated silt and vegetation from the beds and banks of the watercourses, constructed dams and pumped polluted water into tankers for treatment and disposal at a cost of £622,681. The Agency subsequently invoiced Bartoline Ltd, the owner and operator of the factory, for these costs under s.161 of the Water Resources Act 1991. Bartoline also incurred £147,988 in costs in complying with a works notice served by the Environment Agency under s.161A of the 1991 Act.

23.16 Bartoline claimed its costs for remedial works against its public liability policy issued by Royal & Sun Allliance Plc (RSA). The policy provided that RSA agreed to indemnify Bartoline:

> "against legal liability for damages in respect of . . . accidental loss of or damage to Property . . . nuisance trespass to land or trespass to goods or interference with any easement right of air light water or way [during the policy period]."

23.17 RSA denied the claim on the basis that the word "damages" provides cover only for tort claims and not statutory causes of action. HHJ Hegarty Q.C. of the High Court agreed. In his lengthy judgment, he cited

---

[12] *Tesco Stores Ltd v Constable* [2007] EWHC 2088 (Comm); [2007] All E.R. (D) 85 (Sep), QBD.
[13] [2006] EWHC 3598 (QB (Merc)).

Halsbury's description of "damages" as "the pecuniary recompense given by process of law to a person for the actionable wrong that another has done him".[14] He stated that the "essential purpose of [public liability] policies is to provide the indemnity in respect of certain types of tortious liability". He thus concluded that the "established usage" of the word "damages" in a public liability policy is to provide cover for tort claims and not claims arising under legislation such as the Water Resources Act 1991. The High Court's decision was appealed, but settled in 2007 shortly before the hearing. It does not necessarily mean that there is no cover for liabilities for remediating contaminated land under public liability policies which contain the word "damages" in their coverage clauses. As noted above, a court determines the meaning of a word or phrase in the context of the clause in which it appears and the entire policy. The decision does, however, mean that a court would be likely to conclude that many public liability policies do not provide cover for liabilities under Pt IIA or other environmental legislation. An exception could well be a public liability policy which contains Lloyd's Underwriters Non-Marine Association (NMA) clause 1685 (discussed below). Arguably, the coverage clause of a policy which contains a pollution exclusion which writes back cover for remediating contamination must cover the cost of such remediation.

Compensation

The coverage clauses of some public liability policies contain the word **23.18** "compensation" in addition to, or instead of, the word "damages". The word "compensation" may have a broader meaning than the word "damages" depending on the policy wording in which it appears. In the non-environmental case of *Lancashire CC v Municipal Mutual Insurance Ltd*,[15] Simon Brown L.J. (as he then was) rejected a narrow "legalistic" meaning of the word "compensation" in a public liability policy. The insured had contended that the policy provided cover for exemplary as well as compensatory damages. Simon Brown L.J. accepted that "the natural and ordinary meaning of "compensation" in the context of a legal liability to pay damages is one which excludes any element of exemplary damages". He could not accept, however, that the "meaning is wholly clear and unambiguous". He stated that:

> "On the contrary it involves very much a literal, lawyers' understanding of the term and is one which would not command universal acceptance. Many, including no doubt most recipients, would regard 'compensation' to mean instead all damages (of whatsoever nature and however calculated) payable to the victim of a tort."

Simon Brown L.J. thus concluded that the word "damages" in the policy **23.19** at issue included exemplary as well as compensatory damages payable to a claimant in tort. This is, of course, not the same as concluding that the

---

[14] *Halsbury's Laws of England*, Vol. 12(1) (4th edn, 1998) para.802.
[15] [1997] Q.B. 897, CA.

word "compensation" includes statutory as well as tortious damages. It shows, however, that the Court of Appeal was willing to go beyond the legal meaning of the word. However, in the same year that it handed down the decision in *Lancashire CC*, the Court of Appeal cited a 1930s case which narrowly construed the word "damages" in accordance with its legal meaning in the case involving the remediation of the collapsed sewage sludge tip described above.[16]

23.20   In a subsequent decision involving cover for costs incurred by an insured in carrying out remedial works, the Court of Appeal concluded that the public liability policy at issue covered costs incurred by the insured dredging company in removing silt from properties along Southampton Water.[17] The dredging works had resulted in silt in a channel in the estuary being put into suspension and deposited on the affected properties. The owners and occupiers of the properties had alleged that the insured and the port authority were liable in negligence and private nuisance for the damage. The Court of Appeal agreed and concluded that the policy covered costs incurred by the insured and the port authority in removing the silt. The Court of Appeal further concluded that the policy provided cover for costs incurred by the Hampshire Wildlife Trust in carrying out a study of the effect of silt on its nature reserve. The Trust's survey had concluded that the silt would not result in any long-term damage and, therefore, did not need to be removed from the nature reserve. Schiemann L.J. stated that carrying out the survey was in insurers' interests due to property damage having been suspected.

Timing of an occurrence

23.21   The application of Pt IIA to contamination caused by pollution incidents which may have occurred many years before a local authority makes a determination of contaminated land means that appropriate persons may well bring claims for the cost of remedial works against past public liability policies. Public liability policies have a "long tail" of liability. That is, the period for which they provide cover is the period during which bodily injury or property damage occurs, not the period during which a claim is made against the insured for injury or damage. The issue is particularly likely to arise because the vast majority of policies underwritten before 1990 did not exclude cover for gradual pollution.

23.22   Courts in the US have developed four theories to determine the time at which an occurrence takes place under a commercial general liability policy and, thus, the policy or policies which are "triggered" by a claim for bodily injury or property damage due to exposure to a pollutant or contamination. Under the "exposure" theory, policies which are on the risk when an individual or property has been exposed to a contaminant must respond to a claim. Under the "manifestation" theory, the policy which was

---

[16] *Yorkshire Water Services Ltd v Sun Alliance & London Insurance Plc* [1997] 2 Lloyd's Rep. 21, [1997] Env. LR D4, CA (quoting *Hall Brothers Steamship Co Ltd v Young* [1939] 1 K.B. 748, CA ("damages" has a precise meaning to an English lawyer and means "sums which fall to be paid by reason of some breach of duty or obligation").

[17] *Jan de Nul (UK) Ltd v Axa Royale Belge S.A.* [2002] 1 All E.R. (Comm) 767 [2002] 1 Lloyd's Rep. 583, CA. See also para.14.94.

on the risk when the bodily injury or property damage manifested itself or was discovered must respond. Under the "injury-in-fact" theory, policies which were on the risk when actual bodily injury or property damage occurs must respond. Finally, under the "continuous trigger" theory, all policies which are triggered under the exposure, injury-in-fact and manifestation theories must respond.[18]

There is no case under English law which adopts a trigger theory in **23.23** respect of property damage. In *Bolton MBC v Municipal Mutual Insurance Ltd*, a case involving a claim for bodily injury from exposure to asbestos, however, the Court of Appeal affirmed the High Court's rejection of the exposure trigger.[19] The case arose due to Bolton Metropolitan BC (Bolton) having negligently exposed Mr Green, an employee of one of its contractors, to asbestos between 1960 and 1963. A subsequent employer further exposed Mr Green to asbestos between 1965 and 1970 and after 1973 by a subsequent employer. In 1990, Mr Green suffered symptoms of mesothelioma. In January 1991, he was diagnosed with the disease from which he died in November 1991. Between 1960 and 1965, Bolton had a public liability policy from a predecessor of Commercial Union (CU). Between 1979 and 1991, it had a public liability policy from Municipal Mutual Insurance (MMI).

The CU policy indemnified Bolton for: **23.24**

> "[a]ll sums which the Insured shall become legally liable to pay for compensation in respect of . . . bodily injury to or illness of any person . . . occurring . . . during the Period of Indemnity as a result of an accident and happening."

The MMI policy indemnified Bolton for: **23.25**

> "all sums which the Insured shall become legally liable to pay as compensation arising out of . . . accidental bodily injury or illness . . . when such injury illness . . . occurs during the currency of the Policy."

Longmore L.J. rejected the exposure trigger on the basis that Mr Green **23.26** did not suffer an actionable injury during the time in which he was exposed to asbestos. He concluded that Mr Green suffered an actionable injury when the malignant tumour had developed in about 1980 or when identifiable symptoms of mesothelioma first occurred in 1990 to 1991. He thus considered that the appropriate trigger is the injury-in-fact or the manifestation trigger. He did not have to decide which trigger applied due to MMI policies being on the risk during both policy periods. If the *Bolton* case is read across to property damage from contaminated land, the policy which is triggered is the policy on the risk when actual damage to third-party property occurs or the damage is discovered.

---

[18] See generally V. Fogleman, *Environmental Liabilities and Insurance in England and the United States* (Witherbys, 2005), pp. 510–518.

[19] *Bolton MBC v Municipal Mutual Insurance Ltd* [2006] 1 W.L.R. 1492; [2006] All E.R. (D) 66, CA.

23.27   An insurer could argue that its past public liability policies do not cover the cost of remediating contaminated land under Pt IIA because the policies were underwritten before Pt IIA was enacted. A court is, however, unlikely to conclude that a public liability policy does not cover such liabilities simply because the insurer was not aware of them when it underwrote the policy at issue. In a claim for damages due to harm caused by exposure to asbestos, Eady J. commented that an insurer cannot be certain when it issues a policy that:

> "there will not be some development of the law, whether by way of judicial development or by statutory intervention, which will render the assumption of risk less commercially attractive. The question is always whether the legal liability at the time it is established is such as to fall within the scope of the risk insured against."[20]

Pollution exclusions

23.28 In 1990, the Association of British Insurers (ABI) recommended to its members that they exclude cover for gradual pollution in public liability policies. Virtually all public liability policies underwritten since that time have contained a qualified pollution exclusion, that is, an exclusion which bars cover for harm caused by pollution or contamination with the exception of harm caused by a sudden, unexpected and unintended incident.[21] The ABI model pollution exclusion provides that:

> "A   This policy excludes all liability in respect of Pollution or Contamination other than caused by a sudden identifiable unintended and unexpected incident which takes place in its entirety at a specific time and place during the Period of Insurance.
>
> All Pollution or Contamination which arises out of one incident shall be deemed to have occurred at the time such incident takes place.
>
> B   The liability of the Company for all compensation payable in respect of Pollution or Contamination which is deemed to have occurred during the Period of Insurance shall not exceed £. . . in the aggregate.
>
> C   For the purposes of this Endorsement, 'Pollution or Contamination' shall be deemed to mean
>
> (i)   all Pollution or Contamination of buildings or other structures or of water or land or the atmosphere; and
>
> (ii)   all loss or damage or injury directly caused by such Pollution or Contamination."

23.29   Most public liability insurers use the ABI model pollution exclusion or an adaptation of it in their policies.

---

[20] *Phillips v Syndicate 992* [2004] Lloyd's Rep. I.R. 426, QBD.
[21] In contrast, an absolute pollution exclusion bars cover for pollution or contamination absolutely and is occasionally applied by insurers to policies with a high-risk potential.

The other commonly-used pollution exclusion is NMA 1685, which was **23.30** drafted by the Lloyd's Underwriters Non-Marine Association. NMA 1685 provides that:

> "This Insurance does not cover any liability for:
>
> (1) Personal Injury or Bodily Injury or loss of, damage to, or loss of use of property directly or indirectly caused by seepage, pollution or contamination, provided always that this paragraph (1) shall not apply to liability for Personal Injury or Bodily Injury or loss of or physical damage to or destruction of tangible property, or loss of use of such property damaged or destroyed, where such seepage, pollution or contamination is caused by a sudden, unintended and unexpected happening during the period of this Insurance.
>
> (2) The cost of removing, nullifying or cleaning-up seeping, polluting or contaminating substances unless the seepage, pollution or contamination is caused by a sudden, unintended and unexpected happening during the period of this Insurance.
>
> (3) Fines, penalties, punitive or exemplary damages.
>
> This Clause shall not extend this Insurance to cover any liability which would not have been covered under this Insurance had this Clause not been attached."

As with any exclusion which does not expressly reverse the burden of **23.31** proof, an insurer bears the burden of showing that it applies.[22] Case law indicates that the insured has the burden of showing that an exception to the exclusion applies.[23]

No English court has been called on to determine the application, or **23.32** extent of, the ABI model pollution exclusion or NMA 1685. The policy issued to Bartoline by RSA, discussed above,[23a] included a pollution exclusion based on the ABI model exclusion. The exclusion barred legal liability:

> "caused by or arising out of pollution or contamination of buildings or other structures or of water or land or the atmosphere unless the pollution or contamination is caused by a sudden identifiable unintended and unexpected incident which takes place in its entirety at a specific moment in time and place during any Period of Insurance."

Although there was no need to reach a conclusion on the issue, RSA **23.33** agreed that the pollution exclusion would not have barred cover for Bartoline's claim for the cost of remedial works, because it accepted that the fire was a "sudden identifiable unintended and unexpected incident which took place in its entirety at a specific time and place".

---

[22] See *Spinney's (1948) Ltd v Royal Insurance Company Ltd* [1980] 1 Lloyd's Rep. 406, QBD.

[23] See *Rowett, Leakey and Company v Scottish Provident Institution* [1927] 1 Ch. 55, CA.

[23a] See *Bartoline Ltd v Royal & Sun Alliance Insurance Plc* [2006] EWHC 3598 (QB (Merc)), para.23.15 ff.

23.34   One issue which has arisen in claims against public liability policies which contain the ABI exclusion is the meaning of the word "incident", which does not generally appear in public liability policies. For example, an insured might have a secure pit containing liquid hazardous waste on its land, from which the waste escaped during heavy rain and entered groundwater, from which it migrated to a river. If the "incident" was the escape from the pit, it would have been "sudden identifiable unintended and unexpected". If the incident was the gradual entry of the waste into the groundwater or the gradual entry of polluted groundwater into the river, it is likely to have been gradual and coverage would be barred.

23.35   The High Court has concluded that a pollution exclusion which contained the phrase "non-accidental pollution" barred cover for pollution which occurred "over a period of many weeks". The word "accident" was defined to mean "a sudden occurrence which is unintentional and unexpected for the policyholder".[24] Pollution exclusions in public liability policies were construed so as not to bar cover in respect of claims arising from the oil spill from the *Exxon Valdez* in Prince William Sound, Alaska, in 1989. The exclusion in the first case provided that:

> "This contract excludes any loss arising from seepage, pollution or contamination on land unless such risks are insured solely on a sudden and accidental basis."

23.36   The Commercial Court concluded that the exclusion barred cover only in respect of seepage, pollution or contamination from a land-based source, not a vessel.[25] The second coverage action involved construction of the following exclusion:

> "This contract excludes any loss arising from seepage, pollution or contamination on land unless such risks are insured solely on a sudden and accidental basis. This contract also excludes liability in respect of disposal or dumping of any waste materials or substances."

23.37   The Commercial Court concluded that the exclusion did not apply because seaborne pollution occurs at sea rather than on land.[26]

Owned property exclusion

23.38 As discussed above, public liability policies provide cover for claims by third parties against the insured; they do not cover a claim by the insured for damage to its own property. The policies, therefore, typically contain an owned property exclusion which bars cover for damage to property which is owned or occupied by, or is in the care, custody or control of, the insured. If

---

[24] *Jan de Nul (UK) Ltd v N.V. Royale Belge* [2000] 2 Lloyd's Rep. 700, QBD.

[25] *Commercial Union Assurance Co Plc v NRG Victory Reinsurance Ltd* [1998] 1 Lloyd's Rep. 80, QBD, reversed on other grounds [1998] 2 All E.R. 434 [1998] 2 Lloyd's Rep. 600, CA.

[26] *King v Brandywine Reinsurance Co (UK) Ltd* [2004] 2 All E.R. (Comm) 443; [2004] 2 Lloyd's Rep. 670. QBD.

an insured incurs costs in remediating contamination on its own land for the insured's own benefit, the owned property exclusion is highly unlikely to bar cover for the costs depending, of course, on the policy wording. The issue arose in the cases arising from the collapse of Yorkshire Water's sewage sludge tip into the River Colne, described above.[26a] Yorkshire Water's public liability policies barred cover for "any loss of or damage to any property which . . . is owned by . . . or is in the custody or control of [Yorkshire Water]". Humphrey Lloyd Q.C. concluded that Yorkshire Water's public liability policy did not provide cover for losses which arose from the collapse of the tip or associated damage to a pipe because both the collapse and the damage occurred on the insured's own site.[27]

23.39 The owned property exclusion may not bar cover for the cost of remediating polluted groundwater or contaminated soil in order to prevent the pollution migrating to third-party property. In such a case, an insured could contend that the exclusion does not apply because, although a landowner has the right to abstract groundwater beneath its land, it does not have an ownership interest in the groundwater while it is in the ground.[28]

Property policies

23.40 A property policy provides cover for losses resulting from damage to property which is owned or occupied by an insured. There are two types of property policies. An all risks policy provides cover for loss to the property by a peril which is not specifically excluded. A named perils policy specifies the perils which must cause the loss in order for the policy to respond. The matters covered are: fire, riot fire, lightning, aircraft, explosion, riot, civil commotion, malicious damage, earthquake, storm, tempest, flood, burst pipe or escape of oil, impact by own or third party vehicles, and accidental damage. In an all risks policy, the insurer has the burden of showing that an excluded peril has caused the loss. In a named perils policy, the insured has the burden of showing that a specified peril caused the loss.[29]

23.41 Property policies are unlikely to provide cover for the costs of remediating contaminated land for the following reasons. First, a property policy provides cover only in respect of damage to property which is listed in it. Insured property includes buildings but not, as a general rule, land. Thus, if oil from a heating system escapes and causes damage to the structure of a building, the loss should in principle be covered depending, of course, on the terms and conditions of the policy. If the oil seeps into the soil, the cost of remediating it is not typically covered, because soil is not generally insured property.

[26a] See para.23.11.

[27] *Yorkshire Water Services Ltd v Sun Alliance & London Insurance Plc (No. 2)* [1998] Env. L.R. 204, QBD.

[28] *Ballard v Tomlinson* (1885) LR 29 Ch. D. 115, CA.

[29] See *Kelly v Norwich Union Fire Insurance Ltd* [1990] 1 W.L.R. 139; [1989] 2 All E.R. 888, CA (property policy did not cover loss arising from damage to house caused by water entering clay and causing it to heave; insured failed to show that leakage of water, which was specified peril, occurred during policy period).

23.42   Secondly, most property policies since the early 1990s have included a qualified or absolute pollution exclusion. Some qualified pollution exclusions exclude contamination but write back or reinstate cover for losses arising from contamination which results from a peril covered by the policy. A qualified pollution exclusion may also write back cover for damage which results from a covered peril which has resulted from contamination. An example of the exception to the second exclusion is fire damage from heating oil which escapes from a heating system into a basement and ignites, causing damage to the property. Neither exception covers the cost of remediating contaminated land. The existence of a debris removal clause in a property policy does not mean that the policy provides cover for the costs of removing soil which has been contaminated by, say, heating oil from a leaking storage tank. As indicated above, soil is not, as a general rule, insured property. Further, a court may rule that oil is not "debris". In a case arising from the *Exxon Valdez* oil spill, Coleman J. referred to the *Shorter Oxford Dictionary* for the definition of the word "debris". The dictionary defined the word as "the remains of anything broken down or destroyed; ruins, wreck". Coleman J. concluded that, in the context of the contract and its factual matrix, the ordinary meaning of the word "debris" contemplates broken solids rather than a liquid or viscous substance such as oil which has been washed up onto beaches from the sea.[30]

Employers' liability policies

23.43   An employers' liability policy may provide cover to an insured for a claim by an employee who suffers a disease due to having been exposed to contaminants. Businesses have been required to purchase an employers' liability policy since 1972 and to retain copies of past employers' liability certificates so as to facilitate the tracking of past insurers. The policies provide cover against liability for bodily injury or disease sustained by an employee which arises out of and in the course of employment.[31] The mandatory threshold for cover is £5 million; employers often have £10 million in cover.

23.44   Most employers' liability policies have an exposure trigger due to providing cover for bodily injury which is caused to an employee during the policy period. If, therefore, an employee develops a latent disease such as mesothelioma or asbestosis due to exposure to asbestos in the work place, the policies which respond are those which were in force during the employee's exposure to asbestos. Other employers' liability policies have a similar trigger to that in public liability policies. That is, the policies which provide cover are those in force when the employee suffers an actionable injury.

23.45   In the case involving a claim by Bolton against a past policy,[32] discussed above, Longmore L.J. discussed whether the applicable trigger in an employer's liability policy should be the continuous trigger. He stated that:

---

[30] *King v Brandywine Reinsurance Company (UK) Ltd* [2004] 2 All E.R. (Comm) 443 [2004] 1 Lloyd's Rep. 670, QBD.

[31] Employers' Liability (Compulsory Insurance) Act 1969 s.1.

[32] *Bolton MBC v Municipal Mutual Insurance Ltd* [2006] 1 W.L.R. 1492; [2006] All E.R. (D) 66, CA.

"I am far from saying that what has been called this multiple trigger or, sometimes triple trigger theory . . . might not be held, on some future occasion, to be appropriate for employers' liability policies in general, depending on the precise words used. . . . It has been adopted in the United States avowedly for policy reasons in relation to the vastly greater numbers of asbestos-disease sufferers in that country. I see no reason to adopt it in [a case involving a public liability policy] where the same policy considerations are not present."

An employers' liability policy may provide cover for the total amount of **23.46** damages for harm caused by exposure to contaminants. In *Phillips v Syndicate 992*,[33] insurers argued that they were liable for only 72.5 per cent of an award of £205,000 to the family of an employee who had died from mesothelioma. The insured had negligently exposed the employee to asbestos for nine years. Insurers argued that they were not liable for the total amount because their policies were on the risk for only nine of the 13 years of the negligent exposure. Eady J. referred to *Fairchild v Glenhaven Funeral Services Ltd*[34] to conclude that an employer is jointly and severally liable for its material contribution in negligently exposing an employee to asbestos. The employer's insurer which is on risk during the negligent exposure is thus fully liable for the damages. Eady J. rejected the insurers' argument that a generally recognised custom and practice exists, according to which insurers on the risk during an indivisible injury such as meso-thelioma allocate liability between themselves according to time on the risk. He accepted that insurers may have established such a practice, but concluded that it was not a custom or practice between insureds and insurers during the time in which the employee had been exposed to asbestos or had developed mesothelioma.

Directors' and officers' policies

Directors' and officers' (D&O) policies indemnify directors and officers for **23.47** losses arising from legal actions against them which are not covered by policies taken out by their companies and which can, therefore, impact on their personal assets. D&O policies have a claims-made trigger, that is, they provide cover for claims made against a director or officer during the policy period. Since the mid 1990s, some D&O policies have provided a sub-limit of indemnity for costs incurred by the insured in defending criminal or civil environmental-related claims. The policies have not been called on to respond to claims in any great number, however, due to the relatively few actions which have been brought against directors and officers arising out of contaminated land and other environmental issues.

Professional indemnity policies

Professional indemnity policies provide cover for loss arising from the **23.48** alleged fault or negligence of persons who sell their knowledge or skills. The policies, which are underwritten on a claims-made basis, also provide

[33] [2004] Lloyd's Rep. I.R. 426, QBD.
[34] [2003] 1 A.C. 32, HL. See Compensation Act 2006 s.3.

cover for legal defence costs. The main classes of professionals who are at risk of claims due to services regarding contaminated land are solicitors, accountants, surveyors and environmental consultants.

23.49 Solicitors in England and Wales must have at least £2 million of cover from insurers who have been approved by the Law Society to underwrite such cover. The policies must provide cover which is at least as broad as the cover specified in the Law Society's minimum terms and conditions. Insurers are permitted to include only limited exclusions under the minimum terms and conditions; the permitted exclusions do not include a pollution exclusion. It is also rare for such an exclusion to appear in a top-up policy, that is, a policy which provides excess cover above £2 million. Thus, solicitors' professional indemnity policies provide cover for claims which may arise in respect of the solicitor's advice, or failure to provide advice, in respect of contaminated land.

23.50 Similarly, accountants must purchase professional indemnity policies issued by approved insurers. The policies must comply with the minimum terms and conditions set out by the Institute of Chartered Accountants or the Association of Chartered Certified Accountants, as appropriate. The minimum terms and conditions do not permit inclusion of a pollution exclusion. As with solicitors, top-up policies for accountants rarely include a pollution exclusion.

23.51 In contrast to solicitors and accountants, the Royal Institution of Chartered Surveyors (RICS) introduced a pollution exclusion in its RICS-compliant professional indemnity policies for post-1994 policies. The exclusion bars cover for "[a]ny claim or loss (including loss of value) arising directly or indirectly from pollution". The exclusion defines the word "pollution" as "pollution or contamination by naturally occurring or man-made substances, forces or organisms or any combination of them whether permanent or transitory and however occurring". The exclusion does not apply in respect of a claim for negligent structural design.

23.52 Environmental consultants have some professional indemnity cover for contaminated land liabilities in general professional indemnity policies. There is no requirement, however, for them to purchase a professional indemnity policy which provides any cover for contaminated land. Many environmental consultants, including the major consultancies, have purchased specialist insurance policies to provide cover because potential clients often demand that they have the requisite cover before agreeing to instruct them.[35]

Environmental insurance policies

23.53 Due to the uncertainties described above in cover for environmental liabilities in general liability policies, the only effective way to ensure that liabilities arising from contaminated land are insured is to purchase an environmental insurance policy. These policies have become much more flexible than was the case in the early 1990s, when insurers demanded that a potential insured pay for a survey of the environmental condition of its

---

[35] See further, para.23.61ff.

site before deciding whether to issue a policy. The range of policies has also broadened due to the extended range of legislative environmental liabilities and its corollary, the increasing gap in cover for environmental liabilities in public liability and other general liability policies. Further, policy periods have substantially increased and premiums have substantially decreased.

Structure

Environmental insurance policies differ from most other insurance policies. **23.54** The policies are underwritten on a claims-made-and-reported basis, except for contractor's pollution liability cover which is also underwritten on an occurrence basis. In order for a claim to be covered under a claims-made-and-reported policy, the claim against the insured and the claim by the insured to its insurer must be made during the policy period. Some policies have an automatic extended reporting period of up to 60 days and an optional extended reporting period of up to four years, the latter for an additional premium. An insured may receive and report a claim which has arisen from pollution conditions during this period.

Environmental insurance policies for owners and occupiers of land are **23.55** site-specific, that is, they provide cover only for sites which are listed on the policy. Sites may be added to, and deleted from, the policy as the insured acquires and disposes of them during the policy period. Most environmental insurance policies are tailored specifically for the insured's sites or environmental risks. As a result, the wordings of approximately 70 per cent of environmental insurance policies are negotiated. Except for highly complex risks, the policies are not bespoke. Instead, insurers use a specimen policy wording to which endorsements are added. The coverage section of the specimen policy is set out as a menu-type format so as to allow the insured to select the required coverage parts.

Underwriters have a library of standardised endorsements to enable **23.56** them to vary the language in the specimen policy wording and/or schedule. They also manuscript endorsements, as appropriate, to cover risks which are specific to a site. For example, a company which has contaminated a small area of its site with hydrocarbons might wish to purchase insurance for other environmental liabilities arising from its site. Underwriters may manuscript an endorsement to carve out cover for the contaminated area and/or hydrocarbons in respect of the site. If the insured intends to remediate the contaminated area, the endorsement may provide that the policy will cover the cost of any subsequent remedial works after the initial works have been completed.

It is not however necessary for the wordings of all environmental **23.57** insurance policies to be negotiated. A standardised property transfer policy for low risk sites is described below.

Types of policies

Environmental insurance policies are available for: **23.58**

1. on-site and off-site risks from pollution incidents during the policy period;

2. on-site and off-site risks from pre-existing contamination on a site;

3. the risk of cost overruns during the remediation of contaminated land;

4. losses arising from the professional services of environmental consultants and environmental laboratories;

5. losses arising from services carried out by remediation and general contractors;

6. lenders' risks arising from having unknowingly accepted contaminated land which must be remediated as collateral for a loan; and

7. costs incurred by a homeowner due to having purchased a residence on contaminated land which must be remediated.

Off-site liability policies

23.59 Policies which provide cover for off-site liabilities from pollution incidents which take place at an insured site were the first type of environmental insurance policy to be offered for UK risks. Since cover began to be offered for the cost of remediating contamination on-site as well as off-site, the policies have generally been combined so that they provide cover for first-party as well as third-party environmental risks.

Operational risk potential

23.60 Policies for operational risks provide cover for first and third-party bodily injury and property damage as well as the cost of remediating contamination which results from a pollution incident on the insured's site. The policies, which also provide cover for legal defence costs, may be extended to provide cover for additional liabilities including those arising under the Environmental Liability Directive,[36] business interruption, relocation costs, diminution in the value of third-party property and loss in rental income.

Property transfer policies

23.60.1 Property transfer policies have been the most popular environmental insurance policies in the UK since their introduction in 1997. They are specifically designed to provide cover for the cost of remediating contaminated land under Pt IIA as well as providing cover for claims for bodily injury and property damage resulting from the contamination. The insured must not have been aware of the contamination which led to a claim against it when the policy incepted. Alternatively, the insured must have declared the existence of the contamination so as to allow the insurer to decide whether to cover the risk of a claim arising from it. Property transfer policies are triggered by, among other things, a notification that

---

[36] Directive 2004/35/EC of the European Parliament and of the Council on environmental liability with regard to the prevention and remedying of environmental damage. See further Ch.13.

land is contaminated land or by a request from the Environment Agency to remediate water pollution under the Water Resources Act 1991. These policies are largely placed during commercial transactions to back up environmental warranties and indemnities or, in some cases, to transfer risks arising from potentially or actually contaminated land to an insurer, rather than entering into an environmental indemnity to allocate the risks between the seller and the buyer. Policy periods of up to 10 years (with one insurer now offering 15 years) are available. In addition, a renewable one-year policy is available for low risk sites for which a desktop report of the historic and current use of the site has not detected the presence or likelihood of contamination. Due to their low risk nature, such policies are not negotiated.

Stop-loss remediation policies

A stop loss remediation policy, also known as a remediation cost cap policy, **23.61** provides cover for unforeseen costs which may be incurred during the remediation and development of a contaminated site. The costs may arise from the failure of a remedy or a cost overrun due to the discovery of more extensive contamination than contemplated. Their placement involves detailed discussions by environmental consultants for the potential insured and insurers in order to calculate the estimated cost of remedial works. The policies are then drafted to include a deductible which sits above the estimate and a limit of indemnity. The premium is calculated as a percentage of the estimated costs of remediation together with factors such as the amount of the indemnity. Due to the detailed discussions involved, the policies are only suitable for contaminated sites which cost at least £1 million to remediate. Further, due to the amount of time expended by insurers in negotiating the policies, they may charge a fee which is offset against the premium if the policy is placed.

Environmental consultants' policies

Environmental consultants' policies cover losses arising from a consul- **23.62** tant's professional services.[36a] An example of such losses results from a site investigation of St Mary's Island at Chatham Docks, Kent, in preparation for developing the island for residences. The Royal Navy had used the island for several hundred years, among other things, to dump waste including asbestos. The consultants estimated that 363,000 cubic metres of contaminated materials needed to be removed at a cost of £23 million. The remedy, however, entailed the removal of 1,173,486 cubic metres of contaminated materials at a cost of £67.6 million. Following a 77–day hearing, Judge Thornton Q.C. concluded that the environmental consultants had failed to exercise reasonable skill and care by, among other things, failing to carry out a comprehensive environmental survey, failing to excavate a sufficient number of trial pits to take representative samples

---

[36a] Essentially, to claim under the policy there must be a legal liability on the part of the consultant; an insurance policy designed to cover negligent advice may well cover advice given on an unsolicited basis: *Structural Polymer Systems Ltd v Brown (Syndicate 702 at Lloyd's)* (QBD, October 27, 1998, unreported).

and failing adequately to investigate the characteristics of soil to an appropriate depth. The case settled following the judge's provisional award of £18.5 million in damages.[37]

23.63 Environmental consultants' policies generally provide cover for all projects carried out by the consultant during a specified period or for a specific project. Policies for all projects are generally issued annually. The limit of indemnity is in the aggregate. A client of a consultancy, therefore, runs the risk that available insurance cover may have been exhausted by other claims which were made in the same year as that in which the client made a claim. The alternative is to purchase a policy for a specific project and, thereby, ensure that no other claims are made against the policy. The general practice is for the client to pay the premium for such cover. Some insurers are now willing to offer a "round the clock" automatic reinstatement clause, allowing a primary insurer to reinstate cover once excess layers have been exhausted. Likewise, once the primary layer has been exhausted for a second time, the excess layers are automatically reinstated. This can continue for an unlimited number of times, during the policy period, so addressing the risk of exhaustion of cover.

Other policies

23.64 Environmental laboratories may also purchase policies to cover losses arising from their professional services. Cover may be added for legal defence expenses.

23.65 Contractors' pollution liability policies are available to remediation contractors as well as general contractors. The policies are issued on an occurrence basis as well as a claims-made-and-reported basis, with the premium for the former being higher than the premium for the latter. They may be purchased for a set period of time or a specific project.

23.66 A lender's liability policy provides cover to a lender who accepts land as collateral for a loan. The policy, which responds if the borrower defaults and the land must be remediated, provides cover for either the borrower's principal loan balance or the cost of remediating the contamination. Cover is also available for first-party remediation costs, third-party bodily injury and property damage and legal defence costs.

Homeowners' policies

23.67 Homeowners may purchase a policy to cover the risk of their home being located on land which must be remediated under Pt IIA. There are currently two types of cover. The National House-Building Council, through its Buildmark scheme, and Zurich Building Guarantees, through its warranty, provide cover for new and converted homes. Countrywide Legal Indemnities offers the Home Environmental Liability Policy, which is underwritten by Liberty Legal Indemnities at Syndicate 4472 at Lloyd's. The cover includes the cost of remediating contamination under Pt IIA, with an extension for storing the contents of the home and alternative

---

[37] *Urban Regeneration Agency v Mott Macdonald Group Ltd* [2000] 12 Envtl. L. & Mgt. 24, QBD. See further, para.18.18.

accommodation during the remedial works. A similar policy is offered by Hardy Conveyancing Insurances, underwritten by Syndicate 382 at Lloyd's.

Finite risk programmes

23.68 Finite risk programmes are available for the cost of remediating a contaminated site. The programmes combine a funding element (in which funding is provided for remedial works) and an insurance element (in which insurance is provided if the costs of the remedial works exceed a specified amount). Some environmental consultancies have structured finite risk programmes to transfer known and unknown liabilities in remediating contaminated land from the owner or occupier of the land. The consultancy and the owner or operator calculate the amount to remediate the contamination. The consultancy subsequently agrees to carry out the remediation for a fixed price and to assume liability for all known and unknown environmental risks connected with the site, in particular, remediation costs and bodily injury and property damage from contamination. In order to protect itself, the consultancy takes out a long-term insurance policy.

Environmental insurers and brokers

23.69 Four insurance companies currently (2007) provide a wide range of environmental insurance policies for UK commercial risks. They are: ACE Europe Group; AIG Europe (UK) Ltd; Chubb Insurance Company of Europe S.A.; and XL Europe Ltd. Two Lloyd's syndicates (Syndicate 4472) and Hardy Conveyancing (Syndicate 382) have started to insure low-risk sites. Environmental insurance policies should always be placed through a broker who has the appropriate specialist skills. This is because a broker has the necessary expertise and also because a solicitor may be considered to be carrying out insurance mediation activities in the absence of authorisation to do so.[38] The major environmental insurance brokers in London are currently: Aon Ltd; Global Environmental Insurance Partners; Heath Lambert; HSBC Insurance Brokers Ltd; Marsh Ltd; Miles Smith; Tyser & Company Ltd; and Willis Ltd. Other brokers with the requisite specialist expertise are Ensura Ltd and Bridge Insurance Brokers Ltd.

---

[38] See Directive 2002/92 of the European Parliament and of the Council on insurance mediation.

Chapter 24

VALUATION

24.01 It is a rash lawyer who ventures in any detail into the area of valuation of land. However, how land is valued to reflect the presence of contamination is an important aspect of transactions, and therefore this chapter aims to provide a brief discussion by way of orientation. Needless to say, if actual issues of valuation arise, the lawyer will need to consult an appropriately qualified and experienced surveyor.[1]

Valuation, blight and perception of risk

24.02 A decade ago, Paul Syms, in his 1997 book, *Contaminated Land—The Practice and Economics of Redevelopment*,[2] considered issues of risk perception relating to contaminated land. Empirical research conducted at that date, suggested valuers, in general, had a poorly developed perception of the problems associated with contaminated land. The valuation profession at that time appeared to have a fairly poor understanding of site remediation methods and a distrust of innovative technologies; in spite of this, valuers tended to place a relatively low valuation significance on the selection of remediation methods, compared to pre- and post-treatment risk assessments. Various case studies demonstrated that it is possible to redevelop contaminated sites from a variety of past uses to provide modern industrial redevelopments. Such redeveloped sites were considered to be acceptable by occupiers and funding institutions, though it was often necessary to provide the users and financiers with information as to the types of activities previously undertaken on the site and the remedial measures used. There appeared to be little sign of post remediation stigmatisation attributable to the former contaminative use, though in many industrial redevelopment situations the land element may represent less than 25 per cent of the completed value of the project. Stigma was more apparent in the pre-remediation situation, with potential developers in some instances declining the development opportunity or demanding discounts to reflect risk or "stigma". Case studies were also given on residential redevelopment—so far as was known, no potential sales or tenants were lost on any of the developments because of the industrial history of the site or the fact that it had been contaminated. As with the industrial

---

[1] Useful sources of information are the RICS website *(http://www.rics.org.uk)*, the College of Estate Management *(http://www.cem.ac.uk)* and the commercial site *http://www.environmental-surveyors.com)*. See also generally, P. Wyatt, *Property Valuation* (Blackwell Publishing, 2007); also P. Syms and B. Weber, *International Approaches to the Valuation of Land and Property Affected by Contamination*, RICS Foundation Review, RICS Books, 2003.

[2] Blackwell Science, 1997.

developments, the land element attributable to each housing unit was relatively small, and it was not possible to identify any significant reduction in price which could be attributed to stigma. Whilst since this research was carried out the Pt IIA regime has come into force, and there has been an increased awareness generally within the valuation profession of the potential significance of contamination, it would appear that these conclusions still hold good, and that remediated and redeveloped contaminated land will not necessarily carry a significant stigma in valuation terms. This of course is to speak in generalities, and the position on individual sites may vary depending on the state of knowledge and stage of investigation and remediation. It is probably the case that initial perception of a general problem may induce a substantial loss in value ("dread factors").

As understanding increases, so values may rise again to a point where **24.03** they relate to logical factors such as clean-up costs, control measures, delay and contingent liabilities. Not all purchasers will be equally risk-sensitive. A developer with local knowledge may be prepared to bid more for a contaminated site than an institutional investor such as a pension fund, which may have a policy of ruling out investments with a perceived significant risk element. The attitude of mortgage providers will also be relevant: where residential property is identified as contaminated for example, it may become unmortgageable and hence unsaleable until satisfactory remediation has been carried out.[3]

RICS Valuation guidelines

The RICS *Appraisal and Valuation Manual* ("the Red Book") in 1995 stated **24.04** that a failure to report potential contamination which would be apparent to a competent valuer in the course of provision of a valuation was to be considered to constitute a breach of his or her duty of care. At the same time RICS *Guidance Note 2*[4] made a number of points:

1. Valuers need to be aware of the legal framework and to liaise as appropriate with legal advisors.

2. In considering the degree of environmental investigation and assessment to be undertaken, particular regard will need to be paid to the purpose and basis of the valuation.

3. More advice will be required where valuation is needed for an actual or potential transaction, and in particular the valuer should consider whether to recommend "a detailed environment assessment land quality statement". The basis of the work and valuation should be agreed, i.e. assumption that there is no contamination, or reflecting contents of an environmental report, or preliminary enquiries by the valuer to help decide on what basis it is appropriate to proceed.

4. Guidance is given on the relevance of contamination in various respects and further guidance is available in the RICS Guidance

---

[3] See also the discussion of stigma at para.24.10 below.
[4] 12/95 revised, effective from January 1, 1996.

Notice, now *Contamination and Environmental Matter—their implications for property professionals* (effective 1 December 2003).

5. Professional Standard PS4 outlines the appropriate basis of valuation and confirms that unless agreed otherwise in advance, it is expected that all relevant issues will be reflected in the valuation. In most circumstances, possible contamination will be a relevant issue.

6. P5.3 outlines the duties of the valuer in respect of investigations into contamination. A valuer is unlikely to have the knowledge and skills to undertake an environmental audit: he may however employ staff or appoint a suitable consultant.

7. In situations where the valuer considers that site contamination may exist and that further inquiries are necessary in order to assess value, the valuer should discuss with the client the brief to be given to the environmental expert. In particular the valuer will need to brief the expert on the uses (including realistic future uses) which would be most likely to support the highest value on the site.

8. Whilst the valuer should not express an opinion on matters for which he has no professional indemnity insurance cover, failure to report potential contamination which would be apparent to a competent valuer will constitute a breach of his duty of care.

24.05 A note published by the RICS in April 1997 suggested that unless the instructions to the valuer specifically require it, he or she has no obligation to carry out "especially thorough inspections or investigations to establish whether contamination exists or may exist". Indeed the valuer will often have no professional indemnity insurance covering such inspections, investigations and resultant reporting. It also pointed out the possible practical constraints on the extent of inspection and investigation, such as time, occupation of property, possible degree of access, and weather. It went on to say, importantly, that in spite of these factors, where the valuer identifies possible or actual contamination in the course of the inspection, it should be reported, irrespective of the conditions of engagement applying and the assumptions to be made in producing any valuation. The 2003 RICS Guidance Note, *Contamination and Environmental Matters—their implications for property professionals*, suggested the provision of a Property Observation Checklist, which should provide indications of possible contamination identified during inspection, for example spillages, staining or fly-tipping that may indicate poor standards of environmental management, the presence of hazardous materials, or the existence of problematic nearby land uses. Such information may be useful in indicating the need for further investigation and environmental screening in terms of high, medium or low risk, and may be used for example by pension fund trustees in considering whether a property should be included in the holdings of the pension portfolio.

Liability of valuers

24.06 Failure to take account of the possibility of contamination in the context of a property survey or valuation will raise the question of professional negligence. Whilst many surveyors will not have specialist expertise in the field of contaminated land, it is clear that the risks and effects of such contamination are now generally well-known, and on that basis a surveyor who does not at least alert his client to the need for additional specialist advice and draw attention to any indicators of possible contamination encountered must be at risk. Where the surveyor is not instructed to do a full structural survey, there may however be an obligation to follow a "trail of suspicion" where this alerts the surveyor to the need for a further and more comprehensive survey.[4a] It appears that no court has yet had to consider directly the issue of damages where a surveyor is found to be negligent in relation to the identification of contamination. However, on general principles, the correct test to apply is the difference between what the purchaser has paid for the property on the basis of the negligent advice and that sum which the purchaser would have paid had correct advice been given; it is not correct to assess damages on the basis of the cost of works to put the property in the state it would have been in, had the valuation been correct (which might well have involved factoring in the cost of clean-up, as discussed below).[5] This difference of approach may be important, since it is quite conceivable that two tests could produce a widely different result. In many cases the cost of remedial works may greatly exceed the actual effect upon the value of the property, depending upon factors such as the general state of the market and proposed end use. On the other hand, the value test will take into account contingent liabilities (which may result in property having "negative" value) in a way in which the simple cost of remedial works test would not. Even where a building is repaired (or land remediated) there may remain a residual stigma which affects value and is a proper part of damages.[5a]

24.07 In the case of negligent valuations given in the context of loan advances, the leading case is *Swingcastle v Gibson*.[6] Following that case, it is necessary to distinguish two situations: first, where the lender would have lent nothing had the valuation been carried out properly; and, secondly, where the lender would have advanced a lesser amount had the valuation been carried out properly. Either situation may of course apply in the case of contaminated land, depending largely upon the nature of the contamination and its contingent risks and liabilities. In the first case, where the lender would have lent nothing, the damage to be compensated is the difference between the amount of the advance and any capital recovered on repayment or sale, together with consequential expenses such as repossession proceedings against the borrower, and interest at an appropriate rate

---

[4a] *Sneesby v Goldings* (1994) 45 Con L.R. 10 (CA).
[5] *Philips v Ward* [1956] 1 W.L.R. 471; *Watts v Morrow* [1991] 1 W.L.R. 1421. *Gardner v Marsh & Parsons* [1997] 1 W.L.R. 489 (CA); *Hooper Jackson v Patel* [1999] 1 W.L.R. 1792.
[5a] *Prudential Assurance Co Ltd v McBains Cooper* (QBD, TCC, June 27, 2000, unreported).
[6] [1991] 2 A.C. 223; overruling *Baxter v F. W. Gapp & Co* [1939] 2 All E.R. 752. Followed in *Lloyds Bank Plc v Parker Bullen* [1999] E.G.C.S. 107 (July 16, 1999, Ch D); and *Lloyds Bank Plc v Phoenix Beard* (March 11, 1998, QBD).

to reflect the loss of use of the capital sum advanced, credit being given for any interest payments received by the borrower.

24.08   In a case where the effect of a negligent valuation is that the lender advanced more than would otherwise have been the case, it will be necessary to establish the difference in amount, and the lender's damages will be assessed on that basis.[7] It will be for the lender to furnish evidence to prove its case on the correct basis, and this may involve evidence as to the attitude of the lender had it known of the contamination, or possibly by calling evidence from the borrower to show that, had the lender been willing to advance a smaller sum, this would not have been sufficient to enable the borrower to proceed to take up the loan and proceed with the transaction.

Factors relevant to valuation

24.09 Having established the nature, extent and risks of contamination on a site, its potential costs will need to be considered and taken into account by the valuer. These may include, depending on the circumstances:

(a) the cost of any necessary further investigative measures;

(b) the physical cost of clean-up;

(c) any necessary temporary measures to avoid further contamination pending clean-up;

(d) on-going management and monitoring costs, such as groundwater pumping and gas control;

(e) the possible need to redesign the layout and built form of the development, together with any constraints on end use which that may present;

(f) any possible contingent environmental liabilities in respect of contamination;

(g) provision in respect of the risk of liabilities, for example third party insurance (if available) and self insurance or the provisions of a contingency fund;

(h) any necessary works to isolate the site, either to avoid migration of contamination offsite, or to prevent the ingress of contaminants from adjacent land;

(i) the cost of acquiring any rights necessary to undertake such works, where these are off-site;

(j) any impact on services, including the need to divert or reinstate water, gas, drainage or electricity services;

(k) the void period while clean-up is occurring;

---

[7] *Corisand Investments Ltd v Druce & Co* (1978) 248 E.G. 315.

(l) the cost of any future survey work which may be necessary to satisfy a prospective purchaser or finance provider; and

(m) on the positive side, the availability of (if any) of grants or other financial incentives.

The approach of simple "cost to correct" may be inadequate (though, as **24.10** discussed below, it may offer the only readily quantifiable means). It is also important to consider the proposed end use of the property and the extent to which contamination affects the fitness for that use: the effect of contamination on existing use value may differ markedly from the effect on alternative use value. There is also the most nebulous factor, that of "blight" or market perception, the extent of which depends upon the perceived risk of increased future standards for the condition of land and more stringent liability regimes (or the more rigorous application of existing regimes).[8] Stigma has been referred to (in the US context) as[9]:

> "The negative impact that results from public perception that environmental contamination is permanent and represents a continuing risk even after cleanup has been completed. It also refers to the negative result on property values that occurs in properties in close proximity to contaminated sites."

It may have various components including the fear of hidden liabilities, **24.11** lack of mortgageability, the fact that purchasers may prefer to seek a more "trouble-free" property and whether standards of what is an acceptable level or clean-up may change in future. Residual stigma devaluation following clean-up was recognised as a recoverable head of damage by the Court of Appeal in *Blue Circle Industries Plc v Ministry of Defence*.[10]

Application of existing valuation methods

Generally used techniques can be applied to contamination problems, **24.12** though such methods are not always clearly distinct and may raise similar issues. For example, open market value principles may be applicable if there are relevant comparables, though in assessing the "best price" there may be difficulties in relation to the assumption of the "idiot bid" from a reckless or naive purchaser who would pay more than the properly advised purchaser would pay. Logically, if the market in fact comprises such bidders, there is no reason why this evidence should be excluded from the valuer, however misguided their bids might be.[11] For specialised properties,

---

[8] Tim Stapleton, Blundell Memorial Lecture, June 14, 1993. See also T. Richards, *The Valuation and Appraisal of Contaminated Land and Property* (RICS Research, 1996) which refers to the theoretical research in the US on valuation methods

[9] RV Colangelo and RD Miller, *Environmental Site Assessments and their Impact on Property Value: The Appraiser's Role* (Appraisal Institute, 1995), cited by T. Richards, *The Valuation and Appraisal of Contaminated Land and Property* (RICS Research, 1996).

[10] [1999] 2 W.L.R. 295; [1999] Env. L.R. 22 (a case on radioactive contamination under the Nuclear Installations Act 1965).

[11] See E. Martin Sheard, *Valuing Contaminated Land: Asset or Liability? Land Reclamation and Contamination*, 1993, Vol. 1, No. 1, p. 9.

where an open market value is not possible, the depreciated replacement cost (DRC) basis may be applicable. This involves estimating the replacement cost of the asset, e.g. a factory. If the asset is constructed on contaminated land then it will be a difficult issue how clean-up costs (and to what standard) are to be built into the replacement cost: the cost of meeting such requirements could easily fully outweigh or at least make very significant inroads into the total value; this may also be the case with other methods of valuation.[12]

24.13 A problem with contaminated land is that the issues tend to be site specific and there is a lack of comparable transactions. Hence, contaminated land may well lend itself to the residual method of appraisal involving the cost of correction as part of the exercise based on essentially two questions:

  (i) what will be the cost of work to clean-up the land; and

  (ii) what will the land be worth when the work is completed?

Neither of these questions is easy or straightforward. For the first, the valuer must depend on the expertise of other specialists. It can be very difficult to obtain accurate figures in advance for decontamination; this is particularly problematic in the case of grant applications where there will be no "second bite of the cherry". Other factors which will need to be built in include appropriate sums for contingencies, the cost of finance and the developer's profit figure. As to the "after" value, it has to be accepted that even if it is cleaned up to acceptable contemporary standards, the land is still not virgin land and the price it can command will probably reflect this. Some discount is likely to reflect factors such as less flexibility in terms of future uses, the risk of environmental standards changing or of the treatment failing, and general adverse perceptions. Ongoing costs of monitoring and control may be involved and will need to be capitalised. Taking the cost of clean-up and after value together may quite conceivably result in a negative value, depending on market conditions and current perception.

24.14 Valuing let property will also be difficult, particularly given the doubt as to how many common lease terms might operate to allocate liability for contaminative problems.[13] If the legal position is not clear then some allowance for risk will need to be made, whichever interest is being valued.

Lands Tribunal cases

24.15 Issues valuing contaminated land have on occasion been considered by the Lands Tribunal in some cases. In *Proudco v Department of Transport*,[14] the Department compulsorily purchased for the purposes of a road scheme the freehold interest in an area of land forming part of the site of a former

---

[12] See E. Martin Sheard, *Valuing Contaminated Land: Asset or Liability? Land Reclamation and Contamination*, 1993, Vol. 1, No. 1, p. 9.

[13] See Ch.19 generally.

[14] Ref/82/1989; (1991) 31 R.V.R. 103 (V. G. Wellings, Q.C., President).

chemical works. The claimants sought compensation for the land acquired. As at the valuation date the whole site was contaminated by chemical pollution and some radioactivity. It was agreed as a fact that the cost of decontaminating the site (inclusive of fees) could be taken to be £9,900,000. The approach of the Lands Tribunal was to assess the value of the freehold site by means of comparables, ignoring contamination, and then to deduct the agreed cost of decontamination. In relation to a claim for use and occupation of one of the site areas occupied by the Department for 775 days, it was argued by the District Valuer on behalf of the Department that this area could not have been put to any beneficial use, except for the special needs of the Department of Transport, which were to be ignored. On that basis, in his opinion, the plot had no market value in that it could not have been developed by the owner during the period of occupation because removal of the contamination was necessary before development could be carried out. The Lands Tribunal disagreed, on the basis that compensation for use and occupation is not based on the value to the owner, but rather on the basis of a reasonable compensation to the owner for the occupation. In that case, compensation for the area, contaminated as it was, as to be assessed on a daily basis at a nominal rent of £15 per day, resulting in a sum of £11,625.

In *Haddon v Black Country Development Corp*,[15] the Lands Tribunal consid- **24.16** ered the amount of compensation payable on the compulsory acquisition of some six hectares of vacant freehold land at Wednesbury, West Midlands, previously used for the extraction of furnace ash and the deposit of industrial waste materials. The decision contains a helpfully full discussion of the factors affecting valuation and therefore is here discussed at some length. From about 1900 to the 1980 the site had been used for the surface tipping of ash from foundries and iron works. During the 1980s ash was extracted for sale and some 200,000 cubic metres of non-toxic industrial waste were deposited on the site, followed by a degree of levelling and surface covering.

It was agreed as a fact that the void created by the proposed extraction **24.16.1** of ash and other saleable materials from the site would be sufficient to receive 175,000 cubic metres of compacted non-hazardous waste, that it was a practical proposition to re-work the land for ash and that the further void space could therefore be created; and that the estimated cost of £227,778 for the long term monitoring of landfill gas emanating from the site was sufficient. The principal elements of the claimant's suggested figure of £5,760,400 included the value of ash to be extracted, the value of the newly created void which would result from that extraction for waste disposal, and the value for open storage use of the surface which would be created by waste disposal. A s.17 certificate was obtained which included a condition requiring that remedial measures to counter the hazards from any contamination and/or the emission of gases be carried out before any part of the development was commenced. The main forms of contamination highlighted in the expert evidence to the Tribunal related to the pollution and seepage of groundwater and the production of methane gas; it was not disputed that some remedial works were needed if the site was

[15] Ref/166/1991; March 15, 1993, unreported (T. Hoyes, FRICS).

to be reused, both as a practical matter and as a requirement of the s.17 certificate. The real issue between the opposing experts was not so much the degree and technical nature of contamination but whether there was a remedy for it, and if so the cost, immediate and recurring, of effecting that remedy. It was ultimately accepted that despite the past use of the site it did not inhibit the ultimate use for open storage, subject to remedial works being carried out, including ventilation trenches, impermeable capping, treatment of mineshafts, an improved surface water drainage system, long term gas monitoring and continuing maintenance of the ground surface against water penetration and gas leaks. In terms of the general characteristics of the land, it was noted that the site had the advantage of being some 250 metres distant from the nearest dwellings and that it was adjacent to uses which themselves might be regarded as unneighbourly.

24.17　The ultimate decision of the Tribunal in relation to site contamination and remedial measures was that the land was not contaminated to such an extent that the remedial work proposed could not render it fit for open storage use. The "reworking" of the site as proposed was a practical alternative to immediate use for open storage; a new waste repository to current regulations and standards could be formed from on-site materials. However, a prudent purchaser would include a contingency sum in case the clays on site needed supplementing as to quality for the lining of the repositories; this provision should be about 20 per cent and there should be included a further 10 per cent for further possible cost overruns or unforeseen circumstances. The claimant's estimated costs for remedial or safeguarding works were generally accepted, subject to a slight uplift. In relation to the proposed revenues to be achieved from extraction of ash and waste disposal, deductions of 30 per cent were made in each case to reflect the fact that ash extraction and solid waste reception could not be regarded as a "risk free activity". The final amount of compensation determined by the Tribunal was £1,463,000, the acquiring authority to pay the claimant's costs of the reference.

24.18　In *Bromley LBC v London Docklands Development Corp*,[16] the reference concerned the compensation to be paid for the acquisition of vacant and contaminated Thames-side freehold land. Agreement was reached by the parties in respect of all parcels save for some 21 acres at Silvertown in Newham. The experts had approached the valuation of this land in different ways. The Tribunal accepted as the starting value for the land in a remediated condition, but not hard surfaced in tarmac or concrete, freehold with vacant possession for open storage use, a figure of £250,000 per usable acre.

Rating

24.19　The Valuation Office Agency Rating Manual,[17] Vol.4 s.10, deals with contaminated land. This will involve considering the matters affecting the physical state of the land or its physical enjoyment as at the material day[18]

---

[16] Ref 183, 184/1994 (1997), Judge Marder Q.C. (President) and T. Hoyes FRICS (unreported).

[17] 2000, updated. See *http://www.voa.gov.uk/instructions/*.

[18] Local Government Finance Act 1988 Sch.6 para.2(7)(a).

(i.e. the level of contamination) and its effect on value in terms of the hypothetical rental bid. The Manual suggests that there will be a spectrum ranging from cases where a property is largely unaffected, to property which is so severely contaminated that it is incapable of beneficial occupation and hence not rateable. It reflects that fact that the relevant circumstances will include whether it is the landlord or the tenant who would be liable for any remediation required, and any stigma.

24.20 Reference is made to the decision of the Lands Tribunal in *Fusetron Ltd and JGW Coatings Ltd v Whitehouse (Valuation Officer)*,[19] in which the subsoil of two small factory units near Rotherham were affected by arsenic, cyanide and phenol from a former gasworks. It was demonstrated that the units were affected to a greater extent than other properties on the same industrial estate, but the contamination was covered by hard surfacing, which the tenants would not be entitled to disturb. The only basis on which the Tribunal could see that some allowance should be made for contamination was to reflect the fact that the occupier might wish to install plant or machinery which would involve excavations which might disturb the contamination, for which a reasonably well-informed yearly tenant might make some allowance in his rental bid, though not very substantial. This was distinguished from any allowance simply for stigma. On the basis of that case the Manual suggests that a maximum allowance of 10 per cent for contamination should only be given where the ratepayer is able to demonstrate exceptional contamination to the site or the site of a contiguous hereditament. In the majority of cases where the hereditament may have similar contamination to the rest of the estate or district, it advises that no deduction should be given, as the contamination is not exceptional.

24.21 The issue of contamination was the subject of an appeal before the Valuation Tribunal in *Littleales v Roscoe (Valuation Officer)*.[20] The occupier's house was built on the site of the old Dorking Brickworks and was found to be contaminated with fuel oil. It was argued that the house was now worthless since it was not saleable. The appeal in respect of Council Tax was dismissed as invalid, on the basis that the property had been built on the contaminated land in 1983. Thus it existed before the inception of Council Tax, and there had been no material change since the start of the Council Tax Valuation List in 1993.[21] This approach will mean that many such applications for reduction in Council Tax will be unsuccessful.

---

[19] May 20, 1999, M St J Hopper FRICS.
[20] Appeal no.362038197/154C, November 17, 2006. See *http://www.valuation-tribunals.gov.uk*.
[21] See Local Government Finance Act 1993; the Council Tax (Alteration of Lists and Appeals) Regulations 1993 (SI 1993/290).

SECTION 8
COMPARATIVE REGIMES

Chapter 25

SCOTLAND

Introduction[1]

In many respects, the legal framework for addressing contaminated land is **25.01**
similar in Scotland to that in England and Wales. However, in certain
important respects there are differences. It should be noted that both
legislative and administrative power in relation to environmental matters
is devolved, by virtue of the Scotland Act 1998, to the Scottish Parliament
and to the Scottish Executive, which took up their full powers on July 1,
1999. While legislation or common law principles dealing with or relevant
to contaminated land are in some cases similar to that applying in
England, in others they are considerably different. It should never be
assumed that Acts of the Westminster Parliament which once applied to
both England and Scotland continue to apply in the same way. In a number
of cases, they will have been amended both by the Westminster and
Scottish Parliaments with the result that their texts are now substantially
divergent.

Statutory framework for contaminated land

As in England and Wales, in Scotland there is a statutory framework for **25.02**
contaminated land. This is provided for in Pt IIA of the Environmental
Protection Act 1990 (the 1990 Act), which came into force in Scotland on
July 14, 2000, and the regulations and statutory guidance issued under the
Act.[2]

Under Pt IIA of the 1990 Act, local authorities have a duty to inspect **25.03**
their areas from time to time in order to identify contaminated land. Once
a site is designated as contaminated land, the relevant local authority must
issue a remediation notice specifying the actions to be taken regarding the
remediation of the site. Responsibility for enforcement generally lies with
local authorities unless the site in question has been designated as a
special site in which case enforcement lies with the Scottish Environment
Protection Agency (SEPA).

The statutory regime relating to contaminated land is with effect from **25.04**
October 30, 2007 also extended to cover radioactively contaminated land as
a result of The Radioactive Contaminated Land (Scotland) Regulations

---

[1] The authors are indebted to Charles Smith of Brodies LLP for updating and contributing
new material to this chapter.
[2] See, inter alia, Contaminated Land (Scotland) Regulations 2000 (SSI 2000/178); Scottish
Executive Circular 1/2000, July 2000; Contaminated Land (Scotland) Regulations 2005 (SSI
2005/658).

2007. Under these regulations, local authorities are required to notify SEPA where they consider that land may be subject to radioactive contamination. It is then the responsibility of SEPA to inspect the land. Where SEPA considers that the land is subject to radioactive contamination, it is designated as a special site in which case SEPA is the enforcing authority.

25.05   Under Pt IIA of the 1990 Act, SEPA is required to prepare and publish a report on the state of contaminated land in Scotland. No decision has yet been taken on when the first report will be published and at present there is no single source which indicates the extent of contaminated land in Scotland.[3]

Statutory nuisance

25.06 As in England, statutory nuisance is dealt with in Pt III of the Environmental Protection Act 1990. The list of statutory nuisances in both jurisdictions is the same and local authorities are, as in England, subject to a duty to inspect their areas with a view to detecting statutory nuisances. Appeals against abatement notices are to the sheriff court in Scotland. With reference to contaminated land, no matter may constitute a statutory notice to the extent that it consists of, or is caused by, any land being in a contaminated state. Land is defined as being in a "contaminated state" if, and only if, it is in such a condition, by reason of substances in, on or under the land, that (a) significant harm is being caused or there is a significant possibility of such harm being caused or (b) significant pollution of the water environment is being caused or there is a significant possibility of such pollution being caused (see ss.79(1A) and 1B) of the Environmental Protection Act 1990). The term "water environment" is as defined in s.3 of the Water Environment and Water Services (Scotland) Act 2003. That definition encompasses surface water (inland, transitional and coastal), groundwater and wetlands. The legislative intent is that the statutory nuisance regime should not be used to deal with contaminated land as defined for the purposes of Pt IIA of the Environmental Protection Act 1990 ("Pt IIA"). However, given that the definition of contaminated land for the purposes of Pt IIA is restricted and therefore will only capture more serious cases of contaminated land, there is nothing to preclude statutory nuisance being used to address less serious cases of contaminated land.

Water pollution

25.07 Water pollution is governed by the Water Environment and Water Services (Scotland) Act 2003 and the Water Environment (Controlled Activities) (Scotland) Regulations 2005. There is relevance to contaminated land in

---

[3] SEPA mention on their website four possible sources which may provide information on the extent of contaminated land in Scotland. These include public registers under Pt IIA, Pt IIA State of Contaminated Land Report (when published), the Scottish Vacant and Derelict Land Survey and the State of Environment: Scotland's Soil Resource report. See *http://www.sepa.org.uk*.

that a remediation notice under Pt IIA may not be served if the significant harm or the significant pollution of the water environment by reason of which the contaminated land in question is such land is a result of an activity to which the 2005 Regulations apply and enforcement action may be taken in relation to that activity by the relevant regulatory authority, in this case the Scottish Environment Protection Agency (s.78YB(1A) of the Environmental Protection Act 1990).

Waste on land

Waste on land in Scotland is regulated through Pt II of the Environmental **25.08** Protection Act 1990, the Waste Management Licensing Regulations 1994, the Pollution Prevention and Control (Scotland) Regulations 2000 and the Landfill (Scotland) Regulations 2003. Part IIA will not apply in relation to any land in respect of which there is for the time being in force a waste management licence under Pt II of the Environmental Protection Act 1990, except to the extent that any significant harm, or significant pollution of the water environment, by reason of which that land would otherwise fall to be regarded as contaminated land, is attributable to causes other than (a) a breach of the conditions of the licence or (b) the carrying on, in accordance with the conditions of the licence, of any activity authorised by that licence (s.78YB(2) of the Environmental Protection Act 1990).

Similarly, Pt IIA will not apply where the significant harm or pollution of **25.09** the water environment is attributable to the final disposal by deposit of controlled waste and enforcement action may be taken in relation to that activity (s.78YB(2A) of the Environmental Protection Act 1990). A remediation notice may not be served in respect of contaminated land as defined for the purposes of Pt IIA if the significant harm or pollution is attributable to an activity other than the final disposal by deposit in or on land of controlled waste and enforcement action may be taken in relation to that activity (s.78YB(2B) of the Environmental Protection Act 1990). For the purposes of these two exclusions, "enforcement action" means action under reg.19 (enforcement notices) or reg.21 (power of the Scottish Environment Protection Agency to remedy pollution) of the Pollution Prevention and Control (Scotland) Regulations 2000 (s.78YB(2C) of the Environmental Protection Act 1990).

Finally, it is provided that where s.59 of the Environmental Protection **25.10** Act applies (powers to require removal of unlawful deposits of waste) then no remediation notice under Pt IIA may be served in respect of the relevant land by reason of that waste or any consequences of its deposit (s.78YB(3) of the Environmental Protection Act 1990).

Radioactive substances/nuclear installations

Radioactive substances and nuclear installations in Scotland are regulated **25.11** through the Radioactive Substances Act 1993 and the Nuclear Installations Act 1965. As noted above, Pt IIA is extended to radioactive contamination by virtue of the Radioactive Contaminated Land (Scotland) Regulations 2007.

25.12　These Regulations insert new ss.78YB(5)–(9) into the Environmental Protection Act 1990 so as to disapply Pt IIA in respect of radioactive contamination:

　　(a)　within a nuclear site (in terms of the Nuclear Installations Act 1965);

　　(b)　within sites which are nuclear installations and are used by or on behalf of the Secretary of State for Defence;

　　(c)　where action is taken to deal with that contamination in implementation of an emergency plan prepared pursuant to the Radiation (Emergency Preparedness and Public Information) Regulations 2001; and

　　(d)　resulting from a breach of certain duties imposed by the Nuclear Installations Act 1965.

Civil remedies

25.13　In addition to the statutory framework for contaminated land, common law principles can also be relied on in this area of law. Although there are some similarities between Scots and English common law relevant to environmental protection, there are also some significant differences.

　　The Scots law of delict (tort in England) may be relevant to contaminated land situations; in particular the doctrines of nuisance and negligence. Nuisance specifically is relevant in the context of environmental protection due to its connection with heritable (real) property and the remedy of interdict (injunction in England) which is available under this doctrine.

Nuisance

25.14　In Scotland common law nuisance arises where a person uses his property in a manner which causes serious disturbance or substantial inconvenience to another person's enjoyment of land or material damage to this land to an extent which is more than is reasonably tolerable.[4] A claim for interdict can be made to prevent or stop the nuisance and damages may be claimed where loss has occurred as a result of the nuisance. The remedies of damages and interdict correspond to the equivalent English remedies of damages and injunction: there is also the possibility (though the law is undeveloped) of specific implement, which corresponds to a mandatory injunction. Specific implement is generally available as an alternative to damages without special circumstances needing to apply as in English law. However, in the context of nuisance there may be problems with the remedy if, for example, the only way to remedy a relatively minor polluting

---

[4] See *Watt v Jamieson* 1954 S.C. 56; *RHM Bakeries (Scotland) Ltd v Strathclyde RC* 1985 S.L.T. 214; 1985 S.C. (HL) 17; *Kennedy v Glenbelle* 1996 S.L.T. 1186; 1996 S.C. 95.

incident is by disproportionately large expenditure, or where a remedy is impossible. No distinction is drawn in Scots law between private and public nuisance.

One important difference between English and Scots law is that the rule **25.15** of strict liability in *Rylands v Fletcher*[5] does not apply in Scotland.[6] Therefore fault (culpa) requires to be proven in an action of damages in Scotland. However, where interdict is the remedy sought, this is not a requirement.[7] A possible exception to this rule is that where harm is caused by diverting the course of a natural stream, liability may be strict.[8]

Kennedy v Glenbelle[9] recognises four categories of culpa in Scots law. These **25.16** are malice, intent, recklessness and negligence. Conduct which gives rise to a special risk of abnormal damage from which fault may be implied if such damage actually occurs may also fall into this category.[10] Even if the fault in question cannot be specified, the escape of a dangerous substance or thing, or the creation of some other danger that would not have been there but for the act of the defender, will give rise to a strong presumption of fault or negligence if there is no acceptable alternative explanation.[11]

English and Scots law share the doctrine of interference with riparian **25.17** rights to unpolluted water.[12] It is not wholly clear whether this doctrine is part of the law of nuisance in Scotland (and is therefore dependent on fault), or whether it is a branch of law in its own right. Indeed there is some authority to the effect that rights of riparian proprietors to unpolluted water may form part of the law of common interest.[13] However, the more recent view seems to be that nuisance would be the relevant area of law in this instance.[14] It remains to be seen whether Scots Courts would

[5] (1868) L.R. 3 (HL) 330.

[6] *R.H.M. Bakeries (Scotland) Ltd v Strathclyde RC*.

[7] *Logan v Wang (UK) Ltd* 1991 S.L.T. 580 (Outer House) is authority that it is not necessary to plead fault or negligence for an award of interdict.

[8] *Caledonian Railway Co v Greenock Corp* 1917 S.C. (HL) 56. In a subsequent case, it has been noted that such a rule is contrary to a general principle of the law of Scotland, and the rule should not be extended beyond the precise facts of the case: *RHM Bakeries (Scotland) Ltd v Strathclyde RC* 1985 S.C. (HL) 17 at 42; 1985 S.L.T. 214 at 218, per Lord Fraser of Tullybelton. In *Kennedy v Glenbelle* 1996 S.C. 95 at 98, per Lord President Hope, it was noted that *Caledonian Railway Co v Greenock Corp* presented a possible exception to the rule against strict liability in Scotland. However, on the basis of recent research it has also been argued that the case is in fact based on fault. See *Stair Memorial Encyclopaedia*, Reissue Vol.8, Nuisance, 2001 Niall R Whitty (ed.) at para.93 and G D L Cameron "Strict Liability and the Rule" in *Caledonian Railway Co v Greenock Corp.* (2000) 5 S.L.P.Q. 356.

[9] 1996 S.L.T. 1186 at 1188.

[10] 1996 S.L.T. 1186 at 1188.

[11] *Kerr v Earl of Orkney* (1857) 20 D. 298. The principle in this case is in effect similar to *Rylands v Fletcher* as it applies where the defender voluntarily brings onto or creates on his land some new thing, creating a danger not naturally there. The distinction is that there must be a finding of fault, though this can be easily inferred from an especially heavy duty of care in the absence of any exculpating explanation from the defender.

[12] *Young v Bankier Distillery Co* 1893 1 S.L.T. 204; 1893 A.C. 691. Lord Shand notes at p.701 that there is no distinction between English and Scots law regarding the common interest and rights of upper and lower proprietors on the banks of a running stream.

[13] See *Stair Memorial Encyclopaedia*, Vol.18, Property, 1993, para.299; Hume Lectures Vol.III (Stair Soc Vol.15, 1952 G C H Paton (ed.)) p.220; *Bell Principles* s.1106. Although based on nuisance, there is, for example, also reference to common interest in *Duke of Buccleuch v Cowan* (1866) 5 M. 214.

[14] See *Stair Memorial Encyclopaedia*, Reissue Vol.8, *Nuisance*, 2001, Niall R Whitty (ed.) at paras 31 and 79.

follow the House of Lords decision in *Cambridge Water Co Ltd v Eastern Counties Leather Plc*[15] regarding strict liability for interference with groundwater abstraction rights. However, provided this area of law falls under nuisance or otherwise depends on fault, in cases concerning water pollution it seems Scots courts would not follow this decision.

Negligence

25.18 The principles of the law of negligence are broadly the same in the English and Scottish jurisdictions. In Scots law, negligence arises where there has been a failure to comply with a duty of care, the failure results in damage, loss or injury to the person to whom the duty is owed and the harm caused by the failure is reasonably foreseeable.[16] Claims under negligence do not require to be connected to heritable (real) property, but a duty of care must exist for an action to be raised and evidence must be given as to the manner in which this duty has been breached. Alternative pleas of nuisance and negligence have been made in some cases due to the overlap of these doctrines in the context of damages claims, as a result of the similarities between the doctrines of "fault" and "breach of duty".[17] The primary remedy for an action of negligence is damages for any harm or loss suffered.

Property rights

25.19 Property rights are relevant to contaminated land in the context of both title to sue and liability for damage. The Scottish system of real property is somewhat different from that of England and Wales. However, the property regime in Scotland has undergone significant changes in recent years due to the abolition of the feudal system.[18] Whereas under the previous property regime no-one, subject to certain esoteric exceptions, owned land outright, this is no longer the case and simple ownership of heritable property is now possible. The meaning of the term "owner" is therefore now more similar in England and Scotland, but there still remain differences in the two jurisdictions and this is reflected, for example, in the definition of "owner" as relevant to Pt IIA of the 1990 Act, contained in s.78A(9). In Scotland an owner is defined as a person entitled to receive the rent from the land or who would be entitled to receive such rent if the land were let. This includes a trustee, factor, guardian or curator. In respect of public or municipal land, this also includes the persons to whom the management of the land is entrusted. A creditor in a heritable security not in possession of the security subjects is specifically excluded from the scope

---

[15] [1994] 2 AC 264.

[16] *Donoghue v Stevenson* 1932 S.C. (HL) 31.

[17] Such alternative pleas were, for example, made in *Kennedy v Glenbelle* 1996 S.L.T. 1186.

[18] See the Abolition of Feudal Tenure etc. (Scotland) Act 2000. The provisions regarding the abolition of the feudal system of land tenure came into force on November 28, 2004. From this date the system whereby land was held by a vassal on perpetual tenure from a superior was abolished. It is no longer possible to create a feudal estate in land.

of the definition. For the purpose of establishing ownership of land in Scotland, recourse must be made to the Land Register or the Register of Sasines, which are open to the public. The owner of land has essentially similar natural rights to those enjoyed in England. Scots law acknowledges[19]:

> "the undoubted right of the proprietor to the free and absolute use of his own property, but there is this restraint or limitation imposed for the protection of his neighbour, that he is not so to use his property as to create that discomfort or annoyance to this neighbour which interferes with his legitimate enjoyment."

25.20 A lease in Scotland, as in England, is capable of creating a real interest in land, but it is arguable whether a Scots Court would regard the tenant as being the "owner" for the purposes of statutory provisions. It remains to be determined to what extent the Scots Courts would be motivated by other definitions of the word "owner" in other UK statutory provisions as a primary determinant of the liability question.

25.21 While the system of taking security in Scotland is considerably different from that which applies in England, the issue of the possible liability of lenders, receivers, liquidators and administrators for breaches of environmental legislation is probably to be approached in a similar way. It has been held in *Lord Advocate v Aero Technologies Ltd*[20] that receivers may be jointly liable with the company as occupiers for the purposes of the Explosives Acts 1875 and 1923.

---

[19] *Fleming v Hislop* (1886) 13 R. (HL) 43 at 48 per Lord Fitzgerald.
[20] 1991 S.L.T. 134.

Chapter 26

GERMANY

The Federal Soil Protection Act[1]

26.01 Until 1999, soil and groundwater contamination were handled individually by the 16 German federal states (*Länder*), mostly according to their general policies and water laws. With the enactment of the Federal Soil Protection Act,[2] which came into force on March 1, 1999, a uniform standard was introduced for the first time. The Act contains general principles of soil protection and sets out specific obligations of individuals regarding the investigation and remediation of historic contamination. An ordinance sets out threshold values, which are to be used for evaluating contamination risks.[3]

Soil protection laws of the German Länder

26.02 The Federal Soil Protection Act is not a framework statute but fully regulates the responsibility for soil contamination on the federal level. Its entry into force rendered contradictory statutory provisions of the federal states invalid[4] and only leaves a limited leeway for additional state law provisions. These mainly include a few procedural rules such as provisions concerning the establishment of contaminated land registers or notification duties.[5]

Liability for historic contamination

Scope of application

26.03 The Federal Soil Protection Act applies to "detrimental soil changes" and "historic contamination":

(a) Detrimental soil changes are defined as harmful impacts on the soil functions that could cause hazards, significant disadvantages or significant nuisance for individuals or the general public.[6]

---

[1] The authors are indebted to Michael Ramb of Freshfields Bruckhaus Deringer, Berlin, for contributing this chapter, which has involved almost complete re-writing, the applicable law having changed markedly since the first edition in 1994.

[2] Act on Protection against Harmful Changes to Soil and the Clean-up of Contaminated Sites (Federal Soil Protection Act) (BBodSchG) of March 17, 1998, Federal Law Gazette (BGBl.) I, p.502.

[3] Federal Ordinance on Soil Protection and Residual Pollution (BBodSchV) of July 12, 1999, Federal Law Gazette (BGBl.) I, p.1554.

[4] Pursuant to Art.31 of the German Constitution (*Grundgesetz*), federal laws override laws of the German *Länder*.

[5] See s.21 of the Federal Soil Protection Act.

[6] Federal Soil Protection Act s.2(3).

(b) Historic contamination is defined as closed-down waste disposal installations or other properties on which waste has been treated, stored or deposited (former waste disposal sites) as well as properties on which closed-down installations are located and other properties on which environmentally harmful substances have been handled (former industrial sites). Like the concept of detrimental soil change, the definition of historic contamination requires that the contamination causes detrimental soil changes or other actual or potential damage to individuals or to the general public.[7]

The Federal Soil Protection Act may also apply to the contamination of **26.04** surface or ground water if such contamination has been caused by soil contamination (e.g. through infiltration). However, in such cases the Federal Soil Protection Act does not replace water laws entirely but only defines basic liabilities in regard to remediation (e.g. the responsible persons) while the specific remediation targets are governed by the relevant provisions of water laws.

Responsible persons

Compared with the situation before 1999, the Federal Soil Protection Act **26.05** has significantly extended the scope of persons or entities that can be held liable for soil contamination. These persons include:

(a) the polluter;

(b) the universal legal successor (*Gesamtrechtsnachfolger*) of the polluter;

(c) the owner;

(d) the person exercising factual control over the land, e.g. a lessee;

(e) any former owner, provided that he transferred the property after March 1, 1999 and knew or ought to have known the existence of the contamination; or

(f) the person/entity responsible under general principles of commercial or corporate law for the legal entity owning the site.[8]

Unlike other jurisdictions, the concept of lender-liability, under which a **26.06** creditor is responsible for environmental damage caused by the borrower, does not exist in German environmental law. Under the Federal Soil

---

[7] Federal Soil Protection Act s.2(5).

[8] This new liability concept is unknown to traditional environmental law in Germany and was introduced by the Federal Soil Protection Act in 1999. It allows the corporate veil to be pierced in order to prevent corporations from escaping liability for residual pollution through corporate restructuring (e.g. transfer of contaminated assets to a subsidiary). For example, a parent company may be held liable for contaminated land owned by its subsidiary if the subsidiary is under-capitalised, if finances are mixed up with its shareholders' finances, or if both entities form "de facto consolidated companies" (*qualifiziert-faktischer Konzern*).

Protection Act, a lender qualifies neither as a polluter, because he does not directly create a danger through his actions or omissions, nor as a person exercising factual control over the land—because lending money does not give him a significant and determining influence on the location, nature or specific operations of a facility.

26.07 In principle, the authority has full discretion to decide which responsible person it wants to charge with investigation/remediation measures or the costs thereof.[9] This decision is subject to limited judicial review only. In general, the most efficient measure should be taken in order to avert the danger immediately, subject to the principle of proportionality. In addition, the authority may recover the costs of measures it has taken itself in order to avert risks of environmental damage. When recovering such costs, the authorities can choose, as one criterion, the party in the strongest financial position as the liable party.

Scope of remediation

26.08 The Federal Soil Protection Act provides the competent authorities with a variety of instruments in order to address suspected or existing soil contamination. If there are sufficient grounds for suspecting that a detrimental soil change or historic contamination exists, the competent authority may require any of the responsible persons to carry out an inspection at their own expense in order to determine the degree of environmental damage.[10] The specific investigation measures may include the obligation to commission experts and investigating bodies. If there is evidence of a detrimental soil change or historic contamination, the authority is allowed to order decontamination or safeguarding measures. The authorities may require the responsible persons to carry out self-monitoring measures, especially soil and water investigations, and to install and operate measuring stations (even after decontamination has been completed). Moreover, especially in the case of particularly hazardous or widespread contamination, the authorities may order the necessary investigation for decisions regarding the type and extent of the required measures as well as the submission of a remediation plan.

Remediation contract

26.09 The classic instruments of German soil protection law with regard to the remediation of contaminated land are administrative orders by the competent authorities (e.g. a formal investigation or remediation order).

---

[9] A hierarchy or "class" system of responsible persons is unknown to German soil protection law. Rather, the Federal Soil Protection Act assumes that all responsible persons are, in principle, of equal status. In particular, there is no principle of prior-ranking responsibility of the polluter (see Decision of the Higher Administrative Court (VGH) Kassel of January 6, 2006, 6 TG 1392/04). For example, if the polluter is difficult to determine or financially incapable of carrying out remediation, the authority may charge the property owner with remediation. In turn, the property owner may then have a compensation claim against the polluter according to s.24(2) of the Federal Soil Protection Act.

[10] Federal Soil Protection Act s.9(2). In cases where there are mere "clues" for the existence of a detrimental soil change, the competent authority is normally required to clarify the facts itself, see s.9(1) of the Federal Soil Protection Act.

However, "public law contracts" are becoming increasingly important as a flexible instrument to deal with various public law issues. The Federal Soil Protection Act provides for a "remediation-contract" between the environmental authority and the person(s) liable for remediation under the Act.[11] Such a contract may involve third parties (e.g. other responsible parties or future site owners). Once the contract has been made the authorities are bound by the agreed remediation target and cannot require additional works. Only if the inherent basis of the contract is changed may the authority demand an adjustment or the termination of the contract.

Remediation contracts containing provisions affecting third parties may **26.10** require the written consent of the affected third parties. The need for consent is limited to the relevant provisions of the contract. If the contract is agreed without the necessary consent, the third party has the right to challenge the contract.

Statutory compensation claim

As a general rule, the costs for remediation are to be borne by the person **26.11** who is obliged to conduct the respective measures.[12] However, in cases involving several responsible persons, the Federal Soil Protection Act provides for a statutory compensation claim between these various responsible persons, irrespective of their being called to account by the authorities.[13] Where no other arrangements are agreed, the obligation to provide such compensation, and the amount of compensation, depends on the extent to which the hazard or damage was caused primarily by one party or the other. For example, if a property owner who has not caused the contamination is obliged by the competent authorities to carry out remediation, he has a statutory claim of compensation against the polluter.[14]

The statutory claim for compensation pursuant to s.24(2) of the Federal **26.12** Soil Protection Act can be excluded by contract. In 2004, the Federal Supreme Court ruled that such exclusion must be stipulated by explicit contractual terms; moreover, the exclusion is valid exclusively between the contracting parties and not in relation to future purchasers.[15] From a transactional perspective, this means that a vendor must contractually oblige the purchaser to pass on the exclusion of the statutory claim against the vendor to any onward purchasers and subsequent users in order to safeguard against claims by future purchasers based on s.24 (2) of the Federal Soil Protection Act.

---

[11] Federal Soil Protection Act s.13(4).

[12] Federal Soil Protection Act s.24(1).

[13] Federal Soil Protection Act s.24(2).

[14] Claims for compensation pursuant to s.24(2) of the Federal Soil Protection Act become time-barred after three years. The beginning of this three-year period differs depending on whether the authority or a private party has carried out the remediation measures. In the case of an authority taking the measures, the three-year period begins with its collection of the costs; in the case of a private party taking the measures, the three-year period starts on the date the private party becomes aware of the other responsible party. Regardless of such knowledge, claims become time-barred thirty years after the completion of the remediation measures.

[15] Decision of the Federal Supreme Court (BGH) of April 2, 2004 (V ZR 267/03).

Disclosure obligations

26.13 The soil, water and waste laws of the 16 German *Länder* impose a range of disclosure obligations related to soil and groundwater contamination. Depending on the state and statute, there are differences with regard to the persons caught by the disclosure obligation, the required scope of information provided, and the events triggering the obligations.

26.14 Under the state water laws, various persons who deal with substances hazardous to water are obliged to disclose contamination they become aware of. These persons include the operator of a plant, the owner or tenant of land and the owner, user or possessor of the hazardous substance. The disclosure obligations are triggered rather easily, in many instances it is sufficient that a substance hazardous to water is released from a plant and contamination of water or groundwater cannot be excluded.

26.15 Under various state soil protection laws (e.g. Bavaria, Baden-Württemberg; North Rhine-Westphalia), soil contamination or the suspicion thereof must be reported to the authorities by the responsible persons (as defined in the Federal Soil Protection Act). Suspicion exists when the limits set out by the Federal Soil Protection Ordinance are exceeded. In some states, construction companies or builders are under an obligation to report when they encounter hazardous soil contamination in the course of construction measures.[16]

26.16 The Federal Soil Protection Act stipulates disclosure duties only in advanced cases. If the persons liable under the Act are required to carry out self-monitoring measures, the results of these measures must be recorded and disclosed to the authorities upon request. Where a responsible person is required to carry out site investigations or remediation measures, owners of the affected property, as well as other affected authorised users and the affected neighbourhood must be informed about the intended measures.[17] The same duty applies to responsible persons who are required to submit a remediation plan.[18]

It must be considered on a case-by-case basis whether the disclosure obligations are limited by the privilege against self-incrimination. Breach of the disclosure obligation is subject to an administrative fine.

Liability risks related to property transactions

26.17 Public law liability for contaminated land, i.e. the liability of a responsible person towards the competent authorities, cannot be modified by private contracts. A polluter, therefore, cannot transfer his public law liability as polluter onto a purchaser, i.e. he will remain responsible as the polluter of land after the land is sold. However, the parties can stipulate by

---

[16] In addition, there are a few disclosure obligations set by state waste laws with regard to landfills and waste treatment facilities. Their operators (only) are obliged to disclose potentially harmful effects to the environment caused by a disruption or change of operations.

[17] Federal Soil Protection Act s.12.

[18] Federal Soil Protection Act s.13(3).

contractual provisions how any environmental liability is to be shared between them (e.g. the parties may agree on a financial cap, a *de minimis* threshold, a time limit to the buyer's claims other than two years, or sliding scales increasing the buyer's share of liability over time).

The extent of possible liability risks related to property transactions **26.18** depends to a large extent on the nature of the transaction. In share deals, i.e. if the purchaser acquires the shares of the target, the target will be liable for the clean up of any contamination caused as polluter. The same risk arises in mergers, i.e. if the purchaser becomes the legal successor of the target. In such a case, the purchaser may become liable under public and civil law (compensation claims) for any contamination that the target company (or any of its legal predecessors) has ever caused on any former site or adjacent properties.

In asset deals, i.e. if the purchaser acquires the assets of the target, he **26.19** will be liable as the future owner (or occupier) of the land. The Federal Constitutional Court ruled in 2000 that the liability of the landowner is in principle limited to the market value of the site after the completion of remediation measures.[19] The owner's liability may be limited further where the contamination was caused by a natural occurrence, by the public or by an unauthorised third party, and if he did not know about the pollution when he bought the assets.

In addition, with asset deals that took place after March 1, 1999, the **26.20** target company will remain liable as a former owner if it knew or ought to have known about the contamination.

---

[19] Decision of the Federal Constitutional Court (BVerfG) of February 16, 2000 (1 BvR 242/91, 315/99).

Chapter 27

THE NETHERLANDS

Summary

27.01 The Netherlands[1] presents an interesting case-study in the development of legislation on contaminated land.[2] Soil pollution came onto the political agenda in the late 1970s, and there have been some celebrated examples of contaminated sites that have been subject to successful clean-up. These include not only the well-known site at Lekkerkerk (see below) but also the Volgermeerpolder site, used as a landfill since 1927 for the municipality of Amsterdam, and polluted by the disposal of industrial chemicals and pesticides in the 1960s, the Griftpark site at Utrecht and the Kralingen site at Rotterdam. The Dutch Ministry's website suggests that the number of sites in urgent need of clean-up is around 60,000. One particularly serious problem given the geography of The Netherlands is the incidence of polluted aquatic sediments in waterways; in some cases serious problems have occurred through the used of grossly contaminated dredgings to level ground for construction of housing and other development.

27.02 Initially, the remediation of polluted soil was deemed a government task. However, after the start of the first remediation activities, it soon became apparent that the costs for the public would rise to an unacceptable level. In 1998 the Government spent one billion guilders on soil clean-up. One third of that sum came from businesses and private individuals, one from the central Government as part of a scheme under the Soil Protection Act, and a third from other authorities. Despite these serious efforts, it had become clear that soil clean-up was not being tackled fast enough. As a result the Government issued a statement on the review of soil clean-up policy in 1997. This statement presented the objectives of charting the scale of soil pollution nationwide by the year 2005 and efforts to bring the problem under control within 25 years, partly through stepping up private investment by making clean-up standards more realistic and more transparent.

27.03 In addition, it proved difficult to recover the costs of the remediation activities from the parties who had caused the soil pollution. The law has developed so as to draw a clear distinction between "old" and "new" contamination. Thus, under Dutch law, the applicable legal framework depends on the period of time in which the soil pollution was caused. Soil

---

[1] The assistance of André H. Gaastra of Gaastra attorneys at law in updating materials from the first edition is gratefully acknowledged.

[2] The website of the Dutch Environment Ministry, VROM, contains a helpful summary of the policy and legislation, including English translations of the main legislation and key policy documents: see *http://international.vrom.nl/*.

pollution caused prior to the entry into force of the general duty of care towards the soil under the Soil Protection Act, is referred to as "historic soil pollution". The rules applicable to the remediation of historic soil pollution are quite different to the rules applicable to "new pollution". The regime applicable to new pollution is simple, and boils down to a straightforward immediate obligation to take control measures and to remediate. Furthermore, these cases of soil pollution must be reported to the competent authority as soon as possible. The competent authority can, amongst others, issue an order under threat of a penalty if the perpetrator does not fulfil its legal duty of care.

Liability for the clean up of soil pollution is dealt with under civil law. **27.04** The party who causes soil pollution is liable on the basis of tort law vis-à-vis any party who suffers damages. Today, virtually all purchase agreements dealing with the transfer of a business or real estate contain clauses in which the risks pertaining to known or unknown soil pollution are attributed to one of the contracting parties. The Soil Protection Act provides a specific legal basis for actions in tort by the State. On the basis of these provisions, the State can pursue historic polluters for costs incurred relating to soil investigations and remediation activities carried out by the government, and for unjust enrichment as a result of remediation performed for the account of government.

The Soil Clean-up (Interim) Act 1982

Legislation on contaminated land in The Netherlands can be traced back **27.05** to the Soil Clean-up (Interim) Act 1982 (Interim Wet Bodemsane Ring), which was a somewhat hurried response to the incident of soil pollution at Lekkerkeck, near Rotterdam, where toxic chemicals found their way into drinking water serving a housing development. The Act required provincial authorities to draw up each year a clean-up programme to deal with soil contamination, indicating those cases within the province where the soil was contaminated or was in danger of becoming contaminated so as to pose a serious threat to health or the environment and specifying details of investigations or remedial measures to be carried out. The provincial authority was given extensive rights of entry and investigation for the purpose of implementing the programme; the authority could also order any person whose activities it considers wholly or partly responsible for causing contamination to suspend the activities in question or to suspend them if specified requirements were not met.[3] In the case of sites designated for clean up, an order could be made by the Minister of Housing, Physical Planning and Environment against the person with rights to the property on which the source of contamination is situated, to take appropriate measures to eliminate that source or to restrict the contamination or its effects so far as possible.[4] By s.17 of the Interim Act, if the recipient of such an order was likely to suffer financial loss or damage which he could not reasonably be expected to bear in whole or in part, the

---

[3] Soil Clean-up (Interim) Act 1982 s.11(2).
[4] Soil Clean-up (Interim) Act 1982 s.12(1).

provincial authority or Minister had to grant him indemnification to be fixed equitably, insofar as reasonable indemnification had not or cannot be provided by other means.[5] The way in which it was originally envisaged that the Act would work was by the provincial authorities undertaking clean-up operations, funded by the municipalities and by central Government.[6] Legal proceedings under s.21 of the Act would then follow against the person whose unlawful act had caused the contamination in question, to recover costs incurred by the State. However, the Interim Act did not work in this way in practice.

27.06   The first decision on liability under the Interim Act was *State v van Amersfoort* (Dutch Supreme Court, February 21, 1990). It was held that s.21 did not set aside the normal requirements of the law of tort—in particular, a duty owed to the State—as a precondition for recovery. The requirements for liability were subsequently clarified in *State v Akzo Resins* (Supreme Court, April 24, 1992) where it was held that as from January 1, 1975 it was foreseeable to operators who contaminated their own soil that the Government would have to take remedial measures: thus from such a date there was a duty of care owed to the State. This ruling presented practical difficulties of apportionment in cases where the pollution in question occurred both before and after the 1975 date; this was the case in *State v van Wijngaarden*, a Supreme Court decision at the same time as *Akzo Resins*, which was referred back to the court of appeals to determine that issue. The decision absolved Akzo Resins of liability completely, as the pollution concerned spillages of resin solvents between 1954 and 1967. The *Akzo* and *van Wijngaarden* cases concerned own-site contamination, and there remained doubt as to the application of these principles to off-site disposal of wastes: *Staat & Gemeente Ouderkerk v Shell Nederland Raffinaderij BV & Shell Nederland Chemie BV* (Court of Appeal, The Hague November 19, 1992); *State v Philips Duphar* (Court of Appeal Amsterdam, December 1992). In the *Shell-Gouderak* case, the soil in a residential area appeared to be seriously polluted by "drin" pesticides originating from Shell in the 1950s. The contamination was such that a number of houses on the site had to be demolished. In the subsequent claim by the State for clean up costs from Shell, it was held that the principles of the *Azko* case were not relevant to the situation here where the contamination resulted from the transport of wastes for disposal off-site. On the basis of what was known and what could have reasonably been anticipated in the 1950s when the wastes were consigned, Shell was found not to be liable. In the *Duphar* case, it was found that Duphar ought to have been mindful, in the period prior to 1975, of the risks of disposing of chemical waste at a landfill site, but that there was no evidence that this either had been or should have been the case prior to 1970.

27.07   By 1992 some 155 legal actions for cost recovery at contaminated sites had been launched by the Dutch Environment Ministry (VROM) under the 1982 Interim Act. The total costs sought amounted to some Fl 940 million ($520m). Estimates at the time suggested that there were 120,000 contaminated sites in the Nederlands, of which between 30,000 and 60,000

[5] Soil Clean-up (Interim) Act 1982 s.17(1).
[6] Soil Clean-up (Interim) Act 1982 ss.18–20.

would require some degree of clean up.[7] The *Akzo* case, in particular, presented the Government with difficulties in obtaining redress in relation to older historic contamination.

As a matter of practice, however, as in the UK, many clean-ups were **27.08** carried out "voluntarily" by owners or occupiers under express or implicit threat of State action, under the supervision of the authorities. There were some tax advantages to this course.

The Soil Protection Act 1986

The unsatisfactory nature of the 1982 Act's regime led to proposals being **27.09** submitted by the Dutch Government for amendments to the 1982 Act by inserting new provisions into the Soil Protection Act 1986 (Wet Bodembescherming) which entered into force on January 1, 1987. The essential nature of the proposed amendments was to allow investigation and clean-up orders to be made against current owners as well as polluters. Unlike s.21 of the 1982 Act, these new proposals contained no requirement for the Government to prove its interest in the clean-up—the so-called "relativity" principle—thus effectively overruling the *Akzo* and *van Amersfoort* cases. The proposal was heavily criticised by the Dutch business community in view of the strict and retrospective nature of liability. The Government then agreed to modify the rigour of the proposals in relation to the owner by providing that the owner will be held liable only if no polluter with sufficient financial resources can be found, and then subject to a defence where:

1. the owner has not himself caused any pollution;

2. the owner had no legal relationship with the polluter at the time of the pollution; and

3. at the time the owner acquired the property he did not know of the contamination nor should he have known of it.

Further amendments were made to the legislation following fierce **27.10** debate in the Lower House. Powers to issue orders requiring temporary measures were introduced, together with power to issue orders against current and former users of property. Apart from the "innocent owner" defence, a defence was introduced for owners who did not have a considerable share in the pollution; under the defence they may avoid orders on condition that they are prepared to pay a proportional contribution (based on their part of the pollution) to the clean-up costs. At the same time, other legislation was being prepared to prohibit the transfer of contaminated sites and to place obligations on sellers to carry out clean-up operations at the time of transfer, or alternatively to give secured undertakings for clean-up at some date. Against the background of these proposals for new legislation, there was considerable activity involving

---

[7] See also *Soil Protection in the 90s: 10–year planning scenario with specific reference to industrial sites* (Lower House of the States-General 1989–90 Session, 21 557, No.1).

cooperation between industry and Government in voluntary investigation and clean-up—the so-called BSB operation. The advantage for industry of such a scheme lay in the ability to exert influence over timing, strategies and costs. The objective of the BSB scheme was to achieve voluntary clean-up of contaminated sites by industry with the aim of having all such sites cleaned-up within a period of 25 years. The Government's Committee on Clean-up of Industrial Sites was established in 1988 and published its final report on the plan for clean up in June 1991: this involves investigation and prioritisation of sites in actual use.

27.11　An important focus of debate was clean-up criteria and soil protection guidelines. The Soil Clean-Up (Interim) Act 1982 itself contained no criteria for remedial operations. However, immediately after the Act became law, the Environment Ministry issued Guidelines on Soil Clean-up which established the well-known A, B and C levels for the assessment of contamination by a range of substances. The "A" Level (or refence value) constitutes the natural or background level of substances in clean soil. The "B" Level indicates a situation requiring investigation to determine the extent and location of contamination. The "C" Level indicates that clean-up is necessary. The Guidelines were later renamed "Guidelines for Soil Protection" to accord with the approach of the Soil Protection Act 1986. The standards have were reconsidered in the light of recent scientific studies and it was proposed to change the system by abolishing "B" values and by replacing "A" and "C" values with "target levels" and "intervention levels" respectively. Whilst the basic principle of the Dutch approach under the 1982 Act was that of multifunctionality (that is, restoring soil to a level of cleanliness to enable it to be used for any purpose) the rule was never applied inflexibly and in practice the levels for remediation varied on public health, environmental protection and site specific criteria, i.e. specific characteristics of the soil and the current and future use of the site.

The Soil Protection Act 1994

27.12　The 1986 Soil Protection Act was amended by the Soil Protection Act 1994.[8] The essence of the 1994 Act is the incorporation in the 1986 Act of clean-up provisions in a remediation Chapter. The Act requires to be read in conjunction with subordinate legislation on standards of clean-up and soil investigations, and policy documents such as the *Guidelines on Soil Protection*. The Act creates a Technical Soil Protection Committee to advise the Minister.[9] Whilst the Act takes multi-functionality as its starting point for remediation,[10] this is mitigated by the recognition of site specific factors. As well as provisions on clean-up, there is a general duty of care to take all measures that could reasonably be expected to prevent contamina-

---

[8] Usefully described in an article by Gerrit Betlem in [1995] E.E.L.R. 232.
[9] Chapter II.
[10] See s.38, which requires clean up at least to the standard to make the site suitable for the function it will be assigned after decontamination, but also limits to the fullest possible extent the spreading of contaminating substances and limits to the fullest possible extent the need to take measures and impose restrictions on the future use of the soil.

tion or to limit the consequences.[11] Acting in violation of the general duty of care towards the soil is also a criminal offence and even a felony if committed with intent. There are also general duties to notify the Provincial Executive of acts giving rise to contamination of impairment of soil, or of proposed remedial measures.[12] Betlem points out that the approach to clean-up is essentially to place responsibility with private parties, to decentralise administration to provincial authorities, and to provide for uniform procedures and criteria.[13]

A distinction was drawn in the 1994 Act between "old" (pre-January 1, **27.13** 1987) and "new" incidents (occurring after that date) of pollution. All "new" incidents entail liability for clean-up, whereas "old" incidents only involve liability where there is a case of "serious" soil pollution: the criteria for "serious" pollution are intervention values laid down in the *Guidelines on Soil Protection* and corresponding to the former "C" levels. Once soil has been identified as contaminated by these criteria, clean-up orders may be issued if remediation is not undertaken voluntarily: such orders may be issued against the polluter or the owner or lessee. Such orders cannot be issued where clean-up measures have already been undertaken in accordance with the Act, or against an "innocent" owner or occupier: the concept of innocence is defined by reference to absence of involvement in the polluting events and by lack of actual or constructive knowledge at the time of acquisition.[14] Whether the owner/occupier could reasonably have been expected to be aware of continuation raises issues of foreseeability similar to those already ventilated in the Dutch courts in the context of cost recovery by the State. The wording refers to whether the purchaser was at the time of acquiring title "was not aware or could not in all fairness have been aware of the contamination": increasing general awareness of the issue will therefore make this defence more difficult to sustain. The Act does not entail a tiered system of liability; nonetheless it appears that "general principles of proper administration" would require the authority to seek to involve the polluter before turning to the owner or lessee. The potential relevance of Dutch law on unjust enrichment must also be considered in this context.[15] Provisions exist for the recovery of remediation costs by the State: the general principle is that costs can be recovered from the person whose unlawful acts caused the contamination and who has acted unlawfully towards the public body, from anyone who has unfairly benefited from remediation, and also from any other person whose polluting acts led to the contamination and was aware of the hazardous nature of the substances concerned, having regard to common contemporary business practices and reasonable alternatives available.[16] It appears that the new legislation will not affect the existing liability in the general law of tort in relation to incidents of pollution taking place after January 1, 1975.

---

[11] The Soil Protection Act 1994 s.13.
[12] The Soil Protection Act 1994 ss.27 and 28.
[13] The Soil Protection Act 1994 ss.27 and 28.
[14] The Soil Protection Act 1994 s.46.
[15] The Soil Protection Act 1994 s.46.
[16] The Soil Protection Act 1994 s.75.

Change of policy on multi-functionality

27.14 In a speech given in May 1997 by the Dutch Minister for Housing, Spatial Planning and the Environment, Mrs M de Boer, to the Ad Hoc Ministerial Working Group on Contaminated Soil, the Minister signalled an important change of approach in Dutch policy. The scale of the contaminated land problem and the public financial resources devoted to cleaning it up were acknowledged to be vastly greater than anticipated. This resulted in a shift of approach to one which is more market-orientated and relates more to the designated use of the site: this change applies to "historic contamination", i.e. that which occurred before 1987, the year of the Soil Protection Act 1986 coming into force. The shift is from total remediation to a combination of prevention and remediation, and towards integrating remediation more fully into the development process. This policy change obviously took The Netherlands away from its multi-functionality approach, towards a pragmatic approach much more akin to that of the UK's Pt IIA regime. These far-reaching changes to Dutch policy were subsequently brought forward within The Netherlands, and are described in an article by Corn'e van der Wilt.[17] Effectively, the principle of multi-functionality was abandoned where soil pollution is historic—predating the Soil Protection Act 1986. Instead, clean-up measures will be related to the intended use of the land: the principle of "functional clean-up". Other developments emerging at the same time were the making of a distinction between mobile and immobile contamination for the purposes of clean-up standards; the creation of a soil clean-up fund to assist private remedial operations; and the integration of soil clean-up into other societal processes. Overall, the change was a fundamental one, from the initial ambitious goal of total clean-up within one generation, to the objective of leaving "a legacy of manageable proportions". The new approach is formally endorsed in a letter from the Minister of Housing, Spatial Planning and the Environment dated December 3, 1999 to the Lower House of the States-General.[18] This indicates four basic strategic goals:

1. Remediation measures for individual sites will be designed on the basis of an integrated approach, looking at the topsoil and subsoil together and in the light of intended development.

2. The soil will after remediation meet the criteria for use. A distinction is made between residential areas (including residential green areas) and agricultural and nature functions. For residential functions, there is to be a standard approach which consists of the introduction of a surface layer of certain thickness and quality, based on soil-use-specific remediation goals (BGWs) for specified immobile substances. For agricultural and nature functions, there is to be a customised approach. In addition the soil must no longer constitute a source of diffusion of contamina-

---

[17] *Multifunctionality of Soil: The Rise and Fall of a Dutch Principle* [1998] Env. Liab. 18.

[18] Interdepartmental Policy Review: Soil Remediation (1999–2000) No. 25411 (published on VROM website *http://international.vrom.nl/*).

tion, resulting in a "stable end state" where without further physical measures, there will be no further diffusion and the core or seat of the contamination should be removed as far as is possible, within the limits of cost-effectiveness.

3. If remediation operations take a long time, reference points are built in so that adjustments can be made where necessary.

4. The remediation should result in a situation where ongoing care activities for the soil are as limited as possible in terms of extent, intensity and number.

The Government estimated that this approach would lead to an overall **27.15** cost reduction of 35 to 50 per cent compared with the multifunctionality approach.

Further developments

Netherlands policymakers have developed new rules for the purpose of **27.16** enhancing the active remediation of industrial polluted property. Recently, the Soil Protection Act 1994 was amended by the insertion of ss.55a and 55b (special provisions for decontamination of industrial sites) to the effect that owners and long lease holders of industrial real estate can be ordered to remediate in cases of serious pollution that must be remedied urgently, irrespective of whether they are innocent owners. In the case of a transfer of polluted real estate, the former owner or long lease holder remains responsible alongside the new owner for the fulfilment of this obligation until the moment at which the new owner or long lease holder has furnished financial security to the satisfaction of the competent authority. This obligation cannot be avoided by means of a contract. However, certain contractual terms could mitigate the consequences of such liability for the seller.

On the other hand, the State has provided for budgets for the benefit of **27.17** the competent authorities and subsidies for the benefit of some owners and long leaseholders of industrial real estate who intend to remediate in the case of historic serious pollution that must be remedied with due speed.[19] The criteria are such that, in principle, only innocent owners can apply. The case must concern soil pollution that was (partly) caused before January 1, 1975, and a right of ownership or long lease that was acquired before January 1, 1995. Furthermore, the State must not have the intention of taking recourse against the applicant for any damages, on the basis of specific liability provisions in the Soil Protection Act.

Other recent developments[20] have included a 1998 paper outlining policy **27.18** with respect to the development of urban brownfield sites,[21] a revised

---

[19] See ss.76a–76l of the Soil Protection Act, making provision for such budgets and subsidies.
[20] All accessible in English on the VROM website *http://international.vrom.nl/*.
[21] *Urban Brownfields: restructuring and urban economic development* (1998).

Circular on target values and intervention values[22] and a policy document on the re-use of lightly contaminated soils.[23]

---

[22] Circular on target values and intervention values for soil remediation and Annexes A–D (February 4, 2000).

[23] *Policy document: How to deal with contaminated excavated soil* (September 1999).

Chapter 28

USA

This chapter aims to provides a necessarily brief overview of what is a huge **28.01** body of Federal and State statute and case law.[1] Those requiring fuller treatment are recommended to refer to Vol.1 of the comprehensive two-volume work by Valerie Fogleman, *Environmental Liabilities and Insurance in England and the United States*.[2]

Comprehensive Environmental Response, Compensation, and Liability Act

On December 11, 1980, the US Congress enacted the Comprehensive **28.02** Environmental Response, Compensation, and Liability Act (CERCLA),[3] commonly known as Superfund, in response to concern over uncontrolled or abandoned hazardous waste sites, such as Love Canal.[4] CERCLA is the cornerstone of the federal hazardous substance and liability programme, and is primarily implemented by the federal Environmental Protection Agency (EPA). The law created a tax on the chemical and petroleum industries and provided broad Federal authority to respond to releases or threatened releases of hazardous substances from facilities that may endanger public health or the environment. The term "hazardous substance" is defined quite broadly, although it does not include petroleum, natural gas, or their fractions. The tax goes into a Trust Fund, called the Superfund, for cleaning up waste sites. While the Trust Fund can be tapped for clean-up, an extensive liability scheme, described in detail below, allows EPA to recover costs incurred by the Trust Fund. A key purpose of this scheme is "shift[ing] the cost of cleaning up environmental

---

[1] The authors are indebted to Charlotte L. Neitzel of Holme Roberts & Owen LLP, Denver, Colorado, for updating and substantially re-writing this chapter.

[2] 1st edn (London: Witherby & Co Ltd) (2005).

[3] 42 USC §§ 9601–9657.

[4] The Love Canal site at the City of Niagara Falls, New York, resulted from the use of an excavated and uncompleted canal by the Hooker Electrochemical Company, during and after WWII, for the disposal of drummed hazardous wastes, including some 6,900 tons of hexachloride, a carcinogenic substance known as "spent cake". The canal was conveyed in 1953 to the Niagara Falls Board of Education for one dollar, and (contrary to warnings and stipulations of Hooker) the Board built a school on it, as well as selling parts to a real estate speculator for residential housing. The resultant health and safety problems led to the declaration by President Jimmy Carter of two separate Federal state of emergencies (in 1978 and 1980), relocation of over 500 families living in the area and the purchase of their properties with funds allocated by Congress and the State of New York, and closure of the affected school. A full account is provided in Fogleman, *Environmental Liabilities and Insurance in England and the United States* (London: Witherby & Co Ltd) Vol.1, s.16.2.

harm from the taxpayers to the parties who benefited from the disposal of wastes that caused the harm".[5]

28.03 CERCLA has been amended several times since 1980, including by the 1986 Superfund Amendments and Reauthorization Act (SARA), the 1996 Asset Conservation, Lender Liability, and Deposit Insurance Protection Act, and the 2002 Small Business Liability Relief and Brownfields Revitalization Act (Brownfields Amendments).

Liability

28.04 CERCLA s.107 imposes liability on broad categories of persons, called "potentially responsible parties" or PRPs.[6] The four types of PRPs are present owners or operators of facilities, past owners or operators that owned or operated a facility at the time of disposal of a hazardous substance, persons that arranged for treatment or disposal of a hazardous substance at another facility ("generators" or "arrangers"), and transporters that selected the treatment or disposal location.

28.05 The phrase "at the time of disposal" has been extensively litigated. The majority view is that passive leaking or migration does not constitute disposal,[7] although the Fourth Circuit has held that leakage from an underground storage tank could be considered disposal.[8]

28.06 The liability provisions have been interpreted expansively. For example, parent corporations, successor corporations, and shareholders have become liable as owners and operators. In *United States v Bestfoods*,[9] however, the Supreme Court held that CERCLA does not affect the fundamental principle that a parent corporation is not liable for the acts of its subsidiaries simply by virtue of that relationship. The parent may, however, be directly liable if it actually operated the facility by its own directors taking an active role, or by common directors of the parent and subsidiary acting on behalf of the parent. Norms of corporate behavior are relevant in deciding if the degree of control exceeds what might be expected of the parent/subsidiary relationship.

28.07 PRPs can be liable for response costs the government incurs for clean-up, damages to natural resources, the costs of certain health assessments, and injunctive relief where a site may present an imminent and substantial endangerment.[10] EPA may recover response costs only if they are not inconsistent with the National Contingency Plan, which is a set of regulations at 40 Code of Federal Regulations Pt 300. Natural resource damages are for injury to, destruction of, or loss of natural resources, including the reasonable costs of a damage assessment.[11] Natural resources

---

[5] *EPA v Sequa Corp (In the Matter of Bell Petroleum Servs., Inc)*, 3 F.3d 889, 897 (5th Cir. 1993) (citing *United States v Chem-Dyne Corp*, 572 F. Supp. 802, 805–06 (S.D. Ohio 1983).
[6] 42 USC § 9607(a).
[7] See, e.g. *Carson Harbor Village, Ltd v Unocal Corp*, 270 F.3d 863 (9th Cir. 2001, *cert. denied*, 122 S. Ct. 1437, 152 L.Ed. 381 (2002).
[8] *Norad Inc v William E. Hooper & Sons*, 966 F.2d 837 (4th Cir. 1992), *cert. denied sub.nom. Munaw v Nurad, Inc*, 506 US 940 (1992).
[9] 524 US 51 (1998).
[10] 42 USC § 9607(a)(4)(A)–(D).
[11] 42 USC §§ 9601(6), 9607(a)(4)(c).

are defined broadly to include land, fish, wildlife, biota, air, water, ground water and drinking water supplies. The resource must also belong to, be managed by, held in trust by, appertain to, or otherwise be controlled by the United States, any State, an Indian Tribe, a local government, or a foreign government.[12] The measure of damages is the cost of restoring injured resources to their baseline condition, compensation for the interim loss of injured resources pending recovery, and the reasonable costs of a damage assessment.[13] CERCLA does not provide compensation for personal injuries, economic losses, or other damage that may result from exposure to hazardous substances.

28.08 PRPs may be liable retroactively for acts that occurred before Superfund's enactment in 1980. CERCLA liability is strict. A PRP cannot simply assert that it was not negligent or that it was operating according to industry standards. Liability is also "joint and several", meaning that any one PRP may be held liable for the entire clean-up of the site when the harm caused by multiple parties cannot be separated. A PRP may avoid joint and several liability only if it can prove that the harm it caused can be separated from the harm caused by other PRPs. As a practical matter, clean-up is often divided among PRPs using several factors, including fault, volume, and toxicity of the hazardous substances. CERCLA also provides a right of contribution under s.113 of CERCLA for PRPs held jointly and severally liable.[14]

28.09 The involvement of a PRP with a Superfund site typically starts by receipt of a s.104(e)[15] request for information. After EPA identifies the PRPs, it negotiates with them to do the investigation and clean-up themselves or to pay for the clean-up done by another party. CERCLA contains a specific provision, s.122, which codifies settlement procedures.[16] If a PRP does not agree to a negotiated settlement, EPA can issue an administrative order that requires them to do certain work or work with the Department of Justice to pursue the party through the federal court system.

28.10 EPA has an extensive armoury of enforcement options under CERCLA. First, it can issue administrative orders or seek injunctions in court under s.106 directing PRPs to take action where there may be an imminent and substantive endangerment to the public health or welfare or the environment.[17] This section allows a person who complies with an administrative order to seek reimbursement from the Superfund for the reasonable costs of the required response actions if the person can prove that it was not liable and its costs were reasonable or if the response action ordered was arbitrary and capricious. Secondly, if PRPs do not comply with administrative orders willfully and without sufficient cause, they can be liable for fines of up to three times that amount if EPA conducts the clean-up itself. Thirdly, EPA can sue under s.107 to recover the costs of investigation and clean-up, plus interest. Fourthly, EPA can sue under s.107 to recover

---

[12] 42 USC § 9601(16).
[13] 43 CFR Pt 11.
[14] 42 USC § 9613.
[15] 42 USC § 9604(e).
[16] 42 USC § 9622.
[17] 42 USC § 9606.

natural resource damages. Fifthly, it can obtain a federal lien under s.107(l).[18] The lien is subordinate to the rights of any security holder or judgment lien creditor whose interest is perfected under applicable state law before notice of lien is filed in accordance with state law.[19]

28.11 Section 107 provides three very limited defences to CERCLA liability: an act of God, an act of war, or an act or omission of a contractually unrelated third party, where the defendant exercised due care and took appropriate precautions.[20] These defences are unlikely to help most PRPs.

Exemptions and unique PRPs

28.12 Despite CERCLA's broad and harsh liability scheme, certain PRPs are treated more leniently or qualify for exemptions. *De minimis* parties are PRPs that contribute a relatively small amount of waste to a site, generally less than 1 per cent.[21] EPA wants to remove them from discussions with the more significant waste contributors by settling with them early and contributing their payment toward the clean-up. *De micromis* parties are PRPs that contributed a miniscule amount of waste to a site. EPA's policy is that they should not participate in financing the clean-up.[22]

28.13 EPA will generally not identify generators and transporters of municipal solid wastes as PRPs. The 2002 Brownfields Amendments also provide a qualified exemption from Superfund liability to certain residential, small business, and non-profit generators of municipal solid waste.[23] EPA also has a presumptive settlement range for municipalities that are current or past owners and/or operators of co-disposal sites (sites with both municipal solid wastes and hazardous substances) that want to settle their Superfund liability.[24]

28.14 EPA's policy is to not take action against owners of residential property located on or adjacent to Superfund sites. This policy applies to properties that are owned and used exclusively for single family residences of one to four units.[25]

28.15 If a hazardous substance comes on to a property by migrating through the groundwater from a source outside the property, EPA will not take action against the owner of that property that has become contaminated as a result of the migration. EPA may ask the owner to provide access to the property for sampling and clean-up.[26]

[18] 42 USC § 9607(l).

[19] 42 USC § 9607(l)(3).

[20] 42 USC § 9607(b).

[21] 42 USC § 9622(g)(1).

[22] See 42 USC § 9607(o); EPA *Revised Settlement Policy and Contribution Waiver Language Regarding Exempt De Micromis and Non-Exempt De Micromis Parties* (November 11, 2002), http://www.epa.gov/compliance/resources/policies/ cleanup/superfund/wv-exmpt-dmicro-mem.pdf

[23] See 42 USC § 9607(p), *Interim Guidance on the Municipal Solid Waste Exemption Under CERCLA Section 107(p)* (August 20, 2003), http://www.epa.gov/Compliance/resources/policies/cleanup/ superfund/interim-msw-exempt.pdf

[24] See EPA's *Interim Guidance on the Municipal Solid Waste Exemption under CERCLA § 107(p)* (August 20, 2003).

[25] See EPA's *Policy Toward Owners of Residential Property at Superfund Sites* (July 3, 1991), http://www.epa.gov/Compliance/resources/policies/cleanup/superfund/policy-owner-rpt.pdf

[26] See EPA, *Final Policy Toward Owners of Property Containing Contaminated Aquifers* (May 24, 1995), http://www.epa.gov/brownfields/html-doc/aquifer.htm

CERCLA also provides an exemption for certain landowners who qualify **28.16** for the *bona fide* prospective purchaser (BFPP) defence,[27] the contiguous property owner (CPO) defence,[28] or the innocent purchaser defence. The BFPP defence applies only to purchasers (and their lessees) who buy property after January 11, 2002. They must perform "all appropriate inquiry" prior to purchase and may buy knowing, or having reason to know, of contamination on the property. Although BFPPs can avoid liability, EPA can obtain a "windfall lien" on the property for the amount of any increase in fair market value of the property attributable to an EPA clean-up action.[29]

The CPO defence applies to owners of a property that are not the source **28.17** of the contamination. The property must be contiguous to, or otherwise similarly situated to, a facility that is the source of contamination found on the property. CPOs must also perform "all appropriate inquiry" and buy without knowing, or having reason to know, of contamination on the property. If the purchaser does not qualify for a CPO defence because the purchaser knows of contamination on the property, the purchaser can still qualify for the *bona fide* purchaser defence.[30]

Innocent landowners are persons who satisfy certain criteria, including **28.18** all appropriate inquiry and due care,[31] and buy without knowing, or having reason to know, of contamination on the property. The innocent landowner defence is part of the third party defence.

All three landowner defences have common elements.[32] Each must have **28.19** performed "all appropriate inquiry," meaning compliance with the *All Appropriate Inquiries Final Rule*,[33] or the standards set forth in the ASTM E1527–05 *Phase I Environmental Site Assessment Process*.[34] In addition, the defences prohibit affiliation with a liable party. After the property is purchased, owners must comply with land use restrictions and institutional controls, and must take reasonable steps to stop continuing releases, prevent threatened future releases, and prevent or limit exposure. Property owners must also co-operate with persons performing response actions and provide access to the property, comply with information requests and administrative subpoenas, and provide legally required notices.

Prospective Purchase Agreements (PPAs) may also be available under **28.20** limited circumstances to limit Superfund liability for purchasers. As a result of the BFPP defence now available to purchasers, EPA believes that

---

[27] 42 USC §§ 9601(40), 9607(r).

[28] 42 USC § 9607(q)(1)(A).

[29] EPA, *Windfall Lien Guidance: Frequently Asked Questions* (July 16, 2003), *http://www.epa.gov/ Compliance/resources/policies/cleanup/superfund/interim-windfall-lien-faq.pdf*

[30] See EPA, *Contiguous Property Owner Guidance Reference Sheet* (February 5, 2004), *http:// www.epa.gov/Compliance/resources/policies/cleanup/superfund/contig-prop-faq.pdf*; EPA, *Interim Enforcement Discretion Guidance Regarding Contiguous Property Owners*, (March 19, 2003), *http:// www.epa.gov/Compliance/resources/policies/cleanup/superfund/contig-prop.pdf*

[31] 42 USC §§ 9601(35), 9607(b)(3).

[32] See EPA, *Interim Guidance Regarding Criteria Landowners Must Meet in Order to Qualify for Bona Fide Prospective Purchaser, Contiguous Property Owners, or Innocent Landowner Limitations on CERCLA Liability (Common Elements)* (March 6, 2003), *Common Elements Guidance Reference Sheet* (March 6, 2003), *http://www.epa.gov/Compliance/resources/policies/cleanup/superfund/common-elem-ref.pdf*

[33] 70 Fed. Reg. 66,070 (November 1, 2005).

[34] Different standards apply to purchasers who purchased property before January 11, 2002.

in most cases PPAs are unnecessary. EPA, however, will still consider providing a prospective purchaser with a covenant not to sue in limited circumstances where the public interest will be served, such as where a developer agrees to incorporate sustainable development concepts into a project.[35]

28.21 *De minimis* landowner settlements are another means of limiting CERCLA liability. This option applies to innocent landowners who purchased property without actual or constructive knowledge that the property was used for the generation, transportation, treatment, storage, or disposal of hazardous substances.[36] The settlement is available for owners who did not conduct or permit the generation, transportation, storage, treatment, or disposal of hazardous substances and did not contribute to the release or threatened release of hazardous substances through action or omission.

28.22 CERCLA also provides an exemption for lenders.[37] Lenders are exempt from CERCLA liability unless they (a) exercise decision-making control over environmental compliance such that responsibility is undertaken for the handling of hazardous substances or for disposal practices, or (b) exercise control comparable to that of a manager of the property, either in day-to-day decision-making on environmental compliance matters, or in the management of all or substantially all non-environmental operational functions.

28.23 CERCLA also limits the liability of fiduciaries to the assets held in the fiduciary capacity unless the fiduciary can be held responsible, irrespective of its status as a fiduciary, or the fiduciary negligently causes the property to be contaminated.[38]

Response actions

28.24 The CERCLA process starts with discovery of a contaminated site or notification to EPA of possible releases of hazardous substances. Under s.103 of CERCLA,[39] owners and operators of facilities are required to report releases of a hazardous substance in a reportable quantity.

28.25 Superfund authorises both short-term and long-term responses to threats.[40] Short-term responses, called removal actions, address immediate threats to public health and the environment.[41] Generally, the CERCLA programme involves two types of removal actions. The first are "time-critical actions," when EPA determines that less than six months is available before site activities must be initiated. The second are "non-time-

---

[35] EPA, Office of Enforcement and Compliance Assurance Office of Site Remediation Enforcement Environmentally Responsible, Redevelopment & Reuse (ER3) *Frequently Asked Questions and Answers* (December 2005), EPA, *Bona Fide Prospective Purchasers and the New Amendments to CERCLA* (April 31, 2002), *http://www.epa.gov/Compliance/resources/policies/ cleanup/superfund/bonf-pp-cercla-mem.pdf*

[36] 42 USC § 9622(g)(1)(B).
[37] 42 USC § 9601(20)(E).
[38] 42 USC § 9607(n).
[39] 42 USC § 9603.
[40] 42 USC § 9604.
[41] 40 CFR § 300.5.

critical actions," when EPA determines that more than six months is available before on-site activities must begin. Long-term responses, also called remedial actions, involve complex and more contaminated sites that typically require many years for investigation and clean-up.

Once identified, sites are placed on the Comprehensive Environmental **28.26** Response, Compensation, and Liability Information System (CERCLIS), which is EPA's computerised inventory of potential hazardous substance release sites.[42] EPA evaluates the potential for a release of hazardous substances from the site through the following processes.

EPA initially conducts a Preliminary Assessment (PA). A PA is designed **28.27** to distinguish, based on limited data, between sites that pose little or no threat to human health and the environment and sites that pose a threat and require further investigation.[43] If a PA results in a recommendation for further investigation, a Site Inspection (SI) is performed. SI investigators collect environmental and waste samples to determine if hazardous substances have reached nearby targets. Information collected during the PA and SI are used to calculate a Hazard Ranking System (HRS) score.[44] Sites with an HRS score of 28.50 or greater are eligible for listing on the National Priorities List (NPL) and require the preparation of an HRS scoring package.

Sites are placed on the NPL after public comment. Sites on the NPL are **28.28** the most serious sites identified for long-term clean-up.[45] After a site is placed on the NPL, a remedial investigation/feasibility study (RI/FS) is performed many times by the PRPs. The RI typically involves extensive sampling of soils and groundwater and assesses the risk to human health and the environment.[46] The FS evaluates remedial alternatives. Remedial actions can be conducted only at sites listed on the NPL. Sites on the NPL are eligible for clean-up using Superfund Trust money.

Once EPA selects a remedial alternative, it publishes its Proposed Plan **28.29** of Action for public comment.[47] After consideration of public comments, it documents its decision in a Record of Decision (ROD). The ROD contains the site history, site description, site characterisation, community participation, enforcement activities, contamination, and the remedy selected for clean-up.[48]

The next phase in the Superfund process is the Remedial Design/ **28.30** Remedial Action (RD/RA). In the RD phase, the technical specifications for clean-up remedies and technologies are designed. During RA, the construction or implementation phase of clean-up occurs.[49]

After construction completion, several activities are generally still under- **28.31** taken at sites. These include operation and maintenance (O&M), long-term response actions (LTRA), institutional controls and five-year reviews, and deletion from the NPL. These measures are undertaken because many

[42] 40 CFR § 300.5.
[43] 40 CFR § 300.5.
[44] 40 CFR § 300.420(b)(iv).
[45] 40 CFR § 300.425(b), (c).
[46] 40 CFR § 300.430.
[47] 40 CFR § 300.430(f)(3).
[48] 40 CFR § 300.430(f)(5).
[49] 40 CFR § 300.435.

sites allow for restricted uses due to contamination remaining on-site, with institutional and engineering controls limiting unacceptable exposures. Institutional controls, also called land use controls and activity and use limitations, are non-engineered, administrative or legal instruments that minimise the potential for exposure to contamination by limiting land or resource use. They are intended to minimise potential exposure when contamination remaining on-site restricts the unimpeded use of a site or a ground-water aquifer. In addition, many sites with groundwater contamination require ongoing remediation over many years. The primary responsibility for the long-term care belongs with the States for Fund-financed sites, and with viable and responsible PRPs when they assume the lead for clean-up.

28.32   O&M begins after the remedy is determined to be "operational and functional",[50] which is generally up to one-year following completion of construction, and may be required indefinitely for remedies that contain waste on-site or include institutional controls. O&M includes maintaining engineered containment structures, operating leachate and gas collection systems, operating groundwater containment and restoration systems, and maintaining and enforcing institutional controls.

28.33   During LTRA, the Superfund finances groundwater and surface water restoration for Superfund-financed remedies for up to 10 years after the remedy becomes operational and functional.[51] The most common LTRA remedies are groundwater pump and treat and monitored natural attenuation remedies. If clean-up goals are not achieved within the 10 year LTRA period, the system is transferred to the State for continued O&M.

28.34   Five-year reviews are required when hazardous substances or pollutants and contaminants remain on-site above levels that allow for unlimited exposure. Their purpose is to evaluate whether the remedy remains protective of human health and the environment. Five-year reviews are also conducted for sites where completion of remedial action ultimately will allow for unlimited use and unrestricted exposure, but the remedy will take longer than five years to reach clean-up levels. EPA generally conducts these reviews, although EPA can provide funds to a State or Tribe to conduct five-year reviews. EPA can also allow PRPs to conduct studies in support of a five-year review, even though PRPs do not actually conduct the reviews. The findings are documented in a report, which is made available to the public.

28.35   EPA deletes sites from the NPL once all response actions are complete and all clean-up levels are achieved. EPA can delete sites, even when five-year reviews are required. Deletion from the NPL does not preclude eligibility for subsequent response actions. EPA can also delete uncontaminated portions of a site from the NPL.

Private party actions under CERCLA

28.36   Private parties can have a cause of action under CERCLA. In a significant 2004 decision, *Cooper Industries Inc v Aviall Services Inc*,[52] the Supreme Court addressed whether a private party who has not been sued under s.106 or

---

[50] 40 CFR § 300.435(f).

[51] 40 CFR § 300.435(f)(3).

[52] 543 US 157 (2004).

s.107 of CERCLA can nonetheless obtain contribution under s.113(f)(1) of CERCLA.[53] CERCLA s.113(f)(1) provides that any person may seek contribution from any other person who is liable or potentially liable under s.107(a)[54] following any civil action under s.106[55] or s.107(a).[56] The Supreme Court held that a private party could sue under s.113(f)(1) only during or following a civil action under CERCLA s.106 or s.107(a). The United States has clarified, however, that if a party enters into an administrative order on consent or a judicial settlement that resolves liability for response costs or response actions, that would entitle the party to seek contribution.[57] EPA does not believe that *Aviall* addresses the right of non-liable parties to sue for costs under s.107(a). Decisions after *Aviall* are trying to reconcile that decision with the need to encourage voluntary clean-ups. Persons who voluntarily clean-up typically want the right to pursue other PRPs for clean-up.

Resource Conservation and Recovery Act

The Resource Conservation and Recovery Act (RCRA)[58] was enacted in **28.37** 1976 and consists of the Solid Waste Disposal Act of 1965 (SWDA) and the subsequent amendments to it, including the Hazardous and Solid Waste Amendments of 1984 (HSWA). RCRA was passed to address the increasing problem of accumulating wastes and the risks to human health. Subtitle C of RCRA imposed requirements on the generation, transportation, treatment, storage, and disposal of hazardous waste. Subtitle I also addresses underground storage tanks containing petroleum and hazardous substances. In addition, RCRA has other enforcement authorities that are used to force clean-up, such as s.7002 citizen suits and s.7003 imminent and substantial endangerment suits.

Subtitle C hazardous waste programme

The RCRA Subtitle C programme protects human health and the **28.38** environment through two means. First, the programme is designed to prevent environmental problems by ensuring that wastes are well managed from "cradle to grave". Under this programme, the requirements for hazardous waste identification, hazardous waste generators, transporters, treatment, storage, and disposal facilities, hazardous waste recycling and universal wastes, land disposal restrictions, combustion and permits are found in 40 CFR Pts 260–279. Anyone who generates, transports, treats, stores or disposes of hazardous waste, and any entity that produces, burns, distributes, or markets any waste-derived fuels must notify EPA and

---

[53] 42 USC § 9613(f)(1).
[54] 42 USC § 9607(a).
[55] 42 USC § 9606.
[56] 42 USC § 9607(a).
[57] See EPA and the US Department of Justice, *Interim Revisions to CERCLA Removal, RI/FS and RD AOC Models to Clarify Contribution Rights and Protection under s.113(f)* (August 3, 2005).
[58] 42 USC §§ 6901–6992k.

comply with RCRA. Treatment, storage and disposal facilities are required to have a permit. EPA can issue orders for failure to comply, which can impose a civil penalty of up to $27,500 per day for each violation, and require compliance. EPA can also bring civil actions for failure to comply and can bring criminal actions under certain circumstances.[59]

28.39 Second, the programme contains an extensive "corrective action" clean-up programme, similar to a Superfund, for environmental problems caused by the mismanagement of wastes.[60] While similar to Superfund in the extent of investigation and clean-up required, the RCRA Corrective Action Programme differs from Superfund in that corrective action sites tend to have more viable operators and on-going operations that treat, store, or dispose of hazardous waste. EPA can defer the placement of a site on the NPL when the site can be remediated under a corrective action programme.

28.40 EPA has set goals for clean-up of all facilities requiring corrective action. Remediation of the highest priority sites involves numerous steps and often takes years. To stabilise these threatening sites prior to a final remedy, the Corrective Action Programme established two Environmental Indicators (EI): the Human Exposures EI ensures that people near a particular site are not exposed to unacceptable levels of contaminants, and the Ground-water EI ensures that contaminated groundwater does not spread and further contaminate groundwater resources.

28.41 Corrective action may be initiated through the enforcement mechanisms in RCRA, through an RCRA permit, or through agreements with the regulatory authorities. EPA and states with an authorised programme can enforce RCRA or comparable state programmes through administrative or judicial authorities. Under RCRA s.3008(a), EPA can use its general RCRA enforcement authority to compel compliance with clean-up responsibilities required by a Subtitle C permit. Pursuant to RCRA s.3008(h), EPA can order or enter into consent agreements at facilities that manage RCRA hazardous waste under "interim status," meaning that the facilities have not yet received RCRA permits, or at facilities that had or should have had interim status.[61]

28.42 When purchasers are considering purchasing a property that is or may be subject to corrective action, RCRA does not provide the CERCLA defences available to innocent landowners or bona fide prospective purchasers. EPA may, however, consider a Prospective Purchaser Agreement where appropriate. It may also provide a comfort letter[62] that explains its planned involvement at a site.

Subtitle I UST programme

28.43 Subtitle I[63] is the comprehensive programme dealing with underground storage tanks (UST). RCRA authorises states to implement and enforce UST programmes as long as the state programmes are as stringent or

---

[59] 42 USC § 6928.
[60] 42 USC § 6928(h).
[61] 42 USC § 6928(h).
[62] See EPA, *Prospective Purchaser Agreements and Other Tools to Facilitate Cleanup and Reuse of RCRA Sites* (April 8, 2003), *http://www.epa.gov/region04/ead/legal/ppa.html*
[63] 42 USC §§ 6991–6991k.

broader in scope than the federal regulations. This programme covers a large universe, approximately 800,000 tanks nationwide.[64] The Subtitle I programme addresses the problem of leaking USTs (LUSTs) by imposing requirements for: design, construction, and installation; operation; release detection; release reporting; investigation and confirmation of releases; corrective action; closure; and financial responsibilities. Owners of any USTs brought into use after May 8, 1986 must provide notice of the existence of the UST to a designated state agency. For USTs in existence as of May 8, 1986, notification was required by that date. Owners and operators of USTs, with specified exemptions, are subject to this programme. In addition, owners and operators of facilities where USTs are located must ensure that USTs meet the regulatory requirements. USTs are defined to cover tanks that contain a regulated substance, which is defined as a hazardous substance and petroleum.

States generally have authority to issue orders to compel owners or **28.44** operators of leaking USTs to take specific corrective action to carry out investigative studies, take action to fix the tank and clean-up what was leaked, or close the UST. States also have UST trust funds that can be used with deductibles to meet the financial assurance requirement for clean-up of leaks and spills. Owners and operators have to qualify to participate in eligibility for the UST trust funds.

Because the UST programme does not provide a *bona fide* prospective **28.45** purchaser, innocent landowner, or contiguous property owner defence, EPA and some states may be willing to offer prospective purchaser agreements or comfort letters.[65]

EPA has promulgated a rule clarifying when a lender may be exempt **28.46** from petroleum UST liability.[66] The holder of a security interest must not "participate in management of the petroleum UST or engage in petroleum production, refining, and marketing". In addition, the lender may not store petroleum in the UST after foreclosure.[67]

Imminent and Substantial Endangerment Suits and Citizen Suits

RCRA s.7003[68] is an important provision that provides the Federal **28.47** Government with enforcement authority to clean-up solid, as well as hazardous, wastes that may present an imminent and substantial endangerment. Persons who can be sued are ones who have contributed or are contributing to the handling, storage, treatment, transportation, or disposal of solid or hazardous waste that may present a hazard. It has been used in tandem with CERCLA at many sites, particularly when EPA needs an enforcement handle for clean-up of petroleum wastes that are excluded from the "hazardous substance" definition in CERCLA.

---

[64] *http://www.epa.gov/OUST/pubs/20rpt508.pdf.*
[65] EPA Office of Enforcement and Compliance Assurance Office of Site Remediation Enforcement, Environmentally Responsible, Redevelopment and Reuse (ER3) *Frequently Asked Questions and Answers.* (December 2005) (at p.3).
[66] 40 CFR §§ 280.200–280.230.
[67] 40 CFR pt. 280, subpt. I.
[68] 42 USC § 6973.

28.48   RCRA also authorises citizens to sue the same parties as identified in s.7003. Section 7002[69] imposes a 90–day notice requirement before a citizen suit can be commenced unless hazardous waste management regulations have been violated. A citizen suit cannot be brought if a judicial or administrative action is already underway under RCRA s.7003 or CERCLA ss.104 or 106. The Supreme Court has held that s.7002(a)(1)(B) does not provide a monetary remedy when the waste poses no danger to health or the environment at the time of suit, contrasting the provision with CERCLA, which expressly provides for recovery of past clean-up costs.[70]

Oil Pollution Act

28.49 The Oil Pollution Act (OPA) was enacted in response to the *Exxon Valdez* oil spill and provides authority for oil pollution liability and compensation, and for the Federal Government to direct and manage oil spill clean-ups. As with CERCLA, OPA contains provisions to allow the assessment and restoration of natural resources that have been contaminated by the discharge, or threatened discharge, of oil. Responsible parties generally include the owner or operator of a facility or vessel. Similarly to CERCLA, liability is strict and joint and several for damages resulting from a discharge of oil. Removal costs include all costs to remove oil to prevent, minimise, or mitigate the threat of discharge. Categories of compensable damage include injury to property, loss of use of property, injury to or loss of natural resources, loss of taxes, rents and royalties, loss of income, and costs received in providing additional public services.[71]

Brownfields

28.50 Previously used properties that lie abandoned or idle are generally called "Brownfields". EPA and the states have developed programmes to address these properties that may remain unused or underutilised because of actual contamination from past use, or because people fear the property's previous use may have left contamination there. The overall goal is to preserve greenspace, which is uncontaminated land in the United States.

28.51   Probably the most significant programmes to address Brownfields are state voluntary clean-up programmes. Under many voluntary programmes, the state issues a letter saying that the site, on completion of an approved clean-up, is protective of existing and proposed uses and does not pose an unacceptable risk to human health or the environment. These state programmes generally exclude eligibility if the site is subject to clean-up under CERCLA, RCRA, and certain other programmes. EPA has also entered memoranda of agreements with many states that it will not seek enforcement against sites undergoing voluntary clean-up, except under limited circumstances.

---

[69] 42 USC § 6972.
[70] *Meghrig v KFC Western, Inc*, 516 US 479 (1996).
[71] 42 USC §§ 2701 to 2761.

The EPA believes that the 2002 Brownfields Amendments for *bona fide* **28.52** prospective purchasers, contiguous property owners, and innocent landowners help Brownfields to become productive properties.[72] EPA also will consider providing comfort/status letters for unused or underutilised properties, including for RCRA Brownfields properties.[73] These letters can help potential property owners, developers, and lenders better understand EPA's involvement, or likely involvement, at a potentially contaminated property. They can also identify the applicability of a statutory provision or EPA policy toward a specific party or property, describe the clean-up progress at a Superfund or RCRA site, and suggest reasonable steps that should be taken at a site to qualify for a landowner defence. To address Brownfields, EPA's Brownfields Programme provides direct funding for Brownfields assessment, clean-up, revolving loans, and environmental job training.

State programmes and law

Many states have developed their own "mini-Superfund" system of clean- **28.53** up and liability. Most sites are cleaned up under state law, which can be a specific superfund-type law[74] or can be other statutes, such as state water quality laws or hazardous waste laws. All states have state reporting obligations for releases or spills of hazardous materials. Failure to report can expose the persons subject to reporting with significant fines.

State common law addresses when persons exposed to hazardous sub- **28.54** stance pollution can recover against the entities that cause environmental torts. These torts can be based on theories of nuisance, negligence, trespass, and strict liability. Such litigation may attempt to compel the clean-up of pollution or may seek damages for personal injuries, property damage or other losses from exposure to pollution.

A few states have enacted laws that prohibit the transfer of industrial or **28.55** commercial properties until a state agency has been notified of the intended transfer, and has been provided with information regarding the site contaminants. In some cases, the state must approve the transfer, as with the New Jersey Industrial Site Remediation Act (ISRA).[75]

---

[72] EPA, *Brownfields Handouts: How to Manage Federal Environmental Liability Risks* (November 1, 2002), *http://www.epa.gov/Compliance/resources/publications/cleanup/brownfields/handbook/bfhbkcmp. pdf* See also Donald B. Mitchell, Jr, *Brownfields and Small Business Superfund Amendments* [2002] 4 Env Liability 147.

[73] See EPA *Comfort/Status Letters for RCRA Brownfield Properties* (February 15, 2001), *http://www.epa.gov/compliance/resources/policies/cleanup/rcra/comfort-rcra-brwn-mem.pdf*.

[74] See, e.g. the California Hazardous Substance Account Act, Cal. Health & Safety Code §§ 25300–25395.15.

[75] N.J. Stat. Ann. § 13:1K-6, et seq.

Chapter 29

CANADA

GENERAL[1]

29.01 In Canada, as a federal state, jurisdiction over environmental matters is divided between the national government and those of the provinces and territories. Although many environmental impacts are transprovincial, contaminated sites are regulated primarily by the provinces,[2] being considered to be a matter of property and civil rights for Canadian constitutional purposes. The Federal Government has jurisdiction over federal and Aboriginal lands except those under the jurisdiction of the territorial Government of Yukon, all waters in the fishing zones, the territorial sea, and all internal waters of Canada,[3] and therefore regulates contamination issues in such areas. The Federal Government also regulates certain toxic substances on the basis that their management and control are matters of national importance. This regulation of toxic substances also includes their management, storage, import, export and releases.[4]

29.02 Despite some jurisdictional duplication inherent in having two levels of environment ministries, the governments act in a co-ordinated manner. The Federal Government has at times given provinces exclusive control over certain matters, using the concept of equivalency agreements[5] to ensure that national standards are kept as a minimum. However, one must always keep in mind that both national and provincial standards and requirements may apply to a given situation of contamination.

29.03 The environmental role of local governments, which are created by provincial government legislation, has traditionally been limited. Recently, however, provincial governments have amended local government statutes to delegate more powers relating to environmental concerns. Some municipalities have been known to require remediation of contamination extending onto their properties from contaminated sites before granting planning or development approval.

---

[1] Contributed by Paul Wilson, partner at Fasken Martineau DuMoulin LLP and head of the Firm's National Energy and Environmental Group and Julie DesBrisay (summer articled student at Fasken Martineau DuMoulin LLP).

[2] All references to Canada's provinces include the territorial governments.

[3] Fisheries Act, R.S., 1985, c. F-14.

[4] Canadian Environmental Protection Act, 1999, SC 1999, c.33. The list of toxic substances under Federal Government jurisdiction includes, for example, dioxins, chlorofluorocarbons, mercury, benzene, and volatile organic compounds.

[5] Such an agreement indicates that the provincial standards are and must remain at least equivalent to those contained in Federal regulations. It also identifies other crucial aspects of the provincial legislation, such as citizens' requests for information and sanctions and enforcement programs, that are equivalent to Federal legislation.

Legislation

Canadian environmental legislation tends to operate on a command-and- **29.04** control type of system. Canadian statutes comprise a list of prohibitions, powers, and requirements for obtaining approvals, and specify the regulations that may be made under the statute. The details of standards, permitting, and enforcement provisions are contained within regulations enacted by Cabinet. The ministry of environment or other equivalent agency is responsible for contaminated sites regulation and enforcement.

The provinces' contaminated sites regulations are, from a policy stand- **29.05** point, substantially the same across Canada. They generally operate on the basis of the polluter-pays principle. The Directors[6] of the ministries responsible for the environment tend to be given broad regulatory discretion. Among their powers, they are authorised to designate an area as a contaminated site. Following this designation, Directors may issue administrative orders to the person or persons "responsible" for the contamination. This definition varies somewhat across the provinces, but generally includes the persons responsible for the contaminating substance, the current and past owners and occupiers of the contaminated site, and the persons who caused or authorised the pollution, with prescribed exemptions.[7] Liability is therefore based not only on fault, but also on the person's ownership, tenancy, or legal relationship to the land. This can have major consequences for non-polluters, such as developers, though the legislation goes toward avoiding undue liability for some parties, such as innocent purchasers. Generally, secured creditors, receivers, and trustees in bankruptcy receive protection in specified circumstances, as long as they have not "caused" the pollution.

Liability across many of the provinces is generally absolute, joint and **29.06** several, with the opportunity for apportionment of costs among responsible persons. In British Columbia, liability is also retroactive, and applies whether remediation costs are incurred on or off the contaminated site, even if the contaminating substance was not prohibited by legislation or if its introduction was authorised at the time it was released into the environment.[8] Parent corporations may be held to be previous owners or occupiers, and thus liable for contamination.[9] Courts in other jurisdictions have imposed liability on parent corporations by finding direct tort or statutory liability on the part of the parent company simply by virtue of its control over the property.[10]

---

[6] In British Columbia and several other provinces, the Director is the person designated by the minister responsible for the environment to manage the contaminated sites regulatory function of the government.

[7] See, for example, Environmental Management Act, S.B.C. 2003, c. 53 at s. 47, Contaminated Sites Regulations, BC Reg. 375/96 at ss.19–33; Environment Quality Act, RSQ, c.Q-2 at s. 31.43; and Environmental Protection Act, RSO 1990, c.E.19.

[8] Environmental Management Act, SBC 2003, c.53 at s.47.

[9] See *Beazer East Inc v British Columbia (Environmental Appeal Board)* (2000), 36 CELR (NS) 195 (BCSC).

[10] Joseph F. Castrilli, *Pollution Prevention and Environmental Liability: The Evolution of the Law of Toxic Real Estate, Contaminated Lands, and Insurance* in *Environmental Law and Policy* (3rd edn), Elaine Hughes, Alastair R. Lucas & William A. Tilleman, eds (Toronto: Emond Montgomery Publications Ltd, 2003) at p.330.

29.07 Directors' administrative orders may require the responsible person to provide information, conduct investigations, abate the pollution, and/or conduct remediation at the contaminated site. Under provincial legislation, a Director also has the power to issue a proactive order to prevent a situation from continuing where contamination is likely to result. Such orders can be issued to a similarly broad range of persons as remediation orders.

29.08 The legislation in some provinces allows those, including the Director, who incur costs for remediating the site to bring civil actions for cost recovery against the responsible persons. Voluntary remediation may also be undertaken by a responsible person, through an agreement with the Director. Once a contaminated site has been remediated to the satisfaction of the Director, a "certificate" may be issued to ease concerns about future liability. In some provinces, such as British Columbia and Ontario, such certificates have legal significance, providing a degree of protection against future liability, although not a release of liability.

Standards and guidelines

29.09 The Canadian Council of Ministers of the Environment (CCME) has developed a set of standards and guidelines for soil and groundwater contaminants. Some of the provinces have adopted these as regulations; others use them only as guidelines.

British Columbia and the Yukon have the most comprehensive numeric soil and water standards, which vary with land use (i.e. agriculture, residential/parkland, industrial, commercial), and risk factors associated with human and environmental receptors (i.e. drinking water, aquatic life, irrigation use, and livestock).[11] The legislation also allows for risk-based standards to be determined, to the satisfaction of the Director, to be acceptable based on risk to human health and the environment. The remaining provinces' standards have been historically less rule-based, forming part of a more discretionary system. However, numerical standards for soil and groundwater have in recent years been legislated in regulations in some provinces.[12]

29.10 To satisfy civil liability, a polluter may be required to meet a higher standard than that prescribed by the provincial regulations. The owner of a property contaminated by a pollutant migrating from another site may be entitled to have its property remediated to a pristine condition, based on the *Rylands v Fletcher* rule.[13]

Director/officer liability

29.11 There have been instances where directors, officers, and employees have been held personally responsible for environmental offences including those related to contamination of land. The requisite standard of care for

---

[11] See Contaminated Sites Regulations, above note 6 at Schs 4–6; and Yukon's Contaminated Sites Regulations at Schs 1–3.

[12] See, for example, Environment Quality Act, Q–2 A and its regulations and Environmental Protection Act, RSO 1990, c.E.19 and its regulations.

[13] See *Tridan Developments Ltd v Shell Canada Products Ltd* (2002), 57 O.R. (3d) 503 (CA).

directors in matters of environmental issues in Canada was outlined by the Supreme Court of Canada in the hallmark case of *R v Sault Ste-Marie*[14]:

> "The element of control, particularly by those in charge of business activities which may endanger the public, is vital to promote the observance of regulations designed to avoid that danger. This control may be exercised by supervision or inspection, by improvement of his business methods, or by exhorting those whom he may be expected to influence or control ."

The best-known Canadian environmental case where a corporate director was held personally liable is *R v Bata Industries Ltd.*[15] The company director was charged with the regulatory offence of failing to take reasonable care, as a director, to prevent the corporation from causing or permitting a discharge of waste. The director, found not to have fulfilled his requisite inspection duties or to have ensured appropriate training for delegates, was convicted and paid a fine of $6,000 (initially $12,000 but reduced on appeal). **29.12**

Another company's director was similarly convicted for failing to take reasonable care to prevent the corporation from causing or permitting a discharge of waste in *R v Blackbird Holdings*.[16] The company was found to have buried barrels containing contaminants, which degenerated over time and leaked their contents. The Court found that the director had been aware of the burial of the barrels and that they would deteriorate over time, and that he had been "less than frank" with ministry officials inspecting the site. He was convicted and sentenced to a jail term (initially six months, reduced on appeal to 15 days). **29.13**

More recent case law in British Columbia has confirmed director, officer, and employee liability, based solely on their status as directors, officers, or employees in the company owning or occupying the land.[17] Although prison sentences such as that discussed above are rare, they do occur.[18] **29.14**

---

[14] *R. v Sault Ste. Marie (City)* [1978] 2 S.C.R. 1299 at 1322.

[15] *R v Bata Industries Ltd* (1992), 7 C.E.L.R. (NS) 245 (Ont. Prov. Div.).

[16] *R v Blackbird Holdings* (1991), 6 C.E.L.R. (N.S.) 138 (Ont. Prov. Div.), leave to appeal refused (1991), 6 C.E.L.R. (N.S.) 116. See also Dianne Saxe, *The Impact of Prosecution upon Regulatory Compliance by Corporations* (1990) 1 J.E.L.P. 91.

[17] *Lawson v Deputy Director of Waste Management*, 1998–WAS-14(c), 030(a), 034(a) and 1999–WAS-015(a) (Environmental Appeal Board).

[18] See in particular: *R. v Varnicolor Chemical Ltd* (1992), 9 C.E.L.R. (N.S.) 176 (Ont. Prov. Div); *R. v Demacedo*, [1992] B.C.J. No. 2254 (Q.L.) (Prov. Ct.); and *R. v Fontaine*, [1992] B.C.J. No. 2640 (Q.L.) (Prov. Ct.).

Appendix 1

MATERIALS

ENVIRONMENTAL PROTECTION ACT 1990
c.43

PART IIA CONTAMINATED LAND

Editor's Note

As a result of amendments to Pt IIA which have been made in relation to Scotland (or in a few cases England or Wales) only, and because amendments made in respect of the definition of "contaminated land" by the Water Act 2003 have been brought into force for Scotland, but not (as at the date of publication) for England and Wales, the text of Pt IIA now differs significantly as between England and Wales and Scotland. In the interests of clarity, the legislation is reproduced here only with amendments made in relation to England, and with prospective amendments to be made by the Water Act 2003 indicated as footnotes.

Preliminary

78A.—(1) The following provisions have effect for the interpretation of this Part.[1]

(2) "Contaminated land" is any land which appears to the local authority in whose area it is situated to be in such a condition, by reason of substances in, on or under the land, that—

  (a) significant harm is being caused or there is a significant possibility of such harm being caused; or
  (b) pollution of controlled waters is being, or is likely to be, caused[2];

and, in determining whether any land appears to be such land, a local authority shall, subject to subsection (5) below, act in accordance with guidance issued by the Secretary of State in accordance with section 78YA below with respect to the manner in which that determination is to be made.

(3) A "special site" is any contaminated land—

  (a) which has been designated as such a site by virtue of section 78C(7) or 78D(6) below; and
  (b) whose designation as such has not been terminated by the appropriate Agency under section 78Q(4) below.

---

[1] Inserted by the Environment Act 1995, s.57, for certain purposes with effect from September 21, 1995 (SI 1995/1983) and for remaining purposes with effect from April 1, 2000 (SI 2000/340).

[2] Prospectively amended by the Water Act 2003, s.86(2)(a). When this amendment comes into force subs.(2)(b) will read:

  "(b) significant pollution of controlled waters is being caused or there is a significant possibility of such pollution being caused;"

(4) "Harm" means harm to the health of living organisms or other interference with the ecological systems of which they form part and, in the case of man, includes harm to his property.

(5) The questions—

    (a) what harm is to be regarded as "significant",
    (b) whether the possibility of significant harm being caused is "significant",
    (c) whether pollution of controlled waters is being, or is likely to be caused,

shall be determined in accordance with guidance issued for the purpose by the Secretary of State in accordance with section 78YA below.[3]

(6) Without prejudice to the guidance that may be issued under subsection (5) above, guidance under paragraph (a) of that subsection may make provision for different degrees of importance to be assigned to, or for the disregard of,—

    (a) different descriptions of living organisms or ecological systems;
    (b) different descriptions of places; or
    (c) different descriptions of harm to health or property, or other interference;

and guidance under paragraph (b) of that subsection may make provision for different degrees of possibility to be regarded as "significant" (or as not being "significant") in relation to different descriptions of significant harm.[4]

(7) "Remediation" means—

    (a) the doing of anything for the purpose of assessing the condition of—

        (i) the contaminated land in question;
        (ii) any controlled waters affected by that land; or
        (iii) any land adjoining or adjacent to that land;

---

[3] Prospectively amended by the Water Act 2003, ss 86(2)(b), 101(2), Sch.9, Pt.3. When this amendment comes into force subs.(5) will read:

    "(5) The questions—
        (a) what harm or pollution of controlled waters is to be regarded as "significant",
        (b) whether the possibility of significant harm or of significant pollution of controlled waters being caused is "significant",
shall be determined in accordance with guidance issued for the purpose by the Secretary of State in accordance with section 78YA below."

[4] Prospectively amended by the Water Act 2003, s.86(2)(c). When this amendment comes into force subs.(6) will read:

    "(6) Without prejudice to the guidance that may be issued under subsection (5) above, guidance under paragraph (a) of that subsection may make provision for different degrees of importance to be assigned to, or for the disregard of,—
        (a) different descriptions of living organisms or ecological systems, or of poisonous, noxious or polluting matter or solid waste matter;
        (b) different descriptions of places or controlled waters, or different degrees of pollution; or
        (c) different descriptions of harm to health or property, or other interference;
and guidance under paragraph (b) of that subsection may make provision for different degrees of possibility to be regarded as "significant" (or as not being "significant") in relation to different descriptions of significant harm or of significant pollution."

(b) the doing of any works, the carrying out of any operations or the taking of any steps in relation to any such land or waters for the purpose—

   (i) of preventing or minimising, or remedying or mitigating the effects of, any significant harm, or any pollution of controlled waters, by reason of which the contaminated land is such land[5]; or
   (ii) of restoring the land or waters to their former state; or

(c) the making of subsequent inspections from time to time for the purpose of keeping under review the condition of the land or waters;

and cognate expressions shall be construed accordingly.

(8) Controlled waters are "affected by" contaminated land if (and only if) it appears to the enforcing authority that the contaminated land in question is, for the purposes of subsection (2) above, in such a condition, by reason of substances in, on or under the land, that pollution of those waters is being, or is likely to be caused.[6]

(9) The following expressions have the meaning respectively assigned to them—

"the appropriate Agency" means—

(a) in relation to England and Wales, the Environment Agency;
(b) (applies to Scotland only)

"appropriate person" means any person who is an appropriate person, determined in accordance with section 78F below, to bear responsibility for any thing which is to be done by way of remediation in any particular case;
"charging notice" has the meaning given by section 78P(3)(b) below;
"controlled waters"—

(a) in relation to England and Wales, has the same meaning as in Part III of the Water Resources Act 1991 except that "ground waters" does not include waters contained in underground strata but above the saturation zone[7]; and
(b) (repealed—applies to Scotland only)

"creditor" has the same meaning as in the Conveyancing and Feudal Reform (Scotland) Act 1970;
"enforcing authority" means—

(a) in relation to a special site, the appropriate Agency;
(b) in relation to contaminated land other than a special site, the local authority in whose area the land is situated;

---

[5] Prospectively amended by the Water Act 2003, s.86(2)(d). When this amendment comes into force subs.(7)(b)(i) will read:
   "(i) of preventing or minimising, or remedying or mitigating the effects of, any significant harm, or any significant pollution of controlled waters, by reason of which the contaminated land is such land; or"
[6] Prospectively amended by the Water Act 2003, s.86(2)(e). When this amendment comes into force subs.(8) will read:
   "(8) Controlled waters are "affected by" contaminated land if (and only if) it appears to the enforcing authority that the contaminated land in question is, for the purposes of subsection (2) above, in such a condition, by reason of substances in, on or under the land, that significant pollution of those waters is being caused or there is a significant possibility of such pollution being caused. "
[7] Amended by the Water Act 2003, s.86(2)(f), with effect in relation to England from October 1, 2004 (SI 2004/2528).

"heritable security" has the same meaning as in the Conveyancing and Feudal Reform (Scotland) Act 1970;

"local authority" in relation to England and Wales means—

(a) any unitary authority;

(b) any district council, so far as it is not a unitary authority;

(c) the Common Council of the City of London and, as respects the Temples, the Sub-Treasurer of the Inner Temple and the Under-Treasurer of the Middle Temple respectively;

(d) the Council of the Isles of Scilly;

***(applies to Scotland only)

"notice" means notice in writing;

"notification" means notification in writing;

"owner", in relation to any land in England and Wales, means a person (other than a mortgagee not in possession) who, whether in his own right or as trustee for any other person, is entitled to receive the rack rent of the land, or, where the land is not let at a rack rent, would be so entitled if it were so let;

***(applies to Scotland only)

"pollution of controlled waters" means the entry into controlled waters of any poisonous, noxious or polluting matter or any solid waste matter;

"prescribed" means prescribed by regulations;

"regulations" means regulations made by the Secretary of State;

"remediation declaration" has the meaning given by section 78H(6) below;

"remediation notice" has the meaning given by section 78E(1) below;

"remediation statement" has the meaning given by section 78H(7) below;

"required to be designated as a special site" shall be construed in accordance with section 78C(8) below;

"substance" means any natural or artificial substance, whether in solid or liquid form or in the form of a gas or vapour;

"unitary authority" means—

(a) the council of a county, so far as it is the council of an area for which there are no district councils;

(b) the council of any district comprised in an area for which there is no county council;

(c) the council of a London borough;

(d) the council of a county borough in Wales.

Identification of contaminated land[8]

78B.—(1) Every local authority shall cause its area to be inspected from time to time for the purpose—

(a) of identifying contaminated land; and

(b) of enabling the authority to decide whether any such land is land which is required to be designated as a special site.

(2) In performing its functions under subsection (1) above a local authority shall act in accordance with any guidance issued for the purpose by the Secretary of State in accordance with section 78YA below.

---

[8] Inserted by the Environment Act 1995, s.57, for certain purposes with effect from September 21, 1995 (SI 1995/1983) and for remaining purposes with effect from April 1, 2000 (SI 2000/340).

(3) If a local authority identifies any contaminated land in its area, it shall give notice of that fact to—

    (a) the appropriate Agency;

    (b) the owner of the land;

    (c) any person who appears to the authority to be in occupation of the whole or any part of the land; and

    (d) each person who appears to the authority to be an appropriate person;

and any notice given under this subsection shall state by virtue of which of paragraphs (a) to (d) above it is given.

(4) If, at any time after a local authority has given any person a notice pursuant to subsection (3)(d) above in respect of any land, it appears to the enforcing authority that another person is an appropriate person, the enforcing authority shall give notice to that other person—

    (a) of the fact that the local authority has identified the land in question as contaminated land; and

    (b) that he appears to the enforcing authority to be an appropriate person.

Identification and designation of special sites[9]

78C.—(1) If at any time it appears to a local authority that any contaminated land in its area might be land which is required to be designated as a special site, the authority—

    (a) shall decide whether or not the land is land which is required to be so designated; and

    (b) if the authority decides that the land is land which is required to be so designated, shall give notice of that decision to the relevant persons.

(2) For the purposes of this section, "the relevant persons" at any time in the case of any land are the persons who at that time fall within paragraphs (a) to (d) below, that is to say—

    (a) the appropriate Agency;

    (b) the owner of the land;

    (c) any person who appears to the local authority concerned to be in occupation of the whole or any part of the land; and

    (d) each person who appears to that authority to be an appropriate person.

(3) Before making a decision under paragraph (a) of subsection (1) above in any particular case, a local authority shall request the advice of the appropriate Agency, and in making its decision shall have regard to any advice given by that Agency in response to the request.

(4) If at any time the appropriate Agency considers that any contaminated land is land which is required to be designated as a special site, that Agency may give notice of that fact to the local authority in whose area the land is situated.

---

[9] Inserted by the Environment Act 1995, s.57, for certain purposes with effect from September 21, 1995 (SI 1995/1983) and for remaining purposes with effect from April 1, 2000 (SI 2000/340).

(5) Where notice under subsection (4) above is given to a local authority, the authority shall decide whether the land in question—

(a) is land which is required to be designated as a special site, or
(b) is not land which is required to be so designated, and shall give notice of that decision to the relevant persons.

(6) Where a local authority makes a decision falling within subsection (1)(b) or (5)(a) above, the decision shall, subject to section 78D below, take effect on the day after whichever of the following events first occurs, that is to say—

(a) the expiration of the period of twenty-one days beginning with the day on which the notice required by virtue of subsection (1)(b) or, as the case may be, (5)(a) above is given to the appropriate Agency; or
(b) if the appropriate Agency gives notification to the local authority in question that it agrees with the decision, the giving of that notification;

and where a decision takes effect by virtue of this subsection, the local authority shall give notice of that fact to the relevant persons.

(7) Where a decision that any land is land which is required to be designated as a special site takes effect in accordance with subsection (6) above, the notice given under subsection (1)(b) or, as the case may be, (5)(a) above shall have effect, as from the time when the decision takes effect, as the designation of that land as such a site.

(8) For the purposes of this Part, land is required to be designated as a special site if, and only if, it is land of a description prescribed for the purposes of this subsection.

(9) Regulations under subsection (8) above may make different provision for different cases or circumstances or different areas or localities and may, in particular, describe land by reference to the area or locality in which it is situated.

(10) Without prejudice to the generality of his power to prescribe any description of land for the purposes of subsection (8) above, the Secretary of State, in deciding whether to prescribe a particular description of contaminated land for those purposes, may, in particular, have regard to—

(a) whether land of the description in question appears to him to be land which is likely to be in such a condition, by reason of substances in, on or under the land that—

(i) serious harm would or might be caused, or
(ii) serious pollution of controlled waters would be, or would be likely to be, caused; or

(b) whether the appropriate Agency is likely to have expertise in dealing with the kind of significant harm, or pollution of controlled waters, by reason of which land of the description in question is contaminated land.[10]

---

[10] Prospectively amended by the Water Act 2003, s.86(3). When this amendment comes into force subs.(10) will read:
  "(10) Without prejudice to the generality of his power to prescribe any description of

Referral of special site decisions to the Secretary of State[11]

78D.—(1) In any case where—

(a) a local authority gives notice of a decision to the appropriate Agency pursuant to subsection (1)(b) or (5)(b) of section 78C above, but

(b) before the expiration of the period of twenty-one days beginning with the day on which that notice is so given, that Agency gives the local authority notice that it disagrees with the decision, together with a statement of its reasons for disagreeing,

the authority shall refer the decision to the Secretary of State and shall send to him a statement of its reasons for reaching the decision.

(2) Where the appropriate Agency gives notice to a local authority under paragraph (b) of subsection (1) above, it shall also send to the Secretary of State a copy of the notice and of the statement given under that paragraph.

(3) Where a local authority refers a decision to the Secretary of State under subsection (1) above, it shall give notice of that fact to the relevant persons.

(4) Where a decision of a local authority is referred to the Secretary of State under subsection (1) above, he—

(a) may confirm or reverse the decision with respect to the whole or any part of the land to which it relates; and

(b) shall give notice of his decision on the referral—

(i) to the relevant persons; and
(ii) to the local authority.

(5) Where a decision of a local authority is referred to the Secretary of State under subsection (1) above, the decision shall not take effect until the day after that on which the Secretary of State gives the notice required by subsection (4) above to the persons there mentioned and shall then take effect as confirmed or reversed by him.

(6) Where a decision which takes effect in accordance with subsection (5) above is to the effect that at least some land is land which is required to be designated as a special site, the notice given under subsection (4)(b) above shall have effect, as

land for the purposes of subsection (8) above, the Secretary of State, in deciding whether to prescribe a particular description of contaminated land for those purposes, may, in particular, have regard to—
(a) whether land of the description in question appears to him to be land which is likely to be in such a condition, by reason of substances in, on or under the land that—
(i) serious harm would or might be caused, or
(ii) serious pollution of controlled waters would or might be caused; or
(b) whether the appropriate Agency is likely to have expertise in dealing with the kind of significant harm, or significant pollution of controlled waters, by reason of which land of the description in question is contaminated land."

[11] Inserted by the Environment Act 1995, s.57, for certain purposes with effect from September 21, 1995 (SI 1995/1983) and for remaining purposes with effect from April 1, 2000 (SI 2000/340).

from the time when the decision takes effect, as the designation of that land as such a site.

(7) In this section "the relevant persons" has the same meaning as in section 78C above.

Duty of enforcing authority to require remediation of contaminated land etc[12]

78E.—(1) In any case where—

(a) any land has been designated as a special site by virtue of section 78C(7) or 78D(6) above, or
(b) a local authority has identified any contaminated land (other than a special site) in its area,

the enforcing authority shall, in accordance with such procedure as may be prescribed and subject to the following provisions of this Part, serve on each person who is an appropriate person a notice (in this Part referred to as a "remediation notice") specifying what that person is to do by way of remediation and the periods within which he is required to do each of the things so specified.

(2) Different remediation notices requiring the doing of different things by way of remediation may be served on different persons in consequence of the presence of different substances in, on or under any land or waters.

(3) Where two or more persons are appropriate persons in relation to any particular thing which is to be done by way of remediation, the remediation notice served on each of them shall state the proportion, determined under section 78F(7) below, of the cost of doing that thing which each of them respectively is liable to bear.

(4) The only things by way of remediation which the enforcing authority may do, or require to be done, under or by virtue of this Part are things which it considers reasonable, having regard to—

(a) the cost which is likely to be involved; and
(b) the seriousness of the harm, or pollution of controlled waters, in question.[13]

(5) In determining for any purpose of this Part—

(a) what is to be done (whether by an appropriate person, the enforcing authority or any other person) by way of remediation in any particular case,
(b) the standard to which any land is, or waters are, to be remediated pursuant to the notice, or

---

[12] Inserted by the Environment Act 1995, s.57, for certain purposes with effect from September 21, 1995 (SI 1995/1983) and for remaining purposes with effect from April 1, 2000 (SI 2000/340).

[13] Prospectively amended by the Water Act 2003, s.86(4). When this amendment comes into force subs.(4)(b) will read:
   "(b) the seriousness of the harm, or of the pollution of controlled waters, in question"

(c) what is, or is not, to be regarded as reasonable for the purposes of subsection (4) above,

the enforcing authority shall have regard to any guidance issued for the purpose by the Secretary of State.

(6) Regulations may make provision for or in connection with—

(a) the form or content of remediation notices; or
(b) any steps of a procedural nature which are to be taken in connection with, or in consequence of, the service of a remediation notice.

Determination of the appropriate person to bear responsibility for remediation[14]

78F.—(1) This section has effect for the purpose of determining who is the appropriate person to bear responsibility for any particular thing which the enforcing authority determines is to be done by way of remediation in any particular case.

(2) Subject to the following provisions of this section, any person, or any of the persons, who caused or knowingly permitted the substances, or any of the substances, by reason of which the contaminated land in question is such land to be in, on or under that land is an appropriate person.

(3) A person shall only be an appropriate person by virtue of subsection (2) above in relation to things which are to be done by way of remediation which are to any extent referable to substances which he caused or knowingly permitted to be present in, on or under the contaminated land in question.

(4) If no person has, after reasonable inquiry, been found who is by virtue of subsection (2) above an appropriate person to bear responsibility for the things which are to be done by way of remediation, the owner or occupier for the time being of the contaminated land in question is an appropriate person.

(5) If, in consequence of subsection (3) above, there are things which are to be done by way of remediation in relation to which no person has, after reasonable inquiry, been found who is an appropriate person by virtue of subsection (2) above, the owner or occupier for the time being of the contaminated land in question is an appropriate person in relation to those things.

(6) Where two or more persons would, apart from this subsection, be appropriate persons in relation to any particular thing which is to be done by way of remediation, the enforcing authority shall determine in accordance with guidance issued for the purpose by the Secretary of State whether any, and if so which, of them is to be treated as not being an appropriate person in relation to that thing.

(7) Where two or more persons are appropriate persons in relation to any particular thing which is to be done by way of remediation, they shall be liable to

---

[14] Inserted by the Environment Act 1995, s.57, for certain purposes with effect from September 21, 1995 (SI 1995/1983) and for remaining purposes with effect from April 1, 2000 (SI 2000/340).

bear the cost of doing that thing in proportions determined by the enforcing authority in accordance with guidance issued for the purpose by the Secretary of State.

(8) Any guidance issued for the purposes of subsection (6) or (7)' shall be issued in accordance with section 78YA below.

(9) A person who has caused or knowingly permitted any substance ("substance A") to be in, on or under any land shall also be taken for the purposes of this section to have caused or knowingly permitted there to be in, on or under that land any substance which is there as a result of a chemical reaction or biological process affecting substance A.

(10) A thing which is to be done by way of remediation may be regarded for the purposes of this Part as referable to the presence of any substance notwithstanding that the thing in question would not have to be done—

    (a) in consequence only of the presence of that substance in any quantity; or
    (b) in consequence only of the quantity of that substance which any particular person caused or knowingly permitted to be present.

Grant of, and compensation for, rights of entry etc[15]

78G.—(1) A remediation notice may require an appropriate person to do things by way of remediation, notwithstanding that he is not entitled to do those things.

(2) Any person whose consent is required before any thing required by a remediation notice may be done shall grant, or join in granting, such rights in relation to any of the relevant land or waters as will enable the appropriate person to comply with any requirements imposed by the remediation notice.

(3) Before serving a remediation notice, the enforcing authority shall reasonably endeavour to consult every person who appears to the authority—

    (a) to be the owner or occupier of any of the relevant land or waters, and
    (b) to be a person who might be required by subsection (2) above to grant, or join in granting, any rights,

concerning the rights which that person may be so required to grant.

(4) Subsection (3) above shall not preclude the service of a remediation notice in any case where it appears to the enforcing authority that the contaminated land in question is in such a condition, by reason of substances in, on or under the land, that there is imminent danger of serious harm, or serious pollution of controlled waters, being caused.

(5) A person who grants, or joins in granting, any rights pursuant to subsection (2) above shall be entitled, on making an application within such period as may be

---

[15] Inserted by the Environment Act 1995, s.57, for certain purposes with effect from September 21, 1995 (SI 1995/1983) and for remaining purposes with effect from April 1, 2000 (SI 2000/340).

prescribed and in such manner as may be prescribed to such person as may be prescribed, to be paid by the appropriate person compensation of such amount as may be determined in such manner as may be prescribed.

(6) Without prejudice to the generality of the regulations that may be made by virtue of subsection (5) above, regulations by virtue of that subsection may make such provision in relation to compensation under this section as may be made by regulations by virtue of subsection (4) of section 35A above in relation to compensation under that section.

(7) In this section, "relevant land or waters" means—

    (a) the contaminated land in question;
    (b) any controlled waters affected by that land; or
    (c) any land adjoining or adjacent to that land or those waters.

Restrictions and prohibitions on serving remediation notices[16]

78H.—(1) Before serving a remediation notice, the enforcing authority shall reasonably endeavour to consult—

    (a) the person on whom the notice is to be served,
    (b) the owner of any land to which the notice relates,
    (c) any person who appears to that authority to be in occupation of the whole or any part of the land, and
    (d) any person of such other description as may be prescribed,

concerning what is to be done by way of remediation.

(2) Regulations may make provision for, or in connection with, steps to be taken for the purposes of subsection (1) above.

(3) No remediation notice shall be served on any person by reference to any contaminated land during any of the following periods, that is to say—

    (a) the period—

        (i) beginning with the identification of the contaminated land in question pursuant to section 78B(1) above, and
        (ii) ending with the expiration of the period of three months beginning with the day on which the notice required by subsection (3)(d) or, as the case may be, (4) of section 78B above is given to that person in respect of that land;

    (b) if a decision falling within paragraph (b) of section 78C(1) above is made in relation to the contaminated land in question, the period beginning with the making of the decision and ending with the expiration of the period of three months beginning with—

        (i) in a case where the decision is not referred to the Secretary of State under section 78D above, the day on which the notice required by section 78C(6) above is given, or

---

[16] Inserted by the Environment Act 1995, s.57, for certain purposes with effect from September 21, 1995 (SI 1995/1983) and for remaining purposes with effect from April 1, 2000 (SI 2000/340).

      (ii) in a case where the decision is referred to the Secretary of State under section 78D above, the day on which he gives the notice required by subsection (4)(b) of that section;

  (c) if the appropriate Agency gives a notice under subsection (4) of section 78C above to a local authority in relation to the contaminated land in question, the period beginning with the day on which that notice is given and ending with the expiration of the period of three months beginning with—

      (i) in a case where notice is given under subsection (6) of that section, the day on which that notice is given;

      (ii) in a case where the authority makes a decision falling within subsection (5)(b) of that section and the appropriate Agency fails to give notice under paragraph (b) of section 78D(1) above, the day following the expiration of the period of twenty-one days mentioned in that paragraph; or

      (iii) in a case where the authority makes a decision falling within section 78C(5)(b) above which is referred to the Secretary of State under section 78D above, the day on which the Secretary of State gives the notice required by subsection (4)(b) of that section.

(4) Neither subsection (1) nor subsection (3) above shall preclude the service of a remediation notice in any case where it appears to the enforcing authority that the land in question is in such a condition, by reason of substances in, on or under the land, that there is imminent danger of serious harm, or serious pollution of controlled waters, being caused.

(5) The enforcing authority shall not serve a remediation notice on a person if and so long as any one or more of the following conditions is for the time being satisfied in the particular case, that is to say—

  (a) the authority is satisfied, in consequence of section 78E(4) and (5) above, that there is nothing by way of remediation which could be specified in a remediation notice served on that person;

  (b) the authority is satisfied that appropriate things are being, or will be, done by way of remediation without the service of a remediation notice on that person;

  (c) it appears to the authority that the person on whom the notice would be served is the authority itself; or

  (d) the authority is satisfied that the powers conferred on it by section 78N below to do what is appropriate by way of remediation are exercisable.

(6) Where the enforcing authority is precluded by virtue of section 78E(4) or (5) above from specifying in a remediation notice any particular thing by way of remediation which it would otherwise have specified in such a notice, the authority shall prepare and publish a document (in this Part referred to as a "remediation declaration") which shall record—

  (a) the reasons why the authority would have specified that thing; and

  (b) the grounds on which the authority is satisfied that it is precluded from specifying that thing in such a notice.

(7) In any case where the enforcing authority is precluded, by virtue of paragraph (b), (c) or (d) of subsection (5) above, from serving a remediation notice,

the responsible person shall prepare and publish a document (in this Part referred to as a "remediation statement") which shall record—

(a) the things which are being, have been, or are expected to be, done by way of remediation in the particular case; (b) the name and address of the person who is doing, has done, or is expected to do, each of those things; and

(c) the periods within which each of those things is being, or is expected to be, done.

(8) For the purposes of subsection (7) above, the "responsible person" is—

(a) in a case where the condition in paragraph (b) of subsection (5) above is satisfied, the person who is doing or has done, or who the enforcing authority is satisfied will do, the things there mentioned; or

(b) in a case where the condition in paragraph (c) or (d) of that subsection is satisfied, the enforcing authority.

(9) If a person who is required by virtue of subsection (8)(a) above to prepare and publish a remediation statement fails to do so within a reasonable time after the date on which a remediation notice specifying the things there mentioned could, apart from subsection (5) above, have been served, the enforcing authority may itself prepare and publish the statement and may recover its reasonable costs of doing so from that person.

(10) Where the enforcing authority has been precluded by virtue only of subsection (5) above from serving a remediation notice on an appropriate person but—

(a) none of the conditions in that subsection is for the time being satisfied in the particular case, and

(b) the authority is not precluded by any other provision of this Part from serving a remediation notice on that appropriate person,

the authority shall serve a remediation notice on that person; and any such notice may be so served without any further endeavours by the authority to consult persons pursuant to subsection (1) above, if and to the extent that that person has been consulted pursuant to that subsection concerning the things which will be specified in the notice.

Restrictions on liability relating to the pollution of controlled waters[17]

78J.—(1) This section applies where any land is contaminated land by virtue of paragraph (b) of subsection (2) of section 78A above (whether or not the land is also contaminated land by virtue of paragraph (a) of that subsection).

(2) Where this section applies, no remediation notice given in consequence of the land in question being contaminated land shall require a person who is an appropriate person by virtue of section 78F(4) or (5) above to do anything by way of remediation to that or any other land, or any waters, which he could not have been

---

[17] Inserted by the Environment Act 1995, s.57, for certain purposes with effect from September 21, 1995 (SI 1995/1983) and for remaining purposes with effect from April 1, 2000 (SI 2000/340).

required to do by such a notice had paragraph (b) of section 78A(2) above (and all other references to pollution of controlled waters) been omitted from this Part.

(3) If, in a case where this section applies, a person permits, has permitted, or might permit, water from an abandoned mine or part of a mine—

(a) to enter any controlled waters, or

(b) to reach a place from which it is or, as the case may be, was likely, in the opinion of the enforcing authority, to enter such waters,

no remediation notice shall require him in consequence to do anything by way of remediation (whether to the contaminated land in question or to any other land or waters) which he could not have been required to do by such a notice had paragraph (b) of section 78A(2) above (and all other references to pollution of controlled waters) been omitted from this Part.

(4) Subsection (3) above shall not apply to the owner or former operator of any mine or part of a mine if the mine or part in question became abandoned after 31st December 1999.

(5) In determining for the purposes of subsection (4) above whether a mine or part of a mine became abandoned before, on or after 31st December 1999 in a case where the mine or part has become abandoned on two or more occasions, of which—

(a) at least one falls on or before that date, and

(b) at least one falls after that date,

the mine or part shall be regarded as becoming abandoned after that date (but without prejudice to the operation of subsection (3) above in relation to that mine or part at, or in relation to, any time before the first of those occasions which falls after that date).

(6) Where, immediately before a part of a mine becomes abandoned, that part is the only part of the mine not falling to be regarded as abandoned for the time being, the abandonment of that part shall not be regarded for the purposes of subsection (4) or (5) above as constituting the abandonment of the mine, but only of that part of it.

(7) Nothing in subsection (2) or (3) above prevents the enforcing authority from doing anything by way of remediation under section 78N below which it could have done apart from that subsection, but the authority shall not be entitled under section 78P below to recover from any person any part of the cost incurred by the authority in doing by way of remediation anything which it is precluded by subsection (2) or (3) above from requiring that person to do.

(8) In this section "mine" has the same meaning as in the Mines and Quarries Act 1954.

Liability in respect of contaminating substances which escape to other land[18]

78K.—(1) A person who has caused or knowingly permitted any substances to be in, on or under any land shall also be taken for the purposes of this Part to have

[18] Inserted by the Environment Act 1995, s.57, for certain purposes with effect from September 21, 1995 (SI 1995/1983) and for remaining purposes with effect from April 1, 2000 (SI 2000/340).

caused or, as the case may be, knowingly permitted those substances to be in, on or under any other land to which they appear to have escaped.

(2) Subsections (3) and (4) below apply in any case where it appears that any substances are or have been in, on or under any land (in this section referred to as "land A") as a result of their escape, whether directly or indirectly, from other land in, on or under which a person caused or knowingly permitted them to be.

(3) Where this subsection applies, no remediation notice shall require a person—

(a) who is the owner or occupier of land A, and
(b) who has not caused or knowingly permitted the substances in question to be in, on or under that land,

to do anything by way of remediation to any land or waters (other than land or waters of which he is the owner or occupier) in consequence of land A appearing to be in such a condition, by reason of the presence of those substances in, on or under it, that significant harm is being caused, or there is a significant possibility of such harm being caused, or that pollution of controlled waters is being, or is likely to be caused.

(4) Where this subsection applies, no remediation notice shall require a person—

(a) who is the owner or occupier of land A, and
(b) who has not caused or knowingly permitted the substances in question to be in, on or under that land,

to do anything by way of remediation in consequence of any further land in, on or under which those substances or any of them appear to be or to have been present as a result of their escape from land A ("land B") appearing to be in such a condition, by reason of the presence of those substances in, on or under it, that significant harm is being caused, or there is a significant possibility of such harm being caused, or that pollution of controlled waters is being, or is likely to be caused, unless he is also the owner or occupier of land B.[19]

---

[19] Prospectively amended by the Water Act 2003, s.86(5). When this amendment comes into force subss (3) and (4) will read:
"(3) Where this subsection applies, no remediation notice shall require a person—
(a) who is the owner or occupier of land A, and
(b) who has not caused or knowingly permitted the substances in question to be in, on or under that land,
to do anything by way of remediation to any land or waters (other than land or waters of which he is the owner or occupier) in consequence of land A appearing to be in such a condition, by reason of the presence of those substances in, on or under it, that significant harm, or significant pollution of controlled waters, is being caused, or there is a significant possibility of such harm or pollution being caused.
(4) Where this subsection applies, no remediation notice shall require a person—
(a) who is the owner or occupier of land A, and
(b) who has not caused or knowingly permitted the substances in question to be in, on or under that land,
to do anything by way of remediation in consequence of any further land in, on or under which those substances or any of them appear to be or to have been present as a result of their escape from land A ("land B") appearing to be in such a condition, by reason of the presence of those substances in, on or under it, that significant harm, or significant pollution of controlled waters, is being caused, or there is a significant possibility of such harm or pollution being caused, unless he is also the owner or occupier of land B."

(5) In any case where—

    (a) a person ("person A") has caused or knowingly permitted any substances to be in, on, or under any land,

    (b) another person ("person B") who has not caused or knowingly permitted those substances to be in, on or under that land becomes the owner or occupier of that land, and

    (c) the substances, or any of the substances, mentioned in paragraph (a) above appear to have escaped to other land,

no remediation notice shall require person B to do anything by way of remediation to that other land in consequence of the apparent acts or omissions of person A, except to the extent that person B caused or knowingly permitted the escape.

(6) Nothing in subsection (3), (4) or (5) above prevents the enforcing authority from doing anything by way of remediation under section 78N below which it could have done apart from that subsection, but the authority shall not be entitled under section 78P below to recover from any person any part of the cost incurred by the authority in doing by way of remediation anything which it is precluded by subsection (3), (4) or (5) above from requiring that person to do.

(7) In this section, "appear" means appear to the enforcing authority, and cognate expressions shall be construed accordingly.

Appeals against remediation notices[20]

78L.—(1) A person on whom a remediation notice is served may, within the period of twenty-one days beginning with the day on which the notice is served, appeal against the notice—

    (a) if it was served by a local authority in England, or served by the Environment Agency in relation to land in England, to the Secretary of State;

    (b) if it was served by a local authority in Wales, or served by the Environment Agency in relation to land in Wales, to the National Assembly for Wales;

and in the following provisions of this section "the appellate authority" means the Secretary of State or the National Assembly for Wales, as the case may be.

(2) On any appeal under subsection (1) above the appellate authority—

    (a) shall quash the notice, if it is satisfied that there is a material defect in the notice; but

    (b) subject to that, may confirm the remediation notice, with or without modification, or quash it.

(3) Where an appellate authority confirms a remediation notice, with or without modification, it may extend the period specified in the notice for doing what the notice requires to be done.

---

[20] Inserted by the Environment Act 1995, s.57, for certain purposes with effect from September 21, 1995 (SI 1995/1983) and for remaining purposes with effect from April 1, 2000 (SI 2000/340).

(4) Regulations may make provision with respect to—

(a) the grounds on which appeals under subsection (1) above may be made;
(b) [...]
(c) the procedure on an appeal under subsection (1) above.

(5) Regulations under subsection (4) above may (among other things)—

(a) include provisions comparable to those in section 290 of the Public Health Act 1936 (appeals against notices requiring the execution of works);
(b) prescribe the cases in which a remediation notice is, or is not, to be suspended until the appeal is decided, or until some other stage in the proceedings;
(c) prescribe the cases in which the decision on an appeal may in some respects be less favourable to the appellant than the remediation notice against which he is appealing;
(d) prescribe the cases in which the appellant may claim that a remediation notice should have been served on some other person and prescribe the procedure to be followed in those cases;
(e) make provision as respects—

(i) the particulars to be included in the notice of appeal;
(ii) the persons on whom notice of appeal is to be served and the particulars, if any, which are to accompany the notice; and
(iii) the abandonment of an appeal;

(f) make different provision for different cases or classes of case.

(6) This section is subject to section 114 of the Environment Act 1995 (delegation or reference of appeals etc).[21]

Offences of not complying with a remediation notice[22]

78M.—(1) If a person on whom an enforcing authority serves a remediation notice fails, without reasonable excuse, to comply with any of the requirements of the notice, he shall be guilty of an offence.

(2) Where the remediation notice in question is one which was required by section 78E(3) above to state, in relation to the requirement which has not been complied with, the proportion of the cost involved which the person charged with the offence is liable to bear, it shall be a defence for that person to prove that the only reason why he has not complied with the requirement is that one or more of the other persons who are liable to bear a proportion of that cost refused, or was not able, to comply with the requirement.

(3) Except in a case falling within subsection (4) below, a person who commits an offence under subsection (1) above shall be liable, on summary conviction, to a fine not exceeding level 5 on the standard scale and to a further fine of an amount equal to one-tenth of level 5 on the standard scale for each day on which the failure

---

[21] Amended with savings by the Clean Neighbourhoods and Environment Act 2005, ss 104 (for savings see subs.(6)), 107, Sch.5, Pt.10, with effect from August 4, 2006 (SI 2006/1361).
[22] Inserted by the Environment Act 1995, s.57, for certain purposes with effect from September 21, 1995 (SI 1995/1983) and for remaining purposes with effect from April 1, 2000 (SI 2000/340).

continues after conviction of the offence and before the enforcing authority has begun to exercise its powers by virtue of section 78N(3)(c) below.

(4) A person who commits an offence under subsection (1) above in a case where the contaminated land to which the remediation notice relates is industrial, trade or business premises shall be liable on summary conviction to a fine not exceeding £20,000 or such greater sum as the Secretary of State may from time to time by order substitute and to a further fine of an amount equal to one-tenth of that sum for each day on which the failure continues after conviction of the offence and before the enforcing authority has begun to exercise its powers by virtue of section 78N(3)(c) below.

(5) If the enforcing authority is of the opinion that proceedings for an offence under this section would afford an ineffectual remedy against a person who has failed to comply with any of the requirements of a remediation notice which that authority has served on him, that authority may take proceedings in the High Court or, in Scotland, in any court of competent jurisdiction, for the purpose of securing compliance with the remediation notice.

(6) In this section, "industrial, trade or business premises" means premises used for any industrial, trade or business purposes or premises not so used on which matter is burnt in connection with any industrial, trade or business process, and premises are used for industrial purposes where they are used for the purposes of any treatment or process as well as where they are used for the purpose of manufacturing.

(7) No order shall be made under subsection (4) above unless a draft of the order has been laid before, and approved by a resolution of, each House of Parliament.

Powers of the enforcing authority to carry out remediation[23]

78N.—(1) Where this section applies, the enforcing authority shall itself have power, in a case falling within paragraph (a) or (b) of section 78E(1) above, to do what is appropriate by way of remediation to the relevant land or waters.

(2) Subsection (1) above shall not confer power on the enforcing authority to do anything by way of remediation if the authority would, in the particular case, be precluded by section 78YB below from serving a remediation notice requiring that thing to be done.

(3) This section applies in each of the following cases, that is to say—

    (a) where the enforcing authority considers it necessary to do anything itself by way of remediation for the purpose of preventing the occurrence of any serious harm, or serious pollution of controlled waters, of which there is imminent danger;

    (b) where an appropriate person has entered into a written agreement with the enforcing authority for that authority to do, at the cost of that person, that which he would otherwise be required to do under this Part by way of remediation;

---

[23] Inserted by the Environment Act 1995, s.57, for certain purposes with effect from September 21, 1995 (SI 1995/1983) and for remaining purposes with effect from April 1, 2000 (SI 2000/340).

(c) where a person on whom the enforcing authority serves a remediation notice fails to comply with any of the requirements of the notice;

(d) where the enforcing authority is precluded by section 78J or 78K above from including something by way of remediation in a remediation notice;

(e) where the enforcing authority considers that, were it to do some particular thing by way of remediation, it would decide, by virtue of subsection (2) of section 78P below or any guidance issued under that subsection,—

    (i) not to seek to recover under subsection (1) of that section any of the reasonable cost incurred by it in doing that thing; or

    (ii) to seek so to recover only a portion of that cost;

(f) where no person has, after reasonable inquiry, been found who is an appropriate person in relation to any particular thing.

(4) Subject to section 78E(4) and (5) above, for the purposes of this section, the things which it is appropriate for the enforcing authority to do by way of remediation are—

(a) in a case falling within paragraph (a) of subsection (3) above, anything by way of remediation which the enforcing authority considers necessary for the purpose mentioned in that paragraph;

(b) in a case falling within paragraph (b) of that subsection, anything specified in, or determined under, the agreement mentioned in that paragraph;

(c) in a case falling within paragraph (c) of that subsection, anything which the person mentioned in that paragraph was required to do by virtue of the remediation notice;

(d) in a case falling within paragraph (d) of that subsection, anything by way of remediation which the enforcing authority is precluded by section 78J or 78K above from including in a remediation notice;

(e) in a case falling within paragraph (e) or (f) of that subsection, the particular thing mentioned in the paragraph in question.

(5) In this section "the relevant land or waters" means—

(a) the contaminated land in question;

(b) any controlled waters affected by that land; or

(c) any land adjoining or adjacent to that land or those waters.

Recovery of, and security for, the cost of remediation by the enforcing authority[24]

78P.—(1) Where, by virtue of section 78N(3)(a), (c), (e) or (f) above, the enforcing authority does any particular thing by way of remediation, it shall be entitled, subject to sections 78J(7) and 78K(6) above, to recover the reasonable cost incurred in doing it from the appropriate person or, if there are two or more appropriate persons in relation to the thing in question, from those persons in proportions determined pursuant to section 78F(7) above.

---

[24] Inserted by the Environment Act 1995, s.57, for certain purposes with effect from September 21, 1995 (SI 1995/1983) and for remaining purposes with effect from April 1, 2000 (SI 2000/340).

(2) In deciding whether to recover the cost, and, if so, how much of the cost, which it is entitled to recover under subsection (1) above, the enforcing authority shall have regard—

    (a) to any hardship which the recovery may cause to the person from whom the cost is recoverable; and

    (b) to any guidance issued by the Secretary of State for the purposes of this subsection.

(3) Subsection (4) below shall apply in any case where—

    (a) any cost is recoverable under subsection (1) above from a person—

        (i) who is the owner of any premises which consist of or include the contaminated land in question; and

        (ii) who caused or knowingly permitted the substances, or any of the substances, by reason of which the land is contaminated land to be in, on or under the land; and

    (b) the enforcing authority serves a notice under this subsection (in this Part referred to as a "charging notice") on that person.

(4) Where this subsection applies—

    (a) the cost shall carry interest, at such reasonable rate as the enforcing authority may determine, from the date of service of the notice until the whole amount is paid; and

    (b) subject to the following provisions of this section, the cost and accrued interest shall be a charge on the premises mentioned in subsection (3)(a)(i) above.

(5) A charging notice shall—

    (a) specify the amount of the cost which the enforcing authority claims is recoverable;

    (b) state the effect of subsection (4) above and the rate of interest determined by the authority under that subsection; and (c) state the effect of subsections (7) and (8) below.

(6) On the date on which an enforcing authority serves a charging notice on a person, the authority shall also serve a copy of the notice on every other person who, to the knowledge of the authority, has an interest in the premises capable of being affected by the charge.

(7) Subject to any order under subsection (9)(b) or (c) below, the amount of any cost specified in a charging notice and the accrued interest shall be a charge on the premises—

    (a) as from the end of the period of twenty-one days beginning with the service of the charging notice, or

    (b) where an appeal is brought under subsection (8) below, as from the final determination or (as the case may be) the withdrawal, of the appeal,

until the cost and interest are recovered.

(8) A person served with a charging notice or a copy of a charging notice may appeal against the notice to a county court within the period of twenty-one days beginning with the date of service.

(9) On an appeal under subsection (8) above, the court may—

(a) confirm the notice without modification;
(b) order that the notice is to have effect with the substitution of a different amount for the amount originally specified in it; or
(c) order that the notice is to be of no effect.

(10) Regulations may make provision with respect to—

(a) the grounds on which appeals under this section may be made; or
(b) the procedure on any such appeal.

(11) An enforcing authority shall, for the purpose of enforcing a charge under this section, have all the same powers and remedies under the Law of Property Act 1925, and otherwise, as if it were a mortgagee by deed having powers of sale and lease, of accepting surrenders of leases and of appointing a receiver.

(12) Where any cost is a charge on premises under this section, the enforcing authority may by order declare the cost to be payable with interest by instalments within the specified period until the whole amount is paid.

(13) In subsection (12) above—

"interest" means interest at the rate determined by the enforcing authority under subsection (4) above; and
"the specified period" means such period of thirty years or less from the date of service of the charging notice as is specified in the order.

(14) Subsections (3) to (13) above do not extend to Scotland.

Special sites[25]

78Q.—(1) If, in a case where a local authority has served a remediation notice, the contaminated land in question becomes a special site, the appropriate Agency may adopt the remediation notice and, if it does so,—

(a) it shall give notice of its decision to adopt the remediation notice to the appropriate person and to the local authority;
(b) the remediation notice shall have effect, as from the time at which the appropriate Agency decides to adopt it, as a remediation notice given by that Agency; and
(c) the validity of the remediation notice shall not be affected by—

(i) the contaminated land having become a special site;
(ii) the adoption of the remediation notice by the appropriate Agency; or

[25] Inserted by the Environment Act 1995, s.57, for certain purposes with effect from September 21, 1995 (SI 1995/1983) and for remaining purposes with effect from April 1, 2000 (SI 2000/340).

(iii) anything in paragraph (b) above.

(2) Where a local authority has, by virtue of section 78N above, begun to do anything, or any series of things, by way of remediation—

(a) the authority may continue doing that thing, or that series of things, by virtue of that section, notwithstanding that the contaminated land in question becomes a special site; and

(b) section 78P above shall apply in relation to the reasonable cost incurred by the authority in doing that thing or those things as if that authority were the enforcing authority.

(3) If and so long as any land is a special site, the appropriate Agency may from time to time inspect that land for the purpose of keeping its condition under review.

(4) If it appears to the appropriate Agency that a special site is no longer land which is required to be designated as such a site, the appropriate Agency may give notice—

(a) to the Secretary of State, and

(b) to the local authority in whose area the site is situated,

terminating the designation of the land in question as a special site as from such date as may be specified in the notice.

(5) A notice under subsection (4) above shall not prevent the land, or any of the land, to which the notice relates being designated as a special site on a subsequent occasion.

(6) In exercising its functions under subsection (3) or (4) above, the appropriate Agency shall act in accordance with any guidance given for the purpose by the Secretary of State.

Registers[26]

78R.—(1) Every enforcing authority shall maintain a register containing prescribed particulars of or relating to—

(a) remediation notices served by that authority;

(b) appeals against any such remediation notices;

(c) remediation statements or remediation declarations prepared and published under section 78H above;

(d) in relation to an enforcing authority in England and Wales, appeals against charging notices served by that authority;

(e) notices under subsection (1)(b) or (5)(a) of section 78C above which have effect by virtue of subsection (7) of that section as the designation of any land as a special site;

(f) notices under subsection (4)(b) of section 78D above which have effect by virtue of subsection (6) of that section as the designation of any land as a special site;

[26] Inserted by the Environment Act 1995, s.57, for certain purposes with effect from September 21, 1995 (SI 1995/1983) and for remaining purposes with effect from April 1, 2000 (SI 2000/340).

(g) notices given by or to the enforcing authority under section 78Q(4) above terminating the designation of any land as a special site;

(h) notifications given to that authority by persons—

    (i) on whom a remediation notice has been served, or

    (ii) who are or were required by virtue of section 78H(8)(a) above to prepare and publish a remediation statement,

of what they claim has been done by them by way of remediation;

(j) notifications given to that authority by owners or occupiers of land—

    (i) in respect of which a remediation notice has been served, or

    (ii) in respect of which a remediation statement has been prepared and published,

of what they claim has been done on the land in question by way of remediation;

(k) convictions for such offences under section 78M above as may be prescribed;

(l) such other matters relating to contaminated land as may be prescribed;

but that duty is subject to sections 78S and 78T below.

(2) The form of, and the descriptions of information to be contained in, notifications for the purposes of subsection (1)(h) or (j) above may be prescribed by the Secretary of State.

(3) No entry made in a register by virtue of subsection (1)(h) or (j) above constitutes a representation by the body maintaining the register or, in a case where the entry is made by virtue of subsection (6) below, the authority which sent the copy of the particulars in question pursuant to subsection (4) or (5) below—

(a) that what is stated in the entry to have been done has in fact been done; or

(b) as to the manner in which it has been done.

(4) Where any particulars are entered on a register maintained under this section by the appropriate Agency, the appropriate Agency shall send a copy of those particulars to the local authority in whose area is situated the land to which the particulars relate.

(5) In any case where—

(a) any land is treated by virtue of section 78X(2) below as situated in the area of a local authority other than the local authority in whose area it is in fact situated, and

(b) any particulars relating to that land are entered on the register maintained under this section by the local authority in whose area the land is so treated as situated,

that authority shall send a copy of those particulars to the local authority in whose area the land is in fact situated.

(6) Where a local authority receives a copy of any particulars sent to it pursuant to subsection (4) or (5) above, it shall enter those particulars on the register maintained by it under this section.

(7) Where information of any description is excluded by virtue of section 78T below from any register maintained under this section, a statement shall be entered in the register indicating the existence of information of that description.

(8) It shall be the duty of each enforcing authority—

(a) to secure that the registers maintained by it under this section are available, at all reasonable times, for inspection by the public free of charge; and

(b) to afford to members of the public facilities for obtaining copies of entries, on payment of reasonable charges;

and, for the purposes of this subsection, places may be prescribed by the Secretary of State at which any such registers or facilities as are mentioned in paragraph (a) or (b) above are to be available or afforded to the public in pursuance of the paragraph in question.

(9) Registers under this section may be kept in any form.

Exclusion from registers of information affecting national security[27]

78S.—(1) No information shall be included in a register maintained under section 78R above if and so long as, in the opinion of the Secretary of State, the inclusion in the register of that information, or information of that description, would be contrary to the interests of national security.

(2) The Secretary of State may, for the purpose of securing the exclusion from registers of information to which subsection (1) above applies, give to enforcing authorities directions—

(a) specifying information, or descriptions of information, to be excluded from their registers; or

(b) specifying descriptions of information to be referred to the Secretary of State for his determination;

and no information referred to the Secretary of State in pursuance of paragraph (b) above shall be included in any such register until the Secretary of State determines that it should be so included.

(3) The enforcing authority shall notify the Secretary of State of any information which it excludes from the register in pursuance of directions under subsection (2) above.

(4) A person may, as respects any information which appears to him to be information to which subsection (1) above may apply, give a notice to the Secretary of State specifying the information and indicating its apparent nature; and, if he does so—

(a) he shall notify the enforcing authority that he has done so; and

---

[27] Inserted by the Environment Act 1995, s.57, for certain purposes with effect from September 21, 1995 (SI 1995/1983) and for remaining purposes with effect from April 1, 2000 (SI 2000/340).

(b) no information so notified to the Secretary of State shall be included in any such register until the Secretary of State has determined that it should be so included.

Exclusion from registers of certain confidential information[28]

78T.—(1) No information relating to the affairs of any individual or business shall be included in a register maintained under section 78R above, without the consent of that individual or the person for the time being carrying on that business, if and so long as the information—

(a) is, in relation to him, commercially confidential; and
(b) is not required to be included in the register in pursuance of directions under subsection (7) below;

but information is not commercially confidential for the purposes of this section unless it is determined under this section to be so by the enforcing authority or, on appeal, by the Secretary of State.

(2) Where it appears to an enforcing authority that any information which has been obtained by the authority under or by virtue of any provision of this Part might be commercially confidential, the authority shall—

(a) give to the person to whom or whose business it relates notice that that information is required to be included in the register unless excluded under this section; and
(b) give him a reasonable opportunity—
    (i) of objecting to the inclusion of the information on the ground that it is commercially confidential; and
    (ii) of making representations to the authority for the purpose of justifying any such objection;

and, if any representations are made, the enforcing authority shall, having taken the representations into account, determine whether the information is or is not commercially confidential.

(3) Where, under subsection (2) above, an authority determines that information is not commercially confidential—

(a) the information shall not be entered in the register until the end of the period of twenty-one days beginning with the date on which the determination is notified to the person concerned;
(b) that person may appeal to the Secretary of State against the decision;

and, where an appeal is brought in respect of any information, the information shall not be entered in the register until the end of the period of seven days following the day on which the appeal is finally determined or withdrawn.

(4) An appeal under subsection (3) above shall, if either party to the appeal so requests or the Secretary of State so decides, take or continue in the form of a hearing (which must be held in private).

---

[28] Inserted by the Environment Act 1995, s.57, for certain purposes with effect from September 21, 1995 (SI 1995/1983) and for remaining purposes with effect from April 1, 2000 (SI 2000/340).

(5) Subsection (10) of section 15 above shall apply in relation to an appeal under subsection (3) above as it applies in relation to an appeal under that section.

(6) Subsection (3) above is subject to section 114 of the Environment Act 1995 (delegation or reference of appeals etc).

(7) The Secretary of State may give to the enforcing authorities directions as to specified information, or descriptions of information, which the public interest requires to be included in registers maintained under section 78R above notwithstanding that the information may be commercially confidential.

(8) Information excluded from a register shall be treated as ceasing to be commercially confidential for the purposes of this section at the expiry of the period of four years beginning with the date of the determination by virtue of which it was excluded; but the person who furnished it may apply to the authority for the information to remain excluded from the register on the ground that it is still commercially confidential and the authority shall determine whether or not that is the case.

(9) Subsections (3) to (6) above shall apply in relation to a determination under subsection (8) above as they apply in relation to a determination under subsection (2) above.

(10) Information is, for the purposes of any determination under this section, commercially confidential, in relation to any individual or person, if its being contained in the register would prejudice to an unreasonable degree the commercial interests of that individual or person.

(11) For the purposes of subsection (10) above, there shall be disregarded any prejudice to the commercial interests of any individual or person so far as relating only to the value of the contaminated land in question or otherwise to the ownership or occupation of that land.

Reports by the appropriate Agency on the state of contaminated land[29]

78U.—(1) The appropriate Agency shall—

    (a) from time to time, or
    (b) if the Secretary of State at any time so requests,

prepare and publish a report on the state of contaminated land in England and Wales or in Scotland, as the case may be.

(2) A local authority shall, at the written request of the appropriate Agency, furnish the appropriate Agency with such information to which this subsection applies as the appropriate Agency may require for the purpose of enabling it to perform its functions under subsection (1) above.

(3) The information to which subsection (2) above applies is such information as the local authority may have, or may reasonably be expected to obtain, with respect

---

[29] Inserted by the Environment Act 1995, s.57, for certain purposes with effect from September 21, 1995 (SI 1995/1983) and for remaining purposes with effect from April 1, 2000 (SI 2000/340).

to the condition of contaminated land in its area, being information which the authority has acquired or may acquire in the exercise of its functions under this Part.

Site-specific guidance by the appropriate Agency concerning contaminated land[30]

78V.—(1) The appropriate Agency may issue guidance to any local authority with respect to the exercise or performance of the authority's powers or duties under this Part in relation to any particular contaminated land; and in exercising or performing those powers or duties in relation to that land the authority shall have regard to any such guidance so issued.

(2) If and to the extent that any guidance issued under subsection (1) above to a local authority is inconsistent with any guidance issued under this Part by the Secretary of State, the local authority shall disregard the guidance under that subsection.

(3) A local authority shall, at the written request of the appropriate Agency, furnish the appropriate Agency with such information to which this subsection applies as the appropriate Agency may require for the purpose of enabling it to issue guidance for the purposes of subsection (1) above.

(4) The information to which subsection (3) above applies is such information as the local authority may have, or may reasonably be expected to obtain, with respect to any contaminated land in its area, being information which the authority has acquired, or may acquire, in the exercise of its functions under this Part.

The appropriate Agency to have regard to guidance given by the Secretary of State[31]

78W.—(1) The Secretary of State may issue guidance to the appropriate Agency with respect to the exercise or performance of that Agency's powers or duties under this Part; and in exercising or performing those powers or duties the appropriate Agency shall have regard to any such guidance so issued.

(2) The duty imposed on the appropriate Agency by subsection (1) above is without prejudice to any duty imposed by any other provision of this Part on that Agency to act in accordance with guidance issued by the Secretary of State.

Supplementary provisions[32]

78X.—(1) Where it appears to a local authority that two or more different sites, when considered together, are in such a condition, by reason of substances in, on or under the land, that—

---

[30] Inserted by the Environment Act 1995, s.57, for certain purposes with effect from September 21, 1995 (SI 1995/1983) and for remaining purposes with effect from April 1, 2000 (SI 2000/340).

[31] Inserted by the Environment Act 1995, s.57, for certain purposes with effect from September 21, 1995 (SI 1995/1983) and for remaining purposes with effect from April 1, 2000 (SI 2000/340).

[32] Inserted by the Environment Act 1995, s.57, for certain purposes with effect from September 21, 1995 (SI 1995/1983) and for remaining purposes with effect from April 1, 2000 (SI 2000/340).

(a) significant harm is being caused or there is a significant possibility of such harm being caused, or

(b) pollution of controlled waters is being, or is likely to be, caused,

this Part shall apply in relation to each of those sites, whether or not the condition of the land at any of them, when considered alone, appears to the authority to be such that significant harm is being caused, or there is a significant possibility of such harm being caused, or that pollution of controlled waters is being or is likely to be caused.

(2) Where it appears to a local authority that any land outside, but adjoining or adjacent to, its area is in such a condition, by reason of substances in, on or under the land, that significant harm is being caused, or there is a significant possibility of such harm being caused, or that pollution of controlled waters is being, or is likely to be, caused within its area—

(a) the authority may, in exercising its functions under this Part, treat that land as if it were land situated within its area; and

(b) except in this subsection, any reference—

(i) to land within the area of a local authority, or

(ii) to the local authority in whose area any land is situated,

shall be construed accordingly;

but this subsection is without prejudice to the functions of the local authority in whose area the land is in fact situated.[33]

(3) A person acting in a relevant capacity—

(a) shall not thereby be personally liable, under this Part, to bear the whole or any part of the cost of doing any thing by way of remediation, unless

---

[33] Prospectively amended by the Water Act 2003, s.86(6). When this amendment comes into force subss (1) and (2) will read:

"(1) Where it appears to a local authority that two or more different sites, when considered together, are in such a condition, by reason of substances in, on or under the land, that—

(a) significant harm is being caused or there is a significant possibility of such harm being caused, or

(b) significant pollution of controlled waters is being caused or there is a significant possibility of such pollution being caused,,

this Part shall apply in relation to each of those sites, whether or not the condition of the land at any of them, when considered alone, appears to the authority to be such that significant harm, or significant pollution of controlled waters, is being caused, or there is a significant possibility of such harm or pollution being caused.

(2) Where it appears to a local authority that any land outside, but adjoining or adjacent to, its area is in such a condition, by reason of substances in, on or under the land, that significant harm, or significant pollution of controlled waters, is being caused, or there is a significant possibility of such harm or pollution being caused, within its area—

(a) the authority may, in exercising its functions under this Part, treat that land as if it were land situated within its area; and

(b) except in this subsection, any reference—

(i) to land within the area of a local authority, or

(ii) to the local authority in whose area any land is situated,

shall be construed accordingly;

but this subsection is without prejudice to the functions of the local authority in whose area the land is in fact situated."

that thing is to any extent referable to substances whose presence in, on or under the contaminated land in question is a result of any act done or omission made by him which it was unreasonable for a person acting in that capacity to do or make; and

(b) shall not thereby be guilty of an offence under or by virtue of section 78M above unless the requirement which has not been complied with is a requirement to do some particular thing for which he is personally liable to bear the whole or any part of the cost.

(4) In subsection (3) above, "person acting in a relevant capacity" means—

(a) a person acting as an insolvency practitioner, within the meaning of section 388 of the Insolvency Act 1986 (including that section as it applies in relation to an insolvent partnership by virtue of any order made under section 421 of that Act);

(b) the official receiver acting in a capacity in which he would be regarded as acting as an insolvency practitioner within the meaning of section 388 of the Insolvency Act 1986 if subsection (5) of that section were disregarded;

(c) the official receiver acting as receiver or manager;

(d) a person acting as a special manager under section 177 or 370 of the Insolvency Act 1986;

(e) the Accountant in Bankruptcy acting as permanent or interim trustee in a sequestration (within the meaning of the Bankruptcy (Scotland) Act 1985);

(f) a person acting as a receiver or receiver and manager—

(i) under or by virtue of any enactment; or

(ii) by virtue of his appointment as such by an order of a court or by any other instrument.

(5) Regulations may make different provision for different cases or circumstances.

Application to the Isles of Scilly[34]

78Y.—(1) Subject to the provisions of any order under this section, this Part shall not apply in relation to the Isles of Scilly.

(2) The Secretary of State may, after consultation with the Council of the Isles of Scilly, by order provide for the application of any provisions of this Part to the Isles of Scilly; and any such order may provide for the application of those provisions to those Isles with such modifications as may be specified in the order.

(3) An order under this section may—

(a) make different provision for different cases, including different provision in relation to different persons, circumstances or localities; and

(b) contain such supplemental, consequential and transitional provision as the Secretary of State considers appropriate, including provision saving provision repealed by or under any enactment.

---

[34] Inserted by the Environment Act 1995, s.57, for certain purposes with effect from September 21, 1995 (SI 1995/1983) and for remaining purposes with effect from April 1, 2000 (SI 2000/340).

Supplementary provisions with respect to guidance by the Secretary of State[35]

78YA.—(1) Any power of the Secretary of State to issue guidance under this Part shall only be exercisable after consultation with the appropriate Agency and such other bodies or persons as he may consider it appropriate to consult in relation to the guidance in question.

(2) A draft of any guidance proposed to be issued under section 78A(2) or (5), 78B(2) or 78F(6) or (7) above shall be laid before each House of Parliament and the guidance shall not be issued until after the period of 40 days beginning with the day on which the draft was so laid or, if the draft is laid on different days, the later of the two days.

(3) If, within the period mentioned in subsection (2) above, either House resolves that the guidance, the draft of which was laid before it, should not be issued, the Secretary of State shall not issue that guidance.

(4) In reckoning any period of 40 days for the purposes of subsection (2) or (3) above, no account shall be taken of any time during which Parliament is dissolved or prorogued or during which both Houses are adjourned for more than four days.

(5) The Secretary of State shall arrange for any guidance issued by him under this Part to be published in such manner as he considers appropriate.

Interaction of this Part with other enactments[36]

78YB.—(1) A remediation notice shall not be served if and to the extent that it appears to the enforcing authority that the powers of the appropriate Agency under section 27 above may be exercised in relation to—

    (a) the significant harm (if any), and
    (b) the pollution of controlled waters (if any),

by reason of which the contaminated land in question is such land.

(2) Nothing in this Part shall apply in relation to any land in respect of which there is for the time being in force a site licence under Part II above, except to the extent that any significant harm, or pollution of controlled waters, by reason of which that land would otherwise fall to be regarded as contaminated land is attributable to causes other than—

    (a) breach of the conditions of the licence; or

---

[35] Inserted by the Environment Act 1995, s.57, for certain purposes with effect from September 21, 1995 (SI 1995/1983) and for remaining purposes with effect from April 1, 2000 (SI 2000/340).

[36] Inserted by the Environment Act 1995, s.57, for certain purposes with effect from September 21, 1995 (SI 1995/1983) and for remaining purposes with effect from April 1, 2000 (SI 2000/340).

(b) the carrying on, in accordance with the conditions of the licence, of any activity authorised by the licence.[37]

(2A) This Part shall not apply if and to the extent that—

(a) any significant harm, or pollution of controlled waters, by reason of which the land would otherwise fall to be regarded as contaminated, is attributable to the final disposal by deposit in or on land of controlled waste, and

(b) enforcement action may be taken in relation to that disposal.

(2B) A remediation notice shall not be served in respect of contaminated land if and to the extent that—

(a) the significant harm, or pollution of controlled waters, by reason of which the contaminated land is such land is attributable to an activity other than the final disposal by deposit in or on land of controlled waste, and

(b) enforcement action may be taken in relation to that activity.

(2C) In subsections (2A) and (2B) above—

"controlled waste" has the meaning given in section 75(4) of this Act; and "enforcement action" means action under regulation 24 (enforcement notices) or regulation 26(2) (power of regulator to remedy pollution) of the Pollution Prevention and Control (England and Wales) Regulations 2000.[38]

(3) If, in a case falling within subsection (1) or (7) of section 59 above, the land in question is contaminated land, or becomes such land by reason of the deposit of the controlled waste in question, a remediation notice shall not be served in respect of that land by reason of that waste or any consequences of its deposit, if and to the extent that it appears to the enforcing authority that the powers of a waste regulation authority or waste collection authority under that section may be exercised in relation to that waste or the consequences of its deposit.

(4) No remediation notice shall require a person to do anything the effect of which would be to impede or prevent the making of a discharge in pursuance of a consent given under Chapter II of Part III of the Water Resources Act 1991 (pollution offences) or, in relation to Scotland, in pursuance of a consent given under Part II of the Control of Pollution Act 1974.

---

[37] Prospectively amended by the Water Act 2003, s.86(7). When this amendment comes into force subss (1) and (2) will read:

"(1) A remediation notice shall not be served if and to the extent that it appears to the enforcing authority that the powers of the appropriate Agency under section 27 above may be exercised in relation to—
(a) the significant harm (if any), and
(b) the significant pollution of controlled waters (if any),
by reason of which the contaminated land in question is such land.
(2) Nothing in this Part shall apply in relation to any land in respect of which there is for the time being in force a site licence under Part II above, except to the extent that any significant harm, or significant pollution of controlled waters, by reason of which that land would otherwise fall to be regarded as contaminated land is attributable to causes other than—
(a) breach of the conditions of the licence; or
(b) the carrying on, in accordance with the conditions of the licence, of any activity authorised by the licence. "

[38] Inserted by SI 2000/1973, reg.39, Sch.10, para.6, with effect from August 1, 2000.

This Part and radioactivity[39]

78YC.—Except as provided by regulations, nothing in this Part applies in relation to harm, or pollution of controlled waters, so far as attributable to any radioactivity possessed by any substance; but regulations may—

(a) provide for prescribed provisions of this Part to have effect with such modifications as the Secretary of State considers appropriate for the purpose of dealing with harm, or pollution of controlled waters, so far as attributable to any radioactivity possessed by any substances; or

(b) make such modifications of the Radioactive Substances Act 1993 or any other Act as the Secretary of State considers appropriate.

---

[39] Inserted by the Environment Act 1995, s.57, for certain purposes with effect from September 21, 1995 (SI 1995/1983) and for remaining purposes with effect from April 1, 2000 (SI 2000/340).

Contaminated Land (England) Regulations 2006/1380

Citation, commencement, application and interpretation

1.—(1) These Regulations may be cited as the Contaminated Land (England) Regulations 2006 and come into force on 4th August 2006.

(2) These Regulations apply in relation to England only.

(3) In these Regulations, "the 1990 Act" means the Environmental Protection Act 1990.

(4) In these Regulations, unless otherwise indicated—

  (a) any reference to a numbered section is to the section of the 1990 Act which bears that number or, in relation to harm so far as attributable to any radioactivity possessed by any substances, to that section as modified by the Radioactive Contaminated Land (Modification of Enactments)(England) Regulations 2006; and

  (b) in relation to harm, so far as attributable to any radioactivity possessed by any substances, any term defined by the 1990 Act has the meaning given to it by that Act as modified by the Radioactive Contaminated Land (Modification of Enactments)(England) Regulations 2006.

Land required to be designated as a special site

2.—(1) Contaminated land of the following descriptions is prescribed for the purposes of section 78C(8) as land required to be designated as a special site—

  (a) land affecting controlled waters in the circumstances specified in regulation 3;

  (b) land which is contaminated land by reason of waste acid tars in, on or under the land;

  (c) land on which any of the following activities have been carried on at any time—

      (i) the purification (including refining) of crude petroleum or of oil extracted from petroleum, shale or any other bituminous substance except coal; or

      (ii) the manufacture or processing of explosives;

  (d) land on which a prescribed process designated for central control has been or is being carried on under an authorisation, where the process does not solely consist of things being done which are required by way of remediation;

  (e) land on which an activity has been or is being carried on in a Part A(1) installation or by means of Part A(1) mobile plant under a permit, where the activity does not solely consist of things being done which are required by way of remediation;

  (f) land within a nuclear site;

  (g) land owned or occupied by or on behalf of—

      (i) the Secretary of State for Defence;

      (ii) the Defence Council,

     (iii) an international headquarters or defence organisation, or

     (iv) the service authority of a visiting force,

being land used for naval, military or air force purposes;

(h) land on which the manufacture, production or disposal of—

       (i) chemical weapons,

      (ii) any biological agent or toxin which falls within section 1(1)(a) of the Biological Weapons Act 1974 (restriction on development of biological agents and toxins), or

     (iii) any weapon, equipment or means of delivery which falls within section 1(1)(b) of that Act (restriction on development of biological weapons),

has been carried on at any time;

(i) land comprising premises which are or were designated by the Secretary of State by an order made under section 1(1) of the Atomic Weapons Establishment Act 1991 (arrangements for development etc of nuclear devices);

(j) land to which section 30 of the Armed Forces Act 1996 (land held for the benefit of Greenwich Hospital) applies;

(k) land which is contaminated land wholly or partly by virtue of any radioactivity possessed by any substance in, on or under that land; and

(l) land which—

       (i) is adjoining or adjacent to land of a description specified in any of sub-paragraphs (b) to (k); and

      (ii) is contaminated land by virtue of substances which appear to have escaped from land of such a description.

(2) For the purposes of paragraph (1)(b), "waste acid tars" are tars which—

(a) contain sulphuric acid;

(b) were produced as a result of the refining of benzole, used lubricants or petroleum; and

(c) are or were stored on land used as a retention basin for the disposal of such tars.

(3) In paragraph (1)(d), "authorisation" and "prescribed process" have the same meanings as in Part 1 of the 1990 Act (integrated pollution control and air pollution control by local authorities) and the reference to designation for central control is a reference to designation under section 2(4) (which provides for processes to be designated for central or local control).

(4) In paragraph (1)(e), "Part A(1) installation", "Part A(1) mobile plant" and "permit" have the same meanings as in the Pollution Prevention and Control (England and Wales) Regulations 2000.

(5) In paragraph (1)(f), "nuclear site" means—

(a) any site in respect of which, or part of which, a nuclear site licence is for the time being in force; or

(b) any site in respect of which, or part of which, after the revocation or surrender of a nuclear site licence, the period of responsibility of the licensee has not come to an end.

(6) In paragraph (5), "nuclear site licence", "licensee" and "period of responsibility" have the meanings given by the Nuclear Installations Act 1965.

(7) For the purposes of paragraph (1)(g), land used for residential purposes or by the Navy, Army and Air Force Institutes must be treated as land used for naval, military or air force purposes only if the land forms part of a base occupied for naval, military or air force purposes.

(8) In paragraph (1)(g)—

"international headquarters" and "defence organisation" mean, respectively, any international headquarters, and any defence organisation, designated for the purposes of the International Headquarters and Defence Organisations Act 1964;

" service authority" and "visiting force" have the same meanings as in Part 1 of the Visiting Forces Act 1952.

(9) In paragraph (1)(h), "chemical weapon" has the same meaning as in subsection (1) of section 1 of the Chemical Weapons Act 1996, disregarding subsection (2) of that section.

Pollution of controlled waters

3.—The circumstances to which regulation 2(1)(a) refers are where—

(a) controlled waters which are, or are intended to be, used for the supply of drinking water for human consumption are being affected by the land and, as a result, require a treatment process or a change in such a process to be applied to those waters before use, so as to be regarded as wholesome within the meaning of Part 3 of the Water Industry Act 1991 (water supply);

(b) controlled waters are being affected by the land and, as a result, those waters do not meet or are not likely to meet the criterion for classification applying to the relevant description of waters specified in regulations made under section 82 of the Water Resources Act 1991 (classification of quality of waters); or

(c) controlled waters are being affected by the land and—

(i) any of the substances by reason of which the pollution of the waters is being or is likely to be caused falls within any of the families or groups of substances listed in paragraph 1 of Schedule 1 to these Regulations; and

(ii) the waters, or any part of the waters, are contained within underground strata which comprise wholly or partly any of the formations of rocks listed in paragraph 2 of Schedule 1 to these Regulations.

Content of remediation notices

4.—(1) A remediation notice must state (in addition to the matters required by section 78E(1) and (3))—

(a) the name and address of the person on whom the notice is served;

(b) the location and extent of the contaminated land to which the notice relates (in this regulation referred to as the "contaminated land in question"), in sufficient detail to enable it to be identified whether by reference to a plan or otherwise;

(c) the date of any notice which was given under section 78B(3) to the person on whom the remediation notice is served identifying the contaminated land in question as contaminated land;

(d) whether the enforcing authority considers the person on whom the notice is served is an appropriate person by reason of—

    (i) having caused or knowingly permitted the substances, or any of the substances, by reason of which the contaminated land in question is contaminated land, to be in, on or under that land; or

    (ii) being the owner or occupier of the contaminated land in question;

(e) particulars of the significant harm, harm or pollution of controlled waters by reason of which the contaminated land in question is contaminated land;

(f) the substances by reason of which the contaminated land in question is contaminated land and, if any of the substances have escaped from other land, the location of that other land;

(g) the enforcing authority's reasons for its decisions as to the things by way of remediation that the appropriate person is required to do, showing how any guidance issued by the Secretary of State under section 78E(5) has been applied;

(h) where two or more persons are appropriate persons in relation to the contaminated land in question—

    (i) that this is the case;

    (ii) the name and address of each such person; and

    (iii) the thing by way of remediation for which each such person bears responsibility;

(i) where two or more persons would, apart from section 78F(6), be appropriate persons in relation to any particular thing which is to be done by way of remediation, the enforcing authority's reasons for its determination as to whether any, and if so which, of them is to be treated as not being an appropriate person in relation to that thing, showing how any guidance issued by the Secretary of State under section 78F(6) has been applied;

(j) where the remediation notice is required by section 78E(3) to state the proportion of the cost of a thing to be done by way of remediation which each of the appropriate persons in relation to that thing is liable to bear, the enforcing authority's reasons for the proportion which it has determined, showing how any guidance issued by the Secretary of State under section 78F(7) has been applied;

(k) where known to the enforcing authority, the name and address of—

    (i) the owner of the contaminated land in question; and

    (ii) any person who appears to the enforcing authority to be in occupation of the whole or any part of the contaminated land in question;

(l) where known to the enforcing authority, the name and address of any person whose consent is required under section 78G(2) before any thing required by the remediation notice may be done;

(m) where the notice is to be served in reliance on section 78H(4), that it appears to the enforcing authority that the contaminated land in question is in such a condition, by reason of substances in, on or under the land, that there is imminent danger of serious harm or serious pollution of controlled waters being caused;

(n) that a person on whom a remediation notice is served may be guilty of an offence for failure, without reasonable excuse, to comply with any of the requirements of the notice;

(o) the penalties which may be applied on conviction for such an offence;

(p) the name and address of the enforcing authority serving the notice; and

(q) the date of the notice.

(2) A remediation notice must explain—

(a) that a person on whom it is served has a right of appeal against the notice under section 78L;

(b) how, within what period and on what grounds an appeal may be made; and

(c) that a notice is suspended, where an appeal is duly made, until the final determination or abandonment of the appeal.

Service of copies of remediation notices

5.—(1) Subject to paragraph (2), the enforcing authority must, at the same time as it serves a remediation notice, send a copy of it to each of the following persons, not being a person on whom the notice is to be served—

(a) any person who was required to be consulted under section 78G(3) before service of the notice;

(b) any person who was required to be consulted under section 78H(1) before service of the notice;

(c) where the local authority is the enforcing authority, the Environment Agency; and

(d) where the Environment Agency is the enforcing authority, the local authority in whose area the contaminated land in question is situated.

(2) Where it appears to the enforcing authority that the contaminated land in question is in such a condition by reason of substances in, on or under it that there is imminent danger of serious harm or serious pollution of controlled waters being caused, the enforcing authority must send any copies of the notice pursuant to paragraph (1) as soon as practicable after service of the notice.

Compensation for rights of entry etc

6.—Schedule 2 to these Regulations specifies—

(a) the period within which a person who grants, or joins in granting, any rights pursuant to section 78G(2) may apply for compensation for the grant of those rights;

(b) the manner in which, and the person to whom, such an application may be made; and

(c) the manner in which the amount of such compensation is determined;

and makes further provision relating to such compensation.

Grounds of appeal against a remediation notice

2.—(1) The grounds of appeal against a remediation notice under section 78L(1) are any of the following—

(a) that, in determining whether any land to which the notice relates appears to be contaminated land, the local authority—

(i) failed to act in accordance with guidance issued by the Secretary of State under section 78A(2), (5) or (6); or

        (ii) whether by reason of such a failure or otherwise, unreasonably identified all or any of the land to which the notice relates as contaminated land;

(b) that, in determining a requirement of the notice, the enforcing authority—

        (i) failed to have regard to guidance issued by the Secretary of State under section 78E(5); or

        (ii) whether by reason of such a failure or otherwise, unreasonably required the appellant to do any thing by way of remediation;

(c) that the enforcing authority unreasonably determined the appellant to be the appropriate person who is to bear responsibility for any thing required by the notice to be done by way of remediation;

(d) subject to paragraph (2), that the enforcing authority unreasonably failed to determine that some person in addition to the appellant is an appropriate person in relation to any thing required by the notice to be done by way of remediation;

(e) that, in respect of any thing required by the notice to be done by way of remediation, the enforcing authority failed to act in accordance with guidance issued by the Secretary of State under section 78F(6);

(f) that, where two or more persons are appropriate persons in relation to any thing required by the notice to be done by way of remediation, the enforcing authority—

        (i) failed to determine the proportion of the cost stated in the notice to be the liability of the appellant in accordance with guidance issued by the Secretary of State under section 78F(7); or

        (ii) whether, by reason of such a failure or otherwise, unreasonably determined the proportion of the cost that the appellant is to bear;

(g) that service of the notice contravened a provision of subsection (1) or (3) of section 78H (restrictions and prohibitions on serving remediation notices) other than in circumstances where section 78H(4) applies;

(h) that, where the notice was served in reliance on section 78H(4) in circumstances where section 78H(1) or (3) has not been complied with, the enforcing authority could not reasonably have taken the view that the contaminated land in question was in such a condition by reason of substances in, on or under the land, that there was imminent danger of serious harm or serious pollution of controlled waters being caused;

(i) that the enforcing authority has unreasonably failed to be satisfied, in accordance with section 78H(5)(b), that appropriate things are being, or will be, done by way of remediation without service of a notice;

(j) that any thing required by the notice to be done by way of remediation was required in contravention of a provision of section 78J (restrictions on liability relating to the pollution of controlled waters);

(k) that any thing required by the notice to be done by way of remediation was required in contravention of a provision of section 78K (liability in respect of contaminating substances which escape to other land);

(l) that the enforcing authority itself has power, in a case falling within section 78N(3)(b), to do what is appropriate by way of remediation;

(m) that the enforcing authority itself has power, in a case falling within section 78N(3)(e), to do what is appropriate by way of remediation;

(n) that the enforcing authority, in considering for the purposes of section 78N(3)(e) whether it would seek to recover all or a portion of the cost incurred by it in doing some particular thing by way of remediation—

     (i) failed to have regard to any hardship which the recovery may cause to the person from whom the cost is recoverable or to any guidance issued by the Secretary of State for the purposes of section 78P(2); or

     (ii) whether by reason of such a failure or otherwise, unreasonably determined that it would decide to seek to recover all of the cost;

(o) that, in determining a requirement of the notice, the enforcing authority failed to have regard to guidance issued by the Environment Agency under section 78V(1);

(p) that a period specified in the notice within which the appellant is required to do anything is not reasonably sufficient for the purpose;

(q) that the notice provides for a person acting in a relevant capacity to be personally liable to bear the whole or part of the cost of doing any thing by way of remediation, contrary to the provisions of section 78X(3)(a);

(r) that service of the notice contravened a provision of section 78YB (which makes provision regarding the interaction of Part 2A of the 1990 Act with other enactments), and—

     (i) in a case where subsection (1) of that section is relied on, that it ought to have appeared to the enforcing authority that the powers of the Environment Agency under section 27 might be exercised;

     (ii) in a case where subsection (3) of section 78YB is relied on, that it ought to have appeared to the enforcing authority that the powers of a waste regulation authority or waste collection authority under section 59 might be exercised; or

(s) that there has been some informality, defect or error in, or in connection with, the notice, in respect of which there is no right of appeal under the grounds set out in sub-paragraphs (a) to (r).

(2) A person may only appeal on the ground specified in paragraph (1)(d) in a case where—

(a) the enforcing authority has determined that he is an appropriate person by virtue of subsection (2) of section 78F and he claims to have found some other person who is an appropriate person by virtue of that subsection;

(b) the notice is served on him as the owner or occupier for the time being of the contaminated land in question and he claims to have found some other person who is an appropriate person by virtue of that subsection; or

(c) the notice is served on him as the owner or occupier for the time being of the contaminated land in question, and he claims that some other person is also an owner or occupier for the time being of the whole or part of that land.

(3) If and in so far as an appeal against a remediation notice is based on the ground of some informality, defect or error in, or in connection with, the notice, the Secretary of State must dismiss the appeal if he is satisfied that the informality, defect or error was not a material one.

Appeals to the Secretary of State

8.—(1) An appeal to the Secretary of State against a remediation notice must be made to him by a notice ("notice of appeal") which states—

(a) the name and address of the appellant;

    (b) the grounds on which the appeal is made; and

    (c) whether the appellant wishes the appeal to be in the form of a hearing or to be disposed of on the basis of written representations.

(2) The appellant must, at the same time as he serves a notice of appeal on the Secretary of State—

    (a) serve a copy of it on—

        (i) the enforcing authority;

       (ii) any person named in the remediation notice as an appropriate person;

      (iii) any person named in the notice of appeal as an appropriate person; and

      (iv) any person named in the remediation notice as the owner or occupier of the whole or any part of the land to which the notice relates;

    (b) serve on the Secretary of State a statement of the names and addresses of any persons falling within paragraph (ii), (iii) or (iv) of sub-paragraph (a); and

    (c) serve a copy of the remediation notice to which the appeal relates on the Secretary of State and on any person named in the notice of appeal as an appropriate person who is not so named in the remediation notice.

(3) If the appellant wishes to abandon an appeal, he must do so by notifying the Secretary of State in writing and the appeal is then treated as abandoned as from the date on which the Secretary of State receives that notification.

(4) The Secretary of State may refuse to permit an appellant to abandon his appeal against a remediation notice where the notification by the appellant in accordance with paragraph (3) is received by the Secretary of State at any time after the Secretary of State has notified the appellant in accordance with regulation 11(1) of a proposed modification of that notice.

(5) Where an appeal is abandoned, the Secretary of State must give notice of the abandonment to any person on whom the appellant was required to serve a copy of the notice of appeal.

Hearings and local inquiries

9.—(1) Before determining an appeal, the Secretary of State may, if he thinks fit—

    (a) cause the appeal to take or continue in the form of a hearing (which may, if the person hearing the appeal so decides, be held, or held to any extent, in private); or

    (b) cause a local inquiry to be held.

(2) Before determining an appeal, the Secretary of State must act as mentioned in sub-paragraph (a) or (b) of paragraph (1) if a request is made by either the appellant or the enforcing authority to be heard with respect to the appeal.

(3) The persons entitled to be heard at a hearing are—

    (a) the appellant;

    (b) the enforcing authority; and

    (c) any person (other than the enforcing authority) on whom the appellant was required to serve a copy of the notice of appeal.

(4) Nothing in paragraph (3) prevents the person appointed to conduct the hearing of the appeal from permitting any other person to be heard at the hearing and such permission must not be unreasonably withheld.

(5) After the conclusion of a hearing, the person appointed to conduct the hearing must, unless he has been appointed under subsection (1)(a) of section 114 of the Environment Act 1995 (power of Secretary of State to delegate his functions of determining, or to refer matters involved in, appeals) to determine the appeal, make a report in writing to the Secretary of State, which must include his conclusions and his recommendations or his reasons for not making any recommendations.

Notification of Secretary of State's decision on an appeal

10.—(1) The Secretary of State must notify the appellant in writing of his decision on an appeal and must provide him with a copy of any report mentioned in regulation 9(5).

(2) The Secretary of State must, at the same time as he notifies the appellant, send a copy of the documents mentioned in paragraph (1) to the enforcing authority and to any other person on whom the appellant was required to serve a copy of the notice of appeal.

Modification of a remediation notice

11.—(1) Before modifying a remediation notice under subsection (2)(b) of section 78L (appeals against remediation notices) in any respect which would be less favourable to the appellant or any other person on whom the notice was served, the Secretary of State must—

    (a) notify the appellant and any persons on whom the appellant was required to serve a copy of the notice of appeal of the proposed modification;

    (b) permit any persons so notified to make representations in relation to the proposed modification; and

    (c) permit the appellant or any other person on whom the remediation notice was served to be heard if any such person so requests.

(2) Where, in accordance with paragraph (1), the appellant or any other person is heard, the enforcing authority is also entitled to be heard.

Suspension of a remediation notice

12.—(1) Where an appeal is duly made against a remediation notice, the notice is of no effect pending the final determination or abandonment of the appeal.

(2) An appeal against a remediation notice is duly made for the purposes of this regulation if it is made within the period specified in section 78L(1) and the requirements of regulation 8(1) and (2) have been complied with.

Registers

13.—(1) For the purpose of subsection (1) of section 78R (registers) the particulars that must be contained in a register maintained under that subsection are specified in Schedule 3.

(2) The following descriptions of information are prescribed for the purposes of section 78R(2) as information to be contained in notifications for the purposes of section 78R(1)(h) and (j)—

    (a) the location and extent of the land in sufficient detail to enable it to be identified;

(b) the name and address of the person who it is claimed has done each of the things by way of remediation;

(c) a description of any thing which it is claimed has been done by way of remediation; and

(d) the period within which it is claimed each such thing was done.

(3) The following places are prescribed for the purposes of subsection (8) of section 78R as places at which any registers or facilities for obtaining copies must be available or afforded to the public in pursuance of paragraph (a) or (b) of that subsection—

(a) where the enforcing authority is the local authority, its principal office; and

(b) where the enforcing authority is the Environment Agency, its office for the area in which the contaminated land in question is situated.

Revocations

14.—The Contaminated Land (England) Regulations 2000 and the Contaminated Land (England) (Amendment) Regulations 2001 are revoked.

SCHEDULE 1 SPECIAL SITES

1.—The families and groups of substances relevant for the purposes of regulation 3(c)(i) are—

organohalogen compounds and substances which may form such compounds in the aquatic environment;

organophosphorus compounds;

organotin compounds;

substances which possess carcinogenic, mutagenic or teratogenic properties in or via the aquatic environment;

mercury and its compounds;

cadmium and its compounds;

mineral oil and other hydrocarbons;

cyanides.

2.—The formations of rocks relevant for the purposes of regulation 3(c)(ii) are—

Pleistocene Norwich Crag;

Upper Cretaceous Chalk;

Lower Cretaceous Sandstones;

Upper Jurassic Corallian;

Middle Jurassic Limestones;

Lower Jurassic Cotteswold Sands;

Permo-Triassic Sherwood Sandstone Group;

Upper Permian Magnesian Limestone;

Lower Permian Penrith Sandstone;

Lower Permian Collyhurst Sandstone;

Lower Permian Basal Breccias, Conglomerates and Sandstones;

Lower Carboniferous Limestones.

Schedule 2 Compensation for Rights of Entry etc

Interpretation

1.—In this Schedule—

"the 1961 Act" means the Land Compensation Act 1961;

"grantor" means a person who has granted, or joined in the granting of, any rights pursuant to section 78G(2); and

"relevant interest" means an interest in land out of which rights have been granted pursuant to section 78G(2).

Period for making an application

2.—An application for compensation must be made within the period beginning with the date of the grant of the rights in respect of which compensation is claimed and ending on the expiry of whichever is the latest of the following periods—

(a) twelve months after the date of the grant of those rights;

(b) where an appeal is made against a remediation notice in respect of which the rights in question have been granted, and the notice is of no effect by virtue of regulation 12, twelve months after the date of the final determination or abandonment of the appeal; or

(c) six months after the date on which the rights were first exercised.

Manner of making an application

3.—(1) An application must be made in writing and delivered at or sent by pre-paid post to the last known address for correspondence of the appropriate person to whom the rights were granted.

(2) The application must contain, or be accompanied by—

(a) a copy of the grant of rights in respect of which the grantor is applying for compensation, and of any plans attached to that grant;

(b) a description of the exact nature of any interest in land in respect of which compensation is applied for; and

(c) a statement of the amount of compensation applied for, distinguishing the amounts applied for under each of sub-paragraphs (a) to (e) of paragraph 4, and showing how the amount applied for under each sub-paragraph has been calculated.

Loss and damage for which compensation payable

4.—Subject to paragraph 5(3) and (5)(b), compensation is payable under section 78G(5) for loss and damage of the following descriptions—

    (a) depreciation in the value of any relevant interest to which the grantor is entitled which results from the grant of the rights;

    (b) depreciation in the value of any other interest in land to which the grantor is entitled which results from the exercise of the rights;

    (c) loss or damage, in relation to any relevant interest to which the grantor is entitled, which—

        (i) is attributable to the grant of the rights or the exercise of them;

       (ii) does not consist of depreciation in the value of that interest; and

     (iii) is loss or damage of a kind in respect of which compensation for disturbance, or any other matter not directly based on the value of that interest, is payable on a compulsory acquisition;

    (d) damage to, or injurious affection of, any interest in land to which the grantor is entitled which is not a relevant interest, and which results from the grant of the rights or the exercise of them; and

    (e) loss in respect of work carried out by or on behalf of the grantor which is rendered abortive by the grant of the rights or the exercise of them.

Basis on which compensation assessed

5.—(1) The following provisions have effect for the purpose of assessing the amount to be paid by way of compensation under section 78G(5).

(2) The rules set out in section 5 of the 1961 Act (rules for assessing compensation), so far as applicable and subject to any necessary modifications, have effect for the purpose of assessing any such compensation as they have effect for the purpose of assessing compensation for the compulsory acquisition of an interest in land.

(3) No account must be taken of any enhancement of the value of any interest in land, by reason of any building erected, work done or improvement or alteration made on any land in which the grantor is, or was at the time of erection, doing or making, directly or indirectly concerned, if the Lands Tribunal is satisfied that the erection of the building, the doing of the work, the making of the improvement or the alteration was not reasonably necessary and was undertaken with a view to obtaining compensation or increased compensation.

(4) In calculating the amount of any loss under paragraph 4(e), expenditure incurred in the preparation of plans or on other similar preparatory matters must be taken into account.

(5) Where the interest in respect of which compensation is to be assessed is subject to a mortgage—

    (a) the compensation must be assessed as if the interest were not subject to the mortgage; and

    (b) no compensation is payable in respect of the interest of the mortgagee (as distinct from the interest which is subject to the mortgage).

(6) Compensation under section 78G(5) must include an amount equal to the grantor's reasonable valuation and legal expenses.

Payment of compensation and determination of disputes

6.—(1) Compensation payable under section 78G(5) in respect of an interest which is subject to a mortgage must be paid to the mortgagee or, if there is more than one mortgagee, to the first mortgagee and must, in either case, be applied by him as if it were proceeds of sale.

(2) Amounts of compensation determined under this Schedule are payable—

(a) where the appropriate person and the grantor or mortgagee agree that a single payment is to be made on a specified date, on that date;

(b) where the appropriate person and the grantor or mortgagee agree that payment is to be made in instalments on different dates, on the date agreed as regards each instalment; and

(c) in any other case, subject to any direction of the Lands Tribunal or the court, as soon as reasonably practicable after the amount of the compensation has been finally determined.

(3) Any question as to the application of paragraph 5(3) or of disputed compensation must be referred to and determined by the Lands Tribunal.

(4) In relation to the determination of any such question, sections 2 and 4 of the 1961 Act (which provide for the procedure on reference to the Lands Tribunal and costs) apply as if—

(a) the reference in section 2(1) of that Act to section 1 of that Act were a reference to sub-paragraph (3) of this paragraph; and

(b) references in section 4 of that Act to the acquiring authority were references to the appropriate person.

Schedule 3 Particulars Prescribed for the Purpose of Section 78R(1)

Remediation notices

1.—In relation to a remediation notice served by the enforcing authority—

(a) the name and address of the person on whom the notice is served;

(b) the location and extent of the contaminated land to which the notice relates, in sufficient detail to enable it to be identified whether by reference to a plan or otherwise;

(c) the significant harm, harm or pollution of controlled waters by reason of which the contaminated land in question is contaminated land;

(d) the substances by reason of which the contaminated land in question is contaminated land and, if any of the substances have escaped from other land, the location of that other land;

(e) the current use of the contaminated land in question;

(f) what each appropriate person is to do by way of remediation and the periods within which they are required to do each of the things; and

(g) the date of the notice.

Appeals against remediation notices

2.—Any appeal against a remediation notice served by the enforcing authority.

3.—Any decision on such an appeal.

Remediation declarations

4.—Any remediation declaration prepared and published by the enforcing authority under section 78H(6).

5.—In relation to any such remediation declaration—

    (a) the location and extent of the contaminated land in question, in sufficient detail to enable it to be identified, whether by reference to a plan or otherwise; and

    (b) the matters referred to in sub-paragraphs (c), (d) and (e) of paragraph 1.

Remediation statements

6.—Any remediation statement prepared and published by the responsible person under section 78H(7) or by the enforcing authority under section 78H(9).

7.—In relation to any such remediation statement—

    (a) the location and extent of the contaminated land in question, in sufficient detail to enable it to be identified, whether by reference to a plan or otherwise; and

    (b) the matters referred to in sub-paragraphs (c), (d) and (e) of paragraph 1.

Appeals against charging notices

8.—Any appeal under section 78P(8) against a charging notice served by the enforcing authority.

9.—Any decision on such an appeal.

Designation of special sites

10.—In the case of the Environment Agency, as respects any land in relation to which it is the enforcing authority, and in the case of a local authority, as respects any land in its area—

    (a) any notice given by a local authority under subsection (1)(b) or (5)(a) of section 78C, or by the Secretary of State under section 78D(4)(b), which, by virtue of section 78C(7) or section 78D(6) respectively, has effect as the designation of any land as a special site;

    (b) the provisions of regulation 2 or 3 by virtue of which the land is required to be designated as a special site;

    (c) any notice given by the Environment Agency under section 78Q(1)(a) of its decision to adopt a remediation notice; and

    (d) any notice given by or to the enforcing authority under section 78Q(4) terminating the designation of any land as a special site.

Notification of claimed remediation

11.—Any notification given to the enforcing authority for the purposes of section 78R(1)(h) or (j).

Convictions for offences under section 78M

12.—Any conviction of a person for any offence under section 78M in relation to a remediation notice served by the enforcing authority, including the name of the offender, the date of conviction, the penalty imposed and the name of the Court.

Guidance issued under section 78V(1)

13.—In the case of the Environment Agency, the date of any guidance issued by it under subsection (1) of section 78V and, in the case of a local authority, the date of any guidance issued by the Agency to it under that subsection.

Other environmental controls

14.—Where the enforcing authority is precluded by virtue of section 78YB(1) or 78YB(2B) from serving a remediation notice—

(a) the location and extent of the contaminated land in question, in sufficient detail to enable it to be identified, whether by reference to a plan or otherwise;

(b) the matters referred to in sub-paragraphs (c), (d) and (e) of paragraph 1; and

(c) any steps of which the authority has knowledge, carried out under section 27 or by means of enforcement action (within the meaning of section 78YB(2C)), towards remedying any significant harm, harm or pollution of controlled waters by reason of which the land in question is contaminated land.

15.—Where the enforcing authority is precluded by virtue of section 78YB(3) from serving a remediation notice in respect of land which is contaminated land by reason of the deposit of controlled waste or any consequences of its deposit—

(a) the location and extent of the contaminated land in question, in sufficient detail to enable it to be identified whether by reference to a plan or otherwise;

(b) the matters referred to in sub-paragraphs (c), (d) and (e) of paragraph 1; and

(c) any steps of which the enforcing authority has knowledge, carried out under section 59, in relation to that waste or the consequences of its deposit, and in a case where a waste collection authority (within the meaning of section 30(3)) took those steps or required the steps to be taken, the name of that authority.

16.—Where, as a result of a consent given under Chapter 2 of Part 3 of the Water Resources Act 1991 (pollution offences), the enforcing authority is precluded by virtue of section 78YB(4) from specifying in a remediation notice any particular thing by way of remediation which it would otherwise have specified in such a notice,—

(a) the consent;

(b) the location and extent of the contaminated land in question, in sufficient detail to enable it to be identified, whether by reference to a plan or otherwise; and

(c) the matters referred to in sub-paragraphs (c), (d) and (e) of paragraph 1.

Radioactive Contaminated Land (Modification of Enactments) (England) Regulations 2006/1379

Citation, commencement and application

1.—(1) These Regulations may be cited as the Radioactive Contaminated Land (Modification of Enactments)(England) Regulations 2006 and come into force on 4th August 2006.

(2) These Regulations apply in relation to England only.

Interpretation

2.—(1) In these Regulations "Part 2A" means Part 2A of the Environmental Protection Act 1990.

(2) Unless otherwise indicated, any reference to a numbered section is to the section of the Environmental Protection Act 1990 which bears that number.

Extension and modification of Part 2A

3. In so far as not already applied in relation to harm so far as attributable to any radioactivity possessed by any substance, Part 2A applies in relation to and for the purposes of dealing with such harm, and has effect with the modifications made by regulations 5 to 17.

Interpretation of modifications

4.—(1) The definitions set out in the Schedule (which reproduce definitions contained in Article 1 of the Directive) apply for the purpose of the interpretation of the modifications made by these Regulations to Part 2A.

(2) In this regulation and the Schedule, "the Directive" means Council Directive 96/29/Euratom laying down basic safety standards for the protection of the health of workers and the general public against the dangers arising from ionizing radiation, and for the purposes of the Schedule "this Directive" has the same meaning.

(3) In the Schedule, any reference to a numbered "Article" or "Title" is a reference to the Article or Title of that number in the Directive.

Section 78A (preliminary)

5.—(1) Section 78A (preliminary) has effect with the following modifications.

(2) For subsection (2), substitute—

"(2) "Contaminated land" is any land which appears to the local authority in whose area it is situated to be in such a condition, by reason of substances in, on or under the land, that—

(a) harm is being caused; or

(b) there is a significant possibility of harm being caused;

and in determining whether any land appears to be such land, a local authority shall, subject to subsection (5) below, act in accordance with guidance issued by the Secretary of State in accordance with section 78YA below with respect to the manner in which that determination is to be made.".

(3) For subsection (4), substitute—

"(4) "Harm" means lasting exposure to any person resulting from the after-effects of a radiological emergency, past practice or past work activity.".

(4) For subsection (5), substitute—

"(5) The questions—

(a) whether harm is being caused, and
(b) whether the possibility of harm being caused is "significant",

shall be determined in accordance with guidance issued for the purpose by the Secretary of State in accordance with section 78YA below.".

(5) For subsection (6), substitute—

"(6) Without prejudice to the guidance that may be issued under subsection (5) above—

(a) guidance under paragraph (a) of that subsection may make provision for different degrees and descriptions of harm;
(b) guidance under paragraph (b) of that subsection may make provision for different degrees of possibility to be regarded as "significant" (or as not being "significant") in relation to different descriptions of harm.".

(6) For subsection (7), substitute—

"(7) "Remediation" means—

(a) the doing of anything for the purpose of assessing the condition of—

(i) the contaminated land in question; or
(ii) any land adjoining or adjacent to that land;

(b) the doing of any works, the carrying out of any operations or the taking of any steps in relation to any such land for the purpose—

(i) of preventing or minimising, or remedying or mitigating the effects of, any harm by reason of which the contaminated land is such land; or
(ii) of restoring the land to its former state; or

(c) the making of subsequent inspections from time to time for the purpose of keeping under review the condition of the land;

and cognate expressions shall be construed accordingly.

(7A) For the purpose of paragraph (b) of subsection (7) above, "the doing of any works, the carrying out of any operations or the taking of any steps in relation to any such land" shall include ensuring that—

(a) any such area is demarcated;

(b) arrangements for the monitoring of the harm are made;

(c) any appropriate intervention is implemented; and

(d) access to or use of land or buildings situated in the demarcated area is regulated.".

(7) Subsection (8) is omitted.
(8) In subsection (9)—

(a) omit the definitions of "controlled waters" and "pollution of controlled waters"; and

(b) for the definition of "substance", substitute—

"'substance' means, whether in solid or liquid form or in the form of a gas or vapour, any substance which contains radionuclides which have resulted from the after-effects of a radiological emergency or which are or have been processed as part of a past practice or past work activity, but shall not include radon gas or the following radionuclides: Po-218, Pb-214, At-218, Bi-214, Rn-218, Po-214 and Tl-210;".

Section 78B (identification of contaminated land)

6.—(1) Section 78B (identification of contaminated land) has effect with the following modifications.

(2) For subsection (1), substitute—

"(1) Where a local authority considers that there are reasonable grounds for believing that any land may be contaminated, it shall cause the land to be inspected for the purpose of—

(a) identifying whether it is contaminated land; and

(b) enabling the authority to decide whether the land is land which is required to be designated as a special site.

(1A) The fact that substances have been or are present on the land shall not of itself be taken to be reasonable grounds for the purposes of subsection (1).".

Section 78C (identification and designation of special sites)

7.—(1) Section 78C (identification and designation of special sites) has effect with the following modifications.

(2) In subsection (10), for paragraphs (a) and (b), substitute—

"(a) whether land of the description in question appears to him to be land which is likely to be in such a condition, by reason of substances in, on or under the land that serious harm would or might be caused; or

(b) whether the appropriate Agency is likely to have expertise in dealing with the kind of harm by reason of which land of the description in question is contaminated land.".

Section 78E (duty of enforcing authority to require remediation of contaminated land etc)

8.—(1) Section 78E (duty of enforcing authority to require remediation of contaminated land etc) has effect with the following modifications.

(2) In subsection (2), omit "or waters".

(3) For subsection (4), substitute—

"(4) Subject to subsection (4A), the only things by way of remediation which the enforcing authority may do, or require to be done, under or by virtue of this Part are things which it considers reasonable, having regard to—

(a) the cost which is likely to be involved; and

(b) the seriousness of the harm in question.

(4A) Where remediation includes an intervention, that part of the remediation which consists of an intervention may only be considered reasonable—

(a) where the reduction in detriment due to radiation is sufficient to justify any adverse effects and costs, including social costs, of the intervention; and

(b) where the form, scale and duration of the intervention is optimised.

(4B) For the purpose of subsection (4A), the form, scale and duration of the intervention shall be taken to be optimised if the benefit of the reduction in health detriment less the detriment associated with the intervention is maximised.".

(4) In subsection (5), in paragraph (b), omit ", or waters are,".

Section 78F (determination of the appropriate person to bear responsibility for remediation)

9. Subsection (9) of section 78F (determination of the appropriate person to bear responsibility for remediation) has effect with the insertion, after "biological process", of "or radioactive decay".

Section 78G (grant of, and compensation for, rights of entry etc)

10.—(1) Section 78G (grant of, and compensation for, rights of entry etc) has effect with the following modifications.

(2) In subsection (2), for "any of the relevant land or waters", substitute "any relevant land".

(3) In subsection (3), in paragraph (a), omit "or waters".

(4) In subsection (4), omit ", or serious pollution of controlled waters,".

(5) For subsection (7), substitute—

"(7) In this section, "relevant land" means—

(a) the contaminated land in question; or

(b) any land adjoining or adjacent to that land.".

Section 78H (restrictions and prohibitions on serving remediation notices)

11. Subsection (4) of section 78H (restrictions and prohibitions on serving remediation notices) has effect with the omission of ", or serious pollution of controlled waters,".

Section 78J (restrictions on liability relating to the pollution of controlled waters)

12. Section 78J is omitted.

Section 78K (liability in respect of contaminating substances which escape to other land)

13.—(1) Section 78K (liability in respect of contaminating substances which escape to other land) has effect with the following modifications.

(2) For subsection (3), substitute—

"(3) Where this subsection applies, no remediation notice shall require a person—

(a) who is the owner or occupier of land A, and

(b) who has not caused or knowingly permitted the substances in question to be in, on or under that land,

to do anything by way of remediation to any land (other than land of which he is the owner or occupier) in consequence of land A appearing to be in such a condition, by reason of the presence of those substances in, on or under it, that harm is being caused, or there is a significant possibility of harm being caused.".

(3) For subsection (4), substitute—

"(4) Where this subsection applies, no remediation notice shall require a person—

(a) who is the owner or occupier of land A, and
(b) who has not caused or knowingly permitted the substances in question to be in, on or under that land,

to do anything by way of remediation in consequence of any further land in, on or under which those substances or any of them appear to be or to have been present as a result of their escape from land A ("land B") appearing to be in such a condition, by reason of the presence of those substances in, on or under it, that harm is being caused, or there is a significant possibility of such harm being caused, unless he is also the owner or occupier of land B.".

Section 78N (powers of the enforcing authority to carry out remediation)

14.—(1) Section 78N (powers of the enforcing authority to carry out remediation) has effect with the following modifications.

(2) In subsection (1), omit "or waters".

(3) After subsection (1), insert—

"(1A) The enforcing authority shall exercise its power under subsection (1) in any case falling within paragraph (c), (d), (e) or (f) of subsection (3).

(1B) If the Secretary of State thinks fit, he may make available to the enforcing authority a sum or sums of money in respect of costs and expenses incurred or to be incurred by the enforcing authority (or by a person on its behalf) in relation to the exercise of its duty under subsection (1A) provided that—

(a) the amount of such costs and expenses exceeds or is expected to exceed any reasonable provision for such costs and expenses made by the appropriate Agency; and
(b) the total amount made available does not exceed the difference between the amount of such costs and expenses and the amount of such provision.".

(4) In subsection (3)(a), omit ", or serious pollution of controlled waters,".

(5) In subsections (3)(d) and (4)(d), omit "78J or".

(6) For subsection (5), substitute—

"(5) In this section "the relevant land" means—

(a) the contaminated land in question; or
(b) any land adjoining or adjacent to that land.".

Section 78P (recovery of, and security for, the cost of remediation by the enforcing authority)

15. Subsection (1) of section 78P (recovery of, and security for, the cost of remediation by the enforcing authority) has effect with the substitution for "sections 78J(7) and" of "section".

Section 78X (supplementary provisions)

16.—(1) Section 78X (supplementary provisions) has effect with the following modifications.

(2) For subsection (1), substitute—

"(1) Where it appears to a local authority that two or more different sites, when considered together, are in such a condition, by reason of substances in, on or under the land, that—

(a) harm is being caused, or

(b) there is a significant possibility of harm being caused,

this Part shall apply in relation to each of those sites, whether or not the condition of the land at any of them, when considered alone, appears to the authority to be such that harm is being caused or there is a significant possibility of harm being caused.".

(3) For subsection (2), substitute—

"(2) Where it appears to a local authority that any land outside, but adjoining or adjacent to, its area is in such a condition, by reason of substances in, on or under the land, that harm is being caused, or there is a significant possibility of harm being caused within its area—

(a) the authority may, in exercising its functions under this Part, treat that land as if it were land situated within its area; and

(b) except in this subsection, any reference—

(i) to land within the area of a local authority, or

(ii) to the local authority in whose area any land is situated,

shall be construed accordingly;

but this subsection is without prejudice to the functions of the local authority in whose area the land is in fact situated.".

Section 78YB (interaction of Part 2A with other enactments)

17.—(1) Section 78YB (interaction of Part 2A with other enactments) has effect with the following modifications.

(2) For subsection (1), substitute—

"(1) A remediation notice shall not be served if and to the extent that it appears to the enforcing authority that the powers of the appropriate Agency under section 27 above may be exercised in relation to the harm (if any) by reason of which the contaminated land in question is such land.".

(3) In subsections (2), (2A) and (2B), for "significant harm, or pollution of controlled waters" substitute "harm".

(4) After subsection (4), insert—

"(5) Nothing in this Part applies to land which is contaminated land by reason of the presence in, on or under that land of any substances, in so far as by reason of that presence damage to any property occurs, being—

(a) damage caused in breach of any duty imposed by section 7, 8, 9 or 10 of the 1965 Act, or deemed to be so caused by section 12(2) of that Act;

(b) damage which would have been so caused if, in section 7(1)(a) or (b) of the 1965 Act, the words "other than the licensee" or, in section 10(1) of that Act, the words "other than the operator" had not been enacted; or

(c) damage in respect of which any relevant foreign operator or other person is liable under any relevant foreign law, or for which he would be so liable—

    (i) but for any exclusion or limitation of liability applying by virtue of any provision of that law made for purposes corresponding to those of section 13(3) or (4)(a), 15, 16(1) and (2) or 18 of the 1965 Act; or

    (ii) if any such relevant foreign law which does not contain provision made for purposes corresponding to those of section 13(4)(b) of the 1965 Act did contain such provision.

(6) In subsection (5)—
"the 1965 Act" means the Nuclear Installations Act 1965;
"relevant foreign law" and "relevant foreign operator" have the meanings given by the 1965 Act.".

Modification of the Environment Act 1995

18.—(1) In its application in relation to harm so far as attributable to any radioactivity possessed by any substance, the Environment Act 1995 has effect with the modifications mentioned in paragraph (2).

(2) Subsection (15) of section 108 (powers of enforcing authorities and persons authorised by them) has effect with the following modifications—

(a) in the definition of "pollution control functions", in relation to the Agency or SEPA, after paragraph (m), insert—

    "(n) regulations made by virtue of section 78YC of the Environmental Protection Act 1990;"; and

(b) in the definition of "pollution control functions", in relation to a local enforcing authority, after paragraph (c), insert—

"or
(d) by or under regulations made by virtue of section 78YC of the Environmental Protection Act 1990;".".

SCHEDULE
DIRECTIVE DEFINITIONS

Activity (A): the activity, A, of an amount of a radionuclide in a particular energy state at a given time is the quotient of dN by dt, where dN is the expectation value of the number of spontaneous nuclear transitions from that energy state in the time interval dt:

$$A + \frac{dN}{dt}$$

the unit of activity is the becquerel.

Apprentice: a person receiving training or instruction within an undertaking with a view to exercising a specific skill.

Artificial sources: radiation sources other than natural radiation sources.

Becquerel (Bq): is the special name of the unit of activity. One becquerel is equivalent to one transition per second:

$1 \text{ Bq} + 1 \text{ s}^{-1}$.

Dose limits: maximum references laid down in Title IV for the doses resulting from the exposure of workers, apprentices and students and members of the public to ionizing radiation covered by this Directive that apply to the sum of the relevant doses from external exposures in the specified period and the 50–year committed doses (up to age 70 for children) from intakes in the same period.

Emergency exposure: an exposure of individuals implementing the necessary rapid action to bring help to endangered individuals, prevent exposure of a large number of people or save a valuable installation or goods, whereby one of the individual dose limits equal to that laid down for exposed workers could be exceeded. Emergency exposure shall apply only to volunteers.

Exposed workers: persons, either self-employed or working for an employer, subject to an exposure incurred at work from practices covered by this Directive and liable to result in doses exceeding one or other of the dose levels equal to the dose limits for members of the public.

Exposure: the process of being exposed to ionizing radiation.

Health detriment: an estimate of the risk of reduction in length and quality of life occurring in a population following exposure to ionizing radiations. This includes loss arising from somatic effects, cancer and severe genetic disorder.

Intake: the activities of radionuclides entering the body from the external environment.

Intervention: a human activity that prevents or decreases the exposure of individuals to radiation from sources which are not part of a practice or which are out of control, by acting on sources, transmission pathways and individuals themselves.

Ionizing radiation: the transfer of energy in the form of particles or electromagnetic waves of a wavelength of 100 nanometers or less or a frequency of 3 x 1015 Hertz or more capable of producing ions directly or indirectly.

Members of the public: individuals in the population, excluding exposed workers, apprentices and students during their working hours and individuals during the exposures referred to in Article 6(4)(a), (b) and (c).

Natural radiation sources: sources of ionizing radiation from natural terrestrial or cosmic origin.

Practice: a human activity that can increase the exposure of individuals to radiation from an artificial source, or from a natural radiation source where natural radionuclides are processed for their radioactive, fissile or fertile properties, except in the case of an emergency exposure.

Radioactive substance: any substance that contains one or more radionuclides the activity or concentration of which cannot be disregarded as far as radiation protection is concerned.

Radiological emergency: a situation that requires urgent action in order to protect workers, members of the public or the population either partially or as a whole.

Source: an apparatus, a radioactive substance or an installation capable of emitting ionizing radiation or radioactive substances.

Undertaking: any natural or legal person who carries out the practices or work activities referred to in Article 2 of this Directive and who has the legal responsibility under national law for such practices or work activities.

DEFRA Circular 01/2006
Environmental Protection Act 1990

Part IIA: Contaminated Land

1 I have been asked by the Secretary of State for Environment, Food and Rural Affairs to draw your attention to the entry into force of an extended statutory regime for the identification and remediation of contaminated land with effect from 4 August 2006. This extended regime consists of Part 2A of the Environmental Protection Act 1990, as originally introduced on 1 April 2000 together with changes intended chiefly to address land that is contaminated by virtue of radioactivity. The changes are outlined at paragraph 6 to 8 below.

2 For this purpose, the Secretary of State has made the Radioactive Contaminated Land (Enabling Powers) (England) Regulations 2005 (S.I. 2005/3467) and the Radioactive Contaminated Land (Modification of Enactments) (England) Regulations 2006 (S.I. 2006/1379). He has also made the Contaminated Land (England) Regulations 2006 (S.I. 2006/1380), which have been made under sections 78C, 78E, 78G, 78L, 78R and 78X of the Environmental Protection Act 1990. The Environmental Protection Act 1990 (Isles of Scilly) Order 2006 (S.I. 2006/1381) applies Part 2A to the Isles of Scilly only in relation to harm attributable to radioactivity.

3 He has also made the Clean Neighbourhoods and Environment Act 2005 (Commencement No. 2) (England) Order 2006 (S.I. 2006/1361), in order to commence section 104 of the Clean Neighbourhoods and Environment Act 2005, in England. Section 104 amends the arrangements for appeals to remediation notices served by local authorities. Such appeals must be made to the Secretary of State, instead of to the magistrates' court, where a remediation notice is served on or after 4 August 2006. Further details are given in Annex 4.

Purpose of this circular

4 This Circular replaces DETR Circular 02/2000, published in March 2000. It has two functions: first it promulgates the statutory guidance as now amended, which is an essential part of the regime; secondly, it sets out the way in which the extended regime is expected to work, by providing a summary of Government policy in this field, a description of the regime, and a guide to the other relevant Regulations and Commencement Orders.

5 This Circular applies only to England. Responsibility for implementing Part 2A in Scotland and Wales rests with the Scottish Executive and the National Assembly for Wales, respectively.

The main changes in brief

6 The extended regime as described in this Circular will apply to radioactive contamination of land in addition to the contamination covered

previously. Part 2A made provision for the regime to be applied to such radioactive contamination with such modifications as the Secretary of State considers appropriate. Following a consultation exercise in July 2005, the Radioactive Contaminated Land (Enabling Powers) (England) Regulations 2005 were made in January to enable the regime to be extended and guidance issued. The new Statutory Instruments and this Circular complete the process of extension.

7 Apart from the extension to include radioactivity, only one substantive change has been made to the Part 2A regime, concerning the arrangements for appeals against remediation notices served by local authorities. The Secretary of State is now the appellate authority for such appeals. See paragraph 3 above and Annex 4.

8 In respect of radioactivity, details of Government policy and the related changes to the Part 2A regime are set out in the second part of Annex 1 to this Circular.

Statutory guidance

9 The Secretary of State for the Environment, Food and Rural Affairs hereby issues the amendments to statutory guidance in Annex 3 to this circular. This guidance is issued under the following powers:

(a) *The Definition of Contaminated Land*—Chapter A of Annex 3 to this circular sets out guidance issued under section 78A(2) and (5) (as modified) and 78A(2) and (5);

(b) *The Identification of Contaminated Land*—Chapter B of Annex 3 to this circular sets out guidance issued under section 78A(2) and 78B(2);

(c) *The Remediation of Contaminated Land*—Chapter C of Annex 3 to this circular sets out guidance issued under section 78E(5);

(d) *Exclusion from, and Apportionment of, Liability for Remediation*—Chapter D of Annex 3 to this circular sets out guidance issued under section 78F(6) and (7); and

(e) *The Recovery of the Costs of Remediation*—Chapter E of Annex 3 to this Circular sets out guidance issued under section 78P(2).

10 Section 78YA states that before the Secretary of State can issue any guidance under Part 2A, he must consult the Environment Agency and such other persons as he considers it appropriate to consult. Drafts of all the original guidance were published for consultation in September 1996, October 1998 and October 1999. Amendments in respect of the extension of the regime to radioactivity were published for consultation in 2005. The guidance as now amended and contained in Annex 3 to this Circular has been prepared in the light of responses to those consultation exercises.

11 In addition, section 78YA requires the Secretary of State to lay a draft of any guidance he proposes to issue under sections 78A(2) or (5), 78B(2) or 78F(5) or (6) before each House of Parliament for approval under the negative resolution procedure. The original statutory guidance was laid in draft before both Houses on 7 February 2000, and amendments to that guidance were laid in draft before both Houses on 23 May 2006. Annex 3 contains a consolidated version of the statutory guidance and the new amendments.

Financial and manpower implications

12 The financial and manpower implications of the Part 2A regime were addressed in the previous DETR Circular. Additional resources were

provided for local authorities and the Environment Agency. The additional burden of extending the regime to include radioactivity is considered small and provisional funding of £400,000 for local authorities and £333,000 for the Environment Agency has been allocated for 2006/7. On the basis of experience to date, capital requirements are likely to be covered at least in the first few years of the extended regime by existing budgets. New information on need, when available, will be taken into account in future Government spending reviews.

Regulatory Impact Assessment

13 A Regulatory Impact Assessment (RIA) on the original implementation of the Part 2A regime was prepared and published in 2000. A partial RIA for the proposed extension of the regime to include radioactivity was published for consultation in July 2005. Comments received in response to that consultation have been taken into account in the final RIA, which was published on 23 May 2006.

14 Copies of the RIA are available from the address shown in paragraph 15 below or from the Defra website.

Enquiries

15 Enquiries about particular sites and how they may be affected by the regime should be directed, in the first instance, to the local authority in whose area they are situated.

16 DETR Circular 02/2000 *"Contaminated Land"* is revoked, except in relation to formal Part 2A actions currently underway on land which has already been determined as contaminated land.

17 Enquiries about this Circular should be addressed to:

Contaminated Land Branch
Local Environment Quality Division
Defra
Zone 7/D10 Ashdown House
123 Victoria Street
London SW1E 6DE

Phone: (020) 7082 8568
E-mail: landquality.enquiries@defra.gsi.gov.uk
www.defra.gov.uk

Sue Ellis, Assistant Secretary

The Chief Executive
  District Councils
  Unitary Authorities
  London Borough Councils
  The Environment Agency
  Council of the Isles of Scilly
The Town Clerk, City of London

Contents

A STATEMENT OF GOVERNMENT POLICY

The first part of this annex (paragraphs 1 to 64) deals with overall policy, which is substantively unchanged from DETR Circular 02/2000, while the second part (paragraphs 65 onwards) is new and deals specifically with radioactivity, including details of the extension of the regime.

Sustainable development

1 In his foreword to "*A better quality of life: A strategy for sustainable development for the UK,*" the Prime Minister, the Rt Hon Tony Blair MP, said:

"The last hundred years have seen a massive increase in the wealth of this country and the well-being of its people. But focusing solely on economic growth risks ignoring the impact - both good and bad - on people and on the environment. Had we taken account of these links in our decision making, we might have reduced or avoided costs such as contaminated land or social exclusion."

Preventing new contamination

2 Contaminated land is an archetypal example of our failure in the past to move towards sustainable development. We must learn from that failure. The first priority for the Government's policy on land contamination is therefore to prevent the creation of new contamination. We have created a range of regimes aimed at achieving this. Of these, the most significant are:

(a) *Integrated Pollution Control (IPC)*—Part I of the Environmental Protection Act 1990 ("the 1990 Act") placed a requirement on operators of prescribed industrial processes to operate within the terms of permits to control harmful environmental discharges;

(b) *Pollution Prevention and Control (PPC)*—This regime has been introduced to replace IPC, and includes the specific requirement that permits for industrial plants and installations must include conditions to prevent the pollution of soil; and there are also requirements in relation to the land filling of waste;

(c) *Waste Management Licensing*—Part 2 of the 1990 Act places controls over the handling, treatment and disposal of wastes; in the past, much land contamination has been the result of unregulated, or badly-managed, waste disposal activities.

3 Although the prevention of new contamination is of critical importance, the focus of this Circular is on land which has been contaminated in the past. With effect from 4 August 2006, this includes land contaminated by radioactivity (see paragraph 75 below).

Our inherited legacy of contaminated land

4 As well as acting to prevent new contamination, we have also to deal with a substantial legacy of land which is already contaminated, for example by past industrial, mining and waste disposal activities. It is not known, in detail, how much land is contaminated. This can be found out only through wide-ranging and detailed site investigation and risk assessment.

The answer critically depends on the definition used to establish what land counts as being "contaminated".

5 Various estimates have been made of the extent of the problem. In its report Contaminated Land, published in 1993, the Parliamentary Office of Science and Technology referred to expert estimates of between 50,000 and 100,000 potentially contaminated sites across the UK, with estimates of the extent of land ranging between 100,000 and 200,000 hectares. However, the report did note that international experience suggested that only a small proportion of potentially contaminated sites posed an immediate threat to human health and the environment. The Environment Agency estimates that that there may be some 300,000 hectares of land in England and Wales affected to some extent by industrial contamination (ref: Environment Agency *"Indicators for Land Contamination"*—Science report SC030039/SR).

6 The existence of contamination presents its own threats to sustainable development:

(a) it impedes social progress, depriving local people of a clean and healthy environment;

(b) it threatens wider damage to the environment and to wildlife;

(c) it inhibits the prudent use of our land and soil resources, particularly by obstructing the recycling of previously-developed land and increasing development pressures on greenfield areas; and

(d) the cost of remediation represents a high burden on individual companies, home—and other land-owners, and the economy as a whole.

7 In this context, the Government's objectives with respect to contaminated land are:

(a) to identify and remove unacceptable risks to human health and the environment;

(b) to seek to bring damaged land back into beneficial use; and

(c) to seek to ensure that the cost burdens faced by individuals, companies and society as a whole are proportionate, manageable and economically sustainable.

8 These three objectives underlie the "suitable for use" approach to the remediation of contaminated land, which the Government considers is the most appropriate approach to achieving sustainable development in this field.

The "suitable for use" approach

9 The "suitable for use" approach focuses on the risks caused by land contamination. The approach recognises that the risks presented by any given level of contamination will vary greatly according to the use of the land and a wide range of other factors, such as the underlying geology of the site. Risks therefore need to be assessed on a site-by-site basis.

10 The "suitable for use" approach then consists of three elements:

(a) **ensuring that land is suitable for its current use**—in other words, identifying any land where contamination is causing unacceptable risks to human health and the environment, assessed on the basis of the current use and circumstances of the land, and returning such land to a condition where such risks no longer arise ("remediating" the land); the contaminated land regime provides general machinery to achieve this;

(b) **ensuring that land is made suitable for any new use, as planning permission is given for that new use**—in other words, assessing the potential risks from contamination, on the basis of the proposed future use and circumstances, before official permission is given for the development and, where necessary to avoid unacceptable risks to human health and the environment, remediating the land before the new use commences; this is the role of the town and country planning and building control regimes; and

(c) **limiting requirements for remediation to the work necessary to prevent unacceptable risks to human health or the environment in relation to the current use or future use of the land for which planning permission is being sought**—in other words, recognising that the risks from contaminated land can be satisfactorily assessed only in the context of specific uses of the land (whether current or proposed), and that any attempt to guess what might be needed at some time in the future for other uses is likely to result either in premature work (thereby risking distorting social, economic and environmental priorities) or in unnecessary work (thereby wasting resources).

11 Within this framework, it is important to recognise both that the use of any particular area of land may cover several different activities and that some potential risks arising from contamination (particularly impacts on water and the wider environment) may arise independently of the use of the land. In practical terms, the current use of any land should be taken to be any use which:

(a) is currently being made of the land, or is likely to be made of it; and

(b) is consistent with any existing planning permission or is otherwise lawful under town and country planning legislation.

(This approach is explained in more detail in paragraph A.26 of Annex 3 to this Circular and for the extended regime in paragraph A.43.)

12 Regulatory action may be needed to make sure that necessary remediation is carried out. However, limiting remediation costs to what is needed to avoid unacceptable risks will mean that we will be able to recycle more previously-developed land than would otherwise be the case, increasing our ability to make beneficial use of the land. This helps to increase the social, economic and environmental benefits from regeneration projects and to reduce unnecessary development pressures on greenfield sites.

13 The "suitable for use" approach provides the best means of reconciling our various environmental, social and economic needs in relation to contaminated land. Taken together with tough action to prevent new contamination, and wider initiatives to promote the reclamation of previously-developed land, it will also help to bring about progressive improvements in the condition of the land which we pass on to future generations.

14 Within the "suitable for use" approach, it is always open to the person responsible for a site to do more than can be enforced through regulatory action. For example, a site owner may plan to introduce at a future date some new use for the land which would require more stringent remediation, and may conclude that, in these circumstances, it is more economic to anticipate those remediation requirements. However, this is a judgement which only the person responsible for the site is in a position to make.

15 The one exception to the "suitable for use" approach to regulatory action applies where contamination has resulted from a specific breach of an

environmental licence or permit. In such circumstances, the Government considers that it is generally appropriate that the polluter is required, under the relevant regulatory regime, to remove the contamination completely. To do otherwise would be to undermine the regulatory regimes aimed at preventing new contamination.

Action to deal with contamination

Voluntary remediation action

16 The Government aims to maintain the quality of the land in this country and to improve it progressively where it has been degraded in the past. Redeveloping areas where previous development has reached the end of its useful life not only contributes to social and economic regeneration of the local communities but is also an important driver in achieving this progressive environmental improvement.

17 It is, of course, necessary to ensure that when previously-developed land, or any other land, is redeveloped any potential risks associated with contamination are properly identified and remediated. The planning and building control systems, described at paragraphs 41 to 44 below, provide the means of achieving this.

18 There are very few cases where land cannot be restored or adapted to some beneficial use. However, the actual or potential existence of contamination on a site can inhibit the willingness or ability of a developer to do so. The Government is acting in three specific ways to overcome the potential obstacles to the redevelopment of land affected by contamination:

  (a) *by promoting urban regeneration*—substantial support is provided to help bring under used land back into use;

  (b) *by promoting research and development*—the programmes of the science research councils, the Environment Agency, and others aim to increase scientific understanding and the availability and take-up of improved methods of risk assessment and remediation; and

  (c) *by providing an appropriate policy and legal framework*—the "suitable for use" approach ensures that remediation requirements are reasonable and tailored to the needs of individual sites; a significant objective underlying the contaminated land regime is to improve the clarity and certainty of potential regulatory action on contamination, thereby assisting developers to make informed investment appraisals.

Regulatory action

19 The regeneration process is already dealing with much of our inherited legacy of contaminated land. But there will be circumstances where contamination is causing unacceptable risks on land which is either not suitable or not scheduled for redevelopment. For example, there may be contamination on sites now regarded as greenbelt or rural land, or contamination may be affecting the health of occupants of existing buildings on the land or prejudicing wildlife on the site or in its surroundings. We therefore need systems in place both to identify problem sites of this kind and, more significantly, to ensure that the problems are dealt with and the contamination remediated.

20 A range of specific clean-up powers exists to deal with cases where contamination is the result of offences against, or breaches of, pollution

prevention regimes. The main examples of these are described in paragraphs 45 to 54 below.

21 Part 2A of the Environmental Protection Act 1990 provides a framework for the identification and remediation of contaminated land in circumstances where there has not been any identifiable breach of a pollution prevention regime.

22 Although Part 2A itself is relatively recent, it largely replaced existing regulatory powers and duties. Borough and district councils have long-standing duties to identify particular environmental problems, including those resulting from land contamination, and to require their abatement. The origin of these powers is found in the mid-19th century legislation which created the concept of statutory nuisance. They were codified in the Public Health Act 1936 and have most recently been set out in Part 3 of the Environmental Protection Act 1990, which modernised the statutory nuisance regime.

23 In addition, the Environment Agency has powers under Part 7 of the Water Resources Act 1991 to take action to prevent or remedy the pollution of controlled waters, including circumstances where the pollution arises from contamination in the land.

The contaminated land regime

Objectives for the regime

24 The main objective underlying the introduction of the Part 2A contaminated land regime was to provide an improved system for the identification and remediation of land where contamination is causing unacceptable risks to human health or the wider environment, assessed in the context of the current use and circumstances of the land.

25 As stated in paragraph 22 above, the regime broadly reflects the approaches already in place under the statutory nuisance regime and Part 7 of the Water Resources Act 1991. The Government's primary objectives for introducing the regime were:

(a) to improve the focus and transparency of the controls, ensuring authorities take a strategic approach to problems of land contamination;

(b) to enable all problems resulting from contamination to be handled as part of the same process; previously separate regulatory action was needed to protect human health and to protect the water environment;

(c) to increase the consistency of approach taken by different authorities; and

(d) to provide a more tailored regulatory mechanism, including liability rules, better able to reflect the complexity and range of circumstances found on individual sites.

26 In addition to providing a more secure basis for direct regulatory action, the Government considers that the improved clarity and consistency of the regime, in comparison with its predecessors, is also likely to encourage voluntary remediation. This forms an important secondary objective for the Part 2A regime.

27 Companies who may be responsible for contamination, for example on land they currently own or on former production sites, are able to assess the likely requirements of regulators acting under Part 2A. They are then

able to plan their own investment programmes to carry out remediation in advance of actual regulatory intervention.

28 Similarly, the Part 2A regime will assist in the recycling of previously-developed land. The regime cannot be used directly to require the redevelopment of land, only its remediation. However, the Government considers that implementation of the regime will assist developers by reducing uncertainties about so-called "residual liabilities", in particular the perceived risk of further regulatory intervention. In particular it will:

(a) reinforce the "suitable for use" approach, enabling developers to design and implement appropriate and cost-effective remediation schemes as part of their redevelopment projects;

(b) clarify the circumstances in which future regulatory intervention might be necessary (for example, if the initial remediation scheme proved not to be effective in the long term); and

(c) set out the framework for statutory liabilities to pay for any further remediation, should that be necessary.

Outline of Part 2A and associated documents

29 The primary legislation in Part 2A contains the structure and main provisions of the regime. It consists of sections 78A to 78YC. These are modified in relation to radioactivity by the Radioactive Contaminated Land (Modification of Enactments) Regulation 2006. An explanation of how the regime operates is set out in Annex 2 to this Circular.

30 Within the structure of the Part 2A legislation, the statutory guidance set out in Annex 3 to this Circular provides the detailed framework for the following key elements of the regime:

(a) the definition of contaminated land (Chapter A);

(b) the identification of contaminated land (Chapter B);

(c) the remediation of contaminated land (Chapter C);

(d) exclusion from, and apportionment of, liability for remediation (Chapter D); and

(e) the recovery of the costs of remediation and the relief from hardship (Chapter E).

31 The Contaminated Land Regulations made under Part 2A deal with:

(a) the descriptions of land which are required to be designated as "special sites";

(b) the contents of, and arrangements for serving, remediation notices;

(c) compensation to third parties for granting rights of entry etc. to land;

(d) grounds of appeal against a remediation notice, and procedures relating to any such appeal; and

(e) particulars to be contained in registers compiled by enforcing authorities, and the locations at which such registers must be available for public inspection.

32 Annex 4 to this Circular provides a detailed description of the Contaminated Land Regulations. The Modification Regulations and other regulations are described in Annex 5 to this Circular.

Main features of the Part 2A regime

33 The primary regulatory role under Part 2A rests with local authorities:

(a) in Greater London, this means the London borough councils, the City of London and the Temples; and

(b) elsewhere it means the borough or district councils or, where appropriate, the unitary authority.

34 This reflects their existing functions under the statutory nuisance regime, and also complements their roles as planning authorities. In outline, the role of these authorities under Part 2A are:

(a) to cause their areas to be inspected to identify contaminated land;

(b) to determine whether any particular site is contaminated land;

(c) to act as enforcing authority for all contaminated land which is not designated as a "special site" (the Environment Agency will be the enforcing authority for special sites).

35 The enforcing authorities have four main tasks:

(a) to establish who should bear responsibility for the remediation of the land (the "appropriate person" or persons);

(b) to decide, after consultation, what remediation is required in any individual case and to ensure that such remediation takes place, either through agreement with the appropriate person, or by serving a remediation notice on the appropriate person if agreement is not possible or, in certain circumstances, through carrying out the work themselves;

(c) where a remediation notice is served, or the authority itself carries out the work, to determine who should bear what proportion of the liability for meeting the costs of the work; and

(d) to record certain prescribed information about their regulatory actions on a public register.

36 Contaminated land is land which appears to the local authority to be in such a condition, by reason of substances in, on or under the land, that significant harm is being caused, or there is a significant possibility of such harm being caused, or that pollution of controlled waters is being, or is likely to be, caused. The definition is "modified" where harm is attributable to radioactivity (see paragraph 76). The definition is to be applied in accordance with other definitions in Part 2A and statutory guidance set out in this Circular. These definitions and the guidance are based on the assessment of unacceptable risks to human health and the environment in relation to the current use of the land. The regime thus reflects the "suitable for use" approach.

37 Under the provisions concerning liabilities, responsibility for paying for remediation will, where feasible, follow the "polluter pays" principle. In the first instance, any persons who caused or knowingly permitted the contaminating substances to be in, on or under the land will be the appropriate person(s) to undertake the remediation and meet its costs. However, if it is not possible to find any such person, responsibility will pass to the current owner or occupier of the land. (This latter step does not apply where the problem caused by the contamination is solely one of water pollution: this reflects the potential liabilities for water pollution as they existed prior to the introduction of Part 2A.) Responsibility will also be subject to limitations, for example where hardship might be caused; these limitations are set out in Part 2A and in the statutory guidance in this Circular.

38 The Environment Agency has four principal roles with respect to contaminated land under Part 2A. It will:

(a) assist local authorities in identifying contaminated land, particularly in cases where water pollution is involved;

(b) provide site-specific guidance to local authorities on contaminated land;

(c) act as the "enforcing authority" for any land designated as a "special site" (the descriptions of land which are required to be designated in this way are prescribed in the Contaminated Land Regulations); and

(d) publish periodic reports on contaminated land.

Technical material

39 In addition, the Agency carries out technical research and, in conjunction with Defra publishes scientific and technical advice. Key examples are CLR 11 *"Model Procedures for the Management of Land Contamination"* and CLRs 7–10 on Human Health Risk Assessment. Details can be found on the Defra and the Environment Agency websites. Other organisations also offer a range of technical advice documents relating to contaminated land. There is also a procedural guide for local authorities, available from the Chartered Institute of Environmental Health, which is now being modified for the extended regime.

Measuring progress

40 Best Value Performance Indicators were introduced in 2005 which will help to assess overall progress in the task of identifying our inherited legacy of contaminated land and ensuring its remediation. These recognise that Part 2A action is not the sole measure of progress. In addition, information is gathered by the Environment Agency as part of its role in preparing periodic reports on contaminated land.

Interaction with other regimes

Planning and development control

41 Land contamination, or the possibility of it, is a material consideration for the purposes of town and country planning. This means that a planning authority has to consider the potential implications of contamination both when it is developing plans and when it is considering individual applications for planning permission. Planning Policy Statement 23, *"Planning and Pollution Control"*, published by ODPM, and in particular Annex 2 *"Development on Land Affected by Contamination"* sets out policy and practice in detail, including the relationship with Part 2A.

42 In some cases, the carrying out of remediation activities may itself constitute "development" within the meaning given at section 55 of the Town and Country Planning Act 1990, and therefore require planning permission.

43 In addition to the planning system, the Building Regulations (made under the Building Act 1984) requires measures to be taken to protect new buildings, and their future occupants, from the effects of contamination. *"Approved Document Part C (Site Preparation and Resistance to Moisture)"* published in 2004 gives guidance on these requirements.

44 In any case where new development is taking place, it will be the responsibility of the developer to carry out the necessary remediation. In

most cases, the enforcement of any remediation requirements will be through planning conditions and building control, rather than through a remediation notice issued under Part 2A.

Integrated pollution control

45 Section 27 of the Environmental Protection Act 1990 gives the Environment Agency the power to take action to remedy harm caused by a breach of IPC controls under section 23(1)(a) or (c) of the Act. This could apply to cases of land contamination arising from such causes. In any case where an enforcing authority acting under Part 2A considers that the section 27 power is exercisable, it is precluded by section 78YB(1) from serving a remediation notice to remedy the same harm.

Pollution prevention and control

46 There are three main areas of potential interaction between the Part 2A regime and the regime introduced by the Pollution Prevention and Control Act 1999, and the Pollution Prevention and Control (England and Wales) Regulations 2000 ("the PPC regulations"). Schedule 10 paragraph 6 of the PPC regulations amended Part 2A (section 78YB) to ensure an effective interaction between the two regimes.

47 Firstly, there may be significant harm or pollution of controlled waters arising from land for which a permit is in force under the PPC regulations. Under section 78YB(2A), Part 2A does not apply if, and to the extent that, this harm or pollution is attributable to the final disposal by deposit in, on or under land of controlled waste and enforcement action under the PPC regime may be taken in relation to that activity. The land cannot formally be identified as "contaminated land" and no remediation notice can be served.

48 Secondly, under section 78YB(2B), an enforcing authority acting under Part 2A cannot serve a remediation notice if and to the extent that the significant harm or pollution of controlled waters in question is attributable to an activity other than the final disposal by deposit of waste, and enforcement action under the PPC regime may be taken in relation to that activity.

49 If action is needed to deal with a pollution problem in either of these cases, this would normally be addressed by a PPC "enforcement action" - this is either a notice by the PPC regulator under regulation 24, or the use of the regulator's powers to remedy pollution under regulation 26(2) of the PPC regulations. Part 2A does apply if and to the extent that the harm or pollution on a PPC site is attributable to other causes or cannot be the subject of "enforcement action" under the PPC regime.

50 Thirdly, remediation activities may themselves constitute activities or processes which cannot be carried out without a permit issued under the PPC regime.

Waste on land

51 There are three areas of potential interaction between the Part 2A regime and the waste management licensing system under Part 2 of the Environmental Protection Act 1990.

52 Firstly, there may be significant harm or pollution of controlled waters arising from land for which a site licence is in force under Part 2. Where this is the case, under section 78YB(2), the Part 2A regime does not

normally apply; that is, the land cannot formally be identified as "contaminated land" and no remediation notice can be served. If action is needed to deal with a pollution problem in such a case, this would normally be enforced through a "condition" attached to the site licence. However, Part 2A does apply if the harm or pollution on a licensed site is attributable to a cause other than a breach of the site licence, or the carrying on of an activity authorised by the licence in accordance with its terms and conditions.

53 Secondly, under section 78YB(3), an enforcing authority acting under Part 2A cannot serve a remediation notice in any case where the contamination results from an illegal deposit of controlled waste. In these circumstances, the Environment Agency and the waste disposal authority have powers under section 59 of the 1990 Act to remove the waste, and to deal with the consequences of its having been present.

54 Thirdly, remediation activities on contaminated land may themselves fall within the definitions of "waste disposal operations" or "waste recovery operations", and be subject to the licensing requirements under the Part 2 system. Guidance on the meaning of the relevant definitions and the operation of the Part 2 licensing system is provided in DOE Circular 11/94. A number of waste management operations are subject to the permitting regime instead of Part 2 licensing.

Statutory nuisance

55 Until the implementation of the Part 2A contaminated land regime, the statutory nuisance system under Part 3 of the 1990 Act was the main regulatory mechanism for enforcing the remediation of contaminated land.

56 Parliament considered that the Part 2A regime, as explained in the statutory guidance, sets out the right level of protection for human health and the environment from the effects of land contamination. It judged it inappropriate to leave in place the possibility of using another, less precisely defined, system which could lead to the imposition of regulatory requirements on a different basis.

57 From the entry into force of the contaminated land regime in April 2000, most land contamination issues were therefore removed from the scope of the statutory nuisance regime. This is the effect of an amendment to the definition of a statutory nuisance in section 79 of the 1990 Act, consisting of the insertion of sections 79(1 A) and (1B); this amendment was made by paragraph 89 of Schedule 22 to the Environment Act 1995. Any matter which would otherwise have been a statutory nuisance will no longer be treated as such, to the extent that it consists of, or is caused by, land "being in a contaminated state". The definition of land which is "in a contaminated state", and where the statutory nuisance regime is therefore excluded, covers all land where there are substances in, on or under the land which are causing harm or where there is a possibility of harm being caused. Section 40 of the Radioactive Substances Act 1993 disapplies the statutory nuisance provisions of the Environmental Protection Act 1990 to radioactivity, and this remains the position after the extension of the Part 2A regime to include radioactivity.

58 It should also be noted that the statutory nuisance regime continues to apply to the effects of deposits of substances on land which give rise to such offence to human senses (such as stenches) as to constitute a nuisance, since the exclusion of the statutory nuisance regime applies only to harm (as defined in section 78A(4)) and the pollution of controlled waters.

Water Resources Act 1991

59 Sections 161 to 161D of the Water Resources Act 1991 give the Environment Agency powers to take action to prevent or remedy the pollution of controlled waters. The normal enforcement mechanism under these powers is a "works notice" served under section 161A, which specifies what actions have to be taken and in what time periods. This is served on any person who has "caused or knowingly permitted" the potential pollutant to be in the place from which it is likely to enter controlled waters, or to have caused or knowingly permitted a pollutant to enter controlled waters. Where it is not appropriate to serve such a notice, because of the need for urgent action or where no liable person can be found, the Agency has the power to carry out the works itself.

60 There is an obvious potential for overlap between these powers and the Part 2A regime in circumstances where substances in, on or under land are likely to enter controlled waters. The decision as to which regime is used in any case may have important implications, as there are differences between the two enforcement mechanisms.

61 The Environment Agency has policies on the use of Anti-Pollution Works Notices. Details are available from the Environment Agency.

62 The Water Resources Act powers may be particularly useful in cases where there is historic pollution of groundwater, but where the Part 2A regime does not apply. This may occur, for example, where the pollutants are entirely contained within the relevant body of groundwater or where the "source" site cannot be identified.

63 No remediation notice can require action to be carried out which would have the effect of impeding or preventing a discharge into controlled waters for which a "discharge consent" has been issued under Chapter 2 of Part 3 of the Water Resources Act 1991.

Other regimes

64 Other regimes which may have implications for land contamination, or which may overlap with Part 2A, include the following:

(a) *Food Safety*—Part 1 of the Food and Environment Protection Act 1985 gives ministers emergency powers to issue orders for the purpose of prohibiting specified agricultural activities in a designated area, in order to protect consumers from exposure to contaminated food. The 1985 Act provides for ministers to designate authorities for the enforcement of emergency control orders. Following the coming into force of the Food Standards Act 1999, which established the Food Standards Agency, the above powers are exercisable by the Secretary of State. Enforcing authorities under Part 2A should liaise with the Food Standards Agency about any possible use of the powers in Part 1 of the 1985 Act.

(b) *Health and Safety*—The Health and Safety at Work etc Act 1974, the Construction (Design and Management) Regulations 1994 (S.I. 1994/3140) and their associated controls are concerned with risks to the public or employees at business and other premises; risks of these kinds could arise as a result of land contamination. Liaison between Part 2A enforcing authorities and the Health and Safety Executive will help to ensure that unnecessary duplication of controls is avoided, and that the most appropriate regime is used to deal with any problems.

(c) *Landfill Tax*—The Finance Act 1996 introduced a tax on the disposal of wastes, including those arising from the remediation and reclamation of land. However, an exemption from this tax can be obtained where material is being removed from contaminated land in order to prevent harm, or to facilitate the development of the land for particular purposes. An exemption certificate has to be specifically applied for, through HM Revenue and Customs, in each case where it might apply. No exemption certificate will be granted where the material is being removed in order to comply with the requirements of a remediation notice served under section 78E of the 1990 Act. This provides a fiscal incentive for those responsible for carrying out remediation under Part 2A to do so by agreement, rather than waiting for the service of a remediation notice.

(d) *Major Accident Hazards*—The Control of Major Accident Hazards Regulations 1999 (S.I. 1999/743) (COMAH) (as amended by S.I. 2005/1088) require operators of establishments handling prescribed dangerous substances to prepare on-site emergency plans, and the local authorities to prepare off-site emergency plans. The objectives of these emergency plans include providing for the restoration and clean-up of the environment following a major accident. The Health and Safety Executive are responsible for overseeing the COMAH Regulations.

Radioactivity

65 This section of Annex 1 covers both policy in relation to radioactivity and details of the extension of Part 2A to include radioactivity. It sits alongside, and should be read in conjunction with, the preceding more general policy section.

General introduction

66 Under section 78YC of the Environmental Protection Act 1990, the Part 2A regime has not hitherto applied with respect to harm, or water pollution, which is attributable to any radioactivity possessed by any substance. However, section 78YC gives powers to the Secretary of State to make regulations applying the Part 2A regime, with any necessary modifications, to problems of radioactive contamination. There are four sets of regulations which extend Part 2A to include radioactivity. These are described in more detail in Annex 5 to this Circular.

Preventing new radioactive contamination

67 The most significant piece of legislation aimed at preventing the creation of new radioactive contamination is the Radioactive Substances Act 1993 (RSA 93). This Act sets out a prior permitting regime for the keeping and use of radioactive materials and the disposal and accumulation of radioactive waste. It consolidates and replaces the Radioactive Substances Act 1960.

The legacy of radioactive contaminated land

68 Historical contamination of land by radionuclides from anthropogenic activity has in many cases occurred due to a lack of understanding of the hazards posed by radioactive materials at the time. Radioactive substances have been used for a wide variety of purposes since the start of the twentieth century but most have only been subject to regulation since

1963, the year in which the 1960 Radioactive Substances Act came into force. Industrial activities have involved the use of materials containing radioactivity in a variety of different contexts:

(a) where radioactive materials have been employed for their radioactive properties (for example, luminising works);

(b) where radioactive properties are incidental in materials that are used for their non-radioactive properties (for example, gas mantle production); and

(c) where radioactive materials have been inadvertently handled, or escaped accidentally (for example, lead mining).

69 Little information is available on the scale of radioactive contamination outside of nuclear sites. What information is available is subject to large uncertainties. A recent study undertaken on behalf of Defra, the Environment Agency and the Welsh Assembly Government indicated that the likely number of sites in England and Wales where activities took place capable of giving rise to radioactive contamination, if a pollutant linkage was in place, was in the range 100–1000 and most likely to be in the range 150–250[1].

Objectives for extending Part 2A to radioactivity

70 The objectives for the extension of Part 2A to include radioactivity are broadly the same as those for the existing Part 2A regime, namely to provide a system for the identification and remediation of land where contamination is causing lasting exposure to radiation of human beings and where "intervention" is liable to be "justified". This includes applying both the "polluter pays" principle and the "suitable for use" approach.

71 In addition to the objectives set out in paragraphs 24 to 28 above a specific objective for the introduction of radioactivity is to ensure that the UK complies with its obligations to transpose and implement adequately articles 48 and 53 of the Basic Safety Standards Directive (Council Directive 96/29/Euratom) (BSS Directive) which lays down the basic safety standards for the protection of the health of workers and the general public against the dangers arising from ionising radiation[2].

72 In respect of defence sites it should be noted that the legal basis for the extension of Part 2A to include radioactivity is purely domestic law, and not pursuant to the UK's obligations under Euratom.

Non-human receptors

73 The extension of Part 2A to include radioactivity applies only in respect of harm to human health, and not in respect of other receptors or pollution of controlled waters. The Environment Agency have advised that there is no evidence for a widespread risk to protected ecosystems or of pollution from past activities impacting animals or crops and the Government does not consider that there is a need for regulation to address other receptors at this time. This will be kept under review.

74 Water will only be treated as a pathway and not as a receptor. The Water Act 2003 includes a provision, not yet commenced, to amend the current

[1] *Environment Agency "Indicators for Land Contamination"—Science report SC030039/SR* Appendix A. 2005.
[2] OJ No L: 159, 29.06.1996, p.1.

Part 2A definition of pollution of controlled waters to introduce a "significance" test. Consequential amendments to the statutory guidance for non-radioactive contamination will be necessary. Rather than define now what would constitute "significant pollution" for radioactivity, the Government believes it more appropriate to return to the issue at a later date when a significance test for radioactive and non-radioactive contamination can be considered together.

Scope

75 The scope of the extension to the Part 2A regime is largely determined by Title IX of the BSS Directive which is concerned with interventions (see paragraphs 78 to 81 below). That is to say:

(a) it provides for the identification and remediation of radioactive contaminated land which is causing lasting exposure to human beings. Harm to the wider environment or pollution of controlled waters is not included at this time;

(b) it applies only to radioactivity arising from the after-effects of a radiological emergency and substances which have been processed as part of a past practice or past work activity. This includes substances containing artificial radionuclides or processed natural radionuclides. It is not applicable to current practices and natural background radiation is excluded;

(c) it does not apply to radioactive contamination where the operator of a nuclear installation is liable under the Nuclear Installations Act 1965;

(d) it does not apply to radon gas and its short lived decay products which are only a matter of concern within buildings and for which other policy exists;

(e) because of the need to transpose the BSS Directive, the extended regime insofar as it deals with radioactive contamination will apply to the Isles of Scilly.

Main features

76 The main features of the extension of the Part 2A regime to radioactivity are:

(a) A modification[3] of the definition of contaminated land where radioactive contamination is concerned. Section 78A(2) (as modified) defines contaminated land as "any land which appears to the local authority in whose area it is situated to be in such a condition, by reason of substances in, on or under the land, that—

(i) harm is being caused, or
(ii) there is a significant possibility of such harm being caused."

The definition of "harm" (section 78A(4) (as modified)) attributable to radioactivity in respect of human beings is based upon the wording of the Directive. "Harm" is defined as "lasting exposure to any person resulting from the after-effects of a radiological emer-

---

[3] In practice, modification means that when the statutes are being applied in a situation where radioactivity is involved, then they have to be read in the modified form, while in other situations they continue to apply unmodified.

gency, past practice or past work activity". "Harm" should be regarded as being caused where lasting exposure gives rise to radiation doses equal to or in excess of prescribed values set out in the statutory guidance at Annex 3. Lasting exposure is not defined in the Directive but the Government considers it to be exposure that could take place over a protracted period as a result of the nature of the contamination and the use to which land is put.

(b) The duty of a local authority to inspect its area will be restricted to circumstances where there are reasonable grounds for believing land may be contaminated by virtue of radioactivity (section 78B (as modified)).

(c) Any land determined as contaminated land by virtue of radioactivity will be a special site with the Environment Agency acting as the enforcing authority rather than the relevant local authority. Where there is a mixture of radioactive and non-radioactive contamination on a particular site, the Environment Agency will act as the enforcing authority for all the pollutant linkages.

(d) When considering what remediation is reasonable, where remediation includes an intervention (see paragraphs 78 to 80 below), the enforcing authority must consider the cost and harm (including social cost) of any intervention; whether the benefit of the intervention justifies the adverse effects caused by the intervention; and how the intervention can be optimised so that the net benefit can be maximised.

(e) The Environment Agency as the enforcing authority must exercise its power to remediate in certain circumstances where it is necessary for the purposes of the Directive and where there is no other person liable for the remediation (section 78N (as modified)).

Principles and criteria used to extend Part 2A to include radioactivity

77 The system of radiological protection in the UK is based upon the requirements of the BSS Directive, which in turn is based upon the recommendations of the International Commission on Radiological Protection (ICRP). It has been necessary to incorporate some of these into the extension of the Part 2A regime. Radiological protection distinguishes between "**practices**" where radiation exposures can be introduced in a controlled manner, and "**interventions**" dealing with situations where the exposures are already present and the only type of action available is an intervention to reduce them. These are described in more detail below.

Interventions

78 An intervention is defined in the BSS Directive as "a human activity that prevents or decreases the exposure of individuals to radiation from sources which are not part of a practice or which are out of control, by acting on sources, transmission pathways and individuals themselves". It is therefore a type of remedial treatment action as defined in Part 2A and ensures that land is suitable for its current use.

79 Recognising that interventions themselves may cause adverse effects, in radiological protection terms, means that they are only to be undertaken where they will do more overerall good than harm (the principle of justification) (see paragraph 87 below). Furthermore, where an intervention is undertaken it should seek to maximise its net benefit (the principle of optimisation) (see paragraph 88 below).

80 In radiological protection terms, land where contamination by radio-activity is giving rise to exposure to individuals who already occupy the land, might warrant intervention. Under the extension of Part 2A, intervention would seek to reduce the exposure of individuals to radioactivity from land where the intervention will do more good than harm.

81 An example of where an intervention would be considered under the extension of Part 2A would be where an area of land, contaminated by historical uses of radioactivity, has been redeveloped for housing, but where remediation did not take place at the time.

Practices

82 The BSS Directive defines a practice as "a human activity that can increase the exposure of individuals to radiation from an artificial source, or from a natural radiation source where natural radionuclides are processed for their radioactive, fissile or fertile properties, except in the case of an emergency exposure".

83 Assessing the potential risks from contamination on the basis of the proposed future use and circumstances before official permission is given for the development and, where necessary, remediating the land before the new use commences is not a matter for Part 2A; this is the role of the town and country planning and building control regimes.

84 In radiological protection terms where there is a change of use of the land this would be considered a practice because of the potential introduction of new individuals who could be exposed to radiation. Practices are subject to regulatory control, including dose limits and constraints.

85 An example of a practice scenario would be where planning permission for redevelopment of an area of land contaminated with radioactivity is granted subject to effective remediation being undertaken to address the contamination. The Environment Agency (as regulators for the Radioactive Substances Act 1993) would advise the planning authority (which is responsible for controlling the development of land) that options for remediation should be considered to enable an optimal remediation option to be identified. It would also advise that no option should be considered if the residual contamination were to result in doses to individuals in excess of 0.3 millisieverts per year arising from the land. This is consistent with published advice from the Health Protection Agency's Radiation Protection Division[4]. Following this ensures that land is made suitable for any new use, as planning permission is given for that new use.

86 A consequence of the distinction between interventions and practices is that after an intervention, the land could be in a different condition to that which would have arisen if the decision to clean up the land had been taken as part of a redevelopment process. This is because radiological protection philosophy acknowledges that the intervention can itself incur costs (including non-financial and social costs) as well as benefits. This balance needs to be taken into account in deciding whether intervention to reduce the exposure of individuals is justified, and what level of risk reduction the remediation should seek to achieve.

Justification

87 Justification in relation to intervention means ensuring that the reduction in detriment due to radiation is sufficient to justify the adverse effects

[4] NRPB, 1998, Radiological Protection Objectives for Land Contaminated with Radionuclides, Documents of the NRPB 1998, Volume 09, No.2, ISBN 0–85951–416–1.

and costs, including social costs, of the intervention. The principle of justification recognises that an intervention may bring about reduction in doses and other harmful impacts but may incur costs and other adverse effects. It requires that on balance an intervention should do more good than harm. Costs are not restricted to financial costs, but may also include costs to society.

Optimisation

88 Optimisation in relation to intervention means ensuring that the form, scale and duration of the intervention maximises the net benefit, in short, that the intervention option which does the most good is chosen. This is because it is likely that in any particular circumstance there will be a number of options for intervention which are justified. The principle of optimisation means that there is no predetermined end point for remediation that is applicable for all circumstances. In the extension of Part 2A, where a remediation scheme addresses significant pollutant linkages some, but not all, of which relate to lasting exposure, any intervention should be optimised having regard to their benefit in respect of any remedial treatment actions relating to non-radioactive significant pollutant linkages.

Criteria for "harm" and the "significant possibility of harm"

89 The criteria for the determination of whether or not "harm" is occurring are based on levels of effective or equivalent dose at which it is appropriate that the site is investigated and remedial options are considered and where subsequent action is liable to be justified. The criteria set out in paragraph A.41 of Chapter A are doses that exceed one or more of the following:

(a) an effective dose of 3 millisieverts per annum;
(b) can equivalent dose to the lens of the eye of 15 millisieverts per annum; or
(c) an equivalent dose to the skin of 50 millisieverts per annum.

90 Exposures which are not certain to occur are known as potential exposures and are the situations covered by the term "possibility of harm". (Paragraph A.43 of Chapter A). In certain circumstances when dealing with potential exposures it is appropriate to compare the product of the annual dose that could be received and the annual probability of the dose being received with the dose criterion of 3 millisieverts per annum. These circumstances are where the effective doses are less than or equal to 50 millisieverts per annum, and the equivalent doses to the skin and lens of the eye are less than or equal to 50 millisieverts per annum and 15 millisieverts per annum, respectively. These dose levels have been selected in accordance with advice from the Health Protection Agency to avoid the possibility of deterministic effects (for example, burns) arising from highly non-uniform exposure such as that from so-called "hot particles" and to be within the linear range of dose response relationships for stochastic effects such as cancer. In other situations, where these values could be exceeded, a decision on whether the possibility of harm being caused is significant will need to be made on a case by case basis taking into account:

(a) the potential effective dose;

(b) any non-linearity in the dose-effect relationship for stochastic effects;

(c) the equivalent dose to the skin and to the lens of the eye;

(d) the nature and degree of any deterministic effects associated with the potential dose;

(e) the probability of the dose being received and associated uncertainties in the estimation of this probability; and

(f) the duration of the exposure and timescale within which the harm might occur.

Published technical advice

91 The Radioactively Contaminated Land Exposure Assessment (RCLEA) methodology is Defra's recommended approach for the exposure assessment of a site and can be found on the Defra website. It is founded on the Contaminated Land Exposure Assessment (CLEA) approach introduced for the Part 2A regime in 2002. Defra has also published an extension to its Industry Profile series dealing with radioactive contaminated land on its website.

Other regimes

92 Other regimes which may have implications for radioactive land contamination, or which may overlap with the extension of Part 2A, include the following:

(a) *Ionising Radiations Regulations 1999 (IRRs)*—are concerned with the control of exposure to workers and the general public from radiation arising from the use of radioactive materials and radiation generators in work activities. If remediation action is required, the IRRs would require employers to keep exposure to ionising radiation as low as reasonably practicable.

(b) *Radioactive Substances Act 1993 (RSA 93)*—sets out a prior permissioning regime for the keeping and use of radioactive materials and for the disposal and accumulation of radioactive waste. Remediation activities may result in the need for registration and or authorisation under RSA 93.

(c) *Nuclear Installations Act 1965*—sets out a regime of control and liability in relation to nuclear installations. Powers under sections 4 or 5 may be used to deal with contamination within a nuclear site.

ANNEX 2 A DESCRIPTION OF THE REGIME FOR CONTAMINATED LAND

1. Introduction

1.1 Part 2A of the Environmental Protection Act 1990—which was inserted into that Act by section 57 of the Environment Act 1995—provides a regulatory regime for the identification and remediation of contaminated land. In addition to the requirements contained in the primary legislation, operation of the regime is subject to regulations and statutory guidance.

1.1A The regime initially excluded contaminated land by virtue of harm or water pollution attributable to radioactivity possessed by a substance. In August 2006 the regime was extended by new regulations to include land that is contaminated land by virtue of radioactivity. Annex 1 to this Circular describes the main changes. In addition, the statutory guidance issued in 2000 has been amended in line with these changes.

1.1B This annex to the Circular is a revised and updated version of the equivalent text published in DETR Circular 02/2000 ("Contaminated Land"), and takes account of changes which have occurred since then, of which the main ones concern radioactivity. These changes are indicated by highlighted text.

1.2 This annex describes, in general terms, the operation of the regime, "as modified", setting out the procedural steps the enforcing authority takes, and some of the factors which may underlie its decisions at each stage. Where appropriate it refers to the primary legislation, regulations or statutory guidance. However, the material in this annex does not form a part of that statutory guidance, and it should not be taken to qualify or contradict any requirements in the guidance, or to provide any additional guidance. It represents the Department's views and interpretations of the legislation, regulations and guidance. Readers should seek their own legal advice where necessary.

Definitions

1.3 Throughout the text, various terms are used which have specific meanings under the primary legislation, or in the regulations or the statutory guidance. Where this is the case, the terms are printed in SMALL CAPITALS. The Glossary of Terms at Annex 6 to the Circular, which now includes terms related to radioactivity, repeats the most important definitions, or shows where they can be found.

1.4 Unless the contrary is shown, references in this document to

"sections" are to sections of the Environmental Protection Act 1990 (as amended);

"sections (as modified)" are to sections of the Environmental Protection Act 1990 as modified by The Radioactive Contaminated Land (Modification of Enactments) (England) Regulations 2006;

"Contaminated Land Regulations" are references to The Contaminated Land (England) Regulations 2006; and

"Modification Regulations" are references to The Radioactive Contaminated Land (Modification of Enactments) (England) Regulations 2006.

1.4A References to the statutory guidance include the relevant Chapter in Annex 3 to this Circular and the specific paragraph (so that, for example, a reference to paragraph 13 of Chapter B is shown as "*paragraph B.13*"). Such references are to the most relevant paragraph(s): those paragraph(s) must, of course, be read in the context of the relevant guidance as a whole.

2. The definition of contaminated land

The Definition in Part 2A

2.1 Section 78A(2) defines CONTAMINATED LAND for the purposes of Part 2A as:

"any land which appears to the LOCAL AUTHORITY in whose area it is situated to be in such a condition, by reason of substances in, on or under the land, that—

"(a) SIGNIFICANT HARM is being caused or there is a SIGNIFICANT POSSIBILITY of such harm being caused; or

"(b) POLLUTION OF CONTROLLED WATERS is being, or is likely to be, caused".

2.1A Where HARM is attributable to radioactivity, the definition of CONTAMINATED LAND has been modified by regulation 4(a) of the Modification Regulations as:

"any land which appears to the LOCAL AUTHORITY in whose area it is situated to be in such a condition, by reason of substances in, on or under the land, that

"(a) HARM is being caused, or

"(b) there is a SIGNIFICANT POSSIBILITY of such harm being caused".

2.2 These definitions reflect the intended role of the Part 2A regime, which is to enable the identification and remediation of land on which contamination (other than where attributable to radioactivity) is causing unacceptable risks to human health or to the wider environment; or lasting exposure to radiation where action is likely to be justified. The definitions do not necessarily include all land where contamination is present, even though such contamination may be relevant in the context of other regimes. For example, contamination which might cause risks in the context of a new development of land could be a "material planning consideration" under the Town and Country Planning Act 1990.

2.2A HARM attributable to radioactivity is defined more restrictively than other types of harm, being confined to the lasting exposure of human receptors from the after-effects of a radiological emergency or a past practice or past work activity.

2.3 The definition of CONTAMINATED LAND where attributable to radioactivity does not cover any POLLUTION OF CONTROLLED WATERS, although the SECRETARY OF STATE has powers to make regulations to do so. The approach reflects the Government's wish to assess the implications of the Water Framework Directive (2000/60/EC) before considering how a significance test for POLLUTION OF CONTROLLED WATERS might be applied (both where attributable to radioactivity and otherwise).

A pollutant linkage

2.3A The LOCAL AUTHORITY is required to act in accordance with statutory guidance issued by the SECRETARY OF STATE in determining whether land is CONTAMINATED LAND. This is set out at Chapter A of Annex 3 to this Circular. Before the LOCAL AUTHORITY can make the judgement that any land appears to be CONTAMINATED LAND, the authority must satisfy itself that a POLLUTANT LINKAGE exists in relation to the land (*paragraphs A.11 to A.18*). A POLLUTANT LINKAGE requires each of the following to be identified:

(a) a CONTAMINANT;

(b) a RECEPTOR; and

(c) a PATHWAY CAPABLE of exposing a receptor to the contaminant.

2.3B The next step is for the LOCAL AUTHORITY to satisfy itself that the POLLUTANT LINKAGE is a SIGNIFICANT POLLUTANT LINKAGE.

To do this, the LOCAL AUTHORITY must consider the degree of possibility or likelihood of one or more of the following, referring to the definition of CONTAMINATED LAND in paragraphs 2.1 and 2.1A above:

(a) SIGNIFICANT HARM,
(b) POLLUTION OF CONTROLLED WATERS, or
(c) HARM (where attributable to radioactivity).

These are considered in more detail below.

Significant harm

2.4 The definition of CONTAMINATED LAND (other than where attributable to radioactivity) includes the notion of "SIGNIFICANT HARM" and the "SIGNIFICANT POSSIBILITY" of such HARM being caused. The LOCAL AUTHORITY is required to act in accordance with statutory guidance issued by the SECRETARY OF STATE in determining what is "significant" in either context (*section 78A(2) & (5)*). This statutory guidance is set out at Chapter A of Annex 3 to this Circular.

2.5 The statutory guidance explains:

(a) the types of RECEPTOR to which SIGNIFICANT HARM can be caused (HARM to any other type of RECEPTOR can never be regarded as SIGNIFICANT HARM);
(b) the degree or nature of HARM to each of these RECEPTORS which constitutes SIGNIFICANT HARM (*Chapter A, Table A*); and
(c) for each RECEPTOR, the degree of possibility of the SIGNIFICANT HARM being caused which will amount to a SIGNIFICANT POSSIBILITY (*Chapter A, Table B, & paragraphs A.27 to A.33*).

2.6 Before the LOCAL AUTHORITY can make the judgement that any land appears to be CONTAMINATED LAND on the basis that SIGNIFICANT HARM is being caused, or that there is a SIGNIFICANT POSSIBILITY of such harm being caused, the authority must therefore identify a SIGNIFICANT POLLUTANT LINKAGE. This means that each of the following has to be identified:

(a) a CONTAMINANT;
(b) a relevant RECEPTOR; and
(c) a PATHWAY by means of which either:

(i) that CONTAMINANT is causing SIGNIFICANT HARM to that RECEPTOR, or
(ii) there is a SIGNIFICANT POSSIBILITY of such harm being caused by that CONTAMINANT to that RECEPTOR (*paragraphs A. 11 and A.19*).

Pollution of controlled waters

2.7 The LOCAL AUTHORITY is also required to act in accordance with statutory guidance issued by the SECRETARY OF STATE in determining whether POLLUTION OF CONTROLLED WATERS is being, or is likely to be, caused (*section 78A(5)*). This guidance is also set out at Chapter A of Annex 3 to this Circular. Radioactivity is not relevant to assessing whether POLLUTION OF CONTROLLED WATERS may be occurring (see paragraph 2.3 above).

2.8 Before the LOCAL AUTHORITY can make the judgement that any land appears to be CONTAMINATED LAND on the basis that the POLLU-

TION OF CONTROLLED WATERS is being caused or is likely to be caused, the authority must identify a SIGNIFICANT POLLUTANT LINKAGE, where a body of CONTROLLED WATERS forms the RECEPTOR (*paragraphs A.11 and A.19*).

2.9 The POLLUTION OF CONTROLLED WATERS is defined in section 78A(9), by reference to Part 3 (section 104) of the Water Resources Act 1991, and includes "ground waters". Section 78A(9) was amended by section 86 of the Water Act 2003 so that for Part 2A purposes "ground waters" does not include waters contained in underground strata but above the saturation zone (often known as the "unsaturated zone"). This change was brought into force on 1 October 2004 by the Water Act 2003 (Commencement Order No.2, Transitional Provisions and Savings) Order 2004 (S.I. 2004/2528 (C.106)).

2.10 Section 86 of the Water Act 2003, once fully implemented, will, further amend the definition of CONTAMINATED LAND with respect to POLLUTION OF CONTROLLED WATERS, and will also provide powers to issue statutory guidance in respect of this amended definition. As noted at paragraph 2.3 above, it is expected that POLLUTION OF CONTROLLED WATERS by virtue of radioactivity will be considered further at that time. Until this change is implemented, when considering cases where it is thought that very small quantities of a CONTAMINANT might satisfy that definition, it is necessary also to consider the guidance on what remediation it is reasonable to require (see paragraphs 6.30 to 6.32 below).

Harm attributable to radioactivity

2.11 The definition of CONTAMINATED LAND where attributable to radioactivity is based on the notion of "HARM" and the "SIGNIFICANT POSSIBILITY" of such HARM being caused. HARM in this context is defined in section 78A(4) (as modified) as:

"lasting exposure to any person resulting from the after-effects of a radiological emergency, past practice or past work activity".

2.12 The LOCAL AUTHORITY is required to act in accordance with statutory guidance issued by the SECRETARY OF STATE in determining what constitutes HARM and what is a "SIGNIFICANT POSSIBILITY" of such HARM (*section 78A(2)(as modified) & section 78A(5)(as modified)*). This statutory guidance is set out in Chapter A of Annex 3 to this Circular.

2.13 The statutory guidance sets out:

    (a) the dose criteria that determine whether HARM is being caused (*paragraph A.41*);

    (b) the degree of possibility of the HARM being caused which will amount to a SIGNIFICANT POSSIBILITY (*paragraphs A.44 to A.50*);

2.14 Before the LOCAL AUTHORITY can make the judgement that any land appears to be CONTAMINATED LAND on the basis that HARM is being caused, or that there is a SIGNIFICANT POSSIBILITY of such harm being caused, the authority must identify a SIGNIFICANT POLLUTANT LINKAGE. This means that each of the following has to be identified:

    (a) a CONTAMINANT;

    (b) a relevant RECEPTOR (that is, a human being); and

    (c) a PATHWAY by means of which either:

(i) that CONTAMINANT is causing HARM to that RECEPTOR, or

(ii) there is a SIGNIFICANT POSSIBILITY of such harm being caused by that CONTAMINANT to that RECEPTOR (*paragraphs A.44 to A.50*).

2.15 In relation to radioactivity, the definition of a SUBSTANCE in section 78A(9) (as modified) needs to be considered when assessing whether there is a CONTAMINANT present, noting that a SUBSTANCE must contain one or more radionuclides which have resulted from the after-effects of a radiological emergency or which are or have been processed as part of a past practice or past work activity. The definition of a SUBSTANCE excludes radon gas and its short half-life decay products. For the purposes of determining whether a POLLUTANT LINKAGE exists, the LOCAL AUTHORITY may treat two or more SUBSTANCES containing radionuclides as being a single SUBSTANCE (*paragraph A.18A*). This reflects the fact that a number of radionuclides may contribute to the EFFECTIVE DOSE and to the EQUIVALENT DOSE to the lens of the eye and to the skin. These doses need to be assessed in determining whether HARM is being caused (*paragraph A.41*).

2.16 The modified definitions of CONTAMINATED LAND, and of HARM, are only relevant in respect of cases of radioactivity, and are not relevant in other situations.

3. Identification of contaminated land

Inspection of a local authority's area

3.1 Each LOCAL AUTHORITY has a duty to cause its area to be inspected from time to time for the purpose of identifying CONTAMINATED LAND (*section 78B(1)*) other than so far as attributable to radioactivity. In doing so, it has to act in accordance with statutory guidance issued by the SECRETARY OF STATE. This statutory guidance is set out at Chapter B of Annex 3 to this Circular.

3.1A The inspection duty, where it arises in the context of land contamination attributable to radioactivity, is different and a more limited one, as set out in section 78B(1) (as modified). This duty requires that, where a LOCAL AUTHORITY considers that there are REASONABLE GROUNDS for believing that any land may be contaminated by virtue of radioactivity, it shall cause the land to be inspected for the purpose of identifying whether it is CONTAMINATED LAND. Section 78B(1A) states that "the fact that substances have been present on the land shall not of itself be taken to be reasonable grounds. . . ". In fulfilling its duty under section 78B(1) (as modified) and section 78B(1A), the LOCAL AUTHORITY has to act in accordance with statutory guidance issued by the SECRETARY OF STATE. This statutory guidance with reference to radioactivity is set out at Chapter B of Annex 3 to this Circular.

Strategy for inspection: applies other than to radioactivity

3.2 The LOCAL AUTHORITY needs to take a strategic approach to the inspection of its area under section 78(B)(1) (*paragraph B.9*). It is to set out this approach as a written strategy, which it was to publish by July 2001 (*paragraph B.12*). The strategy is to be kept under periodic review (*paragraph B.13*).

3.3 Taking a strategic approach enables the LOCAL AUTHORITY to identify, in a rational, ordered and efficient manner, the land which merits detailed individual inspection, identifying the most pressing and serious problems first and concentrating resources on the areas where CONTAMINATED LAND is most likely to be found.

3.4 The strategy is also to contain procedures for liaison with other regulatory bodies, which may have information about land contamination problems, and for responding to information and complaints from members of the public, businesses and voluntary organisations (*paragraphs B.15 and B.16*).

Reasonable grounds: applies to radioactivity

3.4A The LOCAL AUTHORITY has to inspect land under section 78B(1) (as modified) and section 78 B(1A) where it considers that there are REASONABLE GROUNDS for believing it to be contaminated by virtue of radioactivity. The statutory guidance sets out the requirements for REASONABLE GROUNDS (*paragraphs B.17A to B.17B*). These grounds mean that a LOCAL AUTHORITY needs to be aware of land use which could be capable of giving rise to the dose criteria, or that it has been presented with evidence of a contamination level capable of giving rise to the dose criteria before it considers undertaking detailed individual inspection. The statutory guidance (*paragraph B17.A*) refers to "knowledge of relevant information". In the Government's view, this will not require the LOCAL AUTHORITY to actively review its records compiled before the extended regime came into force.

Inspecting land

3.5 The LOCAL AUTHORITY may identify a particular area of land where it is possible that a POLLUTANT LINKAGE exists. The authority could do so as a result of:

(a) its own gathering of information as part of its strategy;

(b) receiving information from another regulatory body, such as the ENVIRONMENT AGENCY; or

(c) receiving information or a complaint from a member of the public, a business or a voluntary organisation.

3.6 Where this is the case, the LOCAL AUTHORITY needs to consider whether to carry out detailed inspection to determine whether or not the land actually appears to be CONTAMINATED LAND.

3.6A Under the more limited inspection duty for radioactivity, the LOCAL AUTHORITY should carry out detailed inspection where it has reasonable grounds to believe that the land may be contaminated by virtue of radioactivity. When undertaking detailed inspection the LOCAL AUTHORITY should, in the first instance, aim to identify that there is a reasonable possibility both of the presence of a RECEPTOR, and that this RECEPTOR could be exposed to a CONTAMINANT.

3.6B Normally, the LOCAL AUTHORITY will be interested only in land which is in its area. But, under both approaches, if it considers SIGNIFICANT HARM, the POLLUTION OF CONTROLLED WATERS or HARM attributable to radioactivity might be caused within its area as a result of contamination on land outside its area, it may also inspect that other land (*section 78X(2)*).

3.6C The statutory guidance explains what is intended by detailed inspection (*paragraphs B.18 to B.20*). It can include collation and assessment of documentary or other information, visual inspection and limited sampling, and intrusive investigation. Where the LOCAL AUTHORITY is considering HARM attributable to radioactivity, it should have regard to any general guidance and advice issued by the ENVIRONMENT AGENCY on the manner in which to carry out collation and assessment of documentary or other information and visual inspection or limited survey (for example, using hand-held radiation meters) of particular land. The LOCAL AUTHORITY should always make arrangements with the ENVIRONMENT AGENCY for the Agency to carry out any intrusive investigation where the land may be contaminated by virtue of radioactivity (*paragraph B.20(c)*).

3.7 The LOCAL AUTHORITY may already have detailed information concerning the condition of the land. This may have been provided, for example, by the ENVIRONMENT AGENCY or by a person such as the owner of the land. Alternatively, such a person may offer to provide such information within a reasonable and specified time. It may therefore be helpful for the authority to consult the owner of the land and other persons, in order to find out whether information already exists, or could be made available to the authority.

3.8 Where information is already available, or will become available, the LOCAL AUTHORITY needs to consider whether the information provides, or would provide, a sufficient basis on which it can determine whether or not the land appears to be CONTAMINATED LAND. If the information meets this test, the authority does not need to carry out any further investigation of the land (*paragraph B.23*) and will proceed to make a determination on that basis (see paragraph 3.33 below).

3.9 Where the LOCAL AUTHORITY does not have sufficient information, it needs to consider whether to make an inspection of the land. For this purpose it needs to consider whether:

(a) there is a reasonable possibility that a POLLUTANT LINKAGE exists on the land (*paragraph B.22(a)*); and

(b) if the land were eventually determined to be CONTAMINATED LAND, whether it would fall to be designated a SPECIAL SITE (see paragraphs 3.18 to 3.22 below).

3.10 If the answer to the first of these questions is "yes", and the second is "no", the LOCAL AUTHORITY needs to authorise an inspection of the land. It has specific powers to authorise suitable persons to carry out any such investigation under section 108 of the Environment Act 1995. This can involve entering premises, taking samples or carrying out related activities for the purpose of enabling the authority to determine whether any land is CONTAMINATED LAND. In some circumstances, the authorised person can also ask other persons questions, which they are obliged to answer, and make copies of written or electronic records.

3.11 If there is to be an inspection of the land, the LOCAL AUTHORITY needs to consider whether it needs to authorise an intrusive investigation (for example, exploratory excavations) into the land. Under the statutory guidance, the authority should authorise an intrusive investigation only where it considers that it is likely (rather than only "reasonably possible") that a CONTAMINANT is actually present and that, given the current use of the land (as defined at *paragraph A.26*) a RECEPTOR is present or is likely to be present (*paragraph B.22(b)*).

Potential special sites

3.12 Part 2A creates a particular category of CONTAMINATED LAND called "SPECIAL SITES". For any SPECIAL SITE, the ENVIRONMENT

AGENCY, rather than the LOCAL AUTHORITY, is the ENFORCING AUTHORITY for the purposes of the Part 2A regime.

3.13 The descriptions of the types of land which are required to be designated as SPECIAL SITES are set out in the Contaminated Land Regulations (*regulations 2 & 3*; see also Annex 4 to this Circular). The procedure for the designation of a SPECIAL SITE is described at paragraphs 18.1 to 18.34 below, along with other procedural issues relating to SPECIAL SITES.

3.14 The actual designation of a SPECIAL SITE cannot take place until the land in question has been formally identified as CONTAMINATED LAND by the LOCAL AUTHORITY. However, the Government considers it appropriate for detailed investigation of any potential SPECIAL SITE to be carried out by the ENVIRONMENT AGENCY, acting on behalf of the LOCAL AUTHORITY.

3.15 To answer the second of the questions in paragraph 3.9 above, the LOCAL AUTHORITY needs to consider, for any land where the answer to the first question is "yes", whether either:

(a) the land or site is of a type such that it would inevitably be designated a SPECIAL SITE were it identified as CONTAMINATED LAND (for example, because the land has been used at some time for the manufacture or processing of explosives (*regulation 2(l)(c)(ii) of the Contaminated Land Regulations*)), or as land which is wholly or partly CONTAMINATED LAND by virtue of radioactivity (*regulation 2(1)(k) of the Contaminated Land Regulations*); or

(b) the particular POLLUTANT LINKAGE which is being investigated is of a kind which would require the land to be designated a SPECIAL SITE were it found to be a SIGNIFICANT POLLUTANT LINKAGE (for example, where POLLUTION OF CONTROLLED WATERS might stop water for human consumption being regarded as wholesome (*regulation 3 (a) of the Contaminated Land Regulations*)).

3.16 Where either of these circumstances applies, the statutory guidance states that the LOCAL AUTHORITY should always seek to arrange with the ENVIRONMENT AGENCY for that Agency to carry out the detailed investigation of the land (*paragraphs B.28 and B.29*). Where necessary, the LOCAL AUTHORITY will authorise a person nominated by the ENVIRONMENT AGENCY to use the powers of entry conferred by section 108 of the Environment Act 1995 (*paragraph B.30*).

Inspection using statutory powers of entry

3.17 If the premises to be inspected are used for residential purposes, or if the inspection will necessitate taking heavy equipment onto the premises, the authorised person needs to give the occupier of the premises at least seven days notice of his proposed entry onto the premises. The authorised person can then enter the premises if he obtains either the consent of the occupier or, if this is not forthcoming, a warrant issued by a magistrate (*section 108(6) and Schedule 18, Environment Act 1995*).

3.18 In other cases, consultation with the occupier prior to entry onto the premises may still be helpful, particularly so that any necessary health and safety precautions can be identified and then incorporated into the inspection. In some instances, specific consents or regulatory permissions may be needed for access to, or work on, the site.

3.19 In an EMERGENCY, these powers of entry can be exercised forthwith if this is necessary (*section 108(6)*). For these purposes, a case is an EMERGENCY if it appears to the authorised person—

"(a) that there is an immediate risk of serious pollution of the environment or serious harm to human health, or

"(b) that circumstances exist which are likely to endanger life or health "and that immediate entry to any premises is necessary to verify the existence of that risk or those circumstances or to ascertain the cause of that risk or those circumstances or to effect a remedy" (*section 108(15), Environment Act 1995*).

3.20 Compensation may be payable by the LOCAL AUTHORITY for any disturbance caused by an INSPECTION USING STATUTORY POWERS OF ENTRY (*paragraph 6 of Schedule 18 of the Environment Act 1995*).

Objectives for the inspection of land

3.21 The primary objective in inspecting land is to enable the LOCAL AUTHORITY to obtain the information needed to decide whether or not the land appears to be CONTAMINATED LAND.

3.21A Where the LOCAL AUTHORITY is carrying out a detailed inspection because it has REASONABLE GROUNDS to believe the land to be contaminated by virtue of radioactivity, the first step is to identify that there is a reasonable possibility both of the presence of a RECEPTOR, and that this RECEPTOR could be exposed to a CONTAMINANT (*paragraph B.19A*).

3.22 It is not always necessary for the LOCAL AUTHORITY to produce a complete characterisation of the nature and extent of CONTAMINANTS, PATHWAYS and RECEPTORS on the land, or of other matters relating to the condition of the land. The authority may be able to identify, in accordance with the statutory guidance set out at Chapters A and B, one or more SIGNIFICANT POLLUTANT LINKAGES, basing its decision on less than a complete characterisation. Once any land has been identified as CONTAMINATED LAND, fuller investigation and characterisation of identified SIGNIFICANT POLLUTANT LINKAGES can, if necessary, form part of an ASSESSMENT ACTION required under a REMEDIATION NOTICE or described in a REMEDIATION STATEMENT (*paragraphs C.65 and C.66*). The identification of any further SIGNIFICANT POLLUTANT LINKAGES will remain the responsibility of the LOCAL AUTHORITY.

3.23 In some cases, the information obtained from an inspection may lead the LOCAL AUTHORITY to the conclusion that, whilst the land does not appear to be CONTAMINATED LAND on the basis of that information assessed on the balance of probabilities, it is still possible that the land is CONTAMINATED LAND. This might occur, for example, where the mean concentration of a CONTAMINANT in soil samples lies just below an appropriate guideline value for that CONTAMINANT. In cases of this kind, the LOCAL AUTHORITY will need to consider whether to carry out further inspections or pursue other lines of enquiry to enable it either to discount the possibility that the land is CONTAMINATED LAND, or to conclude that the land does appear to be CONTAMINATED LAND. In the absence of any such further inspection or enquiry, the local authority will need to proceed to make its determination on the basis that it cannot be satisfied, on the balance of probabilities, that the land falls within the statutory definition of CONTAMINATED LAND.

3.24 In other cases, an inspection may yield insufficient information to enable the LOCAL AUTHORITY to determine, in the manner described at paragraphs 3.26 to 3.35 below, whether or not the land appears to be CONTAMINATED LAND. In such cases, the LOCAL AUTHORITY will need to consider whether carrying out further inspections (for example, taking more samples) or pursing other lines of enquiry (for example, carrying out or commissioning more detailed scientific analysis of a substance or its properties) would be likely to provide the necessary information. If it is not possible to obtain the necessary information, the LOCAL AUTHORITY will need to proceed to make its determination on the basis that it cannot be satisfied, on the balance of probabilities, that the land falls within the statutory definition of CONTAMINATED LAND. The LOCAL AUTHORITY may, nevertheless, decide that the question should be reopened at some future date, or when further information becomes available.

3.25 A secondary objective in inspecting land is to enable the LOCAL AUTHORITY to identify any CONTAMINATED LAND which is required to be designated as a SPECIAL SITE.

Determining whether land is contaminated land

3.26 Any determination (other than where that determination relates to a situation involving radioactive CONTAMINATED LAND) by the LOCAL AUTHORITY that particular land appears to be CONTAMINATED LAND is made on one or more of the following bases, namely that:

(a) SIGNIFICANT HARM is being caused;
(b) there is a SIGNIFICANT POSSIBILITY of such harm being caused;
(c) POLLUTION OF CONTROLLED WATERS is being caused; or
(d) POLLUTION OF CONTROLLED WATERS is likely to be caused; (*paragraph B.38*).

3.26A Where the determination is made by virtue of the presence of radioactivity (*paragraph B.38*) it is made on the following bases, namely that:

(a) HARM is being caused; or
(b) there is a SIGNIFICANT POSSIBILITY of such harm being caused.

Consistency with other regulatory bodies

3.27 If the LOCAL AUTHORITY is considering whether the land might be CONTAMINATED LAND by virtue of an ECOLOGICAL SYSTEM EFFECT (*Chapter A, Table A*), the authority needs to consult English Nature (*paragraph B.42*).

3.28 Similarly, if the LOCAL AUTHORITY is considering whether land might be CONTAMINATED LAND by virtue of any POLLUTION OF CONTROLLED WATERS, the authority needs to consult the ENVIRONMENT AGENCY (*paragraph B.43*).

3.29 In either case, this is to ensure that the LOCAL AUTHORITY adopts an approach which is consistent with that adopted by the other regulatory bodies, and benefits from the experience and expertise available within that other body.

3.29A When considering whether land might be CONTAMINATED LAND by virtue of HARM attributable to radioactivity or a SIGNIFICANT POSSIBILITY of such harm, the LOCAL AUTHORITY needs to consult with the ENVIRONMENT AGENCY and, for any proposed determination, to provide the ENVIRONMENT AGENCY with a draft record of the determination and have regard to the ENVIRONMENT AGENCY'S advice in response to this draft record (*paragraph B.43A*).

3.30 If the land is covered by a waste management site licence issued under the Environmental Protection Act 1990 or by a Part A PPC permit issued under the Pollution Prevention & Control Act 1999 (as amended) the LOCAL AUTHORITY needs to consider, taking into account any information provided by the ENVIRONMENT AGENCY in its role as the regulator in respect of such licences or permits, whether all of the SIGNIFICANT HARM or POLLUTION OF CONTROLLED WATERS by reason of which the land might be CONTAMINATED LAND is the result of:

(a) a breach of the conditions of the site licence;
(b) activities authorised by, and carried on in accordance with the conditions of, the site licence; or
(c) the final disposal of controlled waste by the deposit in or on land such that enforcement may be taken under the Pollution Prevention and Control (England and Wales) Regulations 2000 (i.e. regulation 24 (enforcement notices) or regulation 26(2) (power of regulator to remedy pollution)).

3.31 If all of the SIGNIFICANT HARM or POLLUTION OF CONTROLLED WATERS falls into any of these categories, the land cannot be identified as CONTAMINATED LAND for the purposes of Part 2A (*section 78YB(2)*). Any regulatory action on the land is the responsibility of the ENVIRON-MENT AGENCY, acting as the regulation authority in the context of both the waste management licensing regime in Part 2 of the Environmental Protection Act 1990 and the Pollution Prevention and Control (England and Wales) Regulations 2000.

3.32 Under other provisions in section 78YB, the land may be identified as CONTAMINATED LAND, but REMEDIATION may be enforced under other regimes rather than under Part 2A (see paragraphs 7.2 to 7.11 below).

Making the determination

3.33 The LOCAL AUTHORITY needs to carry out an appropriate, scientific and technical assessment of the circumstances of the land, using all of the relevant and available evidence. The authority then determines whether any of the land appears to it to meet the definition of CONTAMINATED LAND set out in section 78A(2) and 78A(2) (as modified). Where the authority has received information or advice given by other regulatory bodies referred to in paragraph 3.27 to 3.31 above, it must have regard to that information or advice (*paragraphs B.42 and B.43*).

3.33A Chapter B provides statutory guidance on the manner in which the LOCAL AUTHORITY makes this determination (*Chapter B, Part 4*). This includes guidance on the physical extent of the land which should be covered by any single determination (*paragraphs B.32 to B.36*). Where the determination relates to a situation involving radioactive CONTAMI-NATED LAND the LOCAL AUTHORITY also needs to take account of the ENVIRONMENT AGENCY'S advice on the extent of the land covered by the determination (*paragraph B.43A*).

3.34 There may be cases where the presence of one or more contaminants is discovered on land which is undergoing, or is about to undergo, development. Where this occurs, the LOCAL AUTHORITY will need to consider what action is appropriate under both Part 2A and town and country planning legislation (see Annex 1, paragraphs 41 to 44). Where the LOCAL AUTHORITY is not the local planning authority, the two authorities will need to consult.

3.35 The LOCAL AUTHORITY needs to prepare a written record of any determination that land is CONTAMINATED LAND, providing a summary of the basis on which the land has been identified as such land *(paragraph B.52)*. This will include information on the specific SIGNIFI-CANT POLLUTANT LINKAGE, or linkages, found. Where the CON-TAMINATED LAND is attributable to radioactivity, in preparing this written record, the LOCAL AUTHORITY needs to take account of the ENVIRONMENT AGENCY'S comments on the draft record of determination (see paragraph 3.29A above).

Information arising from the inspection of land

3.36 As the LOCAL AUTHORITY inspects its area, it will generate a substantial body of information about the condition of different sites in its area under both of its inspection duties.

3.37 Where land has been identified as being CONTAMINATED LAND, and consequent action taken, the LOCAL AUTHORITY has to include specified details about the condition of the land, and the REMEDIATION ACTIONS carried out on it, in its REGISTER *(section 78R;* see section 17 of this Annex and Annex 4, paragraphs 71 to 92). Having this information on the REGISTER makes it readily available to the public and to those with an interest in the land.

3.38 But the LOCAL AUTHORITY may also be asked, for example as part of a "local search" for a property purchase, to provide information about other areas of land which have not been identified as CONTAMINATED LAND. This might include, for example, information on whether the authority had inspected the land and, if so, details of any site investigation reports prepared.

3.39 The Environmental Information Regulations 2004 (S.I. 2004/3391) may apply to any information about land contamination. This means that, depending on the circumstances and the particular information requested, the authority may be obliged to provide the information when requested to do so. There are a number of exceptions in the 2004 Regulations where information need not be disclosed, including where disclosure would adversely affect international relations, defence, national security or public safety; the ability of a person to receive a fair trial; and protection of commercial and other confidentiality in specified situations. There is, however, generally a presumption in favour of disclosure.

3.40 Even where land has not been identified as CONTAMINATED LAND, information collected under Part 2A may also be useful for the wider purpose of the LOCAL AUTHORITY and other regulatory bodies, including:

(a) planning and building control functions;
(b) other relevant statutory pollution control regimes (for example, powers to require the removal of illegally-deposited controlled wastes); and
(c) radioactive waste management.

4. Identifying and notifying those who may need to take action

Notification of the identification of contaminated land

Identification of interested persons

4.1 For any piece of land identified as being CONTAMINATED LAND, the LOCAL AUTHORITY needs to establish:

(a) who is the OWNER of the land (defined in section 78A(9));

(b) who appears to be in occupation of all or part of the land; and

(c) who appears to be an APPROPRIATE PERSON to bear responsibility for any REMEDIATION ACTION which might be necessary (defined in section 78F; see paragraphs 9.3 to 9.20 below).

4.2 At this early stage, the LOCAL AUTHORITY may not be able to establish with certainty who falls into each of these categories, particularly the last of them. As it obtains further information, the authority needs to reconsider these questions. It needs to act, however, on the basis of the best information available to it at any particular time.

The notification

4.3 The LOCAL AUTHORITY needs to notify, in writing, the persons set out in paragraph 4.1 above, as well as the ENVIRONMENT AGENCY, of the fact that the land has been identified as being CONTAMINATED LAND *(section 78B(3))*. The notice given to any of these persons will inform them of the capacity—for example, OWNER or APPROPRIATE PERSON—in which they have been sent it.

4.4 The LOCAL AUTHORITY (or, in the case of a SPECIAL SITE, the ENVIRONMENT AGENCY) may, at any subsequent time, identify some other person who appears to be an APPROPRIATE PERSON, either as well as or instead of those previously identified. Where this happens, the relevant authority needs to notify that person that he appears to be an APPROPRIATE PERSON with respect to land which has been identified as CONTAMINATED LAND *(section 78B(4))*.

4.5 The issuing of a notice under either of these headings has the effect of starting the process of consultation on what REMEDIATION might be appropriate. The LOCAL AUTHORITY (or the ENVIRONMENT AGENCY) may therefore wish to consider whether to provide any additional information to the recipients of the notification, in order to facilitate this consultation. The following categories of information may be useful for these purposes:

(a) a copy of the written record of the determination made by the authority that the land appears to be CONTAMINATED LAND *(paragraph B.52)*;

(b) information on the availability of site investigation reports, with copies of the full reports being available on request;

(c) an indication of the reason why particular persons appear to the authority to be APPROPRIATE PERSONS; and

(d) the names and addresses of other persons notified at the same time or previously, indicating the capacity in which they were notified (for example, as OWNER or as APPROPRIATE PERSON).

4.6 The authority will also need to inform each APPROPRIATE PERSON about the tests for EXCLUSION from, and APPORTIONMENT of, liabilities set out in the statutory guidance in Chapter D *(paragraph D.33)*. This will enable those persons to know what information they might wish to provide the authority, in order to make a case for their EXCLUSION from liability, or for a particular APPORTIONMENT of liability.

4.7 The notification to the ENVIRONMENT AGENCY enables the Agency to decide whether:

(a) it considers that the land should be designated a SPECIAL SITE, on the basis that it falls within one or more of the relevant descriptions

(*regulations 2 and 3 of the Contaminated Land Regulations*: see also
paragraphs 7 to 15 of Annex 4);

(b) it wishes to provide site-specific guidance to the LOCAL AUTHOR-
ITY, for example on what REMEDIATION might be required (see
paragraphs 6.8 to 6.9 below); or

(c) it requires further information from the LOCAL AUTHORITY
about the land, in order for the ENVIRONMENT AGENCY to
prepare its national report (*section 78U*).

4.8 If the ENVIRONMENT AGENCY requires any further information from
the LOCAL AUTHORITY, it should request this in writing. The LOCAL
AUTHORITY should provide such information as it has, or can "reasonably be expected to obtain" (*sections 78U(3) & 78V(3)*).

Identifying possible special sites

4.9 Having identified any CONTAMINATED LAND, the LOCAL AUTHOR-
ITY needs to consider whether the land also meets any of the descriptions
which would require it to be designated as a SPECIAL SITE. These
descriptions are prescribed in the Contaminated Land Regulations (*regulations 2 & 3;* see also paragraphs 7 to 15 of Annex 4). If the LOCAL
AUTHORITY concludes that it should designate any land, it will need to
notify the ENVIRONMENT AGENCY.

4.10 The authority needs to reconsider this question whenever it obtains
further relevant information about the land, for example after the
carrying out of any ASSESSMENT ACTION under the terms of a
REMEDIATION NOTICE.

4.11 Description of the procedures for the designation of a SPECIAL SITE,
and the implications of any such designation, are set out in paragraphs
18.1 to 18.34 below.

Role of the enforcing authority

4.12 After the LOCAL AUTHORITY has identified any SIGNIFICANT POL-
LUTANT LINKAGE, thus determined that the land is CONTAMI-
NATED LAND and then carried out the necessary notifications, it is for
the ENFORCING AUTHORITY (that is, the ENVIRONMENT AGENCY
for any SPECIAL SITE and the LOCAL AUTHORITY for any other site)
to take further action.

5. *Urgent Remediation Action*

5.1 Where it appears to the ENFORCING AUTHORITY that there is an
imminent danger of serious HARM, serious POLLUTION OF CON-
TROLLED WATERS, or serious HARM attributable to radioactivity,
being caused as a result of a SIGNIFICANT POLLUTANT LINKAGE
that has been identified, that authority may need to ensure that urgent
REMEDIATION is carried out.

5.2 The ENFORCING AUTHORITY needs to keep this question under
review as it receives further information about the condition of the
CONTAMINATED LAND. It may decide that urgent REMEDIATION is
needed at any stage in the procedures set out below. It is likely that any
REMEDIATION ACTION carried out on an urgent basis will be only a
part of the total REMEDIATION SCHEME for the RELEVANT LAND
OR WATERS, as not all of the REMEDIATION ACTIONS will need to
be carried out urgently.

5.3 The terms "imminent" and "serious" are not defined in Part 2A. The ENFORCING AUTHORITY needs to judge each case on the normal meaning of the words and the facts of that case. However, the statutory guidance in Part 5 of Chapter C sets out a number of considerations relating to the assessment of the seriousness of any HARM or POLLUTION OF CONTROLLED WATERS which may be relevant.

5.4 Where the ENFORCING AUTHORITY is satisfied that there is a need for urgent REMEDIATION, two requirements which normally apply to the service of REMEDIATION NOTICES are disapplied (*sections 78G(4) & 78H(4)*). These are the requirements for:

    (a) prior consultation (*section 78H(1);* see paragraphs 6.10 to 6.17 below); and

    (b) a three month interval between:

        (i) the notification to the APPROPRIATE PERSON that the land has been identified as CONTAMINATED LAND or the land's designation as a SPECIAL SITE, and

        (ii) the service of the remediation notice (*section 78H(3);* see paragraphs 12.4 and 12.5 below).

5.5 However, other requirements in the primary legislation and in the statutory guidance continue to apply, in particular with respect to:

    (a) the standard of REMEDIATION and what REMEDIATION ACTIONS may be required (*section 78E(4) and Chapter C*; see paragraphs 6.18 to 6.29A below); and

    (b) the identification of the APPROPRIATE PERSON and any EXCLUSIONS from, or APPORTIONMENTS of, responsibility to bear the cost of REMEDIATION (*section 78F and Chapter D;* see paragraphs 9.3 to 9.49 below).

5.6 In general where there is a need for urgent REMEDIATION ACTION, the ENFORCING AUTHORITY will act by serving a REMEDIATION NOTICE on an urgent basis (that is, without necessarily consulting or waiting for the end of the three month period referred to in paragraph 5.4(b) above). However, if the ENFORCING AUTHORITY considers that serving a REMEDIATION NOTICE in this way would not result in the REMEDIATION happening soon enough, it may decide to carry out the REMEDIATION itself. The authority has the power to do this only where it considers that:

    (a) there is an imminent danger of serious HARM, serious POLLUTION OF CONTROLLED WATERS, or serious HARM attributable to radioactivity being caused; and

    (b) it is necessary for the authority to carry out REMEDIATION itself to prevent that harm or pollution (*section 78N(3)(a)*).

5.7 These circumstances may apply, in particular, if the ENFORCING AUTHORITY cannot readily identify any APPROPRIATE PERSON on whom it could serve a REMEDIATION NOTICE. There may also be cases where the ENFORCING AUTHORITY considers that urgent REMEDIATION is needed and has already specified the necessary REMEDIATION ACTIONS in a REMEDIATION NOTICE, but the requirements of that notice have been suspended pending the decision in an appeal against the notice (see paragraphs 13.5 to 13.7 below).

5.8 If the ENFORCING AUTHORITY carries out any urgent REMEDIATION itself, it needs to prepare and publish a REMEDIATION STATE-

MENT describing the REMEDIATION ACTIONS it has carried out (*section 78H(7)*). It needs also to consider whether to seek to recover, from the appropriate person, the reasonable costs the authority has incurred in carrying out the REMEDIATION (*section 78P(1) and Chapter E;* see paragraphs 16.1 to 16.11 below).

6. Identifying appropriate remediation requirements

Introduction

6.1 Where any land has been identified as being CONTAMINATED LAND, the ENFORCING AUTHORITY has a duty to require appropriate REMEDIATION. The statutory guidance in Chapter C of Annex 3 to this Circular sets out the standard to which any land or waters should be remediated.

6.2 For the purposes of Part 2A, the term REMEDIATION has a wider meaning than it has under its common usage (*section 78A(7) and 78A(7A)*). It includes ASSESSMENT ACTION, REMEDIAL TREATMENT ACTION and MONITORING ACTION (*paragraphs C.7 and C8*). Part 7 of the statutory guidance at Chapter C of Annex 3 identifies circumstances in which action falling within each of these three categories may be appropriate. Where CONTAMINATED LAND is attributable to radio-activity, a REMEDIAL TREATMENT ACTION may include an INTER-VENTION (*paragraph C.7A*) which reduces or prevents the radiation exposure of individuals (see paragraph 8.28 below).

6.3 In relation to any particular piece of CONTAMINATED LAND, it may be necessary to carry out more than one thing by way of REMEDIATION. To describe the various things which may need to be done, the statutory guidance uses the following terms:

    (a) a "REMEDIATION ACTION" is any individual thing which is being, or is to be done, by way of REMEDIATION;

    (b) a "REMEDIATION PACKAGE" is all the REMEDIATION ACTIONS, within a REMEDIATION SCHEME, which are referable to a particular SIGNIFICANT POLLUTANT LINKAGE; and

    (c) a "REMEDIATION SCHEME" is the complete set or sequence of REMEDIATION ACTIONS (referable to one or more SIGNIFI-CANT POLLUTANT LINKAGES) to be carried out with respect to the RELEVANT LAND OR WATERS.

Phased remediation

6.4 The overall process of REMEDIATION may well be phased, with different REMEDIATION ACTIONS being required at different times. For example, ASSESSMENT ACTION may be needed in order to establish what REMEDIAL TREATMENT ACTION would be effective. Once the results of that ASSESSMENT ACTION are known, the REMEDIAL TREATMENT ACTION itself might then be carried out, with MONITORING ACTIONS being needed to ensure that it has been effective. In another case, there might be a need for different REMEDIAL TREATMENT ACTIONS to be carried out in sequence.

6.5 Wherever the complete REMEDIATION SCHEME cannot be specified in a single REMEDIATION NOTICE or REMEDIATION STATEMENT, and needs to be phased, the process of consulting and determining what particular REMEDIATION ACTIONS are required needs to be repeated for each such notice or statement.

Agreed remediation

6.6 It is the Government's intention that, wherever practicable, REMEDIA-TION should proceed by agreement rather than by formal action by the ENFORCING AUTHORITY. In this context, the authority and the person who will carry out the REMEDIATION may identify by mutual agreement the particular REMEDIATION ACTIONS which would achieve REMEDIATION to the necessary standard (see paragraphs 6.33 to 6.34A below). The REMEDIATION may be carried out without a REMEDIATION NOTICE being served, but with the agreed REMEDIA-TION ACTIONS being described in a published REMEDIATION STATE-MENT (see paragraphs 8.1 to 8.28 below).

6.7 However, where appropriate REMEDIATION is not being carried out, or where agreement cannot be reached on the REMEDIATION ACTIONS required, the authority has a duty to serve a REMEDIATION NOTICE. Any such notice must specify particular REMEDIATION ACTIONS to be carried out and the times within which they must be carried out (*section 78E(1)*).

Site-specific guidance from the environment agency

6.8 The ENVIRONMENT AGENCY has the power to provide site-specific guidance to the LOCAL AUTHORITY, where that LOCAL AUTHOR-ITY is the ENFORCING AUTHORITY for any CONTAMINATED LAND (*section 78V(1)*). It may choose to do so, in particular, where either:

(a) it has particular technical expertise available, for example derived from its other pollution control functions; or

(b) the manner in which the REMEDIATION might be carried out could affect its responsibilities for protecting the water environment.

6.9 In any case where such guidance is given, the LOCAL AUTHORITY has to have regard to it when deciding what REMEDIATION is required (*section 78V(1)*).

Consultation

Remediation requirements

6.10 Before the ENFORCING AUTHORITY serves any REMEDIATION NOTICE it will, in general, need to make reasonable endeavours to consult the following persons with an interest in the CONTAMINATED LAND, or in the REMEDIATION (*section 78H(1)*):

(a) the person on whom the notice is to be served (i.e. the APPROPRI-ATE PERSON);

(b) the OWNER of the land to which the notice would relate; and

(c) any other person who appears to the authority to be in occupation of the whole, or any part of, the land.

6.11 This means that any recipient of a REMEDIATION NOTICE is consulted before the notice is served, at a minimum about the details of what he is being required to do, and the time within which he must do it. However, consultation is not a requirement in cases of urgency (see paragraph 5.4 above).

6.12 In addition to the consultation directly required by section 78H(1), the ENFORCING AUTHORITY is likely to find a wider process of discussion and consultation useful. This could cover, for example:

(a) whether the land should, in fact, be identified as CONTAMINATED LAND; this question might be re-visited, for example, in cases where the land OWNER, or the APPROPRIATE PERSON, had additional sampling information;

(b) what would need to be achieved by the REMEDIATION, in terms of the reduction of the possibility of SIGNIFICANT HARM being caused, or of the likelihood of the POLLUTION OF CONTROLLED WATERS, or of the possibility of HARM attributable to radioactivity being caused and in terms of the remedying of any effects of that harm or pollution; and

(c) what particular REMEDIATION ACTIONS would achieve that REMEDIATION.

6.13 This wider process of discussion may also help:

(a) to identify opportunities for agreed REMEDIATION which can be carried out without the service of a REMEDIATION NOTICE; and

(b) where a REMEDIATION NOTICE is served, to resolve as many disagreements as possible before the service of the notice, thus limiting the scope of any appeal against the notice under section 78L.

Granting of rights

6.14 The ENFORCING AUTHORITY also needs to consult on the rights which may need to be granted to the recipient of any REMEDIATION NOTICE to entitle him to carry out the REMEDIATION. For example, where the APPROPRIATE PERSON does not own the CONTAMINATED LAND, he may need the consent of the OWNER of the land to enter it. Under section 78G(2), any person whose consent is required has to grant, or join in granting, the necessary rights. He is then entitled to compensation (*section 78G and regulation 6 of the Contaminated Land Regulations;* see paragraphs 21 to 38 of Annex 4).

6.15 Except in cases of urgency (see paragraph 5.4 above), the ENFORCING AUTHORITY needs to consult:

(a) the OWNER or occupier of any of the RELEVANT LAND OR WATERS; and

(b) any other person who might have to grant, or join in granting, any rights to the recipient of a REMEDIATION NOTICE (*section 78G(3)*).

Liabilities

6.16 If there are two or more APPROPRIATE PERSONS, the ENFORCING AUTHORITY should make reasonable endeavours to consult each of those persons on any EXCLUSION from, or APPORTIONMENT of, liability (*paragraph D.36*). This allows anyone who might be affected to provide the information on which an EXCLUSION or APPORTIONMENT can be based. In addition to information provided by the APPROPRIATE PERSONS, the authority needs to seek its own information, where this is reasonable (*paragraph D.36*).

6.17 The ENFORCING AUTHORITY may also find it useful to discuss wider questions relating to liabilities with those whom it has identified as being APPROPRIATE PERSONS. For example, they may be able to identify other persons who ought to be identified as APPROPRIATE PERSONS, either in addition or instead.

Identifying an appropriate remediation scheme

6.18 The ENFORCING AUTHORITY'S objective is to identify the appropriate REMEDIATION SCHEME, which will include the REMEDIAL TREAT-MENT ACTION or actions which, taken together, will ensure that the RELEVANT LAND OR WATERS or, in the case of HARM attributable to radioactivity, the RELEVANT LAND, are remediated to the necessary standard (*Chapter C, Part 3*). In some cases, the particular REMEDIA-TION ACTIONS to be carried out may be identified by mutual agree-ment between the authority and the persons who will carry them out. In other cases, that authority has to identify the particular actions itself.

6.19 Where the authority is identifying the actions itself, it is specifically required to ensure that they are "reasonable", having regard to the cost which is likely to be involved and the seriousness of the HARM or of the POLLUTION OF CONTROLLED WATERS or the HARM attributable to radioactivity in question (*section 78E(4), section 78E(4) (as modified) and section78E(4A)*). The authority needs to assess, in particular, the costs involved as against the benefits arising from the REMEDIATION (*para-graph C30;* but see also paragraph 6.37 below).

6.19A In deciding what is reasonable, where REMEDIATION includes an INTERVENTION to deal with HARM attributable to radioactivity, the ENFORCING AUTHORITY needs to consider not only the costs and seriousness of the HARM but also whether the INTERVENTION meets the tests for JUSTIFICATION and OPTIMISATION (*section 78E(4) (as modified)*). The INTERVENTION meets the tests of:

(a) JUSTIFICATION where the benefits of the reduction in health DETRIMENT are sufficient to justify the costs, including the social costs and adverse effects (i.e. the DETRIMENT associated with the INTERVENTION) (*section 78E(4A)(a)*); and

(b) OPTIMISATION where the benefits less the DETRIMENT associ-ated with the INTERVENTION is maximised (*sections 78E(4A)(b) and 78E(4B)*).

6.19B The way in which JUSTIFICATION and OPTIMISATION are to be applied is set out in paragraphs C.43B to C.43J.

6.20 It may be necessary for ASSESSMENT ACTIONS to be carried out before the appropriate REMEDIAL TREATMENT ACTION or actions can be identified (*paragraph C.65*). Where this is the case, the first step will be to identify the appropriate ASSESSMENT ACTION or actions. Once that ASSESSMENT ACTION has been carried out, it will be necessary to complete the identification of the remaining stages of the REMEDIA-TION SCHEME, identifying appropriate REMEDIAL TREATMENT ACTIONS in the light of the information obtained. This may require a sequence of REMEDIATION STATEMENTS or REMEDIATION NOTICES.

6.21 Throughout the process of identifying the appropriate REMEDIATION SCHEME, the ENFORCING AUTHORITY needs to keep under review whether there is a need for urgent REMEDIATION to be carried out (see section 5 of this Annex).

A single significant pollutant linkage

6.22 Where only a single SIGNIFICANT POLLUTANT LINKAGE has been identified on the CONTAMINATED LAND, the ENFORCING AUTHORITY, in conjunction with those it is consulting, needs to consider what is needed, with respect to that linkage, to:

(a) prevent, or reduce the likelihood of, the occurrence of any SIGNIFI-CANT HARM, POLLUTION OF CONTROLLED WATERS, or any HARM attributable to radioactivity; and

(b) remedy, or mitigate, the effect of any such harm or water pollution which has been, or might be, caused.

6.23 The ENFORCING AUTHORITY then needs to identify the REMEDIA-TION PACKAGE which would represent the BEST PRACTICABLE TECHNIQUES of REMEDIATION for that SIGNIFICANT POLLU-TANT LINKAGE. Such techniques will include appropriate measures to provide quality assurance and to verify what has been done.

6.24 The assessment of what represents such BEST PRACTICABLE TECH-NIQUES is made in terms of:

(a) the extent to which the REMEDIATION PACKAGE would achieve the objectives identified in paragraph 6.22 above (*Part 4 of Chapter C*);

(b) whether the package, and the individual REMEDIATION ACTIONS concerned, would be reasonable, having regard to their cost and to the seriousness of the HARM or of the POLLUTION OF CONTROLLED WATERS to which they relate (*Part 5 of Chapter C*); in the case of HARM attributable to radioactivity, where any individual REMEDIATION ACTION is, or is part of, an INTER-VENTION it may only be considered reasonable if the INTERVEN-TION is justified and optimised (*sections 78E(4) (as modified) and 78E(4A) and Part 5 of Chapter C* ; see also paragraph 6.19 above); and

(c) whether the package represents the best combination of prac-ticability, effectiveness and durability (Part 6 of Chapter C).

6.25 Any such REMEDIATION PACKAGE needs to include measures to achieve quality assurance and verification. Where appropriate, such measures may take the form of MONITORING ACTIONS (*paragraphs C.68 and C.69*).

More than one significant pollution linkage

6.26 If more than one SIGNIFICANT POLLUTANT LINKAGE has been identified, the REMEDIATION will have to deal with the SIGNIFICANT HARM, the POLLUTION OF CONTROLLED WATERS, or the HARM attributable to radioactivity resulting from, or threatened by, each of those linkages. However, it may be neither practicable nor efficient simply to consider the REMEDIATION needed with respect to each linkage separately. There may, for example, be cost savings which can be achieved by carrying out particular REMEDIATION ACTIONS which deal with more than one SIGNIFICANT POLLUTANT LINKAGE. In other cases, if the separate REMEDIATION PACKAGES for each of the SIGNIFICANT POLLUTANT LINKAGES were carried out indepen-dently, the individual REMEDIATION ACTIONS might conflict or overlap.

6.27 The ENFORCING AUTHORITY therefore needs to try to identify a REMEDIATION SCHEME which deals with the RELEVANT LAND OR WATERS as a whole, avoids conflict or overlap between the REMEDIA-TION needed for the various SIGNIFICANT POLLUTANT LINKAGES, and does not involve unnecessary expense (*paragraph C.27*). This may result in a REMEDIATION ACTION which replaces, or subsumes, what would otherwise be several separate REMEDIATION ACTIONS in different REMEDIATION PACKAGES.

6.28 The first step in this process is for the ENFORCING AUTHORITY to assess the standard of REMEDIATION to be achieved by the REMEDIATION SCHEME with respect to each SIGNIFICANT POLLUTANT LINKAGE.

6.29 In doing this, the ENFORCING AUTHORITY needs to identify, for each SIGNIFICANT POLLUTANT LINKAGE, the extent to which the relevant SIGNIFICANT HARM, the POLLUTION OF CONTROLLED WATERS, or the HARM attributable to radioactivity should be reduced, and its effects mitigated. The standard for this reduction or mitigation is set by reference to what would be achieved by the BEST PRACTICABLE TECHNIQUES of REMEDIATION for that linkage, if it were the only linkage required to be remediated (*paragraphs C.18 and C.26*). In making this assessment, however, the authority works on the basis of REMEDIATION which could actually be carried out, given the wider circumstances of the land or waters, including the presence of other POLLUTANTS. In other words, in considering what might be achieved in relation to any particular SIGNIFICANT POLLUTANT LINKAGE, the ENFORCING AUTHORITY cannot ignore practical limitations on what might be done that are imposed by other problems on the same site.

6.29A Where there is one or more SIGNIFICANT POLLUTANT LINKAGES attributable to radioactivity, there is an explicit requirement that any INTERVENTION to deal with HARM attributable to radioactivity must meet the requirements of JUSTIFICATION and OPTIMISATION (*sections 78E(4) (as modified) and 78E(4A); paragraphs C.43B to C.43J;* and paragraph 6.19A above). This means that if there is more than one SIGNIFICANT POLLUTANT LINKAGE attributable to radioactivity then these should be considered separately (as in paragraph 6.26 above) and then together, ensuring any proposed INTERVENTION to deal with one or more SIGNIFICANT POLLUTANT LINKAGES is justified and optimised before consideration is given to any possible wider REMEDIATION SCHEME also dealing with SIGNIFICANT POLLUTANT LINKAGES not attributable to radioactivity. Once the wider remediation scheme has been identified, the ENFORCING AUTHORITY needs to check that any INTERVENTION is still justified and optimised for any SIGNIFICANT POLLUTANT LINKAGES attributable to radioactivity (*paragraphs C.43B to C.43J*).

Very slight levels of water pollution

6.30 As stated above (see paragraph 2.9) the definition of "POLLUTION OF CONTROLLED WATERS" is simply the "entry into CONTROLLED WATERS of any poisonous, noxious or polluting matter or any solid waste matter". Radioactivity is not relevant to assessing whether POLLUTION OF CONTROLLED WATERS may be occurring (see paragraph 2.7). Some commentators have suggested that the entry of very small amounts of matter into CONTROLLED WATERS might satisfy this definition, and thus lead to the identification of land as CONTAMINATED LAND. As indicated at paragraph 2.9 above, the definition is to be amended to include a significance test.

6.31 However, in the interim, even if land is identified as CONTAMINATED LAND in this way—on the basis of the actual or likely entry of only a very small amount of a POLLUTANT into CONTROLLED WATERS—this should not lead to the imposition of major liabilities: there are other balances elsewhere in the regime to prevent this. In particular, any REMEDIATION that can be required must be "reasonable", having regard to the cost which is likely to be involved and the seriousness of the POLLUTION OF CONTROLLED WATERS involved (*section 78E(4) and Chapter C, Part 4*). If there is only a very low degree of contamination on any land which gives, or is likely to give, rise to POLLUTION OF CONTROLLED WATERS which is minor in terms of its seriousness, it will be reasonable to incur only a correspondingly low level of expenditure in attempting to remediate that land.

6.32 Nevertheless, the simple fact of land being identified as CONTAMI-NATED LAND in this way may cause its own problems—for example, for landowners. It is therefore important that the circumstances of such cases are clearly entered on the REGISTER kept by the ENFORCING AUTHORITY. If REMEDIATION is not carried out because it would not be reasonable, a REMEDIATION DECLARATION needs to be published by the ENFORCING AUTHORITY (*section 78H(6)*) and entered on its REGISTER (*section 78R(l)(c)*). In this way, a public record is created explaining that no REMEDIATION is required under Part 2A, even though the land has been formally identified as CONTAMINATED LAND.

Assessing remediation schemes proposed by others

6.33 In general, the ENFORCING AUTHORITY needs to adopt a similar approach when it is assessing a REMEDIATION SCHEME proposed by the APPROPRIATE PERSON, the land OWNER or any other person to that which it adopts when itself identifying an appropriate REMEDIA-TION SCHEME (*paragraph C.3(b)*). In deciding whether it is satisfied that such a scheme would be appropriate and sufficient, it needs to consider whether that scheme would achieve a standard of REMEDIATION equivalent to that which would be achieved by the use of the BEST PRACTICABLE TECHNIQUES of REMEDIATION for each SIGNIFI-CANT POLLUTANT LINKAGE (*paragraph C.28*).

6.34 However, the ENFORCING AUTHORITY does not always need to consider whether the proposed scheme would, of itself, be "reasonable" in the sense required by section 78E(4) (i.e. having regard to the cost likely to be involved and the seriousness of the particular harm or water pollution). This is because the person proposing the scheme may wish to carry out REMEDIATION on a wider basis than could be required under the terms of a REMEDIATION NOTICE. For example, the proposed scheme may include works to deal with matters which do not form SIGNIFICANT POLLUTANT LINKAGES, or may involve a more expensive approach to REMEDIATION.

6.34A Where voluntary remediation includes an INTERVENTION to deal with HARM attributable to radioactivity, the ENFORCING AUTHORITY also does not always need to consider whether the proposed scheme would, of itself, be "reasonable" in the sense required by section 78E(4) (as modified) and 78E(4A) for the reasons set out in paragraph 6.34 above. However, it is still necessary for the INTERVENTION to be justified and optimised (*paragraphs C.43B to C.43J*) in the wider context.

6.35 Where an acceptable REMEDIATION SCHEME is proposed by others, and that scheme is likely to proceed without the service of a REMEDIA-TION NOTICE, no such notice needs to be served. In such cases, the procedure set out in section 8 of this Annex will apply.

7. Limitations on remediation notices

7.1 In addition to circumstances where REMEDIATION takes place without the service of a REMEDIATION NOTICE (see section 8 of this Annex), there are a number of restrictions on the service or contents of a REMEDIATION NOTICE. See also paragraphs 51 to 54 and 75(d) of Annex 1 to this Circular on the non-applicability of Part 2A in relation to certain cases involving, respectively, waste management activities and nuclear sites.

Interactions with other statutory remedies

7.2 REMEDIATION cannot be required under Part 2A where the SIGNIFICANT HARM or the POLLUTION OF CONTROLLED WATERS in question results from an offence under the Integrated Pollution Control regime, the Pollution Prevention and Control regime or the waste management licensing regime, and powers are available under the relevant regime to deal with that HARM or POLLUTION OF CONTOLLED [sic] WATERS. REMEDIATION cannot be carried out by the ENFORCING AUTHORITY in such cases (*section 78N(2)*).

7.3 Nevertheless, even in such cases, the ENFORCING AUTHORITY needs to consider whether additional REMEDIATION is required on the RELEVANT LAND OR WATERS under Part 2A, to deal with matters which cannot be dealt with under those other powers.

7.4 If no such additional REMEDIATION is necessary, the ENFORCING AUTHORITY takes no further action, under Part 2A, with respect to the CONTAMINATED LAND in question. However, it then needs to include information about the exercise of these powers on its REGISTER (*Schedule 3, Contaminated Land Regulations;* see also Annex 4, paragraph 83).

Integrated pollution control & pollution prevention and control

7.5 If the SIGNIFICANT HARM or POLLUTION OF CONTROLLED WATERS in question results from the carrying out of a process covered by the Integrated Pollution Control (IPC) regime, the Local Air Pollution Control (LAPC) regime, or the Pollution Prevention and Control (PPC) regime, the regulator may have powers to take enforcement action under those regimes to remedy that HARM or POLLUTION OF CONTROLLED WATERS.

7.6 Section 27 of the Environmental Protection Act 1990 gives the ENVIRONMENT AGENCY the power to carry out remedial steps where:

   (a) an IPC or LAPC process has been carried out either without the necessary authorisation, or in contravention of an enforcement or prohibition notice;
   (b) harm has been caused and it is possible to remedy that harm;
   (c) the SECRETARY OF STATE gives written approval to the exercise of the powers; and
   (d) the occupier of any affected land, other than the land on which the process is being carried out, gives his permission.

7.6A Regulation 24 of the Pollution Prevention & Control (England and Wales) Regulations 2000 (S.I. 2000/1973) gives the relevant regulator the power to serve an enforcement notice where it is of the opinion that an operator has contravened, is contravening or is likely to contravene any condition of his permit, and this may specify both the steps necessary to comply with the permit and the steps that must be taken to remedy the effects of any pollution caused by the contravention. In addition, regulation 26(2) of the PPC Regulations 2000 gives the relevant regulator the power to carry out remedial steps itself, where pollution has been caused and it is possible to take steps towards remedying the effects of the pollution, in cases where:

 (a) the installation or mobile plant has been operated either without the necessary authorisation by a permit, or outside the extent authorised by the permit; or

 (b) there has been a failure to comply with a permit condition, or a contravention of the conditions of a permit; or

 (c) there has been a failure to comply with the requirements of an enforcement notice, a suspension notice, or a closure notice.

7.7A The ENFORCING AUTHORITY, if it considers that the section 27 or regulation 24 or 26(2) powers might apply needs to consider whether it has those powers itself, and if not then it should consult the relevant regulator to find out whether the relevant powers are available to that regulator.

7.7B In any case where the powers under section 27 may be exercised by the ENVIRONMENT AGENCY, a REMEDIATION NOTICE cannot include a REMEDIATION ACTION which would be carried out in order to achieve a purpose which could be achieved by the exercise of those powers (*section 78YB(1)*). Similarly in any case where a PPC enforcement action may be taken—either an enforcement notice under regulation 24 of the PPC regulations, or the use of the powers to remedy pollution under regulation 26(2)—a REMEDIATION NOTICE cannot include a REMEDIATION ACTION which would be carried out in order to achieve a purpose which could be achieved by the exercise of those powers (*section 78YB (2B)*). Nor can an ENFORCING AUTHORITY use its powers under section 78N to carry out remediation.

Waste on land

7.9 The ENVIRONMENT AGENCY (in its capacity as the "waste regulation authority"), and the waste collection authority for the area, have powers under section 59 of the Environmental Protection Act 1990 to deal with illegally-deposited controlled waste. These powers may permit the Agency or authority to remove, or require the removal of the waste, and to take other steps to eliminate or reduce the consequences of the deposit of the waste.

7.10 Section 59 applies where controlled waste has been deposited:

 (a) without a waste management licence being in force authorising the deposit (except where regulations provide an exemption from licensing); or

 (b) in a manner which is not in accordance with a waste management licence.

7.11 If a LOCAL AUTHORITY is the ENFORCING AUTHORITY and it considers that these circumstances might apply, it needs to consult the ENVIRONMENT AGENCY and to consider its position where it is the waste collection authority. If the powers under section 59 may be exercised, any REMEDIATION NOTICE cannot include a REMEDIA-TION ACTION which would be carried out in order to achieve a purpose which could be achieved by the exercise of those powers (*section 78YB(3)*).

7.11A Paragraphs 7.9 to 7.11 above set out the relationship with Part 2A where waste management activities are subject to the PPC regime.

Other precluded remediation actions

Actions which would be unreasonable

7.12 In identifying an appropriate REMEDIATION SCHEME, the ENFORC-ING AUTHORITY may have been precluded from specifying particular

REMEDIATION ACTIONS on the grounds that they would not be reasonable, having regard to their likely cost and the seriousness of the HARM or the POLLUTION OF CONTROLLED WATERS to which they relate. In the particular case of HARM attributable to radioactivity, REMEDIATION ACTIONS may have been precluded taking account of the requirement for JUSTIFICATION and OPTIMISATION (see paragraph 8.28 below). In some cases, such restrictions may lead to a situation in which no REMEDIATION ACTION may be required (see, for one example, paragraph 6.31 above). Alternatively, the preclusion of a particular REMEDIATION ACTION or actions may lead to the adoption of an alternative REMEDIATION SCHEME.

7.13 Where particular REMEDIATION ACTIONS have been precluded because they would not be reasonable the ENFORCING AUTHORITY needs to prepare and publish a REMEDIATION DECLARATION which records:

(a) the reasons why the authority would have specified the remediation actions in a remediation notice; and

(b) the grounds on which it is satisfied that it is precluded from including them in any such notice—that is, why it considers that they are unreasonable (*section 78H(6)*).

7.14 The ENFORCING AUTHORITY also needs to enter details of the REMEDIATION DECLARATION on its REGISTER (*section 78R(l)(c); see paragraphs 17.1 to 17.19 below and Annex 4, paragraph 80*).

Actions which would be contrary to the statutory guidance

7.15 In rare circumstances, there may also be a particular REMEDIATION ACTION which the ENFORCING AUTHORITY would include in a REMEDIATION NOTICE, but it cannot do so because that action is not consistent with the statutory guidance in Chapter C. In any such case, the authority needs to proceed in the same way as if that REMEDIATION ACTION had been precluded on the ground that it was unreasonable (*sections 78E(5) and 78H(6)*).

Discharges into controlled waters

7.16 The ENFORCING AUTHORITY also needs to consider whether any REMEDIATION ACTION in the REMEDIATION SCHEME would have the effect of impeding or preventing any discharge into CONTROLLED WATERS for which consent has been given under Part 3 of the Water Resources Act 1991.

7.17 If this is the case, the ENFORCING AUTHORITY is precluded from specifying the REMEDIATION ACTION in question in any REMEDIATION NOTICE (*section 78YB(4)*). However, it will be good practice for the ENFORCING AUTHORITY to consider in such circumstances whether there is a REMEDIATION ACTION which could address the problems posed by the SIGNIFICANT POLLUTANT LINKAGE without impeding or preventing the discharge.

7.18 However, if a REMEDIATION ACTION cannot be specified because of the restriction in section 78YB(4), the ENFORCING AUTHORITY needs to include information about the circumstances on its REGISTER (*Schedule 3, Contaminated Land Regulations; see also Annex 4, paragraph 84*).

8. Remediation taking place without the service of a remediation notice

8.1 Having identified the appropriate REMEDIATION SCHEME for the RELEVANT LAND OR WATERS, the ENFORCING AUTHORITY needs to consider whether that REMEDIATION is being, or will be, carried out without any REMEDIATION NOTICE being served.

8.2 This might be the case, in particular, where:

(a) the APPROPRIATE PERSON, or some other person, already plans, or undertakes during the consultation process, to carry out particular REMEDIATION ACTIONS (see paragraphs 8.3 to 8.8 below); or

(b) REMEDIATION with an equivalent effect is taking, or will take, place as a result of enforcement action under other powers (see paragraphs 8.9 to 8.17 below).

Volunteered remediation

8.3 The ENFORCING AUTHORITY may be informed, before or during the course of consultation on REMEDIATION requirements, that the APPROPRIATE PERSON or some other person already intends, or now intends, to carry out particular REMEDIATION ACTIONS on a voluntary basis.

8.4 This may apply, in particular, where:

(a) the OWNER of the land has a programme for carrying out REMEDIATION on a number of different areas of land for which he is responsible which aims to tackle those cases in order of environmental priority;

(b) the land is already subject to development proposals;

(c) the APPROPRIATE PERSON brings forward proposals to develop the land in order to fund necessary REMEDIATION; or

(d) the APPROPRIATE PERSON wishes to avoid being served with a REMEDIATION NOTICE.

8.5 Where a development of CONTAMINATED LAND is proposed, an ENFORCING AUTHORITY which is the local planning authority will need to consider what steps it needs to take under town and country planning legislation to ensure that appropriate REMEDIATION ACTIONS are included in the development proposals and that these will ensure that contamination is properly dealt with. (Where the enforcing authority is not the local planning authority, the two authorities will need to consult.)

8.6 In all cases, the ENFORCING AUTHORITY needs to consider the standard of REMEDIATION which would be achieved by the proposed REMEDIATION ACTIONS. If it is satisfied that they would achieve an appropriate standard of REMEDIATION:

(a) it is precluded from serving any REMEDIATION NOTICE (*section 78H(5)(b)*); and

(b) the person who is carrying out, or will carry out, the REMEDIATION is required to prepare and publish a REMEDIATION STATEMENT (*sections 78H(7) & 78H(8)(a);* see paragraphs 8.18 to 8.22 below).

8.7 Even if the ENFORCING AUTHORITY is not satisfied that an appropriate standard of REMEDIATION would be achieved by the REMEDIATION ACTIONS originally proposed, it may be able to persuade the person who made the proposals to bring forward a revised and satisfactory REMEDIATION SCHEME.

8.8 If this is not possible, the ENFORCING AUTHORITY'S duty to serve a REMEDIATION NOTICE may apply *(section 78E(1);* see paragraphs 12.1 to 12.9 below).

Enforcement action under other powers

8.9 Enforcement action under other regulatory powers may already be underway, or could be taken, which would bring about the REMEDIA-TION of the RELEVANT LAND OR WATERS.

8.10 REMEDIATION under Part 2A cannot overlap with enforcement action under section 27 (Integrated Pollution Control and Local Air Pollution Control), section 59 (waste management licensing), regulation 24 or 26(2) (Pollution Prevention & Control which is progressively replacing much of the earlier regimes) (see paragraphs 7.2 to 7.11A above). However, there may be potential overlaps with the applicability of other regimes.

8.11 The ENFORCING AUTHORITY needs to consider whether enforcement could be taken under any other powers, and liaise with the relevant regulatory bodies to find out if it is already in progress or is planned.

8.12 If such enforcement action is in progress, or is planned, the ENFORCING AUTHORITY needs to consider the standard of REMEDIATION which would be achieved as a result of that enforcement action.

8.13 If the ENFORCING AUTHORITY is satisfied that the enforcement action would result in the achievement of an appropriate standard of REMEDIATION:

    (a) it is precluded from serving any REMEDIATION NOTICE (*section 78H(5)(b)*); and

    (b) the person who is carrying out, or will carry out, the action is required to prepare and publish a REMEDIATION STATEMENT (*sections 78H(7) & 78H(8)(a);* see paragraphs 8.18 to 8.22 below).

8.14 If the authority considers that enforcement action could be taken under other powers, but it is not in progress, the authority should liaise with the relevant regulatory body, seeking to ensure that the most appropriate regulatory powers are used.

8.15 The ENFORCING AUTHORITY is required to enter details of the use of these other regulatory powers onto its REGISTER (*Schedule 3, paragraphs 14, 15 and 16 of the Contaminated Land Regulations:* see Annex 4 paragraphs 83 and 84).

8.16 The authority's duty to serve a REMEDIATION NOTICE (*section 78E(1);* see paragraphs 12.1 to 12.9 below) may apply where either:

    (a) enforcement action is not being taken under other powers, and none is intended; or

    (b) the enforcement action under those other powers would not achieve an appropriate standard of REMEDIATION for all of the SIGNIFI-CANT POLLUTANT LINKAGES identified.

8.17 There is a potential for overlap between Part 2A and the works notice powers of the ENVIRONMENT AGENCY (*Section 161A of the Water Resources Act 1991 and the Anti-Pollution Works Regulations 1999*). Where an incidence of actual, or potential, water pollution does fall within the remit of both regimes, ENFORCING AUTHORITIES acting under Part 2A will be under a duty to serve a REMEDIATION NOTICE, whereas the ENVIRONMENT AGENCY is merely granted a power to act under section 161A of the 1991 Act. The ENVIRONMENT AGENCY has policies on the use of Anti-Pollution Works Notices. Details of the current policy approach is available from the ENVIRONMENT AGENCY.

Remediation statements

8.18 In any case where no REMEDIATION NOTICE may be served because appropriate REMEDIATION is taking place, or will take place without any such notice being served, the person responsible for the REMEDIA-TION is required to prepare and publish a REMEDIATION STATE-MENT *(sections 78H(7) & 78H(8)(a))*. This does not apply in the cases described at paragraphs 8.9 to 8.17 above).

8.19 Section 78H(7) requires the following information to be recorded in a REMEDIATION STATEMENT:

"(a) the things which are being, have been, or are expected to be, done by way of REMEDIATION in the particular case;

"(b) the name and address of the person who is doing, has done, or is expected to do, each of those things; and

"(c) the periods within which each of those things is being, or is expected to be done".

8.20 The ENFORCING AUTHORITY is required to enter details of the REMEDIATION STATEMENT onto its REGISTER *(section 78R(1)(c); see* paragraphs 17.1 to 17.19 below and Annex 4, paragraph 80).

8.21 If the person who is required to prepare and publish the REMEDIATION STATEMENT fails to do so, the ENFORCING AUTHORITY has powers to do so itself. This applies after a reasonable time has elapsed since the date on which the authority could have served a REMEDIATION NOTICE, but for the fact that appropriate REMEDIATION was taking place, or was likely to take place, without the service of a notice *(section 78H(9))*.

8.22 In any case of this kind, the ENFORCING AUTHORITY needs to consider whether it should prepare and publish a REMEDIATION STATEMENT itself for inclusion on its REGISTER. If it does so, it is entitled to recover any reasonable costs it incurs from the person who should have prepared and published the statement *(section 78H(9))*.

Reviewing circumstances

8.23 The ENFORCING AUTHORITY needs to keep under review the REMEDIATION which is actually carried out on the RELEVANT LAND OR WATERS, as well as the question of whether any additional REMEDIATION is necessary. If, at any time, it ceases to be satisfied that appropriate REMEDIATION has been, is being, or will be, carried out it may need to serve a REMEDIATION NOTICE.

8.24 The authority may cease to be satisfied if, in particular:

(a) there has been, or is likely to be, a failure to carry out the REMEDIATION ACTIONS described in the REMEDIATION STATEMENT, or a failure to do so within the times specified; or

(b) further REMEDIATION ACTIONS now appear necessary in order to achieve the appropriate standard of REMEDIATION for the RELEVANT LAND OR WATERS.

8.25 If any of the REMEDIATION ACTIONS described in the REMEDIA-TION STATEMENT are not being carried out, the ENFORCING AUTHORITY needs to consider whether:

(a) the REMEDIATION ACTIONS in question still appear to be necessary in order to achieve an appropriate standard of REMEDIA-TION; and

(b) they are still "reasonable" for the purposes of section 78E(4) and section 78E(4) (as modified).

8.26 If both of these apply, and the ENFORCING AUTHORITY is not precluded from serving a REMEDIATION NOTICE for any other reason, the authority will be under a duty to serve a REMEDIATION NOTICE, specifying the REMEDIATION ACTIONS in question. It may do this without any additional consultation, if the person on whom the notice would be served has already been consulted about those actions (*section 78H(10)*).

8.27 Even if the REMEDIATION ACTIONS described in the REMEDIATION STATEMENT are being carried out as planned, the ENFORCING AUTHORITY may consider that additional REMEDIATION is necessary. This may apply, in particular, where:

(a) the REMEDIATION was intended to be phased, and further REMEDIATION ACTIONS can now be identified as being necessary; or

(b) further SIGNIFICANT POLLUTANT LINKAGES are identified, or linkages which have already been identified are discovered to be more serious than previously thought.

8.28 Where it identifies further REMEDIATION as necessary, the ENFORCING AUTHORITY needs to consider how to ensure that the necessary REMEDIATION ACTIONS are carried out. This involves repeating the procedures set out above relating to consultation, and considering whether the additional REMEDIATION will be carried out without a REMEDIATION NOTICE being served. The authority cannot, for example, serve a REMEDIATION NOTICE specifying any additional REMEDIATION ACTIONS unless the person receiving the notice has been consulted on its contents (except in cases of urgency; see paragraphs 5.1 to 5.8 above).

9. Determining Liability

9.1 If the ENFORCING AUTHORITY is not satisfied, at this stage, that appropriate REMEDIATION is being, or will be, carried out without a REMEDIATION NOTICE being served, it needs to consider who might be served with such a notice. This section of this Annex deals with the questions of who appears to be an APPROPRIATE PERSON and, if there is more than one such person, whether any of these should be EXCLUDED from liability and, where necessary, of how the liability for carrying out any REMEDIATION ACTION should be APPORTIONED between the APPROPRIATE PERSONS who remain. Further questions, covered in section 10 of this Annex, need to be considered before the ENFORCING AUTHORITY can decide whether a REMEDIATION NOTICE should be served on anyone.

9.2 Where the ENFORCING AUTHORITY is precluded from serving a REMEDIATION NOTICE by virtue of section 78H(5)(d), because it has the power to carry out the REMEDIATION itself, the authority needs to follow the same processes for determining liabilities, including any EXCLUSIONS and APPORTIONMENTS, in order to determine from whom it can recover its reasonable costs incurred in doing the work (see also paragraphs 16.1 to 16.11 below).

The definition of the "appropriate person"

9.3 Part 2A defines two different categories of APPROPRIATE PERSON, and sets out the circumstances in which persons in these categories might be liable for REMEDIATION.

9.4 The first category is created by section 78F(2), which states that:

"... *any person, or any of the persons, who caused or knowingly permitted the substances, or any of the substances, by reason of which the CONTAMINATED LAND in question is such land to be in, on or under that land is an APPROPRIATE PERSON.*"

9.5 Such a person (referred to in the statutory guidance as a CLASS A PERSON) will be the APPROPRIATE PERSON only in respect of any REMEDIATION which is referable to the particular substances which he caused or knowingly permitted to be in, on or under the land *(section 78F(3))*. This means that the question of liability has to be considered separately for each SIGNIFICANT POLLUTANT LINKAGE identified on the land.

9.6 The second category arises in cases where it is not possible to find a CLASS A PERSON, either for all of the SIGNIFICANT POLLUTANT LINKAGES identified on the land, or for a particular SIGNIFICANT POLLUTANT LINKAGE. These circumstances are addressed in section 78F(4) and (5), which provide that:

"(4) If no person has, after reasonable inquiry, been found who is by virtue of subsection (2) above an appropriate person to bear responsibility for the things which are to be done by way of REMEDIATION, the OWNER or occupier for the time being of the land in question is an APPROPRIATE PERSON.

"(5) If, in consequence of subsection (3) above, there are things which are to be done by way of REMEDIATION in relation to which no person has, after reasonable inquiry, been found who is an APPRO-PRIATE PERSON by virtue of subsection (2) above, the OWNER or occupier for the time being of the CONTAMINATED LAND in question is an APPROPRIATE PERSON in relation to those things."

9.7 A person who is an APPROPRIATE PERSON under sections 78F(4) or (5) is referred to in the statutory guidance as a CLASS B PERSON.

The meaning of "caused or knowingly permitted"

9.8 The test of "causing or knowingly permitting" has been used as a basis for establishing liability in environmental legislation for more than 100 years. In the context of Part 2A, what is "caused or knowingly permitted" is the *presence* of a POLLUTANT in, on or under the land.

9.9 In the Government's view, the test of "causing" will require that the person concerned was involved in some active operation, or series of operations, to which the presence of the pollutant is attributable. Such involvement may also take the form of a failure to act in certain circumstances.

9.10 The meaning of the term "knowingly permit" was considered during the debate on Lords' Consideration of Commons' Amendments to the then Environment Bill on 11 July 1995. The then Minister for the Environment, the Earl Ferrers, stated on behalf of the Government that:

"The test of "knowingly permitting" would require both knowledge that the substances in question were in, on or under the land and the possession of the power to prevent such a substance being there." (House of Lords Hansard [11 July 1995], col 1497)

9.11 Some commentators have questioned the extent to which this test might apply with respect to banks or other lenders, where their clients have themselves caused or knowingly permitted the presence of pollutants. With respect to that question, Earl Ferrers said:

"I am advised that there is no judicial decision which supports the contention that a lender, by virtue of the act of lending the money only could be said to have "knowingly permitted" the substances to be in, on or under the land such that it is contaminated land. This would be the case if for no other reason than the lender, irrespective of any covenants it may have required from the polluter as to its environmental behaviour, would have no permissive rights over the land in question to prevent contamination occurring or continuing." (House of Lords Hansard [11 July 1995], col 1497)

It is also relevant to consider the stage at which a person who is informed of the presence of a pollutant might be considered to have knowingly permitted that presence, where he had not done so previously. In the Government's view, the test would be met only where the person had the ability to take steps to prevent or remove that presence and had a reasonable opportunity to do so.

9.13 Some commentators have, in particular, questioned the position of a person who, in his capacity as OWNER or occupier of land, is notified by the LOCAL AUTHORITY about the identification of that land as being CONTAMINATED LAND under section 78B(3). They have asked whether the resulting "knowledge" would trigger the "knowingly permit" test. In the Government's view, it would not. The legislation clearly distinguishes between those who cause or knowingly permit the presence of pollutants and those who are simply owners or occupiers of the land. In particular, this is evident in sections 78F, 78J and 78K which all relate to the different potential liabilities of OWNERS or occupiers as opposed to persons who have "caused or knowingly permitted" the presence of the POLLUTANTS.

9.14 Similarly, section 78–(1) requires consultation with OWNERS and occupiers for the specific purpose of determining "what shall be done by way of REMEDIATION" and not for the purpose of determining liability. In the Government's view, this implies that a person who merely owns or occupies the land in question cannot be held to have "knowingly permitted" as a consequence of that consultation alone.

9.15 It is ultimately for the courts to decide the meaning of "caused" and "knowingly permitted" as these terms apply to the Part 2A regime, and whether these tests are met in any particular case. However, indications of how the test should be construed can be obtained from case law under other legislation where the same or similar terms are used.

The potential liabilities of owners and occupiers of land

9.16 Only where no CLASS A PERSON can be found who is responsible for any particular REMEDIATION ACTION will the OWNER or occupier be liable for REMEDIATION by virtue solely of that ownership or occupation. OWNERS and occupiers may, of course, be CLASS A PERSONS because of their own past actions or omissions.

9.17 It is ultimately for the courts to decide whether, in any case, it can be said that no CLASS A PERSON has been found. In the Government's view, the context in which the word is used in Part 2A implies that a person must be in existence in order to be found. Section 78F(4) provides that the OWNER or occupier shall bear responsibility only "if no person has, after reasonable inquiry, been found who is an APPROPRIATE PERSON to bear responsibility for the things which are to be done by way of REMEDIATION". A person who is no longer in existence cannot meet that description. Under section 78E(1), the responsibility of an APPRO-PRIATE PERSON for REMEDIATION is established by the service of a REMEDIATION NOTICE. Service implies the existence of the person on whom the notice is served. In general, therefore, this means that a natural person would have to be alive and a legal person such as a company must not have been dissolved. However, it may be possible in some circumstances for the authority to act against the estate of a deceased person or to apply to a court for an order to annul the dissolution of a company.

9.18 Similarly, it is ultimately for the courts to determine what would constitute "reasonable inquiry" for the purposes of trying to find a CLASS A PERSON.

9.19 Section 78A(9) defines the term OWNER as follows:

"in relation to any land in England and Wales, means a person (other than a mortgagee not in possession) who, whether in his own right or as trustee for any other person, is entitled to receive the rack rent of the land, or, where the land is not let at a rack rent, would be so entitled if it were so let".

9.20 The term "occupier" is not defined in Part 2A and it will therefore carry its ordinary meaning. In the Government's view, it would normally mean the person in occupation and in many cases that will be the tenant or licensee of the premises.

The procedure for determining liabilities

9.21 Part 3 of the statutory guidance set out at Chapter D of Annex 3 provides a procedure for the ENFORCING AUTHORITY to follow to determine which of the APPROPRIATE PERSONS in any case should bear what liability for REMEDIATION. That procedure consists of the five distinct stages set out below.

9.22 Not all of these stages will be relevant to all cases. Most sites are likely to involve only one SIGNIFICANT POLLUTANT LINKAGE and thus have only one LIABILITY GROUP. In many cases, such a LIABILITY GROUP will consist of only one APPROPRIATE PERSON. However, more compli-cated situations will arise, requiring the application of all five stages. These steps may appear complex, but they are needed to fulfil the aims of the legislation in implementing the "polluter pays" principle while trying to avoid making APPROPRIATE PERSONS bear more than their fair share of the cost.

First stage—identifying potential appropriate persons and liability groups

9.23 The ENFORCING AUTHORITY will have already identified, on a preliminary basis, those persons who appear to it to be APPROPRIATE PERSONS in order to notify them of the identification of the CONTAMI-NATED LAND (see paragraph 4.1 above).

9.24 At this stage, the authority needs to reconsider this question, and identify all of the persons who appear to be APPROPRIATE PERSONS to bear responsibility for REMEDIATION. Depending on the information it has obtained, it may consider that:

(a) some or all of those who previously appeared to be APPROPRIATE PERSONS still appear to be such persons;

(b) some or all of those persons no longer appear to be APPROPRIATE PERSONS; or

(c) some other persons appear to be APPROPRIATE PERSONS, either in addition to those previously identified, or instead of them.

9.25 An example of circumstances in which the identity of those who appear to be APPROPRIATE PERSONS might change is if the authority had not previously found a person who had caused or knowingly permitted the POLLUTANT to be present (a CLASS A PERSON), but could now do so. At the time it identified the CONTAMINATED LAND, the authority would have identified the OWNER and the occupier of the land as being APPROPRIATE PERSONS. However, these persons would no longer appear to be APPROPRIATE PERSONS, unless they were also CLASS A PERSONS.

9.26 If, as a result of this process of reconsideration, the ENFORCING AUTHORITY identifies new persons who appear to be APPROPRIATE PERSONS, it needs to notify them of the fact that they have been identified as such (*section 78B(4);* see paragraphs 4.3 to 4.6 above).

9.27 The ENFORCING AUTHORITY will have identified one or more SIGNIFICANT POLLUTANTS on the land and the SIGNIFICANT POLLUTANT LINKAGES of which they form part.

A single significant pollutant

9.28 Where there is a single SIGNIFICANT POLLUTANT, and a single SIGNIFICANT POLLUTANT LINKAGE, the ENFORCING AUTHORITY needs to make reasonable enquiries to find all those who have caused or knowingly permitted the SIGNIFICANT POLLUTANT in question to be in, on or under the land (*section 78F(2)*). Any such persons are then "CLASS A PERSONS" and together constitute a "CLASS A LIABILITY GROUP" for the SIGNIFICANT POLLUTANT LINKAGE.

9.29 If no such CLASS A PERSONS can be found, the ENFORCING AUTHORITY needs to consider whether the SIGNIFICANT POLLUTANT LINKAGE of which it forms part relates solely to the POLLUTION OF CONTROLLED WATERS, rather than to any SIGNIFICANT HARM. If this is the case, there will be no LIABILITY GROUP for that SIGNIFICANT POLLUTANT LINKAGE (*section 78J(2)*), and it should be treated as an ORPHAN LINKAGE (see paragraph 11.3 below).

9.30 In any other case where no CLASS A PERSONS can be found for a SIGNIFICANT POLLUTANT, the ENFORCING AUTHORITY needs to identify all of the OWNERS or occupiers of the CONTAMINATED LAND in question. These persons are then "CLASS B PERSONS" and together constitute a "CLASS B LIABILITY GROUP" for the SIGNIFICANT POLLUTANT LINKAGE.

9.31 If the ENFORCING AUTHORITY cannot find any CLASS A PERSONS or any CLASS B PERSONS in respect of a SIGNIFICANT POLLUTANT LINKAGE, there will be no LIABILITY GROUP for that linkage and it should be treated as an ORPHAN LINKAGE (see paragraph 11.3 below).

Two or more significant pollutants

9.32 Where there are several SIGNIFICANT POLLUTANTS, and therefore two or more SIGNIFICANT POLLUTANT LINKAGES, the ENFORC-

ING AUTHORITY should consider each linkage in turn, carrying out the steps set out in paragraphs 9.28 to 9.31 above, in order to identify the LIABILITY GROUP (if one exists) for each of the linkages.

In all cases

9.33 Having identified one or more LIABILITY GROUPS, the ENFORCING AUTHORITY should consider whether any of the members of those groups are exempted from liability under the provisions in Part 2A. This could apply where:

(a) a person who would otherwise be a CLASS A PERSON is exempted from liability arising with respect to water pollution from an abandoned mine (*section 78J(3)*);

(b) a CLASS B PERSON is exempted from liability arising from the escape of a pollutant from one piece of land to other land (*section 78K*); or

(c) a person is exempted from liability by virtue of his being a person "ACTING IN A RELEVANT CAPACITY" (such as acting as an insolvency practitioner) (*section 78X(4)*).

9.34 If all of the members of a LIABILITY GROUP benefit from one or more of these exemptions, the ENFORCING AUTHORITY should treat the SIGNIFICANT POLLUTANT LINKAGE in question as an ORPHAN LINKAGE (see paragraph 11.3 below).

9.35 Individual persons may be members of more than one LIABILITY GROUP. This might apply, for example, if they had caused or knowingly permitted the presence of more than one SIGNIFICANT POLLUTANT.

9.36 Where the membership of all of the LIABILITY GROUPS is the same, there may be opportunities for the ENFORCING AUTHORITY to abbreviate the remaining stages of the procedure for determining liabilities. However, the tests for EXCLUSION and APPORTIONMENT may produce different results for different SIGNIFICANT POLLUTANT LINKAGES, and so the ENFORCING AUTHORITY will need to exercise caution before trying to simplify the procedure in any case.

Second stage—characterising remediation actions

9.37 Each REMEDIATION ACTION will be carried out to achieve a particular purpose with respect to one or more identified SIGNIFICANT POLLU-TANT LINKAGES. Where there is only a single SIGNIFICANT POLLU-TANT LINKAGE on the CONTAMINATED LAND in question, all the REMEDIATION ACTIONS will be referable to that linkage, and the ENFORCING AUTHORITY will not need to consider how the different REMEDIATION ACTIONS relate to different linkages. Therefore the authority will not need to carry out this stage and the third stage of the procedure where there is only a single SIGNIFICANT POLLUTANT LINKAGE.

9.38 However, where there are two or more SIGNIFICANT POLLUTANT LINKAGES on the CONTAMINATED LAND, the ENFORCING AUTHORITY needs to establish, for each REMEDIATION ACTION, whether it is:

(a) referable solely to the SIGNIFICANT POLLUTANT in a single SIGNIFICANT POLLUTANT LINKAGE (a SINGLE-LINKAGE ACTION); or

(b) referable to the SIGNIFICANT POLLUTANTS in more than one SIGNIFICANT POLLUTANT LINKAGE (a SHARED ACTION).

9.39 Where a REMEDIATION ACTION is a SHARED ACTION, there are two possible relationships between it and the SIGNIFICANT POLLU-TANT LINKAGES to which it is referable. The ENFORCING AUTHOR-ITY needs to establish whether the SHARED ACTION is:

(a) a COMMON ACTION—that is, an action which addresses together all of the SIGNIFICANT POLLUTANT LINKAGES to which it is referable, and which would have been part of the REMEDIATION PACKAGE for each of those linkages if each of them had been addressed separately; or

(b) a COLLECTIVE ACTION—that is, an action which addresses together all of the SIGNIFICANT POLLUTANT LINKAGES to which it is referable, but which would not have been part of the REMEDIATION PACKAGE for every one of those linkages if each of them had been addressed separately, because:

(i) the action would not have been appropriate in that form for one or more of the linkages (since some different solution would have been more appropriate);

(ii) the action would not have been needed to the same extent for one or more of the linkages (since a less far-reaching version of that type of action would have sufficed); or

(iii) the action represents a more economic way of addressing the linkages together which would not be possible if they were addressed separately.

A COLLECTIVE ACTION replaces actions that would have been appro-priate for the individual SIGNIFICANT POLLUTANT LINKAGES if they had been addressed separately, as it achieves the purposes which those other actions would have achieved.

Third stage — attributing responsibilities to liability groups

9.40 This stage of the procedure does not apply in the simpler cases. Where there is only a single SIGNIFICANT POLLUTANT LINKAGE, the LIABILITY GROUP for that linkage bears the full cost of carrying out any REMEDIATION ACTION. Where the linkage is an ORPHAN LINKAGE, the ENFORCING AUTHORITY has the power to carry out the REMEDIATION itself, at its own cost, and where the linkage is attributable to radioactivity the ENFORCING AUTHORITY is required to ensure it exercises such power (*section 78N(1B)*; see paragraph 11.3 below).

9.41 Similarly, for any SINGLE-LINKAGE ACTION, the LIABILITY GROUP for the SIGNIFICANT POLLUTANT LINKAGE in question bears the full cost of carrying out that action.

9.42 However, for each SHARED ACTION the ENFORCING AUTHORITY needs to apply the statutory guidance set out in Part 9 of Chapter D, in order to attribute to each of the different LIABILITY GROUPS their share of responsibility for that action.

9.43 After that statutory guidance has been applied to all SHARED ACTIONS, it may be the case that a CLASS B LIABILITY GROUP which has been identified does not have to bear the costs for any REMEDIATION ACTIONS, since the full cost of the REMEDIATION ACTIONS required will have been borne by others. Where this is the case, the ENFORCING AUTHORITY does not need to carry out any of the rest of this procedure with respect to that LIABILITY GROUP.

Fourth stage—excluding members of a liability group

9.44 The ENFORCING AUTHORITY then needs to consider, for each LIA-BILITY GROUP which has two or more members, whether any of those members should be EXCLUDED from liability:

(a) for each CLASS A LIABILITY GROUP with two or more members, the authority applies the statutory guidance on EXCLUSION set out in Part 5 of Chapter D; and

(b) for each CLASS B LIABILITY GROUP with two or more members, the authority applies the statutory guidance on EXCLUSION set out in Part 7 of Chapter D.

Fifth stage — apportioning liability between members of a liability group

9.45 The ENFORCING AUTHORITY next needs to determine how any costs attributed to each LIABILITY GROUP should be apportioned between the members of that group who remain after any EXCLUSIONS have been made.

9.46 For any LIABILITY GROUP which has only a single remaining member, that person bears all of the costs falling to that LIABILITY GROUP. This means that he bears the cost of any SINGLE-LINKAGE ACTION referable to the SIGNIFICANT POLLUTANT LINKAGE, and the share of the cost of any SHARED ACTION attributed to the group as a result of the ATTRIBUTION process set out in Part 9 of Chapter D.

9.47 For any LIABILITY GROUP which has two or more remaining members, the ENFORCING AUTHORITY applies the relevant statutory guidance on APPORTIONMENT between those members. Each of the remaining members of the group will then bear the proportion determined under that guidance of the total costs falling to the group. The relevant APPORTIONMENT guidance is:

(a) for any CLASS A LIABILITY GROUP, the statutory guidance set out in Part 6 of Chapter D; and

(b) for any CLASS B LIABILITY GROUP, the statutory guidance set out in Part 8 of Chapter D.

Agreement on liabilities

9.48 The statutory guidance set out in Part 3 of Chapter D provides the procedure which the ENFORCING AUTHORITY should normally follow. However, two or more APPROPRIATE PERSONS may agree between themselves the basis on which they think costs should be borne, or apportioned between themselves, for any REMEDIATION for which they are responsible. If the ENFORCING AUTHORITY is provided a copy of such an agreement and none of the parties to the agreement has informed the authority that it challenges the application of the agreement, the authority needs to allocate liabilities between the parties to the agreement so as to reflect the terms of the agreement, rather than necessarily reflecting the outcome which would otherwise result from the normal processes of EXCLUSION and APPORTIONMENT (*paragraph D.38*).

9.49 However, the ENFORCING AUTHORITY should not do this if the effect of following the agreement would be to increase the costs to be borne by the public purse. In these circumstances, it should disregard the agreement and follow the five stage process outlined above (*paragraph D.39*).

10. Limits on costs to be borne by the appropriate person

10.1 When the ENFORCING AUTHORITY has APPORTIONED the costs of each REMEDIATION ACTION between the various APPROPRIATE PERSONS, and before proceeding to serve any REMEDIATION NOTICE on that basis, the authority must consider whether there are reasons why any of the APPROPRIATE PERSONS on whom that notice would be served should not be required to meet in full the share of the cost of carrying out the REMEDIATION ACTIONS which has been APPORTIONED to him. The importance of this question is that it may preclude the ENFORCING AUTHORITY fro serving a REMEDIATION NOTICE in respect of those actions on any of the APPROPRIATE PERSONS at all (see paragraph 10.4 below).

10.2 To decide this question, the ENFORCING AUTHORITY needs to consider the hypothetical circumstances which would apply if the authority had carried out itself the REMEDIATION ACTION or actions for which each APPROPRIATE PERSON is liable. Specifically, the authority needs to consider whether, in these hypothetical circumstances, it would seek to recover from each APPROPRIATE PERSON all of the share of the costs which has been APPORTIONED to that person.

10.3 In making its decision, the authority must have regard to:

(a) any hardship which may be caused to the person in question (see paragraphs 10.8 to 10.10 below); and

(b) the statutory guidance in Chapter E of Annex 3 (*section 78P(2)*).

10.4 If the ENFORCING AUTHORITY decides that, in these hypothetical circumstances, it would seek to recover from each APPROPRIATE PERSON all of the share of its reasonable costs APPORTIONED to that person, the authority can proceed to serve the necessary REMEDIATION NOTICES on the basis of its apportionment.

10.5 However, if the ENFORCING AUTHORITY decides, with respect to any REMEDIATION ACTION, that it would seek to recover from any APPROPRIATE PERSON none, or only a part, of that person's apportioned share of the authority's reasonable costs:

(a) it is precluded from serving a REMEDIATION NOTICE specifying that action both on the APPROPRIATE PERSON in question and on anyone else who is an APPROPRIATE PERSON in respect of that action (*section 78H(5)(d)*); and

(b) the authority has the power to carry out the REMEDIATION ACTION in question itself (*section 78N(3)(e); see also paragraphs 11.7 to 11.11 below*).

10.6 Where, in a case of this kind, the ENFORCING AUTHORITY must or decides to exercise its powers and carry out particular REMEDIATION ACTIONS, the authority will be entitled to recover its reasonable costs of doing so when it has completed the work. In deciding how much of those costs it will seek to recover, the authority will need to work on the basis of circumstances as they exist at that point. In practice, however, the decision that the authority has taken on the hypothetical basis described in paragraph 10.2 above will normally settle the questions of limits on the actual recovery of costs. Nevertheless, if there is evidence that the circumstances of the APPROPRIATE PERSON have changed in some relevant respect after the ENFORCING AUTHORITY has made its initial decision on this question, it will need to reconsider its decision as to how much of its reasonable costs it will seek to recover.

10.7 Further details about actual cost recovery are given in section 16 of this Annex.

The meaning of the term "hardship"

10.8 The term "hardship" is not defined in Part 2A, and therefore carries its ordinary meaning — hardness of fate or circumstance, severe suffering or privation.

10.9 The term has been widely used in other legislation, and there is a substantial body of case law about its meaning under that other legislation. For example, it has been held appropriate to take account of injustice to the person claiming hardship, in addition to severe financial detriment. Although the case law may give a useful indication of the way in which the term has been interpreted by the courts, the meaning ascribed to the term in individual cases is specific to the particular facts of those cases and the legislation under which they were brought.

10.10 In deciding whether there would be hardship, and its extent, the matters considered in Chapter E may well be relevant.

11. Remediation Action by the Enforcing Authority

11.1 Before serving any REMEDIATION NOTICE, the ENFORCING AUTHORITY needs to consider whether it has the power to carry out any of the REMEDIATION ACTIONS itself. Where this applies, the authority is precluded from serving a REMEDIATION NOTICE requiring anyone else to carry out that REMEDIATION ACTION (*section 78H(5)*).

The power to carry out remediation

11.2 In general terms, the ENFORCING AUTHORITY has the power to carry out a REMEDIATION ACTION itself in cases where:

(a) the ENFORCING AUTHORITY considers it necessary to take urgent action itself (*section 78N(3)(a) and section 78N(3)(a) (as modified)*: see paragraphs 5.1 to 5.8 above);

(b) there is no APPROPRIATE PERSON to bear responsibility for the action (*section 78N(3)(f)*; see paragraph 11.3 below). The ENFORCING AUTHORITY is required to exercise its powers in these circumstances to deal with HARM attributable to radioactivity;

(c) the ENFORCING AUTHORITY is precluded from requiring one or more persons, who would otherwise be APPROPRIATE PERSONS, to carry out the action (*sections 78N(3)(d) & (e) and section 78N(3)(d) (as modified)*: see paragraph 11.3 below).The ENFORCING AUTHORITY is required to exercise its powers in these circumstances to deal with HARM attributable to radioactivity;

(d) the ENFORCING AUTHORITY has agreed with the APPROPRIATE PERSON that the authority should carry out the REMEDIATION ACTION (*section 78N(3)(b)*; see paragraphs 11.5 to 11.6 below); or

(e) the REMEDIATION ACTION has been specified in a REMEDIA-TION NOTICE, which has not been complied with *(section 78N(3)(c);* see paragraph 15.15 below). The ENFORCING AUTHORITY is required to exercise its powers in these circumstances to deal with HARM attributable to radioactivity.

There is no appropriate person

11.3 The ENFORCING AUTHORITY has the power to carry out a REMEDIATION ACTION if, after reasonable enquiry, it has been unable to find an APPROPRIATE PERSON for that action *(section 78N(3)(f))*. The ENFORCING AUTHORITY is required to exercise its powers to deal with HARM attributable to radioactivity in this case.

The appropriate person cannot be required to carry out remediation action

11.4 The ENFORCING AUTHORITY needs to consider whether it has the power to carry out a REMEDIATION ACTION on the basis that the APPROPRIATE PERSON cannot be required to carry it out. For a REMEDIATION ACTION to deal with HARM attributable to radioactivity, it may in certain circumstances then be required to exercise that power as set out in paragraph 11.2 above. This power applies where:

(a) the ENFORCING AUTHORITY considers that if it carried out the REMEDIATION ACTION itself, it would not seek to recover fully from that APPROPRIATE PERSON the proportion of the costs which that person would otherwise have to bear if the action were included in a REMEDIATION NOTICE *(sections 78N(3)(e) & 78P(2);* see also paragraphs 10.1 to 10.10 above);

(b) the REMEDIATION ACTION is referable solely to one or more SIGNIFICANT POLLUTANT LINKAGES which relate to the POL-LUTION OF CONTROLLED WATERS (and not to any SIGNIFI-CANT HARM or HARM attributable to radioactivity), and either:

(i) the APPROPRIATE PERSON is a CLASS B PERSON *(section 78J(2))*, or

(ii) the APPROPRIATE PERSON is a CLASS A PERSON solely by virtue of his having permitted the discharge of water from a mine which was abandoned before the end of 1999 *(section 78J(3))*;

(c) the SIGNIFICANT POLLUTANT LINKAGE to which the REMEDIATION ACTION is referable is the result of the escape of the POLLUTANT from other land onto the CONTAMINATED LAND in question, and both:

(i) the APPROPRIATE PERSON is a CLASS B PERSON, and

(ii) the REMEDIATION ACTION is intended to deal with SIG-NIFICANT HARM, the POLLUTION OF CONTROLLED WATERS or HARM attributable to radioactivity on land other than the CONTAMINATED LAND in question, to which the POLLUTANT has escaped *(section 78K)*; or

(d) requiring the APPROPRIATE PERSON to carry out the REMEDIA-TION ACTION would have the effect of making him personally liable to bear the costs, and:

(i) he is a "PERSON ACTING IN A RELEVANT CAPACITY" such as an insolvency practitioner *(section 78X(4))*, and

(ii) the REMEDIATION ACTION is not to any extent referable to any POLLUTANT which is present as a result of any act or omission which it was unreasonable for a person acting in that capacity to do or make (*section 78X(3)(a)*).

Written agreement

11.5 Even if none of the grounds set out in paragraph 11.4 above applies, the ENFORCING AUTHORITY may wish to consider whether it would, nonetheless, be appropriate for the authority to carry out a REMEDIATION ACTION itself on behalf of the APPROPRIATE PERSON. This might be appropriate, in particular, in the case of home-owners identified as APPROPRIATE PERSONS.

11.6 If the ENFORCING AUTHORITY considers that it wishes to do this, it needs to seek the written agreement of the APPROPRIATE PERSON for:

(a) the ENFORCING AUTHORITY to carry out the REMEDIATION ACTION itself, on behalf of the APPROPRIATE PERSON; and

(b) the APPROPRIATE PERSON to reimburse the authority for any costs which he would otherwise have had to bear for the REMEDIATION (*section 78N(3)(b)*).

Action by the enforcing authority

11.7 The ENFORCING AUTHORITY'S powers to carry out REMEDIATION under section 78N may be triggered with respect to all of the APPROPRIATE PERSONS for a particular REMEDIATION ACTION, or only with respect to some of them. Whichever is the case, the authority is precluded from including the REMEDIATION ACTION in question in a REMEDIATION NOTICE served on anyone (*section 78H(5)*).

11.8 However, where the ENFORCING AUTHORITY carries out a REMEDIATION ACTION using its powers with respect to urgent action (*section 78N(3)(a)*) or limitations on costs (*section 78N(3)(e)*; see paragraphs 10.1 to 10.6 above), it is entitled to recover its reasonable costs from all of the APPROPRIATE PERSONS for that REMEDIATION ACTION (*section 78P(1)*). In deciding how much of those costs to recover from any particular APPROPRIATE PERSON, the authority must have regard to hardship which may be caused to that person and to the statutory guidance set out in Chapter E of Annex 3 (*section 78P(2)*).

11.9 For example, there may be two APPROPRIATE PERSONS (persons "1" and "2") for a particular REMEDIATION ACTION. The ENFORCING AUTHORITY may consider that the cost which "person 1" would have to bear would cause him hardship. On this basis, the authority has a power to carry out the REMEDIATION ACTION itself, and cannot include that action in a notice served on either of the APPROPRIATE PERSONS (see paragraph 10.5 above). Once the authority has carried out the action, it can recover from "person 2" the same proportion of its costs as a REMEDIATION NOTICE served on him would have specified, and from "person 1" as much of the remainder as would not cause hardship or be inconsistent with the statutory guidance in Chapter E.

11.10 Where the ENFORCING AUTHORITY is precluded from serving a REMEDIATION NOTICE because it has powers under section 78N to carry out the REMEDIATION itself, it will be under a duty to prepare and publish a REMEDIATION STATEMENT recording:

"(a) the things which are being, have been, or are expected to be, done by way of REMEDIATION in the particular case;

"(b) the name and address of the person who is doing, has done, or is expected to do, each of those things; and

"(c) the periods within which each of those things is being, or is expected to be done" (*section 78H(7)*).

11.11 The ENFORCING AUTHORITY must then include details of the REMEDIATION STATEMENT on its REGISTER (*section 78R(l)(c) and regulation 15 of the Contaminated Land Regulations:* see paragraphs 17.1 to 17.19 below and Annex 4, paragraph 80).

12. Serving a remediation notice

12.1 The basis for serving a REMEDIATION NOTICE is that the ENFORCING AUTHORITY considers that there are REMEDIATION ACTIONS, identified as part of the REMEDIATION SCHEME, which:

(a) have not been, are not being, and will not be carried out without the service of a REMEDIATION NOTICE; and

(b) in respect of which the authority has no power under section 78N to carry out itself and for which it is not, itself, the APPROPRIATE PERSON.

12.2 Before serving a REMEDIATION NOTICE, the ENFORCING AUTHORITY needs to decide whether it has made reasonable endeavours to consult the APPROPRIATE PERSON and the other relevant persons (described in paragraph 6.10 to 6.17 above) on the nature of the REMEDIATION which is to be carried out (*section 78H(1)*).

12.3 When the authority is satisfied that it has consulted sufficiently, and subject to the timing requirements outlined in paragraphs 12.4 to 12.5 below, the authority will be under a duty to serve a REMEDIATION NOTICE on each APPROPRIATE PERSON requiring the relevant REMEDIATION ACTION to be carried out (*section 78E(1)*).

Timing of the service of a remediation notice

12.4 The ENFORCING AUTHORITY will have notified each APPROPRIATE PERSON that he appears to be such a person (*section 78B(3) & (4):* see paragraphs 4.1 to 4.6 above). The date of this notification to any person determines the earliest date on which the ENFORCING AUTHORITY can serve a REMEDIATION NOTICE on that person. Except in a case of urgency (see paragraphs 5.1 to 5.8 above), at least three months must elapse between the date of the notification to the person concerned and the service of a REMEDIATION NOTICE on that person (*section 78H(3)(a)*).

12.5 However, later dates apply if the LOCAL AUTHORITY has given notice of a decision that the land is required to be designated a SPECIAL SITE, or if the ENVIRONMENT AGENCY has given an equivalent notice to the LOCAL AUTHORITY (see paragraphs 18.7 and 18.13 below). Once such a notice has been given, the ENFORCING AUTHORITY cannot serve a REMEDIATION NOTICE (except in cases of urgency) until three months have elapsed since:

(a) notice was given by the LOCAL AUTHORITY that the designation of the land as a SPECIAL SITE is to take effect; or

(b) notice was given by the SECRETARY OF STATE that the designation of the land as a SPECIAL SITE is, or is not, to take effect (*sections 78H(3)(b) & (c);* see also section 18 of this Annex).

The remediation notice

12.6 The ENFORCING AUTHORITY must include in any REMEDIATION NOTICE particular information about the CONTAMINATED LAND, the REMEDIATION, the APPROPRIATE PERSON and rights of appeal against the notice. The requirements for the contents of a REMEDIATION NOTICE are formally set out in sections 78E(1) and (3), and regulation 4 of the Contaminated Land Regulations (see Annex 4, paragraphs 16 to 20).

12.7 In any case where there are two or more APPROPRIATE PERSONS for any REMEDIATION ACTION, the ENFORCING AUTHORITY may serve a single REMEDIATION NOTICE on all of those persons. (Acting in this way will make the process of readjusting the APPORTIONMENT of costs after a successful appeal considerably simpler, as the SECRETARY OF STATE will be able to amend the single REMEDIATION NOTICE and the way it affects each of the APPROPRIATE PERSONS; if separate notices are served, this would not be possible, and new notices would have to be served.)

12.8 As well as serving the REMEDIATION NOTICE on the APPROPRIATE PERSONS, the ENFORCING AUTHORITY must send a copy:

   (a) to any person who they have consulted under section 78G(3) about the granting of rights over the land or waters to the APPROPRIATE PERSON;
   (b) to any person who was consulted under section 78H(1); and
   (c) if the ENFORCING AUTHORITY is the LOCAL AUTHORITY, to the ENVIRONMENT AGENCY and if the ENFORCING AUTHORITY is the ENVIRONMENT AGENCY, to the LOCAL AUTHORITY (*regulation 5(1) of the Contaminated Land Regulations*).

12.9 The ENFORCING AUTHORITY is under a duty to include prescribed details of the REMEDIATION NOTICE on its REGISTER (*section 78R(1)(a) and regulation 13 of the Contaminated Land Regulations;* see paragraphs 17.1 to 17.19 below and Annex 4, paragraph 77).

13. Appeals against a remediation notice

13.1 Any person who receives a REMEDIATION NOTICE has twenty-one days within which he can appeal against the notice (*section 78L(1)*). Where a REMEDIATION NOTICE is served on or after 4 August 2006 any appeal is made to the SECRETARY OF STATE.

13.2 The grounds for any such appeal are prescribed in regulation 7 of the Contaminated Land Regulations. Regulations 8–12 of the Contaminated Land Regulations prescribe the procedures for any appeal. These regulations are described in Annex 4 to this Circular.

13.3 If an appeal is made, the REMEDIATION NOTICE is suspended until final determination or abandonment of the appeal (*regulation 12 of the Contaminated Land Regulations*).

13.4 If any appeal is made against a REMEDIATION NOTICE, the ENFORCING AUTHORITY must enter prescribed particulars of the appeal, and the decision reached on the appeal, on its REGISTER (*section 78R(1)(b) and regulation 13 of the Contaminated Land Regulations*).

Action during suspension of a notice

13.5 Where the requirement to carry out particular REMEDIATION ACTIONS is suspended during an appeal, the ENFORCING AUTHOR-

ITY needs to consider whether this makes it necessary for the authority itself to carry out urgent REMEDIATION *(section 78N(3)(a) and section 78N(3)(a) (as modified):* see paragraphs 5.1 to 5.8 above).

13.6 If the ENFORCING AUTHORITY does carry out urgent REMEDIA-TION itself in these circumstances, it does not need to prepare and publish a REMEDIATION STATEMENT, unless the REMEDIATION has not already been described in the original REMEDIATION NOTICE.

13.7 Having carried out any REMEDIATION ACTION, the ENFORCING AUTHORITY needs to consider whether to seek to recover its reasonable costs *(section 78P(1))*. Its ability to do so may, however, be affected by the decision in the appeal against the REMEDIATION NOTICE. For example, it would not be able to recover its costs from the recipient of a notice who successfully appealed on the grounds that he was not the APPRO-PRIATE PERSON.

14. *Variations in remediation requirements*

14.1 It may become apparent, whilst REMEDIATION ACTIONS are being carried out, that the overall REMEDIATION SCHEME for the RELE-VANT LAND OR WATERS is no longer appropriate. For example:

(a) further SIGNIFICANT POLLUTANT LINKAGES may be identi-fied, requiring further REMEDIATION ACTIONS to be carried out; or

(b) a REMEDIATION ACTION which is being carried out may be discovered to be:

(i) ineffective, given the circumstances of the RELEVANT LAND OR WATERS,

(ii) unsafe, in terms of pollution or health and safety risks, given the circumstances of the RELEVANT LAND OR WATERS, or

(iii) unnecessary, in the light of new information about the condition of the land; or

(c) a further REMEDIATION ACTION may be identified which would be reasonable and would achieve a purpose which could not previously be achieved by any reasonable REMEDIATION ACTION.

14.2 If other REMEDIATION ACTIONS are identified as being appropriate, this may require the preparation and publication of a new REMEDIA-TION STATEMENT or the serving of a new REMEDIATION NOTICE.

15. *Follow-up action*

15.1 The ENFORCING AUTHORITY needs to consider whether the REMEDIATION ACTIONS described in the REMEDIATION STATE-MENT or specified in the REMEDIATION NOTICE have been carried out and, if so, whether they have been carried out adequately and satisfactorily. In many cases, the authority will do so on the basis of information generated by the quality assurance and verification pro-cedures included within the REMEDIATION ACTIONS *(paragraphs C.25 and C67)*.

15.2 Whatever it decides, the ENFORCING AUTHORITY also needs to consider whether any further REMEDIATION is appropriate. This applies particularly in circumstances where the completed REMEDIA-

TION ACTIONS form only a single phase of the overall process of REMEDIATION for the RELEVANT LAND OR WATERS. If it decides that further REMEDIATION is appropriate, the authority repeats the procedures set out above for consultation, identifying appropriate REMEDIATION ACTIONS and requiring that REMEDIATION to be carried out by service of a REMEDIATION NOTICE.

Remediation action has been carried out

Notifications of "claimed remediation"

15.3 Any person who has carried out any REMEDIATION which was required by a REMEDIATION NOTICE or described in a REMEDIATION STATEMENT can notify the ENFORCING AUTHORITY, providing particular details of the REMEDIATION he claims to have carried out (*regulation 15(2) of the Contaminated Land Regulations*). The OWNER or occupier of the CONTAMINATED LAND is also entitled to notify the authority.

15.4 If the ENFORCING AUTHORITY receives any notification of this kind, it will be under a duty to include on its REGISTER prescribed details of the REMEDIATION which it is claimed has been carried out (*sections 78R(1)(h) & (j) and regulation 13 of the Contaminated Land Regulations:* see paragraphs 17.1 to 17.19 below and Annex 4, paragraph 81).

15.5 Part 2A provides that the inclusion of an entry of this kind on the REGISTER is not to be taken as a representation by the authority maintaining the REGISTER that the entry is accurate with respect to what is claimed to have been done, or the manner in which it may have been done (*section 78R(3)*).

"Signing off"

15.6 Although Part 2A does not include any formal "signing off" procedure, the ENFORCING AUTHORITY may wish to consider writing to the APPROPRIATE PERSON, confirming the position with respect to any further enforcement action. In a case where a REMEDIATION NOTICE has been served and appears to have been complied with, this could confirm that the authority currently sees no grounds, on the basis of available information, for further enforcement action. In other cases — where a REMEDIATION NOTICE has not been served — the ENFORCING AUTHORITY might confirm that it does not consider that it needs to serve a REMEDIATION NOTICE, which it would need to do if appropriate REMEDIATION had not been carried out.

Remediation has not been carried out

If a remediation statement has not been followed

15.7 If a REMEDIATION ACTION described in a REMEDIATION STATEMENT is not carried out in the manner and within the time period described, the ENFORCING AUTHORITY needs to consider whether it is necessary for a REMEDIATION NOTICE to be served requiring that REMEDIATION ACTION to be carried out.

15.8 The ENFORCING AUTHORITY has a duty to serve such a REMEDIATION NOTICE if:

(a) it considers that appropriate REMEDIATION is not being carried out and it is not satisfied that it will be carried out without the service of a notice; and

(b) it is not precluded for any other reason from serving a notice on the APPROPRIATE PERSON (*section 78H(10)*).

15.9 In these circumstances, the ENFORCING AUTHORITY can serve the REMEDIATION NOTICE without making any further efforts to consult, provided that the REMEDIATION ACTIONS specified in the notice have previously been the subject of consultation with the person in question (*section 78H(10)*).

If a remediation notice is not complied with

15.10 If a REMEDIATION ACTION specified in a REMEDIATION NOTICE is not carried out within the time required, the ENFORCING AUTHORITY needs to consider whether to prosecute the APPROPRIATE PERSON who has failed to comply with the REMEDIATION NOTICE. It will normally be desirable for the authority to inform the APPROPRIATE PERSON that it is considering bringing such a prosecution before it actually does so. This may give that person an opportunity to avoid prosecution by carrying out the requirements of the REMEDIATION NOTICE.

15.11 Part 2A makes it an offence for any person to fail to comply with a REMEDIATION NOTICE "without reasonable excuse" (*section 78M(1)*). The question of whether a person had a "reasonable excuse" in any case is a matter of fact to be decided on the basis of the particular circumstances of that case.

15.12 One defence is specified in Part 2A. This applies where:

(a) the APPROPRIATE PERSON was required by the REMEDIATION NOTICE to bear only a proportion of the cost of the REMEDIA-TION ACTION which has not been carried out; and

(b) that person can show that the only reason why he did not comply with the REMEDIATION NOTICE was that one or more of the other APPROPRIATE PERSONS who should have borne other shares of the cost refused, or were not able, to do so (*section 78M(2)*).

15.13 In general, a person convicted of the offence of non-compliance with a REMEDIATION NOTICE is liable to a fine not exceeding level 5 on the standard scale; at the date of this Circular, that is £5,000. Until either he complies with the REMEDIATION NOTICE, or the ENFORCING AUTHORITY uses its powers to act in default (see paragraph 15.15 below), he is also liable for additional daily fines up of up to one tenth of level 5; that is, at the date of this Circular, £500 (*section 78M(3)*).

15.14 However, where the CONTAMINATED LAND to which the notice relates is INDUSTRIAL, TRADE OR BUSINESS PREMISES, the limit on the fine is higher: the fine may be up to £20,000, with daily fines of up to £2,000 (*section 78M(4)*). Part 2A provides a power to increase those limits by order: the Government's intention is to use that power where necessary to maintain the differential with level 5 on the standard scale.

15.15 In addition, the authority needs to consider whether to carry out the REMEDIATION ACTION itself (*section 78N(3)(c)*). It can decide to do so whether or not it decides to prosecute the APPROPRIATE PERSON. Where the REMEDIATION ACTION is to address HARM attributable to radioactivity, the authority has a duty to carry out such action under section 78(N)(1A)(see paragraph 11.2 above). If it does carry out the REMEDIATION, it is entitled to recover its reasonable costs from the APPROPRIATE PERSON (*section 78P(1) and section 78P(1)* (as modified)).

16. Recovering the costs of carrying out remediation

16.1 In general, where the ENFORCING AUTHORITY has carried out REMEDIATION itself, it is entitled to recover the reasonable costs it has incurred in doing so *(section 78P(1) and section 78P(1) (as modified))*. The ENFORCING AUTHORITY has no power to recover any costs it incurred in inspecting the land to determine whether it was CONTAMINATED LAND.

16.2 In deciding whether to recover its costs and, if so, how much of its costs, the ENFORCING AUTHORITY must have regard to:

(a) any hardship which the recovery might cause to the APPROPRIATE PERSON (see paragraphs 10.8 to 10.10 above) and

(b) the statutory guidance set out in Chapter E of Annex 3 *(section 78P(2); see also paragraphs 10.8 to 10.10 above)*.

16.3 However, the ENFORCING AUTHORITY has no power under section 78P to recover its costs where:

(a) the authority itself was the APPROPRIATE PERSON;

(b) the person who would otherwise have been an APPROPRIATE PERSON for a REMEDIATION ACTION could not have been required to carry out that action under the terms of a REMEDIATION NOTICE, because it related to the POLLUTION OF CONTROLLED WATERS or to the escape of the POLLUTANT from other land *(section 78N(3)(d) and section 78N(3)(d) (as modified))*: or

(c) the authority carried out the REMEDIATION with the written agreement of the APPROPRIATE PERSON *(section 78N(3)(b))*.

16.4 In the first two of these cases, the ENFORCING AUTHORITY has itself to bear the cost of carrying out the REMEDIATION (see paragraphs 16.12 to 16.14 below).

16.5 If the ENFORCING AUTHORITY carries out the REMEDIATION with the written agreement of the APPROPRIATE PERSON *(section 78N(3)(b))*, reimbursement by the APPROPRIATE PERSON will be under the terms of the written agreement.

16.6 If the ENFORCING AUTHORITY decides to recover all or a part of its costs, it needs to consider whether to do so immediately (which will involve an action in the county court or High Court, if payment is not made) or to postpone recovery and, where this is possible, safeguard its right to cost recovery by imposing a charge on the land in question. A CHARGING NOTICE may also be served to safeguard the authority's interests where immediate recovery is intended.

Charging notices

16.7 If the ENFORCING AUTHORITY decides to safeguard its rights to cost recovery by imposing a charge on the land in question, it does so by serving a CHARGING NOTICE *(section 78P(3))*. The authority is entitled to serve a CHARGING NOTICE if the APPROPRIATE PERSON from whom it is recovering its costs is both:

(a) a CLASS A PERSON; and

(b) the OWNER of all or part of the CONTAMINATED LAND *(section 78P(3))*.

16.8 On the same day as the ENFORCING AUTHORITY serves any CHARGING NOTICE, it must send a copy of the notice to every other person who, to the knowledge of the authority, has an interest in the premises capable of being affected by the charge *(section 78P(6))*.

16.9 Any person served with a CHARGING NOTICE, or who receives a copy of it, can appeal against it to a county court *(section 78P(8))*. If any such appeal is made, the ENFORCING AUTHORITY must include prescribed particulars of that appeal on its REGISTER *(section 78R(1)(d);* see paragraphs 17.1 to 17.19 below and Annex 4, paragraph 97). The CHARGING NOTICE itself will not appear on the REGISTER. The power to make regulations on the grounds of appeal against a CHARGING NOTICE and the related procedure has not been exercised. It is therefore for the county court to determine what grounds of appeal it will accept; the ordinary county court procedures for appeals will apply.

16.10 A CHARGING NOTICE can declare the cost to be payable with interest by instalments, within a specified period, until the whole amount is repaid *(section 78P(12)).*

16.11 If the ENFORCING AUTHORITY needs to enforce the charge, it has the same powers and remedies under the Law of Property Act 1925 as if the authority were a mortgagee by deed having powers of sale and lease, of accepting surrenders of leases and of appointing a receiver *(section 78P(11)).*

Central government support to local authorities

16.12 The Department for Environment, Food and Rural Affairs (Defra) runs a programme of support for capital costs incurred by local authorities in dealing with land contamination where they:

  (a) own the land;
  (b) are responsible for its contamination; or
  (c) have other statutory responsibilities for carrying out REMEDIATION, including the use of powers to carry out REMEDIATION under section 78N.

16.13 Support under this programme is not available for work needed solely to facilitate the development, redevelopment or sale of the land. Financial support for remediation in connection with the development or redevelopment of land may be available through other Governmental programmes such as those run by English Partnerships and the regional development agencies.

16.14 All local authorities who are entitled to receive Defra support are invited annually to bid for support from this programme for particular schemes. Schemes are assessed against environmental criteria and prioritised.

16.15 Defra also provides financial support to the ENVIRONMENT AGENCY including works in respect of radioactivity.

16.16 The SECRETARY OF STATE may make available financial support in respect of associated costs and expenses incurred by the ENVIRONMENT AGENCY in carrying out remediation itself to fulfil its duties under section 78N(1 A) (see paragraphs 11.2 to 11.3 above) with respect to radioactivity where these exceed existing provisions (section 78N(1B)).

17. Registers

17.1 Each ENFORCING AUTHORITY has a duty to maintain a REGISTER *(section 78R(1)).* The REGISTER will include details of REMEDIATION NOTICES which have been served and certain other documents in relation to each area of CONTAMINATED LAND for which the authority is responsible. The REGISTER will also include information about the condition of the land in question. For a LOCAL AUTHORITY, the REGISTER must be kept at its principal office. For the ENVIRONMENT

AGENCY, the REGISTER must be kept at the area office for the area in which the land is situated.

17.2 The particular details to be included in each REGISTER are prescribed in regulation 13 of, and Schedule 3 to, the Contaminated Land Regulations (see Annex 4). Neither these Regulations, nor the primary legislation in Part 2A, state when details should be added to the REGISTER. In the Government's view, this implies that they should be added as soon as reasonably practicable after the information they contain is generated; so, for example, the prescribed details of a REMEDIATION NOTICE should be added as soon as reasonably practicable after the service of that notice.

17.3 Before including any information on its REGISTER, the ENFORCING AUTHORITY needs to consider whether that information should be excluded on the basis that:

(a) its inclusion would be against the interests of national security (see paragraphs 17.8 to 17.9 below); or

(b) the information is commercially confidential (see paragraphs 17.10 to 17.19 below).

Copying entries between authorities

17.4 For most areas of CONTAMINATED LAND, the LOCAL AUTHORITY for that area will be the ENFORCING AUTHORITY. However, for particular areas of CONTAMINATED LAND this may not be the case. This applies if:

(a) the CONTAMINATED LAND has been designated a SPECIAL SITE, in which case the ENVIRONMENT AGENCY is the ENFORCING AUTHORITY; or

(b) the land has been identified as CONTAMINATED LAND by the LOCAL AUTHORITY for an adjoining or adjacent area, as a result of SIGNIFICANT HARM, the POLLUTION OF CONTROLLED WATERS or HARM attributable to radioactivity which might be caused in that LOCAL AUTHORITY'S own area (*section 78X(2)*).

17.5 Where this is the case, the ENFORCING AUTHORITY needs to copy all entries it makes into its own REGISTER for the land in question, to the LOCAL AUTHORITY in whose area the land is actually situated (*section 78R(4) & (5)*).

17.6 The LOCAL AUTHORITY which receives these copied entries needs to include them on its own REGISTER (*section 78R(6)*). This means that the REGISTER maintained by any LOCAL AUTHORITY provides a comprehensive set of information about all of the CONTAMINATED LAND identified in its area, whichever authority is the ENFORCING AUTHORITY.

Public access to registers

17.7 Each ENFORCING AUTHORITY is under a duty to keep its REGISTER available for free inspection by the public at all reasonable times (*section 78R(8)(a)*). In addition, it will be under a duty to provide facilities for members of the public to obtain copies of REGISTER entries. It can make reasonable charges for this (*section 78R(8)(b)*).

Exclusion on the grounds of national security

17.8 The ENFORCING AUTHORITY must not include any information on its REGISTER if, in the opinion of the SECRETARY OF STATE, its inclusion would be against the interests of national security (*section 78S(1)*). The SECRETARY OF STATE can give directions to ENFORCING AUTHORITIES specifying information, or descriptions of information, which are to be excluded from any REGISTER or referred to the SECRETARY OF STATE for his determination (*section 78S(2)*). At the date of this Circular, no such directions have been given.

17.9 Any person who considers that the inclusion of particular information on a REGISTER would be against the interests of national security can notify the SECRETARY OF STATE and the ENFORCING AUTHORITY of this. The SECRETARY OF STATE will then consider whether, in his opinion, the information should be included or excluded. The ENFORCING AUTHORITY must not include on its REGISTER any information covered by this kind of notification unless and until the SECRETARY OF STATE determines that it can be included (*section 78S(4)*).

Exclusion on the grounds of commercial confidentiality

17.10 The ENFORCING AUTHORITY must not, without the relevant person's permission, include any information on its REGISTER which:

    (a) relates to the affairs of any individual or business; and
    (b) is commercially confidential to that individual or the person carrying on that business (*section 78T(1)*).

17.11 For these purposes, commercial interests relating to the value of the CONTAMINATED LAND, or to its ownership or occupation, are disregarded (*section 78T(11)*). This means that information cannot be excluded from the REGISTER solely on the basis that its inclusion might provide information to a prospective buyer of the land, thereby affecting the sale or the sale price.

17.12 In addition, the SECRETARY OF STATE can give directions to ENFORCING AUTHORITIES requiring the inclusion of specified information or descriptions of information, notwithstanding any commercial confidentiality, where he considers that the inclusion of that information would be in the public interest (*section 78T(7)*). No such directions have yet been given.

17.13 If the ENFORCING AUTHORITY considers that any information which it would normally include on its REGISTER could be commercially confidential, it must notify the person concerned in writing. The authority then needs to give that person a reasonable opportunity to make representations requesting the exclusion of the information and explaining why the information is commercially confidential (*section 78T(2)*).

17.14 The ENFORCING AUTHORITY then needs to determine, taking into account any representations received, whether the information is, or is not, commercially confidential.

17.15 If the ENFORCING AUTHORITY determines that the information is commercially confidential, that information is excluded from the REGISTER. However, the authority must include on its REGISTER a statement indicating the existence of excluded information of the relevant kind (*section 78R(7)*). This means, for example, that if details of a REMEDIATION NOTICE are excluded, the statement records that the particulars of such a notice have been excluded.

17.16 If the ENFORCING AUTHORITY determines that the information is not commercially confidential, it notifies the person concerned. That person then has twenty-one days in which he can appeal to the SECRETARY OF STATE (*section 78T(3)*). While any appeal is pending, the information is not included on the REGISTER. If the SECRETARY OF STATE determines that the information is commercially confidential, then the information is excluded with a statement about the exclusion being entered on the REGISTER. If the SECRETARY OF STATE determines that the information is not commercially confidential, or if the appeal is withdrawn, the ENFORCING AUTHORITY includes it on its REGISTER seven days afterwards.

17.17 If no appeal is made within twenty-one days of the date on which the ENFORCING AUTHORITY notified the person concerned of its determination, the ENFORCING AUTHORITY enters the information on its REGISTER.

17.18 Where any information is excluded from a REGISTER on the grounds of commercial confidentiality, that exclusion will generally lapse after four years with the information being treated as no longer being commercially confidential (*section 78T(8)*). This means that where information has been excluded, the ENFORCING AUTHORITY will need to put arrangements in place to ensure that information is included on the REGISTER once the four year period has passed.

17.19 However, the person who furnished the information can apply to the ENFORCING AUTHORITY for information to remain excluded. The authority then determines whether the information is still commercially confidential, and acts accordingly. The same arrangements apply for any appeal against this determination as apply in the case of an original determination (*section 78T(9)*).

18. Procedures Relating to Special Sites

Introduction

18.1 Regulations 2 and 3 of the Contaminated Land Regulations, together with Schedule 1 of those Regulations, prescribe various descriptions of CONTAMINATED LAND which are required to be designated as SPECIAL SITES. An explanation of these descriptions is set out in Annex 4 to this Circular.

18.2 The actual designation of any individual site is made by the LOCAL AUTHORITY or, in any case where there is a dispute between the LOCAL AUTHORITY and the ENVIRONMENT AGENCY, by the SECRETARY OF STATE, on the basis that the land meets one or more of these descriptions.

18.3 The effect of any such designation is that the ENVIRONMENT AGENCY takes over from the LOCAL AUTHORITY as the ENFORCING AUTHORITY for that site.

18.4 In carrying out its role as an ENFORCING AUTHORITY, the ENVIRONMENT AGENCY is subject to the same requirements under the primary and secondary legislation and statutory guidance as would be a LOCAL AUTHORITY.

The identification of special sites

Identification by the local authority

18.5 Whenever the LOCAL AUTHORITY has identified any CONTAMINATED LAND, it will need to consider whether that land meets one or more of the descriptions prescribed in the Regulations, and should therefore be designated as a SPECIAL SITE (*section 78C(1)*). It will also need to keep this question under review as further information becomes available.

18.6 If the LOCAL AUTHORITY considers, at any time, that some particular CONTAMINATED LAND might be required to be designated as a SPECIAL SITE, it needs to request the advice of the ENVIRONMENT AGENCY (*section 78C(3)*). If the LOCAL AUTHORITY does not consider that the land might be required to be designated, it does not need to consult the ENVIRONMENT AGENCY. Where the CONTAMINATED LAND is attributable to radioactivity, the LOCAL AUTHORITY will already have provided the ENVIRONMENT AGENCY with a draft record of the determination of whether the land is CONTAMINATED LAND and taken account of the ENVIRONMENT AGENCY'S views (see paragraph 3.33A above).

18.7 The LOCAL AUTHORITY then needs to decide, having regard to any such advice received, whether or not the land is required to be designated (*section 78C(3)*). If it decides that it is, the authority must give notice in writing to:

    (a) the ENVIRONMENT AGENCY;

    (b) the OWNER of the land;

    (c) any person who appears to be the occupier of all or part of the land; and

    (d) each person who appears to be an APPROPRIATE PERSON (*sections 78C(1)(b) & 78C(2)*).

18.8 The ENVIRONMENT AGENCY then needs to consider whether it agrees with the LOCAL AUTHORITY'S decision that the land should be designated.

18.9 If it does not agree, it must notify the LOCAL AUTHORITY within twenty-one days of the LOCAL AUTHORITY'S notification, giving a statement of its reasons for disagreeing (*section 78D(1)(b)*). It also needs to copy the notification and statement to the SECRETARY OF STATE (*section 78D(2)*). The LOCAL AUTHORITY must then refer its decision to the SECRETARY OF STATE (*section 78D(1)*).

18.10 If the ENVIRONMENT AGENCY agrees with the LOCAL AUTHOR-ITY'S decision, or if it fails to notify its disagreement within the twenty-one days allowed, the CONTAMINATED LAND in question will be designated as a SPECIAL SITE (see paragraphs 18.20 to 18.22 below).

Identification by the environment agency

18.11 The ENVIRONMENT AGENCY also needs to consider whether any CONTAMINATED LAND should be designated as a SPECIAL SITE. If at any time it considers that any such land should be designated, it needs to notify in writing the LOCAL AUTHORITY in whose area that land is situated (*section 78C(4)*).

18.12 The ENVIRONMENT AGENCY may take this view on the basis of information received from the LOCAL AUTHORITY or information it obtains itself, for example under its other pollution control functions. However, the basis on which it reaches such a decision must be whether or not it considers that the land meets one or more of the descriptions prescribed in the Contaminated Land Regulations. The ENVIRONMENT AGENCY is not entitled to apply any different tests to those which the LOCAL AUTHORITY would apply.

18.13 The LOCAL AUTHORITY must then decide whether or not it agrees with the ENVIRONMENT AGENCY that the CONTAMINATED LAND should be designated a SPECIAL SITE. Once it has reached a decision, it must notify in writing the persons identified in paragraph 18.7 above of its decision (*section 78C(5)*).

18.14 If the LOCAL AUTHORITY agrees with the ENVIRONMENT AGENCY, the land is designated a SPECIAL SITE (see paragraphs 18.20 to 18.22 below).

18.15 If the LOCAL AUTHORITY disagrees with the ENVIRONMENT AGENCY, the Agency has an opportunity to reaffirm its view that the land should be designated. If it wishes to do this, it must notify the LOCAL AUTHORITY, in writing, within twenty-one days of receiving from the LOCAL AUTHORITY notification of its decision. The Agency must provide a statement of the reasons why it considers the land should be designated (*section 78D(1)(b)*) and send this information to the SECRE-TARY OF STATE (*section 78D(2)*). The LOCAL AUTHORITY must then refer its decision to the SECRETARY OF STATE (*section 78D(1)*).

Referral of decisions to the secretary of state

18.16 If the LOCAL AUTHORITY receives any notification from the ENVIRONMENT AGENCY that the Agency disagrees with a decision it has made concerning the designation or non- designation of any CON-TAMINATED LAND as a SPECIAL SITE, the LOCAL AUTHORITY must refer that decision to the SECRETARY OF STATE.

18.17 In doing so, the LOCAL AUTHORITY must send the SECRETARY OF STATE a statement setting out the reasons why it reached its decision (*section 78D(1)*). It must also notify in writing the persons identified in paragraph 18.7 above of the fact that it has referred its decision to the SECRETARY OF STATE (*section 78D(3)*).

18.18 The SECRETARY OF STATE then decides whether he considers that all, or part, of the CONTAMINATED LAND in question meets one or more of the descriptions prescribed in the Regulations as being required to be designated a SPECIAL SITE. If he decides that some land should be designated, then it is so designated (*section 78D(4)(a)*).

18.19 The SECRETARY OF STATE is under a duty to notify in writing the LOCAL AUTHORITY and the persons identified in paragraph 18.7 above of his decision (*section 78D(4)(b)*).

The actual designation as a special site

18.20 In any case where the LOCAL AUTHORITY'S decision that land should be designated a SPECIAL SITE has not been referred to the SECRE-TARY OF STATE, the notification it gives of that decision takes effect as the designation on the following basis:

(a) if the ENVIRONMENT AGENCY notifies the LOCAL AUTHOR-ITY that it agrees with its decision, the designation takes effect on the day after that notification; or

(b) if no such notification is given, the designation takes effect on the day after a period of twenty-one days has elapsed since the LOCAL AUTHORITY notified the ENVIRONMENT AGENCY of its origi-nal decision (*section 78C(6)*).

18.21 Where a designation takes effect in this way, the LOCAL AUTHORITY must notify in writing the same categories of person as it notified of its original decision (*section 78C(6)*). It must also enter the relevant particu-lars on its REGISTER (*section 78R(1)(e); see paragraphs 17.1 to 17.19 above*).

18.22 In any case where a decision has been referred to the SECRETARY OF STATE, and he decides that some CONTAMINATED LAND should be designated a SPECIAL SITE, the notice he gives of this decision to the LOCAL AUTHORITY and the persons identified in paragraph 18.7 above serves as the actual designation. The designation takes effect on the day after he gives the notification (*sections 78D(5) & (6)*). The LOCAL AUTHORITY and the ENVIRONMENT AGENCY must enter the relevant particulars of the SECRETARY OF STATE'S notification onto their respective REGISTERS (see paragraphs 17.1 to 17.19 above).

Remediation of special sites

18.23 In general, the procedures relating to the REMEDIATION of a SPECIAL SITE are the same as for any other CONTAMINATED LAND, with the exception that the ENVIRONMENT AGENCY is the ENFORCING AUTHORITY, rather than the LOCAL AUTHORITY. In particular, the ENVIRONMENT AGENCY is required to have regard to the statutory guidance on remediation (*Chapter C*) and the recovery of costs (*Chapter E*), and to act in accordance with the statutory guidance on EXCLUSIONS from, and APPORTIONMENT of, liability (*Chapter D*).

18.24 In some cases the designation of a SPECIAL SITE may be made after a REMEDIATION NOTICE has been served or after the LOCAL AUTHORITY has started carrying out REMEDIATION itself.

18.25 If a REMEDIATION NOTICE has already been served, the ENVIRONMENT AGENCY needs to decide whether or not to adopt the existing REMEDIATION NOTICE (*section 78Q(1)*). For example, it may consider that:

    (a) the REMEDIATION ACTIONS specified in the existing notice are still appropriate;

    (b) those REMEDIATION ACTIONS should not be carried out; or

    (c) additional, or alternative, REMEDIATION ACTIONS should be carried out.

18.26 If the ENVIRONMENT AGENCY decides to adopt the REMEDIATION NOTICE, it must notify in writing the LOCAL AUTHORITY which originally served the notice, and the person or persons on whom the notice was served (*section 78Q(1)(a)*). The notice then has effect as if it had been given by the Agency (*section 78Q(1)(b)*). It is also good practice to send a copy of such a notification to anyone else to whom a copy of the original REMEDIATION NOTICE was sent (*regulation 5 of the Contaminated Land Regulations*).

18.27 The adoption of a REMEDIATION NOTICE by the ENVIRONMENT AGENCY means that the Agency has the power to enforce it, bringing a prosecution and carrying out the REMEDIATION itself if the notice is not complied with.

18.28 If the ENVIRONMENT AGENCY does not adopt a REMEDIATION NOTICE, that notice ceases to have effect, and the person on whom it was served is no longer obliged to comply with its requirements. But the ENVIRONMENT AGENCY then needs to decide whether it is required to serve a further REMEDIATION NOTICE. In doing so, it must consult in the same manner as would a LOCAL AUTHORITY for any CONTAMINATED LAND which is not a SPECIAL SITE. Except where urgency is involved, the ENVIRONMENT AGENCY is prevented from serving any REMEDIATION NOTICE until three months have elapsed since the LOCAL AUTHORITY, or the SECRETARY OF STATE, gave notification that the land was designated a SPECIAL SITE (*sections 78H(3)(b) & (c)*).

18.29 In any case where the ENVIRONMENT AGENCY does not adopt a REMEDIATION NOTICE, it is good practice for the Agency to notify the LOCAL AUTHORITY which originally served the notice, any person on whom the notice was served and anyone else to whom a copy of the notice was sent.

18.30 If the LOCAL AUTHORITY has begun to carry out any REMEDIATION itself before the land is designated a SPECIAL SITE, the LOCAL AUTHORITY needs to decide whether to continue carrying out that REMEDIATION (*section 78Q(2)(a)*). Whatever it decides, it is entitled to recover the reasonable costs it incurs, or has already incurred, in carrying out the REMEDIATION, even though it is no longer the ENFORCING AUTHORITY (*section 78Q(2)(b)*).

18.31 As an ENFORCING AUTHORITY, the ENVIRONMENT AGENCY is under a duty to maintain a REGISTER (*section 78R(1)*), with an entry for each SPECIAL SITE. Each time it enters any particulars onto its REGISTER, the ENVIRONMENT AGENCY must send a copy of those particulars to the LOCAL AUTHORITY in whose area the land is situated (*section 78R(4); see paragraphs 17.4 to 17.6 above*). The LOCAL AUTHORITY then must enter those particulars onto its own REGISTER (*section 78R(6)*).

Termination of a designation

18.32 The ENVIRONMENT AGENCY can inspect the SPECIAL SITE from time to time, in order to keep its condition under review (*section 78Q(3)*). In particular, the ENVIRONMENT AGENCY needs to consider whether the land still meets one or more of the descriptions of land prescribed in the Contaminated Land Regulations.

18.33 If it decides that the land no longer meets one or more of those descriptions, it must also decide whether it wishes to terminate that land's designation as a SPECIAL SITE. It is not obliged to terminate the designation as soon as the land ceases to meet any of the descriptions of land prescribed in the Regulations (*section 78Q(4)*). It may choose, for example, to wait until REMEDIATION has been completed on the land.

18.34 If the ENVIRONMENT AGENCY decides to terminate any designation, it must notify in writing the SECRETARY OF STATE and the LOCAL AUTHORITY in whose area the land is situated. The termination takes effect from whatever date is specified by the ENVIRONMENT AGENCY (*section 78Q(4)*). Both the ENVIRONMENT AGENCY and the LOCAL AUTHORITY then need to enter particulars of this notification onto their respective REGISTERS (*section 78R(1)(g)*). It is also good practice to notify everyone else who was notified of the original designation of the land as a SPECIAL SITE (see paragraph 18.7 above).

ANNEX 3

Statutory guidance

This Annex to the Circular contains 5 chapters of statutory guidance issued by the Secretary of State under Part 2A of the Environmental Protection Act 1990. It comprises the guidance issued in March 2000, and further guidance issued by the Secretary of State to accompany modifications made to Part 2A by the Radioactive Contaminated Land (Modification of Enactments) (England) Regulations 2006 so as to apply the regime in Part 2A to include situations where harm is being caused as a result of the presence of radioactivity in, on or under the land. The further guidance is incorporated into the 2000 guidance, and for convenience the additional text is highlighted for ease of reference. This Annex therefore replaces the version in DETR Circular 02/2000, "*Contaminated Land*". The statutory guidance below is signposted at the beginning of each chapter, to indicate which passages are of general application, which concern only matters attributable to radioactivity, and which concern only matters not attributable to radioactivity.

CHAPTER A—THE DEFINITION OF CONTAMINATED LAND

Part 1   Scope of the Chapter

Applies generally.

Part 2 Definitions of Terms and General Material

Applies generally.

Part 3 Significant Harm and the Significant Possibility of Significant Harm

Only applies to situations involving contaminants which are not radioactive.

Part 4 The Pollution of Controlled Waters

Only applies to situations involving contaminants which are not radioactive.

Part 5 Harm attributable to Radioactivity and the Significant Possibility of Harm

Only applies to situations involving contaminants which are radioactive.

Part 1—Scope of the chapter

A.1   The statutory guidance in this Chapter is issued under section 78A(2), (5) and (6) and section 78A(2), (5) and (6) (as modified) of Part 2A of the Environmental Protection Act 1990 and provides guidance on applying the definition of contaminated land.

A.2   "Contaminated land" is defined at section 78A(2) as:

"any land which appears to the local authority in whose area it is situated to be in such a condition, by reason of substances in, on or under the land, that —

"(a) significant harm is being caused or there is a significant possibility of such harm being caused; or

"(b) pollution of controlled waters is being, or is likely to be caused; . . ."

A.2A In relation to harm so far as attributable to radioactivity, the definition of contaminated land has been modified by regulation 5(1) of The Radio-active Contaminated Land (Modification of Enactments) (England) Regulations 2006 ("the Modification Regulations") to read:

"any land which appears to the local authority in whose area it is situated to be in such a condition, by reason of substances in, on or under the land, that —

"(a) harm is being caused, or

"(b) there is a significant possibility of such harm being caused; . . . "

A.3 Section 78A(5) further provides that:

"the questions —

"(a) what harm is to be regarded as "significant"

"(b) whether the possibility of significant harm being caused is "significant"

"(c) whether pollution of controlled waters is being, or is likely to be caused,

"shall be determined in accordance with guidance issued . . . . by the Secretary of State".

A.3A Regulation 5(5) of the Modification Regulations modifies section 78A(5) in relation to harm so far as attributable to radioactivity to provide that:

"the questions —

"(a) whether harm is being caused, and

"(b) whether the possibility of harm being caused is "significant",

"shall be determined in accordance with guidance issued . . . by the Secretary of State. . . ".

A.4 In determining these questions the local authority is therefore required to act in accordance with the guidance contained in this Chapter.

A.5 As well as defining contaminated land, section 78A(2) and section 78A(2) (as modified) further provides that:

"in determining whether any land appears to be such land, a local authority shall . . . . act in accordance with guidance issued by the Secretary of State . . . . with respect to the manner in which that determination is to be made"

A.6 Guidance on the manner in which this determination is to be made is set out in Part 3 of the statutory guidance in Chapter B.

Part 2—Definitions of terms and general material

A.7 Unless otherwise stated, any word, term or phrase given a specific meaning in Part 2A of the Environmental Protection Act 1990 has the same meaning for the purposes of the guidance in this Chapter.

A.7A In relation to harm so far as attributable to radioactivity, unless otherwise stated, any word, term or phrase given a specific meaning in Part 2A of the Environmental Protection Act 1990, as modified by the Modification Regulations, has the same meaning for the purposes of the guidance in this Chapter.

A.8 Any reference to "Part 2A" means "Part 2A of the Environmental Protection Act 1990". In relation to harm so far as attributable to radioactivity, any reference to "Part 2A" means "Part 2A of the Environmental Protection Act 1990, as modified.

A.8A Any reference to a "section" in primary legislation means a section of the Environmental Protection Act 1990, unless it is specifically stated otherwise. Any reference to a "section (as modified)" means a section of the Environmental Protection Act 1990 as modified by the Modification Regulations, unless it is specifically stated otherwise.

A.8B Any reference to "harm so far as attributable to radioactivity" and "other than in relation to harm so far as attributable to radioactivity" means "harm so far as attributable to any radioactivity possessed by any substance" and "other than in relation to harm so far as attributable to any radioactivity possessed by any substance" respectively.

Risk assessment

A.9 The definition of contaminated land is based upon the principles of risk assessment. For the purposes of this guidance, "risk" is defined as the combination of:

    (a) the probability, or frequency, of occurrence of a defined hazard (for example, exposure to a property of a substance with the potential to cause harm); and

    (b) the magnitude (including the seriousness) of the consequences.

A.10 The guidance below follows established approaches to risk assessment, including the concept of contaminant-pathway-receptor. (In the technical literature, this is sometimes referred to as source-pathway-target.)

A.11 There are two steps in applying the definition of contaminated land. The first step is for the local authority to satisfy itself that a "contaminant", a "pathway" (or pathways), and a "receptor" have been identified with respect to that land. These three concepts are defined for the purposes of this Chapter in paragraphs A. 12 to A. 14 below.

A.12 A contaminant is a substance which is in, on or under the land and which has the potential to cause harm or to cause pollution of controlled waters.

A.13 A receptor is either:

    (a) a living organism, a group of living organisms, an ecological system or a piece of property which

        (i) is in a category listed in Table A (see below) as a type of receptor; and

        (ii) is being, or could be, harmed, by a contaminant; or

    (b) controlled waters which are being, or could be, polluted by a contaminant; or

    (c) any person who is, or could be, subject to lasting exposure so far as attributable to radioactivity.

A.14 A pathway is one or more routes or means by, or through, which a receptor:

    (a) is being exposed to, or affected by, a contaminant, or

(b) could be so exposed or affected.

A.15 It is possible for a pathway to be identified for this purpose on the basis of a reasonable assessment of the general scientific knowledge about the nature of a particular contaminant and of the circumstances of the land in question. Direct observation of the pathway is not necessary.

A.16 The identification of each of these three elements is linked to the identification of the others. A pathway can only be identified if it is capable of exposing an identified receptor to an identified contaminant. That particular contaminant should likewise be capable of harming, or, in the case of controlled waters, be capable of polluting that particular receptor.

A.17 In this Chapter, a "pollutant linkage" means the relationship between a contaminant, a pathway and a receptor, and a "pollutant" means the contaminant in a pollutant linkage. Unless all three elements of a pollutant linkage are identified in respect of a piece of land, that land should not be identified as contaminated land. There may be more than one pollutant linkage on any given piece of land.

A.18 For the purposes of determining whether a pollutant linkage exists (and for describing any such linkage), the local authority may treat two or more substances as being a single substance, in any case where:

(a) the substances are compounds of the same element, or have similar molecular structures; and

(b) it is the presence of that element, or the particular type of molecular structures, that determines the effect that the substances may have on the receptor which forms part of the pollutant linkage.

A.18A In relation to harm so far as attributable to radioactivity, for the purposes of determining whether a pollutant linkage exists (and for describing any such linkage), the local authority may treat two or more substances as being a single substance, in any case where they contain radionuclides.

A.19 The second step in applying the definition of contaminated land is for the local authority to satisfy itself that both:

(a) such a pollutant linkage exists in respect of a piece of land; and

(b) that pollutant linkage:

(i) is resulting in significant harm being caused to the receptor in the pollutant linkage,

(ii) presents a significant possibility of significant harm being caused to that receptor,

(iii) is resulting in the pollution of the controlled waters which constitute the receptor,

(iv) is likely to result in such pollution,

(v) is resulting in harm so far as attributable to radioactivity being caused to any person in the pollutant linkage, or

(vi) presents a significant possibility of harm so far as attributable to radioactivity being caused to any person in the pollutant linkage.

A.20 In this Chapter, a "significant pollutant linkage" means a pollutant linkage which forms the basis for a determination that a piece of land is contaminated land. A "significant pollutant" is a pollutant in a "significant pollutant linkage".

A.21 The guidance in Part 3 below relates to questions about significant harm and the significant possibility of such harm being caused. The guidance in Part 4 below relates to the pollution of controlled waters. The guidance in

Part 5 relates to harm so far as attributable to radioactivity and the significant possibility of such harm being caused.

Part 3—Significant harm and the significant possibility of significant harm

A.22 Section 78A(4) defines "harm" as meaning "harm to the health of living organisms or other interference with the ecological systems of which they form part and, in the case of man, includes harm to his property". Section 78A(5) provide that what harm is to be regarded as "significant" and whether the possibility of significant harm being caused is significant shall be determined in accordance with this guidance.

What harm is to be regarded as "significant"

A.23 The local authority should regard as significant only harm which is both:

(a) to a receptor of a type listed in Table A, and
(b) within the description of harm specified for that type of receptor in that Table.

A.24 The local authority should not regard harm to receptors of any type other than those mentioned in Table A as being significant harm for the purposes of Part 2A. For example, harm to ecological systems outside the descriptions in the second entry in the table should be disregarded. Similarly, the authority should not regard any other description of harm to receptors of the types mentioned in Table A as being significant harm.

A.25 The authority should disregard any receptors which are not likely to be present, given the "current use" of the land or other land which might be affected.

A.26 For the purposes of this guidance, the "current use" means any use which is currently being made, or is likely to be made, of the land and which is consistent with any existing planning permission (or is otherwise lawful under town and country planning legislation). This definition is subject to the following qualifications:

(a) the current use should be taken to include any temporary use, permitted under town and country planning legislation, to which the land is, or is likely to be, put from time to time;

(b) the current use includes future uses or developments which do not require a new, or amended, grant of planning permission (but see also paragraph A.34 below);

(c) the current use should, nevertheless, be taken to include any likely informal recreational use of the land, whether authorised by the owners or occupiers or not, (for example, children playing on the land); however, in assessing the likelihood of any such informal use, the local authority should give due attention to measures taken to prevent or restrict access to the land; and

(d) in the case of agricultural land, however, the current agricultural use should not be taken to extend beyond the growing or rearing of the crops or animals which are habitually grown or reared on the land.

TABLE A-CATEGORIES OF SIGNIFICANT HARM

Type of Receptor	Description of harm to that type of receptor that is to be regarded as significant harm
1 Human beings	Death, disease, serious injury, genetic mutation, birth defects or the impairment of reproductive functions. For these purposes, disease is to be taken to mean an unhealthy condition of the body or a part of it and can include, for example, cancer, liver dysfunction or extensive skin ailments. Mental dysfunction is included only insofar as it is attributable to the effects of a pollutant on the body of the person concerned. In this Chapter, this description of significant harm is referred to as a "human health effect".

2 Any ecological system, or living organism forming part of such a system, within a location which is:
• an area notified as an area of special scientific interest under section 28 of the Wildlife and Countryside Act 1981;
• any land declared a national nature reserve under section 35 of that Act;
• any area designated as a marine nature reserve under section 36 of that Act;
• an area of special protection for birds, established under section 3 of that Act;
• any European Site within the meaning of regulation 10 of the Conservation (Natural Habitats etc) Regulations 1994 (i.e. Special Areas of Conservation and Special Protection Areas);
• any candidate Special Areas of Conservation or potential Special Protection Areas given equivalent protection;
• any habitat or site afforded policy protection under paragraph 6 of Planning Policy Statement (PPS 9) on nature conservation (i.e. candidate Special Areas of Conservation, potential Special Protection Areas and listed Ramsar sites); or
• any nature reserve established under section 21 of the National Parks and Access to the Countryside Act 1949.
	For *any* protected location:
	• harm which results in an irreversible adverse change, or in some other substantial adverse change, in the functioning of the ecological system within any substantial part of that location; or
	• harm which affects any species of special interest within that location and which endangers the long-term maintenance of the population of that species at that location.
	In addition, in the case of a protected location which is a European Site (or a candidate Special Area of Conservation or a potential Special Protection Area), harm which is incompatible with the favourable conservation status of natural habitats at that location or species typically found there.
	  In determining what constitutes such harm, the local authority should have regard to the advice of English Nature and to the requirements of the Conservation (Natural Habitats etc) Regulations 1994.
	  In this Chapter, this description of significant harm is referred to as an "ecological system effect".

3 Property in the form of:
• crops, including timber;
• produce grown domestically, or on allotments, for consumption;
• livestock;
• other owned or domesticated animals;
• wild animals which are the subject of shooting or fishing rights.
	For crops, a substantial diminution in yield or other substantial loss in their value resulting from death, disease or other physical damage. For domestic pets, death, serious disease or serious physical damage. For other property in this category, a substantial loss in its value resulting from death, disease or other serious physical damage.
	  The local authority should regard a substantial loss in value as occurring only when a substantial proportion of the animals or crops are dead or otherwise no longer fit for their intended purpose. Food should be regarded as being no longer fit for purpose when it fails to comply with the provisions of the Food Safety Act 1990. Where a diminution in yield or loss in value is caused by a pollutant linkage, a 20% diminution or loss should be regarded as a benchmark for what constitutes a substantial diminution or loss.
	  In this Chapter, this description of significant harm is referred to as an "animal or crop effect".

4 Property in the form of buildings.
  For this purpose, "building" means any structure or erection, and any part of a building including any part below ground level, but does not include plant or machinery comprised in a building.
	Structural failure, substantial damage or substantial interference with any right of occupation.
	  For this purpose, the local authority should regard substantial damage or substantial interference as occurring when any part of the building ceases to be capable of being used for the purpose for which it is or was intended.
	  Additionally, in the case of a scheduled Ancient Monument, substantial damage should be regarded as occurring when the damage significantly impairs the historic, architectural, traditional, artistic or archaeological interest by reason of which the monument was scheduled.
	  In this Chapter, this description of significant harm is referred to as a "building effect".

Whether the possibility of significant harm being caused is significant

A.27   As stated in paragraph A.9 above, the guidance on determining whether a particular possibility is significant is based on the principles of risk assessment, and in particular on considerations of the magnitude or consequences of the different types of significant harm caused. The term "possibility of significant harm being caused" should be taken as referring to a measure of the probability, or frequency, of the occurrence of circumstances which would lead to significant harm being caused.

A.28 The local authority should take into account the following factors in deciding whether the possibility of significant harm being caused is significant:

    (a) the nature and degree of harm;

    (b) the susceptibility of the receptors to which the harm might be caused; and

    (c) the timescale within which the harm might occur.

A.29 In considering the timescale, the authority should take into account any evidence that the current use of the land (as defined in paragraphs A.25 and A.26 above) will cease in the foreseeable future.

A.30 The local authority should regard as a significant possibility any possibility of significant harm which meets the conditions set out in Table B for the description of significant harm under consideration.

TABLE B —SIGNIFICANT POSSIBILITY OF SIGNIFICANT HARM

Descriptions Of Significant Harm (As Defined In Table A)	Conditions For There Being A Significant Possibility Of Significant Harm
1 Human health effects arising from • the intake of a contaminant, or • other direct bodily contact with a contaminant	If the amount of the pollutant in the pollutant linkage in question: • which a human receptor in that linkage might take in, or • to which such a human might otherwise be exposed, as a result of the pathway in that linkage, would represent an unacceptable intake or direct bodily contact, assessed on the basis of relevant information on the toxicological properties of that pollutant. Such an assessment should take into account: • the likely total intake of, or exposure to, the substance or substances which form the pollutant, from all sources including that from the pollutant linkage in question; • the relative contribution of the pollutant linkage in question to the likely aggregate intake of, or exposure to, the relevant substance or substances; and • the duration of intake or exposure resulting from the pollutant linkage in question. The question of whether an intake or exposure is unacceptable is independent of the number of people who might experience or be affected by that intake or exposure. Toxicological properties should be taken to include carcinogenic, mutagenic, teratogenic, pathogenic, endocrine-disrupting and other similar properties.
2 All other human health effects (particularly by way of explosion or fire).	If the probability, or frequency, of occurrence of significant harm of that description is unacceptable, assessed on the basis of relevant information concerning: • that type of pollutant linkage, or • that type of significant harm arising from other causes. In making such an assessment, the local authority should take into account the levels of risk which have been judged unacceptable in other similar contexts and should give particular weight to cases where the pollutant linkage might cause significant harm which: • would be irreversible or incapable of being treated; would affect a substantial number of people; • would result from a single incident such as a fire or an explosion; or • would be likely to result from a short-term (that is, less than 24–hour) exposure to the pollutant.
3 All ecological system effects.	If either: • significant harm of that description is more likely than not to result from the pollutant linkage in question; or • there is a reasonable possibility of significant harm of that description being caused, and if that harm were to occur, it would result in such a degree of damage to features of special interest at the location in question that they would be beyond any practicable possibility of restoration. Any assessment made for these purposes should take into account relevant information for that type of pollutant linkage, particularly in relation to the ecotoxicological effects of the pollutant.
4 All animal and crop effects.	If significant harm of that description is more likely than not to result from the pollutant linkage in question, taking into account relevant information for that type of pollutant linkage, particularly in relation to the ecotoxicological effects of the pollutant.
5 All building effects	If significant harm of that description is more likely than not to result from the pollutant linkage in question during the expected economic life of the building (or, in the case of a scheduled Ancient Monument, the foreseeable future), taking into account relevant information for that type of pollutant linkage.

A.31 In Table B, references to "relevant information" mean information which is:

(a) scientifically-based;

(b) authoritative;

(c) relevant to the assessment of risks arising from the presence of contaminants in soil; and

(d) appropriate to the determination of whether any land is contaminated land for the purposes of Part 2A, in that the use of the information is consistent with providing a level of protection of risk in line with the qualitative criteria set out in Tables A and B.

A.32 In general, when considering significant harm to non-human receptors, the local authority should apply the tests set out in the relevant entries in Table B to determine whether there is a significant possibility of that harm being caused. However, the local authority may also determine that there is a significant possibility of significant harm with respect to a non-human receptor in any case where the conditions in the third, fourth and fifth entries in Table B are not met, but where:

(a) there is a reasonable possibility of significant harm being caused; and

(b) that harm would result from either:

(i) a single incident such as a fire or explosion, or

(ii) a short-term (that is, less than 24–hour) exposure of the receptor to the pollutant.

A.33 The possibility of significant harm being caused as a result of any change of use of any land to one which is not a current use of that land (as defined in paragraph A.26 above) should not be regarded as a significant possibility for the purposes of this Chapter.

A.34 When considering the possibility of significant harm being caused in relation to any future use or development which falls within the description of a "current use" as a result of paragraph A.26(b) above, the local authority should assume that if the future use is introduced, or the development carried out, this will be done in accordance with any existing planning permission for that use or development. In particular, the local authority should assume:

(a) that any remediation which is the subject of a condition attached to that planning permission, or is the subject of any planning obligation, will be carried out in accordance with that permission or obligation; and

(b) where a planning permission has been given subject to conditions which require steps to be taken to prevent problems which might be caused by contamination, and those steps are to be approved by the local planning authority, that the local planning authority will ensure that those steps include adequate remediation.

Part 4—The pollution of controlled waters

A.35 Section 78A(9) defines the pollution of controlled waters as:

"the entry into controlled waters of any poisonous, noxious or polluting matter or any solid waste matter".

A.36 Before determining that pollution of controlled waters is being, or is likely to be, caused, the local authority should be satisfied that a substance is continuing to enter controlled waters or is likely to enter controlled waters. For this purpose, the local authority should regard something as being "likely" when they judge it more likely than not to occur.

A.37 Land should not be designated as contaminated land where:

(a) a substance is already present in controlled waters;
(b) entry into controlled waters of that substance from land has ceased; and
(c) it is not likely that further entry will take place.

A.38 Substances should be regarded as having entered controlled waters where:

(a) they are dissolved or suspended in those waters; or
(b) if they are immiscible with water, they have direct contact with those waters on or beneath the surface of the water.

A.39 The term "continuing to enter" should be taken to mean any entry additional to any which has already occurred.

Part 5—Harm attributable to radioactivity and the significant possibility of harm

A.40 Part 5 applies only so far as the harm or the significant possibility of harm is attributable to radioactivity.

A.40A Section 78A(4) (as modified) defines "harm" as meaning "lasting exposure to any person resulting from the after-effects of a radiological emergency, past practice or past work activity."

A.40B Section 78A(5) (as modified) provides that whether harm is being caused or whether the possibility of harm being caused is "significant" shall be determined in accordance with this guidance.

Whether harm is being caused

A.41 The local authority should regard harm as being caused where lasting exposure gives rise to doses that exceed one or more of the following:

(a) an effective dose of 3 millisieverts per annum;
(b) an equivalent dose to the lens of the eye of 15 millisieverts per annum; or
(c) an equivalent dose to the skin of 50 millisieverts per annum.

A.42 The local authority should disregard any human receptors which are not likely to be present given the "current use" of the land or other land which might be affected.

A.43 For the purposes of this guidance, the "current use" means any use which is currently being made, or is likely to be made, of the land and which is consistent with any existing planning permission (or is otherwise lawful under town and country planning legislation). This definition is subject to the following qualifications:

(a) the current use should be taken to include any temporary use, permitted under town and country planning legislation, to which the land is, or is likely to be, put from time to time;
(b) the current use includes future uses or developments which do not require a new, or amended, grant of planning permission (but see also paragraph A.50 below); and

(c) the current use should, nevertheless, be taken to include any likely informal recreational use of the land, whether authorised by the owners or occupiers or not, (for example, children playing on the land); however, in assessing the likelihood of any such informal use, the local authority should give due attention to measures taken to prevent or restrict access to the land.

Whether the possibility of harm being caused is significant

A.44 The term "possibility of harm" should be taken as referring to a measure of the probability, or frequency, of the occurrence of circumstances which would lead to lasting exposure being caused. In paragraphs A.45 and A.46, the reference to "potential annual effective dose" and "potential annual equivalent dose", refer to doses that are not certain to occur.

A.45 Where:

(a) the potential annual effective dose is below or equal to 50 milli-sieverts per annum; and

(b) the potential annual dose equivalents to the lens of the eye and to the skin are below or equal to 15 millisieverts and 50 millisieverts respectively,

the local authority should regard the possibility of harm as significant if, having regard to any uncertainties, the potential annual effective dose from any lasting exposure multiplied by the probability of the dose being received is greater than 3 millisieverts.

A.46 Where the conditions in A.45 are not met, the local authority should consider whether the possibility of harm being caused is significant on a case by case basis. In deciding whether the possibility of harm being caused is significant, the local authority should take into account relevant information concerning:

(a) the potential annual effective dose;

(b) any non-linearity in the dose-effect relationship for stochastic effects;

(c) the potential annual equivalent dose to the skin and to the lens of the eye;

(d) the nature and degree of any deterministic effects associated with the potential annual dose;

(e) the probability of the dose being received;

(f) the duration of the exposure and timescale within which the harm might occur; and

(g) any uncertainties associated with subparagraphs (a) to (f) above.

A.47 In paragraph A.46, the reference to:

(a) "relevant information" means information which is appropriate, scientifically-based and authoritative;

(b) "stochastic effects" means the type of health effect (the principal one being radiation-induced cancer) where the likelihood of radiation-induced health effects which may be assumed to be linearly proportional to the radiation dose over a wide range of doses and where the seventy of the health effect is not dependent on the level of the dose; and

(c) "deterministic effects" means the type of health effect (such as a radiation-induced cataract of the eye) which occur following a dose of radiation above a certain level, with the severity of the health effect dependent on the level of the dose.

A.48 In considering the timescale in subparagraph A.46(f), the local authority should take into account any evidence that the "current use" of the land (as defined in paragraphs A.42 and A.43) will cease in the foreseeable future.

A.49 The possibility of harm being caused as a result of any change of use of any land to one which is not a "current use" of that land (as defined in paragraph A.43 above) should not be regarded as a significant possibility of harm for the purposes of this Chapter.

A.50 When considering the possibility of harm being caused in relation to any future use or development which falls within the description of a "current use" as a result of subparagraph A.43(b), the local authority should assume that if the future use is introduced, or the development carried out, this will be done in accordance with any existing planning permission for that use or development. In particular, the local authority should assume:

(a) that any remediation which is the subject of a condition attached to that planning permission, or is the subject of any planning obligation, will be carried out in accordance with that permission or obligation; and

(b) where a planning permission has been given subject to conditions which require steps to be taken to prevent problems which might be caused by contamination, and those steps are to be approved by the local planning authority, that the local planning authority will ensure that those steps include adequate remediation.

CHAPTER B—THE IDENTIFICATION OF CONTAMINATED LAND

Part 1 Scope of the Chapter

Applies generally.

Part 2 Definitions of Terms

Applies generally.

Part 3 The Local Authority's Inspection Duty

Paragraphs B.9 to B.18 only apply to situations involving contaminants which are not radioactive. Paragraphs B.17A, B.18A and B.19A only apply to situations involving contaminants which are radioactive. The remaining paragraphs apply generally to all types of contaminants.

Part 4 Determining Whether Land Appears to be Contaminated Land

Paragraphs B.44 to B.51 only apply to situations involving contaminants which are not radioactive. Paragraphs B.51A to B.51H only apply to situations involving contaminants which are radioactive. The remaining paragraphs apply generally to all types of contaminants.

APPENDIX 1. MATERIALS

Part 1—Scope of the chapter

B.1 The statutory guidance in this Chapter is issued under sections 78A(2), 78A(2) (as modified) and 78B(2) of Part 2A of the Environmental Protection Act 1990, and provides guidance on the inspection of its area by a local authority and the manner in which an authority is to determine whether any land appears to it to be contaminated land.

B.2 Section 78B(1) provides that:

"Every local authority shall cause its area to be inspected from time to time for the purpose-

"(a) of identifying contaminated land; and
"(b) of enabling the authority to decide whether any such land is land which is required to be designated as a special site."

B.2A In relation to harm so far as attributable to radioactivity, section 78B(1) (as modified) provides that:

"(1) Where a local authority considers that there are reasonable grounds for believing that any land may be contaminated, it shall cause the land to be inspected for the purpose of-

"(a) identifying whether it is contaminated land; and
"(b) enabling the authority to decide whether the land is land which is required to be designated as a special site.

"(1A) The fact that substances have been present on the land shall not of itself be taken to be reasonable grounds for the purpose of subsection (1)."

B.3 For all cases section 78B(2) further provides that:

"In performing [these] functions . . . . a local authority shall act in accordance with any guidance issued for the purpose by the Secretary of State."

B.4 Section 78A(2) also provides that:

"'Contaminated land' is any land which appears to the local authority in whose area it is situated to be in such a condition, by reason of substances in, on or under the land, that -

"(a) significant harm is being caused or there is a significant possibility of such harm being caused, or
"(b) pollution of controlled waters is being, or is likely to be, caused;

"and, in determining whether any land appears to be such land, a local authority shall, subject to subsection (5), act in accordance with guidance issued by the Secretary of State in accordance with section 78YA with respect to the manner in which that determination is to be made."

B.4A In relation to harm so far as attributable to radioactivity section 78A(2) (as modified) provides that:

"Contaminated land' is any land which appears to the local authority in whose area it is situated to be in such a condition, by reason of substances in, on or under the land, that -

"(a) harm is being caused, or

"(b) there is a significant possibility of such harm being caused;

"and, in determining whether any land appears to be such land, a local authority shall, subject to subsection (5), act in accordance with guidance issued by the Secretary of State in accordance with section 78YA with respect to the manner in which that determination is to be made."

B.5 The local authority is therefore required to act in accordance with the statutory guidance contained in this Chapter.

B.6 The questions of what harm is to be regarded as significant, whether the possibility of significant harm being caused is significant, whether pollution of controlled waters is being or is likely to be caused, and whether harm is being caused and whether the possibility of harm being caused is significant are to be determined in accordance with guidance contained in Chapter A.

Part 2—Definitions of terms

B.7 Unless otherwise stated, any word, term or phrase given a specific meaning in Part 2A of the Environmental Protection Act 1990, or in the guidance at Chapter A, has the same meaning for the purposes of the guidance in this Chapter.

B.7A In relation to harm so far as attributable to radioactivity, unless otherwise stated, any word, term or phrase given a specific meaning in Part 2A of the Environmental Protection Act 1990, as modified by the Modification Regulations, has the same meaning for the purposes of the guidance in this Chapter.

B.8 Any reference to "Part 2A" means "Part 2A of the Environmental Protection Act 1990". In relation to harm so far as attributable to radioactivity, any reference to "Part 2A" means "Part 2A of the Environmental Protection Act 1990, as modified.

B.8A Any reference to a "section" in primary legislation means a section of the Environmental Protection Act 1990, unless it is specifically stated otherwise. Any reference to a "section (as modified)" means a section of the Environmental Protection Act 1990 as modified by the Modification Regulations, unless it is specifically stated otherwise.

B.8B Any reference to "harm so far as attributable to radioactivity" and "other than in relation to harm so far as attributable to radioactivity" means "harm so far as attributable to any radioactivity possessed by any substance" and "other than in relation to harm so far as attributable to any radioactivity possessed by any substance" respectively.

Part 3—The local authority's inspection duty

Strategic approach to inspection

B.9 In carrying out its inspection duty under section 78B(1) the local authority should take a strategic approach to the identification of land which merits detailed individual inspection. This approach should:

(a) be rational, ordered and efficient;

(b) be proportionate to the seriousness of any actual or potential risk;

(c) seek to ensure that the most pressing and serious problems are located first;

(d) ensure that resources are concentrated on investigating in areas where the authority is most likely to identify contaminated land; and

(e) ensure that the local authority efficiently identifies requirements for the detailed inspection of particular areas of land.

B.10 In developing this strategic approach the local authority should reflect local circumstances. In particular it should consider:

(a) any available evidence that significant harm or pollution of controlled waters is actually being caused;

(b) the extent to which any receptor (which is either of a type listed in Table A in Chapter A or is controlled waters) is likely to be found in any of the different parts of the authority's area;

(c) the extent to which any of those receptors is likely to be exposed to a contaminant (as defined in Chapter A), for example as a result of the use of the land or of the geological and hydrogeological features of the area;

(d) the extent to which information on land contamination is already available;

(e) the history, scale and nature of industrial or other activities which may have contaminated the land in different parts of its area;

(f) the nature and timing of past redevelopment in different parts of its area;

(g) the extent to which remedial action has already been taken by the authority or others to deal with land-contamination problems or is likely to be taken as part of an impending redevelopment; and

(h) the extent to which other regulatory authorities are likely to be considering the possibility of harm being caused to particular receptors or the likelihood of any pollution of controlled waters being caused in particular parts of the local authority's area.

B.11 In developing its strategic approach, the local authority should consult the Environment Agency and other appropriate public authorities, such as the county council (where one exists), statutory regeneration bodies, English Nature, English Heritage and the Food Standards Agency.

B.12 The local authority should set out its approach as a written strategy, which it should formally adopt and publish. As soon as its strategy is published, the local authority should send a copy to the Environment Agency.

B.13 The local authority should keep its strategy under periodic review.

B.14 The local authority should not await the publication of its strategy before commencing more detailed work investigating particular areas of land, where this appears necessary.

Contents of the strategy

B.15 Strategies are likely to vary both between local authorities and between different parts of an authority's area, reflecting the different problems associated with land contamination in different areas. The local authority should include in its strategy:

(a) a description of the particular characteristics of its area and how that influences its approach;

(b) the authority's particular aims, objectives and priorities;

(c) appropriate timescales for the inspection of different parts of its area; and

(d) arrangements and procedures for:

    (i) considering land for which it may itself have responsibilities by virtue of its current or former ownership or occupation,

    (ii) obtaining and evaluating information on actual harm or pollution of controlled waters,

    (iii) identifying receptors, and assessing the possibility or likelihood that they are being, or could be, exposed to or affected by a contaminant,

    (iv) obtaining and evaluating existing information on the possible presence of contaminants and their effects,

    (v) liaison with, and responding to information from, other statutory bodies, including, in particular, the Environment Agency and English Nature (see paragraphs B.16 and B.17 below),

    (vi) liaison with, and responding to information from, the owners or occupiers of land, and other relevant interested parties,

    (vii) responding to information or complaints from members of the public, businesses and voluntary organisations,

    (viii) planning and reviewing a programme for inspecting particular areas of land,

    (ix) carrying out the detailed inspection of particular areas of land,

    (x) reviewing and updating assumptions and information previously used to assess the need for detailed inspection of different areas, and managing new information, and

    (xi) managing information obtained and held in the course of carrying out its inspection duties.

Information from other statutory bodies

B.16 Other regulatory authorities may be able to provide information relevant to the identification of land as contaminated land, as a result of their various complementary functions. The local authority should seek to make specific arrangements with such other bodies to avoid unnecessary duplication in investigation.

B.17 For example, the Environment Agency has general responsibilities for the protection of the water environment. It monitors the quality of controlled waters and in doing so may discover land which would appropriately be identified as contaminated land by reason of pollution of controlled waters which is being, or is likely to be, caused.

Reasonable grounds approach to inspection

B.17A Under section 78B(1) (as modified), the trigger for a local authority to cause land to be inspected for the purposes of identifying whether the land is contaminated land, is where it considers that there are reasonable grounds for believing that land may be contaminated. It will have such reasonable grounds where it has knowledge of relevant information relating to:

    (a) a former historical land use, past practice, past work activity or radiological emergency, capable of causing lasting exposure giving rise to the radiation doses set out in paragraph A.41; or

    (b) levels of contamination present on the land arising from a past practice, past work activity or radiological emergency, capable of causing lasting exposure giving rise to the radiation doses set out in paragraph A.41.

B.17B In B.17A references to "relevant information" means information that is appropriate and authoritative and may, for example, include:

    (a) information held by the local authority, including information already gathered as part of its strategic approach to Part 2A as described in paragraphs B.9 to B.14 above or as part of the town and country planning process; or

    (b) information received from a regulatory body, such as the Environment Agency or the Health and Safety Executive.

Inspecting particular areas of land

B.18 Applying the strategic approach to carrying out its inspection duty under section 78B(1) will result in the identification of particular areas of land where it is possible that a pollutant linkage exists. Subject to the guidance in paragraphs B.22 to B.25 and B.27 to B.30 below, the local authority should carry out a detailed inspection of any such area to obtain sufficient information for the authority:

    (a) to determine, in accordance with the guidance on the manner of determination in Part 4 below, whether that land appears to be contaminated land; and

    (b) to decide whether any such land falls within the definition of a special site prescribed in regulations 2 and 3 of the Contaminated Land (England) Regulations 2006, and is therefore required to be designated as a special site.

B.18A Where the local authority is satisfied that there are reasonable grounds under section 78B(1) (as modified) for believing land may be contaminated (in relation to radioactivity), it should carry out a detailed inspection of the land. Subject to the guidance in paragraphs B.22 to B.25 and B.27 to B.30 below, the local authority should carry out a detailed inspection to obtain sufficient information for the authority:

    (a) to determine, in accordance with the guidance on the manner of determination in Part 4 below, whether that land appears to be contaminated land; and

    (b) to decide whether any such land falls within the definition of a special site prescribed in regulation 2 of the Contaminated Land (England) Regulations 2006, and is therefore required to be designated as a special site.

B.19 To be sufficient for the first of these purposes in paragraphs B.18 and B.18A the information should include, in particular, evidence of the actual presence of a pollutant.

B.19A In relation to harm so far as attributable to radioactivity, when undertaking detailed inspection as set out in paragraph B.20 the local authority should in the first instance, aim to identify that there is a reasonable possibility both of the presence of a receptor, and that this receptor could be exposed to a contaminant.

B.20 Detailed inspection may include any or all of the following:

    (a) the collation and assessment of documentary information, or other information from other bodies. In relation to harm so far as attributable to radioactivity, the local authority should have regard to any advice provided by the Environment Agency on the manner in which to carry out such an inspection;

(b) a visit to the particular area for the purposes of visual inspection and, in some cases, limited sampling (for example of surface deposits) or survey (for example using hand held radiation meters). In relation to harm so far as attributable to radioactivity, the local authority should have regard to any advice provided by the Environment Agency on the manner in which to carry out such an inspection; or

(c) intrusive investigation of the land (for example by exploratory excavations). In relation to harm so far as attributable to radioactivity, the local authority should always seek to make arrangements with the Environment Agency for the Agency to carry out such an inspection.

B.21 Section 108 of the Environment Act 1995 and section 108 of the Environment Act 1995 as modified by the Modification Regulations gives the local authority the power to authorise a person to exercise specific powers of entry. For the purposes of this Chapter, any detailed inspection of land carried out through use of this power by the local authority is referred to as an "inspection using statutory powers of entry".

B.22 Before the local authority carries out an inspection using statutory powers of entry, it should be satisfied, on the basis of any information already obtained:

(a) in all cases, that there is a reasonable possibility that a pollutant linkage (as defined in Chapter A) exists on the land; this implies that not only must the authority be satisfied that there is a reasonable possibility of the presence of a contaminant, a receptor and a pathway, but also that these would together create a pollutant linkage; and

(b) further, in cases involving an intrusive investigation,

(i) that it is likely that the contaminant is actually present, and
(ii) given the current use of the land as defined at paragraph A.26 and A.43, that the receptor is actually present or is likely to be present.

B.23 The local authority should not carry out any inspection using statutory powers of entry which takes the form of intrusive investigation if:

(a) it has already been provided with detailed information on the condition of the land, whether by the Environment Agency or some other person such as the owner of the land, which provides an appropriate basis upon which the local authority can determine whether the land is contaminated land in accordance with the requirements of the guidance in this Chapter; or

(b) a person offers to provide such information within a reasonable and specified time, and then provides such information within that time.

B.24 The local authority should carry out any intrusive investigation in accordance with appropriate technical procedures for such investigations. It should also ensure that it takes all reasonable precautions to avoid harm, water pollution or damage to natural resources or features of historical or archaeological interest which might be caused as a result of its investigation. Before carrying out any intrusive investigation on any area notified as an area of special scientific interest (SSSI), the local

865

authority should consult English Nature on any action which, if carried out by the owner or occupier, would require the consent of English Nature under section 28 of the Wildlife and Countryside Act 1981.

B.25 If at any stage, the local authority considers, on the basis of information obtained from a detailed inspection, that there is no longer a reasonable possibility that a particular pollutant linkage exists on the land, the authority should not carry out any further detailed inspection for that pollutant linkage.

Land which may be a special site

B.26 If land has been determined to be contaminated land and it also falls within one or more of the "special sites" descriptions prescribed in regulations made under Part 2A, it is required to be designated as a special site. The Environment Agency then becomes the enforcing authority for that land. It is therefore helpful for the Environment Agency to have a formal role at the inspection stage for any such land.

B.27 Before authorising or carrying out on any land an inspection using statutory powers of entry, the local authority should consider whether, if that land were found to be contaminated land, it would meet any of the descriptions of land prescribed in the Contaminated Land Regulations 2006 as requiring to be designated a special site.

B.28 If the local authority already has information that this would be the case, the authority should always seek to make arrangements with the Environment Agency for that Agency to carry out the inspection of the land on behalf of the local authority. This might occur, for example, where the prescribed description of land in the Regulations relates to its current or former use, such as land on which a process designated for central control under the Integrated Pollution Control regime has been carried out, land which is occupied by the Ministry of Defence, or land which is contaminated land by virtue of radioactive contamination.

B.29 If the local authority considers that there is a reasonable possibility that a particular pollutant linkage is present, and the presence of a linkage of that kind would require the designation of the land as a special site (were that linkage found to be a significant pollutant linkage), the authority should seek to make arrangements with the Environment Agency for the Agency to carry out the inspection of the land. An example of this kind of pollutant linkage would be the pollution of waters in the circumstances described in regulation 3(b) of the Contaminated Land (England) Regulations 2006.

B.30 Where the Environment Agency is to carry out an inspection on behalf of the local authority, the authority should, where necessary, authorise a person nominated by the Agency to exercise the powers of entry conferred by section 108 of the Environment Act 1995 and, in relation to harm so far as attributable to radioactivity, section 108 of the Environment Act 1995 as modified by the Modification Regulations. Before the local authority gives such an authorisation, the Environment Agency should satisfy the local authority that the conditions for the use of the statutory powers of entry set out in paragraphs B.22 to B.25 above are met.

Part 4—Determining whether land appears to be contaminated land

B.31 The local authority has the sole responsibility for determining whether any land appears to be contaminated land. It cannot delegate this responsibility (except in accordance with section 101 of the Local Government Act 1972), although in discharging it the local authority can choose to rely on information or advice provided by another body such as the Environment Agency, or by a consultant appointed for that purpose. This applies even where the Agency has carried out the inspection of land on behalf of the local authority (see paragraphs B.26 to B.30 above).

Physical extent of land

B.32 A determination that land is contaminated land is necessarily made in respect of a specific area of land. In deciding what that area should be, the primary consideration is the extent of the land which is contaminated land. However, there may be situations in which the local authority may consider that separate designations of parts of a larger area of contaminated land may simplify the administration of the consequential actions. In such circumstances, the local authority should do so, taking into account:

   (a) the location of significant pollutants in, on or under the land;
   (b) the nature of the remediation which might be required;
   (c) the likely identity of those who may be the appropriate persons to bear responsibility for the remediation (where this is reasonably clear at this stage); and
   (d) in relation to harm so far as attributable to radioactivity, the views of the Environment Agency concerning the desirability of a separate determination of part of the land.

B.33 If necessary, the local authority should initially review a wider area, the history of which suggests that contamination problems are likely. It can subsequently refine this down to the precise areas which meet the statutory tests for identification as contaminated land, and use these as the basis for its determination.

B.34 In practice, the land to be covered by a single determination is likely to be the smallest area which is covered by a single remediation action which cannot sensibly be broken down into smaller actions. Subject to this, the land is likely to be the smaller of:

   (a) the plots which are separately recorded in the Land Register or are in separate ownership or occupation; and
   (b) the area of land in which the presence of significant pollutants has been established.

B.35 The determination should identify the area of contaminated land clearly, including reference to a map or plan at an appropriate scale.

B.36 The local authority should also be prepared to review the decision on the physical extent of the land to be identified in the light of further information.

Making the determination

B.37 In determining whether any land appears to the local authority to be contaminated land, the authority is required to act in accordance with the guidance on the definition of contaminated land set out in Chapter A. Guidance on the manner in which the local authority should determine whether land appears to it to be contaminated land, by reason of substances in, on or under the land, is set out in paragraphs B.39 to B.51 below.

B.38 There are six possible grounds for the determination, (corresponding to the parts of the definition of contaminated land in section 78A(2) and 78A(2) (as modified)) namely that:

    (a) significant harm is being caused (see paragraph B.44 below);

    (b) there is a significant possibility of significant harm being caused (see paragraphs B.45 to B.49 below);

    (c) pollution of controlled waters is being caused (see paragraph B.50 below);

    (d) pollution of controlled waters is likely to be caused (see paragraph B.51 below);

    (e) harm so far as attributable to radioactivity is being caused (see paragraphs B.51A to B.51F); or

    (f) there is a significant possibility of harm so far as attributable to radioactivity being caused (see paragraphs B.51G to B.51H).

B.39 In making any determination, the local authority should take all relevant and available evidence into account and carry out an appropriate scientific and technical assessment of that evidence.

B.40 The local authority should identify a particular pollutant linkage or linkages (as defined in Chapter A) as the basis for the determination. All three elements of any pollutant linkage (pollutant, pathway and receptor) should be identified. A linkage which forms a basis for the determination that land is contaminated land is then a "significant pollutant linkage"; and any pollutant which forms part of it is a "significant pollutant".

B.41 The local authority should consider whether:

    (a) there is evidence that additive or synergistic effects between potential pollutants, whether between the same substance on different areas of land or between different substances, may result in a significant pollutant linkage;

    (b) a combination of several different potential pathways linking one or more potential pollutants to a particular receptor, or to a particular class of receptors, may result in a significant pollutant linkage; and

    (c) there is more than one significant pollutant linkage on any land; if there are, each should be considered separately, since different people may be responsible for the remediation.

Consistency with other statutory bodies

B.42 In making a determination which relates to an "ecological system effect" as defined in Table A of Chapter A, the local authority should adopt an approach consistent with that adopted by English Nature. To this end, the local authority should consult that authority and have regard to its comments in making its determination.

B.43 In making a determination which relates to pollution of controlled waters the local authority should adopt an approach consistent with that adopted by the Environment Agency in applying relevant statutory provisions. To this end, where the local authority is considering whether pollution of controlled waters is being or is likely to be caused, it should consult the Environment Agency and have regard to its comments before determining whether pollution of controlled waters is being or is likely to be caused.

B.43A In making a determination in relation to harm so far as attributable to radioactivity, the local authority should consult the Environment Agency providing the Environment Agency with a draft record of the determination and have regard to the Environment Agency's advice on the basis for, and the extent of land covered by, the determination before determining land as contaminated land.

Determining that "significant harm is being caused"

B.44 The local authority should determine that land is contaminated land on the basis that significant harm is being caused where:
   (a) it has carried out an appropriate scientific and technical assessment of all the relevant and available evidence; and
   (b) on the basis of that assessment, it is satisfied on the balance of probabilities that significant harm is being caused.

Determining that "there is a significant possibility of significant harm being caused"

B.45 The local authority should determine that land is contaminated land on the basis that there is a significant possibility of significant harm being caused (as defined in Chapter A), where:

   (a) it has carried out a scientific and technical assessment of the risks arising from the pollutant linkage, according to relevant, appropriate, authoritative and scientifically based guidance on such risk assessments;
   (b) that assessment shows that there is a significant possibility of significant harm being caused; and
   (c) there are no suitable and sufficient risk management arrangements in place to prevent such harm.

B.46 In following any such guidance on risk assessment the local authority should be satisfied that it is relevant to the circumstances of the pollutant linkage and land in question, and that any appropriate allowances have been made for particular circumstances.

B.47 To simplify such an assessment of risks, the local authority may use authoritative and scientifically based guideline values for concentrations of the potential pollutants in, on or under the land in pollutant linkages of the type concerned. If it does so, the local authority should be satisfied that:

   (a) an adequate scientific and technical assessment of the information on the potential pollutant, using the appropriate, authoritative and scientifically based guideline values, shows that there is a significant possibility of significant harm; and
   (b) there are no suitable and sufficient risk management arrangements in place to prevent such harm.

B.48 In using any guideline values, the local authority should be satisfied that:

   (a) the guideline values are relevant to the judgement of whether the effects of the pollutant linkage in question constitute a significant possibility of significant harm;
   (b) the assumptions underlying the derivation of any numerical values in the guideline values (for example, assumptions regarding soil conditions, the behaviour of potential pollutants, the existence of pathways, the land-use patterns, and the availability of receptors) are relevant to the circumstances of the pollutant linkage in question;

    (c) any other conditions relevant to the use of the guideline values have been observed (for example, the number of samples taken or the methods of preparation and analysis of those samples); and

    (d) appropriate adjustments have been made to allow for the differences between the circumstances of the land in question and any assumptions or other factors relating to the guideline values.

B.49 The local authority should be prepared to reconsider any determination based on such use of guideline values if it is demonstrated to the authority's satisfaction that under some other more appropriate method of assessing the risks the local authority would not have determined that the land appeared to be contaminated land.

Determining that "pollution of controlled waters is being caused"

B.50 The local authority should determine that land is contaminated land on the basis that pollution of controlled waters is being caused where:

    (a) it has carried out an appropriate scientific and technical assessment of all the relevant and available evidence, having regard to any advice provided by the Environment Agency; and

    (b) on the basis of that assessment, it is satisfied on the balance of probabilities that both of the following circumstances apply:

        (i) a potential pollutant is present in, on or under the land in question, which constitutes poisonous, noxious or polluting matter, or which is solid waste matter, and

        (ii) that potential pollutant is entering controlled waters by the pathway identified in the pollutant linkage.

Determining that "pollution of controlled waters is likely to be caused"

B.51 The local authority should determine that land is contaminated land on the basis that pollution of controlled waters is likely to be caused where:

    (a) it has carried out an appropriate scientific and technical assessment of all the relevant and available evidence, having regard to any advice provided by the Environment Agency; and

    (b) on the basis of that assessment it is satisfied that, on the balance of probabilities, all of the following circumstances apply:

        (i) a potential pollutant is present in, on or under the land in question, which constitutes poisonous, noxious or polluting matter, or which is solid waste matter,

        (ii) the potential pollutant in question is in such a condition that it is capable of entering controlled waters,

        (iii) taking into account the geology and other circumstances of the land in question, there is a pathway (as defined in Chapter A) by which the potential pollutant can enter identified controlled waters,

        (iv) the potential pollutant in question is more likely than not to enter these controlled waters and, when it enters the controlled waters, will be in a form that is poisonous, noxious or polluting, or solid waste matter, and

        (v) there are no suitable and sufficient risk management arrangements relevant to the pollution linkage in place to prevent such pollution.

Determining that "harm so far as attributable to radioactivity is being caused"

B.51A In relation to harm so far as attributable to radioactivity, the local authority should determine that land is contaminated land on the basis that such harm is being caused where:

(a) it has carried out a scientific and technical assessment of the dose arising from the pollutant linkage, according to relevant, appropriate, authoritative and scientifically based guidance on such assessments, having regard to any advice provided by the Environment Agency, and taking into account the requirements of paragraph B.51F;

(b) that assessment shows that such harm is being caused; and

(c) there are no suitable and sufficient risk management arrangements in place to prevent such harm.

B.51B In following any such guidance on the assessment of dose, the local authority should be satisfied that it is relevant to the circumstances of the pollutant linkage and land in question, and that any appropriate allowances have been made for particular circumstances.

B.51C To simplify such an assessment of dose, the local authority may use authoritative and scientifically based guideline values for concentrations of the potential pollutants in, on or under the land in pollutant linkages of the type concerned. If it does so, the local authority should be satisfied that:

(a) an adequate scientific and technical assessment of the information on the potential pollutant, using the appropriate, authoritative and scientifically based guideline values, shows that harm so far as attributable to radioactivity is being caused; and

(b) there are no suitable and sufficient risk management arrangements in place to prevent such harm.

B.51D In using any guideline values, the local authority should be satisfied that:

(a) the guideline values are relevant to the judgement of whether the effects of the pollutant linkage in question constitute harm attributable to radioactivity;

(b) the assumptions underlying the derivation of any numerical values in the guideline values (for example, assumptions regarding soil conditions, the behaviour of potential pollutants, the existence of pathways, the land-use patterns, and the presence of human beings) are relevant to the circumstances of the pollutant linkage in question;

(c) any other conditions relevant to the use of the guideline values have been observed (for example, the number of samples taken or the methods of preparation and analysis of those samples or of radiation surveys);

(d) appropriate adjustments have been made to allow for the differences between the circumstances of the land in question and any assumptions or other factors relating to the guideline values; and

(e) the basis of derivation of the guideline values has taken into account the requirements of paragraph B.51F.

B.51E The local authority should be prepared to reconsider any determination based on such use of guideline values if it is demonstrated to the authority's satisfaction that under some other more appropriate method of assessing the risks the local authority would not have determined that the land appeared to be contaminated land.

B.51F The estimation of an effective dose and an equivalent dose should be undertaken in accordance with Articles 15 and 16 of Council Directive 96/29/EURATOM of 13 May 1996 laying down basic safety standards for the protection of the health of workers and the general public against the dangers arising from ionizing radiation. The estimation of an effective or equivalent annual dose should not include the local background level of radiation from the natural environment.

Determining that "there is a significant possibility of harm so far as attributable to radioactivity being caused"

B.51G The local authority should determine that land is contaminated land on the basis that there is a significant possibility of harm so far as attributable to radioactivity being caused (as defined in Chapter A), where:

(a) it has carried out a scientific and technical assessment of the potential dose arising from the poliutant linkage, according to relevant, appropriate, authoritative and scientifically based guidance on such assessments, having regard to any advice provided by the Environment Agency, and taking into account the requirements of paragraph B.51F;

(b) that assessment shows that there is a significant possibility of such harm being caused; and

(c) there are no suitable and sufficient risk management arrangements in place to prevent such harm.

B.51H In following any such guidance on assessment of the potential dose, the local authority should be satisfied that it is relevant to the circumstances of the pollutant linkage and land in question, and that any appropriate allowances have been made for particular circumstances.

Record of the determination that land is contaminated land

B.52 The local authority should prepare a written record of any determination that particular land is contaminated land. The record should include (by means of a reference to other documents if necessary):

(a) a description of the particular significant pollutant linkage, identifying all three components of pollutant, pathway and receptor;

(b) a summary of the evidence upon which the determination is based;

(c) a summary of the relevant assessment of this evidence; and

(d) a summary of the way in which the authority considers that the requirements of the guidance in this Part and in Chapter A of the guidance have been satisfied.

Chapter C—The remediation of contaminated land

Part 1 Scope of the Chapter

Applies generally.

Part 2 Definitions of Terms

Applies generally.

Part 3 Securing Remediation

Applies generally.

Part 4 The Standard to which Land or Waters should be Remediated

Applies generally.

Part 5 The Reasonableness of Remediation

Paragraphs C.37 to C.43 only apply to situations involving contaminants which are not radioactive. Paragraphs C.43A to C.43J only apply to situations involving contaminants which are radioactive. The remaining paragraphs apply generally to all types of contaminants.

Part 6 The Practicability, Durability and Effectiveness of Remediation

Applies generally.

Part 7 What is to be Done by Way of Remediation

Applies generally.

Part 1—Scope of the chapter

C.1 The statutory guidance in this Chapter is issued under section 78E(5) of Part 2A of the Environmental Protection Act 1990, and provides guidance on the remediation which may be required for any contaminated land.

C.2 Section 78E provides:

"(4) The only things by way of remediation which the enforcing authority may do, or require to be done, under or by virtue of [Part 2A of the Environmental Protection Act 1990] are things which it considers reasonable, having regard to —

"(a) the cost which is likely to be involved; and
"(b) the seriousness of the harm, or pollution of controlled waters, in question.

"(5) In determining for any purpose of this Part —

"(a) what is to be done (whether by an appropriate person, the enforcing authority, or any other person) by way of remediation in any particular case,
"(b) the standard to which any land is, or waters are, to be remediated pursuant to [a remediation] notice, or
"(c) what is, or is not, to be regarded as reasonable for the purposes of subsection (4) above, "the enforcing authority shall have regard to any guidance issued for the purpose by the Secretary of State".

C.2A In relation to harm so far as attributable to radioactivity, section 78E (as modified) provides:

"(4) Subject to subsection (4A), the only things by way of remediation which the enforcing authority may do, or require to be done, under or by virtue of this Part are things which it considers reasonable, having regard to—

"(a) the cost which is likely to be involved; and

"(b) the seriousness of the harm in question.

"(4A) Where remediation includes an intervention, that part of the remediation which consists of an intervention may only be considered reasonable—

"(a) where the reduction in detriment due to radiation is sufficient to justify any adverse effects and costs, including social costs, of the intervention; and

"(b) where the form, scale and duration of the intervention is "optimised".

"(4B) For the purpose of subsection (4A), the form, scale and duration of the intervention shall be taken to be "optimised" if the benefit of the reduction in health detriment less the detriment associated with the intervention is maximised.

"(5) In determining for any purpose of this Part—

"(a) what is to be done (whether by an appropriate person, the enforcing authority, or any other person) by way of remediation in any particular case,

"(b) the standard to which any land is to be remediated pursuant to the notice, or

"(c) what is, or is not, to be regarded as reasonable for the purposes of subsection (4) above,

"the enforcing authority shall have regard to any guidance issued for the purpose by the Secretary of State."

C.3 The enforcing authority is therefore required to have regard to this guidance when it is:

(a) determining what remediation action it should specify in a remediation notice as being required to be carried out (section 78E(1));

(b) satisfying itself that appropriate remediation is being, or will be, carried out without the service of a notice (section 78H(5)(b)); or

(c) deciding what remediation action it should carry out itself (section 78N and section 78N (as modified)).

C.4 The guidance in this Chapter does not attempt to set out detailed technical procedures or working methods. For information on these matters, the enforcing authority may wish to consult relevant technical documents prepared under the contaminated land and radioactive substances research programmes of the Department for Environment, Food and Rural Affairs and the Environment Agency, and by other professional and technical organisations.

Part 2—Definitions of terms

C.5 Unless otherwise stated, any word, term or phrase given a specific meaning in Part 2A of the Environmental Protection Act 1990, or in the statutory guidance in Chapters A or B, has the same meaning for the purposes of the guidance in this Chapter.

C.5A in relation to harm so far as attributable to radioactivity, unless otherwise stated, any word, term or phrase given a specific meaning in Part 2A of the Environmental Protection Act 1990, as modified by the Modification Regulations, has the same meaning for the purposes of the guidance in this Chapter.

C.5B Any reference to "harm so far as attributable to radioactivity" and "other than in relation to harm so far as attributable to radioactivity" means "harm so far as attributable to any radioactivity possessed by any substance" and "other than in relation to harm so far as attributable to any radioactivity possessed by any substance" respectively.

C.6 "Remediation" is defined in section 78A(7) as meaning:

"(a) the doing of anything for the purpose of assessing the condition of—

"(i) the contaminated land in question; or
"(ii) any controlled waters affected by that land; or
"(iii) any land adjoining or adjacent to that land;

"(b) the doing of any works, the carrying out of any operations or the taking of any steps in relation to any such land for the purpose—

"(i) of preventing or minimising, or remedying or mitigating the effects of, by reason of which the contaminated land is such land; or
"(ii) of restoring the land or waters to their former state; or

"(c) the making of subsequent inspections from time to time for the purpose of keeping under review the condition of the land or waters."

C.6A In relation to harm so far as attributable to radioactivity, "remediation" is defined in section 78A(7) (as modified) as meaning:

"(a) the doing of anything for the purpose of assessing the condition of—

"(i) the contaminated land in question; or
"(ii) any land adjoining or adjacent to that land;

"(b) the doing of any works, the carrying out of any operations or the taking of any steps in relation to any such land for the purpose -

"(i) of preventing or minimising, or remedying or mitigating the effects of any harm, by reason of which the contaminated land is such land; or
"(ii) of restoring the land to its former state; or

"(c) the making of subsequent inspections from time to time for the purpose of keeping under review the condition of the land."

C.6B In relation to harm so far as attributable to radioactivity, section 78A (as modified) further provides in subsection (7A):

"For the purpose of paragraph (b) of subsection (7) above, "the doing of any works, the carrying out of any operations or the taking of any steps in relation to any such land" shall include ensuring that—

"(a) any such area is demarcated;
"(b) arrangements for the monitoring of harm are made;
"(c) any appropriate intervention is implemented; and
"(d) access to or use of land or buildings situated in the demarcated area is regulated."

C.7 The definition of remediation given in section 78A and 78A (as modified) extends more widely than the common usage of the term, which more normally relates only to the actions defined as "remedial treatment actions" below.

C.7A "Intervention" is defined in the Schedule to the Modification Regulations as meaning:

"a human activity that prevents or decreases the exposure of individuals to radiation from sources which are not part of a practice or which are out of control, by acting on sources, transmission pathways and individuals themselves." For the purposes of this Chapter, an intervention is taken to be a type of remedial treatment action.

C.8 For the purposes of the guidance in this Chapter, the following definitions apply:

(a) a "remediation action" is any individual thing which is being, or is to be, done by way of remediation;

(b) a "remediation package" is the full set or sequence of remediation actions, within a remediation scheme, which are referable to a particular significant pollutant linkage;

(c) a "remediation scheme" is the complete set or sequence of remediation actions (referable to one or more significant pollutant linkages) to be carried out with respect to the relevant land or waters;

(d) "relevant land or waters" means the contaminated land in question, any controlled waters affected by that land and any land adjoining or adjacent to the contaminated land on which remediation might be required as a consequence of the contaminated land being such land;

(e) an "assessment action" means a remediation action falling within the definition of remediation in section 78A(7)(a) and 78A(7)(a) (as modified) (see paragraphs C.6 and C.6A above);

(f) a "remedial treatment action" means a remediation action falling within the definition in section 78A(7)(b) and 78A(7)(b) (as modified) (see paragraphs C.6 and C.6A above);

(g) a "monitoring action" means a remediation action falling within the definition in section 78A(7)(c) and 78A(7)(c) (as modified) (see paragraphs C.6 and C.6A above);

(h) in relation to harm so far as attributable to radioactivity, "justification" means ensuring that the reduction in detriment due to radiation is sufficient to justify any adverse effects and costs, including social costs, of the intervention;

(i) in relation to harm so far as attributable to radioactivity, "optimisation" means ensuring that the form, scale and duration of the intervention maximises the benefit of the reduction in health detriment less the detriment associated with the intervention;

(j) in relation to harm so far as attributable to radioactivity, "detriment' principally means a health detriment, but may also include other detriments, for example, a detriment associated with blight.

C.9 Any references to "Part 2A" means "Part 2A of the Environmental Protection Act 1990". In relation to harm so far as attributable to radioactivity, any reference to "Part 2A" means "Part 2A of the Environmental Protection Act 1990, as modified."

C.9A Any reference to a "section" in primary legislation means a section of the Environmental Protection Act 1990, unless it is specifically stated otherwise. Any reference to a "section (as modified)" means a section of the Environmental Protection Act 1990 as modified by the Modification Regulations,, unless it is specifically stated otherwise.

C.9B Any reference to "harm so far as attributable to radioactivity" and "other than in relation to harm so far as attributable to radioactivity" means "harm so far as attributable to any radioactivity possessed by any substance" and "other than in relation to harm so far as attributable to any radioactivity possessed by any substance" respectively.

Part 3—Securing remediation

C.10 When the enforcing authority is serving a remediation notice, it will need to specify in that notice any remediation action which is needed in order to achieve remediation of the relevant land or waters to the standard described in Part 4 of this Chapter and which is reasonable for the purposes of section 78E(4) and section 78E(4) (as modified) (see Part 5 of this Chapter). Part 6 of this Chapter provides further guidance relevant to determining the necessary standard of remediation. Part 7 provides guidance on the circumstances in which different types of remediation action may, or may not, be required.

C.11 The enforcing authority should be satisfied that appropriate remediation is being, or will be, carried out without the service of a remediation notice if that remediation would remediate the relevant land or waters to an equivalent, or better, standard than would be achieved by the remediation action or actions that the authority could, at that time, otherwise specify in a remediation notice.

Phased remediation

C.12 The overall process of remediation on any land or waters may require a phased approach, with different remediation actions being carried out in sequence. For example, the local authority may have obtained sufficient information about the relevant land or waters to enable it to identify the land as falling within the definition of contaminated land, but that information may not be sufficient information for the enforcing authority to be able to specify any particular remedial treatment action as being appropriate. Further assessment actions may be needed in any case of this kind as part of the remediation scheme. In other cases, successive phases of remedial treatment actions may be needed.

C.13 The phasing of remediation is likely to follow a progression from assessment actions, through remedial treatment actions and onto monitoring actions. However, this will not always be the case, and the phasing may omit some stages or revisit others. For example, in some circumstances it may be possible for a remedial treatment action to be carried out without any previous assessment action (because sufficient information is already available). But, conversely, in some instances additional assessment action may be found to be necessary only in the light of information derived during the course of a first phase of a required assessment action or the carrying out of required remedial treatment actions.

C.14 Where it is necessary for the remediation scheme as a whole to be phased, a single remediation notice may not be able to include all of the remediation actions which could eventually be needed. In these circumstances, the enforcing authority should specify in the notice the remediation action or actions which, on the basis of the information available at that time, it considers to be appropriate, taking into account in particular the guidance in Part 7 of this Chapter. In due course, the authority may need to serve further remediation notices which include remediation actions for further phases of the scheme.

C.15 However, before serving any further remediation notice, the enforcing authority must be satisfied that the contaminated land which was originally identified still appears to it to meet the definition in section 78A(2) or, in relation to harm so far as attributable to radioactivity, section 78A(2) (as modified). If, for example, the information obtained as a result of an assessment action reveals that there is not, in fact, a significant possibility of significant harm being caused, nor is there a likelihood of any pollution of controlled waters being caused, nor, in relation to harm so far as attributable to radioactivity, is such harm being caused or there is a significant possibility of such harm being caused then no further assessment, remedial treatment or monitoring action can be required under section 78E(1).

Part 4—The standard to which land or waters should be remediated

C.16 The statutory guidance in this Part is issued under section 78E(5)(b) and 78E(5)(b) (as modified) and provides guidance on the standard to which land or waters should be remediated.

The standard of remediation

C.17 The Government's intention is that any remediation required under this regime should result in land being "suitable for use". The aim of any remediation should be to ensure that the circumstances of the land are such that, in its current use (as defined in paragraph A.26 of Chapter A) it is no longer contaminated land (as defined in section 78A(2) or section 78A(2) (as modified)), and that the effects of any significant harm, harm so far as attributable to radioactivity, or pollution of controlled waters which has occurred are remedied. However, it is always open to the appropriate person to carry out remediation on a broader basis than this, if he considers it in his interests to do so, for example if he wishes to prepare the land for redevelopment.

C.18 The standard to which the relevant land or waters as a whole should be remediated should be established by considering separately each significant pollutant linkage identified on the land in question. For each such linkage, the standard of remediation should be that which would be achieved by the use of a remediation package which forms the best practicable techniques of remediation for:

(a) ensuring that the linkage is no longer a significant pollutant linkage, by doing any one or more of the following:

(i) removing or treating the pollutant;
(ii) breaking or removing the pathway; or
(iii) protecting or removing the receptor; and

(b) remedying the effect of any significant harm or pollution of controlled waters or any harm so far as attributable to radioactivity, which is resulting, or has already resulted from, the significant pollutant linkage.

C.19 In deciding what represents the best practicable technique for any particular remediation, the enforcing authority should look for the method of achieving the desired results which, in the light of the nature and volume of the significant pollutant concerned and the timescale within which remediation is required:

    (a) is reasonable, taking account of the guidance in Part 5; and

    (b) represents the best combination of the following qualities:

        (i) practicability, both in general and in the particular circumstances of the relevant land or waters;

        (ii) effectiveness in achieving the aims set out in paragraph C.18 above; and

        (iii) durability in maintaining that effectiveness over the timescale within which the significant harm or pollution of controlled waters or harm so far as attributable to radioactivity may occur.

C.20 Further guidance on how the factors set out in sub-paragraph (b) above should be considered is set out in Part 6. The determination of what in any particular case, represents the best practicable technique of remediation may require a balance to be struck between these factors.

C.21 When considering what would be the best practicable techniques for remediation in any particular case, the enforcing authority should work on the basis of authoritative scientific and technical advice. The authority should consider what comparable techniques have recently been carried out successfully on other land, and also any technological advances and changes in scientific knowledge and understanding.

C.22 Where there is established good practice for the remediation of a particular type of significant pollutant linkage, the authority should assume that this represents the best practicable technique for remediation for a linkage of that type, provided that:

    (a) it is satisfied that the use of that means of remediation is appropriate, given the circumstances of the relevant land or waters; and

    (b) the remediation actions involved would be reasonable having regard to the cost which is likely to be involved and the seriousness of the harm (whether or not attributable to radioactivity) or pollution of controlled waters in question.

C.22A in respect of subparagraph C.22(b), where the remediation of harm involves an intervention, the remediation will only be reasonable if the intervention is justified and optimised as set out in paragraphs C.43B to C.43J below.

C.23 In some instances, the best practicable techniques of remediation with respect to any significant pollutant linkage may not fully achieve the aim in subparagraph C.18(a), that is to say that if the remediation were to be carried out the pollutant linkage in question would remain a significant pollutant linkage. Where this applies, the standard of remediation with respect to that significant pollutant linkage should be that which, by the use of the best practicable techniques:

    (a) comes as close as practicable to achieving the aim in subparagraph C.18(a);

    (b) achieves the aim in subparagraph C.18(b); and

    (c) puts arrangements in place to remedy the effect of any significant harm, pollution of controlled waters or harm so far as attributable to radioactivity which may be caused in the future as a consequence of the continued existence of the pollutant linkage.

C.24 In addition, the best practicable techniques for remediation with respect to a significant pollutant linkage may, in some circumstances, not fully remedy the effect of past or future significant harm, pollution of controlled waters or harm so far as attributable to radioactivity. Where this is the case the standard of remediation should be that which, by the use of the best practicable techniques, mitigates as far as practicable the significant harm, pollution of controlled waters or the effects of harm so far as attributable to radioactivity which has been caused as a consequence of the existence of that linkage, or may be caused in the future as a consequence of its continued existence.

C.25 For any remediation action, package or scheme to represent the best practicable techniques, it should be implemented in accordance with best practice, including any precautions necessary to prevent damage to the environment and any other appropriate quality assurance procedures.

Multiple pollutant linkages

C.26 Where more than one significant pollutant linkage has been identified on the land, it may be possible to achieve the necessary overall standard of remediation for the relevant land or waters as a whole by considering what remediation actions would form part of the appropriate remediation package for each linkage (i.e., representing the best practicable techniques of remediation for that linkage) if it were the only such linkage, and then carrying out all of these remediation actions.

C.27 However, the enforcing authority should also consider whether there is an alternative remediation scheme which would, by dealing with the linkages together, be cheaper or otherwise more practicable to implement. If such a scheme can be identified which achieves an equivalent standard of remediation with respect to all of the significant pollutant linkages to which it is referable, the authority should prefer that alternative scheme.

Volunteered remediation

C.28 In some cases, the person carrying out remediation may wish to adopt an alternative remediation scheme to that which could be required in a remediation notice. This might occur, in particular, if the person concerned wished also to prepare the land for redevelopment. The enforcing authority should consider such a remediation scheme as appropriate remediation provided the scheme would achieve at least the same standard of remediation with respect to each of the significant pollutant linkages identified on the land as would be achieved by the remediation scheme which the authority would otherwise specify in a remediation notice.

Part 5—The reasonableness of remediation

C.29 The statutory guidance in this Part is issued under section 78E(5)(c) and 78E(5)(c) (as modified) and provides guidance on the determination by the enforcing authority of what remediation is, or is not, to be regarded as reasonable having regard to the cost which is likely to be involved and the seriousness of the harm (whether or not attributable to radioactivity) or of the pollution of controlled waters to which it relates.

C.30 The enforcing authority should regard a remediation action as being reasonable for the purpose of section 78E(4) if an assessment of the costs likely to be involved and of the resulting benefits shows that those benefits justify incurring those costs. Such an assessment should include the preparation of an estimate of the costs likely to be involved and of a statement of the benefits likely to result. This latter statement need not necessarily attempt to ascribe a financial value to these benefits. In respect of the remediation of harm so far as attributable to radioactivity, the remediation will only be reasonable where any intervention that forms part of the remediation is justified and optimised (see paragraphs C.43B to C.43J below).

C.31 For the purposes of C.30, the enforcing authority should regard the benefits resulting from a remediation action as being the contribution that the action makes, either on its own or in conjunction with other remediation actions, to:

(a) reducing the seriousness of any harm (whether or not attributable to radioactivity) or pollution of controlled waters which might otherwise be caused; or

(b) mitigating the seriousness of any effects of any significant harm, pollution of controlled waters, or harm so far as attributable to radioactivity.

C.32 In assessing the reasonableness of any remediation, the enforcing authority should make due allowance for the fact that the timing of expenditure and the realisation of benefits is relevant to the balance of costs and benefits. In particular, the assessment should recognise that:

(a) expenditure which is delayed to a future date will have a lesser impact on the person defraying it than would an equivalent cash sum to be spent immediately;

(b) there may be a gain from achieving benefits earlier but this may also involve extra expenditure; the authority should consider whether the gain justifies the extra costs. This applies, in particular, where natural processes, managed or otherwise, would over time bring about remediation; and

(c) there may be evidence that the same benefits will be achievable in the foreseeable future at a significantly lower cost, for example, through the development of new techniques or as part of a wider scheme of development or redevelopment.

C.33 The identity or financial standing of any person who may be required to pay for any remediation action are not relevant factors in the determination of whether the costs of that action are, or are not, reasonable for the purposes of section 78E(4). (These factors may however be relevant in deciding whether or not the enforcing authority can impose the cost of remediation on that person, either through the service of a remediation notice or through the recovery of costs incurred by the authority; see section 78P and the guidance in Chapter E.)

The cost of remediation

C.34 When considering the costs likely to be involved in carrying out any remediation action, the enforcing authority should take into account:

(a) all the initial costs (including tax payable) of carrying out the remediation action, including feasibility studies, design, specification and management, as well as works and operations, and making good afterwards;

(b) any on-going costs of managing and maintaining the remediation action; and

(c) any relevant disruption costs.

C.35 For these purposes, "relevant disruption costs" mean depreciation in the value of land or other interests, or other loss or damage, which is likely to result from the carrying out of the remediation action in question. The enforcing authority should assess these costs as their estimate of the amount of compensation which would be payable if the owner of the land or other interest had granted rights under section 78G(2) or 78G(2) (as modified) to permit the action to be carried out and had claimed compensation under section 78G(5) and regulation 6 of the Contaminated Land (England) Regulations 2006 (whether or not such a claim could actually be made).

C.36 Each of the types of cost set out in paragraph C.34 above should be included even where they would not result in payments to others by the person carrying out the remediation. For example, a company may choose to use its own staff or equipment to carry out the remediation, or the person carrying out the remediation may already own the land in question and would therefore not be entitled to receive compensation under section 78G(5) or 78G(5) (as modified). The evaluation of the cost involved in remediation should not be affected by the identity of the person carrying it out, or internal resources available to that person.

C.37 Other than in respect of an intervention, the enforcing authority should furthermore regard it as a necessary condition of an action being reasonable that:

(a) where two or more significant pollutant linkages have been identified on the land in question, and the remediation action forms part of a wider remediation scheme which is dealing with two or more of those linkages, there is no alternative scheme which would achieve the same purposes for a lower overall cost; and

(b) subject to subparagraph (a) above, where the remediation action forms part of a remediation package dealing with any particular significant pollutant linkage, there is no alternative package which would achieve the same standard of remediation at a lower overall cost.

C.38 In addition, other than in respect of an intervention for any remediation action to be reasonable there should be no alternative remediation action which would achieve the same purpose, as part of any wider remediation package or scheme, to the same standard for a lower cost (bearing in mind that the purpose of any remediation action may relate to more than one significant pollutant linkage).

The seriousness of harm (other than so far as attributable to radioactivity) or of pollution of controlled waters

C.39 When evaluating the seriousness of any significant harm, for the purposes of assessing the reasonableness of any remediation, the enforcing authority should consider:

(a) whether the significant harm is already being caused;
(b) the degree of the possibility of the significant harm being caused;
(c) the nature of the significant harm with respect, in particular, to:

(i) the nature and importance of the receptor,
(ii) the extent and type of any effects on that receptor of the significant harm,

(iii) the number of receptors which might be affected, and

(iv) whether the effects would be irreversible; and

(d) the context in which the effects might occur, in particular:

(i) whether the receptor has already been damaged by other means and, if so, whether further effects resulting from the harm would materially affect its condition, and

(ii) the relative risk associated with the harm in the context of wider environmental risks.

C.40 Where the significant harm is an "ecological system effect" as defined in Chapter A, the enforcing authority should take into account any advice received from English Nature.

C.41 In evaluating for this purpose the seriousness of any pollution of controlled waters, the enforcing authority should consider:

(a) whether the pollution of controlled waters is already being caused

(b) the likelihood of the pollution of controlled waters being caused

(c) the nature of the pollution of controlled waters involved with respect, in particular, to:

(i) the nature and importance of the controlled waters which might be affected,

(ii) the extent of the effects of the actual or likely pollution on those controlled waters, and

(iii) whether such effects would be irreversible; and

(d) the context in which the effects might occur, in particular:

(i) whether the waters have already been polluted by other means and, if so, whether further effects resulting from the water pollution would materially affect their condition, and

(ii) the relative risk associated with the water pollution in the context of wider environmental risks.

C.42 Where the enforcing authority is the local authority, it should take into account any advice received from the Environment Agency when it is considering the seriousness of any pollution of controlled waters.

C.43 In some instances, it may be possible to express the benefits of addressing the harm or pollution of controlled waters in direct financial terms. For example, removing a risk of explosion which renders a building unsafe for occupation could be considered to create a benefit equivalent to the cost of acquiring a replacement building. Various Government departments have produced technical advice, which the enforcing authority may find useful, on the consideration of non-market impacts of environmental matters.

Seriousness of harm attributable to radioactivity

C.43A When evaluating the seriousness of any harm attributable to radioactivity for the purposes of assessing the reasonableness of any remediation, the enforcing authority should consider:

(a) whether the harm is already being caused;

(b) the degree of the possibility of the harm being caused;

(c) the nature of the harm with respect, in particular, to:

(i) the extent and type of effects that may arise from the harm,

(ii) the number of people who might be affected, and

(iii) whether the effects would be irreversible; and

(d) the context in which the effects might occur, in particular the relative risk associated with the harm in the context of wider exposure risks.

Justification and optimisation

C.43B The concepts of justification and optimisation only apply in relation to harm so far as it is attributable to radioactivity and where a remediation involves an intervention. The enforcing authority should ensure that any intervention that forms part of a remediation scheme or remediation package is both justified and optimised.

C.43C The principle of justification recognises that an intervention may bring about reduction in doses and other harmful impacts but may incur costs and other adverse effects. Costs are not restricted to financial costs, but also include costs to society.

C.43D To ensure optimisation, the enforcing authority should choose the option that maximises the net benefit of the intervention, from the interventions that are justified.

C43E For an intervention to be optimised on land affected by both radioactive and non-radioactive significant pollutant linkages, the optimisation should also have regard to the effect of any remedial actions addressing the non-radioactive significant pollutant linkage(s).

C.43F The assessment of whether a potential intervention is justified and optimised should include the preparation of:

(a) an estimate of the financial costs of the intervention, taking into account the guidance in paragraphs C.34 to C.36;

(b) a statement of the social costs and adverse effects (see paragraphs C.43I to C.43J below) associated with the intervention; and

(c) a statement of the benefits (e.g. reduction in radiation exposure) likely to result from the intervention.

C.43G In making an assessment of whether the intervention is justified or optimised, the enforcing authority should:

(a) consult publications of international bodies, including the International Atomic Energy Agency;

(b) apply the approaches of multi-attribute analysis in assessing the balance between the various factors that need to be taken into consideration and the weightings which may be appropriate to assign to the various attributes;

(c) consult with relevant stakeholder groups so as to understand their perceptions of the relative importance of different attributes; and

(d) consider quantitative and qualitative methods as a decision-aid in helping to reveal the key issues and assumptions and allowing an analysis of the sensitivity to various assumptions.

C.43H In assessing benefits and costs, including social costs, the enforcing authority should also consider paragraphs C.55 to C.57 below.

The social costs and adverse effects of remediation

C.43I In relation to harm so far as attributable to radioactivity, the type of social costs and adverse effects to be considered as arising from an intervention mayr for example, include:

(a) social disruption such as vacating property, or limiting its use, or restricting access to it;

(b) doses to remediation workers;

(c) heavy traffic from vehicles, associated with the intervention;

(d) risks:

    (i) to water, air, soil and plants and animals,

    (ii) of nuisance through noise or odours,

    (iii) to the countryside or places of special interest, and

    (iv) to a building of special architectural or historic interest (that is, a building listed under town and country planning legislation or a building in a designated Conservation Area) or a site of archaeological interest (as defined in article 1(2) of the Town and Country Planning (General Permitted Development) Order 1995); and

(e) the generation of waste and, where relevant, the transport and disposal of such waste.

C.43J The enforcing authority should consider both the seriousness of impacts of any social costs and also the likely duration of any impact.

Part 6—The practicability, durability and effectiveness of remediation

C.44 The statutory guidance in this Part is issued under section 78E(5)(b) and 78E(5)(b) (as modified) and is relevant to the guidance given in Part 4 on the standard to which land and waters should be remediated.

General considerations

C.45 In some instances, there may be little firm information on which to assess particular remediation actions, packages or schemes. For example, a particular technology or technique may not have been subject previously to field-scale pilot testing in circumstances comparable to those to be found on the contaminated land in question. Where this is the case, the enforcing authority should consider the effectiveness and durability which it appears likely that any such action would achieve, and the practicability of its use, on the basis of information which it does have at that time (for example information derived from laboratory or other "treatability" testing).

C.46 If the person who will be carrying out the remediation proposes the use of an innovative approach to remediation, the enforcing authority should be prepared to agree to that approach being used (subject to that person obtaining any other necessary permits or authorisations), notwithstanding the fact that there is little available information on the basis of which the authority can assess its likely effectiveness. If the approach to remediation proves to be ineffective, further remediation actions may be required, for which the person proposing the innovative approach will be liable.

C.47 However, the enforcing authority should not, under the terms of a remediation notice, require any innovative remediation action to be carried out for the purposes of establishing its effectiveness in general, unless either the person carrying out the remediation agrees or there is clear evidence that it is likely that the action would be effective on the relevant land or waters and it would meet all other requirements of the statutory guidance in this Chapter.

The practicability of remediation

C.48 The enforcing authority should consider any remediation as being practicable to the extent that it can be carried out in the circumstances of the relevant land or waters. This applies both to the remediation scheme as a whole and the individual remediation actions of which it is comprised.

C.49 In assessing the practicability of any remediation, the enforcing authority should consider, in particular, the following factors:

    (a) technical constraints, for example whether:

        (i) any technologies or other physical resources required (for example power or materials) are commercially available, or could reasonably be made available, on the necessary scale, and

        (ii) the separate remediation actions required could be carried out given the other remediation actions to be carried out, and without preventing those other actions from being carried out;

    (b) site constraints, for example whether:

        (i) the location of and access to the relevant land or waters, and the presence of buildings or other structures in, on or under the land, would permit the relevant remediation actions to be carried out in practice, and

        (ii) the remediation could be carried out, given the physical or other condition of the relevant land or waters, for example the presence of substances, whether these are part of other pollutant linkages or are not pollutants;

    (c) time constraints, for example whether it would be possible to carry out the remediation within the necessary time period given the time needed by the person carrying out the remediation to:

        (i) obtain any necessary regulatory permits and constraints, and

        (ii) design and implement the various remediation actions; and

    (d) regulatory constraints, for example whether:

        (i) the remediation can be carried out within the requirements of statutory controls relating to health and safety (including engineering safety) and pollution control,

        (ii) any necessary regulatory permits or consents would reasonably be expected to be forthcoming,

        (iii) any conditions attached to such permits or consents would affect the practicability or cost of the remediation, and

        (iv) adverse environmental impacts may arise from carrying out the remediation (see paragraphs C.51 to C.57 below).

C.50 The responsibility for obtaining any regulatory permits or consents necessary for the remediation to be carried out rests with the person who will actually be carrying out the remediation, and not with the enforcing authority. However, the authority may in some circumstances have particular duties to contribute to health and safety in the remediation work, under the Construction (Design and Management) Regulations 1994 (S.I. 1994/3140).

Adverse environmental impacts

C.51 Although the objective of any remediation is to improve the environment, the process of carrying out remediation may, in some circumstances, create adverse environmental impacts. The possibility of such impacts may affect the determination of what remediation package represents the best practicable techniques for remediation. In relation to harm so far as attributable to radioactivity such impacts are considered in the justification and optimisation process described in Part 5.

C.52 Specific pollution control permits or authorisations may be needed for some kinds of remediation processes, for example:

(a) authorisations under the Pollution Prevention and Control Act 1999 and its regulations;

(b) site or mobile plant licences under Part 2 of the Environmental Protection Act 1990 (waste management licensing);

(c) abstraction licences under Part 2, or discharge consents under Part 3, of the Water Resources Act 1991; or

(d) authorisations for accumulation and disposal of radioactive waste under the Radioactive Substances Act 1993.

C.53 Permits or authorisations of these kinds may include conditions controlling the manner in which the remediation is to be carried out, intended to prevent or minimise adverse environmental impacts. Where this is the case, the enforcing authority should assume that these conditions provide a suitable level of protection for the environment.

C.54 Where this is not the case, the enforcing authority should consider whether the particular remediation package can be carried out without damaging the environment, and in particular:

(a) without risk to water, air, soil and plants and animals;

(b) without causing a nuisance through noise or odours;

(c) without adversely affecting the countryside or places of special interest; and

(d) without adversely affecting a building of special architectural or historic interest (that is, a building listed under town and country planning legislation or a building in a designated Conservation Area) or a site of archaeological interest (as defined in article 1(2) of the Town and Country Planning (General Permitted Development) Order 1995) (S.I. 1995/418).

C.55 If the enforcing authority considers that there is some risk that the remediation might damage the environment, it should consider whether:

(a) the risk is sufficiently great to mean that the balance of advantage, in terms of improving and protecting the environment, would lie with adopting an alternative approach to remediation, even though such an alternative may not fully achieve the objectives for remediation set out at paragraph C.18 above; or

(b) the risk can be sufficiently reduced by including, as part of the description of what is to be done by way of remediation, particular precautions designed to prevent the occurrence of such damage to the environment (for example, precautions analogous to the conditions attached to a waste management licence).

C.56 In addition, the enforcing authority should consider whether it is likely that the process of remediation might lead to a direct or indirect discharge into groundwater of a substance in either List I or List II of the Schedule to the Groundwater Regulations 1998 (S.I. 1998/1006). (For these purposes, the terms direct discharge, indirect discharge and groundwater have the meanings given to them in the 1998 Regulations.)

C.57 If the enforcing authority considers that such a discharge is likely, it should (where that authority is not the Environment Agency) consult the

Environment Agency, and have regard to its advice on whether an alternative remediation package should be adopted or precaution required as to the way that remediation is carried out.

The effectiveness of remediation

C.58 The enforcing authority should consider any remediation as being effective to the extent to which the remediation scheme as a whole, and its component remediation packages, would achieve the aims set out in paragraph C.18 above in relation to each of the significant pollutant linkages identified on the relevant land or waters. The enforcing authority should consider also the extent to which each remediation action, or group of actions required for the same particular purpose, would achieve the purpose for which it was required.

C.59 Within this context, the enforcing authority should consider also the time which would pass before the remediation would become effective. In particular, the authority should establish whether the remediation would become effective sufficiently soon to match the particular degree of urgency resulting from the nature of the significant pollutant linkage in question. However, the authority may also need to balance the speed in reaching a given level of effectiveness against higher degrees of effectiveness which may be achievable, but after a longer period of time, by the use of other remediation methods.

C.60 If any remedial treatment action representing the best practicable techniques will not fully achieve the standard set out in paragraph C.18 above, the enforcing authority should consider whether additional monitoring actions should be required.

The durability of remediation

C.61 The enforcing authority should consider a remediation scheme as being sufficiently durable to the extent that the scheme as a whole would continue to be effective with respect to the aims in paragraph C.18 above during the time over which the significant pollutant linkage would otherwise continue to exist or recur. Where other action (such as redevelopment) is likely to resolve or control the problem within that time, a shorter period may be appropriate. The durability of an individual remediation action is a measure of the extent to which it will continue to be effective in meeting the purpose for which it is to be required taking into account normal maintenance and repair.

C.62 Where a remediation scheme cannot reasonably and practicably continue to be effective during the whole of the expected duration of the problem, the enforcing authority should require the remediation to continue to be effective for as long as can reasonably and practicably be achieved. In these circumstances, additional monitoring actions may be required.

C.63 Where a remediation method requires on-going management and maintenance in order to continue to be effective (for example, the maintenance of gas venting or alarm systems), these on-going requirements should be specified in any remediation notice as well as any monitoring actions necessary to keep the effectiveness of the remediation under review.

Part 7—What is to be done by way of remediation

C.64 The statutory guidance in this Part is issued under section 78E(5)(a) and provides guidance on the determination by the enforcing authority of what is to be done by way of remediation—in particular, on the circumstances in which any action within the three categories of remediation action (that is, assessment, remedial treatment and monitoring actions) should be required.

Assessment action

C.65 The enforcing authority should require an assessment action to be carried out where this is necessary for the purpose of obtaining information on the condition of the relevant land or waters which is needed:

(a) to characterise in detail a significant pollutant linkage (or more than one such linkage) identified on the relevant land or waters for the purpose of enabling the authority to establish what would need to be achieved by any remedial treatment action or intervention (in relation to harm so far as attributable to radioactivity);

(b) to enable the establishment of the technical specifications or design of any particular remedial treatment action which the authority reasonably considers it might subsequently require to be carried out; or

(c) where, after remedial treatment actions have been carried out, the land will still be in such a condition that it would still fall to be identified as contaminated land, to evaluate the condition of the relevant land or waters, or the incidence of any significant harm or pollution of controlled waters or harm so far as attributable to radioactivity, for the purpose of supporting future decisions on whether further remediation might then be required (this applies where the remediation action concerned would not otherwise constitute a monitoring action).

C.66 The enforcing authority should not require any assessment action to be carried out unless that action is needed to achieve one or more of the purposes set out in paragraph C.65 above, and it represents a reasonable means of doing so. In particular, no assessment action should be required for the purposes of determining whether or not the land in question is contaminated land. For the purposes of this guidance, assessment actions relate solely to land which has already been formally identified as contaminated land, or to other land or waters which might be affected by it. The statutory guidance in Chapters A and B sets out the requirements for the inspection of land and the manner in which a local authority should determine that land appears to it to be contaminated land.

Remedial treatment action

C.67 The enforcing authority should require a remedial treatment action to be carried out where it is necessary to achieve the standard of remediation described in Part 4, but for no other purpose. Any such remedial treatment action should include appropriate verification measures, in the case of harm so far as attributable to radioactivity, remedial treatment action shall if necessary and to the extent of the lasting exposure risk involved, include ensuring that:

(a) any area of land is demarcated;

(b) any appropriate intervention is implemented; and

(c) access to or use of land or buildings situated in the demarcated area is regulated.

C.67A When considering what remedial treatment action may be necessary, the enforcing authority should consider also what complementary assessment or monitoring actions might be needed to evaluate the manner in which the remedial treatment action is implemented or its effectiveness or durability once implemented.

Monitoring action

C.68 The enforcing authority should require a monitoring action to be carried out where it is for the purpose of providing information on any changes which might occur in the condition of a pollutant pathway or receptor, where:

(a) the pollutant, pathway or receptor in question was identified previously as part of a significant pollutant linkage; and

(b) the authority will need to consider whether any further remedial treatment action will be required as a consequence of any change that may occur.

C.69 Monitoring action should not be required to achieve any other purpose, such as general monitoring to enable the enforcing authority to identify any new significant pollutant linkages which might become present in the future. This latter activity forms part of the local authority's duty, under section 78B(1) only to cause its area to be inspected from time to time for the purpose of identifying any contaminated land.

What remediation should not be required

C.70 The enforcing authority should not require any remediation to be carried out for the purpose of achieving any aims other than those set out in paragraphs C.18 to C.24 above, or purposes other than those identified in this Part of this Chapter. In particular, it should not require any remediation to be carried out for the purposes of:

(a) dealing with matters which do not in themselves form part of a significant pollutant linkage, such as substances present in quantities or concentrations at which there is not a significant possibility of significant harm, or harm so far as attributable to radioactivity, nor a likelihood of any pollution of controlled waters being caused; or

(b) making the land suitable for any uses other than its current use, as defined in paragraphs A.25 and A.26 in Chapter A.

C.71 It is, however, always open to the owner of the land, or any other person who might be liable for remediation, to carry out on a voluntary basis remediation to meet these wider objectives.

CHAPTER D—EXCLUSION FROM, AND APPORTIONMENT OFF LIABILITY FOR REMEDIATION

Part 1 Scope of the Chapter

Applies generally.

Part 2 Definitions of Terms

Applies generally.

Part 3 The Procedure for Determining Liabilities

Applies generally.

Part 4 General Considerations Relating to the Exclusion, Apportionment and Attribution Procedures

Applies generally.

Part 5 Exclusion of Members of a Class A Liability Group

Applies generally.

Part 6 Apportionment Between Members of any Single Class A Liability Group

Applies generally.

Part 7 Exclusion of Members of a Class B Liability Group

Applies generally.

Part 8 Apportionment Between the Members of a Single Class B Liability Group

Applies generally.

Part 9 Attribution of Responsibility Between Liability Groups Applies generally.

Applies generally.

Part 1—Scope of the chapter

D.1 The statutory guidance in this Chapter is issued under sections 78F(6) and 78F(7) of the Environmental Protection Act 1990. It provides guidance on circumstances where two or more persons are liable to bear the responsibility for any particular thing by way of remediation. It deals with the questions of who should be excluded from liability, and how the cost of each remediation action should be apportioned between those who remain liable after any such exclusion.

D.2 Section 78F provides that:

"(6) Where two or more persons would, apart from this subsection, be appropriate persons in relation to any particular thing which is to be done by way of remediation, the enforcing authority shall determine in accordance with guidance issued for the purpose by the Secretary of State whether any, and if so which, of them is to be treated as not being an appropriate person in relation to that thing.

"(7) Where two or more persons are appropriate persons in relation to any particular thing which is to be done by way of remediation, they shall be liable to bear the cost of doing that thing in proportions determined by the enforcing authority in accordance with guidance issued for the purpose by the Secretary of State".

D.3 The enforcing authority is therefore required to act in accordance with the guidance in this Chapter. Introductory summaries are included to various parts and sections of the guidance: these do not necessarily give the full detail of the guidance; the section concerned should be consulted.

Part 2—Definitions of terms

D.4 Unless otherwise stated, any word, term or phrase given a specific meaning in Part 2A of the Environmental Protection Act 1990, or in the statutory guidance in Chapters A or B, has the same meaning for the purpose of the guidance in this Chapter.

D.5 In addition, for the purposes of this Chapter, the following definitions apply:

(a) a person who is an appropriate person by virtue of section 78F(2) (that is, because he has caused or knowingly permitted a pollutant to be in, on or under the land) is described as a "Class A person";

(b) a person who is an appropriate person by virtue of section 78F(4) or (5) (that is, because he is the owner or occupier of the land in circumstances where no Class A person can be found with respect to a particular remediation action) is described as a "Class B person";

(c) collectively, the persons who are appropriate persons with respect to any particular significant pollutant linkage are described as the "liability group" for that linkage; a liability group consisting of one or more Class A persons is described as a "Class A liability group", and a liability group consisting of one or more Class B persons is described as a "Class B liability group";

(d) any determination by the enforcing authority under section 78F(6) (that is, a person is to be treated as not being an appropriate person) is described as an "exclusion";

(e) any determination by the enforcing authority under section 78F(7) (dividing the costs of carrying out any remediation action between two or more appropriate persons) is described as an "apportionment"; the process of apportionment between liability groups is described as "attribution";

(f) a "remediation action" is any individual thing which is being, or is to be, done by way of remediation;

(g) a "remediation package" is all the remediation actions, within a remediation scheme, which are referable to a particular significant pollutant linkage; and

(h) a "remediation scheme" is the complete set or sequence of remediation actions (referable to one or more significant pollutant linkages) to be carried out with respect to the relevant land or waters.

D.6 Any reference to "Part 2A" means "Part 2A of the Environmental Protection Act 1990". Any reference to a "section" in primary legislation means a section of the Environmental Protection Act 1990, unless it is specifically stated otherwise.

D.6A Any reference to "harm so far as attributable to radioactivity" means "harm so far as attributable to any radioactivity possessed by any substance".

Part 3—The procedure for determining liabilities

D.7 For most sites, the process of determining liabilities will consist simply of identifying either a single person (either an individual or a corporation such as a limited company) who has caused or knowingly permitted the presence of a single significant pollutant, or the owner of the site. The history of other sites may be more complex. A succession of different occupiers or of different industries, or a variety of substances may all have contributed to the problems which have made the land "contaminated land" as defined for the purposes of Part 2A. Numerous separate remediation actions may be required, which may not correlate neatly with those who are to bear responsibility for the costs. The degree of responsibility for the state of the land may vary widely. Determining liability for the costs of each remediation action can be correspondingly complex.

D.8 The statutory guidance in this Part sets out the procedure which the enforcing authority should follow for determining which appropriate persons should bear what responsibility for each remediation action. It refers forward to the other Parts of this Chapter, and describes how they should be applied. Not all stages will be relevant to all cases, particularly where there is only a single significant pollutant linkage, or where a liability group has only one member.

First stage—identifying potential appropriate persons and liability groups

D.9 As part of the process of determining that the land is "contaminated land" (see Chapters A and B), the enforcing authority will have identified at least one significant pollutant linkage (pollutant, pathway and receptor), resulting from the presence of at least one significant pollutant.

Where there is a single significant pollutant linkage

D.10 The enforcing authority should identify all of the persons who would be appropriate persons to pay for any remediation action which is referable to the pollutant which forms part of the significant pollutant linkage. These persons constitute the "liability group" for that significant pollutant linkage. (In this guidance the term "liability group" is used even where there is only a single appropriate person who is a "member" of the liability group.)

D.11 To achieve this, the enforcing authority should make reasonable enquiries to find all those who have caused or knowingly permitted the pollutant in question to be in, on or under the land. Any such persons constitute a "Class A liability group" for the significant pollutant linkage.

D.12 If no such Class A persons can be found for any significant pollutant, the enforcing authority should consider whether the significant pollutant linkage of which it forms part relates solely to the pollution of controlled waters, rather than to any significant harm or, to any harm so far as attributable to radioactivity. If this is the case, there will be no liability group for that significant pollutant linkage, and it should be treated as an "orphan linkage" (see paragraphs D.103 to D.109 below).

D.13 In any other case where no Class A persons can be found for a significant pollutant, the enforcing authority should identify all of the current owners or occupiers of the contaminated land in question. These persons then constitute a "Class B liability group" for the significant pollutant linkage.

D.14 If the enforcing authority cannot find any Class A persons or any Class B persons in respect of a significant pollutant linkage, there will be no liability group for that linkage and it should be treated as an orphan linkage (see paragraphs D.103 to D.109 below).

Where there are two or more significant pollutant linkages

D.15 The enforcing authority should consider each significant pollutant linkage in turn, carrying out the steps set out in paragraphs D.10 to D.14 above, in order to identify the liability group (if one exists) for each of the linkages.

In all cases

D.16 Having identified one or more liability groups, the enforcing authority should consider whether any of the members of those groups are exempted from liability under the provisions in Part 2A. This could apply where:

    (a) a person who would otherwise be a Class A person is exempted from liability arising with respect to water pollution from an abandoned mine (see section 78J(3));

    (b) a Class B person is exempted from liability arising from the escape of a pollutant from one piece of land to other land (see section 78K or section 78K (as modified)); or

    (c) a person is exempted from liability by virtue of his being a person "acting in a relevant capacity" (such as acting as an insolvency practitioner), as defined in section 78X(4).

D.17 If all of the members of any liability group benefit from one or more of these exemptions, the enforcing authority should treat the significant pollutant linkage in question as an orphan linkage (see paragraphs D.103 to D.109 below).

D.18 Persons may be members of more than one liability group. This might apply, for example, if they caused or knowingly permitted the presence of more than one significant pollutant.

D.19 Where the membership of all of the liability groups is the same, there may be opportunities for the enforcing authority to abbreviate the remaining stages of this procedure. However, the tests for exclusion and apportionment may produce different results for different significant pollutant linkages, and so the enforcing authority should exercise caution before trying to simplify the procedure in any case.

Second stage—characterising remediation actions

D.20 Each remediation action will be carried out to achieve a particular purpose with respect to one or more defined significant pollutant linkages. Where there is a single significant pollutant linkage on the land in question, all the remediation actions will be referable to that linkage, and there is no need to consider how the different actions relate to different linkages. This stage and the third stage of the procedure therefore do not need to be carried out in where there is only a single significant pollutant linkage.

D.21 However, where there are two or more significant pollutant linkages on the land in question, the enforcing authority should establish whether each remediation action is:

(a) referable solely to the significant pollutant in a single significant pollutant linkage (a "single-linkage action"); or

(b) referable to the significant pollutant in more than one significant pollutant linkage (a "shared action").

D.22 Where a remediation action is a shared action, there are two possible relationships between it and the significant pollutant linkages to which it is referable. The enforcing authority should establish whether the shared action is:

(a) a "common action"—that is, an action which addresses together all of the significant pollutant linkages to which it is referable, and which would have been part of the remediation package for each of those linkages if each of them had been addressed separately; or

(b) a "collective action"—that is, an action which addresses together all of the significant pollutant linkages to which it is referable, but which would not have been part of the remediation package for every one of those linkages if each of them had been addressed separately, because:

  (i) the action would not have been appropriate in that form for one or more of the linkages (since some different solution would have been more appropriate),

  (ii) the action would not have been needed to the same extent for one or more of the linkages (since a less far-reaching version of that type of action would have sufficed), or

  (iii) the action represents a more economic way of addressing the linkages together which would not be possible if they were addressed separately.

D.23 A collective action replaces actions that would have been appropriate for the individual significant pollutant linkages if they had been addressed separately, as it achieves the purposes which those other actions would have achieved.

Third stage—attributing responsibility between liability groups

D.24 This stage of the procedure does not apply in the simpler cases. Where there is only a single significant pollutant linkage, the liability group for that linkage bears the full cost of carrying out any remediation action. (Where the linkage is an orphan linkage, the enforcing authority has the power to carry out the remediation action itself, at its own cost, in relation to harm so far as attributable to radioactivity, where the linkage is an orphan linkage, the enforcing authority has a duty to carry out remediation action itself, at its own cost.)

D.25 Similarly, for any single-linkage action, the liability group for the significant pollutant linkage in question bears the full cost of carrying out that action.

D.26 However, the enforcing authority should apply the guidance in Part 9 with respect to each shared action, in order to attribute to each of the different liability groups their share of responsibility for that action.

D.27 After the guidance in Part 9 has been applied to all shared actions, it may be the case that a Class B liability group which has been identified does not have to bear the costs for any remediation actions. Where this is the case, the enforcing authority does not need to apply any of the rest of the guidance in this Chapter to that liability group.

Fourth stage—excluding members of a liability group

D.28 The enforcing authority should now consider, for each liability group which has two or more members, whether any of those members should be excluded from liability:

    (a) for each Class A liability group with two or more members, the enforcing authority should apply the guidance on exclusion in Part 5; and

    (b) for each Class B liability group with two or more members, the enforcing authority should apply the guidance on exclusion in Part 7.

Fifth stage—apportioning liability between members of a liability group

D.29 The enforcing authority should now determine how any costs attributed to each liability group should be apportioned between the members of that group who remain after any exclusions have been made.

D.30 For any liability group which has only a single remaining member, that person bears all of the costs falling to that liability group, that is both the cost of any single-linkage action referable to the significant pollutant linkage in question, and the share of the cost of any shared action attributed to the group as a result of the attribution process set out in Part 9.

D.31 For any liability group which has two or more remaining members, the enforcing authority should apply the relevant guidance on apportionment between those members. Each of the remaining members of the group will then bear the proportion determined under that guidance of the total costs falling to the group, that is both the cost of any single-linkage action referable to the significant pollutant linkage in question, and the share of the cost of any shared action attributed to the group as a result of the attribution process set out in Part 9. The relevant apportionment guidance is:

    (a) for any Class A liability group, the guidance set out in Part 6; and

    (b) for any Class B liability group, the guidance set out in Part 8.

Part 4—General considerations relating to the exclusion, apportionment and attribution procedures

D.32 This Part sets out general guidance about the application of the exclusion, apportionment and attribution procedures set out in the rest of this Chapter. It is accordingly issued under both section 78F(6) and section 78F(7).

D.33 The enforcing authority should ensure that any person who might benefit from an exclusion, apportionment or attribution is aware of the guidance in this Chapter, so that they may make appropriate representations to the enforcing authority.

D.34 The enforcing authority should apply the tests for exclusion (in Parts 5 and 7) with respect to the members of each liability group. If a person, who would otherwise be an appropriate person to bear responsibility for a particular remediation action, has been excluded from the liability groups for all of the significant pollutant linkages to which that action is referable, he should be treated as not being an appropriate person in relation to that remediation action.

Financial circumstances

D.35 The financial circumstances of those concerned should have no bearing on the application of the procedures for exclusion, apportionment and attribution in this Chapter, except where the circumstances in paragraph D.85 below apply (the financial circumstances of those concerned are taken into account in the separate consideration under section 78P(2) on hardship and cost recovery). In particular, it should be irrelevant in the context of decisions on exclusion and apportionment:

(a) whether those concerned would benefit from any limitation on the recovery of costs under the provisions on hardship and cost recovery in section 78P(2); or

(b) whether those concerned would benefit from any insurance or other means of transferring their responsibilities to another person.

Information and decisions

D.36 The enforcing authority should make reasonable endeavours to consult those who may be affected by any exclusion, apportionment or attribution. In all cases, however, it should seek to obtain only such information as it is reasonable to seek, having regard to:

(a) how the information might be obtained;

(b) the cost of obtaining the information for all parties involved; and

(c) the potential significance of the information for any decision.

D.37 The statutory guidance in this Chapter should be applied in the light of the circumstances as they appear to the enforcing authority on the basis of the evidence available to it at that time. The enforcing authority's judgements should be made on the basis of the balance of probabilities. The enforcing authority should take into account the information that it has acquired in the light of the guidance in the previous paragraph, but the burden of providing the authority with any further information needed to establish an exclusion or to influence an apportionment or attribution should rest on any person seeking such a benefit. The enforcing authority should consider any relevant information which has been provided by those potentially liable under these provisions. Where any such person provides such information, any other person who may be affected by an exclusion, apportionment or attribution based on that information should be given a reasonable opportunity to comment on that information before the determination is made.

Agreements on liabilities

D.38 In any case where:

(a) two or more persons are appropriate persons and thus responsible for all or part of the costs of a remediation action;

(b) they agree, or have agreed, the basis on which they wish to divide that responsibility; and

(c) a copy of the agreement is provided to the enforcing authority and none of the parties to the agreement informs the authority that it challenges the application of the agreement;

the enforcing authority should generally make such determinations on exclusion, apportionment and attribution as are needed to give effect to this agreement, and should not apply the remainder of this guidance for exclusion, apportionment or attribution between the parties to the agreement. However, the enforcing authority should apply the guidance to determine any exclusions, apportionments or attributions between any or all of those parties and any other appropriate persons who are not parties to the agreement.

D.39 However, where giving effect to such an agreement would increase the share of the costs theoretically to be borne by a person who would benefit from a limitation on recovery of remediation costs under the provision on hardship in section 78P(2)(a) or under the guidance on cost recovery issued under section 78P(2)(b), the enforcing authority should disregard the agreement.

Part 5—Exclusion of members of a Class A Liability group

D.40 The guidance in this Part is issued under section 78F(6) and, with respect to effects of the exclusion tests on apportionment (see paragraph D.43 below in particular), under section 78F(7). It sets out the tests for determining whether to exclude from liability a person who would otherwise be a Class A person (that is, a person who has been identified as responsible for remediation costs by reason of his having "caused or knowingly permitted" the presence of a significant pollutant). The tests are intended to establish whether, in relation to other members of the liability group, it is fair that he should bear any part of that responsibility.

D.41 The exclusion tests in this Part are subject to the following overriding guidance:

(a) the exclusions that the enforcing authority should make are solely in respect of the significant pollutant linkage giving rise to the liability of the liability group in question; an exclusion in respect of one significant pollutant linkage has no necessary implication in respect to any other such linkage, and a person who has been excluded with respect to one linkage may still be liable to meet all or part of the cost of carrying out a remediation action by reason of his membership of another liability group;

(b) the tests should be applied in the sequence in which they are set out; and

(c) if the result of applying a test would be to exclude all of the members of the liability group who remain after any exclusions resulting from previous tests, that further test should not be applied, and consequently the related exclusions should not be made.

D.42 The effect of any exclusion made under Test 1, or Tests 4 to 6 below should be to remove completely any liability that would otherwise have fallen on the person benefiting from the exclusion. Where the enforcing authority makes any exclusion under one of these tests, it should therefore apply any subsequent exclusion tests, and make any apportionment within the liability group, in the same way as it would have done if the excluded person had never been a member of the liability group.

D.43 The effect of any exclusion made under Test 2 ("Payments Made for Remediation") or Test 3 ("Sold with Information"), on the other hand, is intended to be that the person who received the payment or bought the land, as the case may be, (the "payee or buyer") should bear the liability of the person excluded (the "payer or seller") in addition to any liability which he is to bear in respect of his own actions or omissions. To achieve this, the enforcing authority should:

(a) complete the application of the other exclusion tests and then apportion liability between the members of the liability group, as if the payer or seller were not excluded as a result of Test 2 or Test 3; and

(b) then apportion any liability of the payer or seller, calculated on this hypothetical basis, to the payee or buyer, in addition to the liability (if any) that the payee or buyer has in respect of his own actions or omissions; this should be done even if the payee or buyer would otherwise have been excluded from the liability group by one of the other exclusion tests.

Related companies

D.44 Before applying any of the exclusion tests, the enforcing authority should establish whether two or more of the members of the liability group are "related companies".

D.45 Where the question to be considered in any exclusion test concerns the relationship between, or the relative positions of, two or more related companies, the enforcing authority should not apply the test so as to exclude any of the related companies. For example, in Test 3 ("Sold with Information"), if the "seller" and the "buyer" are related companies, the "seller" would not be excluded by virtue of that Test.

D.46 For these purposes, "related companies" are those which are, or were at the "relevant date", members of a group of companies consisting of a "holding company" and its "subsidiaries". The "relevant date" is that on which the enforcing authority first served on anyone a notice under section 78B(3) identifying the land as contaminated land, and the terms "holding company" and "subsidiaries" have the same meaning as in section 736 of the Companies Act 1985.

The exclusion tests for Class A Persons

Test 1—"excluded activities"

D.47 The purpose of this test is to exclude those who have been identified as having caused or knowingly permitted the land to be contaminated land solely by reason of having carried out certain activities. The activities are ones which, in the Government's view, carry such limited responsibility, if any, that exclusion would be justified even where the activity is held to amount to "causing or knowingly permitting" under Part 2A. It does not imply that the carrying out of such activities necessarily amounts to "causing or knowingly permitting".

D.48 In applying this test with respect to any appropriate person, the enforcing authority should consider whether the person in question is a member of a liability group solely by reason of one or more of the following activities (not including any associated activity outside these descriptions):

(a) providing (or withholding) financial assistance to another person (whether or not that other person is a member of the liability group), in the form of any one or more of the following:

    (i) making a grant,

    (ii) making a loan or providing any other form of credit, including instalment credit, leasing arrangements and mortgages,

    (iii) guaranteeing the performance of a person's obligations,

    (iv) indemnifying a person in respect of any loss, liability or damage,

    (v) investing in the undertaking of a body corporate by acquiring share capital or loan capital of that body without thereby acquiring such control as a "holding company" has over a "subsidiary" as defined in section 736 of the Companies Act 1985, or

    (vi) providing a person with any other financial benefit (including the remission in whole or in part of any financial liability or obligation);

(b) underwriting an insurance policy under which another person was insured in respect of any occurrence, condition or omission by reason of which that other person has been held to have caused or knowingly permitted the significant pollutant to be in, on or under the land in question; for the purposes of this sub-paragraph:

    (i) underwriting an insurance policy is to be taken to include imposing any conditions on the person insured, for example relating to the manner in which he carries out the insured activity, and

    (ii) it is irrelevant whether or not the insured person can now be found;

(c) as a provider of financial assistance or as an underwriter, carrying out any action for the purpose of deciding whether or not to provide such financial assistance or underwrite such an insurance policy as is mentioned above; this sub-paragraph does not apply to the carrying out of any intrusive investigation in respect of the land in question for the purpose of making that decision where:

    (i) the carrying out of that investigation is itself a cause of the existence, nature or continuance of the significant pollutant linkage in question, and

    (ii) the person who applied for the financial assistance or insurance is not a member of the liability group;

(d) consigning, as waste, to another person the substance which is now a significant pollutant, under a contract under which that other person knowingly took over responsibility for its proper disposal or other management on a site not under the control of the person seeking to be excluded from liability; (for the purpose of this sub-paragraph, it is irrelevant whether or not the person to whom the waste was consigned can now be found);

(e) creating at any time a tenancy over the land in question in favour of another person who has subsequently caused or knowingly permitted the presence of the significant pollutant linkage in question (whether or not the tenant can now be found);

(f) as owner of the land in question, licensing at any time its occupation by another person who has subsequently caused or knowingly permitted the presence of the significant pollutant in question (whether or not the licensee can now be found); this test does not apply in a case where the person granting the licence operated the land as a site for the disposal or storage of waste at the time of the grant of the licence;

(g) issuing any statutory permission, licence or consent required for any action or omission by reason of which some other person appears to the enforcing authority to have caused or knowingly permitted the presence of the significant pollutant in question (whether or not that other person can now be found); this test does not apply in the case of statutory undertakers granting permission for their contractors to carry out works;

(h) taking, or not taking, any statutory enforcement action:

(i) with respect to the land, or

(ii) against some other person who appears to the enforcing authority to have caused or knowingly permitted the presence of the significant pollutant in question, whether or not that other person can now be found;

(i) providing legal, financial, engineering, scientific or technical advice to (or design, contract management or works management services for) another person (the "client"), whether or not that other person can now be found:

(i) in relation to an action or omission (or a series of actions and/or omissions) by reason of which the client has been held to have caused or knowingly permitted the presence of the significant pollutant,

(ii) for the purpose of assessing the condition of the land, for example whether it might be contaminated, or

(iii) for the purpose of establishing what might be done to the land by way of remediation;

(j) as a person providing advice or services as described in sub-paragraph (i) above carrying out any intrusive investigation in respect of the land in question, except where:

(i) the investigation is itself a cause of the existence, nature or continuance of the significant pollutant linkage in question, and

(ii) the client is not a member of the liability group; or

(k) performing any contract by providing a service (whether the contract is a contract of service (employment), or a contract for services) or by supplying goods, where the contract is made with another person who is also a member of the liability group in question; for the purposes of this sub-paragraph and paragraph D.49 below, the person providing the service or supplying the goods is referred to as the "contractor" and the other party as the "employer"; this sub-paragraph applies to subcontracts where either the ultimate employer or an intermediate contractor is a member of the liability group; this sub-paragraph does not apply where:

(i) the activity under the contract is of a kind referred to in a previous sub-paragraph of this paragraph,

(ii) the action or omission by the contractor by virtue of which he has been identified as an appropriate person was not in accordance with the terms of the contract, or

(iii) the circumstances in paragraph D.49 below apply.

D.49 The circumstances referred to in paragraph D.48(k)(iii) are:

(a) the employer is a body corporate;

(b) the contractor was a director, manager, secretary or other similar officer of the body corporate, or a person purporting to act in any such capacity, at the time when the contract was performed; and

(c) the action or omissions by virtue of which the employer has been identified as an appropriate person were carried out or made with the consent or connivance of the contractor, or were attributable to any neglect on his part.

D.50 If any of the circumstances in paragraph D.48 above apply, the enforcing authority should exclude the person in question.

Test 2—"payments made for remediation"

D.51 The purpose of this test is to exclude from liability those who have already, in effect, met their responsibilities by making certain kinds of payment to some other member of the liability group, which would have been sufficient to pay for adequate remediation.

D.52 In applying this test, the enforcing authority should consider whether all the following circumstances exist:

(a) one of the members of the liability group has made a payment to another member of that liability group for the purpose of carrying out particular remediation on the land in question; only payments of the kinds set out in paragraph D.53 below are to be taken into account;

(b) that payment would have been sufficient at the date when it was made to pay for the remediation in question;

(c) if the remediation for which the payment was intended had been carried out effectively, the land in question would not now be in such a condition that it has been identified as contaminated land by reason of the significant pollutant linkage in question; and

(d) the remediation in question was not carried out or was not carried out effectively.

D.53 Payments of the following kinds alone should be taken into account:

(a) a payment made voluntarily, or to meet a contractual obligation, in response to a claim for the cost of the particular remediation;

(b) a payment made in the course of a civil legal action, or arbitration, mediation or dispute resolution procedure, covering the cost of the particular remediation, whether paid as part of an out-of-court settlement, or paid under the terms of a court order; or

(c) a payment as part of a contract (including a group of interlinked contracts) for the transfer of ownership of the land in question which is either specifically provided for in the contract to meet the cost of carrying out the particular remediation or which consists of a reduction in the contract price explicitly stated in the contract to be for that purpose.

D.54 For the purposes of this test, payments include consideration of any form.

D.55 However, no payment should be taken into account where the person making the payment retained any control after the date of the payment over the condition of the land in question (that is, over whether or not the substances by reason of which the land is regarded as contaminated land were permitted to be in, on or under the land). For this purpose, neither of the following should be regarded as retaining control over the condition of the land:

(a) holding contractual rights to ensure the proper carrying out of the remediation for which the payment was made; nor

(b) holding an interest or right of any of the following kinds:

(i) easements for the benefit of other land, where the contaminated land in question is the servient tenement, and statutory rights of an equivalent nature,

(ii) rights of statutory undertakers to carry out works or install equipment,

(iii) reversions upon expiry or termination of a long lease, or

(iv) the benefit of restrictive covenants or equivalent statutory agreements.

D.56 If all of the circumstances set out in paragraph D.52 above apply, the enforcing authority should exclude the person who made the payment in respect of the remediation action in question. (See paragraph D.43 above for guidance on how this exclusion should be made.)

Test 3—"sold with information"

D.57 The purpose of this test is to exclude from liability those who, although they have caused or knowingly permitted the presence of a significant pollutant in, on or under some land, have disposed of that land in circumstances where it is reasonable that another member of the liability group, who has acquired the land from them, should bear the liability for remediation of the land.

D.58 In applying this test, the enforcing authority should consider whether all the following circumstances exist:

(a) one of the members of the liability group (the "seller") has sold the land in question to a person who is also a member of the liability group (the "buyer");

(b) the sale took place at arms' length (that is, on terms which could be expected in a sale on the open market between a willing seller and a willing buyer);

(c) before the sale became binding, the buyer had information that would reasonably allow that particular person to be aware of the presence on the land of the pollutant identified in the significant pollutant linkage in question, and the broad measure of that presence; and the seller did nothing material to misrepresent the implications of that presence; and

(d) after the date of the sale, the seller did not retain any interest in the land in question or any rights to occupy or use that land.

D.59 In determining whether these circumstances exist:

(a) a sale of land should be regarded as being either the transfer of the freehold or the grant or assignment of a long lease; for this purpose, a "long lease" means a lease (or sub-lease) granted for a period of more than 21 years under which the lessee satisfies the definition of "owner" set out in section 78A(9);

(b) the question of whether persons are members of a liability group should be decided on the circumstances as they exist at the time of the determination (and not as they might have been at the time of the sale of the land);

(c) where there is a group of transactions or a wider agreement (such as the sale of a company or business) including a sale of land, that sale of land should be taken to have been at arms' length where the person seeking to be excluded can show that the net effect of the group of transactions or the agreement as a whole was a sale at arms' length;

(d) in transactions since the beginning of 1990 where the buyer is a large commercial organisation or public body, permission from the seller for the buyer to carry out his own investigations of the condition of the land should normally be taken as sufficient indication that the buyer had the information referred to in paragraph D.58(c) above; and

(e) for the purposes of paragraph D.58(d) above, the following rights should be disregarded in deciding whether the seller has retained an interest in the contaminated land in question or rights to occupy or use it:

    (i) easements for the benefit of other land, where the contaminated land in question is the servient tenement, and statutory rights of an equivalent nature,

    (ii) rights of statutory undertakers to carry out works or install equipment,

    (iii) reversions upon expiry or termination of a long lease, and

    (iv) the benefit of restrictive covenants or equivalent statutory agreements.

D.60 If all of the circumstances in paragraph D.58 above apply, the enforcing authority should exclude the seller. (See paragraph D.43 above for guidance on how this exclusion should be made.)

D.61 This test does not imply that the receipt by the buyer of the information referred to in paragraph D.58(c) above necessarily means that the buyer has "caused or knowingly permitted" the presence of the significant pollutant in, on or under the land.

Test 4—"changes to substances"

D.62 The purpose of this test is to exclude from liability those who are members of a liability group solely because they caused or knowingly permitted the presence in, on or under the land of a substance which has only led to the creation of a significant pollutant linkage because of its interaction with another substance which was later introduced to the land by another person.

D.63 In applying this test, the enforcing authority should consider whether all the following circumstances exist:

(a) the substance forming part of the significant pollutant linkage in question is present, or has become a significant pollutant, only as the result of a chemical reaction, biological process, radioactive decay or other change (the "intervening change") involving:

    (i) both a substance (the "earlier substance") which would not have formed part of the significant pollutant linkage if the intervening change had not occurred, and

    (ii) one or more other substances (the "later substances");

(b) the intervening change would not have occurred in the absence of the later substances;

(c) a person (the "first person") is a member of the liability group because he caused or knowingly permitted the presence in, on or under the land of the earlier substance, but he did not cause or knowingly permit the presence of any of the later substances;

(d) one or more other persons are members of the liability group because they caused or knowingly permitted the later substances to be in, on or under the land;

(e) before the date when the later substances started to be introduced in, on or under the land, the first person:

(i) could not reasonably have foreseen that the later substances would be introduced onto the land,

(ii) could not reasonably have foreseen that, if they were, the intervening change would be likely to happen, or

(iii) took what, at that date, were reasonable precautions to prevent the introduction of the later substances or the occurrence of the intervening change, even though those precautions have, in the event, proved to be inadequate; and

(f) after that date, the first person did not:

(i) cause or knowingly permit any more of the earlier substance to be in, on or under the land in question,

(ii) do anything which has contributed to the conditions that brought about the intervening change, or

(iii) fail to do something which he could reasonably have been expected to do to prevent the intervening change happening.

D.64 If all of the circumstances in paragraph D.63 above apply, the enforcing authority should exclude the first person (or persons, if more than one member of the liability group meets this description).

Test 5—"escaped substances"

D.65 The purpose of this test is to exclude from liability those who would otherwise be liable for the remediation of contaminated land which has become contaminated as a result of the escape of substances from other land, where it can be shown that another member of the liability group was actually responsible for that escape.

D.66 In applying this test, the enforcing authority should consider whether all the following circumstances exist:

(a) a significant pollutant is present in, on or under the contaminated land in question wholly or partly as a result of its escape from other land;

(b) a member of the liability group for the significant pollutant linkage of which that pollutant forms part:

(i) caused or knowingly permitted the pollutant to be present in, on or under that other land (that is, he is a member, of that liability group by reason of section 78K(1)), and

(ii) is a member of that liability group solely for that reason; and

(c) one or more other members of that liability group caused or knowingly permitted the significant pollutant to escape from that other land and its escape would not have happened but for their actions or omissions.

D.67 If all of the circumstances in paragraph D.66 above apply, the enforcing authority should exclude any person meeting the description in paragraph D.66(b) above.

Test 6—"introduction of pathways or receptors"

D.68 The purpose of this test is to exclude from liability those who would otherwise be liable solely because of the subsequent introduction by others of the relevant pathways or receptors (as defined in Chapter A) in the significant pollutant linkage.

D.69 In applying this test, the enforcing authority should consider whether all the following circumstances exist:

(a) one or more members of the liability group have carried out a relevant action, and/or made a relevant omission ("the later actions"), either

(i) as part of the series of actions and/or omissions which amount to their having caused or knowingly permitted the presence of the pollutant in a significant pollutant linkage, or

(ii) in addition to that series of actions and/or omissions;

(b) the effect of the later actions has been to introduce the pathway or the receptor which form part of the significant pollutant linkage in question;

(c) if those later actions had not been carried out or made, the significant pollutant linkage would either not have existed, or would not have been a significant pollutant linkage, because of the absence of a pathway or of a receptor; and

(d) a person is a member of the liability group in question solely by reason of his carrying out other actions or making other omissions ("the earlier actions") which were completed before any of the later actions were carried out or made.

D.70 For the purpose of this test:

(a) a "relevant action" means:

(i) the carrying out at any time of building, engineering, mining or other operations in, on, over or under the land in question, and/or

(ii) the making of any material change in the use of the land in question for which a specific application for planning permission was required to be made (as opposed to permission being granted, or deemed to be granted, by general legislation or by virtue of a development order, the adoption of a simplified planning zone or the designation of an enterprise zone) at the time when the change in use was made; and

(b) a "relevant omission" means:

(i) in the course of a relevant action, failing to take a step which would have ensured that a significant pollutant linkage was not brought into existence as a result of that action, and/or

(ii) unreasonably failing to maintain or operate a system installed for the purpose of reducing or managing the risk associated with the presence on the land in question of the significant pollutant in the significant pollutant linkage in question.

D.71 This test applies only with respect to developments on, or changes in the use of, the contaminated land itself; it does not apply where the relevant acts or omissions take place on other land, even if they have the effect of introducing pathways or receptors.

D.72 If all of the circumstances in paragraph D.69 above apply, the enforcing authority should exclude any person meeting the description at paragraph D.69(d) above.

Part 6—Apportionment between members of any single Class A liability group

D.73 The statutory guidance in this Part is issued under section 78F(7) and sets out the principles on which liability should be apportioned within each Class A liability group as it stands after any members have been excluded from liability with respect to the relevant significant pollutant linkage as a result of the application of the exclusion tests in Part 5.

D.74 The history and circumstances of different areas of contaminated land, and the nature of the responsibility of each of the members of any Class A liability group for a significant pollutant linkage, are likely to vary greatly. It is therefore not possible to prescribe detailed rules for the apportionment of liability between those members which would be fair and appropriate in all cases.

General principles

D.75 In apportioning costs between the members of a Class A liability group who remain after any exclusions have been made, the enforcing authority should follow the general principle that liability should be apportioned to reflect the relative responsibility of each of those members for creating or continuing the risk now being caused by the significant pollutant linkage in question. (For these purposes, "risk" has the same meaning as that given in Chapter A.) In applying this principle, the enforcing authority should follow, where appropriate, the specific approaches set out in paragraphs D.77 to D.86 below.

D.76 If appropriate information is not available to enable the enforcing authority to make such an assessment of relative responsibility (and, following the guidance at paragraph D.36 above, such information cannot reasonably be obtained) the authority should apportion liability in equal shares among the remaining members of the liability group for any significant pollutant linkage, subject to the specific guidance in paragraph D.85 below.

Specific approaches

Partial applicability of an exclusion test

D.77 If, for any member of the liability group, the circumstances set out in any of the exclusion tests in Part 5 above apply to some extent, but not sufficiently to mean that the an exclusion should be made, the enforcing authority should assess that person's degree of responsibility as being reduced to the extent which is appropriate in the light of all the circumstances and the purpose of the test in question. For example, in considering Test 2, a payment may have been made which was sufficient to pay for only half of the necessary remediation at that time—the authority could therefore reduce the payer's responsibility by half.

The entry of a substance vs. its continued presence

D.78 In assessing the relative responsibility of a person who has caused or knowingly permitted the entry of a significant pollutant into, onto or under land (the "first person") and another person who has knowingly permitted the continued presence of that same pollutant in, on or under that land (the "second person"), the enforcing authority should consider the extent to which the second person had the means and a reasonable opportunity to deal with the presence of the pollutant in question or to reduce the seriousness of the implications of that presence. The authority should then assess the relative responsibilities on the following basis:

(a) if the second person had the necessary means and opportunity, he should bear the same responsibility as the first person;

(b) if the second person did not have the means and opportunity, his responsibility relative to that of the first person should be substantially reduced; and

(c) if the second person had some, but insufficient, means or opportunity, his responsibility relative to that of the first person should be reduced to an appropriate extent.

Persons who have caused or knowingly permitted the entry of a significant pollutant

D.79 Where the enforcing authority is determining the relative responsibilities of members of the liability group who have caused or knowingly permitted the entry of the significant pollutant into, onto or under the land, it should follow the approach set out in paragraphs D.80 to D.83 below.

D.80 If the nature of the remediation action points clearly to different members of the liability group being responsible for particular circumstances at which the action is aimed, the enforcing authority should apportion responsibility in accordance with that indication. In particular, where different persons were in control of different areas of the land in question, and there is no interrelationship between those areas, the enforcing authority should regard the persons in control of the different areas as being separately responsible for the events which make necessary the remediation actions or parts of actions referable to those areas of land.

D.81 If the circumstances in paragraph D.80 above do not apply, but the quantity of the significant pollutant present is a major influence on the cost of remediation, the enforcing authority should regard the relative amounts of that pollutant which are referable to the different persons as an appropriate basis for apportioning responsibility.

D.82 If it is deciding the relative quantities of pollutant which are referable to different persons, the enforcing authority should consider first whether there is direct evidence of the relative quantities referable to each person. If there is such evidence, it should be used. In the absence of direct evidence, the enforcing authority should see whether an appropriate surrogate measure is available. Such surrogate measures can include:

(a) the relative periods during which the different persons carried out broadly equivalent operations on the land;

(b) the relative scale of such operations carried out on the land by the different persons (a measure of such scale may be the quantities of a product that were produced);

(c) the relative areas of land on which different persons carried out their operations; and

(d) combinations of the foregoing measures.

D.83 In cases where the circumstances in neither paragraph D.80 nor D.81 above apply, the enforcing authority should consider the nature of the activities carried out by the appropriate persons concerned from which the significant pollutant arose. Where these activities were broadly equivalent, the enforcing authority should apportion responsibility in proportion to the periods of time over which the different persons were in control of those activities. It would be appropriate to adjust this apportionment to reflect circumstances where the persons concerned carried out activities which were not broadly equivalent, for example where they were on a different scale.

Persons who have knowingly permitted the continued presence of a pollutant

D.84 Where the enforcing authority is determining the relative responsibilities of members of the liability group who have knowingly permitted the continued presence, over a period of time, of a significant pollutant in, on or under land, it should apportion that responsibility in proportion to:

(a) the length of time during which each person controlled the land;

(b) the area of land which each person controlled;

(c) the extent to which each person had the means and a reasonable opportunity to deal with the presence of the pollutant in question or to reduce the seriousness of the implications of that presence; or

(d) a combination of the foregoing factors.

Companies and officers

D.85 If, following the application of the exclusion tests (and in particular the specific guidance at paragraphs D.48(k)(iii) and D.49 above) both a company and one or more of its relevant officers remain as members of the liability group, the enforcing authority should apportion liability on the following bases:

(a) the enforcing authority should treat the company and its relevant officers as a single unit for the purposes of:

(i) applying the general principle in paragraph D.75 above (i.e. it should consider the responsibilities of the company and its relevant officers as a whole, in comparison with the responsibilities of other members of the liability group), and

(ii) making any apportionment required by paragraph D.76 above; and

(b) having determined the share of liability falling to the company and its relevant officers together, the enforcing authority should apportion responsibility between the company and its relevant officers on a basis which takes into account the degree of personal responsibility of those officers, and the relative levels of resources which may be available to them and to the company to meet the liability.

D.86 For the purposes of paragraph D.85 above, the "relevant officers" of a company are any director, manager, secretary or other similar officer of the company, or any other person purporting to act in any such capacity.

Part 7—Exclusion of members of a Class B liability group

D.87 The guidance in this Part is issued under section 78F(6) and sets out the test which should be applied in determining whether to exclude from liability a person who would otherwise be a Class B person (that is, a person liable to meet remediation costs solely by reason of ownership or occupation of the land in question). The purpose of the test is to exclude from liability those who do not have an interest in the capital value of the land in question.

D.88 The test applies where two or more persons have been identified as Class B persons for a significant pollutant linkage.

D.89 In such circumstances, the enforcing authority should exclude any Class B person who either:

(a) occupies the land under a licence, or other agreement, of a kind which has no marketable value or which he is not legally able to assign or transfer to another person (for these purposes the actual marketable value, or the fact that a particular licence or agreement may not actually attract a buyer in the market, are irrelevant); or

(b) is liable to pay a rent which is equivalent to the rack rent for such of the land in question as he occupies and holds no beneficial interest in that land other than any tenancy to which such rent relates; where the rent is subject to periodic review, the rent should be considered to be equivalent to the rack rent if, at the latest review, it was set at the full market rent at that date.

D.90 However, the test should not be applied, and consequently no exclusion should be made, if it would result in the exclusion of all of the members of the liability group.

Part 8—Apportionment between the members of a single Class B liability group

D.91 The statutory guidance in this Part is issued under section 78F(7) and sets out the principles on which liability should be apportioned within each Class B liability group as it stands after any members have been excluded from liability with respect to the relevant significant pollutant linkage as a result of the application of the exclusion test in Part 7.

D.92 Where the whole or part of a remediation action for which a Class B liability group is responsible clearly relates to a particular area within the land to which the significant pollutant linkage as a whole relates, liability for the whole, or the relevant part, of that action should be apportioned amongst those members of the liability group who own or occupy that particular area of land.

D.93 Where those circumstances do not apply, the enforcing authority should apportion liability for the remediation actions necessary for the significant pollutant linkage in question amongst all of the members of the liability group.

D.94 Where the enforcing authority is apportioning liability amongst some or all of the members of a Class B liability group, it should do so in proportion to the capital values of the interests in the land in question, which include those of any buildings or structures on the land:

(a) where different members of the liability group own or occupy different areas of land, each such member should bear responsibility in the proportion that the capital value of his area of land bears to the aggregate of the capital values of all the areas of land; and

(b) where different members of the liability group have an interest in the same area of land, each such member should bear responsibility in the proportion which the capital value of his interest bears to the aggregate of the capital values of all those interests; and

(c) where both the ownership or occupation of different areas of land and the holding of different interests come into the question, the overall liability should first be apportioned between the different areas of land and then between the interests within each of those areas of land, in each case in accordance with the last two sub-paragraphs.

D.95 The capital value used for these purposes should be that estimated by the enforcing authority, on the basis of the available information, disregarding the existence of any contamination. The value should be estimated in relation to the date immediately before the enforcing authority first served a notice under section 78B(3) in relation to that land. Where the land in question is reasonably uniform in nature and amenity and is divided among a number of owner-occupiers, it can be an acceptable approximation of this basis of apportionment to make the apportionment on the basis of the area occupied by each.

D.96 Where part of the land in question is land for which no owner or occupier can be found, the enforcing authority should deduct the share of costs attributable to that land on the basis of the respective capital values of that land and the other land in question before making a determination of liability.

D.97 If appropriate information is not available to enable the enforcing authority to make an assessment of relative capital values (and, following the guidance at paragraph D.36 above, such information cannot reasonably be obtained), the enforcing authority should apportion liability in equal shares among all the members of the liability group.

Part 9—Attribution of responsibility between liability groups

D.98 The statutory guidance in this Part is issued under section 78F(7) and applies where one remediation action is referable to two or more significant pollutant linkages (that is, it is a "shared action"). This can occur either where both linkages require the same action (that is, it is a "common action") or where a particular action is part of the best combined remediation scheme for two or more linkages (that is, it is a "collective action"). This Part provides statutory guidance on the attribution of responsibility for the costs of any shared action between the liability groups for the linkages to which it is referable.

Attributing responsibility for the cost of shared actions between liability groups

D.99 The enforcing authority should attribute responsibility for the costs of any common action among the liability groups for the significant pollutant linkages to which it is referable on the following basis:

(a) if there is a single Class A liability group, then the full cost of carrying out the common action should be attributed to that group, and no cost should be attributed to any Class B liability group);

(b) if there are two or more Class A liability groups, then an equal share of the cost of carrying out the common action should be attributed to each of those groups, and no cost should be attributed to any Class B liability group); and

(c) if there is no Class A liability group and there are two or more Class B liability groups, then the enforcing authority should treat those liability groups as if they formed a single liability group, attributing the cost of carrying out the common action to that combined group, and applying the guidance on exclusion and apportionment set out in Parts 7 and 8 of this Chapter as between all of the members of that combined group.

D.100 The enforcing authority should attribute responsibility for the cost of any collective action among the liability groups for the significant pollutant linkages to which it is referable on the same basis as for the costs of a common action, except that where the costs fall to be divided among several Class A liability groups, instead of being divided equally, they should be attributed on the following basis:

(a) having estimated the costs of the collective action, the enforcing authority should also estimate the hypothetical cost for each of the liability groups of carrying out the actions which are subsumed by the collective action and which would be necessary if the significant pollutant linkage for which that liability group is responsible were to be addressed separately; these estimates are the "hypothetical estimates" of each of the liability groups;

(b) the enforcing authority should then attribute responsibility for the cost of the collective action between the liability groups in the proportions which the hypothetical estimates of each liability group bear to the aggregate of the hypothetical estimates of all the groups.

Confirming the attribution of responsibility

D.101 If any appropriate person demonstrates, before the service of a remediation notice, to the satisfaction of the enforcing authority that the result of an attribution made on the basis set out in paragraphs D.99 and D.100 above would have the effect of the liability group of which he is a member having to bear a liability which is so disproportionate (taking into account the overall relative responsibilities of the persons or groups concerned for the condition of the land) as to make the attribution of responsibility between all the liability groups concerned unjust when considered as a whole, the enforcing authority should reconsider the attribution. In doing so, the enforcing authority should consult the other appropriate persons concerned.

D.102 If the enforcing authority then agrees that the original attribution would be unjust it should adjust the attribution between the liability groups so that it is just and fair in the light of all the circumstances. An adjustment under this paragraph should be necessary only in very exceptional cases.

Orphan linkages

D.103 As explained above at paragraphs D.12, D.14 and D.17 above, an orphan linkage may arise where:

(a) the significant pollutant linkage relates solely to the pollution of controlled waters (and not to significant harm or harm in so far as it is attributable to radioactivity) and no Class A person can be found;

(b) no Class A or Class B persons can be found; or

(c) those who would otherwise be liable are exempted by one of the relevant statutory provisions (i.e. sections 78J(3), 78K, 78K (as modified) or 78X(3)).

D.104 In any case where only one significant pollutant linkage has been identified, and that is an orphan linkage, the enforcing authority should itself bear the cost of any remediation which is carried out.

D.105 In more complicated cases, there may be two or more significant pollutant linkages, of which some are orphan linkages. Where this applies, the enforcing authority will need to consider each remediation action separately.

D.106 For any remediation action which is referable to an orphan linkage, and is not referable to any other linkage for which there is a liability group, the enforcing authority should itself bear the cost of carrying out that action.

D.107 For any shared action which is referable to an orphan linkage and also to a single significant pollutant linkage for which there is a Class A liability group, the enforcing authority should attribute all of the cost of carrying out that action to that Class A liability group.

D.108 For any shared action which is referable to an orphan linkage and also to two or more significant pollutant linkages for which there are Class A liability groups, the enforcing authority should attribute the costs of carrying out that action between those liability groups in the same way as it would do if the orphan linkage did not exist.

D.109 For any shared action which is referable to an orphan linkage and also to a significant pollutant linkage for which there is a Class B liability group (and not to any significant pollutant linkage for which there is a Class A liability group) the enforcing authority should adopt the following approach:

(a) where the remediation action is a common action the enforcing authority should attribute all of the cost of carrying out that action to the Class B liability group; and

(b) where the remediation action is a collective action, the enforcing authority should estimate the hypothetical cost of the action which would be needed to remediate separately the effects of the linkage for which that group is liable. The enforcing authority should then attribute the costs of carrying out the collective action between itself and the Class B liability group so that the expected liability of that group does not exceed that hypothetical cost.

CHAPTER E—THE RECOVERY OF THE COSTS OF REMEDIATION

Part 1 Scope of the Chapter

Applies generally.

Part 2 Definitions of Terms

Applies generally.

Part 3 Cost Recovery Decisions

Applies generally.

Part 4 Considerations Applying Both to Class A & Class B Persons

Applies generally.

Part 5 Specific Considerations Applying to Class A Persons

Applies generally.

Part 6 Specific Considerations Applying to Class B Persons

Applies generally.

Part 1—Scope of the chapter

E.1 The statutory guidance in this Chapter is issued under section 78P(2) of the Environmental Protection Act 1990. It provides guidance on the extent to which the enforcing authority should seek to recover the costs of remediation which it has carried out and which it is entitled to recover.

E.2 Section 78P provides that:

"(1) Where, by virtue of section 78N(3)(a), (c), (e) or (f) . . . the enforcing authority does any particular thing by way of remediation, it shall be entitled, subject to sections 78J(7) and 78K(6). . . , to recover the reasonable cost incurred in doing it from the appropriate person or, if there are two or more appropriate persons in relation to the thing in question, from those persons in proportions determined pursuant to section 78F(7). . .

"(2) In deciding whether to recover the cost, and, if so, how much of the cost, which it is entitled to recover under subsection (1) above, the enforcing authority shall have regard—

"(a) to any hardship which the recovery may cause to the person from whom the cost is recoverable; and

(b) to any guidance issued by the Secretary of State for the purposes of this subsection."

E.2A In relation to harm so far as attributable to radioactivity, section 78P is modified to have effect as if the words "78J and" were omitted.

E.3 The guidance in this Chapter is also crucial in deciding when the enforcing authority is prevented from serving a remediation notice. Under section 78H(5), the enforcing authority may not serve a remediation notice if the authority has the power to carry out remediation itself, by virtue of section 78N. Under that latter section, the authority asks the hypothetical question of whether it would seek to recover all of the reasonable costs it would incur if it carried out the remediation itself. The authority then has the power to carry out that remediation itself if it concludes that, having regard to hardship and the guidance in this chapter, it would either not seek to recover its costs, or seek to recover only a part of its costs.

E.4 Section 78H(5) provides that:

"(5) The enforcing authority shall not serve a remediation notice on a person if and so long as . . .

"(d) the authority is satisfied that the powers conferred on it by section 78N below to do what is appropriate by way of remediation are exercisable. . . "

E.5 Section 78N(3) provides that the enforcing authority has the power to carry out remediation:

> "(e) where the enforcing authority considers that, were it to do some particular thing by way of remediation, it would decide, by virtue of subsection (2) of section 78P . . . or any guidance issued under that subsection,—

>> "(i) not to seek to recover under subsection (1) of that section any of the reasonable cost incurred by it in doing that thing; or
>> "(ii) to seek so to recover only a portion of that cost;. . . ."

E.6 The enforcing authority is required to have regard to the statutory guidance in this Chapter.

Part 2—Definitions of terms

E.7 Unless otherwise stated, any word, term or phrase given a specific meaning in Part 2A of the Environmental Protection Act 1990, or in the statutory guidance in Chapters A, B, C, or D has the same meaning for the purpose of the guidance in this Chapter.

E.8 In addition, for the purposes of the statutory guidance in this Chapter, the term "cost recovery decision" is used to describe any decision by the enforcing authority, for the purposes either of section 78P or of sections 78H and 78N, whether:

(a) to recover from the appropriate person all of the reasonable costs incurred by the authority in carrying out remediation; or
(b) not to recover those costs or to recover only part of those costs (described below as "waiving or reducing its cost recovery").

E.9 Any reference to "Part 2A" means "Part 2A of the Environmental Protection Act 1990". Any reference to a "section" in primary legislation means a section of the Environmental Protection Act 1990, unless it is specifically stated otherwise.

E.9A Any reference to "harm so far as attributable to radioactivity" means "harm so far as attributable to any radioactivity possessed by any substance".

Part 3—Cost recovery decisions

Cost recovery decisions in general

E.10 The statutory guidance in this Part sets out considerations to which the enforcing authority should have regard when making any cost recovery decision. In view of the wide variation in situations which are likely to arise, including the history and ownership of land, and liability for its remediation, the statutory guidance in this Chapter sets out principles and approaches, rather than detailed rules. The enforcing authority will need to have regard to the circumstances of each individual case.

E.11 In making any cost recovery decision, the enforcing authority should have regard to the following general principles:

(a) the authority should aim for an overall result which is as fair and equitable as possible to all who may have to meet the costs of remediation, including national and local taxpayers; and

(b) the "polluter pays" principle, by virtue of which the costs of remediating pollution are to be borne by the polluter; the authority should therefore consider the degree and nature of responsibility of the appropriate person for the creation, or continued existence, of the circumstances which lead to the land in question being identified as contaminated land.

E.12 In general, this will mean that the enforcing authority should seek to recover in full its reasonable costs. However, the authority should waive or reduce the recovery of costs to the extent that the authority considers this appropriate and reasonable, either:

(a) to avoid any hardship which the recovery may cause to the appropriate person; or

(b) to reflect one or more of the specific considerations set out in the statutory guidance in Parts 4, 5 and 6 below.

E.13 When deciding how much of its costs it should recover in any case, the enforcing authority should consider whether it could recover more of its costs by deferring recovery and securing them by a charge on the land in question under section 78P. Such deferral may lead to payment from the appropriate person either in instalments (see section 78P(12)) or when the land is next sold.

Information for making decisions

E.14 In general, the enforcing authority should expect anyone who is seeking a waiver or reduction in the recovery of remediation costs to present any information needed to support his request.

E.15 In making any cost recovery decision, the authority should always consider any relevant information provided by the appropriate person. The authority should also seek to obtain such information as is reasonable, having regard to:

(a) how the information might be obtained;

(b) the cost, for all the parties involved, of obtaining the information; and

(c) the potential significance of the information for any decision.

E.16 The enforcing authority should, in all cases, inform the appropriate person of any cost recovery decisions taken, explaining the reasons for those decisions.

Cost recovery policies

E.17 In order to promote transparency, fairness and consistency, an enforcing authority which is a local authority may wish to prepare, adopt and make available as appropriate a policy statement about the general approach it intends to follow in making cost recovery decisions. This would outline circumstances in which it would waive or reduce cost recovery (and thereby, by inference, not serve a remediation notice because it has the powers to carry out the remediation itself), having had regard to hardship and the statutory guidance in this Chapter.

E.18 Where the Environment Agency is making a cost recovery decision with respect to a special site falling within the area of a local authority which has adopted such a policy statement, the Agency should take account of that statement.

Part 4—Considerations applying both to Class A & Class B persons

E.19 The statutory guidance in this Part sets out considerations to which the enforcing authority should have regard when making any cost recovery decisions, irrespective of whether the appropriate person is a Class A person or a Class B person (as defined in Chapter D). They apply in addition to the general issue of the "hardship" which the cost recovery may cause to the appropriate person.

Commercial enterprises

E.20 Subject to the specific guidance elsewhere in this Chapter, the enforcing authority should adopt the same approach to all types of commercial or industrial enterprises which are identified as appropriate persons. This applies whether the appropriate person is a public corporation, a limited company (whether public or private), a partnership (whether limited or not) or an individual operating as a sole trader.

Threat of business closure or insolvency

E.21 In the case of a small or medium-sized enterprise which is the appropriate person, or which is run by the appropriate person, the enforcing authority should consider:

(a) whether recovery of the full cost attributable to that person would mean that the enterprise is likely to become insolvent and thus cease to exist; and

(b) if so, the cost to the local economy of such a closure.

E.22 Where the cost of closure appears to be greater than the costs of remediation which the enforcing authority would have to bear themselves, the authority should consider waiving or reducing its costs recovery to the extent needed to avoid making the enterprise insolvent.

E.23 However, the authority should not waive or reduce its costs recovery where:

(a) it is clear that an enterprise has deliberately arranged matters so as to avoid responsibility for the costs of remediation;

(b) it appears that the enterprise would be likely to become insolvent whether or not recovery of the full cost takes place; or

(c) it appears that the enterprise could be kept in, or returned to, business even it does become insolvent under its current ownership.

E.24 For these purposes, a "small or medium-sized enterprise" is as defined in the European Commission's Community Guidelines on State Aid for Small and Medium-Sized Enterprises, published in the Official Journal of the European Communities (the reference number for the present version of the guidelines is OJ C213 1996 item 4). This can be summarised as an independent enterprise with fewer than 250 employees, and either an annual turnover not exceeding €50 million, or an annual balance sheet total not exceeding €43 million.

E.25 Where the enforcing authority is a local authority, it may wish to take account in any such cost recovery decisions of any policies it may have for assisting enterprise or promoting economic development (for example, for granting financial or other assistance under section 2(1)(a) of the Local Government Act 2000, including any strategy which it has published under section 4 of that Act concerning the use of such powers).

E.26 Where the Environment Agency is the enforcing authority, it should seek to be consistent with the local authority in whose area the contaminated land in question is situated. The Environment Agency should therefore consult the local authority, and should take that authority's views into consideration in making its own cost recovery decision.

Trusts

E.27 Where the appropriate persons include persons acting as trustees, the enforcing authority should assume that such trustees will exercise all the powers which they have, or may reasonably obtain, to make funds available from the trust, or from borrowing that can be made on behalf of the trust, for the purpose of paying for remediation. The authority should, nevertheless, consider waiving or reducing its costs recovery to the extent that the costs of remediation to be recovered from the trustees would otherwise exceed the amount that can be made available from the trust to cover those costs.

E.28 However, as exceptions to the approach set out in the preceding paragraph, the authority should not waive or reduce its costs recovery:

(a) where it is clear that the trust was formed for the purpose of avoiding paying the costs of remediation; or

(b) to the extent that trustees have personally benefited, or will personally benefit, from the trust.

Charities

E.29 Since charities are intended to operate for the benefit of the community, the enforcing authority should consider the extent to which any recovery of costs from a charity would jeopardise that charity's ability to continue to provide a benefit or amenity which is in the public interest. Where this is the case, the authority should consider waiving or reducing its costs recovery to the extent needed to avoid such a consequence. This approach applies equally to charitable trusts and to charitable companies.

Social housing landlords

E.30 The enforcing authority should consider waiving or reducing its costs recovery if:

(a) the appropriate person is a body eligible for registration as a social housing landlord under section 2 of the Housing Act 1996 (for example, a housing association);

(b) its liability relates to land used for social housing; and

(c) full recovery would lead to financial difficulties for the appropriate person, such that the provision or upkeep of the social housing would be jeopardised.

E.31 The extent of the waiver or reduction should be sufficient to avoid any such financial difficulties.

Part 5—Specific considerations applying to Class A persons

E.32 The statutory guidance in this Part sets out specific considerations to which the enforcing authority should have regard in cost recovery decisions where the appropriate person is a Class A person, as defined in Chapter D (that is, a person who has caused or knowingly permitted the significant pollutant to be in, on or under the contaminated land).

E.33 In applying the approach in this Part, the enforcing authority should be less willing to waive or reduce its costs recovery where it was in the course of carrying on a business that the Class A person caused or knowingly permitted the presence of the significant pollutants, than where he was not carrying on a business. This is because in the former case he is likely to have earned profits from the activity which created or permitted the presence of those pollutants.

Where other potentially appropriate persons have not been found

E.34 In some cases where a Class A person has been found, it may be possible to identify another person who caused or knowingly permitted the presence of the significant pollutant in question, but who cannot now be found for the purposes of treating him as an appropriate person. For example, this might apply where a company has been dissolved.

E.35 The authority should consider waiving or reducing its costs recovery from a Class A person if that person demonstrates to the satisfaction of the enforcing authority that:

(a) another identified person, who cannot now be found, also caused or knowingly permitted the significant pollutant to be in, on or under the land; and

(b) if that other person could be found, the Class A person seeking the waiver or reduction of the authority's costs recovery would either:

(i) be excluded from liability by virtue of one or more of the exclusion tests set out in Part 5 of Chapter D, or

(ii) the proportion of the cost of remediation which the appropriate person has to bear would have been significantly less, by virtue of the guidance on apportionment set out in Part 6 of Chapter D.

E.36 Where an appropriate person is making a case for the authority's costs recovery to be waived or reduced by virtue of paragraph E.35 above, the enforcing authority should expect that person to provide evidence that a particular person, who cannot now be found, caused or knowingly permitted the significant pollutant to be in, on or under the land. The enforcing authority should not regard it as sufficient for the appropriate person concerned merely to state that such a person must have existed.

Part 6—Specific considerations applying to Class B persons

E.37 The statutory guidance in this Part sets out specific considerations relating to cost recovery decisions where the appropriate person is a Class

B person, as defined in Chapter D (that is, a person who is liable by virtue or their ownership or occupation of the contaminated land, but who has not caused or knowingly permitted the significant pollutant to be in, on or under the land).

Costs in relation to land values

E.38 In some cases, the costs of remediation may exceed the value of the land in its current use (as defined in Chapter A) after the required remediation has been carried out.

E.39 The enforcing authority should consider waiving or reducing its costs recovery from a Class B person if that person demonstrates to the satisfaction of the authority that the costs of remediation are likely to exceed the value of the land. In this context, the "value" should be taken to be the value that the remediated land would have on the open market, at the time the cost recovery decision is made, disregarding any possible blight arising from the contamination.

E.40 In general, the extent of the waiver or reduction in costs recovery should be sufficient to ensure that the costs of remediation borne by the Class B person do not exceed the value of the land. However, the enforcing authority should seek to recover more of its costs to the extent that the remediation would result in an increase in the value of any other land from which the Class B person would benefit.

Precautions taken before acquiring a freehold or a leasehold interest

E.41 In some cases, the appropriate person may have been reckless as to the possibility that land he has acquired may be contaminated, or he may have decided to take a risk that the land was not contaminated. On the other hand, he may have taken precautions to ensure that he did not acquire land which is contaminated.

E.42 The authority should consider reducing its costs recovery where a Class B person who is the owner of the land demonstrates to the satisfaction of the authority that:

(a) he took such steps prior to acquiring the freehold, or accepting the grant of assignment of a leasehold, as would have been reasonable at that time to establish the presence of any pollutants;

(b) when he acquired the land, or accepted the grant of assignment of the leasehold, he was nonetheless unaware of the presence of the significant pollutant now identified and could not reasonably have been expected to have been aware of their presence; and

(c) it would be fair and reasonable, taking into account the interests of national and local taxpayers, that he should not bear the whole cost of remediation.

E.43 The enforcing authority should bear in mind that the safeguards which might reasonably be expected to be taken will be different in different types of transaction (for example, acquisition of recreational land as compared with commercial land transactions) and as between buyers of different types (for example, private individuals as compared with major commercial undertakings).

Owner-occupiers of dwellings

E.44 Where a Class B person owns and occupies a dwelling on the contaminated land in question, the enforcing authority should consider waiving or reducing its costs recovery where that person satisfies the authority that, at the time the person purchased the dwelling, he did not know, and could not reasonably have been expected to have known, that the land was adversely affected by presence of a pollutant.

E.45 Any such waiver or reduction should be to the extent needed to ensure that the Class B person in question bears no more of the cost of remediation than it appears reasonable to impose, having regard to his income, capital and outgoings. Where the appropriate person has inherited the dwelling or received it as a gift, the approach in paragraph E.44 above should be applied with respect to the time at which he received the property.

E.46 Where the contaminated land in question extends beyond the dwelling and its curtilage, and is owned or occupied by the same appropriate person, the approach in paragraph E.44 above should be applied only to the dwelling and its curtilage.

The housing renewal grant analogy

E.47 In judging the extent of a waiver or reduction in costs recovery from an owner-occupier of a dwelling, an enforcing authority which is a local authority may wish to apply an approach analogous to that used for applications for housing renovation grant (HRG). These grants are assessed on a means-tested basis, as presently set out in the Housing Renewal Grants Regulations 1996 (S.I. 1996/2890, as amended). The HRG test determines how much a person should contribute towards the cost of necessary renovation work for which they are responsible, taking into account income, capital and outgoings, including allowances for those with particular special needs.

E.48 The HRG approach can be applied as if the appropriate person were applying for HRG and the authority had decided that the case was appropriate for grant assessment. Using this analogy, the authority would conclude that costs recovery should be waived or reduced to the extent that the appropriate person contributes no more than if the work were house renovations for which HRG was being sought. For this purpose, any upper limits for grants payable under HRG should be ignored.

E.49 Where the Environment Agency is the enforcing authority, it should seek to be consistent with the local authority in whose area the contaminated land in question is situated. The Environment Agency should therefore consult the local authority, and should take that authority's views into consideration in making its own cost recovery decision.

Annex 4 Guide to the contaminated land (England) regulations 2006

Introduction

1 This annex provides additional material to help with the understanding of the Contaminated Land (England) Regulations 2006 (S.I. 2006/1380), which are referred to in it as "the Contaminated Land Regulations". The Regulations replace in their entirety the earlier Contaminated Land (England) Regulations 2000, but the differences are relatively minor, and these are included in the description that follows.

2 Cross-references to the other parts of this Circular help to show how the Contaminated Land Regulations relate to the rest of the contaminated land regime.

3 The Contaminated Land Regulations should always be consulted for the precise legal requirements and meanings. What follows is merely an informal guide.

4 The Contaminated Land Regulations set out detailed provisions on parts of the regime which Part 2A of the Environmental Protection Act 1990 leaves to be specified in secondary legislation. In addition to the necessary general provisions, the Regulations deal with five main subjects:

(a) special sites (see paragraphs 7 to 16 below);
(b) remediation notices (see paragraphs 17 to 20 below);
(c) compensation (see in paragraphs 21 to 38 below);
(d) appeals (see paragraphs 39 to 70 below); and
(e) public registers (see in paragraphs 71 to 92 below).

General provisions

5 Regulation 1 contains the usual provisions on citation and references. Any reference to a numbered "section" in this guide refers to that section in Part 2A of the Environmental Protection Act 1990.

6 Since the primary legislation applies to the whole of Great Britain, regulation 1 specifically provides that these regulations apply only to England. The Scottish Executive and the National Assembly for Wales are responsible for any provision made for Scotland or Wales.

Special sites

7 Section 78C(8) provides that land is to be a special site if it is land of a description prescribed in regulations. Regulations 2 and 3, with Schedule 1, provide the necessary descriptions. The procedures related to special sites are described in section 18 of Annex 2 to this Circular.

8 There are four main groups of cases where a description of land is prescribed for this purpose. The individual descriptions of land to be designated are contained in paragraphs (a) to (1) of regulation 2(1). If land is contaminated land and it falls within one of the descriptions, it must be designated as a special site. Otherwise, it cannot be so

designated. The descriptions of land do not imply that land of that type is more likely to constitute contaminated land. They identify cases where, *if* the land is contaminated land, the Environment Agency is best placed to be the enforcing authority.

Water-pollution cases

9 Regulations 2(1)(a) and 3 ensure that the Environment Agency becomes the enforcing authority in three types of case where the contaminated land is affecting controlled waters and their quality, and where the Environment Agency will also have other concerns under other legislation. These cases are set out in regulation 3, and are broadly as follows:

(a) *Wholesomeness of drinking water*: Regulation 3(a) covers cases where contaminated land affects controlled waters used, or intended to be used, for the supply of drinking water. To meet the description, the waters must be affected by the land in such a way that a treatment process or a change in treatment process is needed in order for such water to satisfy wholesomeness requirements. The standards of wholesomeness are currently set out in relation to England in the Water Supply (Water Quality) Regulations 2000 (S.I. 2000/3184 as amended by S.I. 2001/2885) and in relation to Wales in the Water Supply (Water Quality) Regulations 2001 (S.I. 2001/3911), and the Private Water Supplies Regulations 1991 (S.I. 1991/2790). An intention to use water for the supply of drinking water would be demonstrated by the existence of a water abstraction licence for that purpose, or an application for such a licence.

(b) *Surface-water classification criteria*: Regulation 3(b) covers cases where controlled waters are being affected so that those waters do not meet or are not likely to meet relevant surface water criteria. These are currently set out in four sets of Surface Waters (Dangerous Substances) (Classification) Regulations: S.I. 1989/2286, S.I. 1992/337, S.I. 1997/2560 and S.I. 1998/389.

(c) *Major aquifers*: Regulation 3(c) covers cases where particularly difficult pollutants are affecting major aquifers. The Environment Agency will already be concerned both with pollutants of this type and with managing water resources. The list of pollutants is set out in paragraph 1 of Schedule 1. It corresponds to List I of the Groundwater Directive (80/86/EEC). The major aquifers are described in paragraph 2 of Schedule 1 by reference to the underground strata in which they are contained. The British Geological Survey publishes maps which show the location and boundaries of such strata.

10 For the purposes of regulation 3(c), the fact that contaminated land may be located over one of the listed underground strata does not by itself make the land a special site. The land must be contaminated land on the basis that it is causing, or is likely to cause, pollution of controlled waters; the pollution must be by reason of one or more substances from Schedule 1; and the waters being or likely to be polluted must be contained within the strata.

Industrial cases

11 The subsequent items in regulation 2(1) ensure that the Environment Agency is the enforcing agency in respect of contaminated land which is,

or has been, used as a site for industrial activities that either pose special remediation problems or are subject to regulation under other national systems, either by the Environment Agency itself, or by some other national agency. The designation of such sites as special sites is intended to deploy the necessary expertise and to help co-ordination between the various regulatory systems. The descriptions are in respect of:

(a) *Waste acid tar lagoons (regulation 2(1)(b)*: Regulation 2(2) defines what falls into this description. The retention basins (or lagoons) concerned typically involve cases where waste acid tar arose from the use of concentrated sulphuric acid in the production of lubricating oils and greases or the reclamation of base lubricants from mineral oil residues. The description is not intended to include cases where the tars resulted from coal product manufacture, or where these tars were placed in pits or wells.

(b) *Oil refining (regulation 2(1)(c)(i))*: The problems resulting from this are again considered more appropriate for the expertise of the Environment Agency. As for waste acid tar lagoons, activities related to coal are not included.

(c) *Explosives (regulation 2(1)(c)(ii))*: The relatively few sites in this category pose specific problems, which are more appropriately handled by the Environment Agency.

(d) *IPC (Integrated Pollution Control) sites (regulation 2(1)(d))*: Sites which are regulated under Part 1 of the 1990 Act and which have become contaminated will generally be regulated under those powers. But there may be situations where Part 2A powers will be needed. This item ensures that the Environment Agency will be the enforcing authority under Part 2A where it is already the regulatory authority under Part 1. The description therefore refers to a "prescribed process designated for central control". In England, this means a Part A process. This description covers:-

    (i) land on which past activities were authorised under "central control" but which have ceased;

    (ii) land where the activities are continuing but the contamination arises from a non-"central control" process on the land; and

    (iii) land where the contamination arises from an authorised "central control" process but a remediation notice could nevertheless be served. (Section 78YB(1) precludes the service of a remediation notice in cases where it appears to the authority that the powers in section 27 of the 1990 Act may be exercised.)

This description does not cover land where the Part 1 authorisation is obtained in order to carry out remediation required under Part 2A. It also does not cover land which has been contaminated by an activity which ceased before the application of "central controls", but would have been subject to those controls if it had continued after they came into force.

(e) *PPC (Pollution Prevention and Control) sites (regulation 2(1)(e))*: sites which are regulated under the Pollution Prevention and Control Act 2000 which have become contaminated will generally be regulated under those powers. But there may be situations where Part 2A powers will be needed. This item ensures that the Environment Agency will be the enforcing authority under Part 2A where it is already the regulatory authority under PPC. The description therefore refers to a "activity which has been carried on in a Part A(1) installation or by means of a mobile plant under a permit". This description covers:-

   (i) land on which past activities were authorised under a PPC permit but which have ceased;

  (ii) land where the activities are continuing but the contamination arises from an activity on the land but not subject to permitting under PPC; and

 (iii) land where the contamination arises from a permitted activity but a remediation notice could nevertheless be served. (Section 78YB(2A) and (2B) preclude the service of a remediation notice in cases where it appears to the authority that enforcement action under the Pollution Prevention and Control (England and Wales) Regulations may be taken.)

This description does not cover land where the PPC permit is obtained in order to carry out remediation required under Part 2A. It also does not cover land which has been contaminated by an activity which ceased before the application of PPC Part A(1) controls, but would have been subject to those controls if it had continued after they came into force.

 (f) *Nuclear sites (regulation 2(1)(f))*: Regulation 2(5) defines what is to be treated as a nuclear site for this purpose.

Defence cases

12 Regulation 2(1)(g), (i) and (j) ensures that the Environment Agency deals with most cases where contaminated land involves the Ministry of Defence (MOD) estate. Broadly speaking, the descriptions include any contaminated land at current military, naval and airforce bases and other properties, including those of visiting forces; the Atomic Weapons Establishment; and certain lands at Greenwich Hospital (section 30 of the Armed Forces Act 1996). However, off-base housing or off-base NAAFI premises are not included, and nor is property which has been disposed of to civil ownership or occupation. Training areas and ranges that MOD does not own or occupy but may use occasionally do not fall within the descriptions. Regulation 2(1)(h) describes land formerly used for the manufacture, production or disposal of chemical and biological weapons and related materials, regardless of current ownership. In all these cases, the Environment Agency is best placed to ensure uniformity across the country and liaison with the Ministry of Defence and the armed forces.

Radioactivity cases

13 Regulation 2(1)(k) is new and ensures that the Environment Agency deals with cases where the land is contaminated land by virtue of any radioactivity possessed by any substances. This recognises the special case of such contaminants, and the availability of expertise in radioactive substances to the Environment Agency.

Other aspects of special sites

14 *Adjoining/adjacent land (regulation 2(1)(l)*: Where the conditions on a special site lead to adjacent or adjoining land also being contaminated land by

reason of the presence of substances which appear to have escaped from the special site, that adjacent or adjoining land is also to be a special site. This does not apply where the special site is one of the water-pollution cases described in regulations 2(1)(a) and 3. With this exception, the Environment Agency will be the enforcing authority for the adjoining land as well as for the special site that has caused the problem. This approach is intended to avoid regulatory control being split.

15 *Waste management sites*: Land used for waste management activity, such as landfill, is not as such designated as a special site. This is because Part 2 of the 1990 Act and the PPC regime already contains wide powers for the Environment Agency to ensure that problems are tackled. However, such land may fall within one or more of the special site descriptions, for example if pollution of controlled waters is being caused. The interface between Part 2A controls and waste management controls is described at Annex 1, paragraphs 51 to 54.

16 *Role of the Environment Agency*: It remains the task of the local authority to decide, in the first instance, whether land within the description of a special site is contaminated land or not. The work of the Environment Agency as enforcing authority only starts once that determination is made, However, the statutory guidance on the identification of contaminated land says that, in inspecting the land using their powers of entry under s108 of the Environment Act 1995, local authorities should consider whether, if land were determined as contaminated land, it would be a special site. If that is the case, the local authority should always seek to make arrangements with the Environment Agency to carry out any inspections of the land that may be needed, on behalf of the local authority (see Annex 3, paragraphs B.26 to B.30). In the case of land contaminated with radioactivity, the local authority should always seek to make arrangements with the Environment Agency for any intrusive investigation, whether or not section 108 powers are to be used. In addition, in the case of land contaminated with radioactivity, the statutory guidance requires that the Environment Agency is consulted on the draft record of determination.

Remediation notices

17 Section 78E(1) requires a remediation notice to specify what each person who is an appropriate person to bear responsibility for remediation is to do by way of remediation and the timescale for that remediation. Where several people are appropriate persons, section 78E(3) requires the remediation notice to state the proportion which each of them is to bear of the costs of that remediation (see Chapter D of Annex 3). Section 78E(6) then provides that regulations may lay down other requirements on the form and content of remediation notices and the associated procedure.

18 Regulation 4 sets out the **additional** requirements about the content of a remediation notice. The overall intention is to make the notice informative and self-contained. There should be a clear indication of what is to be done; by whom; where; by when; in relation to what problem; the basis for the authority's actions; who else is involved; the rights of appeal; that a notice is suspended if there is an appeal; and other key information.

Copying remediation notices to others

19 As well as serving the remediation notice on the appropriate person or persons, regulation 5 requires the enforcing authority at the same time as

it serves a remediation notice on the appropriate person(s), to send a copy of the notice to:

(a) anyone whom the authority considers to be the owner or occupier of any of the relevant land or waters, and whom they have therefore consulted under section 78G(3)(a) about rights that may need to be granted to enable the work to be done;

(b) anyone whom the authority considers will be required to grant rights over the land or waters to enable the work to be done, and whom they have therefore consulted under section 78G(3)(b) about such rights;

(c) anyone whom the authority considers to be the owner or occupier of any of the land to which the notice relates and whom they have therefore consulted under section 78H(1)about the remediation to be required; and

(d) the Environment Agency where the local authority is the enforcing authority or the local authority where the Environment Agency is the enforcing authority.

20 It will be good practice for the authority to indicate to the recipient in which capacity they are being sent a copy of the notice. Where a remediation notice is served without consultation because of imminent danger of serious harm (see sections 78G(4) and 78H(4)), the copies should be sent to those who would have been consulted if there had not been an emergency.

Compensation for rights of entry etc

21 Under section 78G(2), any person (the "grantor") whose consent is required before any thing required by a remediation notice may be done must grant (or join in granting) the necessary rights in relation to land or waters. For example, an appropriate person may be required to carry out remediation actions upon land which he does not own, perhaps because it has been sold since he caused or knowingly permitted its contamination. Another example may be where access to adjoining land owned or occupied by the grantor's land is needed to carry out the necessary works.

22 The rights that the grantor must grant (or join in granting) are not some special statutory right, but a licence or similar permission of the kind which any person would need to enter on land which they do not own or occupy and carry out works on it.

23 Regulation 6 and Schedule 2 set out a code for compensation payable to those who are required to grant such rights and who thereby suffer detriment. The provisions are closely modelled on those which apply for compensation payable in relation to works required in connection with waste management licences.

Applications for compensation

24 Under paragraph 2 of Schedule 2, applications must be made by grantors within:

(a) twelve months of the date of the grant of any rights;

(b) twelve months of the final determination or abandonment of an appeal, or

(c) six months of the first exercise of the rights,

whichever is the latest.

25 Paragraph 3 requires applications to be made in writing and delivered at or sent by pre paid post to the last known address of the appropriate person to whom the rights were granted. They must include a copy of the grant of rights and any plans attached to it; a description of the exact nature of any interest in the land concerned; and a statement of the amount being claimed, distinguishing between each of the descriptions of loss or damage in the Regulations and showing how each amount has been calculated.

26 Paragraph 4 of the Schedule sets out the various descriptions of loss or damage for which compensation may be claimed. Distinctions are drawn between the grantor's land out of which the rights are granted, any other land of the grantor which might be affected, and other forms of loss. They can be summarised broadly as:

(a) *depreciation*: depreciation in the value of

(i) any relevant interest (that is, the interest in land as a result of holding which the grantor is able to make the grant) which results from the *grant* of the rights; or

(ii) any other interest in land, which results from the *exercise* of the rights;

(b) *disturbance*: loss or damage sustained in relation to the grantor's relevant interest, equivalent to the compensation for "disturbance" under compulsory purchase legislation; this might arise where for example there was damage to the land itself or things on it as a consequence of the exercise of the rights, or a loss of income or a loss of profits resulted from the grant of the right or its exercise;

(c) *injurious affection*: damage to or injurious affection of the grantor's interest in any other land (that is, land not subject to the grant of rights); this again is analogous to the compensation for "injurious affection" under compulsory-purchase legislation; this might arise where the works on the contaminated land had some permanent adverse effect on adjoining land; and

(d) *abortive work*: loss in respect of carried out by, or on behalf of, the grantor which is rendered abortive as result of the grant or the work done under it; this might arise where, for example, access to a newly erected building on the land was no longer possible after the grant of the rights, so that the building could no longer be used (paragraph 5(4) of Schedule 2 ensures that this can include expenditure on drawing up plans etc).

Professional fees

27 Compensation can also be claimed for any reasonable expenses incurred in getting valuations or carrying out legal work in order to make or pursue the application itself (paragraph 5(6) of Schedule 2).

Rules for assessing compensation

28 Paragraph 5 of Schedule 2 ensures that the basic rules in section 5 of the Land Compensation Act 1961 apply to these cases. In particular, this section indicates what is meant by "value" when assessing depreciation.

29 To guard against the possibility of unnecessary things being done on land in order to claim or inflate compensation, paragraph 5(3) requires the value of such things to be ignored in assessing compensation.

Position of mortgagees

30 There may be cases where mortgagees join in with mortgagors in the grant of rights, or grant such rights themselves. This might be because they are a mortgagee in possession, or they may have reserved the right to join in the grant of any rights. In these cases, mortgagees fall within section 78G(5) and are able to obtain compensation in their own right.

31 The effect of paragraph 6(1) of Schedule 2 is that in all cases where there is a mortgage, the compensation is paid to the mortgagee (to the first one, if there *are* several mortgagees), but that it is then applied as if it were the proceeds of sale. This ensures that the mortgagor, or any other mortgagee, will get any appropriate share. Paragraph 5(5) prevents two payments of compensation (i.e. one each to mortgagee and owner) for the same interest in land.

Disputes

32 Disputes about compensation may be referred, by either party, to the Lands Tribunal (paragraph 6(3)). The Tribunal's procedure rules (S.I. 1996/1022) enable the Tribunal, with the consent of the parties, to determine a case on the basis of written representations, without the need for an oral hearing (rule 27). Rule 28 provides for a simplified procedure aimed at enabling certain cases to be dealt with speedily and at minimum expense to the parties. In such cases, the hearing takes place before a single Member of the Tribunal acting as arbitrator. Parties may in straightforward cases, and with the Tribunal's permission, be represented at hearings by a non-lawyer, such as a professional valuer.

Payment

33 Payments are to be made on the date or dates agreed by the parties (paragraph 6(2)) or as soon as practicable after the determination in cases where there is a dispute.

Interest

34 Interest may be payable on compensation, for example where applications take a long time to resolve. The Planning and Compensation Act 1991 makes provision for the calculation of interest on compensation. This has been applied to compensation applications made under the Contaminated Land Regulations by an Order amending Schedule 18 of the 1991 Act (The Planning and Compensation Act 1991 (Amendment of Schedule 18) (England) Order 2002 (S.I. 2002/116). This also provides the date from which interest is to be payable for the various types of compensation.

Other cases

35 Compensation under Part 2A is not available for any loss resulting from remediation work other than in relation to the heads of compensation

specified in the Contaminated Land Regulations. Nor is it available in cases where there is no remediation notice—for example where remediation is carried out voluntarily, without a remediation notice being served. In such cases, there is no requirement for the grant of rights: any rights that are needed must be acquired by negotiation in the usual way.

36 Where a local authority exercises powers of entry under section 108 of the Environment Act 1995 in connection with its contaminated land functions, the relevant compensation provisions are those at Schedule 18 of the 1995 Act.

Role of the enforcing authority

37 Arrangements for compensation under Part 2A are a matter for the grantor and the appropriate persons concerned, and the enforcing authority is not involved. However, it is required to consult those who may have to grant rights and to send them a copy of the remediation notice (see paragraph 19(b) above).

38 In addition, it is good practice for authorities to let those who they have consulted because they may be required to grant rights to the appropriate person(s) know the final outcome of the determination of any appeal against the remediation notice, so that they are alerted to the need to be ready to apply for compensation.

Appeals against remediation notices

39 Remediation notices must include information on the right to appeal against them (see paragraph 18 above). The arrangements for appeals are changed by these Contaminated Land Regulations. In particular, appeals will no longer be made to magistrates. This section of the guide shows how the provisions in Part 2A fit together with the provisions in regulations 7 to 12 and the normal practice of the Department for Environment, Food and Rural Affairs.

Matters affecting appeals generally

Time-limit for appeals

40 Any appeal must be made within twenty-one days of receiving the remediation notice (*section 78L(1)*). There is no provision for extending this time-limit.

The grounds for appeal

41 Any appeal against a remediation notice must be made on one or more of the grounds set out in regulation 7(1). In broad terms, the grounds concern the following matters:

(a) whether the land is contaminated land as defined; this ground may arise either because of failure to act in accordance with the statutory guidance in Chapters A and B of Annex 3 or because the identification is otherwise unreasonable;

(b) what is required to be done by way of remediation; this ground may arise either because of failure to have regard to the statutory guidance in Chapter C of Annex 3 or because the requirements are otherwise unreasonable;

(c) whether an appellant is an appropriate person to bear responsibility for a remediation action; section 78F is relevant;

(d) whether someone else is also an appropriate person for a remediation action; section 78F is relevant; under this ground, the appellant must claim either to have found someone else who has caused or knowingly permitted the pollution or that someone else is also an owner or occupier of all or part of the land;

(e) whether the appellant should have been excluded from responsibility for a remediation action; this ground may arise because of failure to act in accordance with the statutory guidance in Chapter D of Annex 3;

(f) the proportion of cost to be borne by the appellant; this ground may arise either because of failure to act in accordance with the statutory guidance in Chapter D of Annex 3 or because the determination of the appellant's share is otherwise unreasonable;

(g) whether the notice complies with restrictions in the Act on the serving of notices; section 78H(1) and (3) is relevant;

(h) whether the case is one of imminent danger of serious harm from the contaminated land; section 78H(4) is relevant;

(i) whether remediation is taking, or will take, place without a remediation notice; section 78H(5) of the Act is relevant;

(j) whether remediation requirements breach restrictions on liability for pollution of controlled waters; section 78J is relevant;

(k) whether remediation requirements breach restrictions on liability relating to escaping substances; section 78K is relevant;

(l) whether the authority has itself agreed to carry out the remediation at the cost of the person served with the remediation notice; section 78N(3)(b) of the Act is relevant;

(m) whether the authority should have decided that the recipient of the remediation notice would benefit from waiver or reduction of cost recovery on grounds of hardship or in line with the statutory guidance in Chapter E of Annex 3, that it therefore had power itself to carry out the remediation and that it was thus precluded from serving a remediation notice; sections 78N(3)(e) and 78P(1) and (2) are relevant;

(n) whether the authority's powers to remediate were exercisable because this was a case where hardship or the statutory guidance in Chapter E of Annex 3 should lead to a waiver or reduction in cost recovery; this ground may arise either because of failure to have regard to hardship or the statutory guidance in Chapter E or because the decision was otherwise unreasonable; sections 78N(3)(e) and 78P(1) and (2) are relevant;

(o) whether regard was had to site-specific guidance from the Environment Agency; section 78V(1) is relevant;

(p) whether enough time was allowed for remediation; the statutory guidance in Chapter C of Annex 3 to this Circular may be relevant;

(q) whether the notice would make an insolvency practitioner, an official receiver or other receiver or manager personally liable in breach of the limits on such liability; section 78X(3)(a) and (4) is relevant;

(r) whether certain powers under the Integrated Pollution Control system (Part 1 of the Environmental Protection Act 1990) or under the waste management licensing system (Part 2 of that Act) were available to the authority; section 78YB(1), (2A), (2B) (3) and (5) are relevant; the powers concerned are those in section 27 (Part 1) and section 59 (Part 2); and

(s) whether there is some informality, defect or error concerning the notice, not covered above; in an appeal on this ground, the Secretary of State must dismiss the appeal if he is satisfied that the informality, defect or error was not a material one.

Suspension of remediation notice upon appeal

42 Once an appeal has been duly made, the remediation notice concerned is suspended (regulation 12). It remains suspended either until the appeal is finally determined or is withdrawn (abandoned) by the appellant. "Duly made" for this purpose means that an appeal must be made within the time limit, and in accordance with the Contaminated Land Regulations.

Appeals

43 Regulation 8 of the 2000 Contaminated Land Regulations dealt with the procedures for appeals to a magistrates' court. This procedure applied in cases where the remediation notice in question had been served by a local authority. Section 108 of the Clean Neighbourhoods and Environment Act 2005 provides that all appeals against remediation notices are to be made to the Secretary of State. This change takes effect at the same time as the 2006 Contaminated Land Regulations come into force, and applies to all remediation notices served on or after that date. Any earlier remediation notices will remain subject to the previous arrangements, details of which can be found in the former DETR Circular 02/2000.

44 Regulation 8 of the 2006 Contaminated Land Regulations sets out the revised arrangements for appeals. All appeals are to the Secretary of State for the Environment, Food and Rural Affairs.

45 The appellant must appeal by submitting a "notice of appeal" to the Secretary of State. No particular form is prescribed for such a notice of appeal but, in accordance with regulation 8, it must state:

(a) the appellant's name and address;

(b) the grounds of appeal; and

(c) whether the appellant wishes the appeal to be in the form of a hearing, or alternatively have the appeal decided on the basis of written representations.

46 The appellant must at the same time serve a copy of the notice of appeal on

(a) the enforcing authority;

(b) any other appropriate person named in the remediation notice;

(c) any person who is named in the appeal as an appropriate person; this relates to appeal ground (d);

(d) any person named in the remediation notice as the owner or occupier of the land.

47 The appellant must also send to the Secretary of State

(a) a list of the names and addresses of the above persons; these will normally be found in the remediation notice, except for details of any additional person named in the appeal as an appropriate person; and

(b) a copy of the remediation notice.

48 The appellant must also (because they will not have had it previously) serve a copy of the remediation notice on any person named in the appeal as an appropriate person, or as an owner or occupier, who was not named as such in that remediation notice.

49 Appeals to the Secretary of State should be submitted to the Planning Inspectorate. Their current address and telephone number are as follows:

The Planning Inspectorate
Room 4/12 Eagle Wing
Temple Quay House
2 The Square
Temple Quay
BRISTOL BS1 6PN

Tel: 0117 372 8726
Fax: 0117 372 8139
E-mail: environment.appeals@pins.gsi.gov.uk

Initial procedure on an appeal to the Secretary of State

50 Within 14 days of receiving a copy of the notice of appeal, the enforcing authority will notify all others whom the appellant was required to send a copy of the appeal. This notification will ensure that they know there is an appeal, and will make them aware that:

(a) written representations to the Secretary of State may be made within 21 days from the receipt of the enforcing authority's notice;

(b) such representations will be copied to the appellant and the enforcing authority; and

(c) those who make representations will be informed about any public hearing.

51 All written representations made to the Secretary of State at any time throughout the appeal should be dated with the date on which they are submitted.

Delegation to inspectors

52 Most cases will be decided by Inspectors appointed on the Secretary of State's behalf, under the provisions of section 78L(6) which allow for appeal decisions to be delegated to them. References to the Secretary of State in the procedures set out below may be taken to include the inspector, except where the context indicates otherwise.

53 Some cases may, however, be recovered for decision by the Secretary of State. In these "recovered" cases, the Secretary of State will determine the appeal on the basis of a written report from the inspector. In accordance with regulation 9(5), this report must contain conclusions and recommendations, or reasons for not making recommendations.

54 Each appeal will be looked at individually to decide whether it should be "recovered". The categories most likely to be recovered are as follows:

(a) cases involving sites of major importance or having more than local significance;

(b) cases giving rise to significant local controversy;

(c) cases which raise significant legal difficulties; and

(d) cases which raise major, novel issues and which could therefore set a precedent.

55 Other appeal cases may on occasion merit being "recovered" for decision by the Secretary of State.

Deciding an appeal to the Secretary of State

56 A hearing will be arranged if either of the parties asks for that to be done. Otherwise, the appeal will be decided on the basis of written representations, unless the Secretary of State decides, in accordance with regulation 9, that it is desirable to hold a hearing or a public local inquiry.

Written representations

57 If the appeal is being decided by written representations, the procedure will normally run in the spirit of the Town & Country Planning (Appeals) (Written Representations Procedure) (England) Regulations 2000 (S.I. 2000/1628) with further guidance in Annex 1 of DETR Circular 05/2000 *"Planning Appeals: Procedures (Including Inquiries into Called-in Planning Applications)"*. In general the procedure will be as follows:-

Step 1

The Secretary of State will invite the enforcing authority to respond to the grounds of appeal; to provide any other information that it relies on to support its decision to serve the remediation notice within 28 days; and to send the appellant, and any other appropriate person on whom the notice was served, a copy of its response at the same time as it is submitted to the Secretary of State.

Step 2

The appellant, and any other appropriate person on whom the notice was served, will then be given an opportunity to comment on the representations from the enforcing authority. These should be made within 14 days of the date of submission of the authority's representations and must be copied to the authority and any appropriate person on whom the notice was served, at the same time. The Secretary of State will also send to the appellant, any other appropriate person on whom the notice was served and the enforcing authority copies of the representations received under regulation 9 (other than the copy of the enforcing authority response mentioned in step 1 above, which will already have been copied to the appellant and any other appropriate person on whom the notice was served). The Secretary of State will seek their comments, which should also be given within 14 days.

Step 3

Arrangements will be made for an Inspector to visit the appeal site. As far as possible, a mutually convenient time will be arranged. The enforcing authority, the appellant and any other person sent a copy of the notice of appeal under regulation 8(2) will be invited to attend. No representations about the appeal can be made during the visit but must be made in writing under the procedures for making representations and within the appropriate time limits.

58 This procedure is intended to allow the determination of appeals as expeditiously as possible. However, the Secretary of State may in certain exceptional cases set time limits which differ from those above, or may extend a time limit either before or after it has expired. The Secretary of State may also request exchanges of information in addition to those mentioned above.

Hearings

59 Where an appeal is to be decided after a hearing, in accordance with regulation 9(1)–(3), the procedures will follow in the spirit of the Town & Country Planning (Hearings Procedure) (England) Rules 2000 (S.I. 200/1626) adhering to the principles laid out in Annex 2 of DETR Circular 05/2000. The appellant, the enforcing authority and those required to be sent a copy of the notice of appeal under regulation 8(2) will be invited to make representations at the hearing. Other persons may be heard at the discretion of the Inspector. The enforcing authority will inform other persons of the date of the hearing where they have previously expressed an interest in the case.

60 A pre-hearing timetable will be provided for the submission of written statements. Failure to provide this information, within the specified timescales, could lead to hearings being adjourned resulting in unnecessary delays. The conduct of the hearing will be for the Inspector to determine, and will follow the Procedure at the Hearing given at Annex 2(ii) of DOE Circular 05/2000. It may sometimes be necessary to hold a pre-hearing meeting to discuss the nature of the evidence to be given, who is likely to participate and the programme to be adopted.

61 The presumption is that hearings will be held in public. However, a hearing, or any part of it, may be held in private if the Inspector hearing the appeal decides that there are particular and special grounds for doing so, such as reasons of commercial confidentiality, or national security.

Public inquiries

62 The holding of a public local inquiry under regulation 9(1)(b) is expected to be more appropriate for particularly complex or locally controversial cases. A pre-inquiry timetable will be provided for the submission of statements and proofs of evidence. It is important that this is adhered to. Inquiry proceedings are more formal in nature than the majority of hearings. Inquiries will be conducted in accordance with the spirit of The Town & Country Planning Appeals (Determination by Inspectors) (Inquiries Procedure) (England) Rules 2000 (S.I. 2000/1625) for appeals decided by an appointed Inspector and The Town & Country Planning (Inquiries Procedure) (England) Rules 2000 (S.I. 2000/1624) for appeals 'Recovered' for determination by the Secretary of State himself. Further guidance can be found in Annex 3 of DETR Circular 05/2000. The rules require details of the inquiry to be posted locally. As in the case of hearings, it may sometimes be necessary to hold a pre-inquiry meeting.

Abandonment of appeals

63 An appellant who wishes to abandon (withdraw) an appeal must notify the Secretary of State in writing, who will in turn notify all those who have received notice of the appeal in accordance with regulation 8(2) and (5). The appeal is deemed to be abandoned on the day the Secretary of State receives the notice of the abandonment. Abandonment may be refused by the Secretary of State under regulation 8(4) if the appellant has been notified of a modification to the remediation notice under regulation 11.

Notification of appeal decision

64 Regulation 10 requires that the appellant must be notified in writing of the decision on the appeal, and sent a copy of any report made to the

Secretary of State by an inspector. The decision letter, and the report if any, must be copied by the Secretary of State to the enforcing authority and to anyone who was entitled to receive a copy of the notice of the appeal.

65 Details of decision letters on cases will be placed on the register. As long as they do not contain confidential information or trade secrets, copies will also be available for a small charge from the Planning Inspectorate. Further information can also be obtained from the same source.

Award of costs

66 Costs may be awarded where there is a hearing or a public local inquiry. Awards of costs will follow existing general guidance in Department of the Environment Circular 8/93, which governs planning appeals and similar cases. This means that each party will bear their own costs unless there has been unreasonable behaviour leading to unnecessary expense, as described in that Circular. In cases decided by written representations, the parties must meet their own expenses.

Appeals or complaints against the decision

67 There is no statutory right of appeal against a decision made on appeal by the Secretary of State. Once a decision letter has been issued, the decision is final, and the Secretary of State and the inspector can no longer consider any representations or make any further comments on the merits or otherwise of the case. A party to the appeal may be able to seek judicial review of the decision in the High Court. If they consider that there has been maladministration in reaching the decision, they may also ask an MP to take up the matter with the Parliamentary Commissioner for Administration (the Ombudsman), though the Ombudsman cannot re-open the appeal.

68 If anyone has a complaint about the handling of an appeal by the Planning Inspectorate, they should write to the Complaints Officer at the address shown in paragraph 49 above.

Modification of remediation notices

69 Section 78L(2)(b) enables the Secretary of State to modify the remediation notice which is the subject of the appeal. If he proposes to do so in a way which is less favourable to the appellant, or any other appropriate person on whom the notice was served but who may not have appealed, then regulation 11 applies. The Secretary of State must notify those persons of the proposed modification, and also notify any other persons who were required to be sent a copy of the notice of appeal under regulation 8(2) (see paragraph 45 to 48 above). Any of those persons have a right to make representations. The appellant or any other appropriate person on whom the remediation notice was served has a right to be heard, and if this right to be heard is exercised, the enforcing authority (but no other person) also has the right to be heard. The Secretary of State may refuse to permit an appeal to be withdrawn if he has given notice of a proposed modification (regulation 8(4)).

Additional remediation notices to reflect an appeal decision

70 A decision by the Secretary of State to quash or modify a remediation notice on appeal may also have implications for a person who has not

been served with a remediation notice. This might arise where, in particular, an appeal succeeds on the grounds that there is another person who should be held liable instead of or as well as the appellant. In such cases the enforcing authority will need to consider serving a further remediation notice(s) which take(s) into account the appellate authority's decision. Such additional notices would need to fulfil all the relevant requirements of the Act, regulations, and the statutory guidance, in the usual way. They would attract the normal rights of appeal.

Public registers

71 Section 78R requires each enforcing authority to keep a public register. The public register is intended to act as a full and permanent record, open for public inspection, of all regulatory action taken by the enforcing authority in respect of the remediation of contaminated land, and will include information about the condition of land.

72 As records of regulatory activity, registers are broadly similar in purpose to, and part of the suite of, registers kept in relation to other environmental protection controls, including those kept under Part 1 and Part 2 of the Act (IPC etc, and waste regulation); and planning registers kept under the Town and Country Planning Acts, which may also contain valuable information relevant to the condition of land in particular locations.

73 The Agency register is to be kept at the Agency office for the area in question, and the local authority register is kept at the authority's principal office (regulation 13).

Content of the registers

74 Section 78R(1) specifies what material is to be entered on the register. It leaves the details of that material to be prescribed in regulations. These details are set out in Schedule 3.

75 It is good practice to ensure that the register is so organised that all the entries relating to a particular site can be readily consulted in connection with each other.

76 Schedule 3 requires registers to include full particulars of certain matters, rather than copies of the various forms of notice and other documents listed. However, there is no legal objection to authorities placing a copy of the various documents on the register. Any document not placed on the register may, in any case, be accessible under the Environmental Information Regulations 2004 (S.I. 2004/339).

Information to be placed on the register

Information about remediation

77 For a *remediation notice*, the effect of regulation 13 and Schedule 3 is that the following information must be placed on the register:

Site information
(a) the location and extent of the contaminated land sufficient to enable it to be identified; this requirement would ideally be met by

showing its address and the estimated area in hectares, together with a plan to a suitable scale and a National Grid reference;

(b) the significant harm, pollution of controlled waters, or harm attributable to radioactivity by reason of which the land is contaminated land;

(c) the substances by reason of which the land is contaminated land and, if any of the substances have escaped from other land, the location of that other land;

(d) the current use of the land in question;

Remediation information

(e) the name and address of the person on whom the notice is served;

(f) what each appropriate person is to do by way of remediation, and the periods within which they are required to do each of the things;

78 In cases where site investigation reports obtained by or provided to the authority, which relate to the condition of land or any remediation action, are likely to be publicly accessible under the Environmental Information Regulations, it would also be good practice to include a reference to such information. The entry could include:

(a) a description of the information,

(b) the date on which it was prepared,

(c) the person by whom and for whom it was prepared, and

(d) where it is available to be inspected or copied.

79 It is also good practice for the remediation particulars referred to in paragraph 77(f) above to include an indication of whether the action required was "assessment action", "remedial treatment action" or "monitoring action" (see the definitions of these terms in paragraph C.8 above of Chapter C of the statutory guidance, reflecting section 78A(7)).

80 For *remediation declarations, remediation statements* and *notifications of claimed remediation* (that is notifications for the purposes of section 78R(1)(h) or (j)), the requirement is to enter full particulars of the instrument in question, together with the site information described at paragraphs 77(a)-(d) above. This means that the registers should show, in addition to the date of the instrument and the site information, at least:

(a) for *remediation declarations* (see paragraphs 4 and 5 of Schedule 3): the reason why the authority was precluded from specifying a particular remediation action (where, therefore, in the case of pollution of controlled waters, the authority considered that remediation of pollution was precluded on the basis that it would be unreasonable, having regard to the nature of that pollution, the register will show why the authority considered that the contamination was not significant);

(b) for *remediation statements* (see paragraphs 6 and 7 of Schedule 3): the remediation action that has been, is being or will be taken, the timescale for that action and the details of the person who is taking it;

(c) for *notifications of claimed remediation* (see regulation 13(2)) and paragraph 11 of Schedule 3): the remediation action that is claimed to have been taken, the timescale of that action and the details of the person who claims to have taken it.

81 In respect of notifications of claimed remediation, it is open to the person giving the notification to include additional material. In particular, it will be in the interests of both regulators and those giving the notifications to

include, in addition, an indication of what the work carried out was intended to achieve; a description of any appropriate quality assurance procedure adopted relating to what has been claimed to be done; and a description of any verification measures carried out for the purpose of assessing the effectiveness of the remediation in relation to the particular significant harm, pollution of controlled waters or harm attributable to radioactivity to which it was referable.

82 Section 78R(3) makes clear that an entry in the register relating to notifications of claimed remediation in no way represents any endorsement or confirmation by the authority maintaining the register that remediation measures have been carried out nor, therefore, that land is no longer contaminated land. It would be good practice to ensure that this disclaimer is clearly associated with all entries of this kind.

83 *Other environmental controls*: The register is required, by paragraphs 14 and 15 of Schedule 3, to include information in cases of the three situations where a site may be formally identified as contaminated land but is dealt with under certain other controls, instead of under Part 2A (see sections 78YB(1), 78YB(2B) and (3)). These other powers are section 27 in Part 1 of the Environmental Protection Act 1990 (Integrated Pollution Control), enforcement action under Pollution Prevention and Control Regulations and section 59 in Part 2 of the 1990 Act (waste management licensing). In all cases, the register is required to include, in addition to the site information described in paragraphs 77(a)-(d) above particulars of any steps about which the enforcing authority knows that have been taken under those other powers.

84 The register is also required, by paragraph 16 of Schedule 3, to include information about any cases where particular remediation actions cannot be specified in a remediation notice because they would have the effect of interfering with a discharge into controlled waters for which consent has been given under Chapter 2 of Part 3 of the Water Resources Act 1991 (see section 78YB(4)). In addition to the site information described in paragraphs 77(a)-(d) above, the register is required to give particulars of the discharge consent.

Other information

Special sites

85 Where the land is a special site, the register should include the information required in respect of any other site. In addition, under paragraph 10 of Schedule 3, the register is required to include:

(a) the notice designating it as such (given by a local authority under section 78C(1)(b) or 78C(5)(a), or by the Secretary of State under section 78D(4)(b));

(b) an identification of the description of land under which it is a special site (see regulations 2 or 3 and Schedule 1);

(c) any notice given by the appropriate Agency of its decision to adopt a remediation notice;

(d) any notice given by or to the enforcing authority under section 78Q(4) terminating the designation.

Agency site-specific guidance

86 Under paragraph 13 of Schedule 3, the register is required to include the date of any site-specific guidance issued by the Environment Agency

under section 78V(1). Where such site-specific guidance exists, information in it may be required to be available to the public under the Environmental Information Regulations. Where this is likely, it would be good practice to include a reference to where it is available to be inspected or copied.

Appeals against a remediation notice

87 Where a person on whom a remediation notice has been served appeals against that notice, the register is required, under paragraphs 2 and 3 of Schedule 3, to include full particulars of:

    (a) any appeal against a remediation notice, including the date and the name and address of the appellant; and

    (b) the decision on such an appeal.

88 It would also be good practice to include on the register any Court decisions, including an application for judicial review, which may relate to an appeal against a remediation notice.

Appeals against a charging notice

89 Where the owner or occupier of any land appeals to the county court under section 78P(8) against a notice charging costs to be recovered by the enforcing authority on his land, the register is required to contain full particulars of:

    (a) any appeal against a charging notice; including the date and the name and address of the appellant; and

    (b) the decision on such an appeal.

Convictions

90 Under paragraph 12 of Schedule 3, the register is required to include full particulars of any conviction under section 78M (failure to comply with a remediation notice), including the name of the offender, the date of conviction, the penalty imposed, and the name of the Court.

91 Authorities should have regard to the provisions of the Rehabilitation of Offenders Act 1974, under which convictions of individuals can become spent. The Department understands that it would not be unlawful under that Act to retain details of a spent conviction on the register, but nonetheless retention would seem contrary to its spirit. The Department recommends therefore that authorities should regularly review their registers with the aim of identifying and removing spent convictions, although it may be desirable to continue to record that an offence has taken place. In the case of convictions of a body corporate, the 1974 Act does not apply, but it would seem equitable for the same approach to be applied as for the spent convictions of individuals.

Confidentiality

92 Sections 78S and 78T set out restrictions on information to be placed on the register because of considerations of national security or commercial confidentiality. The effect of these provisions is explained in Annex 2, paragraphs 17.8 to 17.19.

ANNEX 5 A GUIDE TO OTHER SUPPORTING LEGISLATION

The Environment Act 1995 (Commencement No.1) Order 1995

1 The Environment Act 1995 (Commencement No.1) Order 1995 (S.I. 1995/1983) brought into force section 57 of the Environment Act 1995 ("the 1995 Act"), in so far as was necessary to enable the Secretary of State to consult on and issue statutory guidance and make regulations.

The Environment Act 1995 (Commencement No.16 and Saving Provision) (England) Order 2000

2 The main effect of the Environment Act 1995 (Commencement No. 16 and Saving Provision) (England) Order 2000 (S.I. 2000/340 (C.8)) was to bring the remainder of section 57 of the 1995 Act into force in England on 1 April 2000. This, in turn, brought the Part 2A regime into force.

3 The Order also brought into force the following amendments to the 1990 Act:

(a) amendments to the definition of a statutory nuisance in section 79, so as to exclude any matter which consists of, or is caused by, land in a contaminated state;

(b) the repeal of the following sections (neither of which ever came into force):

(i) section 61, which would have created specific duties for waste regulation authorities as respects closed landfills, and

(ii) section 143, which would have required local authorities to compile registers of land which may be contaminated; and

(c) an amendment to section 161, relating to the use of the affirmative resolution procedure for any order under the new section 78M(4) (which deals with changes to the maximum level of fines for non-compliance with remediation notices).

4 Article 3 of the Order makes a saving provision with respect to the dis-application of the statutory nuisance regime from land contamination problems. This had the effect of ensuring that any regulatory action which had commenced before 1 April 2000 could continue.

The Radioactive Contaminated Land (Enabling Powers) (England) Regulations 2005

5 The main effect of The Radioactive Contaminated Land (Enabling Powers) (England) Regulations 2005 (S.I. 2005/3467) was to apply the powers in Part 2A of the Environmental Protection Act 1990 to make any regulations or orders, or give directions or issue guidance in respect of radioactive contaminated land.

6 The Regulations were required to come into force in advance of the substantive provisions (contained in the Modification Regulations) extending Part 2A to radioactivity and were necessary to enable the draft statutory guidance and the Contaminated Land (England) Regulations 2006 to be laid before Parliament at the same time as the Radioactive Contaminated Land (Modification of Enactments) (England) Regulations 2006.

The Radioactive Contaminated Land (Modification of Enactments) (England) Regulations 2006

7 The Radioactive Contaminated Land (Modification of Enactments) (England) Regulations 2006 (S.I. 2006/1379) are made pursuant to powers

under Part 2A as modified by the Powers Regulations and make provision for Part 2A of the Environmental Protection Act 1990 to have effect with modifications for the purpose of the identification and remediation of radioactive contaminated land other than where the Nuclear Installations Act 1965 applies or where the Convention on Third Party Liability in the Field of Nuclear Liability applies. In practice, modification means that when the statutes are being applied in a situation where radioactivity is involved, then they have to be read in the modified form, while in other situations they continue to apply unmodified.

8 The Regulations also transpose articles 48 and 53 of Council Directive 96/29/Euratom laying down basic safety standards for the protection of the health of workers and the general public against the dangers arising from ionizing radiation. These articles are concerned with interventions in the case of lasting exposure to ionising radiation.

9 Regulation 5 modifies, amongst others, the definitions of contaminated land, harm, remediation and substances.

10 Regulation 6 provides that a local authority's duty of inspection only applies in relation to land that it has reasonable grounds for believing may be contaminated.

11 Regulations 8 restricts the discretion of an enforcing authority to determine what is reasonable by way of remediation. These include weighing up the benefit of any intervention against the health detriment and costs arising from such intervention and maximising the benefit from such intervention.

12 Regulation 14 requires the enforcing authority to carry out remediation itself in certain circumstances.

13 Regulation 17(4) provides that the modified Part 2A does not apply where the operator of a nuclear installation is liable under the Nuclear Installations Act 1965 or in related circumstances.

14 Regulation 18 ensures that the powers of the Environment Agency or local authority under section 108 of the Environment Act 1995 extend to cover their functions under Part 2A as it applies to harm attributable to radioactivity.

The Clean Neighbourhoods and Environment Act 2005 (Commencement No. 2) (England) Order 2006

15 The main effect of the Clean Neighbourhoods and Environment Act 2005 (Commencement No. 2) (England) Order 2006 (S.I. 2006/1361) is to bring into force on 4 August 2006 in England section 104 of the Clean Neighbourhoods and Environment Act 2005 and Part 10 of Schedule 5 to that Act.

16 The provisions amend section 78L of Part 2A, which relates to appeals against remediation notices, so as to make the appellate authority the Secretary of State in England.

The Environmental Protection Act 1990 (Isles of Scilly) Order 2006

17 The Environmental Protection Act 1990 (Isles of Scilly) Order 2006 (S.I No 2006/1381) applies Part 2A of the Environmental Protection Act 1990 to the Isles of Scilly, in so far as that Part applies in relation to harm attributable to radioactivity. It does not apply to non-radioactive contamination.

18 This Order transposes articles 48 and 53 of Council Directive 1996/29/ Euratom laying down basic safety standards for the protection of the

health of workers and the general public against the dangers arising from ionizing radiation in relation to the Isles of Scilly which is required for full transposition in the UK.

19 The Order also applies the Environment Agency's powers under section 108 Environment Act 1995 to the Isles of Scilly, in so far as those powers relate to Part 2A.

Annex 6 Glossary of Terms

The statutory guidance (and other parts of this Circular) uses a number of terms which are defined in Part 2A of the 1990 Act, associated Regulations, other Acts and Regulations, or in the guidance itself. The meanings of the most important of these terms are set out below, along with a reference to the section in the Act, Regulations, or the Statutory Guidance paragraph in which the relevant term is defined.

Terms which are defined in statutes are shown with underlining.

Animal or crop effect: significant harm of a type listed in box 3 of Table A of Chapter A.

Apportionment: any determination by the enforcing authority under section 78F(7) (that is, a division of the costs of carrying out any remediation action between two or more appropriate persons). *Paragraph D.5(e).*

Appropriate person: defined in section 78A(9) as:

> "any person who is an appropriate person, determined in accordance with section 78F. . . , to bear responsibility for any thing which is to be done by way of remediation in any particular case."

Assessment action: a remediation action falling within the definition of remediation in section 78A(7)(a), that is the doing of anything for the purpose of assessing the condition of the contaminated land in question, or any controlled waters affected by that land or any land adjoining or adjacent to that land. *Paragraph C.8(e).*

Attribution: the process of apportionment between liability groups. *Paragraph D.5(e).*

Building: any structure or erection, and any part of a building including any part below ground, but not including plant or machinery comprised in a building. *Table A.*

Building effect: significant harm of a type listed in box 4 of Table A of Chapter A.

Caused or knowingly permitted: test for establishing responsibility for remediation, under section 78F(2); see paragraphs 9.8 to 9.15 of Annex 2 for a discussion of the interpretation of this term.

Changes to Substances: an exclusion test for Class A persons set out in Part 5 of Chapter D. *Paragraphs D.62 to D.64.*

Charging notice: a notice placing a legal charge on land served under section 78P(3)(b) by an enforcing authority to enable the authority to recover from the appropriate person any reasonable cost incurred by the authority in carrying out remediation.

Class A liability group: a liability group consisting of one or more Class A persons. *Paragraph D.5(c).*

Class A person: a person who is an appropriate person by virtue of section 78F(2) (that is, because he has caused or knowingly permitted a pollutant to be in, on or under the land). *Paragraph D.5(a).*

Class B liability group: a liability group consisting of one or more Class B persons. *Paragraph D.5(c).*

Class B person: a person who is an appropriate person by virtue of section 78F(4) or (5) (that is, because he is the owner or occupier of the land in circumstances where no Class A person can be found with respect to a particular remediation action). *Paragraph D.5(b)*.

Collective action: a remediation action which addresses together all of the significant pollution linkages to which it is referable, but which would not have been part of the remediation package for every one of those linkages if each of them had been addressed separately. *Paragraph D.22(b)*.

Common action: a remediation action which addresses together all of the significant pollution linkages to which it is referable, and which would have been part of the remediation package for each of those linkages if each of them had been addressed separately. *Paragraph D.22(a)*.

Contaminant: a substance which is in, on or under the land and which has the potential to cause harm or to cause pollution of controlled waters. *Paragraph A.12*.

Contaminated land: defined in section 78A(2) as:

"any land which appears to the local authority in whose area it is situated to be in such a condition, by reason of substances in, on or under the land, that—

"(a) significant harm is being caused or there is a significant possibility of such harm being caused, or;

"(b) pollution of controlled waters is being, or is likely to be, caused."

OR with respect to radioactive contamination defined in section 78A(2)(as modified) as

"any land which appears to the local authority in whose area it is situated to be in such a condition, by reasons of substances in, on or under the ground, that:

(a) harm is being caused, or

(b) there is a significant possibility of such harm being caused."

Contaminated Land (England) Regulations 2006: regulations (S.I. 2006/1380) made under Part 2A—described in Annex 4.

Controlled waters: defined in section 78A(9) by reference to Part 3 (section 104) of the Water Resources Act 1991; this embraces territorial and coastal waters, inland fresh waters, and ground waters. Section 78A(9) was amended by section 86 of the Water Act 2003 so that for Part 2A purposes "ground waters" does not include waters contained in underground strata but above the saturation zone as described in paragraph 2.9 of Annex 2.

Cost recovery decision: any decision by the enforcing authority whether:

(a) to recover from the appropriate person all the reasonable costs incurred by the authority in carrying out remediation, or

(b) not to recover those costs or to recover only part of those costs. *Paragraph E.8*.

Current use: any use which is currently being made, or is likely to be made, of the land and which is consistent with any existing planning permission (or is otherwise lawful under town and country planning legislation). This definition is subject to the following qualifications:

(a) the current use should be taken to include any temporary use, permitted under town and country planning legislation, to which the land is, or is likely to be, put from time to time;

(b) the current use includes future uses or developments which do not require a new, or amended, grant of planning permission;

(c) the current use should, nevertheless, be taken to include any likely informal recreational use of the land, whether authorised by the owners or occupiers or not, (for example, children playing on the land); however, in assessing the likelihood of any such informal use, the local authority should give due attention to measures taken to prevent or restrict access to the land; and

(d) in the case of agricultural land, however, the current agricultural use should not be taken to extend beyond the growing or rearing of the crops or animals which are habitually grown or reared on the land. *Paragraph A.26.*

Deterministic effect: type of health effect which occurs following a dose of radiation above a certain level (a 'threshold' level) with the severity of the health effect dependent on the level of the dose. *Paragraph A.47(c)*

Detriment: principally means a health detriment, but may also include other detriments, for example, a detriment associated with blight, *Paragraph C.8(j).*

Ecological system effect: significant harm of a type listed in box 2 of Table A of Chapter A.

Effective (radiation) dose: an energy measure which applies a weighting factor to the equivalent dose to account for the different effectiveness of the dose in causing damage to different human tissues (egg [sic] skin, eyes). It is measured in Sieverts. *Paragraph A.41.*

Equivalent (radiation) dose: an energy measure which applies a weighting factor to the absorbed dose to account for the different effectiveness of various types of radiation (alpha, beta, gamma, neutron) in damaging human tissue. It is measured in Sieverts. *Paragraph A.41.*

Enforcing authority: defined in section 78A(9) as:

(a) in relation to a special site, the Environment Agency;

(b) in relation to contaminated land other than a special site, the local authority in whose area the land is situated.

Escaped Substances: an exclusion test for Class A persons set out in Part 5 of Chapter D. *Paragraphs D.65 to D.67.*

Excluded Activities: an exclusion test for Class A persons set out in Part 5 of Chapter D. *Paragraphs D.47 to D.50.*

Exclusion: any determination by the enforcing authority under section 78F(6) (that is, that a person is to be treated as not being an appropriate person). *Paragraph D.5(d).*

Favourable conservation status: defined in Article 1 of Council Directive 92/43/EEC on the conservation of natural habitats and of wild fauna and flora.

Hardship: a factor underlying any cost recovery decision made by an enforcing authority under section 78P(2). See paragraphs 10.8 to 10.10 of Annex 2 for a discussion of the interpretation of this term.

Harm: defined in section 78A(4) as:

"harm to the health of living organisms or other interference with the ecological systems of which they form part and, in the case of man, includes harm to his property."

OR with respect to radioactive contamination defined in section 78A(4)(as modified) as:

"lasting exposure to any person being resulting from the after effects of a radiological emergency, past practice or past work activity."

Health detriment: defined in the Schedule to the Radioactive Contaminated Land (Modification of Enactments) (England) Regulations 2006 as:

"an estimate of the risk in reduction in length and quality of life occurring in a population following exposure to ionising radiations. This includes loss arising from somatic effects, cancers and severe genetic disorder".

Human health effect: significant harm of a type listed in box 1 of Table A of Chapter A.

Industrial, trade or business premises: defined in section 78M(6), for the purpose of determining the penalty for failure to comply with a remediation notice, as:

"premises used for any industrial, trade or business purposes or premises not so used on which matter is burnt in connection with any industrial, trade or business process, and premises are used for industrial purposes where they are used for the purposes of any treatment or process as well as where they are used for the purpose of manufacturing."

Inspection using statutory powers of entry: any detailed inspection of land carried out through use of powers of entry given to an enforcing authority by section 108 of the Environment Act 1995. *Paragraph B.21.*

Intervention: is a type of remedial action and is defined in the Schedule to the Radioactive Contaminated Land (Modification of Enactments) (England) Regulations 2006 as:

"a human activity that prevents or decreases the exposure of individuals to radiation from sources which are not part of a practice or which are out of control, by acting on sources, transmission pathways and individuals themselves."

Introduction of Pathways or Receptors: an exclusion test for Class A persons set out in Part 5 of Chapter D. *Paragraphs D.68 to D.72.*

Intrusive investigation: an investigation of land (for example by exploratory excavations) which involves actions going beyond simple visual inspection of the land, limited sampling or assessment of documentary information. *Paragraph B.20(c).*

Justification: a radiological protection principle. In the specific case of an intervention, justification means ensuring that the reduction in detriment due to radiation is sufficient to justify any adverse effects and costs including social costs, of the intervention. *Paragraph C.8(h).*

Liability group: the persons who are appropriate persons with respect to a particular significant pollutant linkage. *Paragraph D.5(c).*

Local authority: defined in section 78A(9) as meaning any unitary authority, district council, the Common Council of the City of London, the Sub-Treasurer of the Inner Temple and the Under-Treasurer of the Middle Temple.

Monitoring action: a remediation action falling within the definition in section 78A(7)(c), that is "making of subsequent inspections from time to time for the purpose of keeping under review the condition of the land or waters". *Paragraph C.8(g).*

Optimisation: a radiological protection principle which ensures that the form, scale and duration of the intervention maximises the benefit of reduction in health detriment less the detriment associated with the intervention. *Paragraph C.8(i).*

Orphan linkage: a significant pollutant linkage for which no appropriate person can be found, or where those who would otherwise be liable are exempted by one of the relevant statutory provisions. Paragraphs *D.12, D.14 and D.17.*

Owner: defined in section 78A(9) as:

> "a person (other than a mortgagee not in possession) who, whether in his own right or as trustee for any other person, is entitled to receive the rack rent of the land, or where the land is not let at a rack rent, would be so entitled if it were so let."

Part 2A: Part 2A of the Environmental Protection Act 1990.

Pathway: one or more routes or means by, or through, which a receptor:

> (a) is being exposed to, or affected by, a contaminant, or
> (b) could be so exposed or affected. *Paragraph A.14.*

Payments Made for Remediation: an exclusion test for Class A persons set out in Part 5 of Chapter D. *Paragraphs D.51 to D.56.*

Person acting in a relevant capacity: defined in section 78X(4), for the purposes of limiting personal liability, as any of the following:

> "(a) a person acting as an insolvency practitioner, within the meaning of section 388 of the Insolvency Act 1986 (including that section as it applies in relation to an insolvent partnership by virtue of any order made under section 421 of that Act;
> "(b) the official receiver acting in a capacity in which he would be regarded as acting as an insolvency practitioner within the meaning of section 388 of the Insolvency Act 1986 if subsection (5) of that section were disregarded;
> "(c) the official receiver acting as a receiver or manager;
> "(d) a person acting as a special manager under section 177 or 370 of the Insolvency Act 1986;. . .
> "(f) a person acting as a receiver or receiver and manager under or by virtue of any enactment or by virtue of his appointment as such by an order of a court or by any other instrument."

Pollutant: a contaminant which forms part of a pollutant linkage. *Paragraph A.17.*

Pollutant linkage: the relationship between a contaminant, a pathway and a receptor. *Paragraph A.17.*

Pollution of controlled waters: defined in section 78A(9) as:

> "the entry into controlled waters of any poisonous, noxious or polluting matter or any solid waste matter."

Possibility of harm: relates to radioactive contamination only and is a measure of the probability, or frequency, of the occurrence of circumstances which would lead to lasting exposure being caused. *Paragraph A.44.*

Possibility of significant harm: a measure of the probability, or frequency, of the occurrence of circumstances which would lead to significant harm being caused. *Paragraph A.27.*

Practice: is defined in the Schedule to the Radioactive Contaminated Land (Modification of Enactments) (England) Regulations 2006 as:

> "a human activity that can increase the exposure of individuals to radiation from an artificial source, or from a natural radiation source where natural

radionuclides are processed for their radioactive, fissile or fertile properties, except in the case of an emergency exposure."

Radioactive Contaminated Land (Enabling Powers) (England) Regulations 2005: regulations (S.I. 2005/3467) made under Part 2A and described in Annex 5.

Radioactive Contaminated Land (Modification of Enactments) (England) Regulations 2006: regulations (S.I. 2006/1379) made under Part 2A and described in Annex 5.

Reasonable grounds: relates to radioactive contamination only and sets out the grounds required by a local authority before it can inspect land for the purpose of identifying whether it is contaminated land and whether it should be designated a special site. Grounds are: (Paragraphs B.17Aand B.17B):

(a) a former historical land use, past practice, past work activity or radiological emergency, capable of causing lasting exposure giving rise to the radiation doses of the magnitudes stated; or

(b) levels of contamination present on the land arising from a past work practice, past work activity or radiological emergency, capable of causing lasting exposure giving rise to the radiation doses of the magnitudes stated.

Receptor: either:

(a) a living organism, a group of living organisms, an ecological system or a piece of property which:

    (i) is in a category listed in Table A in Chapter A as a type of receptor, and

    (ii) is being, or could be, harmed, by a contaminant; or

(b) controlled waters which are being, or could be, polluted by a contaminant. *Paragraph A.13;* or

(c) a person subjected to lasting exposure resulting from the after-effects of a radiological emergency, past practice or past work activity *Paragraph A.13.*

Register: the public register maintained by the enforcing authority under section 78R of particulars relating to contaminated land.

Related companies: are those which are, or were at the "relevant date", members of a group of companies consisting of a "holding company" and its "subsidiaries". The "relevant date" is that on which the enforcing authority first served on anyone a notice under section 78B(3) identifying the land as contaminated land, and the terms "holding company" and "subsidiaries" have the same meaning as in section 736 of the Companies Act 1985. *Paragraph D.46.*

Relevant information: information relating to the assessment of whether there is a significant possibility of significant harm being caused, which is:

(a) scientifically-based;

(b) authoritative;

(c) relevant to the assessment of risks arising from the presence of contaminants in soil; and

(d) appropriate to the determination of whether any land is contaminated land for the purposes of Part 2A, in that the use of the information is consistent with providing a level of protection of risk in line with the qualitative criteria set out in Tables A and B of Chapter A. *Paragraph A.31 and A.47.*

Relevant Information: (relating to reasonable grounds) information that is appropriate and authoritative. *Paragraph B.17B.*

Relevant land or waters: the contaminated land in question, any controlled waters affected by that land and any land adjoining or adjacent to the contaminated land on which remediation might be required as a consequence of the contaminated land being such land. *Paragraph C.8(d).*

Remedial treatment action: a remediation action falling within the definition in section 78A (7)(b), that is the doing of any works, the carrying out of any operations or the taking of any steps in relation to any such land or waters for the purpose:

(a) of preventing or minimising, or remedying or mitigating the effects of any significant harm, or any pollution of controlled waters, by reason of which the contaminated land is such land, or

(b) of restoring the land or waters to their former state. *Paragraph C.8(f).*

Remediation: defined in section 78A(7) as:

"(a) the doing of anything for the purpose of assessing the condition of—

"(i) the contaminated land in question;
"(ii) any controlled waters affected by that land; or
"(iii) any land adjoining or adjacent to that land;

"(b) the doing of any works, the carrying out of any operations or the taking of any steps in relation to any such land or waters for the purpose —

"(i) of preventing or minimising, or remedying or mitigating the effects of any significant harm, or any pollution of controlled waters, by reason of which the contaminated land is such land; or
"(ii) of restoring the land or waters to their former state; or

"(c) the making of subsequent inspections from time to time for the purpose of keeping under review the condition of the land or waters."

OR with respect to radioactive contamination defined in section 78A(7)(as modified) as:

"(a) the doing of anything for the purpose of assessing the condition of —

"(i) the contaminated land in question; or
"(iii) any land adjoining or adjacent to that land;

"(b) the doing of any works, the carrying out of any operations or the taking of any steps in relation to any such land for the purpose —

"(i) of preventing or minimising, or remedying or mitigating the effects of any harm by reason of which the contaminated land is such land; or
"(ii) of restoring the land to its former state; or

"(c) the making of subsequent inspections from time to time for the purpose of keeping under review the condition of the land."

Remediation action: any individual thing which is being, or is to be, done by way of remediation. *Paragraph C.8(a).*

Remediation declaration: defined in section 78H(6). It is a document prepared and published by the enforcing authority recording remediation actions which it would have specified in a remediation notice, but which it is precluded from specifying by virtue of sections 78E(4) or (5), the reasons why it would have specified those actions and the grounds on which it is satisfied that it is precluded from specifying them in a notice.

Remediation notice: defined in section 78E(1) as a notice specifying what an appropriate person is to do by way of remediation and the periods within which he is required to do each of the things so specified.

Remediation package: the full set or sequence of remediation actions, within a remediation scheme, which are referable to a particular significant pollutant linkage. *Paragraph C.8(b)*.

Remediation scheme: the complete set or sequence of remediation actions (referable to one or more significant pollutant linkages) to be carried out with respect to the relevant land or waters. *Paragraph C.8(c)*.

Remediation statement: defined in section 78H(7). It is a statement prepared and published by the responsible person detailing the remediation actions which are being, have been, or are expected to be, done as well as the periods within which these things are being done.

Risk: the combination of:

    (a) the probability, or frequency, of occurrence of a defined hazard (for example, exposure to a property of a substance with the potential to cause harm); and

    (b) the magnitude (including the seriousness) of the consequences. *Paragraph A.9*.

Shared action: a remediation action which is referable to the significant pollutant in more than one significant pollutant linkage. *Paragraph D.21(b)*.

Single-linkage action: a remediation action which is referable solely to the significant pollutant in a single significant pollutant linkage. *Paragraph D.21(a)*.

Significant harm: defined in section 78A(5). It means any harm which is determined to be significant in accordance with the statutory guidance in Chapter A (that is, it meets one of the descriptions of types of harm in the second column of Table A of that Chapter).

Significant pollutant: a pollutant which forms part of a significant pollutant linkage. *Paragraph A.20*.

Significant pollutant linkage: a pollutant linkage which forms the basis for a determination that a piece of land is contaminated land. *Paragraph A.20*.

Significant possibility of significant harm: a possibility of significant harm being caused which, by virtue of section 78A(5), is determined to be significant in accordance with the statutory guidance in Chapter A.

Sold with Information: an exclusion test for Class A persons set out in Part 5 of Chapter D. *Paragraphs D.57 to D.61*.

Special site: defined by section 78A(3) as: "any contaminated land—

    "(a) which has been designated as such a site by virtue of section 78C(7) or 78D(6). . . ; and

    "(b) whose designation as such has not been terminated by the appropriate Agency under section 78Q(4). . . ".

The effect of the designation of any contaminated land as a special site is that the Environment Agency, rather than the local authority, becomes the enforcing authority for the land.

Stochastic effect: the likelihood of a radiation-induced health effect which may be assumed to be linearly proportional to the radiation dose over a wide range of doses and where the severity of the health effect is not dependent on the level of the dose. *Paragraph A.47*.

Substance: defined in section 78A(9) as:

> "any natural or artificial substance, whether in solid or liquid form or in the form of a gas or vapour."

OR with respect to radioactive contamination defined in section 78A(9)(as modified) as:

> "whether in solid or liquid form or in the form of a gas or vapour, any substance which contains radionuclides which have resulted from the after-effects of a radiological emergency or which are or have been processed as part of a past practice or past work activity, but shall not include radon gas or the following radionuclides: Po-218, Pb-214, At-218, Bi-214, Rn-218; Po-214 and TI–210."

Appendix 2

FORMS AND PRECEDENTS

Part IIA Forms and Precedents

1. Notice of identification of contaminated land (section 78B(3)).

2. Notice to other appropriate persons of identification of contaminated land (section 78B(4)).

3. Notice of decision that land is required to be designated a special site (section 78C(1)(b)).

4. Notice of decision that land is required to be designated as a special site in response to notice from appropriate Agency (section 78(5)).

5. Notice that decision that land is required to be designated as a special site has taken effect (section 78C(6)).

6. Notice of reference of decision as to special site status to the Secretary of State (section 78D(3)).

7. Notice requesting information.

8. Remediation notice (section 78E(1)).

9. Notice to accompany copies of remediation notice (section 78E(1)).

10. Remediation declaration (section 78H(6)).

11. Remediation statement (section 78H(7)).

12. Application for compensation for the grant of rights (section 78G(5)).

13. Notice of appeal against remediation notice (Secretary of State) (section 78L(1)).

14. Prosecution for failure to comply with remediation notice (section 78M(1))

15. Notice before exercising remediation powers under section 78N.

16. Charging notice under section 78P.

17. Notice of enforcing authority as to possible commercial confidentiality (section 78T(2)).

PRECEDENT 1

NOTICE OF IDENTIFICATION OF CONTAMINATED LAND

Note: Section 78B(3) requires an authority which identifies contaminated land in its area to give notice of that fact to:

(a) *the appropriate Agency;*
(b) *the owner;*
(c) *any person who appears to be in occupation; and*
(d) *each person who appears to be an appropriate person.*

The notice must state by virtue of which paragraph (a)–(d) it is given. The service of notices under the 1990 Act is governed by section 160.

ENVIRONMENTAL PROTECTION ACT 1990, SECTION 78B(3)

To: [NAME AND ADDRESS OF RECIPIENT]:

1. Under section 78B(1) of the Environmental Protection Act 1990 [NAME OF AUTHORITY] has identified the land described in the Schedule to this Notice ("the Land"), situated within the Authority's area, as contaminated land.

2. Notice of that fact is given to you in the capacity indicated below and pursuant to the paragraph of section 78B(3) of the 1990 Act indicated below:

   (A) the appropriate Agency;
   (B) the owner of the Land;
   (C) a person appearing to the Enforcing Authority to be in occupation of [the whole] [part] of the Land;
   (D) a person appearing to the Enforcing Authority to be an appropriate person.
   [DELETE AS APPLICABLE]

3. Because this notice may potentially have financial consequences, you are advised to consult an appropriate independent professional adviser.

4. Should you or your adviser wish to make any representation in response to this notice, or to seek further information, please contact the following as soon as possible:

[NAME OF CONTACT]
at
[ADDRESS, TELEPHONE, FAX]

SCHEDULE
[DESCRIPTION OF THE LAND]

Dated:
[NAME OF AUTHORISED OFFICER]
[NAME AND ADDRESS OF ENFORCING AUTHORITY]

PRECEDENT 2

NOTICE TO OTHER APPROPRIATE PERSONS OF IDENTIFICATION OF CONTAMINATED LAND

Note: Section 78B(4) provides that if after a notice has been given pursuant to section 78B(3)(d) (see Precedent 1) some other person appears to the authority to be an appropriate person, then the authority must give notice to that other person of that fact.

ENVIRONMENTAL PROTECTION ACT 1990, SECTION 78B(4)

To: [NAME AND ADDRESS OF RECIPIENT]:

1. Under section 78B(1) of the Environmental Protection Act 1990 [NAME OF AUTHORITY] has identified the land described in Schedule 1 to this Notice, situated within the Authority's area, as contaminated.

2. The Authority gave notice of that fact on [DATE] to those persons appearing to the Authority to be appropriate persons in relation to that land, more particularly identified in Schedule 2.

3. It now appears to the Enforcing Authority that you are also an appropriate person in relation to that land and this notice is accordingly given to you pursuant to section 78B(4) of the 1990 Act.

4. Because this notice may potentially have financial consequences, you are advised to consult an appropriate independent professional adviser.

5. Should you or your adviser wish to make any representation in response to this Notice, or to seek further information, please contact the following as soon as possible:

[NAME OF CONTACT]
at
[ADDRESS, TELEPHONE, FAX]

SCHEDULE 1
[DESCRIPTION OF THE LAND]

SCHEDULE 2
[PERSONS APPEARING TO BE APPROPRIATE PERSONS]

Dated:
[NAME OF AUTHORISED OFFICER]
[NAME AND ADDRESS OF ENFORCING AUTHORITY]

PRECEDENT 3

NOTICE OF DECISION THAT LAND IS REQUIRED TO BE DESIGNATED AS A SPECIAL SITE

Note: If it appears to a local authority that contaminated land in its area is required to be designated as a special site, it must under section 78C(1)(b) give notice of that decision to the "relevant persons"; that is the appropriate Agency, owner of the land, any person who appears to the local authority to be in occupation of the whole or any part of the land; and each person who appears to the authority to be an appropriate person.

ENVIRONMENTAL PROTECTION ACT 1990, SECTION 78C(1)(b)

To: [NAME AND ADDRESS OF RECIPIENT]:

1. Under section 78C(1)(a) of the Environmental Protection Act 1990 [NAME OF AUTHORITY] has decided that the land described in the Schedule to this Notice being contaminated land situated in its area is land which is required to be designated as a special site.

2. Notice of that decision is given to you pursuant to section 78C(1)(b) as a relevant person as defined in section 78C(2), namely as:

   (A) the appropriate Agency;
   (B) the owner of the land;
   (C) a person appearing to the Authority to be in occupation of [the whole] [part] of the land;
   (D) a person appearing to the Authority to be an appropriate person.
   [DELETE AS APPLICABLE]

3. Should you wish to make any representation in response to this Notice, or to seek further information, please contact the following as soon as possible:

[NAME OF CONTACT]
at
[ADDRESS, TELEPHONE, FAX]

SCHEDULE
[DESCRIPTION OF LAND]

Dated:
[NAME OF AUTHORISED OFFICER]
[NAME AND ADDRESS OF LOCAL AUTHORITY]

PRECEDENT 4

NOTICE OF DECISION AS TO WHETHER LAND IS REQUIRED TO BE DESIGNATED AS A SPECIAL SITE IN RESPONSE TO NOTICE FROM APPROPRIATE AGENCY

Note: By section 78C(4) the appropriate Agency may serve notice on the local authority if it considers that land is required to be designated as a special site. The local authority must then decide whether that is the case, and by section 78C(5) must give notice of its decision to the "relevant persons".

ENVIRONMENTAL PROTECTION ACT 1990, SECTION 7C(5)

To: [NAME AND ADDRESS OF RECIPIENT]:

1. In relation to the land situated in its area and described in the Schedule to this Notice ("the Land") [NAME OF LOCAL AUTHORITY] has received a notice from [NAME OF APPROPRIATE AGENCY] that the Agency considers the Land to be contaminated land which is required to be designated as a special site.

2. The Local Authority has decided that the Land [is land which is required to be designated as a special site] [is not land which is required to be designated as a special site]
[DELETE AS APPLICABLE]

3. This Notice of that decision is given to you pursuant to section 78C(5) as a relevant person as defined in section 78C(2), namely as:

   (A) the appropriate Agency;
   (B) the owner of the Land;
   (C) a person appearing to the Local Authority to be in occupation of [the whole] [part] of the Land;
   (D) a person appearing to the Local Authority to be an appropriate person.
   [DELETE AS APPLICABLE]

4. Should you wish to make any representation in response to this Notice, or to seek further information, please contact the following as soon as possible:

   [NAME OF CONTACT]
   at
   [ADDRESS, TELEPHONE, FAX]

SCHEDULE
[DESCRIPTION OF THE LAND]

Dated:
[NAME OF AUTHORISED OFFICER]
[NAME AND ADDRESS OF LOCAL AUTHORITY]

PRECEDENT 5

NOTICE THAT DECISION THAT LAND IS REQUIRED TO BE DESIGNATED AS A SPECIAL SITE HAS TAKEN EFFECT

Note: Where a Local Authority makes a decision that land is required to be designated as a special site it must give notice of that fact to (inter alia) the appropriate Agency under either section 78C(1)(b) or section 78C(5) of the Act. The Local Authority's decision then takes effect under section 78C(6) either after the expiration of 21 days from such notice, or sooner if the appropriate Agency notifies its agreement to the decision.

By section 78C(6) the Local Authority is required to give a further notice to the "relevant persons" that the decision has taken effect.

ENVIRONMENTAL PROTECTION ACT 1990, SECTION 78C(6)

To: [NAME AND ADDRESS OF RECIPIENT]:

1. In relation to the land situated in its areas and described in the Schedule to this Notice ("the Land") [NAME OF AUTHORITY] decided under [section 78C(1)(b)] [section 78C(5)(a)] of the 1990 Act that the Land is contaminated land which is required to be designated as a special site.

2. Notice of that decision was given to the appropriate Agency on [DATE].

3. In accordance with Section 78C(6) that decision took effect on [DATE].

4. This Notice that the decision has taken effect is given to you pursuant to section 78C(6) as a relevant person as defined in section 78C(2), namely as:

   (A) the appropriate Agency;
   (B) the owner of the Land;
   (C) a person appearing to the Local Authority to be in occupation of [the whole] [part] of the Land;
   (D) a person appearing to the Local Authority to be an appropriate person.
   [DELETE AS APPLICABLE]

5. Should you wish to make any representation in response to this Notice, or to seek further information, please contact the following as soon as possible:

[NAME OF CONTACT]
at
[ADDRESS, TELEPHONE, FAX]

SCHEDULE
[DESCRIPTION OF THE LAND]

Dated:
[NAME OF AUTHORISED OFFICER]
[NAME AND ADDRESS OF LOCAL AUTHORITY]

PRECEDENT 6

NOTICE OF REFERENCE OF DECISION AS TO SPECIAL SITE STATUS TO THE SECRETARY OF STATE

Note: In the event of disagreement between the Local Authority and the appropriate Agency as to whether land should be notified as a special site, the decision is referred by the Local Authority to the Secretary of State under section 78D(1). The Local Authority is required by section 78D(3) to give notice of that fact to the "relevant persons". Responsibility for notifying the relevant persons of the ultimate decision lies with the Secretary of State under section 78(4)(b).

ENVIRONMENTAL PROTECTION ACT 1990, SECTION 78D(3)

To: [NAME AND ADDRESS OF RECIPIENT]:

1. In relation to the land situated in its area and described in the Schedule to this Notice ("the Land") [NAME OF AUTHORITY] gave notice of its decision as to whether the Land is required to be designated as a special site ("the Decision") to [NAME OF AGENCY] pursuant to [section 78C(1)(b)][section 78C(5)(b)] of the 1990 Act.

2. The Agency has given notice to the Local Authority that it disagrees with the Decision.

3. Pursuant to section 78D(1) of the 1990 Act, the Local Authority has referred the Decision to the Secretary of State for determination under section 78D(4) of the 1990 Act.

4. This Notice that the Decision has been referred to the Secretary of State is given to you pursuant to section 78D(3) as a relevant person as defined by section 78C(2) and 78D(7), namely as:

   (A) the appropriate Agency;
   (B) the owner of the land;
   (C) a person appearing to the Authority to be in occupation of [the whole] [part] of the land;
   (D) a person appearing to the Authority to be an appropriate person.
   [DELETE AS APPLICABLE]

5. Should you wish to make any representation in response to this Notice, or to seek further information, please contact the following as soon as possible:

967

[NAME OF CONTACT]
at
[ADDRESS, TELEPHONE, FAX]

SCHEDULE
[DESCRIPTION OF THE LAND]

Dated:
[NAME OF AUTHORISED OFFICER]
[NAME AND ADDRESS OF LOCAL AUTHORITY]

PRECEDENT 7

NOTICE REQUESTING INFORMATION

Note: In practice, before an enforcing authority serves a remediation notice it will be vital to obtain as much information as possible on the relevant circumstances which will affect decisions as to who are the appropriate persons and what should be their apportioned shares of liability. Failure to obtain and assimilate such information may result in a later successful appeal, with wasted expense. The enforcing authority may wish, initially at least, to seek to obtain the information on a voluntary basis, which is the basis on which this notice is drafted. There are however, reserve powers to obtain information on a mandatory basis under section 108 of the Environment Act 1995 or under section 16 of the Local Government (Miscellaneous Provisions) Act 1976. The authority may wish to serve the notice either before or after it has formally identified the land as contaminated.

ENVIRONMENTAL PROTECTION ACT 1990, SECTIONS 78B, E AND F

To: [NAME AND ADDRESS OF RECIPIENT/REGISTERED OFFICE IF COMPANY]

EITHER

[1. Under section 78B(1) of the Environmental Protection Act 1990 [NAME OF ENFORCING AUTHORITY] has identified the land described in the Schedule to this Notice ("the Land"), as contaminated land.]

OR

[1. Pursuant to section 78B(1) of the Environmental Protection Act 1990 [NAME OF ENFORCING AUTHORITY] is considering whether the land described in the Schedule to this Notice ("the Land"), should be identified as contaminated land.]

2. The Enforcing Authority believes that you may have information relevant to the exercise of its duties in relation to the Land.

3. Accordingly, you are requested to provide the following information:

(A)	Are you, or any company in which you have been a shareholder, director, company secretary or manager, the owner of all or part of the Land? If you are the owner of part of the Land please identify the extent of your ownership [on the attached plan].	Yes/No
(B)	Are you, or any company in which you have been a shareholder, director, company secretary or manager, the occupier of all or part of the Land, whether as a tenant or otherwise? If you are the occupier or tenant of part of the Land please identify the extent of your occupation or tenancy [on the attached plan].	Yes/No
(C)	Have you, or any company in which you have been a shareholder, director, company secretary or manager, been an owner of all or part of the Land at any time in the past? If "yes" please give the dates when you were the owner.	Yes/No
(D)	Have you, or any company in which you have been a shareholder, director, company secretary or manager, been an occupier of all or part of the Land at any time in the past, whether as a tenant or otherwise? If "yes"please give the dates when you were in occupation or were a tenant.	Yes/No
(E)	Are there any other persons who are or have been joint owners or joint occupiers with you now or in the past, whether as a tenant or otherwise? If "yes" please provide details.	Yes/No
(F)	Do you know the identity of the present or any former owners of all or part of the Land? If "yes", please provide details.	Yes/No
(G)	Do you know the identity of the present or any former occupiers of all or part of the Land, whether as a tenant or otherwise? If "yes" please provide details.	Yes/No

(H)	Are you aware of the presence of any contaminating substances in, on or under the Land? If "yes", please provide details.	Yes/No
(I)	Are you aware of the identity of any person or persons who may have caused or permitted the Land to be contaminated, for example, by spilling or dumping substances? If "yes" please give details.	Yes/No
(J)	Are you aware of any investigations already carried out as to whether the Land is or may be contaminated? If "yes", please give details and indicate whether any reports or results of such investigations are in your possession or that of any other person.	Yes/No
(K)	What is the nature of the activities which to your knowledge have been carried out on the land?	Yes/No
(L)	Are you aware of any current or previous licence, consent, permission or authorisation held by you or any company or other person involving the introduction on to the land of any substances (such as waste, solvents, oils or chemicals) capable of contaminating the land? If "yes", please give details.	
(M)	Are you aware of any contractual agreements relating to responsibility for contamination present on the Land? If "yes" please give details.	Yes/No
(N)	Are there any other matters you wish to draw to the attention of the Enforcing Authority? Please provide details on a separate sheet if necessary.	Yes/No

Please make your response on the enclosed copy of this Notice, sign and date it and return it within [21] days to the address below. If you are completing the response on behalf of a Company, please indicate in what capacity you are responding and whether you are authorised to do so.

SCHEDULE 1
[DESCRIPTION OF THE LAND]

Dated:
[NAME OF AUTHORISED OFFICER]
[NAME AND ADDRESS OF ENFORCING AUTHORITY]

PRECEDENT 8

REMEDIATION NOTICE

Note: This is a suggested form for a remediation notice under section 78E(1). See generally Chapter 12. Copies of the notice must be sent to each person specified in regulation 5(1) of the Contaminated Land (England) Regulations 2006. There is no prescribed form of notice.

ENVIRONMENTAL PROTECTION ACT 1990, SECTION 78E(1) THE CONTAMINATED LAND (ENGLAND) REGULATIONS 2006

To: [NAME AND ADDRESS OF PERSON OR PERSONS ON WHOM SERVED]:

This Notice is served on you by [NAME OF AUTHORITY] pursuant to section 78E of the Environmental Protection Act 1990 in relation to contaminated land identified as such by the Authority under section 78B(1) [and designated as a special site pursuant to [section 78C] [section 78D]] of the 1990 Act.

This Notice specifies in the Schedule below what you are to do by way of remediation and the periods within which you are to do each of the specified things.

[Where two or more persons are appropriate persons in relation to any particular thing to be done by way of remediation, the Schedule also states the proportion determined under section 78F(7) of the cost of doing those things which each person is liable to bear.]

The further matters required to be stated by the Contaminated Land (England) Regulations 2006 are set out below as Particulars to this Notice.

SCHEDULE

Things required by way of remediation (referring, if necessary, to Annexed specifications)	Period within which each thing is to be done	[Proportion of cost for which each appropriate person is liable]

973

PARTICULARS

(A) Name and address of the person or persons on whom the notice is served:

(B) Location and extent of the relevant land:
[DESCRIBE AND REFER TO PLAN]

(C) Date of the notice given under Section 78B identifying the land as contaminated:

(D) Reason why the person on whom the notice is served is considered to be an appropriate person by the Authority:

    (i) the person caused or knowingly permitted the substances, or any of the substances, by reason of which the land is contaminated land, to be present in, on or under the relevant land;

    (ii) the person is the owner of the relevant land;

    (iii) the person is the occupier of the relevant land.
[DELETE AS APPLICABLE]

(E) Particulars of the significant harm or pollution of controlled waters by reason of which the land is contaminated land:

(F) The substances by reason of which the land is contaminated land [and location of the land from which they have escaped (if applicable)]:

(G) The reasons of the Authority for its decision as to the remediation action required in the Schedule and how the Secretary of State's guidance has been applied:

(H) Whether two or more persons are appropriate persons in relation to the contaminated land in question and if so, the name and address of each such person and the thing by way of remediation for which each bears responsibility:
[Yes] [No]
[IF YES, THE NAME AND ADDRESS OF EACH]

[THE REMEDIATION ACTION FOR WHICH EACH BEARS RESPONSIBILITY]

(I) Whether two or more persons would, apart from section 78F(6), be appropriate persons in relation to a particular remediation action and, if so, the Authority's reasons for determining which of them is to be treated as being an appropriate person, showing how the Secretary of State's guidance has been applied:
[IF YES, THE REASONS]

(J) If proportions of cost are stated in the Schedule, the reasons for the apportionment, showing how the Secretary of State's guidance has been applied:

(K) Whether the Authority knows the name and address of:

    (a) the owner of the relevant land
        [Yes] [No]
        [IF YES, NAMES AND ADDRESSES]

    (b) any person who appears to be in occupation of the whole or part of the relevant land
        [Yes] [No]
        [IF YES, NAME AND ADDRESSES]

(L) Whether the Authority knows the name and address of any person whose consent is required under section 78G of the Act before any thing required by this notice can be done and if so, the names and addresses:
[Yes] [No]
[IF YES, NAMES AND ADDRESSES]

(M) Whether it appears to the Authority that the land is in such a condition by reason of substances in, on or under the land that there is imminent danger of serious harm or serious pollution of controlled waters being caused:
[Yes] [No]

(N) A person on whom a remediation Notice is served may be guilty of an offence for failure, without reasonable excuse, to comply with any of its requirements;

(O) On conviction of an offence for failure to comply with a remediation notice, the offender shall be liable, on summary conviction, to a fine not exceeding £5,000 and to a further fine of £500 for each day on which the failure to comply continues after conviction of the offence and before the Authority begins to exercise its powers to carry out remediation under section 78N. Where a person commits an offence in a case where the contaminated land to which the notice relates is industrial, trade or business premises, the maximum fine on summary conviction is £20,000 and the further daily fine is £2,000;

(P) Name and address of the Authority serving the Notice:

(Q) Date of the Notice:

RIGHT OF APPEAL

    1. A person on whom a remediation Notice is served may appeal to the Secretary of State against the Notice under Section 78L of the 1990 Act. The appeal must be made within a period of 21 days beginning with the day on which the Notice is served.

2. The appeal should be made to the Secretary of State at:

Planning Inspectorate
Room 4/12 Eagle Wing
Temple Quay House
2 The Square
Bristol BS1 6PN
Tel: 0117 372 8726
Email: environment.appeals@Ins.gsi.gov.uk

3. The grounds on which an appeal may be made are set out in regulation 7 of the Contaminated Land (England) Regulations 2006 and are as follows:

[SET OUT GROUNDS (a)–(s) FROM THE REGULATIONS]

4. By regulation 12(1) of the Contaminated Land (England) Regulations 2006 the effect of a duly made appeal is to suspend the Notice so that it is of no effect pending the final determination or abandonment of the appeal.

[SIGNATURE OF AUTHORISED ISSUING OFFICER]
[NAME OF AUTHORISED OFFICER]
[NAME OF ENFORCING AUTHORITY]

PRECEDENT 9

NOTICE TO ACCOMPANY COPIES OF REMEDIATION NOTICE

Note: By Regulation 5 of the Contaminated Land (England) Regulations 2006 when serving a remediation notice the Enforcing Authority must also send a copy of it to the persons specified in the regulation.

ENVIRONMENTAL PROTECTION ACT 1990, SECTION 78E(1) THE CONTAMINATED LAND (ENGLAND) REGULATIONS 2006

To:[NAME AND ADDRESS OF RECIPIENT]:

1. [NAME OF ENFORCING AUTHORITY] has pursuant to section 78E(1) of the Environmental Protection Act 1990 served [a remediation notice] [remediation notices] in relation to contaminated land within its area.

2. The Enforcing Authority is required to send you a copy of the [notice] [notices] by regulation 5(1) of the Contaminated Land (England) Regulations 2006 because:

   (A) you are known to be a person whose consent is required under section 78G before any thing required by the notice can be done;
   (B) you are a person who was required to be consulted under section 78H before the notice was served;
   (C) you are the Environment Agency;
   (D) you are the local authority in whose area the relevant land is situated.
   [DELETE AS APPLICABLE]

3. [A copy] [copies] of the remediation [notice is] [notices are] attached.

4. Should you wish to make any representation in response to this Notice, or to seek further information, please contact the following person as soon as possible:

[NAME OF CONTACT]
at
[ADDRESS, TELEPHONE, FAX]

Dated:
[SIGNATURE OF AUTHORISED OFFICER, IF DESIRED]
[NAME OF AUTHORISED OFFICER]
[NAME AND ADDRESS OF ENFORCING AUTHORITY]

Precedent 10

REMEDIATION DECLARATION

Note: Under section 78H(6) where the enforcing authority is precluded by sections 78E(4) or (5) from specifying a particular thing in a remediation notice (because it is unreasonable in terms of cost or seriousness of harm), the enforcing authority must prepare and publish a remediation declaration referring to the reasons why that thing would otherwise have been specified, and the reason why the authority is precluded from its inclusion in the notice.

ENVIRONMENTAL PROTECTION ACT 1990, SECTION 78H(6)—REMEDIATION DECLARATION

1. [NAME OF ENFORCING AUTHORITY] has identified the land specified in the Schedule to this Declaration, situated within the Enforcing Authority's area, as contaminated land under section 78B of the 1990 Act.

2. There are a number of things which the Enforcing Authority would have included in a remediation notice in relation to the land, were it not precluded from including those things by [section 78E(4)] [section 78E(5)] and [section 78H(5)(a)] of the 1990 Act.

3. Accordingly, the Enforcing Authority is required to prepare and publish this Declaration under section 78H(6) of the 1990 Act.

4. The things which the Enforcing Authority would have included in a remediation notice, and the reasons why it would have specified those things are:

Things that would have been specified	Reasons why they would have been specified

5. The grounds on which the Enforcing Authority is satisfied that it has precluded from specifying each such thing in a remediation notice are:

Things that would have been specified	Grounds on which precluded from specifying each thing

SCHEDULE
(DESCRIPTION OF LAND)

Dated:
[NAME OF AUTHORISED OFFICER]
[NAME AND ADDRESS OF ENFORCING AUTHORITY]

PRECEDENT 11

REMEDIATION STATEMENT

Note: An enforcing authority may be precluded from serving a remediation notice under section 78H(5)(b)–(d) because:

(b) appropriate things are being done or will be done without service of a notice; or

(c) the person on whom the notice would be served is the authority itself; or

(d) the powers conferred on the authority by section 78N to do what is appropriate by way of remediation are exercisable.

In such cases, the "responsible person" (as defined by section 78H(8)) must under section 78H(7) prepare and publish a remediation statement recording the specified matters.

ENVIRONMENTAL PROTECTION ACT 1990, SECTION 78H(7)—REMEDIATION STATEMENT

1. This Statement is prepared by [NAME] as the "responsible person" under section 78H(8) of the 1990 Act in respect of the land specified in the Schedule to this Statement which has been identified by [NAME OF AUTHORITY] as contaminated land under section 78B of the 1990 Act.

2. The Authority has been precluded from serving a remediation notice in respect of the land by section [78H(5)(b)] [78H(5)(c)] [78H(5)(d)] of the 1990 Act and accordingly this Statement is required to be made under section 78H(7) of the 1990 Act.

3. The things which [are being] [have been] [are expected to be] done by way of remediation and the periods within which they are being or are expected to be done, are as follows:

Things by way of remediation	Whether completed, or the period within which each thing is being done or is expected to be done

4. The name and address of the person [who is doing] [who has done] [who is expected to do] each of those things is:

[NAME AND ADDRESS]

SCHEDULE
(DESCRIPTION OF LAND)

Dated:
[NAME AND ADDRESS OF PERSON MAKING STATEMENT]

PRECEDENT 12

APPLICATION FOR COMPENSATION FOR THE GRANT OF RIGHTS UNDER SECTION 78G

Note: Section 78G(2) requires any person whose consent is required in order to comply with a remediation notice to grant, or joint in granting such rights as are necessary. By section 78G(5) such a person may make an application in the prescribed form and within a prescribed period, seeking compensation for the grant of such rights and related matters. The Contaminated Land (England) Regulations 2006 prescribe a period of 12 months from the date of the grant of the right, or six months from the date on which the rights were first exercised for that purpose.

ENVIRONMENTAL PROTECTION ACT 1990, SECTION 78G(5) CONTAMINATED LAND (ENGLAND) REGULATIONS 2006—APPLICATION FOR COMPENSATION

To: [NAME AND ADDRESS OF APPROPRIATE PERSON]

1. On [DATE] rights were granted pursuant to section 78G(2) of the 1990 Act to enable requirements of a remediation notice served under section 78E of the 1990 Act to be complied with [and on [DATE] the rights were first exercised.]

2. In accordance with section 78G(5) of the Act, I/we apply for compensation as a person who granted, or joined in granting, those rights.

3. A copy of the grant [and of the plans attached to it] is annexed to this Application.

4. The exact nature of the interest in land in respect of which compensation is applied for is: [. . .]

5. The amount of compensation applied for is [TOTAL AMOUNT] calculated in relation to paragraph 4 of Schedule 2 to the 2000 Regulations as follows:

   (A) Depreciation in the value of any relevant interest resulting from the grant of the rights [AMOUNT AND CALCULATIONS];

   (B) Depreciation in the value of any other interest in land to which I am entitled, resulting from the exercise of the rights [AMOUNT AND CALCULATIONS];

   (C) Loss or damage in relation to any relevant interest to which I am entitled attributable to the grant of the rights and falling within paragraph 4(c) of Schedule 2 to the Regulations [AMOUNT AND CALCULATIONS];

(D) Damage to, or injurious affection of, any interest in land to which I am entitled which is not a relevant interest, resulting from the grant of the rights or the exercise of them [AMOUNT AND CALCULATIONS];

(E) Loss in respect of work carried out by me or on my behalf which is rendered abortive by the grant of the rights or exercise of them [AMOUNT AND CALCULATIONS];

(F) Reasonable valuation or legal expenses [AMOUNT AND CALCULATIONS].

Dated:

[NAME AND ADDRESS OF APPLICANT]

Precedent 13

NOTICE OF APPEAL AGAINST REMEDIATION NOTICE (SECRETARY OF STATE)

Note: Section 78L of the 1990 Act provides for an appeal against a remediation notice served by the Environment Agency or SEPA to be made to the Secretary of State. By regulation 8 of the Contaminated Land (England) Regulations 2006 such an appeal is by notice, copies of which are to be served on the persons specified at regulation 8(2).

NOTICE OF APPEAL—ENVIRONMENTAL PROTECTION ACT 1990, SECTION 78L(1) CONTAMINATED LAND (ENGLAND) REGULATIONS 2006, REGULATION 8

To:

Planning Inspectorate
Room 4/12 Eagle Wing
Temple Quay House
2 The Square
Bristol BS1 6PN
Tel: 0117 372 8726
Email: environment.appeals@Ins.gsi.gov.uk

Name of Appellant:

Address:

1. The Appellant appeals against the Remediation Notice dated [DATE] served by [NAME OF AGENCY] a copy of which is lodged with this Notice of Appeal.

2. The grounds on which the Appellant appeals against the Remediation Notice are as follows:
   [LIST GROUNDS OF APPEAL]

3. The Appellant wishes the appeal
   [to be in the form of a Hearing]
   [to disposed of on the basis of written representations]

4. The Appellant has served copies of this Notice and of the Remediation Notice on the following persons as required by regulaton 9(2)(a)(ii), (iii) or (iv):
   [LIST NAMES AND ADDRESSES]

Dated:
[NAME OF APPELLANT/AGENT]

PRECEDENT 14

PROSECUTION FOR FAILURE TO COMPLY WITH REMEDIATION NOTICE

Note: By section 78M(1) it is an offence for a person on whom a remediation notice is served to fail, without reasonable excuse, to comply with any of the requirements of the notice.

ENVIRONMENTAL PROTECTION ACT 1990, SECTION 78M(1)

[   ] Magistrates' court (Code)

INFORMATION

Informant: [NAME OF AUTHORITY]

Address:

Defendant:

Address:

Date of offence:

Place of offence:

Statute under which offence charged: section 78M(1) of the Environmental Protection Act 1990.

1. The Defendant is an appropriate person on whom the Authority served a Remediation Notice under section 78E(1) of the 1990 Act dated [DATE] requiring the Defendant to do the things specified in the notice by way of remediation in respect of the contaminated land identified in the notice.

[2. The Defendant appealed against the Remediation Notice which on appeal was upheld on [DATE] subject to the following variations: [VARIATIONS]]

[2. The Defendant appealed against the Remediation Notice but abandoned the appeal on [DATE]]
   [USE/DELETE AS APPLICABLE]

3. The period for compliance with the Remediation Notice expired on [DATE] and since that date the Defendant has failed without reasonable excuse to comply with [any] [the following] requirements of the Remediation Notice:
   [DETAILS OF NON COMPLIANCE]

Statement of Offence

That the said [DEFENDANT] at [PLACE] on [DATE] being a person on
whom [NAME OF AUTHORITY] had served a Remediation Notice, failed
without reasonable excuse to comply with any of the requirements of the
Notice, contrary to section 78M(1) of the Environmental Protection Act
1990.

PRECEDENT 15

NOTICE BY ENFORCING AUTHORITY BEFORE EXERCISING POWERS UNDER SECTION 78N

Note: Section 78N gives power to the enforcing authority, in a range of situations, to do itself what is appropriate by way of remediation to the relevant land or waters. The Act does not require notice to be given by the authority before exercising those powers, but it will be good practice to do so, in particular where the appropriate person has not complied with the remediation notice.

ENVIRONMENTAL PROTECTION ACT 1990, SECTION 78N

To: [NAME OF APPROPRIATE PERSON]
[ADDRESS]

1. [NAME OF ENFORCING AUTHORITY] served a Remediation Notice on you, dated [DATE] requiring you to do those things specified in the Notice in relation to the relevant land specified in the Notice.

2. You have failed to comply with the Remediation Notice in the following respects [LIST REQUIREMENTS OF NOTICE NOT COMPLIED WITH].

3. Accordingly, the Enforcing Authority has power under section 78N(1) and (3)(c) of the 1990 Act to do those things itself.

4. The Enforcing Authority intends to do those things listed in the Schedule to this Notice, the cost of which is indicated in the Schedule. The Enforcing Authority will be entitled under section 78P(1) to recover from you the reasonable cost of doing those things, or such part of the cost as is reasonable having regard to section 78P(2). [In such circumstances the Enforcing Authority may also charge interest on the sums recoverable and may impose a charge on your interest in any premises consisting of or including the contaminated land in question for such sums and accrued interest][1]

5. The Enforcing Authority will not commence the relevant works before [DATE]. Should you wish to make representations in respect of this notice before that date you are advised to contact:
[NAME OF CONTACT]
[ADDRESS, TELEPHONE]

---

[1] Include this sentence only if the appropriate person is a causer and knowing permitter and is an owner of the land.

SCHEDULE
[DETAILS OF PROPOSED WORKS, COST, ESTIMATES]

[NAME OF AUTHORISED OFFICER]
[ADDRESS]

PRECEDENT 16

CHARGING NOTICE UNDER SECTION 78P

Note: Where the enforcing authority exercises its powers under section 78N to carry out remediation itself, it is entitled, in four circumstances (sections 78N(3)(a), (c) (e) and (f)) to recover its reasonable costs incurred from the appropriate person or persons. Under sections 78P(4)–(7) the authority may serve a charging notice on the appropriate person or persons where they are an owner of premises consisting of or including the contaminated land as well as being a causer or knowing permitter. The effect of such Notice is to make the costs carry interest at such reasonable rate as the authority determines, and to make the cost and accrued interest a charge on the owner's interest. A copy of the notice must be served on the same date on every other person who, to the knowledge of the authority, has an interest in the land capable of being affected by the charge.

CHARGING NOTICE—ENVIRONMENTAL PROTECTION ACT 1990, SECTION 78P(4)–(7)

To: [NAME OF OWNER]
[ADDRESS]

1. [NAME OF ENFORCING AUTHORITY] has in exercise of its powers under section 78N(1) of the 1990 Act carried out works by way of remediation ("the Works") to the land identified in Schedule 1 to this Notice. The Works are listed in Schedule 2 to this Notice.

[2. You were informed of the Enforcing Authority's intention to carry out the Works in a Notice dated [DATE] and served on [DATE]].

3. The costs incurred by the Authority in carrying out those works are specified in Schedule 2 to this Notice.

4. The Enforcing Authority has decided pursuant to section 78P(1) and (2) of the 1990 Act that it should recover from you a sum in respect of those costs [being the proportion determined pursuant to section 78F(7) of the 1990 Act, there being more than one appropriate person.]

5. This Notice is served on you pursuant to section 78P(3) as the owner of premises consisting of or including the contaminated land in question, who caused or knowingly permitted the substances by reason of which the land is contaminated to be in, on or under the land.

6. The amount of the cost claimed by the Authority as recoverable is [AMOUNT].

7. The effect of this Notice is as follows:

    (A) the cost will carry interest at [RATE OF INTEREST] from the date of service of this Notice until the whole amount is paid; and

(B) subject to your right to appeal against this notice, the cost and accrued interest shall be a charge on the premises referred to at paragraph 5 above.

[8. The Enforcing Authority has served copies of this Notice on the following persons who, to the knowledge of the Authority, have an interest in those premises capable of being affected by the charge: [NAMES AND ADDRESSES]]

9. You [or such persons] may appeal against this notice to a county court within the period of twenty-one days beginning with the date of service.

SCHEDULE 1
(DESCRIPTION OF THE CONTAMINATED LAND)

SCHEDULE 2
[WORKS CARRIED OUT BY THE ENFORCING AUTHORITY AND COSTS]

Date:
[NAME OF AUTHORISED OFFICER]
[NAME OF ENFORCING AUTHORITY]
[ADDRESS]
[CONTACT NAMES AND
TELEPHONE NUMBER]

PRECEDENT 17

NOTICE BY ENFORCING AUTHORITY AS TO POSSIBLE COMMERCIAL CONFIDENTIALITY

Note: Section 78T(1) provides that no information relating to the affairs of any individual or business shall be included in the public registers without their consent, if and so long as the information is commercially confidential. Section 78T(2) requires an authority who feels that information it has obtained might be commercially confidential to give notice to the person or business concerned.

ENVIRONMENTAL PROTECTION ACT 1990, SECTION 78T(2)

To: [NAME OF RECIPIENT]
                [ADDRESS]

1. [NAME OF AUTHORITY] holds the information, in relation to its functions on contaminated land under Part IIA of the Environmental Protection Act 1990, the general nature of which is given in the Schedule to this Notice. The information is required to be included in the register relating to contaminated land maintained by the Authority under section 78R(1) of the 1990 Act unless the information is excluded under section 78T (exclusion from registers of certain confidential information).

2. It appears to the Authority that the information might be commercially confidential as relating to your affairs or to the affairs of your business. *Note:* Section 78T(1) of the 1990 Act states that information is commercially confidential in relation to any individual or person if its being contained in the register would prejudice to an unreasonable degree the commercial interests of that person. Section 78T(11) of the Act requires prejudice to be disregarded insofar as it relates only to the value of the contaminated land in question or otherwise to the ownership or occupation of that land.

3. You are entitled to object to the inclusion of the information on the register on the grounds that it is commercially confidential and to make representations to the Authority for the purpose of justifying such objection.

992

4. Objection or representations should be made to:

[CONTACT NAME]
[ADDRESS]
[TELEPHONE]
within [PERIOD]² beginning with the date of service of this notice.

SCHEDULE
[THE INFORMATION]³

Date:
[NAME OF AUTHORISED OFFICER]
[NAME OF ENFORCING AUTHORITY]
[ADDRESS]

---

² No period for such representations is prescribed. The authority must give a reasonable opportunity for objections. It is suggested that 21 days should be a reasonable opportunity for this purpose.

³ Because the object of the notice is the possible confidentiality of information, and the Notice itself may reach third parties, the general nature of the information should be stated so as to avoid disclosing its precise substance.

COMMERCIAL PRECEDENTS

The following precedents for dealing with contaminated land in various commercial contexts are given in this Appendix. A variety of drafting styles are offered. Whilst it is hoped that these precedents will provide guidance and ideas, they should not be used dogmatically: practice in the area of contaminated land continues to evolve, as do the exigencies of commercial negotiations, and a degree of flexibility on the part of the drafter is required.

CP1. Enquiries of the local authority and/or Environment Agency regarding possible contamination.

CP2. Enquiries of the seller in property transactions.

CP3. Indemnity on sale of land.

CP4. Access agreement for site investigations.

CP5. Letter to environmental consultant requesting proposal.

CP6. Agreement appointing environmental consultant.

CP7. Collateral warranty by environmental consultant.

CP8. Covenants on sale of part of land.

CP9. Agreement for liability.

CP10. Leasehold covenants.

CP11. Landlord's protection clause: pre-existing contamination.

CP12. Tenant's protection clause: pre-existing contamination.

CP13. Provision in lease giving the tenant the right to terminate the lease in the event of contamination problems and excluding tenant's liability to contribute to such matters.

CP14. Acquisition of a company-information request relating to environmental matters.

CP15. Acquisition of a company-environmental warranties.

CP16. Acquisition of a company-environmental indemnities.

CP17. Company or assets acquisition-contaminated land indemnities.

CP18. Provisions for inclusion in loan facility letter.

CP19. Covenants by mortgagor.

Precedent CP1

ENQUIRIES OF THE LOCAL AUTHORITY AND/OR ENVIRONMENT AGENCY REGARDING POSSIBLE CONTAMINATION

1. Has the property or any nearby property been monitored by the [authority/Agency] or by any person on the [authority's/Agency's] behalf in relation to possible soil contamination? If so, please provide details of such monitoring and confirm whether the results of such monitoring are open to inspection.

2. Has the [authority/Agency] been supplied with information by any other authority, agency or person in relation to possible soil contamination on the property or any nearby property? If so, please provide details of such information and whether such information is open to inspection.

3. Has the [authority/Agency] carried out any investigation in relation to contaminative uses on the property or any nearby property? If so, please provide details of such investigation and confirm whether the information is open to inspection.

4. Has the [authority/Agency] received any complaint relating to contamination or the effects of contamination on the property or on any nearby property? If so, please provide details of such complaint and of any action taken in response.

5. Has the [authority/Agency] ever been asked to advise or comment in relation to public or environmental health, building or planning control in relation to contamination or its effects on the property or any nearby property? If so, please give details of such advice.

6. Has the authority/Agency been requested by any person or body to require preventative or remedial actions to be taken in relation to any land contamination on or in the vicinity of the property, whether on the ground that the contamination creates a risk of human health being adversely affected or that the contamination has caused or there is an imminent threat that it may cause damage to any protected species and/or habitats.

PRECEDENT CP2

ENQUIRIES OF SELLER IN PROPERTY TRANSACTIONS

1. Please confirm that the Property has not been used at any time for any of the following purposes or operations:

burial of diseased livestock;

the extraction, handling, or storage of coal, petroleum or similar materials;

the extraction, handling or storage of mineral ores;

gasworks or coal carbonisation plants;

plants for the treatment of coal, oil or similar materials;

power stations;

electricity sub-stations;

metal production, processing and finishing;

storage and handling of scrap metals;

production and processing of mineral products;

asbestos works;

chemical works;

engineering;

shipbuilding;

explosives or ordnance manufacture or testing;

electrical and electronic component manufacture;

manufacture of pet foods or animal feedstuffs;

processing of animal by-products;

paper and print works;

chemical treatment or coating of timber or timber products;

tanning or leatherworks;

fulling, bleaching or dyeing;

carpet or floor covering manufacture;

processing of natural or synthetic rubber;

marshalling, dismantling, repairing or maintaining railway rolling stock, road transport vehicles, vessels, or aircraft;

sewage treatment;

storage, treatment or disposal of sludge;

treating, keeping, disposing of or depositing waste;

storage or disposal of radioactive materials;

dry cleaning;

educational or research laboratories.

2. If the Property has been used in whole or in part for any of the purposes referred to at (1) above or any other potentially contaminative use, please provide details of such use.

3. Please confirm that properties adjoining or neighbouring the Property, in sufficient proximity to effect the Property, have not been used for any of the purposes referred to at (1) above or otherwise for a potentially contaminative use. If they have been so used, please provide details.

4. Please confirm that no noxious or polluting substances are present in, on or under the Property so as to present a risk of harm to human health or pollution of the environment.

5. If unable to give the confirmation requested at (4) above, please supply details as to the substances, the risks presented by them and any steps taken to remedy the same and any other relevant information.

6. Please confirm that there are not and have not been any underground storage tanks or underground pipework at the Property used to store or transport substances which may cause harm to human health or pollution of the environment; and that all above-ground storage tanks are and have at all times been provided with secondary and (where appropriate) tertiary containment in the form of bunds or other engineered structures.

7. If either of the confirmations requested at (6) above cannot be given, please supply full details of:

(a) the location of such tanks and pipework;

(b) the types of substances stored and transported;

(c) whether the tanks or pipework are currently in use;

(d) if not currently in use, when the use ceased and any steps taken to drain and decontaminate the tank or pipework; and

(e) any known or suspected escapes of substances from the tank or pipework or any corresponding containment facility.

8. Please confirm that the use and condition of the Property complies in all respects with legislation for the protection of human health and the environment and with any orders, notices or directions made or given under such legislation, and that all necessary licences, authorisations and consents have been obtained and remain in effect. Please supply copies of all current licences, authorisations and consents relating to the Property.

9. Please confirm that no notices, orders, claims or demands have been made or given in respect of the Property as a result of the condition of the Property or non-compliance or alleged non-compliance with any legislation as referred to at (8) above and that none are anticipated. If this cannot be confirmed, please provide full details.

10. Please confirm that no waste materials or substances have been disposed of (whether intentionally or otherwise) at the Property. If such confirmation cannot be given, please provide full details of the location and date or dates of disposal and of the nature of the materials or substances and of the disposal operations.

11. Please provide details of how waste, including liquid wastes and effluent, produced on the Property is disposed of.

12. Please confirm that there are no closed or operational waste disposal sites or proposed waste disposal sites within 250 metres of the Property.

13. Please state whether any environmental audit or assessment or site investigation has been undertaken in respect of the Property. Please supply full details of any such investigation which has been undertaken and copies of any reports or results which are in the possession of or control of any member of the Seller group.

14. Please state whether any works have been carried out to treat, remove, isolate or immobilise contamination on the Property or on adjoining or neighbouring property. Please supply full details of any such works and any documentation or contracts in relation thereto which are in the possession or control of any member of the Seller group.

Note:
The list of uses at enquiry (1) is drawn from the first and most comprehensive list of potentially contaminative uses published by the DoE in conjunction with the proposed registers of such uses in 1991.

Precedent CP3

INDEMNITY ON SALE OF LAND

1. The Seller agrees with the Purchaser to indemnify and hold harmless the Purchaser against:

    (a) all claims, judgments, damages, costs, penalties, expenses, losses, demands and actions asserted against or imposed upon the Purchaser at common law or under any Environmental Law arising from or in respect of Contamination;

    (b) all costs and expenses incurred by the Purchaser in complying with any notice, order, direction, injunction or other requirement of any court or any competent authority arising from or in respect of Contamination and made or given under common law or any Environmental Law; and

    (c) all costs incurred by the Purchaser as are reasonably necessary to assess, remove, monitor, neutralise, isolate or otherwise deal with any Contamination so as to cause the Property to be in compliance with the minimum requirements of any Environmental Law.

[in each case where notice of the claim, judgment, damages, costs, penalties, expenses, losses, demands or actions is given to the Seller in writing before the [ ] anniversary of Completion].

2. Within [ ] working days of receiving notice of any claim, judgment, damages, costs, fines,[1] penalties, expenses, losses, demands or actions as referred to at paragraph 1 above, or receiving any notice, order, direction, injunction or other requirement as referred to at paragraph 1 above, or at least [ ] working days before incurring any costs as referred to at paragraph 1 above the Purchaser shall notify the Seller in writing and shall provide the Seller with full details thereof, including copies of all related correspondence and reports of any environmental consultants or similar experts.

3. Upon receiving notice under paragraph 2 above, the Seller shall have the right at any time, but not the obligation, to defend any claim, to contest or comply with any notice, order, direction, injunction or other requirement, or to incur any costs or expenses, and the Purchaser shall afford the Seller all assistance as may be reasonably necessary in respect thereof.

4. If the Seller elects not to act under paragraph 3, the Purchaser shall on a timely basis keep the Seller informed of the conduct and progress of all

---

[1] Though the enforcement of an indemnity in respect of a fine imposed by a court may be contrary to public policy.

claims and of all costs and expenses incurred or proposed to be incurred by the Purchaser and shall provide the Seller with copies of all data, reports, records, pleadings and correspondence in respect thereof, and in particular shall not settle or compromise any claim without giving the Seller at least [10] working days prior notice after which the Seller has either given its written consent to such settlement or has not within such notice period elected to take over the conduct of the claim.

[5. The maximum amount payable in aggregate under the indemnity contained in paragraph 1 shall not exceed [£   ]].

Definitions

"Environmental Law"

means any act or regulation or any notice, direction, imposition, or requirement issued, imposed or directed by any competent authority which relates to the protection of human health or protection of the environment and which is applicable at the date of Completion including any modification or re-enactment thereof [but not to the extent that such modification or re-enactment introduces materially more onerous or stringent requirements in respect of Contamination].

"Contamination"

means contamination of the Property by any substance which, in the quantities or concentration at which it is present on the Property, presents a risk of harm to human health or of pollution of the environment, [ALTERNATIVELY, SPECIFIC SUBSTANCES MAY BE IDENTIFIED] [provided that]:

[(a) the Contamination was present on the Property [before the date of Completion] or [as a result of the acts or omissions of the Seller]; [and

(b) the effects of or risks presented by the Contamination have not been materially increased or exacerbated by the positive acts of the Purchaser or the Purchaser's agents.]

Note:
This precedent is intended as an example of an indemnity which may be used on the sale of property. It has been deliberately kept as simple as possible and such indemnities are likely to vary considerably in their scope, effect and sophistication. It covers not only claims by third parties but also own-site clean-up costs reasonably incurred by the Purchaser. Care will need to be taken to establish exactly what type of contamination is covered and whether the indemnity extends to costs incurred as a result of legislative requirements which become more onerous after Completion. There may be great difficulties in establishing what degree of contamination was present on the property at Completion in the absence of an intrusive environmental investigation, and if the indemnity is worded in such a way that requires this to be determined, then provision for determination by an expert in default of agreement may well be desirable.

Precedent CP4

ACCESS AGREEMENT FOR SITE INVESTIGATIONS

THIS AGREEMENT dated [DATE] is made between:

1. [   ] ("the Owner") and

2. [   ] ("the Interested Party")

Recitals

1. The owner is the owner of land at [DETAILS OF LAND] ("the Property").

2. The Interested Party has expressed an interest in buying/leasing/lending against the Property and has requested access to the Property for the purpose of carrying out investigation as to ground conditions at the Property.

3. The Owner is willing to allow such access by the Interested Party subject to the terms and conditions of this Agreement.

IT IS AGREED AS FOLLOWS:

1. The Owner shall permit [NAME OF INTERESTED PARTY'S CONSULTANT] ("the Consultant") on behalf of the Interested Party to enter the Property on 2 (two) days' notice to the Owner for the purpose of inspecting the Property and of taking samples of soil, strata, building materials, contaminants, groundwater and surface water upon the following terms.

2. The samples shall be taken by the Consultant by means of boreholes [and/or trial pits] at the agreed locations shown on the plan annexed hereto.

3. The Consultant shall exercise the permission to enter the Property and to take samples so as to cause as little damage and disruption as possible and in particular:

   (a) the Interested Party shall make good all damage caused to the Property by the Consultant; and

   (b) neither the Consultant nor the Interested Party shall communicate with any employee of the Owner nor with any person exercising a regulatory function in relation to the Property without the Owner's prior written consent.

4. The Interested Party shall indemnify and hold harmless the Owner against all costs, claims, damages, expenses and loss arising from or in the course of the activities of the Consultant.

5. The Interested Party shall provide the Owner with a copy of the Consultant's report in draft form and shall give the Owner the opportunity (within a period of [ONE WEEK] from being provided with the draft report) to make comments and/or representations upon it. The Interested Party shall provide the Owner with a signed copy of the final report.

6. The Interested Party shall exercise strict control over all copies of the Consultant's draft and final reports and shall ensure that such reports and all related information held by the Consultant and the Interested Party are used solely for the purpose of deciding whether and upon what terms to proceed with the proposed transaction. In particular:

    (a) no more than [NUMBER] copies of any draft or final report shall be produced, each of which shall be numbered consecutively on its face and no further copies shall be made without the prior written consent of the Owner;

    (b) the Interested Party shall not without the prior written consent of the Owner make available to any third party any draft or final report or information contained in or used in the preparation of such report, nor indicate to any third party the existence of any such report or information;

    (c) the Interested Party shall in all other respects treat such reports, draft reports and information as confidential.

7. In the event that proposed transaction with the Interested Party does not proceed for any reason (whether at the decision of the Owner or the Interested Party) the Interested Party shall forthwith deliver to the Owner all copies of final and draft reports of the Consultant, all information in tangible form used in the preparation thereof and all samples of soil or water taken from the Property. The Interested Party shall also ensure that all computer disks containing such reports and information are erased and shall provide the Owner with written confirmation to that effect.

Notes:
1. The main purpose of this agreement is to protect the position of the Seller of Property where a prospective purchaser or other interested party is allowed to conduct physical investigations.

2. It assumes that the Consultants who will carry out the investigations have been appointed by the interested party. However, in some cases there may be advantages in the parties making a joint appointment.

PRECEDENT CP5

LETTER TO ENVIRONMENTAL CONSULTANT REQUESTING PROPOSAL

Dear [CONSULTANT]

Re: Pre-acquisition Contaminated Land Survey
[IDENTIFY PROPERTY]

[NAME OR PURCHASER/TENANT] is currently in negotiation to acquire the [freehold/leasehold] of the property located at [IDENTIFY PROPERTY].

We believe that the current use of the property as [CURRENT USE] has existed since [DATE] when the site was redeveloped by [NAME];

or

The property is currently being developed for [INTENDED USE] by [DEVELOPER] and the development is scheduled to be completed by [DATE].

[PURCHASER/TENANT] wishes to appoint an experienced environmental consultant to undertake an independent investigation into the site's history and condition and provide [PURCHASER/TENANT] with an assessment of the potential environmental liabilities associated with acquisition or funding of the property. In this context [PURCHASER/TENANT] considers environmental liabilities to include costs and expenses to the extent they need to be incurred in order to take preventive or remedial action that the [PURCHASER/TENANT] is obliged or under a duty to take under environmental laws in relation to any contamination at or arising from the property, the potential for any costs, expenses, fines or penalties imposed for breaches of or otherwise arising under environmental legislation, any third party claims relating to the condition of the property either from individuals or regulatory agencies, any costs which could be recovered by any regulatory body with powers to undertake remedial or mitigation works at or in relation to any pollution arising from the property, and any significant capital expenditure which would need to be incurred to upgrade or change plant, equipment or practice on the site in order to prevent or remedy these types of potential environmental liabilities.

[PURCHASER/TENANT] would like to invite you to submit a Proposal for this work which addresses the matters set out below. Following [PURCHASER'S/TENANT'S] acceptance of the Proposal a formal letter of appointment will be issued.

[PURCHASER'S/TENANT'S] solicitors will be making preliminary enquiries before contract requesting copies of all relevant environmental documentation from the Seller. However, at this point [PURCHASER/

TENANT] have identified the following documents which may be relevant to the preparation of the Proposal:

[LIST DOCUMENTS]

Copies of these documents are enclosed herewith. For the avoidance of any doubt, these documents are being provided to you on a strictly confidential basis on the understanding that they will be returned to [PURCHASER/TENANT] forthwith if [PURCHASER/TENANT] does not accept your Proposal.

The Proposal should address the following issues:

1. Scope of work

Identification and review of existing information on the history of the site and its surrounding area including geological, hydrogeological, hydrological, geotechnical, use history data, development documentation and information provided from meetings or discussions with the [engineers/architects/other] for the development. A site visit and walk-over survey by suitably qualified personnel should also be undertaken.

The consultant's report should provide [PURCHASER/TENANT] with an opinion on the following issues:

(a) the likely existence and extent of any contamination of soil or waters at the property or in the surrounding area;

(b) whether in the consultant's professional opinion there are any environmental risks associated with any such contamination or other releases to the environment from the site itself or from adjacent land which could result in [PURCHASER'S/TENANT'S] non-compliance with environmental law or exposure to any significant environmental liability;

(c) whether any site practices in relation to waste management or storage or use of hazardous substances might give rise to future contamination of the site and/or the surrounding area;

(d) wherever possible provide written confirmation of the approach or views of any regulatory authorities (including the Environment Agency, local authority health and planning departments) about the property and the surrounding area; and

(e) that it is either not necessary or appropriate to undertake a further phase of site investigations or, if this is not the case, indicate the nature and cost of any recommended sampling, testing or other investigations necessary or appropriate to enable the consultant to provide the opinions set out above.

The foregoing is provided as guidance as to [PURCHASER'S/TENANT'S] minimum requirements for a pre-acquisition contaminated land survey. However, [PURCHASER/TENANT] will be relying on the consultant's experience and judgment about the necessary or appropriate investigations or techniques for this site and the Proposal should address the issue in full.

For the avoidance of any doubt, although the activities mentioned above do not include sampling and analysis or monitoring, if on the basis of the information already provided you feel that it is necessary and/or appropriate for any such provision to be included in the Proposal at this stage there should be no hesitation in doing so.

[PURCHASER/TENANT] accepts that in undertaking the work you will need to rely from time to time upon work undertaken by others. Whilst it will be acceptable to [PURCHASER/TENANT] for information to be accepted as accurate without further verification, the consultant will be expected to exercise professional judgment in the interpretation of an an assessment of the reliance which can be placed upon such information. The consultant will be required to identify to [PURCHASER/TENANT] as soon as possible any deficiencies or difficulties with such information in order for the situation to be addressed within the overall timescale for the acquisition.

2. Timing and Capacity

[PURCHASER/TENANT] will require at least [seven] clear working days prior to the exchange of contracts to review the final draft of the report. The final draft report (including plans, photos, attachments, etc.) must therefore be in [PURCHASER'S/TENANT'S] and its solicitors' hands by the close of business on [DATE]. We should be grateful if the Proposal could confirm that you will be able to comply with this timetable.

The Proposal should also indicate the individuals who it is proposed will carry out the work and an indication of their experience in this area.

The Proposal should also indicate which laboratories you would consider acceptable for conducting any analysis of samples should that prove necessary and their accreditation details.

3. Production and Form of Report

[PURCHASER/TENANT] would be grateful if you could include in the Proposal an indication of a suggested format for the report.

The consultant will be required to provide a very brief written interim report on [DATE]. However, if during the course of carrying out the work the consultant reaches a definitive view on whether a further phase of investigations will be required or if the accuracy of existing data cannot be safely assumed this should be communicated to [PURCHASER/TENANT] at the earliest opportunity.

Copies of all relevant correspondence and draft reports should be sent to [NAME] at [PURCHASER'S/TENANT'S ADDRESS] and its solicitors [NAME AND ADDRESS OF SOLICITORS] the attention of [NAME]. In the case of the final draft report [PURCHASER/TENANT] may request that it be forwarded directly to [three] other parties.

4. Costs

Please indicate the total cost of carrying out the works indicating the level of your fees, expected level of expenses, costs of any equipment hire, laboratory analysis charges and any other anticipated disbursements.

5. Terms and Conditions

[The work would be undertaken subject to the standard [modifications to your] terms and conditions agreed between [PURCHASER] and yourselves in the letter dated [DATE] a copy of which is attached.]

or

[IN THE CASE WHERE A CONSULTANT WITH WHOM THERE ARE NO EXISTING ARRANGEMENTS IS BEING CONTACTED]

[We would be grateful if you could forward to us a copy of your standard terms and conditions as soon as possible.

You should be aware that the following terms and conditions will be unacceptable to [PURCHASER/TENANT]:

Professional indemnity coverage of less than [£5,000,000][2] for each occurrence to be maintained for a period of less than [six] years;

Total exclusion of liabilities on the part of the consultant including liability for breach of contract or limitations of the amount of liability to the amount of the consultant's fees;

Provisions requiring [PURCHASER/TENANT] to indemnify the consultant for losses associated with the work;

Any further fee for extending reliance on the report to the first purchaser, first tenant or any financial institution with an interest in the Property. In this regard [PURCHASER/TENANT] will require execution of a collateral warranty under seal in favour of each of the foregoing in the form of the relevant draft annexed hereto.

Exclusion of any warranty that in performing the services the consultant has exercised such reasonable skill, care and diligence as may be expected of a properly qualified and competent environmental consultant experienced in carrying out work of a similar nature.]

Please contact [NAME] should you require any further information or wish to discuss the details of this letter.

As timing is quite critical we look forward to receiving a Proposal from you by [DATE]. If you are unable to submit a Proposal for any reason we would be grateful if you would let us know as soon as possible to enable us to make other arrangements.

Yours faithfully

[PURCHASER/TENANT]

Note:
This precedent is intended as an example of a letter inviting a consultant to submit a detailed proposal for a site investigation; it indicates the essential nature of the client's

---

[2] This figure may need to be higher (say, £10,000,000) where the investigations are envisaged as including Phase II (i.e. intrusive) work.

requirements. It can be used either with consultants where agreement has already been reached on contractual terms of engagement or with consultants where there are no existing arrangements. It may be necessary to agree in advance the terms on which collateral warranties will be given by the consultant, and a precedent warranty should be annexed for this purpose (see Precedent 7). The requirements as to terms and conditions of appointment may be controversial, and (depending on the nature of the work) the details given here may not be acceptable to all consultants. Professional indemnity insurance is a particularly difficult area.

Precedent CP6

AGREEMENT APPOINTING ENVIRONMENTAL CONSULTANT

THIS AGREEMENT made the [ ] day of [ ] [ ] BETWEEN

(1) [CLIENT] ("the Client"); and

(2) [CONSULTANT] ("the Consultant")

WITNESSES as follows

Appointment

1. The Client engages the Consultant to provide in relation to the property briefly described in the First Schedule ("the Site") the professional services briefly described in the Second Schedule ("the Normal Services") and the Consultant agrees to provide the Normal Services and the Additional Services mentioned below (together "the Services") subject to and in accordance with the terms of this Agreement.

Care and diligence

2.1 The Consultant has had an opportunity of inspecting the physical conditions (including the sub-surface conditions) and other conditions of or affecting the Site and shall be deemed to have fully acquainted himself with the same and to have obtained all necessary information as to risks, contingencies and all other circumstances which may influence or affect the execution of the Services and no failure on the part of the Consultant to discover or foresee any such condition, risk, contingency or circumstance (whether the same ought reasonably to have been discovered or foreseen or not) shall entitle the Consultant to an addition to the fee stated in the Third Schedule or the addition of fees for Additional Services or to an extension of time and the Consultant should not and shall not be entitled to rely upon any survey report or other document prepared by or on behalf of the Client regarding any such matter as referred to in this clause and the Client makes no representation or warranty as to the accuracy or completeness of any such survey report or document and the Client shall have no liability arising out of or in relation to any such survey, report or document or from any representation or statement whether negligently or otherwise made therein contained.

2.2 The Consultant shall exercise all the skill, care and diligence in the discharge of the Services to be expected of an appropriately qualified and competent environmental consultant experienced in carrying out services of the relevant nature.

Assignment or transfer

3. The Consultant shall not without the prior written consent of the Client (which consent shall be at the absolute discretion of the Client) delegate

any of its obligations in relation to the Services or any part thereof and the Consultant shall be responsible for the acts of any party to whom the Consultant's obligations (or any of them) are delegated whether or not the requisite consent of the Client has been obtained and in particular without limitation the Consultant shall be responsible for the work of any laboratory or other sub-contractor used by the Consultant and approved by the Client and the Client may assign or transfer all or any of the benefit of this Agreement and/or any part share or interest therein.

Normal Services

4. As part of the Normal Services the Consultant shall give to the Client such advice and assistance within the field of its qualifications and competence as may be reasonably required in connection with the Services from time to time by the Client.

Additional Services

5. The Consultant shall if requested by the Client provide in relation to the Site any additional services ("the Additional Services") of reasonably the same nature as the Normal Services.

Fees

6. The sum payable by the Client to the Consultant for the Normal Services shall be the fee stated in the Third Schedule and the Client shall pay the Consultant reasonable additional fees for Additional Services and all fees shall be payable after submission for the Consultant to the Client of the Consultant's final report and satisfactory completion of all the Services.

Expenses and disbursements

7. Unless otherwise expressly agreed in respect of particular expenses and disbursements the fees shall be in full satisfaction of the Client's liability to the Consultant in respect of expenses and disbursements incurred in the provision of the Services.

Period for payment and interest

8. All sums properly due from the Client to the Consultant in accordance with this Agreement shall be paid within thirty working days of the submission by the Consultant of its proper invoices to the Client and any sums remaining unpaid at the expiry of such period of thirty working days shall bear interest after that time such interest to accrue from that time at the rate of [three] per centum per annum above the sterling base lending rate of [NAME OF BANK] from time to time in force.

Value Added Tax

9. All sums due from the Client to the Consultant in accordance with this Agreement are exclusive of Value Added Tax, the amount of which at the

rate and in the manner prescribed by law shall be paid by the Client to the Consultant.

Final report and Consultant's documents

10. The Consultant shall submit its final report to the Client in five copies and each copy of the final report shall include such information, date, drawings, reports, specification, calculations and other similar material as is necessary to enable a reader fully to comprehend the report without reference to any other documents and promptly after completion of the Services the Consultant shall deliver to the Client free of charge one copy of all completed drawings, reports, specifications, calculations and other similar documents relevant to the Services in its possession.

Copyright

11. The copyright in all drawings, reports, specifications, calculations and other similar documents provided by the Consultant in connection with this Agreement shall to the extent they are vested in the Consultant remain vested in the Consultant but the Client and its appointee shall have a royalty-free non-exclusive licence to copy and use such drawings and other documents and to reproduce any designs contained in them for any purpose related to the Site including but without limitation the construction, completion, maintenance, letting, promotion, advertisement, reinstatement, repair and/or extension of the Site and/or of any works or structures for the time being on the Site and the Consultant shall, if the Client so requests and undertakes in writing to pay the Consultant's reasonable copying charges, promptly supply the Client with further conveniently reproducible copies of all such drawings and other documents.

Confidentiality

12. The Consultant shall keep this Agreement and its terms strictly confidential and shall not without the written consent of the Client disclose the existence of this Agreement or any of its terms to anyone and any information concerning this Agreement and/or the Site obtained either by the Consultant or by any person employed by the Consultant in connection with this Agreement is confidential and shall not be used or disclosed by the Consultant or by any such persons except for the purposes of this Agreement.

Professional indemnity insurance

13.1 The Consultant shall maintain professional indemnity insurance covering (inter alia) all liability hereunder in respect of neglects, errors and omissions upon customary and usual terms and conditions prevailing for the time being in the London insurance market and with reputable insurers lawfully carrying on such insurance business in the United Kingdom in an amount of not less than [AMOUNT] pounds for any one occurrence or series of occurrences arising out of any one event for a period beginning now and ending 12 (twelve) years after the completion of the Services provided always that such insurance is available at commercially reasonable rates and the said terms and conditions shall not include any term or condition to the effect that the Consultant must discharge any liability before being entitled to recover from the insurers or any other term or condition which might adversely affect the rights of any person to recover from the insurers pursuant to the Third Parties (Rights Against Insurers) Act, 1930 or any amendment or re-enactment thereof and the Consultant shall not without the prior approval in writing of the Client settle or compromise with the insurers any claim which the Consultant may have against the insurers and which relates to a claim by the Client against the Consultant or by any act or omission lose or prejudice the Consultant's right to make or proceed with such a claim against the insurers.

13.2 Any increased or additional premium required by insurers by reason of the Consultant's own claims record or other acts omissions matters or things particular to the Consultant shall be deemed to be within commercially reasonable rates.

13.3 If such insurance ceases to be available at commercially reasonable rates the Consultant shall promptly notify the Client.

13.4 The Consultant shall fully co-operate with any measures reasonably required by the Client including (without limitation) completing any proposals for insurance and associated documents maintaining such insurance at rates above commercially reasonable rates if the Client undertakes in writing to reimburse the Consultant in respect of the net cost of such insurance to the Consultant above commercially reasonable rates or if the Client effects such insurance at rates at or above commercially reasonable rates reimbursing the Client in respect of what the net cost of such insurance to the Client would have been at commercially reasonable rates.

13.5 As and when reasonably requested to do so by the Client the Consultant shall produce for inspection documentary evidence (including if required by the Client the originals of the relevant insurance documents and/or a letter from the insurer confirming that the policy is in existence and that any policy contains no unusual limitations) that the required professional indemnity insurance is being maintained.

13.6 The above obligations in respect of professional indemnity insurance shall continue notwithstanding termination of this Agreement for any reason whatsoever including (without limitation) breach by the Client.

Collateral warranties

14.1 The Consultant shall within 7 (seven) working days of the Client's request so to do execute in favour of any persons who have entered or shall enter into an agreement for the provision of finance in connection with the Site or any part thereof and/or in favour of any persons who have acquired or shall acquire any interest in or over the Site or any part thereof a Deed in the form annexed as Annex 'A' or a similar form reasonably required by the Client and deliver the same to the Client.

14.2 The above obligation for the provision of a Deed shall continue notwithstanding termination of this Agreement for any reason whatsoever including (without limitation) breach by the Client and any such Deed given after such termination shall be amended by the Client so as to refer to the fact and date of such termination and to omit any obligation to continue to exercise skill care and diligence after such termination.

Proper law and jurisdiction

15. The construction validity and performance of this Agreement shall be governed by English law and the parties agree to submit to the non-exclusive jurisdiction of the English courts.

IN WITNESS whereof the parties have executed this deed in duplicate on the date first stated above

FIRST SCHEDULE

The Site

SECOND SCHEDULE

Normal Services

[As described in:

the Client's request for the Consultant's Proposal dated [   ] ; and

the Consultant's Proposal dated [   ] ;

copies of which are annexed.]

THIRD SCHEDULE

Fees for Normal Services

Note:
This Precedent gives a form of agreement appointing an environmental consultant to carry out agreed works of investigation. Such agreements may be under hand or made by a deed of appointment, as is provided here.

The agreement refers to agreed "Normal Services" but provides the flexibility to incorporate such further work (the "Additional Services") as may become necessary or advisable during the course of the investigation.

An agreement appointing the Consultant may contain provisions for the execution of collateral warranties whereby the Consultant will warrant the results of his environmental investigation to any lender of the property and/or any person acquiring an interest in the site.

Precedent CP7

COLLATERAL WARRANTY BY ENVIRONMENTAL CONSULTANT

THIS AGREEMENT is made the [   ] day of [   ] BETWEEN

(1) [CONSULTANT] ("the Consultant")

(2) [PURCHASER]

("the Purchaser")

WHEREAS

A. The Consultant carries on business as [Environmental Consultants] [Structural and Civil Engineers] and has been appointed as such by [DEVELOPER] ("the Developer") by an agreement ("the Appointment") for the purpose of investigating the history and condition of site of the Development (as hereinafter defined), assessing the nature and extent of contamination and advising on remedial and precautionary measures in relation to such contamination.

B. The Developer [has constructed] [has entered into a building contract with [CONTRACTOR] ("the Contractor") under which (inter alia) the Contractor is to design and build] [DESCRIPTION OF THE DEVELOPMENT]

("the Development")

C. The Purchaser has entered into an agreement with the Developer whereby the Purchaser agrees to purchase the Development from the Developer.

NOW IT IS HEREBY AGREED as follows:

1.1 The Consultant warrants to the Purchaser that it has exercised [and will continue to exercise] reasonable skill care and diligence in the performance of its services to the Developer under the Appointment PROVIDED THAT [the Consultant's liability to the Purchaser under this Agreement for economic and consequential losses suffered by the Purchaser in relation to the Development shall be limited to the reasonable costs of remedying any damage to or defects in the Development which are directly caused by the Consultant's failure to exercise the aforesaid skill care and diligence together with any consequential loss and costs directly attributable to such defects or remedy of such defects and further that] the Consultant shall be entitled in any action or proceedings by the Purchaser under this Agreement to rely on any limitation in the Appointment and to raise the equivalent rights and defence of liability as it would have under the Appointment.

[1.2 The Consultant's liability for costs under this Agreement shall be limited to that proportion of such costs which it would be just and equitable to require the Consultant to pay having regard to the extent of the Consultant's responsibility for the same and on the basis that [NAME OF OTHER CONSULTANTS] shall be deemed to have provided a contractual undertaking to the Purchaser in respect of the performance of their services in connection with the Development and shall be deemed to have paid to the Purchaser such proportion which it would be just and equitable for them to pay having regard to the extent of their responsibility.]

2. The Consultant acknowledges and covenants with the Purchaser that it has exercised all reasonable skill and care in the exercise of its duties and responsibilities in investigating the site for the suitability of the Development and in the preparation of the report entitled [TITLE, DATE AND NUMBER OF REPORT] pursuant to the Consultant's appointment by the Developer and that the Purchaser has relied upon and may continue to rely upon the said report provided that the Consultant shall have no greater duty of care to the Purchaser by virtue of this clause than it would have had if the Purchaser had been named as the Client under such appointment [and provided further that the Consultant's liability to the Purchaser under this clause for economic and consequential losses suffered by the Purchaser in relation to the Development shall be limited to the reasonable costs of remedying any damage to and/or defects in the Development and/or the rebuilding and/or reconstruction of the Development together with any consequential loss and costs directly attributable to any of the aforesaid matters].

3.1 The Consultant shall maintain professional indemnity insurance in the amount of not less than [AMOUNT] for any one occurrence or series of occurrences arising out of any one event for a period of 12 years from the date of [this Agreement] [practical completion of the Development under the said building contract] provided always that such insurance is available at commercially reasonable rates.

3.2 The Consultant shall immediately inform the Purchaser if such insurance ceases to be available at commercially reasonable rates in order that the Consultant and the Purchaser can discuss means of best protecting the respective positions of the Purchaser and the Consultant in the absence of such insurance.

3.3 As and when it is reasonably requested to do so by the Purchaser the Consultant shall produce for inspection documentary evidence that such professional indemnity insurance is being maintained.

3.4 This agreement may be assigned [once by the Purchaser by way of absolute legal assignment to another person taking an assignment of the Purchaser's interest in the Development] without the consent of the Consultant being required [and thereafter may be assigned on one further occasion with the prior written consent of the Consultant (such consent not to be unreasonably withheld or delayed)] and written notice of such assignment shall be given to the Consultant.

4. No action or proceedings for any breach of this Agreement shall be commenced against the Consultant after the expiry of 12 years from the

date [of this Agreement] [practical completion of the Development under the said building contract.]

IN WITNESS whereof the Consultant has executed this Agreement as a Deed the day and year first above written.

Note:
This is an example of a deed of collateral warranty given by a consultant in favour of a purchaser. It contains various optional limitations and alternatives for use where the Development is being sold in the course of construction. It also contains various provisions which the consultant's advisers might seek to have inserted for the protection of the consultant.

Precedent CP8

COVENANTS ON SALE OF PART OF LAND

The Purchaser hereby covenants for itself and its successors in title with the intention to bind the Property and each and every part thereof for the benefit of the Seller's Retained Land and each and every part thereof as follows:

1. Not to use the Property or any part of it for any purpose which may be or become a nuisance (whether or not amounting to a legal nuisance) or an annoyance or obnoxious to the Seller or its successors in title (including tenants and occupiers) to the Retained Land or any part of it or which tends to diminish or lessen the value of the Retained Land or any building erected on any part of it.

2. Not to deposit on the Property any controlled waste as defined in the Environmental Protection Act 1990 or hazardous waste as defined in the Hazardous Waste (England and Wales) Regulations 2005 or radioactive waste as defined in the Radioactive Substances Act 1993 (or any re-enactment thereof) or any other substance (whether from premises used for agriculture within the meaning of the Agriculture Act 1947 or from other sources) or thing which may produce concentrations or accumulations of noxious gases or noxious liquids or other emissions or releases which may cause pollution of the environment or harm to human health.

3. To take all practicable precautions to ensure that no noxious substances are spilled or deposited on the Property or the Retained Land and that contamination of the Property or the Retained Land does not occur.

4. To indemnify and keep indemnified the Seller against all damage or nuisance caused directly or indirectly by the activities of the Purchaser or by the use of the Property to the Seller's Retained Land or the Seller's use of the Retained Land and against all actions claims and demands made against or notices served on the Seller in respect of damage to or pollution of the environment or damage to property or harm to human health caused directly or indirectly by the use of the Property or by any substance thereon whether in liquid or solid form or in the form of gas or vapour or energy[3].

5. To indemnify the Seller and its successors in title for the benefit of the Seller's Retained Land and each and every part thereof against all losses costs expenses claims actions liabilities damages

---

[3] e.g. energy from ionizing or non-ionising radiation

demands proceedings and orders (whether of a statutory or civil nature) which may at any time hereafter arise (whether or not they arise out of an act omission or negligence preceding the date of this Deed) in relation to any matter concerning the state and condition of the Property and adjoining property or any surrounding air space or the substratum of or waters (including groundwaters) associated with the Property or any adjoining property or any claim direction order or fine imposed under any legislation for the protection of human health or the environment (including without limitation the Control of Pollution Act 1974, the Environmental Protection Act 1990, the Water Resources Act 1991, the Water Industry Act 1991 and the Radioactive Substances Act 1993) or any statute modifying amending adding to or replacing the same.

6. Not to discharge or allow to be discharged into any pipe or drain serving the Property and the Seller's Retained Land in common any oil grease deleterious or other harmful matter or substance which might be or become a source of danger or harm or injury to any person or damage the said pipes or drains or any part thereof.

Note:
These covenants may be imposed where the Seller retains adjoining land in order to provide protection against contamination arising from the Purchaser's future activities. They may be supplemented by specific restrictions on certain potentially contaminative activities or the use or storage of certain contaminative substances, if so desired. The Purchaser may, of course, seek reciprocal covenants from the Seller.

PRECEDENT CP9

AGREEMENT FOR LIABILITY

1.1 The Purchaser acknowledges and agrees that:

(a) [it has reviewed or received a copy of [named environmental reports]];

(b) [it has had permission from the Seller to carry out its own investigations into the condition of the Sites];

(c) it has acquired, whether through its own investigations into the condition of the Property or otherwise, information that would reasonably allow it to be aware of the presence of any hazardous substances, contamination or pollution ('Contamination') and the broad measure of its extent and that the Property is "sold with information" within the terms of exclusion test 3 in Part 5 of Chapter D of Annex 3 to DEFRA Circular 01/2006 or any equivalent or similar provisions promulgated at any time;

(d) with regard to the presence or potential presence of any Contamination at the Property, it is not relying and has not relied on any representation, warranty, conduct or statement or silence by the Seller;

(e) the consideration payable for the Property takes into account the amount that is regarded by the Seller and the Purchaser as sufficient to pay for the remediation of the Contamination at the Property, and is intended to constitute a payment made for remediation of the type specified in exclusion test 2 in Part 5 of Chapter D of Annex 3 to DEFRA Circular 01/2006 or any equivalent or similar provisions promulgated at any time.

1.2 The Seller and the Purchaser agree that as between them all liability in relation to any Contamination shall be the sole responsibility of the Purchaser, and shall not in any circumstances be borne in whole or in part by the Seller.

1.3 The Seller and the Purchaser agree that, notwithstanding any confidentiality provisions contained in this Agreement [or any other confidentiality agreement that they have entered into], they will represent to any relevant authority who is making any determination on exclusion, apportionment or attribution of any liability for Contamination that any liability which would have been attributed or apportioned to the Seller (but for this clause) should be attributed or apportioned to the Purchaser, pursuant to paragraph D.38 of Chapter D of Annex 3 to Defra Circular 01/2006 or any equivalent or similar provisions promulgated at any time, and to show the provisions of this clause to any relevant authority that has held, or is threatening or reasonably likely to hold, the Seller liable in relation to any Contamination, and the Seller and the Purchaser shall make known to such authority their agreed intention for the Purchaser to be liable in relation to all Contamination, as provided for above in this clause.

1.4 Each of the Seller and the Purchaser agree not to challenge the application of the agreement set out in this clause.

Note:
This wording is designed to avoid any continuing liability for a Seller post completion in relation to the contaminated land regime set out at Pt IIA of the Environmental Protection Act 1990. It takes account of the provisions of the statutory guidance contained in Annex 3 of Defra Circular 01/2006 Contaminated Land on the exclusion from and apportionment of liability for remediation.

Precedent CP10

LEASEHOLD COVENANTS

1. Reservations

The following rights are reserved:

(a) the right to commission at the Tenant's expense an environmental investigation ("the Second Investigation") similar in nature to the investigation carried out for the purposes of the preparation of the report annexed to this Lease ("the Report") and to be carried out on the Property in the last six months of the term;

(b) the right to enter onto the Property with environmental consultants appointed by the Landlord with or without vehicles and appropriate equipment and machinery on giving reasonable notice for the purpose of carrying out tests and examinations necessary for the preparation of the Second Investigation (the Landlord making good any damage caused thereby) and specifying the remediation works (if any) required to restore the Property to the state and condition specified in the Report.

2. Tenant's Covenants

The Tenant covenants as follows:

(a) to maintain the Property in no worse state and condition than that specified in the Report and to take all practicable precautions to ensure that no noxious substances are spilled or deposited on the Property and that contamination of the Property does not occur.

(b) within one month after service upon the Tenant of notice of remediation to carry out the remediation works (if any) specified in the Second Investigation and if the Tenant shall not within one month after service of such notice or (in case of emergency) immediately after service of such notice commence and thereafter proceed diligently with the execution of such remediation works then to permit the Landlord and all persons authorised by it to enter upon the property and to execute the necessary remediation works the cost of which shall be paid by the Tenant on demand and if not so paid the cost shall be a debt due from the Tenant to the Landlord and be forthwith recoverable by action notwithstanding the expiration or sooner determination of this Lease.

(c) not to deposit on the Property any controlled waste as defined in the Environmental Protection Act 1990 or hazardous waste as defined in the Hazardous Waste (England and Wales) Regulations 2005 or Radioactive Waste as defined in section 18 of the Radioactive Substances Act 1993 or any re-enactment thereof or any other substance (whether from premises used for agriculture within the meaning of the Agricultural Act 1947 or from other sources) or thing which may produce concentrations or accumulations of noxious gases or noxious liquids or any other thing which may cause pollution of the environment or harm to human health.

(d) within 14 days of the occurrence of a Notifiable Event to inform the Landlord of its occurrence and to permit the Landlord to enter and inspect the Property. "Notifiable Event" means the spilling, release or deposit on the Property of any noxious or other substance in a quantity which may cause serious damage to or pollution of the environment or serious damage to property or serious harm to human health.

(e) not to discharge or cause to be discharged into any pipe or drain serving the Property any oil, grease, deleterious or other harmful matter or substance which might cause damage to the environment or be or become a source of danger or harm or annoyance to any person or might cause damage or injury to those pipes or drains or any part thereof.

(f) to indemnify and keep the Landlord indemnified against all actions, claims, costs, damages, judgments, fines, penalties, expenses, losses, and demands in respect of damage to or pollution of the environment or damage to property or harm to human health caused by the Property or any substance thereon whether in liquid or solid form or in the form of gas or vapour or energy.

(g) where expenses for clean-up costs on the Property become a charge on the Property under section 81A of the Environmental Protection 1990 ("the 1990 Act") and such expenses are recovered by the local authority from the tenant under section 81B of the 1990 Act, to waive its statutory right to deduct such expenses from the rent due to the landlord and to pay to the local authority all outstanding clean-up costs as demanded by the local authority in full settlement of such demands irrespective of the amount of rent due to the landlord at any given time.

Notes:
1. So far as the landlord is concerned, the terms of the following usual clauses should be considered carefully so as to protect the reversionary interest:

(1) ensure that the terms of the user covenant are suitable and sufficiently restrictive and include, if appropriate, a restriction on the use and types of equipment on the site;

(2) ensure that there is a sufficient covenant to comply with the provisions of every enactment, instrument, regulation and by-law and notice, order or direction, etc. and that the right to production of copy notices, etc. includes a

right to production of relevant environmental licences (although these will be in the public domain);

(3) *rights of entry and inspection.*

2. In particular, where actual contamination is likely it may be useful to have a soil survey carried out before execution of the lease. The survey report would be attached to the lease like a schedule of repair. The precedent assumes that such an investigation has been carried out. A second investigation can be carried out at the expiration of the lease to assess whether the tenant has caused contamination. The landlord then requires restoration/clean-up on the expiration of the term and the tenant is bound to bring the site up to the standard it was at the beginning of the term. Such provisions will not be suitable for all leases, but may be particularly useful in the case of leases of industrial premises, oil depots and the like.

3. Additional sub-clause (g) below attempts to reverse the effect of s.81B of the Environmental Protection Act 1990 which gives the tenant the power to deduct from rent expenses recoverable from him to relation to statutory nuisance. Whether such a provision is contrary to public policy is arguable: see Johnson v Moreton *[1980] A.C. 37.*

Precedent CP11

LANDLORD'S PROTECTION CLAUSE—PRE-EXISTING CONTAMINATION

1. The Tenant agrees that except as expressly provided in this Lease no representations by or on behalf of the Landlord have been made to the Tenant as to the condition of the Demised Premises, or the applicability or otherwise to the Demised Premises of any requirements under environmental law, or the suitability of the Demised Premises for any purpose whatsoever.

2. The Tenant represents to the Landlord that the Tenant has made its own independent investigation of the Demised Premises and is relying solely on such investigations.

3. The Tenant acknowledges that the Landlord has no experience concerning environmental matters or the requirements of environmental law and that the Tenant is not relying on any representation or assurance by the Landlord with regard to such matters as they affect the Demised Premises.

4. The Tenant unconditionally releases the Landlord from and against any and all liability, whensoever arising, in respect of any liabilities, damage, costs or claims suffered or incurred by the Tenant as a result of the condition of the Demised Premises including, without limitation, the presence of contaminating substances in, on over or under the Demised Premises or any part thereof whether before or during the term hereby granted or any lawful extension thereof and the Tenant covenants to indemnify and hold harmless the Landlord against all liabilities, damages, costs or claims suffered or incurred by the Landlord as a result of such condition of the Demised Premises.

5. It is agreed that the Tenant shall not be excused or released from performance of any of the Tenant's covenants contained in this lease where the performance of such covenants involves work or expenditure to make good, rectify, remove, treat or render harmless contaminating substances present in, on, over or under the Demised Premises (whether before or during the term hereby granted or any lawful extension thereof) or to make good any damage caused by such substances whether on the Demised Premises or elsewhere.

Note:
The object of this provision is to throw the risk of liability arising from the pre-existing soil contamination wholly onto the tenant. Whether it is reasonable to do this will depend on the circumstances, including the length of the term.

Precedent CP12

TENANT'S PROTECTION CLAUSE—PRE-EXISTING CONTAMINATION

1. Notwithstanding the Tenant's covenants in this Lease, the Tenant shall have no liability, in respect of the terms of this Lease or otherwise, as a result of the presence in, on, over or under the Demised Premises or any adjoining or neighbouring property at the date of this Lease of contaminative substances ("Contamination") or as a result of such previous uses of the Demised Premises or any adjoining or neighbouring property as have resulted in the release of contaminative substances ("Contaminative Uses").

2. It is agreed that, without prejudice to the generality of clause 1, the Tenant shall not be required by any of the Tenant's covenants contained in this lease to make good or rectify (or pay to make good or rectify) any defect or want of repair resulting from Contamination or Contaminative Uses (whether at the Demised Premises or elsewhere), nor shall the Tenant be required to rectify, remove, treat or render harmless Contamination or rectify any damage or other adverse consequences of any Contaminative Use.

3. The Landlord shall indemnify and hold harmless the Tenant against all liabilities, damage, costs or claims whensoever arising resulting from Contamination or Contaminative Uses.

Note:
This provision affords the Tenant protection against being held liable (under the terms of the Lease or otherwise) to clean-up or make good pre-existing contamination. The Tenant should be aware that liability in respect of contamination can arise in various ways, for example direct covenant, covenant to comply with statute, covenants as to repair, decoration, service charges, etc. Provisions throwing the risk of such matters onto the Landlord may have a significantly adverse effect on the value of the reversion and may therefore be strongly resisted.

Precedent CP13

PROVISION IN LEASE GIVING TENANT THE RIGHT TO TERMINATE THE LEASE IN THE EVENT OF CONTAMINATION PROBLEMS AND EXCLUDING TENANT'S LIABILITY TO CONTRIBUTE TO COSTS IN SUCH AN EVENT

1. Exclusion of liability to repair

1.1 In this Clause and the following Clause only the following words shall have the following meanings:

"Emissions" shall mean emissions of methane or other gases [or substances or energy] from the soil of the Estate.

"Excluded Occupation" shall mean the Demised Premises are in such a state or condition due to Emissions or Ground Faults that the Tenant cannot make beneficial use or maintain beneficial occupation of the Demised Premises and that such condition is likely to continue for a period in excess of 12 months without remedial works being carried out which are in excess of the Tenant's repairing obligations hereunder as may be varied by this Clause.

"Ground Faults" shall mean landslip, subsidence, settlement or heave.

"Occupation Notice" shall means a notice in writing given by the Tenant to the Landlord that there exists a state of Excluded Occupation.

"the Landlord's Works Option Period" shall mean the period of three months commencing with the date of receipt of the decision of the person appointed in accordance with Clause 1.2 or the date of an agreement between the parties in lieu of reference to the Arbitration Procedure relating to Excluded Occupation.

1.2 Nothwithstanding anything elsewhere in this Lease contained it is hereby agreed and declared between the parties that:

1.2.1 during the period of the first twelve years of the Term the Tenant shall not save to the extent hereinafter in this Clause provided be under any liability to the Landlord or to any other person to carry out or contribute towards the cost of carrying out any works to the Demised Premises or the means of access thereto or to the Estate or to anything therein or serving the same which is attributable to Emissions; and

1.2.3 during the Term the Tenant shall not be under any liability or obligation to carry out or contribute towards the cost of carrying out any works of repair to the Demised Premises or the Estate made necessary or caused by Ground Faults.

PROVIDED THAT:

1.3 Nothing herein contained shall exclude or excuse or prevent the Tenant from complying with its obligations herein contained as to the normal maintenance and repair of the Demised Premises and the equipment installed therein for the protection of the Demised Premises or any other premises from Emissions; and

1.4 Such exclusion hereinbefore contained from the Tenant's liability to repair or contribute to repairs shall not affect the Tenant's obligations to carry out repairs to existing systems, structures or works within the Demised Premises which are designed to protect the Demised Premises or the Estate from Emissions and which are in the nature of routine maintenance works.

2. Tenant's Option to Break

2.1 If during the first 12 years of the Term there exists a state of Excluded Occupation and the Tenant shall give the Landlord an Occupation Notice within three months of the coming into existence of the state of Excluded Occupation THEN unless Excluded Occupation is brought about as a result of the Tenant's failure to observe and perform its obligations hereunder the following provisions shall apply:

2.2 Either the Landlord or the Tenant may require a certificate from an independent surveyor to be agreed upon or appointed in accordance with the Arbitration Procedure certifying whether or not Excluded Occupation exists.

2.3 If the surveyor shall certify that Excluded Occupation exists or the Landlord and the Tenant shall agree that the Excluded Occupation exists the Landlord shall within the Landlord's Works Option Period notify the Tenant in writing whether or not it will carry out such works as may be necessary to end Excluded Occupation.

2.4 If the Landlord shall elect to carry out such works the Landlord shall commence and proceed diligently with such works as soon as practicable thereafter and shall use all reasonable endeavours to complete the same within 12 months.

2.5 If the Landlord shall decline to carry out such works as aforesaid the tenant may by notice in writing at any time within three months after the Landlord's notification under clause 2.1 determine this Lease on giving not less than 14 days' written notice to the Landlord and upon the expiry of such notice this Lease shall cease and determine but without prejudice to the rights and remedies of either party against the other in respect of any antecedent claim for breach of covenant.

2.6 During the period of the Excluded Occupation commencing with the service of the Occupation Notice until the Demised Premises are again rendered fit for occupation and use or until (as the case may be) determination of the Lease the rent payable hereunder or a fair proportion thereof according to the extent to which the Tenant shall have been deprived of occupation shall be suspended and cease to be payable.

2.7 If the Tenant shall not have exercised its option to determine the Landlord may at any time thereafter serve notice upon the Tenant requiring the Tenant to determine the Lease within one month of receipt of such notice and if the Tenant shall not have determined the Lease within such period of one month then upon the expiry of the said period of one month the yearly rent shall thereafter continue to be payable notwithstanding the provisions of clause 2.6.

2.8 If the Tenant shall so determine the Lease the Lease shall cease and determine as provided in clause 2.4 hereof.

3. Relationship to repairing obligations

For the avoidance of doubt nothing in the foregoing clauses 1 and 2 shall be construed as increasing the repairing obligations of the Tenant under this Lease beyond those which would have existed had those clauses not been included herein.

Note:
Such a provision may be useful where, for example, offices or retail premises are constructed on or near a reclaimed waste site. The tenant is allowed to break if the Premises become unusable due to gas emissions or subsidence during the first 12 years of the term and the landlord does not carry out the works necessary to restore them to good order (with rent suspension in the meantime, during such works). The provision also makes it clear that the tenant is not liable to contribute towards any costs arising in respect of subsidence, landslip, settlement or heave.

Precedent CP14

ACQUISITION OF A COMPANY—INFORMATION REQUEST RELATING TO ENVIRONMENTAL MATTERS

In respect of the Company and each of the Subsidiaries (which shall include any former subsidiary, whether or not still in existence or still a subsidiary of the Company) please supply the following particulars:

(a) The full postal addresses of all sites owned or occupied by the Company or any of its Subsidiaries, in each case identified by means of a plan and with details as to the nature of the activities, operations or processes carried on at the site.

(b) So far as is known, the full postal addresses of sites owned or occupied by the Company or any of its Subsidiaries within the last 30 years, in each case identified by means of a plan and with details as to the nature of the activities, operations or practices carried on at each site during the ownership or occupation of the Company or its subsidiaries.

(c) Copies of all statutory authorisations held by the Company and any of its Subsidiaries together with details of any such authorisations applied for.

(d) In relation to all such authorisations, copies of any correspondence with the relevant authorities, notices received from the relevant authorities and any information supplied to the relevant authorities in support of the application for such authorisations.

(e) With regard to all wastes produced by the Company and any of its Subsidiaries, whether solid, liquid or gaseous, particulars of the means by which such wastes are disposed of, including: (i) the names and addresses of the waste carriers and disposal contractors and the sites to which such wastes are disposed of; (ii) details (if known) of the carriers, the contractors and the sites to which such wastes have been disposed of in the past; (iii) copies of existing waste disposal contracts.

(f) Copies of any statements of corporate environmental policy and operating procedures and copies of any environmental audit, investigation or report carried out in relation to the activities, operations and processes of the Company and any of its Subsidiaries, or in relation to any former or existing sites owned or occupied by the Company or any of its Subsidiaries.

(g) Any known breach of Environmental Law by the Company or its Subsidiaries, whether or not such a breach has resulted in prosecution or any other enforcement action or penalty by the relevant authority.

(h) Any known spillages of potentially polluting materials by the Company or its Subsidiaries (wherever occurring) or by any person at any of the Sites owned or occupied by the Company or its Subsidiaries.

PRECEDENT CP15

ACQUISITION OF A COMPANY—ENVIRONMENTAL WARRANTIES

1. Authorisations, etc.

(a) Full particulars are given in the Disclosure Letter of all authorisations, permissions, consents, licences, registrations and agreements held by the Company as are necessary to enable the Company to carry on its business lawfully and effectively in the places and in the manner in which such business is now carried on as specified in the Disclosure Letter and in particular (but without limitation) as are necessary or required: (i) to make all relevant abstractions of water; (ii) to keep, store or hold all relevant substances whether as raw materials, products or wastes; (iii) to carry on all relevant processes and activities; (iv) to construct and maintain all relevant buildings, plant and equipment; and (v) to hold, treat, manage, consign, deposit and dispose of all waste materials, and to discharge and emit other substances, gases and effluents, as the case may be, in the relevant manner. All such authorisations, permissions, consents, licences and agreements have been lawfully obtained and are in full force and effect. No further authorisations, permissions, consents, licences or agreements are necessary.

(b) Save as stated in the Disclosure Letter the Company has complied at all times with all conditions attaching to the authorisations, permissions, consents, licences and agreements referred to above (whether such conditions are imposed expressly or are implied by statute) and the Seller is not aware of any circumstances which would render it impossible for the Company to comply with such conditions in the future.

(c) The Company has received no notice, correspondence or communication in any other form in respect of any of the authorisations, permissions, consents, licences or agreements referred to above revoking, suspending, modifying or varying the same and is not aware of any circumstances which might give rise to such notice, correspondence or communication being received or of any intention on the part of any relevant authority to give or make such notice, correspondence or communication.

(d) The Seller will use all reasonable endeavours to ensure that all relevant authorisations, permissions, consents, licences or agreements are (where necessary) transferred to the Purchaser or, as the case may be, renewed or continued in the name of the Purchaser. In particular, but without limitation, the Seller shall assist the Purchaser in making application to or providing information to any relevant authority for the purpose of such transfer, renewal or continuance.

2. Compliance with Environmental Protection Laws

(a) Save as stated in the Disclosure Letter neither the Company nor any of its officers, agents or employees have committed, whether by act or omission, any breach of statutory requirements for the protection of the environment or of human health or amenity, and have acted at all times in conformity with all relevant codes of practice, guidance, notes, standards and other advisory material issued by any competent authority.

(b) The Company has not received any notice, order or other communication from any relevant authority in respect of the Company's business, failure to comply with which would constitute breach of any statutory requirements or compliance with which could be secured by further proceedings. The Seller is not aware of any circumstances which might give rise to such notice, order or other communication being received or of any intention on the part of such authority to give or make such notice, order or communication.

3. Civil Liability

(a) The Company is not aware of any actual or potential liability on the part of the Company arising from (i) any activities or operations of the Company; or (ii) the state or condition of any properties now or formerly owned or occupied by the Company or facilities now or formerly used by the Company. In particular (but without limitation) such liability includes liability for: (i) injury to persons, including impairment of health or interference with amenity; (ii) damage to land or personal property; (iii) interference with riparian or other proprietory or possessory rights; (iv) public or private nuisance; (v) liability for waste or other substances; and (vi) damage or harm to or impairment of the environment including living organisms.

(b) The Company is not party to any litigation, arbitration or dispute resolution proceedings relating to such actual or potential liability and the Seller is not aware of any such litigation or proceedings pending or being threatened nor of any circumstances or facts likely to give rise to such litigation or proceedings.

(c) The Company is not subject to any injunction or similar remedy or order by a court of competent jurisdiction, or to any undertaking given to such court, in respect of matters referred to in paragraph (a) of this warranty. The Company has not been subject to any such injunction, order or undertaking during the period of [20] years prior to Completion, save as fully particularised in the Disclosure Letter.

(d) Full particulars are given in the Disclosure Letters of all claims made or matters notified (or which should have been notified) to the Company's insurers during the period of [twenty] years prior to Completion in respect of such liability or potential liability as is referred to in paragraph (a) of this warranty.

4. Management, Consignment, and Disposal of Wastes

(a) The Company has at all times taken all necessary steps to ensure proper keeping, treatment, management, consignment and disposal of wastes produced in the course of the Company's business so as to comply with all relevant statutory requirements and duties and in accordance with all relevant codes of practice, guidance notes, notes, standards and other advisory material issued by any relevant authority. For the purposes of this warranty "wastes" includes materials and substances which are wastes to the Company notwithstanding that they may be of value or utility to some other person.

(b) Without prejudice to the generality of the previous words of this warranty, the Company has taken all necessary steps to ensure: (i) that all wastes are and at all times have been consigned only to a properly authorised disposer or carrier for disposal at a facility licensed to receive such wastes and that such disposer or carrier knowingly took over responsibility for the proper disposal or other management of the relevant wastes; (ii) that all such wastes have been properly described; and (iii) that adequate contractual rights of indemnity exist so as to enable the Company to obtain indemnity for any claim arising against the Company in respect of such wastes by reason of breach of statutory duty, lack of due care, or malpractice on the part of the disposer or carrier. Full particulars of all relevant contracts, registrations and licences are given in the Disclosure Letter.

(c) Save as stated in the Disclosure Letter no dispute, claim, or proceedings exists between the Company and any disposer or carrier with regard to the Company's wastes, whether or not yet consigned to such disposer or carrier, and the Seller is not aware of any circumstances which are likely to give rise to such dispute, claim or proceedings.

5. Condition of Sites and Other Land

(a) All sites owned or occupied by the Company are free from any contamination which could give rise (whether on the relevant site or on other land) to any of the following risks: (i) harm to human health or safety; (ii) damage to property or to any protected species or habitats; or (iii) pollution of surface or groundwater or soil. All sites formerly owned or occupied by the Company within the period of [30] years prior to completion were free of such contamination at the time when they ceased to be owned or occupied by the Company.

(b) The Seller is not aware of any circumstances which are such as to require expenditure (whether by the Company or by any other person or authority) on cleaning up or decontaminating any sites owned or occupied by the Company in order to prevent, reduce or mitigate any of the risks referred to in paragraph (a) of this warranty, including investigatory, monitoring, precautionary, preventive or remedial measures.

(c) The Seller is not aware of any circumstances which might give rise to a claim against the Company in respect of expenditure for cleaning up or decontaminating any sites formerly owned or occupied by the Company during the period of [30] years prior to Completion.

(d) Save as stated in the Disclosure Letter no notice or other communication has been received from any relevant authority relating to the physical condition of any site now or formerly owned or occupied by the Company nor is the Seller aware of any circumstances likely to give rise to the service of such notice or communication.

(e) No notice or other communication has been received from any relevant authority as to a proposal for the inclusion of land owned or occupied by the Company within any register of contaminated or potentially contaminated sites and the Seller knows of no intention on the part of any relevant authority to give such notice or communication nor of any investigations by any competent authority or other person which might give rise to such an intention.

(f) No site owned or occupied by the Company has been used for the disposal or deposit of controlled waste during the ownership or occupation of the Company and the Seller is not aware of any such prior use.

(g) No site owned or occupied by the Company is situated in proximity to other land the condition of which is such as could in relation to that site give rise to any of the risks referred to in paragraph (a) of this warranty.

6. Plant and Equipment

All structures, machinery, plant and equipment, whether movable or fixed, provided in connection with the activities, operations and premises of the Company for the protection of human safety, health and amenity, property and the environment, including (without limitation) those for the abatement, arrestment or treatment of polluting substances or emissions, the containment of substances and the prevention of spillages and contamination:

(a) are in good repair and condition and satisfactory working order;

(b) conform with all statutory and other legal requirements;

(c) are capable and will be capable, without further expenditure, of fulfilling the function for which they are designed or intended for the period of six (6) years from Completion.

7. Environmental Information

The Company has at all times supplied to the competent authorities such information and assessments as to the Company's processes, activities, substances, emissions, discharges, wastes and effluents, and as to any incidents involving actual or threatened damage or harm or injury to persons or the environment, as in each case is required by law to be supplied; all such information and assessments given (whether under a legal obligation or otherwise) were correct at the time the information or assessment was supplied and so far as the Seller is aware all information contained on public registers relating to such matters is correct.

8. Internal Policy Assessments and Plans

(a) The Company has complied with any statements of corporate environmental policy and operating procedures.

(b) The Company has properly carried out and made all such assessments, plans, registrations or notifications as are required by law in relation to the Company's substances, processes operations, activities, wastes or incidents (including without limitation those relating to hazardous substances, accident hazards, releases to the environment and noise); proper records have been kept of such assessments, plans, registrations or notifications as the case may be and the Seller knows of no subsequent circumstances which would render such assessments, plans, registrations or notifications incorrect or subject to revision or other amendment.

Note:
This precedent is of general company warranties, some of which cover wider issues than contaminated land. Given the general nature of many warranties, it is difficult and possibly dangerous to try and isolate those dealing specifically with contaminated land. However, where specific indemnities are given, care will be needed to ensure general warranties do not cut across them.

Precedent CP16

ACQUISITION OF A COMPANY—ENVIRONMENTAL INDEMNITIES

The Seller covenants with the Purchaser (for itself and as Trustee for each other member of the Purchaser group which trusteeship the Purchaser acknowledges) and as separate covenants with the Company to indemnify the Company and the Purchaser and hold them harmless against the following:

1. Fines or penalties whenever imposed in respect of any breaches prior to Completion by the Company or its officers, agents or employees of any statutory requirements for the protection of the environment or of human health or amenity.

2. Liability (whenever arising) resulting from; (a) any activities or operations of the Company prior to Completion or; (b) the state or condition prior to Completion of any properties now or formerly owned or occupied by the Company or facilities now or formerly used by the Company. In particular (but without limitation) such liability includes liability for: (i) injury to persons including impairment of health or interference with amenity; (ii) damage to land or personal property; (iii) interference with riparian or other proprietory or possessory rights; (iv) public or private nuisance; (v) liability for waste or other substances; and (vi) damage to or impairment of the environment including living organisms.

3. Losses and costs arising from any order or notice received from a competent authority or made by a court of competent jurisdiction in either case whether before or after Completion in respect of: (a) any activities or operations of the Company prior to Completion; and (b) the state or condition before or after completion of any properties now or formerly owned or occupied by the Company or facilities now or formerly used by the Company insofar as the state or condition prior to Completion was such as to justify such order or notice being given. Such losses and costs include in either case (without limitation): (i) the cost of steps reasonably taken to comply with such order or notice; (ii) losses arising from disruption of the business of the Company including loss of profits; and (iii) the cost of steps reasonably taken to investigate and defend any such order or notice.

4. Expenditure incurred by any authority or any person other than the Purchaser whether before or after Completion in taking remedial or preventive measures in respect of any state of affairs arising from: (a) any activities or operations of the Company prior to Completion; or (b) the state and condition whether before or

1037

after Completion of any property now or formerly owned or occupied by the Company or any facility now or formerly used by the Company insofar as the state or condition prior to Completion was such as to justify such expenditure which and where in either case the Company is subsequently required by law to reimburse such expenditure in whole or in part.

5. Liability whether arising before or after Completion in respect of personal injury, damage to land or personal property, interference with riparian or other proprietory or possessory rights and damage to or impairment of the environment caused in any case by wastes produced by the Company and disposed of by the Company prior to Completion and irrespective of whether such wastes were the sole cause of the injury, damage, interference or impairment (as the case may be).

6. The cost of reasonable measures taken in respect of sites owned or occupied by the Company to prevent or mitigate any risk presented by such site to human health or safety, property, surface or groundwater, soil or protected species or habitats by reason of contamination of or migrating from the site which first arose prior to Completion and including, without limitation, investigatory and monitoring measures.

7. Any reasonable costs, charges and expenses incurred by the Purchaser or Company in connection with any of the above matters or in connection with any action taken in avoiding, verifying, reducing, resisting or settling any such fine, penalty, liability, order, notice, loss, cost or claim.

[Optional Limitation Provisions]

PROVIDED THAT:

(a) The liability of the Seller under this provision shall apply for the period of [ ] years from Completion and after that period shall cease but without prejudice to any rights on the part of the Purchaser or Company which shall have arisen during that period;

(b) The maximum amount of the Seller's liability under this covenant shall be limited to [£] OR the following percentage of the relevant amount;

For the first twelve months after Completion: [ ] per cent

For the second twelve months after Completion: [ ] per cent

For the third twelve months after Completion: [ ] per cent

For the fourth twelve months after Completion: [ ] per cent

and thereafter shall cease.

Note:

This is a precedent for indemnities in a general form, dealing with wider matters than simply contaminated land (though specific reference to the issue is included). The person giving the indemnity will wish to see provisions included as to the giving of notice of claims under the indemnity, the right to take over defence of claims, etc. The Seller may also wish to include other limitations to the effect of limiting the Purchaser's right to claim where the claim was triggered by post-completion acts, such as the Purchaser carrying out intrusive investigations, providing information to regulatory authorities and other third parties, changing the use of the site to a more environmentally sensitive use than that existing at completion, etc.

Precedent CP17

COMPANY OR ASSETS ACQUISITION— CONTAMINATED LAND INDEMNITIES

1. Definitions

Environmental Law

means all present and future rules of common law, acts, regulations, standards or codes having the force of law, applicable rights or obligations under European Community Law, and any notices, directions, impositions or requirements issued, imposed or directed by any competent authority relating to the protection of human health and safety, the protection of property and proprietary rights, or the protection of the environment [and for the avoidance of doubt it is expressly agreed that the term shall include any law introducing materially more onerous or stringent requirements than were applicable at the date of Completion.]

Environmental Conditions

means the state and condition of soil, other strata, surface or sub-surface water, groundwater, all surface and sub-surface structures including, without limitation, mines, adits, drains and sewers, all tips, lagoons, spoil heaps, waste disposal sites whether closed or operational, made ground, and all contaminative or polluting substances and shall include, without limitation, the presence of any Regulated Substance in any environmental medium.

Regulated Substance

means any substance or compound or energy, in whatever form and including commixed substances and waste materials, the presence of which may give rise to requirements for removal, abatement, immobilisation, neutralisation, containment, rendering harmless, or any other form of treatment, remediation or clean-up under any Environmental Law.

Onsite claims

means all losses, claims, judgments, damages, penalties, fines, costs, liabilities, obligations, liens, out of pocket costs or expenses including, without limitation, the costs of investigating or defending any prosecution or claim imposed on, incurred by or asserted against the Purchaser under any Environmental Law in relation to Environmental Conditions at or arising from the Property at the Date of Completion.

Clean-up Costs

means all reasonable costs incurred by the Purchaser in remedying Environmental Conditions at the Property as at the date of Completion including, without limitation, the removal, isolation, containment, neutralisation or treatment of regulated Substances [and including the reasonable cost of investigating, assessing and monitoring such Environmental

Conditions] PROVIDED THAT such costs shall be limited to those necessary in order:

(i) to avoid Onsite Claims arising;

(ii) to render the Property fit for use as [STATE USE];

[(iii) to avoid the risk of harm to the Purchaser, the Purchaser's employees and invitees and the Purchaser's property];

[(iv) to render the Property saleable upon reasonable commercial terms].

2. Indemnity

The Seller covenants to indemnify and hold harmless the Purchaser against:

(a) Onsite Claims; and

(b) Clean-up Costs

arising within the period of [PERIOD] from the date of this Agreement up to a maximum of [AMOUNT] in aggregate for all such Claims and Costs within that period.

3. Indemnity Provisions

3.1 The Purchaser shall notify the Seller in writing of all Onsite Claims made or asserted against the Purchaser. Such modification shall be made as soon as reasonably practicable after receipt of any notice of claim and shall be accompanied by all correspondence and documentation relating thereto. The Seller may, within six weeks of such notification (or any shorter if necessary to allow the Purchaser adequate time to respond to the claim) elect to conduct the response or defence to the claim. The party conducting such response to defence shall keep the other informed of the progress of the claim and shall supply copies of all relevant documents. The other party shall offer all reasonable assistance and cooperation as is necessary for the proper response or defence to the claim. The Purchaser shall not admit liability or compromise the claim without the written consent of the Seller, such consent not to be reasonably withheld or delayed.

3.2 Prior to incurring any Clean-up Costs the Purchaser shall notify the Seller of the Purchaser's intention to do so, together with details of the Costs proposed to be incurred and copies of all relevant reports, data, recommendations, correspondence or other documentation. Within 14 days of receiving such notification the Seller shall either:

(a) notify the Purchaser in writing that the Seller approves the proposed Clean-up Costs; or

(b) notify the Purchaser in writing that the Seller objects to the proposed Clean-up Costs and requires the matter to be referred to arbitration in accordance with the provisions of clause 3.3

3.3 Where the Seller objects to the proposed Clean-up Costs in accordance with Clause 3.2(b) then the issue of whether the Seller is obliged to indemnify the Purchaser against all or part of the Proposed Clean-up Costs shall be referred to an appropriately qualified expert (who shall act as an expert and not as arbitrator) to be agreed by the parties or in default of agreement to be appointed by the President of the Institute of Civil Engineers. [ADD FURTHER STANDARD DISPUTE RESOLUTION PROVISIONS, AS REQUIRED].

Note:
This indemnity is closely focused on contaminated site conditions than the more general indemnity at Precedent 16. It covers not only claims or actions against the Purchaser relating to pre-existing contamination, but also clean-up costs incurred by the Purchaser for certain specified purposes. The Seller may also wish to include other limitations to the effect of limiting the indemnitee's right to claim where the claim was triggered by post-completion acts.

PRECEDENT CP18

PROVISIONS FOR INCLUSION IN LOAN FACILITY LETTER

The obligation of the Bank to allow drawdown hereunder is subject to the fulfilment of the following conditions precedent:

1. The Bank being satisfied that the Borrower has a good and marketable title to the Property free from any matter or restrictions which in the opinion of the Bank materially affect its value as security and that all usual searches and enquiries in relation thereto have been made and that specific enquiries have been made of the Seller as to the presence in, on or under the Property of noxious or other contaminative substances in such concentrations as may cause pollution of the environment or harm to human health and as to the legality of the operations and activities being carried out on the Property and specific enquiries have been made of the local authority as to the registration or likelihood of registration of the Property on the register held pursuant to section 78R of the Environmental Protection Act 1990 and the Bank having no reasonable objection to the replies thereto and the Borrower having deposited with the Bank all deeds and other documents of title (if any).

2. The Borrower having commissioned an environmental investigation of the Property on terms approved in advance by the Bank by consultants approved in advance by the Bank and the Bank being satisfied, having been sent copies of all reports, in draft and in final form, prepared by the consultants in relation to the Property at the same time as such reports are sent to the Borrower, that the reports do not reveal the existence of any circumstances which would materially affect the value of the Property as security.

Note:
The object of this provision is to make it clear that the drawdown of the loan is conditional upon appropriate investigations relating to (inter alia) possible contamination.

Precedent CP19

COVENANTS BY MORTGAGOR

The Mortgagor covenants with the Bank as follows:

1. From time to time and, in any event, within seven days of service by the Bank on the Mortgagor of written notice of investigation, to commission an environmental investigation of the Mortgaged Property on terms approved in advance by the Bank by consultants approved in advance by the Bank and to instruct the consultants to forward to the Bank copies of all reports, whether in draft or in final form, prepared by the consultants in relation to the Mortgaged Property at the same time as such reports are forwarded to the Mortgagor and to implement forthwith all reasonable recommendations made by the consultants as to operational procedures and remediation works and further investigations on the Mortgaged Property and to pay the professional fees of the consultants.

2. To permit the Bank and such consultants as the Bank from time to time in writing for that purpose appoint at all reasonable times during business hours and on 24 hours' written notice to the Mortgagor to enter into and upon the Mortgaged Property with or without vehicles and appropriate equipment and machinery for the purpose of carrying out environmental investigations and forthwith after the service by the Bank of notice of works to implement the reasonable recommendations as to operational procedures and remediation works on the Mortgaged Property made by the consultants and to pay the professional fees of the consultants.

3. Within three days of its occurrence to give full particulars to the Bank of any release, spill or deposit on the Mortgaged Property of any noxious substance in a quantity which would cause serious damage to or pollution of the environment or serious damage to property or serious harm to human health.

4. Within seven days of receipt or notification to give full particulars to the Bank of any correspondence or communication, whether written or verbal, received from any competent authority in connection with any environmental matter including, without prejudice, any notification as to inclusion or possible inclusion of the Mortgaged Property on any part thereof or any register or list of land which is or may be contaminated or which has been or is subject to any contaminative use.

[5. The Mortgagor is unaware of any actual or potential liability on the part of the Mortgagor in respect of the activities carried on at the Mortgaged Property for breach of any legislation having amongst its objectives the protection of the environment or of any actual or potential civil or criminal liability on the part of the Mortgagor for harm to persons or property, nuisance or impairment of the environment resulting from any activities or operations of the Mortgagor or the state or condition of the Mortgaged Property or of any circumstances which might give rise to any such liability in the future.]

Note:
These covenants, for inclusion in a mortgage or charge, are intended to protect the interests of the Lender, by requiring the provision of relevant information by the lender, and by giving rights and obligations as to investigation for contamination and appropriate remedial action. The mortgagee should, however, be aware of the enhanced risk of lender liability which may result from becoming involved in decisions as to clean-up or other remedial action.

INDEX